Attack on the 'Idea of India'
A Decade of Social, Political and Economic Strife

Attack on the 'Idea of India'

A Decade of Social, Political and Economic Strife

PRASANNA MOHANTY

BLACK EAGLE BOOKS
Dublin, USA | Bhubaneswar, India

Black Eagle Books
USA address:
7464 Wisdom Lane
Dublin, OH 43016

India address:
E/312, Trident Galaxy, Kalinga Nagar,
Bhubaneswar-751003, Odisha, India

E-mail: info@blackeaglebooks.org
Website: www.blackeaglebooks.org

First International Edition Published by
Black Eagle Books, 2023

**ATTACK ON THE 'IDEA OF INDIA':
A DECADE OF SOCIAL, POLITICAL AND ECONOMIC STRIFE**
by **Prasanna Mohanty**

Cover & Interior Design: Ezy's Publication

ISBN- 978-1-64560-492-1 (Paperback)
Library of Congress Control Number: 2023952666

Printed in the United States of America

To wife Mousumi and daughter Siddhi, for giving me space and support to work, and friend Dr Trithesh Nandan who read through the entire manuscript, made corrections and provided valuable suggestions.

CONTENTS

Introduction

When Prime Minister Narendra Modi came to power in 2014, one of the first things he did was to institute "Good Governance Day" in 2014, marked on December 25, and "Constitution Day" in 2015, marked on November 26. Both were meant to emphasis his and his government's commitments to good governance and constitutional values. This was decades after India won freedom, on August 15, 1947 (Independence Day) and adopted the Constitution, on January 26, 1950 (Republic Day) – which had marked India's trysts with freedom and constitutional democracy.

Arguably, the previous trysts served Indians well, notwithstanding their many failings and unrealized dreams. By 2014, disillusionment had set in. Ironically, it came soon after economic growth peaked – the GDP growth averaging 7.6% under the 2004-05 series and 6.8% under the 2011-12 GDP series in the decade of FY05 to FY14 when the Congress-led UPA, led by Prime Minister Manmohan Singh, was in office. This is the highest ever growth rate since India became a democracy. But towards the fag end, the decade of high growth turned "job-less" (job creation slowed down[1]), inflation was high and corruption was rampant. Arguably, life was better than ever and aspirations even higher but lack of adequate jobs, inflation and corruption added frustration to the mix – setting the stage for a dramatic change[2].

The Hindu majoritarian Bharatiya Janata Party (BJP), led by Modi as then Gujarat Chief Minister, won absolute majority in the Lok Sabha – ending a quarter century of coalition governments. It promised millions of new jobs, higher growth (which meant double-digit growth at the time) and an end to corruption, among many others. The "Good Governance Day" and the "Constitution Day" added a new charm. The "Good Governance Day" also marks the birthday of Atal Bihari Vajpayee, the first Prime Minister from the BJP and was defined as "participatory, accountable, transparent, responsive government".[3] The new Prime Minister said good governance was "the key to a Nation's progress"; that his government was "committed to providing a transparent and accountable administration… 'Citizen-First' is our mantra"; he also solemnly declared "it has been my dream to bring government closer to our citizens, so that they become active participants in the governance process".[4] The "Constitution Day", which marks the day of adoption of the Constitution of India, began with year-long celebrations to pay "tribute to Dr Ambedkar" (Dr BR Ambedkar), the architect of the Constitution of India.[5]

By now, the list of promises was long, and seductively so: "Achche Din Aayenge" (good days will come); 100 million "manufacturing" jobs in a decade[6]; "minimum government, maximum governance"; "sabka saath, sabka vikas" (inclusive development), to which "sabka vishwas" and "sabka prayas" (winning confidence and cooperation of all) would be added later; "cooperative federalism"; "bhrashtachar-mukt Bharat" (corruption-free India); "open and accountable" government in which people would be "equal and integral part of the decision-making process" etc. What more could the aspirational Indians wish for?

Essentially, these are about high and inclusive growth and good governance. It wasn't as if the previous governments didn't try to deliver on these fronts. His predecessor Manmohan Singh's decade in office (2004-14) saw many groundbreaking works. As Finance Minister in 1991, in the Congress-led coalition government under then Prime Minister Narasimha Rao, Manmohan Singh had liberalized the economy. As Prime Minister for a decade (2004-14), he brought multiple rights-based legislations to ensure "inclusive" growth. The rights-based legislations included the Forest Rights Act of 2006, MGNREG Act of 2005 (rural job guarantee law), National Food Security Act of 2013, Right to Fair Compensation and Transparency in Land Acquisition, Rehabilitation and Resettlement Act (LARR) of 2013, National Rural and Urban Health Missions. He initiated many good governance measures, like the Right to Information (RTI) Act of 2005 and the Pre-legislative Consultation Process (PLCP) of 2014. Then Congress president Sonia Gandhi and her National Advisory Committee (NAC) – a group of rights activists and non-government organizations (NGOs) – had played the lead role in bringing all these changes.[7]

In that sense, Prime Minister Modi's initiatives were continuation of the previous government's policies and practices but carried a new optimism and seemed potent enough to achieve better outcomes (minus the job-less growth, inflation and corruption).

About a decade later, all those promises have turned upside down. There are now serious misgivings about the very survival of India as a constitutional democracy, its syncretic culture, social amity and economic wellbeing of the masses. There is a growing literature on all these subjects – both in India and abroad – deciphering how and why this happened. This book adds to the literature from governance perspective. The logic is simple: (a) as then Gujarat Chief Minister, Modi's best-selling point was his "Gujarat model" of "transformative" changes[8] and after becoming the Prime Minister, he laid particular emphasis on good governance and constitutional values and (b) 'governance' provides the right framework to analyze the entire gamut of social, political and economic (transformative) changes since he came to power.

Two background notes are necessary to get the perspectives right to what follows: One, the concept of 'good governance' and two, the 'idea of India' the Constitution of India embodies.

Why 'Good Governance'

As a concept, 'good governance' was first defined by the World Bank in its 1992 document "Governance and Development"[9] : "Good governance is central to creating and sustaining an environment which fosters strong and equitable development, and it is an essential complement to sound economic policies. Government plays a key role in the provision of public goods. They establish the rules that make markets work efficiently. In order to play this role, they need revenues, and agents to collect revenues and produce the public goods. This in turn requires systems of accountability, adequate and reliable information, and efficiency in resource management and the delivery of public services."

The purpose of good governance, therefore, is unambiguous: Strong and equitable (or inclusive) development. Its *key elements* are the rule of law, accountability and transparency in running public affairs. Good governance matters because its *absence* threatens the very civilizational and democratic progress (liberty, equality and fraternity, among others). The phrase gained prominence in 2015, when the UN launched its 15-year Sustainable Development Goals (SDGs) "to end poverty, protect the planet, and ensure that by 2030 all people enjoy peace and prosperity". It added "zero hunger" (Goal 2) and "reduced inequality" (Goal 10) to its earlier Millennium Development Goals (MDGs). In fact, the SDGs aim at completing the unfinished agenda of the MDGs of ending poverty and ensuring inclusive growth and for which good governance was presented as a key tool. The UN explained[10] that the objective of good governance was "to assist societies to develop on effective government within a democratic system, and to implement sustainable development principles through global partnership".

Another UN document laid out[11] the role and working of government in establishing good governance. It said government must be "epitomized by *predictable, open and enlightened policy making; a bureaucracy imbued with a professional ethos; an executive arm of government accountable for its actions; and a strong civil society* participating in public affairs; and all behaving under the *rule of law*". (*Emphasis added*)

But good governance goes beyond government/state.

A 2011 UN document defined it more broadly[12]: "Governance is a *system of values, policies and institutions* by which a *society manages its economic, political and social affairs through interactions within and among the state, civil society and private sector.* It is the way society organizes itself to make and implement decisions – achieving mutual understanding, agreement and action. It comprises the *mechanisms and processes for citizens and groups to articulate their interests, mediate their differences and exercise their legal rights and obligations.* It is the *rules, institutions and practices* that set the *limits* and provide incentives for individuals, organizations and firms. Governance, including its social, political and economic dimensions, operates at every level of human enterprise, be it the household, village, municipality, nation, region or globe." (*Emphasis added*)

While the multilateral agencies like World Bank and International Monetary Fund (IMF) have set the global economic order (neoliberal economics) since 1980s, the UN, a comity of *193 nations*, has set the global development goals, like the MDGs (2000-2015) and SDGs (2015-2030). So, the two critical sets for delivery of good governance are: (i) system of values, policies and institutions and (ii) role of government/state, civil society and private sector. The failures of good governance are then the failures of both the sets of players in which state/government plays a critical role but isn't the sole arbiter. Surely, by no means "good governance" is the sole preserve of multilateral agencies like the World Bank and the UN – which have been quoted above – but they carry far more significance and legitimacy because most countries in the world *accept and adopt* what they call "good governance".

The 'Idea of India'

What is 'the idea' of India? For the post-independent India, the 'idea of India' is what the Constitution of India has laid down in black and white. The Preamble to the Constitution captures it succinctly and the best to reflect the modern, liberal democracy that the founding fathers envisioned and tried to build.

The original version of the Preamble, adopted in 1950, read[13]: "We the people of India, having solemnly resolved to constitute India into a sovereign democratic republic and to secure to all citizens: justice, social, economic and political; liberty of thought, expression, belief, faith and worship; equality of status and of opportunity; and to promote among them all fraternity assuring the dignity of the individual and the unity of the Nation..."

Note the significance of "we the people of India" and its declaration "to secure" justice, equality, liberty and fraternity to "all citizens".

Also note, three missing words that the amended Preamble carries today – "socialist", "secular" and "integrity" (the first two added after "sovereign" and the last after "unity"). These words were inserted during the Emergency of 1975-77 – a dark phase when constitutional rights were suspended, dissenting voices were jailed and elections were postponed. It lasted 21 months.

While insertion of "integrity" was never an issue, "socialist" wasn't despised until much later when India emerged out of the Nehruvian "socialist era" (starting with mid-1980s' economic reforms and then the 1991's liberalization) but "secular" got the goat of the BJP, a right-wing "nationalist" party championing Hindu supremacy, which came into existence in 1980 but it had a forerunner, the Bharatiya Jana Sangh (BJS) since 1951. The word "secular" or "secularism" got a bad name in the 1990s – when the BJP launched the Ramjanambhoomi-Babri Masjid movement, branded political rivals "pseudo secular" and accused them of practising "pseudo secularism". These words and phrases degenerated into "sickular" and "sickularism" after Prime Minister Modi came to power in 2014.

In 1990, then BJP president LK Advani rolled out a "rath yatra" – riding a Toyota truck converted into a 'rath' or chariot – to claim the 16th century Babri Masjid's land, asserting that it was the original birthplace of Lord Ram, the hero of the epic Ramayana. This was an assertion of Hindu "faith". It led to the masjid's demolition (after having stood there for more than 460 years) on December 6, 1992. In 2019, the Supreme Court legitimized[14] this demolition by awarding the land to Hindus – again, relying on the Hindu "faith", not any material evidence, even while describing the demolition as "egregious violation of the rule of law".

The "rath yatra" and the masjid's demolition had catapulted the BJP into a national political player – and also delivered a decisive blow to India's secularism, social and cultural pluralism and unity-in-diversity credo. From two of the 543 elected seats in the Lok Sabha in 1984, the BJP went on to win 85 seats in 1989, formed governments in Madhya Pradesh (1990), Rajasthan (1990) and Himachal Pradesh (1990) and Uttar Pradesh (1991); it never looked back. Its juggernaut of communal politics keeps rolling[15], first yielding an absolute majority in 2014 with 282 seats and then 303 seats in 2019 (half-way mark is 272).

Under Prime Minister Modi, the BJP's ideological project (of establishing "cultural nationalism" and "Hindu Rashtra", but more of that later) got turbocharged.[16] On the first "Constitution Day" celebration in the Parliament on November 26, 2015 – for which a special parliamentary session was called – then Union Home Minister (now Defence Minister) Rajnath Singh objected to the word "secular"[17] in the Constitution's Preamble (and also to "socialist").

In response, jurist AG Noorani gave a lesson on the Constitution. He wrote:[18] "...secularism is *writ large* in a mosaic of constitutional provisions... first on citizenship (Article 9); on non-discrimination on grounds of religion, race, caste, etc. (Article 15), generally and specifically in public employment

(Article 16); the fundamental rights to freedom of religion individually (Article 25) and collectively (Article 26); ban on discrimination in state-aided educational institutions (Article 29(2)), on taxes for the promotion of religion (Article 27); on religious instruction in them (Article 28) and on exclusion from the general electoral roll on any such ground as well (Article 325). *What does it all add up to but a secular state?" (Emphasis added)*

What Noorani pointed out define the constitutional idea of secularism (as against separation of church and state in the western concept) – which is essentially about (a) *non-discrimination* on the grounds of religion, race, caste (b) *equality* before law and (c) *freedom* in religious practices. These are not unknown but needed to be re-emphasized. But Prime Minister Modi openly flaunts his Hindu identity by building and developing temples, temple corridors and regularly paying visit to Hindu holy places but not those of non-Hindu religions. Amidst the devastating pandemic in 2020, instead of building hospitals, the Prime Minister laid the foundation of the Ayodhya temple[19] and continued with the development of Kashi temple corridor in his constituency, Varanasi.[20] These two incidents effectively put to rest the secular character of the Indian state.

Three more things need to be flagged to explain why the attack on secularism by the BJP and its leaders is inevitable:

(a) The Ramjanambhoomi-Babri Masjid movement sparked country-wide Hindu-Muslim riots for years – killing about 2,000 people during 1990-91[21]; the subsequent demolition in 1992 killing more than 2,000 in its immediate aftermath and the Gujarat riots of 2002 (also linked to it) killing another 1000-2,000 more[22]. This movement made the BJP a national political force that it is today.

(b) Many studies[23] show that communal politics and riots have yielded electoral benefits to the BJP and its forerunner the BJS. Paul R Brass[24], American political scientist known for his works on Indian politics, wrote in 2004: "In many parts of India where Hindu-Muslim riots are endemic, especially in the northern and western states, *institutionalized systems of riot production* (IRS) have been created in the years since independence, which are activated during periods of political mobilisation or at the time of elections. Far from being spontaneous occurrences, the production of such riots involves *calculated and deliberate actions* by key individuals, the conveying of messages, recruitment of participants, and other specific types of activities, especially provocative ones, that are part of a performative repertoire. Moreover, all these actions may require *frequent rehearsals* until the time is ripe, the context is felicitous, and there are no serious obstructions in carrying out the performance." Even the 2014 general elections were preceded by the Muzaffarnagar riots in 2013 (causing a communal polarization that broke the electoral and social bonds between the Jats and the Muslims and also split the alliance between Dalits and Muslims).[25] *(Emphasis added)*

(c)   As Gujarat Chief Minister, Modi became the 'Hindu Hriday Samrat' (king of Hindu's heart) following the 2002 Hindu-Muslim riots[26] and his Hindu majoritarian politics is inalienable part of his charism.[27] He was heralded as India's "first Hindu ruler after 800 years" by a prominent Hindutva leader – ending up in a heated debate in the Parliament in 2015.[28]

Defining Markers of Governance

Most Indians had high expectations from the new Prime Minister to revive high growth and create plentiful jobs. That didn't happen. The economy went into a tailspin[29] much before the pandemic hit in 2020 (FY21). The GDP growth tumbled from 6.4% in FY14 (2011-12 GDP series), which it inherited, to 3.4% in FY20 (much later revised upward to 3.9%). This happened due to several policy-driven disasters, primarily the 'twin shocks' of demonetization in 2016 and the GST in 2017. The pandemic of 2020-21 and its gross mismanagement aggravated the humanitarian and economic crises further; the economy collapsed with the GDP growth plunging to -6.6% in FY21 (first negative growth after *1979* (corresponds to FY1979-80)[30]; later revised upward to -5.8%) – more than double the global fall of -3.1% in the corresponding fiscal of 2020. Millions lost their jobs and small businesses overnight during this period of 2016-2021. India did recover to 9.1% growth in FY22 but it was K-shaped (uneven), slipped to 7.1% in FY23 and is expected to go further down to 6.5%[31] in FY24.

In absence of relevant, credible and current official information on jobs, poverty, hunger and inequality, here are two simple facts to capture the growing economic distress.

* India is feeding *67% households* (75% of rural and 50% of urban)[32] with "free" food grains of 35 kg per household from January 1, 2023. Since the actual beneficiaries are 813.5 million[33] – instead of 955 million as per the population count of 1.43 billion in 2023 (as per the UN DESA[34]) – 141 million are deprived of it. This very population (67%) earlier got "subsidized" ration, as per the National Food Security Act of 2013. When the pandemic struck in 2020, they were given *additional* "free" ration of 5 kg per individual between April 2020 and December 2022. From January 1, 2023, the additional allocation was stopped and all of it was made "free". Over Rs 18.5 lakh crore[35] food subsidy was given in nine years of the Prime Minister (FY15-FY23).

* An analysis of the UN agencies' "State of Food Security and Nutrition in the World 2023" data shows *74% Indians* can't afford a healthy meal[36] –

despite cost of healthy diet increasing the lowest among BRICS nations, including the newly added members.

What about other promises and commitments? The deliveries are exact opposite there too. A good way to present and explain such inversions is to identify the patterns which are pervasive and consistent – let's call those *defining markers of governance* of the post-2014 India. Here are some of the most important ones – not in any particular order.

Fiats as Public Policy

First, top-down, arbitrary and self-serving policies – as against "open and accountable" government in which people would be "equal and integral part of the decision-making process".

Most of these are handed down directly by the Prime Minister, more like the US's post-9/11 "shock-and-awe" military operations – marked by stealth and spectacle.[37] These are either delivered in his national addresses from the Red Fort (on the Independence Day) or at 8 pm national addresses on TV. Some are paradropped through notifications, budget speeches, ordinances and Bills – with the invisible but clear hands of his office, the Prime Minister's Office (PMO) which runs all ministries, mainstream media popularly called 'godi' (lapdog) media and is arguably the most powerful[38] one ever. Invariably, there is no prior consultation, no debate, no parliamentary scrutiny and devoid of logic, evidence, checks and balances. When things go wrong, as they invariably do – inflicting immense and avoidable pain on the people and the economy – there is no admission of failure, no review and no course corrections (save for the withdrawal of the three new farm laws after a year of farmers' protest).

Some of the examples are: Overnight demonetization of 2016 that sucked out 86.9% of high-value currencies and paralyzed all economic activities for months; overnight 24x7 national curfew and complete clampdown on all social and economic activities in 2020 in response to the Covid-19 without planning and preparations; farm and labour laws brought through ordinances during the pandemic lockdown and pushed through the Parliament soon thereafter; overnight abrogation of special status of Jammu and Kashmir (J&K) and its downgrading to two Union Territories in 2019; overnight delegitimization of the elected government of NCT of Delhi in 2021 by declaring its "nominee" Lieutenant Governor as the "government"; overnight declaration of wholesale and indiscriminate privatization of PSUs (in the 2021 budget speech) and so on. The list is too long to be presented here. This is an open invitation to misgovernance and going by the experience so far, it may not be entirely *unintended or alien* to the regime. (Chapters II, X and XI).

Primacy to Private Interest

Second, serving private business interests as against the promised "citizen-first" and the Prime Minister's public vow: "I vow on this soil of my country…I won't let this country be sold off".[39]

Here too there is a long list[40]: A huge spike in yearly write-off of corporate loan defaults (ironically called bank NPAs) since 2015; corporate tax cut of 2019, which brought its peak rate below individual tax rates and delivered amidst fiscal crisis – which didn't lead to the promised higher investment or job creations; the new farm and labour laws brought in 2019 and 2020 which encroached on the interests of farmers and workers; *en masse* and *indiscriminate* sale of public assets in 2021 (irrespective of profit, strategic and economic relevance to private businesses; a public-sector-led Bad Bank (called the National Asset Reconstruction Company Limited (NARCL)"[41] set up in 2021 for acquiring stressed bank loan assets before the intended privatization of banks; "monetisation" of public infrastructure, built with public money, called "National Monetization Pipeline" or NMP) beginning with 2021 etc. (Chapter VII).

In 2023, the central bank, RBI, allowed all banks and financial institutions "compromise settlements" with fraudsters and willful defaulters and give them fresh loans after 12 months.[42] Crony capitalism is flourishing like never before – a kind which may be called "National Champions" model of growth – state-backed, too big to fail, too powerful for normal laws, scrutiny, regulatory oversights and too big to compete with but without the attendant benefits to the economy.[43] Policies are known to be skewed in favour of the rich and against the poor in all democracies, including the best-functioning ones. But it is more skewed in democracies with private money-driven electoral politics like India. The opaque Electoral Bond of 2017 – which allows unaccounted funds from private businesses and foreign entities to political parties – acts as a perfect quid pro quo mechanism to cement politics-business bond. India is doubly exposed to skewed policies since it has the maximum poor (228.9 million)[44]; maximum hungry (233.9 million[45]) and maximum illiterates (287 million adults or 37% of the global total"[46]). All these factors[47] determine the magnitude of the skewed policies favouring the rich. This adds another layer to the challenges to democratic polity. (Chapter VIII).

Conflating PM and Govt to 'Nation'

Third marker is conflating the Prime Minister and his government with "nation" – that is India – which turns his credo of providing "minimum government" on its head.

Although former Prime Minister Indira Gandhi was equated with India by her sycophants and institutions were subservient during the 21-month

Emergency, the sheer scale and pervasiveness now easily surpasses that. Anyone who dares to question or criticize the Prime Minister or his government is branded "anti-national" and raided by the Enforcement Directorate (ED), Central Bureau of Investigation (CBI) and Income Tax Department (ITD).[48] The CBI has had a long history of being used as a political tool to fix rivals and dissent but the ED and IT were weaponized after 2014 and often, all three central agencies work in tandem with state police and anti-terror National Investigation Agency (NIA) and apply stringent laws of sedition and anti-terror UAPA. The ruling establishment's legions of online and offline troll armies, including its official IT Cell and a compliant mainstream media, join in. From political rivals to academics, farmers, lawyers, journalists, comedians, rights activists, students and civil society their list is very long and ever expanding to corner anyone who dares to stand up. Such is the level of democracy that even putting up posters calling for the Prime Minister's removal ("Modi hatao, desh bachao") – a normal and common electoral phenomenon in India in the previous decades – leads to hundreds of FIRs and arrests[49], raids on the printing press and the Delhi Police (under the Union Home Ministry) gets busy removing such posters[50]. (Chapters I and II).

A by-product of this is conflating the Prime Minister with the 'Union of India'. In its affidavit to the Supreme Court in connection with review of sedition law in May 2022, the Ministry of Home Affairs (MHA) pleaded for time in the name of the Prime Minister; stating that since the Prime Minister believed in human rights and was keen to shed the colonial baggage, the government should be allowed to review its position before the constitutionality of the law was decided.[51] The apex court conceded and put it on hold. The Bharatiya Nyaya Sanhita of 2023[52], a bill paradropped in the Parliament in August 2023 as a wholesale replacement of the Indian Penal Code (IPC) of 1860, doesn't mention "sedition" but has Clause 150 – as part of the "offences against the state" – which mirrors the sedition law, expands its scope and increases the punishment from 3-7 years to life imprisonment, making it far more draconian.[53] Even the CBI was emboldened enough file an affidavit before the Supreme Court in the name of the "Republic of India" – in a bail related petition – and the court had to tell it off: "Why have you filed as the 'Republic of India'? You are not representing the Union or the Republic."[54] (Chapter I).

A *symptom* of this is Modi's 'namak'.

Modi's 'Namak': Public Money, Votes for Modi and BJP

Prime Minister Modi's welfare model is best suited to autocracies, not democracies.

While seeking votes in Uttar Pradesh's Hardoi in 2022, the Prime Minister described the *additional* "free" ration given during the pandemic of 2020-2022 as "Modi's namak" (Modi's salt).[55] 'Namak' or 'salt' is a metaphor for personal loyalty and obligations. Although he retracted the statement, this is told to people in multiple ways by his party members who track the beneficiaries for harvesting their votes. This is a far cry from calling himself "Pradhan Sevak" (prime servant of the country)[56] – a variation of the first Prime Minister Jawaharlal Nehru's description of himself as "Pratham Sevak" (first servant)[57].

A part of "Modi's namak" engineering is his *birthday* (September 17) *gifts*. In 2021, his "gift" to the nation was vaccination of 25 million people in a single day – a world record. The vaccination counts a day before was 6.7 million and a day after, 8.8 million.[58] In 2022, he gave two gifts: (a) 8 Cheetahs were introduced in India[59] (in all 20 Cheetahs were introduced, of which six had died due to negligence by August 2023[60]) and (b) personally distributed 75,000 job certificates, which doubled up as "Diwali" gift too, to new government recruits at the "rozgar mela"; his cutouts were installed for the new recruits to take photographs with and thank him for this.[61] By October 2023, he had held such 'mela' *nine times*.[62] No PM has ever taken such personal credit for filling up vacant government jobs.

The Prime Minister also personally releases every single instalment of PM-Kisan (under which farmers get Rs 6,000 a year in three instalments and delayed to *time it* to state elections[63]), flags every single *semi-fast* Vande Bharat AC train (average speed of 63 to 96 kmph[64]), inaugurates new roads, bridges, tunnels, e-files, coffee table books, Twitter (rebranded as 'X') handles – you name it. He is staring at you from everywhere everyday – buildings, highways, newspapers, TV channels, government websites (including Delhi Zoo[65]), vaccine certificates, PDS supplies (packets/bags) and outlets, petrol pumps. All government schemes have been renamed and relaunched after 2014, carrying the prefix "Pradhan Mantri" to put his personal stamp. When the Supreme Court asked the government to provide care for children orphaned by the pandemic, the Prime Minister launched monthly stipend and education loan schemes from his *private fund* his office (PMO) runs, called "PM CARES Fund". This fund is unaccountable (out of the transparency law RTI Act of 2005) but collects huge sums every year from public institutions. (Chapter I)

It is a reflection of this mindset that Union Home Minister Amit Shah asked Tamil Nadu voters to give 25 Lok Sabha seats in 2024 elections[66] as an expression of gratitude to the Prime Minister for installing "Sengol"[67], a legacy of the Chola era, in the new Parliament House. The Prime Minister is permanently in election campaign mode, using *public money* for the partisan political purposes by combining official programmes with address to party workers and election rallies (Chapter X).

The Prime Minister does *excel* in delivery of welfare schemes: "Free" food grains; annual DBT of Rs 6,000 to farmers; farm loan waivers for Uttar Pradesh from the central treasury in 2017 (and eight BJP-ruled states also did so while he criticized Congress-ruled states for the same in 2019 (Chapter VI); free toilets; free medicines for 40% of population; subsidies for housing, fertilizers and LPGs and yet *regularly runs down* all rival political parties for doing the same, calling it "revdi" (freebies) and "revdi culture".[68] That welfare measures are partly also because of his own failures to lift the people out of poverty and provide social security cover also escape his attention.

The vilification of rivals is also a deliberate strategy – to project himself as the only messiah of the poor, get their votes, cultivate a personality "cult" (with public money) while denying such opportunities to political rivals. Two more instances demonstrate this: (a) his government refused to sell rice to the Congress-ruled Karnataka, after the BJP lost the election in 2023, while throwing open its godowns to private businesses repeatedly despite poor response[69], and (b) declaring the entire PDS supply "free" from January 2023, his government denies state governments any role in food subsidy (which they used to provide to further subsidize the centrally subsidized ration).

How the Prime Minister's welfarism is used for harvesting votes was first revealed by his government's first Chief Economic Advisor (CEA) Arvind Subramanian (2014-2018). In his two co-authored studies of 2020 and 2021[70], he described it as "New Welfarism" and wrote it came "laden with calculation" for getting votes. The delivery of only the tangible essentials (easy to deliver, measure and monitor like access to banking for women, electricity, clean cooking fuel and sanitation etc.) *accelerated* but the intangible ones like healthcare and education very critical for development and growth (which might yield results in distant future) *deteriorated*. But how does this translate into votes? These studies mentioned two mechanisms: (i) deploying central agencies (bureaucracy and banks) to deliver the schemes and (ii) strong and persistent messaging from his government to remind voters who was providing the benefits.

From there, the BJP cadre takes over. They brand the beneficiaries as "labharthi" who are identified with the help of government records made available to the party cadre, contacted and tracked during voting. This process helped in beating the strong anti-incumbency against the BJP in four out of five state elections in 2022 – a strategy first adopted in the 2019 general elections[71]. Two credible post-poll surveys showed, massive failures to manage the pandemic, particularly in the 2021 second wave, chronic and severe job crisis, high inflation and mass impoverishment etc. had no impact on the Prime Minister's vote catching ability or the anti-incumbency of the BJP-ruled state governments.[72] These developments show two distressing trends: (a) use of public money for the BJP's votes and (b) blurring of the line between the government and the party.

Yet, if you think the Central government's social sector spending has gone up, you are mistaken.

It was 21% of the total central budget expenditure in FY10 – which fell to 20% in FY20 (pre-pandemic) and remained 20% in FY22 (BE)[73] – despite huge spike due to the "free" ration in 2020 to 2022. The Economic Surveys have stopped giving the centre's social sector expenditure (now comes only combined with states to give an inflated picture). The Ministry of Labour and Employment shows, 94% of workers are in informal sectors – devoid of job security and social security cover. The annual Periodic Labour Force Survey (PLFS) reports show a consistent fall in social security cover even for the salaried/regular wage workers: No social security up from 49.6% in 2017-18 to 53.9% in 2022-23. Worse, India topped the list in the 2023 Global Slavery Index[74] with a 38% rise from 2018 (from 8 million to 11 million) in "modern slavery" – forced labour, forced or servile marriage, debt bondage, forced commercial sexual exploitation, human trafficking, slavery-like practices, and the sale and exploitation of children.

The second area where the government has delivered is "minimum governance" *for private sector*. It has simplified administrative clearances, diluted and deleted a whole lot of safeguards and compliance norms (for environment and CSR) and decriminalized a significant chunk of corporate crimes (in the Companies Act of 2013). It has also been far more generous than any in the past by writing of loans defaults of private corporate entities (called NPAs), gives huge amounts of fiscal and tax concessions (called PLIs and DLIs) and in 2023 did the unthinkable by giving a free pass ("revdi") to fraudsters and willful defaulters mentioned earlier. The Prime Minister will be bequeathing India a dubious legacy. (Chapter VII)

The third area where the government claims to have delivered is in building highways – but this is highly questionable for three reasons:

- From April 2018, highway constructions are counted by the number of lanes[75], unlike in the past when the total linear length was counted (a six-lane road of 1 km becomes 6 km, unlike 1 km previously).

- On March 16, 2023, the Ministry of Road Transport and Highways told the Lok Sabha that "total length of National Highways (NHs) in the country has increased from about 91,287 km in March, 2014 to about 1,45,155 km at present"[76] – addition of 53,868 km). What it forgot to tell was it had told the Rajya Sabha on December 15, 2021[77] that "about 49,087 km of State Roads including SHs have been notified as NHs since 2014-15 till date". Which means, the total addition is only 4,781 km in *nine years*!

- The 2023 report of the Comptroller and Auditor General of India (CAG)[78] exposes gross irregularities in building roads under the "Bharatmala Pariyojana": (a) the Dwarka Expressway's cost went up astronomically high of *Rs 250.77 crore per km* as against the approved cost of Rs 18.2 crore per km by the Cabinet Committee on Economic Affairs (CCEA) and (b) the average cost was pushed up *170.89%* to *Rs 23.89 crore per km* against the CCEA approved cost of Rs 13.98 crore per km. The project is marked by "selection of ineligible bidders, award of works without approved detailed project reports or based on faulty detailed project reports".

Yet another *symptom* of the PM-and-government-as-the-nation is emphasis on duties over rights.

Duty over Rights

The Prime Minister himself repeatedly emphasizes on the citizens duties over their rights.

In January 2022, he said[79]: "We also have to admit that in the 75 years after Independence, a malaise has afflicted our society, our nation and us all. The malaise is that we turned away from our duties and did not give them primacy...People only talked of their rights all these years and fought for them. Speaking of rights may be right to some extent in certain circumstances. But forgetting one's duties completely has played a huge role in keeping India weak." To emphasize on duty, he renamed the iconic Rajpath "Kartavya Path" (Path of Duty) in 2022[80] and the next 25 years (up to 1947) as "Kartavya Kaal"[81] (a period of duty). The Wire listed all the 11 fundamental duties mentioned in the Constitution (duties to abide by the Constitution, respect its ideals and institutions, promote harmony and the spirit of common brotherhood transcending religious, linguistic and regional or sectional diversities etc.) and showed how in each case the Prime Minister had shown scant respect to what he preaches to the citizens.[82]

Emphasis on duty is a marker of authoritarianism, which prefers 'subjects' over empowered citizens capable of questioning and demanding accountability. This goes with extensive surveillance of citizens by the government. "Fundamental duties" were not part of the original Constitution of India. These were introduced during the Emergency of 1975-77 and expanded by the previous BJP-led NDA government in 2002. The fundamental difference between the duties and the rights is that while the former is *non-justiciable* (can't be enforced by law) the latter is (equality before law, non-discrimination, the right to life, freedom of speech and religion, movement etc.) *justiciable* and is of greater importance in a democracy.[83] (Chapter XI)

Taken together (Modi's 'namak', primacy to duties and surveillance), it shows contempt for citizens, constitutional and other democratic values, norms and governance. This goes hand-in-hand with another disturbing development.

Short-changing Accountability and Transparency

Fourth, the Prime Minister evades accountability (answerability) and transparency. He is probably the only democratically elected head of state anywhere in the world, and certainly in India's history, who scrupulously avoids facing open questions from media. Whenever he does talk to media, it is either scripted (written questions given and answers provided, no cross questioning)[84], limited to a selected few often derided as part of the "Godi media"[85] – a play on Modi and 'lapdog' – or to film star Akshay Kumar for sheer entertainment[86].

So much so that even the US media was "sequestered in a van" during the two-day G20 summit in New Delhi in 2023 and denied access to even US President Joe Biden[87] – on which Rs 4,100 crore (more than 400%)[88] was spent just in jazzing up New Delhi alone, as against the budget allocation of Rs 90 crore[89]. Biden finally spilled the beans in Hanoi[90] a day later and said he had raised the issues of civil society, free press and human rights with Prime Minister Modi. The G20 resolution also had a humiliating paragraph (78)[91] for India: "We note the UNGA Resolution A/RES/77/318, particularly its commitment to promote respect for religious and cultural diversity, dialogue and tolerance. We also emphasize that freedom of religion or belief, freedom of opinion or expression, the right to peaceful assembly, and the right to freedom of association are interdependent, inter-related and mutually reinforcing and stress the role that these rights can play in the fight against all forms of intolerance and discrimination based on religion or belief. In this regard, *we strongly deplore all acts of religious hatred against persons, as well as those of a symbolic nature without prejudice to domestic legal frameworks, including against religious symbols and holy books." (Emphasis added)*

He evades responsibility by not addressing issues of national importance inside and outside the Parliament; he has no qualms about misleading the country; his government doesn't allow questions on critical national importance and security to be asked even inside the Parliament. For example, he openly misled the country on the Chinese incursion and grabbing land in the Indian side of the LAC in Ladakh in 2020[92] – leading to a loss of over 1,000 sq km of land.[93] He didn't answer questions on the corruption allegations against business tycoon Gautam Adani and his relationship with him.[94] He didn't speak on his government spying on civilians by using the Israel spyware Pegasus.[95] He never answered questions on the Pulwama blasts of 2019 that killed 40 CRPF jawans and which brought India to the brink of a nuclear war with Pakistan.[96] Apart from these, he never came clean on the demonetization, anti-farmer farm laws, prolonged job and economic crises, every day violence against Muslims, Christians, Dalits, persecution of political rivals, dissenting voices, civil society and free speech etc. Sure, the Prime Minister loves to talk, multiple times a day, 365 days a year, but these are monologues (radio talk, public speeches) and he never takes responsibilities for his mistakes or that of his government ever.

Instead, he keeps blaming the Congress and the first Prime Minister Nehru (1947-1964) for all that ails the country under his watch.[97]

The only two occasions the Prime Minister took open questions – in the UK in 2015 and the US in 2023 – he brushed those aside (narrated a little later). Many have explained his evasions to the "strong leader" image syndrome – which assumes admission to failures makes him weak and vulnerable[98]; his model of politics invented in the days of Gujarat[99] or even his 'idea of India'[100]. It may be a strategic move but goes against his lofty claims of good governance and amounts to shirking responsibility and accountability[101] – decidedly undemocratic. Add to that disabling of all critical institutions of checks and balances by the government – the Parliament, judiciary, media and top official watchdogs like the Comptroller and Auditor General of India (audit), Central Information Commission (transparency), Central Vigilance Commission (CVC), Lokpal (anti-corruption) etc. – and one is looking at the existential crisis for the very Constitution of India that the Prime Minister pretends to hold dear to him.[102]

Politics of Lies, Deceit, Fake News and Propaganda

Fifth, lies, fake news, misinformation, disinformation, alt-truth etc. as key governance tools. A make-believe world that the ruling establishment and its support groups have built follows two Goebbels' propaganda principles: (a) "if you tell a lie big enough and keep repeating it, people will eventually come to believe it" and (b) "accuse the other of that you are guilty".

The Prime Minister himself doesn't shy away from half-truths and whole lies.[103] Mainstream media doesn't fact-check or question him but a number of online media platforms do and routinely exposes those. A good example of this is the Prime Minister's second ever answer to an open question in nine years in office at the White House on June 22, 2023. The question was specifically about "steps you are willing to take to improve the rights of Muslims and other minorities in India to uphold free speech", which was apparently known in advance as he read out a prepared text from two teleprompters on either of his side. It began with a lie (like many others given in the next chapters), contained many more lies, rhetorical discourse on democracy and circular logic to justify it, completely disconnected to the asked question.

The Prime Minister said[104]: "I am actually really *surprised* …as President Biden also mentioned, India and America – both countries, democracy is *in our DNA. Democracy is our spirit. Democracy runs in our veins.* We *live democracy*…when you talk of democracy, if there are no human values and there is no humanity, there are no human rights, then it's not a democracy…*when we live democracy*, then *there is absolutely no space for discrimination*…in India's democratic values, there's *absolutely no discrimination* neither on basis of caste, creed, or age, or any kind of geographic location…" (*Emphasis added*)

Incidentally, his first encounter with open question was in London in 2015 and also related to the anti-democratic impulses of his government: "India is becoming an increasingly intolerant place. Why?" He said another lie: "...we *do not tolerate* such incidents of violence at all. We take strong actions and we will continue to take strong actions and legal actions against such incidents. India is a vibrant democracy which, on the basis of the constitution, *protects every citizen, and the values of every citizen* in accordance with our constitution, and we're committed to that."[105] *(Emphasis added)*

Immediately after denying attack on Muslims in India in the White House in 2023, the Prime Minister went straight to prove himself wrong. In his addressed the US Congress, he said India won freedom "after a thousand years of foreign rule"[106] – alluding to the Muslim period of Indian history. The woman reporter (from the World Street Journal), who had asked the question, was immediately trolled by the BJP's official IT Cell – targeting her *Muslim identity and Pakistan connections*[107] – two red rags and dog whistles to the right-wing troll army. The White House condemned the trolling and said "it's antithetical to the very principles of democracy that".[108] Former President Barak Obama[109] too faced hostile reactions for suggesting, before the Prime Minister's official engagements, that President Biden should tell him about "protection of the Muslim minority in a majority-Hindu India" and cautioned that "if you do not protect the rights of ethnic minorities in India, then there is a strong possibility India at some point starts pulling apart. And we've seen what happens when you start getting those kinds of large internal conflicts".

Assam's Chief Minister Himanta Biswa Sarma of the BJP launched an Islamophobic attack flagging, wrongly, Obama's Muslim identity (he is a Christian).[110] Sarma tweeted: "There are many *Hussain Obama* in India itself. We should prioritize taking care of them".[111] Finance Minister Nirmala Sitharaman joined him, saying Obama as the US had bombed "six Muslim countries" with "more than 26,000 bombs".[112] Defence Minister Rajnath Singh said Obama should "think" how many Muslim countries he had attacked and that India believes in 'Vasudhaiva Kutumbakam' (the entire universe is one family).[113] These are state actors, not fringe elements, never raised such objections when Obama was the US President and exposes the mindset of people at the very top of the government and his party. In his famous 'how-do-you-eat-your-mango' (scripted) interview with film actor Akshay Kumar, the Prime Minister had claimed a "tu-taadi" friendship[114] (informal, like childhood buddies) with Obama but didn't utter a word when Obama was vilified by his own ministers.

But this is to be expected. As Gujarat Chief Minister, he derisively called Pakistan President "Miyan Musharraf" and then ECI JM Lyngdoh "James Michael Lyngdoh" in public rallies to emphasis their Muslim and Christian identity, respectively. His attack on Indian Vice President Hamid Ansari, a scholar and highly regarded diplomat, at the latter's farewell speech in the Parliament in 2017, would go down in history as most undignified and uncalled for in the Parliament's history. Referring to Ansari's diplomatic postings in west Asia (Muslim countries), his involvement with the Aligarh Muslim University and National Commission of Minorities, the Prime Minister said: "You must have been *restless at times*, chafing at (constitutional) constraints. But now that you *have been liberated*, you will have the happy felling of freedom and you will get an opportunity to work, think and talk according to your *basic ideology and instinct.*"[115] Whatever be the provocation, the Prime Minister of India is expected to be dignified and graceful in conducting public affairs. (*Emphasis added*)

A week after the White House engagement saw the police in BJP-ruled Uttarakhand asking Muslims to offer Bakr-Eid namaz *40 km away*[116] from the Hindu temple town of Badrinath and also *40 km away*, near a forest[117] from Purola town (same state). Purola had seen a fake "love jihad"[118] campaign spiralling into Muslim exodus weeks earlier. Of course, *routine mob lynching* and other attacks on Muslims continued unabated[119]; two Gujarat schools even *apologised* for holding Bakr-Eid celebrations at the time[120].

The lies are not only relating to anti-democratic and communal character of the government. It covers a wider canvass. During his same visit to the US in June 2023, the Prime Minister addressed the diaspora and spread more lies: "One new University is coming up in India every week…Every second day, a new college is being opened…Every year one new IIT and one new IIM is being set up in India."[121] Given that he inaugurates every new construction and every single *semi-fast* Vande Bharat train but has never seen doing so for any university or college or IIT exposes the lie. Officially, his government confirmed that he was lying. In an answer to the Rajya Sabha on July 26, 2023[122], the Ministry of Education said "No New IIT or IIM has been opened in last five years" and eight central universities had opened in the past five years – of the total 242 new universities, of which 140 were private ones. But the claims about new universities is just a *claim* – not fact-checked on the ground whether these are functional or not.

As for the IITs, the CAG report of 2023[123] said, of eight new elite IITs approved and set up in 2008 and 2009 (by the previous Congress-led government), only *two IITs had completed Phase-I buildings* (construction of academic buildings, student hostels, residential accommodation for faculty and staff, and laboratories), phase-II (additional facilities) delayed in two and three IITs had not yet initiated Phase-II works by March 2019. The India has 418 accredited universities and 9,062 accredited colleges (Lok Sabha answer of February 13, 2023[124]). Similar lies were told by the Prime Minister[125] and his party[126] in the past too – including about new premier medical institution, the AIIMSs but more about that in Chapter VII (and more about official lies in Chapters II, IV, V, XI and XII).

The Prime Minister doesn't care about higher education and the IITs, IIMs, central universities which continue to have a huge (one-third or more) vacancy of faculty members for years[127], including at the time of he was lying at the White House[128]. Over the years, his government is diluting autonomy of all institutions of excellence, including the IITs and IIMs[129]; premier private sector one like the Tata Institute of Social Sciences (TISS) and other deemed-to-be universities[130]. The means adopted include interferences in their work (IITs), appropriating power to appoint (and dismiss) the head of institutions by amending law (TISS, IIMs). In the case of 20 new IIMs, their assent for amending the law – The Indian Institute of Management (Amendment) Act of 2023 – appropriating power to appoint and dismiss their heads was taken by keeping older IIMs (of Ahmedabad, Bangalore, Kolkata, Indore, Lucknow and Kozhikode) in dark (not inviting to the conclave).[131] Months later, new rules under the amended law was issued empowering the government to *dissolve*[132] the apex decision making body, Board of Governors, of *any IIM* – the highest decision making body – for (a) persistent disobeying of government orders (b) public interest and (c) inability of the Board to perform its duties. The Boards had been deprived of the power to appoint and dismiss the heads (directors) in the amendment by giving the power to the President as the Visitor of the IIMs. This means end of the autonomy for IIMs.

What lies, fake news and propaganda do is obvious. They *derail* debate on genuine issues and concerns; *divert* public attention from crisis; *distort* facts and reality to present a *make-believe world* and, of course, *defame* and undermine all others to project by default (non-existent) superiority and explain away failures – by blaming Muslims for all crises, quieten all dissenting and questioning voices, discredit political rivals, particularly the Congress and the builder of modern India Nehru (multiple fake 'jihads', "anti-national", "tukde-tukde gang", "Khan-market gang" and what you have). At times, such propensities lead to bizarre situations. For example, the Prime Minister asked why Congress leaders Rahul and Priyanka Gandhi don't use 'Nehru' surname (of their maternal great grandfather, which would have been against the established norms and traditional practices) in the Parliament to create a (non-existing) controversy to divert attention from the questions about the alleged corruption by the Adani group and his relationship with its owner Gautam Adani, not answer or evade answerability.[133]

Or the dinner invites to G20 delegates issued in the name of "The President of Bharat" and "The Prime Minister of Bharat"[134] – when the official designations in English carry the word "India" ("Bharat" in Hindi version) – apparently prompted by (a) the need to divert attention from the real issue at stake, which was the possibility of no concrete outcomes and failure to even work out a resolution at the G20 summit[135] and (b) to undermine the traction from the Opposition alliance which calls itself INDIA (Indian National Developmental Inclusive Alliance).[136] In 2015, the government had clearly told the Supreme

Court, in response to a PIL, that there was "no change in circumstances since the Constituent Assembly deliberated the issue to warrant a review"[137] – which was the right stand to take given the historical context[138] in which the Constitution of India declared "India, that is Bharat", not the other way round. Nonetheless, the official booklet uploaded on the G20 website, "Bharat-Mother of Democracy"[139] presents many lies and misleading claims. Three particularly stand out: (i) the Prime Minister is quoted as saying that India "has the distinction of being named as the 'Mother of Democracy' (ii) "Bharat is the official name of the country. It is also mentioned in the Constitution as also in the discussion of 1946-48" and (iii) India has an *unbroken* democratic tradition going back to 6,000 BCE, and includes kings, emperors and also non-monarchical "sanghas" and "ganas" (like "Licchavi Republic") etc. The outright lies are the first two. That India is named as the "Mother of Democracy" is an invention of the current regime. The Constitution says "India, that is Bharat" – not the other way round – and the Constituent Assembly debated and settled that in 1946-48.

The misleading historical claim (popular in the right-wing ecosystem for a long time) in the third has been settled by historians and political scientists. Historian Upinder Singh[140] explains that in India's non-monarchical traditions "political power was circumscribed by widely accepted hierarchies of class, caste and gender" – "very different from modern Indian democracy". Political scientist Ashutosh Varshney[141] goes a step further to explain that "the Hindu-nationalist version of history differs radically from the accounts of professional historians" and seeks to undermine the credentials and significance of Nehru in establishing the *modern democratic India*. Indeed, the Prime Minister had said in the Parliament on February 7, 2018[142]: "I heard them saying that Nehru brought democracy in the country; Congress brought democracy in the country. Oh Kharge Saheb (leader of the Congress Party the Lok Sabha then, now party president), this is really embarrassing...democracy existed even when our country was ruled by the Lichchavi Empire, when there was Buddhism. *Democracy is in our veins and in our tradition*. And the history of Bihar is witness to this. If we look at the ancient history of Lichchavi Empire, there was a system of the Republic in our country *2500 years ago*." *(Emphasis added)*

The same mindset was at work when, in the second half of 2023, 'One-nation-One-Election' (ONOE)[143] idea was re-floated (it was part of the BJP's manifesto for 2014 election). The Prime Minister fanned two more communal agendas (and dog-whistles) – Uniform Civil Code (UCC) and 'Sanatan Dharma' (often used as a synonym of Hindu religion of late) – as he launched election campaigns for a third term. Soon, however, the focus shifted from the UCC to 'Sanatan Dharma' as he not only asked his ministers to engage the Opposition alliance INDIA over this[144] – following its criticism for perpetuating a rigid, discriminatory and exploitative caste system by Tamil Nadu's DMK minister Udainidhi Stalin who compared it to 'malaria' and 'dengue'[145]) he launched a direct attack, accusing the entire INDIA alliance of trying to crush 'Sanatan Dharma' and push back India into 1,000 years of slavery – and asked people to stop this.[146] Christophe Jaffrelot, French political scientist and Indologist traces the origin of the 'Sanatan Dharma' movement to 19th century traditionalist Hindus who formed "Sanatana Dharma Sabha" to *resist social reforms and defend caste system* being attempted by co-religionist 'Arya Samaj'.[147] The issue is likely to linger as the Supreme Court has agreed to hear a plea against Stalin.[148]

All this goes on even as the Prime Minister keeps inventing new slogans every now and then to keep his followers enthralled, perpetually flood public space with drivels to prevent any meaningful debate on any legitimate issue: "Achche Din" (good days) to "Amrit Kaal" (golden period; to make India a 'developed' country by 2047)[149] to "Kartavya Kaal"[150] (period of duty) to "1,000 years of grand future"[151].

Inversion of the Rule of Law

Sixth, collapse of the rule of law – the key bedrock of good governance, along with the other two of accountability and transparency.

The laws are now exclusively for the "others" and manifestly more stringent (like the anti-terror law, sedition and money laundering law) and of questionable legality. The central agencies and police have become manifestly more arbitrary and act as tools of the ruling establishment, rather than custodians of law. Specific laws have been framed to target Muslims – from citizenship (Citizenship Amendment Act of 2019) to food (ban on beef and cattle/cow slaughter) to livelihood (ban on cattle trade, ban on Muslim vendors in Hindu areas, 'land jihad' etc.), marriage (anti-conversion and 'love jihad' (inter-faith marriages targeting Muslim men). In the meanwhile, right-wing mobs and the ruling party members, including those with criminal antecedents and facing serious corruption and other cases but defected to the BJP, are immune from the law.

The Parliament has watched helplessly as a mute spectator. The Supreme Court – the other most powerful constitutional authority – has even assisted in the abuse of law by punishing the justice seekers, rights activist Teesta Setalvad, former Gujarat IPS officers RB Sreekumar and Sanjiv Bhatt and rights activist Himanshu Kumar, by *honouring the government's demands for* such punishment to justice seekers to the court (both the orders were given by two benches led by Justice AM Khanwilkar (Chapters I, II and III).

With the weakening of law and justice system, a new brand of instant retribution (in the name of justice) has also come into being – called "bulldozer justice" which typically targets Muslims.[152] It started from the BJP-ruled Uttar Pradesh in 2020 and spread to other BJP-ruled states of Madhya Pradesh, Gujarat, Assam and even the municipalities under the BJP in the Aam Admi

Party-ruled NCT of Delhi until 2022. Bulldozers are now part of the BJP's election campaign.[153] No less than the Prime Minister himself showcased the bulldozer (JCB machines) when UK premier Boris Johnson visited India in 2022 – amidst bulldozing of shops of Muslims in Delhi's Jahangirpuri.[154] Why do Hindus take their religious processions to Muslim areas and masjids – where they indulge in violent activities – is known well and yet, those are allowed at regular intervals even (shockingly and because of the Muslim hate has been mainstreamed) in non-BJP ruled states like Rajasthan, Bihar, Bengal and Odisha.[155]

Effectively, India is witnessing a classic *mob rule*[156] with numerous right-wing vigilante/militant groups running wild on streets – from forcing Muslims to chant "Jai Shri Ram", the Hindu battle cry associated with riots and lynching, to establish Hindu supremacism, to public lynching in the name of cow protection – with impunity. Many BJP-ruled states like Gujarat, Haryana, Maharashtra, Uttarakhand give official identifications to and work with "gau rakshaks" (cow protectors)[157] – nothing less than a license for mob rule. Calls for Muslim genocide by Hindu religious leaders is par for the course too – despite the Supreme Court repeatedly seeking strong and *suo motu* action from both the BJP-ruled Central and state governments. On one occasion the apex court even said, "This is a complete menace and nothing short of it...We should not end up creating a *Frankenstein* that will gobble (us) up"[158] and at another time: "Is the state impotent? Can't it take timely action against hate speech mongers? If it can't take, why do we have a state at all?"[159] Such observations have had no impact at all. In fact, ethnic cleansing is in progress in many BJP-ruled states, particularly in Manipur (targeting Christian Kukis), Uttarakhand and Haryana (Muslims), and is likely to spread as the 2024 general elections close in. (Chapters III and IV)

Institutional Breakdowns

Seventh, complete institutional breakdown. There are three aspects to this breakdown: *One,* filling key institutions, including constitutional offices, with pliable individuals (Chapter I); *two,* filling these offices with Hindutva ideologues or those driven by this ideology (Chapters VII and XI) and *three, misuse* of official machinery by directing all Central government services to "showcase" and "celebrate" the government's "achievements" during state elections of November 2023 and in the run-up to the general elections of April-May 2024 (Chapter V). The Army has already jumped into the government's bandwagon by directing all soldiers to do "social service" to enhance "nation-building efforts" by talking to people during their annual vacations and giving feedbacks on these efforts (Chapter XI). All this reflect contempt for professional ethics, political neutrality and service rules. Together with the subservient judiciary and media, silenced civil society and a "loyal" middle-class, it has become quite easy for the government to *break* the very core of democracy and democratic governance.

Hate, Violence and Mass Radicalization of Hindu Youth

Eighth, relentless politics of hate-and-violence.

This may be good for the BJP, and hence, the growing normalization of it in politics, law enforcement and judiciary but this has dangerous consequences for Hindus too. Hate and bigotry is seeping deeper and deeper into the society, tearing it apart and dehumanizing the Hindu population – with teachers remorselessly attacking (one woman teacher in Uttar Pradesh's Muzaffarnagar lined up her Hindu students to slap a seven-year-old Muslim student[160] and yet, the apex court had to direct the BJP government to act[161]; another woman teacher in Karnataka's Shivamogga asked two class V Muslim students to go to Pakistan and was transferred by the Congress government immediately[162]); educated professionals in gated communities displaying unheard of animosity towards fellow citizens[163]; cops remorselessly torturing and killing Muslim youths[164]; armed force personnel asking Muslim devotees to chant "Jai Sri Ram"[165] and Hindu youths are getting more and more radicalized[166]. Unemployed Hindu youths are particularly vulnerable to the malaise. Instead of focusing on good education, skilling and employment, a large segment has turned to religious processions to attack Muslims and join the ranks of cow vigilantes in Haryana and Maharashtra[167]. The same amount of hate and bigotry may not be on display against Christians, Dalits and women yet, but that can't be far off.

Having delivered on two of the three "core" and anti-Muslim agenda of the BJP (which his BJP predecessor Vajpayee had to keep aside because he was heading a coalition government) – (a) building a Ram temple at the site of Babri Masjid and (b) abrogation of Article 370 – the Prime Minister brought the third one into political play ahead of the 2024 general election: (c) Uniform Civil Code (UCC).

Exactly four days after he dismissed discrimination against Muslims in the White House, the Prime Minister spoke on the need for UCC[168] *without* a concept note or draft proposal in hand and *without* explaining what exactly he intended to do. Is this about reforms in personal laws, gender justice, uniform application of the rule of law or equality before law or religious freedom? He didn't say but launched a *gratuitous attack* against rival parties in the same breath by accusing them of being pro-Muslim and playing vote bank politics. He also told Muslims how he had *empowered* their women by bringing the 'triple talaq' (instant divorce) law in 2017.

The last bit ('triple talaq') is quite ironical since it criminalized (cognizable and non-bailable) a civil matter (divorce) in 2019.[169] The Supreme Court did declare it unconstitutional in 2017 but didn't make it a criminal offence[170] and *inappropriate* divorce remains a civil offence for all non-Muslims. The legality of this criminalization is still pending before the Supreme Court.[171] It was such communal colours to the UCC debate that the Constituent Assembly, and thereafter, desisted from codifying the UCC and kept it in the Directive Principle (non-justiciable).[172]

Gaming Elections

Nineth, the last hope for Indian democracy has also been seriously compromised with a clear and demonstratable threat to fair play in conducting elections, credibility of the Election Commission of India (ECI) and a growing disconnect between actual performance of the BJP governments and their electoral performance (Chapter X).

Besides, elections have lost their sanctity and the very democracy is threatened with most Opposition leaders facing criminal cases filed by the central agencies like the CBI, ED and ITD and busy fighting court cases and/or undergoing prison terms and their parties financially weakened by the seizure of cash at election time; the BJP's "Operation Lotus" engineering defections and pulling down their governments with or without the help from Governors and the BJP's promise to make India "Congress-mukt" (free of the Congress, the only rival pan-India party) – while the ECI and courts watch silently.

Nonetheless, the Prime Minister keeps telling the world that "democracy is in our DNA", India is the "Mother of Democracy" and a "model of diversity"[173]. The Indian government sold the G20 (rotational) presidentship for an entire year of 2023 as an attempt to build "One Earth, One Family, One Future" and "Vasudhaiva Kutumbakam" (world is one family)[174]. The Prime Minister invited the G20 leaders to come to India to watch the "festival of democracy in the mother of democracy"[175] – but at the same time, even the basic courtesy of inviting Opposition leaders to the dinner for G20 delegates hosted by the President of India was not maintained.[176] His National Security Advisor (NSA) Ajit Doval[177] and his appointee Vice Chancellor of JNU Santishree Dhulipudi Pandit[178] go further to describe India as "Civilizational State" – not a mere democracy. Amitabh Kant, former CEO of government think tank NITI Aayog, even lamented that India has "too much democracy".[179]

Once, talking about the Prime Minister's promise to deliver Rs 15-20 lakh to each Indian by bringing back black money stashed abroad, Union Home Minister Amit Shah (then BJP president) dismissed it as a mere political "jumla" (rhetoric or a slogan) in 2015.[180] But the above examples are not mere political rhetoric or slogans. They can't even be called double-speak or hypocrisy or deception – but something beyond. *They reflect amorality of a different dimension altogether.*

A few questions arise. Why is India witnessing such deep moral and political degradation after 75 years of constitutional democracy? By now Indians should have progressed. Why have they regressed in virtually every aspect?

These are serious questions which need studies and introspection. For a start, here is another defining marker of post-2014 India that needs deeper engagement and understanding.

Hindutva and Governance

Tenth, India is witnessing a new form of governance informed and driven by the ideology 'Hindutva'. To understand this, the BJP's ideological fountainhead, the Rashtriya Swayamsevak Sangh (RSS), and the Hindutva ideology it promotes need to be understood.

The RSS is perhaps the world's largest 'voluntary' organization but it has "no formal membership", it talks of "Hindu, Hindu Rashtra, Hindu Culture".[181] Its website[182] doesn't reveal whether it is a trust, a society or a registered entity. It has numerous affiliated and associated groups, which are active in social, cultural, educational, labour, developmental, political areas and some of which are militant, trained in using weapons; together they are popularly known as "Sangh Parivar".[183] Its ideology is called "Hindutva", which is a political construct, of which Hindu religion is "only a derivative, a fraction, a part" – its very proponent Vinayak Damodar Savarkar wrote so in his eponymous book[184]. Its self-proclaimed goal is "national reconstruction" – a shortcut for homogeneity or imposition of "Hindu culture" and "Hindu Rashtra" – an exclusionary concept in which Muslims and Christians must adopt Hindu way of life and accept to live as second-class citizens. RSS chief Mohan Bhagat keeps insisting that India already is a "Hindu Rashtra".[185] Before joining the BJP – the RSS's political wing – the Prime Minister was a fulltime RSS 'pracharak' (preacher).[186] The BJP came into being in 1980 but as earlier stated, it had a forerunner from 1951-77 – the BJS, which was part of the short-lived Janata Party government (1977-80) after the Emergency ended. The BJP claims, seemingly rightly, that it is the world's largest political party – with over 100 million members way back in 2015.[187]

Ambedkar had clearly seen the dangers from both Hindutva and Hinduism's rigid, discriminatory and exploitative caste system long ago. He warned in his 1946 book "Pakistan or the Partition of India"[188]: "If Hindu Raj does become a fact, it will, no doubt, be the *greatest calamity for this country.* No matter what the Hindus say, Hinduism is a *menace to liberty, equality and fraternity.* On that count it is incompatible with democracy. Hindu Raj must be prevented at any cost." *(Emphasis added)*

Ambedkar had also called out the RSS's "nationalism". In a memorandum to the Constituent Assembly in 1947, he wrote[189]: "Unfortunately for the minorities in India, *Indian nationalism* has developed a new doctrine which may be called the *Divine Right of the Majority to rule* the minorities according to the wishes of the majority. Any claim for the sharing of power by the minority is called communalism, while the *monopolising of the whole power by the majority is called nationalism*. Guided by such political philosophy *the majority is not prepared to allow the minorities to share political power, nor is it willing to respect any convention made in that behalf ...*" *(Emphasis added)*

The RSS's views on the Constitution of India open and well known.

Noorani wrote[190]: "The Rashtriya Swayamsevak Sangh, whose political wing, the Bharatiya Janata Party, is in power at the centre and in many states, never made any secret of its rejection of the constitution of India. Beneath this rejection lies its more openly avowed rejection of India's democratic governance and its national ethos." It is also well documented that the RSS wanted a constitution based on 'Manusmriti' – an ancient Hindu code. Historian Ramchandra Guha[191] recorded how days after the Constituent was adopted in 1949, RSS mouthpiece Organiser wrote in its editorial: "The worst (thing) about the new Constitution of Bharat is that there is nothing Bharatiya about it... (T)here is no trace of ancient Bharatiya constitutional laws, institutions, nomenclature and phraseology in it." It complained about "no mention of the unique constitutional developments in ancient Bharat".

The 'Manusmriti' or the Laws of Manu is known for its orthodoxy, particularly its caste and gender discriminations and meant for a time when kings and queens ruled India. Commenting on it, former Supreme Court judge PB Sawant wrote[192]: "The inherently inhuman, iniquitous and unjust ancient texts like Manusmriti are an anathema to the aims and objectives of our constitution. Dr Ambedkar (chief architect of the Constitution) burnt the MS (Manusmriti) in 1927..." On his part, Ambedkar was scathing in his criticism of Manusmriti and wrote: "At the *root* of the Hindu Social System lies Dharma as prescribed in 'Manusmriti'. Such being the case I do not think it possible to abolish inequality in the Hindu Society *unless the existing foundation of the 'Smriti' religion is removed and a better one laid in its place*. I, however, *despair of the Hindu Society* being able to reconstruct on such a better foundation."[193] *(Emphasis added)*

The RSS didn't even hoist the national tricolour for 52 years at its headquarters in Nagpur on the pretext (which isn't correct) that government regulations didn't allow this, it being a private organization.[194] It did so in 2002, after BJP's Vajpayee had become the Prime Minister for the third time (he headed a 13-day government in 1996, a 13-month government in 1998-99 and then a full-term government in 1999-2004). This came a year after three local activists of Rashtrapremi Yuwa Dal forcibly hoisted the tricolour in the Nagpur premise. These youths were set free in 2013 (of trespassing and other charges)[195].

Political scientist Peter Ronald deSouza explains why the Modi governments' governance failure is *intrinsic* to the Hindutva ideology.[196] He argues, Hindutva is "intrinsically handicapped in running a modern state" as it seeks to redefine the Indian state on the idea of majoritarianism (Hindu Rashtra) through "a politics of othering" ("cultural nationalism"). In the RSS 'shakhas' (daily training camps), where the RSS-BJP cadres have grown up, they have "neither been taught to think about what a modern state requires, nor do they have the imagination". Thus, he explains, when their lack of skills, incompetence and ineptitude are exposed, they unleash the shenanigans now manifest all around in India – demonization of critics and truth tellers as "anti-nationals", weakening of autonomous institutions, propaganda and reliance on pseudo-scientific medicines (more pronounced during the pandemic crisis) etc.

Jaffrelot calls India "de facto majoritarian Hindu Rashtra", "transiting to an "authoritarian Hindu Raj (Hindu nation-state)" in his 2021 book "Modi's India: Hindu Nationalism and the Rise of Ethnic Democracy".[197] He likens the current India to an Israel-type "ethnic democracy" and gives two key reasons for his pessimism about India's immediate future (that is, "electoral defeat of the BJP may not make much of a difference, or, to be more precise, while it is a necessary condition, it may not be sufficient one"): (i) the Sangh Parivar "is so deeply entrenched in the social fabric that it may continue to dictate its terms to the State on the ground – and to rule in the street" and (ii) "the 'deep state' may remain in a position to influence policies and politics even if the BJP is voted out. By "deep state" he means key democratic institution "appear to have become partly dominated by people who don't fully observe constitutional values but share, at least, in part, the worldview of the Sangh Parivar – and in some cases are even connected to them".

Lawyer and author Arvind Narrain says (in his 2022 book "India's Undeclared Emergency")[198] India is "inching towards totalitarianism" – *beyond* the authoritarianism of the Emergency of 1975-77. He flags the rise of "a new kind of State" in which a new "legal framework" was emerging which attempts to make Hindutva ideology "as a part of Indian law" – like the Centre's CAA and stringent anti-cow slaughter, anti-conversion and 'love jihad' laws in the BJP-ruled states. He lists six factors to argue why the current regime goes beyond the Emergency: (i) a clear thread unifying his government's actions to the Hindutva (ii) support of the vast civil society network of the RSS (iii) genuine popularity of the government among the people (iv) supplementary support of the power of the mob (v) brazen attempt to make Hindutva ideology a part of Indian law and (vi) its "naked pro-corporate agenda" with far-reaching changes in the social, economic and political life, which marginalize the concerns of labour, environment and public health.

Narrain distinguishes authoritarian and totalitarian regimes thus: An authoritarian regime is founded on individual leader's cult, which may eventually flounder but not of a totalitarian one which is based on "its popular support with an ideological objective". He argues, the latter, a totalitarian regime, wouldn't collapse so easily.

Similar views have been expressed by others with direct experience of the Emergency. Former IAS officer MG Devasahayam[199] writes: "While the Emergency was brutal and sudden, Modi govt's moves are far more insidious and systemic and will undermine our society for a long time". Nandana and Konarak Reddy write[200]: "A new population of thugs, cutting across all class barriers, infused with the saffron hue, have sprung up in the past few years…" That Indian democracy was always imperfect and the roots of the assaults on liberty and institutions are deep-rooted and historical, is also known and most recently highlighted by Debasish Roy Chowdhury and John Keane in their 2021 book "To Kill a Democracy: India's Passage to Despotism"[201]. However, all those roots (or fissures) have now been laid bare in all their ugliness like never before.

Yet, the question that begs an answer is: Wasn't the regressive turn India has taken expected? After all, Modi's Gujarat record is very well known and exposed repeatedly by investigating journalists Ashish Khetan[202], Rana Ayyub[203], Manoj Mitta[204] and Siddharth Varadarajan[205], apart from Jaffrelot, and also the Supreme Court's various pronouncements on the Gujarat pogrom and its aftermath. The answer is both yes and no.

No, because some of India's brightest minds helped Indians buy the "myths" about him, shielding him from detractors and doomsayers – by pleading for his development credentials in Gujarat, holding that the BJP wasn't a fascist party and that the Prime Minister's office would turn him into a moderate (making him more of a Vajpayee) – only to join the ranks of those they pilloried.[206] The Gujarat model of development turned out to be misleading and a clever marketing exercise[207] and the office of the Prime Minister didn't dim his divisive politics.

Only Jaffrelot[208] was accurate in predicting that Prime Minister Modi would turn to Hindutva if he failed to deliver development and growth. Modi didn't have to wait till he actually crashed the economy through a series of mindless actions (pre-pandemic FY17-FY20) which then collapsed due a large part to gross mismanagement of the pandemic (pandemic FY21).[209] Attack on Muslims had begun right away – leading to the "award wapsi"[210] (return of government awards) in 2015. About 40 leading writers returned their awards to protest against the "climate of intolerance" – the immediate provocations for which were mob lynching of a Muslim man (killed outside Delhi for suspected beef eating) and murder of scholar and rationalist MM Kalburgi (allegedly by right-wing activists). Eight years later, in 2023, a parliamentary panel described the returning of awards as "inappropriate", suggesting that "no award" be given in future without undertaking that they "can't dishonour" the awards "at any point of time in future"[211] – a report which willfully misunderstands[212] the protest against the politics and hate and violence, choice and conscience of writers.

A far more disastrous future awaits India if the government wins a third mandate in 2024 with absolute majority. Journalist Aakar Patel[213] has repeatedly warned that the "end-state" of Hindutva is "not concerned with either nation or Hindus as such, it is occupied by what can be done to minorities". He pointed out that this is in sharp contrast to the goals of Marxists to see the state wither away, in South Asia to align mankind to modernity through the state and in Europe the welfare state.

The bigger threat of Hindutva is to the Constitution of India itself – 'the idea of India' it embodies.

The Constitution already stands undermined in many ways by both *de jure* and *de facto* attacks on it as a dysfunctional Parliament, executive Supreme Court, ineffective Opposition, institutional breakdowns, compromised media and slavish citizens watch on the side. The demand to amend the Constitution is routinely made by the BJP leaders; the last salvo coming from Bibek Debroy, the Prime Minister's chief economic advisor (EAC-PM). Debroy argued for wholesale changes, stating that "amendments will not do if we need to go back to the drawing board and start from first principles"[214]. This was later dismissed as his personal view, not that of the EAC-PM[215]. Congress's P Chidambaram points to the writings on the wall: The BJP is waiting for a two-third majority in the Rajya Sabha (which eludes it so far) to do this.[216]

It isn't clear yet if disaffection with the BJP government has been reached an inflection point or not but surely it is high time it does – if the 'idea of India' has to survive.

Caveats

Five caveats are in order. One, this book records many 'transformative' changes in the post-2014 India, which in itself assumes significance due to the *de facto* and *de jure* censorship/deletion of information. Two, the narrative overlaps because strict compartmentalization of the changes is tough in the face of *360-degree attack on the 'idea of India', 24x7, 365 days a year*. Some critical facts are repeated to give the big picture and ensure that those are not lost sight of. Three, the book doesn't claim to be balanced or neutral. The assumption is simple: Neither is a virtue in the post-2014 India because (a) there can be no balancing between the harsh ground realities and the incessant carpet bombing of alt-truths and propaganda (window dressing of data and a deluge of unsubstantiated claims which will easily fill several books of this size) and (b) the changes are so manifestly regressive and unjust that neutrality would translate into complicity, rather than fairness or accuracy. This assumption, however, has not been used as a ruse to hide facts or deny legitimate claims, rather the attempt is to give a *reality check*. Four, although the book focuses on the decade of Modi government, there are plenty of historical perspectives and comparative analysis – within the obvious limitation of the fact that studies on governance in India are relatively scarce. Five, no claim is made of raising all the right questions or answering them; the endeavour is to draw attention to the existential crisis India is facing and provide food for thought.

Structure of the Book

The book is divided into 12 chapters, each looking at different aspects of the changes that has happened. As the contents are already marked, a very brief outline of these chapters:

Chapter I is about inversion of the rule of law – selective application of law to the "others" (political rivals, Muslims and dissent etc.) and making laws more draconian and arbitrary. Chapters II and III are about the malfunctioning of key institutions of checks and balances – the first about the Parliament, media, citizens and civil society and the second about the Supreme Court. The next three chapters, Chapters IV, V and VI, focus on three Big Bang rhetoric of 'good governance' – 'Sabka saath, sabka vikas', 'minimum government, maximum governance' and 'cooperative federalism', respectively. Chapter VII is about the Big Bang claims about economy – which actually is a command-and-control regime, driven by arbitrary fiats and private business interests. The next two chapters demonstrate the dark sides of this – adverse impacts on the people (Chapter VIII) and the environment (Chapter IX). Chapter X shows why India is about to lose its tag of "electoral autocracy" and turn into a full-fledged autocracy. Chapter XI seeks to understand and explain the most regressive and 'transformative' change – a large segment of citizens, particularly the educated, empowered and vocal middle-class, taking pride in their loyalty and devotion (hero-worship) to the Prime Minister, his government and their Hindu supremacy project. The final chapter, Chapter XII, flags the humongous challenges to the 'idea of India' and provides some food for thought.

***

References

1   Mohanty P, Rebooting Economy 57: When and how will industry take India to next level of growth? Jan 11, 2021; https://www.businesstoday.in/opinion/columns/story/indian-economy-when-and-how-will-industry-take-india-to-next-level-of-growth-284146-2021-01-11

2   Hoffer Eric, The True Believer: Thoughts on the Nature of Mass Movements, Chapter I, pages 3-11, January 2010, first published in 1951; Harper Perennial Modern Classics, https://www.amazon.com/True-Believer-Thoughts-Movements-Perennial/dp/0060505915

3   Good Governance Day, Dec 25, 2014, Department of Electronics and Information Technology (DeitY), Dec 25, 2014; https://www.dropbox.com/s/3kvk06xv8knjv5q/Good%20Governance%20day%202014_DeitY.pdf?dl=0

4   PM's message to the Nation on Good Governance, PMIndia, Dec 25, 2014; https://www.pmindia.gov.in/en/news_updates/pms-message-to-the-nation-on-good-governance/?tag_term=good-governance&comment=disable

5   26th November to be observed as 'Constitution Day', Ministry of Social Justice and Empowerment, Nov 23, 2015; https://pib.gov.in/newsite/PrintRelease.aspx?relid=131806

6   Creation of Jobs under 'Make in India' Campaign, Ministry of Commerce, Mar 18, 2015; https://pib.gov.in/newsite/PrintRelease.aspx?relid=117286

7   Mohanty P, 'An Unkept Promise'

8   Patel Aakar, 'Price of the Modi Years', pages 11-48, Vintage Books, June 2022; https://www.amazon.in/Price-Modi-Years-Aakar-Patel/dp/0670097020

9   Governance and Development, World Bank, 1992; https://documents1.worldbank.org/curated/en/604951468739447676/pdf/multi-page.pdf

10 Description/achievement of initiative, Sustainable Development Goal, UN, 2015; https://sustainabledevelopment.un.org/partnership/?p=1545

11 Good Governance & the Rule of Law, United States Council for International Business, Jan 2015; https://www.uscib.org/docs/Governance%20and%20the%20Rule%20of%20Law.pdf

12 Governance principles, institutional capacity and quality, UNDP, 2011; https://www.dropbox.com/s/i5xf789xufnbk5o/UNDP%208%20Governance%20principles.pdf?dl=0

13 Constitution of India; https://legislative.gov.in/sites/default/files/COI_1.pdf

14 Mohanty P, Ayodhya Verdict Part I: Ayodhya Verdict: Why it would worry us for years to come, Business Today, Nov 15, 2019; https://www.businesstoday.in/latest/economy-politics/story/ayodhya-verdict-supreme-court-ram-temple-why-it-would-worry-us-for-years-to-come-hindus-muslims-238872-2019-11-15; Ayodhya Verdict Part II: Does the evidence add up to ownership of the disputed

land to the Hindus?; https://www.businesstoday.in/latest/economy-politics/story/ayodhya-verdict-does-the-evidence-add-up-to-ownership-of-the-disputed-land-to-the-hindus-and-the-five-acre-land-to-muslims-238831-2019-11-16 & Ayodhya Verdict Part III: SC judgement raises more questions than it answers; https://www.businesstoday.in/latest/economy-politics/story/ayodhya-verdict-sc-supreme-court-judgement-raises-more-questions-than-answers-babri-masjid-ram-janmabhoomi-title-dispute-238811-2019-11-17

15 Sardesai Rajdeep, The Election That Changed India, 2014; https://pdfcoffee.com/2014-the-election-that-changed-indiapdf-pdf-free.html; Verniers Gilles, How the Muzaffarnagar polarisation strategy paid off for the BJP (and why it's being used again), Aug 22, 2014; https://scroll.in/article/675473/how-the-muzaffarnagar-polarisation-strategy-paid-off-for-the-bjp-and-why-its-being-used-again; The BJP in Power: Indian Democracy and Religious Nationalism, edited by Milan Vaishnav, Carnegie Endowment for International Peace, 2019; https://carnegieendowment.org/files/BJP_In_Power_final.pdf; Sardesai Rajdeep,

16 Jha Dhirendra K 2023: RSS conclave revives communal ideals of MS Golwalkar's "We or Our Nationhood Defined", Mar 30, 2023; https://caravanmagazine.in/commentary/rss-conclave-golwalkar-we-or-nationhood-defined-communal-history; Jaffrelot Christophe 2021: Modi's India: Hindu Nationalism and the Rise of Ethnic Democracy, Princeton University Press, Aug 2021, https://www.amazon.in/Modis-India-Nationalism-Ethnic-Democracy/dp/0691206805

17 Rajnath Singh creates furore with his comments on word 'secular' in Constitution, Nov 27, 2015; https://economictimes.indiatimes.com/news/politics-and-nation/rajnath-singh-creates-furore-with-his-comments-on-word-secular-in-constitution/articleshow/49941446.cms?utm_source=contentofinterest&utm_medium=text&utm_campaign=cppst

18 Noorani AG, Constitution and secularism, Frontline, Jan 22, 2016; https://frontline.thehindu.com/the-nation/constitution-and-secularism/article8068322.ece

19 Pradhan Sharat, At Ayodhya Bhoomi Pujan, Modi Became All-in-One; Proper Rituals Not Followed, Allege Pundits, Aug 7, 2020; https://thewire.in/politics/ayodhya-bhoomi-pujan-narendra-modi-priests-pundits7

20 Work at Kashi Vishwanath Corridor catches pace, May 12, 2020; https://www.hindustantimes.com/lucknow/work-at-kashi-vishwanath-corridor-catches-pace/story-eA5YA6QXclewL6FiFW4A3J.html

21 Rajeshwari B, Communal Riots in India A Chronology (1947-2003), Institute of Peace and Conflict Studies Research Paper, Mar 2004; http://nagarikmancha.org/images/1242-Documents-Communal_Riots_in_India.pdf

22 Timeline: Ayodhya holy site crisis, Dec 6, 2012; https://www.bbc.com/news/world-south-asia-11436552

23 Nellis Gareth, Weaver Michael and Rosenzweig Steven C, Do Parties Matter for Ethnic Violence? Evidence From India, Quarterly Journal of Political Science 11(3), October 2016:249-277 (page 267-68) https://www.dropbox.

com/scl/fi/r9neobt5rdjl0dmlvaf1s/Gareth-et-al-2016_BJP-gains-from-riots. pdf?rlkey=4dlfe2ylezu0o916um7fvl2au&dl=0; Ticku Rohit, Riot Rewards? Religious Conflict and Electoral Outcomes, Graduate Institute of International and Development Studies Working Paper No. 19/2015, Jul 2016; https://www. dropbox.com/scl/fi/ttsnhcyhxyavts5patb2l/Rohit-Ticku-2015_riots-benefit-BJP. pdf?rlkey=lj5hvln8fsph8uzfjlq6rfe0w&dl=0

24 Brass Paul R, Development of an Institutionalised Riot System in Meerut City, 1961 to 1982 Economic and Political Weekly, Oct 30, 2004; https://www.paulbrass.com/ attachments/Epwarticle.pdf

25 Verniers Gilles, How the Muzaffarnagar polarisation strategy paid off for the BJP (and why it's being used again), Aug 22, 2014; https://scroll.in/article/675473/how-the-muzaffarnagar-polarisation-strategy-paid-off-for-the-bjp-and-why-its-being-used-again; The BJP in Power: Indian Democracy and Religious Nationalism, edited by Milan Vaishnav, Carnegie Endowment for International Peace, 2019; https:// carnegieendowment.org/files/BJP_In_Power_final.pdf; Sardesai Rajdeep, The Election That Changed India, 2014; https://pdfcoffee.com/2014-the-election-that-changed-indiapdf-pdf-free.html

26 Jaffrelot Christophe, Narendra Modi Between Hindutva and Subnationalism: The Gujarati Asmita of a Hindu Hriday Samrat, May 9, 2016; https://carnegieendowment. org/2016/05/09/narendra-modi-between-hindutva-and-subnationalism-gujarati-asmita-of-hindu-hriday-samrat-pub-66446

27 Vats Vaibhav, Violence Is the Engine of Modi's Politics, Aug 30, 2023; https:// www.theatlantic.com/international/archive/2023/08/narendra-modi-india-gurugram/675171/

28 'First Hindu Ruler in 800 Years': Parliament Storm Over Quote Cited by CPM Leader Mohd Salim, Dec 1, 2015; https://www.ndtv.com/india-news/first-hindu-king-in-800-years-storm-over-quote-cited-by-mohd-salim-1249231

29 Mohanty P, An Unkept Promise: What Derailed the Indian Economy, Chapter I-IV, Sage Publications, Dec 2021; https://www.amazon.in/Unkept-Promise-Derailed-Indian-Economy/dp/9354791867

30 GDP growth (annual %) - India; https://data.worldbank.org/indicator/NY.GDP. MKTP.KD.ZG?locations=IN

31 Monetary Policy Statement, 2023-24 Resolution of the Monetary Policy Committee (MPC) August 8-10, 2023, RBI, Aug 10, 2023; https://www.rbi.org.in/Scripts/BS_ PressReleaseDisplay.aspx?prid=56173

32 National Food Security Act, Ministry of Consumer Affairs, Food & Public Distribution, Jul 2, 2019; https://pib.gov.in/PressReleasePage.aspx?PRID=1576667

33 Ministry of Consumer Affairs, Food & Public Distribution 2022: Free foodgrains to 81.35 crore beneficiaries under National Food Security Act: Cabinet Decision, Dec 23, 2022; https://pib.gov.in/PressReleaseDetailm.aspx?PRID=1886215

34 UN DESA Policy Brief No. 153: India overtakes China as the world's most populous

country, UN DESA, Apr 24, 2023; https://www.un.org/development/desa/dpad/publication/un-desa-policy-brief-no-153-india-overtakes-china-as-the-worlds-most-populous-country/

35   India's Commitment to Food Security: Ensuring Availability and Accessibility for All, Ministry of I&B, May 25, 2023; https://pib.gov.in/PressReleasePage.aspx?PRID=1927190

36   Due to stagnant income levels, 74% in India can't afford a healthy diet: UN agency report | Data, Sept 1, 2023; https://www.thehindu.com/data/as-food-prices-rise-74-in-india-cant-afford-a-healthy-diet-un-agency-report-data/article67256967.ece#:~:text=For%20instance%2C%20in%20India%2C%2074,lower%20than%20many%20comparable%20economies.

37   Kumar Ashwani, The Presidential Prime Minister Narendra Modi, Sept 18, 2017; https://theprint.in/opinion/presidential-prime-minister-narendra-modi/9535/

38   Chowdhury Neerja, How Prime Ministers Decide, page xxi-xxxiii, Aleph Book Company, Jul 2023; https://www.amazon.in/Prime-Ministers-Decide-Neerja-Chowdhury/dp/9390652456

39   Feb 26, 2019; https://www.aajtak.in/literature/poems/story/pm-narendra-modi-readout-prasoon-joshi-poem-main-desh-nahin-jhukane-dunga-644167-2019-02-26

40   Mohanty P, 'An Unkept Promise', Chapter VII-X

41   Frequently Asked Questions regarding Central government guarantee to back Security Receipts issued by National Asset Reconstruction Company Limited for acquiring of stressed loan assets, Ministry of Finance, Sept 16, 2021; https://pib.gov.in/PressReleseDetailm.aspx?PRID=1755466

42   Mohanty P, The flip-side of RBI's "compromise settlement" formula for stressed asset, Jun 13, 2023; https://www.fortuneindia.com/opinion/the-flip-side-of-rbis-compromise-settlement-formula-for-stressed-asset/113023

43   Mohanty P, National champions: Costs and benefits of India's new growth model, Mar 23, 2023; https://www.fortuneindia.com/opinion/national-champions-costs-and-benefits-of-indias-new-growth-model/112005

44   Unpacking deprivation bundles to reduce multidimensional poverty, UNDP-OPHI, Oct 17, 2022; https://hdr.undp.org/content/2022-global-multidimensional-poverty-index-mpi#/indicies/MPI; Unstacking global poverty: Data for high impact action, Jul 11, 2023; https://hdr.undp.org/system/files/documents/hdp-document/2023mpireportenpdf.pdf; Half of the world's poor live in just 5 countries, World Bank, 2019; https://blogs.worldbank.org/opendata/half-world-s-poor-live-just-5-countries#:~:text=The%205%20countries%20with%20the,Congo%2C%20Ethiopia%2C%20and%20Bangladesh.

45   FAO, IFAD, UNICEF, WFP and WHO, The State of Food Security and Nutrition in the World 2023. Urbanization, agrifood systems transformation and healthy diets across the rural–urban continuum. Rome, FAO. https://doi.org/10.4060/cc3017en; https://www.fao.org/3/cc3017en/cc3017en.pdf

46 UNESCO 2014: Teaching and learning: achieving quality for all; EFA global monitoring report, 2013-2014; https://unesdoc.unesco.org/ark:/48223/pf0000225660

47 Mathisen RB 2023: Economic Inequality and Political Power in Norway, University of Bergen, Mar 3, 2023,; https://bora.uib.no/bora-xmlui/bitstream/handle/11250/3050961/drthesis_2023_mathisen.pdf?sequence=2&isAllowed=ye

48 Ganguly Meenakshi 2019: Dissent Is 'Anti-National' in Modi's India, Human Rights Watch, Dec 13, 2019; https://www.hrw.org/news/2019/12/13/dissent-anti-national-modis-india

49 100 FIRs, 6 arrested for pasting posters against PM Narendra Modi across Delhi, Mar 22, 2023; https://economictimes.indiatimes.com/news/india/100-firs-6-arrested-for-pasting-posters-against-pm-narendra-modi-across-delhi/articleshow/98894791.cms?utm_source=contentofinterest&utm_medium=text&utm_campaign=cppst

50 Anti-Modi posters in Capital: 44 FIRs, 4 arrests, Mar 22, 2023; https://indianexpress.com/article/cities/delhi/anti-modi-posters-in-capital-44-firs-4-arrests-8511224/

51 Rao Parsa Venkateshwar Jr 2022: Is there a blurring of distinction between the prime minister and the union government? Leaflet, May 10, 2022; https://theleaflet.in/is-there-a-blurring-of-distinction-between-the-prime-minister-and-the-union-government/

52 Sheriff M Kaunain, Govt says sedition out, new section gets it in, with wider ambit, Aug 12, 2023; https://indianexpress.com/article/india/govt-says-sedition-out-new-section-gets-it-in-with-wider-ambit-8888628/; https://prsindia.org/files/bills_acts/bills_parliament/2023/Bharatiya_Nyaya_Sanhita,_2023.pdf

53 Sinha Chitranshul, Sedition law is not gone, it's set to be more draconian, Aug 12, 2023; https://indianexpress.com/article/opinion/sedition-law-is-not-gone-its-set-to-be-more-draconian-8889139/

54 Anand Utkarsh, You cannot call yourself 'Republic of India' in pleas: SC pulls up CBI, Oct 21, 2023; https://www.hindustantimes.com/india-news/you-cannot-call-yourself-republic-of-india-in-pleas-sc-pulls-up-cbi-101697823661572.html

55 People say can't betray Modi after eating his 'namak': PM, Feb 21, 2022; https://timesofindia.indiatimes.com/city/lucknow/people-say-cant-betray-modi-after-eating-his-namak-pm/articleshow/89712023.cms?utm_source=email&utm_medium=social&utm_campaign=TOIMobile

56 I'm your 'pradhan sewak': Modi tells nation, Aug 15, 2014; https://www.thehindu.com/news/national/I%E2%80%99m-your-%E2%80%98pradhan-sewak%E2%80%99-and-not-%E2%80%98pradhan-mantri%E2%80%99-Modi/article60343724.ece

57 Kumar Ravish, Remembering the legacy of India's first PM from Teen Murti Bhavan, 2014; https://www.youtube.com/watch?v=qzqwssQbMu8

58 CoWin, MoH&FW, https://dashboard.cowin.gov.in/

59 Dickie Gloria and Mehta Tanvi, Modi introduces imported cheetahs to India on his birthday, Sept 17, 2022; https://www.reuters.com/world/india/cheetahs-return-india-after-70-year-absence-2022-09-17/

60 Ninth Cheetah Dies in Kuno National Park, Aug 2, 2023; https://thewire.in/environment/ninth-cheetah-dies-in-kuno-national-park

61 PM Modi kicks off 'Rozgar Mela', says making every effort to deal global economic challenges, PTI, Oct 22, 2022; https://indianexpress.com/article/india/pm-modi-rozgar-mela-jobs-8225120/

62 Bhadoria Sharmila, Rozgar Mela: PM Modi distributes 51,000 appointment letters to paramilitary recruits; calls them Amrit Rakshak, Aug 28, 2023; https://www.livemint.com/news/india/rozgar-mela-pm-modi-congratulates-51-000-new-para-military-recruits-who-receive-appointment-letters-amrit-rakshak-11693199903650.html; Govt boosted employment in traditional as well as emerging sectors: PM Modi, PTI, Oct 28, 2023; https://indianexpress.com/article/india/rozgar-mela-employment-boost-pm-modi-9003467/

63 PM-Kisan payout delayed to time it with polls: Congress, Nov 16, 2023; https://timesofindia.indiatimes.com/india/pm-kisan-payout-delayed-to-time-it-with-polls-congress/articleshow/105245004.cms?from=mdr

64 23 Vande Bharat trains on tracks, but they fail to live up to the promise of speed, Jun 27, 2023; https://www.thehindu.com/news/national/pm-modi-flags-off-five-vande-bharat-trains-but-they-are-not-fast/article67014302.ece

65 National Zoological Park, New Delhi; https://nzpnewdelhi.gov.in/?ln=en

66 T.N. should elect over 25 NDA MPs as thanks for Sengol installation: Amit Shah, Jun 11, 2023; https://www.thehindu.com/news/national/tamil-nadu/tn-must-elect-more-than-25-nda-mps-in-2024-as-gratitude-for-installing-sengol-in-parliament-amit-shah/article66958025.ece

67 Jain Mitu, Fact-Check: The Sengol Was Never Labelled 'Walking Stick', Nor Kept in Anand Bhawan, May 19, 2023; https://thewire.in/politics/fact-check-the-sengol-was-never-labelled-walking-stick-nor-kept-in-anand-bhawan

68 PM Modi says stable government with decisive mandate reason for reforms, Sept 4, 2023; https://indianexpress.com/article/india/pm-modi-lok-sabha-stable-government-mandate-reforms-8922240/; Revdi culture dangerous, must end: PM Modi slams politics of freebies, Jul 17, 2022; https://indianexpress.com/article/cities/lucknow/revdi-culture-dangerous-must-end-pm-modi-slams-politics-of-freebies-8033948/

69 After denying rice to Karnataka, FCI struggles to find bidders in e-auction, Jul 10, 2023; https://www.business-standard.com/india-news/after-denying-rice-to-karnataka-fci-struggles-to-find-bidders-in-e-auction-123071000298_1.html

70 Anand Abhishek, Dimble Vikas and Subramanian Arvind 2020 and 2021: New Welfarism of Modi govt represents distinctive approach to redistribution and inclusion, Dec 22, 2020; https://indianexpress.com/article/opinion/columns/national-family-health-survey-new-welfarism-of-indias-right-7114104/ & New Welfarism and the Child in India: New Evidence from the NFHS, Jan 12, 2021; https://ceda.ashoka.edu.in/new-welfarism-and-the-child-in-india-new-evidence-from-the-nfhs/

71 Sardesai Rajdeep, How Modi Won India, Harper India, 2019; https://www.amazon.in/2019-How-Modi-Won-India/dp/9353573920

72 Mohanty P, The downsides of New Welfarism, Mar 17, 2022; https://www.fortuneindia.com/opinion/the-downsides-of-new-welfarism/107480 & Modi's 'Namak' and the Politics of Welfarism, Mar 14, 2022; https://www.cenfa.org/modis-namak-and-the-politics-of-welfarism/

73 Expenditure on social sector: Turning social safety nets into trampolines, Jun 18, 2023; https://www.business-standard.com/economy/news/story-in-numbers-turning-social-safety-nets-into-the-trampolines-123061800647_1.html

74 Global Slavery Index 2023, ILO, IOM and Walkfree, Jun 2023; https://cdn.walkfree.org/content/uploads/2023/05/17114737/Global-Slavery-Index-2023.pdf

75 Das Gupta Moushumi, Now, new concept to measure length of highways from April 1, Apr 3, 2018; https://www.hindustantimes.com/india-news/now-new-concept-to-measure-length-of-highways-from-april-1/story-Q44qGgFzl4DsAPv5OIG0YI.html

76 Development of national highways, Ministry of Road Transport and Highways, Lok Sabha, Mar 16, 2023; https://pqals.nic.in/annex/1711/AS238.pdf

77 Conversion of state highways into national highways, Ministry of Road Transport and Highways, Rajya Sabha, Dec 15, 2021; https://pqars.nic.in/annex/255/AU2001.pdf

78 Performance Audit on "Implementation of Phase-I of Bharatmala Pariyojana", CAG, Aug 10, 2023; https://cag.gov.in/en/audit-report/details/119177

79 Chidambaram Rebuts PM Modi On Citizens' Right Vs Duties, Urges PM To Read SC's NEET Order, Jan 22, 2022; https://www.republicworld.com/india-news/politics/chidambaram-rebuts-pm-modi-on-citizens-right-vs-duties-urges-pm-to-read-scs-neet-order-articleshow.html

80 India's 75-year journey from Rajpath to Kartavya Path, Sept 9, 2022; https://timesofindia.indiatimes.com/india/indias-75-year-journey-from-rajpath-to-kartavya-path/articleshow/94084000.cms

81 "Amrit Kaal has been named as Kartavya Kaal": PM Modi, Jul 4, 2023; https://economictimes.indiatimes.com/news/india/amrit-kaal-has-been-named-as-kartavya-kaal-pm-modi/articleshow/101478517.cms?utm_source=contentofinterest&utm_medium=text&utm_campaign=cppst

82 Sen Jahnavi and Mukunth Vasudevan, Narendra Modi Says Focus on Duties and Forget Rights, But He's Let India Down on All 11 Duties, Jan 21, 2022; https://thewire.in/government/narendra-modi-says-focus-on-duties-and-forget-rights-but-hes-let-india-down-on-all-11-duties

83 Why Modi's idea of linking rights to duties goes against the Constitution, Oct 14, 2021; https://scroll.in/article/1007654/why-modis-idea-of-linking-rights-to-duties-goes-against-the-constitution; hare Harish, Rights, Duties and the Ramblings of a Nervous Monarch Who Is Weakening India, Jan 25, 2022; https://thewire.in/politics/rights-duties-and-the-ramblings-of-a-nervous-monarch-who-is-weakening-india

84   Full Transcript of PTI's Exclusive Interview with Prime Minister Narendra Modi, PTI, Sept 3, 2023; https://www.ptinews.com/news/big-story/transcript-of-pti-s-exclusive-interview-with-prime-minister-narendra-modi/642493.html; Full text of PM Modi's exclusive interview, PMO, Apr 6, 2019; https://www.hindustantimes.com/india-news/full-text-of-pm-modi-s-exclusive-interview/story-7OqHvrn88TQhqfKutNqF5I.html; Narayan Sanjoy and Gupta Shishir, Full text of PM Narendra Modi's HT interview, Apr 9, 2015; https://www.hindustantimes.com/india/full-text-of-pm-narendra-modi-s-ht-interview/story-mgcimFKvFVOg6vsD1TSbbJ.html

85   PM Narendra Modi's interview with ANI's Smita Prakash, ANI, Feb 10, 2022; https://www.youtube.com/watch?v=1riWlkJc8GM; Upamanyu Kabir, Walia Shelly and Eswar, 'You Fast on Navratri?' Decoding ABP's 'Tough' Questions to Modi, Apr 7, 2019; https://www.thequint.com/opinion/prime-minister-narendra-modi-abp-interview-questions-asked#read-more; Sinha Pratik, PM Modi is asked to recite a recent poetry of his in the @NewsNationTV intvw, May 13, 2019; https://twitter.com/free_thinker/s/1127811843920031744?ref_d%7Ctwterm%5E11278118439200317 44%7Ctwgr%5E2cbd83409246c7ebd17565aae61c047b29ac74a0%7Ctwcon%5Es1_&r ef_url=https%3A%2F%2Fclarionindia.net%2Fcamera-catches-modi-holding-paper-with-questions-answers-during-tv-interview%2F

86   Akshay Kumar said that he interviewed PM Modi as a 'common man': 'Policy related questions would have looked fake', Jun 1, 2022; https://indianexpress.com/article/entertainment/bollywood/akshay-kumar-interview-pm-narendra-modi-common-man-looked-fake-7947011/

87   Judd Donald, White House says India rebuffed requests for more press access ahead of G20 summit, Sept 7, 2023; https://edition.cnn.com/2023/09/07/politics/india-press-access-g20/index.html; Bose Nandita, Biden, Modi discuss rail deal, democracy as U.S. press sidelined, Sept 9, 2023; https://www.reuters.com/world/biden-modi-yellen-meet-before-g20-press-may-be-barred-2023-09-08/

88   Anand Jatin, G20 India Summit: Over Rs 4,100 crore spent on Delhi for G20: where and by whom, Sept 7, 2023; https://indianexpress.com/article/cities/delhi/security-to-roads-lighting-to-signage-citys-expense-bills-for-g20-8928183/#:~:text=At%20 over%20Rs%204%2C000%20crore,as%20per%20the%20records%20of

89   Union Budget 2023: Rs 990 crore allocated for G20 presidency, Feb 2, 2023; https://indianexpress.com/article/business/budget/union-budget-2023-rs-990-crore-allocated-for-g20-presidency-8418567/

90   A Divya, Raised role of civil society, free press & human rights with Modi: Biden in Hanoi, Sept 11, 2023; https://indianexpress.com/article/india/raised-role-of-civil-society-free-press-human-rights-with-modi-biden-in-hanoi-8933886/#:~:text=%E2%80%9CAs%20I%20always%20do%2C%20I,lot%20of%20im-portant%20work%20done%E2%80%9D.s

91   G20 New Delhi Leaders' Declaration, New Delhi, India, 9-10 September 2023; https://www.g20.org/content/dam/gtwenty/gtwenty_new/document/G20-New-Delhi-Leaders-Declaration.pdf

92 PMO issues clarification over PM Modi's comments that no one entered Indian territory, Deccan Herald, May 5, 2022; https://www.deccanherald.com/national/north-and-central/pmo-issues-clarification-over-pm-modis-comments-that-no-one-entered-indian-territory-851761.html

93 Singh Vijaita 2020: China controls 1,000 sq. km of area in Ladakh, Sept 1, 2020; https://www.thehindu.com/news/national/china-controls-1000-sq-km-of-area-in-ladakh-say-intelligence-inputs/article32490453.ece

94 Mahaprashasta Ajoy Ashirwad, In Rajya Sabha Too, PM Modi Doesn't Answer Opposition's Questions About Adani, Feb 9, 2023; https://thewire.in/politics/rajya-sabha-pm-modi-speech-adani

95 Acrimonious Parliament monsoon session concludes early, Aug 9, 2022; https://www.hindustantimes.com/india-news/acrimonious-monsoon-session-concludes-early-101659982475268.html

96 Mathew Liz and CG Manoj, PM told me 'chup raho' on Pulwama, says ex-J&K Gov Malik; Cong calls for answers, Apr 16, 2023; https://indianexpress.com/article/political-pulse/pulwama-attack-satya-pal-malik-pm-modi-congress-8558039/; India, Pakistan came close to a nuclear war, claims former U.S. Secretary of State in new book, Jan 25, 2023; https://www.thehindu.com/news/national/india-pakistan-came-close-to-a-nuclear-war-claims-former-us-secretary-of-state-in-new-book/article66429650.ece

97 'Seven Years In Power, But BJP Is Still Blaming Nehru': Manmohan Singh Blasts PM Modi, PTI, Feb 17, 2022; https://www.outlookindia.com/national/punjab-election-2022-in-power-for-over-seven-years-bjp-is-still-blaming-jawaharlal-nehru-says-ex-pm-manmohan-singh-news-182809

98 Sanghvi Vir, Modi isn't Manmohan, it'll take more than a media frenzy to fire Brij Bhushan, May 4, 2023; https://theprint.in/opinion/sharp-edge/modi-isnt-manmohan-itll-take-more-than-a-media-frenzy-to-fire-brij-bhushan/1554200/

99 Ashraf Ajaz, Biren Singh is the Modi of 2002, Jul 24, 2023; https://www.mid-day.com/news/opinion/article/biren-singh-is-the-modi-of-2002-23299625

100 Sushant Singh, Manipur displays Modi's idea of India, Jun 4, 2023; https://caravanmagazine.in/commentary/manipur-violence-narendra-modi-idea-of-india

101 Patel Aakar, Why Modi Avoids Acknowledging Problems, Jul 24, 2023; https://m.rediff.com/news/column/aakar-patel-why-modi-avoids-acknowledging-problems/20230724.htm

102 Khaitan Tarunabh 2020: Killing a Constitution with a Thousand Cuts: Executive Aggrandizement and Party-state Fusion in India, Walter de Gruyter GmbH, Berlin/Boston, Law & Ethics of Human Rights, Aug 7, 2020; https://www.degruyter.com/document/doi/10.1515/lehr-2020-2009/html

103 Siddharth Arjun, Half truths and whole lies – ten times PM Modi misled the nation in 2017, Jan 10, 2018; https://www.altnews.in/half-truths-whole-lies-ten-times-pm-modi-misled-nation-2017/; Khechar Visoba, Why Does Narendra Modi Lie? Apr 28,

2019; https://thewire.in/politics/why-does-narendra-modi-lie; Pandey Samyak, Modi speech fact-check: From NRC to detention centres, here's where PM went wrong, Dec 23, 2019; https://theprint.in/india/modi-speech-fact-check-from-nrc-to-detention-centres-heres-where-pm-went-wrong/339690/

104 Remarks by President Biden and Prime Minister Modi of the Republic of India in Joint Press Conference, The White House, Jun 22, 2023; https://www.whitehouse.gov/briefing-room/speeches-remarks/2023/06/22/remarks-by-president-biden-and-prime-minister-modi-of-the-republic-of-india-in-joint-press-conference/

105 Joint press conference: David Cameron and Prime Minister Narendra Modi, Nov 12, 2015; https://www.gov.uk/government/speeches/joint-press-conference-david-cameron-and-prime-minister-narendra-modi

106 Address by Prime Minister, Shri Narendra Modi to the Joint Session of the US Congress, PMO, Jun 23, 2023; https://pib.gov.in/PressReleasePage.aspx?PRID=1934649

107 WSJ Reporter Who Asked PM Modi Question About Human Rights Faces Twitter Abuse, Jun 24, 2023; https://thewire.in/media/wsj-reporter-sabrina-siddique-modi-question-human-rights-targeted

108 Press Briefing by Press Secretary Karine Jean-Pierre and NSC Coordinator for Strategic Communications John Kirby, Jun 26, 2023; https://www.whitehouse.gov/briefing-room/press-briefings/2023/06/26/press-briefing-by-press-secretary-karine-jean-pierre-and-nsc-coordinator-for-strategic-communications-john-kirby-17/

109 Liptak Kevin, Obama warns democratic institutions are 'creaky' but Trump's indictment is proof rule of law still exists in US, Jun 23, 2023; https://edition.cnn.com/2023/06/22/politics/barack-obama-interview-cnntv/index.html

110 Obama answers the question: Why are you a Christian? Sept 29, 2010; https://www.reuters.com/article/us-religion-obama-christianity-idUKTRE68R5CU20100928

111 Assam chief minister's attack on Barack Obama shows how Islamophobia is dulling India's soul, Jun 24, 2023; https://scroll.in/article/1051503/assam-chief-ministers-attack-on-barack-obama-shows-how-islamophobia-is-dulling-indias-soul

112 India minister derides Barack Obama for raising religious rights: 'He bombed six Muslim countries', Jun 27, 2023; https://www.independent.co.uk/asia/india/obama-muslims-india-comment-nirmala-sitharaman-b2364236.html

113 Obama should think about how many Muslim countries he attacked: Rajnath Singh, Jun 26, 2023; https://www.indiatoday.in/india/story/obama-on-indian-muslim-how-many-muslim-countries-us-president-attacked-rajnath-singh-2398301-2023-06-26

114 Tu-taadi friends: Modi and Obama, Apr 25, 2019; https://www.telegraphindia.com/india/tu-taadi-friends-modi-and-obama/cid/1689381; Tu Aisa Kyu Karta Hai, Barack Obama Asked PM Modi On Sleeping For 4 Hours Only, ABP News; https://www.youtube.com/watch?v=FI5EakZmOrs

115 PM Modi to Hamid Ansari: You can now follow your basic ideology and instinct, Aug 11, 2017;

http://timesofindia.indiatimes.com/articleshow/60012154.cms?utm_source=contentofinterest&utm_medium=text&utm_campaign=cppst

116 Muslims asked to offer Bakrid namaz 40 km away from Badrinath, Jun 26, 2023; https://www.indiatoday.in/india/story/bakrid-muslims-namaz-40km-away-from-badrinath-uttarakhand-2399228-2023-06-28

117 Uttarakhand: Pushed 40km away, Purola Muslims offer Eid prayers near forest, Jun 30, 2023; https://timesofindia.indiatimes.com/city/dehradun/pushed-40km-away-purola-muslims-offer-eid-prayers-near-forest/articleshow/101377802.cms?from=mdr

118 Uttarkashi: How a 'journalist' and Hindutva groups manufactured the 'love jihad' angle, Jun 17, 2023; https://www.newslaundry.com/2023/06/17/uttarkashi-how-a-journalist-and-hindutva-groups-manufactured-the-love-jihad-angle

119 Maharashtra: Muslim Man Allegedly Lynched To Death By Cow Vigilantes, 6 Arrested, JUn 14, 2023; https://www.outlookindia.com/national/maharashtra-muslim-man-allegedly-lynched-to-death-by-cow-vigilantes-6-arrested-news-294661; 55-year-old lynched by cow vigilantes in Bihar, Jun 30, 2023; https://www.hindustantimes.com/india-news/55yearold-muslim-man-allegedly-lynched-by-cow-vigilantes-in-patna-20-detained-police-step-up-security-101688067157142.html; Halarnkar Samar, New India breaches new lows in race to the bottom, days after Modi's proclamations on democracy, Jul 3, 2023; https://scroll.in/article/1051926/new-india-breaches-new-lows-in-race-to-the-bottom-days-after-modis-proclamations-on-democracy

120 Two Gujarat schools apologise for celebrating Bakrid, Jun 30, 2023; https://www.deccanherald.com/national/west/two-gujarat-schools-apologise-for-celebrating-bakrid-1232614.html

121 "This is the moment, India-US govts have done the groundwork," PM Modi at USISPF, Jun 24, 2023; https://economictimes.indiatimes.com/news/india/this-is-the-moment-india-us-govts-have-done-the-groundwork-pm-modi-at-usispf/articleshow/101229083.cms?utm_source=contentofinterest&utm_medium=text&utm_campaign=cppst

122 IITs, IIMs and new Universities, Rajya Sabha answer, Jul 26, 2023; https://www.dropbox.com/scl/fi/3xvjqfcotzd438ady27qn/RS_2023_IITs-IIMs-Universities.pdf?rlkey=ysfbkwcda2mr7ep5xpjdxs6xc&dl=0

123 What is ailing new IITs? Infrastructure delays, staff shortages, fewer projects, says audit report, Jun 20, 2023; https://scroll.in/article/1051148/what-is-ailing-new-iits-infrastructure-delays-staff-shortages-fewer-projects-says-audit-report

124 Accreditation of Universities, Lok Sabha answer, Feb 13, 2023; https://www.dropbox.com/s/kn6kwd55u2zzjmp/LS_Feb%202023_Univ%20and%20colleges.pdf?dl=0

125 Fact check: Was there really only one university in Ahmedabad district before 2002, as Modi claims? Dec 18, 2022; https://scroll.in/article/1039877/fact-check-was-there-really-only-one-university-in-ahmedabad-district-before-2002-as-modi-claims

126 BJP Claims Centre Set Up 2 Colleges a Day Since 2014, But 74% are Pvt Colleges, Sept 11,

2021; https://www.factchecker.in/fact-check/bjp-claim-colleges-misleading-774330; Fact Check: Did UP have just 12 medical colleges till 2017, as Modi and Adityanath claim? Jul 21, 2021; https://scroll.in/article/1000651/fact-check-did-up-have-just-12-medical-colleges-till-2017-as-modi-and-adityanath-claim

127 Mohanty P, The wheels-within-wheels in central govt vacancies, Aug 4, 2022; https://www.fortuneindia.com/opinion/the-wheels-within-wheels-in-central-govt-vacancies/109199

128 Data | A third of Central University teaching positions lying vacant, Jul 23, 2023; https://www.thehindu.com/data/data-a-third-of-central-varsity-teaching-positions-lying-vacant/article67108773.ece

129 A direct assault on academic autonomy, editorial, Oct 23, 2019; https://www.telegraphindia.com/opinion/the-hrd-ministry-and-research-at-the-iits-a-direct-assault-on-academic-autonomy/cid/1713793; The Indian Institutes of Management (Amendment) Act of 2023, Aug 11, 2023; https://prsindia.org/files/bills_acts/acts_parliament/2023/Indian_Institutes_of_Management_(Amendment)_Act,_2023.pdf

130 TISS head to be picked by govt now, not Tata Trusts-led board, Jul 12, 2023; https://timesofindia.indiatimes.com/city/mumbai/tiss-head-to-be-picked-by-govt-now-not-tata-trusts-led-board/articleshow/101682549.cms?from=mdr

131 Saraswat R, Older IIMs kept in dark, Govt gets say in their affairs via new institutes, Aug 18, 2023; https://indianexpress.com/article/education/older-iims-kept-in-dark-govt-gets-say-in-their-affairs-via-the-new-8877281/

132 Chopra Ritika, Govt identifies three grounds to dissolve IIM Boards: From 'public interest' to 'persistent disobedience', Nov 11, 2023; https://indianexpress.com/article/india/public-interest-to-orders-ignored-govt-gets-power-to-dissolve-iim-boards-9022259/#:~:text=THE%20GROUNDS%20under%20which%20the,board%20to%20perform%20its%20duties.

133 "Why Not Use Nehru Surname?" In Parliament, PM's Latest Attack On Gandhis, Feb 9, 2023; https://www.ndtv.com/india-news/whats-the-shame-in-keeping-nehru-surname-pm-narendra-modi-asks-in-parliament-in-swipe-at-gandhis-3767403

134 A Diya, President of Bharat, Prime Minister of Bharat now official, Govt says India name change talk a rumour, Sept 6, 2023; https://indianexpress.com/article/political-pulse/g20-dinner-invite-president-of-bharat-india-8925337/

135 Singh Sushant, Unlikely Event: The G20 summit is not the crowning glory Modi hoped for, Aug 31, 2023; https://caravanmagazine.in/politics/g20-summit-not-crowning-glory-moment-modi-hoped

136 They hailed Digital India & Start-Up India, but now scared of INDIA: Opposition, Sept 6, 2023; http://timesofindia.indiatimes.com/articleshow/103408873.cms?from=mdr&utm_source=contentofinterest&utm_medium=text&utm_campaign=cppst

137 A Diya, President of Bharat, Prime Minister of Bharat now official, Govt says India name change talk a rumour, Sept 6, 2023; https://indianexpress.com/article/political-pulse/g20-dinner-invite-president-of-bharat-india-8925337/

138 Katju Vivek, India, Bharat and a host of implications, Sept 7, 2023; https://www.thehindu.com/opinion/lead/india-bharat-and-a-host-of-implications/article67278051.ece

139 Bharat the Mother of Democracy; https://ebook.g20.org/ebook/bharatmod/index.html

140 Upinder Singh: Why it may be wrong to ask whether India is the mother of democracy, Aug 20, 2023; https://www.theweek.in/theweek/cover/2023/08/12/indian-historian-upinder-singh-about-non-monarchial-traditions-in-ancient-india.html

141 Varshney Ashutosh, How India's Ruling Party Erodes Democracy, Johns Hopkins University Press, Nov 4, 2022; https://www.dropbox.com/scl/fi/4o21ite7fq39rty6q9pfm/Varshney-2022_How-India-s-Ruling-Party-Erodes-Democracy.pdf?rlkey=bazkjtcaoja314kholcznm5i4&dl=0; Varshney Ashutosh, Denying Nehru his due, Deb 14, 2018; https://indianexpress.com/article/opinion/columns/nehru-modi-gandhi-ambedkar-constitution-electoral-democracy-denying-his-due-5062844/

142 Prime Minister Narendra Modi: Reply on Motion of Thanks to the President's Address (07-02-2018); https://eparlib.nic.in/bitstream/123456789/809843/1/pms_16_14_07-02-2018.pdf

143 Suryawanshi Sudhir, Former President Kovind began 'one nation, one election' spade work in June, Sept 5, 2023; https://www.newindianexpress.com/nation/2023/sep/05/former-president-kovind-began-one-nation-one-election-spade-work-in-june-2611779.html#:~:text=New%20Indian%20Express-,Former%20President%20Kovind%20began%20'one%20nation%2C%20one%20election'%20spade,special%20Parliament%20session%20this%20month.

144 Counter Oppn's remarks on Sanatan Dharma, avoid joining India-Bharat debate: PM Modi tells ministers ahead of G20 summit, PTI, Sept 7, 2023; https://indianexpress.com/article/india/pm-modi-spells-out-dos-and-donts-for-ministers-during-g20-meet-8928250/#:~:text=Prime%20Minister%20Narendra%20Modi%20on,country's%20ancient%20name%2C%20sources%20said.

145 'Sanatana dharma is like malaria and dengue.' Udhayanidhi Stalin's remark sparks huge outcry, Sept 3, 2023; https://www.livemint.com/politics/news/sanatana-dharma-is-like-malaria-and-dengue-udhayanidhi-stalins-remark-sparks-huge-outcry-11693710506807.html

146 Mohan Anand and Naidu Jayprakash, Opposition wants to crush Sanatan, attack us across country, need to stop them: PM, Sept 14, 2023; https://indianexpress.com/article/political-pulse/pm-modi-madhya-pradesh-chhattisgarh-bjp-polls-8939487/

147 Christophe Jaffrelot writes: How Sanatan Dharma was used to defend caste, combat Hindu reform, Sept 27, 2023; https://indianexpress.com/article/opinion/columns/sanatan-dharma-sabha-caste-hierarchy-hindu-reform-dalits-purification-8957653/

148 Das Awstika, Sanatana Dharma Row | Supreme Court Issues Notice To Tamil Nadu Minister Udhayanidhi Stalin, Sept 22, 2023; https://www.livelaw.in/top-stories/supreme-court-udhayanidhi-stalin-sanatana-dharma-row-238418

149 Budget 2023-24 presents vision for Amrit Kaal, Ministry of Finance, Feb 1, 2023; https://pib.gov.in/PressReleaseIframePage.aspx?PRID=1895313; English rendering of PM's reply to the Motion of Thanks to President's address in Rajya Sabha, PMO, Feb 9, 2023; https://pib.gov.in/PressReleseDetailm.aspx?PRID=1897766

150 "Amrit Kaal has been named as Kartavya Kaal": PM Modi, Kul 4, 2023; https://economictimes.indiatimes.com/news/india/amrit-kaal-has-been-named-as-kartavya-kaal-pm-modi/articleshow/101478517.cms?utm_source=contentofinterest&utm_medium=text&utm_campaign=cppst

151 English rendering of Prime Minister, Shri Narendra Modi's address from the ramparts of Red Fort on the occasion of 77th Independence Day, PMO, Aug 15, 2023; https://pib.gov.in/PressReleasePage.aspx?PRID=1948808#:~:text=My%20dear%20family%20members%2C,the%20independence%20of%20the%20country.

152 Why 'Bulldozer baba' Yogi Adityanath keeps using the machine for law and order, Jun 17, 2022; https://theprint.in/opinion/why-bulldozer-baba-yogi-adityanath-keeps-using-the-machine-for-law-and-order/1000182/

153 Sahu Manish, Explained: Not just bulls, how bulldozers made it to election lexicon in UP, Mar 8, 2022; https://indianexpress.com/article/explained/explained-not-just-bulls-how-bulldozers-made-it-to-election-lexicon-in-up-7804167/

154 Outcry in India as Boris Johnson visits JCB plant amid demolitions row, Apr 21, 2022; https://www.theguardian.com/politics/2022/apr/21/boris-johnson-visits-jcb-plant-india-demolitions-row

155 Kumar Sharat, Karauli violence in Rajasthan sparked by planned attack, says FIR, Apr 6, 2022; https://www.indiatoday.in/india/story/karauli-violence-riots-planned-attack-says-injured-rajasthan-cop-1934062-2022-04-06; Post-Ram Navami, fresh violence hits Bihar, Bengal, Apr 3, 2023; http://timesofindia.indiatimes.com/articleshow/99195004.cms?from=mdr&utm_source=contentofinterest&utm_medium=text&utm_campaign=cppst; Fresh violence erupts in Odisha's Sambalpur during Hanuman Jayanti rally, several shops gutted, Apr 15, 2023; https://www.indiatoday.in/india/story/fresh-hanuman-jayanti-violence-erupts-in-odisha-sambalpur-several-shops-gutted-2360226-2023-04-14

156 Opinion: India has suffered greatly under mob rule. Now Trump has unleashed it, too. Jan 8, 2021: https://www.washingtonpost.com/opinions/2021/01/08/trump-capitol-mob-india-modi-political-violence/; Narendra Modi's Reckless Politics Brings Mob Rule to New Delhi, The Wire, Feb 27, 2020; https://thewire.in/communalism/narendra-modi-delhi-riots-mob-violence-bjp

157 Express View on Monu Manesar: The official vigilante, Sept 14, 2023; https://indianexpress.com/article/opinion/editorials/express-view-on-monu-manesar-the-official-vigilante-8938895/

158 Supreme Court calls hate speech 'complete menace', cautions Centre, states, Jan 14, 2023; https://www.hindustantimes.com/india-news/supreme-court-calls-hate-speech-complete-menace-cautions-centre-states-101673636542025.html

159 Is state impotent to take timely action against hate speech mongers, asks SC, Mar 23, 2023; http://timesofindia.indiatimes.com/articleshow/99101001.cms?utm_source=contentofinterest&utm_medium=text&utm_campaign=cppst

160 Gautam Aditi, "I'm Not Ashamed": UP Teacher Who Asked Students To Slap Muslim Classmate, Aug 27, 2023; https://www.ndtv.com/india-news/tripta-tyagi-muslim-student-slapped-up-school-muzaffarnagar-school-video-im-not-ashamed-up-teacher-who-asked-students-to-slap-muslim-classmate-4333022;

161 Slapping of Muzaffarnagar student: SC raises objections over probe, delay in filing FIR; IPS officer to monitor investigation, Sept 26, 2023; https://indianexpress.com/article/india/muzaffarnagar-school-student-slapping-supreme-court-probe-fir-8955152/

162 'Go to Pakistan', Karnataka teacher tells 2 Muslim students, transferred pending departmental inquiry, Sept 4, 2023; https://indianexpress.com/article/cities/bangalore/karnataka-teacher-pakistan-muslim-students-transferred-8922011/

163 Aafaq Zafar, Muslim residents aghast as Hindu neighbours in Noida call the police to stop Ramzan prayers, Apr 1, 2023; https://scroll.in/article/1046631/muslim-residents-aghast-as-hindu-neighbours-in-noida-call-the-police-to-stop-ramzan-prayers

164 Sarkar Alisha Rahman, Muslim passengers among four killed as police officer opens fire inside train in Mumbai, Aug 1, 2023; https://www.independent.co.uk/asia/india/chetan-kumar-rpf-video-railway-constable-shooting-b2385465.html; Roy Rohini, Record Statement of Muslim Man Beaten & Forced To Sing National Anthem: Delhi HC, May 9, 2023; https://www.thequint.com/news/law/northeast-delhi-riots-2020-muslim-man-delhi-police-national-anthem-court-latest-update#read-more

165 Major accused of forcing worshippers to chant 'Jai Shri Ram' at Pulwama mosque, Jun 26, 2023; https://www.telegraphindia.com/india/pulwama-major-accused-of-forcing-worshippers-at-mosque-to-chant-jai-shri-ram-in-kashmir/cid/1947613

166 Halarnkar Samar 2021: The mass radicalisation that India does not acknowledge, Jan 24, 2021; https://scroll.in/article/984915/the-mass-radicalisation-that-india-does-not-acknowledge; Key highlights from the CSDS-KAS Report 'Attitudes, anxieties and aspirations of India's youth: changing patterns' Apr 13, 2017; https://www.kas.de/documents/252038/253252/7_dokument_dok_pdf_48472_1.pdf/2fdad3d0-1a8c-fd74-919b-cf8d9f1761b6?version=1.0&t=1539649329619

167 Yadav Jyoti, Jobless Haryana men have a new mission in Muslim hate. 'They think cow protection is govt job', Aug 22, 2023; https://theprint.in/ground-reports/jobless-haryana-men-have-a-new-mission-in-muslim-hate-they-think-cow-protection-is-govt-job/1724436/; Shantha Sukanya, In Kolhapur, Students Are Transforming Into Communal Mobs: Fact-Finding Team, Sept 9, 2023; https://thewire.in/communalism/in-kolhapur-students-are-transforming-into-communal-mobs-fact-finding-team#:~:text=Several%20educational%20institutions%20across%20Kolhapur,question%20right%2Dwing%20Hindu%20groups.

168 Prime Minister Modi pushes Uniform Civil Code, accuses Opposition of instigating Muslims, Jun 28, 2023; https://indianexpress.com/article/india/prime-minister-

modi-pushes-uniform-civil-code-accuses-opposition-of-instigating-muslims-8689383/#:~:text=Addressing%20BJP%20booth%2Dlevel%20workers,not%20 caring%20for%20their%20welfare.

169 Ara Ismat, A Year Later, Are Instant Triple Talaq Culprits Actually Going to Jail? Oct 23, 2020; https://thewire.in/religion/a-year-later-are-instant-triple-talaq-culprits-actually-landing-in-jail

170 Mustafa Faizan, Why Criminalising Triple Talaq is Unnecessary Overkill, Dec 15, 2017; https://thewire.in/gender/why-criminalising-triple-talaq-is-unnecessary-overkill

171 Sebastian Sheryl, Supreme Court To Hear Batch Of Petitions Challenging Triple Talaq Law In November 2023, Apr 24, 2023; https://www.livelaw.in/supreme-court/supreme-court-triple-talaq-muslim-women-protection-of-rights-on-marriage-act-227052

172 Law Commission of India Consultation Paper on Reform of Family Law, Aug 31, 2018; https://archive.pib.gov.in/documents/rlink/2018/aug/p201883101.pdf

173 Modi Narendra, PM Narendra Modi writes: G20 will reach the last mile, leave no one behind, Sept 7, 2023; https://indianexpress.com/article/opinion/columns/pm-narendra-modi-writes-g20-will-reach-the-last-mile-leave-no-one-behind-8928023/#:~:text=and%20decision%2Dmaking.-,For%20India%2C%20 the%20G20%20Presidency%20is%20not%20merely%20a%20high,that%20is%20 associated%20with%20India.

174 Kapur Devesh, As the G20 summit nears, India is tearing itself apart, Sept 4, 2023; https://www.ft.com/content/dfda7308-475c-45a3-8abb-ef34087a8f57

175 PM Modi invites G20 delegates to witness 'festival of democracy' during 2024 Lok Sabha election, Jun 21, 2023; https://indianexpress.com/article/india/pm-modi-invites-g20-delegates-to-witness-festival-of-democracy-2024-lok-sabha-election-8677937/

176 Sharma Akhilesh, Mallikarjun Kharge Not Invited To G20 Dinner Hosted By President, Sept 8, 2023; https://www.ndtv.com/india-news/congress-chief-mallikarjun-kharge-not-invited-to-g20-dinner-to-be-hosted-by-president-on-saturday-confirms-his-office-4370128

177 A Diya, Ajit Doval: India is a civilisational state where languages, ethnicities and faiths coexist, May 23, 2022; https://indianexpress.com/article/india/ajit-doval-india-civilisational-state-languages-ethnicities-coexist-7932428/

178 Ranjan Prabhas, Opinion: Perils Of Pushing India As A Civilizational State, JUn 15, 2022; https://www.ndtv.com/opinion/perils-of-pushing-india-as-a-civilizational-state-3068738

179 Rattanani Jagdish, Too much democracy: What Niti Aayog chief Amitabh Kant's remarks reveal, Dec 23, 2020; https://www.deccanherald.com/opinion/main-article/too-much-democracy-what-niti-aayog-chief-amitabh-kant-s-remarks-reveal-930779.html

180 Modiji on Rs15L returning to bank accounts was just a political 'jumla': Amit Shah to ABP News, Feb 5, 2015; https://twitter.com/ABPNews/status/563264094820499457?lang=en; Amit Shah calls Modi bluff on black money, Feb 5, 2015; https://www.deccanherald.com/content/458045/amit-shah-calls-modi-bluff.html

181 Basic FAQ on RSS; https://www.rss.org//Encyc/2017/6/3/basic-faq-on-rss-eng.html

182 'Basic FAQ on RSS'

183 Andersen Walter, Damle Shridhar D, Messengers of Hindu Nationalism: How the RSS Reshaped India, C Hurst & Co Publishers, Apr 2019; https://www.amazon.in/Messengers-Hindu-Nationalism-Reshaped-India/dp/1787380254

184 Savarkar, Vinayak Damodar, Hindutva, page 19, Hindi Sahiya Sadan, 2020; https://www.amazon.in/Hindutva-Vinayak-Damodar-Savarkar/dp/9389982111

185 All Indians Are Hindus, India A "Hindu Rashtra": RSS Chief Mohan Bhagwat, PTI, Sept 1, 2023; https://www.ndtv.com/india-news/all-indians-are-hindus-india-a-hindu-rashtra-rss-chief-mohan-bhagwat-4347920; Hindu Rashtra" Concept Being Taken Seriously, But...: RSS Chief Explains, PTI, Oct 5, 2022; https://www.ndtv.com/india-news/hindu-rashtra-concept-being-taken-seriously-but-rss-chief-explains-3404907; Why Hindu Rashtra: K. S. Sudarshan, https://www.archivesofrss.org/why-hindu-rashtra.aspx

186 Jaffrelot Christophe, Modi's India: Hindu Nationalism and the Rise of Ethnic Democracy, Princeton University Press, Aug 2021, https://www.amazon.in/Modis-India-Nationalism-Ethnic-Democracy/dp/0691206805

187 Membership drive: BJP has 10.3 crore members, says party president Amit Shah, May 1, 2015; https://economictimes.indiatimes.com/news/politics-and-nation/membership-drive-bjp-has-10-3-crore-members-says-party-president-amit-shah/articleshow/47116676.cms?from=mdr

188 Ambedkar BR, Pakistan or the Partition of India, page 358, POD Only Publishing, 2020 edition (first published in 1946); https://www.amazon.in/Pakistan-Partition-India-B-R-Ambedkar/dp/8194415314

189 Ambedkar BR, Memorandum on the Safeguards for the Scheduled Castes submitted to the Constituent Assembly on behalf of the All India Scheduled Castes Federation, Mar 15, 3, 1947; https://drambedkar.co.in/wp-content/uploads/books/category2/11states-and-minorities.pdf

190 Noorani, AG, Is Constitution anti-Hindu' or the RSS anti-Indian? Sept 19, 2019; https://www.deccanchronicle.com/opinion/columnists/290919/is-constitution-anti-hindu-or-the-rss-anti-indian.html; Noorani AG, The RSS: A Menace to India, Left Word, New Delhi, 2019; https://www.amazon.in/RSS-G-Noorani/dp/8193466683

191 Guha Ramchandra, Which Ambedkar? RSS can change its mind about Ambedkar. But it needs a frank reckoning with why, how it got here, Apr 21, 2016; https://indianexpress.com/article/opinion/columns/br-ambedkar-2762688/

192 Sawant PB, The Manusmriti and a Divided Nation, The Wire, Nov 16, 2020; https://thewire.in/caste/manusmriti-history-discrimination-constitution

193 Dr Babasaheb Ambedkar: Writings and Speeches, Vol 17, page 236; https://www.marxists.org/archive/ambedkar/writings-and-speeches/Volume_17_01.pdf

194 Sinha Pratik, Did governmental regulations prevent RSS from hoisting national flag for 52 years? Jan 26, 2020; https://www.altnews.in/nationalists-fraudulently-quote-flag-code-excuse-rss-not-hoisting-national-flag-52-years/

195 Activists, who forcibly hoisted tri-colour at RSS premises, freed, Firstpost, Aug 14, 2013; https://www.firstpost.com/india/activists-who-forcibly-hoisted-tri-colour-at-rss-premises-freed-1032849.html

196 deSouza Peter Ronald, The Intrinsic Limits of Hindutva as an Ideology of the Indian State, July 2 issue, 2021; https://www.theindiaforum.in/sites/default/files/pdf/2021/07/02/the-intrinsic-limits-of-hindutva-as-an-ideology-of-the-indian-state.pdf

197 Jaffrelot Christophe, Modi's India: Hindu Nationalism and the Rise of Ethnic Democracy, Princeton University Press, Aug 2021, https://www.amazon.in/Modis-India-Nationalism-Ethnic-Democracy/dp/0691206805

198 Narrain Arvind, 'India's Undeclared Emergency'

199 Devasahayam MG, Modi govt's assault on democracy is more sinister than the Emergency. Look at the differences, Jun 25, 2022; https://theprint.in/opinion/modi-govts-assault-on-democracy-is-more-sinister-than-the-emergency-look-at-the-differences/1005825/

200 Reddy Nandana, Reddy Konark, Emergency then, Emergency now, Jun 28, 2023; https://www.deccanherald.com/opinion/panorama/emergency-then-emergency-now-1232188.html

201 Chowdhury Debasish Roy, Keane John, To Kill a Democracy: India's Passage to Despotism, Oxford University Press, June 2021; https://www.amazon.in/Kill-Democracy-Indias-Passage-Despotism/dp/0198848609

202 Khetan Ashish, Undercover: My Journey into the Darkness of Hindutva, Jan 2021; https://www.amazon.in/Undercover-Journey-into-Darkness-Hindutva/dp/9389152518

203 Ayyub Rana, Gujarat Files: Anatomy of a Cover Up, Mar 2016; https://www.amazon.in/Gujarat-Files-Anatomy-Cover-Up/dp/1943438889

204 Mitta Manoj, Modi and Godhra: The Fiction of Fact Finding, HarperCollins, 2014; https://www.amazon.in/Modi-Godhra-Fiction-Fact-Finding-ebook/dp/B00JJHGGBM

205 Varadarajan Siddharth, Gujarat: The Making Of A Tragedy, Sept 2002; https://www.amazon.in/Gujarat-Making-Tragedy-Siddharth-Varadarajan/dp/0143029010

206 Tripathi Salil, How some of India's brightest minds have bought into the Modi myth, May 11, 2014; https://caravanmagazine.in/vantage/minds-modi-myth; Donthi

Praveen, Political Affairs: The liberals who loved Modi, May 17, 2019; https://caravanmagazine.in/politics/the-liberals-who-loved-modi

207 Patel Aakar, Price of Modi Years, Westland Publications, 2021; https://www.amazon.in/Price-Modi-Years-Aakar-Patel/dp/9391234224

208 'Modi's Plan A will be economy. If that does not work, Hindutva', May 15, 2023; https://scroll.in/article/664475/modis-plan-a-will-be-economy-if-that-does-not-work-hindutva

209 Mohanty P, 'Unkept Promise'

210 Indian writers return awards in protest against 'climate of intolerance', Oct 14, 2015; https://www.theguardian.com/books/2015/oct/14/indian-writers-return-awards-in-protest-against-climate-of-intolerance

211 Parliamentary standing committee on transport, tourism and culture, Rajya Sabha, Jul 24, 2023; https://sansad.in/getFile/rsnew/Committee_site/Committee_File/ReportFile/20/173/351_2023_7_12.pdf?source=rajyasabha

212 Express View on 'award wapsi': Writer's choice, Jul 28, 2023; https://indianexpress.com/article/opinion/editorials/express-view-on-award-wapsi-writers-choice-8864143/s

213 Patel Aakar, How Does the Persecution of Indians Benefit India? Apr 3, 2023; https://thewire.in/communalism/how-does-the-persecution-of-indians-benefit-india

214 Debroy Bibek, There's a case for 'we the people' to embrace a new Constitution, Aug 14, 2023; https://www.livemint.com/opinion/online-views/theres-a-case-for-we-the-people-to-embrace-a-new-constitution-11692021963182.html

215 Bibek Debroy article for new Constitution: PM panel says not our view, Aug 18, 2023; https://indianexpress.com/article/india/bibek-debroy-article-for-new-constitution-pm-panel-says-not-our-view-8897462/

216 BJP will rewrite Constitution if it gets two-thirds majority in RS: Chidambaram, Jun 8, 2022; https://www.thehindu.com/news/national/tamil-nadu/bjp-will-rewrite-constitution-if-it-gets-two-thirds-majority-in-rs-chidambaram/article65505005.ece

Chapter I

When Rule of Law Became Rule by Law

"The rule of law" is the cornerstone of good governance – and of just political or social orders. The UN defines[1] it as "a principle of governance in which all persons, institutions and entities, public and private, including the State itself, are accountable to laws that are publicly promulgated, equally enforced and independently adjudicated, and which are consistent with international human rights norms and standards. It requires measures to ensure adherence to the principles of *supremacy of law, equality before the law, accountability to the law, fairness in the application of the law, separation of powers, participation in decision-making, legal certainty, avoidance of arbitrariness and procedural and legal transparency*". (*Emphasis added*)

Here is a far simpler way of knowing what it means and doesn't.

Former Chief Justice of India (CJI) Justice NV Ramana once explained[2] that a law can't be classified as law unless it imbibes within itself "the ideals of justice and equity". When law is used as a tool for political oppression and enforced unequally it becomes "the rule by law" – which came to public discourse to describe the way British colonial "masters" used law selectively against the Indian "subjects". That is, there were different sets of laws, one for the British "masters" and the other for their "subjects". Thus, the law can be used for delivering justice as well as denying it. Once India gained independence and adopted the Constitution, its citizens ceased to be "subjects" and became "sovereign". Chief architect of the Constitution BR Ambedkar removed all doubts about this when he told the Constituent Assembly in 1948[3] "beyond doubt it (sovereignty) vests with the people". Besides, the Constitution promises equality before law and equal protection of law "within the territory of India" to "any person" (Article 14) and expressly prohibits discrimination "against any citizen on grounds only of religion, race, caste, sex, place of birth or any of them" (Article 15).

There is no gainsaying that India always upheld the rule of law before

2014; the Emergency of 1975-77 is a stark reminder that it didn't, but outside of it, India never witnessed arbitrary use of law and mob rule on a scale and intensity it has since 2014. Laws and rules have also turned more draconian and seemingly unconstitutional, which are then pressed against dissenting and questioning voices, political rivals and minorities, particularly Muslims, Dalits and anyone who dares to stand up. But law is seldom applied to the ruling establishment and its support groups who respect no law.

Weaponizing Law

Sedition Law

The most glaring example of "the rule by law" is the extensive use of colonial era sedition law, Section 124A of the Indian Penal Code (IPC) and the anti-terror Unlawful Activities (Prevention) Act (UAPA) of 1967. The latter was amended in 2004 to turn it into the anti-terror law as well – after repealing the draconian anti-terror law, called the Prevention of Terrorism Act (POTA) of 2002.

Even a casual reading of newspapers would show a sharp spike in *sedition cases* after 2014 and its bizarre application: Stand-up comedian, Munawar Faruqui, booked for a joke he didn't crack (against Hindus)[4]; peaceful protesters demanding scrapping of the discriminatory and seemingly unconstitutional citizenship law Citizenship Amendment Act (CAA) of 2019; doctored videos claiming anti-India and "Pakistan zindabad" slogans were raised – from the arresting JNU student leaders Kanhaiya Kumar, Umar Khalid and Anirban Bhattacharya in 2016[5] to political rivals at political rallies in 2022[6]; cheering for Pakistani cricket team by Kashmiri students[7] (although this happened before 2014 but not as extensively) etc. Siddique Kappan, a journalist from Kerala travelling to report on a gangrape-cum-murder of a Dalit girl in the BJP-ruled Uttar Pradesh's Hathras intercepted, arrested and jailed in October 2020 for 28 months before he got bail – first on the charges of sedition and terrorism and later for money laundering under an equally draconian Prevention of Money Laundering Act (PMLA) of 2002.[8] When the Allahabad High Court granted him bail in the PMLA case in December 2023, it said other than a transfer of Rs 5,000 (yes, you read that right) to the account of his co-accused Atikur Rahman, "no other transaction has been shown in the account of the accused applicant or Atikur Rahman".[9] Rahman, a student activist from Uttar Pradesh assisting Kappan (from faraway Kerala) to reach the crime scene, got bail much later in June 2023, after 32 months in jail. He said they were punished for being "Muslim".[10] Why the jail and such delay in bail for no crime at all will be clear soon. Even Booker Prize winner Arundhati Roy fell victim to it when, in October 2023, the Lieutenant Governor of NCT of Delhi granted sanction to prosecute her for sedition for advocating "azadi" (freedom) for Kashmir 13 years ago in 2010.[11]

A study of sedition cases between 2010 and 2021 by the news portal Article14[12], captured the rise in its abuse. It showed, of 845 sedition cases against 13,222 people during this period, 66% cases against 66.8% individuals were registered during the Modi government (2014-2021). The details show the frivolousness and the targets:

- 27 cases against 3,862 individuals for peaceful protests against the CAA;

- 12 cases against 18 individuals for raising concerns over lack of ventilators, food distribution or migrant labours during the devastating pandemic

- 21 cases against 40 journalists for reporting on the CAA, new farm bills, pandemic management, the Hathras gangrape and murder of a Dalit girl (who was quietly cremated at midnight by the police without the family's consent to remove evidence[13]) and for critical comments on governments.

- More than 106 sedition cases against 167 individuals were filed for social media posts that was considered "anti-national".

- 12 sedition cases were filed against 104 individuals for 'celebrating' India's losses to Pakistan in sports.

- An earlier analysis by the Article14[14] had shown, 96% cases filed against 405 people after 2014 were for criticising politicians and governments – 149 individuals for being criticising Modi and 144 individuals for criticizing BJP's Uttar Pradesh Chief Minister Ajay Singh Bisht better known as Yogi Adityanath (because of his priestly background).

The reliance on the Article14 is because the National Crime Records Bureau (NCRB) started collecting data on sedition cases only from 2014. The Article14 dug up its data from media reports. The following graph captures the trend (no data is available for the pending rates in 2014 and 2015). High pendency of sedition cases points to frivolousness of the cases – an indicator of "process being the punishment"[15] brand of jurisprudence in India which has become the trend after 2014 (see Chapter III).

Graph 1: Spike in sedition cases and pendency

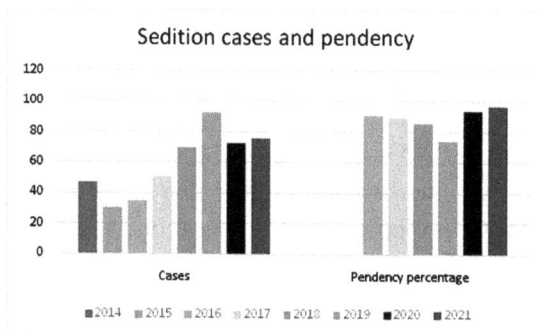

Sedition cases and pendency

2014 ■2015 ■2016 ■2017 ■2018 ■2019 ■2020 ■2021

Source: NCRB reports

This is despite occasional outbursts from higher judiciary and dismissal of the sedition case against journalist Vinod Dua in 2021 by the Supreme Court[16] which said "a citizen has a right to criticize or comment ... so long as he does not incite people to violence against the Government...or with the intention of creating public disorder..." The Delhi High Court granted bail[17] the same year to student activists Natasha Narwal, Devangana Kalita and Asif Iqbal Tanha of "Pinjra Tod" (break the cage) fame, after 13 months in jail for peaceful protest against the CAA but falsely charged for provoking the subsequent Delhi riots of 2020. The court lamented that "the line between the constitutionally guaranteed right to protest and terrorist activity seems to be getting somewhat blurred".

Ironically, the Supreme Court (a vacation bench) declared this Delhi High Court order should not be treated as a precedent two years later on May 2, 2023[18]. It said the bail order "shall not be treated as a precedent and may not be relied upon by any of the parties in any other proceedings" on a twisted logic that "the idea was to protect the state against the use of judgement on the enunciation of law in the bail matter". Why should the apex court protect the state in matters of protection of fundamental rights of individuals would become clear soon (for further clarity read Chapter III).

In 2021, then CJI Ramana spoke harshly against the sedition law, likening it to "a saw" in the hands of a carpenter who he uses it to cut the forest instead.[19] But a year later in 2022, when he had the opportunity to strike the law down, he didn't. Instead, after a prolonged (daily) hearing, he allowed the government to "re-examine and re-consider" the law. This came *after* the Ministry of Home Affairs (MHA) pleaded for time[20] that a "competent forum" would go through it and assured that the Prime Minister was "unequivocally in favour of protection of civil liberties, respect of human rights and giving meaning to constitutionally cherished freedoms" and keen to "shed the colonial baggage". This was a turnaround from the MHA's earlier stand in which it had strongly defended the law and asked the same bench to uphold it.[21] The court put a freeze on the application of the law and also put on hold the judgement.[22]

The MHA's deceptive game would be revealed in 2023.

First came the Law Commission of India report "Usage of the Law of Sedition"[23] in April 2023 (under chairman Justice Ritu Raj Awasthi, a former judge of the Supreme Court) – without anyone's knowledge that this was the "competent forum" the MHA which had been asked to prepare a report. It not only recommended *retaining* the sedition but also *strengthening* it with enhanced punishment. The Law Commission is not a secret body and it is supposed to hold public consultations *before* finalizing any report.

There was no need for this report either. In 2018, the Law Commission of India had released Consultation Paper on 'Sedition'[24] – up on the government's directive – and called it "anachronistic" and needless in a democracy; had cited the UK, from which India inherited the law, abolishing it in 2009 by calling it "arcane". This report (under former Supreme Court judge Justice BS Chauhan) is no longer available on the commission's official website.

In contrast, the 2023 Law Commission report held that the Kedar Nath Singh case of 1962 was "a settled proposition of law" and had qualified the sedition law by adding "with a tendency to incite violence or cause public disorder". This "tendency" was explained as "mere inclination to incite violence or cause public disorder rather than proof of actual violence or imminent threat to violence". There are too many vague words in this formulation, knowing fully well that the space for freedom of expression and right to dissent have been imperiled and the ruling establishment and society have been polarized on communal lines in which the sedition law is being extensively abused, the Law Commission introduced further vagueness and strengthened the sedition law in 2023.

It desists addressing any concerns about the sedition law, including the apprehensions expressed by the Supreme Court. Rather it extensively quoted the National Security Advisor Ajit Doval which are antithetical to democracy and the rule of law. The same Doval had, in 2018[25], called civil society the "invisible enemy" against which India was battling "fourth generation war" and asked the new recruits to elite India Police Service (IPS) to protect "the people" from this enemy. He repeated this in 2021[26] to the IPS recruits too, branding civil society as the "new enemy" posing the "new frontier of war" and said: "The new frontier of war, what you call the fourth-generation warfare, is civil society... that can be...manipulated to hurt the interest of a nation...It's civil society that can be subverted, suborned, divided and manipulated to hurt the interest of a nation. You are there to see this land is fully protected." In fact, on the latter occasion, Doval sought to redefine the rule of law and democracy by running down citizens and giving primacy to government: "The quintessence of democracy does not lie in the ballot box. It lies *in the laws which are made by the people who are elected through those ballot boxes.*" (*Emphasis added*)

The Law Commission's 2023 report also extensively quotes one particular book, Manoj Kumar Sinha and Anurag Deep's "Law of Sedition in India and Freedom of Expression" of 2018, which argues for retaining the sedition and its observations paraphrased ignoring all contrary evidence and views supporting removal of the anti-democratic colonial law and justifying the "tendency" test – an outdated concept which was valid in non-existing context.[27]

Then the penny dropped. On the last day of the monsoon session of Parliament in August 2023, the MHA introduced The Bharatiya Nyaya Sanhita of 2023[28] – a Bill to wholesale replace more than 150 years old Indian Penal Code (IPC) of 1860. It doesn't mention the word "sedition" and hence, Union Home Minister Amit Shah said the sedition law would be "completely repealed"[29] (when passed). But it fools none. Instead of Section 124A, the bill has Clause 150 – as part of the "offences against the state" – which copies the sedition law; makes it more draconian and arbitrary by expanding the scope, vagueness and punishment (from 3-7 years to life imprisonment).[30]

The sedition law had been discarded by the Constituent Assembly in 1940s but the Supreme Court brought it back through the famous Kedar Nath Singh judgement of 1962[31] while limiting its applicability to "acts involving intention or tendency to create disorder, or disturbance of law and order; or incitement to violence". While the Constituency Assembly had rejected it in the context of Article19(1) (freedom of speech and expression), the Kedar Nath Singh judgement inserted it back under Article 19(2) "in the interests of…public order". Jurist AG Noorani called this judgement an entry "by the back door".[32]

The Bharatiya Nyaya Sanhita of 2023 has been referred to a parliamentary panel. Once it comes back to the Parliament and is passed, then someone would have to challenge the far more draconian new sedition law for the Supreme Court to take it up again. It must, however, be pointed it out here that when the farcical case against the stand-up comedian Munawar Faruqui came up before the Supreme Court in April 2023, it didn't quash it but transferred all FIRs against him to Indore in the BJP-ruled Madhya Pradesh – which had first targeted him with the sedition case and arrest.[33]

Anti-terror UAPA

The UAPA of 1967 is equally misused – to *criminalize dissent and protest*.

As pointed out earlier, this law became anti-terror law after the POTA of 2002 – a truly draconian law like its predecessor Terrorist and Disruptive Activities (Prevention) Act (TADA) of 1985 – was repealed. But a 2019 amendment to the UAPA which allowed individuals to be branded terrorists, as against organizations earlier, made it more prone to misuse.[34] While the constitutionality of this amendment is pending (as also the constitutionality of the UAPA), the court overturned, in March 2023, its own 2011 judgement (Arup Bhuyan case) which protected from the executive abuse of it. The 2011 judgement had held that "membership of a banned organization will not incriminate a person unless he resorts to violence or incites people to violence and does an act intended to create disorder or disturbance of public peace by resort to violence". A three-judge bench of the Supreme Court held in 2023 that the 2011 judgement was not good in law.[35] When the 2019 amendment is finally adjudicated (individuals as terrorists) and that of the UAPA in its entirety, this 2023 judgement may have (adverse) bearing on that. One of the most glaring abuses of the anti-terror law is the Bhima-Koregaon or the Elgaar Parishad case – which targeted prominent academics, human rights activists and lawyers from across the country on seemingly false charges. This needs to be told in some details.

Bhima Koregaon or Elgaar Parishad Case

On January 1, 2018, Dalits from across the country gathered at Bhima Koregaon village near Pune, Maharashtra, to celebrate 200 years of a historic win of Dalits (a few hundred Mahar soldiers) led by the British over a massive upper-caste army led by Maharashtra's Peshwas (Brahmins) in 1818. This 2018 congregation was attacked by mobs carrying saffron flags. The first FIR named two Hindutva (radical right) leaders Milind Ekbote and Manohar Bhide as "main conspirators" – which was later confirmed by the Pune police. But instead of arresting and prosecuting them and other attackers, the case was turned on its head by then BJP government of Maharashtra. More than a dozen eminent academics, human rights activists and lawyers (popularly called 'BK-16'[36]) were arrested (starting with 2018) who had participated in another public function the previous evening, called *Elgaar Parishad* ('loud declaration council') as a preparation for the January 1, 2018 celebration. But they were charged with instigating the violence and jailed.[37]

Soon both sedition and terror charges were slapped[38] by accusing BK-16 of plotting to kill the Prime Minister and destabilize the democracy – eerily similar to the Ishrat Jahan fake encounter killings (along with four others) in Gujarat in 2004 when Modi was Chief Minister of Gujarat.[39] The BK-16 case was transferred to anti-terror outfit National Investigating Agency (NIA) and the sedition charges were dropped in 2020.[40] Most accused continue to languish in jail (one died in custody and five got bail) while the actual attackers continue to roam free.[41]

The jailed BK-16 are well known intellectuals and human rights defenders who wrote, spoke and organized peaceful rallies to demand rights for workers, minorities, Dalits and tribals and hence, obvious target of the right-wing BJP regimes. They are: Anand Teltumbde (got bail from the apex court in 2022 after four years in jail[42]), Shoma Sen, Hany Babu, Father Stan Swamy (dead) Mahesh Raut (got bail from the Bombay High Court in September 2023[43]), Varavara Rao (got bail in 2022 from the apex court on health ground[44]), Sudhir Dhawale, Surendra Gadling, Sudha Bharadwaj (who got 'default bail'[45] – a right to bail if chargesheet is not filed within stipulated time – after over three years in jail, from the Bombay High Court in 2021[46]), Gautam Navlakha, Rona Wilson, Sagar Gorkhe, Ramesh Ghaichor, Jyoti Jagtap, Arun Ferreira and Vernon Gonsalves (the last two got bails from the apex court in 2023 after five years in jail; the bail verdict said no evidence was found but was silent on the evidence *planted* against them[47]). Five years have lapsed but trial had not begun by December 2023).[48]

Of them, 84-year-old Father Stand Swamy died in custody in 2021, after repeated denied bail, although the NIA never sought his custody or interrogation.[49] He was denied straw and sipper which he needed because of Parkinson's disease and contacted the Covid-19 virus in jail.[50] This "gratuitous cruelty" shocked the nation and a national daily commented that India was increasingly resembling authoritarian regimes of Hungary, Turkey, Brazil, and the Philippines.[51] But more of the same followed with Navlakha – who was denied spectacles. Such is the bizarre world of law and justice in the BK-16 case that a Bombay High Court judge once questioned why Tolstoy's literacy classic "War and Peace"[52] was found in the house of Veron Gonsalves (who got bail from the apex curt in 2023). The judge later made excuses which turned out to be even more embarrassing for him since it wasn't Tolstoy's but another book with a title that contained this phrase ("War and Peace in Junglemahal"). In fact, books on Mao, Naxal or Marx have been seized and produced "as evidence" in court in a large number of cases across India – betraying strong bias and ignorance of police and other agencies.[53]

In the meanwhile, a series of investigative reports and forensic examinations of evidence revealed that all the evidence (linking them to a banned Maoist outfit and the assassination plot) was planted.

- In 2020, the Amnesty International and Citizen Lab of Toronto University[54] (which exposed the misuse of Israeli military-grade spyware Pegasus in 2021) found nine human rights defenders, most of who were fighting for the release of the BK-16, were unlawfully targeted with a spyware attack using NetWire.

- In 2021, digital forensic firm Arsenal Consulting found at least 10 incriminating letters were planted in the laptop of BK-16's Rona Wilson, *after seizing his laptop*. It later found *22 additional documents* planted in Wilson's computer by the same hacker. Further, the computer of Gadling was later found *infected with NetWire* "nearly two years before his arrest in 2018".[55]

- More evidence surfaced during the Pegasus investigations of 2021. It showed the spyware was used to target BK-16, their family, relatives and associates.[56]

- In 2022, the US-based WIRED[57] revealed involvement of a Pune police officer in planting the evidence (the hackers had "a recovery email address and phone number added as a backup mechanism" of this officer).

All the above evidence has been completely ignored by courts – from the top to the bottom.

The Supreme Court let the BK-16 down in 2018 when it refused to uphold their liberty. It even refused to order forensic examination of evidence (seized electronic devices of the accused) and order an independent investigation (by an SIT). It entirely relied on the "sealed cover" affidavit (secret and not available to the victims) of then Maharashtra's BJP government. The lead author of the judgement was Justice AM Khanwilkar; the other being then CJI Justice Dipak Misra.[58]

In 2019, Justice Khanwilkar, heading another bench, raised the bar for bails in the UAPA cases so high that it is impossible to get bail now – negating the apex court's age-old dictum – "bail is the norm". The bench disallowed "examining merits and demerits" of terror charges and directing lower courts to go by the "broad probabilities" flowing from the materials presented by the police to decide bail. Since an accused is denied opportunity to contest police charges ("elaborate examination or dissection of the evidence is not required to be done" the apex ruled), there is little chance of getting bail. Further, the draconian bail conditions (Section 43D5), which the judgement upheld, says the court can only grant bail if there is "reasonable grounds for believing that the accusation against such person is prima facie true". This leaves no discretion for subordinate courts to give bail.[59]

In another case, not connected to the BK-16, GN Saibaba, a Delhi University professor with over 90% physical disability, is languishing in jail (life sentence) for alleged connections with the banned CPI(Maoist). In October 2022, the Bombay High Court had discharged him and five others in the case – citing absence of valid sanction for the prosecution under the UAPA, which is mandatory under the UAPA – as also the previous anti-terror laws of TADA and POTA – which several Supreme Court judgments had held until then.[60] This Bombay High Court order came on a Friday, October 14, 2022. The very next day, on a Saturday (October 15), then CJI Justice UU Lalit allowed a *special session* of the Supreme Court on a holiday (bench of Justices MR Shaha and Bela M Trivedi). The apex court *immediately* suspended the discharge order saying, among other things, that the question of sanction had not been raised during the trial. Saibaba was put back in jail. Former Supreme Court judge and one of judges in the famous 2018 rebel against then CHI Justice Misra, Madan B Lokur described this development as "unprecedented" and "a new abnormal".[61] On April19, 2023, another Supreme Court bench (Justices MR Shah and CT Ravi Kumar) also set aside the discharge order and asked the Bombay High Court to take a fresh look.[62] Later, the Bombay High Court judge Justice Rohit B Deo *resigned*[63] citing personal reasons. His resignation took the total to 12 High Court judges who have resigned since 2017[64] for various reasons – a worrying development indeed.

The data on UAPA (2016-2020) shows, like the sedition, the cases and arrests have surged. Of 24,134 people arrested, only 212 were convicted and 386 acquitted – taking the pendency of cases to 97.5%. That is, 97.5% of accused are languishing in jail for multiple years because the bail is virtually impossible to get. The conviction rate is abysmally low at 0.9%.[65] The NCRB data for 2021, showed: 814 new cases, 1,621 people arrested and zero conviction.

Graph 2: Surge in UAPA cases and arrests; abysmally low convictions

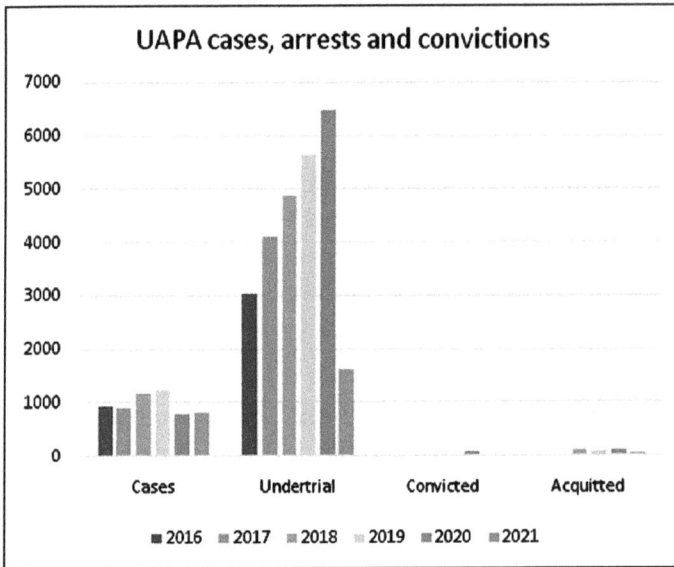

UAPA cases, arrests and convictions

Categories: Cases, Undertrial, Convicted, Acquitted

Legend: ■ 2016 ■ 2017 ■ 2018 ■ 2019 ■ 2020 ■ 2021

Source: Rajya Sabha answer July 2022, NCRB 2022

The practice has caught on. The Telangana government, ruled by a non-BJP Telangana Rashtra Samiti (TRS), for example, slapped UAPA against 152 prominent human rights activists, retired professors and scholars in August 2022 (charged with Maoist links and "take over the power of the democratically elected government at gunpoint"). The accused came to know of it in June 2023 when a human rights organization approached court in connections with FIRs lodged against them over a meeting[66] – two of them were dead for two years, including a retired judge[67]. It shows how *casually* the draconian anti-terror law is being misused.

Misuse of terror laws has a long and dubious history – and hence, the TADA and POTA were allowed to lapse or repealed. But a comparative analysis can't be done since the NCRB doesn't provide TADA and POTA cases. It started tracking the UAPA cases from 2014 as the attack on dissent and minorities began to dramatically rise.[68]

NIA: Perpetual Political Tool

A similar cloud covers the anti-terror outfit, NIA. It strongly opposed Stan Swamy's bail until he died without ever questioning him. What is the purpose of custody? Swamy could have stayed free until the trial ended – which never began – and the judicial pronouncement came. Akhil Gogoi, another rights activist (from Assam), remained in custody for more than a year and half for protesting against the CAA.[69] He got bail as no evidence could be produced. Out on bail, he disclosed that the NIA had offered him bail if he joined the ruling BJP-RSS ahead of the 2021 Assam elections.[70] Tamil Nadu minister and DMK (non-BJP) leader V Senthil Balaji, arrested by the Enforcement Directorate (ED) in 2023 in an alleged corruption charge, was also asked to join the BJP to escape law – his lawyer Kapil Sibal told a Chennai court.[71]

But in 2017, the NIA allowed Pragya Thakur – a terror accused in the Malegaon blasts of 2008 which killed six and injured over 100 in which her bike was allegedly used to plant bombs – to get out on bail on health ground.[72] She contested and won the 2019 general elections, attends the Parliament, plays games and dances at parties but for a long time refused to attend court proceedings on health grounds.[73] She continued to give hate speeches[74], ignoring the Prime Minister's facetious response (not be able to "forgive her with my heart"[75]) to her comment that Mahatma Gandhi's assassin Nathuram Godse was a "patriot".

In fact, the NIA went "soft" on "saffron terror" cases involving Hindu extremist groups immediately after the regime change in 2014, like the Malegaon blasts of 2008.[76] The NIA prosecutor Rohini Salian was the first to blow the whistle in 2015, when she was asked to go soft on the Malegaon blasts of 2008.[77] Incidentally, Thakur's name figures in seven bombings across five states, during 2007 and 2008, killing 119 people, most of whom were Muslim – which were alleged to be executed by the Abhinav Bharat network – along with Aseemanand, former head of the RSS's Vanvasi Kalyan Ashram.[78]

But then, the NIA's use purely as a political tool had been foreseen.

Set up after the Mumbai terror attack of 2008 (26/11), in which 260 plus people were killed, it exclusively focused on "saffron terror" cases. The Congress-led UPA was in power then and all those cases had happened before 26/11: Malegaon blasts of 2006 and 2008, Samjhauta Express blasts of 2007, Ajmer Sharif blasts of 2007, Modasa blast of 2008 and the Sunil Joshi murder case of 2007. The NIA didn't touch terror cases that happened during its time and involved Muslim extremists until 2011. This unifocal targeting of 'saffron' (Hindutva) terror groups had provoked this author[79] to write in 2011: "NIA has been turned into a political tool already…So, what would you expect when the BJP or BJP-led coalition comes to power? Turn NIA on its head. Won't it?"

Journalist Nileena MS[80] traced the transformation of the NIA after the regime change. She wrote: "By later 2014, the NIA was presenting radically divergent conclusions from what it had previously asserted". Many of the "saffron" terror cases were sent back to regular courts – that is, those were no more terror cases – and Hindu extremist organizations behind the bombings mentioned earlier, were not banned. She pointed out that the NIA's remit also expanded to include cases "not strictly within the remit of the NIA, but help legitimize conspiracy theories of the Hindu Right that condemn many forms of dissent as related to terrorism".

A good example of such transfers back from the NIA court is the Nanded blast case of 2006 which is being heard by the district court of Nanded and the CBI is pursuing it. Former RSS member Yashwant Shinde claimed that he was involved in a bomb-making training camp at a resort near Pune, in July 2003, and that there were at least three bomb blasts at mosques in Parbhani, Purna and Jalna, besides the accidental Nanded blast. In his application, he also claimed the same conspiracy also led to the Malegaon blast of 2006; Samjhauta Express blast, Ajmer Sharif blast and Mecca Masjid Hyderabad blast of 2007 and the Malegaon blast of 2008 (in which BJP MP Pragya Thakur is an accused) – in all killing more than 120 people, most of them Muslim. Shinde had earlier argued before the court that he had "personal knowledge of the conspiracy" and said the blast was "hatched by the RSS, VHP and Bajrang Dal". After he was heard for the first time, the judge was changed.[81] When his application was finally rejected in January 2023[82], he had appeared five times before the judge. The ground for dismissal? The CBI's plea that he came forward after "a gap of 16 years" and that "he never approached the CBI nor he gave any information to the investigative agency at any point of time". All these cases were marked as "saffron terror" cases earlier by the NIA – involving Hindutva extremist groups.

The partisan role of the NIA is obvious in all cases of organized terror.

- It ignores all evidence of foul play (planting of evidence) against the BK-16.

- It acted with alacrity and arrested two Muslims, Riaz Akhtari and Ghouse Mohammad, who beheaded a Hindu tailor Kanhaiya Lal in Rajasthan's Udaipur in June 2022 and circulated the video of crime – which was predictably turned into a *poll issue*[83] by the BJP in 2023. The Congress provided numerous photographic evidence and others to show Akhtari, and Talib Hussain Shah, another alleged LeT terrorist arrested from J&K around the same time, the accused were all BJP's minority cell members.[84] The BJP was never questioned.

- It never touched Shambhulal Regar, a Hindu who had hacked and burnt a Muslim in Rajasthan's Rajsamand and also circulated the video of his crime.

- It never acted against coordinated and targeted attack on Muslims since 2014, mob lynching in the name of cow protection (cattle trading and beef eating), attacks on masjids and Muslim localities which is routine and ethnic cleansing in multiple states (see Chapter IV) – not even when a BJP ally writes to it seeking a probe.[85]

Delhi Riots of 2020

Another glaring instance of the misuse of anti-terror law is the Delhi riots of 2020.

In this case, Muslims and their localities were systematically attacked and killed more than 50 people, mostly Muslim men, and their shops and homes torched. Countless videos exist in public domain to show how policemen openly supported marauding mobs from the majority community. Before that, several BJP leaders, including the Prime Minister's cabinet colleague Anurag Thakur, openly called for Muslim genocide (calling out "desh ke gaddaron ko" (to traitors of India) to crowds at public rallies to provoke the inevitable response of "goli maaro saloon ko" (shoot the traitors). Another BJP leader Kapil Mishra took frequent marches shouting the same slogans and according an FIR, carried a gun and led a violent mob during the riots that followed. BJP MP Parvesh Verma warned people at a pubic rally that the protesting Muslims would enter their homes, rape and murder their sisters and daughters. Yet, nothing happened to them.[86] It is worth noting that the riots followed immediately after the BJP lost the election for the NCT of Delhi and was apparently in retaliation against the Muslims for holding protest sit-ins against the discriminatory CAA – which were peaceful and led by old women and students.

Just like the BK-16 case, student activists who were part of peaceful sit-ins and/or called for non-violent protests, including "chakka jam" (blocking roads – a routine political activity all over India) were booked for sedition and terror on the charge of causing the riots. These student leaders included the students of "Pinjra Tod" fame mentioned earlier, JNU scholars Umar Khalid, Shehla Rashid, Sharjeel Imam, Shifa-ur-Rehman and many others. Some like the "Pinjra Tod" members got bail but the rest languish in jail since then *without bail or trial* (except Shehla Rashid due to her pregnancy).

On the other hand, the Delhi High Court's Justice S Muralidhar was targeted for seeking action against the Delhi Police for inaction.[87] He played videos of the BJP leaders' provocative speeches in open court to demonstrate their culpability and the very same midnight he was transferred and asked to report at Punjab and Haryana High Court immediately. Though his transfer had previously been cleared by the apex court, this midnight order was highly unusual. Many investigating reports have exposed the roles the BJP and Delhi Police played in the riots (a large numbers videos had gone viral at that time establishing these links). Investigative reports also showed that the Delhi Police deliberately muddled and skewed investigations against the very victims [88]; Delhi courts found it fabricated evidence, tutored witnesses, and malicious prosecution to subvert justice[89] – while the actual perpetrators roam free.[90] Legendary cop Julio Ribeiro was forced to write to the Delhi Police Commissioner, questioning their probe.[91]

But Justice Muralidhar remained a marked man until his retirement and was not elevated to the apex court despite the Collegium's recommendations and even his transfer from the Odisha High Court to Madras High Court in 2022 was not honoured by the government. In April 2023, the Collegium finally withdrew its recommendation for his elevation citing the delay and arguing that since he was to demit office on 7 August 2023, "leaving less than 4 months' time", the recommendation was being "recalled".[92] Post his retirement, eminent jurist Fali S Nariman, Justice Madan Lokur and senior advocate Sriram Panchu questioned[93] why the Supreme Court Collegium "refused" to bring Justice (retd) Muralidhar to the apex court given his "exemplary record as judge and legal scholar" and "matchless integrity and probity".

The government has blocked the Supreme Court Collegium to appoint judges seen by it as inconvenient in several such cases. Despite occasional outbursts and even leaking information in public to show how the government didn't have a solid case for such action, the Supreme Court failed to assert itself (see Chapter III).[94]

Here is another glaring example of arbitrariness in the Delhi riots case.

In 2022, hearing a sedition case against student activist Umar Khalid, the Delhi High Court took umbrage at his criticism of the Prime Minister and the RSS at a public rally in Maharashtra (unconnected to the Delhi riots), but it didn't decide the sedition charge being heard. This was despite his lawyer pleading that those remarks didn't constitute sedition.[95] After days of hearing the sedition case, the court said it would take it up only after the Supreme Court decided the constitutionality of the sedition law.[96] As mentioned earlier, the Supreme Court didn't do so and passed the ball to the government. Khalid remains in jail for over three years without bail and trial – with even the Supreme Court keeping it hanging for a year.[97]

The same Delhi High Court (but a different bench), however, acted differently when asked to direct the Delhi Police to order FIR and probe against the three BJP leaders (Anurag Thakur, Kapil Mishra and Parvesh Verma) for provoking violence. The court refused, first saying that "if you're saying something *with a smile* then there is no criminality, if you're saying something offensively then criminality".[98] Is this an application of judicial mind? Later, the petitions were dismissed on the plea that the Delhi Police found no evidence of wrong doings by those BJP leaders.[99] In another display of bias against Muslims, in the case of violence caused by Hindutva groups in Delhi's Jahangirpuri during their Ram Navami and Hanuman Jayanti processions (marched to Muslim areas, made provocative speeches, abused and attacked a masjid), the Delhi Police named three main conspirators – all Muslims.[100] *(Emphasis added)*

It must be noted here that the Delhi Police works directly under Union Home Minister Amit Shah – not the Delhi (NCT) government.

NSA, PSA and Section 153A of IPC

Other laws too are misused widely and selectively.

After 2014, the BJP-ruled states have increasingly used the National Security Act (NSA) of 1980, Section 153A of the Indian Penal Code (dealing with spreading communal hatred) and Jammu & Kashmir Public Safety Act (PSA) of 1978 to target Muslims.

For example, a 2021 investigation by Indian Express revealed that the Allahabad High Court called out the abuse of the NSA and quashed 94 out of 120 preventive detention orders between January 2018 and December 2020 in the BJP-ruled Uttar Pradesh. These cases spanned 32 districts and the number one reason to invoke the NSA was allegations of *cow slaughter* (Muslims and Dalits are the targets in such cases). The abuse, the court pointed out, involved "non-application of mind", denial of due process and repeated use of the law to block bail.[101] In 2023, the Supreme Court reacted sharply to invoking the NSA against political rivals and called it "abuse" of law and "non-application of mind[102].

Another draconian law, PSA of 1978, is at play in the troubled state of Jammu & Kashmir – now reduced to two union territories and its special status withdrawn after the President's Rule imposed in 2019. This law is extensively used to send (mostly) Muslims back to jail after they receive bail in earlier cases, including on terror charges. The PSA allows detention without charge. An investigation found that hundreds of people in Jammu & Kashmir, including journalists and human-rights activists, are staying in jail even after courts repeatedly granted bails. It was also found that most charges are not backed by evidence but are frivolous and fanciful, like a crime an accused 'may' commit in future, harbouring 'radical ideology since childhood' and aiding terrorists despite being in jail etc.[103] In cases relating to journalists booked under the PSA, the Jammu and Kashmir High Court not only quashed the charges in one instance and gave bail in another but also questioned why the matter was taken up 11 years later and said detaining government critics under the PSA is "an abuse of the preventive law".[104]

"Hate speech" have become the norm after 2014 but no specific law defines it and *no separate data is collected by the NCRB* (which the Centre confirmed in the Rajya Sabha in July 2022[105]). Cases under Section 153A of the IPC – "promoting enmity between different groups on ground of religion, race, place of birth, residence, language, etc., and doing acts prejudicial to maintenance of harmony" – has seen a *six-fold rise* from 323 in 2014 to 1,804. Most of these cases are from Tamil Nadu, followed by Uttar Pradesh, Telangana, Assam, Andhra Pradesh,

Rajasthan and Karnataka (all more than 100 cases). The religion background of the accused is not known but two-third of the cases were registered in non-BJP ruled states.[106]

The NCRB may not track hate crimes which registered a quantum jump since 2014 but has added a new category of criminal called "anti-national elements" and "jihadi terrorists" since its "Crime in India 2020" report.[107] It doesn't define what these are but perhaps it is enough to align itself with the current government. What will happen when a new governemnt comes? What about the professionalism? These questions don't seem to bother the NCRB or the MHA under which it functions.

The arrest of prominent fact-checker and fake news buster Mohammed Zubair of the Altnews in August 2022 needs special attention for the gross misuse of Section 153A.

Zubair had shared, way back in 2018, a screenshot of 1983 comedy film "Kissi Se Na Kehna" by the legendary filmmaker Hrishikesh Mukherjee. It showed the signboard of a hotel in which "Honeymoon" had been tinkered to "Hanuman" (Monkey God, a Hindu deity standing for celibacy). Zubair's post carried a remark: "Before 2014: Honeymoon Hotel, After 2014: Hanuman Hotel". This screenshot had been shared by many at the time (2018), including a national daily.[108] Notwithstanding the ruse, his arrest was directly linked to his flagging of BJP spokesperson Nupur Sharma's blasphemous remarks against Prophet Muhammed on live TV – which sparked widespread protest in India and abroad and led to her suspension from the party. She, however, was never arrested.[109] Instead, she got police protection after the issue blew up.[110] The Delhi Police told a Delhi court later that she was let go after recording her statement.[111]

The Supreme Court took weeks to grant Zubair bail[112], by which time he was in police and judicial custody for 23 days and five more FIRs had been filed in Uttar Pradesh – all for drawing attention to the blasphemy and hate speeches by Hindu seers in other cases. An SIT was constituted to probe him. He was paraded in Uttar Pradesh and Karnataka in the name of collecting evidence. Among others, Zubair was also charged for describing a firebrand Hindu seer "hate monger". The seer publicly (outside a masjid in Uttar Pradesh) called for rape of Muslim women as a revenge for 'love jihad'. During the seer's bail hearing in the apex court, Additional Solicitor General (ASG) of India called this Hindu seer a "respected" religious leader and added: "When you call a religious leader hate-monger, it raises problems."[113]

Zubair's bail came *a day after* Nupur Sharma was granted protection from legal actions by the very Supreme Court.[114] The court also kept quiet on the other BJP leader Navin Jindal who had supported Nupur Sharma in social media and was thrown out of the party. Days earlier, the court had given prompt protection (the very day of hearing) to pro-government TV anchor from arrest for airing a doctored video of Rahul Gandhi – which falsely linked Rahul Gandhi to the Udaipur lynching of Hindu tailor Kanhaiya Lal mentioned earlier.[115] As we will see in Chapter III, the apex court went out of its way to condemn and seek legal action against justice seekers Teesta Setalvad, RB Sreekumar, Sanjiv Bhatt and Himanshu Kumar in connection with the 2002 Gujarat pogrom and cold-blooded killing of tribals by cops in Chhattisgarh under the BJP government, led by Raman Singh (more in Chapter II). But it sought no action against Nupur Sharma, Navin Jindal or the TV anchor.

It is because of such intransigencies that the Supreme Court's repeated directives to the central and state governments to take tough action against hate speeches directed at Muslims fell on deaf years. It was left to merely recording its helplessness in February 2023: "We have passed so many orders yet nobody is taking action.[116] This was the time when right-wing "Hindu Jan Aakrosh Morcha" was holding a series of public rallies across the BJP-ruled Maharashtra to target Muslims. Over a period of four months, it held 50 public events (by the end of March 2023) in which the themes were usual bogey of 'love jihad' (a conspiracy theory that says Muslim men entice Hindu women by love to convert them into Islam) and 'land jihad' (another conspiracy theory that says masjids have sprouted illegally to grab land) as also public oath of boycotting Muslims from all economic activities.[117]

Zubair's case must be seen in all these contexts playing out.

Ironically enough, the day Zubair was arrested, the Prime Minister was signing a treaty in Germany with G-7 leaders to protect free speech online and offline[118] – a trademark double standard. A few days later, India even committed to shielding journalists and rights activists in talks with the European Union.[119] This was also the time when The Reporters Without Borders (RSF) described the Prime Minister, along with 37 other head of states, as "Press freedom predators"[120] and its entry on him noted that he has been a "predator since taking office" on May 26, 2014. It listed his predatory methods as "national populism and disinformation" and commented: "The violence against journalists, the politically partisan media and the concentration of media ownership – all demonstrate that press freedom is in crisis in the world's largest democracy". In Press Freedom Index, India's rank has tumbled from 133 in 2016 (of 180 countries) to 161 in 2022 and India declared as one of the most dangerous places for media.[121]

Kafka's Law and Agent: PMLA and ED

A new law and agency which have emerged as a potent political weapon – the space which only the CBI occupied so far – to hunt down political rivals is the Prevention of Money Laundering Act (PMLA) of 2002, as amended since then.

It is a draconian and bizarre law – like perhaps no other in the developed world – whose constitutionality is highly questionable. Under it, a person can be raided, arrested and his/her property seized without FIR, warrant or the requirement of being produced before a court in 24 hours – as the normal laws provide. Accused's statement to officials without judicial oversight is also treated as evidence. No bail can be granted without satisfying two additional conditions of (a) giving public prosecutor opportunity to oppose it and (b) the special court satisfied that he/she "is not guilty" and "not likely to commit any offence while on bail". The second (b) is impossible to fulfill in absence of the need for registration of the offence (FIR) and not sharing of such information with the accused, called Enforcement Case Information Report (ECIR). ECIR is equivalent of an FIR, detailing the charges. ECIR is required to be produced only when prosecution complaint or chargesheet is filed – which may take months or years.

Besides, the entire burden of proof is on the accused – inverting the cardinal principle of Indian judicial system: Presumption of innocence until proved guilty. There is yet another dangerous provision – a PMLA case can be slapped with *retrospective effect*, that is, in offences which occurred before the PMLA came into existence. This is because the PMLA crime is considered "a continuing offence", irrespective of time at which the predicate offence was included in its "Schedule". Thus, a person can be incarcerated for a long period and his fundamental rights to life and liberty (Article 21) and equality before law (Article 14) can be suspended without judicial oversight and trial, and without even "Emergency" in place – which is what had happened once in the infamous ADM Jabalpur case of 1976 and the right to life and liberty were suspended for the period of the Emergency.

The Supreme Court upheld the constitutionality of this Kafkaesque law (public policy expert Pratap Bhanu Mehta called it "Kafka's Law")[122]. The court, in its order of July 27, 2022, accepted all of the government's arguments and endorsed that the PMLA is a "special law" and a "complete Code in itself", meaning thereby, it is beyond the due process of law provided under the CrPC/IPC and that it has its own separate and parallel set of mechanism for investigation, inquiry and trial etc. It held that the officials of implementing agency Enforcement Directorate (ED) are "not police officers" and hence, are not subject to normal checks and balances of IPC/CrPC. It also endorsed that the presumption of innocence, is not applicable in the PMLA case by saying "that presumption (innocent until proven guilty) can be *interdicted* by a law made by the Parliament/Legislature". The government had argued that "it cannot be said that presumption of innocence is a constitutional guarantee."[123]

How do you call the PMLA a "special law"?

Its Schedule lists 154 crimes under 30 laws – from the CrPC to laws relating to bonded labour, child labour, juvenile justice, emigration, passport, copyright, trade mark, air and water pollution, corporations etc. This make the PMLA a parallel criminal justice system outside the Constitution of India's ambit. How can any law be constitutional if it suspends fundamental rights to life, liberty and equality before law? In 2017, the very court had held Section 45 of the PMLA – which puts stiff bail conditions mentioned earlier – as "manifestly arbitrary" and "unconstitutional" as they violate Articles 14 and 21. Interestingly, in the 2022 judgement, the court didn't find it odd that the very same Section 45 was *reintroduced* in a 2019 amendment (in defiance of the court ruling). Rather, it approved of it saying that Section 45 "does not suffer from the vice of arbitrariness or unreasonableness" and then upheld its reintroduction by offering an absurd (and unlawful) logic: "It was open to the Parliament to cure the defect noted by this Court so *as to revive the same provision in the existing form*". *(Emphasis added)*

In August 2022, a month later, the Supreme Court did agree to review its judgement upholding the PMLA's constitutionality but not in its entirely. A bench led by then CJI Justice Ramana limited the review to only two provisions – (i) not providing ECIR to the accused and (ii) reversal of burden of proof. Justice Ramana explained that this was because "my brothers are not agreeable" to expanding the scope of the review. The "brothers" here are two other judges (Justices Justice Dinesh Maheshwari and CT Ravikumar) who were also part of the three-judge bench led by Justice Khanwilkar that had delivered the July 2022 verdict (upholding the PMLA's constitutionality). Why were they made members of the review bench and a larger (than three-member) bench was not constituted – which can legitimately overturn a three-judge bench order – are not known. Justice Ramana retired the very next day and thus, another review bench will have to be set up.[124]

However, without any such higher bench, the court ruled in October 2023 that the ED must give in writing or "a copy of the grounds of arrest" at the time of arrest "as a matter of course and without exception", not a mere verbal communication as was the case – during the hearing of a case.[125]

Anyone harbouring illusions about the more stringent PMLA being helpful in reducing money laundering or banking fraud must look at the RBI reports to see the spurt in such cases after 2018 (see Chapter VII). The draconian PMLA was introduced by the previous BJP-led government in 2002. It was subsequently expanded in scope and made more stringent by the subsequent Congress-led and BJP-led governments. Constitutional lawyer Gautam Bhatia commented: "If the UAPA is the executive's weapon of choice to keep inconvenient individuals in jail for years without trial, the Prevention of Money Laundering Act (PMLA) is its political weapon."[126]

Ironically, the Supreme Court upheld the PMLA on the face of massive misuse of it to target the political rivals. Almost every rival political leader and every single rival political party is under ED attack. From Congress leaders Sonia

Gandhi, Rahul Gandhi, P Chidambaram, Karti Chidambaram, DK Shivakumar, relatives and associates of sitting Congress Chief Ministers Charanjit Singh Channi, Kamal Nath and Ashok Gehlot to Nationalist Congress Party's Sharad Pawar, Ajit Pawar, Anil Deshmukh, Nawab Malik to Shiv Sena's Sanjay Rout, Anil Parab, and others to Aam Admi Party's Manish Sisodia, Satyendra Jain (who the CBI later sought to probe for extortion on the notorious jailed alleged conman and extortionist Sukesh Chandrashekar's claim[127] that Jain received protection money, even as the ED case went nowhere) was heading and their Rajya Sabha party colleague Sanjay Singh (CBI raided and questioned AAP Chief Minister Arvind Kejriwal multiple times over the years), along with Telangana Chief Minister K Chandrasekhar Rao's daughter and MLC K Kavitha (also by the CBI) to Trinamool Congress' Abhishekh Banerjee to Rashtriya Janata Dal's Lalu Prasad, Rabri Devi (former RJD Chief Minister) and Bihar's Deputy CM Tejashwi Yadav (also by the CBI) to Jharkhand Mukti Morcha Chief Minister Hemant Soren to Samajwadi Party and CPM leaders, there is hardly a rival political party leader who has been spared.[128]

In none of the cases anything concrete has emerged so far to establish the CBI's bona fide; on the contrary, Ajit Pawar joined the Shiv Sena-BJP government in Maharashtra as Deputy Chief Minister in 2023.

In 2022, the Rajya Sabha was told that as against 112 before 2014, the number of ED raids jumped to 3,010 – 27 times![129] Investigation by the Indian Express revealed that there was 400% rise in ED cases against politicians since 2014, 95% of cases targeting Opposition leaders.[130] But as in the case of sedition and UAPA cases, the conviction rate of ED is *extremely low*. According to the ED's data released by ED – of a total of 5,906 cases since 2005 (up to January 31, 2023), the conviction has been secured only in 24 cases – 0.4% (although it *claimed 96%* by counting only 24 convictions out of 25 cases in which trials have been completed, not a huge number of pending cases)![131]

Months ahead of the November 2023 elections (Madhya Pradesh, Chhattisgarh and Rajasthan), a team of ED officials camped in the Congress-ruled Chhattisgarh with *family members* and carried out many raids. Chief Minister Bhupesh Baghel said[132]: "The ED officers have come to the state with their family, because they know they have to be here till the next Lok Sabha…So, the intention is not to end corruption, but to end the opposition." In June 2023, the ED took possession of 81 assets[133] of Baghel's ex-official, legislators and bureaucrats and seized their assets seized in a coal scam; the same day, the ED searched the houses of Thackeray's close associate Sanjay Rout and son Aditya Thackeray[134] in an alleged Covid-19 scam, along with bureaucrats and others. These were followed by the ED raids on Congress-riled Rajasthan minister Rajendra Yadav and his family.[135] Just ahead of the November 2023 elections in five states, the ED *swooped down* on *top Opposition leaders*[136], along with other central agencies like the CBI, in four states of Chhattisgarh, Rajasthan, Madhya Pradesh and Telangana – not one of these was on a BJP leader or related to money laundering by anyone associated with the BJP-run government – establishing itself as the BJP's political agents. Such raids on the Opposition come with *institutionalized coordination*[137] among the central agencies and the BJP members at the central and state levels – just like the 'Modi's namak' has been institutionalized to create a new vote bank, called "labharthi varg" – obliterating the difference between the government and the political party running it.

Importance of ED Director

It is under ED Director Sanjay Kumar Mishra that the agency became a formidable political tool to target rivals, dissent or anyone who dares to stand up or question the Prime Minister – more powerful, more dreaded (because the law was made more draconian by the government and the apex court and it is virtually unaccountable for very long periods – until trial starts) and grew rapidly in size to overtake the original political tool, the CBI.

His tenure was extended to five years through three extensions, despite repeated adverse rulings by the apex court, violating multiple earlier apex court orders which were aimed at insulating key officers from government interferences.[138] He was first appointed as the ED Director in November 2018, for a period of two years but continued due to multiple "retrospective" extensions through ordinances and amendments.[139] The CBI Director too got similar extensions (taking the tenure to five years).[140] In 2021 (at the end of a three-year term), the Supreme Court upheld the first retrospective extension as "rarest of rare" but asked the government to desist from further extensions.[141]. The government didn't listen. On July 11, 2023, the court finally struck down Mishra's extensions beyond 2021 as "illegal" and marked July 31, 2023 as his last day in office. The order, however, *upheld* retrospective extension of tenures of ED, CBI Directors by three years (taking their terms to five years) by arguing: (a) the "effect" of the judgments of this court could be "nullified" by a legislative act removing the basis of the judgment and (b) such law could be "retrospective".[142]

What came as even more shocking that days later, on July 27, 2023, another bench of the apex court allowed Mishra further extension till September 15 (beyond July 31) "in the larger public and national interest".[143] The larger interest was the government's facile plea that Mishra was needed for the review of ED's works by the Financial Action Task Force (FATF) – a G7 initiative to fight money laundering. This interest would have been served better by improving the effectiveness of ED and the PMLA (higher convictions) – which have been a cause of concern for a full decade.[144] The apex court not only ignored this basic logic but by repeatedly violating its own rulings, it undermined its own authority. Lawyer

Gautam Bhatia wrote[145], "one must now not only wonder whether the SC has any respect for itself and its own orders, but whether it has respect for the rule of law". He warned two direct consequences of the July 27 verdict: (i) "further embolden the executive to treat the Constitution and the law as optional" and (ii) "If the Supreme Court is unable – or unwilling – to enforce its own previous, direct orders (not once, not twice, but many times) in the face of executive recalcitrance, then what hope – if any – ought citizens to have in its ability or willingness to adjudicate cases involving serious and far-reaching constitutional breaches by the executive? Would not such cases and constitutional challenges be effectively turned into a *formality, where the outcome is known, and everyone simply goes through the motions?* We are *aware of jurisdictions where that is the case*; and unfortunately, orders such as today's raise a *disquieting sense* of proximity." (*Emphasis added*)

This is exactly what is already happening in India after 2014 – like the continuation of hate crimes against Muslims while the Modi government and BJP-ruled state governments indulge in whataboutery.[146]

The ED and CBI are investigating agencies for money laundering, black money and corruption. The SC had protected two-year tenure to their Directors in the Vineet Narain case of 1997 to provide "permanent insulation against extraneous influences".[147] But extension of the tenure of their favourite officers to five years turns the very rationale on its head and facilitates abuse of the laws. Consider another parallel development. A two-year limit[148] was put on the extensions for Secretaries of Defence and Home, Intelligence Bureau (IB) and Secretary RAW. In 2023, even this was violated and Home Secretary Ajay Bhalla got fourth extension taking his term to five years.[149] These are bad governance.

In addition to ED, other central agencies, like the CBI, Directorate of Revenue Intelligence (DRI) Income Tax Department (ITD) and Narcotics Control Bureau (NCB) have also been unleashed. The Indian Express found a similar jump in the CBI raids on Opposition leaders. While during the UPA years 60% cases involved Opposition leaders, it jumped to 95% under Prime Minister Modi.[150]

The central agencies get particularly hyper-active in raiding rival political party leaders during the electioneering or just ahead of it – to ensure the BJP candidates get a smooth passage. Occasionally, such raids get awry. For instance, just ahead of the Uttar Pradesh election of 2022, the Directorate General of GST Intelligence (DGGI), based in faraway Ahmedabad (Gujarat), raided perfume maker Piyush Jain of Kanpur (in December 2021) and seized Rs 284 crore in cash 250 kg silver and 25 kg gold.[151] The Prime Minister promptly raised a stink and asked the rival Samajwadi Party (SP) to claim the cash pile.[152] Soon it turned out that this was the wrong P Jain – a BJP supporter, not a SP candidate. So, the right P Jain, the SP's Pushpraj Jain was raided but nothing incriminating was found.[153] Nothing more was heard of it.

Such raids by the central agencies go against Part VII of the Model Code of Conduct (MCC) which puts the onus of conducting a free and fair poll as much on the ruling party, the government as the Election Commission of India (ECI). It says: "The party in power whether at the Centre or in the State or States concerned shall ensure that no cause is given for any complaint that it has used its official position for the purposes of its election campaign..." Such raids also go against the long-held convention of suspending any such actions against politicians during the period of electioneering.[154]

The Prime Minister is quite blasé about such raids by agencies though. Once he said: "These offices work independently. The elections come in between...What can they do? The government has no role in it".[155] Often, such raids are pure vengeance and aimed at poaching rivals, split their parties and overturn their governments. The case of former NCP leader Ajit Pawar (joining the Maharashtra government is classic:

- All corruption cases against the junior Pawar were suspended when he joined the BJP to form a short-lived government in 2019 as Deputy Chief Minister.[156]

- Days later, after he switched back to the NCP, all those cases were revived and central agencies, the ED and IT, raided him and slapped additional charges.[157]

- On June 27, 2023, the Prime Minister gave "Modi's guarantee"[158] at a public function in Bhopal to put all corrupt politicians, including the junior Pawar and other NCP leaders. Five days later, on July 2, 2023, the junior Pawar and other NCP leaders facing corruption charges joined the rebel Shiv Sena-BJP government in Maharashtra; the junior Pawar became Deputy Chief Minister again.[159]

- On September 1, 2023, the ED dropped the junior Pawar's name from the charge sheet filed in connection with the Maharashtra State Cooperative Bank (MSCB) scam case.[160]

There are many such cases of vindictiveness by the government.

- Months after the Aam Admi Party defeated the BJP to win the NCT of Delhi in 2015, Chief Minister Arvind Kejriwal's office was raided by the CBI and his office sealed.[161] The CBI was unleashed on him in 2023 even in the case of renovation of his dilapidated official residence under the state's Public Works Department (PWD)[162] – but never looked into the unwarranted demolition and renovation of the iconic Central Vista and the irregular manners in which it was carried out when thousands of people were perishing to Covid-19 all over the country in 2020 and 2021 due to lack of hospital beds, medicines and equipment.

- In 2019, months after the Congress formed its government in Madhya Pradesh, Chief Minister Kamal Nath's close associates were raided by the IT department.[163] A year later, 22 Congress MLAs, led by Jyotiraditya Scindia, defected to the BJP and the Congress government fell to pave way for a BJP government.

- Trinamool Congress's Mamata Banerjee was targeted after she defeated the BJP in 2021.

- It happened in 2022 in Gujarat when Congress working president of the state Hardik Patel switched to the BJP to *escape* cases slapped against him for leading the 2017 Patel agitations to demand job reservations.[164]

- The Delhi Police (which comes under the Central government) knocked on the door of Rahul Gandhi multiple times after he raised questioned about the allegations against the Adani group and the relationship between the Prime Minister and group promoter Gautam Adani. They wanted to question Gandhi for his old remark about sexual assault on women in Srinagar. The cops wanted to get details about those women.[165]

- Former J&K Governor Satya Pal Malik was questioned by the CBI for five hours soon after he revealed that the Prime Minister told him to "chup raho" (keep quiet) for pointing out serious security lapses leading to the Pulwama blasts of 2019. He was "harassed" by the CBI over an old corruption case he had raised but not the persons accused.[166]

Weaponizing Other Tools

It isn't just the law and central agencies which have been weaponized, a host of other instruments of governance are weaponized too – undermining the rule of law. Here are some examples:

(a) **Courts of Law**: The courts of law have become extended arms of the governments with the Supreme Court not only strengthening draconian laws as explained earlier but also by punishing justice seekers like Setalvad, Sreekumar, Bhatt and Kumar *at behest of the government* (detailed in Chapter III). Gujarat courts, particularly in Ahmedabad, have emerged as the happy hunting grounds for the regime's critics as well as those who expose murky corporate affairs. Here are three examples:

One, top corporate houses have slapped defamation cases and demanded huge amounts of damages to intimidate media investigations. These are called *Strategic Lawsuit Against Public Participation* or SLAPP. The reason being, unlike, say the Delhi High Court's requirement of depositing 10% of the damages sought, Gujarat courts require a maximum court fee of Rs 75,000 under the Gujarat Court-Fees Act of 2004, irrespective of the amount of damages sought.[167] Thus, suits seeking Rs 100 crore and even Rs 5,000 crore in damages were filed against many news organizations (National Herald, The Wire, The EPW).[168]

Two, a Surat court (Gujarat) awarded maximum sentence of two years to Congress leader Rahul Gandhi for defamation in 2023, for an election speech made *in 2019 in Karnataka* (asking "Why do all of them – all these thieves – have Modi, Modi, Modi in their names?"[169]) – which led to his ouster from the Lok Sabha. The court moved so *swiftly* after Gandhi raised questions in the Lok Sabha on the Adani group's alleged corporate frauds and its connections with the Prime Minister in February 2023 that in 20 days, it heard and awarded the sentence. Constitutional lawyer Gautam Bhatia called it "lawfare" (play on law and warfare)[170] – and "completely indefensible".[171] All his appeals for staying the conviction were rejected by all the courts in Gujarat, including the Gujarat High Court – despite *summer vacation* and huge piles of pending cases[172]. When the Supreme Court stayed his conviction in August 2023, it said the trial court gave no "reasons" for the maximum punishment for a "non-cognizable, bailable and compoundable" case and the appellate court and Gujarat High Court didn't consider those aspects while stamping approvals.[173]

Three, justice seeker Teesta Setalvad too was refused bail by all Gujarat courts. While granting her bail, the Supreme Court described the Gujarat High Court's order "totally perverse" and "contradictory".[174]

(b) **Religion:** Hindu religious processions, marking Ram Navami and Hanuman Jayanti, are routinely allowed to go into Muslim localities and masjids to provoke riots, which are then followed by bulldozers to target the Muslim homes and shops. A 2022 study[175] brought to fore how the "routes" of the processions are specifically selected, how violence against Muslims is "systematically planned" followed by "the administrative response as collective punishment" of Muslims in the BJP-ruled states (such processions and riots happened in non-BJP ruled states of Bihar, Odisha and West Bengal in 2022 and 2023[176]). This is over and above specific laws to target Muslims (banning cow slaughter, beef eating, conversion and inter-faith marriages etc.) and state-backed multiple fake 'jihad' campaigns (for more see Chapter IV).

(c) **Mobs:** The ease and impunity with which right-wing organizations associated with the BJP and its large Sangh Parivar have unleashed mob lynching; garlanding of convicted mob lynchers by a Modi's minister Jayant Sinha in 2018[177] and public adulation of convicted mass rapists and killers in the Bilkis Bano case as "Sanskari Brahmins"[178] (cultured Brahmins) – are just the tip of the proverbial iceberg. Right-wing individuals and groups slaughter cows, damaging idols and then blame Muslims[179] or throw pork at masjid[180] to ignite violence; they don't hesitate to lynch even a Hindu police officer[181] in the name of cow protection.

(d) **History:** Textbooks of history[182] are being re-written to create a fake history of Hindu supremacy and delegitimize Muslim identity and culture. These include mass scale deletions – of Mughal history, communal hatred that killed Mahatma Gandhi, 2002 Gujarat pogrom, demolition of the Babri Masjid by the BJP-led mobs, inhuman caste system etc.[183] Such deletions not only reflect the regressive ideology of the ruling establishment[184] but Aditya Mukherjee of the Jawaharlal Nehru University warns[185] genocide follows "erasure of identity of a particular community from our history".

(e) **Fake News, Misinformation, Propaganda:** These are not aberrations but part of the ruling establishment's governance tools and used for various purposes – to target Muslims, build a citizenry who can't differentiate between truth and alt-truth or separate fact and fiction.[186] They also double up as governance – which several subsequent chapters demonstrate.

(f) **Pension:** Increasingly, retired civil servants (IAS, IPS and IFoS)[187], security and intelligence officials[188] and army veterans[189] are being coerced into silence. This is being done either through amendments to the Central Pension Rules or issuing warnings to withhold pensions for airing views without prior permission (even without violating the Official Secrets Act of 1923) and criticising the government policies. If in the process, fundamental rights are violated, federal system is undermined (not consulting or taking consent of states in the case of retired civil servants) so be it.

Immunity for BJP, Supporters and Defectors

But the BJP leaders and their supporters busy spreading hate and violence 24x7, 365 days a year are immune from the law. Other than BJP leaders Thakur, Mishra and Verma, Sharma and Jindal mentioned earlier, there are many such cases. Even if arrested, they get bail easily and roam free, many committing more hate crimes. The list is very long. Here are some key ones.

(i) While Trinamool Congress ministers of West Bengal were arrested their co-accused in the "Narada" bribery case, Mukul Roy, Suvendu Adhikari and Sovan Chattopadhyay who defected to the BJP, were spared.[190]

(ii) BJP Chief Ministers BS Yediyurappa, Himanta Biswa Sarma and Shivraj Singh Chouhan; Central ministers Ramesh Pokhriyal 'Nishank' and Narayan Rane and Bellary's Reddy brothers – all have serious corruption/criminal cases pending against them but they are not raided, arrested or jailed.[191]

(iii) Senior BJP leaders, including Chief Ministers from the party, routinely call for violence but face no action.[192] Some don't shy away from publicly calling for protection of cow vigilantes.[193] Right-wing mobs feel so emboldened that they openly share videos of their violent attacks in social media.[194]

(iv) Union Minister Ajay Mishra Teni's car mowed down a convoy of peacefully protesting farmers in Lakhimpur Kheri, Uttar Pradesh, on October 3, 2021, in which four farmers were killed. He had threatened the farmers for peaceful protests days earlier and publicly admitted that his car was involved in the incidence but Union Home Minister Amit Shah reportedly asked him to continue as a Union Minister.[195] He remains in office.

(v) Teni's son, Ashish Mishra, who was allegedly driving his father's car that mowed down peaceful farmers, was arrested a week after then CJI Justice Ramana intervened. He was released on bail four months later by the Allahabad High Court.[196] When protested, the apex court put him back in jail but in December 2022 (after Justice Ramana's retirement), the apex court was expressing anguish at the slow pace of his trial and demanded to know "how long" could Ashish Mishra be kept in custody.[197] In January 2023, another bench granted him interim bail.[198]

(vi) Haryana's BJP spokesman Suraj Pal Amu roams free after making a series of hate speeches against Muslims, including announcing a reward of Rs 10 crore for beheading the actress and director of film Padmavati.[199]

(vii) Eleven life convicts in the gangrape of pregnant Bilkis Bano and mass murder (14 of her family members, including her three-year daughter), during the 2002 pogrom, walked out of prison on August 15, 2022 – ahead of the Gujarat elections. The "remission" was facilitated by both the Supreme Court and the MHA.[200] The apex court went against its own 2000 order (which called for determining first "whether the offence is an individual act of crime without affecting the society at large" for remission) and asked Gujarat (government) to decide the remission, not Maharashtra where the trial took place and to follow its old 1992 remission policy. The MHA went against its own 2022 guidelines issued weeks earlier banning remission to life convicts and rapists.

The convicts were welcomed with sweets and garlands right outside the jail; a BJP leader who called them "Sanskari Brahmins" won from Godhra in the 2022 state elections.[201] Both the Gujarat government and the Central government had at first refused to even share case files with the Supreme Court – where an appeal was pending by the end of 2023.[202]

(viii) The youths who ran 'Sulli Deal' and then 'Bulli Bai' apps to humiliate Muslim women were out on bail within months. The Delhi Police had delayed action against the 'Sulli Deal' accused, emboldening a re-run, via the 'Bulli Bai' app nearly a year later, and was forced to act as the Maharashtra police (run by then non-BJP government) started arresting suspects.[203]

(ix) The case of BJP MP and former Wrestling Federation of India (WFI) president Brij Bhushan Saran Singh, who has been accused of sexual assault by top several women wrestlers, including a minor (17-year-old) is another case in point. The Delhi Police didn't register the case or arrested him. Solicitor General (SG) Tushar Mehta justified the police inaction saying that a probe was necessary before an FIR is filed and even if it attracted the Protection of Children from Sexual Offences (POCSO) Act of 2012 (involving the minor). The Supreme Court's 2013 judgement, in the Lalita Kumari vs Govt of UP (and the CrPC), had said for a cognizable offence like sexual abuse, FIR must be filed immediately but the court deferred to the SG and then, when the Delhi Police registered the FIRs, the court closed the proceedings[204] expressing satisfaction but didn't question why Singh wasn't arrested. Instead, it directed the wrestlers to approach the Delhi High Court.

Meanwhile, the delays got to the nerves of the minor who withdrew her (POCSO) charge.[205]. The FIRs revealed horrifying acts of sexual predation[206] and the subsequent investigations and charge sheet said the charges to be true[207]. Olympic medallist and one of the lead protesters Vinesh Phogat[208] said she had personally told the Prime Minister about the sexual abuse in 2021 but nothing happened (which was mentioned in the FIR[209]). Singh had told a TV channel in 2022 that he had killed a man (he named the victim)[210] but again, nothing happened. Singh attended the Parliament, was granted exemption[211] from court hearings to do so and got bail[212] without having to face police custody or jail. On the other hand, the women wrestlers were forcibly evicted[213] by the Delhi Police from their dharna at Jantar Mantar when the new Parliament House was inaugurated in June 2023 – which Singh proudly attended.

Journalist Coomi Kapoor wrote[214] that Singh's "extraordinary clout" stemmed from his "direct links with the party high command in Delhi" which used his services for liaising with politicians from rival parties having common interest in wrestling.

(x) Rajvardhan Singh Parmar, national president of Maharana Pratap Sena, was arrested for sexual abuse inside the UP Bhavan, from where he ran his political activities "illegally"; he also stayed at Vithal Patel Bhavan – both meant for accommodation for MPs in the heart of the Lutyens' Delhi.[215]

(xi) No investigation was instituted into multiple viral videos of Union Agriculture Minister Narendra Singh Tomar's son Devendra Singh Tomar allegedly talking about huge cash transfers and deals with multiple individuals during the November 2023 electioneering in Madhya Pradesh – despite repeated demands from Opposition parties – while raids were being conducted against the Congress leaders.[216]

Maximum BJP MPs with Criminal Background

The BJP has maximum number of Lok Sabha members with criminal backgrounds, and their number has gone up from 2014[217] to 2019[218]. Analysis of self-declared election affidavits by the Association for Democratic Reforms (ADR) – a non-profit network working for electoral reforms – shows the BJP has most Lok Sabha members with criminal cases in the current Lok Sabha (2019-2024): 116 MPs, of which 87 have "serious" criminal cases (non-bailable and carry imprisonment of 5 years or more). This is a rise from the previous Lok Sabha (2014-2019) – 98 MPs, of which 63 had serious criminal cases. Here is a comparative picture with the second largest pan-Indian party, the Congress. The Congress has 29 MPs (57% of party MPs) with tainted background, of which 19 have serious criminal cases – up from 8 and 3, respectively, in 2014.[219]

Graph 3: Members of Parliament with criminal records

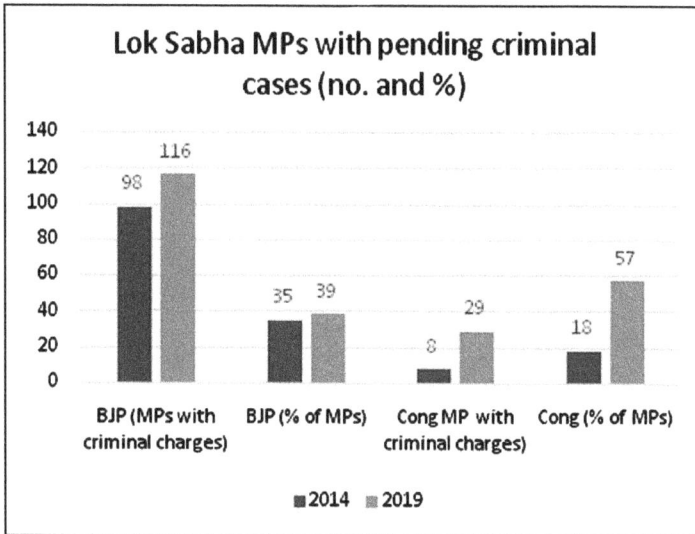

Source: Association for Democratic Reforms

Growing Number of Tainted Ministers

The number of tainted MPs in Modi's cabinet has also jumped from 48 (31%) in 2014 to 68 (39%) in 2019 and 76 (42%) in 2021 (after the reshuffle) – as per the ADR analysis. To expect the Prime Minister to act tough against politicians with criminal background would be naïve – notwithstanding his promise to cleanse politics within a year in the run up to the 2014 elections.[220]

Graph 4: Rising no. of ministers with criminal background

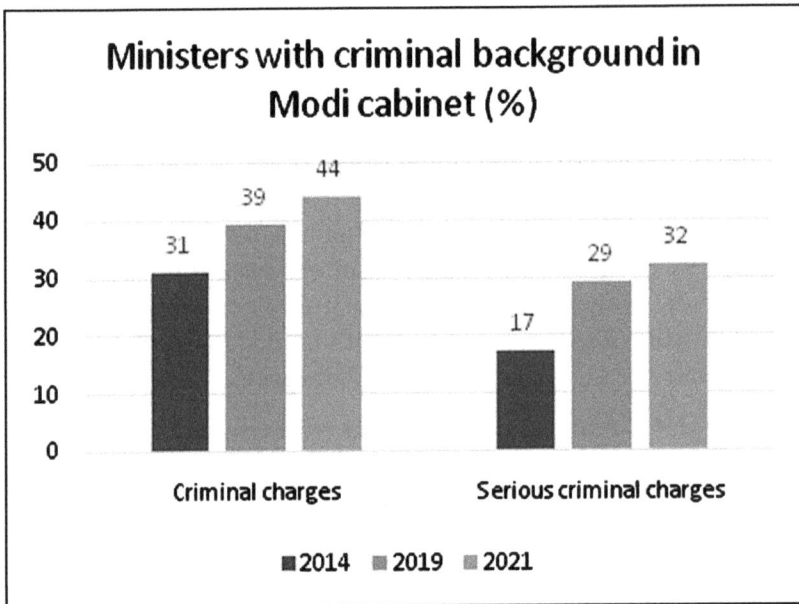

Ministers with criminal background in Modi cabinet (%)

50 — 44
39
40 — 31
32
30 — 29
17
20 —
10 —
0 —

Criminal charges   Serious criminal charges

■ 2014   ■ 2019   ■ 2021

Source: Association for Democratic Reforms

Human Rights: What's That?

At the 28th foundation day of the National Human Rights Commission (NHRC) in October 2021, the Prime Minister said "selective outrage" over human rights was "dangerous" for democracy.[221] This was days after his MoS for Home Ajay Mishra Teni's car mowed down peacefully marching farmers in Lakhimpur Kheri. The Prime Minister also said human rights mattered to people *only* after their basic needs were met (counting fundamental right to life with dignity out of the basic needs). Then NHRC chief Justice Arun Mishra praised the Central government for its human rights record despite the contrary evidence and condemned "new norms" of accusing India of human rights violations at the behest of "international forces". A few weeks later, then Chief of Defence Staff (CDS) General Bipin Rawat[222] joined the chorus stating that the people in Kashmir were saying they would "lynch terrorists" and that this was a "positive sign" and wouldn't amount to violation of human rights. He provided no evidence and no logic for his assertions. As mentioned earlier, NSA Doval has repeatedly branded civil society as the "invisible enemy" with which India was battling the "fourth generation war" as mentioned earlier.

None of these public utterances indicates respect for human rights. Once a powerful body, the NHRC became irrelevant and lost its accreditation with the

UN High Commission for Human Rights (UNHCHR). In 2016, the UNHCHR first deferred accreditation to the NHRC citing its political appointees and failure to ensure gender balance and pluralism. It deferred accreditation for the second time in May 2023 – which means it can't represent India in global forum.[223] The year 2016 had seen the first political appointee to the NHRC[224] – BJP vice president Avinash Rai Khanna as a member of the commission. Its functioning will be obvious from one example. It received 11 complaints of mob violence/arson in Manipur by May 9, 2023 (the first few days when Manipur started burning), yet in the full commission meeting of May 23, 2023, Manipur wasn't discussed at all, instead issues like "forced conversion" were discussed.[225]

Law is What the Govt Fancies

Here are two classic cases – *among many others* already pointed out and detailed in other chapters.

PM CARES Fund

The Prime Minister's Citizen Assistance and Relief in Emergency Situations Fund, or in short PM CARES Fund, was registered as a public trust on March 27, 2020 (FY20) – two days after the pandemic lockdown was announced.[226] Its objective is to provide emergency relief – the same as that of the Prime Minister's National Relief Fund (PMNRF), the official Government of India fund set up in 1948, which is operational and is flush with funds.

Official data shows, when the PM CARES Fund was set up the PMNRF had *unspent* amount of *Rs 4,393 crore* – which the Prime Minister could have utilized. Since then, the unspent amount with the PMNRF has surged: from Rs 4,393 crore in FY20 to Rs 4,927 crore in FY21 to Rs 5,557 crore in FY22.[227] The PM CARES Fund too has large unspent sums: Rs 3,077 crore in FY20, Rs 7,014 crore in FY21 and Rs 5,416 in FY22.[228] In all, in the three fiscals of FY20-FY22, the PM CARES Fund has received Rs 23,198.7 crore, of which foreign funds are Rs 535.4 crore.

The PM CARES trust deed says it is a "public charitable trust" headed by the Prime Minister of India; ministers of defence, home affairs and finance are its trustees (ex-officio) and donations to it is "voluntary". It has government domain name (pmcares.gov.in); is hosted and run by the PMO and carries official symbols (tricolour and Ashokan lions). Ministries, Indian Army, PSUs, government-run universities, private companies donate to it from their CSR and salary funds. Thus, in just four days of FY20, it collected Rs 3,067 crore.[229]

And yet, the PMO refuses to provide answers about the fund's activities under the transparency law, the Right to Information Act (RTI) of 2005 and subject it to public audit or audit by the Comptroller and Auditor General of India (CAG). It has repeatedly told the Supreme Court (in August 2020[230]) and the Delhi High Court (in September 2021[231] and January 2023[232]) that the trust isn't a "public authority" and not subject to the RTI Act. It also told the Delhi High Court in 2021 that "to ensure transparency, the audited report is put on the official website of the Trust along with the details of utilization of funds received by the Trust".

In fact, the Supreme Court was misled into saying, in its August 18, 2020 order that "no Government money is credited in the PM CARES Fund". This is not true. A series of RTI questions to Central PSUs (CPSUs) revealed in the same August 2020[233] that from 'Maharatnas' to 'Navratnas', 39 CPSUs had donated Rs 2,105 crore (65% of Rs 3,077 crore), from their CSR funds, in just four days left for the fiscal. The CPSUs continue to pump their CSR money to the PM CARES Fund – diverting Rs 2,913 crore or 59% of Rs 4,915 crore all listed companies, during FY20-FY22.[234]

The claim that it is voluntary fund is contrary to official communications and ground realities. For example:

- On May 28, 2020, Ministry of Corporate Affairs (MCA) sought CSR funds from companies declaring that "the Government of India has set up".[235] The Companies Act of 2013 was amended to include the fund in its Schedule VII.[236]

- In December 2020, Commissioner of Income Tax (Exemption) wrote in reply to a RTI query: "PM Cares Fund …a body owned by, controlled by and established by the Government of India".[237]

- The Prime Minister personally advised the Ministry of External Affairs (MEA) to publicize the fund and mobilize foreign donations, following which this was done in *27 countries* – a series of RTI queries to embassies revealed.[238]

- On April 2, 2020, a central university, the Indian Maritime University, wrote to Association of Indian Universities for donations.[239]

- Finance Ministry coerced its staff to donate, which said those unwilling must give the reason in writing.[240]

- RTI queries revealed 38 PSUs, including the ailing ONGC, donated *Rs 2,105 crore* from their Corporate Social Responsibility (CSR) funds; 101 PSUs, including the sick BSNL, gave Rs 155 crore from staff salary; armed forces gave Rs 203.7 crore from salary.[241]

- The fund received *Rs 4,316 crore* of CSR fund from corporate entities, public and private, during March-May 2020 and *Rs 85 crore* during March-June 2021.[242]

- Delhi University, which is irregular in paying salary, donated Rs 4 core to the fund.[243]

- The fund enjoys (i) 100% exemption under the Income Tax Act, 1961 and (ii) exempted from the Foreign Contribution (Regulation) Act, enabling foreign donations, as per its website.

As for the self-declared disclosers by the fund[244], it merely provides an account of donations and expenditures which are not verifiable. On the receipt side, the disclosers merely give total amounts under three heads: "voluntary contributors", "foreign contributors" and "interest income" – without identifying the doners or the amount they donated. On the expenditure side, lumpsum amount is mentioned under different heads but without identifying the recipient institutions or states. The only exceptions to the expenditure disclosers are: in FY21, Rs 50 crore were given for two "makeshift" Covid hospitals in Muzaffarpur and Patna and in FY22, Rs 163.99 crore were given for three "makeshift" Covid hospitals in Lucknow, Jammu and Srinagar and to "reactive" a Covid hospital in Delhi Cantt.

Whatever it may be described as, the fund is operated as a private fund but run officially by the PMO and enough reasons exist to investigate its activities or shut it down.[245]

There is yet another reason to worry about the PM CARES Fund. As explained in Introduction, the Prime Minister's "New Welfarism" is highly personalized, has created a new vote bank, called "labharthi varg". This fund is an addition to that – public fund used for building the Prime Minister's image and vote bank for his party. Now, the PM CARES Fund threatens to do more of it. There is yet another downside to it. This is a double whammy. By diverting the CSR fund, not only the CSR's objective of developing "local communities" who suffer adverse consequences of industrial operations (air, water and soil pollutions, loss of community land and forest, displacement of population etc.) is affected, it has hurt fund flows to NGOs too.[246]

Media Censorship: IT Rules of 2021

The same disregard for the rule of law and propriety is reflected in the government's media censorship. It brought the Information Technology (Intermediary Guidelines and Digital Media Ethics Code) Rules of 2021[247], or IT Rules of 2021 for short, to regulate digital news media and media intermediaries like Google, Facebook, WhatsApp and Twitter ('X'). It came after the mainstream media had already been tamed through co-option, coercion and ideological affinity.

The legality of the IT Rules of 2021 was questioned by the Ministry of Information and Broadcasting (I&B), its administrative ministry, and the Intelligence Bureau (IB). They pointed out that the Information Technology Act (IT Act), 2000, under which the rules were being framed at the time, did not cover digital platforms – and hence, no legal basis for IT Rules of 2021. The all-powerful PMO overruled it.[248] The Bombay and Madras High Courts[249] stayed two provisions (1 and 3) of the Rule 9 relating to "Code of Ethics", calling them prima facie against the right to freedom of speech and going beyond the substantive law of the IT Act of 2000 and expressing apprehension that these clauses "may rob the media of its independence and the fourth pillar of democracy may not at all be there". Yet, the IT Rules of 2021 remain in force as the courts didn't strike it down. Petitions challenging its constitutional validity are pending with the apex court and the latter has stayed all proceedings before high courts[250] – *enabling the government* to use it.

In July 2022, the Twitter went to Karnataka High Court to challenge the government seeking to block 1,474 twitter accounts and 175 tweets of political rivals, groups critical of the government and journalists critical of the government by using the IT Rules of 2021 – between February 2021 and 2022. The Twitter alleged, increasingly instructions were being made "without informing" specific tweets, without "proper reasons" and which were "manifestly arbitrary, fail to provide the originators prior notice and are disproportionate in several cases". One of these was for the US's Freedom House's tweet about internet shutdowns in Kashmir. The Twitter said India alone had accounted for 11% of the global legal demands for deleting/blocking tweets during January-June 2021.[251]

Meanwhile, India remains internet shutdown capital of world – another form of information/media censorship – ranking top for the *fifth consecutive time* in 2022 (from 2018 onwards) – even below the war-ravaged Ukraine to a distant second – accounting for 58% of all shutdowns *since 2016*, as documented in the Shutdown Tracker Optimization Project (STOP database).[252] It cost India $184.3 million in 2022 – which went up to $255.2 million in the first five months of June 2023 (less than halfway through the year) as Manipur was added to the list.[253]

IT Rules 2022 and 2023: Further Censorship Without Law

On October 18, 2022, the IT Rules 2022 were brought in by amending the IT Rules of 2021 – to add another layer of media censorship by providing for an executive-controlled adjudication[254] – and further amended the IT Rules of 2021 on April 6, 2023 to set up a censorship board by mandating the government to act as fact-check body on all information relating to itself. These two make the government the prosecutor, the jury and the judge.[255]

The April 6, 2023 notification (i) asked social media intermediaries like Google, Facebook, Twitter to take down posts and block URLs marked as "fake or false misleading information" related to "Government business" or else, they would lose "safe harbour" protections. But it didn't explain what is "fake", "false" or "misleading". This is left for (ii) "the notified *Fact Check Unit* (FCU) of the Central government" to be "identified". So, the government will decide news against it to be blocked without checks and balances.[256] It was challenged in the Bombay High Court; the Centre kept its notification in *abeyance*[257] till September 4, 2023.

Without this FCU, the Centre's communication agency, the Press Information Bureau (PIB) has been fact-checking about media reports on the government affairs since 2019 – and claimed to have receiving *28,380 "actionable queries"*[258] for fact-check since November 2020. The premier fact-checking website Altnews pointed out (a) it is selective and picks only opposition leaders and anti-government contents, not lies spread by the ruling party members or ministers (like Union Home Minister Amit Shah saying that the Russia-Ukraine war was halted for a few hours on Modi's request to facilitate the evacuation of Indian students) – more worryingly because in 2022 it found maximum, 48.1%, misleading statements came from the BJP and its leaders and nearly 41% of instances had "a clear collective target, that target was Muslims". Officially, the BJP had dismissed the leaked PLFS report of 2017-18 showing 45-year high of unemployment rate as "#FakeNews" in January 2019[259] but when the report was finally released after it had secured a second term in May, the data turned out to be true![260] It also found (b) in quite a number of cases the PIB's fact-checks turned out to be false and contrary to facts as confirmed by the government agencies involved; were embarrassing for the government though.[261]

This is censorship without law – through executive rules – quite ironical for a government accused of pioneering fake news, misinformation and disinformation campaigns (propaganda) in India and whose party officially runs (BJP) IT Cell has been repeatedly accused for doing so (Chapter XI).

It will have a "chilling effect on the fundamental right to speech and expression", said the Internet Freedom Foundation.[262] Apart from violating the parliamentary procedures required to expand the scope of the parent legislation, the IT Act of 2000, it violates the Supreme Court ruling in Shreya Singhal vs. Union of India of 2013 of 2015. The 2013 (interim order) struck down Section 66A (punishment for sending offensive messages through communication service, etc.). The 2015 (final) order not only struck down Section 66A, laid down strict procedures for blocking content in general and also under Sections 69A (power to issue directions for blocking information) and 79 (exemption from liability of intermediary in certain cases) – while upholding their validity.[263] At a hearing to stand-up comedian Kunal Kamra's challenge to the FCU, the Bombay High Court said in April 2023 that the IT Rules of 2023 "doesn't have necessary guardrails" and "no protection granted".[264]

Another move to control media is to cap the FDI limit for digital media (while liberalising for the rest) to 26% in 2019. This was a part of the strategy to stifle digital media, as the report of the Group of Ministers (GoM) would reveal in 2021. This capping eventually led to the closure of Huffington Post, a fiercely critical voice, in November 2020. Until 2019, print media and news broadcast television companies had FDI caps of 26% and 49%, respectively, but there was no restriction for digital media.[265]

Next Chapter (II) gives an account of how the government has tamed the mainstream media and intimidated inconvenient journalists and media platforms.

Celebrating "Good Governance Day" and "Constitution Day" makes no sense when the rule of law becomes arbitrary and a weapon to be used against the "others".

***

References

1   The rule of law and transitional justice in conflict and post-conflict societies, Report of the Secretary-General, UN Security Council, Aug 23, 2004; https://www.un.org/ruleoflaw/files/2004%20report.pdf

2   Ramana NV, Rule of Law vs Rule by Law, Indian Express, Jul 2, 2021; https://indianexpress.com/article/opinion/columns/n-v-ramana-pd-desai-memorial-lecture-indian-judiciary-state-rule-of-law-constitution-7385031/

3   Ambedkar BR 1948: Constituent Assembly of India Debates (Proceedings) - Volume VII, Lok Sabha, Nov 15, 1948; http://164.100.47.194/loksabha/writereaddata/cadebatefiles/C15111948.html

4   BBC 2021: Munawar Faruqui: Bail for jailed India comic who did not crack a joke, Feb 5, 2021; https://www.bbc.com/news/world-asia-india-55945712

5   Majumder Sanjoy, Why an Indian student has been arrested for sedition, Feb 15, 2016; https://www.bbc.com/news/world-asia-india-35576855

6   Kumar Abhiskhek 2022: No, 'Pakistan Zindabad' wasn't chanted during nomination rally of Jharkhand Mukhiya candidate, Apr 23, 2022; https://www.altnews.in/media-misreport-jharkhand-mukhiya-candidate-nomination-giridih-panchayat-election-pakistan-zindabad-slogans-raised/

7   Kashmiri students arrested for celebrating Pakistan's cricket win assaulted outside Agra court, Oct 29, 2021; https://scroll.in/latest/1009297/kashmiri-students-arrested-for-celebrating-pakistans-cricket-win-assaulted-outside-agra-court#:~:text=Arsheed%20Yousuf%2C%20Inayat%20Altaf%20Sheikh,neighbouring%20country%20after%20the%20match.

8   Siddique Kappan: Indian journalist released from jail after two years, Feb 2, 2023; https://www.bbc.com/news/world-asia-india-64494426

9   Court No. 10, Criminal misc. bail application No. 13642 of 2022, Allahabad High Court; Dec 23, 2022; https://images.assettype.com/barandbench/2022-12/a879c1f2-8567-429d-baa5-1eb7da0d0410/Sidhique_Kappan_v_ED.pdf

10 Aafaq Zafar, 'We were punished for being Muslim': Atikur Rahman, arrested with Siddique Kappan, is finally free, Jun 23, 2023; https://scroll.in/article/1051390/we-were-punished-for-being-muslim-atikur-rahman-arrested-with-siddique-kappan-is-finally-free

11 Subramaniam Tara and Pandey Tanushree, Indian author Arundhati Roy faces sedition charges over 2010 remarks on Kashmir, Oct 12, 2023; https://edition.cnn.com/2023/10/12/india/india-author-arundhati-roy-sedition-case-intl-hnk/index.html

12 Article14 2022: A decade of darkness: The story of sedition in India, Feb 2022; https://sedition.article-14.com/

13 Pandey Tanushree, Mishra Anuj and Ojha Arvind, Exclusive: UP Police cremate Hathras gangrape victim's body despite family's protest, Sept 30, 2020; https://

www.indiatoday.in/india/story/up-police-takes-hathras-gangrape-victim-s-body-kin-to-village-asks-them-to-cremate-it-overnight-1726773-2020-09-29

14   Article14 2021: Our New Database Reveals Rise In Sedition Cases In The Modi Era, Feb 2, 2021; https://www.article-14.com/post/our-new-database-reveals-rise-in-sedition-cases-in-the-modi-era;

15   Process is the punishment in our criminal justice system: CJI Ramana, Deccan Herald, Jul 16, 2022; https://www.deccanherald.com/national/north-and-central/process-is-the-punishment-in-our-criminal-justice-system-cji-ramana-1127250.html

16   Vinod Dua vs Union of India and others, Supreme Court judgement, Jun 3, 2021; https://main.sci.gov.in/supremecourt/2020/12755/12755_2020_33_1501_28058_Judgement_03-Jun-2021.pdf

17   Natasha Narwal vs State of Delhi NCT, Delhi High Court, Jun 15, 2021; https://www.livelaw.in/pdf_upload/natasha-narwal-bail-order-delhi-high-court-395020.pdf

18   State of NCT of Delhi vs Devangana Kalita, Supreme Court, May 2, 2023; https://main.sci.gov.in/supremecourt/2021/13600/13600_2021_2_9_44099_Order_02-May-2023.pdf

19   Ramana NV, [It] is like giving a saw to the carpenter to cut a piece of wood and he uses it to cut the entire forest itself., Jul 15, 2021; https://www.thehindu.com/app-exclusive/it-is-like-giving-a-saw-to-the-carpenter-to-cut-a-piece-of-wood-and-he-uses-it-to-cut-the-entire-forest-itself/article35336802.ece

20   Sinha Bhadra, Modi govt tells SC it will 're-examine & re-consider' provisions of IPC Section 124A on sedition, May 9, 2022; https://theprint.in/judiciary/modi-govt-tells-sc-it-will-re-examine-re-consider-provisions-of-ipc-section-124a-on-sedition/948958/

21   Sinha Bhadra, Sedition law should be upheld, says attorney general, asks SC for guidelines to stop misuse, May 5, 2022; https://theprint.in/judiciary/sedition-law-should-be-upheld-says-attorney-general-asks-sc-for-guidelines-to-stop-misuse/943506/

22   Rajagopal K, Supreme Court freezes British-era sedition law till it is re-examined, May 11, 2022; https://www.thehindu.com/news/national/sc-asks-centre-states-to-not-file-fresh-firs-in-sedition-cases/article65403622.ece

23   Law commission, Usage of the law of sedition, Report no. 279, Apr 2023; https://cdnbbsr.s3waas.gov.in/s3ca0daec69b5adc880fb464895726dbdf/uploads/2023/06/2023060150.pdf

24   Consultation Paper on "SEDITION", Law Commission of India, GOI, Aug 30, 2018; https://www.thehinducentre.com/incoming/65642923-2018_Law-Commission_Consultation-paper-on-Sedition.pdf

25   Internal security going to be a big challenge for India: NSA Ajit Docal, PTI, Jul 13, 2018; https://economictimes.indiatimes.com/news/defence/internal-security-going-to-be-a-big-challenge-for-india-nsa-ajit-doval/articleshow/49609461.cms

26   Siddiqui Imran Ahmed, NSA Ajit Doval says civil society is 'new frontier of war', Nov 15, 2021; https://www.telegraphindia.com/india/rights-defenders-chide-doval-for-saying-civil-society-is-new-frontier-of-war/cid/1838932

27   Das Saurav, Law Commission's Sedition Report Influenced By 2018 Book That Favours Retention Of Misused, Colonial-Era Law, Jun 12, 2023; https://article-14.com/post/law-commission-s-sedition-report-influenced-by-2018-book-that-favours-retention-of-misused-colonial-era-law-648681a8c8941

28   Sheriff M Kaunain, Govt says sedition out, new section gets it in, with wider ambit, Aug 12, 2023; https://indianexpress.com/article/india/govt-says-sedition-out-new-section-gets-it-in-with-wider-ambit-8888628/;   https://prsindia.org/files/bills_acts/bills_parliament/2023/Bharatiya_Nyaya_Sanhita,_2023.pdf

29   Sedition law to be fully repealed in IPC overhaul: Amit Shah in Parliament, Aug 11, 2023;   https://www.financialexpress.com/india-news/sedition-law-to-be-repealed-amit-shah-lok-sabha-indian-penal-code-bharatiya-nyaya-sanhita-bill-2023/3207686/

30   Rangarajan Lubhyathi, Home Minister Amit Shah Says Sedition Is Dead. But Its Replacement Is More Fearsome Than The Colonial Law Ever Was, Aug 14, 2023; https://article-14.com/post/home-minister-amit-shah-says-sedition-is-dead-but-its-replacement-is-more-fearsome-than-the-colonial-law-ever-was-64d99ff8dc0d8

31   Kedar Nath case1962: SC order in the Kedar Nath Singh vs State of Bihar case, Jan 20, 1962; https://indiankanoon.org/doc/111867/

32   Noorani AG, How a Supreme Court judgment brought back the sedition law in India, Jan 15, 2021; https://frontline.thehindu.com/the-nation/how-a-supreme-court-judgment-brought-back-the-sedition-law-in-india/article33481062.ece

33   Supreme Court transfers all FIRs against Munawar Faruqui to MP, Apr 25, 2023; https://indianexpress.com/article/india/sc-transfers-fir-comedian-munawar-faruqui-indore-8572915/

34   The Unlawful Activities) Prevention Amendment Act, 2019; Gazette of India, Aug 8, 2019; https://egazette.nic.in/WriteReadData/2019/210355.pdf

35   SC 2023: Arun Bhuyan vs State of Assam, Mar 24, 2023; https://main.sci.gov.in/supremecourt/2007/14479/14479_2007_4_1501_43078_Judgement_24-Mar-2023.pdf

36   'Release the Bhima Koregaon 16 Immediately': Nobel Laureates, EU MPs Write to Indian Authorities, Jun 11, 2021; https://thewire.in/rights/bhima-koregaon-arrested-activists-letter

37   Mittal Tusha, Pune Police is diverting the Bhima Koregaon investigation, protecting Bhide, Ekbote: Deputy mayor Siddharth Dhende, Sept 9, 2018; https://caravanmagazine.in/crime/pune-police-is-diverting-the-bhima-koregaon-investigation-protecting-bhide-ekbote-deputy-mayor-siddharth-dhende

38   Chari Mridula, Bhima Koregaon chargesheet 2018: Focus on plot to kill Modi, silence on caste violence, Nov 16, 2018; https://scroll.in/article/902374/bhima-koregaon-chargesheet-focus-on-plot-to-kill-modi-silence-on-caste-violence

39   Ghosh Sohini, Three Gujarat cops accused in Ishrat encounter case discharged by CBI court, Apr 1, 2021; https://indianexpress.com/article/india/ishrat-jahan-fake-encounter-case-cbi-court-discharges-last-three-remaining-accused-7252453/

40   Elgaar Parishad case: NIA frames charges under UAPA against 11, including 9 jailed activists; leaves out sedition, PTI, Feb 4, 2020; https://www.firstpost.com/india/elgaar-parishad-case-nia-frames-charges-under-uapa-against-11-including-9-jailed-activists-leaves-out-sedition-7997951.html

41   Shantha Sukanya, Case Against Hindutva Leaders Ignored, No Justice in Sight for Bhima Koregaon Violence Victims, Sept 26, 2020; https://thewire.in/caste/bhima-koregaon-violence-hindutva-leaders-case

42   Supreme Court confirms bail for Anand Teltumbde: A recap of the Elgar Parishad case, the accused, Nov 26, 2022; https://indianexpress.com/article/explained/sc-confirms-bail-for-anand-teltumbde-elgar-parishad-case-8290006/

43   Joshi Neha, Bhima Koregaon riots: Bombay High Court grants bail to Mahesh Raut; sixth accused to get bail, Sept 21, 2023; https://www.barandbench.com/news/bhima-koregaon-riots-bombay-high-court-grants-bail-mahesh-raut

44   Elgaar Parishad: Supreme Court grants bail to activist Varavara Rao on medical grounds, Aug 11, 2022; https://indianexpress.com/article/india/supreme-court-bail-varavara-rao-bhima-koregaon-8081827/

45   Section 169 of CrPC: Procedure when investigation cannot be completed in twenty-four hours; https://www.indiacode.nic.in/show-data?actid=AC_CEN_5_23_000010_197402_1517807320555&orderno=193#:~:text=(1)%20Whenever%20any%20person%20is,the%20police%20station%20or%20the

46   Court Dismisses NIA's Plea Challenging Default Bail To Sudha Bharadwaj In Bhima Koregaon Case, Dec 7, 2021; https://www.livelaw.in/top-stories/supreme-court-sudha-bharadwaj-default-bail-bhima-koregaon-nia-bombay-high-court-187093,

47   Shantha Sukanya, After 5 Years in Jail, Vernon Gonsalves and Arun Ferreira Get Bail in Elgar Parishad Case, Jul 28, 2023; https://thewire.in/rights/elgar-parishad-bail-vernon-gonsalves-arun-ferreira-supreme-court

48   Choudhury Chitrangada Another Jail Birthday For Youngest In Bhima-Koregaon Case, , Jul 1, 2023; https://www.article-14.com/post/another-birthday-in-jail-for-youngest-bhima-koregaon-accused

49   Modak Sadaf, Stan Swamy dead: NIA didn't seek custody but kept him behind bars, opposed his plea; Jul 6, 2021; https://indianexpress.com/article/india/father-stan-swamy-dead-elgar-parishad-case-nia-probe-7390722/

50   Pandey Geeta, Why is India denying prisoners spectacles and straws? Dec 27, 2020; https://www.bbc.com/news/world-asia-india-55410715

51   Editorial: Repeal UAPA, Jul 8, 2021; https://www.business-standard.com/article/opinion/repeal-uapa-121070801506_1.html

52   Mandhani Apoorva, Not Tolstoy, it was Biswajit Roy's 'War and Peace in

Junglemahal' that HC judge asked about, Aug 29, 2019; https://theprint.in/india/not-tolstoy-it-was-biswajit-roys-war-and-peace-in-junglemahal-that-hc-judge-asked-about/284159/

53   Bhatt Prajwal, When reading books is criminalised: Examining UAPA, sedition cases in India, Jul 25, 2023; https://www.thenewsminute.com/article/when-reading-books-criminalised-examining-uapa-sedition-cases-india-180169

54   India: Human Rights Defenders Targeted by a Coordinated Spyware Operation, Jun 15, 2020; https://www.amnesty.org/en/latest/research/2020/06/india-human-rights-defenders-targeted-by-a-coordinated-spyware-operation/

55   Masih Niha and Slater Joanna, They were accused of plotting to overthrow the Modi government. The evidence was planted, a new report says. Feb 10, 2021; https://www.washingtonpost.com/world/asia_pacific/india-bhima-koregaon-activists-jailed/2021/02/10/8087f172-61e0-11eb-a177-7765f29a9524_story.html; Further evidence in case against Indian activists accused of terrorism was planted, new report says, Apr 20, 2021; https://www.washingtonpost.com/world/2021/04/20/india-bhima-koregaon-activists-report/; Evidence found on a second Indian activist's computer was planted, report says; Jul 6, 2021; https://www.washingtonpost.com/world/2021/07/06/bhima-koregaon-case-india/ & Deb Siddhartha, The unravelling of a conspiracy: were the 16 charged with plotting to kill India's prime minister framed? Aug 12, 2021; https://www.theguardian.com/world/2021/aug/12/bhima-koregaon-case-india-conspiracy-modi

56   Shantha Sukanya, Leaked Data Shows Surveillance Net in Elgar Parishad Case May Have Crossed a Line, Jul 18, 2021; https://thewire.in/rights/elgar-parishad-case-surveillance-pegasus

57   Police Linked to Hacking Campaign to Frame Indian Activists, WIRED, Jun 16, 2022; https://www.wired.com/story/modified-elephant-planted-evidence-hacking-police/

58   Romila Thapar vs Union Of India on 28 September, Supreme Court, 2018; https://indiankanoon.org/doc/52834611/

59   Watali Case 2019: National Investigation Agency vs Zahoor Ahmad Shah Watali on 2 April, 2019, Supreme Court; https://indiankanoon.org/doc/117627977/

60   Lokur Madan B, Strange Case of G.N. Saibaba and the Supreme Court, Another New Abnormal, Oct 19, 2022; https://thewire.in/law/supreme-court-gn-saibaba-discharges-suspend-new-abnormal

61   Lokur Madan B, 'Strange Case'

62   SC Sets Aside Bombay HC Order Discharging G.N. Saibaba in Maoist Links Case, Apr 19, 2023; https://thewire.in/law/sc-sets-aside-bombay-hc-order-discharging-g-n-saibaba-in-maoist-links-case

63   Gokhale Omkar, Bombay High Court judge quits, announces decision in open court, Aug 5, 2023; https://indianexpress.com/article/cities/mumbai/bombay-high-court-justice-rohit-b-deo-resignation-nagpur-bench-open-court-8876242/

64   Benwal Narsi, At least 12 High Court judges have resigned since 2017, Aug 5, 2023; https://www.barandbench.com/news/litigation/at-least-12-high-court-judges-have-resigned-since-2017

65   UAPA cases, Rajya Sabha, Jul 20, 2022; https://pqars.nic.in/annex/257/AU383.pdf

66   Telangana police charged retired UoH Prof Haragopal, OU's Padmaja Shaw, 150 others under UAPA last August; accused 'unaware', Jun 16, 2023; https://thesouthfirst.com/telangana/telangana-police-charged-retired-uoh-prof-haragopal-ous-padmaja-shaw-150-others-under-uapa-last-august-accused-unaware/

67   Maoist link: Dead judge, 151 others in Telangana police FIR, Jun 20, 2023; https://timesofindia.indiatimes.com/city/hyderabad/dead-former-hc-judge-among-152-charged-under-uapa-for-naxal-links/articleshow/101116589.cms

68   India: Government Policies, Actions Target Minorities, Human Rights Watch, Feb 19, 2021; https://www.hrw.org/news/2021/02/19/india-government-policies-actions-target-minorities

69   Tora Agarwala, NIA court discharges Akhil Gogoi in UAPA case, pulls up agency, Jul 1, 2021; https://indianexpress.com/article/north-east-india/assam/nia-discharges-akhil-gogoi-uapa-anti-caa-assam-7384127/

70   Parashar Utpal, Offered bail by NIA for joining RSS, BJP, says jailed Assam activist Akhil Gogoi, Mar 24, 2021; https://www.hindustantimes.com/elections/assam-assembly-election/offered-bail-by-nia-for-joining-rss-bjp-says-jailed-assam-activist-akhil-gogoi-101616558641887.html

71   Sureshkumar, Why don't you join BJP, ED asked TN minister Senthil Balaji: Kapil Sibal, Sept 16, 2023; https://timesofindia.indiatimes.com/city/chennai/why-dont-you-join-bjp-ed-asked-senthil-balaji-sibal/articleshow/103700739.cms?from=mdr

72   Reghunatha Leena Gita, How Pragya Singh Thakur, Sunil Joshi and Aseemanand planned the Samjhauta Express blast, Apr 17, 2019; https://caravanmagazine.in/politics/pragya-singh-thakur-joins-bjp-samjhauta-express

73   Dwary Anurag, Am Unwell, BJP's Pragya Thakur Told Court; Now She's Filmed Dancing, Jul 9, 2021; https://www.ndtv.com/india-news/video-after-basketball-clip-bjps-pragya-thakurs-dance-video-draws-congress-dig-2482694

74   BJP MP Pragya Thakur booked over 'keep knives sharp' speech in Karnataka, Dec 28, 2022; https://www.hindustantimes.com/india-news/bjp-mp-pragya-thakur-booked-for-hate-speech-in-karnataka-s-shivamogga-101672244942071.html

75   Godse remarks: Narendra Modi says he will never be able to forgive Pragya Thakur, May 17, 2019; https://scroll.in/latest/923813/godse-remarks-narendra-modi-says-he-will-never-be-able-to-forgive-pragya-thakur

76   Saigal Sonam, Charges under MCOCA dropped against 8 in Malagaon blast case, Dec 27, 2017; https://www.thehindu.com/news/national/other-states/malegaon-blast-case-mcoca-charges-against-sadhvi-purohit-go/article22287401.ece

77   Gaikwad Rahi, NIA told me to go soft in Malegaon 2008 blast case: Rohini Salian,

Jun 25, 2015; https://www.thehindu.com/news/national/other-states/nia-told-me-to-go-soft-in-malegaon-2008-blast-case-says-special-public-prosecutor-rohini-salian/article7354066.ece

78   MS Nileena, Falling in Line: The National Investigation Agency's loss of credibility, The Caravan, Jul 1, 2022; https://caravanmagazine.in/crime/rise-and-fall-of-nia-hindu-terror-cases-bhima-koregaon?utm_source=mailer&utm_medium=email&utm_campaign=current_issue&utm_id=108

79   Mohanty P, This is NIA, Governance Now, Oct 1-15, 2011; https://www.dropbox.com/s/edcxxcppmtlixy5/This%20is%20NIA..pdf?dl=0

80   MS Nileena 2022, Falling in Line: The National Investigation Agency's loss of credibility, The Caravan, Jul 1, 2022; https://caravanmagazine.in/crime/rise-and-fall-of-nia-hindu-terror-cases-bhima-koregaon?utm_source=mailer&utm_medium=email&utm_campaign=current_issue&utm_id=108

81   Sagar, Judge changed in Nanded blast case on the day of Yashwant Shinde's second hearing, Nov 5, 2022; https://caravanmagazine.in/crime/yashwant-shinde-court-judge-change-vhp-rss-cbi-nanded-blast

82   Sagar, Nanded Blast: Court rejects former RSS man's request to give witness against VHP leader, Feb 19, 2023; https://caravanmagazine.in/crime/nanded-court-rejects-shinde-petition-evidence-against-rss-vhp-milind-parande

83   Khan Hamza, Congress rolls out offensive in Rajasthan as BJP makes Kanhaiya Lal killing a poll issue, Nov 15, 2023; https://indianexpress.com/article/political-pulse/congress-rolls-out-offensive-in-rajasthan-as-bjp-makes-kanhaiya-lal-killing-a-poll-issue-9026425/

84   Congress, BJP in war of words after arrested LeT terrorist linked to saffron party, PTI, Jul 4, 2022; https://www.thehindu.com/news/national/congress-bjp-in-war-of-words-after-arrested-let-terrorist-linked-to-saffron-party/article65596632.ece

85   Odisha BJP Writes To Amit Shah, Seeks NIA Probe Into Sambalpur Violence, PTI, Apr 23, 2023; https://www.outlookindia.com/national/odisha-bjp-writes-to-amit-shah-seeks-nia-probe-into-sambalpur-violence-news-280579

86   Singh Prabhjit, Dead and Buried: Delhi Police ignored complaints against Kapil Mishra, other BJP leaders for leading mobs in Delhi violence, Jun 21, 2020; https://caravanmagazine.in/politics/delhi-police-ignored-complaints-against-kapil-mishra-bjp-leaders-leading-mobs-delhi-violence

87   Bindra Japnam and Sharma Prathma, Row erupts over transfer of judge hours after he pulls up Delhi cops, Feb 28, 2020; https://www.livemint.com/news/india/row-erupts-over-transfer-of-judge-hours-after-he-pulls-up-delhi-cops-11582853787313.html

88   Chander Mani, 11 Ways The Delhi Police Have Muddied The Delhi-Riots Investigation, Sept 13, 2021; https://article-14.com/post/11-ways-the-delhi-police-have-muddied-the-delhi-riots-investigation-613ebb8c99769; Sebastian Manu, Delhi Riots: Damning Observations In Court Orders Raise Questions Over Delhi

Police Probe, Nov 28, 2020; https://www.livelaw.in/columns/delhi-riots-damning-observations-in-court-orders-raise-questions-over-delhi-police-probe-166534; Justice Lokur et al, Uncertain Justice: A Citizens Committee Report on the North East Delhi Violence 2020, Oct 2022; https://theleaflet.in/wp-content/uploads/2022/10/uncertain-justice-citizens-committee-report-on-north-east-delhi-violence-2020.pdf

89   Das Saurav, (part I) Fabricated Evidence, Tutored Witnesses, Malicious Prosecution: How Police Lied & Subverted Path To Justice, Aug 23, 2023; https://article-14.com/post/fabricated-evidence-tutored-witnesses-malicious-prosecution-how-police-lied-subverted-path-to-justice-64e580b7a0b1c; part II: Lying With Impunity: The Challenges Of Prosecuting The Police For Perjury, Aug 24, 2023; https://article-14.com/post/lying-with-impunity-the-challenges-of-prosecuting-the-police-for-perjury--64e6c180a42a9

90   Singh Prabhjit, John Arshu 2020: Crime and Prejudice: The BJP and Delhi Police's hand in the Delhi violence, Caravan, Sept 1, 2020; https://caravanmagazine.in/politics/the-bjp-and-delhi-police-hand-in-the-delhi-violence; Jafri Alishan, Wani Shehlat Maknoon and Varadarajan Siddharth, Delhi 2020, the Real Conspiracy: What the Police Chose Not to See, Feb 28, 2021; https://thewire.in/communalism/delhi-2020-the-real-conspiracy-what-the-police-chose-not-to-see

91   Retd IPS officer Julio Ribeiro questions Delhi riots probe, Sept 13, 2020; https://indianexpress.com/article/cities/delhi/retd-ips-officer-julio-ribeiro-questions-delhi-riots-probe-6593874/

92   Bhatia Gautam, Very disappointing to see the collegium effectively legitimising the executive's pocket veto., Apr 19, 2023; https://twitter.com/gautambhatia88/status/1648738482632769537

93   Nariman Fali S, Lokur Madan B and Panchu Sriram, A question for the collegium: Why was Justice S Muralidhar not brought to the Supreme Court? Aug 19, 2023; https://indianexpress.com/article/opinion/columns/a-question-for-supreme-court-8894242/

94   Sinha Bhadra, After govt delay, SC withdraws proposal to transfer Orissa chief justice to Madras, makes fresh recommendation, Apr 20, 2023; https://theprint.in/judiciary/after-govt-delay-sc-withdraws-proposal-to-transfer-orissa-chief-justice-to-madras-makes-fresh-recommendation/1529037/

95   Sofi Ahsan, Umar Khalid's Amravati speech obnoxious, offensive, says Delhi HC, Apr 22, 2022; https://indianexpress.com/article/cities/delhi/umar-khalids-amravati-speech-offensive-hateful-delhi-hc-7881587/

96   HC defers Umar Khalid's bail appeal: 'Let SC take view on 124A first', Apr 29, 2022; https://indianexpress.com/article/cities/delhi/northeast-delhi-riots-delhi-high-court-umar-khalid-bail-7892907/

97   Supreme Court to hear Umar Khalid's bail petition after four weeks, Sept 12, 2023; https://www.thehindu.com/news/national/delhi-riots-case-sc-admits-former-jnu-student-leader-umar-khalids-plea-fixes-hearing-after-four-weeks/article67298065.ece#:~:text=The%20Supreme%20Court%20on%20Tuesday,Act%20in%20connection%20with%20the

98   Ahsan Sofi, Hate speech case: If said with smile, no criminality, says Delhi HC, Mar 26, 2022; https://indianexpress.com/article/cities/delhi/hate-speech-case-if-said-with-smile-no-criminality-says-hc-7836774/

99   Tripathi Ashish, Shaheen Bagh: Delhi HC dismisses plea for hate speech FIR against Anurag Thakur, other BJP leaders, Deccan Herald, Jun 13, 2022; https://www.deccanherald.com/national/north-and-central/shaheen-bagh-delhi-hc-dismisses-plea-for-hate-speech-fir-against-anurag-thakur-other-bjp-leaders-1117764.html

100   Sur Arnabjit, Jahangirpuri violence: Year on, no trial yet; 44 persons arrested, all but one out on bail, Apr 6, 2023; https://indianexpress.com/article/cities/delhi/jahangirpuri-violence-year-on-no-trial-yet-44-persons-arrested-all-but-one-out-on-bail-8541106/

101   Kaunain Sheriff M 2021: 94 out of 120 orders quashed: Allahabad High Court calls out abuse of NSA in Uttar Pradesh, Indian Express, Apr 7, 2021; https://indianexpress.com/article/express-exclusive/national-security-act-uttar-pradesh-police-detentions-cow-slaughter-ban-7260425/

102   Choudhary Amit A, Supreme Court: Invoking NSA in cases of political nature abuse of law, Apr 12, 2023; http://timesofindia.indiatimes.com/articleshow/99417753.cms?utm_source=contentofinterest&utm_medium=text&utm_campaign=cppst

103   Javed Auqib 2022: As Courts Grant Bail, J&K Govt Uses 43-Year-Old Preventive Detention Law To Keep Hundreds In Jail, May 16, 2022; https://article-14.com/post/as-courts-grant-bail-j-k-govt-uses-43-year-old-preventive-detention-law-to-keep-hundreds-in-jail-6281ae5ba5a64

104   Masood Bashaarat and Sharma Arun, Detaining govt critics is abuse of PSA: Jammu and Kashmir HC quashes journalist's detention, Nov 19, 2023; https://indianexpress.com/article/cities/srinagar/detaining-govt-critics-is-abuse-of-psa-hc-quashes-jk-journalists-detention-9032704/;

105   RS 2022: Increase in attack against minority communities, Rajya Sabha, Jul 27, 2022; https://pqars.nic.in/annex/257/AU1205.pdf

106   Jacob Nidhi 2022, Data Dive: Sixfold Rise in Cases Filed under Hate Speech-Related Law in 7 Years, Jun 21, 2022; https://www.factchecker.in/data-dive/data-dive-sixfold-rise-in-cases-filed-under-hate-speech-related-law-in-7-years-822966

107   Crime in India 2020, National Crime Records Bureau, GOI, Sept 2021; https://ncrb.gov.in/sites/default/files/CII%202020%20Volume%202.pdf

108   Jafri Alishan and Barton Naomi 2022, Kissi Se Na Kehna! Mohammed Zubair Arrested for Tweeting Photo from 1983 Hindi Film, Jun 28, 2022; The Wire; https://thewire.in/communalism/kissi-se-na-kehna-mohammed-zubair-arrested-for-tweeting-photo-from-1983-hindi-film

109   Jain Ayesha, Booked Under Similar Charges, Zubair in Jail But Police Awaits Nupur Sharma, Jun 29, 2022; https://www.thequint.com/news/india/alt-news-zubair-in-jail-nupur-sharma-free#read-more

110   Nupur Sharma and family get Delhi Police protection, June 8, 2022; https://economictimes.indiatimes.com/news/politics-and-nation/nupur-sharma-

and-family-get-delhi-police-protection/articleshow/92067792.cms?utm_
source=contentofinterest&utm_medium=text&utm_campaign=cppst

111 After SC Rebuke, Delhi Police Says Nupur Sharma Was Questioned on June 18,
Jul 1, 2022; https://thewire.in/government/after-sc-rebuke-delhi-police-says-nupur-
sharma-was-questioned-on-june-18

112 Zubair gets bail in all FIRs in UP, SC orders his release by 6 pm today; no bar on
tweeting, Jul 20, 2022; https://www.hindustantimes.com/india-news/sc-grants-bail-
to-mohammed-zubair-in-all-firs-lodged-in-up-101658308266397.html

113 Bajrang Muni, Described by ASG as 'Respectable', Called for Rape of Muslim
Women, Jul 8, 2022; https://thewire.in/communalism/bajrang-muni-zubair-hate-
speech-mass-rape

114 Prophet remarks row: No coercive action against Nupur Sharma, says Supreme
Court, Jul 19, 2022; https://www.thehindu.com/news/national/prophet-remarks-
row-supreme-court-protects-nupur-sharma-from-coercive-action/article65657823.
ece

115 Mahapatra Dhanajay, Supreme Court relief for TV anchor Rohit Ranjan facing
multiple FIRs, Jul 9, 2022; http://timesofindia.indiatimes.com/articleshow/92757074.
cms?utm_source=contentofinterest&utm_medium=text&utm_campaign=cppst

116 Nobody Taking Action Against Hate Speech Despite Orders, Says Supreme Court,
Feb 3, 2023; https://thewire.in/law/supreme-court-action-hate-speech-mumbai

117 Bose Nayonika, Shaikh Zeeshan and Deshpande Alok, 4 months, 50 rallies in
Maharashtra, one theme: 'Love jihad', 'land jihad' and economic boycott, Mar
30, 2023; https://indianexpress.com/article/cities/mumbai/4-months-50-rallies-in-
maharashtra-one-theme-love-jihad-land-jihad-and-economic-boycott-8507077/

118 G7, India and 4 other countries pledge to protect free speech, Jun 28, 2022; https://
www.thehindu.com/news/national/g7-india-and-4-other-countries-pledge-to-
protect-free-speech/article65575574.ece

119 India, EU agree to protect freedom of civil society, Jul 16, 2022; http://timesofindia.
indiatimes.com/articleshow/92908727.cms?utm_source=contentofinterest&utm_
medium=text&utm_campaign=cppst

120 RSF Names PM Modi Among 37 'Predators of Press Freedom' With Kim Jong-un,
Imran Khan, Jul 5, 2021; https://thewire.in/media/rsf-narendra-modi-press-freedom-
predators-kim-jongun-imran-khan-vladimir-putin

121 India slips in World Press Freedom Index, ranks 161 out of 180 countries, May
3, 2023; https://www.thehindu.com/news/national/india-slips-in-world-press-
freedom-index-ranks-161-out-of-180-countries/article66806608.ece

122 Mehta Pratap Bhanu, By upholding PMLA, SC puts its stamp on Kafka's law, Indian
Express, Jul 29. 2022; https://indianexpress.com/article/opinion/columns/pratap-
bhanu-mehta-by-upholding-pmla-sc-puts-its-stamp-on-kafkas-law-8057249/

123 Vijay Madanlal Choudhary vs Union Of India on 27 July, 2022; https://indiankanoon.
org/doc/14485072/

124 Vishwanath Apurva, SC allows PMLA verdict review; flags burden of proof, sharing info, Aug 26, 2022; https://indianexpress.com/article/india/supreme-court-pmla-july-judgment-review-8110656/

125 G Ananthakrishnan, ED must give grounds of arrest in writing to accused: SC, Oct 4, 2023; https://indianexpress.com/article/india/ed-must-give-grounds-of-arrest-in-writing-to-accused-sc-8967241/

126 Bhatia Gautam 2022: The Executive('s) Court: On the Legacy of Justice A.M. Khanwilkar, The Wire, Jul 29, 2022; https://thewire.in/law/justice-khanwilkar-teesta-setalvad-watali-fcra-uapa

127 Anand Jatin, CBI seeks L-G nod to probe 'extortion racket' run by former AAP home minister Satyendra Jain, Nov 13, 2023; https://indianexpress.com/article/cities/delhi/cbi-seeks-lgs-sanction-to-proceed-against-satyendar-jain-in-extortion-matter-9024649/

128 A List of Opposition Leaders Raided or Arrested in the Last Five Years, Jun 1, 2022; https://thewire.in/law/a-list-of-opposition-leaders-raided-or-arrested-since-the-last-five-years; Other links: ED's crackdown on opposition leaders: List of prominent names under probe, May 31, 2022; https://www.indiatoday.in/india/story/ed-scanner-aap-bjp-satyendar-jain-sanjay-raut-chidambaram-1956298-2022-05-31; Masala bonds: ED tightens noose around ex-Kerala FM Thomas Isaac, Aug 29, 2022; https://www.business-standard.com/article/politics/masala-bonds-ed-tightens-noose-around-ex-kerala-fm-thomas-isaac-122082900005_1.html; Sanjay Raut appears before ED, Jul 1, 2022; https://www.theweek.in/news/india/2022/07/01/sanjay-raut-appears-before-ed.html; CBI raids Jodhpur residence of Rajasthan CM Ashok Gehlot's brother Agrasen Gehlot, Jun 17, 2022; https://www.indiatoday.in/india/story/cbi-raids-ashok-gehlot-brother-agrasen-gehlot-jodhpur-1963429-2022-06-17; Day after Shinde's swearing-in, Sharad Pawar says 'received love letter from Income Tax dept', Jul 1, 2022; https://www.indiatoday.in/india/story/income-tax-dept-sends-notice-to-sharad-pawar-over-poll-affidavits-1968887-2022-07-01; Sinha Jignasa, ED gets Sanjay Singh custody, claims Rs 2 crore changed hands at his residence, Oct 6, 2023; https://indianexpress.com/article/cities/delhi/ed-gets-singh-custody-claims-rs-2-cr-changed-hands-at-his-residence-8970462/; In CBI, ED crosshairs over Delhi liquor 'scam', KCR's daughter Kavitha set to be BRS national secy, Feb 10, 2023; https://theprint.in/politics/on-cbi-ed-radar-in-delhi-liquor-scam-kcrs-daughter-kavitha-set-to-be-brs-national-secretary/1365228/; ED records statement of Tejashwi Yadav in land-for-job scam case, Apr 11, 2023; https://www.thehindu.com/news/national/other-states/land-for-jobs-case-bihar-deputy-cm-tejashwi-yadav-appears-before-ed/article66723778.ece

129 ED raids up 27x in 2014-2022 compared to 2004-14: Govt, PTI, Jul 27, 2022; http://timesofindia.indiatimes.com/articleshow/93148727.cms?utm_source=contentofinterest&utm_medium=text&utm_campaign=cppst

130 Tiwary Deeptiman, Since 2014, 4-fold jump in ED cases against politicians; 95% are from Opposition, Sept 21, 2022; https://indianexpress.com/article/express-exclusive/since-2014-4-fold-jump-in-ed-cases-against-politicians-95-per-cent-are-from-opposition-8163060/

131 ED Statistics 2023: KEY DETAILS OF PMLA CASES UP TO 31.01.2023; https://enforcementdirectorate.gov.in/statistics-0

132 MS Nileena, The Enforcers: How the ED became a political tool, Jun 1, 2023; https://caravanmagazine.in/law/ed-political-tool

133 Chhattisgarh coal scam: ED takes possession of 81 assets, Jun 22, 2023; https://timesofindia.indiatimes.com/india/chhattisgarh-coal-scam-ed-takes-possession-of-81-assets/articleshow/101174908.cms

134 ED searches on premises of Raut's & Aaditya's close aides in Covid scam, Jun 22, 2023; https://timesofindia.indiatimes.com/india/ed-searches-on-premises-of-rauts-aadityas-close-aides-in-covid-scam/articleshow/101173772.cms?from=mdr

135 Khan Hamza, ED searches properties of Rajasthan minister, sons; he says no link, Sept 27, 2023; https://indianexpress.com/article/cities/jaipur/ed-searches-properties-of-rajasthan-minister-sons-he-says-no-link-8957808/

136 Tiwary Deeptiman, Multiple ED raids, arrests in cases linked to Opp leaders in 4 poll-bound states in past few months, Oct 27, 2023; https://indianexpress.com/article/political-pulse/prompt-ed-action-in-4-poll-bound-states-in-last-few-months-9001254/

137 Raman P, The Pre-Election Swoop Is the Central Agencies' Latest Trick Against Opposition Leaders, Nov 9, 2023; https://m.thewire.in/article/politics/pre-election-swoop-central-agencies-latest-trick-opposition-leaders?utm=authorlistpage

138 Tweaks in law, extensions to ED chief illegal: Amicus to Supreme Court, Mar 24, 2023; http://timesofindia.indiatimes.com/articleshow/98951963.cms?from=mdr&utm_source=contentofinterest&utm_medium=text&utm_campaign=cppst

139 The CVC (Amendment) Act 2021; https://prsindia.org/files/bills_acts/acts_parliament/2021/The%20Central%20Vigilance%20Commission%20(Amendment)%20Act,%202021.pdf

140 The Delhi Special Police Establishment (Amendment) Ac, 2021; https://prsindia.org/files/bills_acts/acts_parliament/2021/The%20Delhi%20Special%20Police%20Establishment%20(Amendment)%20Act,%202021.pdf

141 Common Cause vs Union of Indian and others, Supreme Court, Sept 8, 2021; https://main.sci.gov.in/supremecourt/2020/26036/26036_2020_5_1501_29937_Judgement_08-Sep-2021.pdf

142 Dr Jaya Thakur vs Union of India and others, Supreme Court, Jul 11, 2023; https://main.sci.gov.in/supremecourt/2022/18592/18592_2022_4_1501_45094_Judgement_11-Jul-2023.pdf

143 Khan Khajida, SC extends ED chief's term till Sept 15 in 'national interest': what is the case, what has court said previously? Jul 28, 2023; https://indianexpress.com/article/explained/explained-law/sc-ed-chiefs-what-is-the-case-sk-mishra-8863630/

144 Jain Meetu, If India Is Serious About FATF Review, ED Director's Term Shouldn't Be its Prime Concern, Jul 28, 2023; https://thewire.in/government/if-india-is-really-concerned-about-fatf-review-ed-directors-term-shouldnt-be-its-prime-concern

145 Bhatia Gautam, The ED Director Judgment – II: The Supreme Court Against the Rule of Law, Jul 27, 2023; https://indconlawphil.wordpress.com/2023/07/27/the-ed-director-judgment-ii-the-supreme-court-against-the-rule-of-law/

146 Raj Kaushik, Govt Whataboutery & Inaction: Why Hate Speech Persists Despite The Supreme Court Wanting To Stop It, Jul 28, 2023; https://article-14.com/post/govt-whataboutery-inaction-why-hate-speech-persists-despite-the-supreme-court-wanting-to-stop-it-64c3372224505#:~:text=They%20sensationalise%20and%20create%20divisions,'t%20act%20in%20time%E2%80%9D.

147 Vineet Narain & Others vs Union Of India & Another, Supreme Court, Dec 18, 1997; https://indiankanoon.org/doc/1203995/

148 Gazette: Fundamental (Amendment) Rules, 2021, Nov 15, 2021; https://images.assettype.com/barandbench/2021-11/d2d2f012-0d8b-4eb4-8e97-9d3bfa2f40f0/Notification_for_Tenure_Extension_of_2_years.pdf

149 In 4th extension, Home Secretary Bhalla gets another year, Aug 5, 2023; https://indianexpress.com/article/india/in-4th-extension-home-secretary-bhalla-gets-another-year-8877328/

150 Tiwary Deeptiman, From 60% in UPA to 95% in NDA: A surge in share of Opposition leaders in CBI net, Sept 21, 2022; https://indianexpress.com/article/express-exclusive/from-60-per-cent-in-upa-to-95-per-cent-in-nda-a-surge-in-share-of-opposition-leaders-in-cbi-net-express-investigation-8160912/

151 Siddiqui Faiz Rahman and Chakraborty Pathikrit, UP: Kanpur perfume trader arrested following recovery of Rs 284 crore, Dec 27, 2021; http://timesofindia.indiatimes.com/articleshow/88510185.cms?utm_source=contentofinterest&utm_medium=text&utm_campaign=cppst

152 Shah Pankaj and Rahman Siddiqui Faiz, 'Take 'credit' for businessman's cash pile,' PM dares SP, Dec 29, 2021; https://timesofindia.indiatimes.com/india/take-credit-for-businessmans-cash-pile-pm-dares-sp/articleshow/88555176.cms

153 Rehman Asad and Sahu Manish, P Jain and P Jain: Tale of 2 perfume merchants raises some stink in UP, Dec 29, 2021; https://indianexpress.com/article/cities/lucknow/p-jain-p-jain-tale-of-2-perfume-merchants-raises-some-stink-in-up-7695439/

154 Mohanty P, Government is equally responsible for ensuring neutrality and level-playing field during elections, India Today, Apr 10, 2019; https://www.indiatoday.in/elections/story/modi-government-elections-lok-sabha-raids-1498312-2019-04-10

155 ED and CBI free, polls come in between, Govt has no role: PM Narendra Modi, Feb 10, 2022; https://indianexpress.com/article/india/ed-and-cbi-free-polls-come-in-between-govt-has-no-role-pm-narendra-modi-7765007/

156 Shiv Sena-NCP-Congress knocks SC door over closing of corruption cases against Ajit Pawar, New Indian Express, Nov 26, 2019; https://www.newindianexpress.com/nation/2019/nov/26/shiv-sena-ncp-congress-knocks-sc-door-over-closing-of-corruption-cases-against-ajit-pawar--2067310.html

157   I-T Dept Raids Maharashtra Deputy CM Ajit Pawar's Premises; 'BJP Afraid,' Says NCP, Oct 17, 2021; https://thewire.in/government/i-t-raids-maharashtra-deputy-cm-ajit-pawars-premises-bjp-afraid-says-ncp

158   PM Modi: This is my guarantee, 'action will be taken against scamsters, their account will be settled', Jun 27, 2023; https://timesofindia.indiatimes.com/videos/toi-original/pm-modi-this-is-my-guarantee-action-will-be-taken-against-scamsters-their-account-will-be-settled/videoshow/101318188.cms

159   Ajit Pawar joins Shinde-Fadnavis Govt: From Chagan Bhujbal to Dilip Walse Patel - These NCP leaders 'defected' with him, Jul 2, 2023; https://www.livemint.com/politics/news/ajit-pawar-joins-shinde-fadnavis-govt-from-chagan-bhujbal-to-dilip-walse-patel-these-ncp-leaders-defected-with-him-11688288598779.html

160   Singh Ashish, Maharashtra State Cooperative Bank Scam: Dy CM Ajit Pawar's Name Dropped From Supplementary Chargesheet, Sept 1, 2023; https://www.freepressjournal.in/mumbai/maharashtra-state-cooperative-bank-dy-cm-ajit-pawars-name-dropped-from-supplementary-chargesheet

161   CBI raids Arvind Kejriwal's office, seals it; Delhi CM calls Narendra Modi a coward and psychopath, News18, Dec 15, 2015; https://www.news18.com/news/politics/cbi-raids-arvind-kejriwals-office-seals-it-delhi-cm-calls-it-narendra-modis-cowardice-1177287.html

162   Manral MS, CBI probes 'irregularities' in renovation of Delhi CM's official residence, Sept 28, 2023; https://indianexpress.com/article/cities/delhi/cbi-probes-irregularities-in-renovation-of-kejriwals-residence-8959296/

163   I-T dept searches properties of MP CM Kamal Nath's aides; huge illegal cash recovered, Apr 7, 2019; https://economictimes.indiatimes.com/news/politics-and-nation/i-t-department-raids-homes-of-kamal-naths-close-aides-huge-amounts-of-cash-reportedly-seized/articleshow/68760307.cms?utm_source=contentofinterest&utm_medium=text&utm_campaign=cppst

164   Face of Patidar quota agitation, one-time critic Hardik Patel joins BJP, Jun 2, 2022; https://www.hindustantimes.com/india-news/face-of-patidar-quota-agitation-one-time-critic-hardik-patel-to-join-bjp-101654141516627.html

165   Delhi Police at Rahul Gandhi's doorstep over 'women being sexually assaulted' remark; he calls it unprecedented, questions process, Mar 19, 2023; https://theprint.in/india/delhi-police-at-rahul-gandhis-doorstep-over-women-being-sexually-assaulted-remark-he-calls-it-unprecedented-questions-process-2/1456177/

166   'Harassment For What I Said on Pulwama': Satya Pal Malik After CBI's Visit to His House, Apr 28, 2023; https://thewire.in/government/satya-pal-malik-cbi-pulwama

167   Sinha Chitranshul, Govt Needs to Amend Law to Stop Defamation SLAPP Suits, Sept 11, 2018; https://www.thequint.com/opinion/civil-defamation-suit-ahmedabad-reliance-civil-procedure-code#read-more

168   Adani Group 'SLAPP' Pushes EPW Editor Out of His Job, Jul 11, 2017; https://thewire.in/media/adani-group-slapps-epw-editor-job; Sinha Chitranshul, Govt

Needs to Amend Law to Stop Defamation SLAPP Suits, Sept 11, 2018; https://www.thequint.com/opinion/civil-defamation-suit-ahmedabad-reliance-civil-procedure-code#read-more

169   Sahu SN, Twists and Turns in Rahul Gandhi's Defamation Trial, Mr 24, 2023; https://www.newsclick.in/twists-and-turns-rahul-gandhis-defamation-trial

170   Bhatia Gautam 2023: A disturbing example of the normalisation of lawfare, The Hindu, Mar 29, 2023; https://www.thehindu.com/opinion/lead/a-disturbing-example-of-the-normalisation-of-lawfare/article66672779.ece

171   Ellis-Petersen Hannah, India's Rahul Gandhi fights 'excessive' defamation case, Apr 9, 2023; https://www.theguardian.com/world/2023/apr/09/indias-rahul-gandhi-fights-excessive-defamation-case

172   Pendency of cases and burdened judiciary, Rajya Sabha, Jul 20, 2023; https://pqars.nic.in/annex/260/AU119.pdf

173   Das Awstika, Supreme Court Stays Conviction Of Congress Leader Rahul Gandhi In 'Modi-Thieves' Defamation Case Which Disqualified Him As MP, Aug 4, 2023; https://www.livelaw.in/top-stories/supreme-court-congress-leader-rahul-gandhi-conviction-stay-criminal-defamation-case-modi-thieves-remark-234384

174   G Ananthakrishnan, Granting bail to Teesta Setalvad, Supreme Court calls Gujarat HC order 'perverse', Jul 20, 2023; https://indianexpress.com/article/india/2002-gujarat-riots-case-sc-grants-bail-to-activist-teesta-setalvad-8848362/

175   Chander Uday Singh for Citizens and Lawyers Initiative, Routes of Wrath: Weaponising Religious Processions, Apr 2023; https://www.livelaw.in/pdf_upload/routes-of-wrath-report-2023-2-465217.pdf

176   Kumar Sharat, Karauli violence in Rajasthan sparked by planned attack, says FIR, Apr 6, 2022; https://www.indiatoday.in/india/story/karauli-violence-riots-planned-attack-says-injured-rajasthan-cop-1934062-2022-04-06; Post-Ram Navami, fresh violence hits Bihar, Bengal, Apr 3, 2023; http://timesofindia.indiatimes.com/articleshow/99195004.cms?from=mdr&utm_source=contentofinterest&utm_medium=text&utm_campaign=cppst; Fresh violence erupts in Odisha's Sambalpur during Hanuman Jayanti rally, several shops gutted, Apr 15, 2023; https://www.indiatoday.in/india/story/fresh-hanuman-jayanti-violence-erupts-in-odisha-sambalpur-several-shops-gutted-2360226-2023-04-14

177   Union minister Jayant Sinha garlands 8 convicted for Ramgarh mob lynching, Jul 16, 2018; https://www.indiatoday.in/india/story/union-minister-jayant-sinha-garlands-8-convicted-for-ramgarh-mob-lynching-1279601-2018-07-06

178   Explained: How BJP won seats in areas with significant Muslim populations, Dec 9, 2022; https://www.firstpost.com/explainers/explained-how-bjp-won-seats-in-areas-with-significant-muslim-populations-11776761.html

179   Hindu Mahasabha workers slaughtered cows to cause communal violence, says UP Police, Apr 8, 2023; https://www.indiatoday.in/india/story/hindu-mahasabha-workers-slaughtered-cows-themselves-to-cause-communal-violence-up-

police-2357323-2023-04-08; Bhattacharya Oishani, 4 Hindus held for Bulandshahr temple vandalism; videos viral with misleading communal claims, https://www.altnews.in/4-hindus-held-for-bulandshahr-temple-vandalism-videos-viral-with-misleading-communal-claims/

180 'Attempt to Provoke Riots': Seven Arrested for Throwing Pork, Abusive Letters Into Ayodhya Mosques, Apr 19, 2022; https://thewire.in/communalism/ayodhya-seven-arrested-for-throwing-pork-abusive-letters-into-mosques

181 Mohanty P, Bulandshahr violence: Governance takes backseat in UP as Yogi Adityanath govt makes mockery of law and order, Dec 19, 2018; https://www.firstpost.com/india/bulandshahr-violence-governance-takes-backseat-in-up-as-yogi-adityanath-govt-mocks-law-and-justice-through-partisan-behaviour-5758001.html

182 Apoorvanand, Why is Modi so scared of history textbooks? Apr 13, 2023; https://www.aljazeera.com/opinions/2023/4/13/why-is-modi-so-scared-of-history-textbooks

183 Mukherjee Aditya and Mukherjee Mridula, Weaponising History: The Hindutva Communal Project, The Wire, Apr 10, 2023; https://thewire.in/history/weaponising-history-the-hindu-communal-project

184 Raghavan Srinath, History in the Service of Hindutva, Feb 27, 2023; https://www.theindiaforum.in/book-reviews/history-service-hindutva

185 Ellis-Petersen Hannah, Indian government accused of rewriting history after edits to schoolbooks, Apr 6, 2023; https://www.theguardian.com/world/2023/apr/06/indian-government-accused-of-rewriting-history-after-edits-to-schoolbooks

186 Chaudhuri Pooja, Amit Malviya: How the ringmaster of BJP's propaganda machinery weaponises misinformation, Feb 10, 2020; https://www.altnews.in/amit-malviya-how-ringmaster-of-bjps-propaganda-machinery-weaponises-misinformation/

187 Yadav Shyamlal, Centre amends rules, can act against IAS, IPS, IFoS pensioners on its own, Jul 20, 2023; https://indianexpress.com/article/india/centre-amends-rules-can-act-against-ias-ips-ifos-pensioners-on-its-own-8849289/s

188 Varadarajan Siddharth, Retired Security Officials Now Need Govt Nod for Any Writing Related to Former Organisation's 'Domain', Jun 2, 2021; https://thewire.in/government/retired-security-officials-now-need-govt-nod-for-any-writing-related-to-former-organisations-domain; Changes in pension rules 'attempt to impose silence' — ex-civil servants write to PM Modi, Jul 17, 2021; https://theprint.in/india/changes-in-pension-rules-attempt-to-impose-silence-ex-civil-servants-write-to-pm-modi/698203/

189 Deshpande Smruti, Army warns veterans against posting 'false narratives' on social media, says pensions could be withheld, Jul 8, 2023; https://theprint.in/defence/army-warns-veterans-against-withholding-pensions-videos-on-social-media-spreading-false-narratives/1660548/

190 Explained: What's Narada Case? Who Are The Ministers Involved? May 18, 2021;

https://www.outlookindia.com/website/story/india-news-explained-what-is-the-narada-bribery-case-know-everything-about-the-leaders-involved/383046

191 Vij Shivam, 7 politicians with corruption charges CBI and ED won't raid, Aug 21, 2019; https://theprint.in/opinion/7-politicians-with-corruption-charges-cbi-and-ed-wont-raid/280173/; CBI did not examine Himanta Biswa Sarma in Saradha scam: Ex-Kolkata top cop to HC, PTI, Jul 23, 2019; https://timesofindia.indiatimes.com/india/cbi-did-not-examine-himanta-biswa-sarma-in-saradha-scam-ex-kolkata-top-cop-to-hc/articleshow/70349359.cms

192 Chakravarty Ipsita, As the prelude to Lakhimpur Kheri shows, the BJP now speaks the explicit language of violence, Scroll, Oct 7, 2021; https://scroll.in/article/1007088/as-the-prelude-to-lakhimpur-kheri-shows-the-bjp-now-speaks-the-explicit-language-of-violence

193 Ensure gau rakshaks are not booked in false cases, Maharashtra Speaker tells police, Jul 3, 2023; https://indianexpress.com/article/cities/mumbai/ensure-gau-rakshaks-are-not-booked-in-false-cases-maharashtra-speaker-tells-police-8687712/

194 Halarnkar Samar, Turning India over to the mob, video by video, Scroll, Mar 27, 2021; https://scroll.in/article/990688/turning-india-over-to-the-mob-video-by-video

195 Tiwary Deeptiman, Lakhimpur Kheri: MoS Ajay Mishra meets Amit Shah; told to resume his routine duties, Oct 7, 2021; https://indianexpress.com/article/cities/lucknow/lakhimpur-kheri-ajay-mishra-amit-shah-meeting-7555495/

196 Union minister's son, accused of running over farmers, gets bail 4 months after arrest; Feb 10, 2022; https://www.indiatoday.in/india/uttar-pradesh/story/lakhimpur-kheri-case-ashish-misra-ajay-misra-1911231-2022-02-10

197 Lakhimpur Kheri violence case: 'How long can we keep Ashish Mishra in custody?', Supreme Court asks, Dec 12, 2022; https://timesofindia.indiatimes.com/city/lucknow/lakhimpur-kheri-violence-case-how-long-can-we-keep-ashish-mishra-in-custody-supreme-court-asks/articleshow/96176056.cms

198 Lakhimpur Kheri violence: Ashish Mishra granted interim bail for eight weeks by Supreme Court, Jan 25, 2023; https://scroll.in/latest/1042543/lakhimpur-kheri-violence-ashish-mishra-granted-interim-bail-for-eight-weeks-by-supreme-court

199 No Police Action Against BJP's Suraj Pal Amu For 'Love Jihad' Hate Speech, Jul 10, 2021; https://www.thequint.com/news/india/no-police-action-for-haryana-bjp-spokesperson-suraj-pal-amu-on-love-jihad-hate-speech

200 Editorial: Error of remission: Gujarat government had more than enough grounds to not release Bilkis case convicts, Aug 17, 2022; https://timesofindia.indiatimes.com/blogs/toi-editorials/error-of-remission-gujarat-government-had-more-than-enough-grounds-to-not-release-bilkis-case-convicts/

201 Explained: How BJP won seats in areas with significant Muslim populations, Dec 9, 2022; https://www.firstpost.com/explainers/explained-how-bjp-won-seats-in-areas-with-significant-muslim-populations-11776761.html

202 Bilkis Bano: Centre, Gujarat refuse to submit files to Supreme Court on convicts' remission; tell Court will challenge order to submit files, Apr 18, 2023; https://www.

barandbench.com/news/litigation/bilkis-bano-centre-gujarat-refuse-submit-files-supreme-court-on-convicts-remission-review

203   'Bulli Bai'-'Sulli Deals' Case: Mumbai Court Grants Bail to 3; All 6 Accused Now Out on Bail, Jun 22, 2022; https://thewire.in/law/bulli-bai-sulli-deals-case-mumbai-court-grants-bail-to-3-all-6-accused-now-out-on-bail

204   Supreme Court Closes Proceedings in Plea by Wrestlers Against Brij Bhushan Singh, May 4, 2023; https://thewire.in/law/supreme-court-closes-plea-wrestlers-brij-bhushan-singh

205   Vishwanath Apurva and Manral Mahender Singh, After 2 statements against him, minor withdraws charges against WFI chief Brij Bhushan, Jun 6, 2023; https://indianexpress.com/article/india/after-2-statements-against-him-minor-withdraws-charges-against-wfi-chief-brij-bhushan-8647463/

206   Sinha Jignasa, Demands for sexual favours, at least 10 cases of molestation detailed in 2 FIRs against Brij Bhushan, Jun 2, 2023; https://indianexpress.com/article/india/demands-for-sexual-favours-at-least-10-cases-of-molestation-detailed-in-2-firs-against-brij-bhushan-8641505/; Manral Mahender Singh, Brij Bhushan offered to buy me supplements if I gave in to sexual advances: wrestler, Jun 2, 2023; https://indianexpress.com/article/india/he-offered-to-buy-me-supplements-if-i-gave-in-to-sexual-advances-wrestler-8641492/

207   Manral Mahender Singh, Photos show WFI chief Brij Bhushan 'making advances', CDRs match location in testimony: Police chargesheet, JUl 12, 2023; https://indianexpress.com/article/india/police-chargesheet-photos-show-brij-bhushan-making-advances-cdrs-match-location-in-testimony-8828323/

208   Khare Vineet, Vinesh Phogat: India wrestler says she told PM Modi about harassment, May 5, 2023; https://www.bbc.com/news/world-asia-india-65478707

209   Prakash Karam, Wrestler told PM Modi of sexual abuse by Brij Bhushan 2 years ago, says FIR, Jun 2, 2023; https://www.tribuneindia.com/news/nation/wrestler-told-pm-modi-of-sexual-abuse-by-brij-bhushan-2-years-ago-says-fir-513663#:~:text=An%20Olympian%20woman%20wrestler%20had,against%20the%20Kaiserganj%20BJP%20M.

210   Watch: When WFI President Brij Bhushan Sharan Singh said on camera that he murdered a person, Jan 19, 2023; https://www.dailyo.in/news/watch-when-wfi-president-brij-bhushan-sharan-singh-said-on-camera-that-he-murdered-a-person-38648

211   Sexual harassment case: Brij Bhushan exempted from court appearance, July 29, 2023; https://www.thehindu.com/news/cities/Delhi/sexual-harassment-case-brij-bhushan-exempted-from-court-appearance/article67133094.ece?utm_source=substack&utm_medium=email

212   Sexual harassment case: Brij Bhushan, Vinod Tomar granted bail by Delhi court, Jul 20, 2023; https://www.thehindu.com/news/national/delhi-court-on-brij-bhushan-bail/article67100943.ece

213   New parliament: PM Modi inaugurates building amid opposition boycott, May 28, 2023; https://www.bbc.com/news/world-asia-india-65718127

214   Kapoor Coomi, Inside Track by Coomi Kapoor | Knock-out clout, May 7, 2023; https://indianexpress.com/article/opinion/columns/knock-out-clout-8595584/

215   At flat meant for MPs in heart of Lutyens' Delhi, a fringe organisation 'ran its ops', Jun 4, 2023; https://indianexpress.com/article/cities/delhi/at-flat-meant-for-mps-in-heart-of-lutyens-delhi-a-fringe-org-ran-its-ops-8644459/

216   Gupta Suchandana, MP: Union minister Narendra Singh Tomar's son in third video row, Cong seeks probe, Nov 15, 2023; https://timesofindia.indiatimes.com/city/bhopal/tomars-son-in-third-video-row-cong-seeks-probe/articleshow/105222074.cms

217   Analysis of Criminal and Financial background details of Lok Sabha 2014 winners, Association for Democratic Reforms (ADR), May 18, 2014; https://adrindia.org/research-and-report/election-watch/lok-sabha/2014/lok-sabha-2014-winners-analysis-criminal-and-finan

218   Lok Sabha Elections 2019 Analysis of Criminal Background, Financial, Education, Gender and other details of Winners, ADR, Jun 3, 2020; https://adrindia.org/content/lok-sabha-elections-2019-analysis-criminal-background-financial-education-gender-and-other

219   17th Lok Sabha: Analysis of Criminal, Financial, and Other background details of Union Council of Ministers, ADR, May 19, 2019; https://adrindia.org/content/17-th-lok-sabha-analysis-criminal-financial-and-other-background-details-union-council

220   17th Lok Sabha: Analysis of Criminal, Financial, and Other background details of Union Council of Ministers, ADR, May 19, 2019; https://adrindia.org/content/17-th-lok-sabha-analysis-criminal-financial-and-other-background-details-union-council; 17th Lok Sabha Analysis of Criminal, Financial, and Other background details of Union Council of Ministers Post Cabinet Expansion on 7th July, ADR, 2021; https://adrindia.org/content/17th-lok-sabha-analysis-criminal-financial-and-other-background-details-union-council

221   Selective outrage violation of rights, hurts country: PM Modi, Oct 13, 2021; https://indianexpress.com/article/india/narendra-modi-human-rights-protests-7567624/

222   Kashmiris now share intel on terrorists, says Gen. Bipin Rawat, Nov 13, 2021; https://www.thehindu.com/news/national/kashmiris-now-share-intel-on-terrorists-says-gen-bipin-rawat/article37475888.ece?homepage=true

223   Vishwanath Apurva and Sharma Harikishan, Global agency affiliated to UN rights body defers NHRC accreditation, May 25, 2023; https://indianexpress.com/article/india/global-agency-united-nations-rights-body-defers-nhrc-accreditation-8627342/

224   Mander Harsh and Bhattacharya Anirban, Politician as Member is Another Nail in the Coffin of the National Human Rights Commission, Nov 15, 2016; https://thewire.in/politics/nhrc-modi-political-appointment

225   Deep Pratyush and Kumar Basant, Complaints, non-compliance, pro-govt stance:

Inside the rise and ruin of India's human rights regime, https://www.newslaundry. com/2023/08/18/complaints-non-compliance-pro-govt-stance-inside-the-rise-and-ruin-of-indias-human-rights-regime#:~:text=That's%20a%20question%20which%20 has,human%20rights%20regime%20in%20India.

226 The trust deed of PM CARES Fund, Mar 27, 2020; https://www.pmcares.gov.in/ assets/donation/pdf/Trust_Deed.pdf

227 https://pmnrf.gov.in/en/about

228 https://www.pmcares.gov.in/en/web/page/about_us

229 The trust deed of PM CARES Fund, Mar 27, 2020; https://www.pmcares.gov.in/ assets/donation/pdf/Trust_Deed.pdf

230 https://main.sci.gov.in/supremecourt/2020/12392/12392_2020_35_1501_23456_ Judgement_18-Aug-2020.pdf

231 PM CARES not govt fund, functions with transparency, Delhi High Court told, Sept 23, 2021; https://www.thehindu.com/news/national/pm-cares-not-govt-fund-functions-with-transparency-delhi-high-court-told/article36625938.ece

232 PM CARES Fund a charitable trust, not controlled by Central or State governments: Central government to Delhi High Court, Jan 31, 2023; https://www.barandbench. com/news/pm-cares-fund-charitable-trust-not-controlled-central-state-governments-central-government-delhi-high-court

233 Yadav Shyamlal, Maharatnas to navratnas: 38 PSUs give Rs 2,105 crore from CSR to PM CARES, Aug 19, 2020; https://indianexpress.com/article/india/maharatnas-to-navratnas-38-psus-give-rs-2105-crore-from-csr-to-pm-cares-6560452/

234 Mampatta Sachin P, Eye on CSR-I: Listed govt firms contributed Rs 2,900 crore to PM CARES, Apr 24, 2023; https://www.business-standard.com/amp/india-news/ listed-govt-firms-paid-over-rs-2-900-crore-to-pm-cares-123042300241_1.html

235 Office Memorandum, Subject: Clarification on contribution to PM CARES Fund as eligible CSR activity under item no. (viii) of the Schedule VII of Companies Act, 2013, Ministry of Corporate Affairs, Mar 28, 2020; https://www.mca.gov.in/Ministry/pdf/ Circular_29032020.pdf

236 Donations by companies to PM-CARES Fund notified as CSR, May 27, 2020; https:// www.business-standard.com/article/companies/donations-by-companies-to-pm-cares-fund-notified-as-csr-says-govt-120052701146_1.html; MCA 2021: Frequently Asked Questions (FAQs) on Corporate Social Responsibility (CSR), Ministry of Corporate Affairs, Aug 25, 2021; https://www.mca.gov.in/Ministry/pdf/FAQ_CSR. pdf

237 PM Cares 'owned, controlled and established' by govt, says Centre, Dec 26, 2020; https://www.hindustantimes.com/india-news/pm-cares-owned-controlled-and-established-by-govt-says-centre/story-IsM4n2ZFtZL0saPwmzmcmN.html

238 Agarwal Poonam, Indian Embassy Websites Publicised PM CARES; Yet No Audit, Why? Dec 15, 2020; https://www.thequint.com/news/india/the-quint-exclusive-indian-embassy-websites-publicised-pm-cares-fund-yet-no-audit

239   Appeal to contribute to PM-CARES Fund/PMNRF due to Covid-19 pandemic, Indian Maritime University, Apr 2, 2020; https://www.imu.edu.in/images/circulars/2020/PM-CARES%20Fund%20COVID%20-%2019.pdf

240   FinMin Tells All Staff, Officers to Donate One Day's Salary Per Month to PM-CARES, Apr 20, 2020; https://thewire.in/government/finance-ministry-staff-donation-pm-cares

241   Yadav Shyamlal, Maharatnas to navratnas: 38 PSUs give Rs 2,105 crore from CSR to PM CARES, Aug 19, 2020; https://indianexpress.com/article/india/maharatnas-to-navratnas-38-psus-give-rs-2105-crore-from-csr-to-pm-cares-6560452/;101 PSUs give Rs 155 crore from their staff salaries to PM fund, Dec 7, 2020; https://indianexpress.com/article/india/101-psus-give-rs-155-crore-from-their-staff-salaries-to-pm-cares-fund-7094510/ & Armed forces gave Rs 203.67 cr from day's salary to PM-CARES Fund, Dec 18, 2020; https://indianexpress.com/article/india/armed-forces-gave-rs-203-67-cr-from-days-salary-to-pm-cares-fund-7109235/

242   CSR spends in FY21 jump 3.62% to Rs 22,000 cr: CRISIL, Aug 25, 2021; https://www.businesstoday.in/latest/economy/story/csr-spends-in-fy21-jump-362-to-rs-22000-cr-crisil-305118-2021-08-25

243   DU Teachers Allege VC Diverted Rs 4-Crore Staff Donations From PMNRF to PM CARES, Apr 22, 2020; https://thewire.in/rights/delhi-university-covid-19-donation-pmcares-yogesh-tyagi

244   PM CARES Fund, Receipt and Payment Accounts (Audited), 20220: https://www.pmcares.gov.in/assets/donation/pdf/Audited%20Statement.PDF; 2021 and 2022: https://www.pmcares.gov.in/assets/donation/pdf/Audited_Statement_2021_22.pdf

245   Sultan Vinay: Unhealthy Secrets: Why the PM CARES fund must be investigated, Aug 31, 2021; https://caravanmagazine.in/government/why-pm-cares-fund-investigated

246   Marfatia Ayesha, In charts: How the PM-Cares fund is hurting India's NGOs, Jul 8, 2020; https://scroll.in/article/966746/in-charts-how-pm-cares-fund-is-hurting-non-profits-in-india

247   IT Rules 2021: Information Technology (Intermediary Guidelines and Digital Media Ethics Code) Rules, 2021; Ministry of Electronics and Information Technology, GOI, Feb 25, 2021; https://www.meity.gov.in/writereaddata/files/Intermediary_Guidelines_and_Digital_Media_Ethics_Code_Rules-2021.pdf

248   Did PMO get its way on India's controversial new IT Rules? Jul 2, 2021; https://themorningcontext.com/chaos/did-pmo-get-its-way-on-indias-controversial-new-it-rules?s=03

249   Bombay HC stays provisions on adherence to 'Code of Ethics' under new IT Rules for digital media, Aug 15, 2021; https://indianexpress.com/article/india/bombay-hc-stays-provisions-of-it-rules-for-digital-media-pertaining-to-adherence-to-code-of-ethics-7453835/; Madras HC stays key clause: 'May rob media of its independence', Sept 17, 2021; https://indianexpress.com/article/india/information-technology-rules-madras-high-court-stays-key-clause-may-rob-media-of-its-independence-7513901/

250 SC stays proceedings before HCs in matters involving challenges to IT Rules, May 9, 2022; https://www.business-standard.com/article/current-affairs/sc-stays-proceedings-before-hcs-in-matters-involving-challenges-to-it-rules-122050900582_1.html

251 Barik Soumyarendra, IT Min ordered to take down 1,474 accounts, 175 tweets: Twitter in petition, Jul 8, 2022; https://indianexpress.com/article/business/social-media-watch-feb-2021-2022-it-min-take-down-accounts-tweets-twitter-8015959/; Twitter takes Centre to court over some orders for takedown of content; https://indianexpress.com/article/technology/social/twitter-pursues-judicial-review-of-indian-content-takedown-orders-report-8010384/

252 Kaskar Zeeshan, India Remains Internet Shutdown Capital of the World for Fifth Year Running: Report, Feb 28, 2023; https://thewire.in/tech/india-remains-internet-shutdown-capital-of-the-world-for-fifth-year-running-report

253 Government Internet Shutdowns Have Cost Over $44 Billion Since 2019, Top10VPN, Jun 16, 2023; https://www.top10vpn.com/research/cost-of-internet-shutdowns/; Cost of India's internet shutdowns in 2023 already exceeds 2022 levels, Jun 18, 2023; https://www.business-standard.com/industry/news/cost-of-internet-shutdowns-in-india-in-2023-so-far-exceeds-2022-levels-123061800429_1.html

254 Panjiar Tejasi and Waghre Prateek, A public brief on the IT Amendment Rules, 2022 a.k.a 'how the government is trying to moderate online speech', Nov 10, 2022; https://internetfreedom.in/public-brief-on-the-it-amendment-rules-2022/

255 P Chidambaram writes: Prosecutor, jury and judge, Apr 16, 2023; https://indianexpress.com/article/opinion/columns/prosecutor-jury-and-judge-8558350/

256 Government Notifies Amendments to the Information Technology (Intermediary Guidelines and Digital Media Ethics code) rules, 2021 for an Open, Safe & Trusted and Accountable Internet, Ministry of Electronics & IT, Apr 6, 2023; https://www.pib.gov.in/PressReleasePage.aspx?PRID=1914358

257 Fact Check Unit for online content will not be notified till Sept 4: Centre tells Bombay HC, Jul 21, 2023; https://indianexpress.com/article/cities/mumbai/centre-bombay-high-court-fact-check-unit-8852063/#:~:text=The%20Centre%20on%20Friday%20extended,Information%20Technology%20(IT)%20Rules.

258 PIB fact-checking unit got over 28,380 'actionable queries' since November '20: Government, Jul 21, 2023; https://timesofindia.indiatimes.com/india/pib-fact-checking-unit-got-over-28380-actionable-queries-since-november-20-government/articleshow/101997150.cms

259 BJP tweet, Jan 31, 2019; https://twitter.com/BJP4India/status/1090903248997822464?ref_src=twsrc%5Etfw%7Ctwcamp%5Etweetembed%7Ctwterm%5E1090903248997822464%7Ctwgr%5Ef30187f50179ecce4121cd7d7c7ee80955ff57c3%7Ctwcon%5Es1_&ref_url=https%3A%2F%2Fwww.thequint.com%2Felections%2Fsocial-dangal%2Funemployment-rate-high-hows-the-jobs-twitter-trends-pm-narendra-modi

260 P Mohanty 2021: An Unkept Promise: What Derailed the Indian Economy, Sage

Publications, Dec 2021; https://www.amazon.in/Unkept-Promise-Derailed-Indian-Economy/dp/9354791867

261   Altnews 2023: IT Rules amendments: Can PIB be given carte blanche to decide what is 'fake'?

Jan   26,   2023;   https://www.altnews.in/it-rules-amendments-can-pib-be-given-carte-blanche-to-decide-what-is-fake/;   https://www.altnews.in/govt-fact-checks-its-own-fact-checking-arm-pib-on-false-news-about-ib-recruitment/?utm_source=website&utm_medium=social-media&utm_campaign=newpost

262   The Internet Freedom Foundation's statement on the notification of the IT Amendment Rules, 2023, Apr 6, 2023; https://internetfreedom.in/statement-on-the-notification-of-the-it-amendment-rules-2023/

263   Ashraf Merrin U, Revisiting Shreya Singhal versus Union of India: A not so bright spot in the free speech jurisprudence of India, Jul 29, 2022; https://theleaflet.in/revisiting-shreya-singhal-versus-union-of-india-a-not-so-bright-spot-in-the-free-speech-jurisprudence-of-india/; Shreya Singhal vs U.O.I on 24 March, 2015, Supreme Court of India; https://indiankanoon.org/doc/110813550/

264   Centre's fact-check rule has no guard rails, says Bombay high court, Apr 25, 2023; http://timesofindia.indiatimes.com/articleshow/99741253.cms?from=mdr&utm_source=contentofinterest&utm_medium=text&utm_campaign=cppst

265   Bal Hartosh Singh 2021, Paranoia about digital coverage led ministers to propose media clampdown, monitoring "negative influencers", Caravan, Mar 4, 2021; https://caravanmagazine.in/politics/paranoia-about-digital-coverage-led-gom-propose-media-clampdown-monitoring-negative-influencers

Chapter II

Institutional Breakdown I: Parliament, Media and Civil Society

Good governance requires robust delivery tools or institutions. In the traditional sense, the "four pillars" of a democracy are executive, legislature, judiciary and media. The roles of the first three pillars are well defined and their powers separated by the Constitution; media, the fourth pillar, is outside this scheme, treated no differently than ordinary citizens. But for the purpose of this chapter and the next, liberty has been taken to focus on four key institutions – the Parliament, Supreme Court, media and citizens. The first one frames laws and policies, but equally importantly, ensures accountability of government; the second interprets, upholds and enforces the Constitution of India – there are other institutions whose autonomy and integrity are important for day-to-day governance and who look up at these two institutions for guidance. The third informs, educates/enlightens and thus, empowers the fourth, citizens – the true "sovereign" who exercise *veto* every five years – of which civil society is an integral part.

All the four institutions are ineffective after 2014, with a governent absolute majority (first time after 1984). For convenience of the narrative, this chapter (Part I) focuses on the Parliament, media and citizens and the next (Part II) on the Supreme Court. Other institutions and instruments of governance are spread over several chapters, including the preceding one.

Parliament of India or 'Divine' Seat of Power?

When Prime Minister Modi entered the Parliament House for the first time in 2014, he bowed down on its steps and called it "the temple of democracy" –

which he would repeat after opening the new Parliament House in June 2023, built at a cost of over $110 million[1] amidst a massive humanitarian crisis that the pandemic of 2020 and 2021 brought and the economy collapsed to -6.6% growth (revised to -5.8% years later). These symbolic gestures (bowing down or calling it "the temple of democracy") is quite ironical since the Parliament has been systematically undermined under his watch – with his active participation.

The new Parliament House is a garish *triangular-shaped* building bulldozed (to use the ubiquitous metaphor for the regime and all BJP-ruled states) into the majestic Lutyens' Delhi (right in front of the *iconic circular building* constructed by the British and which functioned as the Parliament since 1947) with the national emblem, the Ashokan lions, at its top. Even the Ashokan lions are not the "graceful and regally confident" Indians are familiar, but "menacing, teeth-baring and aggressive"[2] – reflecting the all-round distortions to the 'idea of India' that the Prime Minister's "New India" represents. Keeping with the Prime Minister's penchant for pomposity and pretentions, three gates of the new Parliament House are called *Gyan* (Knowledge), *Shakti* (Power) and *Karma (Duty) dwars* (doors) – just like the Rajpath is now called "Kartavya Path" (Path of Duty) and the Race Course Road where his official residence is located called "Lok Kalyan Marg" (Path of Public Welfare).

The Prime Minister strode into the new Parliament House on May 28 2023 carrying a golden sceptre, representing transfer of "divine" right to power and sovereignty, called "Sengol"[3]. This was after he offered the Sengol a "sastang dandavat"[4] (prostration) and accompanied with Hindu priests chanting hymns and performed a "havan" in the Brahminical tradition[5] – completely overshadowing a symbolic sideshow of a multi-faith prayer[6]. At once, all these ceremonial events presented the New Parliament House to the nation as a "divine" seat of power and exclusively Hindu edifice. That India is a constitutionally secular state was officially buried.

This sits well with the fact that the Prime Minister himself claims, on multiple occasions, he is the "God's chosen one"[7] and doing "God's work"[8]; his ministers and party leaders call him "reincarnation" of God[9], "God's gift" to India[10] and claim that people see him as "God"[11]. So, the new Parliament House's connection with divinity is part of the "New India".

This ceremony was timed to the birthday of Hindutva icon VD Savarkar; 20 Opposition parties boycotted it; President of India Draupadi Murmu, the official (non-executive) head of state and a woman, was missing too because she was not invited (in violation of the parliamentary protocol[12]) and the women wrestlers protesting against their sexual harassment by a BJP Member of Parliament Brij Bhushan Saran Singh were forcibly evicted from the Jantar Mantar a few hundred meters away[13]. Delhi's borders were sealed to prevent farmers from joining the wrestlers' protest.[14] Who then filled the empty seats of the new Parliament House?

There was Brij Bhushan Saran Singh for sure and scores of "random" people[15] which shocked even the BJP MPs.

Commenting on the increasing subordination of Parliament to the political executive, constitutional lawyer Gautam Bhatia[16] wondered if the new building represented the parliamentary democracy's turning into "executive democracy". Author Kapil Komireddi provided a historical context to the ceremony. He wrote[17]: "Reprising old rituals and receiving a sceptre from priests will not loft Modi into Nehru's league. Nehru and his comrades prised power from the clenched fists of the most powerful empire in history. Modi pantomimed before an audience of abject yes-men. It was a *fulsome display of the sham that is New India.*" (*Emphasis added*)

The comparison here with Nehru because Modi keeps blaming him for all that ails India now, despite being in office for close to a decade – the rest apportioned to the previous Congress-led UPA government. Modi takes no responsibility or blame for his and his government's actions.

Inauspicious Beginning

The new Parliament building has been mired in controversies for many other reasons too.

The construction began during the humungous pandemic crisis of 2020. It is part of the wholesale demolition and reconstruction of the iconic Central Vista and marked as "essential service"[18] to bypass a ban on all construction activities – at a time when the urgency was to build hospitals to save thousands of people dropping dead due to lack of it and lack of oxygen and other medicines.[19] His government hasn't built a single hospital then or later – the lack of which ended up killing 5.2 million Indians (WHO estimate) in 2020 and 2021 – an *excess death* of 4.7 million over the official estimate – that is, *90% deaths were not even reported.*[20]

The entire project of rebuilding the majestic Central Vista was top-down, with no project report (DPR), no public debate, no open tender and marked by a series of *ad hoc* and *post facto* administrative and legal clearances – which the Supreme Court (a bench led by Justice AM Khanwilkar) let off without qualm.[21] The logic, need, timing and use of money were never explained or examined. Architect Gautam Bhatia[22] said the entire exercise was "cloaked in a veil of secrecy and mired in opaque processes". This was also the time when Indian democracy was downgraded from "free" to "partially free" and called an "electoral autocracy".[23]

The genesis of the new building is in *superstition*. It goes back to 2002, when the BJP-led coalition was in power with Vajpayee as the Prime Minister. Then Lok Sabha Speaker Manohar Joshi, from the BJP's right-wing ally Shiv

Sena, thought the colonial era Parliament House was *cursed* because of certain mishaps (terror attack in December 2001, death of his predecessor GMC Balayogi in a freak helicopter accident and sudden demise of Chairman of Rajya Sabha Krishan Kant, both in 2002).[24] By then the iconic building designed like 'Chausath Yogini' temples embodying tantric traditions and found in Odisha and Madhya Pradesh had served the colonial masters, hosted the Constituent Assembly which debated, passed and adopted the Constitution of India and also hosted the Lok Sabha (and the Rajya Sabha) since 1952.

The idea of a new building was picked up in 2012, during the UPA years, but for a different reason – structural stress – and taken forward in December 2015 – very much during the heady days of honeymoon with the Prime Minister. The reasons were both structural issues and increase in seating capacity for the Lok Sabha in future (there is a 25-year freeze on the number of seats until 2026).[25] But these were never discussed beyond official letters and leakage of the intent. The decision had already been taken to build a new home – by whom and when is not known to the public.

New Delhi suddenly woke to the reality that the government had withdrawn New Delhi's application to the UNESCO for a 'World Heritage City' tag in May 2015 – just a month before the UNESCO was to decide. When protests erupted, the government prevaricated. First it said this tag/status would hamper "infrastructure and construction" plans for New Delhi which nobody knew about[26]; then said it was a "temporary" move.[27] The latter excuse would turn out to an outright lie much later in December 2020, when the Prime Minister turned "Priest King" and presided over a ground-breaking ceremony (called "bhoomipuja") for the new building.[28] The Prime Minister had already played the "Priest King" months earlier for a grand temple in Ayodhya, in August 2020 (a period of national lockdown) and would inaugurate the Kashi temple corridor, the New Parliament House and Bharat Mandapam (which hosted the G20 summit of 2023) in later years.

While inaugurating the new Parliament House in May 2023, the Prime Minister talked about "pride, hope and promise" it evoked and wished for to be "a cradle of empowerment, igniting dreams and nurturing them into reality".[29] But such sentiments are far removed from the ground realities. Under the new regime, the Parliament didn't even debate on the need for the new building, didn't pass it, nor decide to turn the existing building into a museum – just like it never played any role in the pandemic management and didn't debate or clear the massive demolition-and-reconstruction of the Central Vista. To expect the same Parliament under the same Prime Minister – whether in old building or new – to empower people, ignite and nurture their dreams would be too naïve.

The increased seating capacity threatens to open two new political fault-lines: (i) North-South and (ii) Hindu-Muslim. The Lok Sabha seats are based on population and hence, any upward revision would mean rewarding (with more political heft) the backward Hindi heartland (the cow belt which happens to be the Hindutva bastion) with poor record in population control and punishing southern states with better all-round demographic performance. This is one fault-line (north-south).[30]

The other is a pan-India Hindu-Muslim fault-line. The current delimitations in J&K and Assam show, constituencies are redrawn arbitrarily to give Hindus electoral advantage and reduce that of Muslims or completely do away with Muslim-dominated seats altogether by reserving those for Scheduled Castes (see Chapter IV for more). A national exercise under the BJP government in New Delhi is more likely to replicate it nationally.

The building carries a mural of "Akhand Bharat"[31], apparently showcasing the Hindutva's idea of India and includes the territories of smaller neighbours – Nepal, Pakistan and Bangladesh. Such a mural would have been unthinkable under any of the previous governments – far more open, deliberative and conscientious. It came to notice only when the building was inaugurated and caused anxiety in the neighbourhood. When they raised their concerns, the Indian government tried to explain it away that this was a map of the Ashokan empire – dating back to some 300 years before the birth of Christ – and a cultural representation, rather than political.[32] Whether that carried any conviction is another matter, the moot question is: What is the connection between the ancient empire and a modern democracy?

The new building is not even designed to allow free and informal interactions among MPs, ministers, journalists, bureaucrats and occasional guests. It doesn't have a Central Hall like the old building and doesn't allow free access and interactions by separating entrances, lifts, the two Houses and office blocks.[33] The easy access and marked bonhomie that prevailed in the old building before and after 2014 helped in breaking logjams, arrive at compromised solutions and free flow of information. That can't happen anymore.

The first session, a "special session" called in September 2023, saw Indian parliamentary democracy touching many *new lows* – manifestly anti-parliamentary, anti-democratic, hate-filled and regressive – even as it passed a historic law to provide 33% reservations to women in legislatures.

There were three such disturbing incidents.

One, the "special session" was held a few weeks after the monsoon session had ended *without* disclosing its purpose. When the Opposition questioned, the agenda was revealed, listing some routine Bills and topics as a formality[34] as the *only business*[35] it did was the introduction and passage of a law to provide 33% reservation for women in legislative bodies – which had not been listed. The Bill was passed by the Union Cabinet in a veil of secrecy on the very day it was introduced in the Lok Sabha on September 19, 2023.[36] There was no pre-legislative processes or public debate. It was passed the very next day in the Lok Sabha and the day after in the Rajya Sabha – without any scrutiny by a parliamentary panel.[37] The declared Bills and topics were never taken up.

It was a typical "shock-and-awe" spectacle the Prime Minister loves to stage – but the very anti-thesis of how the Indian parliamentary democracy had worked until then.

Two, Ramesh Bidhuri, a BJP MP from *upmarket* South Delhi, used a torrent of abusive and hate-filled language usually targeted at Muslims to a fellow Muslim MP from the Bahujan Samaj Party Danish Ali – while two BJP MPs laughing at the invectives.[38] Beyond expunging the remarks from the parliamentary records, a warning from the Speaker, a reference to the privilege committee and a show cause notice from the party, Bidhuri escaped any real punishment or the possibility – in a Parliament where the Opposition members are routinely suspended and their mikes muted for raising genuine questions against the government. The BJP then sought to justify it saying that Ali provoked Bidhuri first[39] – a typically "action-reaction" (Newtonian) theory[40] to justify violence against Muslims deployed since the 2002 Gujarat pogrom.

A week later, the BJP appointed Bidhuri to lead the party's election campaign in Rajasthan's Tonk district – which has 47% Muslim population (and 50% Hindu) as per the Census 2011[41] – exposing the duplicity around action against him. A furious Opposition described it as a "reward for hate"[42] but there is nothing unexpected here given that the BJP's electoral fortune is driven by its politics of communal hatred and violence (see Introduction and Chapter IV).

Apoorvanand, Delhi University professor and strong critic of the politics of hate, commented[43]: "Bidhuri's appointment also sends a message to the BJP's Hindu voters: that this is what we are. You have to accept us with our uncouthness, obscenity, and perversity. You did it when you elected... You should not expect us to be civilised and a hate spreader at the same time."

The incident marked a new low even for a BJP leader (a long lexicon of communal slurs for Muslims have been invented and used by right-wing parties like the BJP) and has sullied the Parliament's history forever – even though slogans of "Modi, Modi" and "Jai Shri Ram" (the latter is used as a dog-whistle and battle-cry against Muslims, rather than to hail Lord Ram) inside the Parliament are routine now.[44]

Three, the new Parliament House saw visitors to the Rajya Sabha gallery shouting "Modi, Modi" – something that never happened and unimaginable until then. The Opposition demand for strong action against the MPs who facilitated their entry in to the House but no notice was taken.[45] A Parliament session is not political rally and must not be used like one.

Dysfunctional Houses

At the end of the budget session of 2023 (17th Lok Sabha), the PRS Legislative Research[46], a non-profit body, released a comparative study of the Parliament's functioning since 1952 through a series of charts. These charts capture the rot that set in after 2014 (16th and 17th Lok Sabha) and are reproduced below to give a broad picture.

Image: Rapidly declining parliamentary functions

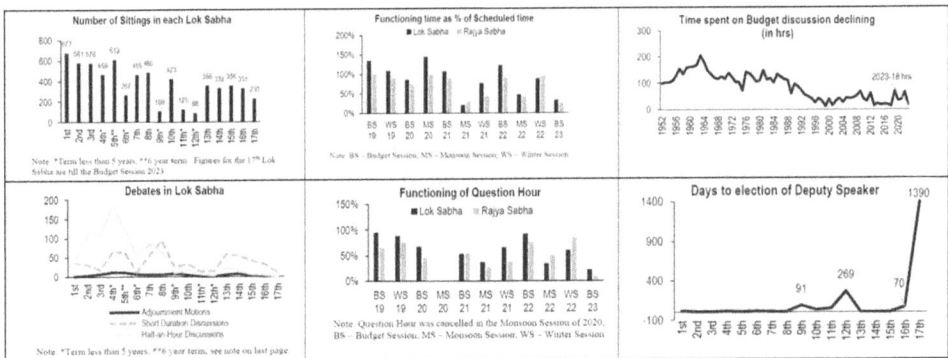

What do these graphs show?

- Of all the Lok Sabhas which completed full five-year term, 16th Lok Sabha (Prime Minister Modi's first term of 2014-2019) had the *lowest sitting days* at 331 a year. With one more year remaining, the 17th Lok Sabha (his second term of 2019-2024) is *likely* to be the shortest ever.

- *Functioning time* for both Lok Sabha and Rajya Sabha is progressively *going down.*

- *Time spent* on budget touching *new low* – the earlier low point in 2000 was during the previous BJP-led NDA government. Budgets were passed without debate twice under the current government (2018, 2023), an unlikely and once-in-a-decade affair – the previous ones being in 2003 and 2014.[47]

- Time for debates on various other issues shrinking to new lows.

- Question hour functioning has worsened.

The subsequent monsoon session of August 2023 continued the trends (and so did the "special session" in the new Parliament House that followed and narrated earlier): The Lok Sabha functioned for 43% of the scheduled time and the Rajya Sabha 55%; 25 Bills were introduced, of which only three were referred to parliamentary committees for scrutiny (which were introduced on the last day without prior disclosure or notice), taking the such Bills in the current Lok Sabha to 17% – lower than the previous three Lok Sabhas; the Lok Sabha passed 9 Bills (out of the total 22 passed) within 20 minutes, two within and another two within two minutes (in all, 20 were passed in less than an hour's discussion); the Rajya Sabha passed 10 Bills within three consecutive days and on eight days, Bills were passed after the Opposition walked out.[48]

There were many more disturbing developments during the monsoon session which reflect the rot that has set in which the graphs and data presented are inadequate to capture. Hence, those developments are flagged at appropriate places later to give better perspective and a fuller picture.

No pre-legislative homework: In order to improve quality of law making, the previous Congress-led government had introduced, in early 2014, Pre-legislative Consultation Process (PLCP).[49] It lays down the process and content – a draft or pre-legislative note giving justification for a legislation, listing essential elements, broad financial implications and assessment of the impact on environment, fundamental rights, lives and livelihoods of the concerned/affected people – which were to be proactively shared and put up in public domain for 30 days. First the government said, in 2019, that no record was being kept to track PLCP compliance[50] and then, in 2022, said it had been done away[51] by using the "leeway" provided in it (using the exemption clause "if not feasible or desirable to do so").

An analysis of the PLCP compliance by a policy watch body Medianama showed[52], during June 2014–May 2019, the government introduced 186 bills in the Parliament, of which 142 (76%) saw *no prior consultations*. The rest 44 were placed in public domain for comments, of which 24 (54.5%) did not bother to adhere to the 30-day deadline. The winter session of Parliament in 2021[53], for example, saw listing of 29 bills (26 new and 3 old) of which 17 had no prior consultations. The list includes abrogation of Article 370, Insolvency and Bankruptcy Code (IBC), cryptocurrency regulation etc. Shockingly, the PCLP, consultations with political parties and public debate on the Electoral Bond was *killed after a meeting with the Prime Minister* on August 21, 2017 – revealed the file notings obtained through the RTI Act of 2005.[54] So much for the Prime Minister's promise of providing "open, accountable, pro-people government" in which all citizens would be "equal and integral part of the decision-making process" etc.[55]

'Money Bill' route for unrelated laws: The Parliament under Prime Minister Modi set a debilitating trend of bringing and passing many critical legislations as 'Money Bill' – unrelated to taxes, borrowings, expenditures and receipts[56] – to *bypass* the Rajya Sabha where the BJP lacked majority. The Rajya Sabha may debate and make recommendations to a 'Money Bill' but it can't amend or pass such a legislation. One such was the Aadhaar law of 2016 which provides for "proof of identity and proof of address for residents of India". The Supreme Court upheld its passing as 'Money Bill' in 2018 but the dissenting judge Justice DY Chandrachud (who became Chief Justice of India in 2022) described this "a fraud on the Constitution"[57] and repeatedly demanded a *review*. Finally, it was referred to a seven-judge bench in 2021 but that bench hasn't been set up yet.[58] Since the Aadhaar card has become *de facto* mandatory for everything under the sun, it poses a great risk as an instrument of surveillance and theft of identity – and with it the loss of money in bank accounts. Another was Electoral Bond of 2017[59] – which amended the RBI Act of 1934, Companies Act of 2013, Representation of People Act of 1951 and Income Tax Act. It introduced *structural corruption* to Indian polity and governance; its constitutionality remains undecided – and yet, the apex court has allowed it to be operationalized. Many amendments, like that to the draconian UAPA and PMLA[60] – which turned those laws more draconian and regressive – were also passed as 'Money Bill'. If held unconstitutional, a whole lot of laws would have to be junked.

Ordinances as laws: This is not new but the current government overtook[61] the previous decade of the Congress-led UPA government in double quick time. From the new farm laws (now withdrawn) to three new labour codes to extending the tenures of ED/CBI Directors to five years and fixing two-year tenures for the Home, RAW, IB and Defence Secretaries etc. many laws were paradropped as ordinances and then bulldozed through the Parliament.

'Shock-and-awe', 'spectacle' but no due diligence and scrutiny: More often than not, all Bills are passed in one day, howsoever significant, with perfunctory debates (like the monsoon session of 20203 passing nine Bills within 20 minutes and four others within 2-3 minutes). Bills being referred to parliamentary panels fell to 25% in the first term (2009-14) and to 17%[62] in in the second (2019-August 2023) – from 71% under the UPA-II (2009-2014) and 60% under UPA-I (2004-2009).[63] No committee meeting was allowed during the pandemic year, not even virtual meetings (unlike developed countries); meetings and their durations are far less than earlier; several standing committees take partisan approach to prevent discussions on key issues which are likely to embarrass the government and dissent notes are not allowed.[64] All the same, the Prime Minister has done his public posturing by calling for "quality debates"[65] in the Parliament. Some examples:

(i)   *Goods and Services Tax (GST)* of 2017: A badly drafted GST law, subsuming in itself indirect taxes (eight imposed by the Central government and nine state governments), was passed at a grand midnight session of the Parliament (akin to August 15, 1947 and branding it as the "second Independence Day") – without preparations and was immediately postponed for two months. It gave the second shock to the economy (already hobbled by the demonetization). *Six years later*, it remains a work-in-progress, with e-verification of vouchers not yet fully implemented[66], flourishing fake-bill business[67] and the notification for setting up GST appellate tribunals[68] being issued in late 2023.

(ii) *Abrogation of Articles 370 an 35A in J&K in -2019:* In August 2019, the special status of Jammu and Kashmir (Articles 370 and 35A) was abrogated overnight and it was downgraded to two union territories (UTs) – for the first time a reorganization led to downgrading a state to UTs. The Presidential order and subsequent legal changes came without prior notice and passed in the Parliament in two days – one day each in the Lok Sabha and Rajya Sabha – even as a stunned Opposition watched helplessly. The rationale for the overnight change was not explained and it was pushed through lies and subterfuge after locking down the entire state.[69] Such special status and privileges are enjoyed by several northeast states, northern hill states and central India tribal belts (Schedule V and VI areas). Since then, the Centre rules those UTs without conducting elections (details in Chapter VI).

(iii) *New farms laws of 2020 and their repeal in 2021:* Overnight ordinances to bring three new farm laws in 2020, amidst the national lockdown, to corporatize farming and farm trade; ram-rodded the respective Bills later through the Parliament during the lockdown. It was withdrawn after more than a year of massive farmers' protests, during which about 700 farmers lost their lives[70], without allowing any debate[71].

(iv) *New labour codes in 2020:* Overnight ordinances to bring three new labour codes in 2020 (the Wage Code had already been legislated in 2019), amidst the national lockdown, and then rushed through the Parliament during the pandemic lockdown. These, along with the Wage Code of 2019, are openly *pro-business and anti-workers* – dilute rights and protections of workers and give more powers to businesses to arbitrarily hire-and-fire and trample workers' rights. Though not withdrawn, protests have ensured that these are on hold (no rules framed).72

(v) Delegitimization of elected government of NCT of Delhi in 2021: In a similar manner, amidst the devastating second pandemic wave in 2021, the government struck again, amending the Government of National Capital Territory of Delhi (GNCTD) Act of 1993 to declare its nominee, the LG, as the "government" of NCT of Delhi – in the place of the elected Legislative Assembly and elected Council of Ministers.[73] In 2023, it took away "services" from the government of NCT through an ordinance and then ratified by the Parliament (amidst the din over Manipur violence and the Opposition's walkout) even as the challenge to the ordinance was pending before the apex court[74] (details in Chapter VI).

(vi) *Wholesale and indiscriminate privatization in 2021:* The 2021 budget announced, out-of-the-blue *en masse* privatization of PSUs – irrespective of whether sick or profit-making – and PSBs to facilitate which a public sector-led Bad Bank was announced to separate their stressed assets. The rationale was never explained – except that the government has no business to be in business.[75]

(vii) "Monetization" of *public assets in 2022*: In 2022 budget, the government announced to handover *brownfield public infrastructures* across the country (roads, railways, power, telecom, mining, aviation, ports etc.) to private players – without prior consultations, debate or parliamentary scrutiny. The objective being mobilization of Rs 6 lakh crore over a period of four years.[76]

(viii) *Wholesale replacement of three criminal laws by wholesale cut and paste and re-arrangement of sections:* In 2023, three Bills were introduced to replace key criminal laws of over 100 years old – the Indian Penal Code (IPC) of 1860, Criminal Procedure Code (CrPC) of 1973 (originally of 1898) and Indian Evidence Act of 1872 – with Hindi titles (the Bharatiya Nyaya Sanhita Bill, 2023 for the IPC, Bhartiya Nagarik Suraksha Sanhita Bill, 2023 for the CrPC and Bharatiya Sakshya Bill, 2023 for the Evidence Act). These were introduced on the *last day* of the Monsoon session of 2023, *without listed* for business.[77] The committee behind framing these, set up in May 2020, operated in *complete secrecy*[78] and two non-members – the SG and ASG – reportedly exerted influence. But the introduction also came with the usual misleading *claims*[79] of wide consultations and was sent to a standing committee.

Early analyses of these bills have thrown up disturbing characteristics – vague/badly defined and drafted provisions with weak guardrails[80], rearrangement of crimes in different clauses (like Section 124A (sedition) becomes Clause 150) which would create confusion about case laws, continuation of draconian colonial provisions incompatible with the constitution vision[81]. It was later cleared by a parliamentary panel in extraordinary haste, in less than two months, without change, despite the Opposition accusing that it was a copy-and-paste job; retained colonial laws but *re-arranged or re-numbered* the sections[82] – which means hundreds of thousands of judges, lawyers, police officers, law teachers and students and general public *re-learning* the old laws and case histories/studies; *all 19 experts* called by the panel *endorsed* the three Bills[83] – defeating the very purpose of such consultations.

It is a classic example of *how not to write laws* – a reflection of both ineptitude and incompetence.

P Chidambaram[84], former Union Home Minister, Congress leader and prominent lawyer who was also part of the parliamentary panel, wrote about the *shoddy job* in all three criminal laws: "We found that 90-95 per cent of the provisions of the *IPC* were cut and pasted in the new draft. As many as 18 chapters out of 26 chapters of IPC (three chapters had only one section each) have been copied in the new Bill...Every one of the 170 sections of *Evidence Act* has been cut and pasted. As much as 95 per cent of *CrPC* has been cut and pasted..." Though the declared objective was to *de-colonize Indian laws* Chidambaram wrote there was nothing anti-colonial about them.

(ix) *Law for women's reservation in legislatures:* The historic law to provide 33% reservations to women in the Lok Sabha and state assemblies – The Constitution (One Hundred and Twenty-eighth Amendment Act, 2023[85] or the "Nari Shakti Vandan Adhiniyam"[86] (Hindi for 'the law worshipping women power') – was passed in the first and a "special session" held in the New Parliament House in September 2023. As mentioned earlier, the purpose of the special session was not disclosed; the Bill appeared suddenly and was passed without scrutiny of any parliamentary panel and passed in a matter of hours. True to the style, this was another *shock-and-awe* operation.

The law carries provisions make it a mere "post-dated cheque": It would come into effect *after* the next Census is held and *after* delimitation of constituencies. These exercises would take at least *eight years* from the starting of a fresh Census (2021 Census is delayed and to start in 2024-25) – going by the past experience – and hence, it is highly unlikely to be implemented in the next general elections of 2029.[87] Delimitation of constituencies (a freeze on it until 2026) is also fraught with additional problem of rewarding the cow belt (Hindi heartland of north) – for the demographic failures (backward and marked by high relatively population growth) – and dis-reward southern states for their demographic successes (more developed and better population control).[88] This is because one-person-one-vote means population determines the number of legislative seats.

Had the government been serious, it could have been implemented right away with constantly updated electoral rolls by identifying seats for women (rotational). Quite clearly, it is a mere political gesture (or "jumla") to influence women voters without actually giving anything. It is for the next two governments to implement it after 2014. Nevertheless, the Prime Minister patted his own back saying "God has chosen me" to deliver it.[89]

The women's reservation exercise began with the introduction of a Bill in 1996 (but not passed); introduced and passed by the Rajya Sabha in 2010 but not by the Lok Sabha over reservations of some parties regarding sub-quota for OBCs. This time near unanimous (except for two Lok Sabha members of the AIMIM who pointed at abysmal numbers of Muslim women in legislatures) – without quota for OBCs (but for the SCs and STs).

No role in policymaking: Given the top-down model of policymaking where even Union Cabinet is not involved, the Parliament has had no role to play in many key policy decisions which have had far-reaching consequences. This includes the pandemic lockdown and its (mis)management – a once-in 100 years' crisis – unlike developed countries like the US. Some examples:

(a) *Dismantling of Planning Commission of India (PCI) in 2014:* The PCI led the re-industrialisation of Independent India as well as helmed the post-reform/liberalization high growth. The Prime Minister announced its death in his national address on August 15, 2014. No alternate plan or vision was in place; the NITI Aayog that replaced it in 2015, is a think tank, most often busy cheer-leading and justifying *post facto* government policies.[90]

(b) *Demonetization of 2016:* One night, at 8 pm, the Prime Minister addressed the nation and declared that in four hours' time, 86.9% of high-value cash would be worthless. This single step began the derailment of India's growth story (first of the 'twin shocks') – and came despite expressed warning from former RBI Governor Raghuram Rajan whose term had expired a few weeks earlier.[91]

(c) *24x7 pandemic lockdown and national curfew in March 2020:* One of the most stringent pandemic lockdowns, along with and 24x7 national curfew, was announced in March 2020 – paralysing social and economic life for months. The Prime Minister announced it at 8 pm national address on TV. The Parliament had no clue, his Cabinet had no role, there was no prior consultations with states and no planning. It was untimely to boot. It devastated the people and the economy and triggered a massive reverse migration that no other country in the world saw.[92] By the time the lockdown was fully withdrawn (Unlock 6.0), it was already November 2020 and a few months later, the second wave hit, bringing more lockdowns (but mercifully by state governments this time).

(d) *"AatmaNirbhar Bharat" relief and stimulus packages of 2020:* Amidst the pandemic lockdown of May 2020, the government announced it without prior consultations, relied on supply-side solutions to a demand-side problem (demand recession), was packed with long-term "reforms" like privatization of public assets and gave official stamp to the unofficial import substitution policy started by it in 2014.[93]

(e) *Corporate tax cut of 2019 and PLIs and DLIs of 2020 and 2021:* In September 2019, amidst a fiscal crisis (states were told the GST Compensation can't be given due to lack of resources), a corporate tax cut of Rs 1.45 lakh crore was given. This was followed by a massive and overnight fiscal incentive for private businesses, called Production Linked Incentive (PLI) scheme, amidst the pandemic lockdown of 2020. Then came the Design Linked

Incentive DLI). The purpose is to boost 'Make in India' but as Finance Minister Nirmala Sitharama revealed in 2022, both were given as demanded by private corporate sector – and yet, has led to neither higher investment nor job creations as promised at the time. Both the tax cut and incentives continue despite lack of results, failures and widespread criticism.[94]

(f) *Expansion of BSF's jurisdiction in 2021:* A simple gazette notification of October 2021[95] expanded the jurisdiction of central paramilitary force, the Border Security Force (BSF), from 15 km to 50 km in border states. In some states, this brought the entire state under the BSF's jurisdiction – Manipur, Mizoram, Tripura, Nagaland and Meghalaya and UTs of J&K and Ladakh. It gobbled up substantial areas of Gujarat, Rajasthan, Punjab, West Bengal and Assam. It sparked strong protest from states but that was ignored (more in Chapter VI).

(g) *"Liberalized" vaccine policy of 2021:* This too came outside the Parliament, turning 50% Covid vaccination into a *for-profit* trade in 2021. It was reduced to 25% after the Supreme Court called it "arbitrary and irrational". Nevertheless, it replaced the tried and tested "universal" and "free" vaccination programme of decades and kept out public sector vaccine makers, which made India self-sufficient and global supplier (60% supply) of vaccines. When shortages hit, the government unilaterally stopped supply of AstraZeneca's Covishield meant for supply to poor countries (COVAX plan), thereby endangering global health. India also went out with a begging bowl for help.[96] Yet, virtually every street corner, highways, petrol pumps has had the Prime Minister's posters claiming "free" vaccine for all and all vaccine certificates carry his photograph, not that of the vaccinated.

No questions allowed: When it matters the most, the government refuses to be answerable to the Parliament.

(i) When questions were asked in the Parliament about the *China's incursion* in 2020 and continued occupation of land on the Indian side of LAC in Ladakh, those (17 questions) were disallowed in "national interest"[97]. Defence expert Sushant Singh called the aversion of the Prime Minister and his government to parliamentary scrutiny "alarming"[98] – given its national security implications.

(ii) When questions were raised about the spying on civilians by using the *Pegasus spyware* in 2021, those too were denied on the plea of it being "sub-judice".[99] The Prime Minister asked his MPs to attack the Opposition[100] for protesting and blocking parliamentary proceedings.

(iii) When *Manipur was burning* in 2023, again the questions were dismissed on the plea of it being "sub-judice"[101]. The Opposition brought no-confidence

motion over the Manipur violence because the Prime Minister refused
to attend the Parliament or give a statement on the situation.[102] Congress
leader Adhir Ranjan Choudhury was suspended for criticizing the Prime
Minister.[103] Manipur MPs weren't allowed to speak.[104] The Prime Minister
didn't answer any questions on Manipur in his response.[105] Journalist Omair
Ahmad wrote it was "naïve" to expect the Prime Minister to speak up on
communal crises and "disavow the very people he has nurtured".[106]

(iv) When questions were asked about the alleged corruption by the *Adani
group* (US-based short seller Hindenburg alleged that the group was
"pulling the largest con job in corporate history" by engaging "in a
brazen stock manipulation and accounting fraud scheme over the course
of decades"[107]) and the Prime Minister's relationship with its proprietor
Gautam Adani, answer was given, no debate was allowed and no probe
was ordered. Instead, the Opposition was called "anti-national" (whatever
the Opposition could say inside the Parliament was during the motion
of thanks to the President's address). The Speaker expunged Congress
leader Rahul Gandhi's questions on the issue in the Lok Sabha (on the
plea that he had provided no evidence).[108] Remarks of Congress President
Mallikarjun Kharge in the Rajya Sabha were deleted a day later[109] with
flimsy explanation that it was done "as per the rules of the House"[110].
During the same parliamentary session, the mikes of Rahul Gandhi[111]
and others, including senior Congress leader Adhir Ranjan Choudhury[112]
were switched off to stop them from responding to allegations from the
ministers and the BJP MPs which were allowed, followed immediately by
adjournments.[113]

In his reply to the debate on the President's address, the Prime Minister
didn't address the questions. Instead, he took potshots at the Nehru-Gandhi
family and claimed how he was proving too big for the entire Opposition ("*ek
akela kitno ko bhari*") and asked why Rahul and Priyanka Gandhis were not using
the Nehru surname (that of their maternal great grand-father and first Prime
Minister Jawaharlal Nehru).[114] Months later, in July 2023, he and his party stitched
a *38-party NDA coalition*[115] to counter the 26-party Opposition coalition, called
INDIA, in preparations for the 2024 elections. To pepper over his neglect of old
NDA allies for years, he said: "I can make mistakes, but I will not do anything
with ill-intention".[116]

No parliamentary probe: The joint parliamentary committee (JPC) probe
went out of lexicon after 2014. No JPC probe was ordered on the demonetization
and Rafale deal in his first term and on the Pegasus scandal, corruption charges
against the Adani group in the second term. The Supreme Court was forced to
announce its own probe panels into the Pegasus and Adani matters but neither
produced any result.[117]

Laws that Kill the Very Laws

Until 2014, Indian laws at times contained what could be called "kill bill" provisions – a provision that rendered the law ineffective or useless. For example, Civil Liability for Nuclear Damage Act of 2010 had a surreptitious line added to Section 7 after being passed by the Lok Sabha and introduced in the Rajya Sabha which read: "Provided that the Central government may, by notification, assume full liability for a nuclear installation not operated by it if it is of the opinion that it is necessary in public interest". This made mockery of liability – effectively creating a situation where the *liability falls on Indians*, not the private company.[118] In 2012, the Land Acquisition, Rehabilitation and Resettlement (LARR) Bill of 2011 *exempted* the Centre from the rehabilitation and resettlement (R&R) liabilities if the land was acquired for "public purpose" and was less than 100 acre in rural areas and less than 50 acres in urban areas[119] – but, fortunately, this was *removed* and the Bill was *redrafted* and passed as "The Right to Fair Compensation and Transparency in Land Acquisition, Rehabilitation and Resettlement Act, 2013".

Now things have changed. In 2015, the government amending the Whistle Blowers Protection Act of 2014 by removing immunity (protection) to the very whistle blowers from prosecution under the Official Secrets Act and prohibited any whistle blower disclosure that contain information which would prejudicially affect the sovereignty, integrity, security, strategic, scientific or economic interests of the state. The amendment was passed by the Lok Sabha but remains pending in the Rajya Sabha.[120]

There are now a series of laws which don't mean what they claim in their preambles. At the risk of repeating the earlier examples, here is how this plays out.

(i) **Aadhaar law of 2016**: The Aadhar (Targeted Delivery of Financial and Other Subsidies, Benefits and Services) Act, 2016, as the name suggests, is for delivery of government services and the Supreme Court also restricted its use to that. Linking this 12-digit unique identity number with other data bases is, therefore, "voluntary".[121] But is mandatory for all practical purposes – through executive orders, in every day practice, by sneaking it in as an *option* or as *mandatory* in various other laws. It is now linked to PAN numbers and income tax returns (ITR), bank accounts, voters identity card, identities of workers (formal or informal), GST, school admissions, births, deaths and registration of property etc. Various laws that have amended to facilitate include the PMLA and the Representation of People Act. In 2023, the Registration of Births and Deaths (Amendment) Act of 2023[122] links the Aadhaar number *mandatorily* with births and deaths (of relatives or reporting person too) and allows this data to be *inter-linked with other databases* – thereby creating a 360-degree database[123] as was exposed in 2020. This has another danger – depriving millions of poor of welfare benefits as has happened with the PDS and MGNREGS beneficiaries.[124]

(ii)   All private services, like mobile phones, banking, health etc., too are linked to the Aadhaar with the official wink. Since all data are *inter-linked* and shared by government agencies with private players, identity theft, stealing money and privacy breach by hacking the Aadhaar data is rampant[125] and Aadhaar itself can be duplicated easily.

(iii)   **Farm laws**: The Farmers (Empowerment and Protection) Agreement on Price Assurance and Farm Services Act, 2020 (withdrawn in 2021 after a year-long protest just ahead of the next round of elections in fice states) was premised on "freedom of choice" to sale "outside the physical premises of markets or deemed markets" so as to facilitate "remunerative prices" through "competitive alternative trading channels". It actually created a parallel and unregulated market for trade outside the state-controlled APMC markets, withdrew the guaranteed MSP, removed state controls, made individual farmers vulnerable to corporate money power and removed all market fee, cess or levy paid by private buyers – which are used to develop the APMC markets and help farmers in distress.[126]

(iv)   **Labour Codes**: The four labour codes of 2019 and 2020 promise welfare of workers but actually dilutes all laws protecting them, excludes millions from its "universal" minimum wages, workplace safety and social protections, makes them more vulnerable to arbitrary hire-and-fire, extends working hours from 8 to 12 hours and dilutes oversight mechanisms.[127] The Central minimum wages remain stuck at *Rs 176* since 2017. This is below the Central government-funded MGNREGS wages – which in turn is substantially lower than all statutory minimum wages of states, except the BJP-ruled Uttar Pradesh.[128] The rules are, however, yet to be framed to operationalize the four Codes.

(v)   **Goods and Services Tax**: The GST of 2017 left out high revenue generating indirect taxes on alcohol, petroleum products and electricity. But the GST was sold as "one-nation-one-tax-one-market" and contains nine tax slabs and instead of being "good and simple" is extremely complex with high compliance burden and highly prone to fake input tax credit (ITC) claims.[129]

(vi)   **Privacy Law of 2023:** Six years after the Supreme Court declared privacy as a fundamental right, the government passed the Digital Personal Data Protection (DPDP) Act of 2023 – without parliamentary scrutiny[130] and parliamentary debate[131]. It was passed amidst the turmoil over the Manipur violence in the monsoon session of the Parliament. It doesn't protect privacy; doesn't even recognize it as fundamental right; gives wholesale exemptions and legal immunity from breach to the government, the executive-controlled regulatory board and private companies dealing with personal data; besides defanging the transparency law, the RTI Act of 2005.[132] Worse, it threatens to establish an "authoritarian" and "arbitrary" legal information regime – argue Aruna Roy and Nikhil Dey, the brain and the force behind the RTI Act.[133]

(vii) **The Forest Conservation (Amendment) Act of 2023**[134]**:** This was also passed without due deliberations, amidst the din over the Manipur violence, by ignoring voluminous objections from various stakeholders and was sent to a *special joint committee* which ignored all objections and endorsed as it is[135] – not to the department-related standing committee which is the norm. It was passed pending a no confidence motion in the Manipur case (mentioned earlier) – which takes precedence over other legislative business as per the parliamentary convention[136]. It replaces the Forest (Conservation) Act, 1980. Instead of "conservation" of forests as its title suggests and wonderfully worded preamble (like "to enable achievement of national targets of Net Zero Emission by 2070 and maintain or enhance the forest carbon stocks through ecologically balanced sustainable development"), it actually facilitates *wholesale diversion and destruction* of forests *by excluding forests clearances*: (i) along railway tracks and public roads for up to 1,000 sqm that lead to habitation or amenities (ii) within *100 km* of international borders for construction of "linear projects of national importance and concerning national securities" (iii) up to 10 ha for construction of security-related infrastructure (iv) up to 5 ha in areas inflicted with left-wing extremism (v) land not notified as forest land in government records on or after 1980 and (vi) "forestry" purpose like zoos and wildlife safaris. This law also undermines the Supreme Court's Godavarman judgement of 1996 which extended definition forest to its "dictionary meaning" (expanding the scope).

(viii) **Jan Vishwas (Amendment of Provisions) Act of 2023**[137]**:** This too was passed without debate in the same monsoon session, *amending 42 laws* across multiple sectors, including agriculture, environment, and media and publication to "further enhance trust-based governance for ease of living and doing business". It hands over power to the executive and keeps courts of law out by *decriminalising criminal offences, waiving off* prosecution and sentencing. One particular amendment, in the Drugs and Cosmetics Act of 1940, hits at the very core of drug quality, creating *distrust*, rather than trust, and undermining public health.[138] This came immediately *after* India-made made cough syrups killed 70 kids in Gambia (2022)[139], 20 deaths reported from Uzbekistan (January 2023)[140] and toxic substances were detected in in Iraq (July 2023)[141]. What was needed, and urgently, was the exact opposite – directing drug companies to follow international (WHO) quality standards and imposing higher penalty for failures, threating delicensing and tightening regulatory oversight. The *full implications* of the

Jan Vishwas law would be clear later, given that 42 laws were amended.

Infiltration of panels: Former BJP member and Rajya Sabha Chairman Jagdeep Dhankar packed 20 parliamentary committees (12 standing committees and eight department-related standing committees) under the House (Rajya Sabha) with his own "personal staff" in 2023. The explanation was to "supplement the staff and officer support" with immediate effect" – without explaining that this is against[142] the House rules.

Unparliamentary lexicon: In 2022, a fresh list of unparliamentary words and phrases was released. These are works and phrases banned from being used. The new list included 'corrupt', 'incompetent', 'dictatorial' and its Hindi 'taanashahi', 'taanashah' (dictator), 'vinash purush' (destroyer), 'anarchist', 'jumlajeevi' (living on 'jumla' or rhetoric), 'hypocrisy', 'snoopgate', 'ashamed', 'abused', 'betrayed', 'drama' etc. When the Opposition protested saying this amounted to "gag order", the Lok Sabha Speaker denied it and said: "Members are free to express their views and no one can snatch that right but it should be as per the decorum of Parliament".[143]

After Bidhuri's invectives against a Muslim MP, those needs to be added to the list.

Using Parliament to Subvert Parliamentary Democracy

The Parliament has been used to pass undemocratic laws by using its majority in the Lok Sabha and various other means in the Rajya Sabha – 'Money Bill' for the Aadhaar law, Electoral Bond and others; subterfuge and taking advantage of disruptions and walkout by the Opposition in the case of abrogation of Articles 370 and 35A, subversion of democratically elected government of NCT of Delhi twice as already mentioned. In the case of the NCT of Delhi, the law taking over the "services" was passed while the legality of the earlier ordinance for this takeover was pending before the apex court.

Lies, Fake News and Diversions

The Parliament's sanctity has been killed through other means too – through outright lies. A few examples:

Citizenship law of 2019: When the communally discriminatory Citizenship Amendment Bill (CAB) of 2019 was being passed in the Parliament, the Prime Minister accused the Opposition of speaking "the very same language used by Pakistan" for opposing it, painted them "anti-national" and his government issued directives to media *not to report public protests against the law.*[144] Outside the Parliament, he told many *lies* about not preparing a National Register for Indian Citizens (NRIC) to identify "doubtful" and illegal" citizens and not building detention centres for them – contrary to official records, allocation of funds for detention centres and gazette notification for the NRIC.[145]

Pandemic crises of 2020 and 2021: While the government gross mismanagement aggravated the economic and humanitarian crises of the pandemic, instead of responding to questions raised by the Opposition, the Prime Minister actually blamed them[146], particularly the Congress and the AAP, in the budget session of 2022, for the distress migration and the spread of Covid-19. Both had resulted from his own top-down, out-of-the-blue and unplanned lockdown on the one hand and the prolonged electioneering in West Bengal and the Kumbh mela.[147] These two parties had actually tried to help the migrants by arranging buses and then paid for their train tickets – which the BJP, the Indian government and the Indian Railways didn't.[148] He called the Congress "tukde-tukde gang" (practicing "divide and rule") and invoked the first Prime Minister Nehru to divert attention from the multiple crises (job crisis, growing impoverishment, inflation etc.) and avoid answerability at the time too.[149] During the far more devastating second wave of the pandemic in 2021, he had simply disappeared for 20 days.[150]

Manipur burning: Manipur was burning for 78 days in ethnic violence, with a civil war between the Meiteis who are predominantly Hindus and the Kukis who are predominantly Christians in May 2023[151] before the Prime Minister spoke up. He and his Home Minister were busy electioneered in Karnataka. Then, the Prime Minister was busy discussing the Russia-Ukraine war with Russian President Vladimir Putin, toured Japan, Papua New Guinea, Australia, the US, Egypt, France and the UAE and spoke on virtually everything else.[152] When he spoke, it was for 30 seconds on Manipur in general ("pain and anger" over "the incident in Manipur")[153] – and after the Supreme Court had taken a strong position on it[154]. In fact, the reaction came after an old video of two Kuki women being stripped and paraded naked (with the help of police[155]) went viral – which came to public domain a few weeks late due to prolonged internet shutdown. In the same breath, the Prime Minister named Congress-ruled Rajasthan and Chhattisgarh (over bad law and order situation in general), which also served as a dog whistle to party leaders. The BJP immediately mounted attacks on Rajasthan, Bihar and West Bengal – all ruled by non-BJP parties – on a loop.[156] Assam Chief Minister (from the BJP) blamed[157] the Congress' "faulty policies" for the Manipur violence. The attack on West Bengal turned out to be misleading[158].

The Prime Minister's comment came just outside the Parliament building – and minutes before the monsoon session of 2023 began. When he was forced to respond to the non-confidence motion moved to bring him into the Parliament, his reply was two-hour-13-minute "blah-sphemy"[159] – as a national daily declared. It shifted the focus from his government's and that of the Manipur (also ruled by the BJP-led coalition with Chief Minister N Biren Singh of the BJP) in containing the violence and full of diatribes against the Congress.[160] Manipur was relegated to the background noise – just as all communal violence and misgovernance are after 2014.

The same monsoon session saw Union Home Minister Amit Shah misleading the Parliament on several occasions. Shah said[161]:

(a) The Prime Minister stopped the Russia-Ukraine war for three days to evacuate Indian students (a repeat of what he and other senior BJP leaders have been telling since 2022, when caught for delayed evacuation of stranded medical students. This had already been dismissed as false[162] by the Foreign Affairs.

(b) Kuki infiltrators from Myanmar caused the ethnic violence in Manipur. The Kuki groups from India and Myanmar refuted this.[163] So did a ground report and an expert[164] – both blaming the Centre and state government for looking the other way. In fact, thousands of Kukis fled to Mizoram[165] and later, the remaining Kukis of Imphal were forcibly evicted[166] to safe places by the state.

(c) J&K is witnessing "improvement" and "normalcy". He had claimed so in 2019 too.[167]. The violence may have reduced but uneasy calm prevails with 5,000 people in jails after 2019[168], independent media outlets shut and journalists jailed[169]. No elections have been conducted for the past four years. Besides, a drug pandemic has hit the Valley as investigating reports [170]says – a manifestation of disturbed social and political life.

(d) Maharashtra woman Kalavati (one of those women who widowed due to farm suicides) and her family were helped by the Central government, not by Rahul Gandhi who had first flagged her plight in the Parliament many years ago. Kalavati called the bluff, describing it as "absolute lie" and said it was Rahul Gandhi alone who had helped her and her family to overcome the crisis.[171]

Ironically, of the three Bills the Home Minister paradropped, one, the Bharatiya Nyaya Sanhita Bill, 2023 proposes a three-year jail for spreading fake news.

Delegitimizing Opposition

The government has tried every trick to make the Opposition irrelevant in the Parliament – which is *systemic*. A few examples.

Deputy Speaker and LoP-mukt Lok Sabha: The 17th Lok Sabha (2019-23) has remained without a Deputy Speaker – a constitutional requirement and which conventionally goes to the Opposition[172] – even after the Supreme Court sought explanations. The government responded by saying that there was no "immediate requirement" or was hindering the functioning.[173] There has just been one instance in the past – for 269 days during the 12th Lok Sabha (1998-99) when the BJP-led NDA government's a 13-month government was in office.

The current regime has also denied another constitutional post, the Leader of Opposition (LoP) given to the numerically largest party from the Opposition benches – the Congress (INC) in this case – since 2014. It not only violates the statues, the Constitution, it also delegitimizes and enfeebles the main political rival inside the Parliament. The Lok Sabha Speaker from his party did this first in 2014 by arguing that the Congress didn't have 10% of seats in the Lok Sabha (its seats numbered 55 then). This betrays either lack of knowledge or deliberate mischief – as this condition *was* meant for "recognizing a Parliamentary Party" as per the Speaker's Directives of 1956. This directive became *redundant* after two specific laws were passed to make LoP a *statutory requirement*. One, Leader of Opposition was defined and provided a statutory status by the Salary and Allowances of Leaders of Opposition in Parliament Act of 1977 (SALOP Act) – as per which the criterion is the "leader in that House of the party in opposition to the Government having the greatest numerical strength", irrespective of strength. Two, the enactment of the 10th Schedule of the Constitution (Anti-Defection Law) in 1985 whereby every party is considered a Parliamentary Party irrespective of its strength in the House.[174]

Thus, LoP is a statutory requirement, not to be decided by the Speaker or by the number of seats. Denial of LoP is, thus, a violation of both the statutes and the Constitution. LoP plays very significant role to play in the Westminster model India adopted. PDT Achary[175], former Lok Sabha secretary general, writes that in the Westminster model, LoP is a "shadow Prime Minister" because she/ he is expected to take over if the government falls and it brings cohesiveness and effectiveness to the opposition's functioning, which is critical for a healthy parliamentary democracy.

LoP also plays a key role in bringing bipartisanship and neutrality to appointment of key institutions of accountability and transparency, like the CVC, CBI, CIC and Lokpal. In contrast, the Aam Admi Party government in Delhi recognizes and grants LoP status to the BJP in spite of it not qualifying by the Lok Sabha Speaker's 10% rule. The practice continues in the Parliament after 2019. This wasn't the first instances though. India didn't have LoP during 1971-77, 1980-84 and 1984-89 – which is, however, no excuse for repeating it.[176]

Rahul Gandhi's disqualification from Lok Sabha: In March 2023, Congress's Rahul Gandhi was disqualified from the Lok Sabha with lightning speed – after a Gujarat court held him guilty of defamation in a highly questionable case. The defamation case was decided swiftly *after*[177] he raised questioned on the corruption charges against the Adani groups and the Prime Minister's relation with its proprietor Gautam Adani. His questions were *deleted* from the parliamentary records.[178] Instead, Gandhi was targeted for telling at his *alma mater* the Harvard University that India's democracy was in danger and that danger came from the BJP, while also saying that "we will deal with our problem, but you must be aware".[179] When his membership was restored in August 2023, his screen time cut by 71%[180] and many of his observations "expunged"[181].

The genesis of the cases is in a statement Gandhi made in 2019 in Karnataka (not in Gujarat): "I have a question. Why do all of them—all these thieves—have Modi, Modi, Modi in their names? Nirav Modi, Lalit Modi, Narendra Modi. And if we search a bit more, many more such Modis will come out." The petitioner was none of the named Purnesh Modi, a BJP legislator and former minister in the Modi's cabinet in Gujarat. Surat chief judicial magistrate (CJM) Harish Hashmukhbhai Varma heard the case and sentenced Gandhi to maximum possible imprisonment of two years. Interestingly, the case was filed in 2019 and was heard by then judicial magistrate AN Dave; Purnesh Modi *strangely* got a stay on the proceedings from the Gujarat High Court in 2022 and then got the stay vacated in February 2023, by when Dave had been replaced with Varma[182] and Gandhi had raised questioned about Adani and Modi.

Verma moved in a tearing hurry. He started hearing it in February 2023, held seven hearings in *20 days* and pronounced the judgement on March 24, 2023 – an incredibly fast for an Indian court, clogged as they are with 40 million cases (average time for deciding a case is 15 years[183]). The official machinery in New Delhi moved *even faster* to get disqualify him in 24 hours and serve eviction notice for his official accommodation in another 12 hours. Very usual indeed.[184]

The Lok Sabha Secretariat's letter[185] of disqualification is problematic. As Achary points out[186], such disqualification is not automatic, notwithstanding the Lily Thomas case judgement of 2013 (disqualification of MPs after conviction and sentencing for minimum of two years under the Representation of People Act of 1951), as the constitutional provisions governing the disqualification of a Member of Parliament are Article 102 and 103.

Article 103[187] provides that it is the President who has the "final" authority on such disqualification, but it also says that before taking such a decision the President "shall obtain the opinion of the Election Commission and shall act according to such opinion" – indicating that (a) the disqualification can't be automatic (b) the President must obtain the opinion of the Election Commission and (c) the Lok Sabha Secretariat has no authority to disqualify. Article 102, governing the grounds for disqualifications of an MP, provides for "so disqualified by or under any law" which, in this case, is the RP Act of 1951. Former bureaucrat Avay Shukla called it "clearly a command performance".[188] Incidentally, CJM Varma was immediately promoted as district judge but the Supreme Court stayed it, along with that of 67 others, saying that it was "illegal and contrary to rules and regulations".[189]

Suspending Opposition members: The Parliament has seen more and more Opposition leaders being silenced through suspensions. The RTI replies[190] from the Parliament to the queries of Surat's RTI activist Sanjeev B Ezhava revealed that between August 3, 2015 and August 10, 2023, *140* Members of Parliament (MPs) had been suspended from the Lok Sabha (92) and Rajya Sabha (48). Not one was from the BJP (0), and maximum were from the Congress (53). This is *more than three times* the total number of MPs suspended during the ten years of the Congress-led UPA years of 2004 to 2014 – only 43. Besides, not one BJP MPs (0) was suspended then, while 53 Congress MPs were suspended during the latter period. This tells its own tell of how the Opposition was being silenced in the Parliament.

That many of the suspensions are "illegal, irrational, unconstitutional"[191] is not exactly unknown. Partisanship shown by the Speaker was mentioned earlier. The Chairman of Rajya Sabha, Jagdeep Dhankhar, also a former BJP leader, has been unusually partisan and harsh towards the Opposition. Once he called CPM MP John Brittas to explain an innocuous newspaper article in which he questioned Home Minister Amit Shah's attack on Kerala during the Karnataka elections[192], going *beyond* his jurisdiction[193] once again. During the Opposition protests and the logjam over the Prime Minister's refusal to give a statement on Manipur, Dhankar expressed his concern over "weaponising of disruptions" in the "temple of democracy".[194]

Both Rajya Sabha Chairman Dhankar and Lok Sabha Speaker refused to intervene and use their offices to bring the Prime Minister to speak on Manipur as the Opposition demanded, instead blaming the them for disrupting proceedings and making unfair demands.[195] They forgot, when their party was in the Opposition during the previous UPA government, their leaders, particularly late Arun Jaitley, used to repeatedly justify disrupting the Parliament saying, "Not allowing parliament to function is also a form of democracy, like any other form" and that the BJP didn't want "to give the government an escape route through debate".[196] Late Jaitley and Sushma Swaraj then as Opposition leaders used to argue that it was the government's *responsibility* to ensure smooth functioning of the House – not that of the Opposition.[197] It was during Dhankar's Rajya Sabha chairmanship that the House's Committee on Privileges said showing disrespect to Rajya Sabha Chair "amounts to breach of privilege".[198]

A big reason for the diminishing role of Parliament is also the weak political opposition. It has been so ineffective, dispirited and invisible that the UK's Financial Times wrote in 2020 that "the annihilation of India's political opposition is almost complete".[199] But it must also be realized that despite the Prime Minister's claim that India is "mother of Democracy" and his officials calling it "Civilizational State" they are the ones who have played a very big role in rendering both the Parliament and the Opposition dysfunctional.

Fawning "Godi" Media

Indian mainstream media – TV news channels and the vast majority of newspapers and magazines with mass reach – has been tamed after 2014 – which is why it has won the sobriquet "Godi media" (a play on Modi and 'lapdog'). The BBC's 2023 documentary on the 2002 Gujarat pogrom contained *three particularly telling comments*[200] on the governance model of then Gujarat Chief Minister Modi.

- It said he was "directly responsible" for the anti-Muslim violence, the VHP and its allies "acted with the support of" and in a "climate of impunity" created by the state government.

- The attack on the train at Godhra "provided the pretext" and "if it had not occurred, another one would have been found".

- Modi said, in an interview which was part of the documentary, that his only "regret" was he couldn't handle the media as well as he ought to have.

The last ("regret") is now a thing of the past. There are several ways in which the Prime Minister and his government have achieved this.

Intimidation is a big weapon (see "media censorship" in Chapter I). The BBC was raided[201] for days in Delhi and Mumbai over tax issues immediately after its documentary on 2002 anti-Muslim pogrom in Gujarat – two-part documentary series "India: The Modi Question". The documentary was *blocked*[202] in India with the government ordering Twitter and YouTube to take down dozens of accounts that had aired the clips on the plea that it was "undermining the sovereignty and integrity of India" and "making unsubstantiated allegations".

Incidentally, British foreign office record obtained through a Freedom of Information Act request in Britain (corresponding to India's RTI Act) revealed in September 2023, that then the BJP-led government of Atal Bihari Vajpayee did not contest its main findings that the pogrom was "pre-planned", that Sangh Parivar outfits like the Vishwa Hindu Parishad (VHP) had played a key role in it and that the Gujarat police had specifically been told not to act against the killers. It only objected to (a) *the leak* of the report at the time and (b) the number of killed ("at least 2000 killed" by them as against India's official figure of 850 dead then, later revised to 1,180 by the Gujarat government in 2009).[203]

There were at least *six such raids*[204] before this on Indian news media for being critical of the Central government:

- The NDTV and the Quaint (the Adani Group took over the NDTV in 2022[205] and acquired 49% stakes in The Quint's sister organization Bloomberg Quint, now BBQ Prime, in March 2023[206]);

- The Dainik Bhaskar and Bharat Samachar (for exposing pandemic mismanagement in 2021 – unclaimed bodies floating in the Ganges in Uttar

Pradesh, buried in its sand banks and lack of medicare in the state's rural areas etc.);

- The NewsClick and Greater Kashmir. Besides, tax officials visited Newslaundry for a 'survey'[207];

- Journalist Rana Ayyub was raided by the ED and tax officials for alleged tax evasion from funds raised for the pandemic relief work[208];

- The Wire was visited by the Delhi Police after their expose of the Pegasus spyware in 2021[209] and

- The Wire was also raided[210] by the Delhi Police in 2022 and the mobile and other electronic devices seized over *planted* articles which had been pulled down and about which it had lodged a complaint with the police.

Besides, in June 2023, the Allahabad High Court stepped in to ban[211] airing of *Al Jazeera*'s film "India …Who Lit the Fuse?" – an investigation into the hate crimes by Hindu nationalist groups against Muslims.

The biggest coordinated attack on independent media was carried out in October 2023 – when the Delhi Police raided 50 locations in Delhi, Delhi NCR and Mumbai in which 46 full-time and part-time journalists, historian Sohail Hashmi, satirist Sanjay Rajoura and scientist D Raghunandan one or other linked to the web portal NewsClick or its programmes, their digital devices (phones, laptops etc.) were seized and two were arrested for terror activities (under the UAPA), conspiracy and promoting enmity (Section 153A of the IPC).[212] Later, in November 2023, hearing the case, the Supreme Court merely described seizure of journalists' devices "a very serious matter" but all it could do was to direct the government to frame "better guidelines"[213] when none exists and remind it that privacy was a fundamental right or such seizure incapacitated media professionals even in their normal functioning as individuals. This was when a petition asking for regulating such search and seizure of digital devices of journalists, academics and lawyers *pending since 2021!*[214] The Delhi Police had earlier seized the devices of The Wire journalists (in 2022). India's law enforcement agencies are known to seize such devices without following any guideline, due diligence, without giving hash value (unique numerical value issued to maintain the integrity of digital data) or cloned copy at the time of seizure and for indefinite period.[215] Unlike India, developed countries have their own strict conditions and additional protocols.[216] In the case of the NewsClick journalists, the Delhi Police even refused to even give a copy of the FIR and had to be told by the court that it was *their right*.[217] This was unheard of development and reflects how the criminal justice system has come to work now.

This was an extension of the ED raid on the NewsClick in 2021 in connection with foreign funding it received. The FIR referred to US businessman Nevile Roy Singham and funding through him for allegedly pushing Chinese propaganda.

This was based on a New York Times report[218] on global funding for Chinese propaganda which also named NewsClick as one of those who received such funding but it provided only one instance of such a propaganda – a video marked "China's history continues to inspire the working classes".

How does this constitute a terror activity or hate crime? Just by citing a *friendship* between NewsClick founder Prabir Purkayastha and Gautam Navlakha [219] – of the same seemingly fake Bhima Koregaon case detailed in Chapter I who languishes in jail/house arrest since 2020 without trial.

But the purpose is clearly – as in all such instances listed – to intimidate journalists who dare to question the government's policies and actions.[220] All the journalists were asked if they had written critical accounts of the government's mishandling of the protests against the CAA of 2019-20, farmers' protest of 2021, Delhi riots of 2020, the pandemic management etc.[221] These incidents were mishandled and reflected the government's ineptitude and incompetence – as has been explained in several chapters (Chapters I, IV, XI) of this book as well as in the author's 2021 book "An Unkept Promise: What Detailed the Indian Economy"[222]. But an admission of it would have apparently been viewed as "anti-national" activity – senior journalist Coomi Kapoor wrote.[223]

But then that was to be expected. While dismissing the China threat as "a pretext to target those who question an increasingly tyrannical government", journalist Hartosh Singh Bal wrote:[224] "The distinction between those who tell the truth and those who cavort for the government has been erased in the public mind. The external environment in which journalists work is toxic. The government has used labels, and the law, to go after those who refuse to side with them and used their prime time anchors to arouse public sentiment against the profession of journalism. Watching the screaming bigotry of television channels, the public has come to ascribe the worst qualities of those they watch to those who do journalism."

This raid took the total notices and raids on media and journalists to 44 (not an exhaustive list) in five years between 2018 and 2023 – 9 by the IT, 15 by the ED and 20 involving the anti-terror investigating agency NIA.[225] It needs to be pointed out that at least four Chinese companies have declared they have or would donate to the Prime Minister's *private fund* "PMCARES Fund" (see Chapter I for details of this fund), including the banned app TikTok and three well-known Indian companies having significant Chinese funding have also made donations to this fund.[226] Does this make the PMO which runs this fund guilty of spreading Chinese propaganda and anti-terror acts? Until the Chinese incursion into India controlled LAC in Ladakh in April 2020, the Prime Minister not only repeatedly *hosted* Chinese President Xi Jinping but also repeatedly *boasted* about his friendship with Jinping calling it "'plus one' friendship").[227]

As pointed out, Mohammed Zubair's arrest in 2022 also marked the day the Prime Minister signed a treaty in Germany with G-7 leaders *to protect free speech* online and offline[228] and a few days later, India *committed* to shielding journalists and rights activists in talks with the European Union.[229] – a trademark double standard of the regime.

The Reporters Without Borders (RSF), a global NGO defending media freedom, has *consistently downgraded* India in its Press Freedom Index rank – from 133 in 2016 fallen to 161 (out of 180) in 2023.[230] In 2021 (when India ranked at 142), it released a list of 37 "Press Freedom Predator" (PFP) in which the Prime Minister of India was one. Headlined "Prime Minister of India since 26 May 2014: Predator since taking office", it said after becoming Gujarat's Chief Minister in 2001, he used the state as a "laboratory for the news and information control", the methods he "deployed" after becoming the Prime Minister in 2014. It has consistently branded India as one the *most dangerous for media;* in 2023 it noticed "the rise of "Godi media" (a play on Modi's name and lapdogs), which "mix populism and pro-BJP propaganda" and said "the old Indian model of pluralist press" is seriously challenged by a combination of harassment and influence".[231]

It listed the following "predatory weapons" of the Prime Minister to control media:

(i)   "Flood" the mainstream media with speeches and information tending to "legitimize" national-populist ideology for which

(ii)   Close ties with billionaire businessmen who own vast media empires – an "insidious strategy" which works in two ways – (a) by visibly "ingratiating" himself with the "owners" of leading media outlets, their journalists know they "risk dismissal" for criticizing the government and (b) "prominent coverage" of his "extremely divisive and derogatory speeches", which often constitute "disinformation", enables the media to achieve "record audience levels" (high TRP). All that is left for government is to neutralise the media outlets and journalists questioning his divisive methods, for which

(iii) A "judicial arsenal" with provisions that pose a major threat to press freedom – risk of life imprisonment under the "extremely vague charge of sedition", a part of which is

(iv)   An army of online trolls known as "yodha" ("warriors") on which he can count on and who wage "appalling hate campaigns" on social media which almost routinely include calls for the journalists to be killed – leading to the killing of Gauri Lankesh in 2017. The work involves quickly branding journalists questioning the Prime Ministers's ideology as "sickular" – a portmanteau of "sick" and "secular" – and are targeted by "bhakt" (devotees) who bring "lawsuits" against them, "defame" them in the mainstream media and "coordinate online attacks" against them – which is "more virulent" if the targets are women journalists, who are labelled as "presstitutes" (Rana Ayyub and Barkha Dutt, for example), were subjected to calls for them to be "gang-raped" and their "personal data" posted online to facilitate attacks.[232]

What the RSF report missed listing is *generous advertisements* to favoured media outlets to ingratiate their owners – and also give exclusive access by appearing at their annual functions/conclaves, which is significant because the Prime Minister neither allows journalists to question him nor engages in two-way dialogue. His is one-way communications (like 'Mann ki Baat', election rallies, national addresses etc.), as is his government's. A Lok Sabha reply of December 2022 revealed that his government spent Rs 6,491 crore during FY15-FY23 (up to December 7, 2022) – Rs 3,260.79 crore in electronic media and Rs 3,230.77 crore in print media in eight years.[233] This works out to be Rs 2.3 crore per day! The total spend on publicity is, however, humongous, given that CPSUs, the BJP-run governments, municipalities and support groups also put up hoardings on roadsides, buildings, petrol pumps etc.

Since many media outlets also run other businesses, they are dependent on the government for administrative clearance and other assistance. Journalist Aakar Patel wrote: "The reliance on the government for licences and for advertising, the popularity of the government's majoritarian ideology and the ownership of large swathes of the media by corporate interests has meant that it has toed the line quite enthusiastically."[236]

The journalists are aware of all this. In fact, a Lokniti-CSDS survey of 2023, "Media in India: Trends and Patterns", revealed[237] that 82% journalists think their employers support the BJP, 80% think the media covers the Prime Minister "too favourably" while 61% said Opposition parties were covered "too unfavourably". It is hardly a secret that India's Big Businesses dominate the media and their private interests have *corrupted*[238] *the media landscape.* Mainstream media has lost its mojo so completely that it even gives fake headlines like stating that India had *ended* China's "adventurism" to give a *false strongman image*[239] to the Prime Minister even as Jaishankar continued to *deny* Chinese land grab. It has also enabled the government to *persecute*[240] inconvenient journalists.

When any news group, howsoever big and powerful (and including The Hindu and Times of India) dared to fallout of line through unfavourable news *swift retaliation*[241] follows by way of cut in ads.

The BJP has an IT Cell operating from its Delhi office – which has allegedly been found churning out misinformation and fake news. The Altnews, the pioneer of fact-checking website in India, started by Pratik Sinha and Mohammed Zubair, has exposed many such misinformation and fake news over the years, which are amplified by many senior ministers on social media, and other right-wing ecosystems.[242] A global study of 2018, "State- Sponsored Trolling: How Governments Are Deploying Disinformation as Part of Broader Digital Harassment Campaigns"[243] found eerie similarity between China's state-run disinformation machinery "50 Cent Army", and this BJP IT Cell – which is run by a mix of *volunteer and paid amateur trolls*. This study, like that of Altnews, flagged how the Prime Minister provides direct leadership as his official Twitter account follows at least *26 troll accounts* who are *serial abusers, sexist bigots, rumour mongers*, and many of them have been *hosted* by him at his official residence too.

The RSF's list also missed the fact that many journalists are not really coerced or scared but are *ideologically aligned* with Hindutva. Those in the media have known it for long. They walked out of the woodwork after 2014. How news coverage and debates are regulated by the government – and hence the copy-cat acts on virtually every issue – is also too well known. For example, a study of 1,779 Republic TV debates revealed in 2020[244] how the channel championed the Prime Minister through "biased" coverage in favour of his government, its policies and the BJP's ideology. Worse, these debates rarely featured most pressing issues like the state of the economy, education and health.

This is true of many other TV channels – who, instead keep spreading communal hatred night after night – as Altnews's Mohammed Zubair[245] has repeatedly exposed year after year. No wonder, multiple scams exposed by the Comptroller and Auditor General of India (CAG) in 2023 evoked no response from the TV anchors[246] – in sharp contrast to what was the case before 2014 when the UPA regime was throughly roasted over such reports.

Its obsequiousness was on full display when the Palestine-Israel conflict started in October 2023. The mainstream media had found no time for six months to go to Manipur as it burnt (and which would have exposed the BJP's "double-engine government's communal politics) but landed in Israel immediately to give a carpet and partisan coverage in favour of Israel (apparently, the Israeli military facilitated their visit, provided hospitality and free visas[247] which explains their "ground reporting" from inside Israel, not Gaza, the "ground zero" at the time and complete absence of the deaths and destructions in Gaza[248]). This is perfectly *aligned* with the Prime Minister's open and partisan support to Israel[249] and a token humanitarian aid to Palestinians[250] (even as India *refused to support* the UN resolution calling for "protection of civilians and upholding legal and humanitarian obligations"[251]) and also the BJP's political campaign to *target domestic Muslims* using the conflict[252] in the run-up to crucial elections in states and the general elections of 2024. India emerged as the *epicentre of hate and misinformation*[253] against Palestinians – in both mainstream and social media. Factchecker Altnews[254] routinely exposes such misinformation campaign originating from India – better known as "Pallywood' narrative, a term pro-

Israel influencers and users use to discredit claims of the deaths and destructions in Gaza, including that of children, by suggesting that Palestinians are play-acting. The BJP-ruled Uttar Pradesh even *banned* expression of any view *contrary to official position* and began *arresting*[255] people for their individual opinions on social media supporting Palestine.

It was such behaviours in the past that had led to an unprecedented development in September 2023 when the 36-party non-BJP alliance INDIA named and shamed 14 anchors to be *boycotted by them*.[256] The BJP cried foul but it had done the same to the NDTV in 2014 (before the takeover by the Adani group) by stating that it "manufactured" tweets "to hurt BJP".[257]

Journalist Seem Chishti[258] rightly pointed out that the "precipitous fall" of the mainstream media is "not about silencing the press alone" but "what is being done is to amplify governmental points of view and propaganda by acts of commission too" and went on to add: "The truth about Indian media being successfully coerced and persuaded to parrot the governmental tune has destroyed the myth of post-Emergency immunity that the big media had been proud to flaunt in the world till eight years ago."

"Positive story" or the positivity narrative is the very anti-thesis of journalism and press. No criticism of government's ineptitude and incompetence and no negative news only helps the government's propaganda of "all's well". In fact, the news media has no business to be in business if it promotes the government propaganda. Yet, mainstream media gives generous help in spreading fake and misleading news and *attack* whoever dares to show the government in poor light (like the women wrestlers protesting against sexual assault by the BJP MP) along with *right-wing Twitter handles*.[259] The ANI, a leading news agency, found a *Muslim angle*[260] to the Manipur stripping of women. The misleading news was taken out after 12 hours, only after it was called out by *the Altnews* but by that time, the damage had already been done, it had gone viral as other news platforms and right-wing ecosystem spread it. This is a typical example of the modus operandi and finding a *Muslims angle* is a routine phenomenon when the government faces embarrassing situations like the *Odisha train accident (connected to nearby masjid)*[261] of 2023 which killed nearly 288 and injured 800 more, violence in the JNU in 2020[262], the *pandemic crisis*[263] of 2020 and virtually everything else (see 'multiple fake jihad' campaigns in Chapter IV). Another trick used is to plant stories using "anonymous sources" – like women wrestlers withdrawing their protests, minor withdrawing POCSO case against BJP MP Brij Bhushan Saran Singh (which later turned out to be true and *under duress*[264] as the law refused to act for a long time) BBC confessing to tax evasion.[265]

The Prime Minister has led from the front to tame media. The night before the overnight, extremely stringent, unpanned and untimely national lockdown was imposed on March 24, 2020 (at 8 pm national address). A Caravan investigative report[266] revealed that the Prime Minister called owners and editors of several print and electronic media outlets and asked them to publish "positive stories" relating to the pandemic and avoid "negativity". The media owners and journalists not only committed to do so but complied! For total control on the news media, a Group of Ministers (GoM) was constituted, with top ministers as members, to prepare strategies to "neutralize" journalists who wrote against the government and monitor "negative influencers". It met *six times during the pandemic lockdown* of 2020 – another investigating report of the Caravan revealed in 2021.[267]

Another investigative report by Morning Context revealed in 2023 that little known TV content monitoring team, called the Electronic Media Monitoring Centre (EMMC), set up in 2008 by the UPA government to monitor TV channels across genres to ensure they comply with standards, has become a tool for surveillance, meet political ends and ensure the Prime Minister and the BJP government look good. It said: "Under the current government, the agency seems to have become a tool for excessive surveillance of TV channels, especially news channels, to track reportage and opinion that are critical of the ruling party."[268] This report pointed out that the EMMC had flagged the MediaOne TV channel (mentioned earlier) during the 2020 communal violence in Delhi, which was taken off the air and in February 2022, the MHA cancelled its broadcast license – which was quashed by the Supreme Court in April 2023.

As "Godi" media started losing credibility, viewership and revenue in 2023[269] (a) the government started giving more ads to online media[270] (b) used social media influencers in 2023 to propagate their views by giving interviews[271] and (c) a constellation of right-wing Hindi YouTubers emerged[272] fast out-performing mainstream news channels in reach, ability to set the news agenda and curate extreme forms of hate speech and Islamophobia. The BJP recruited thousands of influencers across *18 states* to its campaign for 2024.[273]

Access to information is tightly controlled – not even news photographers are allowed in the BJP's official functions and media access to the Parliament is severely restricted after the pandemic of 2020[274], so is the case with the BJP rallies and electioneering – all media coverage is provided by the BJP in news media offices. The NaMo TV (Chapter X) is a prime example how the BJP routinely violates established norms to indulge in ceaselss propaganda even during the 48-hour restrictions on campaigns before polling.

Citizens as 'Bhakts'

One of the *defining markers* of India after 2014 which was not listed in Introduction is a flourishing "Bhakti" (call it devotion, loyalty, obsequiousness, subservience, hero-worship or voluntary servitude) culture. "Bhakti" is driven by faith and has magical power in India which at once negates evidence, logic and scientific quest.

Hindus, as a society, getting visibly more ritualistic and religious (prioritizing 'faith' rather than rational, scientific and questioning mindset) and Hindu youths getting radicalized *en masse* are bad enough. But even worse is a large segment of citizens, particularly highly educated, empowered and vocal middle-class is turning into loyal and devoted supporters of the government and its Hindutva ideology. This is a unique phenomenon in the world – even for countries led by authoritarian and populist demagogues. Economist Pranab Bardhan[275] points out: "The recent spectacular rise of extreme right-wing parties in Italy and Sweden...have revived the puzzle that in the face of economic crisis and rising inequality the working classes are often turning politically right, instead of left. This is as prevalent in developing countries as in the rich countries of North America and Europe. One difference between the two sets of countries (rich countries of North America and Europe and developing ones like India) may be that while in rich countries this trend is markedly among less-educated, older, and more rural workers, in some developing countries, say India, this is also the case for more educated, aspirational urban youth."

These highly educated, professional middle-class people take particular pride in publicly declaring themselves as "Bhakts" (loyal or devoted) to the Prime Minister and defend every action of his and his government – even in the face of evidence of adverse consequences. This is a *lived experience*. Arguably, such regressive outlook never existed in the post-independent India. The ability to speak out against governments and voting them out for non-performance has been lost. The previous UPA regime, which produced the highest-ever growth, hardly ever had a day without strong criticism from those very empowered and vocal middle-class. To believe that the very entitled middle-class is or has become a part of the BJP support base and hence, silent to the Prime Minister's failures, as some seem to do[276], would mean to miss a far more insidious development. Deep down, the middle-class seems to have metamorphosed which needs serious, multi-disciplinary studies to fully unravel because this is a true recipe for "1,000 years of slavery" (to borrow the Prime Minister's favourite phrase about India's past). India may not yet be there but it is very much in the realm of possibility. This phenomenon is so extraordinary that a separate chapter has been devoted to try and understand (Chapter XI).

There is yet another grim aspect to it that must be flagged. The Indian diaspora has seemingly changed too – it's very vocal in support of Hindu majoritarian society and authoritarian politics. Giving an account of this change, scholar Vidya Krishnan writes[277]: "Most of my family and friends in the diaspora champion progressive candidates such as Elizabeth Warren in US elections but throw their weight behind reactionary Indian politicians...They also drag the carcass of caste apartheid wherever they settle." She wrote the US-based people of Indian origin "have learnt to perfectly mimic the language of the oppressed – as people of colour – without ever using that language to speak against oppression back home. This self-obscuring is a dangerous intellectual malady".

Eliminating Civil Society

Yet another *defining marker* not listed in Introduction is systemically elimination of once vibrant civil society.

Systemic attack on civil society began in a big way during the previous Congress-led UPA regime in 2011-12 when the protests against the nuclear plant at Kudanukulam (Tamil Nadu) – being set up with Russian nuclear plants – peaked. But that was a small change compared to what has happened after 2015 – to all except the RSS, the largest NGO which is not even a registered entity, no formal membership[278] and yet gets foreign funding[279] and is not to have been subjected to scrutiny, and other NGOs associated with it. The RSS is building multi-story towers in New Delhi for itself[280] without attracting any attention from tax authorities or the ED.

The key tool to target civil society is through the Foreign Contribution Regulation Act (FCRA) of 2010. Official data shows, of 20,691 licenses cancelled between 2011 and April 29, 2023, 16,745 or 81% were after 2015. There is no record of licenses *suspended or not renewed.*[281] As noted in Chapter 1 ("Human Rights: What is That?"), at the 28th foundation day of the NHRC) in New Delhi in 2021 – a few days after Union Minister (MoS) for Home, Ajay Mishra Teni's car, allegedly driven by his son, mowed down peacefully marching farmers in Lakhimpur Kheri in Uttar Pradesh, drawing all-round condemnations – the Prime Minister made astounding observations. He condemned criticism of his government over human rights violations as "selective outrage" and "dangerous" for democracy. He also said human rights mattered to people *only* after their basic needs were met.

NHRC chief Justice Arun Mishra praised the government for its human rights record, despite ample evidence to the contrary and condemned the "new norms" of accusing India at the behest of "international forces".[282] A few weeks later, the then Chief of Defence Staff (CDS) General Bipin Rawat joined the chorus stating that the people in Kashmir were now saying they would "lynch terrorists" and that this was a "positive sign" and wouldn't amount to violation of human rights. He provided no evidence and no logic for his assertions though.[283] But the truly ominous statement came from the NSA Ajit Doval (see Chapter I). In 2018, Doval branded civil society as "new enemy" and "new frontier of war" and in 2021, not only repeated it but sought to redefine the rule of law and democracy by running down citizens and giving primacy to government – conveniently forgetting that governments are elected to serve people and that all public servants like him and the IPS officers he was addressing, are paid salaries and perks from public money for this very reason. Doval also forgot that civil society has critical role to play in governance, in checking authoritarian drifts of governments and as such criticizing and voting out governments are *constitutionally guaranteed right as well as duty* of citizens. Among others, Aruna Roy[284], former IAS and RTI activist, rightly reminded Doval, a former IPS officer, that civil society was not the enemy, his theory of "fourth generation warfare" undermined the Constitution and would cause a great harm to the nation's security – while reminding him of the oath of office he had taken multiple times in his long career as a government servant.

The FCRA amendment of 2020[285](which came amidst the pandemic crisis) put stiff conditions for NGOs to avail foreign donations: restricted the list of recipients, banned "transfer such foreign contribution to any other person", made it mandatory to open FCRA account only in the designated SBI branch in New Delhi, allowed stopping use of foreign funds and suspend FCRA license on mere suspicion ("reason to believe") without giving on opportunity to be heard or producing evidence ("pending any further inquiry") and extended the period of suspension of license extended from 180 days to 360 days.

The Supreme Court upheld this amendment in 2022 (by bench of Justices AM Khanwilkar, Dinesh Maheshwari and CT Ravikumar). The court's logic for upholding the restrictions is bizarre: "No one can be heard to claim a vested right to accept foreign donation"; need for "insulating the democratic polity from the adverse influence of foreign contribution" and "self-reliant".[286] This argument not only hurts thousands of NGOs doing invaluable development work (some have done pioneering work, like Aruna Roy) in health, education, livelihood, climate change and other areas, particularly in remote parts of the country where government reach is limited or ineffective.

Strangely, the logic of foreign influence, self-reliance etc. were cited by the Supreme Court to justify the restrictions on NGOs while successive governments have openly and pro-actively invite FDIs – the data for which is released every fortnight since 2000 (more than two decades). Besides, the apex court is yet to decide the constitutionality of the really critical amendments of 2016 and 2018 (through the Finance Bills) which removed the ban on foreign contributions/ donations to political parties – thereby legalizing such foreign donations). The earlier ban was to *insulate* Indian democracy and government from foreign influence. These amendments were done after the Delhi High Court found the two leading political parties – the BJP and Congress – guilty of violating the FCRA (Section 4) and also the Representation of People Act of 1951 (Section 29B).[287]

There is no check on the foreign funding to the RSS and in October 2023, the MHA even granted the FCRA license to the Ayodhya temple[288] even as it withdrew that from thousands of NGOs and reputed think tanks and even withdrew tax-exemption[289] status of many. The government has liberalized FDI, more than 86% of which is routed through tax havens and shell companies, and also allows foreign funding for political parties through the opaque Electoral Bond (Chapter X). Both the government and the Supreme Court seem to pretend that such foreign fundings don't compromise economy, governments, political parties, governance and national pride.

The list of NGOs banned for foreign funding includes all the big names – Greenpeace (shutdown operations in 2015), Amnesty International (shutdown operation in 2020), Oxfam India, Commonwealth Human Rights Initiative (CHRI), Centre for Policy Research (CPR), Congress-run two Rajiv Gandhi trusts headed by Sonia Gandhi (for allegedly receiving funds from China)[290] and countless others – many of them critical of the government's policies. Even Mother Teresa's Missionaries of Charity's license was suspended on December 25, 2021 – on the Christmas Day – under mysterious circumstances and later renewed after protests. Donations from US-based Hewlett Foundation, which funds climate awareness campaigns, was banned saying that this was not permissible.[291] The CPR's license was suspended, its offices raided for studies relating to the Adani group's controversial coal mining operation in the Hasdeo forests in Chhattisgarh, among other charges[292]; and then, its FCRA license was taken away and *tax exemption status was canceled*[293]. Similarly, prominent environment lawyer Ritwick Dutta and his NGO, Legal Initiative for Forest and Environment (LIFE), were booked for FCRA violations and charged with using foreign funds to "target and stall" coal projects, the Adani group's projects and for "criticizing government policy" through public media.[294] A third group, R Sreedhar's Environics Trust, too was targeted. All three unconnected think tanks/NGOs (CPR, LIFE and Environics Trust) were raided by the IT simultaneously in September 2022. The Washington Post commented[295] that "each was seen by the government to be a critic of Gautam Adani, one of India's richest men and a political ally of Prime Minister Narendra Modi" and pointed out that all three had opposed the Adani's coal mining in the Hasdeo Arand's virgin and rich forests.

All three lost their tax-exemption status later and the IT department even mentioned their protests against the Adani group's coal mining in its letter as one of the reasons (Oxfam and Environics).[296]

Strange the government never ordered a probe into the corruption allegations against the Adani group by US short seller Hindenburg, nor allowed questions or debate on it in the Parliament (detailed earlier in this chapter). The Supreme Court set up a panel which didn't reach any conclusion and market regulator Security and Exchange Board of India (SEBI) couldn't decide what to do (details in Chapter VII). As the ugly episode was playing out, political scientist Ashutosh Varshney[297] called the present "India's gilded age" (after the America's Gilded Age of 19th century characterized by robber barons).

A group of 86 retired bureaucrats wrote[298] to Union Home Minister, drawing his attention to great works NGOs have done and sought to reverse the government's regressive moves but nothing happened. Then something strange happened during the devastating second wave of the pandemic in May 2021 – when the Indian government went to the world with a begging bowl for help[299]. The Prime Minister sought NGOs' help in sheer desperation. How many came to his rescue is not known but his iron grip on them had already crippled them[300], leaving with little scope to help even if they wished to.

The PMLA Rules 2023, notified in March 2023[301] is also aimed at tighter control on NGOs. This rule makes it mandatory for every bank and financial institution to collect information about financial transactions of NGOs under the money laundering law (PMLA), register details of NGO clients on the NITI Aayog's' Darpan' portal and maintain the record for five years. The *definition of NGOs* has also been amended and linked to the definition of charitable purpose (under Section 2(15) of the Income Tax Act of 1961) to include any entity or organisation, constituted for religious or charitable purposes.

One should never forget that "strong civil society participating in public affairs" is one of the key factors in ensuring good or effective governance[302] and never be allowed to be weakened.

To sum up, three of the four critical institutions to hold the power to account have failed. The performance of the one left out – the Supreme Court of India – is no better as the next chapter would reveal. There are many other institutions – the Governors, Election Commission of India (ECI), SEBI, CAG, Lokpal – and good governance instruments like the RTI Act of 2005 which play critical role and are broken too. But instead of putting all those here, they are part of the other chapters to ensure that they are presented in the right context.

***

References

1   New Parliament building: Timeline, costs incurred, employment generated, May 28, 223; https://www.hindustantimes.com/india-news/new-parliament-building-narendra-modi-timeline-costs-incurred-employment-generated-101685198974352.html

2   Sharma Vibha, Row over angry 'lions' replacing benign ones in national emblem atop new Parliament building, Jul 12, 2022; https://www.tribuneindia.com/news/nation/row-over-angry-lions-replacing-benign-ones-411845

3   Sahu SN, The Sengol Is a Symbol of 'Divine Right' to Power. It Does Not Belong in Parliament., May 27, 2023; https://thewire.in/politics/sengol-divine-right-parliament-people

4   New Parliament Building: PM Modi bows down, does 'Sashtanga Dandavat Pranam' in front of 'Sengol', May 28, 2023; https://zeenews.india.com/video/news/new-parliament-building-pm-modi-bows-down-does-sashtanga-dandavat-pranam-in-front-of-sengol-2614684.html

5   Wankhede Harish S, Parliament Rituals Show Permanency of BJP's Brahmanical Cultural Agenda, Jun 16, 2023; https://thewire.in/politics/new-parliament-brahmanical-cultural-agenda-bjp

6   Multi-Faith Prayer Ceremony Marks New Parliament Building Inauguration, May 28, 2023; https://www.ndtv.com/india-news/multi-faith-prayer-ceremony-marks-new-parliament-building-inauguration-4072705

7   On women's reservation bill, PM Modi's request to Rajya Sabha: 'I urge members…', Sept 19, 2023; https://www.hindustantimes.com/india-news/on-womens-reservation-bill-pm-modis-request-to-rajya-sabha-i-urge-members-101695117036283.html

8   Mehrotra K and Katakey R, Modi Tells India's Hindu Heartland He's Doing God's Work, May 18, 2014; https://www.bloomberg.com/news/articles/2014-05-17/thousands-greet-modi-in-delhi-after-historic-india-win#xj4y7vzkg

9   Seth Maulashree, PM Modi as 'God avatar': UP minister explains, says 'he makes things happen', Nov 1, 2022; https://indianexpress.com/article/political-pulse/the-avatar-of-god-who-makes-things-happen-up-minister-gulab-devi-pm-modi-8237821/

10   Hebbar Nistula, Modi is God's gift to India: Venkaiah, May 20, 2016; https://www.thehindu.com/news/national/Modi-is-God%E2%80%99s-gift-to-India-Venkaiah/article60513878.ece

11   'People see PM Modi as God…': Union Minister Pralhad Joshi hits back at Siddaramaiah, ANI, Apr 20, 2023; https://economictimes.indiatimes.com/news/politics-and-nation/people-see-pm-modi-as-god-union-minister-pralhad-joshi-hits-back-at-siddaramaiah/videoshow/99640950.cms?from=mdr

12   How Modi's Parliament 'Bhoomi Pujan' Breached the Constitution's Basic Structure,

Dec 23. 2020; https://thewire.in/politics/narendra-modi-parliament-bhoomi-pujan-constitution-basic-structure

13   New parliament: PM Modi inaugurates building amid opposition boycott, May 28, 2023; https://www.bbc.com/news/world-asia-india-65718127

14   Stopped at borders from joining wrestlers, UP farmers protest at Ghazipur, May 29, 2023; https://indianexpress.com/article/cities/delhi/stopped-at-borders-from-joining-wrestlers-up-farmers-protest-at-ghazipur-8634036/

15   Kapoor Coomi, Inside Track by Coomi Kapoor: Wrestling troubles, Jun 4, 2023; https://indianexpress.com/article/opinion/columns/wrestling-troubles-8644352/

16   Bhatia Gautam, A parliamentary democracy or an executive democracy, Jun 1, 2023; https://www.thehindu.com/opinion/lead/a-parliamentary-democracy-or-an-executive-democracy/article66916867.ece

17   Komireddi Kapil, Modi's Parliament inaugural was an elaborate mimicry. It displayed the sham that is New India, May 30, 2023; https://theprint.in/opinion/modis-parliament-inaugural-was-an-elaborate-mimicry-it-displayed-the-sham-that-is-new-india/1601291/

18   Lalwani Vijayta, As Covid-19 devastates Delhi, Central Vista project declared an essential service, work continues, Apr 27, 2021; https://scroll.in/article/993385/as-covid-19-devastates-delhi-central-vista-project-declared-an-essential-service-work-continues#:~:text=Currently%2C%20only%20construction%20projects%20which,accessed%20by%20Scroll.in%20shows.

19   Mohanty P, 'An Unkept Promise', Ch II, pages 115-148

20   Mohanty P, 'India has no data to challenge WHO excess Covid deaths' https://www.fortuneindia.com/opinion/india-has-no-data-to-challenge-who-excess-covid-deaths/108072

21   Central Vista Project gets all-clear from Supreme Court in 2:1 verdict, Jan 5, 2021; https://indianexpress.com/article/india/central-vista-project-supreme-court-verdict-new-parliament-buidling-7133176/

22   Bhatia Gautam, Beyond the veils of secrecy, the Central Vista project is both the cause and effect of its own multiple failures, Oct 31, 2020; https://www.thehindu.com/society/beyond-the-veils-of-secrecy-the-central-vista-project-is-both-the-cause-and-effect-of-its-own-multiple-failures/article32980560.ece

23   Rajvanshi Astha, Why India's New Parliament Building Is So Controversial, May 26, 2023; https://time.com/6282819/india-parliament-narendra-modi-controversy/

24   Komireddi Kapil 2020; Modi's ghastly Delhi dream, https://thecritic.co.uk/issues/april-2020/modis-ghastly-delhi-dream/; Dev Atul 2021: Modi's Folly, The New York Review, May 10, 2021; https://www.nybooks.com/online/2021/05/10/modis-folly/

25   Speaker suggests building new Parliament House, Dec 28, 2015; https://timesofindia.indiatimes.com/india/speaker-suggests-building-new-parliament-house/articleshow/50347525.cms

26 Delhi's heritage city dream dashed by government, May 23, 2015; https://www.aljazeera.com/features/2015/5/23/delhis-heritage-city-dream-dashed-by-government

27 Delhi upset with Modi government, wants heritage tag, Jun 4, 2015; https://economictimes.indiatimes.com/news/politics-and-nation/delhi-upset-with-modi-government-wants-heritage-tag/articleshow/47537289.cms?utm_source=contentofinterest&utm_medium=text&utm_campaign=cppst

28 Govt, Jio See Conspiracies by Anti-National 'Gangs', Rivals, Dec 15, 2020; https://www.theindiacable.com/p/the-india-cable-govt-jio-see-conspiracies?utm_campaign=post&utm_medium=web&utm_source=twitter

29 New Parliament building to nurture dreams into reality: PM Modi, ANI, May 28, 2023; https://www.aninews.in/news/national/politics/new-parliament-building-to-nurture-dreams-into-reality-pm-modi20230528114142/

30 Jaffrelot Christophe, Kalaiyarasan A write: Why delimitation could deepen India's North-South faultline, Aug 3, 2023; https://indianexpress.com/article/opinion/columns/christophe-jaffrelot-kalaiyarasan-a-write-why-delimitation-could-deepen-indias-north-south-faultline-8873770/; Modi's new parliament could see Hindi belt gain, South lose power at the Centre, May 27, 2023; https://scroll.in/article/1049779/modis-new-parliament-could-see-hindi-belt-gain-south-lose-power-at-the-centre

31 Tiwary Deeptiman, Yadav Shyamlal, History of the Akhand Bharat idea, and in the imagination of the RSS, June 3, 2023; https://indianexpress.com/article/explained/explained-culture/history-of-the-akhand-bharat-idea-and-in-the-imagination-of-the-rss-8643236/

32 Bhushan Bharat, India's broken dream of 'Akhand Bharat', Jun 9, 2023; https://www.deccanherald.com/opinion/akhand-bharat-pakistan-nepal-bangladesh-bjp-karnataka-kolhapur-1226233.html?utm_source=substack&utm_medium=email

33 Kapoor Coomi, Coffee and politics in Parliament's Central Hall, May 28, 2023; https://indianexpress.com/article/india/coffee-politics-in-parliaments-central-hall-8631649/; Inside Track by Coomi Kapoor: Post-dated cheque, Sept 24, 2023; https://indianexpress.com/article/opinion/columns/women-reservation-bill-journey-bills-passed-in-parliament-ncps-supriya-sule-8953292/

34 Editorial: Misplaced mystery: On the special session of Parliament, the politics, Sept 16, 2023; https://www.thehindu.com/opinion/editorial/misplaced-mystery-the-hindu-editorial-on-the-special-session-of-parliament-the-politics/article67311961.ece

35 Special Session 2023, Legislation: New Bills Introduced: 1, PRS India; https://prsindia.org/sessiontrack/special-session-2023/bill-legislation

36 Prabhu Sunil, Women's Reservation Bill Cleared In Key Cabinet Meeting, Sources Say, Sept 19, 2023; https://www.ndtv.com/india-news/womens-reservation-bill-cleared-in-key-cabinet-meeting-say-sources-4401961

37   Women's Reservation Bill 2023 [The Constitution (One Hundred Twenty-Eighth Amendment) Bill, 2023], PRS India; https://prsindia.org/billtrack/the-constitution-one-hundred-twenty-eighth-amendment-bill-2023#:~:text=The%20Constitution%20(One%20Hundred%20and,state%20legislative%20assemblies%20for%20women.

38   Jha Sanjay K, Lok Sabha: BJP MP Ramesh Bidhuri hurls slurs at BSP's Danish Ali, triggers outrage, Sept 23, 2023; https://www.telegraphindia.com/india/lok-sabha-bjp-mp-ramesh-bidhuri-hurls-slurs-at-bsps-danish-ali-triggers-outrage/cid/1968227

39   Gosh Poulomi, 'Danish Ali provoked, used unpardonable words against PM'; BSP MP rejects charge, Sept 23, 2023; https://www.hindustantimes.com/india-news/danish-ali-provoked-bidhuri-by-unpardonable-words-against-pm-nishikant-dubey-101695485880632.html

40   Varadarajan Siddharth, Modi's 'action-reaction' quote, Oct 27, 2009; https://svaradarajan.com/2009/10/27/modis-action-reaction-quote/

41   Tonk Population 2023, Census India 2011; https://www.census2011.co.in/census/city/85-tonk.html

42   BJP's Ramesh Bidhuri Gets New Role. MP He Abused, Had Predicted... Sept 28, 2023; https://www.ndtv.com/india-news/ramesh-bidhuri-danish-ali-hate-speech-new-role-for-ramesh-bidhuri-who-abused-danish-ali-is-reward-for-hate-4431513

43   Apporvanand, Ramesh Bidhuri's Controversial Appointment Shows Hate Is BJP's Political Currency, Sept 29, 2023; https://m.thewire.in/article/communalism/ramesh-bidhuris-controversial-appointment-shows-hate-is-bjps-political-currency/amp

44   Punwani Jyoti, BJP's new lows and a tradition of communal lexicon, Sept 30, 2023; https://www.newslaundry.com/2023/09/30/bjps-new-lows-and-a-tradition-of-communal-lexicon#:~:text=The%20enemy%20then%20was%20those,symbol%20of%20the%20country's%20heritage.

45   INDIA seeks probe into sloganeering from House gallery, Sept 23, 2023; https://www.thehindu.com/news/national/india-parties-demand-probe-into-women-visitors-who-raised-pro-modi-slogans-in-the-gallery-during-rs-debate/article67338135.ece

46   PRS, Vital Stats: Parliament functioning in Budget Session 2023, Apr 6, 2023, PRS Legislative Research; https://prsindia.org/files/parliament/session_track/2023/vital_stats/Session_Vital-Stats_BS23.pdf

47   Lok Sabha passes Union Budget without debate, Mar 14, 2018; http://timesofindia.indiatimes.com/articleshow/63301079.cms?utm_source=contentofinterest&utm_medium=text&utm_campaign=cppst

48   PRS Vital Stats: Parliament functioning in Monsoon Session 2023; https://prsindia.org/sessiontrack/monsoon-session-2023/vital-stats

49   Decisions taken in the meeting of the Committee of Secretaries (CoS) held on 10th January, 2014, Ministry of Law and Justice; https://lddashboard.legislative.gov.in/sites/default/files/plcp.pdf

50   PLCP Compliance, Lok Sabha, Nov 20, 2019; http://164.100.24.220/loksabhaquestions/annex/172/AU582.pdf

51   Govt takes leeway, skips pre-legislative procedure on bills, Feb 12, 2022; http://timesofindia.indiatimes.com/articleshow/89513634.cms?utm_source=contentofinterest&utm_medium=text&utm_campaign=cppst

52   PS Arun and Patel Sushmita, Democratising Lawmaking: The Tale Of Pre-Legislative Consultation Policy, Aug 15, 2019; https://www.medianama.com/2019/08/223-democratising-lawmaking-the-tale-of-pre-legislative-consultation-policy/

53   Bhatnagar Gaurav Vivek , No Lesson Learnt From Farm Laws, Centre Forgoes Prior Consultation for 17 of 29 Scheduled Bills, Nov 26, 2021; https://thewire.in/government/winter-session-parliament-farm-laws-consultation;   https://twitter.com/policychettan/status/1463144203265871872?ref_   src=twsrc%5Etfw%7Ctwcamp%5Etweetembed%7Ctwterm%5E1463144210492583939%7Ctwgr%5E%7Ctwcon%5Es2_&ref_url=https%3A%2F%2Fthewire.in%2Fgovernment%2Fwinter-session-parliament-farm-laws-consultation

54   Bhardwaj Anjali, In violation of Pre-legislative consultation policy, govt did not make draft of Electoral Bond Scheme public before notifying it. Info obtained under RTI suggests proposal to hold consultations with political parties & seek public comments was scrapped after a meeting with the PM, Oct 30, 2023; https://twitter.com/AnjaliB_/status/1719028025763991968;   https://twitter.com/AnjaliB_/status/1719028025763991968

55   PMO: Quest for Transparency, PMO; https://www.pmindia.gov.in/en/quest-for-transparency/

56   Article 110: The Constitution of India; Indiankanoon.org; https://indiankanoon.org/doc/72095/; Money Bills vs. Other Bills, PRS Legislative Research, December 22, 2015; https://www.prsindia.org/theprsblog/money-bills-vs-other-bills

57   Justice KS Puttaswamy (Retd) vs Union Of India, Supreme Court, September 26, 2018; https://main.sci.gov.in/supremecourt/2012/35071/35071_2012_Judgement_26-Sep-2018.pdf

58   Mandhani Apoorva, Review pleas pending, 7-judge bench not formed — Aadhaar Act validity case languishes in SC, Jan 4, 2021; https://theprint.in/judiciary/review-pleas-pending-7-judge-bench-not-formed-aadhaar-act-validity-case-languishes-in-sc/578834/

59   Mohanty P, General Elections 2019 (Part I): Who is funding the electioneering of our political parties? India Today, Mar 15, 2019; https://www.dailyo.in/politics/lok-sabha-elections-2019-party-funding-electoral-bonds-national-parties/story/1/29910.html

60   CG Manoj, In speeches, PM called for 'quality debates'; in House, Govt pushed 15 Bills in under 10 mins last session, Nov 30, 2021; https://indianexpress.com/article/india/pm-modi-quality-debates-parliament-govt-pushed-15-bills-winter-session-7648106/

61   Chatterji Saubhadra, NDA govt pushes more ordinances than UPA in 10 yrs, Apr 14, 2021; https://www.hindustantimes.com/india-news/nda-govt-pushes-more-ordinances-than-upa-in-10-yrs-101618255988192.html

62   PRS, 'Vital Stats: Parliament functioning in Monsoon Session 2023'

63   Ali Sana and Sharma Ambar, IndiaSpend 2020: Parliamentary Panels' Role, Functioning At All-Time Low, Data Show, September 14, 2020; https://www.indiaspend.com/parliamentary-panels-role-functioning-at-all-time-low-data-show/

64   Ali Sana and Sharma Ambar, IndiaSpend 2020'

65   CG Manoj, 'In speeches, PM called for 'quality debates'

66   Choudhary Shrimi, GST exemptions disrupt input tax credit chain, will complex GST: CBIC chief, Nov 8, 2023; https://www.business-standard.com/economy/news/gst-exemptions-disrupt-input-tax-credit-chain-will-complex-gst-cbic-chief-123110801335_1.html

67   Bahl Advitya, Fake companies and eway bills to spin Rs 10,000-crore GST fraud, Jun 2, 2023; https://timesofindia.indiatimes.com/city/noida/fake-companies-and-eway-bills-to-spin-rs-10000-crore-gst-fraud/articleshow/100690636.cms

68   Sinha Shishir, GST Appellate Tribunals: Govt issues notification to set up 31 State Benches, Sept 15, 2023; https://www.thehindubusinessline.com/economy/gst-appellate-tribunals-govt-issues-notification-to-set-up-31-state-benches/article67310340.ece#:~:text=The%20Centre%20has%20issued%20a,a%20number%20of%20State%20Benches.

69   Mohanty P, Jammu & Kashmir Reorganisation Bill 2019: A rush job raising concerns of democratic propriety, Aug 6, 2019; https://www.indiatoday.in/news-analysis/story/jammu-kashmir-reorganisation-bill-2019-decoded-1577790-2019-08-06;   S Meghnad, Wondering how Amit Shah dismantled #Article370 so fast and furiously? Read this, Aug 5, 2019; https://www.newslaundry.com/2019/08/05/how-amit-shah-narendra-modi-dismantled-article-370-jammu-kashmir

70   Jebaraj Priscilla, 'No record of consultations on farm laws', Jan 11; https://www.thehindu.com/news/national/no-record-of-consultations-on-farm-laws/article33552859.ece

71   Parliament clears Farm Laws Repeal Bill without a debate, Nov 30, 2021; https://www.thehindu.com/news/national/parliament-clears-farm-laws-repeal-bill-without-a-debate/article37762376.ece

72   Mohanty 'An Unkept Promise', Ch VIII

73   The Gazette of India, March 28, 2021; https://www.livelaw.in/pdf_upload/gnctd-amendemnt-bill-391206.pdf

74   Chishti Aiman J, Parliament Passes Delhi Services Bill (GNCTD Amendment Bill), Aug 7, 2023; https://www.livelaw.in/news-updates/parliament-passes-delhi-services-bill-gnctd-amendment-bill-234627#:~:text=The%20Rajya%20Sabha%20

on%20Monday,Lok%20Sabha%20on%20August%2003.

75   Mohanty P 'An Unkept Promise', Ch IX and X.

76   Finance Minister launches the National Monetisation Pipeline, NITI Aayog, Aug 23, 2021; https://pib.gov.in/PressReleseDetail.aspx?PRID=1748297

77   Union Home Minister and Minister of Cooperation, Shri Amit Shah introduces the Bhartiya Nyaya Sanhita Bill 2023, the Bharatiya Nagarik Suraksha Sanhita Bill, 2023 and the Bharatiya Sakshya Bill, 2023 in the Lok Sabha, today, Ministry of Home Affairs, Aug 11, 2023; https://pib.gov.in/PressReleseDetailm.aspx?PRID=1947941; Parliament Session Alert: Monsoon Session: July 20, 2023 – August 11, 2023, PRS Legislative Research, Jul 1, 2023; https://prsindia.org/sessiontrack/monsoon-session-2023/session-alert

78   Das Saurav, How Consultative Was the Framing of the Three Criminal Law Bills, Really? Aug 24, 2023; https://thewire.in/government/how-consultative-was-the-framing-of-the-three-criminal-law-bills-really

79   Manral Mahendra Singh, Before Bills, process of consultations, discussions: Govt, Aug 12, 2023; https://indianexpress.com/article/explained/explained-law/before-bills-process-of-consultations-discussions-govt-8888604/

80   Guruswamy Maneka, Menaka Guruswamy on Centre's criminal code bills: Weakening criminal law's guardrails, Sept 2, 2023; https://indianexpress.com/article/opinion/columns/criminal-code-bills-bharatiya-nyaya-sanhita-criminal-laws-mcoca-ipc-crpc-8920188/; Verma Pranav, Shoddy Drafting Has Left the Government's New Criminal Bills With Glaring Errors, Aug 28, 2023; https://thewire.in/law/criminal-bills-drafting-shoddy-sakshya-nyay-sanhita-ipc-evidence

81   Mustafa Faizan, Faizan Mustafa writes: New penal code falls short of its laudable objectives, Aug 18, 2023; https://indianexpress.com/article/opinion/columns/faizan-mustafa-writes-new-penal-code-falls-short-of-its-laudable-objectives-8889348/; Alam Shahrukh, Proposed Criminal Codes, while trying to break from colonial past, only emulate it, Aug 14, 2023; https://indianexpress.com/article/opinion/columns/parliament-monsoon-session-new-bills-in-parliament-judicial-reforms-8891144/

82   Tiwari Deeptiman, Opposition MPs dissent on criminal law Bills: Copy-paste job, still have colonial spirit, Nov 12, 2023; https://indianexpress.com/article/political-pulse/opp-mps-dissent-on-criminal-law-bills-copy-paste-job-still-have-colonial-spirit-9023326/

83   Vishwanath Apurva, Criminal law Bills: Officials to lawyers, 19 experts heard — all 'welcome initiative', Nov 12, 2023; https://indianexpress.com/article/india/officials-to-lawyers-19-experts-heard-all-welcome-initiative-9023320/

84   P Chidambaram writes: Copy, Cut and Paste 'Reform', Nov 26, 2023; https://indianexpress.com/article/opinion/columns/indian-criminal-laws-reform-9042550/

85   The Constitution (One hundred and Twenty-eighth Amendment) Bill, 2023; https://prsindia.org/files/bills_acts/bills_parliament/2023/Constitution_(128th_Amendment)_Bill_2023.pdf

86   PM hails passage of The Constitution (One Hundred and Twenty-Eighth Amendment) Bill, 2023 in the Lok Sabha, Prime Minister's Office, Sept 20, 2023; https://pib.gov.in/PressReleaseIframePage.aspx?PRID=1959235

87   P Chidambaram writes: Reservation when? After, after, after, Sept 24, 2023; https://indianexpress.com/article/opinion/columns/women-reservation-bill-article-334a-deve-gowda-manmohan-singh-narendra-modi-census-data-8953269/

88   Ninan TN, Penalised for demographic success? Strange case of states south of Godavari, Sept 22, 2023; https://www.business-standard.com/opinion/columns/penalised-for-demographic-success-strange-case-of-states-south-of-godavari-123092200926_1.html

89   On women's reservation bill, PM Modi's request to Rajya Sabha: 'I urge members...', Sept 19, 2023; https://www.hindustantimes.com/india-news/on-womens-reservation-bill-pm-modis-request-to-rajya-sabha-i-urge-members-101695117036283.html

90   Mohanty P, 'An Unkept Promise', ch-1; Desai Nitin 2022: Reforming the NITI Aayog, Business Standard, May 16, 2022; https://www.business-standard.com/article/opinion/reforming-the-niti-aayog-122051601487_1.html

91   Made it clear to government that demonetisation was not a good idea: Raghuram Rajan, PTI, Apr 12, 2018; https://www.thehindu.com/business/Economy/made-it-clear-to-government-that-demonetisation-was-not-a-good-idea-raghuram-rajan/article23513447.ece

92   India Covid-19: PM Modi 'did not consult' before lockdown, Mar 29; https://www.bbc.com/news/world-asia-india-56561095; Mohanty P 'An Unkept Promise', Ch V.

93   Ministry of Finance 2020: Finance Minister announces new horizons of growth; structural reforms across Eight Sectors paving way for Aatma Nirbhar Bharat, PIB, May 16; https://pib.gov.in/PressReleasePage.aspx?PRID=1624536; Mohanty 'An Unkept Promise'

94   Mohanty P, It's time to measure the impact of PLI, DLI schemes, Jun 22, 2023; https://www.fortuneindia.com/opinion/its-time-to-measure-the-impact-of-pli-dli-schemes/113139

95   Gazette notification S.O.416(E), Ministry of Home Affairs (about BSF jurisdiction), Oct 11, 2021; https://egazette.nic.in/WriteReadData/2021/230337.pdf

96   Mohanty 'An Unkept Promise'

97   Rajya Sabha Secretariat Refuses To Answer Swamy's Question On Chinese Crossing LAC; dec 1, 2021: https://www.outlookindia.com/website/story/rajya-sabha-secretariat-refuses-to-answer-swamys-question-on-chinese-crossing-lac/403395; Lahiri Ishadrita, 17 questions on China dismissed by Lok Sabha citing 'national security', Congress' Tewari says, Dec 20, 2021; https://theprint.in/politics/17-questions-on-china-dismissed-by-lok-sabha-citing-national-security-congress-tewari-says/784806/

98 Singh Sushant, Modi's alarming aversion to parliamentary scrutiny over the border crisis in Ladakh, Jun 20, 2020; https://caravanmagazine.in/politics/modi-aversion-parliament-scrutiny-border-ladakh

99 Government disallows question on Pegasus, says matter is sub judice, Aug 6, 2021; https://www.thehindu.com/news/national/government-disallows-question-on-pegasus-says-matter-is-sub-judice/article35768227.ece

100 PM Modi BREAKS his silence over ongoing ruckus in Indian parliament, Jul 27, 2021; https://news.abplive.com/videos/news/india-pm-modi-breaks-his-silence-over-ongoing-ruckus-in-indian-parliament-1472272

101 'Parliament queries on Manipur avoided as subject is sub judice', Jul 28, 2023; https://timesofindia.indiatimes.com/india/parliament-queries-on-manipur-avoided-as-subject-is-sub-judice/articleshow/102184574.cms?from=mdr

102 Rajvanshi Ashtha, Why Modi Is Facing a Rare No-Confidence Vote, Jul 26, 2023; https://time.com/6297996/modi-no-confidence-vote-manipur/

103 Mukhopadhyay Sougata, Irked by his jibes at Modi, House suspends Adhir Chowdhury citing 'unruly' conduct, Aug 10, 2023; https://www.telegraphindia.com/india/irked-by-his-jibes-at-pm-modi-house-suspends-adhir-chowdhury-citing-unruly-conduct/cid/1958152

104 Ghildiyal Subodh, Oppn: Govt didn't let Manipur MPs speak, Aug 11, 2023; https://timesofindia.indiatimes.com/india/oppn-govt-didnt-let-manipur-mps-speak/articleshow/102626046.cms?from=mdr

105 Mahaprashasta Ajoy Ashirwad, In Rajya Sabha Too, PM Modi Doesn't Answer Opposition's Questions About Adani, The Wire, Feb 9, 2023; https://thewire.in/politics/rajya-sabha-pm-modi-speech-adani

106 Ahmad Omair, It Is Naïve to Expect PM Modi to Speak up During Crises, Jul 24, 2023; https://thewire.in/politics/narendra-modi-manipur-gujarat

107 Adani Group: How The World's 3rd Richest Man Is Pulling The Largest Con In Corporate History, Hindenburg Research, Jan 24, 2023; https://hindenburgresearch.com/adani/

108 Rahul Gandhi Speech: What Were the Remarks Expunged by Lok Sabha Speaker? Feb 8, 2023; https://thewire.in/politics/rahul-gandhi-speech-remarks-expunged

109 "Vajpayee Had Used Word": Congress's M Kharge On Remarks Being Deleted, Feb 9, 2023; https://www.ndtv.com/india-news/after-rahul-gandhi-congress-chief-m-kharges-parliament-remarks-deleted-3766716

110 Congress fumes as Kharge's remarks on PM Modi, Adani expunged from Parliament records, Feb 9, 2023; https://www.deccanherald.com/national/congress-fumes-as-kharge-s-remarks-on-pm-modi-adani-expunged-from-parliament-records-1189416.html

111 Mikes in our Parliament are silenced, Rahul Gandhi tells British MPs, Mar 6, 2023; https://economictimes.indiatimes.com/news/politics-and-nation/mikes-in-our-

parliament-are-silenced-rahul-gandhi-tells-british-mps/articleshow/98459353.
cms?utm_source=contentofinterest&utm_medium=text&utm_campaign=cppst

112 Adhir complains to Om Birla: 'My mike in LS muted for last three days… Voice
of Oppn leaders not being heard', Mar 16, 2023; https://indianexpress.com/article/
political-pulse/adhir-ranjan-chowdhury-om-birla-lok-sabha-parliament-8499603/

113 Parliament adjourned after BJP seeks apology from Rahul Gandhi for his remarks
in Britain, Mar 13, 2023; https://scroll.in/latest/1045489/parliament-adjourned-after-
bjp-seeks-apology-from-rahul-gandhi-over-his-remarks-in-britain

114 "Ek akela kitno ko bhari": PM Modi hits back at Congress, opposition parties in
Rajya Sabha, ANI, Feb 9, 2023;

https://www.aninews.in/news/national/politics/ek-akela-kitno-ko-bhari-pm-modi-hits-
back-at-congress-opposition-parties-in-rajya-sabha20230209233848/

115 Coalitions of 'negativity' never successful, says PM Modi, Jul 18, 2023; https://www.
thehindu.com/news/national/nda-a-coalition-of-contributions-not-compulsion-
says-modi/article67095521.ece

116 'Coalition of compulsions': PM Modi on I.N.D.I.A, Jul 19, 2023; https://www.
deccanherald.com/national/national-politics/oppn-must-inspire-confidence-that-
its-goal-is-to-save-constitution-brinda-karat-1238483.html

117 Opposition demands JPC probe into Adani allegations: What is a Joint Parliamentary
Committee

Feb 3, 2023; https://indianexpress.com/article/explained/opposition-jpc-probe-adani-
allegations-what-is-joint-parliamentary-committee-8420654/

118 Mohanty P, Another kill bill clause for nuke non-liability, Aug 28, 2010; https://
www.governancenow.com/news/regular-story/another-kill-bill-clause-nuke-non-
liability

119 Mohanty P, Kill Bill: Discretion in R&R will undo land acquisition law, May 21,
2012; https://www.governancenow.com/news/regular-story/kill-bill-discretion-rr-
will-undo-land-acquisition-law

120 Delay in operationalising Whistle Blowers Protection Act, Ministry of Personnel,
Public Grievances & Pension, Aug 2, 2018; https://pib.gov.in/newsite/PrintRelease.
aspx?relid=181386

121 Aadhaar card linkages with voters ID cards, Rajya Sabha answer, Jul 29, 2021;
https://uidai.gov.in//images/Rajya_Sabha_Unstarred_Qn_No_1189_answered_
on_29_7_2021.pdf; Linking of Aadhaar and Voter ID, Rajya Sabha answer, Jul 27,
2023; https://pqars.nic.in/annex/260/AU909.pdf ; Aadhaar Myth Busters, UIAI;
https://uidai.gov.in/en/my-aadhaar/about-your-aadhaar/aadhaar-myth-busters.
html

122 The Registration of Births and Deaths (Amendment) Act, 2023, Gazette notification,
Aug 11, 2023; https://prsindia.org/files/bills_acts/acts_parliament/2023/
Registration_of_Births_and_Deaths_(Amendment)_Act,_2023.pdf

123 Shrivastava Kumar Sambhav, EXCLUSIVE: Documents Show Modi Govt Building 360 Degree Database To Track Every Indian, Sept 15, 2020; https://www.huffpost.com/archive/in/entry/aadhaar-national-social-registry-database-modi_in_5e6f4d3cc5b6dda30fcd3462

124 Bhardwaj Shrutanaja, Tracking Life & Death: Changes To A 54-Year-Old Law May Exclude Millions Of Poorest Indians & States, Aug 1, 2023; https://article-14.com/post/tracking-life-death-changes-to-a-54-year-old-law-may-exclude-millions-of-poorest-indians-states--64c855e116cf0

125 Mohanty P, Why protecting privacy remains a challenge in India, Jun 21, 2023; https://www.fortuneindia.com/opinion/why-protecting-privacy-remains-a-challenge-in-india/113131

126 Mohanty P, Rebooting Economy XXX: Rural India in far deeper crisis than what govt data claims, Sept 25, 2020; https://www.businesstoday.in/opinion/columns/story/indian-economy-economic-pain-in-rural-india-deeper-than-q1-fy21-data-govt-claim-273802-2020-09-23

127 Mohanty P, 'An Unkept Promise', pages 189-208

128 Thakur Atul, Nagarajan Rema, MNREGS workers subsidised creation of infra assets by Rs 20,000 crore a year, Jan 26, 2022; http://timesofindia.indiatimes.com/articleshow/89125423.cms?utm_source=contentofinterest&utm_medium=text&utm_campaign=cppst

129 Mohanty P, "An Unkept Promise', page 92

130 Barik Soumyarendra and Mathew Liz, Opp seeks House panel study on data privacy report, Govt defends it, unlikely to send it for more dissection, Aug 3, 2023; https://indianexpress.com/article/india/opp-seeks-house-panel-study-on-data-privacy-report-govt-defends-it-unlikely-to-send-it-for-more-dissection-8873959/

131 Digital Personal Data Protection Bill 2023 passed in Rajya Sabha: Key Points, Aug 11, 2023; http://timesofindia.indiatimes.com/articleshow/102579315.cms?utm_source=contentofinterest&utm_medium=text&utm_campaign=cppst

132 Mohanty P, DPDP Bill 2023: Question mark on privacy, more power to govt, Aug 10, 2023; https://www.fortuneindia.com/opinion/dpdp-bill-2023-question-mark-on-privacy-more-power-to-govt/113694

133 Nikhil Dey and Aruna Roy write: Data Protection Bill does not protect us — it attacks our rights, Aug 10, 2023; https://indianexpress.com/article/opinion/columns/nikhil-dey-and-aruna-roy-write-data-protection-bill-does-not-protect-us-it-attacks-our-rights-8880902/

134 The Forest Conservation (Amendment) Act, 2023, Aug 4, 2023; https://egazette.gov.in/WriteReadData/2023/247866.pdf

135 Report of the Joint Committee on the Forest (Conservation) Amendment Bill, 2023, Lok Sabha, Jul 2023; https://prsindia.org/files/bills_acts/bills_parliament/2023/Joint_Committee_Report_on_the_Forest_(Conservation)_Amendment_Bill_2023.

pdf

136   Deuskar Nachiket, Can the Lok Sabha pass bills when a no-confidence motion is pending? Aug 5, 2023; https://scroll.in/article/1053792/can-the-lok-sabha-pass-bills-when-a-no-confidence-motion-is-pending#:~:text=Constitution%20experts%20concur%20that%20there,no%2Dconfidence%20motion%20is%20pending.

137   The Jan Vishwas (Amendment of Provisions) Act, 2023, Aug 11, 2023; https://prsindia.org/files/bills_acts/bills_parliament/2022/Jan%20Vishwas%20(Amendment%20of%20Provisions)%20Bill,%202022.pdf; Highlights of the Bill, PRS India; https://prsindia.org/billtrack/the-jan-vishwas-amendment-of-provisions-bill-2022

138   Thakur Dinesh and Reddy T Prashant, Modi's Jan Vishwas Bill gives the pharmaceutical industry a get-out-of-jail card, Aug 1, 2023; https://www.newslaundry.com/2023/08/01/modis-jan-vishwas-bill-gives-the-pharmaceutical-industry-a-get-out-of-jail-card#:~:text=The%20Jan%20Vishwas%20Bill%20%2C%20which,of%20us%20made%20on%20Twitter.

139   Das Krishna N and Mcallister Edward, Exclusive: Gambia tightens rules for Indian drugs after cough syrup deaths, June 21, 2023; https://www.reuters.com/world/africa/gambia-tightens-rules-indian-drugs-after-cough-syrup-deaths-letter-2023-06-20/#:~:text=At%20least%2070%20children%2C%20most,adulterated%20cough%20syrups%20from%20India.

140   India cough syrup linked to Uzbekistan deaths 'substandard': WHO, Jan 12, 2023; https://www.aljazeera.com/news/2023/1/12/who-alert-on-indian-cough-syrup-linked-to-20-deaths-in-uzbekistan

141   Poison found in Indian-made cough syrup sold in Iraq, tests reveal, Jul 28, 2023; https://www.cnbctv18.com/healthcare/india-iraq-cough-syrup-cold-out-toxic-chemical-poison-world-health-organisation-17367941.htm

142   Barman Sourav Roy, Vice President Jagdeep Dhankhar's personal staff attached to 20 House committees, Mar 9, 2023; https://indianexpress.com/article/political-pulse/vice-president-jagdeep-dhankhar-personal-staff-house-committees-8485598/

143   Full list of 'unparliamentary' words, Jul 14, 2022; https://www.deccanherald.com/national/full-list-of-unparliamentary-words-1126639.html, Jul 14, 2022;

144   Ganguly Meenakshi, Dissent is 'anti-national' in Modi's India – no matter where it comes from, Dec 13, 2019; https://scroll.in/article/946488/dissent-is-anti-national-in-modis-india-no-matter-where-it-comes-from

145   Mohanty P, CAA & NRC II: Here are the myths and facts about all-India National Register of Citizens, Dec 24, 2019; https://www.businesstoday.in/latest/economy-politics/story/caa-nrc-national-register-of-citizens-myths-and-facts-citizenship-amendment-act-modi-amit-shah-govt-241551-2019-12-23; Mohanty P, CAA & NRC III: Who are 'doubtful' citizens NPR seeks to identify?, Dec 24, 2019; https://www.businesstoday.in/latest/economy-politics/story/caa-nrc-iii-who-are-doubtful-citizens-npr-seeks-to-identify-241445-2019-12-24; Pandey Samyak, Modi speech fact-check: From NRC to detention centres, here's where PM went wrong, Dec

23, 2019; https://theprint.in/india/modi-speech-fact-check-from-nrc-to-detention-centres-heres-where-pm-went-wrong/339690/

146 Fadnavis Aditi, PM Narendra Modi blames Congress, AAP for exacerbating Covid crisis, Feb 8, 2022; https://www.business-standard.com/article/politics/pm-narendra-modi-blames-congress-aap-for-exacerbating-covid-crisis-122020800003_1.html

147 Mohanty P, "An Unkept Promise, Ch V.

148 Mohanty P, "An Unkept Promise, Ch V.

149 Mahaprashasta Ajoy Ashirwad, Modi Speech Dodges Economic Distress, Rewrites Govt's COVID Record to Blame Congress, AAP, Feb 8, 2022; https://thewire.in/politics/instead-of-providing-real-answers-modi-uses-parliament-speech-to-lash-out-at-opposition

150 Patel Aakar 2021: Price of Modi Years, Westland Publications, page 361, 2021; https://www.amazon.in/Price-Modi-Years-Aakar-Patel/dp/9391234224

151 Gupta Shekhar, Confounded by Manipur, Jul 22, 2023; https://www.business-standard.com/opinion/columns/confounded-by-manipur-123072101042_1.html

152 Yadav JP, Manipur: PM Modi ends silence, SC asks government to take action against sexual violence, Jul 21, 2023; https://www.telegraphindia.com/india/manipur-pm-modi-ends-silence-sc-asks-government-to-take-action-against-sexual-violence/cid/1953440

153 Too little, too late; mere words won't do: Congress on PM Modi's Manipur video remarks, Jul 20, 2023; https://www.telegraphindia.com/india/too-little-too-late-mere-words-wont-do-congress-on-prime-minister-narendra-modis-manipur-video-remarks/cid/1953334?s=08

154 Manipur: SC steps in, PM breaks silence, Opp wants his statement in Parliament, Jul 21, 2023; https://indianexpress.com/article/india/manipur-sc-steps-in-pm-breaks-silence-opp-wants-his-statement-in-parliament-8851376/

155 Baruah Sukrita, Woman stripped and raped in Manipur speaks: Police were with the mob, they left us with those men, Jul 21, 2023; https://indianexpress.com/article/india/manipur-sexual-assault-mob-video-women-police-8849995/

156 Manipur video: BJP response on a loop, asks what about Rajasthan, West Bengal, Bihar, Jul 23, 2023; https://indianexpress.com/article/political-pulse/manipur-video-bjp-response-on-a-loop-asks-about-rajasthan-west-bengal-bihar-8854842/

157 Manipur's Ethnic Conflicts Have 'Genesis In Faulty Politics' Of Cong: Himanta, PTI, Jul 23, 2023; https://www.outlookindia.com/national/manipur-s-ethnic-conflicts-have-genesis-in-faulty-politics-of-cong-himanta-news-305073

158 Police say no evidence found after BJP alleges panchayat poll candidate paraded naked in Howrah, PTI, Jul 21, 2023; https://www.deccanherald.com/national/east-and-northeast/police-say-no-evidence-found-after-bjp-alleges-panchayat-poll-candidate-paraded-naked-in-howrah-1239437.html

159 The 'record-breaking' blah-sphemy: PM Modi speaks for 2 hours and 13 minutes

in the Lok Sabha, Aug 11, 2023; https://www.telegraphindia.com/india/the-record-breaking-blah-sphemy-pm-modi-speaks-for-2-hours-and-13-minutes-in-the-lok-sabha/cid/1958319

160 Mahaprashast Ajoy Ashirwad, PM Modi's Speech: Shifting Focus From Manipur Violence to Launching a Diatribe Against Congress, Aug 10, 2023; https://thewire.in/politics/pm-modis-speech-shifting-focus-from-manipur-violence-to-launching-a-diatribe-against-congress#:~:text=In%20a%20speech%20that%20lasted,while%20recounting%20his%20government's%20achievements.

161 Nimmo Tai: Amit Shah in Parliament: Modi ji stopped Russia Ukraine war for 3 days, Aug 12, 2023; https://twitter.com/Cryptic_Miind/status/1690235170216103937; Cowpar Amit, 'Russia, Ukraine tanks kept silent for 3 days after Modi's call': Amit Shah, Nov 22, 2022; https://www.hindustantimes.com/elections/gujarat-assembly-election/modi-called-ukraine-pm-russian-prez-to-halt-war-for-3-days-amit-shah-in-gujarat-101669131711141.html

162 Nayak Mahaprajna and Kumar Abhishek, Did Modi halt Ukraine war for evacuating Indians? BJP leaders' claim was refuted by MEA, Feb 24, 2023; https://www.altnews.in/j-p-nadda-falsely-claim-russia-stopped-war-at-pm-modis-phone-call/

163 Outrage mounts over Amit Shah's statement blaming Kukis in Myanmar for Manipur violence, Aug 14, 2023; https://scroll.in/latest/1054312/outrage-mounts-over-amit-shahs-statement-blaming-kukis-in-myanmar-for-manipur-violence#:~:text=All%20the%2010%20Kuki%20MLAs,furnish%20details%20behind%20his%20claims.'

164 Kuthar Greeshma, Fire and Blood: How the BJP is enabling ethnic cleansing in Manipur, Aug 1, 2023; https://caravanmagazine.in/conflict/how-bjp-enabling-ethnic-cleansing-manipur; Thapar Karan, He embraced Meiteis but offended Kukis: Three errors of Amit Shah in handling Manipur crisis, Aug 13, 2023; https://www.telegraphindia.com/india/he-embraced-meiteis-but-offended-kukis-karan-thapar-on-three-errors-of-amit-shah-in-handling-manipur/cid/1958668

165 Singh Bikas, Mizoram government to raise funds for displaced people of Manipur, JUl 3, 2023; https://economictimes.indiatimes.com/news/india/mizoram-government-to-raise-funds-for-displaced-people-of-manipur/articleshow/101464053.cms?utm_source=contentofinterest&utm_medium=text&utm_campaign=cppst

166 Singh Vijaita, Imphal's remaining Kuki families allege forcible eviction, Sept 2, 2023; https://www.thehindu.com/news/national/last-of-the-kuki-zo-families-in-imphal-say-they-have-been-forcibly-evicted-by-security-forces/article67263919.ece

167 'Feel Sad That Home Minister Can Lie Like This': Farooq Abdullah Says He Was Detained, Aug 6, 2019; https://thewire.in/politics/amit-shah-farooq-abdullah-lie-detain-kashmir

168 Bakshi Gursimran K, If there were no protests in Kashmir post-Article 370, it means right people had been put under arrest, Tushar Mehta jokes on Day 13 of hearings, Aug 31, 2023; https://theleaflet.in/if-there-were-no-protests-in-kashmir-post-article-370-it-means-the-right-people-had-been-put-under-arrest-tushar-mehta-jokes-on-day-13-of-the-hearings/

169   Naik Mubashir, 500 Days: Kashmiri Journalist Fahad Shah's Incarceration Is An Exercise In Assumptions & Retribution, Jun 9, 2023; https://article-14.com/post/500-days-kashmiri-journalist-fahad-shah-s-incarceration-is-an-exercise-in-assumptions-retribution--648fbd385207e

170   Sharma Arun and Masood Bashaarat, Drug pandemic in J&K: Networks of terror intersect with drug supply lines, on ground, from sky and online, Aug 20, 2023; https://indianexpress.com/article/express-exclusive/networks-of-terror-intersect-with-drug-supply-lines-on-ground-from-sky-and-online-8900226/; Iqbal Naveed, One addict walks into Srinagar OPD every 12 minutes: Valley's drug pandemic, Aug 20, 2023; https://indianexpress.com/article/express-exclusive/jammu-kashmir-drug-menace-one-addict-walks-into-srinagar-opd-every-12-minutes-8897386/

171   Kalavati Bandurkar refutes Amit Shah claim, says life altered due to Rahul Gandhi, Aug 11, 2023; https://timesofindia.indiatimes.com/city/nagpur/kalavati-refutes-shah-claim-says-life-altered-due-to-rahul/articleshow/102625536.cms?from=mdr

172   Achary PDT 2023: Achary writes: Why Lok Sabha must have a Deputy Speaker, Feb 22, 2023; https://indianexpress.com/article/opinion/columns/missing-in-parliament-8459142/

173   Why the Absence of Deputy Speaker in Lok Sabha for Nearly 4 Years Sets a Bad Precedent, Mar 9, 2023; https://thewire.in/politics/lok-sabha-deputy-speaker-bjp-modi-government

174   Mohanty P, Agenda for new government: A Leader of Opposition, Jun 14, 2019; https://www.indiatoday.in/india/story/agenda-for-new-government-leader-of-opposition-1543236-2019-06-05

175   Achary PDT, Leader of Opposition is a Statutory Position, the '10% Rule' is Not Founded in Law, Jun 1, 2019; https://thewire.in/government/leader-of-opposition-parliament-lok-sabha

176   Mohanty P, Agenda for new government: A Leader of Opposition, Jun 14, 2019; https://www.indiatoday.in/india/story/agenda-for-new-government-leader-of-opposition-1543236-2019-06-05

177   Adani Scandal a National Security Matter and Striking Instance of Cronyism: Rahul Gandhi in LS, Feb 7, 2023; https://thewire.in/politics/adani-scandal-lok-sabha-rahul-gandhi-speech

178   Rahul Gandhi Speech: What Were the Remarks Expunged by Lok Sabha Speaker? Feb 8, 2023; https://thewire.in/politics/rahul-gandhi-speech-remarks-expunged

179   Devasahayam MG, Rahul Gandhi's SOS for India's Collapsing Democracy – Is It a Crime? https://thewire.in/politics/rahul-gandhi-india-democracy, Mar 15, 2023;

180   No-trust motion: Is Sansad TV giving less screen time to Opposition leaders? Aug 10, 2023; https://www.firstpost.com/explainers/no-trust-motion-sansad-tv-opposition-leaders-rahul-gandhi-screen-time-congress-tmc-tickers-parliament-12981302.html

181   In letters to Speaker, Cong MPs demand restoration of Rahul's 'expunged' speech,

call out Sansad TV for 'partisan' behaviour, Aug 10, 2023; https://indianexpress. com/article/india/congress-letter-speaker-expunged-words-rahul-speech-sansad-tv-8885768/

182   Sahu SN, Twists and Turns in Rahul Gandhi's Defamation Trial, Mr 24, 2023; https:// www.newsclick.in/twists-and-turns-rahul-gandhis-defamation-trial

183   Pendency of cases will be curtailed from 15 to 3 years says Dr Veerappa Moily, Ministry of Law and Justice, Jan 14, 2011; https://pib.gov.in/newsite/PrintRelease. aspx?relid=69096

184   Ellis-Petersen Hannah, India's Rahul Gandhi fights 'excessive' defamation case, Apr 9, 2023; https://www.theguardian.com/world/2023/apr/09/indias-rahul-gandhi-fights-excessive-defamation-case

185   Rahul Gandhi disqualified as MP: Read what Lok Sabha notice said, Mar 24, 2023; https://www.indiatoday.in/india/story/rahul-gandhi-disqualified-as-mp-lok-sabha-notice-defamation-case-modi-surname-remark-2350954-2023-03-24

186   No automatic disqualification for Rahul Gandhi: PDT Achary, Mar 24, 2023; https:// www.newindianexpress.com/nation/2023/mar/24/no-automatic-disqualification-for-rahul-gandhi-pdt-achary-2558976.html

187   Article 103 in The Constitution Of India 1949; https://indiankanoon.org/doc/41049/

188   Shukla Avay, Any Party Can Win an Election, But Can BJP Get Away With It Even Before Votes Are Cast? Apr 5, 2023; https://thewire.in/politics/any-party-can-win-an-election-but-can-bjp-get-away-with-it-even-before-votes-are-cast

189   Prakash Satya, 'Contrary to rules': SC stays promotion of Gujarat CJM who convicted Rahul, May 12, 2023; https://www.tribuneindia.com/news/nation/contrary-to-rules-sc-stays-promotion-of-gujarat-cjm-who-convicted-rahul-507219

190   MPs suspended_RTI reply 2023; https://www.dropbox. com/scl/fi/pidkrxe7jlarvql1vbevv/MPs-supended_RTI-2023. pdf?rlkey=y33jcghjmd2zhha2usakqymwo&dl=0

191   Achary PDT, Illegal, irrational, unconstitutional: The problem with recent suspensions of MPs, Aug 14, 2023; https://indianexpress.com/article/opinion/columns/illegal-irrational-unconstitutional-the-problem-with-recent-suspensions-of-mps-8892457/#:~:text=The%20court%20said%2C%20E2%80%9CIf%20the,does%20not%20seem%20to%20hold.

192   Rajya Sabha Chairman Summons John Brittas Over Newspaper Article Critical of Amit Shah, Apr 30, 2023; https://thewire.in/government/rajya-sabha-chairman-summons-john-brittas-over-newspaper-article-critical-of-amit-shah

193   Editorial: Dhankar went out of V-P Dhankar v Opposition: A question of propriety, https://indianexpress.com/article/opinion/editorials/v-p-dhankar-v-opposition-a-question-of-propriety-8459126/

194   Thakur Rajesh Kumar, "There can be no excuse for not allowing the Parliament to function. The absence of the question hour can't be justified," the Vice-President

said., Jul 24, 2023; https://www.newindianexpress.com/nation/2023/jul/24/disruptions-being-weaponised-to-taint-democracy-says-v-p-2598008.html

195   Parliament: RS Chair Says Won't Ask Modi to Speak on Manipur; LS Speaker Stays Away, Aug 3, 2023; https://thewire.in/government/parliament-rs-chair-says-wont-ask-modi-to-speak-on-manipur-ls-speaker-stays-away

196   Disruption: How BJP Is Getting A Taste Of Its Own Medicine, Jul 29, 2021; https://www.outlookindia.com/website/story/india-news-when-the-bjp-disrupted-parliament-and-defended-it/389694

197   Sharma Richa, Opposition puts onus on govt to smoothly run Parliament, Aug 6, 2021; https://www.newindianexpress.com/nation/2021/aug/06/opposition-puts-onus-on-govt-to-smoothly-run-parliament-2340863.html

198   Dash Dipak K, Casting aspersions on Rajya Sabha officers is breach of privilege: Parliamentary panel, Jul 24, 2023; https://timesofindia.indiatimes.com/india/casting-aspersions-on-rajya-sabha-officers-is-breach-of-privilege-parliamentary-panel/articleshow/102064162.cms

199   Kapila Shruti, The annihilation of India's political opposition is almost complete, Aug 16, 2020; https://www.ft.com/content/bf8b2503-a9cf-4506-b947-e476f7656f0c

200   Bal Hartosh Singh, BBC Row: UK report states VHP planned Gujarat violence in advance, Godhra a "pretext", Jan 23, 2023; https://caravanmagazine.in/politics/uk-government-modi-gujarat-2002-riots-report-bbc-documentary; Varadarajan Siddharth, With BBC Tax Raid, the Modi Cult Makes India the 'Smother of Democracy', Feb 17, 2023; https://thewire.in/media/with-bbc-tax-raid-the-modi-cult-makes-india-the-smother-of-democracy

201   Ellis-Petersen Hannah and Waterson Jim, BBC offices in India raided by tax officials amid Modi documentary fallout, Feb 14, 2023; https://www.theguardian.com/world/2023/feb/14/bbc-offices-india-raided-tax-officials-modi-documentary-fallout

202   Ellis-Petersen Hannah, India invokes emergency laws to ban BBC Modi documentary, Jan 23, 2023; https://www.theguardian.com/world/2023/jan/23/india-emergency-laws-to-ban-bbc-narendra-modi-documentarys

203   Ray Ashis, Exclusive: Vajpayee Govt Didn't Object to UK Report That 2002 Riots Were 'Pre-Planned', Cops 'Told Not to Act', Sept 18, 2023; https://thewire.in/diplomacy/exclusive-vajpayee-govt-didnt-object-to-uk-report-that-2002-riots-were-pre-planned-cops-told-not-to-act

204   BBC Not Alone, Here Are Six Indian Media Houses Which Were 'Searched' By Govt Agencies In Recent Times, Feb 15, 2023; https://www.outlookindia.com/national/bbc-not-alone-here-are-six-indian-media-houses-which-were-searched-by-govt-agencies-in-recent-times-news-262346

205   Adani takes control of NDTV, buys promoters at 17 pc premium to open offer price, PTI, Dec 31, 2022; https://indianexpress.com/article/business/adani-control-ndtv-promoters-17-pc-premium-offer-price-8352948/

206   Gautam Adani acquires 49% in Quintillion Business Media for Rs 48 crore, PTI, Mar 28, 2023; https://indianexpress.com/article/business/companies/adani-acquires-49-per-cent-quintillion-business-media-for-rs-48-crore-8522385/

207   Tax 'surveys' conducted at NewsClick, Newslaundry offices in Delhi, Sept 10, 2021; https://amp.scroll.in/latest/1005108/income-tax-department-conducts-surveys-at-offices-of-newsclick-newslaundry?__twitter_impression=true

208   Did not use public funds for self: Journalist Rana Ayyub after Enforcement Directorate attachment, New Indian Express, Feb 11, 2022; https://www.newindianexpress.com/nation/2022/feb/11/did-not-use-public-funds-for-self-journalist-rana-ayyub-after-enforcement-directorate-attachment-2418332.html

209   Not just another day at the office for @thewire_in after #PegasusProjectPoliceman, Jul 23, 2021; https://twitter.com/svaradarajan/status/1418513671764865024

210   Delhi Police search The Wire editors' houses, seize e-devices, Nov 1, 2022; https://www.newindianexpress.com/nation/2022/nov/01/delhi-police-search-the-wire-editors-houses-seize-e-devices-2513637.html

211   India court bars airing of Al Jazeera documentary, June 16, 2023; https://www.aljazeera.com/news/2023/6/16/india-court-bars-airing-of-al-jazeera-documentary#:~:text=A%20court%20in%20India%20has,from%20airing%20the%20film%20India%20%E2%80%A6

212   Sinha Jignasa, NewsClick founder-editor among 2 held under UAPA, 46 questioned in crackdown on news portal, Oct 4, 2023; https://indianexpress.com/article/cities/delhi/delhi-police-newsclick-journalist-searches-china-funding-8966029/#:~:text=NewsClick%20founder%2Deditor%20Prabir%20Purkayastha,in%20crackdown%20on%20news%20portal

213   Seizure of journalist's devices very serious, come up with better guidelines: SC to Govt, Nov 8, 2023; https://indianexpress.com/article/india/seizure-of-journalists-devices-come-up-with-better-guidelines-sc-to-govt-9017810/

214   Supreme Court Circulates Interim Guidelines for Seizure of Devices, Nov 13, 2023; https://thewire.in/rights/supreme-court-circulates-interim-guidelines-for-seizure-of-devices

215   Philipose Pamela, Backstory: It's Time Journalists Woke Up to Their Digital Security, Nov 11, 2023; https://thewire.in/media/backstory-its-time-journalists-woke-up-to-their-digital-security

216   'Supreme Court Circulates Interim Guidelines'

217   Thakur Nirbhay, Hand FIR copy to NewsClick, court tells cops; 10 journalists questioned, Oct 6, 2023; https://indianexpress.com/article/india/hand-fir-copy-to-newsclick-court-tells-cops-10-journalists-questioned-8970471/s

218   Hvistendahl Mara, Fahrenthold David A, Chutel Lynsey and Jhaveri Ishaan, A Global Web of Chinese Propaganda Leads to a U.S. Tech Mogul, Aug 5, 2023; https://www.nytimes.com/2023/08/05/world/europe/neville-roy-singham-china-

propaganda.html

219 Goyal Prateek, Gautam Navlakha, farm stir, Kashmir map: In Delhi cops' application for NewsClick founder custody, Oct 4, 2023; https://www.newslaundry. com/2023/10/04/gautam-navlakha-farm-stir-kashmir-map-in-delhi-cops-application-for-newsclick-founder-custody

220 Explained: What Are the Stories Done By Journalists Raided By the Delhi Police Today? Oct 3, 2023; https://thewire.in/media/explained-what-are-the-stories-done-by-journalists-raided-by-the-delhi-police-today

221 Goyal Prateek, Gautam Navlakha, farm stir, Kashmir map: In Delhi cops' application for NewsClick founder custody, Oct 4, 2023; https://www.newslaundry. com/2023/10/04/gautam-navlakha-farm-stir-kashmir-map-in-delhi-cops-application-for-newsclick-founder-custody

222 Mohanty P, 'An Unkept Promise', Ch I and VII

223 Kapoor Coomi, Inside track by Coomi Kapoor: Back to the drawing board, Oct 8, 2023; https://www.financialexpress.com/opinion/inside-track-by-coomi-kapoor-back-to-the-drawing-board/3266010/

224 Bal Hartosh Singh, Malice in Modiland: China threat is a pretext to target those who question an increasingly tyrannical government, Oct 4, 2023; https:// caravanmagazine.in/media/newsclick-raids-china-funding-uapa-journalist-arrests

225 Sodhi Tanishka, At least 44 times over 5 years: The NIA, ED and I-T 'crackdown' on the media, May 5, 2023; https://www.newslaundry.com/2023/05/05/at-least-44-times-over-5-years-the-nia-ed-and-i-t-crackdown-on-the-media

226 Fact Check: Have Chinese Companies Really Donated to the PM CARES Fund? Jun 29, 2020; https://thewire.in/politics/fact-check-have-chinese-companies-really-donated-to-the-pm-cares-fund; Now banned TikTok gave Rs 30 crore to PM CARES Fund, Jul 7, 2020; https://www.businesstoday.in/technology/news/story/pm-cares-fund-received-rs-30-crore-from-now-banned-tiktok-262711-2020-06-30

227 My friendship with Xi Jinping is 'plus one': PM Narendra Modi, PTI, May 16, 2015; https://economictimes.indiatimes.com/news/politics-and-nation/my-friendship-with-xi-jinping-is-plus-one-pm-narendra-modi/articleshow/47310465.cms?utm_source=contentofinterest&utm_medium=text&utm_campaign=cppst

228 G7, India and 4 other countries pledge to protect free speech, Jun 28, 2022; https:// www.thehindu.com/news/national/g7-india-and-4-other-countries-pledge-to-protect-free-speech/article65575574.ece

229 India, EU agree to protect freedom of civil society, Jul 16, 2022; http://timesofindia. indiatimes.com/articleshow/92908727.cms?utm_source=contentofinterest&utm_medium=text&utm_campaign=cppst

230 India; https://rsf.org/en/country/india; World Press Freedom Rank of India from 2002 to 2022; https://www.statista.com/statistics/1364514/india-press-freedom-ranking/

231   India, RSF, 2023; https://rsf.org/en/country/india

232   RSF 2021: Prime Minister of India since 26 May 2014: Predator since taking office, https://rsf.org/en/protagonist-narendra-modi

235   Rs 8.54 Lakh an hour, Rs 2.05 Cr a day, every day since 2014: Modi govt's advertisement spending. Know all details inside, Dec 13, 2022; https://www.thedispatch.in/rs-8-54-lakh-an-hour-rs-2-05-cr-a-day-every-day-modi-govts-advertisement-spending-know-all-details-inside/#google_vignette

236   Aakar Patel | Fact-checking' by govt & the truth: Sweeping powers to curb dissent? Apr 11, 2023; https://www.deccanchronicle.com/opinion/columnists/100423/aakar-patel-fact-checking-by-govt-the-truth-sweeping-powers.html

237   Sodhi Tanishka, Lokniti-CSDS media survey: 82 percent of journalists think their employers support the BJP, Jul 27, 2023; https://www.newslaundry.com/2023/07/27/lokniti-csds-media-survey-82-percent-of-journalists-think-their-employers-support-the-bjp; Indian Media: Trends and Patterns Aug2023; https://lokniti.org/media/upload_files/Media%20in%20India-%20Trends%20and%20Patterns%20(1).pdf

238   Bal Hartosh Singh, Private Interest Journalism, How conglomerates corrupt the Indian media landscape, Dec 2, 2022; https://caravanmagazine.in/media/big-media-corrupts-journalism

239   India stood up to China's LAC adventurism, 'delegitimised' Pakistan terror: EAM S Jaishankar, Jun 9, 2023; https://timesofindia.indiatimes.com/india/india-stood-up-to-chinas-lac-adventurism-delegitimised-pak-terror-eam-s-jaishankar/articleshow/100859884.cms?from=mdr

240   Krishnan Vidya, To playing violins in the void, Dec 23, 2022; https://caravanmagazine.in/media/modi-media-2022-journalism-burden; Jaswal Srishti, Monitor reporter's trial opens: Why India treats journalists as terrorists, Apr 19, 2023; https://www.csmonitor.com/World/Asia-South-Central/2023/0419/Monitor-reporter-s-trial-opens-Why-India-treats-journalists-as-terrorists

241   Ghosal Devjyot, Modi government freezes ads placed in three Indian newspaper groups, Jun 28, 2019; https://www.reuters.com/article/india-media-idINKCN1TT1R6

242   Chaudhuri Pooja, Amit Malviya: How the ringmaster of BJP's propaganda machinery weaponises misinformation, Feb 10, 2020; https://www.altnews.in/amit-malviya-how-ringmaster-of-bjps-propaganda-machinery-weaponises-misinformation/; Jawed Sam, Fake News Round-up, November 2017 – BJP IT Cell head Amit Malviya is the star, Dec 6, 2017; https://www.altnews.in/fake-news-round-november-2017-bjp-cell-head-amit-malviya-star/; Sinha Prateek and Chaudhuri Pooja, Who runs Kreately? – Alt News investigates the factory of hate and misinformation, Apr 10, 2021; https://www.altnews.in/who-runs-kreately-alt-news-investigates-the-factory-of-hate-and-misinformation/?utm_source=website&utm_medium=social-media&utm_campaign=newpost; Chaudhuri Pooja, The year that was: Misinformation trends of 2020, Jan 5, 2021; https://www.altnews.in/the-year-that-

was-misinformation-trends-of-2020/; Jawed Sam, Hall of shame – Serial abusers, sexist bigots, rumour mongers followed by PM Modi on Twitter, Sept 7, 2017; https://www.altnews.in/hall-shame-serial-abusers-sexist-bigots-rumour-mongers-followed-pm-modi-twitter/

243 Nyst Carly and Monaco Nik, State-sponsored Trolling, Institute for the Future, California, 2018; https://cgt.columbia.edu/wp-content/uploads/2018/11/Politics-of-Visual-Arts-Recommended-Reading.pdf

244 Jaffrelot Christophe and Jumle Vihanf, One-Man Show: A study of 1,779 Republic TV debates reveals how the channel champions Narendra Modi, Christophe Jaffrelot and Vihang Jumle, Dec 15, 2020; https://caravanmagazine.in/media/republic-debates-study-shows-channel-promotoes-modi-ndtv

245 Zubair Mohammed, One of the world's richest man has invested in hate in India., Dec 31, 2022; https://twitter.com/zoo_bear/status/1609187348251832321

246 Jha Sanjay K, Silence over CAG exposing scams: "great momory loss on CAG: Jha Sanjay K, 'PM should shut down CAG': Congress takes swipe at Narendra Modi government over 'seven scams', Aug 17, 2023; https://www.telegraphindia.com/india/pm-should-shut-down-cag-congress-takes-swipe-at-narendra-modi-government-over-seven-scams/cid/1959433

247 Philipose Pamela, Backstory: It's Time Journalists Woke Up to Their Digital Security, Nov 11, 2023; https://thewire.in/media/backstory-its-time-journalists-woke-up-to-their-digital-security

248 TV Newsance 230: Israel Palestine conflict, Indian media at ground zero, Oct 14, 2023; https://www.newslaundry.com/2023/10/14/tv-newsance-230-israel-palestine-conflict-indian-media-reports-from-ground-zero

249 Bikhchandani Raghav, 'People of India stand firmly with Israel', Modi reiterates after receiving call from Netanyahu, Oct 10, 2023; https://theprint.in/india/people-of-india-stand-firmly-with-israel-modi-reiterates-after-receiving-call-from-netanyahu/1798614/

250 Israel-Hamas War: India sends humanitarian aid to Palestine, PTI, Oct 22, 2023; https://www.newindianexpress.com/nation/2023/oct/22/israel-hamas-war-india-sends-humanitarian-aid-to-palestine-2626253.html

251 India Refuses to Back Landslide UN General Assembly Call for Humanitarian Truce in Gaza, Oct 28, 2023; https://thewire.in/world/india-refuses-to-back-landslide-un-general-assembly-call-for-humanitarian-truce-in-gaza

252 Deb Abhik, How the BJP is using the Israel-Palestine conflict for domestic gain, Oct 9, 2023; https://scroll.in/article/1057325/how-the-bjp-is-using-the-israel-palestine-conflict-for-domestic-gain

253 Khan Mohammad Asif, India is the epicentre of hate and misinformation against Palestinians, Nov 10, 2023; https://www.middleeastmonitor.com/20231110-india-is-the-epicentre-of-hate-and-misinformation-against-palestinians/; Jones Marc Owen, Analysis: Why is so much anti-Palestinian disinformation coming from India? Oct

16, 2023; https://www.aljazeera.com/news/2023/10/16/analysis-why-is-so-much-anti-palestinian-disinformation-coming-from-india

254   Majumder Shinjinee, Disinformation, falsehoods flood social media as Israel-Hamas conflict escalates into full-blown war, Oct 12, 2023; https://www.altnews.in/disinformation-falsehoods-flood-social-media-as-israel-hamas-conflict-escalates-into-full-blown-war/; Bhattacharya Oishani, Woman caressing the face of a dead child: Pro-Israel users give 'Pallywood' spin to harrowing video on X, Nov 11, 2023; https://www.altnews.in/woman-caressing-the-face-of-a-dead-child-pro-israel-users-give-pallywood-spin-to-harrowing-video-on-x/

255   Sahu Manish, UP cleric held for Palestine posts, doctor booked for anti-minority comments, Oct 16, 2023; https://indianexpress.com/article/cities/lucknow/up-cleric-held-for-palestine-posts-doctor-booked-for-anti-minority-comments-8983368/#:~:text=DAYS%20AFTER%20Uttar%20Pradesh%20Chief%20Minister%20Yogi%20Adityanath,cleric%20has%20been%20identified%20as%20Suhail%20Ansari%20%2823%29.

256   Sharma Nootan and Sharma Unnati, 'Being targeted, not boycotted' — what 14 blacklisted anchors have to say about INDIA's ban on them, Sept 15, 2023; https://theprint.in/politics/being-targeted-not-boycotted-what-14-blacklisted-anchors-have-to-say-about-indias-ban-on-them/1763614/

257   Tweet being manufactured by a channel in order to hurt BJP, Mar 8, 2014; https://www.bjp.org/pressreleases/press-boycott-ndtv

258   Chishti Seema, Precipitous Fall in Press Freedom, Economic and Political eekly, Vol 57, May 21, 2022; https://www.epw.in/journal/2022/21/comment/precipitous-fall-press-freedom.html

259   As wrestlers intensified their protest, some TV 'news' anchors came out with their 'toolkit' to defame the movement. No surprises there., Jun 4, 2023; https://twitter.com/newslaundry/status/1665229392963080194; Goyal Prateek, 'Toolkit gang, urban naxals': How right-wing Twitter is campaigning against the wrestlers' protest, Jun 1, 2023; https://www.newslaundry.com/2023/06/01/toolkit-gang-urban-naxals-how-right-wing-twitter-is-campaigning-against-the-wrestlers-protest

260   Bhattacharya Oishani, Manipur shocker: Misreport by ANI sets off false communal claim; Abdul Hilim's arrest not related to viral video case, Jul 21, 2023; https://www.altnews.in/manipur-video-misreport-by-ani-sets-off-false-communal-claims-on-social-media-none-of-the-4-arrested-so-far-is-a-muslim/

261   Majumdar Shinjinee, Social media users add communal spin to Odisha train mishap, falsely describe temple near tracks as a mosque, Jun 3, 2023; https://www.altnews.in/social-media-users-add-communal-spin-to-odisha-mishap-falsely-describe-temple-near-tracks-as-a-mosque/

262   Patel Jignesh, Muslim student from JNU falsely blamed for 'masterminding' violence at the university, Jan 7, 2020; https://www.altnews.in/muslim-student-from-jnu-falsely-blamed-for-masterminding-violence-at-the-university/

263   Jain Ritika, Covid-19: How fake news and Modi government messaging fuelled India's latest spiral of Islamophobia, Apr 21, 2020; https://scroll.in/article/959806/covid-19-how-fake-news-and-modi-government-messaging-fuelled-indias-latest-spiral-of-islamophobia

264   Vishwanath Apurva, Manral Mahendra Singh, After 2 statements against him, minor withdraws charges against WFI chief Brij Bhushan, Jun 7, 2023; https://indianexpress.com/article/india/after-2-statements-against-him-minor-withdraws-charges-against-wfi-chief-brij-bhushan-8647463/

265   BBC's 'confession' and wrestler protests: Three news items, three sources – and all three were wrong? Jun 7, 2023; https://www.newslaundry.com/2023/06/07/bbcs-confession-and-wrestler-protests-three-news-items-three-sources-and-all-three-were-wrong

266   Sagar, Speaking Positivity to Power: Hours before lockdown, Modi asked print-media owners, editors to refrain from negative COVID coverage, Mar 31, 2020; https://caravanmagazine.in/media/hours-before-lockdown-modi-asked-print-media-owners-editors-refrain-negative-covid-coverage

267   Bal Hartosh Singh 2021: Paranoia about digital coverage led ministers to propose media clampdown, monitoring "negative influencers", Caravan, Mar 4, 2021; https://caravanmagazine.in/politics/paranoia-about-digital-coverage-led-gom-propose-media-clampdown-monitoring-negative-influencers

268   Tiwari Ayush 2023: How the Modi government 'monitors' the media, Apr 20, 223; https://themorningcontext.com/chaos/how-the-modi-government-monitors-the-media/?utm_source=The%20Morning%20Context&utm_campaign=c743b142f3-EMAIL_CAMPAIGN_2022_10_13_01_35_COPY_01&utm_medium=email&utm_term=0_932343683d-c743b142f3-211273364

269   Farooqui Javed, Broadcast industry scrambles for answers as overall TV viewership declines, Jul 18, 2022; https://www.exchange4media.com/media-tv-news/broadcast-industry-scrambles-for-answers-as-overall-tv-viewership-declines-121378.html

270   Government Ads Have Shifted Away From Newspapers, Broadcasters: Report, May 11, 2023; https://thewire.in/media/government-ads-have-shifted-away-from-newspapers-broadcasters-report

271   Deuskar Nachiket, Why are so many Indian politicians giving interviews to social media influencers? Jul 30, 2023; https://scroll.in/article/1052678/why-are-so-many-indian-politicians-giving-interviews-to-social-media-influencers

272   Madhav Neel and Jafri Alishan, Clicks and Bait: How a constellation of far-right Hindi YouTubers determine what you see on your TV, Dec 2, 2022; https://caravanmagazine.in/media/youtube-facebook-right-wing-hate-speech-ecosystem-yogi-adityanath-yati-narsinghanand

273   Sodhi Taniska, BJP's social media push: Outreach efforts span 18 states, thousands of influencers, Jul 31, 2023; https://www.newslaundry.com/2023/07/31/bjps-social-media-push-outreach-efforts-spans-18-states-1000s-of-influencers?utm_

source=substack&utm_medium=email

274 Today is the first day of the Winter Session of 2021. This is also the 5th session when reporters have been deliberately kept out of the Press Gallery, Press Club of India, Nov 29, 2021: https://twitter.com/PCITweets/status/1465217021960855552

275 Bardhan Pranab, Working class politics: A global puzzle, Nov 21, 2022; https://www.business-standard.com/article/opinion/working-class-politics-a-global-puzzle-122112101073_1.html

276 Ali Asim, Citizen activism that is missing from the wrestling ring, Jun 5, 2023; https://www.thehindu.com/opinion/lead/citizen-activism-that-is-missing-from-the-wrestling-ring/article66931429.ece

277 Krishnan Vidya, The hypocrisy of the Indian diaspora is overwhelming, Oct 25, 2022; https://caravanmagazine.in/communities/hypocrisy-indian-diaspora-overwhelming

278 Basic FAQ on RSS; https://www.rss.org//Encyc/2017/6/3/basic-faq-on-rss-eng.html

279 An unnoticed fact: the RSS, India's biggest NGO, gets foreign funding too, Jun 13, 2014; https://scroll.in/article/667071/an-unnoticed-fact-the-rss-indias-biggest-ngo-gets-foreign-funding-too

280 After BJP, RSS constructing massive New Delhi office with 'donations', NH and IANS, Dec 28, 2019; https://www.nationalheraldindia.com/india/after-bjp-rss-constructing-massive-new-delhi-office-with-donations

281 Mohanty P, Apex court's FCRA order a big blow to NGOs, grassroot development work, Fortune India, Apr 19, 2022; https://www.fortuneindia.com/opinion/apex-courts-fcra-order-a-big-blow-to-ngos-grassroot-development-work/107833

282 Selective outrage violation of rights, hurts country: PM Modi, Oct 13, 2021; https://indianexpress.com/article/india/narendra-modi-human-rights-protests-7567624/

283 Kashmiris now share intel on terrorists, says Gen. Bipin Rawat, Nov 13, 2021; https://www.thehindu.com/news/national/kashmiris-now-share-intel-on-terrorists-says-gen-bipin-rawat/article37475888.ece?homepage=true

284 Roy Aruna, Civil society is not the enemy, Nov 19, 2021; https://indianexpress.com/article/opinion/columns/ajit-doval-nsa-fourth-generation-warfare-constitution-7628080/

285 The FC (Regulation) Amendment Act, 2020, Ministry of Law and Justice, Sept 28, 2020; https://fcraonline.nic.in/home/PDF_Doc/fc_amend_07102020_1.pdf

286 Noel Harper and others vs Union of India and another, Supreme Court, Apr 8, 2022; https://main.sci.gov.in/supremecourt/2021/10824/10824_2021_3_1501_34940_Judgement_08-Apr-2022.pdf

287 Mohanty P, Apex court's FCRA order a big blow to NGOs, grassroot development work, Apr 19, 2022; https://www.fortuneindia.com/opinion/apex-courts-fcra-order-a-big-blow-to-ngos-grassroot-development-work/107833

288 Jain Bharti, MHA grants FCRA approval to Ram temple trust, Oct 19, 2023; http://timesofindia.indiatimes.com/articleshow/104535090.cms?utm_source=contentofinterest&utm_medium=text&utm_campaign=cppst

289 Mittal Sumedha, I-T dept revokes tax exemption status of 4 NGOs, letters to two mention protests against Adani, Oct 14, 2023; https://www.newslaundry.com/2023/10/14/i-t-dept-revokes-tax-exemption-status-of-4-ngos-letters-to-two-mention-protests-against-adani#:~:text=The%20Income%20Tax%20department%20has%20revoked%20the%20tax,exemption%20was%20reportedly%20revoked%20about%20two%20weeks%20ago.

290 Centre cancels FCRA licences of two NGOs headed by Sonia Gandhi, PTI, Oct 23, 2022; https://www.business-standard.com/article/current-affairs/rajiv-gandhi-foundation-s-fcra-licence-cancelled-for-violating-law-122102300116_1.html

291 Mohanty P, 'Apex court's FCRA order a big blow'

292 Bhardwaj Ashutosh, Is There an Adani Link to Modi Govt's Actions Against the Centre for Policy Research? Mar 4, 2023; https://thewire.in/rights/is-there-an-adani-link-to-modi-govts-actions-against-the-centre-for-policy-research

293 Sarin Ritu, First FCRA, now think tank CPR loses its tax-exempt status, Jul 6, 2023; https://indianexpress.com/article/india/first-fcra-now-think-tank-cpr-loses-its-tax-exempt-status-8779945/#:~:text=Four%20months%20after%20its%20license,had%20for%20almost%20five%20decades.

294 Rajpurohit Shivnarayan, 'Used foreign funds to oppose Adani project': I-T report on Ritwick Dutta, Apr 27, 2023; https://www.newslaundry.com/2023/04/27/used-foreign-funds-to-oppose-adani-project-i-t-report-on-ritwick-dutta

295 Shih Gerry, Mehrotra Karishma and Gupta Anant, India cracks down on critics of coal, Jun 5, 2023; https://www.washingtonpost.com/world/2023/06/05/india-coal-adani-modi-crackdown/

296 Mittal Sumedha, I-T dept revokes tax exemption status of 4 NGOs, letters to two mention protests against Adani, Oct 14, 2023; https://www.newslaundry.com/2023/10/14/i-t-dept-revokes-tax-exemption-status-of-4-ngos-letters-to-two-mention-protests-against-adani#:~:text=The%20Income%20Tax%20department%20has%20revoked%20the%20tax,exemption%20was%20reportedly%20revoked%20about%20two%20weeks%20ago.

297 Ashutosh Varshney writes: What government-Adani relationship says about Indian capitalism, Feb 16, 2023; https://indianexpress.com/article/opinion/columns/ashutosh-varshney-government-adani-relationship-indian-capitalism-8442387/

298 FCRA needs 'drastic overhaul' to make it more accessible, ex-bureaucrats urge Amit Shah, Jul 5, 2023; https://scroll.in/latest/1052074/fcra-needs-drastic-overhaul-to-make-it-more-facilitating-ex-bureaucrats-urge-amit-shah

299 52 countries helped India during second wave of Covid-19 pandemic: Centre, IANS, Jul 22, 2021; https://timesofindia.indiatimes.com/india/52-countries-helped-india-during-second-wave-of-covid-19-pandemic-centre/articleshow/84647250.cms

300 Yamunan Sruthisagar, Modi wants NGOs to help fight Covid-19. But their hands are tied by rules his government introduced, May 4, 2021; https://scroll.in/article/993897/modi-wants-ngos-to-help-fight-covid-19-but-their-hands-are-tied-by-rules-his-government-introduced

301 PMLA Rules 2023, Mar 7, 2023; https://egazette.nic.in/WriteReadData/2023/244194.pdf

302 Good Governance & the Rule of Law, United States Council for International Business, Jan 2015; https://www.uscib.org/docs/Governance%20and%20the%20Rule%20of%20Law.pdf

Chapter III

Institutional Breakdown II: Supreme Court

W hat this chapter tells may shock some – given the trust the Supreme Court evokes – or may not. But before proceeding, a historic perspective and a reference to a particular episode to set the tone.

The first one is the historic perspective of the Indian Supreme Court provided by former Chief Justice of Delhi High Court Justice AP Shah in an article of 2022, titled "From Lodha to Ramana: The Chief Justices of the Modi era".[1] He divided its judicial history into "three periods", but actually mentioned four, and flagged a constant "rebalancing of power" between the judiciary and the executive.

He wrote: "When we examine the evolution of the Indian Supreme Court and the office of the CJI, it is a classic example of a constant shifting and rebalancing of power between the judiciary and the executive. When the *executive was powerful*, usually through a single party majority, as with the Indira Gandhi and Rajiv Gandhi-led governments, the judiciary practically succumbed to the executive's control. However, when *relatively weaker coalition governments* were elected, the judiciary restored powers to itself." *(Emphasis added)*

About the latest period since 2014, the third, he wrote: "This rebalancing is playing out again now. Since 2014, the executive is once again a single party majority under the Narendra Modi-led BJP government. Consequently, the judiciary's powers are weaker than before, and the executive is back in control. We see a rise in autocratic tendencies of the executive, through the slow destruction of democratic institutions, the misuse of investigating agencies, communal polarisation, and a gradual chipping away at constitutional protections available to citizens, all of which a weak judiciary is unable or disinclined to tackle."

About the two earlier periods, Justice Shah had written:

- "From 1950 to 1971, the Chief Justice had complete authority over judicial appointments, and the recommendation of the Chief Justice would always be followed, even to the extent of powers of a veto."

- "Between 1971 and 1993, strong single party governments occupied the Centre, and the executive insisted on appointing 'committed judges' to the Supreme Court, in a clear attempt at court packing. Multiple supersessions took place, with the executive exercising prerogative in appointing Chief Justices, and the seniority convention was openly flouted. The shocker came with the decision in the first judges' case in 1981 (SP Gupta), where it was held that the opinion of the Chief Justice of India would not be binding on the government. With the second judge's case in 1993, and around when Justice MN Venkatachaliah took over as the CJI, the trend reversed and the judiciary practically wrested the power of appointments back from the executive. Judicial primacy and the collegium's creation happened in this period, and while the collegium has since acquired considerable notoriety for being arbitrary and undemocratic, it still occupies the field today."

The *judicial* period he mentioned (but didn't list) is the one from 1993 and 2013 when India had coalition governments at the Centre – which was actually between 1989 and 2013 – about which he wrote (in the first quote) when "the judiciary restored powers to itself".

Note, the first period of 1950-1971 coincides substantially (up to 1964) with the term of the first Prime Minister of India Jawaharlal Nehru – the institution builder and maker of the modern, liberal democratic India.

Coming back to the contemporary period, "since 2014", in another article in 2022 Justice Shah lamented[2] that "the only institution capable of stopping the death of democracy is aiding it", pointing at its multiple failures to check "elected autocrats" weaponizing institutions to use them as political ammunition, compelling the media and the private sector into silence and redrafting rules to suit their interests over those of their political opponents. He described the apex court as "weak", has "lost its way" and seemingly unwilling to "deal with real-world problems".

Here is the episode mentioned at the beginning.

A significant phenomenon was witnessed in the aftermath of Bhopal gas tragedy of 1984 – when a strong Central government was in office under Prime Minister Rajiv Gandhi, followed by a long spell of relatively weak coalition governments. Virtually every single top lawyer in India either advised or fought on the side of the Union Carbide in its legal battle against the victims of the disaster. This author drew up a list titled "Bhopal's Hall of Shame"[3] in 2010 about those and also various court rulings relating to the case. Why did so many top judges and lawyers did what they did in this case may not be a mystery but certainly demands introspection – which is best left to the bar and the bench at this point in time.

The Revolt of 2018

The Supreme Court had a massive meltdown in January 2018[4] – a first in its history – when four senior-most judges openly revolted against then CJI Justice Dipak Misra (2017-18).

The revolting judges warned people that the very democracy of India was under threat "unless this institution is preserved and it maintains its equanimity, democracy will not survive in this country". They particularly flagged arbitrary assignment of cases ("with no rational") by the CJI, implying "forum shopping" or handing over cases to selective benches knowing the outcome in advance, and expressed unhappiness with "certain judicial orders" which they said "adversely affected the overall functioning of the court". They explained they were forced to go public with their concerns because the CJI refused to listen to them.

One of the cases that triggered the revolt was the mystery surrounding death of a CBI judge BH Loya, who was hearing the extra-judicial killings of Sohrabuddin Shaikh, his wife Kauser Bi and friend Tulsiram Prajapati (in 2005) in which then Gujarat Home Minister Amit Shah, now Union Home Minister, was the prime accused. Justice Misra headed bench (with Justices DY Chandrachud and AM Khanwilkar) dismissed the demand for independent probe, relying on the Maharashtra government's controversial report dismissing there being foul play in the death. This report cited four judicial officers claiming to have been with judge Loya before his death and that the death was due to natural causes.[5] The probe was disallowed despite multiple flaws in and unreliability of that report.[6]

There were several cases involving Justice Misra as the CJI which had spread disquiet. He headed he bench that denied fundamental rights to the BK-16 members (Bhima-Koregaon case) and refused an independent probe into it in 2018 (along with Justice Khanwilkar, while Justice Chandrachud dissented).[7] He led the bench that upheld the Aadhaar law's passage as 'Money Bill' in 2018 (along with Justices AK Sikri, Khanwilkar and Ashok Bhushan, while Justice Chandrachud dissented)[8]; another bench doubted its correctness and requested for a seven-judge bench – which is pending since 2019.[9] Justice Misra became the first serving CJI to face *impeachment* – which was disallowed by the Rajya Sabha chairman Venkaiah Naidu – for his many omissions and commissions. The list included illegal gratification in medical college cases, administratively and judicially dealing with it although his name involved and rejecting an SIT probe into it, 'forum shopping', acquiring land on false affidavit in Odisha etc.[10] Justice Kurien Joseph – one of the four revolting judges – made a sensational claim later alleging that Justice Misra was "remote controlled" from outside[11]; Justice Misra's omissions and commissions[12] had already dented his credibility.

For many, Justice Misra (then as the Supreme Court judge) would also be remembered for unleashing a nation-wide frenzy through a *bizarre order* of November 2016 (along with Justice Amitava Roy) which made it mandatory for cinema halls to play the national anthem, for audience to stand up and thereby, instill "a sense of committed patriotism and nationalism". It took him *two years* (actually 15 years as his first such order in the same case had come in 2003 as the judge of Madhya Pradesh HC[13], along with Justice A Srivastava) to realize that it isn't his job to preach "committed patriotism and nationalism" but to apply judicial mind and uphold the constitutional values and correct himself in 2018 ("not mandatory, but optional or directory")[14] as the CJI (others in this bench were Justices Khanwilkar and Chandrachud).

Things didn't improve after Justice Ranjan Gogoi (2018-19), one of the revolting judges, took charge from Justice Misra or under the leadership of next CJI Justice SA Bobde (2019-21). In fact, it got worse. As the CJI, Justice Gogoi headed the five-judge bench that unanimously delivered *wholly illogical* and *unjustified* Ayodhya verdict of 2019; didn't decide the constitutionality of the Electoral Bond of 2017 but allowed it to be sold openly; completed the National Register of Citizens for Assam (NRC) knowing well its impact on communalizing politics ahead of the 2021 Assam elections (drove it in "urgent – almost messianic – manner") and sat on judgement over his own sexual harassment case.[15]

As the CJI, Justice Bobde continued the trend of abdicating constitutional responsibility. Constitutional lawyer and author Gautam Bhatia[16] summed up his tenure thus: "...his tenure saw *further acceleration of trends* begun under his predecessors: that of the Supreme Court, in effect, turning into an *Executive Court* (a court aligned to state's interest, imagine and think like the way the executive does, oblivious to their blatant abuse of power, not as independent authority applying its judicial mind).The difference is that under his predecessors, there were still occasions when the Supreme Court continued to act like a "court", as we understand it. Under CJI Bobde, there was very little evidence of that." *(Emphasis added)*

Justice Bobde's tenure is known for several questionable judicial actions and inactions. The constitutionality of several laws were *kept pending*: (i) Electoral Bond (ii) abrogation of Article 370 and degrading J&JK to two UTs (iii) Rohingyas were allowed to be deported to Myanmar where they were facing genocidal war, ignoring India's commitment to protect persecuted refugees (iv) the government's gross pandemic mismanagement in 2020 and 2021, which led to an unprecedented distress migration and avoidable deaths (due to lack of oxygen and hospital beds) went unaddressed and (v) instead of deciding the constitutionality of three new farms laws that sparked countrywide protest for a year, a committee was set up to examine those laws, and the laws' operation was suspended for one-and-half years, before which the government withdrew them.[17]

Justice Bobde's record of upholding fundamental rights raised more concerns. While hearing the habeas corpus petition in 2020 seeking release of Kerala journalist Siddique Kappan (arrested and slapped with sedition while going to cover the Hathras gang rape and murder case), Justice Bobde refused to intervene, loftily declaring, "We are trying to cut down the Article 32 jurisdiction, we do not appreciate this". This was appalling because days earlier, the court (Justices Chandrachud and Indira Banerjee) had immediately intervened and granted bail to TV anchor Arnab Goswami – infamous as part of the fawning "Godi" media (Chapter II) – in a case unrelated to journalistic work (in a criminal case).[18] As the "master of the roaster", Justice Bobde would have assigned the case. He did the same in several other such cases.[19] The poor record of the court showed up in a reply to the RTI query which revealed that 58 habeas corpus petitions were pending while he was the CJI, the oldest being from 2015.[20]

Two things need to be pointed out here.

One, about Article 32. It guarantees right to move the apex court for enforcement of all fundamental rights, including right to equality (Article 14), right against discrimination (Article 15), right to freedom (Article 19) and right to life and personal liberty (Article 21). Habeas corpus writs, seeking release of people imprisoned or detailed unlawfully, is a key instrument to ensure these rights.[21] The criticality of Article 32 was explained by none other than Ambedkar himself. To the Constituent Assembly, he said: "If I was asked to name any particular article in this Constitution *as the most important* – an article *without which this Constitution would be a nullity* – I could not refer to any other article except this one. It is the *very soul* of the Constitution and the *very heart* of it and I am glad that the House has realised its importance".[22] At that time, it was Article 25. (*Emphasis added*)

As a lawyer earlier and then a judge, former CJI Justice Bobde must be familiar with the above.

Two, Justice Bobde was part of the nine-judge bench of 2017 which overturned the infamous ADM Jabalpur case relating to *habeas corpus* – which had suspended fundamental rights to life and liberty (Article 21) during the period of Emergency of 1975-77. The nine-judge bench hearing the Aadhaar law in the Puttaswamy case[23](led by then CJI JS Khehar and included Justice Chandrachud, son of late YV Chandrachud who was part of the ADM Jabalpur judgement of 1976 and the longest serving CJI between 1978 and 1985) observed: "It would be preposterous to suggest that a democratic Constitution without a Bill of Rights would leave individuals governed by the state without either the existence of the right to live or the means of enforcement of the right. The right to life being inalienable to each individual, it existed prior to the Constitution and continued in force under Article 372 of the Constitution." Justice Bobde wouldn't have forgotten it.

Incidentally, Kappan walked out on *bail after two years and four months* to reveal the misuse of law, bigotry, brutality of the Uttar Pradesh police.[24] A month later in March 2023, the SC/ST special court acquitted all four accused of rape and murder in the Hathras case; indicting only one for culpable homicide not amounting to murder with this logic: "As the victim was interacting even after eight days of the incident, it cannot be stated that the accused wanted to kill her...the evidence doesn't prove that she was raped".[25] In effect, no gangrape and no murder had happened!

When Justice CV Ramana (2021-2022) took over, hopes were raised after a long time that the apex curt would do what it is supposed to do–but, unfortunately, belied. The hopes were raised because Justice Ramana intervened in many critical cases like, setting up an expert committee to examine the *Pegasus* surveillance after the government refused to answer (but the panel's report remains a secret and its key findings read out by the court didn't provide a closure to the case[26], more about it in Chapter XI); he promised to hear the constitutionality of Electoral Bond, pending since 2018 (but didn't and retired[27]); took *suo motu* cognizance and directed action against Ashish Mishra, son of Union Minister (MoS) for Home Ajay Mishra Teni, and also sent him back to jail after the Allahabad High Court gave him bail ahead of the Uttar Pradesh elections in 2022[28]; objected to "sealed cover" affidavits (but didn't make the Pegasus report public)[29] and ordered that no state can withdraw criminal cases without High Court's permission, when he found state governments were doing so in a large number of cases.[30]

There was no movement on six cases of national importance during his tenure and 53 fresh cases that required review by constitution benches remained unaddressed – just as was the case during the previous three CJIs.[31] Commenting on the court's failures in the previous few years, leading public intellectual Pratap Bhanu Mehta had written in 2020: "The Indian Supreme Court was never perfect. It has had its dark periods before. But the signs are that it is slipping into judicial barbarism in the senses described above (overwhelming appearance of arbitrariness in judicial decision-making). This phenomenon is not just a matter of individual judges or individual cases. It is now a *systematic phenomenon* with deep institutional roots. It is also part of a global trend, of a piece with developments in Turkey, Poland and Hungary, where the judiciary aids this kind of democratic barbarism."[32] In 2022, when Justice Ramana was the CJI and after the arrests of justice seeker Setalvad, fact-checker Zubair and the apex court's mishandling of defections in the Shiv Sena in Maharashtra (more on it in Chapter VI), he wrote, his use of "judicial" in "judicial barbarism" (in 2020) was "superfluous".[33]

After the PMLA judgement of 2022 (Chapter I), Mehta wrote the apex court had become "even more executive minded than the executive". Bhatia wrote: "Justice Khanwilkar's constitutional law judgments is: "for the State, anything; for the individual, the law": it is the philosophy not just of the executive court, but of the executive('s) court."

These were very harsh words indeed – but reflect the contemporary impressions the apex court has created for itself.

When Justice Chandrachud became the CJI (2022-24), the same hopes were ignited once again. With more than a year to go before his tenure ends (November 2024), it is too early to write about it. But the attacks on him by pro-BJP troll armies (branding him "internal enemy, a foreign agent, and a threat to democracy"[34]) point to an uneasy relationship with the ruling establishment.

Executive Court

When the rule by law was changing into the rule by law and mob rule, the apex court should have stepped in but it didn't – thereby letting down the Constitution and "we the people". Apart from Justice Shah, many others have also studied the judicial system during Prime Minister Modi's regime.

Jeffrelot, in his 2021 book "Modi's India"[35], described it as "judicial national authoritarianism at the expense of secularism". He marked the evolution of two distinct phases: (a) "the 2015-16 war of attrition" when the government battled with the Supreme Court to gain upper hand in judicial appointments (marked by then CJI Justice TS Thakur (2015-17) breaking down in public, in front of the Prime Minister in April 2016, because of continued high vacancy in judiciary[36]) and (b) "from truce to surrender, 2017-20" when the court and the Collegium gave in and avoided verdicts that were "likely to result in conflicts" with the government.

Sociologist Nandini Sundar's 2023 study "The Supreme Court in Modi's India"[37] marks out three strong features: (i) "an unwillingness to hear major constitutional issues that might challenge the regime" (ii) "judgments that serve as an advertorial for the regime, reinforcing an antiminority ideological orientation, justifying the government's actions, and promoting Modi's personality cult" and (iii) "By outsourcing several political decisions to a seemingly disinterested and neutral judiciary, the Modi government has been far more successful than it would have been if it had imposed those decisions purely by legislative majority. In turn, by addressing a variety of political issues as purely procedural matters and not addressing them as constitutional questions, the courts have *collaborated in the delegitimization of dissent and reinforced the claims of the Modi regime.*" (Emphasis added)

New Jurisprudence

To understand the shifts in judicial behaviour, a few distinct patterns of jurisprudence need to be highlighted. There are atleast *11 of those*:

(i)   'Clean chit' jurisprudence, in which corruption and other criminal cases are closed without investigation and trial.

(ii)   'Sealed cover' jurisprudence, in which government affidavits are sought and accepted in sealed over and orders are passed but are not available to litigants or public – and thus, goes against natural justice.

(iii)   'Fait accomplice' or 'Head-in-the-sand' jurisprudence, in which apparently flawed and constitutionally suspect laws are kept undecided but allowed to operate.

(iv)   'Inverted' jurisprudence, in which justice seekers are targeted by the court.

(v)   'Enabling executive' jurisprudence, in which legal checks are removed and executive is facilitated to abuse/misuse law.

(vi)   'Dharma' or 'theocratic' jurisprudence, in which validity for law is traced not to the Constitution but to ancient Hindu texts.

(vii)   'Forum shopping' jurisprudence, in which cases are allotted to benches knowing the outcome in advance.

(viii) 'Secrecy' jurisprudence, in which the findings of the court's own panel is not revealed.

(ix)   'Illegal but permissible' jurisprudence, in which acts declared illegal is allowed to be perpetuated in 'national interest' or some other excuse.

(x)   'Tebbit test' jurisprudence, in which a litigant has to first prove his national loyalty.

(xi)   'Limited applicability' jurisprudence, in which non-existing law is decided but its subsequent reincarnation in far more regressive and draconian form remains pending.

Now, some illustrations on these.

'Clean-chit' Jurisprudence

Former Additional Solicitor General Indira Jaising (2009-2014) defines 'clean chit' jurisprudence as one which *doesn't require due process* of law or *trials* to ascertain charges/allegations. She wrote, it came to prominence when the Special Investigation Team (SIT), set up by the apex court to probe the 2002 Gujarat pogrom, concluded that there was no "larger conspiracy" in the killings and thus giving a clean chit to the Gujarat government. The same approach was visible, she pointed out, in dismissing a plea challenging the acquittal of Amit Shah, then Gujarat Home Minister, in the extra-judicial killings of Sohrabuddin Shaikh *et al* mentioned earlier, by saying that the petitioner was not an "affected person". Thus, closing the door for questioning the acquittal of Shah as the Bombay High Court had earlier dismissed a PIL challenging his acquittal.[38]

Three big corruption scandals hit after 2014: The Birla and Sahara bribery cases of 2015 and Rafale fighter jet deal of 2016. In the first two, documents seized by the IT department showed huge sums were paid to politicians, including Modi as Gujarat Chief Minister, by the two business groups (Birla and Sahara). The court dismissed the demand for probe for both saying "loose sheets of papers are wholly irrelevant as evidence".[39] In a similar case, famously known as the Jain Hawala case of 1997[40], the apex court had not only ensured smooth investigations but mandated a series of measures to ensure independence of CBI and its Director through minimum tenures of two years.

In the Rafale case, France opened judicial probe in July 2021 after its premier investigating agency, Agence Française Anticorruption (AFA), found evidence of kickbacks in 2021.[41] India's CBI had documents showing kickbacks but it didn't probe.[42] The apex court dismissed pleas for an FIR and investigation into the deal in 2018, burying the corruption charges. In 2023, a French court sought India's *cooperation*[43] in the case. Incidentally, India got the critical *anti-corruption clauses removed*[44] from the deal. An investigating report of the Caravan, published in November 2023[45] showed the government was in possession of explosive documents, christened "The Gupta Papers", telling a saga of kickbacks in defence deals over two decades, including in the Rafale case for which an alleged middleman was compensated mostly "in the form of offset projects", but both the ED and CBI ignored these to cover up of the Rafale case.

'Sealed cover' Jurisprudence

The "sealed cover" figured prominently in the BK-16 case (mentioned in Chapter I), NRC drive in Assam[46] and also in the Rafale judgement of 2018, among others. It is particularly epidemic in civil rights cases to which "national security" is brought in and the court indulges the government[47] – a clear *denial of natural justice* because litigants/victims don't get access to the claims/explanations.

In the Rafale case, it was found that the government had misled the court in "sealed cover" affidavit by claiming that it got clean chits from (i) the CAG and (ii) a parliamentary panel (PAC) which examined the CAG report. These false claims became public via the judgement of 2018. The government then rushed to the court for corrections. The court agreed, thus, coming to know of the misleading government claims but neither allowed a probe nor reviewed its judgement.[48] Later, the CAG produced a "redacted" report in February 2019 – withholding "commercial details" like pricing of the fighter jets which would have nailed the corruption (inflated price by over 2.5 billion Euro[49]). The CAG report itself said this happened for the *first time* in its history and yet handed over a clean chit to the government exactly as the "sealed cover" had told the court months earlier (another example of "command performance").[50]

Neither the CAG nor the apex court was as accommodative of the previous Congress-led UPA government. In fact, both acted tough then. The CAG exposed the financial irregularities in the 2G spectrum and coal block allocations, among others.[51] The apex court then cancelled both in 2012 and 2014, respectively.[52] Meanwhile, the number of CAG reports on the Central government has come down drastically from 55 in 2015 to just 14 in 2020 – a 75% fall – thus, undermining fiscal and financial accountability of the government.[53] Unlike the previous Congress-led UPA government, not all CAG reports are tabled in the Parliament either – and the number of CAG reports not tabled by the government goes to 33![54] Some accountability and transparency is this.

Former CJI Justice Ramana had objected to "sealed cover" affidavits but didn't make the Pegasus report public; his successor Justice Chandrachud too scoffed at 'sealed cover' affidavits multiple times (for example, the government ban on Malayalam TV Channel, MediaOne in 2022[55], including the government's offer to suggest names in the court-appointed Adani probe panel[56]. But he actually sought the Adani panel's report[57] and Manipur government's report on arms recovery (looted from armoury)[58] in sealed cover. The demonetization hearing and judgement in his tenure, was entirely a sealed cover business.[59]

Its Adani panel gave a wishy-washy report of no consequence, setting a *bad precedence*[60] (details in Chapter VII). Here is how ineffective Supreme Court appointed probe panels have been in the past two decades. Journalist Saurav Das[61] examined six SC-appointed panels, all on highly sensitive issues of the day, and found those were marked by "secrecy, ineffectiveness or arbitrary behaviour":

- 2018 panel on prison reforms is yet to produce a report.

- Reports of three panels never made public: (i) Pegasus snooping, 2021 (ii) conspiracy against former CJI Ranjan Gogoi, following the sexual harassment charge against him, 2019 and (iii) six reports of the SIT on black money, 2011.

- Panel on three farm laws, 2021, was inconsequential. The day the panel was constituted, the court stayed the operation of the laws. The report was never used by the government, which withdrew the laws in December 2021 on its own. The panel had caused a public uproar as all its four members were known public supporters of those farm laws.[62]

- The panel on deforestation, 2002, has delivered multiple reports but India continues to lose forest land to non-forestry projects.

And yet, the court appointed panels[63] on Manipur to monitor the CBI probe into violence and provide relief to victims but the later panel appointed 12 experts for assistance which didn't even have a Manipuri in it.[64]

It is relevant to recall the fate of Supreme Court-appointed SIT in the Gujarat pogrom of 2002. On the big question of complicity of the state government, it concluded that there was no "prosecutable evidence" against him and others[65] – the precise charge which had prompted the Supreme Court to describe then Gujarat government as "The modern Day 'Neros'".[66] Former CBI Director RK Raghavan, who headed the panel, was appointed High Commissioner of Cyprus in 2017 – usually Indian Foreign Services are appointed to such posts.[67] The significance of this will soon become clearer. Cyprus is a top-ranking tax haven, ranked 14 in the Tax Justice Network's Corporate Tax Haven Index[68], and pumps in huge amounts of FDI inflow into India, ranking 10 among top FDI investing countries[69].

'Fait Accompli' or 'Head-in-the- sand' Jurisprudence

This amounts to endorsing apparently flawed laws without testing their constitutionality and without putting them on hold – that is, allowing their operation. This makes constitutionality of laws and the very Constitution irrelevant. The list is very long:

(a) In the case of PM CARES Fund, the court refused to entertain an appeal against the Allahabad High Court's order rejecting the challenge to its constitutionality.[70]

(b) Legality of the sedition law remains pending.

(c) Abrogation of Articles 370, 35A and degradation of J&K to UTs. Hearings began in 2023, remains inconclusive.[71]

(d) Amendment declaring the Centre's nominee LG as the "government" of NCT of Delhi – in the place of elected assembly and council of ministers.

(e) The opaque Electoral Bond, which introduced systemic/structural corruption into the body politic. The court had sought and received information in "sealed cover" in 2019 but never opened it nor decided its legality.[72] It was finally taken up *five years later in October 2023* (details in Chapter X).

(f) 2019 amendment to the anti-terror UAPA declaring individuals as terrorists, as against groups earlier.[73]

(g) Resurrection of "single directive" in 2018.

(h) The IT Rules of 2021, 2022 and 2023.

(i) New farm laws of 2020.[74]

(j) The CAA of 2019, which discriminates Muslims.[75]

(k) The triple talaq law criminalizes only Muslim men's act of incorrect method of divorcing wives – but not non-Muslim men.[76] The court had struck it down in 2017, following which a law was passed in 2019 and ever since then, petitions challenging it are pending.[77]

(l) The Sabarimala judgement of 2018 allowing Hindu women entry into the Kerala temple. It was challenged by Hindutva groups, following which it was clubbed with unrelated cases and referred to a seven-judge bench, which is yet to be constituted – *effectively* putting it on hold.[78]

(m) In the 'hijab' case, it passed a split verdict in 2022, thereby kicking the can ahead.[79] A three-judge bench to hear it has not been constituted.

(n) The Aadhaar law, passed as 'Money Bill', was validated by the court in 2018 but this validity was doubted by another five-judge bench and referred to a seven-judge bench. The bench is yet to be constituted.[80]

(o) Bringing political parties within the ambit of transparency law, RTI Act of 2005, was clubbed with Electoral Bond and is pending since 2019.[81]

(p) The court scoffed at mob rule and mob lynchings, asked the Centre and states in 2018 to make appropriate laws. The Centre ignored it; it prevented states of Rajasthan, Manipur and West Bengal from doing too by withholding the Presidential consent.[82] Its nominee, Governor, returned such a law back to the government in Jharkhand.[83] The court hasn't yet enforced its order.

(q) Constitutionality of foreign funding to political parties, which was allowed by amending the FCRA – post-2024 Delhi High Court indictment (Chapter II).

(r) Targeted bulldozing of Muslim homes and shops in Delhi, Uttar Pradesh, Madhya Pradesh and Gujarat by the BJP-ruled states and municipalities is dealt with soft hands and in piecemeal. The court did intervene in Delhi's Jahangirpuri and Uttar Pradesh but refused to take up the illegality of such overnight demolitions – without notice, without checking documents and calling for explanations – expressing its inability to pass omnibus order to stop the open illegality.[84]

(s) The hearings in the remission of 11 convicts in the Bilkis Bano case dragged on for more than a year (pending until December 2023).

(t) It has allowed various high courts to drag on the Central Information Commission (CIC) order of 2016 directing the PMO to reveal the Prime Minister's educational qualifications.[85] A fake degree means the Prime

Minister's election would be invalidated.

In September 2023, the Supreme Court's record showed there were 462 *cases pending* before constitution benches of five-judges (306 cases), seven-judge bench (21 cases) and nine-judge (135 cases). The list is going up. If three-judge benches (584 cases) are counted, the pending cases go up to 1,046.[86] Add to this a large number of pending habeas corpus petitions (challenging arbitrary detentions) – 58 in 2021 (not disclosed on the official website) – and denial of justice to BK-16, Umar Khalid and thousands of other victims of deliberate misuse of law to target political rivals, dissent and Muslims since 2014.

The apex court hasn't exactly set high standards in putting its own house in order either.

(i) Former CJI Dipak Misra heard his own case in the illegal gratification case – one of the reasons for his impeachment move in 2018 (mentioned earlier)[87].

(ii) It didn't probe corruption charges against its own judges and politicians that former Arunachal Pradesh Chief Minister Kalikho Pul had named and detailed in his suicide note in 2016; in 2021, the court dismissed a petition seeking a CBI inquiry into this matter.[88]

(iii) It also obstructed natural justice in the sexual harassment case against then sitting CJI Justice Ranjan Gogoi by holding an opaque and farcical investigation and giving a clean chit to him. It was the victim, a court staff, who lost her job, arrested and even tortured in police custody. And then, after the clean chit to Justice Gogoi, her job was restored with full back wages – suggesting that she was not on the wrong and that she was doubly victimized.[89]

'Inverted' Jurisprudence: Putting Justice Seekers 'in the Dock'

The fourth category is 'inverted' jurisprudence in which the very justice seekers are put "in the dock" by the apex court and the accused given a free pass. It began with the Zakia Jafri case in June 2022.

Zakia Jafri is the widow of Ahsan Jafri, a former Congress MP who was killed during the 2002 Gujarat pogrom along with about 70 others. She was seeking review of the SIT's 'clean chit' to the Gujarat government for "larger conspiracy". The apex court (a bench headed by Justice Khanwilkar) not only dismissed the plea and gave a clean chit to the SIT and thereby, to the Gujarat government, it attacked co-petitioner and justice seeker Teesta Setalvad – journalist and activist who played a key role in bringing justice to the riot victims – and two police officers, former DGP RB Sreekumar and former IPS officer Sanjiv Bhatt, both of whom had pointed fingers at the involvement of Gujarat government in the post-Godhra pogrom of 2002.

The court charged Setalvad, Sreekumar and Bhatt of having "ulterior design" to "keep the pot boiling" and said they should be *"in the dock and proceeded with in accordance with law"* for abuse of the judicial process. It also added: "At the end of the day, it appears to us that a *coalesced effort of the disgruntled officials of the State of Gujarat along with others was to create sensation by making revelations which were false to their own knowledge.* The falsity of their claims had been fully exposed by the SIT after a thorough investigation."[90] *(Emphasis added)*

Legal fraternity was aghast and pointed out that natural justice demanded that the three should have been given *prior notices and heard* before being indicted.[91] The judgement marked a reversal of what the apex court had done until then to secure justice for the victims of the 2002 pogrom. It set up the SIT in 2009 (which submitted its report to local courts in 2012) and shifted the trials of many cases to Maharashtra to prevent Gujarat's interference. Its 2004 order was highly critical of the Gujarat government's handling of investigations and trials, commenting that there was "ample evidence…glaringly demonstrating subversion of justice delivery system", "investigation appears to be perfunctory and anything but impartial without any definite object of finding out the truth and bringing to book those who were responsible for the crime". It's description of the state's top executives was scathing: "The modern Day 'Neros' were looking elsewhere when Best Bakery and innocent children and helpless women were burning, and were probably deliberating how the *perpetrators of the crime can be saved or protected.* Law and justice become flies in the hands of these "wanton boys".[92] *(Emphasis added)*

Following the judgement, the Gujarat government promptly lodged an FIR, set up a new SIT to probe the three justice seekers and arrested them. Like in the case of BK-16 and many others, the law was turned on its heads.[93] Sreekumar and Bhatt continue to be in jail; Setalvad got bail from the apex court[94]. Incidentally, the third person who had given evidence to an unofficial fact-finding panel about this collusion of Gujarat government in the post-Godhra pogrom of 2002 – Haren Pandya of the BJP, former Gujarat Home Minister (1998-2001) and then Revenue Minister before he resigned in August 2002 – was found shot dead in seemingly mysterious circumstances in Ahmedabad in 2003.[95]

Multiple accounts of eyewitness Azam Khan pointing to the probable *link* between Pandya's killing and the extrajudicial killings of Sohrabuddin *et al* (2005) – the latter frequently figures in this chapter – exist. Khan, an associate of Sohrabuddin and a key witness in his extrajudicial killing (along with wife and friend), who has been in official custody for long, has revealed this link to a Mumbai trial court, to the CBI and even the Supreme Court was told about it.[96] But instead of ordering fresh investigation to prevent miscarriage of justice, which senior advocate Prashant Bhushan's Centre for Public Interest Litigation (CPIL) had sought (also by Pandya's family), the apex court (Justices Arun Mishra and Vineet Saran) not only dismissed it ("No ground for further reinvestigation or investigation is made out in the matter.") but *imposed a fine of R 50,000* on the CPIL in 2019 for wasting the court's time.[97]

The Zakia Jafri case was followed with another judgement seeking action against justice seeker Himanshu Kumar in July 2022 (by a bench of Justices Khanwilkar and JB Pardiwala).[98]

Kumar had sought a probe into the Dantewada killings of September and October 2009 involving paramilitary forces, Chhattisgarh police and 'Salwa Judum' commandos. The killings had followed the massacred of 76 paramilitary CRPF personnel by Maoists in April 2009. The petition demanding a probe into the retaliatory killing was filed in 2009 – 13 years ago. The court not only kept it pending for so long and refused a probe, it also endorsed the government's demand for legal action against Kumar. The court imposed a penalty of Rs 5 lakh and sought action against him "in accordance with law" and added: "…we leave it to the State of Chhattisgarh/CBI (Central Bureau of Investigation) to take appropriate steps in accordance with law as discussed above in reference to the assertions made in the interim application. We clarify that it shall not be limited only to the offence under Section 211 of the IPC. A case of criminal conspiracy or any other offence under the IPC may also surface. We may not be understood of having expressed any final opinion on such action/proceedings. We leave it to the better discretion of the State of Chhattisgarh/CBI to act accordingly keeping in mind the seriousness of the entire issue."

Both the court directives to punish the justice seekers (Setalvad *et al* and Himanshu Kumar) came *after* the Central government asked for it during the hearings (both the benches were led by Justice Khanwilkar who also made it virtually *impossible to get bail in the UAPA and PMLA* cases and upheld other draconian provisions in them as detailed in Chapter I).

Such failures on multiple fronts (not upholding fundamental rights to life, liberty and equality before law, siding with the government, not deciding legality of laws, attacking justice seekers etc.) have earned the apex court sobriquets like "Executive Court" and "Orwellian Court".[99] Ironically, at other times, the apex court refuses to enter the executive's domain – honouring separation of power – which may appear fine at first glance but is very problematic when citizens are "facing executive excesses without legislative control" – as political scientist Suhas Palshikar[100] once pointed out.

'Enabling executive' jurisprudence

The previous chapter elaborated how the UAPA and PMLA have been made more draconian by the Supreme Court by allowing executive to abuse these laws and facilitate persecution (process is punishment) of dissent and political rivals. The 'head-in-the-sand' jurisprudence subhead lists a large number of cases where the constitutionality of the laws is pending but the government is allowed freely to abuse those laws – the IT Rules, abrogation of Article 370, 'LG' as the 'government' of NCT Delhi, Electoral Bond, PM CARES Fund etc. (except sedition). The previous sub-section on targeting justice seekers by the apex court – as wished by the executive – is a blatant act that can be described as *killing fundamental rights* and turning "innocent until proven guilty" jurisprudence on its head.

These are the very anti-thesis of what the highest constitutional court in the land is supposed to be – which is *to uphold the rule of law, protect fundamental rights, test constitutionality of laws and uphold the Constitution of India.*

'Dharma' or 'theocratic' jurisprudence

The court has played a key role in turning India and Indian government into Hindu majoritarian – both socially and politically – by tracing laws not to the Constitution of India but to ancient Hindu religious texts.

G Mohan Gopal, former director of the Bengaluru's National Law School, flagged this in his February 2023 speech "Theocratic Judges Who Find Source of Law in Religion than Constitution Increased".[101] His central argument is that the Modi government is seeking to establish a *theocratic state* by 2047, *not by overthrowing* the Constitution but through the *re-interpretation* of the Constitution as a Hindu document (through judicial interpretations) – as Nandini Sundar also pointed, mentioned earlier. He averred this from looking at the number of judges appointed to the Supreme Court and identifying how many were "constitutionalists" (rely exclusively on the Constitution) and how many were "theocratic" or "committed" to go outside of the Constitution and look at religious texts as the source of law. The latter assessment was based on the judicial pronouncements alone, he stressed.

Of the 56 appointed during the ten years of the Congress-led UPA and 55 in nine years of the current regime, Gopal found *six* in the former but *nine* in the latter period were constitutionalists (the rise in their numbers was due to the Collegium's awareness and resistance to the regime's theocratic or ideological agenda "bent upon destroying the Constitution", he said). But the number of "theocratic" judges were *zero* in the former but *nine* in the latter period – of which five were in the bench at the time (February 2023).

Gopal said there was a two-strategy to this *theocratic project* – first, appointment of judges open to looking beyond the Constitution and at religious sources for interpretation of law and second, appointment of judges who identify the "theological sources" for law. He cited two cases where religious texts, rather the Constitution guided the judgements – the Ayodhya verdict of 2019 and the 'hijab' verdict of 2023.

Citing the 'hijab' case, he pointed out that the judgement equated "dharma" with the Constitution and "dharma" with "Sanatan Dharma" (another name used for Hindu religion by the current regime, highlighted in Introduction). That is how, he said, in Karnataka schools "homa" ('havan' or offerings to the fire god) is allowed but not 'hijab'; 'homa' is dharma but 'hijab' is 'religion' – as if all religions are not about 'dharma'. The judgement also interpreted the constitutional term 'secular' in the Constitution's Preamble not as "dharma nirapeksh" but "panth nirapeksh". ("Panth" refers to sect and "nirapeksh" means neutral.) As pointed out in Introduction, the constitutional concept of secularism is very different from the western and Hindutva concepts.

At that time, the BJP-ruled Karnataka planned to introduce Bhagawat Gita, like Gujarat, in school curriculum but not Bible, Quran, Guru Granth Sahib or other religious texts with its then education minister saying that Gita isn't a religious text like the Bible and Quran as it talked about "values and life" and not religious practices.[102] In October 2022, the Supreme Court delivered a *split verdict* with one judge upholding the state's authority to ban 'hijab' while the other called it a matter of choice that can't be stifled by the state – thereby seeking a larger bench to hear it.[103] That is still pending.

This interpretation of the word 'secular' by the court is in line with the RSS-BJP interpretation[104] which is averse to the very idea of secularism as *non-discrimination* on the grounds of religion, race, caste, sex or place of birth.

This marks the other big failure of the apex court – assisting in undermining Indian secularism, explained in some detail later.

'Forum shopping' jurisprudence

The 2018 revolt by the Supreme Court judgement brought 'forum shopping' to public discourses – involving CJI's administrative power as the "master of the roaster". At the time, the focus was more on the CBI judge BH Loya's mysterious death, illegal gratification in the medical colleges case – both involving then CJI Misra who also heard the reviews and dismissed them. Then CJI Gogoi presided over a court that dealt with his own alleged sexual harassment of a female employee in 2019, calling it a "bigger plot" to "deactivate the office or [the] CJI" – after four news reports the allegations.[105] During 2019-2020, Justice Arun Mishra heard cases involving the Adani group, a crony capitalist with close links to the government. A series of investigating reports by Abir Dasgupta and Paranjoy Guha Thakurta found all *seven cases* during this period went in favour of the Adani group.[106] Senior advocate Dushyant Dave wrote to the judges, pointing out the irregular manner in which the Adani related cases were being listed and heard by Justice Mishra.[107] Then in 2022, then CJI UU Lalit constituted an extraordinary bench on a Saturday – a holiday for the court – to stay former Delhi University professor GN Saibaba's discharge in a Maoist link case (see Chapter I).

The spectre of abuse of "master of the roaster" was raised again in May 2023, when CJI Chandrachud constituted a bench headed by him (with Justices PS Narasimha and Pardiwala) to hear the government's application to "recall" a default bail order of April 26, 2023 in which a two-judge bench (Justices Krishna Murari and CT Ravikumar)[108] had ruled *for the right to default bail* if incomplete chargesheet is filed "with the purpose of scuttling the right to default bail". Days earlier, on April 10, 2023, another two-judge bench (Justices MR Shah and Ravikumar)[109] had ruled *against the right to* default bail by stating that if it was not sought during the first extension for investigation, the right is forfeited. After the government sought a recall of the April 26, 2023 order, another two-judge bench led by CJI Justice Chandrachud (with Justice Pardiwala) did something strange. It directed all bail applications filed on the basis of the April 26 judgement to be "deferred beyond 4 May 2023"[110] – thereby effectively putting a stay without a review of another two-judge bench. Later, it was put before a three-judge bench (the third being Justice PS Narasimha) which is yet to hear it.[111]

'Secrecy' jurisprudence

As pointed out earlier ('sealed cover' jurisprudence), news portal Article14's analyses showed of six court-appointed panels, before the one on the Adani group in the past two decades, were marked by "secrecy, ineffectiveness or arbitrary behaviour".

'Illegal but permissible' jurisprudence

The Ayodhya verdict of 2019, mentioned earlier, is perhaps the starting point of the apex court calling something "illegal" and then legalizing it in the same judgement. The demolition of the Babri masjid was called "illegal" but it was legalized and the guilty (Hindutva groups) were rewarded. In May 2023, a five-judge bench (led by CJI Chandrachud) unanimously decided[112] that the Maharashtra Governor's 2022 call for a trust vote was "illegal" in absence of "objective material and reasons" to justify its action and also the treatment of the rebel Shiv Sena as the "real" Shiv Sena "illegal" but ruled that "the status quo ante cannot be restored because Mr Thackeray did not face the floor test and tendered his resignation". Thackeray had to resign because a vacation bench of the very court had allowed the trust vote – which Thackeray had refused to take and resigned (see Chapter VI for more). The third major case is the extension to ED Director Sanjay Kumar Mishra, granted in July 2023, despite having ruled earlier extensions "illegal" on multiple times (see Chapter I). But these are not the only such instances, there are more.

'Tebbit test' jurisprudence

September 2023 saw an extraordinary demand from the Supreme Court. While the hearing on abrogation of Article 370 was on, Solicitor General Tushar Mehta sought (to divert attention) and got the court to direct litigant Mohammad Akar Lone, a National Conference leader and a veteran legislator (J&K Assembly and Lok Sabha), to file an affidavit declaring *his allegiance* to the Constitution and also declaring that J&K is an inalienable part of India – in connection with an old and obscure alleged remark of his in defence of Pakistan (in the J&K Assembly in 2018). The directive came from then CJI Justice Chandrachud who had said earlier that "the Constitution works even if you don't believe in it".[113]

'Limited applicability' jurisprudence

On September 11, 2023, the Supreme Court delivered a judgement on the applicability of infamous "single directive" (Section 6A of the Delhi Special Police Establishment Act (DPEA) of 1946) during the period of 2003-2014 (which was the reference for this case and *pending since 2007*).[114]

First introduced in 1969 to the CBI mandating prior sanction to investigate government servants of joint secretary and above levels ("decision making level"), the "single directive" was reissued in 1988, after the Bofors scandal hit and became a big issue – both by then Congress governments. It was struck down in 1997 (in the Vineet Narain case involving the Jain hawala diaries) but was resurrected in 2003 by then BJP-led NDA government of Vajpayee. It was again struck down in 2014 (11 years later) arguing (like in 1997) that it "thwarts an independent, unhampered, unbiased, efficient and fearless inquiry/investigation to track down the corrupt public servants" and also violates equality of law or all (Article 14).

The current judgement deals with the applicability of this "single directive" when it was in operation (2003-2014) and says, once a law is declared unconstitutional (in 2014) it "can be applied retrospectively" (from 2003). It is applicable only to the old pending cases. The problem is, in 2018, the government resurrected the "single directive" in a new form – as Section 17A of the Prevention of Corruption Act (PCA) of 1988 – requiring prior government sanction to investigate any government official – retired or serving. It no longer violates discrimination (Article 14) but makes corruption investigation impossible if the government doesn't wish it. The CBI is governed by the DPEA of 1946 but primarily investigates corruption cases under the PCA of 1988, hence, the "single directive" remains equally effective.[115] The Supreme Court's latest judgement mentions Section 17A of the PCA of 1988 – but ignores it saying that "not germane to the reference order". The challenge to Section 17A is also pending since 2018 – allowing the government to deliver "investigation-mukt" Bharat (probe-free Inia) so far as corruption goes (Chapter V).

What is objectionable in the September 2023 judgement? That the far more draconian and arbitrary version of law is allowed to remain operational. Soon, one may expect a similar judgement relating to the sedition law (124A of the IPC) – which isn't called 'sedition', becomes Clause 150 in the Bharatiya Nyaya Sanhita of 2023[116] introduced out-of-the-blue in August 2023 to replace the entire IPC and it is part of "offences against the state". This reincarnation is far more draconian and arbitrary – with expanded scope, vagueness and punishment.[117]

But, so what? Going by the dominant trend, the chances are that the worse version of the sedition law will be allowed to come into force – without deciding its constitutionality for long, thereby sanctioning abuse of the judicial system.

Court & Secularism

There have been several apex court judgements which have harmed the cause of secularism and inflame communal conflicts. The Ayodhya verdict[118] delivered in 2019 is one such. It ended the Ramjanambhoomi movement with the court delivering the Babri masjid land to Hindus. Delivered *unanimously* by a five-judge bench, the court didn't uphold the rule of law or the Constitution as the order declared (a) the demolition of the 464-year-old Babri masjid in December 1992 as "egregious violation of the rule of law" (b) the clandestine placing of an idol inside the masjid in 1949 had "led to the desecration of the mosque and the ouster of the Muslims otherwise than by the due process of law" and (c) the Muslims had been "wrongly deprived of a mosque". Yet, it gave the Babri masjid land to the law breakers (Hindus) to build a temple and asked 5-acre of land to be given to the victims (Muslims) *outside Ayodhya* to build their masjid.[119]

Worse, this verdict legitimized violation of the constitutional secularism by the state (government) by asking (d) the Central government to "formulate a scheme", set up a trust and "make necessary provisions in regard to the functioning of the trust" the mandate of which (trust) is "construction of a temple". It (e) didn't ask the Central or the Uttar Pradesh government to similarly assist building the masjid. Then CJI Justice Gogoi and his four brother judges (including Justice Chandrachud who is believed to have authored the entire Ayodhya verdict[120] and included Justice S Abdul Nazeer) forgot that the Indian state, the vey apex court and the Constitution of India guiding both the state and the court are "secular" in character and must not been seen discriminating on the basis of religion.

As a result of this blatantly unsecular and unconstitutional verdict, no one told the Prime Minister to stop from holding "bhoomi puja" for the construction of the Ayodhya temple or the President of India not to *donate Rs 5 lakh* (then President Ram Nath Kovind was the first one to do so) to the temple trust (but not for the masjid). President Kovind was followed by Madhya Pradesh Chief

Minister Shivraj Singh Chouhan from the BJP, who donated Rs 1 lakh[121]. They all forgot about their constitutional oath and duty (dharma).

The verdict (f) made no attempt to ensure the guilty of demolishing the masjid were punished either. All accused in the demolition case were acquitted subsequently by a CBI court. Incidentally, in the Ismail Faruqui case of 1994[122], the apex court had ruled that the Babri masjid was *not essential to Islam* by arguing that "unless the place has a particular significance for that religion so as to form an essential or integral part thereof" its land can be acquired. The context was acquisition of the masjid land after it was demolished by Hindutva groups led by the BJP in 1992.

India witnesses the Prime Minister, Home Minister and Chief Ministers from the BJP openly building religious statues, developing temple corridors, holding Hindu festivals, rituals and functions with public money – openly flaunting their Hindu faith – without extending same courtesies to non-Hindu religious institutions, festivities, rituals and practices.

In 2022, the court not only failed to stop fresh mandir-masjid conflicts but allowed to raise its ugly head again. The court did this by allowing a local court in Uttar Pradesh to hearing the Kashi's Gyanvapi masjid-Vishwanath temple issue. In the Ayodhya verdict, the apex court had spoken gloriously about the Places of Worship (Special Provisions) Act of 1991 – the objective of which is "to prohibit conversion of any place of worship and to provide for the maintenance of the religious character of any place of worship as it existed on the 15th day of August, 1947, and for matters connected therewith or incidental thereto", except the Babri masjid case. The court had then said that this 1991 law "imposes a *non-derogable obligation* towards enforcing our commitment to secularism" and that "the law is hence a legislative instrument designed to *protect the secular features* of the Indian polity, which is one of the *basic features of the Constitution*". (*Emphasis added*)

But in the Gyanvapi masjid case – in which Hindus demand worship right in the Kashi's masjid on the plea that a temple existed there more than 350 years ago and that a "Shivling" still exists under the masjid – a three-judge bench led by CJI Justice Chandrachud, who was part of the Ayodhya verdict and presumably wrote it, along with Justices Surya Kant and PS Narasimha, allowed a court to open up a new conflict. For this, the court found a new logic to bypass the 1991 law by observing: "We have dealt with the provisions (of the Places of Worship Act, 1991) in our Ayodhya verdict. The ascertainment of the religious character of the place of worship is not expressly barred."[123] Incidentally, Justice Narasimha had fought the Ayodhya case as a lawyer for a Hindu petitioner.[124]

This order has given a fresh lease of life to a series of old litigations about Hindu claims on masjids and tombs in various parts of the country despite the

1991 law: Agra's Taj Mahal, Mathura's Shahi Idgah Masjid (Krishna temple), Delhi's Qutub Minar and Dhar's Bhojshala complex.[125] Not just that, the very 1991 law has been allowed to be challenged.[126] The Kashi and Mathura cases have gathered more significance – which is in keeping with the BJP's old claim going back to the days of the Ayodhya movement of 1980s and 1990s: "*Ayodhya-Babri sirf jhaanki hai, Kashi-Mathura ab baaqi hai*"[127] (Ayodhya is just a glimpse, Kashi and Mathura are yet to come)". The Gyanvapi case has witnessed "near identical petitions"[128] set off for claiming the Babri masjid by the right-wing groups in 1950s.

Then, just as it had passed the legal baton to the Uttar Pradesh courts in the Kashi's Gyanvapi case, the apex court passed the Sri Krishna Janmabhoomi-Shahi Idgah case (Mathura) to the Allahabad High Court in July 2023.[129] Both the cases would fester for long – undermining the 1991 law.

The court has let down Muslims in multiple ways. It has failed to check "bulldozer justice" – open and unchecked illegal use of state power targeting Muslims as punitive and retribution against protests in BJP-ruled states – since 2020.[130] It became the electoral tool for the BJP and continues unabated in Uttar Pradesh, Madhya Pradesh, Gujarat, Assam. When the BJP-ruled municipality targeted Muslims of Delhi's Jahangirpuri – immediately after Hindutva mobs attacked their houses and masjid during their Ram Navami and Hanuman Jayanti processions in 2022 – the court did stay it but failed to address the lawlessness and persecution of Muslims in the cow belt as bulldozers continued to demolish Muslim shops and houses overnight – without notice, without checking documents or calling for explanations. It failed to pass omnibus order to provide *substantive justice*.[131]

The court also failed to check open hate speech and crime against Muslims – which saw a new resurgence after 2014. It did direct the central and state governments repeatedly to take *suo motu* cognizance of hate speeches, beginning with October 2022[132], but that made little difference as the BJP leaders and Hindutva groups continued to indulge in such violence, even repeatedly calling for Muslim genocide. Same is the case with fake encounters often targeting Muslims. A petition, filed in 2007 by journalist BG Verghese (now dead) and lyricist Javed Akhtar, seeking probe into extra judicial killings in Gujarat. In the last hearing in April 2023, the Gujarat government refused to share the details, questioning the locus of the petitioners.[133] Meanwhile, the Uttar Pradesh government, another BJP-ruled state, boasts of carrying out more than 10,000 encounters killing 179 people in six years.[134]

Right, the apex court's journey to de-legitimise India's constitutional secularism didn't begin in 2019 but goes a long way back.[135] But one old case is particularly disturbing. That is the 1995 ('Hindutva') judgement[136] in which a bench led by late Justice JS Verma (who authored the judgement and was the

CJI later during 1997-98) first equated Hindutva with Hinduism and then called Hindutva "a way of life" for Indians, not a mere religion. It never occurred to the judge that the same is true ("a way of life") of all other religions in the world – and not really an intelligent thing to say at a time and in a country in which religious hatred and violence was being used to capture political power (in itself violation of the Constitution) by a leading political party.

This pronouncement was gratuitous (*obiter dicta* in legal parlance) to boot!

The case being heard wasn't about Hindutva or Hinduism at all but legality of seeking votes in the name of religion (by the late Shiv Sena founder Bala Saheb Thackeray), which is expressly forbidden in the Representation of People Act of 1951 and is marked a "corrupt practice". The judgement, in fact, upheld the law (disapproving use of religion in electioneering) and that should have been the end of the matter. But the needless pronouncement on Hindutva gave (a) a fresh sail to Hindutva's communal politics – which had been sunk after the Babri masjid's demolition in 1992 and (b) by declaring Hinduism and Hindutva not religion but "a way of life" it also gave a license to the BJP to openly use religion in politics and electioneering. Since then, the court has been asked to review late Justice Verma's pronouncements multiple times, the last being in 2016[137], but it never did.

In January 2017, 22 years after the pronouncement and four years after his death, his daughter Shubhra Verma said[138] Justice Verma had regretted this pronouncement because it was misunderstood and twisted for political purpose: "He always had a regret about being misunderstood after 1995 and how for their own purposes, a group of politicians had twisted the spirit of his judgment. He practised the most inclusive principles in his life, keeping us away from all rituals, with no burden, and letting us be. He spoke often of how in Satna, his old family friends, Muslims, had taken refuge in their home when communal fires raged during partition."

Historically speaking, Aakar Patel[139] and Ajaz Ashraf[140] have pointed to a long list of Supreme Court verdicts and observations for Muslims to feel *let down*.

Questionable Judgements

The above examples are not the only ones in which the Supreme Court has failed the Constitution and "we the people of India". There are numerous such instances.

One of these is upholding the 10% EWS quota[141] – quota in educational institutions and government jobs for economically weaker sections (EWS) among *upper castes*. This judgement violates the very objective of reservations introduced in the Constitution, allowed in legislative bodies, education and government jobs – 'affirmative action' to uplift backward classes who have suffered historic discrimination, deprivation and exploitation at the hands of upper castes which is sanctified by *Hindu religion.*

The apex court had *struck down* this 10% EWS quota in jobs, first made in 1990, in the *1992 Indra Sawhney case.*[142] But it upheld it in 2022. Justice Pardiwala, one of the three judges who wrote the majority view (3-2) for Justices Dinesh Maheshwari and Bela M Trivedi, observed that "reservation should not continue for an indefinite period of time so as to become a vested interest", that "the new concept of economic criteria…may go a long way in eradicating caste-based reservation" and that this "may be perceived as a first step in the process of doing away with caste-based reservation."

Going by the economic criteria set out – family income below Rs 8 lakh per year, family owning less than 5 acres of agricultural land etc. – *more than 90% Indian households qualify* for it. Can this be called "affirmative", "positive discrimination" or "reservation"?[143] Besides, the same judgement quotes the *Sinho Commission Report* to point out that the maximum poor comes from the underprivileged and backward classes – 38% of the SCs, 48.4% of the STs, and 33.1% of the OBCs are below poverty line (BPL), as against a mere 18.2% of the upper castes falling under the 'general category'. Further, how will the EWS quota end caste-based reservation? With this legal clearance, the reservation goes beyond 49% – violating the limit set in the Indra Sawhney case – which this judgement undermined.

Another is the demonetization judgement of January 2023.[144]

The court upheld its "legality", that is, the government is empowered to demonetize, by a 4-1 verdict (Justices S Abdul Nazeer, BR Gavai, AS Bopanna and V Ramasubramanian in favour and Justice BV Nagarathna the dissenting). But it glossed over more critical elements – the economic "wisdom or soundness" and "procedural" flaws – which too were to be decided and must to establish accountability and transparency in governance, institutional integrity (also independence) and democratic checks and balances. This judgement leaves the space for encore of *rash, mindless and arbitrary* demonetization-like policymaking that began the derailment of Indian economy – a dangerous situation to have in a totalitarian regime. The judgement also *relied entirely on 'sealed cover'* documents to decide that both the "wisdom" and the "procedural" matters were alright. It didn't formally ask for all the critical documents relating to the decision making in sealed covers but made it *de facto* so by asking for these documents, which the petitioners had asked to be made public, *after completing the hearing.* These documents including the government's letter asking for the RBI's approval, agenda and minutes of the RBI Board which approved it, cabinet note, cabinet decision and minutes of the cabinet meeting etc.

The judgement conveniently skipped the "wisdom" part by stating that it is "best left to the wisdom of the experts"; even the dissenting one says the policy was in "the best intentions" and for a "noble objects for the betterment of the Nation". Some of the above documents and other evidence demonstrate that nothing could be farther from truth. The government had dismissed all expert opinions and violated the procedure by imposing its wish on the RBI. More than enough evidence existed at the time of the judgement to show the lack of economic wisdom and the incalculable harm it caused (cash was rationed for months, all economic activities came to stand still overnight as 86.9% cash was banned and their replacement took many months, millions of jobs and small businesses were shut immediately and some permanently). It also came *six years too late* – a *perfect case* of 'fait accompli' jurisprudence.[145]

The consequence of this rank bad judgement (which failed to fix accountability and rational policymaking) was visible soon enough – on May 19, 2023 the RBI withdrew Rs 2,000 notes with "immediate effect" while declaring that it "will continue to be legal tender" nonetheless.[146] This was a clear indication that there was a *hidden agenda* (as in the case of demonetization) since none of its arguments for this withdrawal – the purpose of re-monetization already fulfilled, these notes are not being commonly used, its life-span is four to five years and its printing had stopped etc. – makes any economic sense at all.[147]

The 'Agnipath' judgement of 2023 is yet another such instance.

The CJI Justice Chandrachud-led bench (with Justices Narasimha and Pardiwala) dismissed pleas against this hairbrained scheme of recruiting to defence forces by stating: "There is no *vested right* (to be appointed in the armed forces) here. The High Court has said the government *cannot act arbitrarily*. But it is not really a decision which is weighed in by any extraneous circumstances or any arbitrary reasons." The court was actually hearing a challenge to the Delhi High Court verdict which declared 'Agnipath' a "well-thought-out policy decision" and "in national interest". Given that India is witnessing a prolonged and severe job crisis, millions of youths prepare for defence services for several years, thousands had qualified all tests since 2019 but were not recruited using the pandemic as an excuse and then all eligible candidates (many waiting for appointment letters) were dumped as this new scheme of recruitment was launched, for the apex court to say that there is "no vested right" to be appointed is not plain insensitivity but illogical.[148]

It was another top-down decision, without prior consultations – not with independent experts, youths, even Parliament. It provides *short-term contracts* of four years in armed forces *without pension and any social security* at the end of which only 25% will be picked up for "regular" or permanent soldering jobs – compromising professionalism and national security. It also jeopardizes social peace as 75% 'Agniveer', trained in organized killing, enter into society every four years – which lacks capacity to provide jobs and is torn apart in communal frenzy with the Hindu majoritarian groups targeting Muslims[149] (also see Chapter XI).

Here are two other instances in which the apex court failed.

- It *abdicated* its responsibility in the women wrestlers' sexual abuse case by passing the baton to the Delhi High Court even when the accused the BJP MP Brij Bhushan Saran Singh roams free (Chapter I).

- It *refused* to act and *directed*[150] the civil society initiative, Association for Democratic Reforms or ADR, to approach the Election Commission for violation of its own orders on *cleansing politics of criminals* – knowing fully well that the Election Commission has lost its way after 2014.

- The festering ethnic conflict in Manipur has as much to do with the apex court's long silence as it was seized with the matter when the violence broke out in May 2023 after the Manipur High Court's directive to the state to provide reservation to Hindu Meitei as "scheduled tribes". It took suo motu cognizance only after the video of two women being paraded naked came to public domain in July 2023.[151]

Good Judgements

It would, however, be wrong to say that the Supreme Court has done no good at all. There are good judgements though not too many to count.

- It declared privacy as a fundamental right in 2017 (led by then CJI Justice Khehar and Justices Chelameswar, Bobde, RK Agrawal, Rohinton Fali Nariman, AM Sapre, Chandrachud (author), SK Kaul and Nazeer).[152]

- In the case Vinod Dua (Justices UU Lalit and Vineet Saran), it upheld a journalist's right to criticize the government and quashed the sedition charge (although a large number of such cases are pending and freedom of expression is not protected as the previous chapter shows).

- It quashed the 2022 ban on the Malayalam TV channel MediaOne (CJI Justice Chandrachud and Justice Hima Kohli) by the Information and Broadcasting Ministry saying that 'national security' claim can't be made "in a cavalier manner" or "in thin air" and denial of security clearance to it produces "a chilling effect" on free speech, particularly press freedom. The I&B Ministry had banned it without disclosing the reasons to the TV channel but told the court in 'sealed cover' its two objections: (i) it was funded by Jamaat-e-Islami Hind and (ii) its "anti-establishment stance on various issues 'including UAPA, Armed Forces (Special Power) Act, developmental projects of the Government, encounter killings, Citizenship (Amendment) Act, CAA/NPR/NRC". The court found "no nexus" between the material provided in 'sealed cover' and "the inference drawn from such material" and criticized the Central government for using 'national security' as "a tool to deny citizens remedies that are provided under the law", adding that "this is not compatible with the rule of law."[153] Constitutional lawyer Bhatia commented, the four-pronged proportionality test laid down in the judgement makes a valuable contribution to the proportionality jurisprudence, although it is so complex as to make it very much a case of "the proof of the pudding".[154]

Sinecure for Judges & Lawyers

New precedent has also been set in giving political offices to the apex judges by the government.

In 2014, months after Prime Minister Modi came to power, Justice P Sathasivam, who had retired as the CJI just six months earlier, was appointed as Governor of Kerala. This was *a first for India* given that Justice Sathasivam had dealt with, as the apex court judge, the extra-judicial killings of Sohrabuddin *et al* in the earlier stage and had quashed an FIR against Amit Shah – hence, it sparked a huge debate over the impartiality and autonomy of the highest court of the land.[155] He wasn't the first apex court judge to be a Governor. There were two in the past: Justice S Fazl Ali (Governor of Odisha and Assam) during 1952 to 1959, and Justice Fathima Beevi (Governor of Tamil Nadu). But in the latter cases, there are no scandals. Justice Ali became a Governor soon after retirement but that was a different era – an era of setting up the democratic structure – and Justice Beevi was made Governor five years after retirement.[156]

Three judges in the Ayodhya bench got post-retirement sinecure.

- In 2020, Justice Gogoi was nominated to the Rajya Sabha by the government, months after retirement, again raising the same questions.[157] Interestingly, Justice Gogoi doesn't care to attend the Parliament or ask questions[158] – after having claimed he wanted to raise issues pertaining to the judiciary and the northeast region. His *maiden speech* was in 2023 to defend taking away of the elected Delhi government's powers and handing it over to the "nominated" LG during which he *questioned*[159] the "basic structure" of Constitution doctrine which he had cited in support of multiple times as a judge.

- In 2021, his brother judge in the Ayodhya bench, Justice Ashok Bhushan, was made head of the National Company Law Appellate Tribunal (NCLAT) in 2021 four months after retirement.[160]

- In 2023, another brother judge Justice Nazeer was appointed Governor of Andhra Pradesh – the second case – a month after his retirement.[161] Justice Nazeer was part of the bench that delivered the Puttaswamy (privacy right), Ayodhya, triple talaq (in which he dissented) and demonetization verdicts (detailed earlier).

Controversial Justice Arun Mishra was appointed chairman of the NHRC soon after retirement in 2021. He is known for many questionable judgements in high-profile cases – Sahara-Birla diaries; the Haren Pandya murder case (mentioned earlier); the medical college bribery case; amendments to Scheduled Castes and Scheduled Tribes (Prevention of Atrocities) Act; turf war between two senior CBI officers; directed eviction of forest dwellers and tribals whose claims over land were rejected under the Forest Rights Act of 2006 – and publicly called the Prime Minister a "versatile genius" months before retirement. He also defended India's poor human rights records as NHRC chairman, instead of protecting such rights.[162] He had also delivered orders favouring the Adani group in all cases (mentioned earlier).

This is part of the story. The other is appointing lawyers who have defended Union Home Minister Amit Shah.

- Former CJI Lalit had defended Shah in the extra-judicial killings of Sohrabuddin Shaikh *et al*.[163] Justice Lalit had defended his appearances for Shah stating that it was "inconsequential as the lead counsel was Mr Ram Jethmalani".[164] He also defended the extraordinary bench he constituted (GN Saibaba case in 2022), first saying "I was not aware because the registry officials simply came to me and said that there is a bench to be formed"[165] and then, saying that he had not told the judges the "nature of the matter", "parties involved", "kind of matter" and "why the matter was to be listed the next day".[166]

- Justice Narasimha represented the Hindu parties in the Ayodhya verdict and soon thereafter was directly appointed to the highest court.

- In Gujarat, two judges who heard and dismissed the appeals by Rahul Gandhi in the defamation case in 2023 – Justice Hemant M Prachak of the Gujarat High Court was one of the lawyers defending former BJP minister Maya Kodnani, an accused in the 2002 Gujarat riot case and Judge Robin Paul Mogera of the Surat sessions court was Amit Shah's lawyer in the extra-judicial killings of Sohrabuddin *et al* until 2014 when the case was with the CBI.[167] Incidentally, the Surat judge, Judicial Magistrate Harish Hasmukhbhai Varma who sentenced Rahul Gandhi to two years' imprisonment was, promptly promoted as a district judge, which was later stayed by the apex court (along with 67 others) for multiple improprieties.

Such appointments of lawyers are not necessarily and *per se* unfair or unjust but it must be kept in mind that justice should not only be done but also *seen* to be done. Antecedents of judges do create doubts in the minds of petitioners and people.

Government and Collegium Tussle

That the government was manipulating appointments to higher judiciary became clear when then CJI Justice TS Thakur (2015-17) broke down in public, in the presence of Prime Minister Modi, in April 2016.[168] He cited high vacancies and mounting pending cases – not a new phenomenon but no CJI had cried in public in such sheer desperation. This was ominous and would become more pronounced later with judges considered inconvenient by the government being kept out of the apex court.

Justice Akil Kureshi's was a glaring case. As a judge of the Gujarat High Court (in 2010), he had sent Amit Shah, then state's Home Minister, to the CBI custody in the killings of Sohrabuddin *et al.* Justice Kureshi never made it to the Supreme Court[169] and the CBI court acquitted Shah and all other accused in the case later.[170]

A month after Justice Thakur's broke down, in May 2016, the court struck down (by 4-1 by a bench by Justice JS Khehar)[171] the National Judicial Appointments Commission (NJAC) Act of 2014, which envisaged an *equal say* of politicians and civil society in the appointment and transfer of judges in the higher courts – a reform initiated by the previous UPA government with a Bill in 2013. The court decided to continue with the "Collegium System", in which judges appoint judges though subject to the government's final nod.[172] This led to a conflict and during the tenure at has made no difference as the numerous cases cited above. But the conflict saw no Collegium recommendation for Supreme Court appointments during CJI Justice HL Dattu's 14-month tenure (2014-2015).[173] It happened again in CJI Justice Bobde's 14-month tenure because of the deadlock over Justice Kureshi's elevation since Collegium member Justice RF Nariman insisted on his inclusion. After Justice Bobde's term ended, the Collegium recommended fresh names – without Justice Kureshi's.[174]

There have been several such instances.

In January 2023 – five years after the famous revolt by the Supreme Court judges – the court broke another tradition (to stop the government's non-cooperation) and made public the government's objections to the Collegium's recommendation for appointment of lawyers Saurabh Kirpal, Somasekhar Sundaresan and R John Sathyan to high courts. These documents revealed that the Kirpal's recommendation was pending for *more five years* because the government objected to his being *gay* (now it is easy to understand why the government vigorously opposed and succeeded in blocking legalization of gay (same-sex) marriage – which the apex court (a bench led by CJI Justice Chandrachud) deferred to, refused to allow and asked *the government to make a law in October 2023*[175], knowing fully well that the government is opposed to such marriages – to the *delight* of Solicitor General Tushar Mehta[176]) and his Swiss wife being a security risk. The Collegium dismissed both (dismissing security threat by saying that the external intelligence agency RAW's communication "do not reflect any apprehension") and reiterated his appointment.[177] Similarly, the Collegium dismissed objections to Sundaresan (social media comments critical of government policies and initiatives) and Sathyan (critical comments on the Prime Minister) and reiterated their recommendations.[178] But, despite such public shaming, the government didn't appoint them.

A few months later, in April 2023, the Collegium succumbed and *recalled* its recommendation to transfer Justice S Muralidhar from Odisha High Court to Madras High Court as the government kept it pending and his retirement was just four months away.[179] Justice Muralidhar is the same Delhi High Court judge who had directed the Delhi Police to register FIRs against senior BJP leaders for provoking violence ahead of the 2020 Delhi riots (killing more than 50, mostly Muslims, and destroying houses, shops) and was transferred to Punjab and Haryana High Court hours later, at midnight (Chapter I).

In September 2023, the Supreme Court was livid but gave an ultimatum to clear the pending *70* Collegium recommendations of promotions and transfers in high courts since November 2022.[180] In October 2023, the court invoked the rarely used the "silence is approval" clause in the Memorandum of Procedure (MoP) – which governs the mechanism for appointment of judges – to recommend appointment of three high court judges to the Union Law Minister. The clause says, if state authorities don't respond to the high court chief justice's proposals for six weeks, the Union Law Minister should presume they have nothing to add and proceed.[181]

Despite all this, the government wants a representation in the Supreme Court Collegium and a direct say in the appointment to higher judiciary.[182] Law Minister Kiren Rijiju and Vice President Jagdeep Dhankar (former BJP leader) have repeatedly attacked the court and the Collegium. So much so that the Bombay Lawyers' Association even filed petitions in the apex court against both for showing scant regard and lack of faith in the apex court.[183] Weeks before he was replaced as Law Minister, Rijiju had mounted an unprecedented attack on retired Supreme Court judges in March 2023 for speaking out against the government on policies and practices by publicly declaring that "three or four" retired judges were part of an "anti-India" gang and "will have to pay a price".[184]

There is, however, no disputing that the Collegium system means judges appoint themselves; the process is opaque and arbitrary. Several retired judges have spoken against it over the years[185] while many others began supporting it given the high-handedness of the regime, including CJI Justice Chandrachud[186] but judicial reform is not in the agenda any more.

High Courts: Questionable Verdicts

It isn't just the apex court which is failing, the problem with the judiciary runs wide – particularly in high courts. Many are talking and giving outright regressive rulings. Some examples.

- At least two high courts, Delhi High Court and Karnataka High Court, have taken exceptions to critical comments on the Prime Minister. The Delhi High Court, in 2022, objected to Umar Khalid for using "jumla" (rhetoric) to describe the Prime Minister's action and reminded him of "Lakshman rekha" (limit to criticism).[187] The Karnataka High Court[188] said, in 2023, constitutional functionaries like Prime Minister "cannot be insulted for having taken a policy decision" and asked that students shouldn't be taught to criticise government policies. These high courts forgot that an elected Prime Ministers *must to be criticized in a democracy* and ignored the fact that calling Prime Ministers "chor" (thief)[189] *inside and outside the Parliament* has been part of India's political and electoral narratives for long.

- Delhi High Court, in 2022, refused probe against three BJP leaders (Anurag Thakur, Parvesh Verma and Kapil Mishra, the first continues to be a minister), for publicly provoking the Delhi riots of 2020, first saying that "if you're saying something *with a smile* then there is no criminality, if you're saying something offensively then criminality"[190] and then dismissing the plea saying that the Delhi Police found no evidence of wrong doings by those BJP leaders.[191]

- Delhi High Court, in 2023, gave a free hand to event organizers to organize events in which hate speeches are likely to be made on the plea that organizers of public meetings can't be held liable for hate speeches delivered by a participant – knowing fully well how a series of events have been organized in Delhi and all over India where hate speech and genocide calls for Muslims were given.[192]

- A Delhi High Court judge set a new record of sorts by delivering 65 verdicts on her last working day.[193]

- Gujarat High Court fined Arvind Kejriwal Rs 25,000 in April 2023 for seeking the Prime Minister's MA degree (in "Entire Political Science") for "making mockery of the very intent and purpose of the RTI Act" and quashed the *seven-year-old* order of the Central Information Commission (CIC) to provide the information.[194] This is not only a mockery of legal rights but also the electoral law which provides for disqualification in case of wrong declarations in electoral affidavits. The Prime Minister has declared he passed MA from the Gujarat University in 1983 in his electoral affidavits of 2014 and 2019.[195]

- Gujarat High Court, in June 2023, refused to allow abortion of a 17-yr-old rape survivor, asked her to go to shelter home; the same court had, at an earlier hearing of the case, had suggested to her advocate to "read the Manusmriti" (Hindu religious text, see Introduction) and remarked that girls would already have had their first child by the age of 17 before the 21st century.[196]

- Gujarat High Court, in 2023, denied bail to a Congress leader accused of making derogatory remarks on Facebook against the Prime Minister and for anti-India, pro-Pakistan comment, saying that people staying in India must be "faithful".[197]

- Allahabad High Court, in 2023, sought "kundli" (horoscope or 'birth chart' as per astrology) of the rape victim from the astrology department of Lucknow University to examine if she was a 'mangalik' (considered inauspicious for married life). This was after the accused claimed that he refused to marry after learning that she was 'mangalik'. The Supreme Court, fortunately, stayed it after CJI Justice Chandrachud intervened.[198]

- Allahabad High Court, in 2023, granted bail to a man accused of raping his live-in partner saying that "changing partners every season cannot be considered the hallmark of a healthy society" and it is "very difficult" for women coming out of live-in relationships to find a partner for marriage.[199]

- Jaipur High Court, in 2017, having recommended that the cow be declared the national animal of India and the judge went on to share a baffling view on national bird peacock outside the court. He described both the species as "pious" and added: "The peacock is a lifelong brahmachari (celibate). It never has sex with the peahen. The peahen gets pregnant after swallowing the tears of the peacock."[200]

- Allahabad High Court, in 2023, sought a ban on cow slaughter stating that cow is divine and as per 'puranas' (Hindu religious text), anyone who kills cows or allows others to kill them is deemed to rot in hell.[201] A sessions court of Tapi in Gujarat, had said in January 2023 in connection with illegal trafficking of cows that cow dung stops radiation, cow urine cures illness etc.[202]

- Gujarat High Court, in 2023, ordered that once an FIR was quashed media should *delete news articles reporting it*[203] – even after the court was told that the news of quashing the FIR was published too. The court argued that it could harm the reputation and goodwill of the person. This order ignores that investigations and trials may not always be fair (witness turning hostile is not alien to Indian courts). On July 28, 2023, a special CBI court *acquitted gangster Chhota Rajan after 26 years*[204] saying there was no evidence against him for plotting to kill trade union leader Datta Samant. Does it mean, all newspapers must remove all news items related to the killing charges against Rajan?

- Punjab and Haryana High Court, in 2023, changed the bench that took *suo motu* cognizance of the illegal demolition of Muslim houses and shops in Gurgaon's Nuh, slammed the Haryana government and described its action as "ethnic cleansing". The case was assigned to a new bench ahead of the second hearing.[205]

Once in 2022, CJI Justice Chandrachud said subordinate judiciary is scared to do justice ("a sense of fear of being targeted for granting bail in heinous cases"[206]). True, high courts and subordinate courts refuse to uphold liberty of individuals, forcing complainants to go the Supreme Court for relief even when not needed[207] – as in the case of Rahul Gandhi, Teesta Setalvad, Zubair, and BK-16 accused.

What about the Supreme Court itself? It has been dragging its feet for long to decide bail for (a) Umar Khalid (in jail without bail and trial for *over three years* – since his arrest on September 13, 2020 – for advocating peaceful protest against the CAA).[208] Having heard Khalid's case for months (the Delhi High Court rejected his bail plea in October 2022[209]), it issued fresh notice[210] to the government on October 31, 2023.

It has also dragged its feet for months[211] in the case of (b) AAP leader and former Deputy CM of Delhi (NCT) Manish Sisodia seeking interim bail to attend an ailing wife, after being in jail for *over eight months* without bail and trial since his arrest in the alleged irregularities in the liquor policy by the ED on March 9, 2023 (after the CBI arrested him on February 26, 2023 – a day before he was to present the budget. The bench of Justices Sanjiv Khanna and SVN Bhatti asked the ED to *argue its case better* having found no evidence to implicate him – rather than granting bail! It asked the ED twice in the first week of October 2023: "Where is the evidence against Sisodia? This will fall flat"; other observations/questions included, Sisodia never received fund, Sisodia is not part of the money trail, how would the ED then bring him under the money laundering law, the ED's claims about the money trail is based only on an approver's claims (the ED case is that Sisodia got illegal money from a liquor lobby).[212]

This is as clear an indication as any that the ED is on a *roving and fishing expedition* [213] selectively using a draconian law as senior Supreme Cort advocate Sanjay Hegde commented. Hegde also pointed out how it went against the apex court's observation of April 5, 2023 while *dismissing*[214] the plea of *14 Opposition* parties who had complained of misuse of the ED: "Come back with a concrete case, where there has been a specific instance or instances of the agencies being used to selectively target leaders. On the basis of the law that we have laid down, we can evolve general principles with respect to the facts of the case." But when

214 of Attack on the 'Idea of India'

the specific case came up, the court did a summersault. An aside. The Congress moved the Election Commission of India about such misuse of central agencies for years in vain (see Chapters V, X and IX.)

And then, the *very same bench* (Justices Sanjiv Khanna and SVN Bhatti) *hearing the same liquor policy case*, but hearing the bail plea in connection with the CBI's charges (bribery) denied him bail on October 30, 2023 – instead of *telling off* the ED, the CBI and the government of India for selective abuse of law to *trap* rival political leaders – that is, if the ED doesn't get him, the CBI will – as the bail order demonstrated.

The bail order said while certain aspects of the case were doubtful, it found one charge "tentatively supported" by material and evidence – that of "the excess amount of 7% commission/fee earned by the wholesale distributors" of Rs 338 crore, which constitute an offence "relating to a public servant being bribed", adding that "as per the DoE (that is, ED), these are proceeds of crime". But before denying the bail, the court didn't forget to note: "Detention or jail before being pronounced guilty of an offence should not become punishment without trial." And then added that Sisodia was free to seek bail again "in case of change in circumstances, or in case the trial is protracted and proceeds at a snail's pace in next three months".[215]

Here it needs to be pointed out that there was yet another question from the same bench (bench of Justices Sanjiv Khanna and SVN Bhatti) on the same day in the first week of October 2023 during which it had questioned the ED about evidence against Sisodia. That question was why the Aam Admi Party (AAP) had not been made a party to the money laundering case. It later clarified that it was merely posing a question and the idea was not to implicate the AAP.[216] But before the month was out, the ED summoned[217] the AAP national convenor and Delhi Chief Minister Arvind Kejriwal to appear before it – which it had not done since the case was taken up by the CBI in August 2022; the ED stepped in later (as "predicate" offence). Incidentally, Additional Solicitor General S V Raju is appearing for both the CBI and the ED.

Coming back to Sisodia, nearly nine months after his arrest, in November 2023, a Delhi court granted Sisodia just *six hours* of time to mee his wife – against a bail plea for five days. His wife suffers from multiple sclerosis for the past five years. Earlier in the year, the Delhi High Court had granted him *seven hours* to meet his wife at home but he had to return back to jail because his wife had been taken to hospital by then and his time had run out.[218]

Such is the justice delivered by the Indian judicial system in the 'New India' passing through 'Amrit Kaal' (golden time).

***

References

1   Shah AP 2022: From Lodha to Ramana, Sept 20, 2022; https://www.thehindu. com/opinion/op-ed/from-lodha-to-ramana-the-chief-justices-of-the-modi-era/ article65909662.ece

2   Shah AP 2022: The Only Institution Capable of Stopping the Death of Democracy Is Aiding it, Sept 18, 2022; https://thewire.in/law/supreme-court-rights-uapa-bjp-nda-master-of-roster

3   Mohanty P, Bhopal's Hall of Shame: The power people who 'gassed' the victims, Jun 12, 2010; https://www.governancenow.com/news/regular-story/bhopals-hall-shame

4   India Supreme Court judges: Democracy is in danger, Jan 12, 2018; https://www.bbc. com/news/world-asia-india-42660391

5   Supreme Court Dismisses Petitions Seeking Probe Into Judge Loya's Death, Apr 19, 2018; https://thewire.in/law/supreme-court-judge-loya-probe-petition-dismissed

6   Saxena Nikita, Dev Atul, Takle Niranjan 2018: Death of Judge Loya: Government letter concealed from the Supreme Court detailed purpose of Loya's visit to Nagpur and arrangements for his stay, Caravan, Jun 12, 2018; https://caravanmagazine.in/ vantage/death-of-judge-loya-government-letter-concealed-supreme-court-detailed-purpose-of-loya-visit-nagpur-arrangements

7   Why Justice Chandrachud Thinks an SIT, Not Maha Police, Should Probe Bhima Koregaon Case, Sept 28, 2018; https://thewire.in/rights/justice-chandrachud-bhima-koregaon-maharashtra-police-activists-arrests

8   Constitutionality of Aadhaar Act: Judgment Summary, Sept 26, 2018; https://www. scobserver.in/reports/constitutionality-of-aadhaar-justice-k-s-puttaswamy-union-of-india-judgment-in-plain-english/

9   Ahmed Areeb Uddin, From CAA to mob lynching: Important issues still pending before the Supreme Court in 2022, Bar and Bench, Jan 8, 2022; https://www. barandbench.com/columns/caa-mob-lynching-important-issues-pending-supreme-court-in-2022

10 Full text: Opposition lists five charges against CJI Dipak Misra as it moves impeachment motion, Apr 20, 2018; https://scroll.in/latest/876340/full-text-opposition-lists-five-charges-against-cji-dipak-misra-as-it-moves-impeachment-motion; Venkaiah Naidu Rejects Impeachment Motion Against CJI Dipak Misra, Apr 23, 2018; https://thewire.in/law/venkaiah-naidu-rejects-impeachment-motion-against-cji-dipak-misra

11 Dipak Misra was 'remote-controlled' by an external source: Justice Joseph, Dec 3, 2018; https://www.business-standard.com/article/current-affairs/dipak-misra-was-remote-controlled-by-an-external-source-justice-joseph-118120301018_1.html

12 Bhatia Gautam, A Look Back at Chief Justice Dipak Misra's Errors of Commission and Omission, Oct 3, 2018; https://thewire.in/law/supreme-court-chief-justice-dipak-misra;

13   Shyam Narayan Chouksey vs Union Of India (UOI) And Ors. on 24 July, 2003, Madhya Pradesh High Court; https://indiankanoon.org/doc/1836522/

14   Shyam Narayan Chouksey vs Union Of India on 9 January, Supreme Court, 2018; https://indiankanoon.org/doc/81046706/

15   Bhatia Gautam, The Troubling Legacy of Chief Justice Ranjan Gogoi, Mar 16, 2020; https://thewire.in/law/chief-justice-ranjan-gogoi-legacy; John Arshu, His Own Judge: Ranjan Gogoi's desperate bid to set the record straight, Caravan, Mar 1, 2022; https://caravanmagazine.in/books/former-cji-ranjan-gogoi-autobiography

16   Bhatia Gautam, Mouse Under the Throne: The Judicial Legacy of Sharad A Bobde, Apr 24, 2021; https://thewire.in/law/mouse-under-the-throne-the-judicial-legacy-of-sharad-a-bobde

17   Supreme Court suspends implementation of three farm laws, forms committee, Jan 13, 2021; https://economictimes.indiatimes.com/news/politics-and-nation/supreme-court-suspends-implementation-of-three-farm-laws-forms-committee/articleshow/80226707.cms?from=mdr

18   Arnab Goswami gets bail from Supreme Court in abetment to suicide case, Nov 11, 2020; https://www.indiatoday.in/india/story/supreme-court-grants-bail-to-arnab-goswami-1740103-2020-11-11

19   Trivedi Divya, Supreme Court's contrasting views on petitions under Article 32 raise the hackles of experts, Dec 18, 2020; https://frontline.thehindu.com/the-nation/article-32-and-the-supreme-court-contrasting-views-on-it-raises-legal-experts-hackles/article33213187.ece

20   58 Habeas Corpus petitions pending before Supreme Court, oldest is from 2005: RTI response, Bar and Bench, Feb 22, 2021; https://www.barandbench.com/news/litigation/58-habeas-corpus-petitions-pending-before-supreme-court-oldest-2005-rti

21   Sachdev Vakasha, What is Article 32 & Can SC 'Discourage' Petitions Under It? Nov 24, 2020; https://www.thequint.com/explainers/article-32-constitution-of-india-why-does-cji-want-to-discourage-supreme-court-jurisprudence

22   Fertilizer Corporation Kamgar Union, Sindri & Ors Vs. Union of India & Ors, Supreme Court, 1980; https://www.latestlaws.com/latest-caselaw/1980/november/1980-latest-caselaw-220-sc/

23   Justice KS Puttaswamy (retd) and another vs Union of India And Others, Supreme Court, August 24, 2017; https://main.sci.gov.in/supremecourt/2012/35071/35071_2012_Judgement_24-Aug-2017.pdf /

24   Tantray Shahid and Singh Amrita, My heart is my first court, there I am innocent: Siddique Kappan, Feb 17, 2023; https://caravanmagazine.in/interview/journalist-siddique-kappan-hathras-uapa-up-police

25   Court sentences one to life term in Hathras case; 3 accused acquitted, Mar 3, 3023; https://www.hindustantimes.com/india-news/court-sentences-one-to-life-term-in-hathras-case-3-accused-acquitted-101677783457238.html

26 Varadarajan Siddharth, The Supreme Court on Pegasus: Two Short Steps Away From the Truth, Aug 26, 2022; https://thewire.in/law/pegasus-spyware-supreme-court-truth

27 Supreme Court agrees to hear case against electoral bonds, Apr 6, 2022; https://economictimes.indiatimes.com/news/india/supreme-court-agrees-to-hear-case-against-electoral-bonds/articleshow/90671587.cms?utm_source=contentofinterest&utm_medium=text&utm_campaign=cppst

28 Supreme Court cancels Ashish Mishra's bail in Lakhimpur Kheri case, Apr 18, 2022; https://www.tribuneindia.com/news/nation/sc-cancels-bail-granted-to-ashish-mishra-in-lakhimpur-kheri-violence-case-387363

29 Editorial: Supreme Court's red flagging of sealed cover jurisprudence is welcome. It must now decisively curtail this practice, Mar 17, 2022; https://indianexpress.com/article/opinion/editorials/supreme-courts-red-flagging-of-sealed-cover-jurisprudence-is-welcome-7823350/

30 Anand Utkarsh, States cannot withdraw cases against MPs, MLAs without HC nod: SC, Aug 11, 2021; https://www.hindustantimes.com/india-news/states-cannot-withdraw-cases-against-mps-mlas-without-hcnodsc-101628582060399.html

31 Das Saurav, Lots Of Speeches, But No Action In Cases Of National Importance: The Legacy of Chief Justice Ramana, Aug 24, 2022; https://article-14.com/post/lots-of-speeches-but-no-action-in-cases-of-national-importance-the-legacy-of-chief-justice-ramana-63058720be481

32 Mehta Pratap Bhanu, SC was never perfect, but the signs are that it is slipping into judicial barbarism, Indian Express, Nov 18, 2020; https://indianexpress.com/article/opinion/columns/supreme-court-arnab-goswami-bail-article-32-pratap-bhanu-mehta-7055067/

33 Mehta Pratap Bhanu, By upholding PMLA, SC puts its stamp on Kafka's law, Indian Express, Jul 29. 2022; https://indianexpress.com/article/opinion/columns/pratap-bhanu-mehta-by-upholding-pmla-sc-puts-its-stamp-on-kafkas-law-8057249/

34 Pro-BJP accounts lead trolling of CJI Chandrachud, researchers show, May 30, 2023; https://scroll.in/article/1050055/pro-bjp-accounts-lead-social-media-attacks-on-cji-chandrachud-researchers-show#:~:text=Such%20efforts%20were%20evident%20in,to%20object%20to%20his%20nomination.

35 Jaffrelot Christophe, Modi's India: Hindu Nationalism and the Rise of Ethnic Democracy, pages 278-298, Princeton University Press, Aug 2021, https://www.amazon.in/Modis-India-Nationalism-Ethnic-Democracy/dp/0691206805

36 An overworked Chief Justice TS Thakur breaks down in front of Modi, Apr 24, 2016; http://timesofindia.indiatimes.com/articleshow/51964732.cms?utm_source=contentofinterest&utm_medium=text&utm_campaign=cppst

37 Sundar Nandini, The Supreme Court in Modi's India, abstract, UC Berkley, 2023; https://escholarship.org/uc/item/313700c7

38   Jaising Indira, Amit Shah and the Toxic Consequences of 'Clean Chit' Jurisprudence, The Wire, Aug 3, 2016; https://thewire.in/politics/amit-shah-toxic-consequences-clean-chit-jurisprudence

39   Simha Vijay, Birla-Sahara case: Only an investigation can settle the unanswered questions, Scroll, Mar 17, 2017; https://scroll.in/article/831125/birla-sahara-case-only-an-investigation-can-settle-unanswered-questions

40   Vineet Narain & Others vs Union Of India & Another on 18 December, 1997, Supreme Court; https://indiankanoon.org/doc/1203995/

41   'Rafale Papers': France opens judicial probe into fighter deal with India, new revelations emerge, Jul 2, 2021; https://www.mediapart.fr/en/journal/international/020721/rafale-papers-france-opens-judicial-probe-fighter-deal-india-new-revelations-emerge; 'Rafale Papers': the explosive documents in France-India jets deal, Apr 8, 2021; https://www.mediapart.fr/en/journal/international/080421/rafale-papers-explosive-documents-france-india-jets-deal & Sale of French Rafale jet fighters to India: how a state scandal was buried, April 4, 2021; https://www.mediapart.fr/en/journal/international/040421/sale-french-rafale-jet-fighters-india-how-state-scandal-was-buried?utm_source=facebook&utm_medium=social&utm_campaign=Sharing&xtor=CS3-66

42   Gunasekar Arvind and Jain Srinivasan, New Rafale Twist: Papers Show Agencies Didn't Act On Alleged Kickbacks, Nov 9, 2021; https://www.ndtv.com/india-news/new-rafale-twist-papers-show-agencies-didnt-act-on-alleged-kickbacks-2604385

43   Philippin Tann, Rafale Papers: how Indian tycoon sought help of Macron and finance minister over tax bill, Jul 12, 2023; https://www.mediapart.fr/en/journal/international/120723/rafale-papers-how-indian-tycoon-sought-help-macron-and-finance-minister-over-tax-bill

44   Ram N, Government waived anti-corruption clauses in Rafale deal, Feb 11, 2019; https://www.thehindu.com/news/national/government-waived-anti-corruption-clauses-in-rafale-deal/article61543440.ece

45   MS Nileena, The Gupta Papers: How the Modi government is covering up two decades of defence corruption to save the Rafale deal, Nov 2, 2023; https://caravanmagazine.in/reportage/gupta-papers-rafale-deal-agusta-westland-sushen-gupta

46   Bhatia Gautam, The Troubling Legacy of Chief Justice Ranjan Gogoi, Mar 16, 2020; https://thewire.in/law/chief-justice-ranjan-gogoi-legacy

47   Bhatia Gautam, Proportionality, Sealed Covers and the Supreme Court's Media One Judgment, Apr 6, 2023; https://thewire.in/law/supreme-court-media-one-sealed-cover-analysis

48   Rafale verdict: Government asks SC to correct error, says court misinterpreted wording, Dec 16, 2018; https://www.hindustantimes.com/india-news/rafale-verdict-government-files-application-to-correct-factual-error/story-p8bb1oGyjrlaj13KYuoyEK.html

49   Bal Hartosh Singh, Payload: PM Modi cleared Rafale deal at over €2.5 billion higher than first benchmark price, Dec 14, 2018; https://caravanmagazine.in/government/rafale-modi-approved-price-billions-higher-benchmark

50   Performance Audit Report on Capital Acquisition in Indian Air Force, Report No. 3 of 2019, Comptroller and Auditor General of India, 2019; https://www.dropbox.com/s/7aipjissy4eb1yn/CAG%202019%20Rafale%20report.pdf?dl=0

51   Supreme Court scraps UPA's 'illegal' 2G sale, Feb 2, 2012; https://www.thehindu.com/news/national/supreme-court-scraps-upas-illegal-2g-sale/article2853159.ece

52   Supreme Court quashes allocation of 214 coal blocks, Sept 24, 2014; https://www.thehindu.com/news/national/supreme-court-quashes-allocation-of-all-but-four-of-218-coal-blocks/article6441855.ece

53   Vikram Kumar, CAGed? Top audit body's reports on Centre's money management down by 75 per cent, March 7, 2021: https://www.newindianexpress.com/thesundaystandard/2021/mar/07/caged-top-audit-bodys-reports-on-centres-money-management-down-by-75-per-cent-2273200.html

54   Chishti Seema, Precipitous Fall in Press Freedom, Economic and Political eekly, Vol 57, May 21, 2022; https://www.epw.in/journal/2022/21/comment/precipitous-fall-press-freedom.html

55   Editorial: Supreme Court's red flagging of sealed cover jurisprudence is welcome. It must now decisively curtail this practice, Mar 17, 2022; https://indianexpress.com/article/opinion/editorials/supreme-courts-red-flagging-of-sealed-cover-jurisprudence-is-welcome-7823350/

56   Adani-Hindenburg row: SC no to govt's sealed cover names for panel, Feb 17, 2023; https://www.business-standard.com/article/current-affairs/adani-row-sc-refuses-to-accept-centre-s-suggestion-to-form-expert-panel-123021700892_1.html

57   Vishal Tiwari vs Union of India and others, Supreme Court, Mar 2, 2023; https://main.sci.gov.in/supremecourt/2023/5354/5354_2023_1_1501_42639_Judgement_02-Mar-2023.pdf

58   Mahapatra Dhananjay, Give report on arms recovery in sealed cover, SC tells Manipur, Sept 7, 2023; http://timesofindia.indiatimes.com/articleshow/103444111.cms?from=mdr&utm_source=contentofinterest&utm_medium=text&utm_campaign=cppst

59   Mohanty P, Why demonetisation verdict raises more questions than answers, Jan 4, 2023; https://www.fortuneindia.com/opinion/why-demonetisation-verdict-raises-more-questions-answers/111008

60   Dalal Sucheta, Adani Stock Saga: Clean Chit by SC Committee Raises Questions & Creates a Worrying New Template for Investigation, May 23, 2023; https://www.moneylife.in/article/adani-stock-saga-clean-chit-by-sc-committee-raises-questions-and-creates-a-worrying-new-template-for-investigation/70867.html?utm_source=substack&utm_medium=email

61   Das Saurav 2023: Why Supreme Court Decision To Probe The Adani-Hindenburg Matter Is Good News For The Govt, Mar 6, 2023; https://article-14.com/post/why-supreme-court-decision-to-probe-the-adani-hindenburg-matter-is-good-news-for-the-govt-64054c5a44b8ff

62   Menon Aditya, All 4 Members of SC Appointed Committee Support Govt's Farm Laws, Jan 12, 2021; https://www.thequint.com/news/politics/supreme-court-committee-members-support-farm-laws-ashok-gulati-anil-ghanwat

63   G Ananthakrishnan, Supreme Court intervenes in Manipur, names probe monitor, panel of ex-judges, Aug 8, 2023; https://indianexpress.com/article/india/manipur-violence-sc-commences-hearing-state-proposes-district-level-sit-probe-cases-8880736/

64   Mahapatra Dhanjay, No Manipuri among 12 experts to help panel appointed by SC, Aug 23, 2023; https://timesofindia.indiatimes.com/india/no-manipuri-among-12-experts-to-help-panel-appointed-by-sc/articleshow/102959872.cms?from=mdr

65   Citing lack of intent, SIT lets Modi off riots hook, Feb 10, 2012; https://www.thehindu.com/news/national/citing-lack-of-intent-sit-lets-modi-off-riots-hook/article2876151.ece

66   Zahira Habibullah H Sheikh vs State of Gujarat, Supreme Court, 2004; https://indiankanoon.org/doc/105430/

67   Former CBI Director RK Raghavan Named Indian Envoy to Cyprus, Aug 31, 2017;https://www.thequint.com/news/india/rk-raghavan-made-indian-high-commissioner-to-cyprus

68   Cyprus, corporate tax haven index rank 14; Tax Justice Network; https://taxjustice.net/country-profiles/cyprus/

69   Quarterly fact sheet on FDI inflow (from Apr 2000 to June 2023), Department for Promotion of Industry and Internal Trade; https://dpiit.gov.in/sites/default/files/FDI_factsheet_June_23.pdf

70   PM-CARES Fund: SC refuses to entertain plea against HC order, Mar 26, 2022; https://indianexpress.com/article/india/pm-cares-fund-sc-refuses-to-entertain-plea-against-hc-order-7836785/

71   Ahmed Areeb Uddin 2022: From CAA to mob lynching: Important issues still pending before the Supreme Court in 2022, Bar and Bench, Jan 8, 2022; https://www.barandbench.com/columns/caa-mob-lynching-important-issues-pending-supreme-court-in-2022

72   Jalihal Shreegireesh, Agarwal Poonam, Jha Somesh 2022: Debunking a 'Sealed' Myth: Only 17 Political Parties Of 105 In EC List Got Electoral Bonds, Article14, Jun 6, 2022; https://article-14.com/post/debunking-a-sealed-myth-only-17-political-parties-of-105-in-ec-list-got-electoral-bonds-629d7a3bd1d5a

73   Ahmed Areeb Uddin 2022: From CAA to mob lynching: Important issues still pending before the Supreme Court in 2022, Bar and Bench, Jan 8, 2022; https://www.

barandbench.com/columns/caa-mob-lynching-important-issues-pending-supreme-court-in-2022

74 Supreme Court suspends implementation of three farm laws, forms committee, Jan 13, 2021; https://economictimes.indiatimes.com/news/politics-and-nation/supreme-court-suspends-implementation-of-three-farm-laws-forms-committee/articleshow/80226707.cms?utm_source=contentofinterest&utm_medium=text&utm_campaign=cppst

75 Ahmed Areeb Uddin 2022: From CAA to mob lynching: Important issues still pending before the Supreme Court in 2022, Bar and Bench, Jan 8, 2022; https://www.barandbench.com/columns/caa-mob-lynching-important-issues-pending-supreme-court-in-2022

76 Supreme Court agrees to examine validity of practice of talaq-e-hasan, May 5, 2023; http://timesofindia.indiatimes.com/articleshow/99996805.cms?from=mdr&utm_source=contentofinterest&utm_medium=text&utm_campaign=cppst

77 Sebastian Sheryl, Supreme Court To Hear Batch Of Petitions Challenging Triple Talaq Law In November 2023, Apr 24, 2023; https://www.livelaw.in/supreme-court/supreme-court-triple-talaq-muslim-women-protection-of-rights-on-marriage-act-227052

78 Sabarimala case: Supreme Court upholds referring religious questions to larger Bench, frames 7 questions of law, Feb 10, 2010; https://www.thehindu.com/news/national/sabarimala-case-supreme-court-upholds-referring-religious-questions-to-larger-bench-frames-7-questions-of-law/article61633368.ece

79 Aishat Shifa vs state of Karnataka, Supreme Court, Oct 13, 2022; https://main.sci.gov.in/supremecourt/2022/8344/8344_2022_6_1501_38867_Judgement_13-Oct-2022.pdf

80 Ahmed Areeb Uddin 2022: From CAA to mob lynching: Important issues still pending before the Supreme Court in 2022, Bar and Bench, Jan 8, 2022; https://www.barandbench.com/columns/caa-mob-lynching-important-issues-pending-supreme-court-in-2022

81 Bhatnagar Gaurav Vivek, Matter Being 'Sub Judice' Not Grounds for Denying Information Under RTI: CIC, Jun 11, 2021; https://thewire.in/government/matter-being-sub-judice-not-grounds-for-denying-information-under-rti-cic

82 Centre returns anti-lynching bills of Rajasthan, Manipur; seeks clarification, PTI, 15 March, 2022; https://theprint.in/india/centre-returns-anti-lynching-bills-of-rajasthan-manipur-seeks-clarification/874676/; Singh Vijaita, Anti-mob lynching bills passed by 4 Assemblies at various levels of non-implementation, Feb 15, 2022; https://www.thehindu.com/news/national/anti-mob-lynching-bills-passed-by-4-assemblies-at-various-levels-of-non-implementation/article65052872.ece

83 Kant Vishal, Jharkhand governor returns anti-lynching bill, asks state to revisit definition of 'mob', Mar 18, 2022; https://www.hindustantimes.com/india-news/jharkhand-guv-returns-anti-lynching-bill-asks-state-to-revisit-definition-of-mob-101647542130365.html

84   Bhatia Gautam 2022: Demolitions: In Ignoring Open Illegality, is the Supreme Court Becoming an Orwellian Court? The Wire, Jul 14, 2022; https://thewire.in/law/is-the-supreme-court-on-the-way-to-becoming-george-orwells-court

85   Supreme Court rejects Kejriwal's plea in PM Modi degree defamation case, PTI, Aug 25, 2023; https://www.hindustantimes.com/india-news/supreme-court-rejects-kejriwals-plea-in-pm-modi-degree-defamation-case-101692963168758.html;   PM Modi degree row: Gujarat court refuses to quash summons against Arvind Kejriwal, Sanjay Singh, PTI, Sept 15, 2023; https://www.newindianexpress.com/nation/2023/sep/15/pm-modi-degree-row-gujarat-court-refuses-to-quash-summons-against-arvind-kejriwal-sanjay-singh-2614915.html;   Thaplial Nupur, Delhi High Court Refuses To Advance Hearing Of RTI Case On PM Modi's BA Degree, JUl 10, 2023; https://www.livelaw.in/high-court/delhi-high-court/delhi-high-court-2017-pm-modi-ba-degree-case-232320

86   Coram wise pending cases, National Judicial Data Grid, Supreme Court of India, accessed on September 17, 2023, https://njdg.ecourts.gov.in/scnjdg/

87   Full text: Opposition lists five charges against CJI Dipak Misra as it moves impeachment motion, Apr 20, 2018; https://scroll.in/latest/876340/full-text-opposition-lists-five-charges-against-cji-dipak-misra-as-it-moves-impeachment-motion

88   SC refuses to order CBI probe into death of ex-Arunachal CM Kalikho Pul, Apr 29, 2021; https://www.thehindu.com/news/national/sc-refuses-to-consider-plea-seeking-cbi-probe-into-death-arunachal-pradesh-ex-cm-kalikho-pul/article34440243.ece

89   John Arshu 2022: His Own Judge: Ranjan Gogoi's desperate bid to set the record straight, Caravan, Mar 1, 2022; https://caravanmagazine.in/books/former-cji-ranjan-gogoi-autobiography

90   Zakia Ahsan Jafri vs State of Gujarat and another, Supreme Court, Jun 24, 2022; https://main.sci.gov.in/supremecourt/2018/34207/34207_2018_3_1502_36189_Judgement_24-Jun-2022.pdf

91   Gurmat Sabah, Absence of Notice by SC Violates Legal Norms: Legal Experts on Teesta Setalvad, Sreekumar Arrests, The Wire, Jun 28, 2022; https://thewire.in/law/supreme-court-notice-teesta-sreekumar

92   Zahira Habibullah H Sheikh vs State of Gujarat, Supreme Court, 2004; https://indiankanoon.org/doc/105430/

93   Jha Vaibhav, New SIT to probe Sreekumar, Setalvad, Bhatt for criminal conspiracy, forgery, Jun 27, 2022; https://indianexpress.com/article/cities/ahmedabad/new-sit-probe-sreekumar-setalvad-bhatt-criminal-conspiracy-forgery-7992667/

94   Rajagopal Krishnadas, Activist Teesta Setalvad to continue on bail, says Supreme Court, Jul 20, 2023; https://www.thehindu.com/news/national/supreme-court-grants-bail-to-activist-teesta-setalvad/article67097554.ece

95   Ray Ashis, Exclusive: Vajpayee Govt Didn't Object to UK Report That 2002 Riots Were 'Pre-Planned', Cops 'Told Not to Act', Sept 18, 2023; https://thewire.in/

diplomacy/exclusive-vajpayee-govt-didnt-object-to-uk-report-that-2002-riots-were-pre-planned-cops-told-not-to-act; A Midnight Meeting On Feb 27 And A Murdered Minister, Feb 5, 2022; https://www.outlookindia.com/magazine/story/a-midnight-meeting-on-feb-27-and-a-murdered-minister/235982

96   CBI and another vs Mohd Parvez Abdul Kayuum etc., Supreme Court, Jul 5, 2019; https://main.sci.gov.in/supremecourt/2011/37430/37430_2011_4_1501_14733_Judgement_05-Jul-2019.pdf; Jose Vinod K, Narendra Modi's shadow lies all over the Haren Pandya case, Jul 6, 2019; https://caravanmagazine.in/politics/haren-pandya-narendra-modi-murder-case-supreme-court; Ayyub Rana, An appeal to the Supreme Court after its Haren Pandya judgment: Examine the "Gujarat Files" tapes as evidence, Jul 11, 2019; https://caravanmagazine.in/law/appeal-supreme-court-haren-pandya-examine-gujarat-files-rana-ayyub-evidence?fbclid=IwAR2KH8Bs7b7ePBAkPJn_WwsDpeSyYbYrRIR3g-2CkNgaYeLg--090aZ0zKo; Mahaprashasta Ajoy A, The Story of Azam Khan, Endangered Keeper of Deadly Secrets from Haren Pandya to Sohrabuddin, Nov 14, 2018; https://thewire.in/rights/azam-khan-witness-haren-pandya-sohrabuddin-sheikh-vanzara; DG Vanzara gave contract to Sohrabuddin to kill ex-minister Haren Pandya: Witness, Nov 4, 2018; https://www.asianage.com/india/all-india/041118/dg-vanzara-gave-contract-to-sohrabuddin-to-kill-ex-minister-haren-pandya-witness.html?fbclid=IwAR23-OgQbrzUw-5qqhc4UD7OIAwxCZc3eMHWlLF3bIg-t3GNExYaA5k8FGY

97   CBI and another vs Mohd Parvez Abdul Kayuum etc., Supreme Court, Jul 5, 2019; https://main.sci.gov.in/supremecourt/2011/37430/37430_2011_4_1501_14733_Judgement_05-Jul-2019.pdf; Jha Prem Shankar, The Shadow of Haren Pandya's Case Lies Long Over Justice Arun Mishra, Aug 30, 2020; https://m.thewire.in/article/law/haren-pandya-case-justice-arun-mishra/amp?__twitter_impression=true

98   Himanshu Kumar and others vs State of Chhattisgarh and others, Supreme Court order of Jul 14, 2022; https://main.sci.gov.in/supremecourt/2009/32715/32715_2009_3_1501_36329_Judgement_14-Jul-2022.pdf

99   Bhatia Gautam 2022: The Executive('s) Court: On the Legacy of Justice A.M. Khanwilkar, The Wire, Jul 29, 2022; https://thewire.in/law/justice-khanwilkar-teesta-setalvad-watali-fcra-uapa; Bhatia Gautam 2022: Demolitions: In Ignoring Open Illegality, is the Supreme Court Becoming an Orwellian Court? The Wire, Jul 14, 2022; https://thewire.in/law/is-the-supreme-court-on-the-way-to-becoming-george-orwells-court

100   Suhas Palshikar on wrestlers' protest: The Indian system failed these young women, and society failed itself, Jun 6, 2023; https://indianexpress.com/article/opinion/columns/suhas-palshikar-on-wrestlers-protest-the-indian-system-failed-these-young-women-and-society-failed-itself-8647274/

101   Theocratic Judges Who Find Source Of Law In Religion Than Constitution Have Sharply Increased: Dr Mohan Gopal, 18 Feb 2023; https://www.livelaw.in/top-stories/theocratic-judges-who-find-source-of-law-in-religion-than-constitution-have-sharply-increased-dr-mohan-gopal-221925

102   Bhagavad Gita is not a religious book like the Bible and Quran, says Karnataka

education minister, Apr 28, 2022; https://scroll.in/latest/1022813/bhagavad-gita-is-not-a-religious-book-like-the-bible-and-quran-says-karnataka-education-minister

103 Aishat Shifa vs state of Karnataka, Supreme Court, Oct 13, 2022; https://main.sci.gov.in/supremecourt/2022/8344/8344_2022_6_1501_38867_Judgement_13-Oct-2022.pdf

104 Pande Mrinal 2015: What Lies Behind the Hairsplitting Over Dharma, Panth and Secularism, Nov 27, 2015; https://thewire.in/politics/what-lies-behind-the-hairsplitting-over-dharma-panth-and-secularism

105 Chief Justice Says Sexual Harassment Charge Part of 'Bigger Plot' to 'Deactivate' Him, Apr 20, 2019; https://thewire.in/law/supreme-court-special-sitting-cji-ranjan-gogoi-allegations

106 Dasgupta Abir, Thakurta Paranjoy Guha 2020: Justice Arun Mishra's Final 'Gift' of Rs 8,000 Crore to Adani, Sept 7, 2020; https://www.newsclick.in/Justice-Arun-Mishra%27s-Final-Gift-of-8000-Crore-to-Adani

107 Dave Dushyant 2019: Why Were Adani's Cases Listed and Heard by Justice Arun Mishra in a Tearing Hurry?, Aug 16, 2019; https://thewire.in/law/why-were-adanis-cases-listed-and-heard-by-justice-arun-mishra-in-a-tearing-hurry

108 Ritu Chhanaria vs Union of India and others, Supreme Court, Apr 26, 2023; https://main.sci.gov.in/supremecourt/2023/6873/6873_2023_13_1501_44023_Judgement_26-Apr-2023.pdf

109 Qamar Ghani Usmani vs The State of Gujarat, Supreme Court, Apr 10, 2023; https://main.sci.gov.in/supremecourt/2022/33056/33056_2022_4_1509_43314_Judgement_10-Apr-2023.pdf

110 SLP: Directorate of Enforcement vs Manpreet Singh Talwar, May 1, 2023; https://main.sci.gov.in/supremecourt/2023/18272/18272_2023_1_808_44060_Order_01-May-2023.pdf

111 https://main.sci.gov.in/supremecourt/2023/18272/18272_2023_1_49_44212_Order_04-May-2023.pdf

112 Subhash Desai vs Principal Secretary, Governor of Maharashtra & Ors., Supreme Court, May 11, 2023; https://main.sci.gov.in/supremecourt/2022/20234/20234_2022_1_1502_44512_Judgement_11-May-2023.pdf

113 Express View: Supreme Court slips, lowers its bar by asking an MP to file a loyalty affidavit, Sept 7, 2023; https://indianexpress.com/article/opinion/editorials/express-view-on-supreme-court-demanding-akbar-lone-affidavit-with-due-respect-8928020/

114 CBI vs RR Kishore, Supreme Court, Sept 11, 2023; https://main.sci.gov.in/supremecourt/2007/415/415_2007_2_1501_46897_Judgement_11-Sep-2023.pdf

115 Mohanty P, Agenda for new government: Insulating anti-corruption architecture, Jun 14, 2019; https://www.indiatoday.in/india/story/agenda-for-next-government-insulating-anti-corruption-architecture-1542034-2019-06-04

116   Sheriff M Kaunain, Govt says sedition out, new section gets it in, with wider ambit, Aug 12, 2023; https://indianexpress.com/article/india/govt-says-sedition-out-new-section-gets-it-in-with-wider-ambit-8888628/;   https://prsindia.org/files/bills_acts/bills_parliament/2023/Bharatiya_Nyaya_Sanhita,_2023.pdf

117   Rangarajan Lubhyathi, Home Minister Amit Shah Says Sedition Is Dead. But Its Replacement Is More Fearsome Than The Colonial Law Ever Was, Aug 14, 2023; https://article-14.com/post/home-minister-amit-shah-says-sedition-is-dead-but-its-replacement-is-more-fearsome-than-the-colonial-law-ever-was-64d99ff8dc0d8

118   M Siddiq versus Mahant Suresh Das & Ors, Supreme Court, Nov 9, 2019; https://www.sci.gov.in/pdf/JUD_2.pdf

119   Mohanty P 2019: Ayodhya Verdict I: Ayodhya Verdict: Why it would worry us for years to come, Business Today, Nov 15, 2019; https://www.businesstoday.in/latest/economy-politics/story/ayodhya-verdict-supreme-court-ram-temple-why-it-would-worry-us-for-years-to-come-hindus-muslims-238872-2019-11-15; Ayodhya Verdict II: Does the evidence add up to ownership of the disputed land to the Hindus?; https://www.businesstoday.in/latest/economy-politics/story/ayodhya-verdict-does-the-evidence-add-up-to-ownership-of-the-disputed-land-to-the-hindus-and-the-five-acre-land-to-muslims-238831-2019-11-16 & Ayodhya Verdict III: SC judgement raises more questions than it answers; https://www.businesstoday.in/latest/economy-politics/story/ayodhya-verdict-sc-supreme-court-judgement-raises-more-questions-than-answers-babri-masjid-ram-janmabhoomi-title-dispute-238811-2019-11-17

120   Mahapatra Dhanajay, Author of Ayodhya verdict not named, but it bears Chandrachud's imprint, Nov 10, 2019; https://timesofindia.indiatimes.com/india/author-of-ayodhya-verdict-not-named-but-it-bears-chandrachuds-imprint/articleshow/71989381.cms

121   President Kovind donates Rs 5 lakh for Ram temple construction as fund-raising drive kicks off, Jan 15, 2021; https://indianexpress.com/article/india/president-kovind-donates-rs-5-lakh-for-ram-temple-construction-7147458/

122   Dr M Ismail Faruqui Etc, Mohd vs Union Of India And Others on 24 October, 1994; https://indiankanoon.org/doc/37494799/

123   Ascertaining of religious character of place of worship not barred under 1991 law: SC, May 20, 2022; https://theprint.in/india/ascertaining-of-religious-character-of-place-of-worship-not-barred-under-1991-law-sc/964608/

124   Anand Utkarsh 2022: How SC judges hearing Gyanvapi case were associated with Babri matter, Hindustan Times, May 17, 2022; https://www.hindustantimes.com/india-news/how-sc-judges-hearing-gyanvapi-case-were-associated-with-babri-matter-101652756376204.html

125   Ahmed Areeb Uddin, Gyanvapi Mosque & Similar Litigation Illegal Under A 31-Year-Old Law, Yet Courts Keep Hearing Cases, May 19, 2022; https://article-14.com/post/gyanvapi-mosque-similar-litigation-illegal-under-a-31-year-old-law-yet-courts-keep-hearing-cases-628574e5b0b3f

126 Places of Worship Act: SC refuses fresh pleas, allows intervention applications, Jul 30, 2022; https://indianexpress.com/article/india/places-of-worship-act-sc-refuses-fresh-pleas-allows-intervention-applications-8060012/

127 Setalvad Teesta, 'Kashi-Mathura Baaqi Hain': Why the Ayodhya Verdict Won't Offer Any Respite From Saffron Hatred, Oct 20, 2019; https://thewire.in/communalism/ kashi-mathura-baaki-hain-why-the-ayodhya-verdict-wont-offer-any-respite-from-saffron-hatred

128 Jha Dhirendra, Near identical petitions in the Gyanvapi case follow the pattern of Ayodhya suits, Sept 28, 2022; https://caravanmagazine.in/commentary/petitions-in-the-gyanvapi-case-follow-the-pattern-of-ayodhya-suits

129 Better if high court adjudicates Krishna Janmabhoomi case: Supreme Court, Jul 22, 2023; http://timesofindia.indiatimes.com/articleshow/102026881.cms?from=mdr&utm_ source=contentofinterest&utm_medium=text&utm_campaign=cppst

130 Mittal Tusha 2023: The demolition of dissent in India, Apr 14, 2023; https://www. codastory.com/authoritarian-tech/india-bulldozers-muslim-neighborhoods/

131 Bhatia Gautam, Demolitions 2022: In Ignoring Open Illegality, is the Supreme Court Becoming an Orwellian Court? Jul 14, 2022; https://thewire.in/law/is-the-supreme-court-on-the-way-to-becoming-george-orwells-court

132 Take suo motu action against hate speeches, register cases immediately: Supreme Court, Oct 21, 2022; https://www.telegraphindia.com/india/take-suo-motu-action-against-hate-speeches-register-cases-immediately-supreme-court/cid/1893465

133 In Supreme Court, Gujarat Refuses To Share Details Of Alleged Fake Encounters, Apr 1, 2023; https://www.ndtv.com/india-news/in-supreme-court-gujarat-refuses-to-share-details-of-alleged-fake-encounters-3936823

134 179 killed in over 10,000 encounters in UP in 6 years, Mar 16, 2023; https:// economictimes.indiatimes.com/news/india/179-killed-in-over-10000-encounters-in-up-in-6-years/articleshow/98711064.cms?utm_source=contentofinterest&utm_ medium=text&utm_campaign=cppst

135 Patel Aakar 2021: Price of Modi Years, Westland Publications, 2021; https://www. amazon.in/Price-Modi-Years-Aakar-Patel/dp/9391234224

136 Ramesh Prabhoo case 1995: Dr. Ramesh Yeshwant Prabhoo vs Shri Prabhakar Kashinath Kunte & others, Supreme Court, Dec 11, 1995; https://indiankanoon.org/ doc/925631/

137 Supreme Court says it won't reconsider 1995 judgment defining Hindutva as way of life, Oct 25, 2016; http://timesofindia.indiatimes.com/articleshow/55045616. cms?utm_source=contentofinterest&utm_medium=text&utm_campaign=cppst

138 Chishti Seema, Why, 22 years on, the SC's 'Hindutva judgment' remains elephant in room, Jan 3, 2017; https://indianexpress.com/article/explained/gujarat-riot-nhrc-religion-elections-vote-bank-supreme-court-why-22-years-on-the-scs-hindutva-judgment-remains-elephant-in-room-4456258/

139   Patel Aakar, Our Hindu Rashtra: What It Is. How We Got Here, Ch 9, Dec 2020; https://www.amazon.in/Our-Hindu-Rashtra-What/dp/9389648890

140   Ashraf Ajaz, Why Muslims feel let down by Supreme Court, Aug 14, 2023; https://www.mid-day.com/news/opinion/article/why-muslims-feel-let-down-by-supreme-court-23303489

141   Janhit Abhiyan vs Union of India, Supreme Court, Nov 7, 2022; https://www.scobserver.in/wp-content/uploads/2021/10/EWS-Reservations-Judgment.pdf

142   Indra Sawhney Etc. Etc vs Union Of India And Others, Supreme Court, Nov 6, 1992; https://indiankanoon.org/doc/1363234/

143   Mohanty P, EWS Quota: Can targeting 90% of Indians be called reservation, affirmative action or positive discrimination? Nov 10, 2022; https://www.cenfa.org/ews-quota-10/

144   Vivek Narayan Sharma vs Union of India and others, Supreme Court, Jan 2, 2023; https://main.sci.gov.in/supremecourt/2016/37662/37662_2016_3_1501_40708_Judgement_02-Jan-2023.pdf

145   Mohanty P, Why demonetisation verdict raises more questions than answers, Jan 4, 2023; https://www.fortuneindia.com/opinion/why-demonetisation-verdict-raises-more-questions-answers/111008

146   ₹2000 Denomination Banknotes – Withdrawal from Circulation; Will continue as Legal Tender, RBI, May 19, 2023; https://www.rbi.org.in/Scripts/BS_PressReleaseDisplay.aspx?prid=55707

147   Mohanty P, Are top banks getting their economics wrong? Jun 28, 2023; https://www.fortuneindia.com/opinion/are-top-banks-getting-their-economics-wrong/113197; Kumar Arun, Rs 2,000 Banknotes and the Mysteries of This Mini-Demonetisation, May 20, 2023; https://thewire.in/economy/rs-2000-rbi-demonetisation

148   Mohanty P, 'Agnipath' ground realities harsh and unforgiving, Jun 23, 2022; https://www.fortuneindia.com/opinion/agnipath-ground-realities-harsh-and-unforgiving/108692; Mohanty P, Budget 2023: Why India Needs A Jobs Policy, Jan 4, 2023; https://www.fortuneindia.com/long-reads/budget-2023-why-india-needs-a-jobs-policy/111005

149   Singh Sushant, Tour of Duty model could add to majoritarian violence and affect army efficiency, Apr 21, 2022; https://caravanmagazine.in/security/tour-of-duty-pensions-lead-to-majoritarian-violence-hindutva-army-efficiency

150   ADR seeks action against parties for contempt of SC order on candidates with criminal record, Jun 20, 2023; https://indianexpress.com/article/india/adr-seeks-action-against-parties-for-contempt-of-sc-order-on-candidates-with-criminal-record-8673455/

151   Dushyant Dave Writes: On Manipur, Supreme Court Must Be More Proactive, Jul 22, 2023; https://www.livelaw.in/top-stories/manipur-violence-supreme-court-response-fundamental-rights-233395

152 Justice KS Puttaswamy (retd) and another vs Union Of India And Others, Supreme Court, August 24, 2017; https://main.sci.gov.in/supremecourt/2012/35071/35071_2012_Judgement_24-Aug-2017.pdf/

153 Madhyamam Broadcasting Limited vs Union of India and others, Supreme Court, Apr 5, 2023; https://main.sci.gov.in/supremecourt/2022/6825/6825_2022_1_1501_43332_Judgement_05-Apr-2023.pdf

154 Bhatia Gautam, Proportionality, Sealed Covers and the Supreme Court's Media One Judgment, Apr 6, 2023; https://thewire.in/law/supreme-court-media-one-sealed-cover-analysis

155 SC relief for Narendra Modi aide Amit Shah, Apr 9, 2013; http://timesofindia.indiatimes.com/articleshow/19451140.cms?utm_source=contentofinterest&utm_medium=text&utm_campaign=cppst; Ex-CJI Sathasivam is Governor, jurists say it may lead to more 'political intervention', Sept 4, 2014; https://indianexpress.com/article/india/india-others/ex-cji-sathasivam-appointed-kerala-governor/

156 Retired SC Judge S. Abdul Nazeer Made Andhra Pradesh Governor, Had Delivered Ayodhya Temple Judgment, Feb 12, 2023; https://thewire.in/government/retired-sc-judge-s-abdul-nazeer-appointed-as-governor-of-andhra-pradesh

157 In Unprecedented Move, Modi Government Sends Former CJI Ranjan Gogoi to Rajya Sabha, Mar 16, 2020; https://thewire.in/law/cji-ranjan-gogoi-rajya-sabha-nomination

158 "I Go When I Feel Like": Justice Gogoi On Rajya Sabha Attendance, Dec 10, 2021; https://www.ndtv.com/india-news/justice-gogoi-on-poor-attendance-i-go-to-rajya-sabha-when-i-feel-like-2644997

159 Vishwanath Apurva and CG Manoj, Delhi services bill: RS MP Gogoi questions basic structure, Justice Gogoi had quoted it, Aug 8, 2023; https://indianexpress.com/article/india/delhi-services-bill-perfectly-legitimately-valid-ranjan-gogoi-in-rajya-sabha-8881181/

160 Justice Ashok Bhushan takes charge as Chairperson of National Company Law Appellate Tribunal, Nov 9, 2021; https://government.economictimes.indiatimes.com/news/governance/justice-ashok-bhushan-takes-charge-as-chairperson-of-national-company-law-appellate-tribunal/87599560

161 Retired SC Judge S. Abdul Nazeer Made Andhra Pradesh Governor, Had Delivered Ayodhya Temple Judgment, Feb 12, 2023; https://thewire.in/government/retired-sc-judge-s-abdul-nazeer-appointed-as-governor-of-andhra-pradesh

162 Nine months after he retired from SC, Justice Arun Mishra is NHRC chief, Indian Express, Jun 3, 2021; https://indianexpress.com/article/india/justice-arun-mishra-nhrc-chairman-7340811/

163 Why the criticism of UU Lalit's appointment as India's next chief justice is flawed, Aug 10, 2022; https://scroll.in/article/1030045/why-the-criticism-of-uu-lalits-appointment-as-indias-next-chief-justice-is-flawed

164 "Appeared For Amit Shah But...": Ex Chief Justice UU Lalit To NDTV, Nov 14, 2022;

https://www.ndtv.com/india-news/appeared-for-amit-shah-but-ex-chief-justice-uu-lalit-on-controversial-case-3515730

165 Ex-CJI Lalit Breaks Silence on Urgent Hearing in GN Saibaba's Case, Nov 13, 2022; https://www.thequint.com/news/india/ex-cji-uu-lalit-breaks-silence-on-urgent-hearing-against-gn-saibabas-acquittal

166 Former CJI UU Lalit clears air on listing of activist Saibaba's case in SC on holiday, Nov 14, 2022; https://economictimes.indiatimes.com/news/india/former-cji-uu-lalit-clears-air-on-listing-of-activist-saibabas-case-in-sc-on-holiday/articleshow/95493337.cms?utm_source=contentofinterest&utm_medium=text&utm_campaign=cppst

167 HC Judge Hearing Rahul Gandhi's Appeal in Defamation Case Was Maya Kodnani's Lawyer, Apr 30, 2023; https://thewire.in/law/gujarat-high-court-judge-hemant-prachak-rahul-gandhi-maya-kodnani

168 An overworked Chief Justice TS Thakur breaks down in front of Modi, Apr 24, 2016; http://timesofindia.indiatimes.com/articleshow/51964732.cms?utm_source=contentofinterest&utm_medium=text&utm_campaign=cppst

169 Akil Kureshi: A Justice, denied, Aug 29, 2021; https://indianexpress.com/article/india/a-justice-denied-7475880/

170 Amit Shah Was Not on Trial But Sohrabuddin Judge Gives Him Clean Chit Nonetheless, Dec 29, 2018; https://thewire.in/rights/amit-shah-was-not-on-trial-but-sohrabuddin-judge-gives-him-clean-chit

171 Rajagopal Krishnadas, SC Bench strikes down NJAC Act as 'unconstitutional and void', May 23, 2016; https://www.thehindu.com/news/national/Supreme-Court-verdict-on-NJAC-and-Collegium-system/article60384480.ece

172 SC Bench strikes down NJAC Act as 'unconstitutional and void', May 23, 2016; https://www.thehindu.com/news/national/Supreme-Court-verdict-on-NJAC-and-Collegium-system/article60384480.ece

173 CJI's final push for collegium to appoint 1st SC judge in his tenure, Mar 18, 2021; https://www.hindustantimes.com/india-news/cjis-final-push-for-collegium-to-appoint-1st-sc-judge-in-his-tenure-101616009551294.html

174 Justice Kureshi, Who Sent Amit Shah to CBI Custody in 2010, Finds no Place in SC Collegium, Aug 19, 2021; https://www.newsclick.in/justice-kureshi-amit-shah-CBI-custody-2010-place-SC-collegium

175 Vishwanath Apurva, Supreme Court's marriage equality judgment unpacked: Two views on four key issues, Oct 19, 2023; https://indianexpress.com/article/explained/explained-law/scs-marriage-equality-judgment-unpacked-two-views-on-four-key-issues-8988049/

176 Solicitor General Tushar Mehta welcomes SC verdict on same-sex marriage, ANI, Oct 17, 2023; https://www.aninews.in/news/national/general-news/solicitor-general-tushar-mehta-welcomes-sc-verdict-on-same-sex-marriage20231017170948/ 1

177 This file relates to reconsideration of the proposal for appointment of Shri Saurabh

Kirpal, Advocate as Judge of the Delhi High Court, Supreme Court of India, Jan 18, 2023; https://main.sci.gov.in/pdf/Collegium/19012023_105547.pdf

178 SC Reiterates Saurabh Kirpal's Appointment as Judge, Rejects Govt Objections About Sexuality, Jan 19, 2023; https://thewire.in/law/saurabh-kirpal-appointment-supreme-court-collegium-reiterate

179 Citing delay by Centre, SC recalls proposal to transfer Justice S Muralidhar to Madras HC, Apr 20, 2023; https://scroll.in/latest/1047682/citing-delay-by-centre-sc-recalls-proposal-to-transfer-justice-s-muralidhar-to-madras-hc

180 G Ananthakrishnan, 70 Collegium proposals pending: Supreme Court says will monitor, not be quiet, Sept 27, 2023; https://indianexpress.com/article/india/collegium-recommendations-pending-sc-govt-delay-appoiantment-transfer-hc-judges-8956932/

181 Mahapatra Dhananjay, Supreme court invokes 'silence is approval' clause to name 3 judge picks, Oct 13, 2023; https://timesofindia.indiatimes.com/india/supreme-court-invokes-silence-is-approval-clause-to-name-3-judge-picks/articleshow/104382059.cms

182 Govt writes to CJI, wants its representatives on Supreme Court collegium, Jan 16, 2023; http://timesofindia.indiatimes.com/articleshow/97015515.cms?utm_source=contentofinterest&utm_medium=text&utm_campaign=cppst

183 Appeal filed in Supreme Court against remarks by Vice-President, law minister on judiciary, Collegium, Mar 28, 2023; http://timesofindia.indiatimes.com/articleshow/99069416.cms?from=mdr&utm_source=contentofinterest&utm_medium=text&utm_campaign=cppst

184 Some Retired Judges Are Part of 'Anti-India Gang', Says Law Minister Kiren Rijiju, Mar 18, 2023; https://thewire.in/law/kiren-rijiju-judges-rahul-gandhi-anti-india-gang

185 Collegium system failed: Law panel chief, Jul 26, 2014; https://timesofindia.indiatimes.com/india/collegium-system-failed-law-panel-chief/articleshow/39013084.cms ; Thakur Pradeep, Collegium lacks transparency, needs reforms: Justice Shah, Nov 28, 2016; https://timesofindia.indiatimes.com/india/collegium-lacks-transparency-needs-reforms-justice-shah/articleshow/55656623.cms ; Collegium's opacity is injurious to the institution's health, editorial, Nov 24, 2023; https://indianexpress.com/article/opinion/editorials/collegiums-opacity-is-injurious-to-the-institutions-health-9039926/

186 Collegium system not perfect but best available: CJI Chandrachud, PTI, Mar 18, 2023; https://www.thehindu.com/news/national/collegium-is-the-best-system-we-have-developed-says-chief-justice-of-india-chandrachud/article66635107.ece

187 'Is Word Jumla Against PM Proper': HC Bats for 'Lakshman Rekha' for Criticism of Govt, Apr 28, 2022; https://thewire.in/law/umar-khalid-delhi-high-court-jumla-lakshman-rekha

188 'Don't Teach Children to Criticise Govt Policies': HC While Quashing Bidar Sedition

Case, Jul 7, 2023; https://thewire.in/law/karnataka-hc-school-should-not-teach-students-criticise-govt-policies

189   Chor-vs-chor lines drawn in Parliament, Dec 18, 2018; https://www.telegraphindia.com/india/chor-vs-chor-or-thief-vs-thief-lines-drawn-in-parliament/cid/1679324

190   Hate speech case: If said with smile, no criminality, says Delhi HC, Mar 26, 2022; https://indianexpress.com/article/cities/delhi/hate-speech-case-if-said-with-smile-no-criminality-says-hc-7836774/

191   Shaheen Bagh: Delhi HC dismisses plea for hate speech FIR against Anurag Thakur, other BJP leaders, Deccan Herald, Jun 13, 2022; https://www.deccanherald.com/national/north-and-central/shaheen-bagh-delhi-hc-dismisses-plea-for-hate-speech-fir-against-anurag-thakur-other-bjp-leaders-1117764.html

192   Thapliyal Nupur, Organizer Of Public Meeting Can't Be Held Liable For Hate Speech Delivered By A Participant, Mere Presence Not Enough: Delhi High Court, Jul 21, 2023; https://www.livelaw.in/high-court/delhi-high-court/delhi-high-court-organizer-public-meeting-vicarious-liability-hate-speech-233307

193   Mathur A, On her last day, Delhi High Court judge delivers 65 verdicts in fast-tracked criminal cases, Jun 27, 2023; https://www.indiatoday.in/law/story/delhi-high-court-judge-delivers-65-verdicts-fast-tracked-criminal-cases-day-before-retirement-2398545-2023-06-27

194   Delhi CM Arvind Kejriwal fined Rs 25k as Gujarat HC junks CIC's PM Modi degree order, Apr 1, 2023; https://timesofindia.indiatimes.com/india/delhi-cm-arvind-kejriwal-fined-rs-25k-as-gujarat-hc-junks-cics-pm-modi-degree-order/articleshow/99156608.cms

195   PM Modi lists Rs 2.5 crore worth assets, MA degree from Gujarat University in election affidavit, PTI, Apr 26, 2019; https://indianexpress.com/elections/narendra-modi-assets-lok-sabha-election-affidavit-ma-degree-5696234/

196   17-yr-old rape survivor to move to shelter home as Gujarat HC refuses abortion plea, Jun 20, 2023; https://indianexpress.com/article/cities/ahmedabad/rape-survivor-pregnancy-termination-plea-gujarat-high-court-8673544/

197   Upadhyay Sparsh, 'People Staying In India Must Be Faithful To It': Gujarat HC Denies Bail To Congress Leader Accused Of Making FB Posts Against India, Prime Minister, Jun 9, 2023; https://www.livelaw.in/high-court/gujarat-high-court/gujarat-high-court-people-faithful-india-denies-bail-congress-leader-fb-posts-anti-indian-prime-minister-230363#:~:text=The%20Gujarat%20High%20Court%20on,bench%20of%20Justice%20Nirzar%20S.

198   After CJI's intervention, SC stays Allahabad HC order seeking answer on rape victim's 'manglik' status, Jun 4, 2023; https://indianexpress.com/article/india/sc-stays-allahabad-hc-direction-to-examine-if-rape-victim-is-manglik-8643802/

199   Rehman Asad, 'Systematic design to destroy institution of marriage': Allahabad HC slams live-in relationships, Sept 1, 2023; https://indianexpress.com/article/india/middle-class-morality-india-allahabad-hc-bail-man-accused-raping-live-in-partner-8919698/

200 Singh Harsha Kumari, Peacocks Don't Have Sex, Says Judge Who Recommended Cow As National Animal, Jun 1, 2017; https://www.ndtv.com/india-news/peacock-dont-have-sex-says-judge-who-recommended-cow-as-national-animal-1706363

201 Ban Cow Slaughter, Declare Them 'Protected National Animal': Allahabad HC, Mar 4, 2023; https://www.outlookindia.com/national/ban-cow-slaughter-declare-protected-national-animal-allahabad-hc-news-267200

202 Cow dung stops radiation, urine cures illness, says judge in Tapi district, Agencies, Jan 25, 2023; https://timesofindia.indiatimes.com/city/surat/atomic-radiation-cannot-affect-cow-dung-houses/articleshow/97295770.cms?from=mdr

203 Once FIR is quashed, media must delete articles regarding filing of FIR since they harm reputation: Gujarat High Court, Jul 26, 2023; https://www.barandbench.com/news/once-fir-is-quashed-media-must-delete-articles-regarding-filing-of-fir-since-they-harm-reputation-gujarat-high-court#:~:text=Once%20a%20First%20Information%20Report,High%20Court%20observed%20on%20Wednesday.

204 26 years after Datta Samant killing, CBI court acquits Chhota Rajan, JUl 28, 2023; https://indianexpress.com/article/cities/mumbai/gangster-chhota-rajan-acquitted-murdering-labour-union-leader-datta-samant-8865549/

205 Nuh-Gurugram Demolitions: Bench Of Punjab & Haryana High Court Hearing Suo Motu Case Changed Ahead Of Hearing Tomorrow, Aug 10, 2023; https://www.livelaw.in/top-stories/nuh-gurugram-demolitions-bench-of-punjab-haryana-high-court-hearing-suo-motu-case-changed-ahead-of-hearing-tomorrow-234918

206 Judges Reluctant To Grant Bail For Fear Of Being Targeted: Chief Justice, ANI, Nov 20, 2022; https://www.ndtv.com/india-news/chief-justice-of-india-dy-chandrachud-says-judges-fear-of-being-targeted-for-granting-bail-3536696

207 Banerjee Soutik, Audacity, Rule of Law & Teesta Setalvad: Why Must Road to Liberty Go Through SC? Jul 22, 2023; https://www.thequint.com/opinion/audacity-rule-of-law-teesta-setalvad-why-must-road-to-liberty-go-through-supreme-court

208 Das Awstika, Supreme Court Adjourns Umar Khalid's Bail Plea in Delhi Riots Larger Conspiracy Case; To Hear After Four Weeks, Sept 12, 2023; https://www.livelaw.in/top-stories/supreme-court-umar-khalid-delhi-riots-larger-conspiracy-case-237561

209 Delhi HC Denies Bail To Umar Khalid: What Transpired In Court Till Now, Oct 18, 2022; https://www.outlookindia.com/national/delhi-hc-denies-bail-to-jnu-scholar-umar-khalid-news-230784

210 Umar Khalid's plea challenging UAPA provisions: SC issues notice to Centre, Nov 1, 2023; https://indianexpress.com/article/cities/delhi/umar-khalids-plea-challenging-uapa-provisions-sc-issues-notice-to-centre-9008276/

211 SC to hear bail plea of Manish Sisodia on October 4, Sept 16, 2023; https://www.newindianexpress.com/cities/delhi/2023/sep/16/sc-to-hear-bail-plea-of-manish-sisodiaon-october-4-2615418.html

212 G Ananthakrishnan, SC questions ED on money laundering matter: 'Where is the

evidence against Sisodia? This will fall flat', Oct 6, 2023; https://indianexpress.com/article/cities/delhi/sc-questions-ed-on-money-laundering-matter-where-is-the-evidence-against-sisodia-this-will-fall-flat-8970463/; Kumar Ashmit, Delhi Liquor Case | As Manish Sisodia remains in jail for 8 months, SC tells ED there's no visible money trail leading to him, Oct 5, 2023; https://www.cnbctv18.com/india/supreme-court-sc-observes-no-money-trail-leading-to-aap-manish-sisodia-delhi-liquor-scam-highlights-17962151.htm

213 Hegde Sanjay, The Curious Case of Supreme Court's Denial of Bail to Manish Sisodia, Nov 10, 2023; https://thewire.in/law/curious-case-denial-bail-manish-sisodia-supreme-court

214 'Guidelines Exclusively for Politicians?': SC Turns Down Petition on 'Misuse' of Central Agencies, Apr 5, 2023; https://thewire.in/law/guidelines-exclusively-for-politicians-sc-turns-down-opposition-petition-on-agency-misuse

215 Manish Sisodia vs CBI, Supreme Court, Oct 30, 2023; https://main.sci.nic.in/supremecourt/2023/26668/26668_2023_3_1501_47839_Judgement_30-Oct-2023.pdf

216 'Question not to implicate anyone', SC clarifies question on making AAP an accused during Sisodia bail hearing, Oct 5, 2023; https://www.deccanherald.com/india/delhi/question-not-to-implicate-anyone-sc-clarifies-question-on-making-aap-an-accused-during-sisodia-bail-hearing-2713882

217 Delhi CM Kejriwal summoned by ED in excise case, asked to appear on November 2, Oct 30, 2023; https://www.thehindubusinessline.com/incoming/delhi-cm-kejriwal-summoned-by-ed-in-excise-case-asked-to-appear-on-november-2/article67478066.ece

218 Delhi court allows Manish Sisodia to meet ailing wife today, Nov 11, 2023; https://timesofindia.indiatimes.com/city/delhi/delhi-court-allows-manish-sisodia-to-meet-ailing-wife-today/articleshow/105136106.cms

Chapter IV

Rhetoric as Governance I:
'Sabka Saath, Sabka Vikas'

Set aside how the World Bank and UN define good governance. Take a close look at what the Prime Minister has promised to deliver: "Sabka saath, sabka vikas" (inclusive governance or unity and development of all) to which he later added "sabka vishwas" and "sabka prayas" (confidence and cooperation of all); "minimum government, maximum governance"; "cooperative federalism"; "bhrashtachar-mukt Bharat" (corruption-free India); "open, accountable, pro-people government" in which all citizens would be "equal and integral part of the decision-making process" etc.[1] These are far more earthy, appealing and Big Bang in dimensions. What more could one ask for?

Except, the promises haven't been delivered – but turned on their heads. These are mere slogans or political rhetoric, masquerading as good governance. There is a complete delink between official policy statements and pronouncements and policy practices, official deliveries on the ground. This chapter provides a *reality check* against the promised "Sabka saath, sabhka vikas" – which went a notch higher, especially during India's G20 (rotational) presidentship in 2023 to claim the Prime Minister's *grand vision* of good governance with new slogans, "Vasudhaiva Kutumbakam" and its English variation, "One Earth, One Family, One Future". The next two chapters do more reality checks on two other big promises – Chapter V on "minimum government, maximum governance" and Chapter VI on "cooperative federalism".

Muslims on Target

One of the most astoundingly hypocritical and anti-people moves the Prime

Minister made after winning the second term in 2019 was to start a National Register of Indian Citizens (NRIC), asking all Indians to *prove their citizenship*[2] – which no other government ever did. The stated objective is to *identify* "doubtful citizens" – without defining what this means (and leaving it to lowly officials to determine) – and to put them in "detention centres" which his government started building immediately after coming to power in 2014.[3]

Had the NRC been restricted to border districts or areas known for high influx of outsiders it would have made sense. But it is meant for the entire population, except Assam which already has it (which has a unique history of civil strife over migrations from the present-day Bangladesh and its redrawing of the boundaries post-independence of 1947) since 1951 and was updated in 2018 by then CJI Justice Gogoi[4] but the BJP rejected it because it excluded a large number of Hindus[5], contrary to their expectations. For the rest of the country, NRIC (or NRC for convenience) was to kickstart in (April-September) 2020, along with the Census for 2021 – both deferred to post-2024 general elections.

This move threw up many disturbing questions.

1. If all Indian citizens are "doubtful citizens", what is the legitimacy of the 2014 and 2019 elections that brought the Prime Minister to office?

2. Is there any evidence to suggest growing infiltration in recent times? The Census 2011 data shows that isn't the case. The number of outsiders residing in India saw a rapid fall in recent decades and those staying in India for less than a year was less than 200,000; 1 to 4 years and 5 to 9 years less than 5,00,000 each.[6]

3. Given Assam's bad experience with NRC (driven through 'sealed cover' jurisprudence by the Supreme Court) – very punishing for poor, illiterates and inter-state migrants to produce documents, inflicting unimaginable hardship – should this be extended to the entire country?

4. That the entire population is expected to provide a series of documents to prove their *bona fide* and that of their parents and grand-parents when the battle for the Prime Minister's educational degrees is being fought at virtually every level of institutions and judiciary all across the country since 2016 – without any success (Chapter III) – is truly heartbreaking, to say the least.

It was clear from the beginning that Muslims were the target but the BJP officially talked about Muslim 'infiltrators'.

Then BJP president and now Home Minister Amit Shah left nothing to imagination in his famous "chronology"[7] speech during the 2019 electioneering. He said, after winning the elections his government would *first* pass Citizenship Amendment Bill (CAB) to exclude Muslim refugees from getting citizenship, *then* bring NRIC/NRC to *filter out* "infiltrators" or "termites" (Bangladeshi Muslims). It is highly unlikely that Shah didn't know that weeks earlier the Asian Development Bank (ADB) had reported that Bangladesh was about to overtake India in per capita income and as such it makes little sense for Bangladeshis to "infiltrate" into India and the IMF later confirmed that Bangladesh indeed overtook India (in per capita income), even if for a short time.[8]

Shah's chronology also turned out to be true.

The CAB was passed and became the Citizenship Amendment Act (CAA) of 2019. The law provides citizenship on the *basis of religion* to refugees facing religious persecution in their home countries in Afghanistan, Bangladesh and Pakistan. But it excludes other neighbours – China (Buddhist Tibetans, who have faced political repression), Sri Lanka (Hindu Tamils) and Myanmar (Muslim Rohingyas) from where refugees have come to India to escape religious persecution. In Pakistan, the Ahmadis (Muslim) face religious persecution but are excluded. This law is a clear violation of Article 14[9] of the Constitution which guarantees "equality before law" and "equal protection of the laws" to "*any person…within the territory of India*". But since the Supreme Court hasn't decided its constitutionality yet, the sword hangs. *(Emphasis added)*

The CAA-NRC sparked the famous Shaheen Bagh protest in Delhi, led by elderly Muslim women and students waving the tricolour, singing the national song and reading the Preamble of the Constitution in late 2019 – which found resonance across the country (from Sikhs, Hindus and others). The Delhi polls were due in early February 2020. Unnerved, the government started spreading lies. The Prime Minister declared in December 2019 that there was no move to prepare a national NRC and "no discussion" on it had ever taken place. Now Home Minister, Shah took it further and said that there was "no link" between the National Population Register (NPR) to be prepared and the NRC.[10]

The truth was different. The gazette notification for the NPR had come six months' earlier on July 31, 2019. Subsequently, the Union Cabinet approved Rs 3,941 crore for it. What is NPR? It has no independent existence in any India law; it exists *only* in the 2003 Rules under the Citizenship Act of 1955 (brought during the earlier BJP-led government under Vajpayee) and the purpose of this is to prepare the NRC. So, the NPR is nothing but preparing for the NRC. The gazette notification for the NPR was also notified under this very 2003 Rules.[11]

Both the CAA and NRC were put on hold as the pandemic struck but continues to be raised, particularly the NRC, at the time of elections to threaten Muslims and as a dog-whistle for Hindutva followers. In August 2023, the MHA sought eighth's extension to frame the rules for the CAA which was legislated in December 2019.[12] But that is not the end to the government's hypocrisy.

The government passed a law criminalizing "triple talaq" in 2019 (see

Introduction) and hailed the Supreme Court's 2016 order allowing Muslim women entry into the Mumbai's Haji Ali Dargah – both in the name of "empowerment of women". But when the same Supreme Court allowed Hindu women entry into the Sabarimala temple in Kerala in 2018, all hell broke loose. The BJP took out massive rallies for days; Amit Shah threatened the Kerala government against enforcing the court order and reprimanded the apex court by saying "you should issue orders that can be implemented, not the ones that break the faith of people..."[13] The pressure tactics worked. Instead of dismissing review petitions against the Sabarimala order, the court effectively stayed it by referring the review petitions, first to a five-judge bench and then to a nine-judge bench, after clubbing it with other unrelated religious matters. There is no sign of the nine-judge bench.[14]

Politics inevitably involves double-speak/hypocrisy. Outright lies, half-truth, mis-directions are also not aliens. But when these become the defining marker of a government it *leads to trust deficit*, not to speak of breakdown of governance[15] and which became endemic after 2014[16].

Methods in Madness: 360-Degree Attack

The attacks on Muslims are relentless and virulent, in both real and virtual worlds, and they live in perpetual fear. Their life has completely changed, many adopting Hindu names and dress codes just to survive (avail jobs and rented houses).[17] These attacks are multi-pronged.

(a) Destabilize their citizenship through the CAA-NRC.

(b) Erase their identity and heritage by changing Muslim names of streets, cities, railway stations, districts, deleting Mughal period from history textbooks. Union Minister and "Sadhvi" (woman saint) Niranjan Jyoti publicly called Muslims "haramzada"[18].

(c) Delegitimize their identity, religious practices and food through draconian laws banning beef eating, cow slaughter, "love jihad" (banning Muslim men from marrying Hindu women), "recovery" of damages to public properties by Muslims during riots or protests (BJP-ruled Uttar Pradesh, Madhya Pradesh and Haryana have brought such laws[19]).

(d) Damage their livelihood by denying access to markets in Hindu areas.

(e) Segregate their neighbourhoods and force to live in "unlivable" ghettos (like the Naroda Patia victims living on the Ahmedabad outskirts[20]).

(f) Deny political representation (by not giving space in elections, governments and through delimitations). Although the BJP is the largest party, enjoys absolute majority in the Lok Sabha and runs more than a dozen states it has completely isolated Muslims who constitute 14.2% of the population (172 million, as per Census 2011). It has over 400 MPs in the Parliament and over 1,000 MLAs and runs governments alone or in coalition in more than a dozen states/UTs – but no Muslim MPs, no Muslim Minister anywhere. It got a lone Muslim MLA in Tripura in September 2023 and nominated four MLCs in Uttar Pradesh in April 2023.[21]

(g) Terrorize by unleashing and empowering right-wing mobs and vigilante groups and using police and civic authorities to *bulldoze* ("bulldozer justice") their homes and shops on cooked up pretexts (dangerous building, protesting or attacking Hindus) and without following the due process of law – as a form of *collectively punishment*[22]. Bulldozers rolled out to target former JNU student activist Afreen Fatima[23] days after local and global protests sparked over BJP spokesperson Nupur Sharma's blasphemous remarks against Prophet Muhammed; bulldozers hogged the streets and posters during the BJP's election campaign in Uttar Pradesh in 2022[24]; in Madhya Pradesh, the police and civic authorities even brought along *drum beaters* in 2023[25].

(h) Denial of social development and education with the number of beneficiaries sharply declining.[26] This is unconnected with a pre-matric scholarship scam exposed by the Indian Express in Jharkhand and Bihar in November 2020.[27]. Budgets for their welfares are stagnant and the actual spending fallen abysmally (to 14% of fund allocations in FY23[28]).

(i) Dehumanize and demonize Muslims through propaganda (malicious and fake narratives) Bollywood films like Kashmir Files and Kerala Story – all declared tax-free by the BJP-ruled states. The screening of these films marked hate speeches, oath taking to attack Muslims inside theatres to actual attacks[29] outside. The Prime Minister promoted and supported[30] the Kerala Story during the Karnataka elections in 2023 and BJP Chief Ministers endorsed, publicly watching it.[31]

(j) Ethnic cleansing of primarily Muslims but also Christians in the BJP-ruled states of Uttarakhand, Haryana and Manipur and attacks on lifestyle and livelihood of Muslims in J&K and Lakshadweep.[32]

Such attacks on Muslims have been well documented by many scholars (Aakar Patel[33], Christophe Jaffrelot[34], Mukul Kesavan[35], Rononjoy Sen[36]) and human rights bodies (bipartisan US federal government agency USCIRF[37] and independent human rights watchdogs like Amnesty International[38] and Human Rights Watch *HRW)[39]) – pointing to a *de facto* and in many ways a *de jure*, Hindu Rashtra in action. The country witnesses a *new ploy* virtually every other day to attack Muslims: 'hijab', 'halal' meat, loudspeakers calling for 'azaan', offering 'namaz' on streets or inside housing societies, marches to Muslim localities to abuse and provoke violence during Hindu festivals of Ram Navami and Hanuman Jayanti, 'dharm sansads' (religious assembly) by Hindu seers where call for Muslim genocide are routine. Offering 'namaz' in public places is fraught with severe punishment (arrested and fines of Rs 5 lakh)[40] while schools are shut, national, state highways and other public roads, parks etc. blocked for weeks to give a free pass to and host Hindu 'kanwariyas' – millions carrying Ganga water during an entire monsoon month – including rose petals showers from the sky[41]. Muslim-run non-vegetarian food stalls and meat shops are shut during Hindu festivals.

Hindu religious processions need special mention because it is a tried and tested weapon of right-wing groups.

Hindu Processions to Masjids

Journalist Ajaz Ashraf[42] traced the history of riots to demonstrate how Hindu religious processions are a tried and tested technique to engineer riots. In 2022, violent Hindu processions were taken out across nine states.[43] A new study of such violence in 2022 ("Routes of Wrath: Weaponising Religious Processions"[44]) showed the "single most factor" was the "route" of the procession – allowing Hindus to pass through or by Muslim dominated areas – pointing to "distinct" and "eerie" patterns in which violence is "systematically planned", which included the "nature of instigation", the "tactics of mobilizing the majority" and the "administrative response as collective punishment". Yet, more such processions were taken out in 2023, sparking violence in Bihar, West Bengal and Odisha (repeated over several rounds) – all non-BJP ruled states as fresh round of elections loomed.[45] Two such processions, within a week, were allowed in Delhi's trouble spot Jahangirpuri in April 2023 but fortunately, went without violence.[46]

Ashutosh Varshney and Bhanu Joshi[47] mined the "Varshney-Wilkinson Dataset on Hindu-Muslim Violence in India, 1950-95" to find that the attack on Muslims through such processions is a "relatively new phenomenon" – of 1,192 riots during this period, there were only 9 (0.001%) riots relating to Ram Navami procession. This, they explained, was because Ram wasn't always a symbol of majoritarian power and domination; the metamorphosis began in the late 1980s.

The other requiring special mention is fake 'jihad' campaigns.

Multiple Fake Jihads Campaigns

The most convenient and potent communal weapon of the BJP and its support groups is fake campaigns accusing Muslims of 'jihad' – religious war by the followers of Islam against non-Islam followers. It is actually a *dog-whistle* to create fear and paranoia in Hindus about threats from Muslims. Essentially, its origin in India is traced to 'love jihad' – an Islamophobic conspiracy theory[48] (but equally applies to Christians) invented by the right-wing organizations like Sri Ram Sena and Vishwa Hindu Parishad (VHP) in 2009 (in Kerala) and then more got added to the list.

But to understand how such fake campaigns to create fear and paranoia about Muslims in a *de facto* Hindu Rashtra is going on one must note the "duality" that plays out simultaneously (co-exists) in the Hindu-Muslim binary: Hindu supremacy co-existing with Hindu "khatre mein hai" (Hindus are threatened).

Journalist Tusa Mittal captured this duality well in her essay of 2023, "Theatre of Destruction: How bulldozers became part of the Hindu nationalist lexicon in India"[49]. She wrote: "India's Modi years have also been marked with a telling duality – the discourse of Hindu supremacy coexisting with the idea of Hindu victimhood, of a historical, civilizational injustice to Hindus perpetrated by Muslims, from as far back as the Mughals and continuing to this day. In this imagination, Hindus are both the true, rightful claimants of the Indian land, and simultaneously victims of assault at the hands of Muslims. *The bulldozer is where these two narratives seamlessly meet*. It has resonance as a symbol of dominance and finally, of payback. The conflict has been framed in a manner in which the Hindu Right needs a narrative of victory over Muslims. The bulldozer is the symbol of that political and cultural victory." (*Emphasis added*)

The list of 'jihads' is *ever expanding* to keep this *threat from Muslims alive*. More than enough evidence exists to show that 'love jihad' is a fake right-wing campaign[50] to target Muslims. Here are many more 'jihad' campaigns from them to keep Indian society and polity *perpetually on the edge* since 2014:

(i) 'Jihadi terrorists': A new invention; after cow vigilantism was encouraged through a ban on cow slaughter in 2017[51] and mob lynching went unchecked, two new crime categories "anti-national elements" and "jihadi terrorists" were added to "Crime in India 2020" report of the National Crimes Record Bureau (NCRB).[52]

(ii) 'Thook jihad': The pandemic of 2020 saw Muslims being blamed for spreading the virus through 'thook jihad'[53] ('thook' for spitting). The conspiracy theory is that Muslims spit on people and things to spread the virus and it began with the Tablighi Jamaat (more in Chapter XI). What is seen by the paranoid right-wing Hindutva groups is blowing of air on food or a person by Muslims *after reciting verses* from the Quran *as a blessing* for prosperity and well-being.[54]

(iii) 'Land jihad': Here in comes the bulldozer. The BJP-ruled states routinely accuse Muslims of land grab and their houses, shops and masjids are bulldozed without legal processes and was first noticed after the protests against the CAA in 2019-2020.[55]

(iv) 'Mazar' and 'madrasa' jihad: Uttarakhand government launched a war on what it calls 'mazar jihad'[56] with Chief Minister Pushkar Singh Dhami (from the BJP) asking authorities to demolish 'mazar' that have come up on illegally-occupied land, adding that over a thousand such illegal structures had been erected in the state. Assam, under Chief Minister Himanta Biswa Sarma (of the BJP who coined the misleading "Hussain Obamas" for the former US President who is a Christian), pioneered many new 'jihad' campaigns, apart from championing the old ones ('love jihad' and 'land jihad'), one is 'madrasa jihad'[57]. Many 'madrasas' were demolished on the charge of being built on encroached land ('land jihad') and allegedly teaching and fostering Muslim fundamentalism ('madras jihad'). After the Gyanvapi masjid (17th-century mosque built by Aurangzeb in Varanasi) controversy erupted in 2022, *thousands of masjids* have been targeted[58] by right-wing groups. On his part, Sarma also said all madrasas (religious schools) would be *shut*[59] as those are not needed in modern times but went back to launch 'education' jihad campaign – calling Muslim students "Ajmal's people" and alleging that they were stealing engineering and medical seats from Hindus.[60] "Ajmal" comes from prominent businessman and legislator from Assam who provides coaching facilities to students.

(v) 'Flood jihad': The annual floods in Assam took a new turn in 2022 when Muslims were accused of waging a jihad by engineering floods in Hindu majority areas by damaging flood protections, which actually led to arrests of Muslims.[61]

(vi) 'Fertilizer jihad': Sarma himself launched a campaign for natural farming in June 2023 but called it a "fight against fertilizer jihad" and named areas dominated by vegetable growers who are Bengali Muslim to make his targets clear.[62] Sarma also launched a crackdown against child marriage in 2023. Instead of preventing it, thousands of already married couples, their children and family members were arrested. An Indian Express report[63] showed, 62.24% of those arrested were Muslims while the rest were Hindus and from other communities.

(vii) 'Vyapar jihad': BJP-ruled Uttarakhand saw a fake[64] 'love jihad' metamorphose into a 'land jihad' in which Muslims houses and shops were marked with 'x' and they forced to flee as Hindu business community got together in Purola in 2023, gaining another variation called 'vyapar jihad'.[65] Such was the hate generated that a BJP leader had to cancel his daughter's marriage with a Muslim man.[66]

(viii) 'Gaming jihad': A fake media campaign which posits that Hindu boys were being "lured to believe" that by memorising the Quran's 'aayats' (verses) they can win online games and that by adopting Islam, miracles will happen in their lives.[67]

(ix) 'Momo' (meat) jihad: In 2017, a campaign was launched against meat-filled momos becoming ubiquitous in most part of the country but it soon faded out[68] because no Muslim angle could be established – momo is a delicacy of Tibet and north-eastern states.

Special mention is also required for 'Muslim angle' phenomenon and various innovative ways invented.

'Muslim Angle' and Innovative Attack

Fake campaigns against Muslims include finding a 'Muslim angle' to a disaster or crisis – and then blame Muslims for it. A few examples:

(a) The pandemic outbreak of 2020 and 2021 was blamed on Muslims (see Chapter XI for details).[69]

(b) The Odisha train accident of 2023 saw an ISKCON (Hindu) temple near the accident site wrongly (deliberately) identified as a masjid and holding it responsible for the accident.[70] When that failed, a non-existent Muslim station master was blamed.[71] The government also helped by giving the accident a conspiracy twist and ordered a CBI inquiry, which luckily ruled out conspiracy[72] – *after* the Commission of Railway Safety (CRS)'s probe said so and pointed to lapses in signaling system[73]. Train accidents of this kind (not involving bomb explosion, removal of fish-plates, hijacking etc.) is the job of the CRS, which has the right skillsets and more than 150 years of institutional experience), not the CBI which has a historic reputation of being a political tool.

(c) In the Manipur stripping and parading of Kuki women case, a Muslim link was invented (a Muslim man arrested in an unrelated case in unrelated district).[74]

(d) The 2020 attack on JNU students by right-wing mob was also blamed on a Muslim student.[75]

There are other innovative ways to dehumanize/demonize Muslims too.

(i) The Prime Minister identified Muslim protesters (against the CAA) by their clothes in 2019[76] and made other public speeches at the time that generated ill-will against Muslims[77]. It was his government's ban on cattle/cow slaughter in 2017 which had sparked a fresh cow vigilantism (mentioned earlier).

(ii) Union Home Minister Amit Shah describes Muslims as "Alia, Malia Jamalia" to suggest Muslim infiltration and inaction of the previous Congress governments and branding Muslims as terrorists.[78]

(iii) Maharashtra Deputy CM Fadnavis calls them "Aurangzeb ki aulad".[79] It is a state where uploading Mughal emperor Aurangzeb's image is a criminal offence and leads to arrests.[80]

(iv) Teachers are arrested and sacked for making students sing Muhammad Iqbal's immortal poem "Lab Pe Aati Hai Dua".[81] A principal was suspended for conducting Islamic prayer.[82] A school's recognition was suspended for allowing 'hijab' and 'scarf' as "optional"[83].

(v) "Marry Kashmiri girls" and "buy land in Kashmir" campaigns were launched soon after Article 370 was revoked in 2019.[84]

(vi) The Indian Railways sought and carried out part demolition of masjids as "encroachment" in 2023 – which are claimed to be much older than the Railways itself and had even donated land to it.[85]

(vii) Minor Muslim boys put on riot trials to recover damages in Madhya Pradesh[86]– under a law similar to the BJP-ruled Uttar Pradesh and Haryana.

(viii) Officially naming Muslims in FIRs when the aggressors are Hindus, like the VHP's "Shobha Yatra" vandalising the Dhuldoyawad Masjid and Hazrat Kalu Shahid Dargah in Vadodara in 2023 but the state police's FIR mentions *only Muslims, not Hindu.*[87] Often police don't register cases against Hindus (and Muslims don't find lawyers as in the Nuh riots 2023)[88].

(ix) Victimise Muslims *twice over* by letting the attacks on them happen and then, turning criminal prosecution against the very victims by repeatedly fabricating evidence and getting caught and yet nothing happens to the Delhi Police in the Delhi riots of 2022. It merrily keeps doing the same year after year.[89]

(x) 'Saffron' terror accused are *shielded*[90] – which is very dangerous as anyone familiar with the subject would tell – by the topmost leaders (in the case of Pragya Thakur, for example) and the anti-terror agency NIA (see Chapter I).

(xi) The Hindutva hatred for Muslims has now *gone global.*[91]

Well, not all ways of persecuting Muslims are exhausted yet. It isn't possible given the extraordinary hypocrisy of the BJP. For example, while conversion from Hindus to non-Hindu is a crime, non-Hindus converting to Hinduism is no crime and is called "ghar wapsi" (returning home), organized routinely by right-wing groups. Yet another is, slaughtering buffalo, eating its meat or exporting it are legitimate too and eating cow meat (beef) is allowed in the BJP-ruled north-eastern states and Kerala (where it has no footprint) too, with "beef feasts" organized at election times by the BJP there – forgetting that their "gau mata" for votes and power. The BJP has no qualms of their "gau mata" abandoned in huge numbers, posing traffic menace on highways and causing deaths in Gujarat and Madhya Pradesh[92] and damaging crops in Uttar Pradesh (forcing the Prime Minister to promise to find solution to stay cattle problem during election time[93]). In fact, one of the very first things that the BJP-ruled Uttar Pradesh did after coming to power in 2017 was to launch an *ambulance service exclusively for cows*[94], but not humans – in the state known as a 'BIMARU' (sick) state, along with three other cow-belt, Hindi heartland states of Bihar, Madhya Pradesh and Rajasthan, in India known for its backwardness and lack of healthcare facilities.

In 2023, when the demand was for a country-wide census on the Other Backward Classes (OBCs) – this state announced a *cow census* on a *priority basis*[95] instead and geo-tag them, particularly the strays. It also *banned* manufacture, sale, storage and distribution of *halal-certified products* in the state with immediate effect, ironically, in the name of "public health" but excluding food products made for export. An FIR was also registered against firms issuing such certificates, their owners and managers etc. alleging absurd crimes such as "anti-national conspiracy", "funding notified terrorist organisations and organisations involved in anti-national activities" and for "conspiring to incite large-scale riots by messing with public faith."[96]

Delimitation to Reduce Muslim Representation

Apart from denying Muslim representation in legislatures and council of ministers the BJP has sought to disempower them politically through the delimitation exercise.

It began with J&K after the abrogation of its special status in 2019 to reduce the chances of Muslims getting elected. The Hindu majority Jammu gets higher number of Assembly seats (up from 37 to 43) but Muslim majority Kashmir saw addition of just one seat (46 to 47) – redrawn on the basis of outdated 2001 Census – not 2011 Census as is the case with other states (Assam, Manipur, Nagaland, Arunachal Pradesh) which underwent simultaneous delimitations.[97] The Lok Sabha seats have also been redrawn arbitrarily, ignoring geographical contiguity, in a way to give Hindus more electoral influence. As part of this dilution of Muslim representation, the Centre decided to give voting rights to those "ordinarily" residing in J&K (like the rest of India but unlike to territories given special status), which expects to add 25 lakh voters to 76 lakh voter-base (35.5% addition).[98]

Then in 2023, the delimitation of Assam was accomplished which *reduced Muslim representation*[99] by (i) basing on 2001 Census, not the latest 2011 Census - Muslims were 30.9% in 2001 which went up to 34.22% (ii) several Muslim dominated seats done away with or mixed with majority Hindu constituencies (iii) as the CM said, 110 of 126 Assembly seats go to indigenous people (read Hindu) – up by 19 seats – currently Assam has 31 Muslim legislators, none from the BJP (v) *five assembly seats* which always elected Muslim candidates were made *reserved seats*[100] for SCs (from six to eight) and STs (from 16 to 19). This may well happen all over India when the Parliamentary and Assembly seats are increased after the 2026 deadline ends – the new Parliament House has higher seats keeping that in mind.

Call for Muslim Genocide

The attacks on Muslims got so vicious in 2022 that Gregory Stanton, president of the US-based Genocide Watch (who had predicted Rwanda genocide five years before it happened) warned the world of an impending Muslim genocide in India by *mobs*. He said: "We don't say that the next stage – that is extermination – has begun yet. Our view is that it is a huge danger in India because it won't be the State that carries out any genocide, *it will be mobs*." He even asked the US Congress "to pass a resolution that warns genocide should not be allowed to occur in India".[101]

The warning followed Hindu religious leaders calling for Muslim genocide openly in Delhi and Haridwar at "dharm sansad" (religious congregation) in which many repeat offenders participated – in the run-up to the Uttar Pradesh elections in 2022.[102] This was also the time when BJP Chief Minister of Uttar Pradesh Yogi Adityanath unleashed a hate campaign. The Wire analyzed his publicly available speeches (November 2021 to first week of February 2022) to find "over 100 distinct instances" which had "straightforward hate speech, anti-Muslim dog-whistling, an emphasis on anti-Muslim policy and legislation, the targeting of the opposition as a proxy for Muslims, and a chilling focus on Hindu supremacist rhetoric".[103] The warning didn't stop the genocide calls. During a Supreme Court hearing (Altnews' Mohammed Zubair) Additional Solicitor General SV Raju described one such hate monger Hindu seer "respected religious leader"[104].

None of it should surprise because the BJP owes its political and electoral fortunes to the hate-Muslim campaigns, particularly the one that ended with the Babri Masjid's demolition in 1992. It has since then kept the communal pot boiling for sustenance and growth. Many studies (multi-year) have unanimously concluded that communal riots exclusively benefit the BJP electorally and hurts the Congress (Nellis *et al*[105], Iyer & Shrivastava[106], Rohit Ticku[107]). Even the second mandate in 2019[108] owes it to the Pulwama blasts of February 2019 – which was blamed on Pakistan and India's own security failures that then Governor Satya Pal Malik repeatedly flagged was ignored and told to shut up[109] – triggering Hindu consolidation. Shocking as it may seem to outsiders, there is no official probe report, at least not in public, to know what exactly happened and why.

Just for the record, the US-based 'Hindutva Watch' which tracks attack on minorities analyzed anti-Muslim hate speeches in the first half of 2023 (no comparative study for previous years) to say (i) hate speeches spiked around elections (ii) 80% hate speech events took place in BJP-ruled states.[110] In 2018, the NDTV news channel had found 500% rise in hate speech by *high-ranking* politicians ("VIP hate speech"[111]) in the four years between May 2014 and April 2018 – compared to the previous five years of the Congress-led UPA II (2009-2014). It went through 1,300 articles, cross-referenced with other hate speech trackers and examined 1,000 tweets of politicians and public figures. It said: "…it seems not a day, or a week goes by without some senior politician – a member of Parliament, minister, MLA or even Chief Minister making a hateful comment, be it in the language of bigotry or calling for violence. The rise in use of social media by politicians has only amplified this disturbing trend." No prize for guessing: "90% of hateful comments made during the NDA's current terms are by BJP politicians."

Often, therefore, the Prime Minister and his government keep silent on communal attacks. When it becomes too hot – like the derogatory remarks against the Prophet by a party spokesperson Nupur Sharma in 2022, drawing ire of Arab countries – blatant *double speaks* begin. For example, on that occasion, the BJP issued a statement claiming that it (a) "respects all religions" (b) "strongly denounces insult of any religious personalities of any religion" (c) is "strongly against any ideology which insults or demeans any sect or religion" and (d) "India's Constitution gives right to every citizen to practice any religion of his/her choice and to honour and respect every religion"[112].

The MEA blamed it on "fringe elements" and declared "strong action has already been taken against those who made the derogatory remarks".[113] This was a lie since Nupur Sharma was an official BJP spokesperson and she was never arrested or faced prosecution. The Supreme Court played a questionable role. First it slammed Delhi Police for "not taking substantive action" in the FIR against her, following which the police said it had questioned her about a fortnight ago and let her go.[114] By then, the police had given her security cover (and hence knew where she was).[115] Thereafter, the Supreme Court first issued orders protecting her from arrest[116] and then dismissed plea for her arrest[117].

The Prime Minster has spoken against attacks on Muslims on a few occasions – all of which reflect duplicity (which is very understandable and obviously intended), rather than meaningful or consequential. Here are some randomly picked instances.

1. In 2014, in response to his minister "sadhvi" Niranjan Jyoti's open and repeated description of Hindus as "Ramzada" (Ram's children) and Muslims as "Haramzada" (bastards), he *reportedly* said (in a closed-door meeting, not in public and can't be verified) such comments were "not acceptable" and asked party MPs to refrain from giving a bad name to the government and the party.[118] Later, in response to a parliamentary

logjam due to the Opposition's protests, he asked them (in the Parliament) to forgive and forget and accept her apology.[119] She was never sacked and continues to be a Union Minister in his second term. Often hate speech makers are rewarded.[120] An analysis by the Association for Democratic Reforms (ADR) analysis of October 2023 showed[121], of 107 sitting MPs and MLAs who had declared registered cases of hate speech, 42 were from the BJP.

2. In 2015, he blamed mob lynching on "non-state actors" in vague terms ("Intolerant non-state actors now control large territories where they are unleashing barbaric violence on innocent people.").[122] In 2016, he told his party workers in response to flogging of Dalits (hate crime emanating from rigid and Brahminical caste system that is part of right-wing activities) in Gujarat's Una saying: "If you want to attack Dalits, *attack me first*. If you want to fire at Dalits, fire the first bullet at me..."[123] He didn't call to stop such violence or promise strong action.

3. On February 26, 2020, he *tweeted* for peace and harmony in Delhi *three days* after the Delhi riots of 2020 had started (February 23-27[124]) and almost ran its course ("I appeal to my sisters and brothers of Delhi to maintain peace and brotherhood *at all times*. It is important that there is calm and normalcy is restored at the earliest.").[125] His own policy (CAA), anti-Muslim pronouncements had built the base for the riots, his minister and party leaders had directly provoked the attacks ('*desh ke gaddaron ko, goli marro...*'), one of whom also led the riots as per an FIR (see Chapter I).

4. In January 2023, he *reportedly* told party leaders (in a closed-door meeting, not in public and can't be verified): "No one should make unnecessary comments that would overshadow the hard work we do."[126] Be that as it may, it related to Shah Rukh Khan's film "Pathaan" and by the time this statement came out in newspapers, a prolonged campaign against it by BJP leaders[127] and right-wing groups (against the lead actress for wearing saffron colour bikini) had boomeranged and it made many major records in box office collections in India and abroad[128].

The Prime Minister's prolonged silence on the equally prolonged communal violence in Manipur (in 2023) and yet, the persistent attempts by the Opposition and others asking him to speak provoked journalist Omair Ahmad to write that it "baffles me" that people are so "naïve" as to expect him to speak up on such matters and thereby "disavow the very people he has nurtured" in his political career since 2002.[129]

Jaffrelot[130] had forewarned that if the Prime Minister failed to deliver on the economic front, he might fall back on "Hindutva-based polarisation strategy". Two of the three main communal agenda of the BJP (and its ideological fountainhead the RSS) have already been fulfilled: (a) building a Ram temple in Ayodhya is nearing competition and (b) Article 370 has been abrogated. The third (c) Uniform Civil Code (UCC) has been pushed to the front by him and his party-ruled states (Uttarakhand, Himachal Pradesh, Gujarat, Karnataka).[131] But in view of the forthcoming 2024 general elections, the BJP launched "Modi Mitra" to woo 'Pasmanda' Muslims (most backward and constituting 85% Muslims[132]). This was despite the BJP repeatedly declaring that it does not need Muslim votes in Gujarat and Uttar Pradesh and refused to field them in elections. The Prime Minister asked his party MPs to celebrate the 2023 "Rakshadbandhan" with Muslim women.[133] The BJP also launched a new country-wide "affection" dialogues ("sneh samabad") with Muslims (and Christians)[134] which may end after the polling.

It may not be out of place to recall what the Auschwitz Museum had tweeted in 2018[135]: "When we look at Auschwitz we see the end of the process. It's important to remember that the Holocaust actually did not start from gas chambers. This hatred gradually developed from words, stereotypes & prejudice through legal exclusion, dehumanisation & escalating violence." The US State Department noted that the US holocaust museum considers India as having "potential for mass killing" – which the government dismissed as "misinformation", "motivated and biased commentary"[136] as it continues to *live in denial*[137].

There can't be a joke crueler than "Sabka saath, sabka vikas".

The attack on Muslims is particularly shocking because they are the *poorest* among all religious groups in India, worse than even the SCs and STs in many aspects. They have also been the victims of *institutionalized discrimination* for a very long time – as the Sachar Committee report of 2006 had shown.[138] The recent survey on higher education for 2020-21 showed while enrolment increased for all other groups (upper caste, SCs, STs, OBCs), that of Muslims fell by 8% from 2019-20 (by 179,147) – which is unprecedented level of absolute decline that no group has seen in the recent past.[139]

On Target: All Except Right-wing Groups

By no means such attacks are limited to Muslims. The targets are ever expanding and includes anyone who dares to question or criticize the Prime Minister, his government and their totalitarian approach and communal politics. Name and they are there: Non-Hindu religions; non-upper caste Hindus like Dalits and Adivasis; students, teachers, farmers, civil society, women and women wrestlers... The list is endless.

The USCIRF's annual report of 2023[140] asked the US administration for the *fourth consecutive year* to declare India a "country of particular concern" and said: "In 2022, religious freedom conditions in India continued to worsen. Throughout the year, the Indian government at the national, state, and local levels promoted and enforced religiously discriminatory policies, including laws targeting religious conversion, interfaith relationships, the wearing of hijabs, and cow slaughter, which negatively impact *Muslims, Christians, Sikhs, Dalits, and Adivasis* (indigenous peoples and scheduled tribes). The national government also continued to suppress critical voices – particularly religious minorities and those advocating on their behalf – including through surveillance, harassment, demolition of property, and detention under the Unlawful Activities Prevention Act (UAPA) and by targeting nongovernmental organizations (NGOs) under the Foreign Contribution Regulation Act (FCRA)." It added: "Throughout the year, destruction of property – including places of worship in predominantly Muslim and Christian neighborhoods – continued...Social media platforms continued to facilitate widespread disinformation, hate speech, and incitement of violence toward religious minorities." The Human Rights Watch (HRW)[141] and Amnesty International[142] have also been flagging the rising human rights violations, including in Jammu & Kashmir – attack on dissent, massive surveillance, severe crackdown on human rights activists and group (NGOs), courts undermining right to fair trial and delays etc. after Modi became the Prime Minister. *(Emphasis added)*

The attack on Christians saw a massive uptick after 2014.[143] The United Christian Forum (UCF), a Delhi-based civil society group, recorded a rise of four times in attacks on Christians during 2012-2022 – rising to disconcerting highs after 2014.[144] It turned very vicious during the Christmas of 2021 – again, ahead of the crucial Uttar Pradesh elections – and in Karnataka. The New York Times said about the incidents in Karnataka: "Anti-Christian vigilantes are sweeping through villages, storming churches, burning Christian literature, attacking schools and assaulting worshipers. In many cases, the police and members of India's governing party are helping them, government documents and dozens of interviews revealed. In church after church, the very act of worship has become dangerous despite constitutional protections for freedom of religion."[145] The BJP's rise in Karnataka is entirely driven by its communal politics, not development, in any case.[146] The Manipur's ethnic conflict (Hindu vs Christians) saw 254 churches and 132 temples burnt – as per the police.[147]

In 2021, the Minorities Commission reported a rise in complaints from *Sikhs, Buddhists and Parsis* of attacks.[148] In fact, the Indian society has been on the slow boil with mob violence at the ground and hate speech from the top.[149]

When the Prime Minister was asked about the attacks on minorities in India at the White House in June 2023, he said there is "absolutely no discrimination" on basis of caste, creed, or age, or any kind of geographic location – which was, of course a blatant lie as explained in 'Introduction' (others too called that out[150]).

Foreign Affairs Minister S Jaishankar went a step ahead in response to a similar question on September 29, 2023 in the same Washington DC: "What is the test really of fair and good governance or of the balance of a society? It would be whether in terms of the amenities, the benefits, the access, the rights, do you discriminate or not…I defy you to show me discrimination. In fact, the more digital we have become, the more faceless the governance has become. Actually, it's become fairer."[151]

Of course, Jaishankar wouldn't look at facts – *systemic* attack or *the pivot* of the BJP's politics – or the facts staring at the face for nearly a decade[152] but Pratik Sinha[153], founder of Altnews which pioneered busting fake news in India, nailed the glib talk around non-discrimination in governance (in response of Jaishankar's challenge) best. He wrote: "This is a *templated answer that BJP has chosen to respond to all questions concerning minorities – that social welfare is extended to everyone.* The whole party apparatus of BJP, from top to bottom, is involved in dehumanising Muslims in India through disinformation and hate speech, and you can't simply get away by claiming that a *poor Muslim also gets access to ration.*" *(Emphasis added)*

Liberal Women

Women, particularly educated, liberated and empowered ones, have always been targeted by the conservative right-wing groups (a display of "Hindutva masculinity"[154]). Right-wing women's groups too attack such women to protect Hindu 'sanskriti' (culture) from western influences. Celebrating the Valentine's Day, sitting or going out with male friends attract swift punitive actions.[155] Top BJP and RSS leaders are known for their misogyny. They often ask Hindu women to confine to home, take care of husbands and produce more children to ward-off dangers from Muslims.[156] Prime Minister once indirectly referred to then Congess president Sonia Gandhi as "Congress ki vidhwa"[157] (widow of the Congress) at a public rally, likened then Congress MP Renuka Chowdhury to "Suparnkha" (an evil mythological character) inside the Parliament[158] and Congress MP Shashi Tharoor's wife a "50-crore-rupee girlfriend"[159].

It is not surprising a parliamentary panel said, in its December 2021 report, that the government's "Beti bachao, Beti padhao" (save and educate girls) scheme had spent 79% of its budget on *publicity* alone during 2016-2019[160], although the NITI Aayog claimed in 2021 that the "Beti bachao, Beti Padhao" is a success story[161]. According to the Ministry of Women and Child Development, sex ratio has been falling since 2020 in more than a dozen states.[162] Yet another shocker: According to a parliamentary answer of 2023, *more than 13.13 lakh girls and women went missing in three years between 2019 and 2021*[163] – and yet, it didn't make any visible impact at all on the government.

This misogyny was reflected in the "Sulli Deals"[164] – online campaigns putting liberal and educated Muslim women on 'online sale' on social media (Github App). By using their publicly available photographs, hundreds of fake profiles were created and offered these women as "deals of the day", describing them as "sulli", a derogatory slang for Muslim women. The Delhi Police didn't act for months. Meanwhile, an organized attempt was made to blame a Muslim youth.[165] Six months later, in January 2022, it resurfaced as "Bulli Bai" deal on the same Gitbub App, this time auctioning Muslim women journalists. It was the Mumbai police under then non-BJP government that began a crackdown[166], forcing the Delhi Police to act. But the alt-right *network*[167] that supports them remains untouched.

Other prominent instances include the Bilkis Bano and Hathras cases detailed in earlier chapters. There are many such cases. In the Kathua rape and murder case of 2018, a Muslim child was raped and killed in which the accused were Hindus. Then BJP ministers of J&K took out marches in support of the accused.[168] Hindutva outfits, the VHP and Bajrang Dal have sat in dharna in support of multiple rape convict Asaram Bapu.[169] Ram Rahim, another religious guru, convicted in two rape-cum-murder cases and sentenced to 20 years, is granted regular *paroles* (ranging from 21 days to 40 days at a time), *particularly to celebrate his birthday*[170] and help during *state elections*[171] by the Haryana's BJP government – 182 days in 2022 and 2023 alone. In the case of sexual abuse of women wrestlers, the initial probe ordered by the government was headed by Olympic medal winner and then BJP MP Mary Kom who *justified*[172] the accused's action and sought video evidence of sexual misconduct. When the women wrestlers resumed their dharna in April 2023, the International Olympic Committee (IOC) supported them and sought swift action[173] but PT Usha, the first women president of the Indian Olympic Association (appointed by the new regime) met and *chastised*[174] the protesters saying that their protests lowered India's image and their protests amounted to indiscipline. No women MPs of BJP, usually very vocal and shrill during the UPA regime over crimes against women, never uttered a word in angst.

In the case of women wrestlers' charge of sexual abuse by a BJP MP and then president of the Wrestling Federation of India (WFI) Brij Bhushan Saran Singh, Union Minister Meenakshi Lekhi *ran*[175] when her comment was sought; Women and Child Welfare Minister Smriti Irani and other BJP MPs kept their silences[176]; the National Women's Commission (NCW), merely saying she had sought a report[177] from the Delhi Police after it was questioned. The mainstream media and the middle class barely stirred, except for certain farmers' "khaps" making it a Jat issue (some the victims being Jats). Political scientist Suhas Palshikar lamented[178] how such attitude reflected co-option and polarisation of the society in which the government was not called to question. Neither the rule of law nor public pressure was seen in such a critical issue. It ended with the accused roaming free while all the while, even after being indicted by the police probe and chargesheet was filed confirming sexual abuse. For the first time, the WFI was *suspended*[179] by the United World Wrestling (UWW) for not holding elections in time – which meant Indian wrestlers were to participate in the World Championships in September as neutrals and not under the national flag. Why does the BJP defend someone accused of sexual abuse? Mukul Kesavan wrote in the context of Singh[180]: "The Sangh rallied around Singh because in its deepest being, it is a patriarchal, misogynistic organisation hardwired to discipline recalcitrant women. Just as the Sangh Parivar uses the idea of a 'love jihad' to police the partner choices of Hindu women, it used the Delhi Police to teach successful, articulate, disobedient women a lesson: rebellion doesn't pay; learn to be pliable clients."

More of the same happened when the video of naked Kuki women of Manipur being paraded and molested surfaced in July 2023. The BJP's firebrand women MPs not just kept quiet but led by Irani, raised a storm over an *imaginary* "flying kiss"[181] by Rahul Gandhi in the Parliament during the debate on a no-confidence motion in August 2023. The no-confidence motion was to force the Prime Minister to come to the Parliament and give a statement on the Manipur situation (burning for more than two-and-half months), including the atrocities on Kuki women. The BJP women MPs, in fact, filed a complaint with the Speaker against Rahul Gandhi's "indecent" and "inappropriate" gesture towards Irani (a patently false claim as the video showed) and demanded strong action. The media, as always, joined in to keep the focus on this ridiculous episode.[182]

The crux is, the BJP keeps quiet and even supports the accused in crime against women if the accused happens to be a Hindu. The Prime Minister maintains his trademark silence. He had a minister in the first term, Nihalchand Meghwal, who was summoned by a court in a rape case and yet, when he was dropped in 2018 reshuffle[183] it wasn't for his criminal background but for alleged poor performance.[184] This (ministerial non-performance) is ironical since most ministers are unknown individuals, seldom come out in public or are known to have any say in policymaking or running their own ministries.

This is a such a perverse development in India. Recall how the 'Nirbhaya' case of 2012, when the Congress-led UPA was in power, jolted people and politics. A massive public protest erupted in New Delhi for many weeks; Manmohan Singh acknowledged the monstrosity of the crime, accepted the protests as legitimate, didn't blame Opposition parties for similar crimes in the BJP-ruled states and promised prompt action[185]. The accused were held, tried and hanged[186], the rape law was made more stringent (including death sentence); the POCSO Act of 2012 (Protection of Children from Sexual Offences)[187] had come months earlier to address growing sexual crime against children.[188]

Incidentally, the BJP has the maximum number of legislators (MPs and MLAs) with crimes against women – 44 of the total 134 – and rape cases – 7 of the toral 18 – as per the Association for Democratic Reforms report of 20203.[189]

Caste Subjugation

Ironically, Dalits (earlier known as "untouchables") are often foot soldiers of Hindutva during riots (they played active role in the 2002 Gujarat anti-Muslim pogrom, for example) and also the victims of its cow vigilantism (along with Muslims). It is often their search for acceptance within the Hindu society that gravitates Dalits towards Brahmins running the conservative right-wing outfits – the very forces which have historically victimized them through the rigid caste systemin.[190] The Una (Gujarat) flogging incident of 2016, mentioned earlier, best exemplified it.[191] In Gujarat, anything can trigger attacks on Dalits – for sporting moustache, wearing sunglasses, good clothes, riding horse, playing DJ music etc.[192]

Tribals, or Adivasis, attract similar harsh treatment from right-wing. A BJP leader urinated[193] on a tribal in Madhya Pradesh. The "Pathalgarhi movement" of Jharkhand – a tribal tradition of erecting stone slabs to demarcate their villages' jurisdiction, declaring autonomy and self-rule as the Fifth Schedule of the Constitution grants – was crushed by the BJP government headed by a non-tribal Raghubar Das (2014-2019). The BJP came to power supporting a separate homeland for tribals – but booked 30,000 people[194], mostly Adivasis, under severe sections of law, including sedition to crush the Pathalgarhi movement. President of India Draupadi Murmu, a tribal from neighbouring Odisha, was then the Governor of Jharkhand (2015-2021).[195]

Protesters: Students, Farmers and Others

Students of Delhi Jawaharlal Nehru University (JNU), Jamia Millia Islamia (JMI) and Aligarh Muslim University (AMU) protesting against the CAA became anti-national, "tukde-tukde" gang and urban naxals[196] in 2019-2020. In the JMI, they were beaten by police, in the JNU, they and their faculty members were allegedly attacked by police-backed ABVP (RSS's youth wing) goons. The Delhi Police reportedly switched off lights to facilitate this attack inside the JNU campus and was seen escorting the mob out afterwards in viral videos.[197] Komal Sharma (seen in the videos) was one of the attackers, identified by the Delhi Police[198] as ABVP member and the ABVP admitted. In the case of AMU, police entered the campus without authorization, used military grade stun grenade against peaceful students and shouted "Jai Shri Ram" – the battle cry of right-wingers.[199] Despite adequate video evidence of all these incidents, no action was taken either on cops or the mob.[200] Campuses have turned *saffron*[201] too with the right-wing students and teachers running the affairs.

The attack on students had begun with then JNU's student union president Kanhaiya Kumar (associated with Leftist group AISF) in February 2016 – in connection with a protest against the hanging of Afzal Guru, who had been convicted in the Parliament attack case of 2001, during which anti-India slogans were alleged to have been made. Kumar was arrested, charged with sedition (along with Umar Khalid) and then Union Home Minister Rajnath Singh said anti-India slogans won't be tolerated[202] – which the Delhi Police confirmed to be fabricated[203] a year later. That it was fabricated was public knowledge a few days after his arrest through forensic examinations and some of the BJP leaders had even apologized and withdrawn their allegations.[204] The BJP affiliated lawyers beat him up in the Patiala House court [205] while being escorted by the Delhi Police. The Delhi High Court (Justice Pratibha Rani)[206] gave him bail in March 2016 but seemed to take the allegations seriously, and began her bail order with a Bollywood song on patriotism, compared the doubtful slogans (some of the BJP leaders had apologized by then) with "gangrene" for which, the bail order said, "amputation is the only treatment".

Such is the distrust in campus and academic *unfreedom* that a premier private university Ashoka University has seen resignations of its Vice Chancellor Pratap Bhanu Mehta and Assistant Professor Sabyasachi Das. Mehta had to resign in 2021 for his articles which were critical of the government policies and Das in 2023 for his paper flagging electoral 'manipulations' in 2019 general elections which gave it the second term – which upset the management with the BJP protesting against them.[207] Karan Sangwan, a law teacher of edtech platform 'Unacademy' was sacked[208] for saying in a private video criticizing three criminal bills (wholesale replacement of the IPC, CrPC and Evidence Act) and asking 'vote for educated person' in 2023 for breaching 'code of conduct' without giving a chance to explain. Days after folk singer Neha Singh Rathod sang "UP Mein Ka Ba Part 2" in 2023, her husband Himanshu Singh was *asked to quit*[209] Drishti IAS, a prominent coaching institute for civil services; this was after she was accused of creating disharmony. The South Asian University (SAU) asked its students enrolling for 2023 academic session to give a "General Declaration" stating that they wouldn't join agitation, strike, participate in activity that has a "tendency to disturb peace" and also declare that they are not suffering from "psychiatric or psychological disorder" – the very opposite of its vision of providing "liberal and human education".[210] 2022 saw 16 fellows *resign*[211] from the University of Melbourne's Australia India Institute because of lack of academic freedom when the Indian High Commission interfered in their public event about *violence against Muslims* in India.

The farmers' protest against 2020 pro-corporate farm laws saw a vicious attack on them too, particularly the Sikh farmers who lead it. They were branded anti-national, terrorists and called 'Khalistanis'. Fake Sikh profiles came up across social media platforms to sabotage genuine voices and "alter perceptions on important issues around Sikh independence, human rights and values".[212] Home Minister Amit Shah and cricket and Bollywood celebrities attacked fiercely when climate activists Greta Thunberg, singer Rihanna and US Vice President's niece Meena Harris tweeted in favour of farmers.[213] The BJP workers even attacked peaceful farmers at Singhu border and the UP Police tried to evict them from the Ghazipur border.[214] Junior Union Home Minister Ajay Mishra Teni's vehicle was used, allegedly driven by his son, to mow down four peaceful farmers marching in protest in Lakhimpur Kheri. There was attempt to sabotage farmers protest when a Punjab leader Deep Sandhu[215] (now dead) associated with the BJP's top leaders, hoisted a flag on the Red Fort on January 26, 2021. Sandhu set up the Sikh separatist outfit Waris Punjab De, which under his successor Amritpal Singh raised the spectre of Sikh militancy rising again, demanding 'Khalistan' in 2023, was arrested under the National Security Act (NSA).[216] This has led to suspicions that the BJP government might have been involved with the Waris Punjab.[217]

Ethnic Cleansing

A natural progression of a communally divisive politics of the regime is ethnic cleansing. It is more visible in some BJP-ruled states and less so in others but it is systemic – no mistaking that. All these states happen to be "double-engine" governments of the BJP. From Jammu and Kashmir to Uttarakhand, Haryana, Assam, Manipur and elsewhere, the Hindutva agenda of establishing a uniform 'Hindu Rashtra' is marching ahead. Multiple fake 'jihad' campaigns listed earlier are used for the purpose – along with selective "quota" politics (Manipur and Jammu and Kashmir) and NRC coming into picture (Assam and Manipur). The genesis is very much in Gujarat, the first laboratory of the Hindutva experiment that started decades ago. As Aakar Patel has described, it is simply by coercion by Hindutva mobs, who mark Muslim shops and houses with 'x' (crossed) for attacks and eviction and applying laws like the 'Disturbed Areas Act' to segregate Muslims.[218]

In J&K, this began with the abrogation of Article 370 and Article 35A and downgrading it to two UTs in 2019. As part of this, outsiders were allowed and allotted land and Hindu youths were encouraged to "marry Kashmiri girls" and "buy land in Kashmir"[219]; that it *didn't pick up*[220] pace as expected is a different matter. It continues through the delimitation exercise and voting rights to "ordinarily" residents – as explained earlier. In Uttarakhand's Purola town, right-wing groups of the VHP, Bajrang Dal, Hindu Yuva Vahini and others like Hindu traders' body, give open call to Muslims to vacate their houses and shops (marked 'x') and give hate speeches – with the tacit support of police and state government.[221] It is a *century-old project*[222] of the Hindu right to exclude Muslims from Uttarakhand in the quest for a Hindu holy land.

In Haryana, even the Punjab and Haryana High Court used the phrase "ethnic cleansing" to describe the BJP government's use of law and order as a ruse[223] to selectively bulldoze Muslims houses and shops without following the law – after five days of unrestrained bulldozing. By then, for days VHP and Bajrang Dal and other right-wing mobs and Hindu-dominated "panchayats" (which is illegal and the officer who issued notice to them was immediately *transferred*[224]) and Hindu "mahapanchayats"[225] asked Muslims to vacate Haryana and "banned" their entry. The Haryana govt had allowed a Hindu religious procession, *Braj Mandal Yatra*[226] – mobs marching through Muslims areas carrying guns – provoked by fugitive Monu Manesar who wasn't arrested for allegedly killing Junaid and Nasir in February 2023 – and not only didn't allow Rajasthan Police not to arrest but lodged FIRs against the Rajasthan Police as Chief Minister *Ashok Gehlot* revealed[227]. Monu Manesar of the Bajrang Dal and a designated cow protector of BJP-ruled Haryana, is the prime accused in the mob lynching of Junaid and Nasir (who were then burnt in their vehicle) in February 2023 for suspected cattle smuggling. He was let go by the Haryana police just before Junaid and Nasir were burnt to death.[228] Local Hindus mobilized 'mahapanchayat' to protest against any attempt to arrest him.[229] He resurfacing at the time of the Nuh violence in June 2023, untouched.[230] He was finally arrested in September 2023 – long after the murders and the communal violence had subsided – for a social media post by the Haryana police.[231]

In Manipur, having spent two months amidst the raging civil war between predominantly Hindu Meiteis and Christian Kukis, the Caravan's Greeshma Kuthar leaves nothing to imagination about how ethnic cleansing is in full flow[232]: "...I found the Biren Singh government and the Meitei mobs it enables using most of the coercive practices listed by the committee, including murder, torture, arbitrary arrest, extrajudicial executions, sexual assault, displacement of civilians, attacks on civilian areas, the use of civilians as human shields, and the destruction and theft of personal property. The result was a state caught in a humanitarian crisis of the BJP government's own making, with the demonisation of a community being followed by wanton violence against it, leaving it facing an uncertain future of starvation, permanent displacement and possible expulsion from the state." Kukis have been forced to flee with the *active support*[233] from the BJP-run state government with the BJP's "double-engine" government effectively *apportioning*[234] areas of Meiteis and Kukis for control. Manipur began burning *after* the High Court asked the state to give tribal status (ST) to Meiteis[235] and the Centre approved *NRC drive* (to identify outsiders)[236] in April 2023 – providing the spark to the old but subdued ethnic conflict.

The 2013 Muzaffarnagar riots (between Jats and Muslims) and Muslim exodus – which preceded the Prime Minister's win in the 2014 general elections and the 2023 Gurgaon's Nuh (Meo Muslims) riots and exodus of Muslims – just ahead of the 2024 general elections – has one thing in common. For the previous two decades these places had not seen communal riots. The J ats and Muslims of western Uttar Pradesh are known to have lived in peace for long and have shared economic interests and social parity.[237] The Meo Muslims are known to have shared tight bonds and socio-cultural life with Hindus for centuries.[238] Right-wing groups broke new grounds by causing communal violence which didn't exist until then.

In Assam, the ethnic cleansing has a long history – beginning with the NRC in 1950s, which was reignited after *driven* by then CJI Ranjan Gogoi in "urgent – almost messianic – manner"[239] in 2019. Most of the fake jihad campaigns are now in Assam under the BJP government – as detailed earlier. The Assam agitations were not communal, it was the RSS which *turned it communal.* Shekhar Gupta wrote about this in 2018[240]: "RSS changed Assam's political fault line from *anti-outsider to anti-migrant* to *anti-Muslim* infiltrator". *(Emphasis added)*

Who are then left under the umbrella of "Sabka saath, sabka vikas"? All the right-wing organizations, their troll armies, mobs and 'Bhakts' – all of who share a visceral hatred for Muslims, Christians, other minorities, women and Dalits and also whoever dares to question the Prime Minister, his government and party and demand accountability from them.

How the rhetoric of "sabka saath, sabka vikas" has turned out to be a *sick joke* is well reflected in the fact that more and more ordinary Indians are fleeing the country in sheer desperation – despite facing deaths and hardships. Between November 2022 and September 2023 (less than a year), *97,917 Indians were arrested* by the US authorities for illegally entering it – a five-fold rise since 2019 – of which about 45,000 said this was due to the "fear in their own country". The economic hardship is another reason – as 730 of the arrested were unaccompanied minors. Ironically, most of those fleeing India are from the Prime Minister's home state of Gujarat (along with Punjab) where his party has been in power continuously for *nearly three decades* – since 1995.[241] Increasingly, business tycoons are also fleeing India after 2014 – after swindling huge sums of bank loans under the watch of a Prime Minister who claims to have made India corruption-free with his oft-repeated rhetoric: "Na khaunga, na khane doonga" (I will neither indulge in corruption, nor allow others to do so). (see Chapter VII).

***

References

1   PMO: Quest for Transparency, PMO; https://www.pmindia.gov.in/en/quest-for-transparency/

2   Mohanty P, CAA, NPR-NRIC V: Does India really need these nation-wide exercises? Business Today, Jan 14, 2020; https://www.businesstoday.in/latest/economy-politics/story/caa-npr-nric-does-india-really-need-these-nation-wide-exercises-illegal-migrants-citizenship-242772-2020-01-13

3   Mohanty P, CAA & NRC III: Who are 'doubtful' citizens NPR seeks to identify? Business Today, Dec 24, 2019; https://www.businesstoday.in/latest/economy-politics/story/caa-nrc-iii-who-are-doubtful-citizens-npr-seeks-to-identify-241445-2019-12-24

4   Azad Abdul Kalam, Assam NRC: A History of Violence and Persecution, Aug 15, 2018, https://thewire.in/rights/assam-nrc-a-history-of-violence-and-persecution

5   "Conspiracy To Keep Hindus Out": Assam BJP Leaders Unhappy With NRC List, Aug 31, 2019; https://www.ndtv.com/india-news/assam-nrc-final-list-conspiracy-to-keep-hindus-out-assam-bjp-leaders-unhappy-with-nrc-list-2093492

6   Mohanty P, CAA, NPR-NRIC V: Does India really need these nation-wide exercises? Business Today, Jan 14, 2020; https://www.businesstoday.in/latest/economy-politics/story/caa-npr-nric-does-india-really-need-these-nation-wide-exercises-illegal-migrants-citizenship-242772-2020-01-13

7   Amit Shah: First we will pass the Citizenship Amendment bill…Tweet of May 1, 2019; https://twitter.com/AmitShah/status/1123581776415399937?ref_src=twsrc%5Etfw%7Ctwcamp%5Etweetembed%7Ctwterm%5E112358177641 5399937%7Ctwgr%5E%7Ctwcon%5Es1_&ref_url=https%3A%2F%2Fscroll. in%2Farticle%2F947436%2Fwho-is-linking-citizenship-act-to-nrc-here-are-five-times-amit-shah-did-so

8   Mohanty P, India struggles but Bangladesh's GDP rides high on manufacturing, export boom, Oct 30, 2019; https://www.businesstoday.in/latest/economy-politics/story/india-struggles-but-bangladesh-gdp-rides-high-on-manufacturing-export-boom-235110-2019-10-30; Sinha Shishir, Per capita GDP for Bangladesh higher than India till 2022, May 7, 2023; https://www.thehindubusinessline.com/news/world/per-capita-gdp-for-bangladesh-higher-than-india-till-2022/article66823548.ece

9   Article 14, Constitution of India 1949; https://indiankanoon.org/doc/367586/

10   No talks on nationwide NRC right now, PM Modi was right, says Amit Shah, Dec 24, 2019; https://www.indiatoday.in/india/story/no-talks-on-nationwide-nrc-now-amit-shah-interview-1631224-2019-12-24

11   Mohanty P, CAA & NRC IV: NPR has no independent existence; it exists only in the NRIC context, Business Today, Dec 26, 2019; https://www.businesstoday.in/latest/economy-politics/story/caa-and-nrc-iv-protests-national-population-register-only-exists-in-the-nric-context-modi-govt-amit-shah-241373-2019-12-26

12   Singh Vijaita, Home Ministry seeks eighth extension to frame CAA rules, Aug 8, 2023; https://www.thehindu.com/news/national/home-ministry-seeks-eighth-extension-to-frame-caa-rules/article67169456.ece

13   Mohanty P, Sabarimala row: BJP and Congress undermining Constitution's secular values without a second thought for country's future, Firstpost, Nov 10, 2018; https://www.firstpost.com/india/sabarimala-row-bjp-and-congress-undermining-constitutions-secular-values-without-a-second-thought-for-countrys-future-5530371.html

14   Sabarimala case: Supreme Court upholds referring religious questions to larger Bench, frames 7 questions of law, Feb 10, 2020; https://www.thehindu.com/news/national/sabarimala-case-supreme-court-upholds-referring-religious-questions-to-larger-bench-frames-7-questions-of-law/article30780943.ece

15   Khechar Visoba, Why Does Narendra Modi Lie? Apr 28, 2019; https://thewire.in/politics/why-does-narendra-modi-lie

16   Penkar Ahan, Fact Check: The lies and misdirections of the Modi government during the coronavirus lockdown, Jun 13, 2020; https://caravanmagazine.in/politics/fact-check-the-modi-administrations-statements-on-the-lockdown-were-filled-with-misdirections-and-lies

17   Ghosh Rohit, The Myriad Things Indian Muslims Are Changing To Survive Overt & Covert Hostility In Their Changing Country, Mar 27, 2023; https://www.article-14.com/post/the-myriad-things-indian-muslims-are-changing-to-survive-overt-covert-hostility-in-their-changing-country--6420a1fd73768; Ramani Priya, 'First They Came For Our Lifestyle, Then Our Livelihoods, Now Our Right To Life', Dec 30, 2021; https://article-14.com/post/-first-they-came-for-our-lifestyle-then-our-livelihoods-now-our-right-to-life--61cd5032dddd1

18   Haramzada and 4 other controversial comments that Narendra Modi govt found difficult to defend, Dec 4, 2014; https://indianexpress.com/article/political-pulse/five-controversial-comments-that-modi-govt-found-difficult-to-defend/

19   Singh Ratna and Ahmed Areeb Uddin, Demolitions As Collective, Illegal Punishment, With Mainly Muslim Properties Destroyed After Riots, Apr 25, 2022; https://article-14.com/post/demolitions-as-collective-illegal-punishment-with-mainly-muslim-properties-destroyed-after-riots-6265a9ad591d8

20   Rahman Aquilur, Kumar Vipul, 20 Years After Gujarat Riots, Muslim Survivors From Naroda Patiya Live Near A Mountain Of Trash, Jan 13, 2023; https://article-14.com/post/20-years-after-gujarat-riots-muslim-survivors-from-naroda-patiya-live-near-a-mountain-of-trash--63c080d93c6ea

21   Bhatnagar Gaurav Vivek, In One Month's Time, BJP Will Have No Muslim Representatives in Parliament, Assemblies, Jun 6, 2022; https://thewire.in/government/in-one-months-time-bjp-will-have-no-muslim-representatives-in-parliament-assemblies; BJP now eyes road to Muslim hearts via Legislative Council, Apr 8, 2023; https://indianexpress.com/article/political-pulse/bjp-muslim-legislative-council-up-8541856/

22 Bhatia Gautam, Demolitions as state-sanctioned collective punishment, Aug 11, 2023; https://www.thehindu.com/opinion/lead/demolitions-as-state-sanctioned-collective-punishment/article67180107.ece

23 Aafaq Zafar, India activist Afreen Fatima says her house bulldozed 'illegally', Jun 13, 2022; https://www.aljazeera.com/news/2022/6/13/act-of-vendetta-afreen-fatima-on-her-house-bulldozed-in-india

24 In response to Akhilesh Yadav's jibe, bulldozers line up at UP CM Yogi's Sultanpur rally venue, Feb 27, 2022; https://www.indiatoday.in/elections/uttar-pradesh-assembly-polls-2022/story/akhilesh-yadav-jibe-bulldozer-yogi-adityanath-rally-sultanpur-1918183-2022-02-26

25 Kakvi Kashif, Why Former Police Chiefs, Judge Say Arrest Of 3 Muslim Teens, Demolition of Their Home By MP Govt Is Illegal, Jul 26, 2023; https://article-14.com/post/why-former-police-chiefs-judge-say-arrest-of-3-muslim-teens-demolition-of-their-home-by-mp-govt-is-illegal--64c079ad46ab8#:~:text=Former%20Madras%20High%20Court%20Justice%20Chandru%20concurred%20with%20Rahman's%20view,the%20thumb%20of%20the%20majority%E2%80%9D. /

26 Union Government Discontinues MANF Scholarship for Minority Communities, Dec 9, 2022; https://thewire.in/education/manf-minority-smriti-irani-sachar-committee

27 Angad Abhishek, Jharkhand scholarship scam: Fraud went on unchecked even as red flags were waved in Centre and state, Nov 3, 2020; https://indianexpress.com/article/india/jharkhand-scholarship-scam-fraud-hemant-soren-6915609/; Scholarship scam spreads to Bihar, ropes in school from Punjab too, Nov 5, 2022; https://indianexpress.com/article/india/scholarship-scam-bihar-punjab-jharkhand-6950793/

28 Utilisation of funds, Mar 23, 2023, Lok Sabha 2023; https://pqals.nic.in/annex/1711/AU3903.pdf

29 Sharma Supriya, How 'Kashmir Files' added to communal fires in Khargone that ended with bulldozer injustice, Apr 29, 2022; https://scroll.in/article/1022860/how-kashmir-files-added-to-communal-fires-in-khargone-that-ended-with-bulldozer-injustice; Ali Jehangir, Students Suspended After 'The Kerala Story' Stokes Communal Violence at GMC Jammu Campus, May 16, 2023; https://thewire.in/communalism/gmc-jammu-violence-the-kerala-story

30 PM Narendra Modi supports The Kerala Story, says Congress "kneeled down before terrorism", May 8, 2023; https://economictimes.indiatimes.com/news/politics-and-nation/pm-narendra-modi-supports-the-kerala-story-says-congress-kneeled-down-before-terrorism/articleshow/100017655.cms?utm_source=contentofinterest&utm_medium=text&utm_campaign=cppst

31 The Kerala Story: BJP CMs show their support by turning up to watch the film, May 13, 2023; https://indianexpress.com/article/political-pulse/the-kerala-story-bjp-cms-show-their-support-8606964/

32 Rajsekhar M, Marooned: Praful Patel's war on Lakshadweep, Jun 2, 2022; https://caravanmagazine.in/politics/praful-khoda-patel-lakshadweep-economy-protests

33 Patel Aakar 2021: Price of Modi Years, Westland Publications, 2021; https://www.amazon.in/Price-Modi-Years-Aakar-Patel/dp/9391234224

34 Jaffrelot 'Modi's India'

35 Kesavan Mukul, Maiming India: The regime's mimicry of Pakistan in rewriting India's history; Apr 16, 2023; https://www.telegraphindia.com/opinion/maiming-india-the-regimes-mimicry-of-pakistan-in-rewriting-indias-history/cid/1929997#.ZDu53yhQNRU.twitter

36 Sen Rononjoy, The politics of naming and renaming public spaces in India, Mar 1, 2021; https://www.hindustantimes.com/opinion/the-politics-of-naming-and-renaming-public-spaces-in-india-101614520459026.html

37 USCIRF 2023: International Religious Freedom, 2023 annual report, India segment; https://www.uscirf.gov/sites/default/files/2023-05/2023%20Annual%20Report.pdf

38 The state of the world's human rights, Amnesty International, 2022, https://www.amnesty.org/en/wp-content/uploads/2022/03/WEBPOL1048702022ENGLISH.pdf

39 India: Government Policies, Actions Target Minorities, Human Rights Watch, 2021; https://www.hrw.org/news/2021/02/19/india-government-policies-actions-target-minorities

40 Poddar Umang, Public worship is everywhere in India – so how are arrests being made for namaz? Jul 26, 2022; https://scroll.in/article/1028964/public-worship-is-everywhere-in-india-so-how-are-arrests-being-made-for-namaz; Muslim residents aghast as Hindu neighbours in Noida call the police to stop Ramzan prayers, Apr 1, 2023; https://scroll.in/article/1046631/muslim-residents-aghast-as-hindu-neighbours-in-noida-call-the-police-to-stop-ramzan-prayers

41 Watch: Kanwariyas showered with flower petals from chopper by top official in UP, Jul 25, 2022; https://www.hindustantimes.com/india-news/watch-kanwariyas-showered-with-flower-petals-from-chopper-by-top-official-in-up-101658753693985.html

42 Ashraf Ajaz, History of how Sangh Uses Religious Processions to Spark Riots, Apr 13, 2022; https://www.newsclick.in/history-how-sangh-uses-religious-processions-spark-riots

43 Ram Navami-Hanuman Jayanti clashes: 'India has reached stage of perpetual violence', Apr 5, 2023; https://thefederal.com/news/ram-navami-hanuman-jayanti-clashes-india-has-reached-stage-of-perpetual-violence/

44 Singh Chander Uday, Routes of Wrath: Weaponising Religious Processions, Citizens & Lawyers Initiative, Apr 2023; https://www.livelaw.in/pdf_upload/routes-of-wrath-report-2023-2-465217.pdf;

New Report Finds 'Distinct', 'Eerie' Patterns in Hanuman Jayanti, Ram Navami Rallies in April 2022, https://thewire.in/communalism/new-report-finds-distinct-eerie-patterns-in-hanuman-jayanti-ram-navami-rallies-in-april-2022;,

45   Post-Ram Navami, fresh violence hits Bihar, Bengal, Apr 3, 2023; http://timesofindia.indiatimes.com/articleshow/99195004.cms?from=mdr&utm_source=contentofinterest&utm_medium=text&utm_campaign=cppst;   Fresh violence erupts in Odisha's Sambalpur during Hanuman Jayanti rally, several shops gutted, Apr 15, 2023; https://www.indiatoday.in/india/story/fresh-hanuman-jayanti-violence-erupts-in-odisha-sambalpur-several-shops-gutted-2360226-2023-04-14

46   Under Delhi Police eye, Jahangirpuri observes Hanuman Jayanti; Apr 7, 2023; https://indianexpress.com/article/cities/delhi/under-delhi-police-eye-jahangirpuri-observes-hanuman-jayanti-8543254/

47   Ashutosh Varshney and Bhanu Joshi write: Ram Navami violence — it wasn't always so, Apr 8, 2023 https://indianexpress.com/article/opinion/columns/ram-navami-violence-it-wasnt-always-so-8544515/

48   'Love Jihad' is an Islamophobic Campaign: Why Honour is about Controlling Women's Bodies, Economic and Political Weekly (Engage), 2020; https://www.epw.in/sites/default/files/engage_pdf/2020/12/14/157730.pdf

49   Mittal Tusa, Theatre of Destruction: How bulldozers became part of the Hindu nationalist lexicon in India, May 16, 2023; https://caravanmagazine.in/politics/bulldozers-hindu-india

50   Singh Chander Uday, Busting The Myth Behind 'Love Jihad' Laws Made By Eleven States, Jan 8, 2023; https://hindutvawatch.org/busting-the-myth-behind-love-jihad-laws-made-by-eleven-states-column-by-cu-singh-senior-advocate-livelaw/; Ara Ismat, Exclusive: UP Police Report Contradicts Adityanath Claim of 'Rise in Love Jihad', Nov 23, 2020; https://thewire.in/communalism/up-police-report-adityanath-love-jihad-cases; Kaskar Zeeshan, Watch: Not a Single 'Love Jihad' Case in Front of Maharashtra's Interfaith Marriage Panel, Mar 26, 2023; https://thewire.in/communalism/watch-not-a-single-love-jihad-case-in-front-of-maharashtras-interfaith-marriage-panel

51   Venkatesan Rashmi, Laws Prohibiting Cow Slaughter Are Creating Both Vigilantes and Victims, Sept 15, 2017; https://thewire.in/politics/cow-slaughter-laws-vigilantes-victims

52   Crime in India 2020, National Crime Records Bureau, GOI, Sept 2021; https://ncrb.gov.in/sites/default/files/CII%202020%20Volume%202.pdf

53   Jafri Alishan, Thook Jihad? No, India is Drowning in the Cesspool Our Reigning Spit Experts Have Created, Feb 8, 2022; https://thewire.in/communalism/thook-jihad-no-india-is-drowning-in-the-cesspool-our-reigning-spit-experts-have-created

54   Chaudhuri Pooja, Fact check: Does this video show a cleric spitting on food? Nov 9, 2021; https://www.altnews.in/fact-check-does-this-video-show-a-maulana-spitting-on-food/

55   Mittal Tusa, 'Theatre of Destruction'

56   Is mazar jihad real or weapon to polarize? Apr 7, 2023; https://www.indiatoday.in/programme/india-first/video/is-mazar-jihad-real-or-weapon-to-polarize-2357229-2023-04-07

57   "Madrassas Being Used As Terror Hub": Assam Chief Minister On Demolitions, Aug 9, 2022; https://www.ndtv.com/india-news/madrassa-demolished-in-assams-barpeta-district-chief-minister-himanta-biswa-sarma-confirms-3296413

58   Ellis-Petersen Hannah, Thousands of mosques targeted as Hindu nationalists try to rewrite India's history, Oct 30, 2022; https://www.theguardian.com/world/2022/oct/30/thousands-of-mosques-targeted-as-hindu-nationalists-try-to-rewrite-indias-history

59   CM Himanta Biswa Sarma: No need for madrasas, will shut all in Assam, Mar 18, 2023; https://www.newindianexpress.com/states/karnataka/2023/mar/18/cm-himanta-biswa-sarma-no-need-for-madrasas-will-shut-all-in-assam-2557042.html

60   'Ajmal's people' will take all medical, engineering seats if Assam doesn't prioritise education: Himanta, Jun 23, 2023; https://indianexpress.com/article/india/ajmal-people-medical-engineering-seats-assam-doesnt-prioritise-education-himanta-8682752/; 'Ajmal's people' will take all seats if we do not prioritise education, says Assam CM, Jun 24, 2023; https://scroll.in/latest/1051479/ajmals-people-will-take-all-seats-if-we-do-not-prioritise-education-says-assam-cm

61   Assam: Muslims falsely accused of waging 'flood jihad', Aug 3, 2022; https://www.bbc.com/news/world-asia-india-62378520

62   Baruah Sukrita, A new weapon in Assam CM Himanta Sarma's arsenal: 'fertiliser jihad', Jun 11, 2023; https://indianexpress.com/article/political-pulse/assam-cm-himanta-sarma-fertiliser-jihad-bengali-muslim-8656703/

63   Baruah Sukrita, Overnight crackdown, tip-offs from sources: Behind the 916 child marriage arrests in Assam, Oct 3, 2023; https://indianexpress.com/article/india/assam-child-marriage-crackdown-arrest-8966223/

64   Pritam Anmol, Uttarkashi: How a 'journalist' and Hindutva groups manufactured the 'love jihad' angle, Jun 17, 2023; https://www.newslaundry.com/2023/06/17/uttarkashi-how-a-journalist-and-hindutva-groups-manufactured-the-love-jihad-angle

65   Jafri Alishan, Cross Marks on Doors, Cries of Extermination: How Uttarakhand Became Our Hate Speech Capital, Jun 12, 2023; https://thewire.in/communalism/uttarakhand-hate-speech-jihad-anti-muslim

66   BJP leader puts off daughter's wedding to Muslim man after protests, says: 'My responsibility is also towards my people', May 23, 2023; https://indianexpress.com/article/india/cancelling-daughters-wedding-muslim-man-protests-bjp-leader-8621542/

67   Goyal Prateek and Shaikh Tarmeem, The truth behind 'gaming jihad': How media skipped facts to manufacture a story, Jun 19, 2023; https://www.newslaundry.com/2023/06/19/the-truth-behind-gaming-jihad-how-media-skipped-facts-to-manufacture-a-story

68   BJP's Ramesh Arora wants momos banned, claims 'killer dumplings' worse than alcohol, drugs, Jun 29, 2017; https://www.firstpost.com/india/bjp-leader-ramesh-arora-wants-momos-banned-claims-killer-dumplings-worse-than-alcohol-drugs-3759269.html

69   Apoorvanand, How the coronavirus outbreak in India was blamed on Muslims, Apr 18, 2020; https://www.aljazeera.com/opinions/2020/4/18/how-the-coronavirus-outbreak-in-india-was-blamed-on-muslims

70   Majumder Shinjinee, Social media users add communal spin to Odisha train mishap, falsely describe temple near tracks as a mosque, Jun 3, 2023; https://www.altnews.in/social-media-users-add-communal-spin-to-odisha-mishap-falsely-describe-temple-near-tracks-as-a-mosque/

71   Bhattacharya Oishani and Bhattacharya Indradeep, Rly staff have joined Balasore accident probe, reports of 'absconding' false. And the station master's name is not Sharif, Jun 6, 2023; https://www.altnews.in/rly-staff-have-joined-balasore-accident-probe-reports-of-absconding-false-and-the-station-masters-name-is-not-sharif/

72   Balasore tragedy: CBI arrests 3 railway staffers, invokes culpable homicide, Jul 8, 2023; https://timesofindia.indiatimes.com/india/balasore-tragedy-cbi-arrests-3-railway-staffers-invokes-culpable-homicide/articleshow/101582490.cms?from=mdr

73   Lapses in Signalling, Telecom Departments Led to Balasore Train Mishap, Finds Probe by Railways, Jul 1, 2023; https://thewire.in/government/commissioner-of-railway-safety-signaling-operations-staff-balasore-tragedy

74   Bhattacharya Oishani, Manipur shocker: Misreport by ANI sets off false communal claim; Abdul Hilim's arrest not related to viral video case, Jul 21, 2023; https://www.altnews.in/manipur-video-misreport-by-ani-sets-off-false-communal-claims-on-social-media-none-of-the-4-arrested-so-far-is-a-muslim/

75   Patel Jignesh, Muslim student from JNU falsely blamed for 'masterminding' violence at the university, Jan 7, 2020; https://www.altnews.in/muslim-student-from-jnu-falsely-blamed-for-masterminding-violence-at-the-university/

76   Citizenship Act: Protestors 'creating violence can be identified by their clothes', claims Modi, Dec 15, 2019; https://scroll.in/latest/946901/citizenship-act-protestors-creating-violence-can-be-identified-by-their-clothes-claims-modi

77   Sagar, Delhi Violence Unmasked | Part Two: How Modi's speeches fomented hate, aided Hindutva mobilisation against anti-CAA protesters, Mar 1, 2021; https://caravanmagazine.in/politics/part-two-how-modi-speeches-fomented-hate-aided-hindutva-mobilisation-against-anti-caa-protesters

78   Rao Vidhatri, Alia-Malia-Jamalia: How a Gujarati phrase became a jibe against UPA govt, Jun 13, 2023; https://indianexpress.com/article/political-pulse/alia-malia-jamalia-amit-shah-upa-govt-8659435/

79   Express View on Devendra Fadnavis's communal rhetoric: Dogwhistle in Mumbai, Jun 10, 2023; https://indianexpress.com/article/opinion/editorials/devendra-fadnavis-aurangzeb-ki-aulad-kolhapur-communal-tension-8655090/

80   Aurangzeb on WhatsApp profile pic gets Maharashtra man detained, Jun 12, 2023; https://timesofindia.indiatimes.com/city/navi-mumbai/aurangzeb-on-w/a-profile-pic-gets-maharashtra-man-detained/articleshow/100921415.cms?from=mdr

81   Aafaq Zafar, Jailed, suspended, fired: How teachers in UP have paid a price for Hindutva campaigns against a song, May 15, 2023; https://scroll.in/article/1048880/

82   Smart Pallavi and Rajpur Sagar, Principal suspended, booked over claims of college event luring students towards Islam, Jun 14, 2023; https://indianexpress.com/article/cities/mumbai/principal-suspended-booked-over-claims-of-college-event-luring-students-towards-islam-8659611/

83   Sikdar Shubhomoy, M.P. government suspends recognition of school caught in 'compulsory hijab' row, Jun 3, 2023; https://www.thehindu.com/news/national/other-states/mp-government-suspends-recognition-of-school-caught-in-compulsory-hijab-row/article66924676.ece

84   'I'll help you buy land, find Kashmiri girls to marry', Aug 8, 2019; https://www.deccanherald.com/national/national-politics/ill-help-you-buy-land-find-kashmiri-girls-to-marry-752791.html

85   Akhtar Sadia, Railways issue notice to religious places in Delhi over 'encroachments' on its land, Jul 23, 2023; https://www.hindustantimes.com/cities/delhi-news/northern-railway-issues-notice-calling-for-removal-of-religious-structures-on-its-land-101690052091987.html

86   Jalihal Shreegireesh, Under New Madhya Pradesh Law, 12-year-old Muslim Boy On Trial Before Tribunal To Recover Riot Damage, Oct 17, 2022; https://article-14.com/post/under-new-madhya-pradesh-law-12-year-old-muslim-boy-on-trial-before-tribunal-to-recover-riot-damage-634c614a55ad6

87   Aswani Tarushi, Changed Procession Route, Provoking Muslims: Ram Navami Followed a Familiar Pattern in Gujarat, Apr 18, 2023; https://thewire.in/communalism/gujarat-vadodara-ram-navami-anti-muslim

88   Raj Kaushik, In Riot-Torn Nuh, A Muslim Man Has Found It Impossible To Get His Complaint Registered, Aug 14, 2023; https://article-14.com/post/in-riot-torn-nuh-a-muslim-man-has-found-it-impossible-to-get-his-complaint-registered--64d5951c03420#:~:text=Nuh%2C%20Haryana%3A%20Ten%20days%20after,who%20he%20accused%20of%20pelting

89   Bhalla Vineet, Delhi Police has been caught fabricating evidence for 2020 riots cases – but faces no consequences, Sept 12, 2023; https://scroll.in/article/1055170/delhi-police-has-been-caught-fabricating-evidence-for-2020-riots-cases-but-faces-no-consequences; Chander Mani, 11 Ways The Delhi Police Have Muddied The Delhi-Riots Investigation, Sept 13, 2021; https://article-14.com/post/11-ways-the-delhi-police-have-muddied-the-delhi-riots-investigation-613ebb8c99769; Sebastian Manu, Delhi Riots: Damning Observations In Court Orders Raise Questions Over Delhi Police Probe, Nov 28, 2020; https://www.livelaw.in/columns/delhi-riots-damning-observations-in-court-orders-raise-questions-over-delhi-police-probe-166534; Justice Lokur et al, Uncertain Justice: A Citizens Committee Report

on the North East Delhi Violence 2020, Oct 2022; https://theleaflet.in/wp-content/uploads/2022/10/uncertain-justice-citizens-committee-report-on-north-east-delhi-violence-2020.pdf

90   Swain Ashok, Why saffron terror is not a myth, May 20, 2016; https://scroll.in/article/808306/why-saffron-terror-is-not-a-myth

91   Sen Somdeep, Hindu nationalists now pose a global problem, Sept 16, 2022; https://www.aljazeera.com/opinions/2022/9/26/violent-hindu-extremism-is-now-a-global-problem

92   Form policy to curb stray cattle menace: Gujarat HC, Jul 12, 2023; http://timesofindia.indiatimes.com/articleshow/101681110.cms?from=mdr&utm_source=contentofinterest&utm_medium=text&utm_campaign=cppst; Stray cattle, a major problem on MP roads, Jul 24, 2023; http://timesofindia.indiatimes.com/articleshow/102066187.cms?from=mdr&utm_source=contentofinterest&utm_medium=text&utm_campaign=cppst

93   PM Modi Promises To Solve Issue Of Stray Cattle In UP, PTI, Feb 20, 2022; https://www.ndtv.com/india-news/up-polls-2022-prime-minister-narendra-modi-promises-to-solve-stray-cattle-issue-in-up-2779249

94   Safi Michael, Blues and moos: Indian state launches cow ambulance service, May 8, 2017; https://www.theguardian.com/world/2017/may/08/cow-ambulances-indias-latest-scheme-to-protect-revered-animal

95   UP: Yogi government to conduct census of cows in three categories, ANI, Nov 6, 2023; https://www.aninews.in/news/national/general-news/up-yogi-government-to-conduct-census-of-cows-in-three-categories20231106213432/

96   Rashid Omar, UP's Crackdown Against Halal Products: A 'Criminal Case' and a Ban, Nov 19, 2023https://thewire.in/communalism/ups-crackdown-against-halal-products-a-criminal-case-and-a-ban

97   Delimitation Commission for J&K, Assam, Manipur, Arunachal, Nagaland Formed, Mar 7, 2020; https://thewire.in/government/delimitation-commission-jk-assam-manipur-arunachal-nagaland

98   Ali Jehangir, Dangers of adding 25 lakh to 76 lakh voter base; Jehangir Ali, J&K Regional Parties Go Into a Huddle as EC Expects Two Million New Voters; Aug 19, 2022; https://thewire.in/government/jammu-kashmir-regional-parties-election-commission-new-voters

99   Zaman Rokibuz, Why the Election Commission's Assam delimitation proposal is being seen as communal, Jun 27, 2023; https://scroll.in/article/1051522/why-the-election-commissions-assam-delimitation-proposal-is-being-seen-as-communal; Agarwala Tora, Assam delimitation draft: What changes it proposes, why it has led to protests, Jun 27, 2023; https://indianexpress.com/article/explained/explained-politics/assam-delimitation-draft-what-changes-it-proposes-why-it-has-led-to-protests-8687267/

100   Kalita Prabin, 5 Assam minority bastions now reserved SC/ST seats, Aug 12, 2023;

http://timesofindia.indiatimes.com/articleshow/102662945.cms?from=mdr&utm_source=contentofinterest&utm_medium=text&utm_campaign=cppst

101   Joshua Anita, India at risk: Rwanda killings predictor sounds genocide warning, Jan 20, 2022; https://www.telegraphindia.com/india/india-at-risk-rwanda-killings-predictor-sounds-genocide-warning/cid/1848331; Thapar Karan, Full Text | As PM, Modi Has a Moral Obligation To Denounce Hate Speech: Gregory Stanton, The Wire, Jan 21, 2022; https://thewire.in/communalism/full-text-gregory-stanton-karan-thapar-narendra-modi-haridward-hate-speech-genocide-india

102   Hindutva leaders call for killing of Muslims at Haridwar and Delhi events, Dec 24, 2021; https://scroll.in/latest/1013435/videos-of-seers-calling-for-killing-of-muslims-hindu-rashtra-spark-anger

103   Fatima Madeeha, Barton Naomi and Jafri Alishan, 100+ Instances of Hate Speech, Religious Polarisation, Hindutva Supremacy in Adityanath's Poll Speeches, Mar 3, 2022; https://thewire.in/communalism/100-instances-of-hate-speech-religious-polarisation-hindutva-supremacy-in-adityanaths-poll-speeches

104   Hate Speech: What Bajrang Muni, Yati Narsinghanand, Anand Swaroop Said In The Past, Jul 8, 2022; https://www.boomlive.in/news/bajrang-muni-das-rape-threat-muslim-women-hate-speech-mohammed-zubair-supreme-court-18453

105   Nellis, Gareth & Weaver, Michael & Rosenzweig, Steven C., 2016. "Do Parties Matter for Ethnic Violence? Evidence From India," Quarterly Journal of Political Science, now publishers, vol. 11(3), pages 249-277, October.

106   Iyer Sriya, Shrivastava Anand 2015, Religious Riots and Electoral Politics in India, University of Cambridge, https://docs.iza.org/dp9522.pdf

107   Ticku, Rohit, Riot Rewards? Religious Conflict and Electoral Outcomes (May 1, 2016). Graduate Institute of International and Development Studies Working Paper No. 19/2015, Available at SSRN: https://ssrn.com/abstract=2803978 or http://dx.doi.org/10.2139/ssrn.2803978

108   Menon Aditya, Lokniti-CSDS post poll survey, the 2019 Lok Sabha election, Sept 1, 2020; https://www.thequint.com/news/politics/narendra-modi-hindutva-lok-sabha-election-results-2019-csds-survey-muslims-sikhs#read-more

109   Mathew Liz and CG Manoj, PM told me 'chup raho' on Pulwama, says ex-J&K Gov Malik; Cong calls for answers, Apr 16, 2023; https://indianexpress.com/article/political-pulse/pulwama-attack-satya-pal-malik-pm-modi-congress-8558039/

110   Najafizada Eltaf, Modi's Party Linked With Most Hate Speech in India, Report Finds, Sept 25, 2023; https://www.bloomberg.com/news/articles/2023-09-25/modi-s-party-linked-with-most-hate-speech-in-india-report-finds

111   Jaiswal Nimisha, Jain Sreenivasan and Singh Manas P, Under Modi Government, VIP Hate Speech Skyrockets - By 500%, Apr 19 2018; https://www.ndtv.com/india-news/under-narendra-modi-government-vip-hate-speech-skyrockets-by-500-1838925

112   BJP Press release, Jun 5, 2022; https://www.bjp.org/pressreleases/press-release-bjp-national-general-secretary-shri-arun-singh-7

113   Embassy of India, Doha, Press release, Jun 5, 2022; https://indianembassyqatar.gov.in/s?id=eyJpdiI6IlROam5DNHRlY3pHNGs4Sm4zdFk3UGc9PSIsInZhbHVlIjoiXC9pSk1lXC9WWEdNWFAwdmkwWHZjR21RPT0iLCJtYWMiOiJjZmMwMjEyYzlhMGQ1YTc3YmZkNGVkY2JhYTkzZmJjMjczNDZjYTRkMzRmNWMxYTQxMDdhNTc2ZGGYyYzRiODdjIn0=

114   After SC Rebuke, Delhi Police Says Nupur Sharma Was Questioned on June 18, Jul 1, 2022; https://thewire.in/government/after-sc-rebuke-delhi-police-says-nupur-sharma-was-questioned-on-june-18

115   Delhi Police gives security to suspended BJP spokesperson Nupur Sharma, Jun 7, 2022; http://timesofindia.indiatimes.com/articleshow/92052913.cms?utm_source=contentofinterest&utm_medium=text&utm_campaign=cppst

116   SC: Nupur Sharma can't be arrested till August 10, Jul 20, 2022; https://economictimes.indiatimes.com/news/india/sc-nupur-sharma-cant-be-arrested-till-august-10/articleshow/92989352.cms?utm_source=contentofinterest&utm_medium=text&utm_campaign=cppst;

117   SC grants protection to Nupur Sharma from arrest in FIRs on Prophet row, issues notices to govt, Jul 19, 2022; https://www.hindustantimes.com/india-news/sc-grants-protection-nupur-sharma-from-arrest-in-firs-on-prophet-row-101658221934978.html

118   Modi disapproves of Minister Sadhvi Jyoti's remarks, Dec 2, 2014; https://www.thehindu.com/news/national/Modi-disapproves-of-Minister-Sadhvi-Niranjan-Jyoti%E2%80%99s-remarks/article60321875.ece

119   Parliament live: Logjam over Sadhvi's remarks ends after chairman reads out resolution, Dec 8, 2014; https://www.firstpost.com/politics/parliament-live-logjam-over-sadhvis-remarks-ends-after-chairman-reads-out-resolution-1820325.html

120   Patel Aakar, The 'Haramzada' Manoeuvre, Feb 4, 2022; https://www.outlookindia.com/website/story/the-haramzada-manoeuvre/292805

121   Analysis of Sitting MPs/MLAs with Declared Cases Related to Hate Speech, ADR, Oct 3, 2023; https://adrindia.org/content/analysis-sitting-mpsmlas-declared-cases-related-hate-speech

122   Non-state actors unleashing violence on innocent people: PM Modi, Sept 4, 2015; https://indianexpress.com/article/india/india-others/ideologies-opposed-to-dialogue-cause-violence-pm-modi/

123   Attack me, shoot me if you want, but don't attack Dalits: PM Modi, Aug 8, 2016; https://www.hindustantimes.com/india-news/attack-me-but-don-t-attack-dalits-pm-modi-in-hyderabad/story-VaCQhXHjePtJzXcSvpWIbM.html

124   Dutta Alisha and Tewari Samridhi, 2020 Delhi riots: three years later, the scars remain, Feb 23, 2023; https://www.thehindu.com/news/cities/Delhi/2020-delhi-riots-3-years-later-the-scars-remain/article66542087.ece

125   Pandey Neelam, PM Modi appeals for peace in riot-hit Delhi, but BJP leaders' tweets are far from pacifying, Feb 26, 2020; https://theprint.in/politics/pm-modi-appeals-for-peace-in-riot-hit-delhi-but-bjp-leaders-tweets-are-far-from-pacifying/371608/

126   Mathew Liz, Unnecessary comments, like those on films, overshadow our hard work: PM Modi, Jan 19, 2023; https://indianexpress.com/article/political-pulse/refrain-from-making-unnecessary-comments-against-films-pm-modi-to-party-workers-8388649/

127   Effigy of SRK burnt in protest against Pathaan movie in Indore, Dec 15, 2022; https://www.indiatoday.in/india/story/effigy-of-shah-rukh-khan-burnt-protest-against-pathaan-movie-indore-besharam-rang-song-2309291-2022-12-15

128   Pathaan box office: Every major record that Shah Rukh Khan's blockbuster film has broken, in India and worldwide, Feb 2, 2023; https://indianexpress.com/article/entertainment/bollywood/pathan-collection-pathaan-box-office-records-list-shah-rukh-khan-blockbuster-8419674/

129   Ahmad Omair, It Is Naïve to Expect PM Modi to Speak up During Crises, Jul 24, 2023; https://thewire.in/politics/narendra-modi-manipur-gujarat

130   'Modi's Plan A will be economy. If that does not work, Hindutva', May 15, 2015; https://scroll.in/article/664475/modis-plan-a-will-be-economy-if-that-does-not-work-hindutva

131   Uttarakhand, Gujarat, Himachal Pradesh and now Karnataka: How BJP is advancing its UCC agenda, May 2, 2023; https://indianexpress.com/article/political-pulse/with-karnataka-four-states-counting-how-bjp-is-advancing-its-ucc-agenda-8585940/

132   Explained | Who Are Pasmanda Muslims, Why Is BJP Wooing Them, And Will It Work?, Oct 19, 2022; https://www.thequint.com/explainers/explained-pasmanda-muslims-bjp-vote-meeting-atrocities-lynchings-why-what-who#read-more

133   Celebrate Rakshabandhan with Muslim women: PM Modi to BJP MPs, Aug 2, 2023; https://timesofindia.indiatimes.com/india/celebrate-rakshabandhan-with-muslim-women-pm-modi-to-bjp-mps/articleshow/102328679.cms?from=mdr

134   Anand Jatin, 'Affection Dialogues': here's BJP's plan for nationwide outreach to minorities, Oct 21, 2023; https://indianexpress.com/article/cities/delhi/in-minority-outreach-for-ls-polls-bjp-to-hold-affection-dialogues-8992992/

135   Aushwitz Museum, Nov 27, 2018; https://twitter.com/AuschwitzMuseum/status/1067175336184606720?ref_src=twsrc%5Etfw

136   US State Dept Highlights 'Continued Targeted' Attacks on Minorities; India Calls Remarks 'Motivated', May 16, 2023; https://thewire.in/world/us-state-department-india-minorities-modi-visit

137   If there was violence against Muslims in India, would their population be growing, says Nirmala Sitharaman, IANS, Apr 11, 2023; https://m.tribuneindia.com/news/nation/india-has-2nd-largest-muslim-population-in-world-nirmala-sitharamans-reply-to-reports-on-violence-against-minorities-496350

138   Parkar Priya, Summary of Sachar Committee Report, PRS Legislative Research; Dec 7, 2006; https://prsindia.org/files/policy/policy_committee_reports/1242304423--Summary%20of%20Sachar%20Committee%20Report.pdf

139   Jaffrelot Christophe and Kalaiyarasan A, Muslims in higher education: A sobering tale, May 8, 2023; https://indianexpress.com/article/opinion/columns/lower-in-higher-education-8598739/

140   International Religious Freedom, 2023 USCIRF annual report, India segment; https://www.uscirf.gov/sites/default/files/2023-05/2023%20Annual%20Report.pdf

141   India: Government Policies, Actions Target Minorities, Human Rights Watch, Feb 19, 2021; https://www.hrw.org/news/2021/02/19/india-government-policies-actions-target-minorities

142   The state of the world's human rights, Amnesty International, 2022, https://www.amnesty.org/en/wp-content/uploads/2022/03/WEBPOL1048702022ENGLISH.pdf

143   A Look At Recent Attacks Against Christians In India, Mar 13, 2023; https://www.outlookindia.com/national/a-look-at-recent-attacks-against-christians-in-india-news-269813

144   Sen Jahnavi, Data: Rise in Attacks on Christians in India, Up Four Times in 11 Years (2012-2022), Sept 9, 2023; https://thewire.in/communalism/data-rise-in-attacks-on-christians-in-india-up-four-times-in-11-years-2012-2022

145   Arrests, Beatings and Secret Prayers: Inside the Persecution of India's Christians, Dec 2021; https://www.nytimes.com/2021/12/22/world/asia/india-christians-attacked.html?referringSource=articleShare

146   Kuthar Greeshma, All Santhosh's Men: The BJP's re-engineering of Karnataka, May 1, 2023; https://caravanmagazine.in/politics/bl-santosh-and-bjp-reengineered-karnataka-culture-rss-brahminical-vision

147   Barua Sukrita, Manipur violence: 175 deaths so far, 4,786 houses burnt, say police, Sept 15, 2023; https://indianexpress.com/article/north-east-india/manipur/manipur-violence-deaths-houses-burnt-police-8941007/

148   Bhatnagar Gaurav Vivek, Minorities Commission Sees Rise in Complaints From Sikhs, Buddhists and Parsis, Nov 30, 2021; https://thewire.in/government/minorities-commission-sees-rise-in-complaints-from-sikhs-buddhists-and-parsis

149   Inamdar Vedika and George Pooja, Slow Boil: Patterns in everyday acts of public violence in Modi's India, Jun 1, 2022; https://caravanmagazine.in/politics/public-violence-modi-india

150   Sherwani Arfa Khanum, Modi's White Lie in the White House, Jun 25, 2023; https://thewire.in/communalism/modi-discrimination-muslims-question-inequality

151   "I defy you to show me discrimination..." Jaishankar on minorities in India, ANI, Sept 29, 2023; https://www.aninews.in/news/world/us/i-defy-you-to-show-me-discrimination-jaishankar-on-minorities-in-india20230929221807/?amp=1

152   Questioned on Minorities, Jaishankar Says 'Show Me Discrimination'. The Facts

He Can See., Sept 29, 2023; https://m.thewire.in/article/rights/questioned-on-minorities-jaishankar-says-show-me-discrimination-the-facts-he-can-see/amp; Sherwani Arfa Khanum, Modi's White Lie in the White House, Jun 25, 2023; https://thewire.in/communalism/modi-discrimination-muslims-question-inequality

153 Questioned on Minorities, Jaishankar Says 'Show Me Discrimination'. The Facts He Can See., Sept 29, 2023; https://m.thewire.in/article/rights/questioned-on-minorities-jaishankar-says-show-me-discrimination-the-facts-he-can-see/amp

154 Subramanian Sujatha, Is Hindutva Masculinity on Social Media Producing A Culture of Violence against Women and Muslims? Economic & Political Weekly, Vol. 54, Issue No. 15, 13 Apr, 2019; https://www.epw.in/engage/article/hindutva-masculinity-social-media-producing-violence-against-women-muslims#.YQZEflwdhno.gmail

155 Flock Elizabeth, The War on Valentine's Day in India, The Atlantic, Feb 14, 2018; https://www.theatlantic.com/international/archive/2018/02/protecting-valentines-day-in-india/553244/

156 5 Times Mohan Bhagwat, RSS Supremo, Stirred Controversy, The Quint, Feb 14, 2018; https://www.thequint.com/news/india/rss-chief-mohan-bhagwat-army-women-controversial-statements#read-more; related links: Produce more children, RSS tells Hindu couples, Aug 22, 2016; https://www.thehindu.com/news/national/other-states/Produce-more-children-RSS-tells-Hindu-couples/article14582028.ece; 7 controversial statements of Yogi Adityanath on women, minorities, Asianet, Mar 31, 2018; https://newsable.asianetnews.com/india/7-controversial-statements-of-yogi-adityanath-on-women-minorities

157 Congress slams PM Modi for 'widow' comment, Dec 10, 2018; https://indianexpress.com/article/india/congress-slams-pm-narendra-modi-for-widow-comment-sonia-gandhi-5485811/

158 That 'Surpanakha' moment: Renuka Chowdhury threatens to sue PM Modi, says will courts act, Mar 27, 2023; https://indianexpress.com/article/political-pulse/renuka-chowdhury-pm-narendra-modi-surpanakha-moment-8517926/

159 Narendra Modi calls Shashi Tharoor's wife '50-crore-rupee girlfriend', Oct 29, 2012; https://timesofindia.indiatimes.com/india/narendra-modi-calls-shashi-tharoors-wife-50-crore-rupee-girlfriend/articleshow/17008278.cms

160 Beti Bachao, Beti Padhao | 80% of funds spent on media campaigns, says Parliamentary Committee, Dec 10, 2021; https://www.thehindu.com/news/national/beti-bachao-beti-padhao-whopping-80-of-funds-spent-on-media-campaigns-says-parliamentary-committee/article37922778.ece

161 Review of Beti Bachao Beti Padhao (BBBP) Scheme, MoWCD, Feb 2021; https://pib.gov.in/PressReleasePage.aspx?PRID=1695199#:~:text=As%20per%20the%20evaluation%20report,practices%20and%20community%2Dlevel%20initiatives.

162 Madhukalya Amrita, Over dozen states saw decline in sex ratio since 2020: Govt, Jul 24, 2023; https://www.deccanherald.com/national/jamia-millia-islamia-to-get-medical-college-international-campus-1239948.html

163   13.13 Lakh Girls, Women Went Missing in India in 2019-2021, Most From MP: Govt Data, Jul 31, 2023; https://thewire.in/women/13-13-lakh-girls-women-went-missing-in-india-in-2019-2021-most-from-mp-govt-data

164   Sulli Deals: The Indian Muslim women 'up for sale' on an app, Jul 10, 2021; https://www.bbc.com/news/world-asia-india-57764271

165   Sulli Deals: Organised attempt to blame a Muslim youth for the app, Nov 15, 2021; https://www.altnews.in/sulli-deals-organised-attempt-to-blame-a-muslim-youth-for-the-app/?utm_source=website&utm_medium=social-media&utm_campaign=newpost

166   For Bulli Bai App, Bengaluru Student Arrested, Uttarakhand Woman Detained, Jan 4, 2022; https://www.ndtv.com/india-news/bulli-bai-app-case-engineering-student-vishal-jha-arrested-by-mumbai-police-over-auction-of-muslim-women-on-social-media-2687886

167   Why Trads, India's Alt Right, remain untouched online despite hate crimes, Scroll, May 13, 2022; https://scroll.in/article/1023789/why-trads-indias-alt-right-remain-untouched-online-despite-hate-crimes

168   Kathua rape case: 2 BJP ministers attend rally in support of accused, Mar 4, 2018; https://www.indiatoday.in/india/story/kathua-rape-case-2-bjp-ministers-attend-rally-in-support-of-accused-1181788-2018-03-04

169   VHP, Bajrang Dal stage dharna in support of Asaram, Aug 27, 2013; https://timesofindia.indiatimes.com/city/chandigarh/vhp-bajrang-dal-stage-dharna-in-support-of-asaram/articleshow/22083197.cms?from=mdr

170   Ram Rahim Again Granted 30-Day Parole, 7th Time In 2.5 Years; Rape Convict To Celebrate His Birthday In Baghpat, Jul 20, 2023; https://www.freepressjournal.in/india/rape-convict-ram-rahim-again-granted-30-day-parole-7th-time-in-25-years; Rape, murder convict Dera chief Gurmeet Ram Rahim Singh out on 30-day parole; 2nd this yr, 4th in 2 yrs, Jul 21, 2023; https://indianexpress.com/article/cities/chandigarh/dera-chief-gurmeet-ram-rahim-singh-30-day-parole-stay-up-ashram-8850343/

171   Sura Ajay, A poll pattern to Dera chief freedom stints? Nov 22 2023; http://timesofindia.indiatimes.com/articleshow/105397040.cms?utm_source=contentofinterest&utm_medium=text&utm_campaign=cppst

172   Koshie Nihal, Wrestlers' protest: 'Panel asked us for audio, video proof… member said Brij Bhushan Singh like father figure', May 16, 2023; https://indianexpress.com/article/sports/sport-others/wrestlers-protest-sexual-harassment-case-panel-asked-us-for-audio-video-proof-member-said-bhushan-sharan-singh-like-father-figure-8611220/

173   IOC steps in, supports wrestlers: (May 28) treatment very disturbing, protect athletes, conduct unbiased probe, Jun 1, 2023; https://indianexpress.com/article/sports/sport-others/wrestlers-protest-global-olympics-body-steps-in-very-disturbing-protect-athletes-8637663/

174 Dwivedi Sandeep, An idol crumbles: How PT Usha missed the podium again, Apr 30, 2023; https://indianexpress.com/article/sports/sport-others/wrestlers-protest-pt-usha-misses-it-again-8582060/

175 Watch: BJP MP Meenakshi Lekhi starts running when questioned on wrestlers' protest, May 31, 2023; https://www.newslaundry.com/2023/05/31/watch-bjp-mp-meenakshi-lekhi-starts-running-when-questioned-on-wrestlers-protest

176 Srivastava Nitin Kumar, 'Silent, as always': Sena MP slams Smriti Irani, NCW over wrestlers' protest, May 14, 2023; https://www.indiatoday.in/india/story/wrestlers-protest-write-to-smriti-irani-nirmala-sitharaman-wfi-chief-2379134-2023-05-14

177 NCW chief seeks report from Delhi Police on sexual harassment charges against WFI head, Apr 27, 2023; https://www.deccanherald.com/india/ncw-chief-seeks-report-from-delhi-police-on-sexual-harassment-charges-against-wfi-head-1213449.html,

178 Suhas Palshikar on wrestlers' protest: The Indian system failed these young women, and society failed itself, Jun 6, 2023; https://indianexpress.com/article/opinion/columns/suhas-palshikar-on-wrestlers-protest-the-indian-system-failed-these-young-women-and-society-failed-itself-8647274/

179 Bose Shuvaditya, Explained: WFI Suspended – But Why? What Does It Mean for Indian Wrestlers? Aug 26, 2023; https://www.thequint.com/explainers/wfi-suspended-reason-what-led-to-this-what-it-means-indian-wrestlers-explained#read-more

180 Kesavan Mukul, Existential terror, Jun 4, 2023; https://www.telegraphindia.com/opinion/existential-terror-the-bjps-fear-of-the-agency-of-articulate-women/cid/1942132

181 Zubair Mohammed, This is the video of Rahul Gandhi just before @smritiirani spoke, Aug 9, 2023; https://twitter.com/zoo_bear/status/1689201435874086912

182 TV Newsance 222: TV News' fixation with Rahul's flying kiss, Newsclick and real Godi media exposé, Aug 12, 2023; https://www.newslaundry.com/2023/08/12/tv-newsance-222-tv-news-fixation-with-rahuls-flying-kiss-newsclick-real-godi-media-expos

183 Modi's cabinet reshuffle: From Rajasthan, a Jat for a Jat, and SC for an SC balancing act, Aug 20, 2018; https://indianexpress.com/article/opinion/web-edits/modis-cabinet-expansion-from-rajasthan-a-jat-for-a-jat-and-sc-for-an-sc-balancing-act-2894929/

184 Daniyal Shoaib, Why has women's safety stopped having any political impact in the Modi age? May 8, 2023; https://indiafix.stck.me/post/82830/Why-has-womens-safety-stopped-having-any-political-impact-in-the-Modi-age

185 Delhi gang-rape case: PM Manmohan Singh appeals for calm, vows to protect women, Dec 24, 2012; https://economictimes.indiatimes.com/news/politics-and-nation/delhi-gang-rape-case-pm-manmohan-singh-appeals-for-calm-vows-to-protect-women/articleshow/17739603.cms?utm_source=contentofinterest&utm_medium=text&utm_campaign=cppst

186   Smriti Irani Hails Hanging Of Nirbhaya Convicts, Says 'It's A Message To Everyone', Mar 20, 2020; https://www.republicworld.com/india-news/politics/smriti-irani-hails-hanging-of-nirbhaya-convicts-says-it-is-a-message.html

187   Protection of Children from Sexual Offences Act, 2012, Ministry of Law and Justice, Jun 19, 2012; https://wcd.nic.in/sites/default/files/POCSO%20Act%2C%202012.pdf

188   Sengar Shweta, Death Penalty To POCSO Act: How Nirbhaya & Kathua Rape Cases Changed Indian Criminal Laws, Dec 8, 2021; https://www.indiatimes.com/news/india/death-penalty-pocso-act-nirbhaya-kathua-rape-cases-criminal-laws-556266.htmlt

189   Analysis of sitting MPs/MLAs with Declared Cases Related to Crimes against Women, ADR, Aug 10, 2023; https://adrindia.org/content/analysis-sitting-mpsmlas-declared-cases-related-crimes-against-women

190   Kanungo Pralay, Co-opting Dalits into the Hindutva Fold, Economic & Political Weekly, May 19, 2007; https://www.epw.in/journal/2007/20/book-reviews/co-opting-dalits-hindutva-fold.html; Meghwanshi Bhanwar, 2020: I Could not be Hindu: The Story of a Dalit in the RSS, Navayana Publishing, 2020; https://www.amazon.in/Could-Not-Be-Hindu-Story/dp/8189059939

191   Chauhan Chetan, In state after state, cow protection vigilantes pick on Dalits, Muslims, Jul 29, 2016; https://www.hindustantimes.com/india-news/in-state-after-state-cow-protection-vigilantes-pick-on-dalits-muslims/story-F1CFAkyduCopAY5lYlN4LL.html

192   Ghosh Sohini, To be young and Dalit in a Gujarat village, Jun 27, 2023; https://indianexpress.com/article/cities/ahmedabad/to-be-young-and-dalit-in-a-gujarat-village-8685976/

193   Madhya Pradesh: Home of Indian man who urinated on tribal worker demolished, Jul 6, 2023; https://www.bbc.com/news/world-asia-india-66106342

194   Anwar Tarique, Jharkhand: Every 10th Adivasi in Khunti Dist Charged with Sedition for Resorting to 'Pathalgarhi', Jul 22, 2019; https://www.newsclick.in/jharkhand-every-10-adivasi-khunti-dist-charged-sedition-resorting-pathalgarhi

195   Profile of the President, https://presidentofindia.nic.in/Profile

196   A violent attack on academic freedom: Letters, Jan 9, 2020; https://www.theguardian.com/world/2020/jan/09/a-violent-attack-on-academic-freedom

197   Khan Jamshed Adil and Jain Nitin, JNU Tapes: Police turned off the lights, ABVP activist reveals how Delhi cops helped mob in violence, India Today, Jan 10, 2020; https://www.indiatoday.in/india/story/jnu-tapes-police-turned-off-the-lights-abvp-activist-reveals-how-delhi-cops-helped-mob-in-violence-1635789-2020-01-10

198   JNU violence: Police name masked woman in video, ABVP admits she is a member, Jan 15, 2022; https://scroll.in/latest/949945/jnu-violence-police-name-masked-woman-in-video-abvp-admits-she-is-its-member; JNU: Students across India protest against campus attack, Jan 6, 2020; https://www.bbc.com/news/world-asia-india-51004204

199 Report on AMU violence: 'Cops raised Jai Shri Ram slogans, admin failed in its duty', Dec 25, 2019; https://indianexpress.com/article/india/report-on-amu-violence-cops-raised-jai-shri-ram-slogans-admin-failed-in-its-duty/

200 22 months on, no headway in JNU violence probe, Nov 16, 2021; http://timesofindia.indiatimes.cbrom/articleshow/87724650.cms?utm_source=contentofinterest&utm_medium=text&utm_campaign=cppst

201 Iznallah and Aparna, Saffron Spillovers in Educational Spaces: An Insider's View from IIT Bombay, Jun 7, 2023; https://thewire.in/communalism/iit-bombay-saffron-kerala-story-love-jihad-social-media

202 Kanhaiya Kumar arrest: The FIR filed by Delhi Police in sedition case, Feb 17, 2016; https://indianexpress.com/article/india/india-news-india/kanhaiya-kumar-arrest-the-fir-filed-by-delhi-police-in-sedition-case/

203 A year on, Delhi Police lack evidence to charge ex-JNUSU president Kanhaiya Kumar for sedition: Report, Mar 1, 2017; https://indianexpress.com/article/india/kanhaiya-kumar-sedition-a-year-on-delhi-police-lack-evidence-to-charge-ex-jnusu-president-kanhaiya-kumar-report-4549115/

204 Fact check: The video of Kanhaiya Kumar shouting for 'azadi' – it's doctored, Feb 18, 2016; https://scroll.in/article/803776/fact-check-the-video-of-kanhaiya-kumar-shouting-for-azadi-its-doctored; Forensic experts say Kanhaiya video was doctored, Feb 20, 2016; https://www.indiatoday.in/india/delhi/story/forensic-experts-say-kanhaiya-video-was-doctored-309626-2016-02-19

205 JNU row: Kanhaiya Kumar beaten up by lawyers at Patiala House Court, sent to 14 days of judicial custody, Feb 17, 2016; https://indianexpress.com/article/india/india-news-india/jnu-delhi-police-kanhaiya-kumar-patiala-house-court-india-news/

206 Kanhaiya Kumar vs State of NCT of Delhi, Delhi High Court, Mar 2, 2016; https://sabrangindia.in/sites/default/files/files/301714554-Delhi-High-Court-s-Bail-Order-for-JNU-President-Kanhaiya.pdf

207 Author of Paper on Possible 'Manipulation' in 2019 Polls Quits Ashoka University, Aug 14, 2023; https://thewire.in/education/author-of-paper-on-possible-manipulation-in-2019-polls-quits-ashoka-university

208 Kissu Sagarika, 'Vote for educated person' — how a video turned Unacademy teacher Karan Sangwan's life 'upside down', Aug 20, 2023; https://theprint.in/india/vote-for-educated-person-how-a-video-turned-unacademy-teacher-karan-sangwans-life-upside-down/1721623/

209 Murari Krshan, Singer Neha Singh's husband told to 'quit job', after her police notice for UP mein ka ba song, Feb 24, 2023; https://theprint.in/india/singer-neha-singhs-husband-told-to-quit-job-after-her-police-notice-for-up-mein-ka-ba-song/1395099/

210 Express View on South Asian University undertaking: Campus unfreedom, Aug 1, 2023; https://indianexpress.com/article/opinion/editorials/express-view-on-south-asian-university-undertaking-campus-unfreedom-8870095/

211   Chakravarty Gargee, In Australia, debate continues about claims Indian High Commission interfered in academic institute, Apr 17, 2022; https://scroll. in/article/1021985/in-australia-debate-continues-about-claims-indian-high-commission-interfered-in-academic-institute

212   Fake social media profiles targeting Sikhs exposed, Nov 24, 2021; https://www.bbc. com/news/world-asia-india-59338245

213   Farmers' protest: Why did a Rihanna tweet prompt Indian backlash? Feb 3, 2021; https://www.bbc.com/news/world-asia-india-55914858

214   Kaur Pawanjot, Day of Clashes With 'BJP-Sponsored Goons' Bolsters Farmers' Resolve, Jan 30, 2021; https://thewire.in/agriculture/day-of-clashes-with-bjp-sponsored-goons-bolsters-farmers-resolve; Are the 'Locals' Taking on Farmers at Singhu Border BJP Workers?, Jan 30, 2021; https://www.thequint.com/news/india/ are-supposed-locals-at-singhu-border-actually-bjp-workers-social-media-aman-kumar-krishan-dabas

215   Who Is Deep Sidhu – the Actor Who Hoisted Nishan Sahib at Red Fort, Feb 9, 2023; https://www.thequint.com/news/india/who-is-deep-sidhu-actor-nishan-sahib-red-fort#read-more; Arora Kusum, Who Are Deep Sidhu and Lakha Sidhana, and Why Are Farmers' Unions Angry With Them? Jan 28, 2021; https://thewire.in/politics/ deep-sidhu-lakha-sidhana-farmers-unions

216   Amritpal Singh: Who is he and why was he arrested? Apr 23, 2023; https:// www.aljazeera.com/news/2023/4/23/amritpal-singh-who-is-he-and-why-was-he-arrested

217   Fair C Christine, Conspiracy Theories Swirl Around Sikh Separatist Amritpal Singh Sandhu, May 1, 2023; https://foreignpolicy.com/2023/05/01/amritpal-singh-sandhu-sikh-separatism-punjab-india-conspiracy-theories/

218   Patel Aakar, Our Hindu Rashtra: What It Is. How We Got Here, Westland, Dec 2020; https://www.amazon.in/Our-Hindu-Rashtra-What/dp/9389648890

219   Mohanty P, Rebooting Economy 42: How will changes to land laws in Jammu and Kashmir help, and whom?, Nov 2, 2020; https://www.businesstoday.in/ latest/economy-politics/story/indian-economy-how-will-changes-to-land-laws-in-jammu-and-kashmir-help-and-whom-277373-2020-11-02

220   185 Outsiders Bought Land In Jammu And Kashmir In Last 3 Years: Centre, Apr 5, 2023; https://www.ndtv.com/india-news/185-outsiders-bought-land-in-jammu-and-kashmir-in-last-3-years-centre-3922369

221   Tapasya and Gairola Hemant, Meet Uttarakhand leaders targeting Muslims, while police turn a blind eye, Jun 12, 2023; https://www.reporters-collective.in/trc/meet-uttarakhand-leaders-targeting-muslims-while-police-turn-a-blind-eye;   Zubair Mohammed, You see below outcome because there was no action by Uttarakhand Police, Jun 11, 2023; https://twitter.com/zoo_bear/status/1667924937741590529

222   Mittal Tusha and Jafri Alishan, Driving Muslims out of "Devbhoomi"" The Sangh's quest for a Hindu holy land, Aug 1, 2023; https://caravanmagazine.in/politics/bjp-

rss-create-hindu-holy-land-dev-bhoomi-uttarakhand-muslim-ethnic-cleansing

223   Sura Ajau, 'Ethnic cleansing by state?' HC halts Nuh demolitions, Aug 8, 2023; https://timesofindia.indiatimes.com/city/chandigarh/ethnic-cleansing-by-state-hc-halts-nuh-demolitions/articleshow/102518670.cms?from=mdr

224   Rewari DC, who issued showcause notices over Muslim entry ban in villages, transferred, Aug 20, 2023; https://indianexpress.com/article/chandigarh/rewari-dc-who-issued-notices-over-muslim-entry-ban-transferred-8900337/

225   Sandhu Kamaljit Kaur, Haryana violence: 50 panchayats issue letters barring entry of Muslim traders, Aug 9, 2023; https://www.indiatoday.in/india/story/after-nuh-clashes-50-haryana-panchayats-issue-letters-barring-entry-of-muslim-traders-2418403-2023-08-09

226   Mishra Dheeraj, Nuh: Mahapanchayat says yatra to resume on August 28, wants guns for 'self-defence', Aug 14, 2023; https://indianexpress.com/article/india/nuh-mahapanchayat-says-yatra-to-resume-on-august-28-wants-guns-for-self-defence-8891335/

227   On Haryana's Offer To Help Arrest Monu Manesar, Ashok Gehlot's Response, Aug 4, 2023; https://www.ndtv.com/india-news/ashok-gehlot-slams-haryana-government-over-offer-to-arrest-monu-manesar-4267635

228   Ara Ismat, Who is Monu Manesar? Feb 20, 2023; https://frontline.thehindu.com/the-nation/profile-who-is-monu-manesar-bajrang-dal-activist-gaukrakshak/article66524348.ece

229   At mahapanchayat in Manesar, a warning for Rajasthan police: Arrest Monu at own risk, Feb 24, 2023; https://indianexpress.com/article/cities/delhi/hindu-mahasabha-haryana-warning-for-rajasthan-police-arrest-monu-manesar-8458588/

230   Went on pilgrimage, not hiding from cops, claims Monu Manesar, who is a suspect in Nasir-Junaid murder case, Jun 16, 2023; https://indianexpress.com/article/cities/delhi/went-on-pilgrimage-not-hiding-from-cops-claims-monu-manesar-who-is-a-suspect-in-nasir-junaid-murder-case-8665548/

231   Raj A and Bhatia V, Arrested in Haryana for social media post, Monu Manesar handed over to Rajasthan in murder case, Sept 13, 2023; https://indianexpress.com/article/cities/delhi/monu-manesar-detained-nuh-haryana-violence-8936317/

232   Kuthar Greeshma, Fire and Blood: How the BJP is enabling ethnic cleansing in Manipur, Aug 1, 2023; https://caravanmagazine.in/conflict/how-bjp-enabling-ethnic-cleansing-manipur

233   Choudhury Angshuman, Targeting of Kukis the main reason behind Manipur violence, Jun 27, 2023; https://frontline.thehindu.com/the-nation/marginalisation-of-kukis-the-main-reason-behind-manipur-violence/article67000979.ece

234   Mashal Mujib and Raj Sushsini, Could Ethnic Conflict in India Become an Issue Modi Cannot Ignore? Jul 30, 2023;https://www.nytimes.com/2023/07/30/world/asia/india-manipur-modi.html

235 Manipur violence: Trouble long brewing, ST status for Meiteis issue just the spark, PTI, May 5, 2023; https://www.deccanherald.com/india/manipur-violence-trouble-long-brewing-st-status-for-meiteis-issue-just-the-spark-1216069.html

236 "Centre's approval required to introduce NRC in Manipur": CM Biren Singh, Apr 1, 2023; https://www.aninews.in/news/national/general-news/centres-approval-required-to-introduce-nrc-in-manipur-cm-biren-singh20230401064459/,

237 Mody Anjali, Politicians and Politics that Stoked Latent Communal Tensions in Muzaffarnagar, Jan 15, 2015; https://caravanmagazine.in/vantage/politicians-politics-communal-tensions-muzaffarnagar

238 Mander Harsh, Who lit the fires in Nuh? Aug 17, 2023; https://scroll.in/article/1054316/who-lit-the-fires-in-nuh

239 Bhatia Gautam, The Troubling Legacy of Chief Justice Ranjan Gogoi, Mar 16, 2020; https://thewire.in/law/chief-justice-ranjan-gogoi-legacy

240 Gupta Shekhar, Assam's 35-year saffronisation, Aug 3, 2018; https://theprint.in/opinion/writings-on-the-wall/assams-35-year-saffronisation/93004/

241 97,000 Indians, mostly from Punjab and Gujarat, arrested in 1 year trying to enter US illegally, PTI, Nov 3, 2023; https://www.tribuneindia.com/news/diaspora/97-000-indians-mostly-from-punjab-and-gujarat-arrested-trying-to-enter-us-illegally-between-in-2022-2023-559096

Chapter V

Rhetoric as Governance II: 'Minimum Government, Maximum Governance'

Previous chapters have demonstrated how his government doesn't really answer to the description of "minimum government, maximum governance". It is a near decade (2014-2023) of command-and-control regime with top-down policies, inversion of the rule of law, suppression of dissent, attack on political rivals, institutional breakdowns, communal strife and centralization of power vis-à-vis state governments. In fact, all evidence points to "maximum government, minimum governance". The Prime Minister and his office (PMO) have emerged very powerful – not only rivaling but outstripping that of former Prime Minister Indira Gandhi. This is not a healthy sign for any democracy.

But before going further on the maximum government and its minimal governance, here are some performance indicators for a larger perspective.

The World Bank's Worldwide Governance Indicators (WGI)[1] evaluates governance on six parameters: Control of corruption, government effectiveness, political stability and absence of violence/terrorism, regulatory quality, rule of law and voice and accountability. It aggregates data from more than 30 think tanks, international organizations, nongovernmental organizations, and private firms and is essentially about *perceptions*. How does India fare in this assessment? The following graphs capture India's scores on each parameter between 1996 and 2022 (for which data is available).

To appreciate the scores better, a backgrounder: New Delhi had coalition governments from 1996 to 2014; the Prime Minister came to power in May 2014 with absolute majority after a decade of the Congress-led coalition government (2004-2014) and six years of the BJP-led coalition governments (1998-2004) and during 1996-1998, there were three coalition governments for a period of 13 days, 324 days and 332 days.

Graph: India's performance in World Bank's WGI

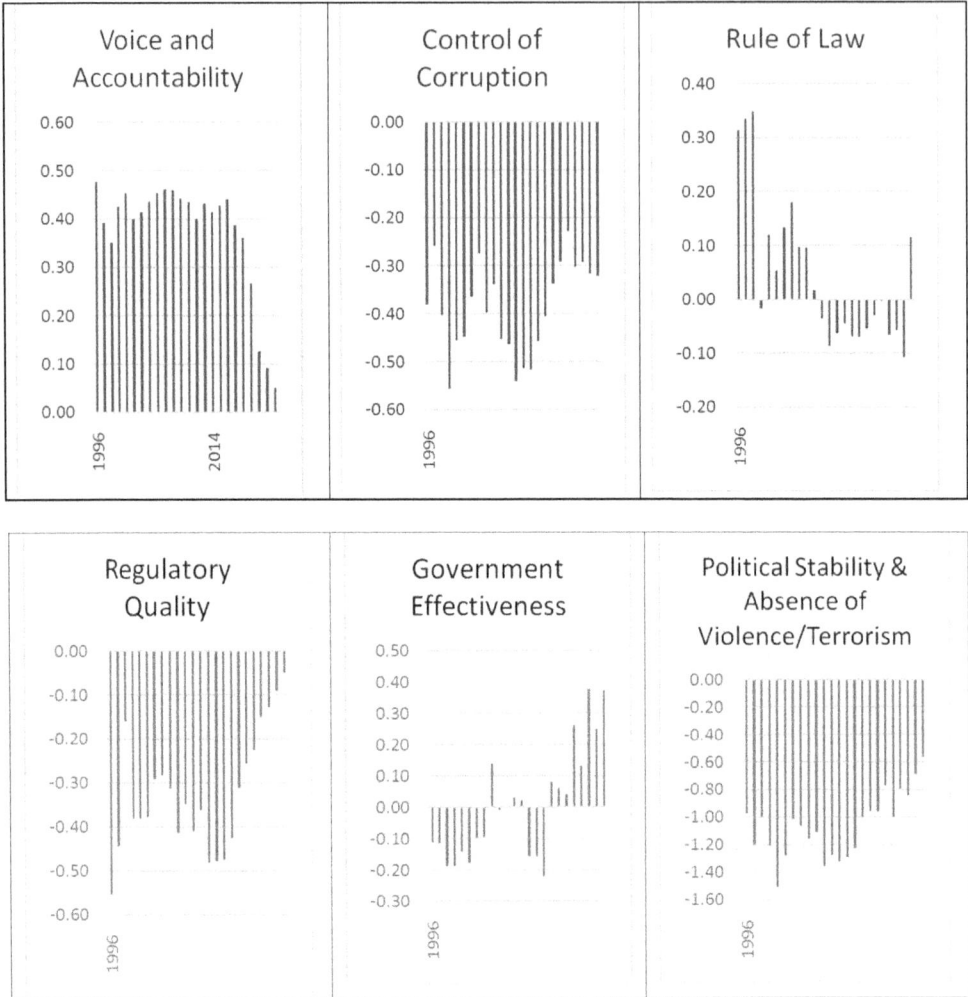

Source: Daniel Kaufmann and Aart Kraay (2023). Worldwide Governance Indicators, 2023 Update (www.govindicators.org), Accessed on 10/9/2023

What the graphs show are:

- Voice and accountability: Rapidly sinking after 2014, and is at the lowest since 1996.

- Corruption control: After an initial dip following the change in government in 2014, it is going up again.

- Rule of law: It has remained in the negative zone for long, hitting the lowest level before improving in 2022.

- Regulatory quality: Consistent improvement.

- Government effectiveness: Not so consistent but improvement nonetheless.

- Political stability and absence of violence/terrorism: Rapid improvement.

Going by the very definitions[2] of these parameters and measurements ("perceptions"), a strong and popular government in office for a decade is likely to perform better in certain parameters as the government does – given that it came after 18 years of coalition governments (since 1996, in this context). These are: Political stability and absence of violence/terrorism ("likelihood of political instability and/or politically motivated violence, including terrorism"), government effectiveness ("quality of public services, the quality of the civil service and the degree of its independence from political pressures, the quality of policy formulation and implementation, and the credibility of the government's commitment to such policies") and regulatory quality ("ability of the government to formulate and implement sound policies and regulations that permit and promote private sector development.").

Had governance been good, it would have certainly reflected in the scores of the three other parameters: Voice and accountability, corruption control and rule of law – which isn't the case. Besides, it isn't really easy to capture India's reality through perceptions. For example, how do you capture corruption when there is zero probe against the government and ruling party members with the central agencies running after only the rival political leaders and dissent? How do you capture accountability or transparency when the government suppresses or doesn't collect critical data, churns out discredited data (listed in Chapter VII); refuses to answer questions of national important, including national security, inside or outside the Parliament (Chapters Introduction, II, IV, V and XII) and fills the public space (both real and virtual worlds) with endless fake news and propaganda (Chapter XI) and when the judiciary, media and citizens are unwilling or unable to hold the government to account (Chapters II, III, XI)?

There is yet another set of data measuring the state of governance – which is more specific and better measured – which shows the utter failure of the government on all fronts. Aakar Patel in his book "Price of the Modi Years"[3] tracks and lists more than 50 global governance indicators to show India's performance under the Prime Minister. It shows, India's scores and global rankings fell sharply in all indicators after 2014 – except for the odd ones like the now defunct World Bank's doing business index (DBI) and innovation index (reason cited was number of start-ups). These include the democracy indices of the V-Dem, Economist Intelligence Unit, Freedom House's Freedom index; the UN Human Development Index, Cato Human Freedom Index, Global Gender

Gap Index, Smart Cities Index, Access Now Tracker (internet shutdowns), global RTI ratings, World Air Quality Index, Yale Environmental Performance Index, World Press Freedom Index, Fraser Institute's Global Economic Freedom Index etc.

These indicators tell their own story but don't really explain the Whys and Hows. For that, read on.

Maximum Government: PM-PMO

As mentioned earlier, the PM-PMO has emerged very powerful after 2014 – far more than even of Prime Minister Indira Gandhi who put the democracy on suspended animation for 21 months by imposing the Emergency during 1975-77. It is because its writ runs large – tightly controlling the government, the ruling party and the mainstream media.

Here is a brief backgrounder on the evolution of the PMO.

In her book 2023 "How Prime Ministers Decide", journalist Neerja Chowdhury writes that when first Prime Minister Jawaharlal Nehru was in office (1947-64), it was called the Prime Minister's Secretariat (PMS) – a nomenclature that continued till 1977. Nehru had just one joint secretary in his PMS – MO Mathai, his private secretary. His successor Lal Bahadur Shastri brought in LK Jha as secretary in the PMS – who grew more powerful than the cabinet secretary, the head of bureaucracy. It was his successor Indira Gandhi who made the PMS all powerful – brought in deputy minister Dinesh Singh and later all-powerful secretary PN Haksar. Her successor Morarji Desai renamed it as PMO – but downgraded its role. The PMO under PV Narasimha Rao (1991-96) and Manmohan Singh (2004-2014) were rather subdued. The really powerful PMO officials who influenced government's policymaking were Haksar and Brajesh Mishra – the latter principal secretary to Prime Minister Atal Behari Vajpayee (1998-2004) and also National Security Advisor (NSA).

The Prime Minister has retired bureaucrats in his PMO, Nripendra Misra (in the first term and in the second heads the trust building the Ayodhya temple), PK Mishra (in both terms) and his NSA Ajit Doval (both terms) – all holding the rank of Cabinet ministers[4] – and as such, equivalent in status to other Cabinet ministers and higher than ministers of state (MoS). This status also takes them far above the Cabinet Secretary – the head of bureaucracy – in the order of precedence[5]. Given that most ministers in his Cabinet are political lightweights, remain out of sight and are virtually unknown to the public and journalists alike, the PM-PMO has complete dominance. Here is an example of how irrelevant ministers are. When a BJP MP Rajkumar Ranjan Singh's house in Imphal was attacked during the Manipur violence in June 2023[6], it came as a big surprise that he is also the MoS for External Affairs and Education! Imagine the kind of collective responsibility and accountability of the ministers and their role in decision making when most of them don't appear in public, don't explain or take questions on the functioning of their ministries. The only other powerful minister in the Cabinet is Union Home Minister Amit Shah and only very few, like the Finance Minister, Defence Minister and External Affairs Minister, are familiar faces.

With sanctioned (2018) civilian posts of 511 – as per a Rajya Sabha reply of 2020[7] – Prime Minister Modi's PMO is inexplicably large. In fact, it has more staff than the Cabinet Secretariat's 359 (sanctioned posts) and several ministries and departments – like the Coal Ministry (424), Ministry of Parliamentary Affairs (149), Department of School Education and Literacy (446) and nearly as many as the Department of Rural Development (515).

Congress president Mallikarjun Kharge[8] once wrote the Prime Minister was no longer first among equals, but the sole Chief Executive, like that in the USA and the morphing of the PMO into an "independent Executive force" was a perversion of the cabinet system. This isn't an exaggeration as this book shows. This is also diametrically opposite to the Manmohan Singh's mechanism of Group of Ministers (GoMs) and Empowered GoMs (eGoMs) to decide all important policy matters, none of which was headed by him (of 37, Pranab Mukherjee, a political heavyweight who became the President of India later headed 24)[9] – which was abandoned once Modi assumed power.

Appointments to Key Offices

The PM-PMO exercises their powers through several ways, the most important one being the power to appoint key officials.

All top officials appointed through the Appointments Committee of the Cabinet (ACC) are selected by the PM-PMO. For the first time in India's history, the ACC was turned into a two-member body consisting of Prime Minister and Home Minister – from a three-member one; the third being the minister concerned (when appointing to ministries) – in December 2014.[10] This means no minister has a say on appointments to his/her ministry. Then Home Minister was cut off in 2014 as most proposals to the ACC came carrying the instruction that "approval of the Home Minister will be obtained *ex post facto* in the ACC".[11]

The Prime Minister directly orders officials, bypassing his ministers. A classic example was the 2021 directive from the Prime Minister to bureaucrats to prepare a 60-point action plan for the country[12] –linking birth certificates to citizenship, linking job clause to trade pacts, promoting 'family database design', drafting a single environment law subsuming all other related laws in the sector etc. The entire central bureaucracy is run by a small coterie of trusted officers, mostly from his Gujarat days.[13] State Chief Ministers are often bypassed by the Prime Minister and instructions are directly issued to state officials. Though this practice was first started by former Prime Minister Rajiv Gandhi, it became more frequent and pervasive after 2014. Such instructions cover a wide array of activities, including pandemic management, crime control and other administrative matters.[14]

The result of overtly powerful PM-PMO is a weakened accountability and transparency. These appointments extend from high constitutional offices to other critical institutions like banking regulator RBI, government auditor CAG, anti-corruption watchdog Lokpal, transparency watchdog Central Information Commission (CIC), election regulator ECI, human rights body NHRC etc. Environment watchdog set up by the Supreme Court in 2002, the Central Empowered Committee (CEC), was the latest to fall victim in September 2023 – which sans non-government members.[15]

Drawing attention to such appointments, Tarunabh Khaitan of Melbourne Law School wrote in 2020[16]: "The Modi government has worked systematically to either cripple these institutions to prevent them from performing their accountability-seeking function (often by simply refusing to fill vacancies) or pack them with party ideologues to ensure their institutional capture"; the mode of operation was "subtle, indirect, and incremental, but also systemic". He called it "killing a Constitution with a thousand cuts". Former RBI Governor Raghuram Rajan was once provoked enough to warn in 2019: "India has become too big an economy to be run from the top (PM and PMO). And unfortunately, the experience so far is that it simply doesn't work".[17]

Leader of Opposition (LoP), a post that has been denied to the Congress since 2014, is part of several key appointments. How such appointments are made without a LoP? Here are a few instances.

- For the appointment of Lokpal, the apex anti-corruption watchdog, LoP was substituted with "leader of the single largest party in Lok Sabha" – as then CJI Justice Ranjan Gogoi had directed in 2017[18]. But Congress leader Mallikarjun Kharge, who qualified for it, was invited to the selection committee as "special invitee" – which carries no decision-making power. Hence, Kharge boycotted it and the Lokpal was selected and appointed in 2019 without his participation.[19]

- In 2020, when Sanjay Kothari was appointed as CVC, the Congress' Adhir Ranjan Chowdhury went in as the leader of the single largest party and objected to the selection of Kothari – pointing out that his (Kothari's) name was not in the shortlist of the search committee. He revealed that though the Prime Minister accepted that the procedure had been vitiated, the appointment went though, making a mockery of the process.[20]

- The appointment of Rakesh Asthana as the Commissioner of Delhi Police was even more curious. First the government tried to appoint him as the CBI Director in May 2021. But then CJI Justice Ramana, a member of the selection panel, opposed it by citing the Supreme Court order in the Prakash Singh vs Union of India 2006 case that forbids appointment of an official having less than six months of service left to a post which carries a minimum tenure of two years.[21] In July 2021, Asthana was appointed as the Commission of Delhi Police with overnight change in his cadre and extension in service as he was about to retire – violating the very Supreme Court judgement then CJI had cited. What changed? The CJI is not a member of the selection committee for this post (unlike the Director of CBI). The Delhi High Court[22] dismissed challenges to Asthana's appointment on the ground that (a) Delhi had witnessed challenging law and order situations having international ramifications and hence the Centre's choice of an experienced officer is appropriate and that (b) the Supreme Court order mandating two-year term is "intended to apply only to the appointment of a State DGP", not for Delhi's Police Commissioner.

The extensions to the Directors of ED and CBI and Home Secretary and the government's veto in the appointments to the ECI, CVC and other key positions – through ordinances and legislations – have eliminated scope for LoP or CJI from selections and appointments to key offices.

What happens when a bureaucrat falls out of line?

The retribution is swift. Two examples. In August 2023, the CAG audit reports exposed corruption and other financial irregularities in the highway projects ('Bharatmala Pariyojana') and health insurance (Ayushman Bharat). These were unusual reports (the findings are detailed later), from the CAG after the regime change in 2014 (very unlike the previous Congress-led UPA government which had seen the CAG exposing corruption in coal block allocations, 2G spectrum allocation etc. The very next month, September 2023, three CAG officers from the Indian Audit and Accounts Service (IA&AS) – two in charge of these reports and another initiated the audit of the Ayushman Bharat scheme – were *transferred*, but it was clubbed with other transfers to give the mask of a 'routine' reshuffle.[23]

The second is the hounding of Election Commissioner Ashok Lavasa and his family (wife, sister and son) in 2019 through multiple probes against them (even the ED was called in) for flagging blatant and repeated violations of the electoral model code (MCC) by the Prime Minister and then BJP president now Union Home Minister Amit Shah during the 2019 general elections. His is a constitutional post (but the government makes the appointments) and was to head the Election Commission soon, but he was forced to resign. His case is detailed in Chapter X.

And what happens to the officers who do as they are asked to? As in the case of ED Director Sanjay Kumar Mishra detailed in Chapter I shows, laws are changed, court battles are fought to keep them in office for years after retirement. Chapter III also gives some such examples and more are listed in this chapter.

In October 2023, the PM-PMO touched a *new low*. The Department of Personnel and Training (DoPT), which is under the PM-PMO, issued a *secret order* (not available in public domain but came to public knowledge when the Finance Ministry's instructions to its officials were made public by the Congress) which directed all 12 central services – from the IAS to IES, IT, Customs, Excise, Audit and Accounts, Forest, Postal, Telecom etc. – to launch a country-wide campaign as "rath pravaris" ("special officers") and take out specially-fitted "raths" (vehicles) on "rath yatras" (christened "Viksit Bharat Sankalp Yatra") to "showcase" the the government's "achievements".[24] The order said: "In order to coordinate for the preparations, planning, execution, monitoring of the Rath Yatra, it has been decided to deploy joint secretaries, directors, deputy secretaries of the Government of India as district rath prabharis (special officers). In this regard, it is requested that a requisite number of officers from various services, deputed across the country, may be nominated by the respective cadres." These "rath yatras" would cover all 765 districts covering 2.69 lakh gram panchayats between November 20, 2023-January 25, 2024 – coinciding with high-stake elections in five states and run-up to the 2024 general elections (April-May 2024).

Such a directive turns bureaucrats into the BJP's political workers/agents and politicizes them (public servants) who are politically neutral and not expected to become political agents/workers – a clear violation of the service rules. The wordings of the directive leave nothing to imagination about the Prime Minister's drive to build a "committed bureaucracy". Recall the BJP's "rath yatras" in 1990s that led to the demolition of the Babri masjid in 1992 and catapulted it into a national political player. The Prime Minister personally hands over appointment letters, directly and/or virtually, to all public servants since 2022 and showcases such "rozgar melas" as a personal "gift" from him; uses welfare schemes to seek votes for himself and his party (Introduction and Chapter XI). He is also on a permanent campaigning mode by misusing *public functions and public money* for electioneering 24x7, 365 days a year since 2014 (Chapter X).

The Congress complained to the Prime Minister and the Election Commission (ECI). The Prime Minister didn't care to respond, the ECI merely stopped in the states going for elections in November 2023 but allowed in all other states – without addressing the issue of turning public servants into private poll agents of the BJP, objecting to the officials being designated as "prabharis", their campaigns being called "rath yatras" and the forthcoming general elections of 2024.[25] On the other hand, BJP president JP Nadda brazened it out by saying that public service delivery is the duty of government.[26] But later, the government renamed the "prabharis" as "nodal officers".[27]

It must be pointed out that former Prime Minister Indira Gandhi's election from Rae Bareilly in 1971 was countermanded by the Allahabad High Court in June 1975; she was disqualified for elections for six years – which led to the imposition of the Emergency of 1975-77 – because of *misuse of official machinery*. Those misuses were minor in comparison: (a) her personal secretary Yashpal Kapoor, a government servant, had assisted her in her campaign for a few days before resigning from his official position and (b) the Uttar Pradesh officials had set up election rostrums or stages for her rallies.[28]

This apart, in May 2023, the Indian Army issued a strange order to all Command Headquarters directing[29] that all soldiers going on annual leave are expected to do "social service" to enhance "nation-building efforts" by talking to people about the government's welfare programmes and giving back written feedback to the government about it (Chapter XI).

The Prime Minister's transgressions are systematic, routine and subversive of all norms of good governance. The ECI, however, has repeatedly failed to rise to the occasion, making a mockery of electoral governance (more about it in Chapter X).

PMO's writ over the BJP

The PMO's remit runs in his party too.

Former CBI Director Alok Verma[30] alleged, in 2018, that the PMO actively collaborated with the CBI to frame RJD leader Lalu Prasad in the IRCTC scam and pulldown the JD(U)-RJD coalition government in Bihar in 2017. The government was replaced with a coalition of the JD(U)-BJP. During the Bihar elections of 2020, an investigative report alleged possible role of the PMO in collecting funds for the BJP.[31] The government's "one-nation-one fertilizer" policy of 2022[32] mandates all fertilizers bags to carry "Bhartiya Janurvarak Pariyojna" – the first three letters resembling the party's name (BJP), which is further highlighted and printed in the party's saffron colour in the bags. The 'NaMo' app[33], the official app of the Prime Minister, began a fundraising drive for the BJP in the names of government schemes, obliterating the distinction between the government and the party. The use of Israeli spyware Pegasus (more in Chapter XI) against political rivals, bureaucrats, rights activists, journalists, businessmen, even members of higher judiciary and ECI further reflects that more than the security concerns of state, it is the desire to perpetuate the BJP's power and rule that drove the government – *blurring* the line between the government and the party.[34] The same *institutional coordination* between the government and the BJP workers and leaders is also seen when central agencies raid and decapacitate rival political parties round the year, more so during the electioneering; when welfare schemes are delivered (creating the vote bank "labharthi varg") – as pointed out earlier. The trend continued with the launch of "Namo Bharat" train service[35] in 2023.

NK Singh, chairman of the 15th Finance Commission, was one of the first ones to notice excessive centralisation of power in the PM-PMO in 2017 but sought to rationalise it by writing[36]: "The historic mandate of a single -party government was Modi-Centric. It is his reputation and credentials which secured the decisive mandate of the government. The final accountability rests with him. The apparatus of government including the PMO must sub-serve this overarching objective."

A symptom of this is the extraordinary cases of two conmen claiming PMO links, Sanjay Rai 'Sherpuria' and Kiran Bhai Patel – both of whom were nabbed in 2023. Veteran journalist P Raman[37] writes that there are over a dozen such conmen (lists many of those) and points out that India "never ever witnessed such a surge of conmen claiming links with the Prime Minister's Office (PMO)". He explains that "conmen thrive in situations where decisions are guided by one individual's preferences"; under relatively transparent governance "political dynamics determined official decisions" and provides "little role for conmen".

Zero accountability & Transparency

The demonetization of 2016 is a good example of all that is wrong with the governance model. Former Vice President Venkaiah Naidu described it as a "new cultural revolution" project of the Prime Minister to bring behavioural change[38] (is it "voluntary servitude" or slavery?)

It began with a big lie.

The government notification said that the demonetization was "recommended" by the central bank RBI. The lie was nailed once the minutes[39] of RBI's Central Board of Directors, which approved it, was accessed through the RTI after several years of effort in 2019[40] (by the CHRI – whose FCRA license has now been cancelled).

The minutes said the proposal had come from the Finance Ministry on November 7, 2016, which was taken up and approved on November 8, 2016 (the next day in Delhi, not at the RBI's headquarter in Mumbai). It revealed the government's three arguments for demonetization were: (a) significant growth in bank notes of Rs 500 and Rs 1,000, implying growth in black money (b) shadow economy grew from 20.7% in 1999 to 23.2% in 2007 and (c) counterfeiting is on the rise and at Rs 400 crore.

The RBI directors rejected the first two, explaining that the mismatch wasn't stark if adjusted for inflation and that the quantum of fake currency of

Rs 400 crore (as against Rs 15.4 lakh crore of those currency notes) was "not very significant". It pointed out that "most of the black money is held *not in the form of cash but in the form of real sector assets such as gold or real-estate* and... this move would not have a material impact on those assets." As for the third argument ("shadow economy"), it didn't even respond – reflecting the frivolous nature of the claim. *(Emphasis added)*

Why did the RBI approve it then?

The minutes disclosed it: "The Board was *assured*...the proposed step also presents a big opportunity to take the process of *financial inclusion and incentivizing use of electronic modes of payment* forward as people see the benefits of bank accounts and electronic means of payment over use of cash". These were *not the stated objective* of the demonetization at all. The objectives spelt out by the Prime Minister himself were different: *elimination of black money, counterfeit currencies and terror funding.*[41] None of these objectives was achieved as cash component kept growing, no black money was detected and the government never claimed even in its justifications to the Supreme Court that terror funding was impacted; the Supreme Court order of 2023 observed that the RBI acquiesced and did "as desired by the government"; the court itself faltered, failed to hold the government to account and gave *post facto* approval to it (six years too late and in spite of more than adequate evidence to the contrary).[42] *(Emphasis added)*

There was no accountability either.

The Parliament had no role to play in the policy; the Union Cabinet was told minutes before the announcement. The Prime Minister reportedly told his Cabinet that "I have done all the research and, if it fails, then I am to blame"; the sudden announcement startled even senior officers.[43] But the Prime Minister didn't take the blame. Not even after seeking 50 days from the people to prove himself right or else face punishment at any "chowk".[44] He refused to answer questions in the Parliament in 2016[45]; when he did in 2017, it had no substance[46] and then he lied[47] in 2020 that all objectives have been met: (i) tax/GDP ratio drastically improved (ii) made India a lesser cash-based economy (iii) helped reduce black money, increase tax compliance, "boost to transparency" and (iv) it has been "greatly beneficial towards national progress". All the claims were contrary[48] to what the official statistics showed then – and later[49].

There was more. The 2019 report of the Parliamentary Standing Committee on Finance[50], which examined demonetization, described it "ill-conceived" but it was junked as the ruling BJP members[51] with a clear majority in the panel refused to adopt it. The then Chief Economic Advisor Arvind Subramanian described demonetization as a "massive, draconian monetary shock" that plunged GDP for the next 7 quarters.[52] Former RBI Governor Raghuram Rajan revealed in his book

"I Do What I Do" that he had "orally" rejected the proposal when mooted to him in February 2016. Later, through a note, the RBI outlined the potential costs and benefits, outlined the preparations and time needed should the government over-rule and go for it and also mentioned the adverse consequences. His successor Urjit Patel cleared the demonetization nonetheless. The result was for all to see: Long queues outside banks for months as cash was rationed and millions of jobs and businesses were lost overnight.

The Supreme Court failed too.

In its verdict in 2023 (six years later), it confined to the legality of the government's order, upheld it but gave a free pass on the economic "wisdom" of the decision by saying that it was "best left to the wisdom of the experts" – while all evidence showed the government acted *contrary* to all such expert views/advices. The court gave a clean chit on "procedural" matters – for which it relied on "sealed cover" documents (asking for the documents *after* hearings were over). The court failed to fix accountability and paved the way for more irrational, opaque and policy making in future.[53]

The pandemic saw even more lack of transparency and accountability. All powers were centralized overnight by invoking the National Disaster Management Act (NDMA) of 2005 and imposing a stringent 24x7 national curfew. Critical epidemiological data were removed[54] – which showed prevalence of new infections in 10 hotspots. The Bloomberg's investigation[55] blamed the government for errors, inaction and also the politics of controlling information flow which sent the far more deadly Delta variant (which had emerged in India), killing millions around the world in the second wave. The second wave of 2021 saw a massive shortages of oxygen cylinders which led to at least 619 deaths[56] across the country. Several high courts stepped in, but not the Supreme Court, and yet, the government lied about the oxygen and medicine shortages[57] even while going global with begging bowl[58] for help.

It told the Parliament that there was no death due to lack of oxygen[59] and then passed the blame on states for not reporting it[60]. It didn't disclose that states didn't give the data because its communique didn't list such an information.[61] It lied about vaccine shortages and then unilaterally stopped supply[62] of AstraZeneca's Covishield (for which India was given a production license to be supplied to poor countries (COVAX plan), endangering global health and yet, the Prime Minister asked state governments to hold "tika utsav"[63] (vaccine festival).

The government also lied about *excess Covid deaths* and dismissed the WHO data showing *4.74 million* excess deaths in 2020 and 2021 – over and above the government's reported 0.48 million deaths.[64] In short, India missing 90% of Covid deaths! Prabhat Jha[65], one of the world's most highly regarded epidemiologists, and ground reports confirmed the WHO estimates, rather than the government's claims.[66] The government had refused to even collect data on deaths during the distress migration in 2020 – 971 non-Covid deaths were reported then (migrants collapsing due to exhaustion, road and train accidents etc.)[67] – and refused to pay compensation to their families on this very ground.

The Pegasus lock-jam of the Parliament in 2021 saw senior government officials refusing to attend the scheduled meeting of a parliamentary panel on IT to avoid answering questions about the illegal nature of surveillance; the BJP members of the panel, though present, refused to sign the register to ensure the panel didn't meet due to lack of quorum.[68]

Emasculating RTI Act – The Transparency Watchdog

The Right to Information Act (RTI) of 2005 revolutionized accountability and transparency in governance as official information became accessible to ordinary citizens. A 2010 study by the Yale University showed that use of the RTI "is almost as effective as bribery in helping the poor to secure access to a basic public service".[69] This law has been enfeebled through various mechanisms.

A major blow came through the 2019 amendment and the rules under it.[70] These changes diminished the status of the transparency watchdogs, Chief Information Commissioner (CIC) and Information Commissioners (ICs) at the central and state levels. At the Centre, from being equivalent to Chief Election Commissioner (CEC) and Election Commissioners (ECs), who in turn, are equivalent to Supreme Court judges in status, salary and other service conditions, information commissioners (CIC and ICs) were reduced to "fixed" salary bracket of Rs 2.5-2.25 lakh per month. This reduces them to government servants subject to government hierarchy and protocols and therefore, can't be expected to issue orders to officers of equivalent salary grades or above. Their term was reduced from five years to three. At state level, from being equivalent in status to the Supreme Court judges, their status was reduced to "fixed" salary of Rs 2.25 lakh per month and a three-year tenure. They are thus handicapped in enforcing RTI Act on officers of equivalent or higher salary grade.[71]

In 2023, the government introduced (in the Rajya Sabha) the Chief Election Commissioner and Other Election Commissioners (Appointment, Conditions of Service and Term of Office) Bill, 2023, to cut down the status of ECI and ECs from that of SC judges to Cabinet Secretary.[72]

The government *never fills* the vacancies of ICs or CIC *without* citizens approaching the Supreme Court. The selection criteria and appointment process remain opaque in spite of the apex court's express directives in 2019: (i) begin the appointment process 1 to 2 month before a vacancy occurs (ii) expand the choice of candidates to outside the bureaucracy (iii) make the process transparent by making all relevant information accessible to public and (iv) "make the criteria for short-listing the candidates public so that it is ensured that short-listing is done on the basis of objective and rational criteria". The selection criteria and process have not been made public yet, vacancies continue and the vacant posts are routinely filled with retired government officers who are unlikely to act independently.[73] In fact, in October 2023, the Supreme Court lamented that the RTI Act was fast becoming "a dead letter law" after finding that huge vacancies continue to plague central and state information commissions.[74]

But given the state of judiciary in post-2014 India (Chapter III), high courts are also playing a key role in undermining the transparency law. A study of 18 pending cases in the Delhi and other high courts by *Article14*[75] showed long delays, frequent adjournments and lengthy court proceedings are pushing cases into oblivion, acting as a deterrent for people to exercise their rights to know and pursue the cases. High courts are found to order stays of the information commissions' order at the first instance – without even hearing the other side – hurting transparency and accountability.

On the face of it, the official reports show the responses under the RTI Act have improved but this presents a misleading picture as a large number of applications for important information are routinely rejected using the excuse of national security, particularly Section 8 of the RTI Act which exempts disclosure on the grounds of national security, strategic, scientific or economic interests of the government etc.[76] Here is an example. In August 2021, the CIC rejected the RTI query on overnight abrogation of Article 370 and downgrading of Jammu and Kashmir to two union territories. The query sought "copy of all papers along with file notings, list of ministers who attended cabinet meeting and all other attachments and enclosures from the file regarding decision taken in the cabinet meeting". It also sought copy of all correspondences between Government of India and Government of Jammu and Kashmir about it since August 5, 2019. The Home Ministry and the Cabinet Secretariat refused to provide answers. The CIC refused to act as the watchdog of transparency and rejected the appeal citing the same Section 8 even when Section 8(1)(i) says information about cabinet decisions can "be made public after the decision has been taken, and the matter is complete, or over".[77]

The example of the PM CARES Fund has been provided in Chapter I. It is a private fund, run by the PM-PMO from their office, with government domain name (pmcares.gov.in), carries India's official symbols (tricolour and Ashokan lions) and collects public fund. Yet, the PMO refuses to answer questions about it saying that it is out of the ambit of RTI Act because it is not a public authority. As for smaller everyday corruptions, the Transparency International[78] had said India had the highest bribery rate in Asia in its report of November 2020. It said: "India has the highest overall bribery rate (39%) and the highest rate of citizens using personal connections (46%), following India, Indonesia and China have the second and third highest rates of people using personal connections with 36% and 32% respectively." This was a survey of 17 Asian countries.

Living in Denial and Bravado

The government lives in perpetual denial – which has already been flagged in the case of the Rafale deal, the devastating impacts of demonetization and pandemic mismanagement, economic slowdown and job crisis and widespread surveillance on civilian by using the Pegasus spyware. It is an endless list: breach of privacy that former Twitter CEO Jack Dorsey flagged (with MeiTY Minister Rajiv Chandrasekhar replying that privacy "is not a fundamental right" – which is not ignorance but a deliberate lie[79]; the Hindenburg report on the Adani group's alleged corruption and the Prime Minister's personal connection with Gautam Adani[80]; BBC documentary on 2002 Gujarat pogrom[81]; global reports on rising hunger and corruption, worsening press freedom (RSF), social security and democracy (V-Dem, EIU)[82]; worsening human rights reports (reports of the USCIRF, Amnesty Internal, HRW) [83].

At the same time, the Prime Minister and his government don't dare to stand up to China and openly talk about its incursion into the India side of LAC in 2020 and consolidating its position with troops and constructions. The Prime Minister denied the Chinese incursion and didn't even name China as the aggressor. He told the nation: "*Na koi wahan hamari seema mein ghus aaya hai, na hi koi ghusa hua hai, na hi hamari koi post kisi dusre ke kabze mein hain*" (No one has intruded and nor is anyone intruding, nor has any post been captured by someone).[84] Foreign Affairs Minister S Jaishankar made a feeble excuse[85]: "Look, they (China) are the bigger economy. What am I going to do? As a smaller economy, I am going to pick up a fight with the bigger economy?". The government prevented the US from "mentioning China in any US-India communication or any Quad communication"[86] and allowed itself be outmanoeuvred[87].

Now, India keeps pleading with China to hand back its patrolling rights and China keeps refusing (19th meeting of corps commanders by August 2023)[88] – although disengagement have taken place in some areas. India has lost 26 patrolling points, out of 65 in Ladakh[89] and over 1,000 sq km of land along the LAC[90]; China has kept on consolidating *its troops* and *infrastructure* along the LAC.[91] The talks between corps commanders look so farcical because neither the Prime Minister has withdrawn his words nor his government refuted him. And yet, Union Home Minister repeatedly keeps projecting the Prime Minister as a powerful leader who stopped the Russia-Ukraine war for three days, first at a public rally in Gujarat in 2022[92] and then in the Parliament in 2023[93]. The Ladakh SP's report that flagged the loss of 26 patrol points was taken down and no civilian or journalist is allowed anywhere near the ground zero since 2020.

At times, the government not only keeps silence but attacks whistleblowers.

A good example is the Pulwama terror attack of 2019 on the CRPF. The whistleblower is none other than then Governor of J&K Satya Pal Malik – an appointee of the current regime (he was also BJP-appointed Governors of Goa, Meghalaya and Bihar). In 2023, Malik repeated[94] what he had raised in 2019 – multiple security lapses/failures which led to it: (i) the government refused to airlift jawans (ii) left all "8-10 link roads" connecting to the road the jawans took unmanned (allowing the explosive laden vehicle to ram the convoy and, more sensationally (for the first time he said he was revealing) (iii) after the attack, the Prime Minister and his NSA asked him to *"chup raho"* (shut up).

The government played up the terror attack by blaming it on Pakistan in the 2019 general elections – despite the Election Commission's specific orders against invoking defence forces for electioneering (Chapter X). The Prime Minister, his NSA and the Defence Ministry – all have refused to respond to Malik's charges. But that wasn't the end of the matter. The CBI soon went after him, first questioning him for five hours for his old corruption charges against the Reliance and RSS leader Ram Madhav in an insurance scheme for the Kashmiri government officials. But neither the Reliance nor Ram Madhav was questioned – forcing Malik to call his questioning a "harassment"[95]. Days later, the CBI raided[96] his ex-aides (the complainant's side) in connection with the same insurance case and again spared those he had pointed fingers at. In the meanwhile, there is no official probe report revealing why the intelligence lapses happened and who is to be blamed for the Pulwama tragedy. Malik further alleged the Prime Minister was only interested in winning elections.[97]

Malik isn't alone. The government has left all whistle blowers out in the cold – to end whistle blowing all together.

Whistle Blowers Protection Out, 'Citizens' Charter' Lost Way

Accountability and transparency call for protections to RTI activists who are often attacked and killed by the corrupt. The CHRI tracker shows, 106 activists have been killed, 7 committed suicide and 375 assaulted, harassed or threatened until August 2023.[98]

This is why the Whistle Blowers Protection Act of 2014 was passed and notified by the previous Congress-led regime. Instead of implementing it, the government sought to dilute it through The Whistle Blowers Protective (Amendment) Bill of 2015. The amendment proposed (a) to remove immunity (protection) to whistle blowers from prosecution under the Official Secrets Act and (b) prohibits any whistleblower disclosure that contain information which would prejudicially affect the sovereignty, integrity, security, strategic, scientific or economic interests of the state. The amendments were brought without public consultation and sparked protests.[99] It has been pending in the Rajya Sabha since then and the law is yet to be operational.[100]

Another instrument for good governance is a grievance redressal mechanism, or Citizens' Charter, to ensure timely delivery of services. A Bill to ensure this, The Right of Citizens for Time Bound Delivery of Goods and Services and Redressal of their Grievances Bill of 2011 (Citizens Charter), which had already been examined and approved (with multiple recommendations to improve its impact and efficiency) by a parliamentary committee[101], was allowed to lapse with the 15th Lok Sabha. The Prime Minister promised[102] to revive it but didn't.

Investigation-mukt Bharat (Probe-Free India)

One of the key issues that catapulted the BJP to power in 2014 was corruption. The Prime Minister promised "zero corruption", bring back black money stashed abroad and give Rs 15-20 lakh to each Indians. The BJP's 2014 election manifesto[103] promised to "set-up an effective Lokpal institution" (anti-corruption watchdog that the "India Against Corruption" movement had sought) and declared "corruption at any level will be dealt with firmly and swiftly". A year after coming to power, then BJP president Amit Shah described the Prime Minister's promise to deliver Rs 15-20 lakh to every Indian as a political "jumla" (political rhetoric signifying nothing).[104] On the other two promises – zero corruption and bringing black money from abroad – the government has failed to deliver too.

Corruption itself has been made invisible – by dispensing with investigations into corruption allegations altogether. As pointed out in previous chapters, no probe was ordered into the (a) Birla and Sahar bribery cases involving, among others, Modi as Gujarat Chief Minister (b) the Rafale jet deal of 2016 despite documentary evidence of corruption (c) allegations of corruption against the Adani group in 2023 – not just not probed, no question was allowed in the Parliament, no parliament scrutiny (JPC) was allowed and the government agencies (ED, CBI, SFIO etc.) didn't cooperate with the Supreme Court-appointed probe panel (Chapter VII). Add to the list (d) no probe into the illegal surveillance of civilians through the Israeli spyware Pegasus (Chapter XI) and (e) the suicide-note of former Arunachal Pradesh Chief Minister Kalikho Pul, which blamed corruption in politics and the highest judiciary in 2016 and identified the persons who sought bribes from him were never probed; the apex court refused to even probe it[105] in 2021 (Chapter III). This is not an exhaustive list, more will follow.

The Rafale defence deal case needs to be told in some detail – given how the Bofors deal of 1980s had unmade former Prime Minister Rajiv Gandhi a couple of years after winning the highest ever majority in the Lok Sabha in 1984 (over

400 seats). First the government told the Supreme Court that the Rafale contract papers had been stolen[106] from the Defence Ministry – with a view to implicate the petitioners under the Official Secrets Act – only to retract it[107] when the lies were nailed. The probe into this deal is very important also because it compromised the national security[108] by drastically reducing the number of fighter jets from 126 to 36, while paying more money that originally being negotiated (higher by over 2.5 billion Euro than first benchmark price[109]).

The current strength of fighter squadrons is down to 30 from the required 42 squadrons – which would go further down as "the total technical life of most of the existing squadron is expiring and consequently the squadron strength is progressively depleting" – said a parliamentary panel in March 2022.[110] The Centre placed 83 Light Combat Aircraft (LCA Mk-IA) – which has little 'Make in India' component to begin with – to *compensate* but as anyone familiar with the troubled LCA project of the Hindustan Aeronautics Limited (HAL) knows the LCA Mk-1A is still in the development stage in 2022 and would need at least a couple of years' testing to qualify for production and delivery.[111] Another parliamentary panel report of December 2018[112] had pointed out that two LCA Mk-1 squadrons inducted into the IAF recently had to be given "53 concessions/ permanent waivers" by the IAF since these jets failed to meet its specified operational requirements called "Air Staff Requirement" (ASR).

Then the bubble around the indigenously developed Tejas burst when the Centre signed a deal to install GE Aerospace engines[113] in the next stage of development Mk-2 fighter jets. The LCA project is a complete failure. In 2023, the government entered into a deal with the US's GE Aerospace to build and supply engines for Mk-2 jets in June 2023[114] with the very same HAL which was cut off from the Rafale deal in 2016 in favour of an Anil Ambani's company with no previous experience, but by now Anil Ambani's entire empire had collapsed – exposing the government's ineptitude – and was left with no choice.

Other no-probe cases:

(f) **MQ-9B Drone deal**: During the Prime Minister's 2023 US tour, the government signed a deal to buy 31 MQ-9B drones from a private US company and after a hue and cry, the Ministry of Defence called charges of overpriced deal without prior approval of the Cabinet Committee of Security (CCS)[115] as "speculative" and the prices are "subject to negotiations"[116]. Nevertheless, "government sources" said that it would be "27% lower" for India[117] – just as was said about the Rafale India. The Congress alleged India signed the deal at more than double the cost (Rs 110 million each) at which the US ($ 56.5 million each) and much higher than a host of countries have acquired.[118] Whether there will be a probe into this is yet to be seen.

(g) **Banking frauds and NPA write-offs**[119]: During the current regime, writing-off corporate loan defaults as NPAs made a quantum jump – a total of Rs 14.6 lakh crore during FY15-FY23 – which is 24 times more than in the previous nine years of the UPA government. Corporate loan defaulters also include banking frauds and willful defaults (those who can pay but don't) – many of whom fled India. It sunk or jeopardized several banks and non-banking financial institutions – like the PMC Bank, Punjab National Bank, ICICI Bank, Yes Bank, Lakshmi Vilas Bank, IL&FS, HDIL, DHFL etc. Another defining aspect of these scandals was shell companies (which the Prime Minister claimed had been wiped out months earlier due to his (dubious) demonetization and subsequent drives against corruption) *tumbled out by hundreds* – more would tumble out as the Adani group came under intense scrutiny in 2023, anti-corruption-crusader Ramdev's Patanjali group and tax haven Cyprus (Cyprus Confidential) detailed in Chapter VII). The NPA write-offs not only continues without probe or attempt to check fraudsters and willful defaulters but the RBI brought a scheme in 2023, called "Framework for Compromise Settlements and Technical Write-offs" to allow compromise settlements with them (which entails high hair-cuts) and make them eligible for fresh loans after 12 months – a veritable invitation to more banking frauds and willful defaults! The banks are then recapitalized with more public money and/or bailed out with public money (PSBs and PSUs like the LIC). Since most frauds (68% of bank money) involve public sector banks (PSBs), it is a massive loss of public money. The question that arises is: Why should a government do this unless there is a quid pro quo? What is the quid pro quo? Is it the opaque Electoral Bonds or commissions on written-off loans? Public has no knowledge because there has never been any investigation to this massive loss of public money.

(h) **The IBC loss**[120]: The 'big ticket' reform Insolvency and Bankruptcy Code (IBC) of 2016 has failed to achieve its objective – to free stuck-up capital and promote entrepreneurship – and is bleeding the economy with a total yield of *17.6%* of the "admitted claims" during FY18-FY23 (a haircut of 82.4%), with *75% of the firms* ending in scrap sale. This is far worse than the previous FRBM regime which yielded 25% and which the IBC replaced. Yet, there is no attempt to study what ails it – like, lack of political will, poor regulatory culture and gaming of the system which makes it a happy hunting ground for a few businesses close to the government and tax haven entities – or redraft it. Interestingly, such is the environment of laxity and impunity that personal guarantors went to court to challenge the IBC provision bringing them into the ambit, *introduced only in 2019*; which the apex court *greenlighted*[121] in November 2023.

(i) **Corporate Tax Cut**[122]: Corporate tax cut of September 2019 led to revenue loss of Rs 2.28 lakh crore in two fiscals of FY20 (Rs 1.02 lakh crore) and FY21 (Rs 1.28 lakh crore) – as the Parliament has been told. There is no evidence of direct benefits from it to the economy since corporates used it for "debt servicing, build-up of cash balances and other current assets rather than restarting the capex cycle" as per the RBI's annual report of 2019-20. Yet, there is no scrapping it.

(j) **PLI and DLI incentives**[123]: Continuous expansion of the PLIs and DLI without studying their impacts on the economy and without trying to decipher why the manufacturing's share is *stuck at 17-18% of the GDP for 16 years*. India claims to have used the PLI to boost export of mobile phones but it is merely assembling, not manufacturing, and importing components by greater values, thereby raising trade deficits. The Micron's chip unit in Gujarat – for which Rs 16,000 of public money (70% of the total cost of this private project) is to be given – is an assembling unit.[124]

(k) **Ayushman Bharat (AB-PM-JAY) scandal:** This scheme, launched in 2018, is a scaled-up model of the failed 'Rashtriya Swasth Bima Yogjana' (RSBY), abandoned by the previous UPA government for its multiple failures. It provides insurance-based healthcare to bottom 40% which *failed spectacularly*[125], before and after the pandemic hit (most of the money goes to private hospitals, people pay part of treatment, although it is free and cashless scheme and public hospitals are known to deny the benefits to the poor). The Comptroller and Auditor General of India (CAG) report of 2023[126] revealed a mindboggling scam:

- 22.78 lakh beneficiary accounts have no names ("name column is blank").

- 7.5 lakh accounts linked to one mobile phone number (9999999999) and 1.4 lakh to another (8888888888).

- Size of family "11 to 201 members" in *43,197 households*.

- 3,446 patients "who died in previous admission" were paid Rs 6.9 crore.

- More than 13,000 beneficiaries paid "part of their treatment" from own pocket.

- In 11 states/UTs, "transaction before inception of the scheme" and "surgery *after* discharge of patient" were found.

- *78,396 claims* of 48,387 patients were found to have been admitted in "multiple hospitals during the same period of hospitalisation".

Since all phone numbers are linked to the Aadhaar identity, none of it could have been possible without official collusion. The Health Ministry *dismissed it* (through an "unnamed" official, another characteristic of the government)[127] saying that mobile numbers are not used in validation process, only to contradict itself by stating: "AB-PMJAY identifies the beneficiary through *Aadhaar identification* wherein the beneficiary undergoes the process of mandatory Aadhaar based e-KYC." (*Emphasis added*)

(l) **Bharatmala Pariyojana (PPP) project**: A CAG report of 2023 found[128], under this PPP project launched in 2017 to build 74,942 km of national highways, "significant changes made in the scope of projects and cost estimates as well as richer project specifications adopted" (a) the Dwarka Expressway's cost went up astronomically high of *Rs 250.77 crore per km* as against the approved cost of R 18.2 crore per km by the Cabinet Committee on Economic Affairs (CCEA) and (b) the overall average cost of the entire project was pushed up *170.89%* to *Rs 23.89 crore per km* against the CCEA approved cost of Rs 13.98 crore per km. The BP project is marked by irregularities like "selection of ineligible bidders, award of works without approved detailed project reports or based on faulty detailed project reports". No probe has been ordered.

In pre-2014 India, during the 'corrupt' Congress-led UPA regime, corruption allegations led to deals getting cancelled by the government or Supreme Court (Antrix-Devas mobile service deal, 2G spectrum and coal block allocations); ministers resigned and were sent to jail (Telecom Minister A Raja, for example, who was later acquitted); government's top auditor, CAG, parliamentary committees and government appointed High-Level Committees (like, in the case of Commonwealth Game corruption charges) probed corruption allegations and roundly panned the government for financial misappropriations.

India entered into a no-inquiry regime in 2014, and hence, no resignations or jails happen. Those are things of the past. In fact, all corruption investigations are focused on Opposition parties. When a tainted Opposition leader joins the BJP, he/she gets a free pass and all investigations are dropped instantly – a trick also used to engineer defections and pulldown Opposition-ruled state governments (Chapters I, VI and X)

(m) **Organized crime:** Mob lynching and other organized violence against minorities and Dalits continues unbated but none of the security agencies, including the NIA, have probed into it or exposed the real organization providing moral and material support (including legal).

Anticorruption Architecture Defanged

To make corruption involving government and organizations associated with it invisible and targeting political rivals, one of the tools used is to *defang* the very anti-corruption architecture.

One of the first things the new government did after coming to power in 2014 was to amend the law governing the Lokpal, the apex anti-corruption watchdog, to knock out its key pillar to fight corruption – *Section 44* of the original Lokpal law[129] which mandated (statutory) disclosure of assets and liabilities by all public servants in a time-bound manner (annually) and in a prescribed format which were then to be made public. The Lokpal and Lokayuktas (Amendment) Act of 2016[130] was passed within 24 hours of its introduction in the Parliament, without making its content public; it reduced Section 44 to a *single sentence*, giving the Central government all power to decide the manner of such disclosures ("as may be prescribed") and struck down the statutory powers given to Lokpal in the matter. The amendment also empowered the government to make the rules "retrospectively".

Anyone familiar with the fight against corruption in India would realize how this makes Lokpal a toothless body. Then came a bigger "kill bill" provision. The Prevention of Corruption Act (PCA) of 1988 was defanged by introducing the infamous "single directive" in 2018 to make prior government sanction mandatory for investigating agencies *before* starting any corruption investigation against any official. Such a provision earlier existed in the DPSEA of 1946 governing the CBI and had been struck down by the Supreme Court on multiple occasions. The earlier "single directive" prevented any inquiry against officers of joint secretary and above levels without prior government approval (to protect decision makers from arbitrary targeting); the 2018 amendment extended it to all government officials under the PCA. The "single directive" disables the CBI, the anti-corruption agency under the PCA and also the investigating body under the Lokpal.[131]

Such is the hypocrisy over "zero tolerance" to corruption that the government also removed Section 13(1)(d) of the PCA 2018[132] – expanded the "criminal misconduct by a public servant" to include use of "corrupt or illegal means", "abuse" of position to hold "any valuable thing or pecuniary advantage" himself or someone else on his behalf "without any public interest". Its repeal means significantly narrowing down criminal conduct[133] under this law. The regime also removed disqualification of MPs on the ground of corruption in 2015 from the Representation of People Act of 1951 – the Act 9 of 2003[134] (more in Chapter X).

Corruption really doesn't matter to the government. Just two days before the allegedly corrupt politicians from the NCP, led by Ajit Pawar, joined his party-ruled Maharashtra government in 2023, the Prime Minister had thundered at a public rally in Madhya Pradesh, talking about "Modi's guarantee" to put all corrupt politician in jail[135]; he had earlier called the NCP "Naturally Corrupt Party".[136] And a few days later, the Prime Minister continued unabated, describing the Congress as "loot ki dukaan" and "jhoot ka bazaar"[137], the Congress-ruled Chhattisgarh government "as an ATM"[138], called the K Chandrasekhar Rao government of Telangana as the "most corrupt"[139]. Later, on October 3, 2023, he even declared at an *official function-cum-election rally* in Telangana's Nizamabad: "Koi bhrashtachari mere bagal me baith kar mera taap sahan nahin kar sakta hai"[140] (No corrupt can sit beside me and tolerate my (righteous) heat) to explain the absence Chief Minister KC Chandrashekar Rao from the rival party, the Bharat Rashtra Samithi (BRS), who had been boycotting him – and paint him as corrupt. No word can truly express the sheer mendacity given that scores of politicians declared corrupt by him and his party have joined them and been rewarded (see Chapter I).

After joining the BJP all the allegedly corrupt politicians become holy cows as they get immunity from legal actions. Ajit Pawar had learnt this earlier as the corruption cases against him were withdrawn when he first joined the BJP government in Maharashtra in 2019[141] (which fell in 24 hours) and those cases were revived in 2022, the ED and IT raided him again and fresh charges were added[142] when the BJP-rebel Shiv Sena government returned to power. Presumably, all corruption cases would now be put on hold till he is now part of the BJP government.

Lokpal of India: Missing in Action

Having weakened the very anti-corruption architecture, the government (i) refused to appoint the Lokpal for four years until 2019 – despite repeated reprimand from the Supreme Court and threat of contempt (ii) didn't frame rules and formats for filing complaints for two more years until 2020 and (iii) hasn't appointed a director of inquiry for conducting preliminary inquiry. The selection of the Lokpal was without the participation of the LoP as required by the law and the processes was completely opaque – undermining the trust in the institution.[143]

The government refused to disclose the minutes of the selection committee meeting for the Lokpal under the RTI. Strangely, the government's plea was upheld by the Central Information Commission (CIC)[144], raising questions about the transparency watchdog's complicity. The selection of Lokpal is critical because it is empowered to investigate corruption cases against the high and mighty, including present and former Prime Ministers. The Lokpal's power was further diluted through the Rules of 2020[145] which said, in case of sitting or former Prime Minister the preliminary inquiry shall be held "in camera", and "if the Lokpal comes to the conclusion that the complaint deserves to be dismissed, the records of the inquiry shall not be published or made available to anyone" – as per Section 14a(ii) of the law, read with the Lokpal (Complaint) Rules of 2020.

The Lokpal of India's official website shows, it received 1,427 complaints in 2019-20. Of this, 1,219 cases (85%) were "beyond jurisdiction", 77 were closed for various reasons and only in case of 3 status/inquiry reports were pending. In 2020-21, the number of complaints fell to 110. Of this, preliminary inquiry was ordered in 30 cases and the rest were closed at or after preliminary examination/inquiry. In 2021-22, there were just 30 complaints (up to July 2021 – not updated thereafter until August 2023)[146], of which 11 had been rejected, preliminary inquiry ordered in 7. In July 2022, media reported the first Lokpal order to the CBI to investigate the bullet train project chief Satish Agnihotri for graft, leading to his sacking.[147]

The Lokpal woke up from its *deep slumber* to suddenly order a CBI investigation into the alleged "cash-for-query" scam against Mahua Moitra of the Trinamool Congress leader who has been asking tough questions on the Adani group's business in November 2023.[148] This brings the Lokpal into the league of the ED, CBI and IT to target only political rival of the Central government.

The government claims the fall in cases with the Lokpal is evidence of no corruption – as Jitendra Singh, Minister of State for Personnel and PMO, said in 2021.[149] The fact, however, remains that not one important corruption case is known to have been taken up by the Lokpal – other than the Agnihotri case mentioned earlier. Corruption crusader Prashant Bhushan dismisses the Lokpal as a "Jokpal".[150]

But that is to be expected.

During his 12 years as Gujarat's Chief Minister, Modi didn't appoint (since 2003) or allow the Lokayukta (on the state's statute book since 1986) – the apex anti-corruption watchdog in states – to function. In 2011, when the Governor appointed Justice AR Mehta bypassing him, he was humiliated and forced to resign.[151] Finally, the state appointed a Lokayukta in 2013, who retired in 2018. After a gap of two years, another one was appointed in 2020. That the Gujrat Lokayukta is only on paper, completely non-functional is self-evident. One clear indication is its official website – blank except for half a dozen photos and names and photos of four Lokayuktas, sans profiles, any information on its cases, not even a single annual report since 1988.[152] It is not known, or heard to have, taken up or cracked any corruption case.

CBI: From 'Caged Parrot' to Unleashed Hound

The CBI is the premier anti-corruption investigating agency. It is notorious for inefficiency with the Supreme Court describing it a "caged parrot" during the UPA regime. Its blatant political misuse worsened after 2014, leading to an unprecedent move by *nine states* to withdrew general consent to it to investigate in their territories by March 2022[153] – reflecting the state of "cooperative federalism", another tall claim.

Appointments to the CBI has raised serious questions about propriety and suitability of the candidates. Rakesh Asthana's first appointment as Special Director was when he being probed by the very CBI for multiple corruption cases. Later, CBI Director Alok Verma pressed corruption and bribery charges against him. (Asthana also complained against Verma, leading to an ugly spat and the midnight transfer of both). Then, the government tried to appoint Asthana as the CBI Director in 2021 but failed (as mentioned earlier). Verma's midnight removal in 2021 was apparently because of the fears that he might order a probe into the controversial Rafale deal detailed in the previous chapter. The transfer was held as illegal and squashed by the apex court but the government hounded him, he was subject to surveillance through the Pegasus (long with Asthana) and when he quit, he was denied pension.[154]

The Supreme Court saw a couple of ridiculous assertions from the Centre. First, in 2021, the Centre filed an affidavit telling the Supreme Court that the West Bengal government had *no power*[155] to stop the CBI from probing cases in the state after it had withdrawn the general consent. The second was in 2023, when the CBI filed an affidavit declaring itself to be of the "Republic of India" – in a bail related petition – forcing the court to question its status[156] and then the government told the apex court that the CBI was a separate legal entity and it had no control over it ("separate legal entity outside the Union of India")[157].

The Central Vigilance Commission (CVC) Act of 2003, which empowers it to oversee the CBI's functioning (corruption investigations under the PCA), became toothless even before 2014. Under Modi, its credibility received a big setback with the appointment of former chairperson of the Central Board of Direct Taxation (CBDT) KV Chowdary. Chowdhary's non-investigation into the Birla and Sahara bribery cases mentioned earlier had cast serious doubts on his credibility. His role in the enquiry into the allegations (by Asthana) of corruption against Verma also saw the latter calling into question Chowdary's integrity.[158]

All of the above narratives show that the anti-corruption crusade the Prime Minister promised is a charade and it is well-nigh impossible to deliver inclusive, accountable, transparent and corruption-free government.[159] The manifestation of this failure is in the pervasive *mob rule* earlier talked about.[160]

What Happened to Black Money?

The Prime Minister doesn't talk about bringing black money stashed abroad any more, in spite of a series of investigative reports, in the interim, identifying and naming many corporate bigwigs, famously known as the *Panama Papers, Paradise Papers* and *Pandora Papers*.[161] In the meanwhile, banking and corporate frauds have significantly spiked. As mentioned earlier, the NPA write-offs spiked 24 times during the regime to Rs 14.6 lakh crore during FY15-FY23 (for context and explanations, see Chapter VII).

Meanwhile, the Swiss bank deposits of Indians, which the Prime Minister had proclaimed to be black money and promised to bring back in the run up to the 2014 elections, nearly doubled from 1.81 billion Swiss Franc in 2014 to 3.83 billion (Rs 30,500 crore) in 2021 – a 14-year high.[162] To this news the government reacted by telling the Lok Sabha[163]: "There is no official estimate of amount of money deposited by Indian citizens and companies in Swiss banks." India gets regular update about Swiss accounts from the Swiss government as per the international agreement following the 2007-09 financial crisis. In fact, a few months after the denial, India received the *fourth trench* of documents on Swiss accounts.[164]

Worse, the deputy chief of the government-appointed SIT on black money, (retired) Justice Arijit Pasayat was found to have misreported Rs 1.06 crore of earnings and had opted for an "amnesty" scheme to escape IT raids and prosecution for tax evasion.[165] This SIT submitted six reports between 2014-2017[166] but none of these reports has been made public either by the government or by the Supreme Court. The government even denied that it has any information on tax haven-based shell companies (used for channelling unaccounted money) and no India law even defines shell companies. This was in sharp contrast to the Prime Minister's declaration[167] in his national day address on August 15, 2017 that his government had shut thousands of empty corporate shells. In fact, the Hindenburg's allegations on the Adani group's tax haven connections and accounting frauds showed shell companies and tax havens are *flourishing*[168].

Meanwhile, Dr John Brittas, CPI-M Member of Parliament who had sought information on the government's action against shell companies, was summoned days later by Vice President Jagdeep Dhankar and asked to give a written explanation after an oral explanation in an unconnected case (an innocuous opinion piece in a newspaper as earlier mentioned in Chapter II).

Given such a dismal record of the regime, political scientist Suhas Palshikar's description of the government's governance model as "bulldozer governance"[169] – for routinely discarding procedures and shunning all forms of accountability – sounds more apt.

***

References

1   Worldwide Governance Indicators 2023, World Bank, Daniel Kaufmann and Aart Kraay (2023); https://databank.worldbank.org/source/worldwide-governance-indicators#

2   Worldwide Governance Indicators: Overview (with definitions and data sources); https://www.govindicators.org/

3   Patel Aakar, Price of the Modi Years, Westland Publications, 2021; https://www.amazon.in/Price-Modi-Years-Aakar-Patel/dp/9391234224

4   Tewari Ruhi, The perks Ajit Doval, Nripendra Misra & PK Mishra are entitled to under Cabinet rank, Jun 12, 2019; https://theprint.in/india/governance/the-perks-ajit-doval-nripendra-misra-pk-mishra-are-entitled-to-under-cabinet-rank/249127/

5   Updated copy of the Table of Precedence, President's Secretariat; https://www.mha.gov.in/sites/default/files/table_of_precedence.pdf

6   Singh Bikash, Union minister's house set on fire in violence-hit Manipur, Jun 16, 2023; https://economictimes.indiatimes.com/news/politics-and-nation/union-ministers-house-set-on-fire-in-violence-hit-manipur/articleshow/101052297.cms?utm_source=contentofinterest&utm_medium=text&utm_campaign=cppst

7   Vacant posts in central services, Unstarred question no. 1713, Rajya Sabha, Mar 5, 2020; https://www.dropbox.com/s/1ybk8e3wkdyzw3b/RS_Vacancies%202020_PMO%20511.pdf?dl=0

8   Kharge Mallikarjun, The PMO Has Morphed Into an Independent Executive Force – Where Is the Cabinet?, Nov 26, 2023; https://thewire.in/books/pmo-modi-mallikarjun-kharge-book-excerpt

9   Pranab Mukherjee is UPA II's Mr Fixit, May 17, 2012; https://timesofindia.indiatimes.com/india/pranab-mukherjee-is-upa-iis-mr-fixit/articleshow/13178699.cms; Mohanty P, How about GoM for good governance? May 11, 2011; https://www.governancenow.com/views/columns/how-about-gom-good-governance

10 Composition of the Cabinet Committees (as on 03.12.2014), Cabinet Secretariat, Dec 3, 2014; https://documents.doptcirculars.nic.in/D2/D02eod/PDF/Composition%20of%20ACC%20-%20as%20reconstituted%20on%2003.12.2014.pdf

11 Home Minister is quietly cut out of senior officers' appointments, Aug 13, 2014; https://indianexpress.com/article/india/india-others/home-minister-is-quietly-cut-out-of-senior-officers-appointments/

12 PM action plan: Single environment Act, birth certificate for citizenship, jobs clause in FTAs; The Indian Express, Oct 19, 2021; https://indianexpress.com/article/india/pm-action-plan-environment-act-birth-certificate-citizenship-jobs-clause-ftas-7578973/

13 6 years on, PM Modi's core team is in the grip of IAS, IPS, IRS officers from Gujarat, Oct 5, 2020; https://theprint.in/india/governance/6-years-on-pm-modis-core-team-is-in-the-grip-of-ias-ips-irs-officers-from-gujarat/514820/

14   PM Modi attends DGP meet; cyber crime, Maoism in focus, The Indian Express, Nov 21, 2021; https://indianexpress.com/article/india/pm-modi-dgp-meet-cyber-crime-maoism-7633557/; PM Modi interacts with state and district officials on the COVID-19 situation, May 20, 2021; https://ddnews.gov.in/national/pm-modi-interacts-state-and-district-officials-covid-19-situation; States on board Gati Shakti, govt looks to cut project time, Jul 9, 2022; https://indianexpress.com/article/business/economy/states-on-board-gati-shakti-govt-looks-to-cut-project-time-8018273/

15   Nitnaware Himanshu, Experts irked over revised structure of Central Empowered Committee, Sept 8, 2023; https://www.downtoearth.org.in/news/environment/experts-irked-over-revised-structure-of-central-empowered-committee-91628

16   Khaitan Tarunabh 2020: Killing a Constitution with a Thousand Cuts: Executive Aggrandizement and Party-state Fusion in India, Walter de Gruyter GmbH, Berlin/Boston, Law & Ethics of Human Rights, Aug 7, 2020; https://www.degruyter.com/document/doi/10.1515/lehr-2020-2009/html

17   Indian economy is now too big to be run from PMO: Raghuram Rajan, Oct 14, 2019; https://theprint.in/economy/indian-economy-big-pmo-raghuram-rajan/305447/

18   Can't keep hanging, pick Lokpal without Leader of Opposition: SC, Apr 28, 2017; https://indianexpress.com/article/india/cant-keep-hanging-pick-lokpal-without-leader-of-opposition-supreme-court-4631260/

19   India's First Lokpal Appointed: Justice Pinaki Chandra Ghose as Chief, 8 Members, Mar 20, 2022; https://thewire.in/government/indias-first-lokpal-appointed-justice-pinaki-chandra-ghose-as-chief-8-members

20   Adhir Ranjan Chowdhury writes to PM objecting to CVC appointment, India Today, Mar 9, 2020; https://www.indiatoday.in/india/story/adhir-ranjan-chowdhury-pm-modi-cvc-1653878-2020-03-09; President's secretary Sanjay Kothari appointed Central Vigilance Commissioner, Apr 25, 2020; https://economictimes.indiatimes.com/news/politics-and-nation/presidents-secretary-sanjay-kothari-appointed-central-vigilance-commissioner/articleshow/75372424.cms?utm_source=contentofinterest&utm_medium=text&utm_campaign=cppst

21   Centre's Top Choices for New CBI Chief Dropped After CJI Ramana's Opposition, May 25, 2021; https://thewire.in/government/centres-top-choices-for-new-cbi-chief-dropped-after-cji-ramanas-opposition

22   No irregularity, illegality in appointment Rakesh Asthana as Police Commissioner, says HC, Oct 12, 2021; https://economictimes.indiatimes.com/news/india/hc-dismisses-plea-challenging-appointment-of-rakesh-asthana-as-delhi-police-commissioner/articleshow/86958949.cms?utm_source=contentofinterest&utm_medium=text&utm_campaign=cppst

23   Dasgupta Sravasti, Officers In Charge of CAG Reports on Ayushman Bharat Graft, Bharatmala Cost Irregularities Transferred, Oct 11, 2023; https://thewire.in/government/officers-cag-reports-ayushman-bharat-bharatmala-transferred

24   Gupta Moushumi Das, I-T to customs, officers of 12 services to be deployed as 'rath

prabharis' to showcase 9 yrs of Modi govt, Oct 22, 2023; https://theprint.in/india/i-t-to-customs-officers-of-12-services-to-be-deployed-as-rath-prabharis-to-showcase-9-yrs-of-modi-govt/1814215/; A Divya and Nath Damini, Viksit Bharat Sankalp Yatra: EC tells govt to ensure no govt scheme yatra in poll-bound states, Oct 26, 2023; https://indianexpress.com/article/political-pulse/viksit-bharat-sankalp-yatra-rath-prabharis-9001070/; Pisharoty Sangeeta Barooah, Modi Government Move to Turn Government Officers into 'Rath Prabharis' Stirs Storm, Oct 22, 2023; https://thewire.in/government/modi-government-move-to-turn-government-officers-into-rath-prabharis-stirs-storm

25   A Divya and Nath Damini, Viksit Bharat Sankalp Yatra: EC tells govt to ensure no govt scheme yatra in poll-bound states, Oct 26, 2023; https://indianexpress.com/article/political-pulse/viksit-bharat-sankalp-yatra-rath-prabharis-9001070/

26   Kharge writes to PM on 'politicising of bureaucracy, Armed Forces'; Nadda hits back, Oct 23, 2023; https://indianexpress.com/article/political-pulse/kharge-pm-politicising-of-bureaucracy-armed-forces-nadda-hits-back-8995114/; Express View: BJP's rath prabhari circular — the bureaucracy must be neutral and independent, Oct 25, 2023; https://indianexpress.com/article/opinion/editorials/officer-and-prabhari-8998014/; CG Manoj, In complaints to EC, Congress seeks campaign ban on Amit Shah, Himanta Sarma; action on 'rath prabhari' row, Oct 25, 2023; https://indianexpress.com/article/political-pulse/ec-congress-seeks-campaign-ban-on-amit-shah-himanta-sarma-action-rath-prabhari-row-8999505/

27   A Divya and Nath Damini, 'Viksit Bharat Sankalp Yatra'

28   Pisharoty Sangeeta Barooah, Modi Government Move to Turn Government Officers into 'Rath Prabharis' Stirs Storm, Oct 22, 2023; https://thewire.in/government/modi-government-move-to-turn-government-officers-into-rath-prabharis-stirs-storm; Indira Nehru Gandhi vs Shri Raj Narain & Anr on 7 November, 1975, Supreme Court; https://indiankanoon.org/doc/936707/

29   Chhina MAS, Do social service on leave, be ambassadors for nation-building: Army to its soldiers, Sept 2, 2023; https://indianexpress.com/article/cities/chandigarh/do-social-service-on-leave-be-ambassadors-for-nation-building-army-to-its-soldiers-8920298/; When on leave... do social service, promote govt schemes: Army advises jawans, Sept 4, 2023; https://www.hindustantimes.com/india-news/army-encourages-soldiers-to-undertake-social-service-during-leave-contribute-to-nation-building-effort-101693765707394.html

30   Rakesh Asthana, Sushil Modi and PMO Worked Together to Book Lalu: CBI Director, Nov 18, 2018; https://thewire.in/government/lalu-prasad-cbi-rakesh-asthana-alok-verma

31   Agarwal Poonam 2020: PMO collecting funds for BJP for Bihar election, The Quint, Oct 30, 2020: https://www.thequint.com/amp/story/news/india/can-pmo-use-government-machinery-to-collect-donations-for-bjp-bhartiya-janta-party

32   Explained: The One Nation One Fertiliser scheme, the Govt's logic, and some immediate risks, Aug 25, 2022; https://indianexpress.com/article/explained/

everyday-explainers/one-nation-one-fertiliser-scheme-explained-risks-challenges-drawbacks-8111071/

33   Ahmed Z Shabbir 2022: 'NaMo' app that raises funds for BJP uses names of govt schemes: Is this legal? News Minute, Mar 14, 2022; https://www.thenewsminute.com/article/namo-app-raises-funds-bjp-uses-names-govt-schemes-legal-161893

34   Shrivastava Kabeer 2021: In India, the Use of Pegasus Tells Us the Line Between State and Party Has Blurred, The Wire, Aug 2, 2021; https://thewire.in/politics/pegasus-expose-blurred-lines-state-party-national-security

35   PM Modi Inaugurates 'Namo Bharat', India's 1st Regional Rapid Train Service, Oct 20, 2023; https://www.ndtv.com/india-news/pm-modi-inaugurates-namo-bharat-indias-1st-regional-rapid-train-service-4498814

36   Singh NK 2017: The PMO Under Modi Takes Unprecedented Shape, NDTV, Jun 1, 2017; https://www.ndtv.com/opinion/the-pmo-under-modi-takes-unprecedented-shape-767404

37   Raman P, What the Clutch of Conmen Faking Links to the PMO Says About Modi's Governance Style, Jul 3, 2023; https://thewire.in/politics/pmo-conmen-modi-governance-style

38   Naidu Venkaiah, The New Cultural Revolution, Nov 29, 2016; https://indianexpress.com/article/opinion/columns/demonetisation-effect-rbi-economy-gdp-4400464/

39   Pdf of "Minutes of Central Board of Directors", RBI, Nov 8, 2016; https://www.humanrightsinitiative.org/download/DeMon%201stattachment.pdf

40   RBI compelled to disclose demonetisation meeting minutes after CIC's penalty cause notice under RTI Act, Commonwealth Human Rights Initiative (CHRI), Feb 16, 2019; https://www.humanrightsinitiative.org/blog/rbi-compelled-to-disclose-demonetisation-meeting-minutes-after-cics-penalty-show-cause-notice-under-rti-act

41   Text of Prime Minister's address to the Nation, Prime Minister's Office, Nov 8, 2016; https://pib.gov.in/newsite/PrintRelease.aspx?relid=153404

42   Mohanty P, Why demonetisation verdict raises more questions than answers, Jan 4, 2023; https://www.fortuneindia.com/opinion/why-demonetisation-verdict-raises-more-questions-answers/111008

43   Who knew about Modi's secret demonetisation plan? Mint, Dec 10, 2016; https://www.livemint.com/Politics/PZJjaYlbSXITq8gIrZePnL/How-closely-guarded-was-Narendra-Modis-demonetisation-plan.html; Backroom story of demonetisation: From PMO to RBI, how it all played out, Oct 7, 2019; https://www.business-standard.com/article/economy-policy/backroom-story-of-demonetisation-from-pmo-to-rbi-how-it-all-played-out-117110700044_1.html

44   PM Modi on demonetisation: Bear pain for 50 days, then punish me, Nov 14, 2016; https://indianexpress.com/article/india/india-news-india/demonetisation-of-rs-500-rs-1000-notes-pm-modi-bear-pain-for-50-days-then-punish-me-4373933/

45   Narendra Modi won't reply to demonetisation debate in Parliament: Venkaiah, Nov 17, 2016; https://www.thehindu.com/news/national/Narendra-Modi-won%E2%80%99t-reply-to-demonetisation-debate-in-Parliament-Venkaiah/article16644649.ece

46   Modi's defence of demonetisation in Parliament fails to resonate with Opposition, Feb 8, 2017; https://www.hindustantimes.com/india-news/modi-s-defence-of-demonetisation-in-parliament-fails-to-resonate-with-opposition/story-Y1V0VKpVC74DOQRviLx7IO.html

47   Demonetisation helped to reduce black money, increase tax compliance and given a boost to transparency: PM, Nov 8, 2020; https://pib.gov.in/PressReleseDetail.aspx?PRID=1671214

48   Mohanty P, Rebooting Economy 48: Do tax numbers show a healthier economy? Nov 26, 2020; https://www.businesstoday.in/opinion/columns/story/indian-economy-do-tax-numbers-show-a-healthier-economy-economic-growth-279744-2020-11-26

49   Mohanty P, 'Why demonetisation verdict...'

50   Status of unaccounted income/wealth both inside and outside the country - A critical analysis, Standing Committee on Finance (2018-19), Sixteenth Lok Sabha, Mar 28, 2019; https://eparlib.nic.in/bitstream/123456789/785330/1/16_Finance_73.pdf

51   BJP MPs obstruct adoption of parliamentary panel's report that was critical of demonetisation, Aug 28, 2018; https://scroll.in/latest/892175/bjp-mps-obstruct-adoption-of-parliamentary-panels-report-that-was-critical-of-demonetisation

52   'Demonetisation was a massive, draconian, monetary shock', says Arvind Subramanian in his new book; November 28, 2018; https://www.livemint.com/Industry/PL1a49BBpiMN2r2VRhvOrN/demonetisation-arvind-subramanian-book-of-counsel-modi-jaitl.html

53   Mohanty P, 'Why demonetisation verdict...'

54   How Covid numbers were hushed up, Sept 20, 2020; https://www.telegraphindia.com/india/how-covid-numbers-were-hushed-up/cid/1792482

55   Kay Chris and Pandya Dhwani, How Errors, Inaction Sent a Deadly Covid Variant Around the World, Dec 27, 2021; https://www.bloomberg.com/news/features/2021-12-29/how-delta-variant-spread-in-india-deadly-errors-inaction-covid-crisis

56   Pandey Kiran, Passing the buck: No deaths due to lack of oxygen reported by states, Centre says, Jul 20, 2021; https://www.downtoearth.org.in/news/health/passing-the-buck-no-deaths-due-to-lack-of-oxygen-reported-by-states-centre-says-78047

57   No shortage of Covid vaccines, oxygen, medicines: Harsh Vardhan, New Indian Express; Apr 18, 2021; https://www.newindianexpress.com/states/karnataka/2021/apr/18/no-shortage-of-covid-vaccines-oxygen-medicinesharsh-vardhan-2291464.html

58   Mohanty 'An Unkept Promise'

59   No deaths due to lack of oxygen reported during second Covid wave: Centre, Jul 21, 2021; https://www.indiatoday.in/coronavirus-outbreak/story/covid-second-wave-lack-shortage-liquid-medical-oxygen-lmo-deaths-health-ministry-response-parliament-1830549-2021-07-20

60   Pandey Kiran, 'Passing the buck'

61   Bedi Aneesha, Why states/UTs didn't report Covid deaths due to lack of O2 despite 'oxygen shortage' crisis, Jul 27, 2021; https://theprint.in/health/why-states-uts-didnt-report-covid-deaths-due-to-lack-of-o2-despite-oxygen-shortage-crisis/703387/

62   Chowdhury Debasish Roy, Modi Never Bought Enough COVID-19 Vaccines for India. Now the Whole World Is Paying, May 28, 2021; https://time.com/6052370/modi-didnt-buy-enough-covid-19-vaccine/

63   Coronavirus India Highlights: PM Modi asks CMs to focus on micro-containment, Indian Express, Apr 9, 2021; https://indianexpress.com/article/india/india-coronavirus-second-wave-live-updates-lockdown-curfew-rules-cases-deaths-vaccination-7262037/

64   Mohanty P, India has no data to challenge WHO excess Covid deaths, May 9, 2022; https://www.fortuneindia.com/opinion/india-has-no-data-to-challenge-who-excess-covid-deaths/108072

65   Watch: WHO-Linked Epidemiologist Prabhat Jha on India's Disputed COVID Death Numbers, May 11, 2022; https://thewire.in/health/watch-who-linked-epidemiologist-prabhat-jha-on-indias-disputed-covid-death-numbers

66   Gujarat's Real Covid Tragedy Revealed: Data Suggests At Least 2.8 Lakh Excess Deaths During Pandemic, Aug 17, 2021; https://www.reporters-collective.in/projects/gujarats-real-covid-tragedy-revealed-data-suggests-at-least-2-8-lakh-excess-deaths-during-pandemic

67   No Data, No Problem: Centre in Denial about Migrant Worker Deaths and Distress, Stranded Workers Action Network (SWAN), Sept 2020; https://thewire.in/rights/migrant-workers-no-data-centre-covid-19-lockdown-deaths-distress-swan

68   Editorial: Disregarding Parliament: Govt officials cannot be allowed to ignore committees, Aug 2, 2021; https://www.business-standard.com/article/opinion/disregarding-parliament-121080201623_1.html

69   Peisakhin Leonid and Pinto Paul, Is Transparency an Effective Anti-Corruption Strategy? Evidence From a Field Experiment in India, Yale University, 2010; https://isps.yale.edu/research/publications/isps10-029

70   The Right to Information (Amendment) Act, Aug 1, 2019; https://egazette.nic.in/writereaddata/2019/209696.pdf; Rules under the RTI (Amendment) Act of 2019, Oct 24, 2019; https://egazette.nic.in/WriteReadData/2019/213438.pdf; https://prsindia.org/theprsblog/tenure-and-salaries-cic-and-ics-under-right-information-rules-

2019#:~:text=The%20CIC%20and%20ICs%20(at%20the%20central%20level)%20
shall%20receive,receive%20a%20pay%20of%20Rs.

71   Tenure and salaries of CIC and ICs under the Right to Information Rules, 2019,
     PRS Legislative Service, Oct 29, 2019; https://prsindia.org/theprsblog/tenure-and-
     salaries-cic-and-ics-under-right-information-rules-2019#:~:text=The%20CIC%20
     and%20ICs%20(at%20the%20central%20level)%20shall%20receive,receive%20
     a%20pay%20of%20Rs

72   The CEC and Other ECs (Appointment, Conditions of Service and Term of Office)
     Bill, 2023; https://prsindia.org/files/bills_acts/bills_parliament/2023/Bill_Text_
     Chief_Election_Commissioner_and_other_Election_Commissioners_Bill_2023.pdf

73   Anjali Bhardwaj and others vs Union of India and others, Writ petition
     (2018), Supreme Court, Feb 15, 2019; http://judicialreforms.org/wp-content/
     uploads/2019/02/15968_2018_Judgement_15-Feb-2019.pdf; Bhardwaj Anjali, Johri
     Amrita, 'Corruption-Free India' Under BJP Government Is Just a Sham, The
     Wire, Dec 9, 2020; https://thewire.in/government/corruption-free-india-modi-
     government-sham-reveals-study-transperancy-international

74   Mahapatra Dhananjay, Right to Information Act fast becoming a dead letter,
     says SC, Oct 31, 2023; http://timesofindia.indiatimes.com/articleshow/104835119.
     cms?utm_source=contentofinterest&utm_medium=text&utm_campaign=cppst

75   Das Saurav, 17 Years After India's Landmark Information Law Was Passed, India's
     Courts Are Undermining That Right, Nov 8, 2023; https://article-14.com/post/17-
     years-after-india-s-landmark-information-law-was-passed-india-s-courts-are-
     undermining-that-right-654afcbc09b5b

76   Nayak Venkatesh, Hiding in the name of national security, Jul 18, 2021; https://
     www.deccanherald.com/opinion/panorama/hiding-in-the-name-of-national-
     security-1009901.html; 1 Out of Every 3 RTIs Is Rejected Using Section 8 (1), Says
     CIC Annual Report 2019-20, Moneylife.in, Apr 28, 2021; https://www.moneylife.
     in/article/1-out-of-every-3-rtis-is-rejected-using-section-8-1-says-cic-annual-
     report-2019-20/63685.html

77   Yadav Shyamlal, Art 370: CIC rejects disclosure plea, cites security, strategic
     interests, Indian Express, Aug 14, 2021; https://indianexpress.com/article/india/art-
     370-cic-rejects-disclosure-plea-cites-security-strategic-interests-7452898/

78   India records highest rate of bribery in Asia: survey, Nov 26, 2020; https://www.
     thehindu.com/news/national/india-records-highest-rate-of-bribery-in-asia-survey/
     article33184156.ece

79   Mohanty P, Why protecting privacy remains a challenge in India, Jun 21, 2023;
     https://www.fortuneindia.com/opinion/why-protecting-privacy-remains-a-
     challenge-in-india/113131

80   Constitution of Committee to Investigate Adani Group, Lok Sabha answer, Mar
     13, 2023; https://www.livelaw.in/pdf_upload/au1932-463151.pdf; Budget session
     concludes; productivity suffers due to daily adjournments, disruptions, PTI, Apr 6,

2023; https://theprint.in/india/budget-session-concludes-productivity-suffers-due-to-daily-adjournments-disruptions/1502934/

81   BJP slams BBC's 'venomous' reporting on India, says I-T department should be allowed to do its work, DHNS, Feb 15, 2023; https://www.deccanherald.com/india/bjp-slams-bbcs-venomous-reporting-on-india-says-i-t-department-should-be-allowed-to-do-its-work-1191095.html

82   Kudrati Mohammed, From Hunger To Press Freedom: Global Reports The Govt Disagrees With, JUl 30, 2022; https://www.boomlive.in/explainers/hunger-press-freedom-happiness-democracy-index-disgree-parliament-lok-sabha-rajya-sabha-18673

83   Remarks by President Biden and Prime Minister Modi of the Republic of India in Joint Press Conference, The White House, Jun 22, 2023; https://www.whitehouse.gov/briefing-room/speeches-remarks/2023/06/22/remarks-by-president-biden-and-prime-minister-modi-of-the-republic-of-india-in-joint-press-conference/

84   Narendra Modi Didn't Watch His Words on Chinese Intrusion So PMO 'Censors' Official Video, Jun 25, 2020; https://thewire.in/government/narendra-modi-china-video-pmo-censor

85   Military veterans slam Modi's '56-inch chest' boast, S Jaishankar's comment on China, Feb 24, 2023; https://www.telegraphindia.com/india/military-veterans-slam-modis-56-inch-chest-boast-s-jaishankars-comment-on-china/cid/1918541

86   India asked Washington not to bring up China's border transgressions: Former US ambassador, Mar 2, 2022; https://scroll.in/latest/1018580/india-asked-washington-not-to-mention-chinas-border-transgressions-former-us-ambassador-to-india

87   Singh Sushant, Out of Control: How China outmanoeuvred the Modi government and seized control of territory along the LAC, Oct 1, 2022; https://caravanmagazine.in/security/india-china-ladakh

88   India, China hold 19th round of Corps Commander-level talks to end LAC stand-off, Aug 14, 2023; https://www.thehindu.com/news/national/india-china-hold-19th-round-of-corps-commander-level-talks-to-end-lac-stand-off/article67195006.ece

89   Singh Sushant, Full text of report on India's loss of access to 26 patrolling points on Ladakh border, Jan 26, 2023; https://caravanmagazine.in/security/full-text-sp-ladakh-india-lost-access-patrolling-points-china-border

90   Singh Vijaita, China controls 1,000 sq. km of area in Ladakh, Sept 1, 2020; https://www.thehindu.com/news/national/china-controls-1000-sq-km-of-area-in-ladakh-say-intelligence-inputs/article32490453.ece

91   Dutta Amrita N, Following Galwan clashes, China ramped up troop presence, infra along LAC in 2022, says Pentagon, Oct 22, 2023; https://indianexpress.com/article/india/following-galwan-clashes-china-ramped-up-troop-presence-infra-along-lac-in-2022-says-pentagon-8994076/

92   Cowpar Amit, 'Russia, Ukraine tanks kept silent for 3 days after Modi's call': Amit Shah, Nov 22, 2022; https://www.hindustantimes.com/elections/gujarat-assembly-election/modi-called-ukraine-pm-russian-prez-to-halt-war-for-3-days-amit-shah-in-gujarat-101669131711141.html

93   Nimmo Tai: Amit Shah in Parliament: Modi ji stopped Russia Ukraine war for 3 days, Aug 12, 2023; https://twitter.com/Cryptic_Miind/status/1690235170216103937

94   Pulwama, Modi, Corruption: Full Explosive Transcript of Satya Pal Malik's Viral Interview, Apr 16, 2023; https://thewire.in/politics/satya-pal-malik-full-interview-pulwama-modi; Why PM Modi's 'Tum Ab Chup Raho' to Satya Pal Malik Is a Telling Indictment, Apr 21, 2023; https://thewire.in/politics/why-pm-modis-tum-ab-chup-raho-to-satya-pal-malik-is-a-telling-indictment

95   'Harassment For What I Said on Pulwama': Satya Pal Malik After CBI's Visit to His House, Apr 28, 2023; https://thewire.in/government/satya-pal-malik-cbi-pulwama

96   CBI Raids Locations Linked to Two of Satya Pal Malik's Aides, May 17, 2023; https://thewire.in/politics/cbi-raids-locations-linked-to-two-of-satya-pal-maliks-aides

97   Barman Sourav R, Satyapal Malik says 'BJP can go to any extent to win 2024,' party hits back — 'he should be OTT writer', Aug 2, 2023; https://theprint.in/politics/satyapal-malik-says-bjp-can-go-to-any-extent-to-win-2024-party-hits-back-he-should-be-ott-writer/1697204/

98   CHRI Tracker: Hall of Shame: Mapping attacks on RTI users, Commonwealth Human Rights Initiative; http://attacksonrtiusers.org/

99   Activists Urge Rajya Sabha MPs Not to Pass Amended Whistleblowers Bill as Is, Jul 17, 2017; https://thewire.in/law/rajya-sabha-whistle-blowers-act-amendments

100   Delay in operationalising Whistle Blowers Protection Act, Ministry of Personnel, Public Grievances & Pension, Aug 2, 2018; https://pib.gov.in/newsite/PrintRelease.aspx?relid=181386

101   The Right of Citizens for Time Bound Delivery of Goods and Services and Redressal of their Grievances Bill, 2011 (Citizens Charter), PRS Legislative Research; https://prsindia.org/billtrack/the-right-of-citizens-for-time-bound-delivery-of-goods-and-services-and-redressal-of-their-grievances-bill-2011-citizens-charter; Standing Committee Report Summary: Citizen Charter Bill, 2011; https://prsindia.org/files/bills_acts/bills_parliament/2011/SCR_Summary-Citizen_Charter_Bill,_2012.pdf

102   Provisions of UPA-era bill may see light of the day through a new window, Nov 30, 2020; https://economictimes.indiatimes.com/news/politics-and-nation/provisions-of-upa-era-bill-may-see-light-of-the-day-through-a-new-window/articleshow/79498586.cms?utm_source=contentofinterest&utm_medium=text&utm_campaign=cppst

103   BJP election manifesto 2014; http://library.bjp.org/jspui/bitstream/123456789/252/1/bjp_lection_manifesto_english_2014.pdf

104   Modiji on Rs 15L returning to bank accounts was just a political 'jumla':

Amit Shah to ABP News, Feb 5, 2015; https://twitter.com/ABPNews/status/563264094820499457?lang=en; Amit Shah calls Modi bluff on black money, Feb 5, 2015; https://www.deccanherald.com/content/458045/amit-shah-calls-modi-bluff.html

105   SC refuses to order CBI probe into death of ex-Arunachal CM Kalikho Pul, Apr 29, 2021; https://www.thehindu.com/news/national/sc-refuses-to-consider-plea-seeking-cbi-probe-into-death-arunachal-pradesh-ex-cm-kalikho-pul/article34440243.ece

106   Rafale contract documents stolen from Defence Ministry, Attorney General Venugopal tells SC, Mar 6, 2019; https://www.thehindu.com/news/national/rafale-documents-stolen-from-defence-ministry-a-g-kk-venugopal-tells-sc/article26445025.ece

107   Rafale Documents Not Stolen, Petitioners Used Photocopies, Attorney General Clarifies, Mar 9, 2023; https://www.ndtv.com/india-news/rafale-documents-not-stolen-petitioners-used-photocopies-attorney-general-clarifies-2004890

108   Mohanty P, Fewer Rafale jets leave gaps in national security, Fortune India, Apr 4, 2022; https://www.fortuneindia.com/opinion/fewer-rafale-jets-risk-to-national-security-parliamentary-panel/107648

109   Bal Hartosh Singh, Payload: PM Modi cleared Rafale deal at over €2.5 billion higher than first benchmark price, Dec 14, 2018; https://caravanmagazine.in/government/rafale-modi-approved-price-billions-higher-benchmark

110   Standing Committee on Defence, Demand for Grants (Demand No. 21 and 22), Mar 2022; http://164.100.47.193/lsscommittee/Defence/17_Defence_27.pdf

111   'Light Combat Aircraft MK-1A to take flight in June', Jan 9, 2022; https://www.thehindu.com/news/national/light-combat-aircraft-mk-1a-to-take-flight-in-june/article38200517.ece

112   Public Accounts Committee 2018-19, Design, development, manufacturing and introduction of Light Combat Aircraft (LCA), Dec 14, 2018; https://eparlib.nic.in/bitstream/123456789/783969/1/16_Public_Accounts_114.pdf

113   GE Aerospace signs MoU with HAL, to produce fighter jets for Tejas Mk2, Jun 22, 2023; https://www.livemint.com/news/india/ge-aerospace-signs-mou-with-hal-to-produce-fighter-jet-engines-for-tejas-mk2-11687425054827.html

114   Jet engine deal powers ties between India and US, Jun 22, 2023; https://indianexpress.com/article/india/jet-engine-deal-india-us-8680662/

115   Defence Ministry approves MQ-9 Reaper drone deal with US, final clearance to be given by CCS, Jun 15, 2023; https://economictimes.indiatimes.com/news/defence/defence-ministry-approves-mq-9-reaper-drone-deal-with-us-final-clearance-to-be-given-by-ccs/articleshow/101016307.cms?utm_source=contentofinterest&utm_medium=text&utm_campaign=cppst

116   Acquisition of MQ-9B drones: Speculative reports uncalled for, Ministry of Defence,

Jun 25, 2023; https://pib.gov.in/PressReleaseIframePage.aspx?PRID=1935160

117 Average cost offered by US for MQ-9B drones 27 per cent less for India, negotiations yet to begin: Sources

Jun 29, 2023; https://economictimes.indiatimes.com/news/defence/average-cost-offered-by-us-for-mq-9b-drones-27-per-cent-less-for-india-negotiations-yet-to-begin-sources/articleshow/101369387.cms?utm_source=contentofinterest&utm_medium=text&utm_campaign=cppst

118 Congress questions high cost of US drone deal; corruption in Opp party's DNA, says BJP, Jun 29, 2023; https://indianexpress.com/article/india/pawan-khera-press-conference-pm-modi-amit-malviya-drones-fir-8690170/

119 Mohanty P, NPAs: RBI must name and shame fraudsters, wilful defaulters, Jul 31, 2023; https://www.fortuneindia.com/opinion/npas-rbi-must-name-and-shame-fraudsters-wilful-defaulters/113563

120 Mohanty P, Poor run for IBC continues. What ails it? May 30, 2023; https://www.fortuneindia.com/opinion/poor-run-for-ibc-continues-what-ails-it/112852#:~:text=Everything%20that%20could%20go%20wrong,seems%20to%20have%20been%20gamed&text=The%20Insolvency%20and%20Bankruptcy%20Code,FY23%20shows%20a%20minor%20uptick.

121 Srivats KR, Relief for lenders. Supreme Court clears the path for personal guarantor insolvency , Nov 9, 2023; https://www.thehindubusinessline.com/economy/supreme-court-clears-the-path-for-personal-guarantor-insolvency/article67517656.ece

122 Mohanty P, Is India back to 'license raj'? Aug 15, 2023; https://www.fortuneindia.com/opinion/is-india-back-to-license-raj/113736

123 Mohanty P, It's time to measure the impact of PLI, DLI schemes, Jun 22, 2023; https://www.fortuneindia.com/opinion/its-time-to-measure-the-impact-of-pli-dli-schemes/113139; Mohanty P, Is PLI helping India's manufacturing? Sept 26, 2022; https://www.fortuneindia.com/opinion/is-pli-helping-indias-manufacturing/109789

124 Mohanty P, 2 Chinese roadblocks to India's semiconductor ambition, Jul 31, 2023;https://www.fortuneindia.com/opinion/2-chinese-roadblocks-to-indias-semiconductor-ambition/113560

125 Mohanty P, Coronavirus Lockdown VI: How India's insurance-led private healthcare cripples its ability to fight COVID-19, Apr 17, 2020; https://www.businesstoday.in/latest/economy-politics/story/coronavirus-lockdown-india-health-insurance-private-healthcare-public-hospitals-covid19-254637-2020-04-14; Early lessons from India's health insurance scheme, Pradhan Mantri Jan Arogya Yojana, Apr 29, 2021; https://www.brookings.edu/blog/future-development/2021/04/29/early-lessons-from-indias-health-insurance-scheme-pradhan-mantri-jan-arogya-yojana/;   MP: Only 18k of over 5.31 lakh eligible under Ayushman Bharat got free COVID-19 treatment, The Week, Jun 22, 2021; https://www.theweek.in/news/india/2021/06/22/

mp-only-18k-of-over-531-lakh-eligible-for-ayushman-bharat-got-free-covid-19-treatment.html; Upadhyay Ankita, 'They lied, told us Ayushman Bharat clearance would take months': Patients duped by doctor at top Central hospital, Jul 21, 2023; https://indianexpress.com/article/express-exclusive/they-lied-told-us-ayushman-bharat-clearance-would-take-months-patients-duped-by-doctor-at-top-central-hospital-8849192/

126   Performance Audit of Ayushman Bharat-Pradhan Mantri Jan Arogya Yojana, CAG, Aug 8, 2023; https://cag.gov.in/en/audit-report/details/119060

127   Kaur Banjot, Treatment for the Dead, Discharge Before Surgery and the Many Problems of Ayushman Bharat, Aug 10, 2023; https://thewire.in/government/ayushman-bharat-cag-report-pmjay-corruption

128   Performance Audit on "Implementation of Phase-I of Bharatmala Pariyojana", CAG, Aug 10, 2023; https://cag.gov.in/en/audit-report/details/119177

129   Lokpal and Lokayuktas Act, 2013, Gazette notification, Jan 1, 2014; https://prsindia.org/files/bills_acts/bills_parliament/The_Lokpal_and_Lokayuktas_Act,_2013.pdf

130   Lokapl and Lokayukta (Amendment) Act, 2016, Gazette notification, Jul 30, 2016; https://prsindia.org/files/bills_acts/bills_parliament/Lokpal%20and%20Lokayuktas%20(Amendment)%20Act,%202016_0.pdf;

131   Mohanty P, Agenda for new government: Insulating anti-corruption architecture, India Today, Jun 4, 2019; https://www.indiatoday.in/india/story/agenda-for-next-government-insulating-anti-corruption-architecture-1542034-2019-06-04

132   Section 13(1)(d) in The Prevention of Corruption Act, 1988; https://indiankanoon.org/doc/1101716/

133   The Prevention of Corruption Act of 1988 (post-2018 amendment) https://www.indiacode.nic.in/bitstream/123456789/9317/1/corruptiona1988-49.pdf

134   The repealing and amending Act, 2015, Ministry of Law and Justice, May 13, 2015; https://prsindia.org/files/bills_acts/acts_parliament/2015/the-repealing-and-amending-act,-2015.pdf

135   Opposition can only guarantee corruption, says PM; cites laundry list of scam allegations, Jun 28, 2023; https://economictimes.indiatimes.com/news/politics-and-nation/opposition-can-only-guarantee-corruption-says-pm-cites-laundry-list-of-scam-allegations/articleshow/101314560.cms?utm_source=contentofinterest&utm_medium=text&utm_campaign=cppst; 'NCP Behind Scams Worth Rs 70,000 Crore': PM Modi's 'Ghotala Metre' Attack On Opposition; India Today; https://www.youtube.com/watch?v=qcBhu-S_7Io

136   Sharad Pawar's swipe at PM Modi: He alleged corruption, now welcomes, Jul 3, 2023; https://indianexpress.com/article/cities/pune/not-worried-go-to-people-rebuild-party-pawar-jibe-modi-8697555/

137   PM Modi in poll-bound Rajasthan: Congress means loot ki dukaan, jhooth ka bazaar, Jul 9, 2023; 3; https://indianexpress.com/article/india/pm-in-poll-bound-

rajasthan-cong-means-loot-ki-dukaan-jhooth-ka-bazaar-8819099/

138   Congress sees Chhattisgarh as an ATM: Modi, Jul 8, 2023; https://indianexpress. com/article/india/congress-sees-chhattisgarh-as-an-atm-modi-8814022/

139   PM Modi calls KCR govt 'most corrupt', BRS says he 'habitually lies' during Telangana visits, Jul 8, 2023; https://indianexpress.com/article/cities/hyderabad/ pm-modi-kcr-govt-corrupt-brs-habitually-lies-telangana-visits-8816530/

140   Mishra Arpit, Oct 3, 2023; https://bharat.republicworld.com/amp/india-news/ politics/no-corrupt-person-can-sit-next-to-me-said-pm-narendra-modi-attacks-kcr-telangana

141   Maharashtra: ACB drops 9 corruption cases against Ajit Pawar, Nov 25, 2019; https://www.livemint.com/politics/news/maharashtra-acb-drops-9-corruption-cases-against-ajit-pawar-11574686848053.html

142   'MSCB fraud' case linked to Ajit Pawar to be probed by EOW again, Oct 20, 2022; https://indianexpress.com/article/cities/mumbai/mscb-fraud-case-linked-to-ajit-pawar-to-be-probed-by-eow-again-8214762/; I-T Dept Raids Maharashtra Deputy CM Ajit Pawar's Premises; 'BJP Afraid,' Says NCP, Oct 17, 2021; https://thewire. in/government/i-t-raids-maharashtra-deputy-cm-ajit-pawars-premises-bjp-afraid-says-ncp

143   Mohanty P, Agenda for next government: A Lokpal that inspires trust, June 4, 2019; https://www.indiatoday.in/india/story/agenda-for-next-government-a-lokpal-that-inspires-trust-1542374-2019-06-04

144   Centre need not disclose Lokpal selection committee minutes, rules CIC; Feb 10, 2021,   https://www.thehindu.com/news/national/centre-need-not-disclose-lokpal-selection-committee-minutes-rules-cic/article33796767.ece

145   Lokpal Rules 2020: Lokpal (Complaint) Rules, 2020, DoPT circular, G.S.R.148(E); http://documents.doptcirculars.nic.in/D2/D02ser/Lokpal-03032020raXKt.pdf;   It's official: Complaint against any PM will go to Lokpal full bench, no explanation if rejected, Mar 4, 2020; https://indianexpress.com/article/india/complaint-against-prime-minister-narendra-modi-lokpal-rules-6298117/

146   Lokpal of India: Complaints Statistics; http://lokpal.gov.in/?menu_bar?complaints_statistics?0301; https://www.lokpal.gov.in/pdfs/cs_2021_2022.pdf

147   Bullet train project chief sacked amid graft case, Jul 8, 2022; https://indianexpress. com/article/india/bullet-train-project-chief-sacked-amid-graft-case-8015928/

148   'Cash-for-query' row: CBI begins probe into Lokpal complaint on Mahua, Nov 25,   2023;   https://indianexpress.com/article/india/cbi-to-probe-cash-for-query-allegations-against-mahua-moitra-after-lokpals-nod-9042265/

149   Complaints to Lokpal reducing; shows there is hardly anything to complain against now: MoS for Personnel and PMO Jitendra Singh; Aug 5, 2021; https://economictimes. indiatimes.com/news/politics-and-nation/complaints-to-lokpal-reducing-shows-there-is-hardly-anything-to-complain-against-now-mos-for-personnel-and-pmo-

jitendra-singh/articleshow/85068662.cms?utm_source=contentofinterest&utm_medium=text&utm_campaign=cppst

150 Bhushan Prashant, Lokpal to Jokepal: The Lokpal has no credibility or authority, which is why it is futile to refer cases, National Herald, Aug 13, 2021; https://www.nationalheraldindia.com/india/lokpal-to-jokepal-the-lokpal-has-no-credibility-or-authority-which-is-why-it-is-futile-to-refer-cases

151 Lokayukta on Modi govt: Can't work with 'my way or highway' mindset, Aug 7, 2013; https://www.rediff.com/news/report/lokayukta-on-modi-govt-cant-work-with-my-way-or-highway-mindset/20130807.htm

152 Government of Gujarat; https://lokayukta.gujarat.gov.in/aboutlokayuktaoffice

153 Explained: What is 'general consent' for the CBI, now withdrawn by Meghalaya? Mar 5, 2022; https://indianexpress.com/article/explained/what-is-general-consent-for-cbi-now-withdrawn-by-meghalaya-7800997/;https://lokpal.gov.in/pdfs/cs_2021_2022.pdf

154 Bhatnagar Gaurav V, Illegally Sacked, Spied Upon and Denied Pension, Former CBI Chief Now Faces RTI Stonewalling, Apr 1, 2022; https://thewire.in/rights/alok-verma-former-cbi-director-rti-cases

155 Rajagopal Krishnadas, Bengal can't bar CBI, Centre tells Supreme Court, Oct 22, 2021; https://www.thehindu.com/news/national/west-bengals-power-to-withhold-consent-to-cbi-is-not-absolute-centre-to-sc/article37121312.ece

156 Anand Utkarsh, You cannot call yourself 'Republic of India' in pleas: SC pulls up CBI, Oct 21, 2023; https://www.hindustantimes.com/india-news/you-cannot-call-yourself-republic-of-india-in-pleas-sc-pulls-up-cbi-101697823661572.html

157 CBI a separate entity, have no control over it, Govt tells Supreme Court, Nov 10, 2023; https://indianexpress.com/article/india/crime/cbi-a-separate-entity-have-no-control-over-it-govt-tells-supreme-court-9020965/

158 The murky past of central vigilance commissioner KV Chowdary, Nov 23, 2018;https://caravanmagazine.in/government/murky-past-central-vigilance-commissioner-kv-chowdary

159 Manor James, Narendra Modi's Power and Cult Endanger the BJP, Sept 3, 2021; https://thewire.in/politics/narendra-modis-power-and-cult-endanger-the-bjp

160 Opinion: India has suffered greatly under mob rule. Now Trump has unleashed it, too., Jan 8, 2021: https://www.washingtonpost.com/opinions/2021/01/08/trump-capitol-mob-india-modi-political-violence/; Narendra Modi's Reckless Politics Brings Mob Rule to New Delhi, Feb 27, 2020; https://thewire.in/communalism/narendra-modi-delhi-riots-mob-violence-bjp

161 After Panama, it's Pandora: facing regulatory heat, elite Indians find new ways to ringfence wealth in secret havens, Oct 4, 2021; https://indianexpress.com/article/express-exclusive/pandora-papers-exclusive-how-elite-indians-ringfence-wealth-7550012/

162 Indian money parked in Swiss banks rise to 14-year high, Jun 17, 2022; https://

www.cnbctv18.com/india/indian-funds-in-swiss-banks-rise-to-14-year-high-swiss-national-bank-snb-13849052.htm

163   Money deposited in Swiss Banks, Lok Sabha, Jul 25, 2022; http://164.100.47.194/Loksabha/Questions/QResult15.aspx?qref=40039&lsno=17

164   Swiss bank account details shared with India for 4th time under agreed framework, Oct 10, 2022; https://www.livemint.com/news/india/swiss-bank-account-details-shared-with-india-for-4th-time-under-agreed-framework-11665399925315.html

165   Sarin Ritu, I-T flagged 'misreporting' of Rs 1.06-cr, black money SIT judge opted for amnesty scheme, Indian Express, https://indianexpress.com/article/express-exclusive/i-t-flagged-misreporting-rs-1-06-cr-black-money-sit-judge-amnesty-scheme-7970050/

166   Measures taken by Government to Control and Curb Parallel Economy and Unaccounted Transactions, Dec 19, 2017; https://pib.gov.in/PressReleasePage.aspx?PRID=1513203

167   PMIndia: PM's address to the Nation from the ramparts of the Red Fort on the 71th Independence Day, Aug 15, 2017; https://www.pmindia.gov.in/en/news_updates/pms-address-to-the-nation-from-the-ramparts-of-the-red-fort-on-the-71th-independence-day/

168   Mohanty P, Games shell companies and tax havens play, Feb 28, 2023; https://www.fortuneindia.com/macro/games-shell-companies-and-tax-havens-play/111745

169   Suhas Palshikar writes: The rise of bulldozer governance, Aug 12, 2023; https://indianexpress.com/article/opinion/suhas-palshikar-writes-rise-bulldozer-governance-8887752/

Chapter VI

Rhetoric as Governance III: 'Cooperative Federalism'

This chapter looks at the Centre-states relations after the Prime Minister promised to bring "cooperative federalism" – from political, administrative and fiscal perspectives. The term didn't exist in the BJP's 2014 election manifesto[1] but it existed, couched in a different language: "place centre-state relations on an "even keel through the process of consultation"; "evolve a model of national development, which is driven by the states"; "Team India" to include chief ministers and other functionaries as "equal partners"; "ensure fiscal autonomy of states"; create 'Regional Councils of States' (RCS); revive "moribund forums like 'National Development Council' (NDC) and 'Inter-State Council' (ISC) etc.

The Prime Minister used the term first in February 2015, while addressing Chief Ministers at the first Governing Council of NITI Aayog meeting. He asked them[2] to work with the Centre "to forge a *model of cooperative federalism,* whereby the Centre and the States – "TEAM INDIA" – to resolve differences, and chart a common course to progress and prosperity...in the spirit of 'Sabka saath, sabka vikas'...in promoting governance initiatives, in a spirit of "cooperative, competitive federalism".

A historic perspective: It was the Sarkaria Commission[3] set up in 1983 (submitted its reports in 1998) to resolve the centre-state relations which first used the term "cooperative federalism" to advocate that "inter-governmental relations" would have to be worked on the principles of cooperative federalism – since this is "the diffused pattern of distribution of governmental functions between the Union and the States, and the manner in which the administration and enforcement of most Union laws is secured through the machinery of the States", adding that several other features of the Constitution of India "reinforce this conclusion".

In that sense, the Prime Minister reintroduced the term. But as this chapter shows, it is mere slogan and it has been violated in the letter and spirit – arguably, far more than any time in the past, save for the invocation of Article 356 to impose President's Rule in states. And certainly, there is no sign of the promise the Prime Minister made in February 2015 – after dismantling the Planning Commission in 2014 by denouncing its centralised planning ("one-size-fits-all" solutions) and fund allocations.

Federalism has been undermined in various ways – (A) Fiscally (B) Administratively and (C) Politically. But before exploring federalism in the Modi regime a look at what are its claims for "cooperative federalism". At least three developments are cited for this claim: (a) 14th Finance Commission (FC) award, raising states' share of the divisible pool of tax from 32% to 42% in 2015 (b) dismantling of the PCI in 2014, and its replacement with the NITI Aayog in 2015 to end centralized planning and fund allocations and (c) Goods and Services Tax (GST) and GST Council in 2017. These claims essentially have two components – fiscal and development planning.

A. Fiscal Centralization: FCs and Fiscal Devolution

The Centre has centralized fiscal resources in multiple ways.

First, it is short-changing states in tax devolutions awarded by the Finance Commissions – a constitutional body. The 14th Finance Commission (FC) accepted a long-pending demand of states to increase their tax shares in December 2014. During the previous 13th FC, many states, including Gujarat under Modi, had sought 50% share but were disappointed when the share went up by a tiny margin – from 30.5% to 32%.[4] The 14th FC report[5] dramatically raised it to 42% for the period of 2015-20.

After that, the Prime Minister rushed to claim personal credit. He wrote letters to Chief Ministers in February 2015[6]: "…we have wholeheartedly accepted the recommendations of the 14th Finance Commission, although it puts a tremendous strain on the Centre's finances…This is all towards the fulfilment of *my promise of cooperative federalism.* As you have already seen, we have decided to involve states in discussing and planning national priorities…This is our strategy to take the country to a faster and yet inclusive growth trajectory through *cooperative federalism which is real and true federalism.*" *(Emphasis added)*

Nothing could be further from truth. The 14th FC was set up by the previous Congress-led UPA government in 2013. After Prime Minister Modi took over, his finance ministry strongly *opposed* raising states' shares. In its memorandum in September 2014 (detailed in the 14th FC report) pleaded for the exact opposite – a higher tax share for itself by seeking to centralize more development programmes it runs in states. The Centre's *four key arguments* were:

i.   It "underlined increasing demands on the Union's resources on account of expenditure commitments on items in the Union List, such as defence, internal security and energy security".

ii. "Emphasised the need for the Union Government to retain fiscal space for its development agenda".

iii. "Justified the need for the Union Government's intervention in State subjects…suggested that the Union Government should have a greater role in the design and implementation of such projects".

iv. "Also argued that the Union Government has an obligation to ensure welfare programmes, particularly for backward States, to address inter and intra-State disparities".

But the 14th FC ignored all and raised the devolution from 32% to 42%. It listed *four reasons* to explain why it did so:

a.   States are not entitled to the growing Cess and Surcharge the Centre collects.

b.   More direct transfer gives states more flexibility to plan their capital and other expenditures.

c.   States' need higher revenue expenditure now that plan and non-plan distinction is gone.

d.   More fiscal space is available with the Centre.

The new government did well to accept the awards but it had little choice.

PDT Achary, former Secretary General of the Lok Sabha (2005-10), explains that although Article 280[7] of the Constitution provides for the FC, it doesn't spell out that its awards are mandatory; it is a long-established convention for governments to accept the awards and act accordingly. The official website of the FC, in its FAQ[8], spells out two specific modalities of implementation of the awards: (i) "Those to be implemented by an order of the President: The recommendations relating to distribution of Union Taxes and Duties and Grants-in-aid fall in this category" and (ii) "Those to be implemented by executive orders: Other recommendations to be made by the Finance Commission, as per its Terms of Reference" or TOR. The FC's report is submitted to the President who then forwards it to the government. Going by the first modality of implementation of its tax devolution awards, the Centre has no discretionary power.

When the 15th FC (2021-26) was constituted in 2018[9] by the government, it sparked an *unprecedented* protest from states because its terms of reference (TOR) imposed certain conditions that go against the spirit of cooperative federalism. Three TOR entries in particular were distressing for states – which had asked the FC to

(a) Keep in mind "the impact on the fiscal situation of the Union Government of substantially enhanced tax devolution to States following recommendations of the 14th FC, coupled with the continuing imperative of the national development programme including New India-2022".

(b) Use population data of 2011 (not that of 1971 Census as is usual).

(c) Spell out "conditions that GoI may impose on the States while providing consent under Article 293(3) of the Constitution" – which refers to states' powers to borrow).

What do these TOR entries mean?

• The first TOR entry reflects the Centre's discomfort with higher tax devolution by the 14th FC and attempted to *nudge* the 15th FC to adopt a particular stance – "New India-22" that the NITI Aayog's India@75 had spelt out, putting higher emphasis on central sector schemes (CSs) and centrally sponsored schemes (CSSs), which essential perform states' functions (various development and welfare programmes).

• The second TOR entry hurts the states which have performed better in population control and is contrary to the established norm of policymaking not to reward states which have performed poorly. It also contradicts another entry in the TOR which asks for using measurable performance-based incentives for states, such as "efforts and Progress made in moving towards replacement rate of population growth". Expectedly, several states from south and east, which have controlled population growth better, objected to the TOR for the first time, reflecting a *trust deficit* between the Centre and states.[10]

• The third TOR entry implies putting conditions on states' borrowing, as against no such condition for borrowing up to 3% of GSDP fiscal deficit – as per the Fiscal Responsibility and Budget Management (FRBM) Act of 2003.

In the midst of the pandemic crisis, in October 2020 (the same month that the 15th FC report came agreeing to performance-based incentives for borrowing by states), the Centre *imposed* stiff and unprecedented conditions of carrying out four "reforms": (i) 'one nation one ration' system (ii) improvement in ease of doing business (iii) power sector reforms and (iv) urban local body reforms – for 1% additional borrowing.[11] For the record, the 14th FC had given a choice to states to select the population base (1971 or 2011 Census). Of 29 states, 13 had opted for 1971 Census, 9 for 2011 Census and 7 wanted no weightage to population.[12]

The 15th FC report[13] submitted in October 2020, *reducing* the states' share from 42% to 41% – citing downgrading of Jammu & Kashmir to two union territories (under the administrative control of the Centre) to take care of the Centre's burden. The overnight change in the status of Jammu & Kashmir is in itself a *marker* of turning cooperative federalism on its head.

The significance of FC awards needs to be understood before examining how these have been honoured by the regime.

The Centre transfers resources both "unconditionally" through the FC awards and "conditionally" through various central schemes and programmes. The aggregate transfers exceed 60% of the central resources (from tax and non-tax revenues). The 14th FC favoured the states' demand for more "unconditional" transfers (through its awards) as it argued that tax devolution (from the divisible pool) should be the *primary route of transfer* of resources because it is formula-based, and thus, conducive to sound fiscal federalism. Besides, a higher "unconditional" devolution (in the aggregate tax transfers) does not impose additional fiscal burden on the Centre.

Actual Tax Devolution

Is the Centre devolving more tax to states? No. Budget documents show while the devolution has increased with higher FC awards, the gap between the FC awards and actual devolution has increased sharply. The following graphs captures that growing gap as well as the asymmetric rise in the Centre's tax kitty (the reasons for which will be clear soon).

Graph 1: Tax devolution to states and gap from FC awards

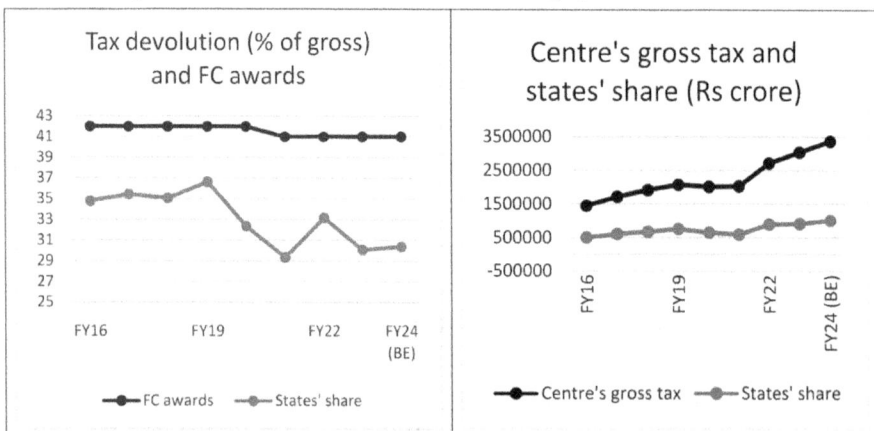

Source: Union budgets of 2021, 2022 and 2023

How was the situation before 2014? It was much better.

The average tax devolution was 25.9% and 27.9% of the Centre's gross tax revenue during the 12ᵗʰ and 13ᵗʰ FC periods, respectively – when the awards were 31% and 32%. In the 14ᵗʰ FC period, the tax devolution rose to 34.9%, when the award was 42%, and fell to 20.7.5% during FY21-FY24 when the 15ᵗʰ FC award was 41%. The *departure* (or gap) in devolution were 5.1 and 4.1 percentage points in 12ᵗʰ and 13ᵗʰ FC periods – which jumped to 7.1 and 10.3 percentage points during the 14ᵗʰ and 15ᵗʰ FC periods, respectively.

This then is the *first* way states are being short-changed and the Centre is hurting rather than furthering cooperative federalism (fiscal). The *second* is not sharing the disinvestment and privatization proceeds.

Denying Share of Disinvestment and Privatization

Two, the Centre is denying states their share of non-tax revenues too.

It collects *non-tax* revenue through disinvestment (stake sale) and privatization (strategic sale in which control passes to private entity) of public assets (Central PSUs). The proceeds go entirely to the Consolidated Fund of India (CFI) as it has not been made a part of the 'divisible pool'. During eight years of FY15-FY23, the Centre has collected Rs 5.1 lakh crore through disinvestment and privatization – a sharp rise from Rs 1.2 lakh crore during the previous 10 years of the UPA (FY05-FY14). The Centre needs to share this too. Several states, like Chhattisgarh, Jharkhand and Tamil Nadu have sought.[14] Tamil Nadu sought a share of Rs 2,383 crore the Centre raised by off-loading its entire 66.7% stake in the Chennai-based Kamarajar Port Limited (KPL) in FY20. After all, states play a critical role in building up Central PSUs and should be compensated when these are disposed of partially or fully. The 14ᵗʰ FC had recommended division of such proceeds arguing that "many of states have provided land, power and water at concessional rates as well as other incentives such as tax concessions". Unlike the 14ᵗʰ FC, the 15ᵗʰ FC was *silent*.[15]

Rise of Cesses and Surcharges

Third, the Centre is imposing more and more Cess and Surcharge, which are not part of the divisible tax pool, and hence, are not shared with states.

Cess and Surcharge are meant for *specific purposes* in special conditions or needs and have existed for long. Post 2014, they have grown significantly. They are now imposed on most items: education, health, crude oil, bidi, sugar, automobiles, environment, clean energy, infrastructure, road and infrastructure (on motor spirit and highspeed diesel), GST compensation, exports, Swachch

Bharat, Krishi Kalyan, textile and textile machinery etc. The 2021 budget added another Cess: Agriculture Infrastructure and Development Cess (AIDC), which is imposed on a host of items like gold, alcoholic beverages, soyabean, apples, coal, fertilizers, pulses on customs side and petrol and diesel on excise side. Surcharge covers social welfare, corporate tax, income tax, tobacco products, health and education, motor spirit etc.

Of all the Cess and Surcharge only the GST Compensation Cess is shared with states. In fact, this Cess is meant to compensating states for the shortfall in state GST (SGST) after the GST was adopted in 2017. The Centre was to pay Compensation for a period of five years with this Cess. Midway through, the Centre declared it wouldn't because of fiscal constraints. That was *a lie* because in the very same September 2019, it announced a corporate tax cut of Rs 1.45 lakh crore. It went on to ask states to borrow from market to meet the shortfall, unmindful of the "cooperative federalism" and violation of its own law, The GST (Compensation to States) Act of 2017 – which guaranteed the compensation. Then good sense prevailed, it borrowed from the RBI to give loan to states. It borrowed Rs 1.59 lakh crore in FY21 and Rs 1.1 lakh crore in FY22. It will collect this from the GST Cess, which would now continue beyond the mandated June 30, 2022, until June 30, 2026 but no GST Compensation would be paid. The states, however, would continue to have a shortfall in SGST and that may prove to be the GST's undoing.[16]

In the meanwhile, data shows how Cess and Surcharge have surged (graph below).[17]

Graph 2: Surging Cess and Surcharge

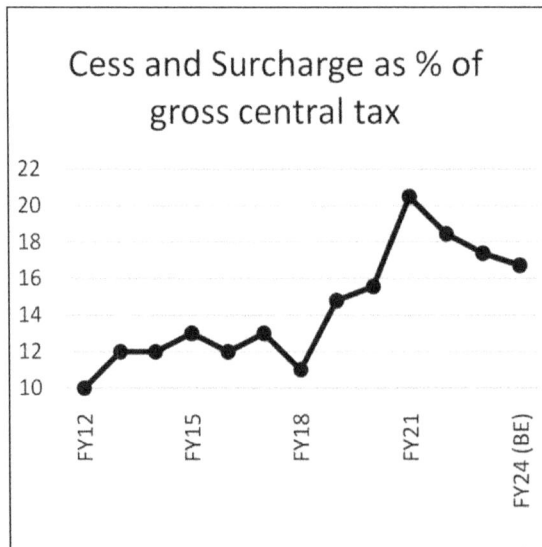

Source: PRS India study 2021 and Rajya Sabha reply 2023

The Centre misappropriates these Cess and Surcharge.

The 2020 CAG report[18] said, the Centre was misappropriating Cess and Surcharge collection and not using those for the specific purpose they are meant to. This included GST Compensation Cess too. The CAG found the Centre *misappropriated Rs 47,272 crore* of GST Cess in FY18 and FY19 by transferring to the CFI – which is not allowed. That is, Rs 47,272 crore was *not given to states* for which it is meant for. But when the Centre was asked to pay the GST Compensation from the CFI, after it stopped it for FY21, it told the Parliament that there was no such provision.[19] How did it then misappropriate the GSR Cess into the CFI? That was never explained.

The CAG reported that "out of the Rs 2,74,592 crore received from 35 Cesses, levies and other charges in 2018-19, only *Rs 1,64,322 crore* had been transferred to Reserve Funds/Boards" and the rest was retained in the CFI. That is, *40% of Cess and Surcharge was misappropriated* by the Central government in FY19.

More Central Schemes & Double-Engine Growth

Fourth, proliferation of central schemes, which mean more direct interference in states' domain and 'one-size-fits' solution for all – which the Prime Minister as Gujarat Chief Minister opposed.

The pandemic saw the Centre adding new central schemes, rather than devolve more funds, like the Pradhan Mantri Garib Kalyan Yojana (PM-GKY), which encompassed several others like Garib Kalyan Anna Yojanat (PM-GKAY) providing "free" ration of 5 kg for ration card holders and Garib Kalyan Rojgar Abhiyan (PM-GKRY) providing jobs to migrant workers.[20] It then encashed these schemes in state elections (explained in Introduction).

The Centre has also been using these as a political tool. For example, in the run up to the West Bengal elections in 2021, West Bengal complained that it was kept out of the PM-GKRY (jobs to migrants) and put up as a bait – if the BJP was voted to power. The Telegraph explained it[21]: "Federalism is predicated upon the principle of cooperation. This element has gone missing in the Centre-state relationship in recent times. This *erosion of trust and collaboration* would undermine public welfare to a great extent." In 2023, the West Bengal government would hold sit-ins in Delhi and Kolkata (outside the Governor's residence) to complain against pending MGNREGS dues – even as the Centre would deny it.[22] The Prime Minister and his party keep seeking votes for a "double-engine" government and growth – that is, votes for the BJP in states – which violates "co-operative federalism". There are many instances of discriminations against states on party line. During the devastating second wave of the pandemic, vaccine allocation was highly skewed against states run by rival parties in violation of the criteria laid out[23]: (a) extent of infection (number of active Covid cases) (b) performance (speed of administration) and (c) wastage of vaccine. This was done to help Gujarat and discriminate against Kerala (ruled by the Left Front).

Ashoka University[24] analyzed data relating to caseload and vaccine allocations and found a gross mismatch. Vaccine allocation was lowest for Maharashtra, which witnessed maximum cases (violating the first criterion), so was the case with Kerala and Delhi. All three states are run by the non-BJP parties then (Maharashtra is back in the NDA fold with the BJP being accused of splitting two rival parties, the Shive Sena and the NCP, in 2022 and 2023). They got less than 5 vaccines per case. In contrast, Gujarat, homes state of Prime Minister and run by the BJP, received the maximum, 30.6 vaccines per case. This *partiality* towards Gujarat is evident in the way the Vedanta-Foxconn's semiconductor plant was *shifted out*[25] of the Opposition-ruled Maharashtra to Gujarat in 2022 and the Micron's semiconductor assembling plant was also declared at *Gujarat's Sanand*[26] on the day the Prime Minister met its CEO in June 2023.

The Centre particularly discriminated the Left Front-ruled Kerala. Kerala had higher case count than Gujarat, its "performance", the second criterion, was far better than Gujarat and in "wastage" (third criterion), it recorded "zero wastage" – which the Central government acknowledged[27]. But Gujarat got the vaccine cake.[28] The 2021 CAG report[29] pointed to how the Centre is directly funding development schemes in Gujarat – again a violation of the government directive (of April 1, 2014) mandating all central assistance for central schemes be given to states, not implementing agencies. The Centre is not only bypassing state and directing funding implementing agencies but it went up by 358% – *from Rs 2,542.77 crore in 2015-16 to Rs 11,659.35 crore* in 2019-20. Such transfers don't get reflected in state's financial accounts, thus distorting its true fiscal health.

As explained earlier, the FC awards are important because it devolves fiscal resources "unconditionally", giving more flexibility to states for their use. The Central Sector Schemes (CS), which are fully funded by the Centre and Centrally Sponsored Schemes (CSSs), which are partly funded (90% to 60%), are the "conditional" transfers which carryout programmes in states' domain to address developmental gaps. As against thw Prime Minister's promise, the fiscal allocations for CS and CSS have gone up. This is also a *reversal of the earlier trend*[30] of cutting down such schemes and handing over the funds to states.

All new central schemes (mostly old ones renamed and re-launched) come prefixed with "Pradhan Mantri" (Prime Minister), for his own *branding*[31], like, the Swachch Bharat (2014), Fasal Bima Yojana (2016), Ujwala (2016), North East Special Infrastructure Development Scheme (2017), Ayushman Bharat (2018), PM-Kisan (2019) etc. These schemes encroach on states' territories. Then, as explained earlier, these are sold to voters as a personal benevolence. The PM-Kisan was introduced through the vote-on-account budget of 2019, just ahead of the general elections and violated the established conventions of *not presenting a full budget* ahead of general elections. The Ayushman Bharat (PM-JAY) is the *failed and abandoned* RSBY and has failed again (Chapter V). Nonetheless, keeping with the infatuation with governance-by-rhetoric, the failed Ayushman (long life) primary healthcare centres (PHCs) were re-christened as "Ayushman Arogya Mandir"[32] (temple of health and long life) in late 2023.

The following graph maps the growth in CS and CSS. (NB: The pre-FY16 budget data is not comparable as classifications were different).

Graph 3: CS and CSS jump to 50% in pandemic FY21

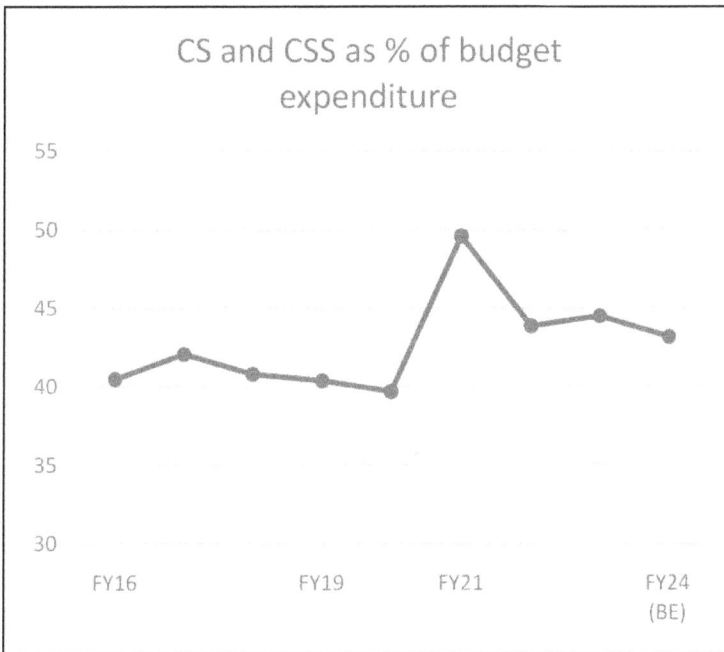

Source: Budget documents

GST & GST Council

Fifth, short-changing states on the GST.

States, rather than the Centre, demonstrated the best form of cooperative federalism in 2017 when they gave up most of their rights to indirect taxes by opting for the Goods and Services Tax (GST) in 2017. They lost more in terms of fiscal autonomy. The 15th FC said the subsumed indirect taxes in the GST accounted for 35% of the gross tax revenue of the Centre but 44% of the "own tax revenue" of states. States accepted the GST *after* the Centre promised to compensate (GST Compensation) for their tax loss and also an annual 14% hike in it for *five years* – both of which was incorporated in the GST (Compensation to States) Act of 2017 – from 2017 to 2022. But the Centre *renegaded and stopped paying* GST Compensation in the last two years in violation of the 2017 statute. The Centre first asked states to borrow the shortfall and then took loans – Rs 1.59 lakh crore in FY21 and Rs 1.1 lakh crore in FY22 – to pay the compensations.[33]

The GST Cess, which the Centre imposed to pay the compensation, now continues until 2026 to repay the loans but no compensation was to be paid from July 2022 onwards. States will continue to incur the shortfall. The 15th FC had estimated the SGST shortfall of "about ₹7.1 lakh crore" between 2017 and 2022. Finance Ministry think tank, National Institute of Public Finance and Policy (NIPFP), estimated the average annual share of *compensation in SGST was 34% for 18 states during FY18-FY21*. This means, discontinuation of the compensation will deprive 34% of the SGST for states. For Punjab, GST compensation constituted 92.83% of SGST, followed by Goa with 59.8%, Chhattisgarh with 48.3%, Karnataka with 43%, Odisha with 39.8% and Gujarat with 39.5%. These states will face very *high tax revenue shocks*. The NIPFP had a dire warning about states' ability for capital expenditure: "Our analysis shows that for majority of states the share of SGST collection (with GST compensation receipts) in GSDP do not show much increase during 2017-21 as compared to the share of revenue that is subsumed into GST in GSDP during 2015-17."[34]

Not to forget, the role of states in the GST Council, which regulates the GST regime, is *marginal* as the Centre has voting right of 33% and a veto power to boot, while individual states just 2%, big or small – that is, *the Centre is equal to 17 states in voting rights*. Often, opposition-ruled states are kept out of crucial committees[35] and their demands shot down or ignored. For example, at the June 2021 GST Council meet, the Centre shot down a majority demand to exempt Covid-related essentials – medical oxygen, ventilators, ventilator masks, cannula and helmet, testing kits, inflammatory diagnostic kits etc. – from the GST.[36] Instead, the Centre reduced tax only for six months. Even when India begged for support from foreign countries for Covid management in 2021, it prioritized tax over saving lives by holding up supplies at airports for days to decide tax rates while scores were dropping dead every day for the lack of oxygen and other essentials.[37] When, in June 2022, many states, including those ruled by the BJP, demanded extending GST Compensation the Centre *imperiously ignored it*.[38]

The GST regime remains a work-in-progress six years down the line. A tribunal to adjudicate disputes (GSTAT) was approved by the Union Cabinet in January 2019[39] but it was the *50th GST Council*[40] meet in July 2023 that it was approved. It will take a while for it to become actually functional.

Why States Need Greater Tax Autonomy

The case for states to be fiscally more empowered can't be overstated. Here are *five* major reasons why so.

1. States spend far more on capex than the Centre to boost growth. Official statistics show, during 12 years of FY12-FY23, the share of Centre and state in capex was 36:64. But states' tax base is much low compared to the Centre, in fact, just the opposite of the capex ratio. The share of states' "own tax revenue" and the Centre gross tax is 62:38. In terms of percentage of GDP, Centre's gross tax receipts averaged 10.5% while states' "own tax revenue" was 6.3% during the same period. These trends are mapped in the following graphs.

Graph 4: Capex and Tax resources of Centre and states

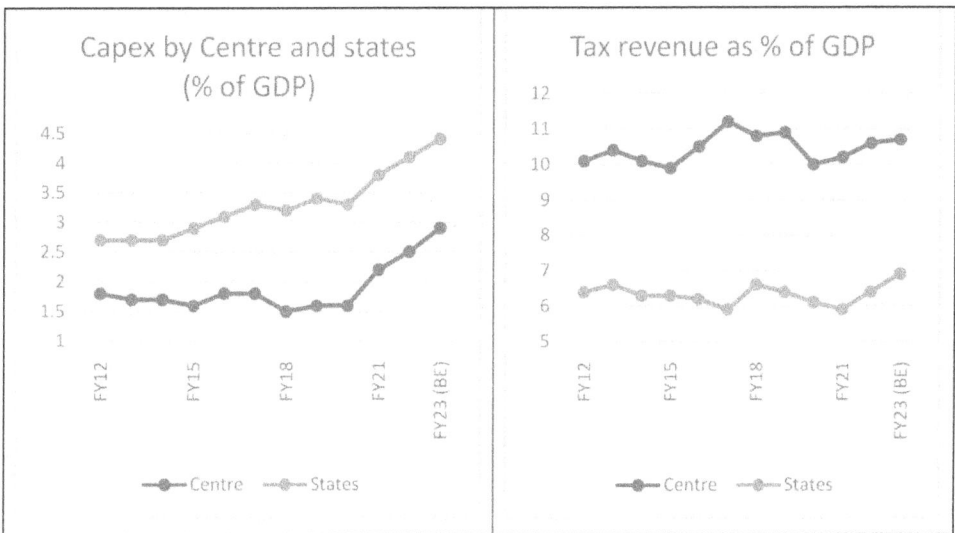

Source: Economic Survey 2020-21 to 2022-23; RBI and 2023 budget

2. Centre generates more tax because of its exclusive rights to direct taxes like corporate tax, income tax from non-corporate entities; exclusive indirect taxes like Customs; Cess and Surcharge, plus it collects other indirect taxes like Excise (as do states). States gave up most of their indirect tax rights while opting for the Goods and Services Tax in 2017 (except on items like petroleum and petroleum products, alcohol for human consumption and electricity).

3. States are far more fiscally responsible. During 12 years between FY12 and FY23, the annual average fiscal deficit of the Centre is 5% of the GDP, while for states it is much less at 2.8% of the GDP. The Fiscal Responsibility and Budget Management (FRBM) Act of 2003 puts the limit at 3% for both. The following graph maps the fiscal deficit trends.

Graph 5: Comparative fiscal deficits of Centre and states

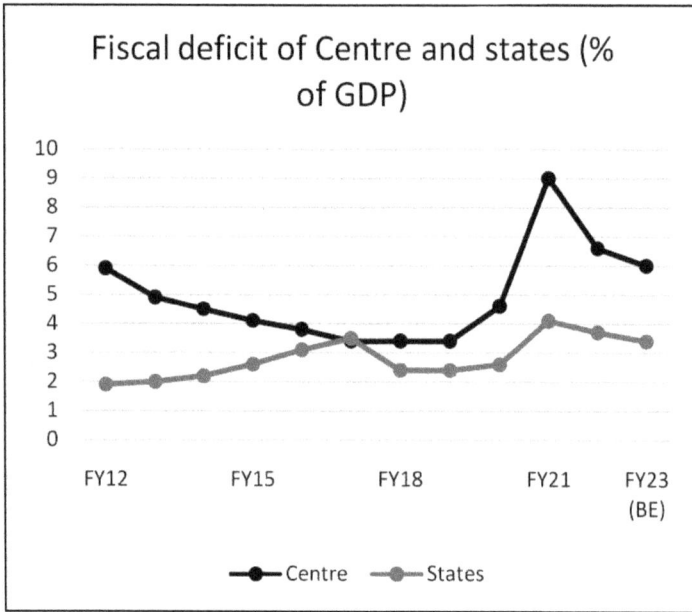

Fiscal deficit of Centre and states (% of GDP)

Source: Economic Survey of 2021-2023

4. In spite of this, the Centre has tightened the noose on states by setting tougher fiscal deficit targets. The 2021 budget[41] set two different standards: For states, fiscal deficit target ("suggested") was set at 3% *(of GSDP) by 2023-24*, from 3.2% in FY20 and limited states' borrowing at 4% of GSDP for FY22. But for itself, the Centre put a fiscal deficit target of *4.5% (of GDP) by 2025-26*.

5. As mentioned earlier, states will continue to have SGST shortfalls after FY23 with no hope for compensation as the Centre refused to extended it beyond June 30, 2022 – despite strong demand from several states – but it put conditions of four measurable reforms for 1% additional borrowing. Finance Ministry think tank, National Institute of Public Finance and Policy (NIPFP), in its report of July, 2022[42] showed the average annual share of compensation in SGST was 34% for 18 states during FY18-FY21 – pointing to the extent of shortfall.

States need greater fiscal space too.

Many states are bigger than European countries in geography and population. Having conceded most of the indirect tax rights to the Centre by adopting the GST, they are hamstrung to generate resources. Besides, the GST's cooperative federalism has turned into "coercive" federalism when the Prime Minister *named and shamed* Opposition-run governments and asked them to cut oil taxes to bring the retail prices down without doing so himself. This was unfair since the Centre collected 61% of all oil taxes collected between FY15 to FY23, as against states' combined collection of 39% (PPCA[43]). The Rs 1.3 lakh crore interest-free loans to state (for 50 years), budgeted in FY24, is a poor substitute as it keeps state dependent on the Centre. By mid-way through the year, only Rs 56,415 crore had been sanctioned to 16 States (under 'Special Assistance').[44]

How was the previous UPA different from the current situation?

There are three essential differences between the two:

- Centralization of indirect tax (GST), robbing states of their tax resources.

- CS and CSS were being cut down and more funds were being handed to states, which has reversed and

- Disinvestment proceeds were very little and privatization – whereby a PSU is permanently handed over to private business – was non-existent earlier, as against after 2014.

Apart from short-changing states in fiscal devolution, cooperative federalism has been violated administratively and politically.

B. Administrative Centralization

The centralization process didn't start with the GST but with the demonetization of 2016 – which derailed the entire economy. The Prime Minister didn't consult states – the actual implementors – then nor while locking down (pandemic) the entire country with four hours' notice in March 2020 (by invoking the NDMA of 2005). The same happened with the unilateral "liberalized" vaccine policy, passing the responsibility of 25% vaccination to states without consulting them – which was reversed after the Supreme Court called it "arbitrary and irrational". The same had also happened with the new farm laws of 2020 (later withdrawn), although agriculture is a state subject, and encroached on their powers limited.

Further, the Planning Commission of India was dismantled in 2014 to end centralized planning and "one-size-fits-all" development but it was replaced with the National Institution for Transforming India (NITI) Aayog in 2015 without consultations with states. The NITI Aayog's mandate[45] is to transform India, among others, by (a) evolving a shared vision of national development priorities, sectors and strategies and (b) to foster cooperative and competitive federalism. A Cabinet resolution envisioned promotion of *participative citizenry, mechanism to formulate credible plans at local levels, encourage partnerships between key stakeholders, create systemic processes for collaborations* etc. for the Aayog.

The reverse has happened on the ground:

(a) More CS and CSS, development means more centralized and "one-size-fits-all" solutions. The Chief Ministers' sub-committee recommendations of 2015[46] on restructuring CSSs (passing all non-core schemes to states, for instance) remain unimplemented.

(b) Growing list of the Centre's *one-nation-one-policy* format, described as "one nationism" by Yamini Aiyar and Louise Tillin[47]:" one-nation-one-identity card (Aadhaar), one-nation-one tax (GST), one-nation-one-grid (energy), one-nation-one-mobility card (RuPay), one-nation-one-election, one-nation-one-ration card, one-nation-one-digital payment (e-RUPI), one-nation-one-vaccine app (CoWin).

(c) The Inter-state Council (ISC), a permanent and constitutional body (Article 263) to improve Centre-state relations was set up in 1990, has met just once after 2014, in 2016.[48] It used to meet regularly earlier (10 meetings before 2016).

(d) The National. Development Council (NDC) – which met annually to approve the central and state budgets – was scrapped and the NITI Aayog was supposed to provide an alternate platform, but that hasn't happened. The states have been pleading for a "credible institution" for a policy dialogue with the Centre, as NDC remains defunct, but no such attempt has been made.[49]

(e) Five "Zonal Councils" of states (east, west, north, south and central) set up by Pandit Nehru for "cooperative working", last met in 2005-07 of the UPA.[50]

(f) The NITI Aayog's engagement with states is through *indices and rankings*, which has changed little in the Centre-state relations. Rather, Aiyar and Tillin[51] point out, the Aayog has *helped in further centralization* through programmes like "Aspirational Districts" for developing poor districts driven by it, rather than states, and which allows the Central government to *bypass states* to *directly deal* with district administrations. The claims of *competing models* of state governments (competitive federalism) is gone. Former RBI Governor YV Reddy wrote[52] that the Aayog "suffers from wide mandate and diffused focus"; it hasn't even been designed to further centre-state cooperation (the PCI was doing that earlier, howsoever flawed), thereby leaving an *institutional vacuum* occupied by central ministries.

Tillin[53] points out that the *decentralization trend* seen in 1990s and 2000s *reversed* to *re-centralization* in all sorts of ways after 2014 – administrative, legal and political powers. During the earlier decades states had developed a certain character. The Bihar election of 2020 saw the Prime Minister and his party seeking votes in the name of "double-engine government" – at the Centre and states – for better growth. Later, the same happened elsewhere – West Bengal and Uttar Pradesh, for example. She described this (double-engine growth) as "a *far cry* from the idea of cooperative federalism". Nevertheless, many states stood up to the Centre and at least seven states withdrew from the Centre's Fasal Bima Yojana and instituted their own schemes.[54] Tillin[55] had earlier explained that the cooperative federalism talk was actually *a ruse* "consistent with a move to *re-empower the Centre* to set policy agendas and incentivise states to carryout central missions". She cited the parallel with the US in 1950s and 1960s when the phrase cooperative federalism was "often used as a *rhetorical device to allay fears about centralization*".

There are more examples of centralization after 2014.

(i) The Centre repeatedly denies Chief Ministers of non-BJP parties to go abroad and interact with foreign governments and citizens.[56] Visiting foreign dignitaries no longer meet Opposition leaders – as has been an age-old practice.

(ii) Opposition-ruled state Kerala was devastated by floods and it agreed to receive a Rs 700 crore financial assistance from the UAE but the Centre didn't allow it saying, India didn't need foreign aid.[57] It did give Rs 600 crore of aid but demanded Rs 33 crore for flood relief and airlifting assistances.[58]

(iii) All Opposition-ruled state ministers and ruling party leaders (only) are routinely raided, arrested and their assets seized by the central agencies (ED, CBI, Income Tax). A whole team of *ED officials with family*[59] camped in Congress-ruled Chhattisgarh for months, ahead of the 2023 assembly elections, and did exactly that – raids, arrests and seizure of assets. The raids *rapidly increased*[60] to target Opposition leaders in Delhi, Rajasthan, Tamil Nadu, West Bengal and Telangana as the November-December 2023 state elections and the 2024 general elections drew closer.

(iv) **Imposition of Hindi**: The Centre is imposing Hindi[61] on states despite knowing the decades of conflict over this, particularly with non-Hindi speaking southern states. Both Prime Minister and Home Minister call for making Hindi the national language (Hindi and English are the official languages while 22 languages are recognized as "scheduled languages" in the Constitution). They use Hindi in their official communications. All government reports, legislations, even Cabinet notes, come fully or partially in Hindi – including the titles of the three bills making wholesale changes in the criminal laws of IPC, CrPC and Evid3ence Act. The Centre has declared to make Hindi compulsory in Northeastern region up to class X. This is despite the Madras High Court's 2021 direction[62] not to do so, especially while dealing with non-Hindi speaking states, and warning about the dangers of spreading "linguistic fanaticism". Yet, in 2023, the government removed "All India Radio" from the official radio services to keep its Hindi version "Akasvani" – notwithstanding that the All India Radio has many regional language versions too.[63]

(v) **Driving out English**: English is the link language, particularly when connecting to south India. English is being edged out through other means: The National Education Policy (NEP) of 2023 and through changes in the UPSC exams. This would not only hit the education and job prospect of millions of youths, especially in well-paying MNCs, it would end up eliminating the advantage that made India a IT power and the IT services became the driving force of exports.[64] To further weaken English advantage, Home Minister Amit Shah-led parliamentary committee *recommended in 2022*[65] that Hindi should mandatorily be for all technical and non-technical educations, including in central universities. Given that India has zero contribution to technology and non-technology advancements and Hindi lacks the vocabulary, this would *completely ruin higher education* in India. Around the same time, Shah unveiled Hindi textbooks for MBBS students[66] in the BJP-ruled Madhya Pradesh. By this time the BJP knew its BJP's move to introduce Engineering education in Hindi in Gujarat – from the 2022 academic session – had no takers and which would continue in 2023 too[67].

(vi) **Taking over border areas**: On October 11, 2021, the Centre delivered another shock to cooperative federalism. *Without consulting states and without explaining why*, it issued a gazette notification[68] expanding the jurisdiction of the central paramilitary force, the Border Security Force (BSF). In some border states, the entire area was brought under BSF's jurisdiction and in others its jurisdiction was increased from 15 km to 50 km. It said "the whole of the area comprised in the States of Manipur, Mizoram, Tripura, Nagaland and Meghalaya and Union Territories of Jammu and Kashmir and Ladakh and so much of the area comprised within a belt of fifty kilometers in the States of Gujarat, Rajasthan, Punjab, West Bengal and Assam, running along the borders of India". It sparked immediate protests from border states like Punjab and West Bengal[69], run by rival political parties, as a substantial territory now came under the BSF, and by proxy, the Centre. In West Bengal, it was estimated that one-third of the territory would now be the Centre's control.[70] Days later, the MHA *dismissed*[71] their concerns saying: "The extension of territorial jurisdiction of BSF would *result in better and more effective control on trans-border crimes* in conjunction and co-operation with State Police." Coinciding with this, BSF DG Pankaj Singh[72] made a facile argument that it "could be" due to "demographic change" in border states (due to "agitations in certain states and there have been many revolts") – not clarifying but apparently referring to protests against the Centre's communal agenda of CAA-NRC.

What did the Supreme Court do when Punjab challenged it? CJI Justice Chandrachud dismissed it saying that it was "only a preventive power", "the power of investigation is not taken away", "nothing is taken away from the Punjab police" on December 1, 2023, while hearing the matter.[73]

(vii) **Taking over rivers and dams:** It took over management of the Krishna and Godavari projects from riparian states of Andhra Pradesh and Telangana in July 2021.[74] For this, it used a controversial provision in the Andhra Pradesh Reorganization Act of 2014[75] – which carved out Telangana from Andhra Pradesh. The said provision, Section 84(1), reads: "(1) The Central government shall, on and from the appointed day, constitute an Apex Council for the supervision of the functioning of the Godavari River Management Board and Krishna River Management Board." The operative word is "supervision", not complete take-over, as has been done. The Centre transferred management of 31 irrigation projects on the Krishna basin and 71 on Godavari to the Krishna and Godavari River Management Boards (KRMB and GRMB) on the plea of long-standing inter-state disputes. It empowered itself for appointments to the boards and disqualified all engineers and other personnel from the two states from holding any position but imposed all liabilities arising out of the boards' functioning on these states.

Law professor Sridhar Acharyulu[76] argued that the Andhra Pradesh Reorganization Act of 2014 didn't authorize the Centre to usurp state power. "Deciding jurisdiction or regulation does not mean taking over the assets and all controls depriving the riparian states of their rights over the rivers running through their states", he wrote. The matter would now be decided in court. The planning has been long. The Centre passed two bills in the Lok Sabha for the purpose – Dam Safety Bill, 2019 and Inter-State River Water Disputes (Amendment) Bill 2019 for the purpose. The first was passed and notified in 2021, dismissing the Opposition's charge that it was "unconstitutional", "anti-federal" and that it should be examined by a parliamentary panel.[77] The second lapsed This Bill lapsed with the dissolution of the Lok Sabha in 2019.[78]

India has 5,254 large dams and another 447 under construction.[79] States' key objections to the Dam Safety Bill of 2019[80] were three: (i) Water being state subject, their power is being appropriated in the name of dam safety by establishing National Committee on Dam Safety (NCDS) and National Dam Safety Authority (NDSA) (ii) both NCDS and NDSA would be controlled by the centre; in NCDS, its chairman, 10 members and three experts (nominated by the centre) would be Central government representatives while states will have only seven "rotational" members and while NDSA would be headed by a Central government representative and the centre would "provide such number of officers and other employees as it may consider necessary" for the functioning of the authority and (iii) the Centre to control a dam owned by one state but located in another to prevent conflicts, which a state like Tamil Nadu does – it claims to own, operate and maintain four dams located in Kerala, namely, the Mullaperiyar, Parambikulam, Thunakkadavu and Peruvaripallam dams, through pre-existing agreement with Kerala. Dam Bill 2019.

To the Centre's credit, it did amend the Forest Act of 1927 in 2017[81] to strike bamboo out as "tree" formally. While gram panchayats had been granted the rights to harvest bamboo and it was treated as "minor forest produce"[82] by the previous UPA governments and in states, the necessary amendment in the law had not been made. But that has made no material difference since no other gram panchayat has received such a right after 2014. In fact, not just forest rights but forests are being deleted to promote private business interests (see Chapter IX).

C. Political Centralization

Political centralization is equally ruthlessly pursued by several means – other than using central agencies as partisan political tools. These include:

(i)   Misusing the office of Governors to pulldown Opposition-ruled states or hoist a BJP government even without majority and engineering defections and splitting the rival political parties ("Operation Lotus").

(ii)   President rule imposed unfairly on Opposition-ruled states (Congress-ruled Arunachal Pradesh and Uttarakhand in 2016) but not in BJP-ruled Manipur where the Supreme Court said constitutional order had *broken down*[83]. In the case of Arunachal Pradesh and Uttarakhand, the governments were *wrongly dismissed*[84] by using obliging Governors' reports of constitutional breakdown, which were then *reversed* by the Supreme Court. The Arunachal Pradesh event turned tragic as it led to the suicide of its Chief Minister Kalikho Pul – who implicated several high-profile judges and politicians in his suicide note for seeking bribes to restore his government, but this was never probed either by the government or by the Supreme Court (Supreme Court judges and officials were implicated in it too).[85]

(iii)   Taking away constitutional and democratic rights of elected government – as in the case of J&K and NCT of Delhi.

(iv)   Fostering and allowing to fester communal/ethnic conflicts in states to polarize votes in its favour – like in Manipur (ethnic violence and NRC), Assam (NRC), Lakshadweep (attack on Muslim culture by the BJP-appointed Lieutenant Governor[86]) and Goa (attack on Portuguese culture[87]). These are in addition to demographic changes and ethnic cleansing (Chapter IV) going on in J&K, Uttarakhand and Haryana. All these developments add more dangerous dimension to the divisive politics – endanger internal security and invite enemy nations to get a foothold. The government has now created a new enemy in China due to its own failures, and also caused distrust with other neighbours through its Big Brother attitude (Chapter XI).

Misuse of Governors and "Operation Lotus"

Misuse of Governor's office and "Operation Lotus" – organizing defections and splits in the Opposition ranks to steal their mandate and install BJP governments in states – go hand-in-hand in most cases. This is now a routine – the very anti-thesis of the Prime Minister's claim of championing "cooperative federalism".

The very first move of the government did after Modi became the Prime Minister was to sack Governors in May 2014.[88] Although this was not the first such instance, the move was against the BJP's stated stand in the Parliament in 2004 when it had opposed a similar move by the Congress-led government and had approached the Supreme Court. But that was forgotten. Worse, such patently illegal order (also against cooperative federalism) was carried out through the then Home Secretary Anil Goswami[89], who called up Governors on phone to seek their resignations. No less than *eight* Governors resigned[90] within days (Uttar Pradesh, Goa, Maharashtra, West Bengal, Kerala, Nagaland, Chhattisgarh and Mizoram (after being transferred to Nagaland); one more, Kamla Beniwal (Governor of Gujarat during Modi's last term as chief minister), was first transferred to Mizoram and then sacked.

This violates the 2010 Supreme Court order[91] which ruled: "A Governor cannot be removed on the ground that he is out of sync with the policies and ideologies of the Union Government or the party in power at the Centre. Nor can he be removed on the ground that the Union Government has lost confidence in him. It follows therefore that *change in government at Centre is not a ground for removal of Governors* holding office to make way for others favoured by the new government."

Ironically, this ruling came in response to a PIL filed by BJP MP BP Singhal in 2004, when the Governors of Uttar Pradesh, Gujarat, Haryana and Goa were sought to be removed. Ironically too, Uttarakhand Governor Aziz Qureshi filed a PIL in the apex court in 2014 citing the same to stop his sacking but nothing more was heard about it. He was then transferred to Mizoram and then sacked[92] – a trick tried with the Gujarat Governors.[93]

The government made wholesome changes and appointed 26 Governors and 7 Lieutenant Governors (LGs) who are known to be associated with the BJP. It was during this exercise that former CJI Justice Sathasivam was appointed as Governor of Kerala sparking questions about judicial independence and autonomy.[94] Here are some such instances:

- **Maharashtra 2019, 2022 and 2023**: The Centre and its appointed Governor installed its leader Devendra Fadnavis as Chief Minister at early morning swearing-in even without a majority on its side (a hung assembly) in November 2019.[95] The Centre did this by imposing first the President's Rule by invoking *Rule 12*[96] of the Government of India (Transaction of Business) Rules of 1961 – which allows revocation of President's Rule *without* Cabinet approval, if the Prime Minister "deems it necessary". Hartosh Singh Bal called this (and the manner in which Article 370 was abrogated also in 2019) "Modi-Shah governance model" of "stealth, self-aggrandizement and stupidity".[97]

Fadnavis was forced to resign in hours because he didn't have the majority, for which he had brought rival NCP leader Ajit Pawar to his side and sworn-in him as deputy CM. Thus came the Shiv Sena-led Maha Vikas Aghadi (MVA) government with Udhav Thackeray as the Chief Minister (with Congress support). In 2022, the Thackeray's party was split and the rebels joined the BJP to pull down this government. In this toppling, not just the Governor but also central agencies and the Supreme Court played critical roles. The Governor had kept 12 seats in the legislative council and the Speaker's post vacant for more than a year[98]; his call for a trust vote was declared "illegal" by the Supreme Court (as "objective material and reasons" to justify it didn't exist) by a bench headed by CJI Justice Chandrachud in 2023.

The rebel Sena leaders were hounded by the ED and CBI[99] and so was NCP leaders, including its president Sharad Pawar[100]; the apex court's vacation bench (headed by Justices Surya Kant and JB Pardiwala) had earlier in June 2022 (a) *extended* the time to decide the question of *disqualification* of the rebels (Shinde group) in the Assembly and (b) allowed the trust vote in the interim. Thackeray resigned, instead of taking a floor test. In 2023, Justice Chandrachud-led bench found[101] the Governor on the wrong and the treatment of the rebel Shiv Sena as the "real" Shiv Sena (appointment of its members as the legislature party leader and chief whip) "illegal" but said it, "the status quo ante cannot be restored because Mr Thackeray did not face the floor test and tendered his resignation". Commenting on this judgement, constitutional lawyer Gautam Bhatia wrote[102] the "original sin" was the two "interim" orders from the vacation bench but the CJI-led bench found nothing wrong.

In the interim, the Election Commission, in a controversial move, recognised the "Shinde faction" as the "real Shiv Sena" – which remains contentious[103] and pending before the Supreme Court.[104] The disqualification question is pending in the Assembly – forcing the apex court to direct the Speaker to decide it by December 31, 2023.[105]

Meanwhile, July 2023 saw more drama as the NCP split with Ajit Pawar going back to join the Shinde-Fadnavis government. Many of his key members and their kin, including himself and Praful Patel, were in the net of central agencies for corruption.[106] Here comes the Prime Minister's "jumla" governance: Two days earlier, he had thundered "Modi's guarantee" to put in jail all corrupt politician in which he had alleged the NCP leaders (and other rivals like the Congress) were directly involved in corruption cases amounting to Rs 70,000 crore ("who looted the poor and the country").[107] He had earlier called the NCP "Naturally Corrupt Party").[108]

- **Goa, Manipur, 2017**: In 2017, after state elections in these two states, the BJP was invited to form the government by the Governor despite not being the single largest party or part of the pre-poll alliance. *Mass defections* from the Congress and other parties followed to keep the BJP in office.[109]

- **Bihar 2017**: Opposition-ruled Bihar government was toppled in 2017 by splitting the JD(U)-RJD coalition; Chief Minister Nitish Kumar from the JD(U) resigned suddenly and then equally suddenly declared forming a new government in coalition with the BJP – midway through the term. It raised many questions which remain unanswered. A few months later, in 2018, RJD leader Lalu Prasad Yadav[110] was sentenced to jail in the fodder scam. At that time another scam came to public notice: siphoning of Rs 700-1,000 crore during the previous JD(U)-BJP government, in which NGO Srijan Sahayog Mahila Vikas Samiti[111], known for its close proximity to top leaders of JD(U)-BJP government, emerged as a key player. It saw no such high-profile arrests and went out of public glare. Nitish Kumar hit the reset botton again in 2022 and formed the government with the RJD by dumping the BJP.

- **Karnataka 2018, 2019**: Like in Maharashtra in 2019, Karnataka saw the BJP come to power without majority – in which the Governor came handy – but it couldn't prove its majority and fell.[112] One year later, the BJP was back in power after a wholesale defection of Opposition legislators. Later, the Pegasus investigations of 2021[113] revealed the possibility of the military-grade spyware playing a role in the fall of the Opposition's government. Later, Congress won the 2023 elections and its Deputy CM DK Shivakumar revealed[114], he had refused to defect to the BJP in 2019 and chose to go to jail instead. He faces *multiple cases*[115] filed by the ED and CBI and has gone to join by then. During the 2023 elections, Prime Minister equated Hindu god Hanuman with the right-wing militant group Bajrang Dal[116] known for its communal and violent activities and the Congress had sought to ban it. But the Prime Minister sought vote in the name of "Jai Bajrang Bali" (EC didn't react given that it is violation of model code and the Constitution of

India) and said the Congress was seeking secession of Karnataka. (The BJP asked the ECI to deregister Congress even when Sonia Gandhi's speech, which was the basis for this, didn't call for any secession.[117]). Such was the vicious fight from the BJP that Union Home Minister Amit Shah warned of *riots*[118] if the Congress came to power – all the while ignoring that Manipur was burning for weeks in ethnic violence.[119]

- **Madhya Pradesh 2020**: A massive defection in the ranks of the Congress led to its government's fall in one-and-half years and the BJP came back to power in 2020. Jyotiraditya Scindia[120], Congress leader from the prominent political family of Scindias, joined the BJP with 22 Congress MLAs – who had resigned from the Assembly to reduce the Congress government to minority.[121] Scindia was rewarded with a cabinet berth in 2021 even though the Prime Minister routinely runs down political dynasta as "the biggest threat to democracy" – a fake claim since the BJP has far more dynasts of its own and those defected from the Congress, NCP and other parties.[122]

The list of Governors and Lieutenant Governors creating problems for non-BJP ruled government is long and very disconcerting. They seem to forget their constitutional responsibilities and limits to act as super Chief Ministers. Here are some such examples:

- **Tamil Nadu** Governor RN Ravi on his own sacked a minister Senthil Balaji after the latter was targeted by the ED without the necessary prior recommendation of the Council of Ministers and then kept his patently unconstitutional act it on hold, *after* his blunder was pointed out, saying he was seeking *legal advice*[123] on this illegal act. He has not only held up many Bills passed by the state, some for three years, without any justification (as revealed by the RTI query) but has been caught lying about it too.[124]

- **Puducherry** LG Kiran Bedi never let the elected Congress government to work in peace or pursue its policies without her interference. In February 2021, two months ahead of the 2021 elections, she was recalled[125] as she was considered a liability for the BJP's poll prospects. Soon, half-a-dozen legislators – five from the Congress, including two ministers and one from the DMK – resigned from the government and the Congress government fell.[126] The BJP formed a coalition government, for the first time in the UT, after fresh elections.

- Governor of **West Bengal** Jagdeep Dhankar (now Vice President of India) interfered and played overtly partisan politics to keep the ruling Trinamool Congress (TMC) government of Mamata Banerjee on tenterhooks. In February 2022, the confrontation took an ugly turn as Mamata blocked[127] Dhankar on Twitter protesting against his "unethical and unconstitutional" statements and accusing him of treating government officials like "his servants". As mentioned earlier, the Centre had started harassing the state government after the BJP lost the 2021 elections. Its investigating agency, the CBI, selectively arrested some TMC leaders (as mentioned earlier) and then issued orders to immediately recall the state chief secretary and report in New Delhi immediately, without seeking the state's consent or consulting it[128], something it did with the AAP-ruled NCT of Delhi after losing the 2015 elections.

- **Kerala** Governor Arif Mohammad Khan has a running feud with the LDF government led by Pinarayi Vijayan, assuming himself to be an authority above and superior to the elected government – trampling on most fundamental democratic principles.[129] He is sitting on eight Bills for long[130], despite reminders and meetings provoking Vijayan to talk of approaching the apex court. This is despite the apex court directive to Governor to act and not sit over Bills.[131]

- Muslim-dominated union territory of **Lakshadweep** is on a boil for several months after Praful Khoda Patel, Modi's home minister in Gujarat, was appointed Administrator in December 2020. He imposed the *Hindutva agenda* on the Muslim-dominated territory through ban on cow slaughter and removing meat from school meals. He proposed preventive detention law, while crime is very low in the UT, handing over land for tourism development and allow liquor sales. He has disrupted trade and businesses and has fired one-third of all government employees, about 3,000, holding temporary and casual work. Since the state is the biggest employer and the local economy is too small to absorb them, their households have cut down in expenses, its shops, hotels and other businesses have tanked.[132]

- **Punjab**: Governor Banwarilal Purohit threatened Chief Minister Bhagwant Mann (of the AAP government) to recommend imposing central rule and launch criminal proceedings if the questions he raised on the sale of drugs and addictions were not answered – equating it with breakdown in constitutional order.[133]

- **Manipur**: The BJP-ruled state ("double engine" government) has been burning for months since May 2023 in ethnic clashes – open gun battles between different groups is routine; close to 6,000 weapons have been looted from the armoury and close to 100 bodies are lying in mortuary for five months[134]; the state police is fighting the Assam Rifles in a clear indication of rifts in controlling violence (an unprecedented development for India[135]) and more than 50,000 people have already fled or were shifted for their safety by security forces. There can't be a clearer case of breakdown in law and order and constitutional governance. Yet, its Governor Anusuiya Uikey has said nothing beyond that she is "deeply concerned" and that the state government doesn't listen to her.[136] Nobody knows if she has sent a report recommending central rule or expressing her concerns.

- **Telangana**: The K Chandrashekar Rao government (of Bharat Rashtra Samithi (BRS), not an ally of the BJP) went to the Supreme Court to complain against Governor Tamilsai Soundararajan for sitting on Bills. The court told the Governor, in April 2023, to act promptly and read out proviso 1 of Article 200 to emphasis on "as soon as possible": "The Governor may, as soon as possible, after the presentation to him of the bill for assent, return the bill if it is not a money bill."[137]

As more and more Opposition-ruled states approached the Supreme Court, a CJI Justice Chandrachud-led bench asked all Governors to "stop" this and "must act" beforehand and do some "soul searching" as they are not "elected representatives of the people" – while hearing the AAP-run Punjab government's complaints.[138] Less than a week later, Tamil Nadu Governor RN Ravi returned 10 Bills for the government to reconsider and two forwarded to the President.[139]

With the "Operation Lotus" (lotus is its party symbol), the old 'Aya Ram, Gaya Ram' culture (of late 1960s, 1970s and early 1980s) is back to Indian polity – effectively ending the anti-defection law of 1985 (which allowed one-third of party to merge with another without disqualification) and its amendment in 2003 (which raised the bar to two-third of a party and the defectors must get themselves re-elected) which had virtually stopped it. In the case of Madhya Pradesh (after one-and-half years) and Puducherry (towards the end of the term) for example, the defectors from the Congress resigned from the Assemblies because the number was not on their side – reducing the government to a minority and thus, the governments fell. They were then given tickets by the BJP for re-election – thus, circumventing the number games.

Such is the BJP's fearsome reputation for splitting political rivals using money, central agencies and other methods that the Congress government of Rajasthan shifted its MLAs to Jaisalmer in 2020 while the rival faction led by Sachin Pilot camped in a Alwar resort.[140] The governments of AAP in NCT of Delhi and Jharkhand Mukti Morcha-led coalition in Jharkhand held trust votes in 2022 just to ensure their MLAs had not been poached.[141]

The Association for Democratic Reforms (ADR), an election watchdog, analysed defection of MLAs between 2016 and 2021 (before March 11, 2021) which showed the BJP benefited from it the most. In all, 44.9% of defecting MLAs joined the BJP. The Congress lost the maximum – 42%.[142]

Graph 6: Defections: Advantage to the BJP

Defection of number of MLAs from 2016 to Mar 2021

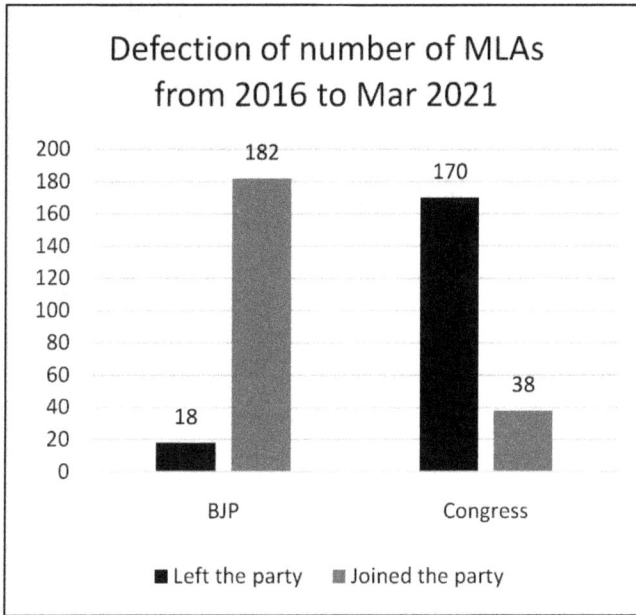

Source: ADR, March 11, 2021

Killing Democracy through Law and Parliament

The Parliament has been misused to kill democracy. Two key instances are that of the J&K and NCT of Delhi – which were reduced to *vasal states*.

Disempowerment and disembodiment of J&K

In August, 2019, the government disempowered, dismembered and downgraded J&K.[143] The state's special status under Article 370 and Article 35A, was abrogated overnight and the Parliament passed the Jammu & Kashmir Reorganisation Act of 2019 to reduce it to two union territories – which are governed through the Central government's administrator. This was fulfilment of the Hindutva's one big political goals (other than the ultimate goal of building a Hindu Rashtra) – of the three it set out long ago, the other two being building a grand Ram temple at the at the Babri Masjid site in Ayodhya and bringing a Uniform Civil Code (UCC). The goal to build the temple in Ayodhya would be facilitated through the Supreme Court order in November 2019.

The abrogation of Article 370 began with a series of *big lies and subterfuge.*[144]

In 2018, the BJP suddenly pulled out[145] of its three-year-old coalition government in the state as a junior partner of the People's Democratic Party

(PDP) on *flimsy ground*, described vaguely as the "situation" was untenable and the alliance was "untenable", but never explained what these meant. The state was placed under the Governor's rule and then the President's rule (beyond six months).[146] Then a *false alarm* of terror strike was raised three days ahead of August 5, 2019 – the day Article 370 was abrogated – to cancel the Amarnath pilgrimage, issue prohibitory orders, suspend internet services and deploy more army in the state. At midnight of August 4-5, top Opposition leaders, including three former chief ministers, one was who was Mehbooba Mufti who had led the PDP-BJP coalition government between 2016-2018, were put under house arrest. The entire state and its people were locked down (which continue for a long time); about 4,000 people were arrested[147], including politicians, lawyers, journalists and others were arrested – over 1,000 under the anti-terror UAPA[148].

Then Congress chief whip in Rajya Sabha Bhubaneswar Kalita *defected*[149] to the BJP the night before August 5, along with two other Rajya Sabha members from other parties. Kalita sent his resignation in the morning of August 5, just ahead of the Centre's final strike. His resignation meant he couldn't issue whip to Congress members to vote against the government's move on the critical day. Kalita joined the BJP and was rewarded with a Rajya Sabha seat.

On the morning of August 5, a Presidential order was issued revoking Article 370, that granted special status to the state, *without any explanation*. Similar special status remains intact in more than a dozen states, granted under Article 371 (northeast states) and Article 244 (in the Fifth and Sixth Schedule areas), covering a large part of the country (central, north and northeast). Besides, the government had also entered into a peace agreement with the Naga insurgents by then promising them "special status" – separate constitution and flag.[150]

This Presidential order[151] is a bunch of legal obfuscations of doubtful constitutionality:

- It equates J&K's "Constituent Assembly" (whose "recommendation" is necessary for a Presidential Order under Article 370(3) to revoke Article 370[152]) to its non-existent "Legislative Assembly" (already dissolved in 2018).

- It then equates the non-existent Legislative Assembly to "the Governor of Jammu and Kashmir" (as the state was under the administrative control of a Governor then).

- Then, it "construed" the "government" of the state to include "references to the Governor of Jammu and Kashmir acting on the advice of his Council of Ministers" (non-existent Council of Ministers).

Put it simply, the President's order *denied J&K peoples' voice*, reflected through their Legislative Assembly; conflated the people's voice to the *opinion of the Centre's nominee, the Governor*. All this meant, the Centre became the people of

J&K and gave *consent to itself* for the purpose of revoking Article 370. It is like the formulation from the Alice in Wonderland: *"I'll be judge, I'll be jury", Said cunning old Fury: "I'll try the whole cause, and condemn you to death."*

With the Presidential order went out Article 35A[153], which had been included in the Constitution's Appendix I, not in the main text. It granted special privileges and rights to the permanent residents of the state and debarred non-residents from buying land or property, getting a government job and voting rights. More than 20 petitions challenging these moves were kept pending for four years until August 2023 when the Supreme Court took it up for hearing (was pending until the second week of October 2023), without explaining the delay (but keeping with the apex court's reluctance to stand up to the government in a large number of cases listed in Chapter III). Four years down the line, no Assembly election has been held (not even with the five states which went to polls in November 2023) and the Centre rules it as a vasal state. However, the government told the Supreme Court in 2023 that it abrogated Article 370 due to the Pulwama attack of 2019).[154]

In the meanwhile, the Centre's delimitation exercise (redrawing Assembly and Lok Sabha seats)[155] has produced the expected outcome: boosting the electoral influence of Hindus and diluting that of Muslims by discarding the core determinant of it, population. The exercise was circumcised by pre-assigning (in the reorganisation law) a larger rise in assembly seats to Hindu majority Jammu (from 37 to 43) than Muslim majority Kashmir (46 to 47). This means Jammu with 44% population gets 48% seats and Kashmir with 56% population gets 52% seats, as per Census 2011. This also means a failure to adhere to the Census of 2011 that was mandated by the J&K Reorganisation Act, 2019 – downgrading it. It is quite another matter that for four states, Assam, Manipur, Nagaland, Arunachal Pradesh, undergoing simultaneously delimitations, the population base is Census 2001[156] as per the Delimitation Act of 2002, not Census 2011. Besides, the Lok Sabha seats have been redrawn arbitrarily, ignoring geographical contiguity, in a way to give Hindus more electoral influence. Later, the Centre decided to give voting rights to those "ordinarily" residing in J&K (like rest of India but unlike under the special status to the territory), which expects to add 25 lakh voters to 76 lakh vote-base (35.5% addition)[157] – sparking fear that the BJP would easily displace local parties and capture power on its own.

All these patently unlawful activities have ended up further deepening the distrust of Muslim-dominated Kashmir with the Centre and given a fresh spurt to communal divide within the state. Contrary to the government's claims of peace and development, J&K remains chained and the political process muted. It tops in the internet shutdowns between 2012 to June 2023.[158] This disrupts everyday life – education, employment and social activities. Independent media outlets have been shut and journalists jailed[159] and more than 5,000 are in jails[160] after

2019. Ahead of the government's final clampdown in August 2019, it had shut down trade[161] between India and Pakistan through Uri overnight. Thousands of jobs have been lost, trading and other businesses remain closed turning the town's life upside down causing immense distress. Such social, political and economic disruptions have perpetuated violence; the incidents of stone pelting and deaths may have gone down but violence endures[162], particularly targeted killings of Kashmiri Hindus and non-Kashmiris in the Valley have gone up. There is also a new crisis – that of drugs. A series of Indian Express investigating reports show[163] there is a dramatic rise in seizure of heroin and arrests; one drug addict walking in to the Srinagar hospital every 12 minutes. Perpetual conflicts create psychological scars leading to such developments.

Delegitimization of NCT of Delhi

Ironically, the AAP government of NCT of Delhi had welcomed and voted in favour of the abrogation of Article 370 in 2019 even as it was fighting for full statehood for its territory[164] – without suspecting that the same fate would befall it. Amidst the devastating second pandemic wave in 2021, the Centre struck – it amended the Government of National Capital Territory of Delhi (GNCTD) Act of 1993 to declare its nominee, the LG, as the "government" of NCT of Delhi – in the place of the elected Legislative Assembly and elected Council of Ministers.[165] It is a patently unconstitutional act and is pending before judicial review in the Supreme Court since then. Curiously, even as the Supreme Court kept the constitutional validity of this amendment pending (before another bench), it paved the way for the Centre to takeover "services" of the NCT of Delhi. But before that some background information.

The AAP government has virtually been paralysed after the BJP lost the Delhi election in 2015.[166] First the CBI raided Chief Minister Arvind Kejriwal and his office was sealed and then successive LGs are used to make the government functioning difficult – something that had *not happened*[167] until then (after 1993 when Delhi got its limited statehood). The LG started appointing key officials, including chief secretary, without consulting the state government. The LG blocked all major policies and laws, including at least *14 crucial bills*, passed by the Delhi Assembly (8 of which were never returned to the Assembly).[168] These included Delhi Jan Lokpal Bill, Delhi Right of Citizen to Time-Bound Delivery of Services Amendment Bill, Delhi School Verification of Accounts and Refund of Excess Fee Bill (to fix accountability of profiteering private schools). He also clipped the wings of state's anti-corruption bureau (ACB).

At the core of these interference was the MHA notification of May 21, 2015[169] which made two key changes: (i) the LG was empowered to exercise exclusive powers relating to public order, police, land and services and services matters

(ii) allowing the LG to act "in his discretion" by ignoring the elected government – virtually paralysing it by controlling the entire bureaucracy (appointments, transfers etc.). By taking over services, the notification allowed the Centre (that is LG) to take over the GNCTD's Anti-Corruption Bureau (ACB), which threatened action against corrupt officers.

The subsequent eight years saw the GNCTD challenge it in the Delhi High Court and Supreme Court without any result. Finally, a five-member bench headed by CJI Justice Chandrachud delivered an unanimous judgement on May 11, 2023.[170] It didn't invalidate the notification and made all the right noises about constitutional democracy, "triple chain of command" (civil service officers accountable to ministers; ministers accountable to Parliament/Legislature and Parliament/Legislature accountable to the electorate), the ideals of responsible and representative government and the *sui generis* character of the GNCTD. But it also *paved the way*[171] for the subsequent *ordinance* eight days later on May 19, 2023[172], replacing the notification of May 21, 2015 – and took away the "services" (in addition to the existing control over police, public order and land). The ordinance set up a three-member "National Capital Service Authority" headed by the Chief Minister but with two officers under the Centre's control – thereby, effectively neutralizing the elected Chief Minister.

The Supreme Court judgement *paved the way* for the ordinance and then the amendment by stating that: (a) "Parliament has legislative competence over all matters in List II and List III in relation to NCTD (state list and concurrent list, respectively), except those expressly excluded even as concluding that (b) the Centre's power can't be "read to further exclude the legislative power" of the GNCTD and (c) the GNCTD "ought to have control" over services but "subject to exclusion of subjects which are out of its legislative domain". At the same time, it also concluded that (d) the GNCTD "has legislative and executive power over "Services" and yet (e) the exercise of rule-making power under the proviso to Article 309 "does not oust" the legislative power of the appropriate authority (Centre) to make laws "over Entry 41 ("services") of the State List.

The May 19, 2023 ordinance just did that – corrected the anomaly of the May 2015 notification. All this happened while the constitutional validity of it was pending before the apex court, the government passed it in the Parliament in August 2023, Then, it was passed by the Parliament in 2023 (amidst the din over Manipur violence and Opposition's walkout).[173] And then, the Centre took control of the entire bureaucracy of the NCT Delhi – even as a challenge was pending before the Supreme Court. The Supreme Court let the Central government grab the power when the latter *unilaterally* decided to give extension to chief secretary (CS) Naresh Kumar despite strong objections from the elected government. The court first asked the government to prepare a panel of five officers, questioned the *obsession* with an individual officer[174] (just as the case with ED Director Sanjay

Kumar Mishra detailed in Chapter I) and then allowed a *six-month extension*[175] to the CS.

Until the current regime, all the previous governments of the NCT of Delhi (of the BJP and Congress) functioned smoothly (when the NDA I and UPA I and II were in power at the Centre) and controlled the bureaucracy; even in matters relating to public order, police and land which were with the Centre, there was hardly any conflict. But things changed dramatically after Modi came to power. Nothing seems to matter or deter it – the democratic/constitutional propriety or conventions. It didn't allow even humanitarian services like doorstep delivery of ration during the pandemic crisis – even as the government used "free" and "subsidized" ration, branded as a gift from the Prime Minister and carried his images on the packets, to win elections in Uttar Pradesh and three other states in 2022 (see Introduction). The Delhi High Court, which too has been hearing the "services" matter for years, kept changing its position before finally disallowing it in May 2022, stating that the LG didn't permit it.[176]

This happened despite the fact that (and violated) the Supreme Court's *2018 order* on the Centre-GNCTD conflict (five-member bench led by then CJI Justice Dipak Misra and included Justice Chandrachud) had said[177] "*the real authority to take decisions resides in the Council of Ministers*, which owes ultimate responsibility to the people, through a legislature to whom the Council is responsible. Collective responsibility and the aid and advice doctrine must not be construed as disjunctive but together constitute integral parts of the discourse in ensuring the strength of and commitment to democracy". It had also said that "the Lieutenant Governor of Delhi is *bound by the aid and advice of the Council of Ministers of Delhi*". (Emphasis added)

Delhi now has a third LG, Saxena, who continues to breath down the necks of the elected government, acting like the real elected government. Together with the Centre the LG even delayed the 2023 budget on frivolous ground of high allocation for advertisement (actual allocation Rs 550 crore) and relatively low funding for infrastructure (Rs 22,000 crore) and other development initiatives – provoking Chief Minister Arvind Kejriwal to now-famous comment "illiterates (ruling the country) from top to bottom".[178] This was the apparent provocation for Kejriwal to later regale the Delhi Assembly with the story of a "Chauthi Pass Raja" (Uneducated King) – a dig at the Prime Minister, which repeated in public rallies.[179] This led to a *meme fest* in social media about uneducated leaders and appeals not to vote for such leaders. One of them was law teacher Karan Sangwan (mentioned in Chapter IV) of edtech platform Unacademy who was *sacked*[180] for asking people to 'vote for educated person' in August 2023.

Undeterred, just a day before Delhi's finance minister and Deputy Chief Minister Manish Sisodia was to present the budget, he was *arrested*[181] by the CBI, which *directly works under the Prime Minister* (who heads the Ministry of

Personnel, Pension & Public Grievances) in the alleged irregularities relating to the previous year's liquor policy and then by the ED and he has been languishing in jail since then (see Chapter III for more about it).

'Revdi' (Freebie) Attack on Opposition-ruled States

The Prime Minister wants to play the sole "messiah" of the poor with no space for anyone else. While he takes entire credit and seeks votes in lieu of his welfare schemes (public money) – like "new welfarism", "Modi's 'namak'" and "free", instead of "subsidized", ration to 67% of households since January 2023 (which cuts out states from chipping in with their bits to subsidize ration) have already been explained; Rs 6,000 to all farmers under the PM-Kisan scheme since 2019, huge amounts of fiscal and tax incentives like the PLIs and DLIs since 2020 to industry, writing off corporate loan defaults of even fraudsters and willful defaulters since 2014, corporate tax cut of 2019 etc. (detailed in the next chapter) – he names and shames Opposition-ruled states and rival political leaders for their welfare measures as a matter of routine.

His first attack came in 2019 and continued in 2022 and 2023. It is not just hypocrisy but also a propaganda technique to discredit Opposition-ruled states and political rivals – given the context in which such attacks are mounted but with the confidence that he has the monopoly in public messaging with a pliant media to ensure that monopoly.

The one of January 2019 came immediately *after* the BJP lost elections in three important states a month earlier (December 2018) – in Rajasthan, Madhya Pradesh and Chhattisgarh – all of which the Congress won. All political parties had fought the elections with competitive promises of welfares and populist schemes. It was just *ahead* of the (April-May) 2019 general elections. Once the 2019 elections were over and he secured a second term, the issue was forgotten. This is a trend that would be repeated twice more, but first flashback to January 2019.

In January 2019, the Prime Minister denounced the farm loan waivers announced by Congress-ruled states of Rajasthan, Madhya Pradesh and Chhattisgarh (as promised during the campaigning). He called those "politics of lies and deceit"[182], "lollipops" and "political stunt" while *denying* he or his party ever did that (an outright lie)[183]. This was strange since he had repeatedly assured (a prelude to the "Modi's guarantee" that would become his catch phrase later) farm loan waivers during the Uttar Pradesh Assembly elections in February 2017: "I will make sure that the first cabinet decision after forming (BJP) government in Lucknow will be to waive loans given to farmers in Uttar Pradesh".[184]

The RBI would spring to support the Prime Minister later in September 2019 with "Report of the Internal Working Group to Review Agriculture

Credit"[185] which dismissed farm loan waivers "not the panacea" for farmers or farm distress, and worse: "In fact, they destroy the credit culture which may harm the farmers' interest in the medium to long term and also squeeze the fiscal space of governments to increase productive investment in agriculture infrastructure." The farm loan waivers are *paid for* by state and Central governments, whichever announces it, and hence, banks don't lose money. *In contrast*, the RBI never raised a finger at the huge corporate loan defaults being written off as bank NPAs by the government year after year since 2014 as a routine exercise – which is a net loss for banks, far more damaging to the credit culture and fiscal management of the country far more very severely.[186]

Another development had taken place by then. Then Congress president Rahul Gandhi had proposed a minimum income guarantee (MIG) scheme called 'NYAY' – a transfer Rs 6,000 per month (Rs 72,000 a year) to 50 million poor families.

The mainstream media launched a scathing attack on the Congress by raising two questions: Will India's fiscal condition allow farm loan waivers or 'NYAY'? How the beneficiaries of 'NYAY' be identified?

These questions were superfluous for four reasons:

(a) Six BJP-ruled states had already announced farm loan wavers, fully or partially – Uttar Pradesh (2016, 2017), Rajasthan (2017, Feb 2018), Maharashtra (2016), J&K (2017), Chhattisgarh (2015) and Assam (2018)[187] – and *two more* had announced sops for farmers, Jharkhand (2018)[188] giving Rs 5,000 to all small and marginal farmers and Gujarat waived off farmers' power bills (2018)[189].

(b) Economic Survey of 2016-17 (of the Modi government) had already proposed a MIG scheme, called Universal Basic Income (UBI), to cover 75% *of the population*, calculated the cost and identified the source of funding.[190]

(c) By then, the government was writing off huge amounts of corporate loan *defaults* – amounting to Rs 3.98 lakh crore during FY15-FY18 (RBI reports more about which is in Chapter VII).

(d) The Ayushman Bharat (PM-JAY), launched in 2018, was covering 40% of the poorest families with health insurance cover on the basis of Social Economic and Caste Census (SECC) of 2011 – and the same data could have been used for identifying the rest.[191]

The debate ended with the Central government declaring Rs 6,000 per year to farmers by announcing the PM-Kisan scheme in the 'vote-on-account' budget on February 1, 2019 – a clear violation of the budgeting norms. The media which had gone ballistic days earlier, conveniently forgot to ask those very questions.

In 2022, the RBI set the stage for the Prime Minister by producing two reports in June[192] and July 2022[193] – both of which severely criticized states for "non-merit freebies", warning that these posed Sri Lanka like "financial risks". It flagged their other fiscal profligacies like "off-budget" borrowing going up to "4.5% of the GDP", while their "own tax revenue" was on a "slowdown". These reports skipped "non-merit" freebies of the Central government or its off-budget borrowings and debts. The Finance Ministry think tank National Institute of Public Finance and Policy (NIPFP)'s August 2022 report[194] *contradicted* the RBI with a comprehensive study of state government finances. The RBI was all along wrong, selectively using data to paint a wrong picture and was forced to correct itself through another report in January 2023[195] – *profusely commending* states for their sound fiscal management (no mention of freebies, off-budget borrowing and debt but noted that *19 states/UTs were revenue surplus*) despite their fiscal space shrinking due to fiscal centralization explained earlier and the pandemic constraints but without apologizing for its earlier cavalier and political reports. The RBI knew all along that states have fiscally *outperformed* states in every single fiscal parameter, at least in the entire 2011-12 GDP series until FY22 (which continues).[196]

In the meanwhile, in July 2022, the Prime Minister launched his attacks on Opposition-ruled states, introducing derogatory words like "revdi" and "revdi culture" for welfare schemes and continued for months as the next round of elections in Gujarat, Himachal Pradesh loomed.[197] The BJP had lost only one of the five states that had gone to election in 2022 (detailed in Introduction) – the Aam Admi Party (AAP) winning Punjab. The AAP was contesting the forthcoming Gujarat elections and promised free electricity and water – just as it promised in Punjab and had not only promised but delivered in Delhi (NCT of Delhi). The Congress too promised welfare schemes, as did the BJP.

Just two example to illustrate how BJP leaders lure voters. Union Minister Smriti Irani offered sugar at Rs 13 per kg during the 2019 general elections mentioned earlier "on behalf of Prime Minister Modi".[198] Union Home Minister Amit Shah asked voters to vote for the BJP and take away *two free LPG cylinders*[199] in the 2022 Uttar Pradesh elections. Both are violation of election codes (MCC) and yet no action was taken against them.

The 2022 debate saw the Supreme Court coming into the picture (an old petition was revived to time the Prime Minister's diatribe). It conducted daily hearings in August 2022 – to which the Election Commission of India (ECI) and Finance Commission (FC) were dragged in. But nothing came out of it all.

The apex court referred the matter to a three-judge bench to take it forward – which is yet to be constituted.[200] The ECI asked political parties to disclose the cost of freebies they announce[201] – which is not even feasible because 'revdi' (freebie) hasn't been defined by anyone and nobody knows what exactly it stands for. It has many qualifiers like 'rational' and 'irrational' (used by the apex court), 'merit' and 'non-merit' (used by the RBI), 'populist' or otherwise (used by the FC), 'unwarranted' and 'wasteful' (used by others); budget documents and the Economic Survey reports use terms like 'subsidies' when it is the poor and 'stimulus', 'tax incentive' and 'revenue foregone' when it is for corporate entities, partnership firms, trusts and high net-worth individuals (HNIs).

The very existence of these qualifying terms underlines that freebies *per se* are a necessity in India because it is home to maximum poor (228.9 million[202]) and maximum hungry (224.3 million[203]) in the world. Nonetheless, good fiscal management calls for eternal vigilance. However, once the elections in Gujarat and Himachal Pradesh elections ended, the debate was buried.

The Finance Commission is not even a permanent body and the 15th FC (mentioned earlier) did nothing more than bring a new term "populist" without defining it and coined a new phrase, "high-powered inter-governmental group", for fiscal monitoring – instead of 'fiscal council' the previous FCs had sought for the same purpose.

After the BJP lost election in Karnataka in 2023 – despite the Prime Minister and Union Home Minister stationed there for long as Manipur burnt – and the next round of state elections looked (Rajasthan, Madhya Pradesh, Chhattisgarh and others going to polls in November-December 2023), the Prime Minister launched another attack in September 2023. In an interview, he again talked about 'revdi' and 'revdi culture' and warned[204] that "financially irresponsible policies and populism may give political results in the short term but will extract a great social and economic price in the long term"; "those who suffer those consequences the most are often the poorest and the most vulnerable". This was followed by a wave of media reports on states' fiscal affairs.[205] As he continued daily campaigning for the state elections in October-November 2023, he blasted the Opposition parties for promising more "revdi", kept silence on his party's government and party in doing the same and worst of all, declared to extend "free" ration to 67% of Indians for *five more years* on November 6, 2023[206] – of course, *without consent or approval* of Council of Ministers[207], which cleared it *23 days later* on November 29, 2023[208]. The Prime Minister's "revdi" discourse can't even be called a double-speak, duplicity or hypocrisy, given that such talk is routine and part of the 'New India' governance model – as every single chapter of this book demonstrates, bringing to mind an observation credited to Rene Descartes' "To know what people really think, pay regard to what they do, rather than what they say" (or even the 2018 animated film The Spiderman: "Don't watch the mouth. Watch the hands").

Like on the two earlier occasions, this debate is more likely to remain seasonal, political, partisan and inconclusive. The Supreme Court issued a fresh notice to the Chief Ministers of Rajasthan and Madhya Pradesh over their announcement of election freebies ahead of the November 2023 elections.[209]

But since, this debate is essentially about fiscal management (freebies, off-budget borrowing and debt), it must to be debated and fixed. But for that the following five steps are needed:

(i) 'Freebie' needs to be defined.

(ii) Limits to freebies must be set – as percentage of revenue or fiscal deficits.

(iii) Accounting standards and disclosure norms for off-budget borrowings must be spelt out.

(iv) 'Fiscal council' must be set up to redefine standards and monitor fiscal management since the CAG is not good enough as a watchdog and Inter-state Council (ISC) and National Development Council (NDC) – both are non-functional after 2015 – must be revived.

(v) Empowerment of 'fiscal council' to set new standards on fiscal deficit and debt since the FRBM Act of 2003 is too old and irrelevant for the current situations as the global standard setting body, the International Monetary Fund (IMF), is seeking an *upward revision*.[210]

Now look at the three key elements of the fiscal components and how the central and state governments perform.

As for 'revdi' (freebies), the RBI's June 2022 report said states had declared "freebies" of 0.1-2.7% of their respective GSDP. Economist Sudipto Mundle (chairman of the Centre for Development Studies) estimated the Central government's "unwarranted subsidies" accounted for 6% of the GDP – far too higher than states' – even without counting corporate tax cut, NPA write offs, PLIs and DLIs, fertilizer subsidy etc. all of which go to big corporate entities.

As for off-budget borrowings, the Central government has been suppressing it year after year, despite providing "statement of extra budgetary resources (EBRs)" – or "statement 27" in the "expenditure profile" – from FY20.[211] Here is a good example. Its "statement 27" of FY24 (BE)[212] shows, between FY17-FY22 (six fiscals), off-budget borrowings amounted to a mere Rs 1.39 lakh crore. But the FY22 budget document[213] showed, the revised estimate (RE) for FY21 for food and fertilizer subsidies were Rs 5.56 lakh crore – against the budgeted Rs 1.86 lakh crore – an excess of Rs 3.7 lakh crore but the entire off-budget borrowings declared for six fiscals of FY17-FY22 was just Rs 1.39 lakh crore!

The huge discrepancies were explained by Delhi-based think tank, Centre for Social and Economic Progress (CSEP), published a study on off-budget borrowings in June 2023, "An Analysis of Off-Budget Borrowings by Indian Governments and their Legal Context".[214] For this study, the CSEP relied on the CAG audit reports because it said budget documents didn't give proper accounts (due to "non-standard accounting"). About the Central government's disclosures, it said: "The CAG audits from 2020-2022 of the union government point out the *inadequacies* of Statement 27, which include *deficiency in the format, and incomplete and non-disclosure of certain entities' debt."* About states, it said, their disclosures are (i) "highly understated" and suffer from additional deficiencies like (ii) for states like Madhya Pradesh, Uttarakhand and Gujarat (all BJP-ruled states) "no data is available at all" and (iii) for many other states, data is "not consistently available for the last few years". *(Emphasis added)*

As for debt, the FRBM Act of 2003 (post 2018 amendment) sets different yardsticks for centre and state government – 40% of the GDP for the former and 20% for the latter (totaling 60% of the GDP). The current levels of debts are:

- States' debts in FY23 (BE) were 29.5% of the GDP (RBI's January 2023 report) – 9.5 percentage points higher than the limit.

- The Centre's debt in FY23 (BE) was 59% of the GDP (Economic Survey 2022-23) – 19 percentage higher than the limit. In absolute numbers, the Centre's debt went up three times – from Rs 56.7 lakh crore in FY14 (50.5% of the GDP).

Denying Rice to States

The Congress won the Karnataka elections in 2023. It had promised five big welfare schemes and implemented it on day 1 in office.[215]

It needed rice from the Central government since the latter procures food grains for public distribution (PDS) and runs the godowns (FCI). By then, the Central government cut off states completely from the PDS supply. It refused to sell rice to Karnataka citing stock constraints – but just as the BJP president JP Nadda had warned the Karnataka voters that if not voted back, the Prime Minister would not give his "ashirwad" (blessings).[216]

The FCI godowns were overflowing with rice stock and the Central government needed to sell them. It opened the FCI's rice stocks for "open market" sale – at a lower price than what Karnataka was offering[217] and yet, there were "no takers"[218]. It explicitly *barred state governments*[219] from participating in the "open market" sale of rice which were meant only for corporate entities to make ethanol. Realizing the vendetta politics and trouble in future, Karnataka demanded that the 16th Finance Commission (which was about to be set up) shouldn't have the term of reference (TOR) that of the 15th Finance Commission had – which tied-up devolution of funds to states' "control or lack of it in incurring expenditure on populist measures".[220]

Now consider another development.

Addressing civil servants was on the Civil Services Day in 2022, the Prime Minister told them to keep a watch on political parties to check misuse of taxpayers' money to create vote banks and ensure that it was used only in national interest.[221] Presumably, he and his government are not to be watched because he and his party have used public money in giving "free" ration (called "Modi's 'namak'") which was encashed by creating a "labharthi varg" – an exclusive vote bank for himself and the BJP – in the 2022 state elections (Introduction). Besides, the Prime Minister is in a permanent (24x7, 365 days) campaign mode – using public money for votes for himself and the party by mixing official tours with political campaigns (Chapter X).

'Saam, Daam, Dand, Bhed'

The BJP is fond of quoting *Chanakya's* four methods of achieving an objective: *saam, daam, dand and bhed* (persuade, bribe, punish, exploit secrets). Apart from others, Amit Shah[222] as the BJP president had famously said in 2018 that Modi's governance model was based on these four methods.

It never occurred to the BJP and its leaders that Chanakya was an ancient philosopher and royal advisor, his methods were meant for kings and their subjects – completely unsuitable for a democratic order in which governments are voted in and out every five years based on their performance and in which Prime Minister is a public servant, not a king.

The Centre-state relations have always been strained – particularly between the rival party-run governments. Since 1980, two commission, the Sarkaria Commission of 1983 and the (MM) Punchhi Commission of 2005, were set up to recommend measures to improve the relationship. But both reports have gathered dust. The Punchhi Commission was set up[223] because the Sarkaria Commission report was two decades old then, which gave its report in 2010. Thirteen years later, after having worked on it for five years, the government told the Rajya Sabha in March 2023 that it was initiating the process for getting fresh comments from states.[224] This brings back the situation to square one.

As a Chief Minister of Gujarat for 12 years before becoming the Prime Minister (the second one after HD Deve Gowda) and having expressed his unhappiness against the Congress-led government in New Delhi, he was expected to do better but he has brought it to a new low. Neither his claim of heralding "cooperative federalism" nor India being the "Mother of Democracy" and "democracy is *in our DNA*" carries credibility.

***

References

1   BJP election manifesto 2014; http://library.bjp.org/jspui/bitstream/123456789/252/1/
      bjp_lection_manifesto_english_2014.pdf

2   PM chairs first meeting of Governing Council of NITI Aayog, Feb 8, 2015; https://
      pib.gov.in/newsite/PrintRelease.aspx?relid=115246

3   Sarkaria Commission report, Chapter III: Administrative Relations, 1998; https://
      interstatecouncil.gov.in/wp-content/uploads/2015/06/CHAPTERIII.pdf

4   Unhappy with finance panel recommendations, Asim calls meeting, Feb 26, 2010;
      https://indianexpress.com/article/cities/kolkata/unhappy-with-finance-panel-
      recommendations-asim-calls-meeting/

5   Fourteenth Finance Commission Report, 2015-20, Dec 15, 2014; https://
      fincomindia.nic.in/writereaddata/html_en_files/oldcommission_html/fincom14/
      others/14thFCReport.pdf

6   PM: Our Government has decided to devolve maximum money to states and
      allow them the required freedom to plan the course of states' development,
      Prime Minister's Office, PIB, Feb 24, 2015; https://pib.gov.in/newsite/PrintRelease.
      aspx?relid=115722

7   Article 280 in The Constitution of India 1949; https://indiankanoon.org/doc/559924/

8   FC FAQ: Finance Commission of India, https://fincomindia.nic.in/ShowContentOne.
      aspx?id=8&Section=1

9   Fifteenth Finance Commission: Terms of Reference, Finance Ministry, GOI,
      2018;   https://fincomindia.nic.in/writereaddata/html_en_files/fincom15/
      TermsofReference_XVFC.pdf

10   Venkataraman J, The Hindu explains: why the 15th Finance Commission has riled
      some States, Mar 29, 2018; https://www.thehindu.com/news/national/the-hindu-
      explains-why-the-15th-finance-commission-has-some-states-riled/article23384141.
      ece; Isaac Thomas TM, An open letter to Finance Ministers, May 14, 2018;
      https://www.thehindu.com/opinion/op-ed/an-open-letter-to-finance-ministers/
      article23874674.ece

11   Mohanty P, A case for greater GST autonomy to states, Fortune India, Jun 6,
      2022; https://www.fortuneindia.com/opinion/a-case-for-greater-gst-autonomy-to-
      states/108459

12   NIPFP 2019: Indian Fiscal Federalism at the Crossroads: Some Reflections,
      NIPFP Working Paper No 260, Apr 30, 2019; https://www.nipfp.org.in/media/
      medialibrary/2019/05/WP_260_2019.pdf

13   XV Finance Commission Report, 2021-26, Oct 2020; https://fincomindia.nic.in/
      writereaddata/html_en_files/fincom15/Reports/XVFC%20VOL%20I%20Main%20
      Report.pdf

14   Chhattisgarh, Jharkhand Seek Share In Revenue When Airports Are Privatised,

Apr 25, 2022; https://www.ndtv.com/india-news/chhattisgarh-jharkhand-seek-share-in-revenue-when-airports-are-privatised-2917430

15   Mohanty P, Why states are denied share of CPSE sale proceeds? Fortune India, Jan 7, 2022; https://www.fortuneindia.com/opinion/why-states-are-denied-share-of-cpse-sale-proceeds/106663

16   Mohanty P, A case for greater GST autonomy to states, Fortune India, Jun 6, 2022; https://www.fortuneindia.com/opinion/a-case-for-greater-gst-autonomy-to-states/108459

17   Funds collected from cesses and surcharges, Rajya Sabha, Mar 21, 2023; https://www.dropbox.com/scl/fi/0qrb4x5dwhtw8w8lp8a4v/RS_Surcharge-Cess-Mar-2023.pdf?rlkey=ngdzeu7mqld46o73jr4sj2cn5&dl=0; Tiwari Suyash and Surya Saket, State of state finances, PRS Legislative Research, Nov 2021; https://prsindia.org/files/budget/budget_state_finance_report/2021/State%20Finances%202021-22.pdf

18   Report No.4 of 2020 - Accounts of the Union Government - Financial Audit, For 2018-19; Comptroller Auditor General of India, GOI, Sept 23, 2020; https://cag.gov.in/webroot/uploads/download_audit_report/2020/Report%20No.%204%20of%202020_Eng-05f808ecd3a8165.55898472.pdf

19   CAG: Centre broke the law, used funds for GST compensation elsewhere, Sept 25, 2020; https://indianexpress.com/article/india/cag-centre-broke-the-law-used-funds-for-gst-compensation-elsewhere-6609749/

20   Finance Minister announces Rs 1.70 Lakh Crore relief package under Pradhan Mantri Garib Kalyan Yojana for the poor to help them fight the battle against Corona Virus, Mar 26, 2020; https://pib.gov.in/PressReleaseIframePage.aspx?PRID=1608345

21   Strain shows: Cooperative federalism twaddle, Jun 23, 2020; https://www.telegraphindia.com/opinion/strain-shows-cooperative-federalism-twaddle-in-india/cid/1782957

22   Union Minister flags 'discrepancies' in use of funds; TMC slams 'lies', Oct 8, 2023; https://indianexpress.com/article/cities/kolkata/union-minister-flags-discrepancies-in-use-of-funds-tmc-slams-lies-8973002/#:~:text=UNION%20MINISTER%20Sadhvi%20Niranjan%20Jyoti%20on%20Saturday%20countered,the%20past%20nine%20years%20are%20%E2%80%9Cindicative%E2%80%9D%20of%20that.

23   Government of India announces a Liberalised and Accelerated Phase 3 Strategy of Covid-19 Vaccination from 1st May, Ministry of Health and Family Welfare, Apr 19, 2021; https://pib.gov.in/PressReleasePage.aspx?PRID=1712710

24   Agarwal Sonal and Bhardwaj Ankur, Covid Vaccination Program: Not a Rosy Picture, Centre for Economic Data & Analysis, Ashoka University, Apr 27, 2021; https://ceda.ashoka.edu.in/covid-vaccination-program-not-a-rosy-picture/

25   Mohanty P, It's time to measure the impact of PLI, DLI schemes, Jun 22, 2023; https://www.fortuneindia.com/opinion/its-time-to-measure-the-impact-of-pli-dli-schemes/113139

26   PM Modi meets Micron CEO Sanjay Mehrotra, talks about semiconductor manufacturing, Jun 22, 2023; https://www.businesstoday.in/technology/news/story/pm-modi-meets-micron-ceo-sanjay-mehrotra-talks-about-semiconductor-manufacturing-386611-2023-06-22; Micron Announces New Semiconductor Assembly and Test Facility in India, Micron Technology, Jun 22. 2023; https://investors.micron.com/news-releases/news-release-details/micron-announces-new-semiconductor-assembly-and-test-facility; Mohanty P, 2 Chinese roadblocks to India's semiconductor ambition, Jul 31, 2023; https://www.fortuneindia.com/opinion/2-chinese-roadblocks-to-indias-semiconductor-ambition/113560

27   Russia's Sputnik V has been approved for emergency use in India Ministry of Health and Family Welfare, Apr 13, 2021; https://pib.gov.in/PressReleseDetail.aspx?PRID=1711558

28   Coronavirus | States, Centre spar over vaccine wastage, May 27, 2021; https://www.thehindu.com/news/national/coronavirus-states-centre-spar-over-vaccine-wastage/article34661604.ece

29   Government of Gujarat Report No. 1 of the year 2021 - State Finances Audit Report of the Comptroller and Auditor General of India for the year ended 31 March 2020, Sept 28, 2021; https://cag.gov.in/webroot/uploads/download_audit_report/2020/SFAR%20English%202019-20-06156deacd8a530.37244727.pdf

30   Reforms galore: Restructuring of central schemes, Jun 29, 2013; https://www.business-standard.com/article/economy-policy/reforms-galore-restructuring-of-central-schemes-113062500699_1.html; Report of the Committee on restructuring of centrally sponsored schemes (CSS), 2011; http://14.139.60.153/bitstream/123456789/1401/1/REPORT%20OF%20THE%20COMMITTEE%20ON%20RESTRUCTURING%20OF%20CENTRALLY%20SPONSORD%20SCHEMES%20%28CSS%29.pdf

31   Aiyar Yamini, How Modi is skewing Centre-State ties, Deccan Herald, Oct 11, 2020; https://www.deccanherald.com/opinion/how-modi-is-skewing-centre-state-ties-900319.html; North Aiyar Yamini & Tillin Louise, "One nation", BJP, and the future of Indian federalism, India Review, 19:2, 117-135, https://doi.org/10.1080/14736489.2020.1744994; PM Modi approves new central scheme to plug infras gaps for the Northeast, Dec 16, 2017; https://economictimes.indiatimes.com/news/economy/infrastructure/pm-modi-approves-two-new-schemes-for-north-east/articleshow/62094855.cms?utm_source=contentofinterest&utm_medium=text&utm_campaign=cppst

32   Ayushman Bharat Health And Wellness Centres Renamed As "Ayushman Arogya Mandir", PTI, Nov 26, 2023; https://www.ndtv.com/india-news/ayushman-bharat-health-and-wellness-centres-renamed-as-ayushman-arogya-mandir-4607833

33   Mohanty P, Revenue shock to hit state capex as GST compensation ends, Fortune India, Jul 8, 2022; https://www.fortuneindia.com/opinion/revenue-shock-to-hit-state-capex-as-gst-compensation-ends/108867

34   Mohanty P, Revenue shock to hit state capex as GST compensation ends, Fortune

India, Jul 8, 2022; https://www.fortuneindia.com/opinion/revenue-shock-to-hit-state-capex-as-gst-compensation-ends/108867

35 Congress CMs protest against exclusion from GoM on GST waiver for COVID-19 products, June 1, 2021; https://www.thehindu.com/news/national/cong-ministers-omission-from-gom-on-gst-exemption-to-covid-19-relief-material-deliberate/article34698358.ece

36 Centre, not States, has resources to reduce tax: Palanivel Thiaga Rajan, Aug 2, 2022; https://www.thehindu.com/news/national/tamil-nadu/centre-not-states-has-resources-to-reduce-tax-palanivel-thiaga-rajan/article65717333.ece

37 Mohan Geeta, A long wait: Indian diaspora sends Covid aid, but it gets stuck in the process, India Today, May 4, 2021; https://www.indiatoday.in/coronavirus-outbreak/story/a-long-wait-indian-diaspora-sends-covid-aid-but-it-gets-stuck-in-the-process-1798879-2021-05-04

38 GST compensation in limbo: Group of ministers on slabs rejig gets 3 more months, Jun 30, 2022; https://www.financialexpress.com/economy/gst-compensation-in-limbo-group-of-ministers-on-slabs-rejig-gets-3-more-months/2577429/

39 Cabinet approves creation of the National Bench of the Goods and Services Tax Appellate Tribunal (GSTAT), Union Cabinet, Jan 23, 2019; https://pib.gov.in/Pressreleaseshare.aspx?PRID=1561067

40 Paliwal Mariya, 50th GST Council Recommends Notification Of GST Appellate Tribunal By The Centre With Effect From 01.08.2023, Jul 12, 2023; https://www.livelaw.in/tax-cases/50th-gst-council-notification-gst-appellate-tribunal-232560

41 Budget Speech, Finance Minister, GOI, Feb 1, 2021; https://www.indiabudget.gov.in/doc/Budget_Speech.pdf

42 Mukherjee Sacchidanand, Revenue Assessment of Goods and Services Tax (GST) in India, Working Paper 385, National Institute of Public Finance and Policy (NIPFP), Jul 2022; https://www.nipfp.org.in/media/medialibrary/2022/07/WP_385_2022.pdf

43 Contribution of Petroleum Sector to Exchequer, PPAC; https://ppac.gov.in/prices/contribution-to-central-and-state-exchequer

44 Centre approves Rs. 56,415 crore to 16 States for Capital Investment, Ministry of Finance, Jun 26, 2023; https://pib.gov.in/PressReleaseIframePage.aspx?PRID=1935378#:~:text=Under%20the%20scheme%2C%20special%20assistance,1%20lakh%20crore.

45 Objectives and Features, NITI Aayog 2015, https://www.niti.gov.in/objectives-and-features

46 Report of the sub-group of chief ministers on rationalization of centrally sponsored schemes, Oct 2015; https://www.niti.gov.in/sites/default/files/2019-08/Final%20Report%20of%20the%20Sub-Group%20submitter%20to%20PM.pdf

47 Aiyar Yamini & Tillin Louise, "One nation", BJP, and the future of Indian federalism, India Review, 19:2, 117-135, https://doi.org/10.1080/14736489.2020.1744994

48   Inter-state Council Secretariat, MHA, https://interstatecouncil.gov.in/isc-meetings/

49   Without planning commission, states & Centre need forum for policy dialogue - N.K. Singh, Dec 11, 2020; https://theprint.in/economy/without-planning-commission-states-centre-need-forum-for-policy-dialogue-n-k-singh/565158/

50   Zonal Council, MHA; https://www.mha.gov.in/en/page/zonal-council

51   Aiyar Yamini & Tillin Louise, "One nation", BJP, and the future of Indian federalism, India Review, 19:2, 117-135, https://doi.org/10.1080/14736489.2020.1744994

52   Reddy YV and Reddy GR, Indian Fiscal Federalism, OUP, 2019; https://india.oup.com/product/indian-fiscal-federalism-9780199493623

53   Interview: Louise Tillin on how the Modi era upended conventional thinking about Indian federalism, Scroll, Nov 21, 2020; https://scroll.in/article/978931/interview-louise-tillin-on-how-the-modi-era-upended-conventional-thinking-about-indian-federalism

54   Why Did 7 States, including Gujarat, Bihar, Back Out Of PM Crop Insurance Scheme? Parl Panel Asks Govt, Aug 10, 2021; https://www.news18.com/news/india/why-did-7-states-including-gujarat-bihar-back-out-of-pm-crop-insurance-scheme-parl-panel-asks-govt-4067984.html

55   Tillin Louise, Indian Federalism, OUP, 2019; https://india.oup.com/product/indian-federalism-9780199495610?

56   Ranjan Alok, Kejriwal's Singapore visit: When Opposition CMs were denied permission to travel abroad, Jul 19, 2022; https://www.indiatoday.in/india/story/arvind-kejriwal-singapore-visit-clearance-opposition-chief-ministers-denied-permission-centre-1977415-2022-07-19

57   Kerala wants aid from UAE, Centre says no, Aug 23, 2018; https://timesofindia.indiatimes.com/india/kerala-wants-aid-from-uae-centre-says-no/articleshow/65508030.cms

58   Koshi Sneha Mary, Kerala Government Gets Huge Bill For Flood Relief, Airlifting Ops, Nov 30, 2018; https://www.ndtv.com/kerala-news/kerala-floods-2018-kerala-government-asked-to-foot-bill-for-airlifting-during-floods-1955512

59   MS Nileena, The Enforcers: How the ED became a political tool, Jun 1, 2023; https://caravanmagazine.in/law/ed-political-tool

60   Are Central Agency Raids on Opp Politicians Politically Motivated Ahead of 2024 Elections, Oct 5, 2023; https://www.timesnownews.com/videos/times-now/shows/are-central-agency-raids-on-opp-politicians-politically-motivated-ahead-of-2024-elections-blueprint-video-104192075

61   Amit Shah's Hindi remark triggers 'imposition' debate: Understanding India's history of language politics, Apr 11, 2022; https://www.firstpost.com/india/amit-shahs-hindi-remark-triggers-imposition-debate-understanding-indias-history-of-language-politics-10542311.html

62   S Venkatesan vs Minister Of State For on 19 August, 2021, Madras High Court, Aug 19,2021; https://indiankanoon.org/doc/80094082/

63   Express View: Let All India Radio co-exist with Akashvani, May 6, 2023; https://indianexpress.com/article/opinion/editorials/express-view-let-all-india-radio-co-exist-with-akashvani-8594099/

64   Mohanty P, Future of Indian trade is in services exports, Apr 18, 2023; https://www.fortuneindia.com/opinion/future-of-indian-trade-is-in-services-exports/112303

65   Sultan Parvez, Indian languages mandatory in all institutions, recommends Amit Shah-led panel, Oct 9, 2022; https://www.newindianexpress.com/thesundaystandard/2022/oct/09/indian-languages-mandatory-in-all-institutions-recommendsamit-shah-led-panel-2506150.html

66   Amit Shah releases textbooks in Hindi for MBBS students in Madhya Pradesh, PTI, Oct 17, 2022; https://www.indiatoday.in/education-today/news/story/amit-shah-releases-textbooks-in-hindi-for-mbbs-students-in-madhya-pradesh-2286136-2022-10-17

67   Sharma Ritu, No takers for GTU's Gujarati medium engg courses, again, Oct 22, 2023; https://indianexpress.com/article/cities/ahmedabad/no-takers-for-gtus-gujarati-medium-engg-courses-again-8994270/

68   Gazette notification S.O.416(E), Ministry of Home Affairs (about BSF jurisdiction), Oct 11, 2021; https://egazette.nic.in/WriteReadData/2021/230337.pdf

69   BSF area expanded, Punjab, Bengal call it intrusion on rights, Oct 14, 2021. https://indianexpress.com/article/india/mha-bsf-jurisdiction-bengal-punjab-assam-gujarat-7570560/

70   Changes in BSF Law to Bring One-Third Area in West Bengal Under Central Agency, Oct 19, 2021; https://thewire.in/rights/changes-in-bsf-law-to-bring-one-third-area-in-west-bengal-under-central-agency

71   Jurisdiction of BSF, Lok Sabha, Nov 30, 2021; http://loksabhaph.nic.in/Questions/QResult15.aspx?qref=28854&lsno=17

72   BSF DG's remark on demographic change to justify a wider berth in border areas is flawed, disturbing, The Indian Express, Dec 2, 2021; https://indianexpress.com/article/opinion/editorials/bsf-powers-jurisdiction-extended-border-issue-7651593/

73   Extending BSF jurisdiction doesn't take away powers of Punjab Police, says SC, Dec 2, 2023; https://indianexpress.com/article/india/extending-bsf-jurisdiction-doesnt-take-away-powers-of-punjab-police-says-sc-9050767/

74   Ministry of Jal Shakti, Notification SO 2842 (E), Gazette of India, Jul 15, 2021; https://static.pib.gov.in/WriteReadData/specificdocs/documents/2021/jul/doc202171641.pdf

75   Andhra Pradesh Reorganization Act of 2014, Gazette notification, Mar 1, 2014; https://www.aplegislature.org/documents/12524/17895/APRegACT2014.pdf/8505fe86-f67b-41a7-ac8f-571f58090586

76   Acharyulu Sridhar, Whether Act 2014 authorised Centre to takeover rivers? Primepost, Aug 11, 2021; https://www.primepost.in/does-the-act-allow-centre-to-

take-over-rivers/; How the Centre's water management boards can spell doom for Andhra Pradesh, Telangana, Down To Earth, Jul 30, 2021; https://www.downtoearth.org.in/news/water/how-the-centre-s-water-management-boards-can-spell-doom-for-andhra-pradesh-telengana-78205

77   After protests, Rajya Sabha clears dam bill, Lok Sabha sees 117% productivity, Dec 3, 2021; https://timesofindia.indiatimes.com/india/after-protests-rajya-sabha-clears-dam-bill-lok-sabha-sees-117-productivity/articleshow/88060257.cms

78   Mohanty P, The Inter-State River Water Disputes (Amendment) Bill 2019: Stoking fears of centralising resolution mechanism, India Today, Jul 31, 2019;   https://www.indiatoday.in/india/story/interstate-river-water-disputes-bill-2019-1575531-2019-07-31; The Inter-State River Water Disputes (Amendment) Bill   2019,   https://prsindia.org/files/bills_acts/bills_parliament/Inter-State%20River%20Water%20Disputes%20(Amendment)%20Bill,%202019.pdf

79   Dam Safety Organisation, Central Water Commission; http://www.cwc.gov.in/damsafety/home

80   Mohanty P, Dam Safety Bill 2019: Why it evokes opposition from other stakeholders, India Today, Aug 2, 2019; https://www.indiatoday.in/india/story/dam-safety-bill-2019-why-evokes-opposition-stakeholders-1576391-2019-08-02; The Dam Safety Bill, 2019 as introduced in Lok Sabha; https://prsindia.org/files/bills_acts/bills_parliament/Dam%20Safety%20Bill,%202019.pdf

81   The   Indian   Forest   (Amendment)   Act,   2017,   Gazette   notification, Jan   5,   2017;   https://upload.indiacode.nic.in/showfile?actid=AC_CEN_16_0_00013_192716_1523350029217&type=notification&filename=gazette_notification_indian_forest_(amendment)_act,_2017.pdf

82   Mohanty P, MSP for minor forest produce: 15 years too late, Governance Now, Apr 14, 2011; https://www.governancenow.com/views/columns/msp-minor-forest-produce-15-years-too-late

83   Mahapatra Dhananjay, Constitutional machinery broke down in Manipur from May to July: Supreme Court, Aug 2, 2023; https://timesofindia.indiatimes.com/india/constitutional-machinery-broke-down-in-manipur-from-may-to-july-supreme-court/articleshow/102328486.cms?from=mdr

84   Christophe Jaffrelot writes: BJP is chipping away at India's federalism, Jun 23, 2023; https://indianexpress.com/article/opinion/columns/christophe-jaffrelot-writes-bjp-is-chipping-away-at-indias-federalism-8680814/

85   Hindu 2021d: SC refuses to order CBI probe into death of ex-Arunachal CM Kalikho Pul, Apr 29, 2021; https://www.thehindu.com/news/national/sc-refuses-to-consider-plea-seeking-cbi-probe-into-death-arunachal-pradesh-ex-cm-kalikho-pul/article34440243.ece

86   After Kashmir, Delhi Sets Sights On Another Muslim-Majority Region, Article14, May 26, 2021; https://www.article-14.com/post/after-kashmir-delhi-sets-sights-on-another-muslim-majority-region; Rajsekhar M, Marooned: Praful Patel's war on

Lakshadweep, Caravan, Jun 2, 2022; https://caravanmagazine.in/politics/praful-khoda-patel-lakshadweep-economy-protests

87   Rai Arpan, Indian state leader says traces of centuries-long Portuguese rule should be 'wiped away', Jun 8, 2023; https://www.independent.co.uk/asia/india/goa-portuguese-rulers-pramod-sawant-wiped-b2353775.html; Portuguese destroyed temples, wipe away their signs: Goa CM Pramod Sawant, Jun 8, 2023; https://www.hindustantimes.com/cities/others/goas-chief-minister-blames-portuguese-for-temple-destruction-plans-to-erase-colonial-signs-in-state-s-new-journey-101686048827880.html Let Goa be, TOI editorial, Jun 9, 2023; https://timesofindia.indiatimes.com/blogs/toi-editorials/let-goa-be/

88   Kumar Sanjay (CSDS), Governors in the firing line, Jul 7, 2014; https://www.thehindu.com/opinion/lead/Governors-in-the-firing-line/article11255891.ece

89   Governor's resignation: RK Singh backs Anil Goswami's move for asking for resignations, Jun 21, 2014; https://m.economictimes.com/news/politics-and-nation/governors-resignation-r-k-singh-backs-anil-goswamis-move-for-asking-for-resignations/articleshow/36912626.cms?_oref=cook; Home secretary admits to suggesting Uttarakhand governor to quit, Oct 15, 2014; http://timesofindia.indiatimes.com/articleshow/44826819.cms?utm_source=contentofinterest&utm_medium=text&utm_campaign=cppst

90   Sheila Dikshit becomes the 8th governor to resign after Modi became PM, Aug 26, 2014; http://timesofindia.indiatimes.com/articleshow/40921143.cms?utm_source=contentofinterest&utm_medium=text&utm_campaign=cppst

91   BP Singhal vs Union of India & Anr, Supreme Court, May 7, 2010; https://indiankanoon.org/doc/1471968/

92   Mizoram Governor Aziz Qureshi sacked, Mar 29, 2015; https://indianexpress.com/article/india/india-others/mizoram-governor-aziz-qureshi-sacked/

93   Sheila Dikshit becomes the 8th governor to resign after Modi became PM, Aug 26, 2014; http://timesofindia.indiatimes.com/articleshow/40921143.cms?utm_source=contentofinterest&utm_medium=text&utm_campaign=cppst

94   Dhavan Rajeev, From Goa to Manipur, Modi's Governors Have Sabotaged Democracy, Mar 23, 2017, https://thewire.in/politics/modis-governors-goa-manipur; Dhavan Rajeev 2020, The Revolving Door for Ranjan Gogoi Does the Supreme Court and Parliament No Credit, Mar 25, 2020; https://thewire.in/law/the-revolving-door-for-ranjan-gogoi-does-the-supreme-court-and-parliament-no-credit

95   Devendra Fadnavis sworn in as Maharashtra Chief Minister after Ajit Pawar ditches uncle Sharad Pawar, Nov 23, 2019; https://www.thehindu.com/news/cities/mumbai/devendra-fadnavis-takes-oath-as-maharashtra-cm-ajit-pawar-as-deputy-cm/article61615444.ece

96   The Government of India (Transaction of Business) Rules, 1961; https://cabsec.gov.in/writereaddata/transactionofbusinessrulescomplete/completeaobrules/english/1_Upload_2214.pdf

97   Bal Hartosh Singh, The Modi-Shah model of governance—stealth, self-aggrandisement and stupidity, Nov 30, 2019; https://caravanmagazine.in/politics/modi-shah-model-of-governance

98   Explained: As Maharashtra political crisis continues, a look at why the Assembly is without a Speaker, Jun 28, 2022; https://www.firstpost.com/politics/explained-as-maharashtra-political-crisis-continues-a-look-at-why-the-assembly-is-without-a-speaker-10844821.html

99   Joshi Yogesh, Central probing agencies a common thread among some rebel Sena leaders, Jun 24, 2022; https://www.hindustantimes.com/cities/pune-news/central-probing-agencies-a-common-thread-among-some-rebel-sena-leaders-101656092905184.html; Shaikh Jeeshan, Rebel Sena leaders, MLAs in Eknath Shinde camp facing ED, IT heat: Sarnaik, Jadhav, Gawali, Jun 24, 2022; https://indianexpress.com/article/political-pulse/rebel-sena-leaders-mlas-in-shinde-camp-facing-ed-it-heat-sarnaik-jadhav-gawali-7986497/

100 After ED books him, NCP's Sharad Pawar says 'never been to jail, will be pleased to go', Sept 25, 2019; https://www.hindustantimes.com/mumbai-news/after-ed-books-him-ncp-s-sharad-pawar-says-never-been-to-jail-will-be-pleased-to-go/story-3PTIMH3zlujTgsnAI2FR2N.html; Sharad Pawar meets PM Modi, says raised ED action on Sanjay Raut, Apr 7, 2022; https://www.hindustantimes.com/india-news/pawar-meets-modi-says-raised-ed-action-on-raut-101649271573195.html

101 Subhash Desai vs Principal Secretary, Governor of Maharashtra & Ors., Supreme Court, May 11, 2023; https://main.sci.gov.in/supremecourt/2022/20234/20234_2022_1_1502_44512_Judgement_11-May-2023.pdf

102 Bhatia Gautam, The Supreme Court's Maharashtra Political Crisis Judgment – I: To Be Hoisted on Someone Else's Petard, May 11, 2023; https://indconlawphil.wordpress.com/2023/05/11/the-supreme-courts-maharashtra-political-crisis-judgment-i-to-be-hoisted-on-someone-elses-petard/?utm_source=substack&utm_medium=email

103 Explained: How the Election Commission recognised Eknath Shinde's faction as the real Shiv Sena, Feb 21, 2023; https://scroll.in/article/1044266/explained-how-the-election-commission-recognised-eknath-shindes-faction-as-the-real-shiv-sena

104 Uddhav Thackeray Faction Moves Supreme Court Challenging ECI Order Recognising Eknath Shinde As Official 'Shiv Sena, Feb 20, 2023; https://www.livelaw.in/top-stories/uddhav-thackeray-faction-moves-supreme-court-challenging-eci-order-recognising-eknath-shinde-as-official-shiv-sena-222002

105 Tripathi Ashish, SC gives Maharashtra Speaker till Dec 31 to decide on disqualification petitions against Sena MLAs, Jan 31 for NCP, Oct 30, 2023; https://www.deccanherald.com/india/maharashtra/sc-gives-maharashtra-speaker-till-dec-31-to-decide-on-disqualification-petitions-against-sena-ncp-mlas-2747813

106 4 of 9 NCP MLAs, kin in graft dock: What will ED, agencies do now, Jul 3, 2023; https://indianexpress.com/article/cities/mumbai/cases-against-ncp-leaders-cabinet-ministers-shinde-fadnavis-maharashtra-government-8697138/

107 Opposition can only guarantee corruption, says PM; cites laundry list of scam allegations, Jun 28, 2023; https://economictimes.indiatimes.com/news/politics-and-nation/opposition-can-only-guarantee-corruption-says-pm-cites-laundry-list-of-scam-allegations/articleshow/101314560.cms?utm_source=contentofinterest&utm_medium=text&utm_campaign=cppst; 'NCP Behind Scams Worth Rs 70,000 Crore': PM Modi's 'Ghotala Metre' Attack On Opposition; India Today; https://www.youtube.com/watch?v=qcBhu-S_7Io

108 Sharad Pawar's swipe at PM Modi: He alleged corruption, now welcomes, Jul 3, 2023; https://indianexpress.com/article/cities/pune/not-worried-go-to-people-rebuild-party-pawar-jibe-modi-8697555/

109 Dhavan Rajeev, From Goa to Manipur, Modi's Governors Have Sabotaged Democracy, Mar 23, 2017, https://thewire.in/politics/modis-governors-goa-manipur; Dhavan Rajeev 2020, The Revolving Door for Ranjan Gogoi Does the Supreme Court and Parliament No Credit, Mar 25, 2020; https://thewire.in/law/the-revolving-door-for-ranjan-gogoi-does-the-supreme-court-and-parliament-no-credit

110 44 Years in Politics, Yet Lalu Prasad Yadav's Relevance in Bihar Remains Undiminished, New Indian Express, Apr 10, 2021; https://thewire.in/politics/44-years-in-politics-yet-lalu-prasad-yadavs-relevance-in-bihar-remains-undiminished

111 ED attaches over Rs 4-crore assets in Bihar's Srijan money laundering case, Jun 30, 2021; https://www.newindianexpress.com/nation/2021/jun/30/ed-attaches-over-rs-4-crore-assets-in-bihars-srijan-money-laundering-case-2323591.html; How a Bihar NGO siphoned off crores in govt funds under govt nose — with some help, Indian Express, Aug 21, 2017: https://indianexpress.com/article/india/bihars-srijan-scandal-700-crore-part-i-how-a-bihar-ngo-siphoned-off-crores-in-govt-funds-under-govt-nose-with-some-help-4803269/

112 Karnataka Live | Yeddyurappa resigns; Kumaraswamy to become CM on Wednesday, May 19, 2018; https://www.thehindu.com/elections/karnataka-2018/karnataka-assembly-floor-test-live-updates/article23934015.ece; 'Aaya Ram, Gaya Ram': A contemporary history of defections to the BJP, The Week, Mar 12, 2020; https://www.theweek.in/news/india/2020/03/12/aaya-ram-gaya-ram-a-contemporary-history-of-defections-to-the-bjp.html

113 Leaked Snoop List Suggests Surveillance May Have Played Role in Toppling of Karnataka Govt in 2019, Jul 20, 2021; https://thewire.in/politics/karnataka-government-toppling-pegasus-spyware-surveillance

114 DK Shivakumar: I chose jail over BJP's offer of joining them and becoming the Deputy CM, May 10, 2023; https://twitter.com/bhatia_niraj23/status/1656358642059460614

115 Sharma Aman, 8 Cases Filed by CBI, ED, IT & 1 ED Summon — What Blocks DK Shivakumar's Way to Karnataka CM Chair, May 17, 2023; https://www.news18.com/explainers/ed-cbi-cases-against-dk-shivakumar-blocks-karnataka-cm-7843831.html

116 Aakar Patel | What was behind Cong K'taka win: The questions that need to be asked, May 16, 2023; https://www.deccanchronicle.com/opinion/columnists/150523/aakar-patel-what-was-behind-cong-ktaka-win-the-questions-that-ne.html

117 'Sovereignty' row: BJP tells EC to deregister Cong, act against Sonia; speech transcript shows she didn't use word, May 8, 2023l; https://indianexpress.com/article/political-pulse/bjp-complains-ec-sonia-gandhis-sovereignty-karnataka-remark-8598037/

118 Karnataka Will See Riots if Congress Comes to Power, Says Amit Shah at Rally, Apr 26, 2023; https://thewire.in/communalism/karnataka-will-see-riots-if-congress-comes-to-power-says-amit-shah-at-rally

119 Manipur ethnic gulf widens, big relocation on: Security officials, May 30, 2023; https://timesofindia.indiatimes.com/city/imphal/manipur-ethnic-gulf-widens-big-relocation-on-security-officials/articleshow/100607090.cms

120 Jyotiraditya Scindia rewarded for delivering Madhya Pradesh to BJP, PTI, Jul 7, 2021; http://timesofindia.indiatimes.com/articleshow/84205417.cms?utm_source=contentofinterest&utm_medium=text&utm_campaign=cppst

121 Menon Aditya, Madhya Pradesh: Why Did Kamal Nath Govt Fall & What Happens Next? Mar 20, 2020; https://www.thequint.com/news/politics/madhya-pradesh-kamal-nath-resigns-shivraj-chouhan-jyotiraditya-scindias

122 Dynastic politics biggest enemy of democracy, 'fake Samajwadi' denotes 'parivarvad', says PM Modi, Feb 9, 2022; https://economictimes.indiatimes.com/news/politics-and-nation/dynastic-politics-biggest-enemy-of-democracy-fake-samajwadi-denotes-parivarvad-says-pm-modi/articleshow/89458154.cms?utm_source=contentofinterest&utm_medium=text&utm_campaign=cppst

123 Tamil Nadu Governor puts order sacking jailed minister Senthil Balaji on hold, to consult AG, Jun 30, 2023; https://www.financialexpress.com/india-news/tamil-nadu-governor-puts-order-sacking-jailed-minister-senthil-balaji-on-hold-to-consult-agnbsp/3148860/

124 Contradicting TN Governor's Claim, RTI Response Reveals 13 Bills Pending Before Him, Jun 26, 2023 https://thewire.in/government/thirteen-bills-pending-before-tn-governor-despite-his-earlier-claims

125 Ignominious Exit Aside, Kiran Bedi's Term as Puducherry LG Greatly Helped the BJP, The Wire, Feb 23, 2021: https://thewire.in/politics/kiran-bedi-ignominious-exit-as-puducherry-lg-help-bjp

126 Puducherry CM resigns; Speaker rules trust vote defeated, The Hindu, Feb 22, 2021; https://www.thehindu.com/news/cities/puducherry/puducherry-cm-narayanasamy-loses-trust-vote/article33900712.ece

127 Mamata blocks Governor Dhankar on Twitter: 'He abuses me, officers', Feb 1, 2022; https://indianexpress.com/article/cities/kolkata/mamata-banerjee-blocks-governor-jagdeep-dhankar-twitter-7749956/

128 West Bengal will not release chief secretary, Mamata Banerjee tells Modi, May 31,

2021; https://scroll.in/latest/996208/west-bengal-chief-secretary-unlikely-to-report-to-centre-today-state-yet-to-issue-release-order

129 Menon Kesava, How conflicts between Governors and State governments are playing out, Dec 1, 2022; https://frontline.thehindu.com/politics/how-conflicts-between-governors-and-state-governments-are-playing-out/article66188258.ece

130 Philip Shaju, 8 Bills awaiting Governor assent, Pinarayi govt mulls moving SC, Sept 28, 2023; https://indianexpress.com/article/cities/thiruvananthapuram/8-bills-awaiting-governor-assent-pinarayi-govt-mulls-moving-sc-8959336/

131 Thomas A, Supreme Court reminds governors not to delay assent to bills, Apr 25, 2023; https://www.hindustantimes.com/india-news/supreme-court-reminds-state-governors-to-give-assent-to-bills-as-soon-as-possible-to-avoid-delay-and-defeat-of-parliamentary-democracy-101682363717007.html

132 After Kashmir, Delhi Sets Sights On Another Muslim-Majority Region, Article14, May 26, 2021; https://www.article-14.com/post/after-kashmir-delhi-sets-sights-on-another-muslim-majority-region; Rajsekhar M, Marooned: Praful Patel's war on Lakshadweep, Caravan, Jun 2, 2022; https://caravanmagazine.in/politics/praful-khoda-patel-lakshadweep-economy-protests

133 Vasudev K, Punjab row: Governor warns CM with case, Central rule, Aug 26, 2023; https://indianexpress.com/article/cities/chandigarh/president-punjab-gov-banwarilal-purohit-bhagwant-mann-8909017/

134 96 Unclaimed Bodies, 5,668 Weapons Looted: State Data On Manipur Violence, Sept 15, 2023; https://www.ndtv.com/india-news/manipur-violence-in-numbers-175-dead-96-unclaimed-bodies-5-668-weapons-looted-4391476?pfrom=video-read

135 Singh Vijaita, Manipur Police register criminal case against Assam Rifles, Aug 9, 2023; https://www.thehindu.com/news/national/manipur-police-file-criminal-case-against-assam-rifles/article67172647.ece

136 Thapar Karan, Watch | Manipur Governor 'Deeply Concerned' by Violence But Ignored by Biren Govt: Brinda Karat, Aug 14, 2023; https://thewire.in/video/watch-manipur-violence-governor-biren-singh-brinda-karat

137 Thomas A, Supreme Court reminds governors not to delay assent to bills, Apr 25, 2023; https://www.hindustantimes.com/india-news/supreme-court-reminds-state-governors-to-give-assent-to-bills-as-soon-as-possible-to-avoid-delay-and-defeat-of-parliamentary-democracy-101682363717007.html

138 G Ananthakrishnan, Governors must act before state govts come to SC: CJI Bench on Punjab govt plea on pending Bills, Nov 7, 2023; https://indianexpress.com/article/india/sc-updated-status-punjab-govt-plea-against-guv-delay-nod-bills-9015573/

139 Nair Shilpa, Tamil Nadu Assembly readopts all 10 bills that Governor RN Ravi had returned, Nov 18, 2023; https://www.indiatoday.in/india/story/tamil-nadu-assembly-session-mk-stalin-governor-rn-ravi-returned-bills-for-assent-2464393-2023-11-18

140 Congress shifts Rajasthan MLAs to Jaisalmer hotel; BJP takes a dig, PTI, Jul

31, 2020; http://timesofindia.indiatimes.com/articleshow/77288959.cms?utm_source=contentofinterest&utm_medium=text&utm_campaign=cppst

141   Soren government in Jharkhand to seek trust vote on Monday to dispel 'uncertainty', Sept 4, 2022; https://timesofindia.indiatimes.com/india/soren-government-in-jharkhand-to-seek-trust-vote-on-monday-to-dispel-uncertainty/articleshow/93975922.cms

142   Analysis of Re-contesting MPs and MLAs Who Changed Parties-Pan-India Since 2016, Association for Democratic Reforms, Mar 11, 2021; https://adrindia.org/content/analysis-re-contesting-mps-and-mlas-who-changed-parties-pan-india-2016

143   Jammy and Kashmir Reorganization Act, 2019, Aug 9, 2019; https://egazette.nic.in/WriteReadData/2019/210407.pdf

144   Wondering how Amit Shah dismantled #Article370 so fast and furiously? Read this, Aug 5, 2019; https://www.newslaundry.com/2019/08/05/how-amit-shah-narendra-modi-dismantled-article-370-jammu-kashmir; Ali Asim, Why Does the BJP Get Away With Lies? Aug 14, 2019; https://thewire.in/politics/bjp-kashmir-terrorist-threat-lie-article-370

145   Jammu-Kashmir: BJP pulls out of Mehbooba Mufti government, says alliance with PDP untenable, Jun 19, 2018; https://indianexpress.com/article/india/bjp-pdp-alliance-break-up-narendra-modi-mehbooba-mufti-amit-shah-jammu-and-kashmir-government-5223787/

146   About 4,000 people arrested in Kashmir since August 5: govt sources to AFP, Aug 18, 2019; https://www.thehindu.com/news/national/about-4000-people-arrested-in-kashmir-since-august-5-govt-sources-to-afp/article61582905.ece

147   About 4,000 people arrested in Kashmir since August 5: govt sources to AFP, Aug 18, 2019; https://www.thehindu.com/news/national/about-4000-people-arrested-in-kashmir-since-august-5-govt-sources-to-afp/article61582905.ece

148   J&K: More Than 2,300 Arrested Under UAPA Since 2019, Nearly 50% Still In Custody, Aug 15, 2021; https://thewire.in/rights/jk-more-than-2300-arrested-under-uapa-since-2019-nearly-50-still-in-custody

149   Night before Centre's August 5 move, BJP reached out to Congress chief whip in Rajya Sabha; he quit next morning, Aug 7, 2021: https://indianexpress.com/article/india/abrogation-of-article-370-night-before-centres-august-5-move-bjp-reached-out-to-congress-chief-whip-in-rs-he-quit-next-morning-7440572/lite/?__twitter_impression=true

150   Mohanty P, Rebooting Economy 42: How will changes to land laws in Jammu and Kashmir help, and whom?, Business Today, Nov 2, 2020; https://www.businesstoday.in/latest/economy-politics/story/indian-economy-how-will-changes-to-land-laws-in-jammu-and-kashmir-help-and-whom-277373-2020-11-02

151   The Constitution (Application to Jammu and Kashmir) Order, 2019, Aug 5, 2019; https://egazette.nic.in/WriteReadData/2019/210049.pdf

152   Article 370 in The Constitution Of India 1949; https://indiankanoon.org/doc/666119/

153   Article 35A: Constitution: The Constitution of India, Ministry of Law and Justice; https://legislative.gov.in/sites/default/files/coi-4March2016.pdf

154   Mahapatra Dhananjay, Pulwama terror strike forced govt to decide on scrapping Article 370: SG tells Supreme Court, Aug 29, 2023; https://timesofindia.indiatimes.com/india/pulwama-terror-strike-forced-govt-to-decide-on-scrapping-article-370-sg-tells-supreme-court/articleshow/103149619.cms

155   Drabu Haseeb A, J&K delimitation exercise sets a dangerous precedent, Indian Express, Dec 31, 2021; https://indianexpress.com/article/opinion/columns/jk-delimitation-exercise-sets-a-dangerous-precedent-7698697/

156   Delimitation Commission for J&K, Assam, Manipur, Arunachal, Nagaland Formed, Mar 7, 2020; https://thewire.in/government/delimitation-commission-jk-assam-manipur-arunachal-nagaland

157   Ali Jehangir, Dangers of adding 25 lakh to 76 lakh voter base; Jehangir Ali, J&K Regional Parties Go Into a Huddle as EC Expects Two Million New Voters; Aug 19, 2022; https://thewire.in/government/jammu-kashmir-regional-parties-election-commission-new-voters

158   Pradeep Nimisha S, Kill switch. India is second in the world in internet shutdowns in H1CY23, Jul 31, 2023; https://www.thehindubusinessline.com/data-stories/data-focus/india-is-second-in-the-world-in-internet-shutdowns-in-h1cy23/article67131027.ece

159   Naik Mubashir, 500 Days: Kashmiri Journalist Fahad Shah's Incarceration Is An Exercise In Assumptions & Retribution, Jun 9, 2023; https://article-14.com/post/500-days-kashmiri-journalist-fahad-shah-s-incarceration-is-an-exercise-in-assumptions-retribution--648fbd385207e

160   Bakshi Gursimran K, If there were no protests in Kashmir post-Article 370, it means right people had been put under arrest, Tushar Mehta jokes on Day 13 of hearings, Aug 31, 2023; https://theleaflet.in/if-there-were-no-protests-in-kashmir-post-article-370-it-means-the-right-people-had-been-put-under-arrest-tushar-mehta-jokes-on-day-13-of-the-hearings/

161   Shabir Zaid B, Debt, Distress & Antidepressants: Thousands Struggle To Recover From A J&K Trade Route Closed 4 Years Ago, Aug 21, 2023; https://article-14.com/post/debt-distress-antidepressants-thousands-struggle-to-recover-from-a-j-k-trade-route-closed-4-years-ago-64e2d26386a39

162   Javeed Auqib, Soap Star, Social Rebel, Family Provider: In Kashmir, An Executed Daughter & The Absence Of Closure, Aug 11, 2023; https://article-14.com/post/soap-star-social-rebel-family-provider-in-kashmir-an-executed-daughter-the-absence-of-closure-64d59c2f2398e

163   Sharma Arun and Masood Bashaarat, Drug pandemic in J&K: Networks of terror intersect with drug supply lines, on ground, from sky and online, Aug 20, 2023; https://indianexpress.com/article/express-exclusive/networks-of-terror-intersect-

with-drug-supply-lines-on-ground-from-sky-and-online-8900226/; Iqbal Naveed, One addict walks into Srinagar OPD every 12 minutes: Valley's drug pandemic, Aug 20, 2023; https://indianexpress.com/article/express-exclusive/jammu-kashmir-drug-menace-one-addict-walks-into-srinagar-opd-every-12-minutes-8897386/

164   Arvind Kejriwal, who wants full statehood for Delhi, supports J&K becoming two UTs, Aug 5, 2019; https://www.indiatoday.in/india/story/we-hope-this-will-bring-peace-arvind-kejriwal-supports-govt-on-article-370-1577380-2019-08-05

165   The Gazette of India, March 28, 2021; https://www.livelaw.in/pdf_upload/gnctd-amendemnt-bill-391206.pdf

166   Centre trying to cripple Delhi govt to avenge poll loss: Kejriwal, Jul 30, 2015; https://www.hindustantimes.com/delhi/centre-trying-to-cripple-delhi-govt-to-avenge-poll-loss-kejriwal/story-Uvwc9B2vk8nF1M6PJw2wpK.html

167   Delhi Deadlock: How it Was Under Sheila Dikshit and What Changed After Arvind Kejriwal Came to Power, Feb 14, 2019; https://www.news18.com/news/india/delhi-deadlock-how-it-was-under-sheila-dikshit-and-what-changed-after-arvind-kejriwal-came-to-power-2035781.html

168   Delhi: Passed in Assembly, 14 bills stuck with L-G, govt depts, Sept 5, 2019; https://indianexpress.com/article/cities/delhi/passed-in-assembly-14-bills-stuck-with-l-g-govt-depts-5966994/

169   Ministry of Home Affairs Notification, SO 1368(E), May 21, 2015; https://www.mha.gov.in/sites/default/files/video_87.pdf

170   GNCTD vs Union of India, Supreme Court, May 11, 2023; https://main.sci.gov.in/supremecourt/2016/29357/29357_2016_1_1501_44512_Judgement_11-May-2023.pdf

171   Khetan Ashish, Did the Supreme Court Truly Give the Delhi Government a 'Big Win'? May 15, 2023; https://thewire.in/law/supreme-court-delhi-government-union-centre

172   The GNCTD (Amendment) Ordinance, 2023; https://hindi.oneindia.com/downloads/2023/5/245962.pdf

173   Chishti Aiman J, Parliament Passes Delhi Services Bill (GNCTD Amendment Bill), Aug 7, 2023; https://www.livelaw.in/news-updates/parliament-passes-delhi-services-bill-gnctd-amendment-bill-234627#:~:text=The%20Rajya%20Sabha%20on%20Monday,Lok%20Sabha%20on%20August%2003.

174   SC asks Centre to suggest names of 5 officers for Delhi chief secretary, PTI, Nov 24, 2023; https://www.business-standard.com/india-news/sc-asks-centre-to-suggest-names-of-5-officers-for-delhi-chief-secretary-123112400925_1.html; 'Are you stuck with one person?': SC on Centre's proposal to extend tenure of Delhi Chief Secy Naresh Kumar, Nov 29, 2023; https://indianexpress.com/article/cities/delhi/sc-centres-proposal-extend-tenure-chief-secy-naresh-kumar-9045998/

175   Anand Utkarsh, SC gives nod for six-month extension to Delhi chief secy, Nov 30,

2023; https://www.hindustantimes.com/india-news/sc-gives-nod-for-six-month-extension-to-delhi-chief-secy-101701284085008.html

176   No L-G nod, HC sets aside Delhi Govt's doorstep ration scheme, May 19, 2022; https://www.tribuneindia.com/news/nation/no-l-g-nod-hc-sets-aside-delhi-govts-doorstep-ration-scheme-396281

177   Government of NCT of Delhi vs Union of India and others, Supreme Court, Jul 4, 2018; https://main.sci.gov.in/supremecourt/2016/29357/29357_2016_Judgement_04-Jul-2018.pdf

178   "Illiterates From Top To Bottom": Arvind Kejriwal Amid Delhi Budget Row, Mar 21, 2023; https://www.ndtv.com/india-news/illiterates-from-top-to-bottom-arvind-kejriwal-amid-delhi-budget-row-3880438

179   Arvind Kejriwal's jibe at PM Modi, calls him 'chauthi pass Raja...'Mirror Now, Apr 18, 2023; https://www.youtube.com/watch?v=cexQAqdJXPA; At AAP rally, Kejriwal narrates the story of an 'uneducated king', PTI, Jun 11, 2023; https://www.theweek.in/news/india/2023/06/11/at-aap-rally-kejriwal-narrates-the-story-of-an-uneducated-king.html

180   Kissu Sagarika, 'Vote for educated person' — how a video turned Unacademy teacher Karan Sangwan's life 'upside down', Aug 20, 2023; https://theprint.in/india/vote-for-educated-person-how-a-video-turned-unacademy-teacher-karan-sangwans-life-upside-down/1721623/

181   Manish Sisodia, top Delhi minister, arrested on corruption charge, Deb 27, 2023; https://www.aljazeera.com/news/2023/2/27/dirty-politics-top-delhi-minister-arrested-in-liquor-probe

182   Chinna Man Aman Singh, Congress fooling farmers with loan waiver promise: Narendra Modi, Jan 5, 2019; https://indianexpress.com/article/india/congress-fooling-farmers-with-loan-waiver-promise-narendra-modi-5522512/

183   "Political Stunts": PM Modi On Farm Loan Waiver In Congress-Ruled States, Jan 2, 2019; https://www.ndtv.com/india-news/political-stunts-pm-modi-on-farm-loan-waiver-in-congress-ruled-states-1971055

184   Uttar Pradesh elections: Modi promises loan waiver for farmers, slams Akhilesh for crime stats, Feb 16, 2017; https://www.indiatoday.in/assembly-elections-2017/uttar-pradesh-assembly-election-2017/story/uttar-pradesh-elections-narendra-modi-hardoi-loan-waiver-farmers-961006-2017-02-16

185   Report of the Internal Working Group to Review Agricultural Credit, RBI, Sept 13, 2019; https://rbidocs.rbi.org.in/rdocs/PublicationReport/Pdfs/WGREPORT101A17FBDC144237BD114BF2D01FF9C9.PDF

186   Mohanty P, Usurious ways of out-of-line SBI branch; practice rampant in banks, Dec 10, 2021; https://www.fortuneindia.com/opinion/usurious-ways-of-out-of-line-sbi-branch-practice-rampant-in-banks/106350

187   Waiving off Agricultural loan, Ministry of Agriculture & Farmers Welfare, Jul 24, 2018; https://pib.gov.in/PressReleasePage.aspx?PRID=1539828 Report of the

Internal Working Group to Review Agricultural Credit, RBI, Sept 13, 2019; https://www.rbi.org.in/Scripts/PublicationReportDetails.aspx?UrlPage=&ID=942; Verma Lalmani, Dec 11 effect? Jharkhand 3rd BJP state to announce aid to farmers, Dec 22, 2018; https://indianexpress.com/article/india/dec-11-effect-jharkhand-3rd-bjp-state-to-announce-aid-to-farmers-raghubar-das-5504780/; Assam government approves ⊚600 crore farm loan waiver, PTI, Dec 18, 2018; https://www.livemint.com/Politics/BYsmP9e4ok0cLqimG3pQiI/Assam-government-approves-Rs-600-crore-farm-loan-waiver.html; Singh Harsha K, Polls Ahead, Vasundhara Raje Announces 8,000-Crore Farm Loan Waiver, Feb 13, 2018; https://www.ndtv.com/india-news/rajasthan-budget-2018-vasundhara-raje-announces-farm-loan-waiver-that-will-cost-rs-8000-crore-1811923

188   Verma Lalmani, Dec 11 effect? Jharkhand 3rd BJP state to announce aid to farmers, Dec 22, 2018; https://indianexpress.com/article/india/dec-11-effect-jharkhand-3rd-bjp-state-to-announce-aid-to-farmers-raghubar-das-5504780/

189   Langa Mahesh, Gujarat writes off farmers' power bills, Dec 18, 2018; https://www.thehindu.com/news/national/other-states/gujarat-writes-off-farmers-power-bills/article25776176.ece;

190   Mohanty P, How does Rahul Gandhi plan to finance his 'Minimum Income Guarantee to every poor' scheme? Can this be done? Jan 29, 2019; https://www.dailyo.in/politics/rahul-gandhi-minimum-income-guarantee-scheme-non-performing-assets-29177

191   Mohanty P, 'How does Rahul Gandhi plan to finance'

192   RBI Bulletin June 2022; https://rbidocs.rbi.org.in/rdocs/Bulletin/PDFs/RBIJUNEBULLETIN2022BC3DC495560D430E9D6E7A0122FF225E.PDF

193   RBI Bulletin July 2022; https://rbidocs.rbi.org.in/rdocs/Bulletin/PDFs/RBIJULYBULLETIN202267BBAD9D5BDB477F9A644D27F58FD3DB.PDF

194   Mukherjee Sacchidananda, Analysis of State Budgets 2022-23 of Major States in India, NIPFP Working Paper No. 386; Aug 3, 2022; https://www.nipfp.org.in/media/medialibrary/2022/08/WP_386_2022.pdf

195   State Finances: A Study of Budgets of 2022-23, RBI, Jan 2023; https://rbidocs.rbi.org.in/rdocs/Publications/PDFs/0STATEFINANCE2022233E17F212337844888755EFDBCC661812.PDF; Mohanty P, States' fiscal space rapidly shrinking, here's why..., Feb 15, 2023; https://www.fortuneindia.com/opinion/states-fiscal-space-rapidly-shrinking-heres-why/111603s

196   Mohanty P, Centre vs states: Who's fiscally more profligate? Jul 26, 2022; https://www.fortuneindia.com/opinion/centre-vs-states-whos-fiscally-more-profligate/109074#:~:text=The%202022%20budget%20document%20shows,3.7%25%20for%20the%20corresponding%20years.; Mohanty P, A case for greater GST autonomy to states, Jun 6, 2022; https://www.fortuneindia.com/opinion/a-case-for-greater-gst-autonomy-to-states/108459

197   Revdi culture dangerous, must end: PM Modi slams politics of freebies, Jul 17,

2022; https://indianexpress.com/article/cities/lucknow/revdi-culture-dangerous-must-end-pm-modi-slams-politics-of-freebies-8033948/; PM Modi slams 'revdi culture', says a large section wants its end, Oct 23, 2022; https://indianexpress.com/article/cities/bhopal/pm-modi-slams-revdi-culture-says-a-large-section-wants-its-end-8225638/

198 Bid adieu to 'missing MP', Irani asks Amethi voters, offers sugar at Rs 13 a kg as deal sweetener, Apr 21, 2019; https://www.businesstoday.in/pti-feed/story/bid-adieu-to-missing-mp-irani-asks-amethi-voters-offers-sugar-at-rs-13-a-kg-as-deal-sweetener-191740-2019-04-21

199 Jaiswal Anuj, Vote for BJP, celebrate Holi with a free gas cylinder, says Amit Shah in UP rally, Feb 15, 2022; https://timesofindia.indiatimes.com/india/vote-for-bjp-celebrate-holi-with-a-free-gas-cylinder-says-amit-shah-in-up-rally/articleshow/89591559.cms

200 List plea on freebies before three-judge bench at the earliest: SC, Nov 2, 2022; https://economictimes.indiatimes.com/news/politics-and-nation/list-plea-on-freebies-before-three-judge-bench-at-the-earliest-sc/articleshow/95238735.cms?from=mdr

201 Vaidyanathan Iyer P, Election Commission wants parties to disclose cost of 'revdi', and how it will be funded, Oct 4, 2022; https://indianexpress.com/article/political-pulse/election-commission-quantify-revadi-promises-freebies-political-parties-polls-8189249/

202 Unpacking deprivation bundles to reduce multidimensional poverty, UNDP-OPHI, Oct 17, 2022; https://hdr.undp.org/content/2022-global-multidimensional-poverty-index-mpi#/indicies/MPI; Unstacking global poverty: Data for high impact action, Jul 11, 2023; https://hdr.undp.org/system/files/documents/hdp-document/2023mpireportenpdf.pdf; Half of the world's poor live in just 5 countries, World Bank, 2019; https://blogs.worldbank.org/opendata/half-world-s-poor-live-just-5-countries#:~:text=The%205%20countries%20with%20the,Congo%2C%20Ethiopia%2C%20and%20Bangladesh.

203 Global Hunger Index 2022 scores; https://www.globalhungerindex.org/pdf/en/2022.pdf; The state of food security and nutrition in the world, FAO, IFAD et al 2022; https://www.fao.org/3/cc0639en/cc0639en.pdf

204 Full Transcript of PTI's Exclusive Interview with Prime Minister Narendra Modi, Sept 3, 2023; https://www.ptinews.com/news/big-story/transcript-of-pti-s-exclusive-interview-with-prime-minister-narendra-modi/642493.html

205 Study: States may have breached debt ceilings, Sept 7, 2023; https://timesofindia.indiatimes.com/business/india-business/study-states-may-have-breached-debt-ceilings/articleshow/103335843.cms?from=mdr; Politics of handouts: Freebies walk thin line between welfare and wasteful, Sept 10, 2023; https://www.business-standard.com/politics/politics-of-handouts-freebies-walk-thin-line-between-welfare-and-wasteful-123091000501_1.html; https://timesofindia.indiatimes.com/business/india-business/freebies-vs-welfarism-as-supreme-court-mulls-over-matter-rbi-raises-red-flags/articleshow/103322782.cms?from=mdr

206   As Modi extends free ration scheme for 5 more years, Congress says it indicates economic distress, inequality, Nov 6, 2023; https://indianexpress.com/article/political-pulse/narendra-modi-extends-free-ration-scheme-congress-says-economic-distress-inequality-9014095/

207   Dash Dipak K, Grain subsidy to cost government 11L crore over 5 years, Nov 7, 2023; https://timesofindia.indiatimes.com/india/grain-subsidy-to-cost-government-11l-crore-over-5-years/articleshow/105023700.cms?from=mdr

208   Free Foodgrains for 81.35 crore beneficiaries for five years: Cabinet Decision, Ministry of Consumer Affairs, Food & Public Distribution, Nov 29, 2023; https://pib.gov.in/PressReleaseIframePage.aspx?PRID=1980689

209   Sharma Padmakshi, Supreme Court Issues Notice To Rajasthan & Madhya Pradesh On Plea Challenging Chief Ministers Announcing, Oct 6, 2023; https://www.livelaw.in/top-stories/supreme-court-issues-notice-to-rajasthan-madhya-pradesh-on-plea-challenging-chief-ministers-announcing-election-freebies-239484

210   Mohanty P, Beware! IMF's rethink on debt-to-GDP, fiscal deficit limits has consequences, Mar 11, 2022; https://www.fortuneindia.com/opinion/beware-imfs-rethink-on-debt-to-gdp-fiscal-deficit-limits-has-consequences/107414

211   Budget speech (2021-22), Feb 1, 2021; https://www.indiabudget.gov.in/budget2021-22/doc/Budget_Speech.pdf

212   Statement 27: Expenditure Profile 2023-24; https://www.indiabudget.gov.in/doc/eb/stat27.pdf

213   Budget at a glance, 2021-22; https://www.indiabudget.gov.in/budget2021-22/doc/Budget_at_Glance/budget_at_a_glance.pdf

214   Gupta Shruti and James Kevin, An Analysis of Off-Budget Borrowings by Indian Governments and their Legal Context, CSEP Working Papr 53, Jun 2023; https://csep.org/wp-content/uploads/2023/06/Off-Budget-Borrowings-2.pdf

215   TA Johnson, On Day 1, Karnataka Cabinet clears 5 promises, to cost Rs 50k crore per year, May 21, 2023; https://indianexpress.com/article/cities/bangalore/on-day-1-karnataka-cabinet-clears-5-promises-to-cost-rs-50k-cr-per-yr-8620448/#:~:text=On%20Day%201%2C%20Karnataka%20Cabinet,Bangalore%20News%20%2D%20The%20Indian%20Express

216   Ataulla Naheed, Karnataka pays the price with rice, Jul 2, 2023; https://www.nationalheraldindia.com/india/karnataka-pays-the-price-with-rice

217   India's FCI sells 170 lt rice as recycled PDS rice rules cheaper, Jul 6, 2023; https://www.thehindubusinessline.com/economy/agri-business/only-170-tonnes-out-of-386-lt-rice-sold-in-fci-auction-wheat-offtake-improves/article67048166.ece#:~:text=Food%20Corporation%20of%20India%20(FCI,cent%20in%20the%20first%20round.

218   Sharma Harikishan, No takers in FCI rice e-auction, Centre hints at tweaking policy, Jul 11, 2023; https://indianexpress.com/article/india/no-takers-in-fci-rice-e-auction-centre-hints-at-tweaking-policy-8825013/

219   Sharma Harikishan, States barred from buying FCI rice under open market, supply for ethanol rises, Jul 27, 2023; https://indianexpress.com/article/india/states-barred-from-buying-fci-rice-under-open-market-supply-for-ethanol-rises-8862258/

220   Moudgal Sandeep, Drop 'penalties' for populist schemes, Karnataka tells Centre. Aug 14, 2023; https://timesofindia.indiatimes.com/india/drop-penalties-for-populist-schemes-karnataka-tells-centre/articleshow/102705342.cms?from=mdr

221   Sharma Harikishan, See if a party is raising black money via policy shift: PM Modi to bureaucrats, Apr 22, 2023; https://indianexpress.com/article/india/civil-services-day-modi-bureaucrats-public-money-8568893/

222   Amit Shah in Pune, says 'Chanakya niti' is Modi's principle, Jul 9, 2018; https://www.hindustantimes.com/pune-news/amit-shah-in-pune-says-chanakya-niti-is-modi-s-principle/story-OcnQ4naRlsNFkd4yzE6IGO.html

223   The Commission of Centre-state relations; MHA, 2005; https://www.mha.gov.in/sites/default/files/2022-08/CCSRelation120508%5B1%5D.pdf

224   Barman Sourav Roy, 5 yrs after Punchhi panel work 'completed', Centre set to invite state views again, Mar 1, 2023; https://indianexpress.com/article/political-pulse/punchhi-panel-work-centre-state-views-8472376/

Chapter VII

Command-and-Control Economy

In Introduction, it has been pointed out that the current regime has vastly improved the delivery of welfare schemes ("new welfarism") and building of highways. The only other area where it can legitimately claim success in the delivery of "minimum governance" or "ease of doing business" or "trust-based governance" for private businesses. But the government's economic regime best answers to the description of being a "command-and-control" one – which is the focus of this chapter and a *defining marker* (not listed in Introduction).

Here, the "trust-based governance" needs to be explained because this is a new coinage – first used in the 2022 budget speech. Finance Minister Nirmala Sitharaman foregrounded it with a sentence worth re-reading: "For the Amrit Kaal, the next phase of Ease of Doing Business (EODB 2.0) and Ease of Living, will be launched. In our endeavour to improve productive efficiency of capital and human resources, we will follow the idea of 'trust-based governance'."[1] Then she explained what "trust-based governance" means: "This new phase will be guided by an active involvement of the states, digitization of manual processes and interventions, integration of the central and state-level systems through IT bridges, a single point access for all citizen-centric services, and a standardization and removal of overlapping compliances. Crowdsourcing of suggestions and ground level assessment of the impact with active involvement of citizens and businesses will be encouraged."

She then added that after coming to power in 2014, her government had reduced over *25,000 compliances* and repealed *1,486 Central laws* for improve both productive efficiency of capital and *human resources*. In her 2023 budget speech[2], she recorded further improvements and promised more: "For enhancing ease of doing business, more than *39,000 compliances* have been reduced and more than *3,400 legal provisions* have been decriminalized. For furthering the trust-based governance, we have introduced the *Jan Vishwas Bill* to amend 42 Central Acts." The Jan Vishwas Act of 2023[3] that followed further decriminalized about a hundred corporate offences by amending 42 Central laws, which include the Air (Prevention and Control of Pollution) Act of 1981 and Environment (Protection) Act, 1986. This emphasis should not surprise. Traditionally, the BJP has been a "Brahmin-Bania" party (upper castes and traders), until Prime Minister Modi expanded its base, deepened politics-business nexus through a virulent form of crony capitalism and opaque Electoral Bond.

But 'Modinomics' is far from being liberal (neoliberal) or 'market' determined/driven as the government would like to project. There is little economic logic, evidence, planning or preparation in economic policies and the adverse consequences simply don't matter. Hence, there is no scope for course corrections. Many have tried to make sense of it. Journalist Sagar[4] drew parallel with RSS's trade union leader and founder of Swadeshi Jagaran Manch Dattopant Thengadi's book "Third Way"[5] to highlight the blending of Hindutva's religious thinking and 'swadeshi' economic concepts. "According to Thengadi's ideal model", Sagar wrote, "an industrial structure should be "financed by commoners," "utilized by consumers," "coordinated by Parliament," "assisted by state," and ultimately "governed by Dharma." Economist Prabhash Ranjan wrote[6] the Prime Minister is "no champion of the free market". Some economists call it *voodoo economics*[7] for good reasons. There is, however, a method to it. Read on to find.

From 'Swadeshi' to Private Wealth Creators

When Vajpayee, the first Prime Minister from the BJP, came to head a coalition government (NDA-I) in late 1990s-early 2000s, his party was strongly opposed to the Congress' pro-reforms and liberalized economics; it had its 'swadeshi" model (self-reliant) which was suspicious of globalization, foreign investment and multinationals but the very first budget it presented in 1998, by then Finance Minister Yashwant Sinha, took to the Congress route. When asked why, Sinha had explained then that once in government, they were better informed about the state of economy and did what the situation demanded. From the beginning, the Modi government took forward this pro-reform and liberalized policies but with a *twist*. This twist was so subtle at the beginning that it took years to decipher.

Immediately after coming to power the government had turned inwards ('swadeshi') in one important way: Reinstating the failed import substitution policy of 1960s and 1970s. It took then Chief Economic Advisor (CEA) Arvind Subramanian to blow the whistle on it – in 2020 with fellow economist Shoumitro Chatterjee in their paper "India's Inward (Re)Turn: Is it Warranted? Will it Work?"[8]

He had quit his job two years earlier. The import substitution policy erected trade barriers by raising tariff; it was officially acknowledged and became part of the "AatmaNirbhar Bharat" mission launched amidst the pandemic lockdown of 2020.

With the import barrier came a flurry of policies and practices billed variously as "master stroke" or "surgical strike" – dismantling of the Planning Commission, demonetization, Insolvency and Bankruptcy Code (IBC), GST, national pandemic lockdown, NPA write offs, corporate tax cuts, fresh incentives to industry called Production Linked Incentive (PLIs) and Design Linked Incentives (DLIs), new farm laws, new labour codes and finally the failed license-permit raj (in 2023) dismantled in 1980s and 1990s.[9] None of it has served the economy well or likely to. In fact, the irrational demonetization, botched GST and mismanagement of the pandemic inflicted immense and avoidable pain on the people and the economy[10]; the new farms laws were withdrawn, the new labour codes are yet to be operationalized and the outcome of the others would be clear soon.

The Prime Minister never hid his pro-business approach but it went up several notches higher a year before the pandemic hit. He called private businesses "wealth creators". In his national address on August 15, 2019, he said[11]: "We should stop viewing our Wealth Creators with suspicion: they deserve greater respect. Greater wealth creation will lead to greater distribution and help in the welfare of poor people.". The context wasn't explained then but would become clear during the *2020 pandemic lockdown* when the stated policy of disinvestment and privatization (or "strategic disinvestment") of sick PSUs was changed to allow *en masse* and *indiscriminate* sale of public assets, along with a string of reforms – except for a few in the "strategic sectors". In *August 2021* (just after the second wave of the pandemic) came the National Monetization Pipeline (NMP) – envisaging handing over all public built infrastructure to private business to run. Both reflect the Prime Minister's oft-repeated philosophy of "opportunity-in-crisis"[12] – in this case, *en mass* privatization during the pandemic crisis. Until then, the Prime Minister loved to take public vows in public rallies by reciting poet and lyricist Prasoon Joshi's poem "saugandh mujhe is mitti ki, main desh nahin bikne doonga"[13] (I vow to this soil of my country I will not let this country to be sold), which was also the BJP *theme song* in the 2014 elections.

The only justification the Prime Minister ever offered for this shift is: The government has no business to be in business.[14] Finance Minister Nirmala Sitharaman warned[15] the Parliament that "unless wealth creators create wealth" there would be nothing to re-distribute among the poor. When the Opposition interpreted it as promotion of crony capitalism, BJP MP KJ Alphonse said[16] India should "worship" Mukesh Ambani and Gautam Adani – the two richest Indians running infrastructure conglomerates – as wealth and job creators. There is *no evidence* of such private wealth creators sharing their wealth with the poor or creating enough jobs to fill the gaps.[17] Philanthropy is very patchy and limited as against what is seen in western countries[18] and to add to the trouble, the corporate social responsibility (CSR) has been *significantly diluted* (Chapter I). Private businesses are also *solely responsible* for India's banking stress (loan defaults and NPAs) – contributing 98.6% to the entire NPAs during FY03-FY20[19], are increasingly fleeing India with their wealth and bank loans[20] and those making huge profits are doing so by cutting jobs and wages[21] and 'predatory' pricing[22].

Here is one good example.

The Gautam Adani's rise coincides with that of the Prime Minister. From an obscure businessman of Gujarat, Adani rose to be the richest Indian and third richest in the world and his group became the largest conglomerate (in market capitalization) in India in 2022.[23] Then came the US-based short seller Hindenburg's report in January 2023[24] – alleging that the Adani group was "pulling the largest con job in corporate history" and is engaged "in a brazen stock manipulation and accounting fraud scheme over the course of decades". The group lost about $100 billion in less than 10 days.[25] Adani has been a close ally from the Prime Minister's Gujarat days[26]; his aircrafts were used for the 2014 campaign[27] and also used to fly to take charge in New Delhi in May 2014.[28] Adani lost his position as the richest individual[29] and his group slid back to No. 3 in India (in market capitalization) – after the Tatas and the Reliance (Mukesh Ambani group)[30]. The group is too big, nevertheless. It runs infrastructure, controlling 30% of freight through a dozen shipping ports, 23% of airline passengers through seven airports, operates the biggest generators of private electricity and holds 30% of grains in its warehouses[31], besides building highways, developing real estate, investing big in green energies and running media outlets. But what is its *contribution to the Indian economy*? Too insignificant to count. Here is why.

(a) In terms of jobs, with 23,000 employees, it is too small for the Reliance (3.43 lakh) and even smaller for the Tata (9.35 lakh) – as per the disclosures in their respective websites.[32]

(b) In terms of net profits, not one Adani company figures in the top 100 companies, while several of those from the (Mukesh) Ambani and Tata figure at the top.[33]

(c) In terms of tax payment, none of its companies come in the top 30 companies (unlike the Reliance and Tata group companies).[34]

So, the Adani group has done very well for itself, but it contributes little to Indian's prosperity. His is part of a new growth paradigm better known as 'National Champions' – crony capitalism by another name in the Indian context and another *defining marker* of the post-2014 era– which is unlikely to work for the people's wellbeing or work wonders that South Korean and Chinese equivalents have done.

'National Champions' and Crony Capitalism

Private businesses have enjoyed state patronage, both before and after the 1991 liberalization. They get cheap land (often acquired on their behalf by governments using emergency provisions), cheap electricity and mines, tax holidays, incentives in normal times and fiscal stimulus, bail outs during crises, write-off loans defaults (NPAs) etc. What changed is the sheer magnitude and the expanse. So much so that the first Chief Economic Advisor (CEA) of the Modi government, Arvind Subramanian, flagged the spectacular rise of 'As' – the Gautam Adani and Mukesh Ambani groups – as dominant players in farm trade and green energy, causing *anxiety*[35] among farmers and others. Some may argue that both during the licence-permit raj and the subsequent liberalized era India witnessed cronyism, which is true but with an important difference: Cronyism began to recede after liberalization and new entities like the Infosys, TCS and Wipro emerged as truly global players as trade barriers fell.[36] But before going forward, here is a caveat: The purpose this chapter is not to undermine the significance of private businesses in India's growth and development in any way but to warn against its *dark sides* of crony capitalism.

That India has a 'National Champions' model of growth became a subject of global discussion after the Hindenburg report on the Adani group came in early 2023. There is no official word on it; economists and political scientists have taken note of the government's overt policies and cues from similar global experiences to qualify it as such. Scholar Milan Vaishnav[37] of the US-based Carnegie Endowment for International Peace (CEIP), best explained this model as one which Modi "honed" as Gujarat Chief Minister (2001 to 2014) and which "premised on the state giving a set of favoured corporations concessions on land, on capital, on tax, on environmental and building clearance in exchange for setting up shop", which he then "scaled up" at national level as the Prime Minister.

'National Champions' usually means a government promoting a few private business groups to implement its development priorities or push growth – ending up with a few oligopolistic conglomerates in line with Indonesia's 'National Champions', South Korean 'Chaebols' or China's SOEs. By the very concept, 'National Champions' are state-backed, too big to fail (TBTF), too powerful for normal laws, scrutiny, regulatory oversights and too big to compete with.[38]

A host of economists and political scientists went on to flag the dark sides of this model of India. Economist Nauriel Roubini[39], who had accurately warned about the 2007-09 Global Recession, recognized that "in some ways" such concentration of economic power with private conglomerates had served India well, but he warned: "...the dark side of this system is that these conglomerates have been able to capture policymaking to benefit themselves.

This has had two broad, harmful effects: it is stifling innovation and effectively killing early-stage startups and domestic entrants in key industries; and it is changing the government's Make in India programme into a counterproductive, protectionist scheme." He reminded, "the Asian financial crisis of the 1990s demonstrated that, over time, the partial capture of economic policy by crony capitalist conglomerates will hurt productivity growth by hampering competition, inhibiting Schumpeterian "creative destruction" and increasing inequality."

Political scientist Ashutosh Varshney wrote[40] the Indian model resembled the South Korean 'Chaebols' but with clear differences. South Korea produced global leaders like Samsung, Hyundai and LG and its model worked because they were "heavily international trade-oriented", competed with world best producers, international competition provided a "disciplinary check" on their businesses, generating "huge efficiencies"; they produced cell phones, computers, electronics, semiconductors and auto, capturing significant global export markets for their country. That is, there was competition and incentives for innovation. In contrast, he wrote, the Adani group is "mostly in non-tradable sectors" and the efficiency gains that came from international trade were "missing".

Former RBI Deputy Governor Viral Acharya wrote a paper "Replete with Contradictions, Brimming with Opportunities, Saddled with Challenges"[41] in March 2023 to point out how India's "Big 5" companies – the Reliance, Tata, Birla, Adani and Bharti groups – were *profiteering* by misusing their market dominance. He sought their dismantling ("dismantle or reduce the market power of Indian conglomerates"), no less. His data showed that post-1991 liberalization, the Indian Big 5 have not only expanded their footprint in more and more sectors but increased their share in total assets of the non-financial sectors from 10% in 1991 to nearly 18% in 2021 – while the share of the next big five business groups fell from 18% in 1992 to less than 9%. "In other words, Big-5 grew not just at the expense of the smallest firms, but also of the next largest firms", he found. About their profiteering, he wrote, their "rising market power is coincident with rising markups since 2016", adding: "Markups (profiteering) fell gradually from early 1990s until 2013, but started rising steadily and significantly thereafter, scaling in 2021 the high level of 1.4 in 1990s, and even when capacity utilization in the Indian industry was low during the pandemic due to collapse of aggregate demand." Markup refers to artificial hike in price; Acharya measured by the *rise in price relative to 1% rise in input cost*.

He presented the following two graphs in support of his arguments – which are reproduced here. *Image 1* shows the rise in market share of Big-5 vis-à-vis the next 5 companies across industries and Image 2 the rise in markups by the Big-5 vis-à-vis the next 5 companies.

Image 1: Rising market share of Big-5 vis-à-vis the next 5 across industries

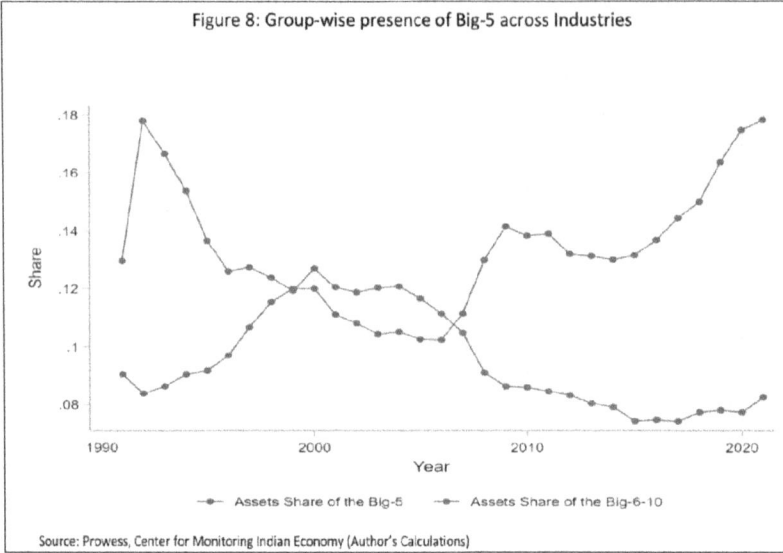

Figure 8: Group-wise presence of Big-5 across Industries

Source: Viral Acharya's 2023 paper, 'Replete with Contradictions, Brimming With Opportunities, Saddled with Challenges'

Image 2: Rising profiteering (markup in prices) by Big-5 vis-à-vis next 5

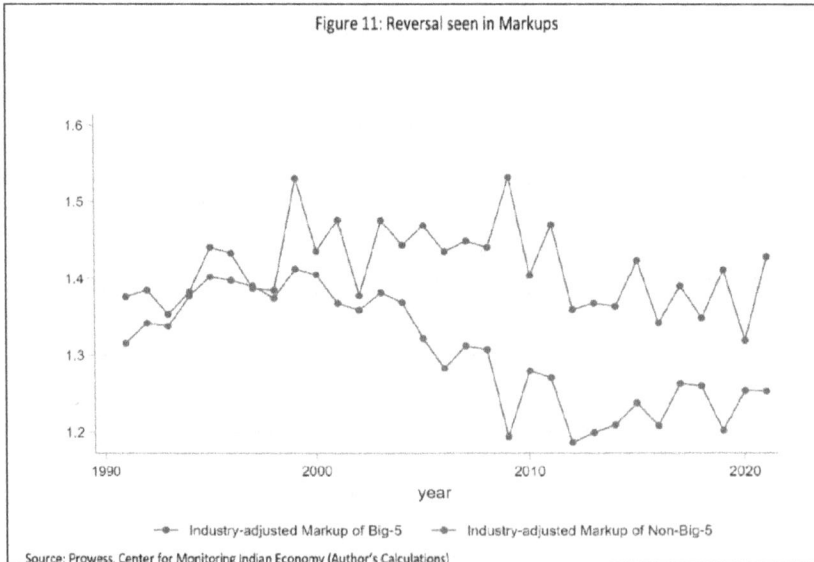

Figure 11: Reversal seen in Markups

Source: Viral Acharya's 2023 paper, 'Replete with Contradictions, Brimming With Opportunities, Saddled with Challenges'

While Acharya, who now teaches in the US, could figure it out and explain why "core" (non-food and non-fuel) prices were going up in India even while the input costs were going down in 2022 and 2023 – profiteering by the Big-5. But the RBI couldn't. It merely expressed its wonderment at this phenomenon, in one of its reports in 2023[42], without even trying to understand, let alone explain.

Economists in the US and Europe called this phenomenon "sellers' inflation"[43] or "greedflation[44] – a global phenomenon in 2022 and 2023 – something that baffled[45] the US and European bankers as until 2022, it would have been "heretical" to even suggest profiteering as a cause of inflation. The global world has come to believe since 1970s that inflation is caused either due to (i) excess aggregate demand in relation to capacity (Keynesian) or (ii) too much money chasing too few goods (monetarist or neoliberal). When input cost goes up, both the interpretations restrict themselves to "purely a matter of inflated wages" – that is, there is "no role for profits or the power of firms to set prices" – as economists Isabella M Weber and Evan Wasner[46] explained.

Primacy to Private Cronies

In 2019, news portal Newsclick (which was raided by the Income Tax Department and ED in 2021 and 2023[47]) had tracked *18 deals*[48] the Anil Ambani group and the Adani group signed –while accompanying the globe-trotting Prime Minister on his tours. These deals spanned *16 countries* and in the areas of defence, logistics and power. At the time the Opposition was asking the Prime Minister if he was business development managers of private companies.[49]

One such was the Rafale jet deal of *7.8 billion Euro* between the governments of India and France (Dassault) in 2016. Anil Ambani, who was part of the Prime Minister's delegation, walked away with an offset contract of Rs 21,000 crore for his company *Reliance Defence* – incorporated two weeks before this contract[50] despite having no experience or expertise in fighter jets whatsoever. In contrast, the tried and tested public sector entity Hindustan Aeronautical Limited (HAL), which was pushed out, has been building fighter aircrafts for 60 years, including the Sukhois and LCAs (Tejas). In 2018, French President Francois Hollande, who was in power at the time, said the Indian government proposed the Anil Ambani-led Reliance Defence as offsets partner for Dassault. "We did not have a say. The Indian government proposed this service group, and Dassault negotiated with Ambani. We did not have a choice, we accepted the interlocutor that was given to us", he was quoted as saying.[51] Later in 2023, it was revealed that Ambani had sought tax waiver (tax claim of 151 million Euro) for his French subsidiary – which was finally *cut down*[52] to 6.6 million Euros. By then, the fate of Dassault Aviation's Rafale *joint venture* (with Reliance Aerostructure Limited (RAL)[53] had *collapsed*[54] because of the latter's *inability to make the required investments*.

In 2019, Anil Ambani was *pleading bankruptcy,* to avoid paying Rs 550 crore to Ericsson (which challenged it raising the Rafale deal)[55] and told a UK court in 2021 that his investments had collapsed and his net worth was "zero"[56] to plead inability to pay $925 million loaned by three Chinese banks on his *personal guarantee.* The *Pandora Papers* of 2021[57] – an investigation by the International Consortium of Investigative Journalists (ICIJ) into wealth hidden in tax havens – revealed that the *bankrupt* Anil Ambani had stashed away *$1.3 billion* in a complex web of secret offshore companies. Now the Rafale project is jeopardized.

In one such trip of 2015, both the Reliance Power (Anil Ambani group) and Adani Power signed MoUs in *Bangladesh* to set up power plants and export coal-fired power from India. An official statement of Ministry of Foreign Affairs (MEA) recorded the Prime Minister's direct involvement, on June 7, 2015[58]: "He (Modi) requested Prime Minister Hasina for facilitating the entry of Indian companies in the power generation, transmission and distribution sector of Bangladesh."

It is part of those MoUs with Bangladesh that the Adani Group signed a power purchase agreement (PPA) in 2017 for supply of coal-fired powered from the group's Godda plants in Jharkhand. The PPA remained shrouded in secrecy until Bangladesh cried foul about unfair pricing and sought revision in 2023.[59] At the heart of the conflict is tax incentives the Adani Group receives from the government of India which isn't factored-in in the cost of supply and the provision that Bangladesh would pay a certain amount as capacity and maintenance charges, regardless of whether it generates any electricity.[60] One of the Adani's Godda plant (800 MW of 1,600 MW) started supplying power to Bangladesh in April 2023.[61]

The project is controversial for other reasons too. *One,* the Godda plants are the first-of-its-kind Special Economic Zone (SEC) in India – to exclusively export power to another country – which was approved in 2019. It enjoys a host of fiscal and non-fiscal incentives apart from direct and indirect tax benefits.[62] *Two,* the Godda project has been at the heart of conflicts with local tribals unhappy at the unfair means in which their villages were acquired by the Adani group. The forest and village land were acquired allegedly bypassing the Forest Rights Act of 2006 and laws to protect environment and tribals' oter special rights.[63]

Another was the Adani group's acquisition of the Carmichael coal mining and railway projects in *Australia.* Newsclick recorded that Gautam Adani accompanied the Prime Minister to Brisbane in 2014. It wrote: "Adani and State Bank of India Chairperson Arundhati Bhattacharya signed a memorandum of understanding (MoU) for a Rs 6,200-crore loan for what was claimed to be the world's "largest greenfield coal mining project" which is currently embroiled in several controversies." Interestingly, the state-run SBI rushed to a heavily indebted Adani group by announcing funding $1 billion (the net debt of the group stood at \$13 billion in 2014[64]) after several global banks had refused to lend to the group because of environmental concerns[65].

Similar linkage between the Prime Minister and Adani came from *Sri Lanka* in 2022 – *outside* of the 18 cases tracked by the Newsclick. MMC Ferdinando, chairman of Sri Lanka's Ceylon Electricity Board (CEB), told their parliamentary panel in 2020 that he was told by President Rajapaksa about the Prime Minister pressuring him to give the wind power project directly to the Adani group (500 MW renewable energy project in Sri Lanka's Mannar district). President Rajapaksa denied the claim and a day later, Ferdinando retracted his statement and resigned.[66] In September 2023, news broke that the Sri Lankan government wants to convert it to government-to-government deal to get around the legal difficulty of having given the contract without open tendering.[67]

Yet another case is that of Adani group's ventures in Israel after 2017. Modi is the first Prime Minister of India to visit Israel and change India's traditional foreign policy on the Palestine-Israel conflict. The Adani group signed a joint venture with an Israel company in 2018 on drones and acquired Israeli Haifa port in 2023[68] – which is proposed to be connected in the Middle East corridor announced during the G20 summit in New Delhi in 2023. A New York Times investigation[69] revealed in 2022, that during this visit (NSA Ajit Doval was part of the visit) India had acquired the notorious military-grade spyware Pegasus used for spying on civilians as part of a "package of sophisticated weapons and intelligence gear worth roughly \$2 billion".

How Adani Acquired Airports: From *no experience* in aviation or running airports, the Adani group won the bid to control and run all six top-earning public airports[70] across the country (run by the public sector Airport Authority of India) in a single go 2019 – when they were privatized. Through this (airports of Ahmedabad, Lucknow, Jaipur, Mangaluru, Guwahati and Thiruvananthapuram), it became the *largest* private airport operator overnight. This happened despite *strong objections* from the Finance Ministry and NITI Aayog over building a *private monopoly* – which preferred not to handover more than two airports to a single private operator.[71] The lease period too was extended to 50 years – from earlier 30 years.

A year later in 2020, the Adani group acquired the Mumbai International Airport and also got the ownership of the upcoming Navi Mumbai Airport from the GVK Group and other minor partners[72] – taking its tally to *8 airports*. Investigations[73] revealed that just a month before the GVK gave up its bid for the Mumbai airports (it had developed the Mumbai one and was building the Navi Mumbai one) after, in June 2021, the CBI filed FIR for financial irregularities in the development of the Mumbai international airport and in July 2021, the Enforcement Directorate (ED) registered a case of money laundering basing on this FIR. For the record, two years later, amidst the Adani-Hindenburg heat, the

GVK denied that it handed over the Mumbai airports under pressure.[74] In the case of the Navi Mumbai airport, the SBI underwrote its entire debt requirement of Rs 12,770 crore in 2022.[75]

In the case of Jaipur airport, a special notification was used to give exemption from GST (18%) for the transfer of operations, management and development as a "going concern" – contrary to what was ruled in the case with the Ahmedabad and Lucknow airports.[76] During the previous UPA regime, the development and operations of the Delhi and Mumbai international airports had been given to private companies (GMR and GVK, respectively) for 30 years – which was increased to 50 years.

Too many coincidences

There are many instances of political connections facilitating specific policies to allow rent-seeking and profiteering to the select few.

Here are some.

(i)   On July 31, 2023, the Reliance launched JioBook. Four days later on August 3, the government announces *immediate and overnight ban* (another top-down policy) on imports of laptops, personal computers, tablets etc. on the plea that now "valid licence for restricted imports" is needed – *without* giving reason (but "national security risk" was forwarded unofficially as the reason, while admitting that not a single such complaint has been received[77] and readying this as the reason when the US and China complained it to the WTO[78]). The JioBook is "manufactured" in China[79], not India – in effect, giving license only to the Reliance to import laptops, PCs and tablets from abroad (back to pre-1991 License Raj[80]). It created immediate chaos as *90% of all domestic sales*[81] are imported, forcing the DGFT to put it *on hold* for three months. The Reliance Jio had used *predatory pricing*[82] to kill competition in telecom and emerge as the dominant player in 2016.

(ii)   The government's launch of "National Green Hydrogen Mission"[83] on March 21, 2022, for which Rs 20,000 crore was later allocated – *without*[84] even a policy framework in place "to support establishment of Green Hydrogen ecosystem". Around the time, the Adani group[85] and the Ambani group[86] unveiled their plans to make India a hydrogen hub.

(iii)   In August 2021, *corporate monk* Ramdev (Ramkrishna Yadav) declared his foray into palm oil plantation in Assam, Tripura and other northeastern states, through his acquired company Ruchi Soya. Seven days later, the government announced a Rs 11,040 crore National Mission on Edible Oils-Oil Palm (NMEO-OP)[87] to boost domestic production of palm oil in northeastern states and Andaman and Nicobar Islands.

The story Ramdev owning the Ruchi Soya and turning its fortune around is an interesting tale. In 2019, the Ruchi Soya went to bankruptcy for its inability to pay a debt of over Rs 12,146 crore; of this, financial creditors, led by public sector's State Bank of India (SBI) owed Rs 9,384.75 crore. Ramdev's Patanjali group bought it for Rs 4,350 with the banks led by SBI taking a haircut of Rs 5,291.56 crore (56.4%). Some of the same banks, led by the very same SBI, then lent Rs 3,233 crore to Ramdev's Patanjali to buy the same Ruchi Soya. In short, public banks lost 56.4% of the loans to the Ruchi Soya but pumped in money to Ramdev's firm to buy the very same bankrupt company.[88]

With a 99% ownership by the Patanjali (0.97% public holding), the Ruchi Soya's stocks zoomed 8,764% in one year, to attract adverse comments from market regulator SEBI[89] to rethink its policy about public shareholding for firms emerging from bankruptcy. In, April 2022, the Patanjali became *completely debt free*[90] by paying back its loans from money raised through follow-on public offering (FPO). It prompted two investigative journalists probing the matter to describe it as "an instructive example of nationalized banks, regulatory institutions and tribunals enabling massive wealth accumulation".[91]

Ramdev was also part of the anti-corruption movement led by Anna Hazare (who completely disappeared from public life and anti-corruption crusade once Modi became the Prime Minister) and Arvind Kejriwal (who floated the Aam Admi Party later and became Delhi's Chief Minister) that helped Modi to come to power in 2014. In 2023, investigating reports by The Reporters' Collective[92] revealed another facet of the transformation of the anti-corruption crusader into a business tycoon. These reports alleged his Patanjali group used "a web of dubious shell companies" to funnel money to buy Aravalli forestland and sell it as real estate – making "super-profits" even as the "Haryana government blocked multiple legal routes to protect the Aravalli's forest lands".

His rise has been *dramatic*[93] – from a yoga guru to a business tycoon in a very short period. He has built a business empire in herbal (ayurvedic) medicines, food and other consumable products and sells them as "swadeshi" products with generous help from the BJP-ruled states. No less than the Prime Minister publicly endorsed his company Patanjali which received more than $46 million in discounts for land acquisitions in states controlled by the BJP.[94] The pandemic year saw the Centre clearing his herbal concoction of questionable utility, Coronil, and his ministers promoting it for Covid "management" and then as a definitive "cure" for Covid without credible evidence.[95] Several of his products has failed quality tests[96]; he has made many fake claims of curing cancer, homosexuality, HIV[97], produce "male child"[98] (all of which he was forced to recant); his advertisement not only mislead about his own drugs but keep trashing modern medicine for which he has been fined and reprimanded by courts, warned and his advertisements pulled down on several occasions[99]. Even the Supreme Court warned his Patanjali group to fine Rs 1 crore fine for each false claim in its ads and asked the government to come up with measures to address misleading medical ads[100] but Ramdev remained defiant and denied making any false claims.[101]

(iv) Instances and allegations of *raids* by central agencies (CBI/ED) and those going for bankruptcy proceedings having ended up with certain business groups close to the government has been documented.[102]

(v) An investigating report alleged that the Adani group influenced lifting the stocking limits for food grains for corporates in 2020 – amidst the pandemic lockdown.[103] It now has exclusive agreements with the Food Corporation of India (FCI) to store grains and is fast establishing is monopoly – taking it away from the FCI – with generous help from the BJP-ruled government.[104]

(vi) A key member of the Adani Green Energy Limited, Janardhan Choudhary, is now a member of the MoEFF's Expert Appraisal Committee (EAC) for hydro projects which recommended in favour of its project and the minutes showed he participated in it, though he denied doing so.[105]

(vii) Another investigating report alleged that the Vedanta group quietly lobbied the government to dilute environmental safeguards regulating the oil and mining industries during the pandemic.[106]

'National Champions' model disproportionately empowers some politically and financially, kills competition and innovation. Competition and innovations played major roles not just in making South Korea's Chaebols and China's state-owned enterprises (SoEs)[107] for their extraordinary technological and manufacturing successes; China turned into the global hub of manufacturing and leads the world in cutting-edge technologies critical for current and future progress. On the other hand, India's 'National Champions' model and other policies have killed competition – as Acharya (mentioned earlier) demonstrated. Worse, Acharya and Raghuram Rajan, in their 2020 paper "Do we really need Indian corporations in banking?"[108] had warned India against "authoritarian cronyism" – while opposing entry of big industrial houses into banking, particularly in an economy marked by close political-business nexus, cheap money flow, debt-fueled private sector growth and bad governance. They were polite. During the pandemic, Nikkei[109] specifically warned in 2021 that the Prime Minister runs the risk of turning India into Russia-type "gangster capitalists" as a "clutch of billionaire cronies is growing richer at everyone else's expense". The Economist[110] wrote in 2020 how the fortunes of private companies like the Adani group skyrocketed at the cost of others using "political influence and privileged access to capital".

In the meanwhile, India has seen many of its regional tycoons falling by wayside (including GVK which built the new Mumbai now gone to the Adani group) and many others. The centralised political funding through the Electoral Bond has diminished their (regional tycoons') role and influence in politics and policies. Coupled with the current version of crony capitalism (conglomerates cutting down competitor in different sectors) has helped the to centralize more money power.[111]

A good indicator of the rise in crony capitalism is Economist's Crony Capitalism Index. As per its 2023 report, India ranked 10 in 2022 – up from 9 out of 22 countries in 2014 – with wealth from crony-capitalist sectors rising from 5% to 8% of its GDP over a decade, which is far higher than the global rise. India is among four countries contributing to over 60% of the increase in crony capitalist's wealth, the others being the US (ranked 26), China (ranked 26) and Russia (ranked 1).[112] The Credit Suisse's Global Wealth Reports show Indian billionaires' wealth has risen sharply. It started listing India in the top 10 countries with high (USD) dollar millionaire (physical and financial wealth) presence from 2018. Its reports say Indian dollar millionaires numbered 7.25 lakh in 2018, 9.12 lakh in 2019, 6.89 lakh in 2020 and 7.96 lakh in 2021. In 2026, its report said, India could "more than double" to 1.6 million (16.32 lakh) dollar millionaires.[113]

The pandemic year of 20201 saw the wealth of Mukesh Ambani and Gautam Adani soaring while millions lost their lives and livelihoods. The Hurun Global Rich List of 2022 said Ambani added $20 billion to take his wealth to $103 billion and Adani added $49 billion – more than the net addition of wealth by the top three global billionaires Elon Musk, Jeff Bezos and Bernard Arnault.[114] India abolished wealth tax in 2016 when the world was waking up to rising inequality and debating the possibility of imposing higher wealth tax – which French economist Thomas Piketty's "Capital in the Twenty-First Century" flagged.

Ironically, the Economic Survey of 2019-20[115] devoted a full chapter to explain the difference between "pro-business" and "pro-crony" policies. It said the former increases competition, generates "greater wealth" which "enhances welfare for all citizens" while the latter is more into "extracting rents", siphoning off wealth ("willful default") from banks, destroying "value in the economy" and may end up hurting social welfare. It cited economic evidence (churning in the composition of firms in the Sensex to argue for "pro-business" policies which led to "rapid emergence of new firms, new ideas, new technologies and new operating processes". But those lessons have been completely ignored.

The results of the skewed policies – on the people and the environment – are presented in the next two chapters.

Why 'National Champions' are Untouchables

The very concept of 'National Champions' makes it too powerful for normal laws, scrutiny, regulatory oversights. The Hindenburg-Adani saga demonstrates just that.

The Hindenburg had raised 88 questions – relating to allegations of accounting and financial irregularities, related party transactions, round-tripping, stock manipulations, violation of 25% public float etc. All of which the Adani group denied in writing.[116] Its spokesperson came draped in the national flag to declare that it was "a calculated attack on India"[117]. The Hindenburg responded[118] that "Adani failed to specifically answer 62 of our 88 questions" and that "fraud cannot be obfuscated by nationalism".

Not just the Hindenburg a series of investigating reports alleged irregularities and undue favours to the Adani group. Some of these are:

(a) In September 2022, the Bloomberg[119] flagged offshore "silent soldiers" who, it alleged, acted as "Adani's fortune drivers" and "deserve some scrutiny".

(b) In March 2023, London's Financial Times[120] alleged the Adani group received 45.4% of its total FDIs $5.7 billion during 2017-2022, from "opaque overseas entities with connections to group". The government responded with (a) Indian laws don't define "offshore shell company" and (b) "data/details regarding offshore shell companies owned by Indian citizens is not available".[121] But until then, it was screaming from rooftops that 2,38,223 shell companies had been "struck off" between 2018-2021[122]; the Prime Minister himself claimed 1.75 lakh of shell companies had been struck off[123].

(c) In October 2023, London's FT[124] further alleged that its analysis of customs records "supports" longstanding claims that the Adani group had been "inflating fuel costs using offshore middlemen" for billions of dollars of (imported) coals, leading to millions of Indians overpaying for electricity.

(d) In February and March 2023, the Forbes[125] and Morning Context[126] alleged the group's acquisition of Swiss-based Holcim's cement businesses in India – Ambuja Cements and ACC Ltd – which made the group the second largest cement player in the Indian market was through a Mauritius-based entity owned by Vinod Adani. After this, the Adani group admitted that the elder brother of Gautam Adani was part of the "promoters of various listed entities within the Adani group".[127] The group had earlier denied[128] the Hindenburg's charges that Vinod Adani was a promoter and "controlled" a vast network of offshore entities located tax havens of Mauritius, Cyprus, the UAE, Singapore, and several Caribbean Islands, directly or "surreptitiously" moved funds to the group. Later, Vinod Adani resigned as director of three companies connected to Adani's coal mine in Australia.[129]

(e)   The Cyrus Confidential[130] investigations of November 2023 threw up the name of Vinod Adani again as one of 66 Indians who benefitted from "golden passport" scheme of tax haven Cyprus.

(f)   In April 2023, the Morning Context[131] alleged that if the group's offshore funds (accused of related-party transactions) were removed the public float of the Adani Enterprises fell to 10% and that of Adani Transmission "effectively" about 7-8%". In May 2023, the public-float manipulation gained more weight as global index services provider MSCI cut down the Adani Total Gas's free-float from 25% to 14% and that of Adani Transmission from 25% to 10% and dropped both entities from the MSCI India Index.[132]

(g)   The Indian Express investigations of March 2023[133] alleged the Adani group's defence joint venture had a Mauritius-based shadowy company (Elara India Opportunities Fund) holding public shares in its group companies and accused of round-tripping and market manipulation in Adani stocks – is also a promoter entity that has a Rs 590 crore contract with the Indian government. It is strange that the government has no idea about this company – thereby, compromising national security.

The government kept mum on all this.

These are in addition to a host of other such investigating reports by the Indian media spread over several years which alleged the government benefitted Adani group companies in various ways – including arbitrary allocation of coal blocks in violation of the Supreme Court's 2014 order cancelling the coal block allocations, undue tax benefits, CPSUs partnering with the group in various business ventures shoring up its finances when it was heavily indebted.[134]

The government's response to the Hindenburg's allegations was contrary to what a democratic and accountable government is expected to do.

It answered no questions in the Parliament and didn't allow debate or probe by its agency ("No Sir"[135] was its cryptic response in the Lok Sabha) or a parliamentary scrutiny (JPC). The government passed the burden to the market regulator SEBI and also said the Directorate of Revenue Intelligence (DRI) had concluded its probe (imports of power equipment by the Adani group) and submitted its report to judicial authorities but the DRI's investigations into coal imports by the Adani group from Indonesia (alleged over-priced) was incomplete.[136] It also passed the buck to the Supreme Court, which had ordered a probe panel because the government refused to do so.

Government supporters branded the Hindenburg "anti-Indian" out to make money by short-selling.[137] That short-selling is globally recognized as an *efficient tool* to discipline financial markets, ensure liquidity and promote corporate governance practices was ignored[138] even when the Hindenburg said seven listed Adani Group companies were over-priced by *85%*. In the previous three years, the Adani stocks skyrocketed to incredible heights – ranging from 1,500% for Adani Transmission to 5,000% for Adani Green, while their peers could manage moderate increases.[139]

The Supreme Court-appointed panel (SC panel) failed – as was expected – to produce a meaningful report. It reached at no conclusion and said in its report of March 2, 2023[140]:

(i)   SEBI had "drawn a blank" on the "ultimate" owners of 42 entities (12 of them FPIs) invested in the Adani group to get a fix on the minimum shareholding or 25% public float (further probe was on). These entities are based in *seven tax havens* – the Cayman Islands, Malta, Curacao, British Virgin Islands, Bermuda, Ireland and the UK.

(ii)   "No scope for an adverse comment" on "regulatory failure" in related-party transactions because the SEBI changed the definitions of related-party and related-party transactions in November 2021 with "deferred" prospective (further probe was on).

(iii)   "Not possible" to conclude (SEBI's) regulatory failure on price manipulation, as no evidence of "artificial" or coherent pattern of "abusive" trading (or "wash trades") to influence Adani stocks' prices was found.

(iv)   Further probes by the SEBI could be "a journey without a destination" since the challenges were too daunting.

(v)   Its (panel's) attempts to get assistance from international securities firms and banks drew a blank as "none" was "desirous of engaging" in the matter

(vi)   The CBDT and ED had refused to cooperate with the SEBI in investigation. The CBDT said it can't conduct a "roving and fishing expedition" without specific, verifiable and actionable intelligence is given by the SEBI. The ED said, "without prior registration of an offense under the PMLA" it can't probe.

(vii)   A probe by multi-agency Financial Stability and Development Council *under the government* could help.

In September 2023, a petition was filed pointing out the "conflict of interests" of two members of the panel for their alleged links with the Adani group and sought it to be reconstituted and the matter relooked into.[141]

The SC panel missed the point that the government had refused to probe (which explains why the CBDT and ED didn't cooperate with the panel). As for its suggestion of a multi-agency probe, it didn't recon that Multi-Agency Group (MAG) probes into the revelations of the Panama Papers (2016)[142], Paradise Papers (2017)[143], Pandora Papers (2021)[144] – of money laundering, tax evasions, hiding money and assets in tax havens, use of shell companies – have produced no report, or at least known to public, reflecting futility of such an exercise. Moreover, since the Pandora Papers[145] had revealed how the wealthy (including loan defaulters pleading bankruptcy in courts) continued to *ring-fence* and salted their wealth in tax havens, the MAG is no deterrent. In fact, the Paradise Papers of 2017 had revealed two of the 13 offshore entities linked with the Adani group was in public domain for six years and yet, the SEBI, CBDT, SFIO, ED and the SC panel had drawn a blank[146] – indicating the problem is with the government's lack of will or effort to fight corruption.

In fact, the SC panel set a *bad precedence and template*[147] for investigations by raising more questions than answers, failing to produce a meaningful report and thereby, letting off the government without a closure to the episode.

And then the market regulator SEBI *failed to produce* its findings too – even as it said it was tracking 12 FPIs who hold stocks in the Adani companies[148] by the end of August 2023 – despite receiving multiple extensions from the court and despite multiple investigating reports from India and abroad giving enough information.

On the face of it, the SEBI had harmed its own case through two regulatory changes (the SEBI has legislative powers) – as the SC panel disclosed.

(i)   In December 2018 it amended[149] the SEBI (FPIs) Regulations of 2014[150] *substituting* "ultimate" owners of FPIs with "beneficial" owners (as per the PMLA of 2002).

(ii)   In November 2019[151] it *deleted* the need for FPIs to disclose "opaque structure". The 2014 regulation was specifically meant to lift the corporate veil on "ultimate" owners and "opaque" structures. Hence, although the SEBI had begun its investigations into 42 entities (including 12 FPIs) since October 2020, it had drawn a lank.

The SC panel drew attention to this, described it as a "piquant" and "a chicken-and-egg" situation and commented: "It appears that the legislative policy stance of SEBI on the ownership structure of FPIs has moved in one direction while the enforcement by SEBI is moving in the opposite direction." Hence, it's conclusion that the SEBI's probe "can become a perpetual one".

It is still a mystery why the SEBI didn't reverse its amendments after October 2020 or even after January 2023 (when the Hindenburg report came). As for the ED, surely it probed and later found *12 short sellers had benefited* from the Adani group shares at the time[152]; it had nothing to say about the corruption allegations against the Adani group. The ED has built up a formidable reputation for itself as the government's primary tool to raid and round up Opposition leaders and dissenting voices (like the NewsClick and other media houses).

Meanwhile, in August 2023, the Deloitte resigned as the auditor of Adani group's ports business, citing the group's failure to set up independent inquiry into the Hindenburg's allegations of financial irregularities inhibited its ability to scrutinize potential related-party transactions.[153] This development raised doubts about the group's clean chit to itself. Then in September 2023, further investigating reports pointed to further irregularities.

(a) The Mint alleged that six out of eight offshore funds located in tax havens Bermuda and Mauritius had shut shop *after* the SEBI initiated investigations in 2020 in the past few years[154]– and hence, going forward there would be no meaningful report or action from the SEBI.

(b) The Organized Crime and Corruption Reporting Project (OCCRP), a global network of investigative journalists, alleged that two men who secretly invested in the Adani group have close ties to the Adani family (raising questions about violations of SEBI's rules on free float). But it found no evidence of the "source" of the funds. These were published by The Guardian[155] and Financial Times[156].

Persecution and Prosecution for Pointing Fingers at Adani group

What is even more reprehensive is a seemingly coordinated attack on politicians, NGOs and journalists who have pointed fingers at the Adani group's alleged wrong doings. Here are some instances:

• Rahul Gandhi was expeditiously convicted by a Gujarat court in a defamation, as narrated in Chapter II, and expelled from the Lo Sabha soon after raising questions about the Prime Minister's relations with the Adani group – following the Hindenburg report in January 2023. Trinamool Congress MP Mahua Moitra, who asked tough questions and spoke against the Adani group's business dealings also faced a coordinated attack and accused of "cash-for-query" and the Lok Sabha's Ethics Committee questioned her relations with a businessman in this connection – which she described as "vastraharan"[157] (disrobing, aka the Mahabharat story of Draupadi) for being subjected to "undignified questions" about her personal life.

The panel found her guilty and recommended her *expulsion* from the Lok Sabha in extraordinary hurry (within weeks) while the BJP's Ramesh Bidhuri, who abused and made hate-filled language inside the Parliament against Muslim MP Danish Ali didn't even *bother to respond*[158] to the summons issued by the same Ethics Committee for months and nothing happened to him. Then the *virtually dead* Lokpal and ordered a CBI investigation[159] into the case.

• Gujarat police served notices on two Indian journalists Ravi Nair and Anand Mangnale in connection with their investigating reports published in the OCCRP website alleging that the Adani group's offshore fundings were linked to the promoters constituting a criminal offence.[160] It also launched inquiry against two India-based journalists of the Financial Times Benjamin Nicholas Brooke Parkin and Chloe Nina Cornish (both UK citizens) *unconnected*[161] to the newspaper's investigating report on the Adani group's offshore funding in collaboration with the OCCRP and The Guardian. It turned out that they were refused FIR copies; the Gujarat police was acting on behalf of an "investor" in the Adani group with dubious past (banned by the SEBI from trading for three years in a case of "alleged price rigging") and that it had no jurisdiction.[162]

- Nair had also been summoned by the Gujarat police in July 2022 in a defamation case lodged by the Adani group for articles about how the group was set to become India's largest private airport operator, its network of offshore investors, and the dangers of private monopolies controlling infrastructure facilities.[163] Another journalist Paranjoy Guha Thakurta also faces defamation case filed in a Gujarat court, for which non-bailable arrest warrants was issued in 2021, for his articles on the Adani group but the Supreme Court merely ordered restreaint orders against the Gujarat police.[164]

- In October 2023, Ravi Nair and Anand Mangnale were *alerted*[165] by the Apple that their iPhones might have been targeted by "state-sponsored" hackers allegedly using Pegasus spyware. Given the Israel supplier NSO's claim that the Pegasus spyware was given *only to governments* to fight terror and drug menace, not to private entities, it pointed to the involvement of the Central government agencies (see details in Chapter XI).

- The Washington Post[166] said the simultaneous IT raids on three NGOs – CPR, LIFE and Environics Trust (see Chapters II and IX) – in September 2022 was linked to their opposition to the Adani group's coal mining in Chhattisgarh's Hansdeo Arand virgin forests and that they were "seen by the government to be a critic of Gautam Adani".

Market regulator SEBI's Failures

The SEBI has done a commendable job of developing and improving regulatory oversight of India's capital market, but it has had many failures to its belt. It is also one of the most powerful capital market regulators in the world with power to arrest, raid, seizure, disgorgement and legislation. A 2022 comprehensive study[167] of its enforcement actions by Devendra Damle of Finance Ministry think tank National Institute of Public Finance and Policy (NIPFP) and Bhargavi Zaveri-Shah of the National University of Singapore is revealing. It looked into the SEBI enforcement orders spanning a decade between January 2011 and December 2020 and examined 8,032 orders (out of 9,048 during the period). Its key findings are:

(a)   In 80% cases, SEBI found violation complaints true.

(b)   Majority of orders (69%) were monetary sanctions, followed by non-monetary sanctions (25%) and settlement orders (6%).

(c)   3/4th enforcement actions were against "unregulated" entities – those "not SEBI-licensed intermediaries and are "largely market participants, insiders and listed companies". A "significant proportion" of these are settlement orders.

(d)   To issue show cause notices, SEBI "typically" took "more than 3 years" (from the day of complaint) or a mean of 1,534 days (more than four years), which went beyond 15 years in extreme cases.

(e)   To issue orders (from the notice), monetary penalties (by AOs) took 548 days, non-monetary sanctions (by WTMs) 943 days and settlement (by AOs) 779 days. This is after (mean) 1,534 days to issue notice.

(f)   Longer time for WTMs for non-monetary sanctions – 2,477 days (1,534 + 943) or nearly 7 years from the date of complaint – is a bigger concern as it may turn "futile" the SEBI's powers to "pre-empt misconduct or remedy the consequences of misconduct". The delays in more serious cases were due to "complexity of violations", not the complexity of the issues involved.

This study didn't delve into individual cases but there are reports suggesting its failures in dealing with big and powerful entities and called a "reluctant regulator".[168]

Why Is it a Command-and-Control Economy?

Having explained the 'National Champions' model and the overt crony capitalism, it is now easier to explain why the economic regime answers to the description of "command-and-control". Look at a series of economic policies unveiled since 2014, some of which has no apparent connections with either this model or 'Make in India' mission:

(i)   **Import substitution** policy beginning with 2014: The liberalised trade policy, which served India well for three decades, was *reversed* without anyone getting even a whip of it. In their expose in 2020, Chatterjee and Subramanian[169] said "for three decades a stellar export performance has played a critical role in India's overall growth" and reversing it was "akin to killing the only goose that can lay eggs" due to the constraints on public, corporate and household balance sheets. Trade data shows, they have *proven right* – with exports falling far more than imports and trade deficit rising (data a little later)[170].

(ii)   **Demonetization of 2016 and GST of 2017**: The twin shocks that derailed the Indian growth story because of the flawed ideas and implementations without due diligence and despite warnings. In 2023, RBI withdrew Rs 2,000 notes introduced after the demonetization – while declaring such notes to continue as "legal tender" – on absurd logic which the top PSB, State Bank of India supported for its non-existent wisdom ("precision strike")[171]. The GST remains as big a muddle as it ever was (see Chapter VI).

(iii) **High oil tax since 2015**: As the Brent prices fell to half of previous years, oil taxes went up and so did retail oil prices – despite full de-control. After the Russia-Ukraine war in 2022, India imports a bulk of cheap oil from Russia and emerged as a top exporter of this cheap Russian oil to Europe. None of it benefitted ordinary Indians but private businesses and the government (more in Chater VIII).[172]

(iv) **Predatory pricing**: Not just oil, telecom, flight and train tickets and inflation fueled by the Big 5 through 'sellers' inflation' or 'greedflation' show predatory pricing has *official sanctions*.[173]

(v) **Tax arbitrariness**: The BJP condemned the 2012 retrospective tax – tax on business deals prior to 2012 involving asset takeover in tax havens – as "terror tax" but the Modi regime used the same law until 2021 to pursued tax in *17 cases* by fighting at international tribunals. The end came *a month after* India was *humiliated by oil major Cairn Energy* which obtained a French tribunal order in July 2021 to seize about *20 Indian properties* in central Paris, worth more than $1.2 billion. India fought and lost the case.[174] This meant Indian properties across the world were now vulnerable to Cairn Energy and other multinationals in the crosshair. Cairn Energy had sought seizure of the Air India's assets in the US, as did the Devas Multimedia and India was forced to appeal to the US court for *sovereign immunity*.[175] After being forced to withdraw it, the Prime Minister did his usual double-speak. He told Indian corporate leaders that he was "fixing mistakes of the past" and hoped this will strengthen "the trust" between industry and government.[176]

(vi) **Rising NPA write-offs**: Corporate bank defaults have skyrocketed and so is their write-offs but neither is studied or explained by the RBI or the government. Instead, the blame has been passed on to the previous government and Raghuram Rajan who began the banking clean up as RBI Governor (detailed later).

(vii) **Incentives for banking frauds**: Banking frauds too have skyrocketed but instead of checking it, the RBI and the Centre have allowed "compromise settlements" with fraudsters and willful defaulters by making them eligible for fresh loans (detailed later).

(viii) **Big-ticket IBC reform of 2016 is new blackhole:** This has proved to be a big scam, benefiting selected few, hobbling banking and the economy as a whole, with worse than ever recovery of capital and credit. But there is little rethink on it – thereby, reflecting official sanctions. Journalist Andy Mukherjee argues[177] that it is the IBC that needs rescuing now.

(ix) **Corporate tax cut of 2019:** It came amidst severe resource crunch, cut down corporate tax collection drastically – a loss of Rs 1.02 lakh crore in FY20 and Rs 1.28 lakh crore in FY21 – but no corresponding gain to the economy as corporates used it for "debt servicing, build-up of cash balances and other current assets rather than restarting the capex cycle" as per the RBI's annual report of 2019-20.[178] Corporate tax cuts are known to surge income inequality.[179]

(x) **Subsidized manufacturing:** Despite a host of incentives for manufacturing, including 'Make in India', a wide-ranging, long-standing and excruciatingly long list of tax incentives to boost production and exports of manufacturing goods, manufacturing share is stuck at 17-18% of the GDP for 17 years since FY07 and job share remains low at 11.4% in 2022-23 (PLFS) – from 8.8% in 1950-51.

Here is the list of such incentives: import substitution, PLIs, 'Make in India', GST, tax holidays and ither tax incentives by way of SEZs, special tax rates, exemptions, deductions, rebates, deferrals, NPA write offs, export incentives like EOUs, Deemed Export Benefit Scheme, Advance Authorization Scheme, Duty Drawback, DFIA, ECGC, MEIS, RoDTEP, RoSCTL, EPCG etc. Highly subsidized manufacturing may improve domestic capacity but it threatens to perpetuate such incentives and make them globally uncompetitive – as Raghuram Rajan, Viral Acharya and others keep warning against. Assembled mobile phones are working up trade deficits.

Wonder of wonders, a Russian company got the contract to manufacture the Prime Minister's showcase Vande Bharat trains, in a joint venture with the Railways' PSU in March 2023.[180]

(xi) **State and regulatory capture:** Growing cronyism and 'National Champions' model has led to state and regulatory captures – as evidenced in predatory pricing, irrational trade policies, incentives to bank fraud, unrestrained NPA write offs. Two highly regulated sectors – aviation and telecom now effective has a duopoly – from multiple players during the previous regime. Competition has been killed and consumers disadvantaged.

(xii) **Ease of Doing Business Fiasco:** The government achieved another success – dramatic rise in India's ranking in the World Bank's Ease of Doing Business Index (DBI) from 142 in 2014 to 63 in 2019. Thereafter, the World

Bank's DBI itself collapsed due to allegations of data manipulation.[181] Here is a *secret* most Indian don't know.

In October 2017 – immediately after the twin shocks of demonetization and GST which derailed the economy – India's rank jumped 130 to 100. When questioned closely, Junaid Ahmad, World Bank's Country Director in India, told The Hindu[182] that its data didn't capture demonetization (November 2016) and GST (July 2017). By not capturing their impact, the DBI ranking masked the harsh ground realities. Ahmed said these impacts would be reflected in next year's ranking. But next year, in 2018, India's rank jumped 23 places to 77 and in 2019 to 63 even as India slipped into a prolonged slowdown with 3.4% growth in FY20 (corresponding fiscal). It is reasonable to consider that Ahmed's promise remained unfulfilled.

The main objective of DBI is to attract higher FDI inflows. The inflow did improve in absolute numbers but if the rate of growth is compared, it fell from average of 25.5% during the 13 fiscals of FY02-FY14 to 8.4% in 9 fiscals of FY15-FY23 (dropped to -16% in FY23).[183] Two other facts worth noting. Russia too gamed the DBI and its rank fell 50 during 2015-2019 but its FDI inflow share was 0.5% to 1.5% – much lower than average of 2.6% in the previous 7 years of 2008-2014. China didn't and its rank remained above 80, averaging 88.8 during 2008-2015 but its FDI inflow share was 14.2% but when its rank fell below 80 during 2016-2019, its FDI inflow share average lower at 11.2%.[184] The Russia and China case demonstrates that there is little correlation between DBI ranking and FDI inflows.

So, what is the basis for chasing EODB 2.0 – which is same as DBI?

The growth in the FDI inflows is far off the levels before FY15 (average of 25.5% during FY02-FY14) despite further liberalization after FY15 (average of 8.4%) and in FY23, the total FDI inflows (including re-invested earnings) to India fell by (-)16% to a decade low, and FDI equity fell by (-) 22%.[185] Since FDIs are long-term commitments, this is preferred over FPI inflows – which goes into stock markets, fickle and fled in a major way in FY22. This is because FDIs don't depend on DBI ranking alone, if at all. There are other factors at play, like institutional quality (administrative and regulatory mechanisms, rule of law, accountability, dispute resolution etc.)[186] Further, a 2023 Study of DBI showed: (i) improvements in DBI scores didn't raise per capita GDP (ii) in the short-run, improved DBI scores were associated with lower GDP and (iii) DBI may have hindered more substantive economic reforms.[187]

(xiii) Privatization of profit, socialization of lose: Writing off corporate loan defaults as NPAs is the best example of this phenomenon. Privatization of profitable PSUs at throwaway prices (detailed later) is another example. There are others. In 2018, oil PSU ONGC took over[188] Gujarat's bankrupt and scam-tainted Gujarat State Petroleum Corporation (GSPC) – which ran up a liability of Rs 20,000 crore on non-existent oil discovery when Modi was Chief Minister. The takeover allegedly benefited a *private partner*[189] of the GSPC for which it had run up a huge debt. In August 2023, the Arunachal Pradesh government dumped 12 "unviable" private hydro projects on PSUs – namely, NHPC, NEEPCO, and Satluj Jal Vidyut Nigam.[190]

There are more examples of the command-and-control regime which couldn't be explained in bullet points and need proper elaboration.

Privatization: Handing Over Public Wealth to Private Cronies

The reason for privatization of PSUs is not lost on anyone and is very much line with Noam Chomsky's "standard technique of privatization": "defund, make sure things don't work, people get angry, you hand it over to private capital."[191]

After 2014, the government adopted five ways to defund CPSUs[192]:

(a)   Making CPSUs to pay for disinvestment in other CPSUs (limited stock sales) and privatization (handing over management control), which often entailed borrowing from market – making PSU giants like ONGC, NTPC and PFC indebted and fragile.

(b)   Transfer of maximum dividends and cash surplus to the government.

(c)   Making CPSUs to donate to a private and opaque fund PMCARES Fund run by the Prime Minister – from their CSR funds and even salary accounts during the pandemic lockdown. A 2023 report[193] said, CPSUs had contributed 59.3% of funds from listed companies to the PM CARES Fund.

(d)   Making oil CPSUs to fund *statues and temples*. A CAG report[194] said oil PSUs paid *Rs 926.8 crore* in FY16 and FY17 for the Sardar Patel's statue in Gujarat alone. During the devastating second wave of the pandemic, the oil PSUs donated *Rs 100 crore* to "redevelop" Badrinath Dham shrine, instead of building hospitals and oxygen plants.[195] When the Ayodhya temple was being built, more public institutions, like the Central Building Research Institute (CBRI) and Inter-University Centre for Astronomy and Astrophysics (IUCAA) of Pune were engaged in its design[196] – instead of designing modern scientific institutions.

(e)   Diverting CSR fund (mandatory spending of 2% average net profits of three years under the Companies Act of 2013) hurts ameliorative works for communities adversely impacted by industrial activities (displacement, environmental damage etc.). The corporate efficiency, innovative ideas, management skills and better outcomes – everything is lost.[197]

Further, CPSUs have been filled with people connected to the BJP's ideology and retired bureaucrats. Several RTI queries in 2021[198] revealed that 86 of 172 (50%) Independent Directors (IDs) appointed to *98 CPSU boards* have close links with the party and its ideology and 46 other IDs appointed to 40 CPSUs were retired bureaucrats. This data pertained to 146 CPSUs. Such appointments make institutions "pliant to the executive", which defeats the very purpose of IDs who are meant to bring fairness, transparency and ethical corporate governance. Alarmed about the induction of retired bureaucrats, government think tank Indian Institute of Corporate Affairs (IICA) said in 2019[199]: "The selection of Independent Directors for PSUs has *not remained independent.* Instead of experienced domain experts, preference is being given to ex -IAS or recently to political affinity so the whole idea of ID has been vitiated." *(Emphasis added)*

But this is part of the story. It goes hand-in-hand with non-appointment of Independent Directors in most *listed* CPSUs. In December 2022, the CAG reported that of 72 *listed* CPSUs, 59 (82%) were without the mandated Independent Directors – including all 'Maharatna' ones like Coal India, NHPC, MTNL and REC which had not appointed any.[200]

As for privatization of CPSUs, it goes against the government's stated policy, redrafted by the government after 2014. The Disinvestment Policy[201] declares PSUs as "the wealth of the Nation", promises to ensure this wealth rests with the people by "promote public ownership" and declares that the proceeds would be put in the National Investment Fund (NIF) for seven specific capital expenditure purposes. What has been done are exact the opposite and the CAG reports[202] have found the government failed to achieve any of its objectives.

The policy does talk of "strategic disinvestment" whereby management control is given to private players but the idea has always been to do this for sick PSUs, not profitmaking ones. This was changed during the pandemic lockdown, allowing wholesale privatization, except 3 to 4 in each of four strategic sectors: Atomic Energy, Space and Defence; Transport and Telecommunications; Power, Petroleum, Coal and other Minerals and Banking, Insurance and Financial Services in 2021. Quietly, profit-making PSUs were also allowed to be sold. The government simply told the Parliament: "In February, 2021, the Government has notified the New Public Sector Enterprise ("PSE") Policy. Profitability/Loss of the CPSE is not a relevant criterion for disinvestment."[203]

Investigating reports[204] have revealed that many key ministries opposed such wholesale sale of PSUs – from health to fertilizer to defence, shipping and coal – pointing out the adverse impacts but they were ignored. The second term saw several controversial privatizations, except only one went through – the long ailing official airline Air India in 2022. It was handed back to its original owner, the Tatas, after 68 years of its nationalization and entailed writing off of Rs 61,000 crore of legacy debts and other liabilities.[205] Other privatizations saw PSUs getting sold for *very cheap.*

(i) **Central Electronics Limited (CEL).** It is a profit-making entity developing critical frontier technologies for defence and space and quite apparently, of strategic interest to India. It was sold for Rs 210 crore in FY22 to a minor finance company named Nandal Finance and Leasing with no background in science and technology and which is owned (99.96%) by a home décor company, Premier Furniture and Interiors. At the time of the sale, the CEL had declared a profit of Rs 136 crore (for FY21), had pending orders of Rs 1,592 crore, which would alone have generated a profit of Rs 730 crore (going back past records) and owned 50 acre of prime land on Delhi's outskirts worth Rs 440-660 crore. Yet, its market price was fixed at a low of Rs 194. The buyers are found to be connected to the BJP.[206] When its employees went to court, the privatization was *terminated*.[207]

(ii) **DNH (Dadra Nagar Haveli) Power Distribution Corporation**: It had posted a profit of Rs 229 crore for FY21 – up from Rs 114 crore in FY20 – but its reserve price was pegged at a lowly Rs 151 crore. It was sold off to Gujarat-based Torrent Power for Rs 550 crore.[208]

(iii) **Pawan Hans Limited (PHL)**: The government sold off 51% of its stakes in this public sector "maharaja" of helicopter services. The PHL provides logistic support to the oil PSU ONGC in its offshore operations, besides providing access to remote areas (islands and hilly areas), carries out difficult tasks (in fighting Maoists in Gadchiroli forests) and emergency rescue and relief operations. Again, it is of strategic important and owned 43 helicopters. It was sold off for a pittance, Rs 211 crore, to a consortium of questionable credentials. The remaining 49% stakes with the ONGC was also to be sold to the same entity at the same rate. The government put the sale on hold immediately after an investigating report[209] revealed that the consortium is led by a financial company based in tax haven Cayman Islands which had defaulted in payment in another acquisition case and for which the NCLT had sanctioned it weeks earlier. This should have rendered this company ineligible. Its privatization was called off in July 2023[210] – due to doubtful integrity of their private buyers (also that of the CEL).[211]

(iv) In 2023, further privatization was put on hold after the Hindenburg report generated turmoil hit and the finances of two key potential buyers (of profit-making monopolies of Container Corporation of India and metal importing NMDC), Gautam Adani and Anil Agarwal of the Vedanta, came under scrutiny for high debts.[212]

The privatization drive began during the earlier BJP-led government under Prime Minister Vajpayee during early 2000s. It had seen mired in controversy for various omissions and commissions, like selling off PSUs dirt cheap, without valuing operational and reserved mines, huge tracts of developed and undeveloped land, fully developed townships, plants and machinery etc. The official auditor CAG had thoroughly exposed these deals.[213]

One of those came back to haunt the government in 2022.

(v) **Hindustan Zinc Limited (HZL)**: The Vajpayee government had handed over the Sterlite Opportunities & Ventures (SOVL) in 2002. In November 2021, the Supreme Court asked the CBI to register an FIR into the gross irregularities in this deal after it was found that (i) the SEBI had disqualified the SOVL from participating in the bidding (ii) CAG had objected to selling HZL's shares at Rs 40.51 when the market rate was Rs 119.1 "resulting in a loss of about Rs 650 crore" (iii) CBI found the global advisor which had used "discounted cash flow", instead of "asset valuation" method that a government-appointed committee had recommended, to drastically reduce the value of HZL, had *disappeared and untraceable* and (iv) the global asset valuer had "failed to consider" various assets and properties, including three operational mines, to the tune of Rs 80,000 crore. The CBI finally registered an FIR five months later in 2022, after having opposed it in the court.[214] It is the long saga of corruption charges that prevented the stake sale of the remaining 26% in the HZL.

Here is how much the Indian government has earned from disinvestment and privatization of PSUs since 1992 – when it was forced by the World Bank-International Monetary Fund duo to privatize public assets for bailing it out from a foreign exchange crisis. Notice the sharp rise after Modi came to power, and also the subsequent fall.

Graph 1: Proceeds from disinvestment and privatization

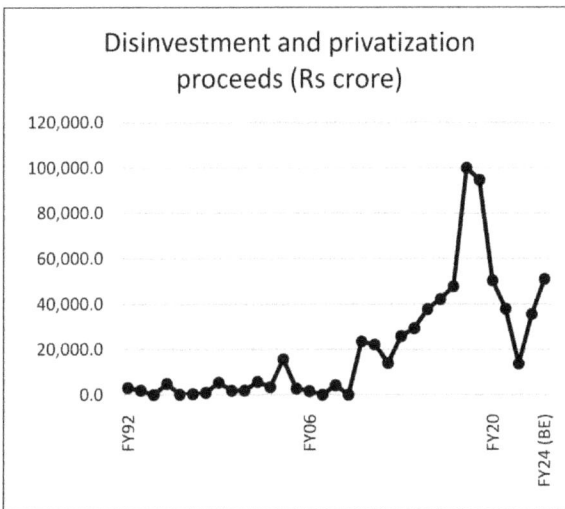

Source: DIPAM, Budget FY24

There is an interesting twist to this process.

All disinvestment and privatization proceeds have gone to meet fiscal deficits – which remains elevated and beyond the officially mandated limit. The proceeds were never deposited in the NIF, which the policy mandates, but went to the Consolidated Fund of India (CFI). The proceeds are also *not shared* with state governments[215], which have contributed immensely by providing cheap land and electricity, tax concessions etc.

National (Asset) Monetization Pipeline (NMP)

Another method of handing over public assets to private businesses is the "National Monetisation Pipeline" (NMP)[216] announced in August 2021. It envisages (as per the NITI Aayog[217]) wholesale handing over of existing roads, railways, power, telecom, mining, aviation, ports etc. built with public money for the next 25-30 years to generate Rs 6 lakh crore in four years. These include: 26,700 km of roads, 28,608 ckt km of power transmission assets, 6 GW of hydel and renewable power assets, 8,154 km of natural gas pipelines, 3,930 km of petroleum products pipeline, 210 LMT (lakh metric ton) of warehousing assets, 400 railway stations, 90 passenger train operations, 265 goods sheds, Konkan Railway and Dedicated Freight Corridor, 2.86 lakh km of Bharatnet Fiber and 14,917 BSNL, MTNL towers, 25 airports etc.

There is little economic logic to the NMP when private investments have stalled for years. Private business putting money in brownfield projects mean (a) cut in investment in new projects that boost growth and create jobs and (b) private buyers will impose rents to repay the money given to the government (Rs 6 lakh crore) and also earn a profit – thereby collecting *high rent from public* to use the very infrastructure they paid to build. Interestingly, the NMP came after the Prime Minister made grand announcements of infrastructure investment plans of Rs 100 lakh crore or more for three consecutive years – in 2019, 2020 and 2021 in his national addresses.[218] In 2022, the NMP was extended to social sector.[219] By the end of FY23, the NMP had generated Rs 1.14 lakh crore, 19% of the target.[220]

Why PSUs Matter

It is often forgotten that PSUs were first set up by the first Prime Minister Nehru after the 200 years of colonial rule de-industrialized India. Private sector was nascent, unwilling and incapable of long-term investments in big industries and infrastructure that India needed. The Bombay Plan of 1944[221], prepared by the industrial doyens like JRD Tata, JD Birla and others, had called for state-led and planned re-industrialization and development of India in which private sector was willing to subject itself to state-control. This model was later rolled out through the five-year plans.

That PSUs have served India well is known.

It provided capital goods, infrastructure, jobs, incomes and helmed India's growth for decades. Ajay Shankar, ex-secretary to Department of Industrial Policy and Promotion (DIPP) and Prof Sushil Khanna of IIM-Kolkata[222] warned against indiscriminate privatization stating that it compromises India's sovereignty and economic freedom, threaten its energy security and strategic assets. They pointed out how the Chinese state-owned enterprises (SOEs) have made China the economic superpower. They pointed out how India had already compromised its economic and strategic interests by neglecting its PSUs: "The government's refusal to support PSEs at critical moments has left *wide gaps in key industrial capabilities*. With the collapse of HMT, India is *forced to import* 80 per cent of its machine tools, the bedrock of manufacturing. The *undermining of the pharmaceutical PSEs* like IDPL and HAL, once India's pride, makes it dependent on active ingredients from China. The government's reluctance to support BHEL has *flooded* the Indian power sector with Chinese equipment. Moreover, India is largely *absent in emerging technologies* like solar wafers, computer chips or EV batteries. India *needs to imitate China* in establishing new PSEs in strategic and emerging industries, which require patient capital and greater risk."

PSUs are significant for many other reasons too: They provide jobs to the underprivileged (reservation or "affirmative action"); ensure competition critical for efficiency and productivity enhancement and counter private monopolies and create more public wealth. Many other studies have shown that PSUs perform better than their private sector peers in a wide range of parameters, including higher returns on capital.[223] India's globally reputed public sector vaccine makers supplied 60% of global vaccines until the government kept those out of the Covid vaccine programme and turned India's universal vaccination to a for-profit trade up to 50% at first and then to 25% after the Supreme Court called it "arbitrary" and irrational".[224]

In recent times, PSUs are on the decline. Official data shows: (i) CPSU jobs have fallen by 2.7 lakh in the past decade – from 17.3 lakh in March 2013 to 14.6 lakh in March 2022 – which led by 'Maharatna' and 'Ratna' companies like the ONGC, IOC, GAIL, Coal India, SBI etc. and (ii) contractual and casual workers increased from 19.5% to 42.6% during the same period.[225] As on June 2023, *six of 11* PSBs had no chairman, some for *more than two years*.[226]

Rising Bank Frauds and NPA Writ-offs

There has been a quantum jump in writing off corporate loan defaults since 2014 as banks' NPAs (SCBs) – went up dramatically from a mere Rs 61,039 crore in nine years of FY06-FY14 to Rs 14.6 lakh crore during the first nine years of FY15-FY23 – 24 times (graph below)! About 68% of this is by public sector banks (PSBs).

Such write-offs include banking frauds that either led to collapse or caused massive setbacks to a large number of banking and non-banking institutions like the PMC Bank, Punjab National Bank, ICICI Bank, Yes Bank, Lakshmi Vilas Bank, IL&FS, HDIL, DHFL etc. The banking frauds have risen dramatically – on number and amounts (graph below). Many corporate tycoons have fled the country with bank loans under the Prime Minister's watch – Vijay Mallya, Mehul Choksi, Nirav Modi, Jatin Mehta, Sandesara brothers (who run flourishing business in Africa and suspected to be doing business with Indian oil PSUs[227]). The ED listed *36 such businessmen* who have fled.[228] It is impossible to believe that none of the banks and government agencies had any inkling of their massive crimes – as they had defaulted/evergreened loans and got citizenships abroad with government clearances.[229]

Of those who didn't flee, Rishi Agarwal of Gujarat-based ABG Shipyard was accused of over Rs 22,000-crore banking fraud. It was known to the CBI and ED since 2019 when his fraud was identified but action began in 2022. The Yes Bank promoter Rana Kapoor is accused of multiple loan and money laundering scams that led to the bank's collapse in 2020 and hit 17 banks in all. The DHFL promoters Kapil Wadhawan and brother Dheeraj Wadhawan, accused of "biggest" banking scam of Rs 34,615 crore[230], bought business jet, floated offshore companies (like Anil Ambani) – the Pandora Papers had revealed. Even bigger was the case of Chitra Ramakrishna, former MD and CEO of the largest stock exchange NSE, and others, is astounding. She was removed from the NSE in 2016 for "co-location scam" and abuse of power. She had been found passing critical and internal "confidential" information to an "unknown" Himalayan yogi, a certain Paramahansa, who remains unidentified. The SEBI and CBI acted against her six years later in 2022.[231]

The following two graphs uses the RBI data and Lok Sabha answer[232] to show how dramatically banking frauds (banks and financial institutions or FIs involving Rs 1 lakh and above) and NPA write-offs have zoomed together – which can't be just a coincidence or due to business failures (as is obvious from the facts presented earlier).

Graph 2 and 3: Skyrocketing banking frauds and the NPA write-offs

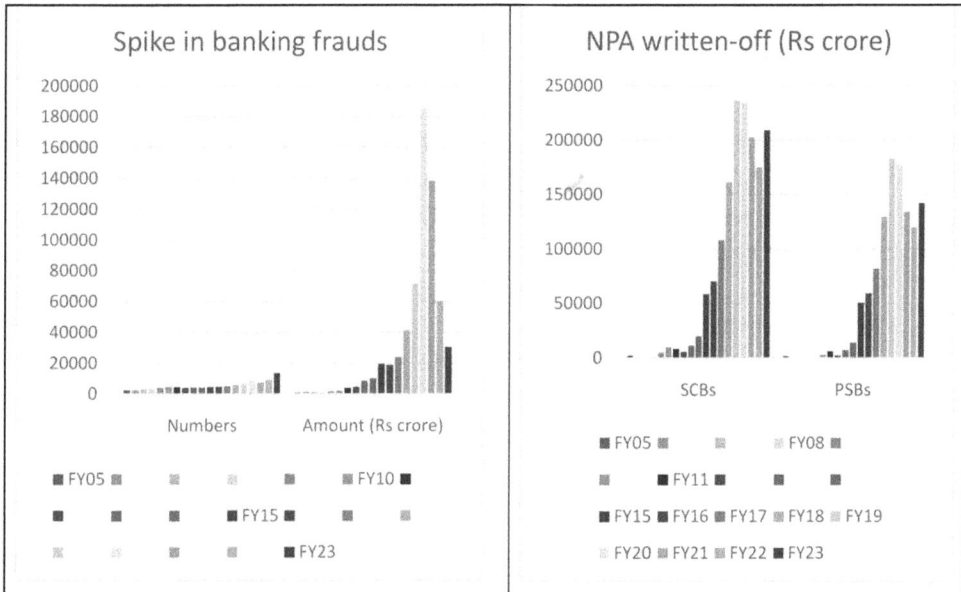

Spike in banking frauds | NPA written-off (Rs crore)

Source: RBI database (above Rs 1 lakh in case of banking frauds) and LS reply for NPA write off

And yet, the RBI is *incentivizing banking frauds and willful defaults* (the later are those who can pay but don't) by issuing "Framework for Compromise Settlements and Technical Write-offs" on June 8, 2023. It allows and empowers all financial institutions to offer "compromise settlements" with such dubious debtors. Even more shocking, it permits such debtors to avail fresh loans after 12 months. This is beyond any logic, especially in view of the facts that:

(a)   The number of banking frauds jumped 17 times during the nine fiscals of FY15-FY23 to 5,88,744 – from 34,198 in the previous nine years of FY04-FY14; the amount involved nearly doubled (1.9 times) to ₹65,812 crore during the nine years of FY15-FY23 – as against ₹34,904 in the previous nine years of FY06-FY14 (RBI data).

(b)   By December 2022, 15,778 of willful defaulters had accumulated debts of Rs 3.4 lakh crore (as per the RBI registered Transunion Cibil).

(c)   The SEBI has classified 120 companies as "untraceable", out of 692 cases in the 'difficult to recover' category, with dues of Rs 73,287 crore (as of March 2023[233]).

(d)   The problems with "compromised settlements" are both heavy haircuts and no "recovery" (as in the case of NPA write-offs). In any case, the "recovery" by SCBs is not much – 16.6% during the five years of FY18-FY22 (as per a Rajya Sabha reply of March 28, 2023).

(e)   Yet, the RBI refuses to disclose the name of these fraudsters and willful defaulters because credit information is "confidential" – instead of naming and shaming them in public.[234]

Also keep in mind the following:

(f)   There is a *flood* of Indians giving up citizenship and *fleeing*. Their number is up from 1,22,819 in 2011 (pre-Modi) to 1,31,405 in 2015 (after the "Achhe Din" promise set in) to 2,25,620 in 2022 and 87,026 till June 2023 (halfway mark) as the Lok Sabha was told[235] – exposing how wrong the Prime Minister was to tell Indian diaspora in Shanghai in 2015 that before he came to power in 2014, Indians were "ashamed of being born Indian".[236] Such migrations often (about 30%) entail investment of $300,000-3,000,000 in many countries that offer "residence-by-investment" or "citizenship-by-investment" programmes.[237]

(g)   Ironically, the Prime Minister's many "wealth creators" salt away bank loans and other properties in tax havens as revealed by the Panama Papers, Paradise Papers and Pandora Papers; the latest to join the rank was investigating reports called *Cyprus Confidential*[238] in 2023 reflecting more of the same (tax evasion, havens, shell companies, salting away assets etc.).

(h)   Indian corporates are *debt-driven* and *debt-ridden*. The Credit Suisse's "India Corporate Health Tracker" of August 2019 showed that barring a few, all big private business houses were "chronically stressed" (interest cover ratio of less than 1 for a period of 1 to 12 quarters). Spread across infrastructure, manufacturing, telecom, power, metals, textiles etc. the debts of these chronically stressed companies were rising from Rs 8.9 lakh crore in FY17 to Rs 9.1 lakh crore in FY18 and Rs 10.2 lakh crore in FY19.[239] There has been no updates on this (at least not available in public domain).

What does the government do?

It keeps blaming the previous governments and the man who began the bank asset clean up.

The Prime Minister himself blamed, in 2023, the NPA crisis to "phone banking scam" during the previous UPA government (which was replaced nine years ago in 2014)[240] even as bank loans and frauds have skyrocketed under him and the RBI is incentivizing it.

The Economic Survey of 2020-21 blamed former RBI Governor Raghuram Rajan (2013-16) – the one who began the cleaning up banking stressed assets with his Asset Quality Review (AQR) of 2015. Union Minister Rajeev Chandrashekhar said Rajan was to be blamed for the entire economic crisis. Even the argument that the NPA crisis had the genesis in exuberance of bank loans during the UPA years doesn't wash because that was also the period of highest ever growth.

Secondly, a series of economic misadventures of the Prime Minister regime derailed growth the GDP plunged to 3.4% in FY20 (later retrospectively raised to 3.9%).[241] Additionally, the bank frauds, write off of NPAs and further policy to give loans to fraudsters and willful defaulters demonstrate complicity, rather than incompetence and ineptitude.

Arbitrary Trade Policies and Practices

Indian trade practices have become highly unpredictable – completely unconnected with its trade policy or what goes by it. The import substitution began in 2014 but was officially acknowledged only in 2020. The Prime Minister gave a call then for "Vocal for Local" and "Local for Global". In 2022, he asked Indians to reduce "slavery to foreign goods"[242] – to mark 75 years of Independence – even though he is personally fond of top-notch luxury brands of foreign origin (Maybach sunglasses, Movado watch, Mont Blanc pen, apart from his long list of imported official cars and planes).[243]

By 2023, India was already the "tariff king"[244]; the WTO found India *guilty*[245] of raising import duty of 7.5-20% tax on imports of ICT products while the WTO rates were 'zero'; his top advisor and former NITI Aayog Vice Chairman Arvind Panagariya had expressed *amazement*[246] that the Centre was pursuing a policy without evidence and no analysis "whatsoever"; trade data shows[247] both exports and imports fell sharply – disabling the export engine of growth.

Graph 4: India's falling exports, rising imports

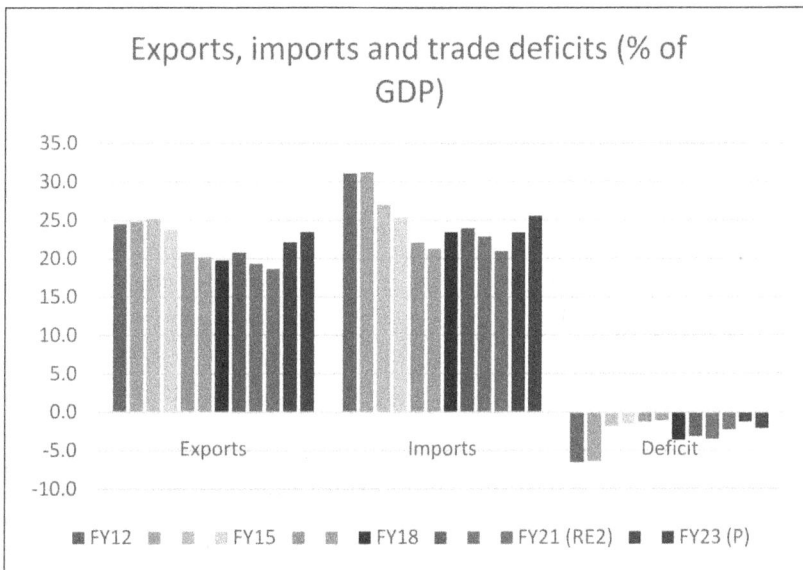

Source: MoSPI, Jan 2023 and May 2023

Former RBI governor Viral Acharya[248] listed four negative impacts of higher import tariffs: (a) high tariff on agriculture (above 35%) with its low efficiency (employing over 40% workers but generating 15% of the GDP) "prevents a market-based rotation of jobs" from low-skilled o high-skilled (b) makes Indian goods costly and globally uncompetitive (c) makes imported goods costlier in India (such as for iPhones), forcing Indians to go for inferior domestic products and keeping inflation higher and (d) disincentivizes investments in efficiency and builds up market concentration. Ashoka Mody[249] has pointed how India's short-sighted trade policy is depriving it of major gains from multinationals' search for alternate home under their China+1 strategy – as most prefer to "friend-shorting" or "near-shoring". Instead of open competition, India is more relying on subsidized manufacturing (Production Linked Incentives or PLIs).

There are several such arbitrariness in trade:

(i) While it is the services which is *driving* trade and generating *trade surplus*, the focus is *entirely* on merchandise goods which continues to generate huge trade deficits. Even basic information is not available on services exports and the Foreign Trade Policy (FTP) of 2023 doesn't mention it; it merely focuses on process improvement (ease of doing business), rather than product improvements and expanding trade ties.[250]

(ii) India is also going *exclusively* for bilateral FTAs (except trade talks with the EU), shunning multilateral FTAs (RCEP, IPEF ad CPTPP) *without any evidence of efficacy* of such an approach – not even the *three documents* which is supposed to be *guided it* says so[251]. This is all the more reprehensible in view of "geoeconomic fragmentation" is intensifying and the world is gravitating to two major blocs – the US and Europe and Russia-China – with everything pointing to the fact that India would fail to integrate with global value chains (GVCs) in its protectionist zeal. An IMF paper warns that "geoeconomic fragmentation" would hit trade, technology transfer and investment flows. As mentioned earlier, in FY23, the total FDI inflows fell by 16% – lowest in a decade – and FDI equity fell by 22% due to global turmoil.

(iii) Now diplomatic chill and other policy intransigencies are holding up bilateral FTAs. The one with the UK is stuck because India insists on free access to its labour market while it has categorically ruled out any change in its immigration policy. The diplomatic chill over the killing of Canadian citizen and alleged terrorist Hardeep Singh Nijjar on its soil has stalled the bilateral FTA. The trade talks with the EU are stuck due to two factors: (i) the EU's proposed carbon tax and (ii) the WTO's adverse ruling in May 2023 against India's tariff barrier of 7.5-20% on ICT products as against the WTO mandate of 0% tax – in which the complainants included Japan and Taiwan also. Though trade negotiations have progressed with Australia, a "comprehensive" deal is expected only by the end of 2023.[252]

(iv)   The strained diplomatic and trade ties with China (over the latter's incursion and control of land on the India side of the LAC in Ladakh) will work against India for several reasons: (i) China is the dominant global producer and supplier of raw materials for chips and advanced electronics – gallium and germanium and (ii) China dominates the global supply of lithium and lithium-ion batteries essential for EVs and mobile phones.[253] Besides, China is (iii) the second largest economy after the US (iv) the global leader in manufacturing (28.7% of global manufacturing output in 2019, as against 16.8% of the next in the list, the US) (v) the global leader in the export of goods (14.3% of the global share in 2020, as against 8.1% of the second leader, the US and (vi) also the global technology leader – leading in 37 of 44 "crucial technology fields spanning defence, space, robotics, energy, environment, biotechnology, artificial intelligence (AI), advanced materials and key quantum technology areas" because it has established "stunning lead in high-impact research".[254] India may be the fifth largest economy but has no claims in any of the other areas that makes China what it is today.

(v)   India *unilaterally* pulled out of 68 bilateral investment treaties (BITs) in 2017 and it is renegotiating them again as these are essentially part of FTAs and critical to join GVCs too.[255] Now BITs have run into *trouble*[256] because India is averse to international arbitrations and wants to exhaust "local remedies" as pre-condition (given the Cairn Energy seizing India's foreign assets explained earlier). This is without justification since most international arbitrations have actually benefited the Indian government, rather than the investors (274 cases in favour vs 212 against[257]).

(vi)   India is actually damaging its *services exports* by seeking to displace English in education through the New Education Policy (NEP) of 2022 and recruitments through the UPSC exams – by putting *equal emphasis* on 22 non-English Indian languages and *removing* English skills as pre-requisite to qualify for taking top grade job exams.[258]

(vii)   There is no knowing when import and exports are restricted or banned (for wheat, rice, sugar and other commodities) – which ends *predictability and stability*[259] that drive trade. In 2022, the coal mix was suddenly changed to allow 30% imported coal for all thermal plants – *unilaterally invoking emergency power* (requiring no consent of buyer states). Imported coal was 10 times costlier at the time. The burden shifted to public – either directly or in state subsidies. In FY23, coal imports jumped 30% in volume and 56.8% in value (USD) – draining out forex reserve. Who benefitted? Obviously, the private firms importing coal.[260]

Big Bang Claims

No account on Indian economy would be complete without Big Bang schemes and spectacular (often redundant) targets. A few examples.

(i) **100 million jobs:** The Prime Minister and his government promised 100 million "manufacturing" jobs under 'Make in India' in 10 years in March 2015.[261] The government showcases payroll data (EPFO) as evidence of formal job creations and makes big claims (like 1.5 million new jobs every month). The EPFO's annual reports show, a net addition of *8.7 million* regular PF contributors (or 8.7% of promise 100 million) in the six fiscals since then (FY16 to FY22) – from 37.6 million in FY16[262] to 46.3 million in FY22[263].

(ii) **Rs 100 lakh crore infrastructure spending:** The Prime Minister promised to invest Rs 100 lakh crore in infrastructure in three national addresses, in 2019, 2020, 2021 – when the GDP size was just Rs 137-150 lakh crore (at constant prices) – with three different names but when, finally, it was unveiled (the "Gati Shakti") in October 2021 (FY22)[264], it was just a *digital platform* linking all infrastructure ministries for better coordination. There was no mention of Rs 100 lakh crore investment or jobs. In fact, a month earlier in August 2021, a new plan was launched to handover public infrastructure to private businesses to run (NMP)[265] to generate Rs 6 lakh crore for the government in the next four years. By the end of FY23, the NMP had generated Rs 1.14 lakh crore, or 19% of the target.[266]

(iii) **100 Smart Cities:** In 2014, the Prime Minister unveiled Smart Cities Mission to build 100 Smart Cities, which turned out to be renamed urban renewal programme of the previous government (JNNURM). Not only not one single Smart City has been set up, going by the devastations caused by monsoon rains in Delhi, Mumbai and dozens of cities in plains and hills, this mission has turned into a bad joke.[267]

(iv) **1,000 years' vision of development:** From the promise of 'Achche Din' to 'Amrit Kaal' the Prime Minister finally said, in 2023, that he was laying the foundation for the next *1,000 years*[268] – contrasting it against 1,000 years of "slavery" under the Muslim rule. The Mughals and other Muslim rulers came from outside but lived and died in India. On the global stage, India didn't do bad in those times – many scholars have pointed out how the Indian living standards may have been "on a par with the developing parts of Western Europe" before it was colonized by the British[269], including British economist Angus Maddison's book "The World Economy: A Millennial Perspective"[270] gives a good account of it.

(v) **$5-30 trillion economy and third largest economy:** Amidst rising poverty, hunger and job crisis caused directly by the Prime Minister's top-down and arbitrary policies, he claims to be building $5 trillion economy (the target years keeps extending)[271] and his ministers promise $30 trillion[272] economy by 2047. The Prime Minister gave "Modi's guarantee"[273] that India would become the 3rd largest economy in his third term, after having already turned it into the fifth largest economy – all based on *fudged GDP*[274] and unreliable data[275]. He has given *countless* guarantees – doubling farmers' income by 2022, ending hunger and poverty, giving Rs 15-20 lakh in each Indian after bringing back black money in 100 days etc. but not one has been delivered.[276] Just days after he thundered another "Modi's guarantee" in 2023 to put all corrupt politicians, his party *inducted*[277] many of those into its Maharashtra government, one becoming Deputy Chief Minister.

(vi)   **134 million lifted out of poverty:** The Prime Minister also claimed that 134 million Indian had been *lifted out of poverty*[278] during his rule – based on *dubious calculations*[279] by government think tank NITI Aayog and economists keep making fake claims of near zero poverty (0.8% of population)[280] and "a jobful economy"[281] – when India is home to most of the poor and hungry in the world and job crisis is worse than ever (see Chapter VIII for details).

(vii) **Institutes of Eminence (IOE):** In 2017, his government announced setting up *Institutes of Eminence* (IOE)[282] to improve India's global ranking in educational institutions. It *ended up* giving such titles to *non-existing private institutes*[283] – and was left with no choice but to acknowledge the old IITs and other institutions of excellence set up by Nehru or in his time.

(viii) **Moon landing:** When the Chandrayaan-3 landed on the moon in August 2023, the Prime Minister claimed it as a success of his 'Make in India'[284] – pretending not to know that it was a project of the ISRO set up by the Congress in the early decades of Independence (Its official website says[285]: "ISRO was previously the Indian National Committee for Space Research (INCOSPAR), set up by the Government of India in 1962, as envisioned by Dr Vikram A Sarabhai. ISRO was formed on August 15, 1969 and superseded INCOSPAR with an expanded role to harness space technology. DOS (Department of Space) was set up and ISRO was brought under DOS in 1972."). The Chandrayaan-3 cost just Rs 615 crore. Contrast this to his 'Make in India' roads which cost *Rs 250.77 crore per km* (against the sanctioned Rs 18.2 crore) and yet, no probe is ordered.[286]

(ix)   **Vande Bharat trains:** The Prime Minister personally flags off every single semi-fast luxury Vande Bharat train as a 'Make in India' achievement, even as (i) the Railways cut 25% on tickets for AC and executive class due to low occupancy[287] (ii) the wheels and axles of these trains are *imported from China*[288] and (iii) a *Russian company*[289] has got the contract to make these trains. Its high-profile (direct association with the Prime Minister) has meant the timetable of regular and faster trains like the Rajdhani and

Shatabdi are derailed. Worse, the Railways said, in response to RTI queries, that it *doesn't* keep profit-and-loss account of this train service![290] The Railways has been spending huge amounts on just flagging these trains. In an RTI reply, it said it *spent Rs 2.6 crore to flag just two* such trains.[291]

(x) **500 million skilled youth**: The Pradhan Mantri Kaushal Vikas Yojana (PMKVY) was launched in 2015 (old UPA era scheme) to skill 500 million youths, and two years later in 2017, it had proved a failure and was *abandoned* .[292] There are no reliable information as the government occasionally provides mere dashboard information.[293]

(xi) **Direct benefit transfer (DBT) saves trillions of rupees:** The government has used the DBT to identify and build its vote bank called "labharthi varg" (class of beneficiaries) – while claiming it to be good governance tool. The Finance Minister's claim that it saved Rs 2.73 lakh crore since 2014[294] is a typical example for which no evidence exists nor provided.

(xii) **"2 crore (20 million) "lakhpati didis":** His latest promise is to create 20 million 'millionaire' women in rural areas through women self-help groups.[295] Women in self-help groups are associations of very poor rural women being given *micro loans* through microfinance institutions (MFIs) to survive on small businesses. The Prime Minister knows and it isn't his ignorance speaking.

(xiii) **15 new premier health institutions, the AIIMS, started since 2014:** A fact check reveals construction hasn't started in three – including the AIIMS Darbhanga and the AIIMS Madurai about which the Prime Minister himself and his government claimed to be doing good work. Construction has started in six and classes have started in 12 from temporary campuses. Many don't have OPDs or IPDs. In short, not one of the 15 is fully functional.[296]

(xiv) **New IIT and new IIM every year and new universities every week:** Introduction pointed out, this claim by the Prime Minister is false as his government's reply to the Parliament shows, no new IIT or IIM had been opened. As for new universities every week, his government's reply said 242 new universities were opened, of which 58% were in private sector – but whether these are functional remains to be fact-checked.

(xv) **74 New airports after 2014**: This claim by Civil Aviation Minister Jyotiraditya Scindia[297] turns out to be highly exaggerated from the ministry's own records which reveals that only 11 have been built from the scratch, while *15 have fallen into disuse* due to the collapse of almost 50% routes launched under the subsidized Regional Connectivity Scheme (RCS).[298]

(xvi) **Manufacturing chips:** The government claims that the US's Micron is setting up "India's first manufacturing plant" while the agreement signed for the project is actually for an assembling facility (under the scheme "Assembly, Testing, Marking and Packaging (ATMP)"). For this *private project*, 70% money (total cost $2.75 billion) will be public money (Centre's 50% and Gujarat's 20%) as incentives.[299]

(xvii) **India is manufacturing hub for mobile phones:** The government claims its incentive scheme (PLI) has led to manufacturing of smart phones, but former RBI Governor Raghuram Rajan and his colleagues analyzed trade data to bust that myth and say India was merely assembling phones.[300]

But these are not the only signs that the Modinomics is failing.

- **Stagnant growth in GDP and per capita income**: Growth was slowing down before the pandemic hit and the recovery is K-shaped. Per capita GDP growth is *falling behind* the GDP growth pointing to uneven growth and rise in income inequality.[301] The World Bank's database shows Indians are *one of the poorest* in the world with a per capita income of $2,3886 (current USD, 2022), while the global average is $12,647.5 – 5.3 *times* higher.[302]

- **Tax base sharply shrinks by 54% in 7 years**: The latest income tax data presented to the Lok Sabha on July 24, 2023[303] shows a shocking development: The number of people declaring *taxable income fell by 54%* in seven years – *from 48.6 million in FY16 to 22.4 million in FY23.* This is due to a sharp rise in the number of people declaring *zero tax liability* – up from 29 million in FY20 to 51.6 million in FY23. This can't be explained fully due to an increase in taxable limits by Rs 2 lakh after 2014. The massive loss of income (from job and business losses) caused by the twin shocks of demonetization and GST, the pandemic economic shutdowns of 2020 and 2021 and the subsequent K-shaped recovery would have played a big role – which need more data and studies to figure out. Tax-to-GDP ratio remains unchanged (10-11% during the past 12 fiscals beginning with FY12 and budgeted at 11% for FY24). Tax return data for FY15-FY23[304] had shown a sharp increase in income inequality as it impacted most those in the lowest income slab (Rs 0-5 lakh) and their numbers fell. None of this is a sign of healthy or equitable economic growth (graph in the next chapter).

- **Growth drivers are stalling:** None of the two earlier developments is surprising because all the four growth engines have stalled in the past 12 fiscals between FY12 and FY23 – private consumption (PFCE), government expenditure (GFCE), private capital investment (private GFCF available until FY22) and net exports. One of these, net exports, continues to be *negative*. If 'exports' is taken as the fourth growth engine, the status is no better.

How does India reach the Prime Minister's promised "Amrit Kaal" and "developed" nation by 2047? The RBI[305] said India would take 13 years (by FY35) to recover from the pandemic loss alone – if it grows at 7.5% during FY24-FY35 – while the GDP growth during the past 11 years between FY13 and FY23 is just 5.7% (so is the case during FY15-FY23)!

Graph 5: All four growth engines stalled

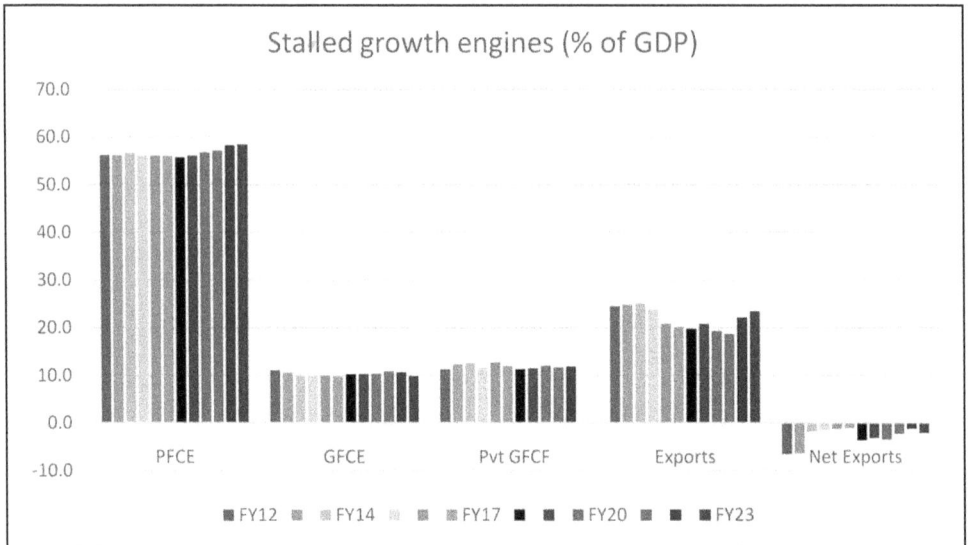

Source: National Accounts Statistics

(i)   **Private investment stuck:** The government has been very accommodative of the demands from private businesses – corporate tax cut in 2019 and PLIs and DLIs.[306] Despite this, private investment, *private GFCF* has fallen from the peak of 16.8% of the GDP in FY08, amidst the Great Recession of 2007-09 (2011-12 GDP back series data, current prices) to 10% in FY22 (up to which the National Account Statistics data is available). The trend remains downward midway through FY24 – shows other data ("envisaged" investment).[307] This fall has nothing to do with corporate profits as despite historic high corporate profits in the pandemic FY21 corporate tax hit a historic low (below income tax collection) and there was massive loss of jobs and wage cut in the corporate world. An analysis showed, the "stellar rise" in corporate profits in FY21 and FY22 accompanied with the slowest growth in capex (growth in "fixed assets") in the previous six fiscals at 2.3% in FY22 and corporate profits doesn't even have anything to do with sales or revenue growth (which explain the "sellers' inflation" or "greedflation" explained earlier)![308] Total GFCF (government and private) too has fallen – at 28.7% of the GDP in nine fiscals of FY15-FY23, from 33.7% in the previous nine fiscals of FY06-FY14 (current prices). All this is because of low demand and high unutilized capacity.

(ii)   **Corporate wealth goes to the top**: Crony capitalism and vitiation of competition has led to wealth concentrating at the very top – and shifting from PSUs to private corporates. An analysis of corporate profits[309] showed in FY05, six out of top 10 and 12 out of top 20 most profitable firms were PSUs which declined to three and seven, respectively, by H1 of 2022. It also showed that in FY05 the share of top 20 firms in total corporate profits was 55.8%, which dipped to 52% in FY11 and then went up to 72% in FY20. The pandemic saw their share dip to 62.4% in FY21 but in H1 of FY22, it was up again at 65%. This concentration of profits at the top was accompanied with a disturbing trend: small and public sector firms struggling to make profits. Another analysis[310] showed, in three years of FY20-FY22, top 20 listed companies pocketed 80% profits (moving average) in the NIFTY as compared to around 40% a decade ago due to digitization, new business models and taxation policies etc. Business portal CMIE's analysis for FY21[311]

Such lop-sided growth is one of the reasons for data fudging, data suppression, data vacuum, fake claims and unrealistic claims (of building a $5 to $30 trillion economy, fifth largest economy, developed country at the end of "Amrit Kaal" in 2047 etc.).

Data Fudging, Suppression & Vacuum

A big casualty is India's once-globally reputed and pioneering statistical system. Back in 1972, American statistician W Edwards Deming wrote[312]: "No statistician ever had more influence on the entire profession and on government statistical offices the world over." More recently, in 2005, economists Angus Deaton and Valerie Kozel wrote[313] "most countries can only envy India's its statistical capacity". But in March 2019, 108 eminent national and international economists and sociologists were fervently appealing to the government to restore that credibility.[314]

Various tricks have been employed to achieve the synthesis of tall claims and data: (a) data fudging (b) junking inconvenient data (c) creating data vacuum by not collecting critical data or not releasing if collected (d) presenting unverifiable (dashboard) data (e) raising questions on methodology and surveys of the government itself and (f) peddling misleading, fake/absurd economic theories.

Data fudging: The most reprehensible data fudging is that of the new GDP series of 2011-12 series, introduced in January 2015 – which then CEA Arvind Subramanian said overestimated the GDP growth by *2.5 to 3.7 percentage points* per year during 2011-12 and 2016-17[315] – based on his study of 17 high frequency economic indicators. The new GDP series relied on a secret and untested MCA-21 database (self-populated by industry) for mapping manufacturing and services – which remains *deeply flawed*[316] nearly a decade later. The GDP continues to be *overestimated by about 3 percentage points* in 2023 – as a number of economists, like Ashoka Mody, Arvind Subramanian and Josh Felman and Arun Kumar, have demonstrated in 2023.[317]

Its back series data was released three years later in November 2018 – after *cutting down*[318] high growth during the earlier UPA regime. The new GDP series suddenly made India the fastest growing major economy in the world in 2015 – which *evaporated* in the pandemic 2020[319] – and served the purpose of maintaining the pretense of higher growth. This data fudging meant that India witnessed the highest growth in the past decade in FY17 (8.3%) – ignoring the 9.1% growth in FY22 which came on the low base of FY21 (which saw negative growth for the first time after 1979 (FY1979-80[320]). This high growth of 8.3% in FY17 was when the disastrous demonetization hit.

In the new GDP series, agriculture is doing far better, particularly after the pandemic hit in 2020, but the fact that tight stock limits, frequent bans and restrictions on export of various agriculture produce like non-basmati rice, wheat, sugar, onion, pulses etc. in the name of fighting inflation, and continued high inflation in food items, are clear indications that the agriculture harvest data is fudged to inflate the GDP numbers and paint a rosier picture.[321] This was finally admitted to by the government in 2023 that the crop yield estimates are unreliable and has adversely impacted its policymaking and plans.[322]

Junking inconvenient data or creating data vacuum: A few examples:

(i)   2017-18 MPCE was not made public because the government said the data quality was suspect. This was a *big lie*[323] – the very expert committee which the government said had raised the quality issue and sought its scrapping *denied* and *asserted* that the data was robust. The last MPCE was in 2011-12 – over a decade old. The absence of this data means (a) the headline inflation data, CPI (and also WPI), is based on over a decade old data of 2012. This also means that the RBI's inflation targeting is based on very old and unreliable data (consumption patterns keep changing). Besides (b) the National Account (proxy for income) for poverty estimation can't be done.

(ii)   7th Economic Census, launched in 2019 and completed in 2021, hasn't been released yet[324]. The 6th Economic Census (2013-14) was published in 2016 – about a decade old.

(iii)   Census 2021, for the first time in Indian history (since 1881), has been put on hold and pushed to 2024-25.[325] The Census is key to policymaking in the areas of health, education, employment, welfare and others – but is over 12 years old now.

(iv)   Other old data – Unincorporated Enterprises (non-farm) survey of 2015-16, Index of Industrial Production (IIP) of 2011-12, Input-Output table of 2008-09, Tendulkar poverty line of 2004-05, Unorganized Sector Statistics report was last published in 2012 but it is not clear which year the assessment was made that informal economy contributes "about 50% of the national product".

(v)   Non-release of caste data of 2011 SECC, raising data quality issue. The real objective is to suppress it and hence, the government has refused to collect caste data in the 2021 Census by offering lame excuses like it was too late to incorporate it the framework.[326]

(vi)   No data on shell companies operating from tax havens – as the government said after the Hindenburg report hit in 2023.

(vii)   Although India challenged the WHO's estimate of *4.74 million excess deaths* due to the pandemic in 2022, it didn't have the Civil Registration System (CRS) data for 2021 to do this – nor made available for more than a year later.[327] During the pandemic in 2020 and 2021, the Ministry of Health and Family Welfare provided dashboard data which didn't tell the daily or total cases of the Covid-19 infections. The daily cases were embedded in a link on the next page – which was replaced daily, removing the previous day's data. It was private trackers like the John Hopkins' or Our World in Data one used to keep an account.[328]

(viii)   No hate crime and mob lynching of Muslims by right-wing militant groups, since the NCRB stopped collecting such data in 2017[329] and media was forced to shut down their hate crime trackers (Hindustan Times and IndiaSpend)[330]. A country that doesn't value democratic order and secularism harms its economic progress (see Chapter XII)

(ix)   None died of oxygen shortage in 2021, no migrant died during the massive reverse migration in 2020, no data on job loss of migrants, no farmer died during year-long protest in 2021-22 etc. – earning the government the sobriquet "No Data Available" government.[331]

(x)   No data on actual tax payers, from different income groups, and how much tax they pay is released – only the returns filed are given – hiding the ground realities.

Dashboard data: Official data are presented in dashboards – which can't be verified. Data released by departments often don't match the NSSO surveys. Kundu and Mohanan[332] tell how in pre-2014 India the mismatch between the National Sample Surveys (NSSs) and departmental information used to cross-check and study data to explain the gaps, which was discontinued to provide a rosier-than-reality picture about everything – education, health, sanitation, jobs – further damaging the credibility of Indian statistical system and official data. Reading or making sense of official data is now a near impossible task.

Data pages are frequently recast (wholesale) in design, locations and links or URLs, nomenclatures and compositions (different headlines and elements within it) and tables (different numbers) – leaving no trace of the earlier data. Many a times the relevant and routine data are not even uploaded or can't be found. This is particularly true for all critical websites like the parliamentary question-answers, RBI database, the National Accounts Statistics (MoSPI) and labour surveys (PLFS). Most government documents are scanned or photocopies, disabled for search; carry raw data which don't reveal basic information (like totals) and can't be copied or transferred to excel sheets (including budget documents and parliamentary committee reports). Reading official statistics and reports are so daunting that it calls for extraordinary courage and persistence. The data suppression is so ridiculous that here is a simple test: Try to find out annual headline inflation number (CPI) of India from any official source, be it the MoSPI or the RBI – you will simply not get it.

Absurd data and Economics: If data manipulations and tall claims don't work, then absurdities are peddled as economic theory:

(a)   In 2022, the Finance Ministry said (i) inflation doesn't hit the poor but the rich and (ii) lower inflation leads to "redistribution of income".[333]

(b)   In 2023, the SBI Research made an absurd claim that withdrawal of Rs 2,000 notes would boost consumption and GDP growth because it would remain a legal tender. This was after the RBI said it was withdrawing the note because (a) it was issued to re-monetize after demonetization (oxymoronic) (b) printing of these notes stopped in FY19 (c) its life-span was 4-5 years and (d) stock of banknotes in other denominations was adequate. To compound the confusion, it said that the withdrawn notes "will continue to be legal tender".[334]

(c)   NITI Aayog has developed its own indices and produces shoddy papers. Its report on SDG said poverty, hunger and income inequality declined in most states during the two waves of the pandemic crisis – without explaining how. Its multidimensional poverty index (MPI) claimed 135 million Indians were lifted out of poverty from highly questionable NFHS-5 data of 2019-21.[335]

Misleading claims: Convoluted calculations and exaggerated claims like near zero poverty (0.8%)[336] and jobful economy[337] are not usual and often come from people in powerful positions. Of late, questions have been raised about the official surveys and methodologies by the government's economists.[338] Irrespective of the merit of it, creating further doubts about data quality nine years only ends up preparing a fertile ground for more fake and misleading claims.

All such data manipulations make the government's accountability *non sequitur* and *non-est*. In fact, the central problem with the statistical system is the government's emphasis on "positivity" and controlling the narrative to show it in good light – a shorthand for falsehood and propaganda (see Chapter II and IX) – which has created the credibility crisis[339] in the Indian statistical system.

To sum up, the Prime Minister's command-and-control economic regime has ended up benefitting selected private businesses (cronies) and brought mass impoverishment and hunger to the masses. Until such a regime continues, there is no hope for a brighter future for most Indians.

***

References

1   Finance Minister's Budget speech, Feb 1, 2022; https://www.indiabudget.gov.in/doc/bspeech/bs202223.pdf

2   Finance Minister's budget speech, Feb 1, 2023; https://www.indiabudget.gov.in/doc/budget_speech.pdf

3   The Jan Vishwas (Amendment of Provisions) Act, 2023, Aug 11, 2023; https://egazette.gov.in/WriteReadData/2023/248047.pdf

4   Sagar, Scriptural Economy: Modi's Atmanirbhar Bharat is a thinly veiled blueprint of the RSS's "Hindu Economics", Jul 23, 2020; https://caravanmagazine.in/politics/narendra-modi-atmanirbhar-bharat-rss-hindu-economics-rashtra

5   Dattopant Thengadi, Third Way, Sahitya Sindhu Prakashan, 1998; https://www.amazon.in/THIRD-WAY-DATTOPANT-THENGADI/dp/8186595031

6   Ranjan Prabhash, What's So Neoliberal About Narendra Modi's India Anyway?, Jul 28, 2018; https://thewire.in/political-economy/neoliberalism-modi-bjp-congress-india

7   Guruswamy Mohan, Why Gurumurthy has to employ voodoo economics to defend demonetisation (and attack Manmohan Singh), Dec 15, 2016; https://scroll.in/article/824190/why-gurumurthy-has-to-employ-voodoo-economics-to-defend-demonetisation-and-attack-manmohan-singh; Subramanya Rupa, Opinion: Modi has failed to reform India's economy. Populist tricks are all he has left., Jan 15, 2019; https://www.washingtonpost.com/opinions/2019/01/15/modi-has-failed-reform-indias-economy-populist-tricks-are-all-he-has-left/

8   Chatterjee Shoumitro and Subramanian Arvind, India's Inward (Re)Turn: Is it Warranted? Will it Work? Ashoka Centre for Economic Policy, Oct 2020; https://www.ashoka.edu.in/static/doc_uploads/file_1603091486.pdf

9   Mohanty P, Is India back to 'license raj'? Aug 15, 2023; https://www.fortuneindia.com/opinion/is-india-back-to-license-raj/113736

10   Mohanty P, 'An Unkept Promise', Ch III-XI

11   The Prime Minister, Shri Narendra Modi addressed the nation from the ramparts of the Red Fort on the 73rd Independence Day, Aug 15, 2019; https://pib.gov.in/PressReleseDetailm.aspx?PRID=1582103

12   Covid crisis an opportunity, time for bold decisions and investments: Modi, PTI, Jun 11, 2020; https://timesofindia.indiatimes.com/india/covid-19-crisis-should-be-turned-into-an-opportunity-for-self-reliant-india-pm-modi/articleshow/76316166.cms

13   Feb 26, 2019; https://www.aajtak.in/literature/poems/story/pm-narendra-modi-readout-prasoon-joshi-poem-main-desh-nahin-jhukane-dunga-644167-2019-02-26,

14   Government Has "No Business To Be In Business": PM Narendra Modi, Feb 24, 2021; https://www.ndtv.com/india-news/government-has-no-business-to-

be-in-business-pm-narendra-modi-2377787; Government has no business to do business: PM Narendra Modi, Feb 9, 2022; https://www.businesstoday.in/latest/economy/story/government-has-no-business-to-do-business-pm-narendra-modi-322064-2022-02-09

15   FM underlines role of pvt sector; says bending Covid curve, Budget will help sustain revival, Feb 14, 2021; https://indianexpress.com/article/business/economy/fm-nirmala-sitharaman-private-sector-budget-economy-revival-covid-7187730/

16   We should worship job creators like Adani, Ambani, says BJP MP, Feb 10, 2022; https://www.thehindu.com/news/national/we-should-worship-job-creators-like-adani-ambani-says-bjp-mp/article38408523.ece

17   Mohanty P, Rebooting Economy 68: How private wealth creators are serving Indian economy and people, Feb 21, 2021; https://www.businesstoday.in/opinion/columns/story/rebooting-economy-68-how-private-wealth-creators-are-serving-indian-economy-and-people-288805-2021-02-19

18   Daniyal Shoaib, Azim Premji aside, why are India's ultra rich so tight-fisted when it comes to philanthropy?, Jul 11, 2015; https://scroll.in/article/740220/azim-premji-aside-why-are-indias-ultra-rich-so-tight-fisted-when-it-comes-to-philanthropy; Mapstone Michael, Indian billionaires are failing to help the country's poor – but it's more complicated than you think, Jun 11, 2019; https://www.independent.co.uk/voices/india-billionaire-wealth-philanthropy-poverty-charity-nilekani-a8953326.html

19   Mohanty P, Rebooting Economy 67: Set the record straight before setting up a Bad Bank, Feb 15, 2021; https://www.businesstoday.in/opinion/columns/story/rebooting-economy-67-set-the-record-straight-before-setting-up-a-bad-bank-287585-2021-02-14

20   Mohanty P, NPAs: RBI must name and shame fraudsters, wilful defaulters, Jul 31, 2023; https://www.fortuneindia.com/opinion/npas-rbi-must-name-and-shame-fraudsters-wilful-defaulters/113563

21   Mohanty P, Pricing Power Behind High Inflation? May 8, 2023; https://www.fortuneindia.com/long-reads/pricing-power-behind-high-inflation/112581

22   Mohanty P, West is vigilant about predatory pricing, India not, JUn 16, 2023; https://www.fortuneindia.com/opinion/west-is-vigilant-about-predatory-pricing-india-not/113069#:~:text=The%20most%20glaring%20case%20is,Paris%20flight%20on%20the%20day).

23   Adani group overtakes Reliance in market cap; trails Tata, Aug 23, 2022; https://www.fortuneindia.com/investing/adani-group-overtakes-reliance-in-market-cap-trails-tata/109386

24   Adani Group: How The World's 3rd Richest Man Is Pulling The Largest Con In Corporate History, Hindenburg Research, Jan 24, 2023; https://hindenburgresearch.com/adani/

25 Adani: How the billionaire's empire lost $100bn in days, Feb 2, 2023; https://www.bbc.com/news/world-asia-india-64494466

26 Travelli Alex, Gautam Adani's Rise Was Intertwined With India's. Now It's Unraveling. Feb 4, 2023; https://www.nytimes.com/2023/02/04/business/adani-modi-india.html

27 Fleet of 3 aircraft ensures Modi is home every night after day's campaigning, Apr 22, 2014; http://timesofindia.indiatimes.com/articleshow/34069525.cms?utm_source=contentofinterest&utm_medium=text&utm_campaign=cppst

28 Modi flies into brand cloud, May 24, 2014; https://www.telegraphindia.com/india/modi-flies-into-brand-cloud/cid/182148

29 Forbes: The world's real-time billionaires; https://www.forbes.com/real-time-billionaires/#2d0d2bf93d78

30 Tata, Reliance most valued business groups, Mar 13, 2023; https://economictimes.indiatimes.com/markets/stocks/news/tata-reliance-most-valued-business-groups/articleshow/98591916.cms?utm_source=contentofinterest&utm_medium=text&utm_campaign=cppst

31 Roy Arundhati, Modi's model is at last revealed for what it is: violent Hindu nationalism underwritten by big business, Feb 18, 2023; https://www.theguardian.com/commentisfree/2023/feb/18/narendra-modi-hindu-nationalism-india-gautam-adani

32 Adani Group: https://www.adani.com/about-us#:~:text=Adani%20Group%20is%20a%20diversified,has%20a%20pan%2DIndia%20presence.; Reliance:https://www.ril.com/getattachment/3de565d6-3a54-4243-b40b-02f6a25679c2/AnnualReport_2021-22.aspx; Taya Group: https://www.tata.com/about-us

33 Money Control; https://www.moneycontrol.com/stocks/marketinfo/netprofit.php?optex=BSE&opttopic=&group=A&indcode=All

34 Top 100 taxpaying companies, Money Control: https://www.moneycontrol.com/stocks/marketinfo/tax/bse/index.html

35 Shrivastava Bhuma, Pradhan Bibhudatta and Sanjai PR, How Mukesh Ambani, Gautam Adani were caught in crossfire over farming laws, Jan 17, 2021; https://www.business-standard.com/article/economy-policy/how-mukesh-ambani-gautam-adani-were-caught-in-crossfire-over-farming-laws-121011700060_1.html

36 Mohanty P, Budget 2022: Dismantle protectionism and crony capitalism for growth, Jan 24, 20https://www.fortuneindia.com/budget-2022/budget-2022-dismantle-protectionism-and-crony-capitalism-for-growth/106824

37 Economist 2023, Why Adani Group's troubles will reverberate across India, Feb 9, 2023; https://archive.is/PwvQc

38 Mohanty P, National champions: Costs and benefits of India's new growth model, Mar 23, 2023; https://www.fortuneindia.com/opinion/national-champions-costs-and-benefits-of-indias-new-growth-model/112005

39   Roubini Nouriel, India is a big global player – but there are problems it must tackle, Feb 12, 2023; https://www.theguardian.com/business/2023/feb/22/india-modi-government-economic-growth-nouriel-roubini

40   Ashutosh Varshney writes: What government-Adani relationship says about Indian capitalism, Feb 16, 2023; https://indianexpress.com/article/opinion/columns/ashutosh-varshney-government-adani-relationship-indian-capitalism-8442387/

41   Acharya Viral, Replete with Contradictions, Brimming with Opportunities, Saddled with Challenges, Mar 30-31, 2023; https://www.brookings.edu/wp-content/uploads/2023/02/BPEA_Spring2023_EM-Panel_Acharya_unembargoed_updated.pdf

42   RBI's March 2023 bulletin; https://rbidocs.rbi.org.in/rdocs/Bulletin/PDFs/RBIMARCH2023BULLETIN73EB5BC739844D19A4EC2D89CFAEF1D7.PDF

43   Weber Isabella M, Wasner Evan, Sellers' Inflation, Profits and Conflict: Why can Large Firms Hike Prices in an Emergency? University of Massachusetts Amherst, March 2023; https://scholarworks.umass.edu/cgi/viewcontent.cgi?article=1348&context=econ_workingpaper

44   Daniel Will, 'We may be looking at the end of capitalism': One of the world's oldest and largest investment banks warns 'Greedflation' has gone too far, Apr 6, 2023; https://fortune.com/2023/04/05/end-of-capitalism-inflation-greedflation-societe-generale-corporate-profits/

45   Mohanty P, West is vigilant about predatory pricing, India not, Jun 16, 2023; https://www.fortuneindia.com/opinion/west-is-vigilant-about-predatory-pricing-india-not/113069#:~:text=The%20most%20glaring%20case%20is,Paris%20flight%20on%20the%20day).

46   Weber Isabella M, Wasner Evan, 'Sellers' Inflation'

47   ED attaches flat linked to NewsClick editor-in-chief Prabir Purkayashta, Aug 9, 2023; https://www.hindustantimes.com/india-news/ed-attaches-newsclick-editor-s-flat-in-money-laundering-probe-charge-sheet-expected-soon-101691560513699.html

48   Singh Vivashwan, The 'Beneficiaries' of Modi's Globetrotting: Adani and Ambani, Apr 1, 2019; https://www.newsclick.in/%E2%80%98Beneficiaries%E2%80%99-Modi%E2%80%99s-Globetrotting-Adani-Ambani

49   Is Modi a PM or business development manager of Ambani, Adani: Sidhu, Apr 20, 2019; https://www.business-standard.com/article/news-ani/is-modi-a-pm-or-business-development-manager-of-ambani-adani-sidhu-119042000368_1.html

50   Two weeks before Rafale announcement, Anil Ambani met French Defence officials, Feb 12, 2019; https://indianexpress.com/article/india/two-weeks-before-rafale-announcement-anil-ambani-met-french-defence-officials-5579069/

51   Rafale offsets deal: Anil Ambani was Indian government's choice, says Francois Hollande, Sept 22, 2018; https://economictimes.indiatimes.com/news/politics-and-

nation/indian-govt-proposed-reliance-defence-as-partner-in-rafalefrench-media-quoting-hollande/articleshow/65903420.cms

52   Philippin Tann, Rafale Papers: how Indian tycoon sought help of Macron and finance minister over tax bill, Jul 12, 2023; https://www.mediapart.fr/en/journal/international/120723/rafale-papers-how-indian-tycoon-sought-help-macron-and-finance-minister-over-tax-bill

53   Official website of Reliance Infrastructure; https://www.rinfra.com/defence

54   Dassault Aviation's Rafale joint venture with Anil Ambani likely to be dissolved, Jul 13, 2023; https://www.newindianexpress.com/nation/2023/jul/13/dassault-aviations-rafale-joint-venture-with-anil-ambanilikely-to-be-dissolved-2594310.html

55   How does Anil Ambani have money for Rafale deal but not for paying dues, asks Ericsson lawyer, Feb 13, 2019; https://scroll.in/latest/913105/how-does-anil-ambani-have-money-for-rafale-deal-but-not-for-paying-dues-asks-ericsson-lawyer

56   From riches to rags: Anil Ambani pleads poverty, says his net worth is zero, Feb 8, 2020; https://www.business-standard.com/article/companies/from-riches-to-rags-anil-ambani-pleads-poverty-says-his-net-worth-is-zero-120020701929_1.html

57   What 'bankrupt' Anil Ambani didn't tell: his $1.3-billion web of offshore firms, Oct 4, 2021; https://indianexpress.com/article/express-exclusive/anil-ambani-pandora-papers-7550155/

58   MEA, GOI, Joint Declaration between Bangladesh and India during Visit of Prime Minister of India to Bangladesh- " NotunProjonmo – Nayi Disha", Jun 7, 2015; https://www.mea.gov.in/incoming-visit-detail.htm?25346/Joint+Declaration+between+Bangladesh+and+India+during+Visit+of+Prime+Minister+of+India+to+Bangladesh+quot+Notun+Projonmo++Nayi+Dishaquot

59   Bangladesh seeks new terms for Adani coal electricity deal, Feb 7, 2023; https://www.washingtonpost.com/world/2023/02/07/adani-bangladesh-electricity-coal-discount/

60   'Was PM Modi Directly Involved in Adani's Bangladesh Power Deal?: TMC MP Asks EAM, Feb 17, 2023; https://thewire.in/government/adani-bangladesh-modi-jawhar-sircar-jaishankar

61   Adani's Goda plant starts power supply to Bangladesh, Apr 9, 2023; https://www.livemint.com/industry/energy/adanis-godda-plant-starts-power-supply-to-bangladesh-11681048727204.html

62   Govt approves Adani Power's Rs 14,000 cr Jharkhand SEZ project, Mar 3, 2019; https://economictimes.indiatimes.com/industry/energy/power/govt-approves-adani-powers-rs-14000-cr-jharkhand-sez-project/articleshow/68240390.cms?utm_source=contentofinterest&utm_medium=text&utm_campaign=cppst

63   Dirty Tricks and Coercion Used to Acquire Land for Adani's Godda Power Plant,

Jul 22, 2020; https://www.newsclick.in/Dirty-Tricks-Coercion-Acquire-Land-Adani-Godda-Power-Plant

64   Adani steps up Australia coal plans ahead of Modi visit, No 14, 2014; https://www.reuters.com/article/adani-ent-australia-coal-idUSL3N0T126820141112

65   Menon Aditya, Modi's Achhe Din: Selfie with Abbott, coal mine for Adani? DilyO, India Today Group, Nov 20, 2014; https://www.dailyo.in/politics/modis-achhe-din-selfie-with-abbott-coal-mine-for-adani/story/1/722.html

66   Sri Lanka Adani Row: Official Quits After Alleging Link To PM Modi, Jun 14, 2022; https://www.ndtv.com/india-news/sri-lanka-adani-row-energy-official-quits-after-alleging-link-to-pm-narendra-modi-3063344

67   Subramanian Nirupama, To Legalise Power Project Given to Adani Without Tender, Sri Lanka Wants it Turned Into Govt-to-Govt Deal, Sept 4, 2023; https://thewire.in/south-asia/to-legalise-power-project-given-to-adani-without-tender-sri-lanka-wants-it-turned-into-govt-to-govt-deal

68   'Reflection of Trust Towards India': Israeli Envoy Defends Adani's Haifa Port Deal, Feb 22, 2023; https://thewire.in/diplomacy/reflection-of-trust-towards-india-israeli-envoy-defends-adanis-haifa-port-deal

69   The Battle for the World's Most Powerful Cyberweapon, Jan 28, 2022; https://www.nytimes.com/2022/01/28/magazine/nso-group-israel-spyware.html

70   PPP development of airports first conceived in UPA II regime, Nov 17, 2018; https://www.newindianexpress.com/nation/2018/nov/17/ppp-development-of-airports-first-conceived-in-upa-ii-regime-1899530.html

71   Mukul Pranav, Sasi Anil, Finance Ministry and Niti Aayog had raised red flags before Adani's clean sweep of six airports, Indian Express, Jan 15, 2021; https://indianexpress.com/article/business/adani-airports-finance-ministry-niti-aayog-7146853/; Nair Ravi, Thakurta Paranjoy Guha, How Adani Will Become India's Largest Private Airport Operator, Sept 2, 2020; https://www.newsclick.in/How-Adani-Will-Become-India%27s-largest-Airport-Operator

72   Adani Group buys 74% stake in Mumbai international airport, Aug 31, 2020; https://scroll.in/latest/971805/adani-group-buys-74-stake-in-mumbai-international-airport

73   Mukul Pranav, Sasi Anil, Finance Ministry and Niti Aayog had raised red flags before Adani's clean sweep of six airports, Indian Express, Jan 15, 2021; https://indianexpress.com/article/business/adani-airports-finance-ministry-niti-aayog-7146853/; Nair Ravi, Thakurta Paranjoy Guha, How Adani Will Become India's Largest Private Airport Operator, Sept 2, 2020; https://www.newsclick.in/How-Adani-Will-Become-India%27s-largest-Airport-Operator

74   Adani issue: GVK refutes Rahul Gandhi's claim on pressure to sell Mumbai airport, Feb 8, 2023; http://timesofindia.indiatimes.com/articleshow/97708740.cms?utm_source=contentofinterest&utm_medium=text&utm_campaign=cppst

75   Adani Group completes financial closure for Navi Mumbai airport, Mar 29, 2022; https://www.livemint.com/companies/news/adani-group-completes-financial-closure-for-navi-mumbai-airport-11648571932835.html

76   '18% GST on Adani's staff cost dues to AAI', Apr 24, 2023; https://timesofindia.indiatimes.com/business/india-business/18-gst-on-adanis-staff-cost-dues-to-aai/articleshow/99714171.cms?from=mdr

77   Mohanty P, 'Is India back to 'license raj'?'

78   Barik Soumyarendra and Magazine Aanchal, As US, China red flag laptop import measure, India to take 'security' line, Oct 19, 2023; https://indianexpress.com/article/business/economy/as-us-china-red-flag-laptop-import-measure-india-to-take-security-line-8989711/

79   JioBook, Amazon; https://www.amazon.in/JIO-NB1112MM-BLU-JioBook/dp/B0CCDRPGD8

80   Mohanty P, 'Is India back to 'license raj'?'

81   Gupta Surajit Das, Personal computer firms to seek 3-month reprieve from import curbsm Aug 4, 2023; https://www.business-standard.com/industry/news/pc-companies-to-seek-three-month-reprieve-from-import-restrictions-123080300692_1.html

82   Mohanty P, West is vigilant about predatory pricing, India not, Jun 16, 2023; https://www.fortuneindia.com/opinion/west-is-vigilant-about-predatory-pricing-india-not/113069

83   National Hydrogen Mission, Ministry of New and Renewable Energy, Mar 21, 2022; https://static.pib.gov.in/WriteReadData/specificdocs/documents/2023/jan/doc2023110150801.pdf

84   Cabinet approves National Green Hydrogen Mission, MN &RE, Jan 4, 2023; https://pib.gov.in/PressReleasePage.aspx?PRID=1888547

85   Adani And TotalEnergies To Create The World's Largest Green Hydrogen Ecosystem, Jun 14, 2022; https://www.adani.com/newsroom/media-release/adani-and-totalenergies-to-create-the-worlds-largest-green-hydrogen-ecosystem

86   Ambani's $75 billion plan aims to make India a hydrogen hub, Jan 31, 2022; https://timesofindia.indiatimes.com/business/india-business/ambanis-75-billion-plan-aims-to-make-india-a-hydrogen-hub/articleshow/89236627.cms

87   Oil palm mission: Govt cleared despite red flags by top forestry institute, Aug 23, 2021; https://indianexpress.com/article/india/oil-palm-mission-govt-cleared-despite-red-flags-by-top-forestry-institute-7466071/

88   Standard Chartered Bank, DBS Bank vs Ruchi Soya Industries, National Company Law Tribunal, Mumbai, Jul 24, 2019; https://ibbi.gov.in//uploads/order/9fe19063d2ab4fcebae37607485e0f5c.pdf; IBBI 2019: Insolvency and Bankruptcy News, July-Sept 2019; https://www.ibbi.gov.in/uploads/publication/

cff2db5cfaa42ed5aad9544b04bfac8b.pdf; Dasgupta & Nair 2022: Dasgupta Abir, Nair Ravi, Backed by Nationalised Banks, How Ramdev's Patanjali got Rich Through Ruchi Soya, Mar 30, 2022; https://www.newsclick.in/backed-nationalised-banks-how-ramdevs-patanjali-got-rich-through-ruchi-soya

89   Insolvency Resolution Process (CIRP), Security and Exchange Board of India, Aug 19, 2020; https://www.sebi.gov.in/sebi_data/meetingfiles/dec-2020/1608621922552_1.pdf

90   Completely Debt Free After Paying 2,925 Crore Loans: Ruchi Soya, PTI, Apr 9, 2022; https://www.ndtv.com/business/ruchi-soya-repays-entire-loans-of-rs-2-925-crore-2872128#:~:text=Baba%20Ramdev%27s%20Patanjali%20Ayurved-led%20Ruchi%20Soya%20has%20recently,Ltd%2C%20tweeted%20that%20Ruchi%20Soya%20has%20become%20debt-free.

91   Dasgupta & Nair 2022: Dasgupta Abir, Nair Ravi, Backed by Nationalised Banks, How Ramdev's Patanjali got Rich Through Ruchi Soya, Mar 30, 2022; https://www.newsclick.in/backed-nationalised-banks-how-ramdevs-patanjali-got-rich-through-ruchi-soya

92   Jalihal Shreegireesh and Tapasya, Patanjali Group spawned dubious shell companies for lucrative real estate business, part I, Nov 22, 2023; https://www.reporters-collective.in/trc/baba-ramdevs-real-estate; As Haryana kept Aravallis unprotected, Patanjali quietly traded forestland, part II, Nov 23, 2023; https://www.reporters-collective.in/trc/as-haryana-kept-aravallis-unprotected-patanjali-quietly-traded-forestland

93   Worth Robert F, The Billionaire Yogi Behind Modi's Rise, Jul 26, 2018; https://www.nytimes.com/2018/07/26/magazine/the-billionaire-yogi-behind-modis-rise.html

94   Sharma Betwa, Meet The Doctor Who Challenged Patanjali's Misleading Advertisements & Won, May 19, 2023; https://www.article-14.com/post/meet-the-doctor-who-challenged-patanjali-s-misleading-advertisements-won-64665d83e8557

95   Coronavirus: The misleading claims about an Indian remedy, BBC, Mar 2, 2021; https://www.bbc.com/news/56172784

96   Ramdev's Patanjali products fail quality test, RTI inquiry finds, May 13, 2017; https://www.hindustantimes.com/india-news/baba-ramdev-s-patanjali-products-fail-uttarakhand-quality-test/story-bXo4XySEajw7ZDby4GISML.html

97   Cancer, HIV, COVID: Patanjali's Long List of Murky, Unproven Cures, May 23, 2021; https://www.thequint.com/news/webqoof/patanjali-ramdev-coronil-and-the-long-list-exaggerated-unproven-cures#read-more

98   Ramdev Baba drug 'Putrajeevak Beej' promises male child, May 1, 2015; https://www.financialexpress.com/industry/controversy-hits-ramdev-drug-promising-birth-of-male-child-hits-modis-beti-bachao-campaign/68323/

99   Baba Ramdev's Patanjali Fined ₹ 11 Lakh For Misleading Advertisements, Dec

15, 2016; https://www.ndtv.com/india-news/baba-ramdevs-patanjali-fined-rs-11-lakh-for-misleading-advertisements-1637974; SC pulls up Ramdev, says must restrain from abusing other systems of medicine, Aug 24, 2022; https://www.hindustantimes.com/india-news/sc-pulls-up-ramdev-says-must-restrain-from-abusing-other-systems-of-medicine-101661240945398.html; Sharma Betwa, Meet The Doctor Who Challenged Patanjali's Misleading Advertisements & Won, May 19, 2023; https://www.article-14.com/post/meet-the-doctor-who-challenged-patanjali-s-misleading-advertisements-won-64665d83e8557

100   Supreme Court warns Ramdev's Patanjali of Rs 1 crore fine for each false claim in its advertisements, Nov 22, 2023; https://scroll.in/latest/1059443/supreme-court-warns-patanjali-of-rs-1-crore-penalty-for-each-false-advertisement

101   'Ready for death penalty if...': Baba Ramdev on SC warning Patanjali over 'misleading' ads, Nov 22, 2023; https://www.businesstoday.in/latest/story/ready-for-death-penalty-if-baba-ramdev-on-sc-warning-patanjali-over-misleading-ads-406745-2023-11-22

102   Companies competing with Adani for prized assets faced CBI, ED raids: Cong, PTI, Aug 5, 2023; https://www.business-standard.com/politics/companies-competing-with-adani-for-prized-assets-faced-cbi-ed-raids-cong-123080500284_1.html; Mohanty P, Poor run for IBC continues. What ails it? May 30, 2023; https://www.fortuneindia.com/opinion/poor-run-for-ibc-continues-what-ails-it/112852

103   Jalihal Shreegireesh, Adani Group complained against farm law. Gov't diluted it to allow hoarding by corporates, Aug 16, 2023; https://www.reporters-collective.in/trc/adani-group-complained-against-farm-law-govt-diluted-it-to-allow-hoarding-by-corporates

104   FCI inks pact with Adani Group for construction of 2 silos, PTI, Jun 9, 2016; https://economictimes.indiatimes.com/news/economy/agriculture/fci-inks-pact-with-adani-group-for-construction-of-2-silos/articleshow/52672814.cms?from=mdr; Gayatri Geetanjali, After CLU grant, Adani Group setting up silos for FCI in Panipat, Dec 10, 2020; https://www.tribuneindia.com/news/haryana/after-clu-grant-adani-group-setting-up-silos-for-fci-in-panipat-182181

105   Mazoomdaar Jay, Adani Green advisor in hydel appraisal committee of Environment Ministry, Nov 14, 2023; https://indianexpress.com/article/india/adani-green-advisor-in-hydel-appraisal-committee-of-moef-9025521/

106   Deshmane Akshay, Inside Indian Energy and Mining Giant Vedanta's Campaign to Weaken Key Environmental Regulations, Aug 31, 2023; https://www.occrp.org/en/investigations/inside-indian-energy-and-mining-giant-vedantas-campaign-to-weaken-key-environmental-regulations#:~:text=Mining%20and%20oil%20giant%20Vedanta%20ran%20a%20covert,them%20using%20what%20experts%20say%20are%20illegal%20methods.

107   Mohanty P, Budget 2023: What gives China immunity from extreme poverty, but not India? Dec 28, 2022; https://www.fortuneindia.com/budget-2023/budget-2023-what-gives-china-immunity-from-extreme-poverty-but-not-india/110924

108   Acharya Viral and Rajan Raghuram, Do we really need Indian corporations in banking, New York University, Dec 2020, http://pages.stern.nyu.edu/~sternfin/vacharya/public_html/pdfs/acharya-rajan.pdf

109   Modi risks turning India into a nation of gangster capitalists, Nikkei Asia, Feb 5, 2021; https://asia.nikkei.com/Opinion/Modi-risks-turning-India-into-a-nation-of-gangster-capitalists

110   India's super-rich are getting much richer; Even as the economy shrinks by a tenth, Dec 3, 2020; https://www.economist.com/asia/2020/12/03/indias-super-rich-are-getting-much-richer

111   Damodaran Harish, Real power is with Centre, which holds the purse-strings in these fiscally-challenging times, Indian Express, Dec 5, 2020; https://indianexpress.com/article/opinion/columns/narendra-modi-politics-economy-farmers-protest-7092116/

112   India #10 on 'crony capitalism' index — how 'The Economist' ranked 43 biggest economies, May 11, 2023; https://theprint.in/economy/india-10-on-crony-capitalism-index-how-the-economist-ranked-43-biggest-economies/1563224/

113   Global Wealth Report 2022: Leading perspectives to navigate the future, Credit Suisse, https://www.credit-suisse.com/about-us/en/reports-research/global-wealth-report.html

114   Gautam Adani adds $49 bn wealth in 2021, higher than Jeff Bezos, Elon Musk, Mar 16, 2022; https://indianexpress.com/article/business/gautam-adani-adds-49-bn-wealth-in-2021-higher-than-bezos-musk-7823016/

115   Economic Survey 2019-20, Volume 1, Chapter 3; https://www.indiabudget.gov.in/budget2020-21/economicsurvey/index.php

116   Adani response, Jan 29, 2023; https://www.adani.com/-/media/Project/Adani/Invetsors/Adani-Response-to-Hindenburg-January-29-2023.pdf

117   Adani Group says Hindenburg fraud claim 'calculated attack on India', Jan 30, 2023; https://www.bbc.com/news/business-64448880

118   Our Reply To Adani: Fraud Cannot Be Obfuscated By Nationalism Or A Bloated Response That Ignores Every Key Allegation We Raised, Jan 29, 2023; https://hindenburgresearch.com/adani-response/

119   Mukherjee Andy, Gautam Adani and his fortune drivers deserve keener spotlight, scrutiny, Sept 23, 2022; https://www.business-standard.com/article/companies/gautam-adani-and-his-fortune-drivers-deserve-keener-spotlight-scrutiny-122092300102_1.html

120   Financial Times, Indian data reveals Adani empire's reliance on offshore funding, Mar 21, 2023; https://www.ft.com/content/a01c8930-005d-48e1-8a52-cbd0850cbbff?shareType=nongift

121   Rajya Sabha reply, Mar 21, 2023; https://www.dropbox.com/s/rg6lhet5eb0ooze/RS_No%20info%20on%20offshore%20shells.pdf?dl=0

122 Ministry of Corporate Affairs: Government identified 2,38,223 companies as shell companies between 2018-2021, Rajya Sabha, Jul 27, 2021; https://www.pib.gov.in/PressReleasePage.aspx?PRID=1739583

123 PMIndia: PM's address to the Nation from the ramparts of the Red Fort on the 71th Independence Day, Aug 15, 2017; https://www.pmindia.gov.in/en/news_updates/pms-address-to-the-nation-from-the-ramparts-of-the-red-fort-on-the-71th-independence-day/

124 McCrum Dan, Cook Chris, Sheppard David and Harlow Max, The mystery of the Adani coal imports that quietly doubled in value, Oct 12, 2023; https://www.ft.com/content/7aadb3d7-4a03-44ba-a01e-8ddd8bce29ed

125 Exclusive: New Investigation Reveals Gautam Adani's Older Brother As Key Player In Adani Group's Biggest Deals, Feb 28, 2023; https://www.forbes.com/sites/giacomotognini/2023/02/28/exclusive-new-investigation-reveals-gautam-adanis-older-brother-vinod-adani-as-key-player-in-adani-groups-biggest-deals/?sh=2837138b7dea

126 Morning Context, The Adani group does not own Ambuja Cements and ACC, Mar 13, 2023; https://themorningcontext.com/business/the-adani-group-does-not-own-ambuja-cements-and-acc

127 Vinod Adani owns Ambuja Cements and ACC, Mar 16, 2023; https://www.cnbctv18.com/business/companies/acc-ambuja-cements-ownership-vinod-adani-hindenburg-research-related-party-16172791.htm

128 Vinod Adani Is Part of Promoter Group: Adani Group's U-Turn on Gautam's Elder Brother, Mar 16, 2023; https://thewire.in/business/vinod-gautam-adani-u-turn

129 Adani's Billionaire Brother Starts to Retreat as Scrutiny Builds, Apr 25, 2023; https://www.bloomberg.com/news/articles/2023-04-25/who-is-vinod-adani-gautam-s-billionaire-brother-faces-scrutiny#xj4y7vzkg?leadSource=uverify%20wall

130 Sarin Ritu, Vinod Adani, Pankaj Oswal among 66 Indians who got golden passport, Nov 16, 2023; https://indianexpress.com/article/express-exclusive/vinod-adani-pankaj-oswal-among-66-indians-who-got-golden-passport-9026977/

131 Upadhyay Jayshree P, Why do these foreign funds love Adani Group companies? Apr 26, 2023; https://themorningcontext.com/business/why-do-these-foreign-funds-love-adani-group-companies Copyright © The Morning Context

132 MSCI drops Adani Transmission, Adani Total Gas from MSCI India Index in quarterly review, May 12, 2023; https://www.financialexpress.com/market/msci-drops-adani-transmission-adani-total-gas-from-msci-india-index-in-quarterly-review/3084058/

133 Singh Sandeep, Sarin Ritu, Key Adani investor Elara co-owner with Adani in defence firm, Mar 16, 2023; https://indianexpress.com/article/business/companies/key-adani-investor-elara-co-owner-with-adani-in-defence-firm-8497439/; Mauritius-Based Key Investor in Adani is Also Co-Owner of a Group Defence

Firm: Report, Mar 15, 2023; https://thewire.in/business/elara-adani-group-defence-firm-co-owner

134 Rajshekhar M, Adani's Acquisitions (part III): Why India Needs to Keep Track of the Costs, Aug 26, 2023; https://thewire.in/business/adanis-acquisitions-india-needs-to-keep-track-costs; part II: Adani's Acquisitions: Inside the Company's Growth Machine; https://thewire.in/business/adani-acquisitions-inside-the-companys-growth-machine; part III: Adani's Acquisitions: The 'Inorganic Strategy' Behind the Purchase of Gangavaram Port, https://thewire.in/business/adanis-acquisitions-the-inorganic-strategy-behind-the-purchase-of-gangavaram-port; Rajshekhar M, A Journalistic History of the Adani Group, Feb 1, 2023; https://thewire.in/business/adani-rise-reading-list; MS Nileena, Coalgate 2.0: The Adani Group reaps benefits worth thousands of crores of rupees as the coal scam continues under the Modi government, Mar 1, 2018; https://caravanmagazine.in/reportage/coalgate-2-0

135 Lok Sabha answer on Constitution of Committee to Investigate Adani Group, Mar 13, 2023; https://www.livelaw.in/pdf_upload/au1932-463151.pdf7

136 Lok Sabha answer on Investigation into Adani Group of Companies, Mar 13, 2023; https://www.livelaw.in/pdf_upload/au1889-463150.pdf

137 Month after Hindenburg's bombshell report, Adani stocks in shambles; group loses over Rs 12 lakh crore m-cap; Feb 24, 2023; https://www.livemint.com/market/stock-market-news/month-after-hindenburg-s-bombshell-report-adani-stocks-in-shambles-group-loses-over-rs-12-lakh-cr-m-cap-11677238532189.html

138 Mohanty P, Why Hindenburg report, short-selling are a blessing in disguise, Mar 13, 2023; https://www.fortuneindia.com/opinion/why-hindenburg-report-short-selling-are-a-blessing-in-disguise/111872

139 Basu Debashis, Adani stocks: What price rigging? May 23, 2023; https://www.business-standard.com/opinion/columns/adani-stocks-what-price-rigging-123052100876_1.html

140 Report of the expert committee, SC panel, Mar 2, 2023; https://www.dropbox.com/s/4y0jl8op8upa99m/SC%20panel%20report_Original.pdf?dl=0

141 Adani case: Plea claims conflict of interest in court-appointed panel, Sept 19, 2023; https://www.newindianexpress.com/business/2023/sep/19/adani-case-plea-claims-conflict-of-interest-in-court-appointed-panel-2616235.html

142 Panama Papers 2016: What is Panama Papers? Here is everything you need to know; https://indianexpress.com/photo-news/india/panama-papers-india-full-coverage-names-list-documents-companies/

143 Paradise Papers 2017: Biggest data leak reveals trails of India's corporates in global secret tax havens; https://indianexpress.com/article/india/paradise-papers-indian-corporates-black-money-4923999/#:~:text=The%20Paradise%20Papers%20is%20the,714%20Indians%20in%20the%20tally.

144 Pandora Papers 2021: After Panama, it's Pandora: facing regulatory heat, elite

Indians find new ways to ringfence wealth in secret havens; https://indianexpress.com/article/express-exclusive/pandora-papers-exclusive-how-elite-indians-ringfence-wealth-7550012/

145   After Panama, it's Pandora: facing regulatory heat, elite Indians find new ways to ringfence wealth in secret havens, Oct 4, 2021; https://indianexpress.com/article/express-exclusive/pandora-papers-exclusive-how-elite-indians-ringfence-wealth-7550012/; Probe gathers pace, IT notices sent to Indians, NRIs in Pandora; notices supervised by panel set up by govt, The Indian Express, Nov 16, 2021; https://indianexpress.com/article/india/it-notices-to-indians-nris-pandora-papers-7624699/

146   Mazoomdaar Jay, Two offshore funds in Hindenburg's Adani report were on I-T radar, May 30, 2023; https://indianexpress.com/article/india/two-offshore-funds-in-hindenburgs-adani-report-were-on-i-t-radar-8635698/

147   Dalal Sucheta, Adani Stock Saga: Clean Chit by SC Committee Raises Questions & Creates a Worrying New Template for Investigation, May 23, 2023; https://www.moneylife.in/article/adani-stock-saga-clean-chit-by-sc-committee-raises-questions-and-creates-a-worrying-new-template-for-investigation/70867.html?utm_source=substack&utm_medium=email

148   SEBI to SC: Probe on to track owners of 12 FPIs who hold stake in Adani Group firms, Aug 26, 2023; https://indianexpress.com/article/business/sebi-tells-supreme-court-it-has-completed-adani-probe-8909443/

149   Securities and Exchange Board of (Foreign Portfolio Investors) (Third Amendment) Regulations, 2018, Dec 31, 2018; https://www.sebi.gov.in/legal/regulations/dec-2018/securities-and-exchange-board-of-foreign-portfolio-investors-third-amendment-regulations-2018_41532.html

150   SEBI (Foreign Portfolio Investors) Regulations, 2014 [Last amended on March 6, 2017], Apr 18, 2017; https://www.sebi.gov.in/legal/regulations/apr-2017/sebi-foreign-portfolio-investors-regulations-2014-last-amended-on-march-6-2017-_34690.html

151   Operational Guidelines for FPIs, DDP and Eligible FIs; https://www.sebi.gov.in/sebi_data/commondocs/nov-2019/Operational%20Guidelines%20for%20FPIs,%20DDPs%20and%20EFIs%20revised_p.pdf

152   Sarin Ritu, Hindenburg report probe: Short selling in Adani shares led to 'gains' for 12 firms, ED to SEBI, Aug 30, 2023; https://indianexpress.com/article/business/hindenburg-report-probe-short-selling-in-adani-shares-led-to-gains-for-12-firms-ed-to-sebi-8913806/

153   Chakraborty Sayan, Deloitte quits as auditor of Adani Group's ports business, Aug 14, 2023; https://asia.nikkei.com/Business/Companies/Adani-Group/Deloitte-quits-as-auditor-of-Adani-Group-s-ports-business

154   Sood Varun and Burugula Pavan, Six of eight funds used to invest in Adani Group stocks now closed, Sept 5, 2023; https://www.livemint.com/companies/news/6-of-8-funds-used-to-invest-in-adani-shut-11693937876487.

html#:~:text=BENGALURU%20%2C%20NEW%20DELHI%20%3A%20Six%20 of,posing%20a%20challenge%20for%20the

155   Ellis-Petersen and Goodley Simon, Modi-linked Adani family secretly invested in own shares, documents suggest, https://www.theguardian.com/world/2023/ aug/31/modi-linked-adani-family-secretly-invested-in-own-shares-documents-suggest-india

156   McCrum Dan and Reed John, Secret paper trail reveals hidden Adani investors, Aug 30, 2023; https://www.ft.com/content/8d46b435-9725-46d4-80be-2cb3e276c4c9

157   CG Manoj and Mathew Liz, My vastraharan at meeting, panel chief conduct shameful: Moitra to Speaker after walkout with Opp, Nov 3, 2023; https:// indianexpress.com/article/political-pulse/unethical-personal-questions-mahua-moitra-storms-out-of-lok-sabha-ethics-panel-meet-9010675/

158   Pathak Vikas, As Mahua Moitra panel wraps up, progress on Ramesh Bidhuri row under wraps, Nov 14, 2023; https://indianexpress.com/article/political-pulse/ mahua-moitra-panel-ramesh-bidhuri-row-9025270/

159   'Cash-for-query' row: CBI begins probe into Lokpal complaint on Mahua, Nov 25, 2023; https://indianexpress.com/article/india/cbi-to-probe-cash-for-query-allegations-against-mahua-moitra-after-lokpals-nod-9042265/

160   Summons over Adani report: SC directs no coercive action be taken against 2 journalists, Nov 10, 2023; https://indianexpress.com/article/india/summons-adani-report-sc-2-journalists-9021813/

161   Mittal Sumedha, 'No jurisdiction', a dubious complainant: Why FT journalists moved SC against police notices, Nov 11, 2023; https://www.newslaundry. com/2023/11/11/no-jurisdiction-a-dubious-complainant-why-ft-journalists-moved-sc-against-police-notices#:~:text=Since%20the%20notices%20were%20 not,no%20jurisdiction%20to%20summon%20persons%E2%80%9D.

162   Mittal Sumedha, 'No jurisdiction'

163   Sodhi Tanishka, 'Arrest warrant' against journalist for 'defaming' Adani Group, Jul 26, 2022; https://www.newslaundry.com/2022/07/26/arrest-warrant-against-journalist-for-defaming-adani-group

164   'Drop Arrest Warrant against Paranjoy Guha Thakurta': Demands Committee to Protect Journalists, Jan 23, 2021; https://www.newsclick.in/drop-arrest-warrant-paranjoy-guha-thakurta-demands-committee-protect-journalists

165   Phone of journalist who reported on Adani Group targeted with Pegasus spyware, says reporters' group, Nov 8, 2023; https://scroll.in/latest/1058813/phone-of-journalist-who-reported-on-adani-group-targeted-with-pegasus-spyware-says-reporters-group

166   Shih Gerry, Mehrotra Karishma and Gupta Anant, India cracks down on critics of coal, Jun 5, 2023; https://www.washingtonpost.com/world/2023/06/05/india-coal-adani-modi-crackdown/

167   Damle Devendra and Zaveri Bhargavi, Enforcement of Securities Laws in India: An Empirical Overview., Sept 19, 2022; https://papers.ssrn.com/sol3/papers.cfm?abstract_id=4198772

168   Dalal Sucheta, SEBI: Reluctant Market Regulator Needs To Press the Reset Button, Mar 23, 2023; https://www.moneylife.in/article/sebi-reluctant-market-regulator-needs-to-press-the-reset-button/70210.html; What about National Pride When SEBI Is Repeatedly Embarrassed by Overturned Orders in Major Scams? Feb 11, 2023; https://www.moneylife.in/article/what-about-national-pride-when-sebi-is-repeatedly-embarrassed-by-overturned-orders-in-major-scams/69780.html; A Study on Role of Sebi in Indian Capital Market, International Journal of Pure and Applied Mathematics, Vol 119 No. 17 2018; https://acadpubl.eu/hub/2018-119-17/1/69.pdf

169   Chatterjee Shoumitro and Subramanian Arvind, India's Inward (Re)Turn

170   Mohanty P, Is protectionism helping or harming India's exports? May 30, 2023; https://www.fortuneindia.com/opinion/is-protectionism-helping-or-harming-indias-exports/112851

171   Mohanty P, Are top banks getting their economics wrong? Jun 28, 2023; https://www.fortuneindia.com/opinion/are-top-banks-getting-their-economics-wrong/113197

172   Mohanty P, 'Is protectionism helping or harming India's exports?'

173   Mohanty P, West is vigilant about predatory pricing, India not

174   Cairn Energy gets right to seize Indian assets in tax row, Jul 8, 2021; https://www.bbc.com/news/business-57742080

175   India asks US court to reject Cairn Energy's $1.2 billion suit; cites 'sovereign immunity', Business Today, Aug 17, 2021; https://www.businesstoday.in/latest/corporate/story/india-asks-us-court-to-reject-cairn-energys-12-billion-suit-cites-sovereign-immunity-304409-2021-08-17

176   CII meet: Fixing mistakes of past, retrospective tax move will build trust, says PM Modi, Aug 12, 2021; https://indianexpress.com/article/business/economy/cii-meet-fixing-mistakes-of-past-retrospective-tax-move-will-build-trust-says-pm-modi-7449594/

177   Mukherjee Andy, It's bankruptcy that needs a rescue in India, May 24, 2023; https://www.livemint.com/opinion/columns/its-bankruptcy-that-needs-a-rescue-in-india-11684899949758.html

178   Mohanty P, 'Is India back to 'license raj'?'

179   Nallareddy Suresh, Ethan Rouen and Juan Carlos Suárez Serrato, "Corporate Tax Cuts Increase Income Inequality." Harvard Business School Working Paper, No. 18-101, May 2018; https://www.hbs.edu/ris/Publication%20Files/18-101%20Rouen%20Corporate%20Tax%20Cuts_0a4626be-774c-4b9a-8f96-d27e5f317aad.pdf

180 Contract for making 120 Vande Bharat trains awarded to Russian major-rail-rail PSU JV, Mar 30, 2023; http://timesofindia.indiatimes.com/articleshow/99123827. cms?from=mdr&utm_source=contentofinterest&utm_medium=text&utm_campaign=cppst

181 Chaudhary Archana, World Bank Probes Irregularities in Ease of Business Report Data, BloombergQuint, Aug 28, 2020; https://www.bloombergquint.com/global-economics/world-bank-probes-irregularities-in-ease-of-business-report-data

182 Impact of GST on India's ranking will be seen next year: Junaid Ahmad, Oct 31, 2017; https://www.thehindu.com/business/Economy/impact-of-gst-on-indias-ranking-will-be-seen-next-year-junaid-ahmad/article19956734.ece

183 Quarterly fact sheet on FDI inflow (from Apr 2000 to June 2023), Department for Promotion of Industry and Internal Trade; https://dpiit.gov.in/sites/default/files/FDI_factsheet_June_23.pdf

184 Ease of Doing Business, https://tradingeconomics.com/country-list/ease-of-doing-business; OECD Data on FDI inflows, https://data.oecd.org/fdi/fdi-flows.htm

185 DPIIT FDI Statistics; https://dpiit.gov.in/publications/fdi-statistics

186 Sabir S, Rafique A and Abbas K, Institutions and FDI: evidence from developed and developing countries. Financial Innovation 5, 8 (2019). https://doi.org/10.1186/s40854-019-0123-7

187 Adhikari Tamanna and Whelan Karl, Did raising doing business scores boost GDP? Journal of Comparative Economics, Apr 13, 2023; https://www.karlwhelan.com/Papers/JCE.pdf

188 Mohanty P, Rebooting Economy 68: How private wealth creators are serving Indian economy and people, Feb 21, 2021; https://www.businesstoday.in/opinion/columns/story/rebooting-economy-68-how-private-wealth-creators-are-serving-indian-economy-and-people-288805-2021-02-19

189 Showcase of Gujarat Model: The GSPC Fraud, Dec 5, 2017; https://www.newsclick.in/showcase-gujarat-model-gspc-fraud

190 Karmakar Rahul, Unviable Arunachal hydro projects have been dumped on Central PSUs, say experts, Aug 13, 2023; https://www.thehindu.com/news/national/unviable-arunachal-hydro-projects-have-been-dumped-on-central-psus-say-experts/article67190744.ece

191 The State-Corporate Complex: A Threat to Freedom and Survival, Apr 7, 2011 lecture at University of Toronto; https://chomsky.info/20110407-2/

192 Mohanty P, An Unkept Promise: What Derailed the Indian Economy, page 239-240, Sage Publications, Dec 2021; https://www.amazon.in/Unkept-Promise-Derailed-Indian-Economy/dp/9354791867

193 Mampatta Sachin P, Eye on CSR-I: Listed govt firms contributed Rs 2,900 crore to PM CARES, Apr 24, 2023; https://www.business-standard.com/amp/india-news/listed-govt-firms-paid-over-rs-2-900-crore-to-pm-cares-123042300241_1.html

194   CAG 2018: Report of the Comptroller and Auditor General of India for the year ended 31 March 2017, Report No.18 of 2018 (CPSEs), Aug 7, 2018; https://cag.gov.in/cag_old/sites/default/files/audit_report_files/Report_No_18_of_2018_-_Compliance_Audit_on_General_Purpose_Financial_Reports_of_Central_Public_Sector_Enterprises_of_Union_Government__Commercial.pdf

195   IOC, ONGC, GAIL, other oil PSUs commit Rs 100 cr for redevelopment of Badrinath Dham shrine, PTI, May 6, 2021; https://www.businesstoday.in/latest/economy-politics/story/ioc-ongc-gail-other-oil-psus-commit-rs-100-cr-for-redevelopment-of-badrinath-dham-shrine-295167-2021-05-06

196   Verma Lalmani, Ayodhya idol: Behind tin-sheet curtains, three sculptors in a secretive race for best Ram Lalla sculpture, Oct 1, 2023; https://indianexpress.com/article/india/ayodhya-idol-ram-lalla-mandir-modi-temple-up-8962773/

197   Report of the High Level Committee on CSR, 2015; https://www.mca.gov.in/Ministry/pdf/CSRHLC_13092019.pdf

198   How independent are Independent Directors of PSUs? Half from BJP, Jul 2, 2021; https://indianexpress.com/article/india/how-independent-are-independent-directors-of-psus-half-from-bjp-7380271/; An Express Investigation: Not politicians alone, ready perch for bureaucrats too in PSU boards, https://indianexpress.com/article/india/not-politicians-alone-ready-perch-for-bureaucrats-too-in-psu-boards-7381904/; Khaitan Tarunabh, Killing a Constitution with a Thousand Cuts: Executive Aggrandizement and Party-state Fusion in India, Walter de Gruyter GmbH, Berlin/Boston, Law & Ethics of Human Rights, Aug 7, 2020; https://www.degruyter.com/document/doi/10.1515/lehr-2020-2009/html

199   Research Report on 'Discipline of Independent Directors: Form Code to Contribution', Indian Institute of Corporate Affairs, 2019; https://iica.nic.in/images/ID%20Research%20Report%2013_03_19.pdf

200   82% listed CPSEs don't have mandated independent directors: CAG report, Dec 29, 2022; https://www.business-standard.com/article/companies/82-listed-cpses-don-t-have-mandated-independent-directors-cag-report-122122901102_1.html

201   Disinvestment Policy, Department of Investment and Public Management, GOI, 2021; https://dipam.gov.in/disinvestment-policy#:~:text=(a)%20Disinvestment%20through%20minority%20stake%20sale&text=Already%20listed%20profitable%20CPSEs%20(not,or%20a%20combination%20of%20both.   National Investment Fund, May 2022, DIPAM; https://www.dipam.gov.in/national-investment-fund

202   Disinvestment in CPSEs, CAG Report No. 18, 2019; Chapter VII; https://cag.gov.in/uploads/download_audit_report/2019/Chapter_8_Disinvestment_in_CPSEs_of_Report_No_18_of_2019_General_Purpose_Financial_Reports_of_Central_Public_Sector_Enterprises.pdf; CAG 2020: Union Government Accounts of the Union Government No. 4 of 2020 (Financial Audit), CAG, Sept 23, 2020; https://cag.gov.in/webroot/uploads/download_audit_report/2020/Report%20No.%204%20of%202020_Eng-05f808ecd3a8165.55898472.pdf

203 Privatisation/disinvestment of profit and loss making PSUs, Rajya Sabha answer, Feb 9, 2021; https://pqars.nic.in/annex/253/AU867.pdf

204 Jha Somesh, Privatisation Files: Modi's Flagship Policy Faces Pushback From Key Ministries, BloombergQuint, Mar 24, 2021; https://www.bloombergquint.com/business/privatisation-files-modis-flagship-policy-faces-pushback-from-key-ministries-bq-exclusive & https://www.thequint.com/news/india/modi-government-ministries-oppose-privatisation-push#read-more

205 Government settles over Rs 61,000 crore Air India debt, other liabilities before transfer to Tatas, Jan 27, 2022; https://economictimes.indiatimes.com/industry/transportation/airlines-/-aviation/government-settles-over-rs-61000-crore-air-india-debt-other-liabilities-before-transfer-to-tatas/articleshow/89162597.cms

206 Rajshekhar M, Finance Firm Buying Public Sector Central Electronics Ltd. for Cheap Has Links to BJP Leaders, Mar 8, 2022; https://thewire.in/political-economy/central-electronics-bjp-cel-sharda-nandal

207 Government terminates privatisation of Central Electronics Limited, Sept 29, 2022; https://www.thehindubusinessline.com/economy/government-terminates-privatisation-of-central-electronics-limited/article65949876.ece

208 Rajshekhar M, 'Finance Firm Buying Public Sector'; Mohanty P, Why profitable strategic PSU CEL's sale leaves scientists aghast, Fortune India, Jan 5, 2022; https://www.fortuneindia.com/opinion/why-profitable-strategic-psu-cels-sale-leaves-scientists-aghast/106614

209 Nair Ravi, Dasgupta Abir and Thakurta Paranjoy Guha, Pawan Hans Sale: Cayman Firm in Winning Bid Flayed By NCLT for Failure to Pay, Show Funding Plan, The Wire, May 16, 2022: https://thewire.in/business/pawan-hans-sale-cayman-firm-nclt

210 Winning bidder unfit, govt calls off privatisation of Pawan Hans, Jul 4, 2023; https://timesofindia.indiatimes.com/business/india-business/winning-bidder-unfit-govt-calls-off-privatisation-of-pawan-hans/articleshow/101470469.cms?from=mdr

211 Govt drops plan to sell Pawan Hans, Central Electronics, Aug 29,2022; https://www.financialexpress.com/industry/govt-drops-plan-to-sell-pawan-hans-central-electronics/2647288/

212 With Adani, Agarwal under scrutiny, India's privatisation drive stalled, May 23, 2023; https://www.business-standard.com/economy/news/with-adani-agarwal-under-scrutiny-india-s-privatisation-drive-stalled-123052300145_1.html

213 Mohanty P, An Unkept Promise: What Derailed the Indian Economy, Sage Publications, Dec 2021; https://www.amazon.in/Unkept-Promise-Derailed-Indian-Economy/dp/9354791867; Report No. 17 of 2006 for the period ended March 2005 Performance Audit of - Disinvestment of Government Shareholding in Selected PSUs during 1999-2003, Comptroller and Auditor General of India; 2006; https://cag.gov.in/en/old-audit-reports/view/13768

214 Mohanty P, Why the distress sale of PSUs amidst booming govt revenue? Fortune

India, May 6, 2022; https://www.fortuneindia.com/opinion/why-the-distress-sale-of-psus-amidst-booming-govt-revenue/108058

215   Mohanty P, Disinvestment strategy: Centre's love; CAG's hate! Fortune India, Jan 6, 2022; https://www.fortuneindia.com/opinion/disinvestment-strategy-centres-love-cags-hate/106635

216   Finance Minister launches the National Monetisation Pipeline, Niti Aayog, Aug 23, 2021; https://pib.gov.in/PressReleseDetail.aspx?PRID=1748297

217   National Monetisation Pipeline, Vol II: Asset Pipeline, Aug 23, 2021; https://www.niti.gov.in/sites/default/files/2021-08/Vol_2_NATIONAL_MONETISATION_PIPELINE_23_Aug_2021.pdf

218   Modi repeats same Rs 100 lakh crore infrastructure plan in three I-Day speeches in a row, Aug 16, 2021; https://amp.scroll.in/latest/1002917/modi-repeats-same-rs-100-lakh-crore-infrastructure-plan-in-three-i-day-speeches-in-a-row?__twitter_impression=true

219   Govt to extend PM Gati Shakti project to social sector damaging health, education further, Dec 2, 2022; https://www.livemint.com/economy/pm-gati-shakti-to-be-implemented-for-social-sector-projects-dpiit-secy-11670000881390.html

220   Assets worth Rs 26,000 crore monetised in FY23: NITI Aayog, Feb 23, 2023; https://economictimes.indiatimes.com/news/economy/finance/assets-worth-rs-26000-crore-monetised-in-fy23-niti-aayog/articleshow/98188784.cms?utm_source=contentofinterest&utm_medium=text&utm_campaign=cppst

221   Memorandum Outlining A Plan of Economic Development for India, JNU, 1944; http://www.isec.ac.in/Plan_%20of_%20economic_%20development_%20for_%20India.pdf

222   Shankar Ajay, Khanna Sushil, Why India must strengthen its public sector, Indian Express, Sept 28, 2021; https://indianexpress.com/article/opinion/columns/indias-public-sector-privatisation-economic-freedom-7532870/

223   Mohanty P, Budget 2022: Why PSUs should be valued, not private monopolies, Fortune India, Jan 24, 2022; https://www.fortuneindia.com/opinion/budget-2022-why-psus-should-be-valued-not-private-monopolies/106835

224   Mohanty P, An Unkept Promise: What Derailed the Indian Economy, Sage Publications, Dec 2021; https://www.amazon.in/Unkept-Promise-Derailed-Indian-Economy/dp/9354791867

225   Central PSU jobs down 2.7 lakh over past decade: Govt data, Jun 16, 2023; http://timesofindia.indiatimes.com/articleshow/101027898.cms?from=mdr&utm_source=contentofinterest&utm_medium=text&utm_campaign=cppst; Podishetty Akash, Why are top PSU companies not hiring?, Aug 17, 2022; https://www.business-standard.com/podcast/current-affairs/why-are-top-psu-companies-not-hiring-122081700041_1.html

226   Chairman posts vacant in six of 11 public sector banks, some for two years, Jun

21, 2023; https://www.business-standard.com/industry/banking/non-executive-chairman-post-vacant-in-six-out-of-11-public-sector-banks-123062100563_1.htmls

227 Are fugitive Sandesara brothers selling oil to India via UK companies? TNN, Aug 3, 2023; https://timesofindia.indiatimes.com/india/are-fugitive-sandesara-brothers-selling-oil-to-india-via-uk-companies/articleshow/84991700.cms

228 Mohanty P, Rebooting Economy XIII: Why Indian corporates are debt-ridden, Business Today, Aug 5, 2020; https://www.businesstoday.in/opinion/columns/story/indian-economy-npas-why-indian-corporates-are-debt-driven-non-performing-assets-269182-2020-08-05#:~:text=India%20faces%20a%20fresh%20threat,the%20COVID%2D19%20pandemic%20hit

229 What is PNB scam, May 18, 2018; https://www.business-standard.com/about/what-is-pnb-scam; related link: Mehul Choksi got citizenship last year, India made no objection: Antigua, Aug 4, 2018; http://timesofindia.indiatimes.com/articleshow/65264744.cms?utm_source=contentofinterest&utm_medium=text&utm_campaign=cppst

230 CBI books DHFL in 'biggest' banking fraud of Rs 34,615 crore; 17 banks hit, Jun 23, 2022; https://www.business-standard.com/article/companies/cbi-books-dhfl-former-cmd-and-director-in-rs-34-615-crore-bank-fraud-case-122062200611_1.html

231 Mohanty P, SEBI's stunning about-turn, Fortune India, Feb 21, 2022; https://www.fortuneindia.com/opinion/sebis-stunning-about-turn/107189#:~:text=In%20a%20stunning%20order%2C%20apex,%E2%80%9D%20instead%20of%20%E2%80%9Cmandatory%E2%80%9D

232 Corporate Loan, Aug 7, 2023, Lok Sabha answer; https://www.dropbox.com/scl/fi/xg0hqt9bsxmehm4nzvdvp/LS_NPA_Writeoff_Aug2023.pdf?rlkey=u0d2f4uhyw3ncjinekks21io0&dl=0

233 Difficult to recover dues: SEBI lists 120 companies as 'untraceable', Aug 9, 2023; https://indianexpress.com/article/business/banking-and-finance/difficult-to-recover-dues-sebi-lists-120-companies-as-untraceable-8882963/

234 Mohanty P, 'NPAs: RBI must name and shame fraudsters'

235 Renunciation of Indian citizenship, Lok Sabha, Jul 21, 2023; https://www.dropbox.com/scl/fi/s3247svyi7zorto2ajrf6/LS_17.5-lakh-Indians-give-up-citizenship.pdf?dl=0&rlkey=7wzosb8jbo01murilqapvrazf

236 Twitter roasts Modi for saying people were ashamed to be born Indian till one year ago, May 19, 2015; https://scroll.in/article/728501/twitter-roasts-modi-for-saying-people-were-ashamed-to-be-born-indian-till-one-year-ago

237 Mohanty P, Rebooting Economy 68: How private wealth creators are serving Indian economy and people, Business Today, Feb 19, 2021; https://www.businesstoday.in/opinion/columns/story/rebooting-economy-68-how-private-wealth-creators-are-serving-indian-economy-and-people-288805-2021-02-19

238 Sarin Ritu and Yadav Shyamlal, Cracking Cyprus Confidential: EU state gave investors tax haven, secrecy – and a golden passport, Nov 15, 2023; https://indianexpress.com/article/express-exclusive/cracking-cyprus-confidential-eu-state-gave-investors-tax-haven-secrecy-and-a-golden-passport-9026642/; Sarin Ritu, Vinod Adani, Pankaj Oswal among 66 Indians who got golden passport, Nov 16, 2023; https://indianexpress.com/article/express-exclusive/vinod-adani-pankaj-oswal-among-66-indians-who-got-golden-passport-9026977/; Mazoomdaar Jay, From Down Under to Switzerland via Dubai, Pankaj Oswal, wife hit a hurdle in Cyprus, Nov 16, 2023; https://indianexpress.com/article/express-exclusive/from-down-under-to-switzerland-via-dubai-pankaj-oswal-wife-hit-a-hurdle-in-cyprus-9028349/; Cyprus Confidential: Shining a light on tax evasion, Editorial, Nov 20, 2023; https://indianexpress.com/article/opinion/editorials/cyprus-confidential-shining-a-light-on-tax-evasion-9033989/

239 Mohanty P, Rebooting Economy XIII: Why Indian corporates are debt-ridden, Business Today, Aug 5, 2020; https://www.businesstoday.in/opinion/columns/story/indian-economy-npas-why-indian-corporates-are-debt-driven-non-performing-assets-269182-2020-08-05#:~:text=India%20faces%20a%20fresh%20threat,the%20COVID%2D19%20pandemic%20hit

240 Mohanty P, NPAs: RBI must name and shame fraudsters, wilful defaulters, Jul 31, 2023; https://www.fortuneindia.com/opinion/npas-rbi-must-name-and-shame-fraudsters-wilful-defaulters/113563

241 Mohanty P, NPAs: RBI must name and shame fraudsters, wilful defaulters, Jul 31, 2023; https://www.fortuneindia.com/opinion/npas-rbi-must-name-and-shame-fraudsters-wilful-defaulters/113563

242 PM Modi calls for reducing "slavery to foreign goods" in 75th year of Independence, May 6, 2022; https://economictimes.indiatimes.com/news/india/pm-modi-calls-for-reducing-slavery-to-foreign-goods-in-75th-year-of-independence/articleshow/91366453.cms?utm_source=contentofinterest&utm_medium=text&utm_campaign=cppst

243 Maybach sunglasses, Movado watch: Expensive items owned by bougie birthday boy PM Modi, Free Press Journal, Sept 17, 2020; https://www.freepressjournal.in/india/maybach-sunglasses-movado-watch-expensive-items-owned-by-bougie-birthday-boy-pm-modi

244 Acharya Viral, India at 75: Replete with Contradictions, Brimming with Opportunities, Saddled with Challenges, Mar 30-31, 2023; Brookings Paper, https://www.brookings.edu/wp-content/uploads/2023/02/BPEA_Spring2023_EM-Panel_Acharya_unembargoed_updated.pdf1

245 India- Tariff treatment on certain goods in the ICT sector, WTO, Apr 17, 2023; https://www.wto.org/english/tratop_e/dispu_e/582r_e.pdff

246 Panagariya Arvind, Custom that costs us dear: Import duties are going up since 2018-19. There's been no economic analysis to justify this, Aug 10, 2022; https://timesofindia.indiatimes.com/blogs/toi-edit-page/custom-that-costs-us-dear-

import-duties-are-going-up-since-2018-19-theres-been-no-economic-analysis-to-justify-this/

247 Mohanty P, Budget 2022: Dismantle protectionism and crony capitalism for growth, Jan 24, 2022; https://www.fortuneindia.com/budget-2022/budget-2022-dismantle-protectionism-and-crony-capitalism-for-growth/106824; Mohanty P, Future of Indian trade is in services exports, Apr 18, 2023; https://www.fortuneindia.com/opinion/future-of-indian-trade-is-in-services-exports/112303

248 Acharya Viral, 'India at 75'

249 Mody Ashoka, India's Boom Is a Dangerous Myth, Mar 29, 2023; https://www.project-syndicate.org/commentary/india-economy-boom-is-a-myth-actually-failing-most-people-by-ashoka-mody-2023-03

250 Mohanty P, Future of Indian trade is in services exports, Apr 18, 2023; https://www.fortuneindia.com/opinion/future-of-indian-trade-is-in-services-exports/112303

251 Mohanty P, Is protectionism helping or harming India's exports? May 30, 2023; https://www.fortuneindia.com/opinion/is-protectionism-helping-or-harming-indias-exports/112851

252 Mohanty P, What is hurting India's exports engine, Sept 30, 2023; https://www.fortuneindia.com/opinion/what-is-hurting-indias-exports-engine/114293

253 Mohanty P, 2 Chinese roadblocks to India's semiconductor ambition, Jul 31, 2023; https://www.fortuneindia.com/opinion/2-chinese-roadblocks-to-indias-semiconductor-ambition/113560

254 Mohanty P, Paying for Russian oil in Yuan will hurt globalisation of Rupee, Jul 12, 2023; https://www.fortuneindia.com/opinion/paying-for-russian-oil-in-yuan-will-hurt-globalisation-of-rupee/113351#:~:text=Indian%20refiners%20paying%20in%20Chinese%20Yuan%20for%20Russian,followed%20by%20France%20%2829%25%29%20and%20the%20US%20%2811%25%29.

255 Mohanty P, FTP 2023: Can it navigate the new world order? Apr 24, 2023; https://www.fortuneindia.com/opinion/ftp-2023-can-it-navigate-the-new-world-order/112141

256 Suneja Kirtika, Commerce Ministry backs tweaks to bilateral investment treaty, Jul 11, 2023; https://economictimes.indiatimes.com/news/economy/foreign-trade/commerce-ministry-backs-tweaks-to-bilateral-investment-treaty/articleshow/101677494.cms?utm_source=contentofinterest&utm_medium=text&utm_campaign=cppst

257 Out of alignment: India should accept international arbitration, Jul 13, 2023; https://www.business-standard.com/opinion/editorial/out-of-alignment-123071301037_1.html

258 Mohanty P, 'Future of Indian trade is in services exports'

259 Mohanty P, 'Future of Indian trade is in services exports'

260   Mohanty P, 'Is protectionism helping or harming India's exports?'

261   Ministry of Commerce, Creation of Jobs under 'Make in India' Campaign, Mar 18, 2015; https://pib.gov.in/newsite/PrintRelease.aspx?relid=117286

262   EPFO annual report 2015-16, page 13; https://www.epfindia.gov.in/site_docs/Annual_Report/Annual_Report_2015-16.pdf

263   EPFO 69th annual report 2021-22, page 46; https://www.epfindia.gov.in/site_docs/Annual_Report/Annual_Report_2021-22.pdf

264   Prime Minister launches PM Gati Shakti, Prime Minister's Office, Oct 13, 2021: https://pib.gov.in/PressReleasePage.aspx?PRID=1763576; Explained: Connecting ministries for infrastructure projects, Oct 16, 2021; https://indianexpress.com/article/explained/pm-gatishakti-infrastructure-development-projects-7574071/

265   Finance Minister launches the National Monetisation Pipeline, Niti Aayog, Aug 23, 2021; https://pib.gov.in/PressReleseDetail.aspx?PRID=1748297; National Monetisation Pipeline, Vol II: Asset Pipeline, Aug 23, 2021; https://www.niti.gov.in/sites/default/files/2021-08/Vol_2_NATIONAL_MONETISATION_PIPELINE_23_Aug_2021.pdf

266   Assets worth Rs 26,000 crore monetised in FY23: NITI Aayog, Feb 23, 2023; https://economictimes.indiatimes.com/news/economy/finance/assets-worth-rs-26000-crore-monetised-in-fy23-niti-aayog/articleshow/98188784.cms?utm_source=contentofinterest&utm_medium=text&utm_campaign=cppst

267   Meghnad S, Whatever happened to SMART cities? Apr 8, 2019; https://www.newslaundry.com/2019/04/08/whatever-happened-to-smart-cities; Mohanty P, Dharavi: Challenges of rebuilding economically viable cities, Jul 18, 2023; https://www.fortuneindia.com/opinion/dharavi-challenges-of-rebuilding-economically-viable-cities/113420

268   English rendering of Prime Minister, Shri Narendra Modi's address from the ramparts of Red Fort on the occasion of 77th Independence Day, PMO, Aug 15, 2023;   https://pib.gov.in/PressReleasePage.aspx?PRID=1948808#:~:text=My%20dear%20family%20members%2C,the%20independence%20of%20the%20country.

269   Sullivan Dylan and Hickel Jason, How British colonialism killed 100 million Indians in 40 years, Dec 2, 2022; https://www.aljazeera.com/opinions/2022/12/2/how-british-colonial-policy-killed-100-million-indians

270   Maddison Angus, The World Economy: A Millennial Perspective, page OECD 2002;   https://theunbrokenwindow.com/Development/MADDISON%20The%20World%20Economy--A%20Millennial.pdf

271   Sharma Saurav, From $5 tn to a developed nation: What PM Modi said about Indian economy in last 5 Independence Day speeches, Aug 14, 2023; https://www.businesstoday.in/latest/story/from-5-tn-to-a-developed-nation-what-pm-modi-said-about-indian-economy-in-last-5-independence-day-speeches-394148-2023-08-14

272   Hindustan Times Leadership Summit 2022: India will become $30-trillion economy by 2047, says Goyal, Nov 13, 2022; https://www.hindustantimes.com/india-news/hindustan-times-leadership-summit-2022-india-will-become-30-trillion-economy-by-2047-says-goyal-101668288005116.html

273   The Many Economic Guarantees and Promises of the Modi Government, Jul 27, 2023; https://thewire.in/economy/the-many-economic-guarantees-and-promises-of-the-modi-government#:~:text=%E2%80%9CIndia's%20Gross%20Domestic%20Product%20was,first%20and%20second%20positions%20respectively.

274   Mohanty P, 'An Unkept Promise', Ch II.

275   Mody Ashoka, India's Fake Growth Story, Sept 6, 2023; https://www.project-syndicate.org/commentary/india-growth-rate-flawed-accounting-ignores-growing-problems-by-ashoka-mody-2023-09; Mody Ashoka, India's Boom Is a Dangerous Myth, Mar 29, 2023; https://www.project-syndicate.org/commentary/india-economy-boom-is-a-myth-actually-failing-most-people-by-ashoka-mody-2023-03?barrier=accesspaylog; Modi can't prove India is 5th largest economy. Data will fail him, Aug 22, 2023; https://theprint.in/the-fineprint/modi-cant-prove-india-is-5th-largest-economy-data-will-fail-him/1724092/

276   The Many Economic Guarantees and Promises of the Modi Government, Jul 27, 2023; https://thewire.in/economy/the-many-economic-guarantees-and-promises-of-the-modi-government

277   PM Narendra Modi biggest patron of corruption: AAP after Ajit Pawar joins NDA govt in Maharashtra Jul 2, 2023; http://timesofindia.indiatimes.com/articleshow/101438292.cms?from=mdr&utm_source=contentofinterest&utm_medium=text&utm_campaign=cppst

278   English rendering of Prime Minister, Shri Narendra Modi's address from the ramparts of Red Fort on the occasion of 77th Independence Day, PMO, Aug 15, 2023; https://pib.gov.in/PressReleasePage.aspx?PRID=1948808#:~:text=My%20dear%20family%20members%2C,the%20independence%20of%20the%20country.

279   Mohanty P, Data war on India lifting 135-140 million out of poverty

280   Bhalla Surjeet, Bhasin Karan and Virmani Arvind, Pandemic, Poverty, and Inequality: Evidence from India, IMF, Apr 5, 2022; https://www.imf.org/en/Publications/WP/Issues/2022/04/05/Pandemic-Poverty-and-Inequality-Evidence-from-India-516155

281   Bhalla Surjit, A 'jobful' economy: 2019-22 saw India's fastest ever phase of employment growth, with women being the main beneficiaries, Mar 19, 2023; https://timesofindia.indiatimes.com/blogs/toi-edit-page/a-jobful-economy-2019-22-saw-indias-fastest-ever-phase-of-employment-growth-with-women-being-the-main-beneficiaries/

282   Government has taken various initiatives to improve the global ranking of Indian education institutions – Education Minister, Ministry of Education, Sept 17, 2020; https://www.pib.gov.in/PressReleseDetailm.aspx?PRID=1655699

283   Chopra Ritika, For private campuses, Institution of Eminence tag gift-wrapped in red tape, Mar 29, 2023; https://indianexpress.com/article/express-exclusive/for-private-campuses-institution-of-eminence-tag-gift-wrapped-in-red-tape-8522548/

284   PMaddressesTeamISROonsuccessofChandrayaan-3,PMO,Aug26,2023;https://pib.gov.in/PressReleaseIframePage.aspx?PRID=1952360#:~:text=%E2%80%9CThe%20success%20of%20Chandrayaan%203,moon%20missions%20of%20every%20country.

285   About ISRO; https://www.isro.gov.in/profile.html

286   Mohanty P, Chandrayaan-3: 'Make in India's' moment of reckoning, Aug 31, 2023; https://www.fortuneindia.com/enterprise/chandrayaan-3-make-in-indias-moment-of-reckoning/113927

287   Low-occupancy sectors: Indian Railways to offer up to 25% fare cut in AC chair car, executive class, Jul 9, 2023; https://indianexpress.com/article/india/low-occupancy-sectors-rlys-to-offer-up-to-25-fare-cut-in-ac-chair-car-executive-class-8819295/

288   Government plans PLI for train-part manufacturers, Aug 16, 2023; https://government.economictimes.indiatimes.com/news/smart-infra/government-plans-pli-for-train-part-manufacturers/102762289

289   Contract for making 120 Vande Bharat trains awarded to Russian major-rail-rail PSU JV, Mar 30, 2023; http://timesofindia.indiatimes.com/articleshow/99123827.cms?from=mdr&utm_source=contentofinterest&utm_medium=text&utm_campaign=cppst

290   Deshmukh Vinita, Vande Bharat Express: No Profit & Loss Record Maintained, Railways Reply Under RTI, Oct 5, 2023; https://www.moneylife.in/article/vande-bharat-express-no-profit-and-loss-record-maintained-railways-reply-under-rti/72190.html

291   Railways spent Rs 2.6 crore to arrange PM Modi events in Chennai, Thiruvananthapuram to flag off two Vande Bharat trains, Jul 12, 2023; https://timesofindia.indiatimes.com/city/chennai/railways-spent-rs-2-6-crore-to-arrange-pm-modi-events-in-chennai-thiruvananthapuram-to-flag-off-two-vande-bharat-trains/articleshow/101692374.cms?from=mdr

292   Mallapur Chaitanya, High targets and wasted funds: The problems with the Skill India programme, JUl 26, 2017; https://scroll.in/article/844871/high-targets-and-wasted-funds-the-problems-in-the-skill-india-programme; Nanda Prashant K, Govt abandons goal of training 500 million people in new skils by 2022, Jun 7, 2017,   2023;   https://www.livemint.com/Politics/mhdopSWAv59UtBaRlJPZQK/Govt-abandons-goal-of-training-500-million-people-in-new-ski.html

293   Government committed to equip workers with employable skills and knowledge in mission mode, Ministry of Finance, Jan 31, 2023; https://pib.gov.in/PressReleseDetailm.aspx?PRID=1894912

294   Singh Nikesh, DBT helps govt save Rs 2.73 trillion since 2014: FM Nirmala

Sitharaman, Aug 14, 2023; https://www.business-standard.com/economy/news/dbt-has-helped-govt-save-rs-2-73-trillion-since-2014-fm-nirmala-sitharaman-123081400886_1.html

295   PM's address from the ramparts of Red Fort on the occasion of 77th Independence Day, PMIndia, Aug 15, 2023; https://www.pmindia.gov.in/en/news_updates/pms-address-from-the-ramparts-of-red-fort-on-the-occasion-of-77th-independence-day/

296   Sadhwani Garima, 15 New AIIMS Since 2014: What's Their Status in 2023? We Looked at Data, Aug 19, 2023; https://www.thequint.com/fit/15-aiims-announced-since-2014-data-shows-current-status-not-fully-functional#read-more

297   Number of airports gone up 100% in India: Scindia, Jan 8, 2023; https://www.livemint.com/news/india/number-of-airports-gone-up-100-in-india-scindia-11673156444180.html

298   Chandra Jagriti, Turbulence hits UDAN scheme, 50% routes grounded, Jul 29, 2023; https://www.thehindu.com/news/national/some-rcs-routes-collapse-airports-fall-into-disuse/article67136014.ece

299   Mohanty P, '2 Chinese roadblocks to India's semiconductor ambition'

300   Mohanty P, It's time to measure the impact of PLI, DLI schemes, Jun 22, 2023; https://www.fortuneindia.com/opinion/its-time-to-measure-the-impact-of-pli-dli-schemes/113139

301   Mohanty P, What latest tax data says about income inequality, Feb 28, 2023; https://www.fortuneindia.com/opinion/what-latest-tax-data-says-about-income-inequality/111744

302   GDP per capita (current US$), World Bank; https://data.worldbank.org/indicator/NY.GDP.PCAP.CD

303   Income tax returns, Lok Sabha answer, Jul 24, 2023; https://www.dropbox.com/scl/fi/032fc56yy5ynyu407ridb/LS_tax-categories_Jul-2023.pdf?rlkey=90cwy3e6zuxmvwmlsgxxxr6k7&dl=0

304   Mohanty P, 'What latest tax data says about income inequality'

305   Report on currency and finance 2021-22, RBI, Apr 2022; https://rbidocs.rbi.org.in/rdocs/Publications/PDFs/RCF202122_FULLB5D854DD796948889FF5099C22CD6893.PDF

306   FM asks why industry is not investing: the answer is simple, Sept 26, 2022; https://www.livemint.com/opinion/online-views/fm-asks-why-industry-is-not-investing-the-answer-is-simple-11664166990041.html; Mohanty P, Is India's capex cycle on revival path?, Aug 31, 2022; https://www.fortuneindia.com/opinion/is-indias-capex-cycle-on-revival-path/109477

307   Mohanty P, Is private investment in the economy on revival path? Oct 17, 2023; https://www.fortuneindia.com/opinion/is-private-investment-in-the-economy-on-revival-path/114485

308   Mohanty P, What will deliver 'strong' growth in FY24? Nov 30, 2023; https://www.fortuneindia.com/opinion/what-will-deliver-strong-growth-in-fy24/114896

309   Profit concentration in India Inc rises amid private sector growth, Nov 25, 2022; https://www.business-standard.com/article/companies/profit-concentration-in-india-inc-rises-amid-private-sector-growth-121112500070_1.html

310   Rajhansa Nandita and Mukherjea Saurabh, India's 20 Largest Profit Generators Are Earning 80% Of the Nation's Profits, Jan 12, 2023; https://thewire.in/economy/winner-takes-all-in-indias-new-improved-economy

311   Vyas Mahesh, Widespread superlative profits, CMIE, Jun 13, 2022; https://www.cmie.com/kommon/bin/sr.php?kall=warticle&dt=20220613152550&msec=960

312   Bhattacharya P, India's Statistical System

313   Deaton Angus and Kozel Valerie; Data and Dogma: The Great Indian Poverty Debate, OUP, 2005; https://www.princeton.edu/~deaton/downloads/deaton_kozel_great_indian_poverty_debate_wbro_2005.pdf

314   An Appeal from 108 Economists & Social Scientists across the World"; Mar 14, 2019; https://cdn-live.theprint.in/wp-content/uploads/2019/03/1552578453615_Press-Release-14-3-2019-Economic-Statistics-in-Shambles.pdf

315   Subramanian Arvind, India's GDP Mis-estimation: Likelihood, Magnitudes, Mechanisms, and Implications, Harvard University, June 29, 2019; https://www.hks.harvard.edu/centers/cid/publications/faculty-working-papers/india-gdp-overestimate

316   Sidhartha, Resolve MCA-21 issues, government tells LTI Mindtree, Jul 11, 2023; https://timesofindia.indiatimes.com/business/india-business/resolve-mca-21-issues-govt-tells-lti-mindtree/articleshow/101651306.cms?from=mdr

317   Mohanty P, GDP growth: Headwinds in financial assets, tax filings hurt average Indian, Oct 18, 2023; https://www.fortuneindia.com/opinion/gdp-growth-headwinds-in-financial-assets-tax-filings-hurt-average-indian/114504; Mody Ashoka, India's Fake Growth Story, Sept 6, 2023; https://www.project-syndicate.org/commentary/india-growth-rate-flawed-accounting-ignores-growing-problems-by-ashoka-mody-2023-09; Subramanian Arvind and Felman Josh, Is the economy surging or decelerating: Understanding India's growth rate, Sept 14, 2023l; https://www.business-standard.com/opinion/columns/understanding-india-s-growth-rate-is-economy-accelerating-or-decelerating-123091400756_1.html; Kumar Arun, Understanding GDP Growth Through Discrepancies and Why the Major Push Is Not Visible, Sept 5, 2023; https://thewire.in/economy/understanding-gdp-growth-through-discrepancies-and-why-the-major-push-is-not-visible

318   Mohanty P, 'An Unkept Promise', pages 51-54

319   Mohanty P, Budget 2023: Is India ready to face global recession? Jan 18, 2023; https://www.fortuneindia.com/opinion/budget-2023-is-india-ready-to-face-global-recession/111202

320   GDP growth (annual %) - India; https://data.worldbank.org/indicator/NY.GDP.MKTP.KD.ZG?locations=IN

321   Express View on stock limits on wheat: Going backwards, Sept 18, 2023; https://indianexpress.com/article/opinion/editorials/express-view-on-stock-limits-on-wheat-going-backwards-8944434/

322   Mohanty P, What is hurting India's exports engine, Sept 30, 2023; https://www.fortuneindia.com/opinion/what-is-hurting-indias-exports-engine/114293

323   Jha Somesh, Consumer spend survey: Panel didn't flag quality issues, ask for scrapping, Nov 21, 2019; https://www.business-standard.com/article/economy-policy/consumer-spend-survey-panel-didn-t-flag-quality-issues-ask-for-scrapping-119112001535_1.html

324   Magazine Aanchal, Economic census: Parliamentary panel questions ministry over delay in results, Jul 27, 2023; https://indianexpress.com/article/business/economy/economic-census-parliamentary-panel-questions-ministry-over-delay-in-results-8864102/

325   Census to be delayed again, deadline for freezing administrative boundaries pushed to January 1, 2024, Jul 3, 2023; https://indianexpress.com/article/india/census-delayed-deadline-administrative-boundaries-pushed-8697397/

326   Mohanty P, Why is the Centre afraid of caste data and the census? Jun 10, 2022; https://www.cenfa.org/why-is-the-centre-afraid-of-caste-data-and-the-census/

327   Mohanty P, India has no data to challenge WHO excess Covid deaths, May 9, 2022; https://www.fortuneindia.com/opinion/india-has-no-data-to-challenge-who-excess-covid-deaths/108072

328   Mohanty P, Rebooting Economy XXII: Why is India reluctant to provide unemployment allowance? Aug 29, 2020; https://www.businesstoday.in/opinion/columns/story/why-is-india-reluctant-to-provide-unemployment-allowance-to-its-organised-unorganised-workforce-271603-2020-08-29

329   Bhardwaj Ananya, NCRB stopped collecting data on lynching, hate crime as it was 'unreliable', govt tells LS, Dec 21, 2021; https://theprint.in/india/governance/ncrb-stopped-collecting-data-on-lynching-hate-crime-as-it-was-unreliable-govt-tells-ls/785201/

330   FactChecker pulls down hate crime database (HT and IndiaSpend), IndiaSpend editor Samar Halarnkar resigns, Sept 12, 2019; https://scroll.in/latest/937076/factchecker-pulls-down-hate-crime-watch-database-sister-websites-editor-resigns

331   NDA is 'No Data Available' govt with no accountability: Rahul Gandhi, Jul 23, 2022; https://indianexpress.com/article/india/nda-is-no-data-available-govt-with-no-accountability-rahul-gandhi-8047312/

332   Kundu Amitabh, Mohanan PC, Data Discrepancies, EPW, Vol 58, No 21, May 27, 2023; https://www.epw.in/tags/data-discrepancies

333   Mohanty P, When Finance Ministry takes to fakery, Centre for Financial Accountability, May 16, 2022; https://www.cenfa.org/when-finance-ministry-takes-to-fakery/

334   Mohanty P, 'Are top banks getting their economics wrong?'

335   Mohanty P, Data war on India lifting 135-140 million out of poverty, Aug 16, 2023; https://www.fortuneindia.com/opinion/data-war-on-india-lifting-135-140-million-out-of-poverty/113738

336   Bhalla Surjeet, Bhasin Karan and Virmani Arvind, Pandemic, Poverty, and Inequality: Evidence from India, IMF, Apr 5, 2022; https://www.imf.org/en/Publications/WP/Issues/2022/04/05/Pandemic-Poverty-and-Inequality-Evidence-from-India-516155

337   Bhalla Surjit, A 'jobful' economy: 2019-22 saw India's fastest ever phase of employment growth, with women being the main beneficiaries, Mar 19, 2023; https://timesofindia.indiatimes.com/blogs/toi-edit-page/a-jobful-economy-2019-22-saw-indias-fastest-ever-phase-of-employment-growth-with-women-being-the-main-beneficiaries/

338   Shamika Ravi writes: Our national surveys are based on faulty sampling, Jul 7, 2023; https://indianexpress.com/article/opinion/columns/shamika-ravi-writes-our-national-surveys-are-based-on-faulty-sampling-8799300/; Sanyal Sanjeev, Chauhan Srishti, How a handful measures the world, Jun 16, 2023; https://timesofindia.indiatimes.com/blogs/toi-edit-page/how-a-handful-measures-the-world/

339   Bhattacharya P, India's Statistical System: Past, Present, Future, Jun 28, 2023; https://carnegieendowment.org/2023/06/28/india-s-statistical-system-past-present-future-pub-90065

Chapter VIII

Economic Burden Shifts to Poor

Out-and-out crony capitalism and 'National Champions' model have predictable consequences: Economic burden has shifted to poor, further impoverishing them. There is multiple evidence for this: A sharp fall in taxpayers in the lowest income group (Rs 0-5 lakh), a sharp fall in people reporting taxable income, rise in poverty, hunger and inequality, a sharp fall in household savings to 50-year low, high fuel tax, predatory pricing keeping inflation high etc. It is often said that that bad economics makes for good politics – which is to say token welfare schemes for the poor to get their votes without improving their long-term economic wellbeing while the real economic benefits go to the rich, making them richer. India is no stranger to this phenomenon. Eventually it is the poor who is burdened. This chapter shows how this is more so now than any time in the past.

This goes against Article 38[1] of the Constitution which says: "State to secure a social order for the promotion of welfare of the people: (1) The State shall strive to promote the welfare of the people by securing and protecting as effectively as it may a social order in which *justice, social, economic and political, shall inform all the institutions of the national life,* (2) The State shall, in particular, strive to *minimize the inequalities in income, and endeavor to eliminate inequalities in status, facilities and opportunities,* not only amongst individuals but also amongst groups of people residing in different areas or engaged in different vocations." *(Emphasis added)*

It has already been explained (Introduction) how targeted and efficient delivery of welfare schemes ("new welfarism") and targeted political campaigns around "free" food, cash transfers for LPGs, farmers etc. have created a new vote bank called "labharthi varg". These are keys to blunting the impact of impoverishment.[2] But there are dark sides to it: (i) as against the Congress-led UPA regime's rights-based schemes to ensure inclusive growth (listed in Introduction), the Prime Minister brought in cash-transfers as "revdis" (freebies) for votes and temporary relief which bring no lasting improvement in the fortunes of the masses and (ii) health, education, job creations and long-term financial wellbeing of ordinary citizens, which require vision, planning and strategies get completely sidelined.[3] In the meanwhile, there is no let-up in sloganeering: "Achche Din", "Ease of Living"[4] , "Amrit Kaal", "Kartavya Kaal", "1,000 years of grand future", "Jan Vishwas" laws and Big Bang claims detailed in the previous chapters.

How Tax Burden Shifts to Poor

What happens when tax incentives for corporate entities keep rising, like the corporate tax cut of September 2019 (FY20) amidst a fiscal crisis, the PLIs and DLIs and a host of other incentives to manufacture and export goods the previous chapter listed? The peak base rate for corporate entities has fallen from 30% to 22% (without exemptions) for existing manufacturing units and the minimum alternate tax from 25% to 15% for new manufacturing units. "Effective tax rate" (minus all tax incentives) – not available for FY22 and FY23 – for corporates making profit before tax (PBT) of over Rs 500 crore is 19%. It ranges from 22.5% to 24.8% – lower for corporates with more PBT and higher for those with less PBT (maximum of 24.8% for those registering PBT of Rs 0-1 crore.[5]

In contrast, the peak tax rate for individuals remains 30% (taxable slab of Rs 15 lakh and above without exemptions) – 5 percentage points higher than for corporate entities. It must also be noted that corporate entities are taxed on their "profits", that is, *after deduction of expenses* while individuals pay tax on their "incomes" *without deduction of expenses.*[6]

Oil Tax Burden

The oil taxes went up incessantly during 2015-2021 even as international crude price crashed and remained low during 2015-2021. This was in spite of the fact that oil prices were "fully" decontrolled by the current regime in 2014, as against "partial" one in the previous UPA regime.[7] During 2015-21, the Brent price was about half of what it was in earlier years – from annual average of over $100/barrel in FY12, FY13 and FY14 to $58.5 during FY15-FY21. During this period, the Central government raised several indirect taxes on fuel – Excise, Customs, IGST, CGST, Service Tax, Cess, Royalty, Surcharge, Dividend etc. In 2022, the Brent prices went up following the Russia-Ukraine war; the rise in taxes stopped for petrol and diesel but LPG (cylinders) and CNG (compressed gas to households) continued to rise. This happened when India was importing a bulk of its oil cheaply from Russia – at $60 per barrel when the crude was over $110. Who gained? The three top gainers were three private companies – Reliance Industries and Nayara Energy and an unknown Mumbai-based company Gatik Ship Management. Indian emerged as top exporter of oil to Europe. Oil PSUs gained too but not ordinary Indians.[8]

Between FY15 and FY23, the Central government moped up Rs 31.6 lakh crore and states Rs 19.9 lakh crore – taking the total to Rs 51.4 lakh crore[9] – from the higher oil tax and dividend. Oil tax alone has gone up by 241% from FY15 to FY23. This is way too high than what the UPA had collected when the crude price was soaring before 2014-15 – at annual average of Rs 3.4 lakh crore, it is more than double that of Rs 1.4 lakh crore during FY12-FY14[10].

Graph 1: Rising revenue from oil tax

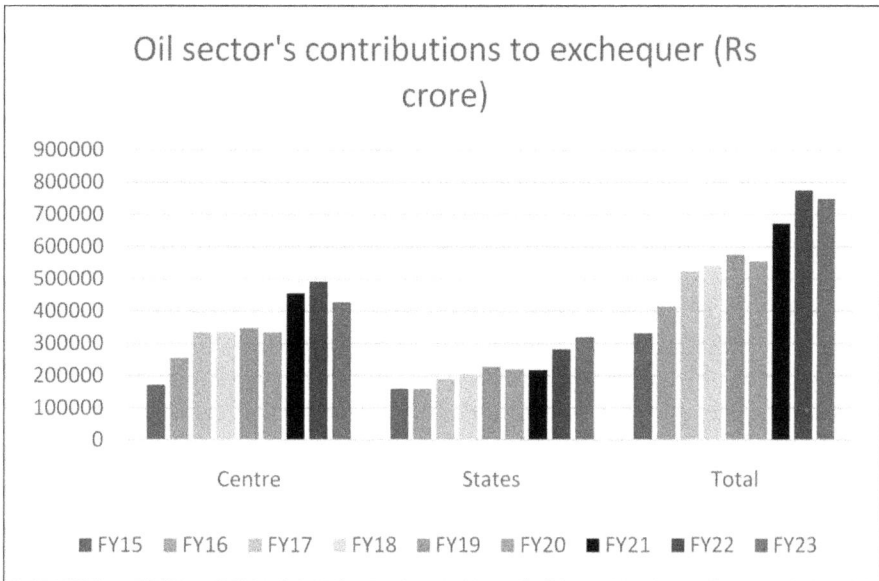

Source: Petroleum Planning and Analysis Cell, GOI

In defending high oil tax, Finance Minister Sitharaman misled the country first in August 2021 by blaming states for the raising retail prices of petrol and petroleum products and then calling it a "trickery" of the previous Congress-led UPA government for burdening the Centre with "oil bonds" – which actually *insulated* people from rising crude and kept the retail prices low.[11] Thereafter, she blamed it on the Russian-Ukraine war.[12]

Were the states to be blamed? No. States lost indirect tax rights when they accepted the GST in 2017 and compared to the Central government, states collected Rs 19.9 lakh crore, against the Central government's Rs 31.6 lakh crore during FY15-FY23. Did the previous UPA government put the "oil bond" burden? Yes but no because the new government paid very little outstanding "oil bond". Budget documents show, the outstanding oil bonds in FY14 was Rs 1.34 lakh crore – a year before the new government came. By FY22, the outstanding was Rs 1.21 lakh crore – which meant it had paid only Rs 13,500 crore or 0.5%, while collecting Rs 27.3 lakh crore in oil taxes during FY15-FY22!

Image 1: Outstanding oil bonds, Budget 2021-22

			Receipt Budget, 2021-2022					59
								(In ₹ Crores)
			As at the end of					
Name of Loan	Earliest date of maturity	1950-1951	2016-2017	2017-2018	2018-2019	2019-2020	Revised 2020-2021	Budget 2021-2022
2 E - SPECIAL SECURITIES ISSUED TO OIL MARKETING COMPANIES IN LIEU OF CASH SUBSIDY								
8.13% GOI spl. Bonds,2021	16.10.2021	..	5000.00	5000.00	5000.00	5000.00	5000.00	
7.75% GOI spl. Bonds,2021	28.11.2021	..	5000.00	5000.00	5000.00	5000.00	5000.00	
8.20% GOI spl. Bonds,2023	10.11.2023	..	22000.00	22000.00	22000.00	22000.00	22000.00	22000.00
8.01% GOI spl. Bonds,2023	15.12.2023	..	4150.00	4150.00	4150.00	4150.00	4150.00	4150.00
8.20% GOI spl. Bonds,2024	12.02.2024	..	5000.00	5000.00	5000.00	5000.00	5000.00	5000.00
8.20% GOI spl. Bonds,2024	15.09.2024	..	10306.33	10306.33	10306.33	10306.33	10306.33	10306.33
6.35% GOI spl. Bonds,2024	23.12.2024	..	22000.00	22000.00	22000.00	22000.00	22000.00	22000.00
7.95% GOI spl. Bonds,2025	18.01.2025	..	11256.92	11256.92	11256.92	11256.92	11256.92	11256.92
8.40% GOI spl. Bonds,2025	28.03.2025	..	9296.92	9296.92	9296.92	9296.92	9296.92	9296.92
8.40% GOI spl. Bonds,2026	29.03.2026	..	4971.00	4971.00	4971.00	4971.00	4971.00	4971.00
6.90% GOI spl. Bonds,2026	04.02.2026	..	21942.00	21942.00	21942.00	21942.00	21942.00	21942.00
8.00% GOI spl. Bonds,2026	23.03.2026	..	10000.00	10000.00	10000.00	10000.00	10000.00	10000.00
Total			130923.17	130923.17	130923.17	130923.17	130923.17	120923.17

High oil tax is a direct burden on the poor. Here is how.

A government sponsored survey of 2014[13] showed: (a) *61.4% of petrol is consumed by two-wheelers* (b) 13% diesel is consumed by agriculture and (c) 70% of diesel, 99.6 % of petrol are consumed by transport sector. The first one shows high tax on fuel is a direct burden on the poor who use two-wheelers and the other two raises the cost of travel (by bus and train), food and other essentials. High fuel tax, when crude price has fallen but not passed on to consumers (as continued to happen even as international crude prices fell in 2023 and the cheap Russian oil brought windfall gains to oil marketing companies, not only feeds inflation, it cuts down households' disposable income.

High GST Collections

Ordinary people are burdened by high GST too – as an indirect tax, the impact on the rich and the poor is equal but the ability to pay is not. The government takes particular pride in high GST collection – a rise of *116%* between FY18 and FY24 (BE) – and yet in July 2022, the government imposed 5% GST on food items consumed by the poor and exempted earlier – on pre-packaged *unbranded* food items like wheat, rice, curd, lassi, puffed rice, mutton and fish in. This was when the GST on luxury items had been cut down from 28% to 12-18%. Sitharaman said it was approved by all states but Keral refuted and said it wanted the GST on luxury items to be restored back to 28%.[14]

If other states agreed to tax on these food items it was only because having sacrificed most of their indirect tax rights while adopting the GST (eight central and nine state indirect taxes were subsumed into in 2017) and the GST Compensation discontinued from the same July 2022 they were left with little choice. A higher GST collection would mean they would get more (their share) – as against a *loss of 34%*[15] from the discontinuation of the GST Compensation.

High GST is both bad taxation and bad economics – it violates the cardinal principles of capacity to pay and equity. Advanced economies collect more direct tax and less indirect tax for these reasons. India does the reverse – giving tax cuts and incentives to rich individuals and corporate entities (more profit they make less "effective tax" they pay). Six years down the line, the GST and its IT infrastructure remain a work-in-progress, riddled with systemic loopholes because of which fake GST claims keep mounting every year – reflecting a broken system.[16]

The poor is also targeted by banks (SCBs) – which have written off Rs 14.6 lakh crore of corporate loans by branding those as NPAs without battling an eyelid during FY15-FY23. Banks have collected huge amounts as penalty for not maintaining minimum balance and additional ATM withdrawal charges and SMS service charges. They collected Rs 35,587.68 crore during FY18-FY23 on these accounts, as the government told the Rajya Sabha in August 2023.[17] An earlier reply to the Lok Sabha had revealed that banks had collected Rs 10,391.4 crore during FY16-FY19 (up to September 2018)[18]. This is remarkable since the government has shown extraordinary sensitivity to the rich: (i) abolished wealth tax in 2015 (b) (b) reduced maximum surcharge on high net-worth individuals (HNIs) from 37% to 25% in the 2023 budget (c) put on hold[19] a 20% levy on payment of over Rs 7 lakh through international debit and credit cards and (d) lowered GST on luxury goods in 2022.

It is also pertinent to note that the tax burden on the poor is more because the government has been wasting public money on *vanity projects* (without valid reasons or urgency) – building more statues and temples, developing temple corridors, a bullet train corridor on a route with 40% occupancy rate, demolishing and rebuilding most part of the majestic and iconic heritage buildings of the Central Vista and Pragati Maidan. Some of these are:

- Building "world's tallest statue" of Sardar Patel in Gujarat at a cost of Rs 3,000 crore[20] using public money by *diverting huge funds* from public sector units and also building *temples, temple corridors* with public money.[21]

- Starting the first bullet train with a loan of Rs 100,000 crore from Japan on the unviable and loss making (Rs 10 crore a month) route of Ahmedabad-Mumbai with more than 40% seat vacancy.[22]

- Demolishing *iconic* Pragati Maidan structures and rebuilding them at a cost of Rs 3,000 crore.[23]

- Demolishing *majestic* Central Vista of New Delhi and rebuilding it at estimated cost of Rs 20,000 crore during the pandemic lockdown, which includes building brand new Parliament House, new residents for the Prime Minister and Vice President – without a project report and without following established norms of administrative and legal approval processes.[24] The money and effort could have been deployed to build crumbling public health infrastructure during the pandemic, instead.

Compare this with the Indian Space Research Organization (ISRO) which landed Chandrayan-3 on the moon in August 2023. It cost a mere Rs 610 crore.[25] The credit for setting up the ISRO goes to the same the Congress governments of early decades of independence.[26] The PM hogged as much space as the Chandrayan-3 that day but his government had cut down the budget for space science by 32%[27] in the 2023 budget.

But how does one know that the tax burden has *actually* shifted to the poor? It shows up in various other indicators: (a) Tax data (b) household savings (c) poverty and hunger and (d) unemployment numbers etc.

(a) 54% fall in Taxable Income in 7 Years; Poor hit the Most

The best tax data is not the total number of returns (ITRs) filed but the number of ITRs declaring *taxable income* (total ITRs filed minus ITRs showing zero tax liability). The IT department's *annual data* shows the number of ITRs declaring *taxable income* was 48.6 million (3.8% of population) in FY16 (pre-demonetization)[28] and 48.9 million (3.8% of population) in FY17 (demonetization fiscal)[29] (demonetization fiscal). Their number fell to 22.4 million (1.6% of population) in FY23 as the Lok Sabha answer of July 24, 2023[30] showed.

This is *massive fall* in taxable income ITRs – by *more than half* (53.9%) from FY16 and FY17. It couldn't have happened by a rise in taxable limit of Rs 2 lakh (other tax incentives remain virtually unchanged) from the pre-2014 period alone. As the above data shows, the impact of the twin shocks of demonetization of 2016 and GST of 2017, the pandemic economic shutdowns in 2020 and 2021 and the subsequent K-shaped pandemic recovery is obvious.

The ITR data *including zero tax liability* filers (total ITRs) giving *income group-wise* data[31] provides how the different income groups have been impacted. These data provide six income groups: up to Rs 5 lakh, Rs 5-10 lakh, Rs 10-20 lakh, Rs 20-50 lakh, Rs 50 lakh-1 crore and above Rs 1 crore. (For convenience, Rs 5-10 lakh is taken while it is Rs 500,001 to Rs 10 lakh, and so on). This data for six fiscals of FY18-FY23 shows:

- Those in the lowest income category (up to Rs 5 lakh) have suffered badly – their numbers falling from 52.55 million in FY18 to 49.78 million in FY23.

The *average growth* in their numbers (five fiscals) is -0.4%. They matter most as they *constitute (average) 80% of total ITRs (76.6% in FY23)* – and a sign of *mass impoverishment*.

- The *average growth* (five fiscals) for all other income categories is positive – 5.4% for Rs 5-10 lakh and 10.3% to 13.5% for the rest (higher income) categories.

- As percentage of the population, the ITRs are *stagnant* – 5% in FY18, 4.9% each in FY19 and FY20, 5.3% in FY21, 4.6% in FY22 and 5% in FY23. Thus, the taxbase (ITR) has remained *stagnant*.

Graph 2 and 3: ITRs with 'taxable income' and income group-wise growth in

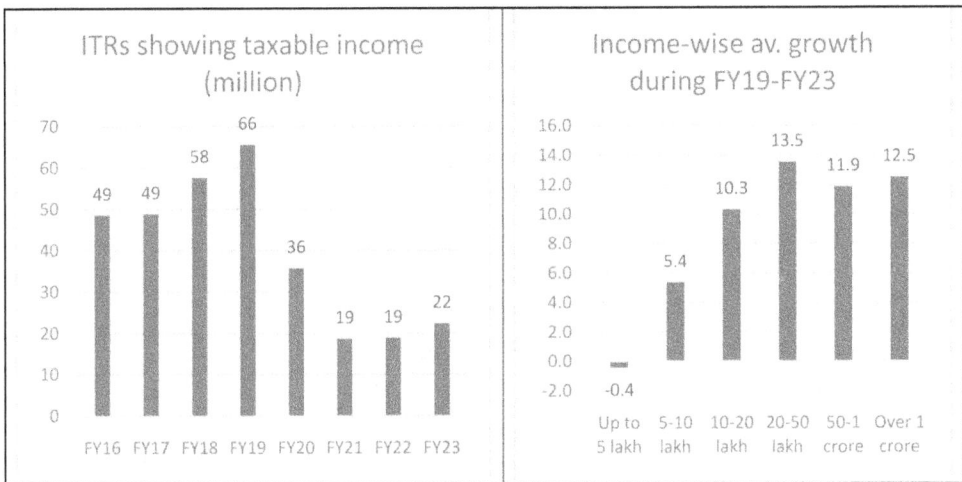

total ITRs

Source: ITD's annual reports (FY16-FY19) and LS reply (FY20-FFY23) and e-file data (second graph)

Regressive Tax System

India's tax system has been *regressive for a long time* in any case – in which indirect tax is the main source of tax revenue – putting a higher burden on general public, rather than taxing people on the basis of their (higher) income.

The RBI database shows, in the general government (centre and states) tax revenue, indirect tax has always been higher than direct tax. The gap between the two touched a low of -2 percentage points in FY10 but has widened since then.[32]

Graph 4: Direct and indirect tax revenue

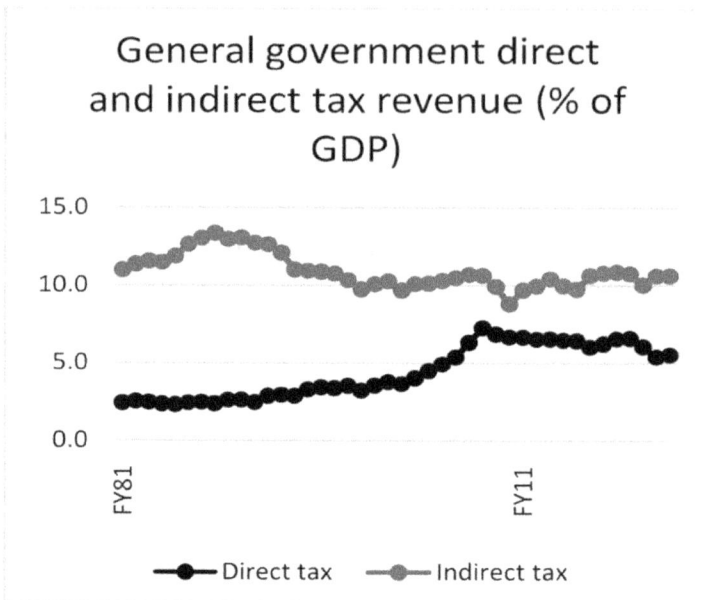

Source: RBI database

Going by the last ten fiscals of FY13-FY22, the ratio of direct-indirect tax stands at 37:63 – reverse of the OECD average of 68:32[33]. India's tax-to-GDP remains below par, at 12-18% during 1980-81 to 2021-22, peaking at 17.9% in FY08.[34] This is despite the demonetization of 2016 and GST of 2017, both of which were supposed to increase tax efficiency and base. The OECD average, in sharp contrast, is 33% in the past five years[35].

In fact, the Central government's tax-to-GDP remains confined to 10-11% of the GDP since FY12. From a high of 11.2% in FY17 and FY18 (demonetization and GST fiscals), it dipped to 9.8% in the pre-pandemic FY20 – when the corporate tax cut of Rs 1.45 lakh crore was announced. It led to a straight loss of Rs 2.28 lakh crore in two fiscals of FY20 and FY21.[36] In fact, this corporate tax cut led to income tax collection surpassing that of corporate tax for the first time in FY21 the 2011-12 GDP series. In FY23 (RE) and FY24 (BE), it remains 11.1%.

(b) Household Financial Health: Back to 1970s

On September 18, 2023, the RBI released the latest data on financial health of households.[37] It shows, *net* financial assets of households dropped sharply from 11.5% of the GDP in FY21 to 7.2% in FY22 and 5.1% in FY23. Going by its data, available since 1970-71, this fall (5.1% in FY23) is a *47-year low!* The last time it went below 5.1% was in *1975-76* when it was 4.7%; the next low was *5.2% in 1977-78*.

This is a huge fall. In 16 out of 18 fiscals between 1993-94 and 2010-11, net financial assets averaged 10.8%, peaking at 12% in FY10. After FY11, the only fiscal it touched double-digit was in FY21 (11.5%) – the pandemic fiscal in which the GDP growth plunged to -5.8% – and then dropped to 5.1% in FY23 when the GDP growth was 7.2%.

The fall in net financial assets is due to a *sharp* rise in financial *liabilities*. The latest RBI data shows, liabilities fell from 3.9% of the GDP in FY21 to 3.8% in FY22 but went up to 5.8% in FY23. In the past 53 fiscals for which the RBI provides data (since 1970-71) *only twice* financial liabilities crossed 5% – 5.1% in FY06 and 6.6% in FY07.

The growing impoverishment of households has been known for years and yet, no attention has been paid. Here are five more official datasets to demonstrate this.

(i)   The NSSO's 2017-18 household consumption expenditure survey (MPCE) showed a fall in 'real' expenditure – but it was junked on misleading claims (that an experts committee questioned the data quality[38]). No MPCE survey has been taken up thereafter.

(ii)   The MoSPI data shows, *net household savings* (financial and physical assets) has fallen from *23.6% of the GDP in FY12 (25% in FY09 and FY10) to 19.7% in FY22* (up to which data is available). Household savings constitute *64% of gross domestic savings (gross capital formation), during FY12-FY22*.

(iii) *Net* physical assets have fallen from 16.3% to 12% of the GDP during the same period.

(iv)   The RBI data shows bank credit outflow *inverted* in FY20 – "personal loans" for consumption overtaking that to industry, large industry and services and continues to do so in FY24.

What is driving personal loans?

Analysis of personal loans during FY19-FY23 shows[39], it is driven mainly by (a) housing loans (49.3%) and (b) "other personal loans" (25.9%) – which includes health emergencies, which entails such "catastrophic" expenditure that 60 million Indians are pushed into poverty every year in normal times, as the Ayushman Bharat (PM-JAY) document of 2018 says.

Other components of 'other personal loans" include loans for wedding, home renovation, travel, festival and pension loans etc. for which no disaggregated data is available. The other components of personal loans are for vehicles (12.2%), credit card payment (4.4%), education (2.7%) and loans against gold jewellery (1.9%).

The significant fall in people reporting taxable income and household assets mean the consumption demand and fund availability for investments in the economy would continue to fall – cutting down growth prospects further.

(c) Poverty, Hunger & Inequality Soar

Beginning with the pandemic in 2020, focus turned to rising poverty in India and the world. The Pew Research[40] which showed *75 million* Indians – accounting for 60% of the global rise in absolute poverty – were impoverished due to the pandemic in 2020 and the Indian *middle class shrunk by 32 million.* The World Bank 2022 (November)[41] report said India added 79% or 56 million of new "extreme poor" (per capita per day expenditure of $2.15 at 2017 PPP) to the global addition of 71 million. The CE360 Survey 2021[42] of Mumbai-based think tank PRICE confirmed the findings saying that the poorest 20% Indian households lost (-) 53% of annual income in FY21, from their levels in 2015-16 – during which the richest 20% saw their household income grow 39%.

Graph 5: Fall in income in 2021 over 2016

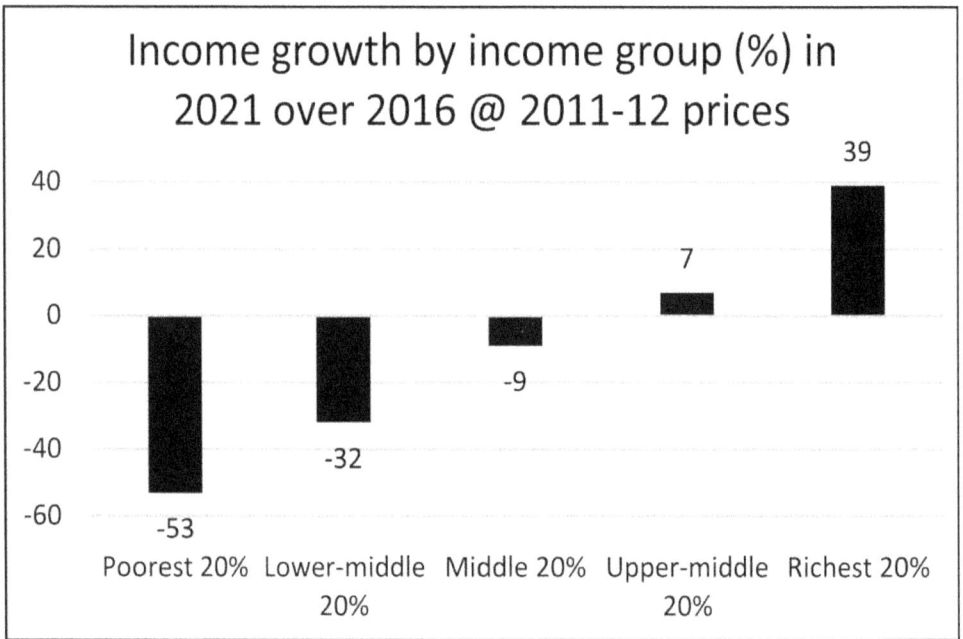

Source: PRICE's ICE360 survey

And then, beginning with April 2022, came a series of India-specific reports claiming that India had lifted millions out of poverty during and immediately before the pandemic. First off-the-block were the IMF and World Bank.

The authors of the IMF report "Pandemic, Poverty, and Inequality: Evidence from India"[43] were economists Surjeet Bhalla, Karan Bhasin and Arvind Virmani. Their report covered 2011-2020 and they said extreme poverty ($1.9 per capita per day expenditure) had been virtually wiped out of India in the pandemic year of 2020 (FY21). Their main findings were: Extreme poverty in 2019 (pre-pandemic FY20) was 1.4% – a decline of *10.8 percentage points* since FY12 – which further declined to *0.8%* in 2020 (pandemic fiscal of FY21) due to food "transfers" ("free" over and above "subsidized" ration to 67% households), without which it would have been 2.48%.

There are at least four issues with this assessment.

- The IMF report justifies junking of the consumer expenditure survey (MPCE) of 2017-18 on the ground that an expert committee had questioned its data quality but used the same government agency NSSO's MPCE of 2011-12 as its *base*. Unbeknownst to the (Indian) authors, the said expert committee had actually *refuted*[44] this charge floated by the government to junk the 2017-18 finding that poverty went up for the first time in 40 years, with the 'real' consumption expenditure *falling*[45].

- It used consumption data for post-2011-12 years from the 2011-12 GDP series (PFCE) – which maps consumption of *all Indians, rich or poor*, except government consumption (GFCE) and doesn't tell which income segment group consumes how much. Besides, if then Chief Economic Advisor (CEA) Arvind Subramanian didn't trust the 2011-12 GDP series (introduced in 2015), stating that it *overestimated* the GDP growth by *2.5 percentage points* during 2012-2016, it is strange for the IMF team to have selectively relied on the very GDP series data for PFCE. Add frequent retrospective revisions in the GDP series and there is no knowing what the reality is. For example, the highest GDP growth since FY13 was 8.3% in FY17 – the year of demonetization that paralyzed the entire economy.

- It also assumed that all 67% households received full quota of PDS supply (and used its money value for poverty calculations). Going by the strong and repeated *censure*[46] of the government by the Supreme Court for its failures to provide PDS to millions of workers who migrated in distress from urban to their rural homes with family, this seems highly unlikely.[47] Besides, the IndiaSpend[48] found government data showed 1.4 million of 54 million inter-state migrants got ration annually during 2019-2023 under the one-nation-one-ration (ONORC) scheme.

- Free and/or subsidized ration can *avert hunger – not poverty.* Poverty gets reduced *only by raising income.* So, using PDS supply underestimates poverty.

The World Bank report, "Poverty in India Has Declined over the Last Decade but Not as Much as Previously Thought"[49], was authored by Sutirtha Sinha Roy and Roy Van Der Weide. It covered 2011-2019 and said: Poverty (at $1.9) declined from 22.5% in 2011 (FY12) to 10.2% in 2019 (FY20) – a drop of 12.3 percentage points but it *didn't explain why this happened.* The data it used is questionable: It used the same MPCE of 2011-12 as the base and then used private business portal CMIE's CPHS data to estimate poverty in FY20, even while admitting that the latter is not comparable with the NSSO's MPCE data and tweaked it. The CPHS data is known to *underestimate*[50] poverty vis-à-vis other surveys because of its urban bias (more well-off population)– which the CMIE had *admitted and promised*[51] to look into in 2021.

It must be pointed out here that both these IMF and World Bank reports are *statistical constructs and projections* – not based on actual data or survey. They had no choice because the Indian government has no MPCE data after 2011-12 and the last poverty line estimates (the Tendulkar poverty line) is from 2004-05.

Then in October 2022 came the UNDP-OPHDI's Multi-dimensional Poverty Index (MPI) report (an abridged version of its was published in July 2023)[52]. It claimed *140 million* Indians were lifted out of poverty ($1.9 per capita per day expenditure) during 2015-16 and 2019-21. In total, it said India lifted 415 million Indians out of poverty during 2005-06 and 2019-21 (*275 million* lifted out during 2005-06 and 2015-16).

What data it used? It was only the health survey data of NFHS-5 of 2019-21. The MPI measures multiple deprivations – on three parameters of education, health and standard of living. The UNDP-OPHDI relied on one single data, that of health survey (NFHS-5), because no data exists on the two others. It found poverty had fallen (from 55.1% in 2005-06 to 27.7% in 2015-16) to *16.4%* in 2019-21.

The same data sources (NFHS-4 and NGHS-5) were used by the NITI Aayog to claim in July 2023 that "135 million have exited multi-dimensional poverty" during 2015-16 and 2019-21 in its report "National Multidimensional Poverty Index: A Progress Review 2023".[53] In this, the Aayog claimed the poverty had fallen from 24.95% in 2015-16 to *14.96%* in 2019-21 – different from the UNDP-OPHDI. The difference is significant (a fall by 9.99 percentage for the Aayog and 11.3 percentage for the UNDP-OPHDI) and the reason for this are: (a) They used different methodologies and (b) two additional indicators (taking the total to 12) were used by the Aayog – maternal health and bank account.

Two eminent Indian economists[54] with extensive working knowledge of the Indian economy have objected to the Aayog's methods and indicators. Pronab Sen, who heads the new Standing Committee on Statistics, said: "The way the MPI is structured, it is *almost impossible to show a decrease* in these indicators over a period of time". C Rangarajan said: "The MPI takes into account bank accounts, which do not indicate welfare. Bank accounts *will keep increasing over a period*. Therefore, it needs to be discussed how relevant some of these indicators are." *(Emphasis added)*

There are many problems with the NFHS-5 data. These are:

- Notice, NFHS-5 is for 2019-21 – not 2019-20 or 2020-21 which is a standard practice in India and world over. Also notice, 2019-20 was pre-pandemic and 202-21 was the pandemic year or what economists call an *unusual year*. Why did the NFHS-5 mix the data of a normal year data with that of an abnormal year? The obvious explanation is that the government wanted to *hide* the true impact of the pandemic on health, education and living standard – all of which were *severely hit*.

- The Aayog report (page 4) reads: "It is *important to note* that the poverty estimates presented in this report *may not fully assess the effects* of the COVID-19 pandemic on poverty, since *more than 70% of the data (NFHS-5) was collected before the pandemic*. At the same time, this report *does not capture* the economic and social progress the country has made in the last two years." This is corroborated by the UNDP-OPHDI's MPI report of 2022 (page 19) but missing from its abridged version released in 2023) which reads: "The effects of the COVID-19 pandemic on poverty India cannot be fully assessed because *71 percent of the data* from the 2019/2021 Demographic and Health Survey for the country were collected *before the pandemic*." The question that arises is: Since most of the NFHS-5 data ("more than 70%" or "71%") is on the pre-pandemic 2019-20, could it represent 2019-20 or 2020-21? The answer is: No. That means, both the UNDP-OPHDI and NITI Aayog reports are flawed. *(Emphasis added)*

The Aayog had prepared a baseline MPI report on November 24, 2021[55] – which was based on the NFHS-4 of 2015-16 when the NHFS-5 of 2019-21 data was already public. The NFHS-4 data were released in two trenches – phase I in December 2020[56] and phase II on the same day as the Aayog's MPI of 2021 – *November 24, 2021*[57] but the raw data (to work with) would have been available for months before that. Why was the *baseline* MPI of 2021 prepared on the old NFHS-4 of 2015-16 data is not known.

India is home to not only most poor but most hungry in the world too.

The UNDP-OPHDI reports on MPI mentioned earlier says India has "by far the largest number of poor people worldwide" at *228.9 million* in 2021 (income level of $1.9 at 2011 PPP) and "India still has the *highest number* of poor children in the world (97 million, or 21.8 percent of children ages 0–17 in India)."

The World Bank's database also shows Indians are *one of the poorest* in the world with a per capita income of $2,3886 (current USD, 2022), while the global average is $12,647.5 – *5.3 times* richer or higher in income.[58]

The UN's Food and Agriculture Organization (FAO)-led assessment, "The State of Food Security and Nutrition in the World (SOFI) 2023"[59], showed India is home to the maximum hungry, *233.9 million* or 16.6% of globally undernourished population in 2022 – which is up from 224.3 million or 27% of the global undernourished during 2019-2021[60]. An analysis of its data shows, 74% Indians can't afford a healthy diet due to stagnant income.[61] In the Global Hunger Index (GHI) of 2023 – which measures *multidimensional* hunger taking into account undernourishment, child stunting, child wasting and child mortality – India presents a highly distressing picture. Although its multidimensional hunger score improved marginally from 29 in 2022 to 28.5 in 2023 – it is far higher than known poor countries and neighbours like Rwanda and neighbours Nepal, Pakistan, Myanmar and Bangladesh. India continued to rank far below them and it fell further from 107 to 111 (of 125 countries) in this one year. What this mean is that while other countries have reduced their multidimensional hunger faster, India's *stalled* (in fact, reversed between 2014-2022) and has a long way to go. The graph (in the next page) shows the relative progress of these countries.

The Indian government did *dismiss*[62] both reports, like in the previous years' reports and like other global indicators showing India's worsening performance in various areas. But this is an unjustified quibble because both use the very same Indian government's (highly flawed) NHFS-5 of 2019-21 detailed earlier, with an additional survey (sample size 3,000) to project the proportion of population undernourishment. But then, India has a huge data vacuum – no household consumption survey (MPCE) after 2011-12 – to reflect the state of undernourishment and poverty level of the population. Why did it junk the MPCE of 2017-18 with *a big lie* (mentioned earlier)?

The graph (in the next page) shows the stark reality the Indian government is unwilling to accept. Don't forget, 67% of Indian households are being fed with "free" additional ration to the "subsidized" ration since April 2020 when the pandemic lockdown was underway and "free" ration (not "subsidized" any more) from January 2023. If Indians are well-fed, why such a huge "free" food distribution – which the government takes pride in telling people at the time of electioneering? Why this new vote bank called "labharthi varg"?

Graph 6: India losing fight against hunger

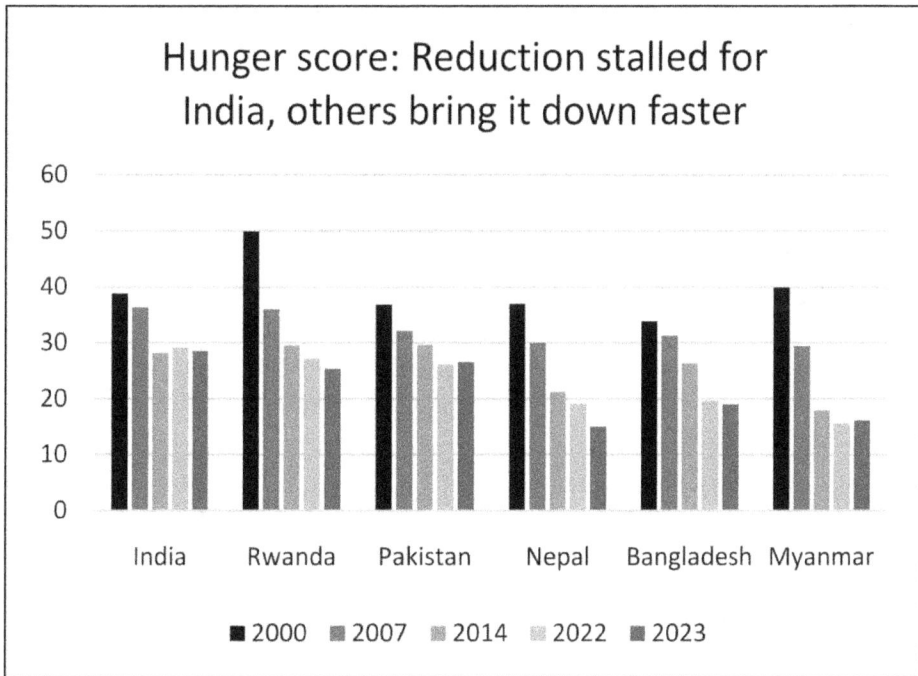

Hunger score: Reduction stalled for
India, others bring it down faster

Source: Global Hunger Index 2022 and 2023

Not just that, India is home of *maximum illiterates*. A 2014 UNESCO report[63] had said India has the "largest population of illiterate adults, 287 million amounting to 37% of the global total".

It has worst *maternal deaths record*: A UN report of May 2023[64] said India tops the list of 10 countries in most maternal deaths, stillbirths and neonatal deaths in 2020 – at 17% of the global total or 0.8 million.

India tops the list in *slavery* too: The 2023 Global Slavery Index[65] shows India coming at the top with a 38% rise in "modern slavery" since 2018 (from 8 million to 11 million) – which is defined as forced labour, forced or servile marriage, debt bondage, forced commercial sexual exploitation, human trafficking, slavery-like practices, and the sale and exploitation of children).

Most Unequal in World

The World Inequality Report 2022[66] shows this to be true on multiple fronts:

• **Income inequality**: India stands out as "a poor and very unequal country, with an affluent elite". While the top 10% and top 1% hold 57% and 22% of total national income, respectively, the bottom 50% share has gone down to 13% in 2020. In 2021, the top 10% income share is estimated at 49%.

- **Wealth Inequality**: This is even worse. The bottom 50% owns "almost nothing" (6% of total wealth), the middle-class is relatively poor (29.5% of total wealth), while the top 10% and top 1% owned 65% and 33% of total wealth in 2021, respectively.

- **Gender Inequality**: The female labour income share is equal to 18% — significantly lower than the average in Asia (21%, excluding China). The value is one of the lowest in the world, slightly higher than then average share in West Asia (15%).

- **Carbon Inequality**: India is low carbon emitter with the average per capita consumption of 2 tCO2e (ton of carbon dioxide equivalent) comparable with sub-Saharan African countries. The bottom 50%, middle 40% and top 10% consume 1,2 and 9 tCO2e/capita, respectively. The top 10% has the maximum carbon footprint.

Many other evidence points to such growing inequality and concentration of income and wealth at the top. Growth in per capita has trailed that of GDP (constant prices) in the entire 2011-12 GDP series. While the GDP grew by 83.2%, the per capita income grew by 61.6% – indicating that *average Indian's income* has not grown as much as the economy. There are many high-frequency indicators that point to *inversions* – pointing to impoverishment of the masses, concentration of wealth and income at the top and a K-shaped (unequal) growth other than those mentioned earlier (tax, household savings, poverty, hunger etc.). Some of these are[67]:

(i) Sales of SUVs and luxury cars have overtaken entry level cars since FY22; sales of two-wheelers remain far below the FY19 level.

(ii) Sales of affordable houses (below Rs 40 lakh) are *going down below* the mid-segment and luxury houses – shifting the focus away from affordable houses.

(iii) Premium segment smartphone sale is seeing far robust growth and (iv) FMCG sales sluggish in rural areas compared to urban areas.

(iv) Number of passengers travelling by rail (poorer segment) in FY23 (April 2022 to February 2023) at 5,864 million[68] was substantially less *than* 8,439 million in the pre-pandemic FY19[69] (improving from 3,519 million in FY22[70]). Train speed is gradually slowing down[71]; more and more sleeper and second-class coaches are being replaced with AC coaches in Northern, Central and Western Railways by the day[72] even as overcrowding of sleeper and second-class coaches continue at festival times. Data showed train safety funds remain unused, anti-collision "Kavach" system not installed in most routes and a CAG report found safety fund diverted to buy *Foot massagers, crockery and jackets*.[73]

(v) Although more Indians are travelling by air (richer segment) but 1% Indians account for 45% of flights.

This inequality was not always so.

French economists Lucas Chancel and Thomas Piketty, who studied income inequality in India and also helmed the World Inequality Report of 2022, said the Nehruvian socialism era (1950s to mid-1980s) had substantially reduced inequality but the trend "reversed" in *the mid-1980s* when "pro-business, market deregulation policies were implemented". Today, the Nehruvian socialism is much-maligned because of this ideological shift. The following three graphs have been taken from their book "From British Raj to Billionaire Raj?"[74] *An aside:* Few realise that India never saw the quantum jump in its growth, not even in the post-liberalized era, that the socialist Nehruvian era saw – the GDP growth jumped to 4.1%, which is *4.6 to 5.1 times*[75] the pre-independence era growth of 0.8-0.9% - the truly "Golden Period" of Indian economy.

Image 2, 3 and 4: (From Left): Fall in income of Bottom 50%, Surge in income of Top 10% but fall in that of Middle 40% and Surge in income of Top 1%

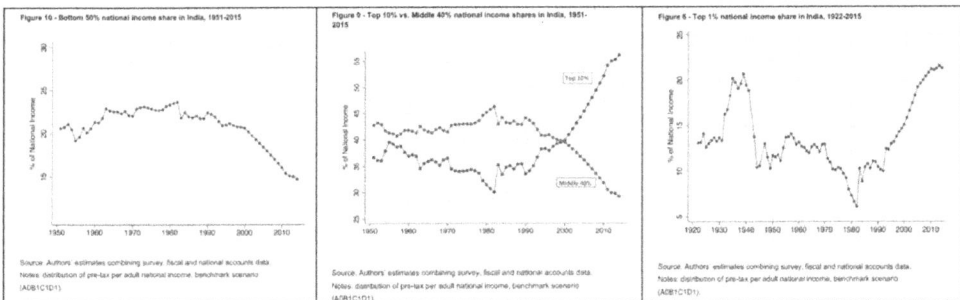

Source: From British Raj to Billionaire Raj?" (Chancel & Piketty 2017)

Chancel and Piketty also pointed out that income inequality of India and China was "at similar levels" in the early 1980s and it grew at a similar pace till the mid-2000s. While it stabilized in China thereafter, the rise continued in India. This "difference", they explained, was *likely* due to "differences in national policies, rather than mechanical forces". Piketty had earlier written, "inequality is neither economic nor technological; it is ideological and political".[76]

How do poverty, hunger, illiteracy, inequality etc. matter?

RB Mathisen of University of Bergen (Sweden), in his 2023 study "Economic Inequality and Political Power in Norway"[77] shows, the factors that make policies skewed in favour of the rich and against the poor are very much these ones – high economic inequality, poor education level, money rather than political and intellectual agency influencing elections. No wonder, India has a *command-and-control economy* now.

(d) Chronic and Prolonged Job Crisis

Jobs are what redistributes wealth and income. India transitioned from 'job-less' growth under the UPA government – when total jobs went up but manufacturing jobs were lost – to 'job-loss' growth under the new regime when jobs were lost.

The government's own PLFS reports of 2017-18 (which was first junked and then released after the regime secured its second term in 2019) revealed a 45-year high unemployment rate of 6.1% during 2011-12 and 2017-18. The Azim Premji University's analysis of this PLFS report's unit-level data showed *9 million jobs were lost* "for the first time in India's history".[78] Another study of the Azim Premji University (2021)[79] said during the pandemic year of 2020 India lost 100 million jobs to the lockdown, of which *15 million* were lost permanently.

A 2022 Bloomberg report[80] analyzed business portal CMIE's data showed *more than half* of the 900 million Indians of legal working age – roughly the population of the US and Russia combined – *stopped looking* for jobs because there aren't any to look for. It showed labour participation rate had dropped from 46% to 40% in five years of 2017 to 2022 and that only 9% of Indian women are employed or looking for jobs. Labour economists Mehrotra & Parida[81] said the government had inherited 10 million unemployed which had grown to 40 million by 2022. Another indication of job loss is shut down of 19,687 MSMEs[82] (a major source of employment) in three years of 2020-23.

India is now witnessing a reverse "structural transformation" (or reverse Lewisian transformation) with workers going back to agriculture. The annual PLFS reports of *2017-18 to 2022-23,* shows:

- Agriculture's share of jobs jumped to 45.8%, from 44.1%.

- Manufacturing's share dropped to 11.4% from 12.1%.

- Services' share to fell to 41.9%, from 42.8%.

That is, jobs moved away from formal to informal and high productive, high income to low productive, low income and vulnerable ones – increasing precarity of workers. It reflects worsening job crisis.

- Best-quality jobs, "regular wages/salaried", fell to 20.9%, from 22.8%.

- Bad quality jobs, "casual" also fell to 21.8%, from 24.9%.

  Where are workers going?

They are shifting to "self-employment" – (a) "own account" workers and employers or (b) "helper in household enterprise" (officialese for *unpaid* worker).

- Self-employment went up from 52.2% to 57.3%.

- Unpaid workers (total) went up from 13.6% (of the total workforce) to 18.3%.

- Unpaid women workers went up rapidly – up from 31.7% of total women workers to 37%.

The Ashoka University's Centre for Economic Data and Analysis (CEDA) and CMIE study[83] confirmed the above trends and pointed out that during FY17-FY21, manufacturing jobs *halved* ("declined by 46%"), pushing workers to migrate to low-paying and low-productive agriculture and self-employment. It is to this worsening of employment condition and Prime Minister's causal approach to job creation, best reflected in his 2018 remark during a TV interview that earning Rs 200 per day by selling "pakoda" is also employment that has led to alternate expression to "Modinomics", called "pakodanomics".[84]

The PLFS reports, however, show all the headline numbers improving – employment rate (WPR), labour participation rate for men and women (LFPR) and for women (FLFP) and unemployment rate (UR). How did this happen when millions of jobs and small businesses were lost overnight – first due to the demonetization of 2016, then the GSYT of 2017 and the pandemic lockdowns of 2020 and 2021? The PLFS reports don't explain that.

Even then, at worker-population ratio (WPR) for all ages (in current weekly status or CWS which is the global standard and used by the OECD countries) of 38% in 2022-23 (up from 32.7%), it is awfully low. The OECD average (for 15-64 years) is far higher at 70%.[85] In LFPR (which reflects those working in total labour force, which includes those looking or jobs), India's number in 2022-23 stood at 40% – up from 35.9%. The FLFP went up from 15.8% to 23.7%. The OECD average for LFPR and FLFP is around 70% or more.[86] Since the rise in India's FLFP is fueling the ranks of unpaid women workers, it is not a good development.

What about wages and social security cover? The PLFS data gives plenty of bad news[87]:

- Average 'real' wage for regular wages/salaried is negative (-) 2.9% and for self-employed negative (-) 1.8%. It marginally improved for casual workers to positive (+) 0.6%.

- "No social security" (one of PF/pension; gratuity; healthcare/maternity benefits etc.) *rising* – from 49.6% to 53.9%.

Development economist Jean Dreze used the PLFS and other data sources to show that since 2014, there has been a virtual stagnation in wages across India with the poorest communities earning less.[88]

The government's bet on higher GDP growth and incentives to manufacturing (PLIs and DLIs) to create jobs has predictably failed. Not only the GDP growth petered out even before the pandemic hit, manufacturing is producing less jobs in India and globally due to technological advancement and higher capital intensity. A 2018 study by Azim Premji University[89] showed in 1970s and 1980s of India, when the GDP growth was 3-4%, the employment growth was 2% but since 1990s and particularly in 2000s the GDP growth had accelerated to 7% but the employment growth had slowed down to 1% or less. The ratio of employment growth to GDP growth was now less than 0.1. In its latest report of 2023, the Azim Premji University says[90] post-pandemic unemployment rate is lower than it was earlier but "it remains above 15% for graduates and more worryingly it touches a huge 42% for graduates under 25 years".

MGNAREGA and NFSA To Rescue

The chronic and severe job crisis was reflected in the extraordinary jump in the rural job guarantee scheme MGNREGS. This scheme provides menial and below statutory minimum wages of states (all states, except Uttar Pradesh) because of which, a Times of India's analysis[91] showed the MGNREGS workers subsidized Rs 42,000 crore of infrastructure assets in two years of 2020 and 2021.

Rural households who availed such works went up from 48 million in FY16 (pre-demonetization) to 75.5 million in FY21 (pandemic) and came down to 61.9 million in FY23. Individuals' number went up from 72.3 million in FY16 to 111.9 million in FY21 and then to 87.6 million in FY23.[92] Going by the 167.9 million rural households (2011 Census), this means 45% households worked for the low-wage menial work in FY21. Consider the fact that 55% of total agriculture workforce is landless (Census 2011), this is not surprising.

Yet, it continues to provide 50 days or less of work (though guaranteed to provide 100 days and in drought years 150 days) and remains under-funded with large pending bills year after year and allocations were drastically cut in FY24 – by -31.5% from the FY23 (RE). This is not surprising since the Prime Minister had condemned this in 2015 by calling it a "living monument" of UPA's failure.[93] A comparative study[94] of the scheme during 2014-2020 and the UPA years of 2008-14 showed the coverage was reduced as fewer person-days of employment were generated, fewer households received 100 days of guaranteed work and financial allocations declined as percentage of GDP (by 0.47% on average). Besides, every trick in the book was used to undermine this right, like introducing 'National Mobile Monitoring System' digital app to monitor attendance, wage payments channeled through the Aadhaar Based Payment System (ABPS) when this linkage was officially declared to cover only 43% of cardholders and plagued by multiple systemic failures.[95]

Worse, the Centre "deleted" job cards of *15 million and 52 million* in FY22 and FY23[96], respectively, in the name of fake and duplicate job cards, "not willing to work" and others.

It was, however, this scheme and the National Food Security Act (NFSA) of 2013 – which the government's top think tank NITI Aayog wanted (against all evidence of its need) to curtail in 2021[97] – came to the rescue of people during the pandemic fiscals of FY21 and FY22. The "subsidized" ration under the NFSA Act was made "free" from January 1, 2023 for 67% of total households (75% rural and 50% urban) – reflecting the growing poverty.

Another reason for the failure to create jobs is to change the track. From promising 10 million jobs a year in 2015, (a) the PM equated selling "pakoda" (fried snacks) and earning Rs 200 a day with employment in 2018 (b) his government sold the rise in start-ups to claim "job seekers have become job creators" (which employs a large number of low-paying gig workers and which began to unravel in 2022 with the "funding winter") and (c) then the PM promised, in July 2022, to *fill 1 million jobs* lying vacant in Central government ministries and departments for eight years under his very watch. These vacancies, however, don't include large number of vacancies that exist in central PSUs, defence and paramilitary forces.[98]

All the above factors get reflected in another dataset.

The number of suicides due to economic distress, by unemployed, self-employed and daily wagers, apart from farmers, is growing rapidly. The National Crime Records Bureau (NCRB) data shows suicides by self-employed and daily wagers jumped to 38% of total suicides in 2021 – up from 32% in 2020. Daily wagers' death counted for 25.6% in 2021. The sharp spikes in these suicides due to economic distress which has been captured in the following graph.

Graph 7: Surge in suicides by different groups

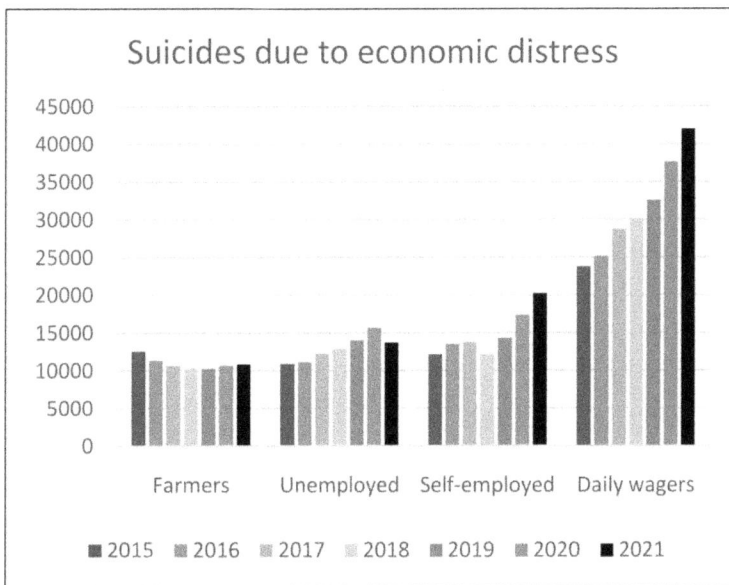

Source: NCRB reports

An interesting aspect of suicide data is that while farmers' suicide dominated headlines earlier (to hide which the government stopped publishing NCRB data altogether in 2017 and 2018), suicides by self-employed and daily wagers have far outnumbered year after year and yet, doesn't cause public uproar or national debate.

What this chapter tells is that the skewed pro-business policy of the government has led to the economic burden shifting to the masses – impoverishing them further. If the masses are getting poorer a high GDP growth only means enrichment of the top 10% or the top 1% of population. For an economy to grow, two critical factors are consumption demand and availability of household savings for investment – more so since private investment remains very low for a considerable period, forcing the government to push capex, which in turn depends on household savins for its capex push (65% of gross capital formation). This means a setback for household demands and household savins as drivers of growth.

The other impact is the burden shifting to environment – which the next chapter focuses on.

***

References

1   Article 38 in The Constitution Of India 1949; https://indiankanoon.org/doc/1673816/

2   Kishore Roshan, Terms of Trade | Why are the fuel hike protests confined to Parliament? Jun 19, 2023; https://www.hindustantimes.com/opinion/terms-of-trade-why-are-the-fuel-hike-protests-confined-to-parliament-101648201919042.html

3   Mohanty P, The downsides of New Welfarism, Mar 17, 2022; https://www.fortuneindia.com/opinion/the-downsides-of-new-welfarism/107480

4   Finance Minister's Budget speech, Feb 1, 2022; https://www.indiabudget.gov.in/doc/bspeech/bs202223.pdf

5   Statement of revenue impact of tax incentives under the central tax system, Annex-7, Budget 2023-2024; https://www.indiabudget.gov.in/doc/rec/annex7.pdf

6   Corporate tax rates slashed to 22% for domestic companies and 15% for new domestic manufacturing companies and other fiscal reliefs, Sept 19, 2019; https://pib.gov.in/PressReleaseIframePage.aspx?PRID=1585641 & New Personal Income Tax Regime heralds significant relief, especially for Middle Class Taxpayers, Feb 1, 2019; https://pib.gov.in/PressReleseDetailm.aspx?PRID=1601463

7   Deregulation of Diesel and Natural Gas Pricing, Ministry of Petroleum & Natural Gas, Dec 22, 2014; https://pib.gov.in/newsite/PrintRelease.aspx?relid=113867

8   Mohanty P, Is protectionism helping or harming India's exports? May 30, 2023; https://www.fortuneindia.com/opinion/is-protectionism-helping-or-harming-indias-exports/112851; Paying for Russian oil in Yuan will hurt globalisation of Rupee, Jul 12, 2023; https://www.fortuneindia.com/opinion/paying-for-russian-oil-in-yuan-will-hurt-globalisation-of-rupee/113351

9   Contribution of Petroleum Sector to Exchequer (FY15-FY23), PPAC; https://ppac.gov.in/prices/contribution-to-central-and-state-exchequer

10   Contribution of Petroleum Sector to Ex-Chequer (FY12-FY15), PPAC, 2015; http://ppac.org.in/WriteReadData/userfiles/file/RS_5_Cont_to_Exch.pdf

11   Oil bonds aim to 'insulate' customers: Experts see 'scope for fuel cess cuts', Aug 19, 2021; https://indianexpress.com/article/business/oil-bonds-aim-to-insulate-customers-experts-see-scope-for-fuel-cess-cuts-7460442/

12   Finance Minister Blames Ukraine War For Steepest Fuel Price Hike On Record, Mar 30, 2022 https://www.ndtv.com/business/finance-minister-blames-ukraine-war-for-steepest-fuel-price-hike-on-record-2851800

13   70% of Diesel, 99.6 % of Petrol consumed by Transport Sector, Ministry of Petroleum & Natural Gas, Jan 28, 2014; https://pib.gov.in/newsite/printrelease.aspx?relid=102799;   https://www.ppac.gov.in/WriteReadData/Reports/201411110329450069740AllIndiaStudyonSectoralDemandofDiesel.pdf

14   Decision to levy GST on packaged food was taken with all states on board, claims

Nirmala Sitharaman, Jul 19, 2022; https://scroll.in/latest/1028613/decision-to-levy-gst-on-packaged-food-was-taken-with-all-states-on-board-claims-nirmala-sitharaman

15   Mukherjee Sacchidananda, Revenue Assessment of Goods and Services Tax (GST) in India, NIPFP, Jul 6, 2022; https://www.nipfp.org.in/publications/working-papers/1984/

16   Tax officials unearth Rs 19.5K cr GST evasion, Jul 22, 2023; https://www.magzter. com/stories/newspaper/Business-Standard/TAX-OFFICIALS-UNEARTH-195K-CR-GST-EVASION, Jul 22, 2023; GST officers bust 304 syndicates involving Rs 25,000 cr fake ITC claims, Jul 2, 2023; https://indianexpress.com/article/business/gst-officers-bust-304-syndicates-involving-rs-25000-cr-fake-itc-claims-8696504/

17   High service charges levied by SCBs, Rajya Sabha answer, Aug 8, 2023; https://pqars.nic.in/annex/260/AU2136.pdf

18   Rawat Mukesh, In 4 years, banks fined you more than what Vijay Mallya and Nirav Modi owe them, Dec 31, 2018; https://www.indiatoday.in/business/story/what-banks-charge-for-minimum-balance-extra-atm-transactions-1418865-2018-12-29

19   Magazine Aanchal, Decision put on hold, credit card use abroad not to attract TCS, Jun 29, 2023; https://indianexpress.com/article/business/banking-and-finance/decision-put-on-hold-credit-card-use-abroad-not-to-attract-tcs-8691435/

20   Govt spent Rs 3,000 cr on Patel statue, Rs 2.64 cr more in advertising it, Jan 16, 2019; https://www.business-standard.com/article/current-affairs/govt-spent-rs-3-000-cr-on-patel-statue-rs-2-64-cr-more-in-advertising-it-119011600405_1.html

21   Report of the Comptroller and Auditor General of India for the year ended 31 March 2017, Report No.18 of 2018 (CPSEs), Aug 7, 2018; https://cag.gov.in/cag_old/sites/default/files/audit_report_files/Report_No_18_of_2018_-_Compliance_Audit_on_General_Purpose_Financial_Reports_of_Central_Public_Sector_Enterprises_of_Union_Government__Commercial.pdf; IOC, ONGC, GAIL, other oil PSUs commit Rs 100 cr for redevelopment of Badrinath Dham shrine, PTI, May 6, 2021; https://www.businesstoday.in/latest/economy-politics/story/ioc-ongc-gail-other-oil-psus-commit-rs-100-cr-for-redevelopment-of-badrinath-dham-shrine-295167-2021-05-06

22   As Modi plans a bullet train, RTI query reveals 40% seats on Mumbai-Ahmedabad trains go vacant, Oct 31, 2017; https://www.indiatoday.in/india/story/bullet-trains-narendra-modi-government-mumbai-ahmedabad-1078662-2017-10-31

23   Iconic Pragati Maidan makeover on anvil; to cost around Rs 3,000 crore, Nov 12, 2015; https://economictimes.indiatimes.com/news/economy/infrastructure/iconic-pragati-maidan-makeover-on-anvil-to-cost-around-rs-3000-crore/articleshow/49756296.cms

24   Centre Defends Rs 20,000 Crore Central Vista Project, Tells SC 'It Saves Money, Doesn't Waste It', Nov 2, 2020; https://www.news18.com/news/india/centre-defends-rs-20k-cr-central-vista-project-tells-sc-it-saves-money-not-wastes-it-3038003.html

25 Das Yudhajit Shankar and Gupta Rahul, Is Chandrayaan-3 a waste of money? This is what data says, https://www.indiatoday.in/science/chandrayaan-3/story/isro-moon-landing-is-chandrayaan-3-vs-other-space-missions-cost-analysis-2425382-2023-08-23

26 Genesis, Indian Space Research Organization; https://www.isro.gov.in/genesis.html

27 Budget 2023 | Department of Space gets Rs 12,500 crore, 8% less than previous year, Feb 1 2023; https://www.thehindu.com/business/budget/budget-2023-department-of-space-gets-12500-crore-8-less-than-previous-year/article66458858.ece

28 Income Tax Return Statistics Assessment Year 2016-17, Income Tax Department, Oct 2018; https://incometaxindia.gov.in/Documents/Direct%20Tax%20Data/Income-tax-statistics-i-t-return-ay-2016-17-v1.pdf

29 Income Tax Return Statistics Assessment Year 2017-18, Income Tax Department, Oct 2018; https://incometaxindia.gov.in/Documents/Direct%20Tax%20Data/Income-tax-statistics-i-t-return-ay-2017-18-v1.pdf

30 Income tax returns, Lok Sabha answer, Jul 24, 2023; https://www.dropbox.com/scl/fi/032fc56yy5ynyu407ridb/LS_tax-categories_Jul-2023.pdf?rlkey=90cwy3e6zuxmvwmlsgxxxr6k7&dl=0

31 Category and Total Income Range Wise filing count, e-Filing, Income Tax Department; https://www.incometax.gov.in/iec/foportal/statistics-data

32 Direct and indirect tax revenues of central and state governments, RBI, https://dbie.rbi.org.in/BOE/OpenDocument/1608101727/OpenDocument/opendoc/openDocument.faces?logonSuccessful=true&shareId=0

33 OECD 2022: Revenue statistics; https://www.oecd.org/tax/tax-policy/revenue-statistics-highlights-brochure.pdf

34 Author's calculation based on RBI data

35 OECD 2022: Revenue statistics; https://www.oecd.org/tax/tax-policy/revenue-statistics-highlights-brochure.pdf

36 Mohanty P, Is India back to 'license raj'? Aug 15, 2023; https://www.fortuneindia.com/opinion/is-india-back-to-license-raj/113736

37 No. 50 (a): Flow of Financial Assets and Liabilities of Households - Instrument-wise, RBI, Sept 18, 2023; https://rbidocs.rbi.org.in/rdocs/Bulletin/PDFs/50AT_180920231942F33367ED4E19B02A328F75B484AB.PDF

38 https://www.fortuneindia.com/opinion/data-war-on-india-lifting-135-140-million-out-of-poverty/113738

39 Deployment of bank credit by major sectors, RBI, https://cimsdbie.rbi.org.in/BOE/OpenDocument/2306011537/OpenDocument/opendoc/openDocument.jsp?logonSuccessful=true&shareId=3

40   In the pandemic, India's middle class shrinks and poverty spreads while China sees smaller changes, March 18, 2021; https://www.pewresearch.org/fact-tank/2021/03/18/in-the-pandemic-indias-middle-class-shrinks-and-poverty-spreads-while-china-sees-smaller-changes/

41   Poverty and shared Prosperity: Correcting Course, World Bank, 2022, https://www.worldbank.org/en/publication/poverty-and-shared-prosperity

42   ICE360 2021, Annual Household income 2021 vs 2016 @ 2011-12 prices; https://www.ice360.in/product/annual-household-income-2021-vs-2016-2011-12-prices/?type=lightbox

43   Bhalla Surjeet, Bhasin Karan and Virmani Arvind, Pandemic, Poverty, and Inequality: Evidence from India, IMF, Apr 5, 2022; https://www.imf.org/en/Publications/WP/Issues/2022/04/05/Pandemic-Poverty-and-Inequality-Evidence-from-India-516155

44   https://www.business-standard.com/article/economy-policy/consumer-spend-survey-panel-didn-t-flag-quality-issues-ask-for-scrapping-119112001535_1.html

45   Jha Somesh, Consumer spend sees first fall in 4 decades on weak rural demand: NSO data, Nov 15, 2019; https://www.business-standard.com/article/economy-policy/consumer-spend-sees-first-fall-in-4-decades-on-weak-rural-demand-nso-data-119111401975_1.html

46   Paliath Shreehari, A Year After Exodus, No Reliable Data Or Policy On Migrant Workers, Mar 24, 2021; https://www.indiaspend.com/governance/migrant-workers-no-reliable-data-or-policy-737499; SC asks states, UTs to implement 'one nation, one ration card' scheme, PTI, Jun 12, 2021; https://www.business-standard.com/article/current-affairs/sc-asks-states-uts-to-implement-one-nation-one-ration-card-scheme-121061200046_1.html

47   Paliath Shreehari, A Year After Exodus, No Reliable Data Or Policy On Migrant Workers, Mar 24, 2021; https://www.indiaspend.com/governance/migrant-workers-no-reliable-data-or-policy-737499; SC asks states, UTs to implement 'one nation, one ration card' scheme, PTI, JUn 12, 2021; https://www.business-standard.com/article/current-affairs/sc-asks-states-uts-to-implement-one-nation-one-ration-card-scheme-121061200046_1.html

48   Paliath Shreehari and Iqbal Nushaiba, Why Ration Card Portability Scheme Is Mostly Limited To Delhi, Jul 5, 2023; https://www.indiaspend.com/governance/why-ration-card-portability-scheme-is-mostly-limited-to-delhi-867957

49   Sinha Roy, Sutirtha and Van Der Weide Roy, Poverty in India Has Declined over the Last Decade But Not As Much As Previously Thought, Apr 2022; https://openknowledge.worldbank.org/entities/publication/2c93123f-dbbc-58fa-b70f-1e247ecab589

50   Dreze Jean and Somanchi Anmol, "Bias it is": CMIE chief's defence of CPHS survey elicits fresh critical response from Jean Drèze, Anmol Somanchi, Jun 27, 2021; https://economictimes.indiatimes.com/opinion/et-commentary/bias-it-is-cmie-chiefs-defence-of-cphs-survey-elicits-fresh-critical-response-from-jean-drze-anmol-somanchi/articleshow/83889707.cms

51   Sanyal Salil, Sources of Biases in the Consumer Pyramids Household Survey, Oct 1, 2021; https://www.theindiaforum.in/letters/sources-biases-consumer-pyramids-household-survey?utm_source=website&utm_medium=organic&utm_campaign=Letters&utm_content=Homepage e

52   Unpacking deprivation bundles to reduce multidimensional poverty, UNDP-OPHI, Oct 17, 2022; https://hdr.undp.org/content/2022-global-multidimensional-poverty-index-mpi#/indicies/MPI; Unstacking global poverty: Data for high impact action, Jul 11, 2023; https://hdr.undp.org/system/files/documents/hdp-document/2023mpireportenpdf.pdf; Half of the world's poor live in just 5 countries, World Bank, 2019; https://blogs.worldbank.org/opendata/half-world-s-poor-live-just-5-countries#:~:text=The%205%20countries%20with%20the,Congo%2C%20Ethiopia%2C%20and%20Bangladesh.

53   National Multidimensional Poverty Index: A Progress Review 2023, NITI Aayog, Jul 17, 2023; https://niti.gov.in/sites/default/files/2023-07/National-Multidimentional-Poverty-Index-2023-Final-17th-July.pdf

54   Dhasmana Indivjal, Multidimensional poverty estimates: Is India measuring poverty accurately? Jul 29, 2023; https://www.business-standard.com/economy/news/multidimensional-poverty-estimates-is-india-measuring-poverty-accurately-123072500717_1.html

55   National Multidimensional Poverty Index Baseline Report, Based on NFHS-4 (2015-16), NITI Aayog, Nov 24, 2021; https://www.niti.gov.in/sites/default/files/2021-11/National_MPI_India-11242021.pdf

56   Fact Sheet: Key Indicators: 22 States/UTs from Phase-I, Ministry of Health and Family Welfare, Dec 2020; https://main.mohfw.gov.in/sites/default/files/NFHS-5_Phase-I.pdf

57   NFHS-5 2019-20: Compendium of Fact Sheets, Key Indicators: India and 14 States/UTs (Phase-II), 2023; https://main.mohfw.gov.in/sites/default/files/NFHS-5_Phase-II_0.pdf; Union Health Ministry releases NFHS-5 Phase II Findings, Ministry of Health and Family Welfare, Nov 24, 2023; https://www.pib.gov.in/PressReleasePage.aspx?PRID=17745333

58   GDP per capita (current US$), World Bank; https://data.worldbank.org/indicator/NY.GDP.PCAP.CD

59   FAO, IFAD, UNICEF, WFP and WHO, The State of Food Security and Nutrition in the World 2023. Urbanization, agrifood systems transformation and healthy diets across the rural–urban continuum. Rome, FAO. https://doi.org/10.4060/cc3017en; https://www.fao.org/3/cc3017en/cc3017en.pdf

60   FAO, IFAD, UNICEF, WFP and WHO, The State of Food Security and Nutrition in the World; https://www.fao.org/3/cc0639en/cc0639en.pdf

61   Due to stagnant income levels, 74% in India can't afford a healthy diet: UN agency report | Data, Sept 1, 2023; https://www.thehindu.com/data/as-food-prices-rise-74-in-india-cant-afford-a-healthy-diet-un-agency-report-data/article67256967.ece

62   Measurement of over 7 Crore children shows wasting at about one-third of that used in Global Hunger Index, Ministry of Women and Child Development, Oct 12, 2023; https://www.pib.gov.in/PressReleaseDetailm.aspx?PRID=1967164

63   UNESCO 2014: Teaching and learning: achieving quality for all; EFA global monitoring report, 2013-2014; https://unesdoc.unesco.org/ark:/48223/pf0000225660

64   Improving maternal and newborn health and survival and reducing stillbirth: Progress Report 2023, May 2023, WHO, UNICEF, UNFPA, https://cdn.who.int/media/docs/default-source/mca-documents/nbh/stillbirth/enap-epmm-midpoint-status-report-_08052023.pdf?sfvrsn=6b1f1c6c_3

65   Global Slavery Index 2023, ILO, IOM and Walkfree, Jun 2023; https://cdn.walkfree.org/content/uploads/2023/05/17114737/Global-Slavery-Index-2023.pdf

66   World Inequality Report 2022, https://wir2022.wid.world/www-site/uploads/2021/12/WorldInequalityReport2022_Full_Report.pdf

67   Mohanty P, What gets missed in India's growth indicators, May 4, 2023; https://www.fortuneindia.com/opinion/what-gets-missed-in-indias-growth-indicators/112555; Aggarwal Raghav, Demand for luxury homes overtakes affordable ones for first time in India, Oct 4, 2023; https://www.business-standard.com/industry/news/demand-for-luxury-homes-overtakes-affordable-ones-for-first-time-in-india-knight-frank-123100400372_1.html; Three years on, Indian Railways' passenger traffic remains below pre-pandemic numbers, Apr 13, 2023; https://economictimes.indiatimes.com/industry/transportation/railways/three-years-on-indian-railways-passenger-traffic-remains-below-pre-pandemic-numbers/articleshow/99458137.cms?utm_source=contentofinterest&utm_medium=text&utm_campaign=cppst; Air India, IndiGo: New record as 456,000 Indians take flights in a day, May 2, 2023; https://www.bbc.com/news/world-asia-india-65334390; Indus Valley Annual Report 2023; https://www.slideshare.net/amione/indus-valley-annual-report-2023

68   Magnitude of rail passengers, Ministry of Railways, Mar 17, 2023; https://sansad.in/getFile/annex/259/AU2058.pdf?source=pqars

69   Indian Railways, annual report 2018-19; https://indianrailways.gov.in/railwayboard/uploads/directorate/stat_econ/Annual-Reports-2019-2020/Indian-Railways-Annual%20-Report-Accounts%20-2019-20-English.pdf

70   Indian Railways, annual report 2021-22; https://indianrailways.gov.in/railwayboard/uploads/directorate/stat_econ/pdf/Indian%20Railways%20Annual%20Report%20%26%20Accounts%20English%202021-22_web_Final.pdf

71   Passenger trains in India are getting slower, and your trips longer, Nov 15, 2023; https://www.business-standard.com/india-news/passenger-trains-in-india-are-getting-slower-and-your-trips-longer-123111500536_1.html

72   Radhakrishnan Vignesh, Varghese Rebecca and Loganathan Sonikka, Why increasing AC coaches and reducing Sleeper and Second Class is a problem for commuters | Data, Nov 24, 2023; https://www.thehindu.com/data/why-increasing-ac-coaches-and-reducing-sleeper-and-second-class-a-problem-for-commuters-data/article67562053.ece

73 Sharma Milan, Funds allocated, not utilised: Govt data shows why no Kavach on route of Odisha train accident, Jun 5, 2023; https://www.indiatoday.in/india/story/odisha-train-accident-zero-money-spent-kavach-southeast-zone-govt-data-2388937-2023-06-05; CAG Report Shows Indian Railways Misused Safety Fund to Buy Foot Massagers, Crockery, Jackets, Jun 10, 2023; https://thewire.in/government/cag-report-shows-indian-railways-misused-safety-fund-to-buy-foot-massagers-crockery-jackets

74 Chancel and Piketty 2017 and 2019: Indian Income Inequality, 1922-2015: From British Raj to Billionaire Raj? 2017 and 2019; International Association for Research in Income and Wealth; https://wid.world/document/chancelpiketty2017widworld/; http://piketty.pse.ens.fr/files/ChancelPiketty2019RIW.pdf

75 Mohanty P, 'An Unkept Promise', Chapter VI, page 162

76 Piketty Thomas, Capital and Ideology, Harvard University Press, Mar 2020, https://www.amazon.in/Capital-Ideology-Thomas-Piketty/dp/0674980824

77 Mathisen RB 2023: Economic Inequality and Political Power in Norway, Mar 3, 2023, University of Bergen; https://bora.uib.no/bora-xmlui/bitstream/handle/11250/3050961/drthesis_2023_mathisen.pdf?sequence=2&isAllowed=ye

78 Mohanty P, Budget 2023: Why India Needs A Jobs Policy, Jan 4, 2023; https://www.fortuneindia.com/long-reads/budget-2023-why-india-needs-a-jobs-policy/111005

79 State of Working India 2021, Azim Premji University, May 5, 2021; https://cse.azimpremjiuniversity.edu.in/state-of-working-india/swi-2021/

80 Beniwal Vrishti, Majority of India's 900 Million Workforce Stop Looking for Jobs, Bloomberg, Apr 25, 2022; https://www.bloomberg.com/news/articles/2022-04-24/majority-of-india-s-900-million-workforce-stop-looking-for-jobs

81 Mehrotra Santosh, Giri Tuhinsubhra, Claims vs reality: India's bleak job picture, Deccan Herald, Feb 13, 2022; https://www.deccanherald.com/specials/claims-vs-reality-indias-bleak-job-picture-1080938.html

82 Closed MSMEs, Lok Sabha, Jul 20, 2023; https://www.dropbox.com/scl/fi/s91dqx26qghxjpbyqfxqi/LS_MSMEs-shut-20k-3-years.pdf?rlkey=wm3ozvdbgwiavuzcp7cfhvzgp&dl=0

83 CEDA-CMIE Bulletin: Manufacturing employment halves in 5 years, CEDA, Ashoka University and CMIE, May 6, 2021; https://ceda.ashoka.edu.in/ceda-cmie-bulletin-manufacturing-employment-halves-in-5-years/

84 Mehrotra Santosh and Parida Jajati, 'Pakoda' Employment Has Increased Poverty Over the Last Eight Years, Oct 14, 2021; https://thewire.in/economy/pakoda-employment-has-increased-poverty-over-the-last-eight-years; Khan Aaqib Raza, PM Modi's 'Pakodanomics': What do Informal Sector Workers Think? Feb 8, 2018; https://www.thequint.com/videos/news-videos/prime-minister-modi-street-vendors-pakoda-employment-comment; Rao V Venkateswara, Pakodanomics is the new economics, May 1, 2023; https://www.deccanherald.com/opinion/pakodanomics-is-the-new-economics-1214538.html;

85   Labour Market Situation, OECD - Updated: October 2023; https://www.oecd.org/sdd/labour-stats/labour-market-situation-oecd-updated-october-2023.htm; OECD employment and labour force participation rates reach record highs in the fourth quarter of 2022, Apr 2023; https://www.oecd.org/sdd/labour-stats/labour-market-situation-oecd-04-2023.pdf

86   Mohanty P, PLFS 2022-23: Good news, bad news, and the unanswered questions, Oct 26, 2023; https://www.fortuneindia.com/macro/plfs-2022-23-good-news-bad-news-and-the-unanswered-questions/114576

87   Mohanty P, 'PLFS 2022-23'

88   Dreze Jean, Since 2014, the poorest communities are earning less, May 25, 2023; https://indianexpress.com/article/opinion/columns/since-2014-the-poorest-communities-are-earning-less-8625367/s

89   State of Working India, Azim Premji University, 2018; https://cse.azimpremjiuniversity.edu.in/wp-content/uploads/2019/02/State_of_Working_India_2018-1.pdf

90   State of Working India 2023, Azim Premji University, Sept 2023; https://publications.azimpremjiuniversity.edu.in/5166/1/State_of_Working_India_2023.pdf

91   Thakur Atul, Nagarajan Rema, MNREGS workers subsidised creation of infra assets by Rs 20,000 crore a year, Jan 26, 2022; http://timesofindia.indiatimes.com/articleshow/89125423.cms?utm_source=contentofinterest&utm_medium=text&utm_campaign=cppst

92   MGNAREGA At a Glance, https://mnregaweb4.nic.in/netnrega/all_lvl_details_dashboard_new.aspx?Fin_Year=2023-2024&Digest=WJEEpOm1k0Ptz2KJJGSoqA

93   'Living monument' to Modi's doublespeak, May 5, 2017; https://www.telegraphindia.com/india/living-monument-to-narendra-modis-doublespeak/cid/1773784

94   Narayan Swati, A slow death, Jun 7, 2023; https://www.telegraphindia.com/opinion/a-slow-death-the-nrega-has-been-repeatedly-undermined/cid/1942838

95   Dreze Jean, Making Aadhaar-Based Payments Compulsory for NREGA Wages Is a Recipe for Disaster, Feb 16, 2023; https://thewire.in/rights/aadhaar-payments-compulsory-nrega

96   Deletion of names under MGNREGS, Lok Sabha answer, Jul 25, 2023; https://www.dropbox.com/scl/fi/w23fc8rsknhnosfyvp835/LS_MGNREGS-deletions_2023.pdf?rlkey=i8cwoiomg10eyawurnf84vh58&dl=0

97   To cut subsidy bill, Niti paper says lower coverage of food security law, Feb 28, 2021; https://indianexpress.com/article/india/to-cut-subsidy-bill-niti-paper-says-lower-coverage-of-food-security-law-7207884/

98   Mohanty P, The wheels-within-wheels in central govt vacancies, Aug 4, 2022; https://www.fortuneindia.com/opinion/the-wheels-within-wheels-in-central-govt-vacancies/109199

Chapter IX

Economic Burden Shifts to Environment

One of the very first things the Prime Minister did after coming to power in May 2014 was to rename the Ministry of Environment and Forests (MoEF) as Ministry of Environment, Forest and Climate Change (MoEFCC) (May 28, 2014).[1] This was a message that he and his government were serious about climate mitigation but that wasn't to be. Immediately thereafter, a series of executive orders and green clearances followed, allowing polluting industries to continue by paying penalty and diverting forest land for non-forest use without due diligence. These executive orders would be made statutory later. Parallelly, all rights of tribals and other forest dwelling communities over their forests, forest resources and minor minerals were bypassed. All these moves would enable a free pass to private businesses to exploit natural resources and boost growth while noble slogans like "One Earth, One Family, One Future"[2], "living in harmony with nature"[3] and official website 'LiFE' (Lifestyle for Environment)[4] claiming to bring sustainable lifestyle would flood public discourse as cover fires.

Dazzling to Deceive

A few examples of what followed after the MOEF became MoEFCC:

(a)   In July 2014, the National Board for Wildlife (NBWL) headed by the Prime Minister – the premier decision-making body on matters relating to wildlife – was reconstituted nominating only one NGO working in the field of conservation, against five, and two independent experts from the field of wildlife against 10. Following this, the Supreme Court restrained the NBWL from taking decisions in August 2014[5] and later, in November 2014, lifted it on the assurance that it had been reconstituted to give adequate representations to independent experts – paving the way for over 100 projects the NBWL had cleared.[6]

(b)   By July 18, 2014, green clearances had been given to *five mega projects* with far reaching consequences for environment and forests[7] – including two highly polluting coal-based power plants: the Adani Ports' SEZ in Gujarat; two coal mining projects, Coal India's Tikak block in Assam and Reliance Power's Chhatrasal block in Madhya Pradesh; GAIL's gas-based power plant in Madhya Pradesh and a state highway renovation project in Assam.

(c)   In August 2014, the PMO asked the green ministry to relax norms and speed up clearances for road constructions for areas up to *100 kms* from international borders.[8]

(d)   In August 2014, a panel under former Cabinet Secretary TSR Subramanian was set up to review all green laws – Environment Protection Act (EPA) of 1986, Forest Conservation Act (FCA) of 1980, Wildlife Protection Act (WPA) of 1972, Water (Prevention and Control of Pollution) Act of 1974 and Air (Prevention and Control of Pollution) Act of 1981 and Indian Forest Act (IFA) of 1927 – to *fast-track green clearances*. It was given two months' time and in November 2014, the panel gave its report proposing a new "umbrella" law to streamline the processes.[9]

(e)   In early September 2014, the Prime Minister changed his older view on climate change. From recognizing it as a threat, he was saying that it was a *myth*. He told students in a TV show (on "Teacher's Day"): "Climate has not changed. We have changed. Our habits have changed. Our habits have got spoiled. Due to that, we have destroyed our entire environment". He told a national daily: "Climate change? Is this terminology correct? The reality is this that in our family, *some people are old*...They say this time the weather is colder. And, people's ability to bear cold becomes less." These were in variance with his earlier view (2011): "Climate change is definitely affecting the future generations which, as of now, have no voice on the actions of present generation." After he changed his views, The Guardian explained: "So what changed? Modi has *dismantled* a number of environmental protections, clearing the way for *new coal mines* and other *industrial projects*. He also *blocked funds to Greenpeace and other environmental groups* and is known to be *vehemently anti-NGOs*."[10] (*Emphasis added*)

By mid-September 2014, eminent environmentalist Sunita Narain was in deep pain.[11] She wrote that in two months till July end, forest clearance had been granted to over *92 projects*, diverting *1,600 ha* of forests; the green ministry was (i) speeding up clearances by amending the Environmental Impact Assessment (EIA) notification to delegate powers to states "with the full knowledge that the state agencies lack capacity and accountability" (contrary to making "informed decisions") and (ii) wherever possible, the provision of holding public hearings or taking gram sabhas' consent was being "diluted or even removed". She also noted that green clearances were bad enough during the previous UPA government (with less than 3% projects getting rejected on environmental concerns), the system was designed to obstruct and prevaricate, not scrutinise and assess environmental damage. What changed? She explained: "In some ways the NDA is doing what the UPA did but *without any pretence.*" *(Emphasis added)*

This is a pattern – piety and noble sentiments followed by their violations – which would repeat itself in later years. But piety and noble sentiments have their usefulness. In October 2018, the Prime Minister received the UN's highest environmental honour, the UNEP Champion of the Earth award, for "his pioneering work in *championing* the International Solar Alliance and for his *unprecedented pledge* to eliminate all single-use plastic in India by 2022".[12] The UN may be surprised to know India announced a *ban* on "manufacture, import, stocking, distribution, sale and use" of "identified" single-use plastic (SUP) only *from* July 1, 2022[13] – a few months before the deadline (presumably December 31, 2022) to "eliminate" it was to end. A few months later, German broadcaster Deutsche Welle wrote: "But India, which uses about 14 million tons of plastic annually, has *not issued any advisory to stop the use* of SUPs, and *no penalties have been imposed* following the ban. SUP products continue to be *available as usual*".[14] It said India was struggling to find alternative to SUPs and establish effective waste management system. *(Emphasis added)*

By now, the government had taken a series of steps to fast-tract environment and forest clearances to projects with minimum fuss. Having installed a "single-window" green clearance system, it took this to a notch higher.

In fact, a couple of months before the UN award was announced, the Prime Minister had, in August 2018, launched 'PARIVESH' or Pro-Active and Responsive facilitation by Interactive, Virtuous and Environmental Single-window Hub – ironically on the World Biofuel Day – a single-window Integrated Environmental Management System.[15]

It was billed as "more of a facilitator, than a regulator" and meant for "online submission, monitoring and management of proposals submitted by Project Proponents to the Ministry of Environment, Forest and Climate Change (MoEFCC), as well as to the State Level Environmental Impact Assessment Authorities (SEIAA), to seek various types of clearances (e.g., Environment, Forest, Wildlife and Coastal Regulation Zone Clearances) from Central, State and district-level authorities". That is, all-in-one project approval – and its real implications would become clear much later.

Meanwhile, pieties continued. On Mahatma Gandhi's birth anniversary of

October 2, 2021, the Prime Minister invoked the Father of the Nation to advise Indians to adopt "lifestyle that is in harmony with nature". The same day, however, the MoEFCC issued a "consultative paper"[16] proposing wholesale exemptions for a range of infrastructure activities from the Forest (Conservation) Act (FCA) of 1980[17] – forgetting that its job is to protect environment and forests and mitigate climate change. A few days later, it was learnt that the Prime Minister had asked his senior bureaucrats to prepare a "single environment law"[18] – subsuming all other laws relating to environmental protections (from environment clearances for diversion of land and forests to air-water-soil pollutions etc. for mining and other industrial/infrastructure projects) – to ensure green clearances were faster and least cumbersome.

A month later, on November 2, 2021, the Prime Minister travelled Glasgow to attend the COP26 meet and invoke the Mahatma again[19] – expressing his faith in peaceful co-existence with nature, advising the world leaders to be "mindful" rather than pursue "mindless and destructive consumption".

But over the next few days at the COP26, the Indian delegation would refuse to commit to 'net zero' by 2050, push its limit to 2070 and refuse to commit to "phase out" coal (one of the most polluting).[20]

And then, what pieties often do, happened in May 2022.

The Prime Minister was on a visit to Denmark. There he told the Indian diaspora that India had "no role in damaging" environment and asked them to tell their Denis friends to visit India to see this for themselves – his "living in harmony with nature" philosophy or 'LiFE', the "sustainable" development model, at work.[21]

The next month, in June 2022, the global Environmental Performance Index of 2022 (EPI)[22] was released, listing India at the bottom – 180th position among 180 countries – as the "least sustainable" country. This was a progressive fall from 155 rank in 2014 (when the Prime Minister assumed charge) because of "low scores across a range of critical issues". The index is based on the latest scientific insights and environmental data which includes 40 performance indicators for improving environmental health, protecting ecosystem vitality, and mitigating climate change. Who continued to top the list for best environmental management? It was the same Denmark.

India no longer hears of public hearings, approvals by 'gram sabha', public debates on environment, forests, dangers of climate change and its mitigation or about the Forest Rights Act (FRA) of 2006 and Panchayats (Extension to Scheduled Areas) Act (PESA) of 1996 – rather their absence is becoming more conspicuous[23]. These are from the pre-2014 India.

License to Pollute

Following the footsteps of the previous BJP-led NDA government, the current regime also pushed *ex post facto* green clearances to highly polluting industries. In January 2016, the National Green Tribunal (NGT)[24] had struck down the earlier executive order of 2002 as "is illegal, void and inoperative". It said the executive order of 2002 "cannot override the provisions of the Environment (Protection) Act of 1986". The 1986 law governs environment clearances for which a study (a *self-certification* exercise as it is carried out by project proponents) as per the Environment Impact Assessment (EIA) notification of 1994 – a procedural law – is mandatory.

The EIA provides detailed guidelines to assess the impact of a project on air, water and soil, human displacement and diversion of forests and cutting down of trees etc. The EIA of 1994 was replaced in 2006 and a draft was floated in 2020 but not approved or notified.

The government and the affected industries challenged the NGT's 2016 order in the Supreme Court. The court (a bench of Justices Chandrachud and Ajay Rastogi)[25] upheld the main ruling and declared *ex post facto* environment clearance "unsustainable in law" in April 2020 but *struck down* two key elements of the NGT order (i) revocation of green clearances to the polluting industries and (ii) immediate closure of the polluting industries (three pharmaceutical companies operating in Gujarat's Ankaleshwar Industrial Area) on the argument that these elements violated "the principle of proportionality" – thereby, handing over the polluting industries as *fait accompli* – by imposing a penalty of Rs 10 crore on each polluting industry. Like in the Ayodhya verdict of 2019 (Chapter III) and the Lafarge judgement of 2011 (explained later), this judgement too relied on "the doctrine of proportionality" and Article 142 of the Constitution (discretionary power of the apex court) to side with the lawbreakers.

Nevertheless, this apex court judgement of April 2016 recognized that the polluting pharma units "operated without valid environmental clearances (ECs) for several years" before or after the EIA of 1994, they operated "in an unregulated and in defiance of the law" and that some of the environmental damages they caused "would be irreversible". These units did not have the legal authorisation under the laws governing air, water and hazardous wastes even before the EIA notification of 1994 – that is, they were operating without legal sanction.

This judgement relied on a similar *fait accompli* judgement, famously known as the Lafarge case of 2011 (three-member bench led by then CJI Justice SH Kapadia). French company Lafarge operated a cement plant in Bangladesh for which limestone was given from Meghalaya's Khasi hills. The project got environment clearance in 2001 on the basis of a *rapid* EIA (single season study) report which gave false information – that the proposed mining area (100 ha) was a "wasteland", "covered with rocks" with "low botanical and floral diversity" and "no likelihood of any wildlife presence" which later turned out to be "natural and virgin forest" with "thick natural vegetation cover".[26]

In the meanwhile, the government had, in March 2017, issued an amnesty to polluting industries to provide *ex post facto* clearances to projects set up in violation of the EIA of 2006 (which had replaced the 1994 one by then). The government got away by telling the Madras High Court that this was a *one-time* measure and wouldn't be repeated.[27] But, amidst the national pandemic lockdown in 2020, a draft EIA was issued to replace that of the 2006 – to make the one-time amnesty a permanent one. Following strong opposition from activists and repeated reprimands from the Delhi High Court, this draft was put on hold.

Then came another executive order in February 19, 2021, to grant *ex post facto clearance* to projects under construction or operational without prior environmental clearance under the Coastal Regulation Zone (CRZ) Notification 2011. This was stayed by the Bombay High Court in May 2021.[28] Then the government issued another executive order, a "standard operating procedure" (SoP) in July 2021[29], allowing polluting industries to get *ex post facto* clearances by paying a penalty. The Madras High Court stayed this.[30]

These stays didn't deter the government, nor did the opposition to the draft EIA of 2020 (formally, its consultation period was extended by two years till October 2022). The pandemic crisis of 2020 and 2021 saw more changes putting green laws on the chopping block.[31]

The MoEFCC issued a series of executive orders, called Office Memorandums (OMs), and changed rules and draft notifications to mirror the draft EIA of 2020 to *dilute and eliminate* green protections. One report of 2022[32] tracked and listed some of these: These OMs allowed (i) *ex post facto* clearances and removed prior appraisal or public consultations (ii) green nod allowed in "good faith" – and expansion of 30 coal mines were given clearances despite poor compliance (iii) did away with clearances for expansion of airport terminals within the existing area, highways within 100 km of border areas and ropeway projects – for all of which the MoEFCC suggested that SoPs be followed during construction and (iv) self-certification was allowed in draft building construction environment management rules – notified, taking it way from the government scrutiny.

Another 2022 report[33] listed some more: (v) New guidelines of May 2021 passed forest clearances to states for "critical infrastructure projects" in the Maoist impacted districts, those relating to defence and security projects in border areas (instead of the ministry's forest advisory committee) (vi) April 20, 2022 draft notification (which exempted green clearance for border roads) delegated environmental appraisal of non-coal mining, river valley and thermal power projects to state (as the draft EIA 2020 had sought) and (vii) April 12, 2022 draft notification extended environmental clearances granted to hydropower projects for 13 years, to nuclear projects for 15 years and mining projects for up to 50 years (under the EIA 2006, the validity of prior environmental clearance granted to a river valley project was 10 years, for mining a maximum of 30 years and seven years for other projects).

But soon, these would become redundant as the government finally passed a law to give statutory backing. Remember, all this was happening despite the NGT order of 2016 and the Supreme Court order of 2020 ruling that *ex post facto* clearances are "illegal, void and inoperative" and "unsustainable in law".

License to Kill Forests and Rights of Tribals

After India got the rotational G20 presidentship, the Prime Minister unveiled its theme in November 2022: "Vasudhaiva Kutumbakam" and "One Earth, One Family, One Future". The PMO issued a statement to explain what it meant: "Essentially, the theme affirms the value of all life – human, animal, plant, and microorganisms – and their interconnectedness on the planet Earth and in the wider universe. The theme also spotlights LiFE with its associated, environmentally sustainable and responsible choices, both at the level of individual lifestyles as well as national development, leading to globally transformative actions resulting in a cleaner, greener and bluer future."[34]

For the next one year until the summit in New Delhi September 2023, the government showcased these as its governing philosophy through hoardings, banners, ads in newspapers and TV channels, government websites etc. But all this while it was working on a law to undermine forests by removing legal protections: The Forest Conservation (Amendment) Bill 2023 to modify the Forest (Conservation) Act of 1980.

The Bill was introduced on May 29, 2023 and the same day referred to a special "joint" committee (JPC) set up on the very day – not the Parliamentary Standing Committee on Science, Technology, Environment and Forest, which is the true domain of this Bill and is chaired by Congress leader Jairam Ramesh. Ramesh protested[35] against a "hopelessly one-sided" committee, packed with the ruling party members, but the government was not impressed. Unusually fast for any parliamentary panel, this one gave its report in less than two months, on July 20, 2023[36] – rejecting voluminous objections from state governments, environment experts, lawyers, tribal groups, activists and endorsing the government's Bill without changes. The Bill was passed by the two Houses of the Parliament in one day each – without due deliberations and amidst disruptions over the Manipur violence.

The preamble of the Bill (and the Act)[37] makes for fascinating reading:

"Whereas, the importance of forests is to be realised to enable achievement of *national targets of Net Zero Emission* by 2070 and *maintain or enhance the forest carbon stocks* through ecologically balanced sustainable development; and whereas, Nationality Determined Contribution targets of the country envisage creating carbon sink of additional 2.5 to 3.0 billion tons of $CO2$ equivalent by 2030; and whereas, the country envisages an *increase in the forest and tree cover* to one-third of its land area... enhancing forest based economic, social and environmental benefits, including *improvement of livelihoods for forest dependent communities...*" *(Emphasis added)*

But its provisions undermine all three big objectives in its preamble:

(i)   Definition of forest has been changed to cover only "declared or notified" and "recorded" forests until 1980. This overturns the Supreme Court's expanded definition in the *Godavarman* judgement of 1996 (Justices JS Verma and BN Kripal)[38] – which used the dictionary meaning of forest to protect forest. Large tracts of forested areas are known not to have been declared/notified/recorded as forest in official records. This judgement directed states to identify such forest patches and declare them as forest. Some states did, some didn't.

(ii) Gives wholesale *exemptions* from green clearances by *excluding* forest land (i) along railway tracks and public roads for up to *1,000 sqm* that lead to habitation or amenities (ii) within *100 km* of international borders, LACs and LOCs for construction of "linear projects of national importance and concerning national securities" (iii) up to *10 ha* for construction of security-related infrastructure (iv) up to *5 ha* in areas inflicted with left-wing extremism (v) "forestry" purpose include zoos and wildlife safaris and (vi) private plantations, reforestations.

(iii) Appropriates all powers by insertion of Section 3C which reads: "The Central government may, from time to time, issue such directions, to any authority under the Central government, State Government or Union territory Administration, or to any organisation, entity or body recognised by the Central government, State Government or Union territory Administration, as may be necessary for the implementation of this Act.".

How will the change in definition of forests impact?

The restricted definition makes *more than one-fourth* of forests shown in the latest State of Forest Report of 2021, which was released in 2023, liable to be diverted and destroyed. Here is how. The "Statement of Clause-by-Clause consideration of the Forest (Conservation) Amendment Bill, 2023 by the Joint Committee on the Forest (Conservation) Amendment Bill, 2023"[39] shows, apprehensions were raised to the JPC about exclusion of large tracks of forests, which the JPC recorded: "Approximately, 27.62 percent of our forests (recorded forest), out of the total forest area, will fall beyond the scope of the Act". In response to this, the MoEFCC *confirms* it and says: "The India's State of the Forest Report of the Forest Survey of India mention that about 5,16,630 sq km of the forests of India are *within* Recorded Forest Areas (notified forest areas) while 1,97,159 sq km of forests *lie outside* Recorded Forest Areas" – which works out to be exactly 27.62% of forest cover kept *outside the ambit* of the new law.

And then, the MoEFCC adds two bizarre sentences to its statement to the JPC contradicting itself and confirming the fears while denying both at the same time: "Provisions of the Act are applicable on the revenue forest land, private forest land and other land *recorded* as forest in the records. Therefore, observations that 27.62% of the forest will fall beyond the scope of the Act is *not tenable." (Emphasis added)*

But the JPC is satisfied and gives a free pass – reflecting that it didn't apply its mind at all.

Similar is the case with the threat to the rights of tribals and other forest living communities under the FRA of 2006, the PESA of 1996 and land acquisition law LARR of 2013 – by way of insertion Section 3C in the new law. The JPC document records it and then records another bizarre explanation from the MoEFCC which simply denies without providing any logic, such as Section 3C doesn't abrogate states' powers, don't infringe or abrogate the rights under the FRA, PESA and LARR or facilitate corporate houses to take control of forest land. The MoEFCC also denies that the new law would facilitate private businesses to take control of forest land.

To understand what is happening in reality, *four* additional developments must be taken into count.

One, in June 2022, the Forest (Conservation) Rules of 2022[40] were notified allowing the MoEFCC to give forest clearances *without (a) settling forest rights* and (b) *prior consents* of "gram sabha" as the Forest Rights Act (FRA) of 2006 and the Panchayats (Extension to the Scheduled Areas) Act (PESA) of 1996 provide and (c) *passed* the responsibility to states, *post facto* the final clearance from its end (MoEFCC).

The FRA and PESA give absolute power to tribals and other forest-swelling communities – through their 'gram sabha' – to decide the fate of the forests they live in, and also minor minerals, and these being the central laws, mandate the MoEFCC to *first* settle these rights and take *prior approvals* of tribals settle these matters before giving clearance to divert forest or any other minerals. In short, the FC Rules of 2022 violate two central laws brought in to undo the "historic injustices" (denying their rights over their resources) to tribals and other forest dwelling communities by the previous UPA government.

What the Rules of 2022 do is to give *automatic* green clearances – recall the 'PARIVESH' the Prime Minister had launched on the World Biofuel Day in 2018 – without following any law, rule or processes governing forests.

It also means that the proverbial 'Sword of Damocles' hangs over states – all blames for violating the central laws of the FRA and PESA would be on states but not on the MoEFCC or the Central government – which brought the two laws and empowered those laws to "override" all other existing laws! And there is no reason to believe that the FC Rules of 2022 would be changed.

In the meanwhile, from September 2022, the 'PARIVESH' website stopped providing details on environment, forest, wildlife and coastal regulation zone clearances and also on the environmental impacts of projects; the MoEFCC is believed to have decided to provide such information only under the RTI Act of 2005.[41]

Two, the Rules of 2022 was actually to overcome the government's failed move to weaken the third-tier of democracy – village panchayats or 'gram sabha' – with a view to undermine the FRA and the PESA. It had circulated a draft Indian Forest (Amendment) Bill of 2019[42] to make *wholesome changes* in the Indian Forest Act of 1927 – a colonial era legislation which allowed the colonial masters to use forests as they pleased. The draft proposed to re-establish state power over forests and forest produce by undermining the FRA and the PESA. It sought to empower forest bureaucracy to manage "village forest", record forest rights, suspend forest rights and also use fire-arms with immunity from prosecution in line with the much-abused Armed Forces (Special Powers) Act of 1958 (AFSA). Fierce protests from civil rights activists ensured that the draft bill was withdrawn in November 2019.[43]

Three, on June 30 and July 1, 2022, the MoEFCC notified a proposal to "decriminalize" (dilute) three key environment laws – Environment Protection Act of 1986, Air (Prevention and Control of Pollution) Act of 1986 and Water (Prevention and Control of Pollution) Act of 1974 – to facilitate the ease of doing business. This means violations of these laws – like not ensuring safeguards for hazardous substances – would attract only monetary fine and which will be adjudicated by the Central government bureaucrats (executive power), not independent body or judicial authorities.[44] This proposal was legislated through the Jan Vishwas (Amendment of Provisions) Act of 2023[45] – passed in August 2023 along with the Forest Conservation (Amendment) Act of 2023.

How the FRA and the PESA have helped dramatically improve the life of tribal communities and other forest dwellers and bring them prosperity – by granting individual and community forest rights and rights over minor minerals – are known and present a hope for about *275 million such people*[46] who depend partly or fully on forests for livelihood. The case of Gadchiroli's Menda-Lekha village[47] – the first village to get forest rights over bamboo in 2011 – and also Gadchiroli's Parasvihir village[48] in which a family of five own 144 hectare of forests as community forest right, beginning with 2016, are inspiring. Minimum support price (MSP) for minor forest produces[49], first attempted in 2011 but later abandoned[50] due to protests from some states would also help. But there is little effort to grant these rights and support now. Until June 2022, *only 50%*[51] of individual and community forest rights claims were granted.

Four, the Forest Conservation (Amendment) Act of 2023 law was immediately followed by the government notification, in September 2023, setting up a permanent new Central Empowered Committee (CEC) – in place of the ad hoc one set up by the Supreme Court in 2002 as a watchdog for the protection of environment and forests. It had independent experts who produced several reports pointing out the Central government's mishandling of environment and forests and made valuable policy recommendations. The new permanent body has no non-government representations[52]– thus, making it an executive body which is unlikely to stand up against the government, particularly after the MoEFCC turned completely opaque after September 2022.

Bad Recordkeeping of Forests

It isn't as if India's record keeping of forests or afforestation or compensatory afforestation was very good before 2014. In fact, India's official State of Forest Reports (SFRs) present a highly inflated picture – primarily because of the very definition of forest it uses – a 10% canopy cover on a plot of one hectare, irrespective land use or ownership. This leads to bizarre results. A ground verification of the latest SFR of 2021 by a group of Indian Express reporters led by Jay Mazoomdaar[53] showed how unlikely patches are counted as 'forest' – private plantation on encroached and cleared reserve forests, tea gardens, betal nut clusters, village homesteads, roadside trees, urban housing area, VIP residences (Lutyens' bungalows), parts of educational and medical institutes (RBI building, AIIMS, IIT) etc.

Tapasya and Nitin Sethi Nitin[54] analyzed official records to point out that average net addition of 2,146 sq km of forest cover is shown every year during 1987-2021 – but details reveal that while average of 2,594 sq km of very dense and moderately dense forest turned into scrub or barren lands every two years, average of 1,907 sq km of scrub or non-forest land have also turned into very dense or moderately dense forest during every two years. The latter forces them to ask: "How does a near-barren piece of land turn into a dense or extremely dense patch of forest in merely two years?" Besides, they point out that the forest cover figures presented at international platforms don't match with the ones presented in the State of Forest reports.

India's record in compensatory afforestation (CA) is extremely disappointing. Mazoomdaar's investigations[55] showed it "neither compensates nor forests", 60% funds remain unused. Yet, the MoEFCC approved a bizarre CA plan in November 2022 while secretly giving nod to the mega Greater Nicobar Island project of Rs 72,000 crore – spread over 160 sq km area – and comprises of international container transshipment terminal, military-civil dual use airport, solar power plant and an integrated township etc.

The project is at the southern tip of India – part of the Andaman Nicobar Islands – to be taken up in a public-private-partnership (PPP) mode. It is billed as "strategic" for national security but there was no debate in the Parliament or in public. The NGT stayed its environment clearance (EC) and set up a panel to revisit the clearance in April 2023.[56] Two environmentalists Kanchi Kohli and Manju Menon of the CPR dug up documents to point out that there is a CA plan to mitigate diversion of 130.75 sq km of forests and felling of 8 lakh trees in this project. This afforestation would be carried out either in the mainland state of Haryana or Madhya Pradesh – by handing over non-forest/degraded forest land to forest departments.

How will the virgin, tropical and dense forests of Greater Nicobar Island can be replaced with afforestation thousands km away in the mainland Haryana or Madhya Pradesh – or create equivalent carbon sink or as a climate mitigation measure – is not clear yet.

In the meanwhile, India is losing forest cover fast. The Rajya Sabha was told in April 2023[57] that in *five years between April 1, 2018 March 31, 2023,* India diverted *over 88,903 hectare of forest land* – more than Mumbai and Kolkata put together – for non-forestry purpose; of this, over 19,424 ha was for roads, 18,847 ha for mining, 13,344 ha for irrigation, 9,469 ha for transmission lines and 7,630 ha for defence projects.

Inviting Land Subsidence

Here is how allowing a *free pass* to roads (maximum forest land diverted for this as mentioned earlier) has caused havoc with life in ecologically fragile Himalayan region.

A mega road-widening project (10m roads spanning about 900 km) to promote Hindu pilgrimage by building wider all-weather roads, called Char Dham Highway Development Project (CDHDP) in Uttarakhand, was started in *2016* in the upper Himalayas of the fragile Uttarakhand where catastrophic flash floods, glacier bursts and cloud bursts and landslides destroy roads and kill hundreds every few years (2013[58], 2019[59] and 2021[60] and 2023[61]). These events cause massive devastations because of heavy constructions along the rivers, a series of dams and run-of-the-river hydroelectric projects the debris of which are dumped in riverbeds.

The CDHDP was cleared without due diligence, ignoring environment laws and warnings from experts and even a Supreme Court's September 2020 directive limiting the width of the carriageway to 5.5 metres.[62] When questioned by the Supreme Court in November 2021, the government *openly lied and misled* it by citing *national security* – alluding to the Chinese incursion into the India side of LAC and build-up in the area – to stress on the need to transport missiles like BrahMos and other critical equipment. Attorney General (AG) KK Venugopal pleaded[63], "we are vulnerable" and "have to do whatever we can". None reminded him that China hadn't intruded into the India side of the LAC when the Char Dham project began in 2016, it did so four years later in 2020 – and in Ladakh – when then Chief of Defence Staff (CDS) General Bipin Rawat was mobilizing Indian Airforce and Navy to shower rose petals from the sky[64] to honour healthcare workers fighting the pandemic.

Nobody told the AG either that the Indian Air Force is eminently capable of flying BrahMos missiles and it had inducted a squadron of *Sukhoi-30 MKI fighter planes* with the capability of carrying these missiles, which it demonstrated too – at its Thanjavur airbase more than one-and-half years earlier in January 2020.[65] In August 2021, Air Chief Marshal (retd) BS Dhanoa was boasting[66], and so did the Indian Air Force, that India's adversaries would think twice before starting a war as the IAF held a major edge in the region – integrated with fighter jets capable of carrying a variety of missiles, including BrahMos. Not just the Sukhoi-30s but India had acquired Boeing's *Apache and Chinook helicopters and a modern fleet of transport aircraft* and that India already had integrated its formidable missile arsenal with the IAF fleet.

The Supreme Court (a bench of Justices Chandrachud, Surya Kant and Vikram Nath), in its December 14, 2021 order[67] *allowed* widening the all-weather roads to 10 m (from 5.5 m it had cleared earlier), driven by the security concerns which was added later, knowing fully well that these roads had skipped environmental assessments, approvals and violated various environmental laws. It also noted, among other things, that the CDHDP had been *split to 53 patches of less than 100 km each* for evading environment assessment and clearances – and that the government had admitted that *125 landslides had been triggered along the project's routes due to this project until then.*[68] What more evidence the court needed to stop it?

The fears turned out to be true.

An important pilgrim site, Joshimath, partially collapsed in January 2023, creating panic and requiring shifting of population. It has been sinking for years which was accelerated due to mega projects like the NTPC's Tapovan-Vishnugad Hydro Power Project (cleared against the environment ministry's 2014 expert panel advice) and tourist infrastructure like the Char Dham project which has sparked widespread landslides as mentioned earlier.[69] When a ISRO report showed a "rapid subsidence" of nearly 5.4 cm in the 12 days around that time and 9 cm during April-November 2022, it was immediately taken down and a general gag order was put in place.[70] The report of an expert panel set up to study the reasons has been kept secret – despite the Uttarakhand High Court's objections.[71]

Similar panic was created in various other parts of Uttarakhand – Uttarkashi, Nainital, Rudra Prayag, Bageshwar, Tehri Garhwal in 2023.[72] Following these events, a new Office Memorandum (OM) was issued in February 2023 putting riders on the July 2022 OM which had exempted environment clearances, prior study of ecology (fragility) and land management.[73]

It isn't only about "all-weather" roads or power projects alone but also indiscriminate constructions and *sand mining*[74] – all-round failure of state and Central governments, industries and courts who have short-changed green laws.[75] Himachal Pradesh, the adjoining hilly state, has also fallen victim to indiscriminate construction and "all-weather" roads being built. When it was hit by floods in 2023, more than 1,200 roads were blocked due to landslides, erosion and damage, some got washed away.[76] Sand mining is a major problem for the country – even outside the hills. A *Deutsche Welle* report said, illegal sand mining is rampant in India – changing the riverine ecosystems and lands which were once very fertile.[77]

Air Pollution: No Policy, No Control

Consider the state of air pollution reflected in various reports:

- India has 39 of world's 50 most polluted cities in the world – as per the fifth World Air Quality Report[78] – with both New Delhi and 'greater' Delhi (NCR) figuring are the top 10.

- A 2022 medical journal *Lancet's* report[79] said, 93% of India had higher air pollution level than the WHO's 2021 norms for safe air.

- A 2020 medical journal *Lancet's* report[80] said air pollution killed *1.67 million in India in 2019*, accounting for 17·8% of the country's total deaths.

- A parliamentary panel too had flagged lack of quality data on air pollution in small cities and towns.[81]

- The University of Chicago's annual study of 2023 said[82]: "Of all the countries in the world, India faces the greatest health burden from air pollution due to the large number of people its high particulate pollution concentrations affect." The level of PM2.5 has increased to more than 10 times the WHO norms by 2021; average Indian would lose 5.3 years and those in norther plain (the most polluted in India) 8 years of life expectancy – if the WHO norms are not met. Delhi being "the most polluted megacity in the world" with annual average PM2.5 level *more than 25 times* the WHO norm, its residents' loss would be far greater – *11.9 years*. Of all air pollutants, PM2.5 (particle size of 2.5 microns or smaller) are the focus of air pollution studies as these are the ones that enter lungs and other parts of body easily and deeply, posing serious threat to life.

Yet, there is no national policy to control air pollution – or for that matter, water and soil pollution. As mentioned earlier, none is expected because it's primary focus is to bypass green laws, fast administrative and legal hurdles and in case of polluting industries, *post facto* green clearances through penalty – as reflected in the Jan Vishwas (Amendment) Act and the Forest Conservation (Amendment) Act of 2023.

Amidst a heated debate on air pollution in Delhi-NCR cities in 2020, aggravated by farmers of Punjab, Haryana and western Uttar Pradesh burning stubble after the winter harvesting, the government first kept quiet and then sprang a surprise when questioned by the Supreme Court. True to its style, it brought an ordinance to set up a permanent commission over and above all pollution control boards in the region without debate, attempt to understand the past failures or consulting experts.

The ordinance was reissued in 2021 and then passed by the Parliament in August 2021 – passed without debate and amidst disruptions by the Opposition parties over the Pegasus surveillance scandal. Called The Commission for Air Quality Management in National Capital Region (CAQM) and Adjoining Areas Act of 2021[83], it provides for a 30-member commission. It is highly centralized, burdened with bureaucrats and seeks to keep the judiciary out – especially the Supreme Court appointed monitoring committee working for over two decades and which had played a pioneering role in pollution control. Sections 22 and 23 says no civil court would have jurisdiction on the commission's orders, except the NGT, and no suit or legal can be initiated against it.

This law's failure was exposed a few months later, in the winters of 2021. As air pollution worsened, the Supreme Court stepped in to monitor the commission's work, directed the government to set up a Task Force to check polluting activities and then asked the commission to seek opinion of general public and experts regarding permanent solution to air pollution.[84] The government had not paid attention to the essentials: How will the commission be effective when pollution control boards and the Supreme Court-appointed Environment Pollution (Prevention and Control) Authority (EPCA) had failed for years?

In 2023, the Supreme Court again lambasted[85] *state governments* (NCT of Delhi and neighbouring states of Punjab, Haryana, Uttar Pradesh and Rajasthan) and pollution control authorities as air pollution spiked in Delhi-NCR despite no "winter inversion" (cold winter air sinking and trapping pollutants close to earth's surface), it being unusually warmer winter in October and stubble burning had halved (45%) in Punjab. Not just India but worldwide, 2023 has been warmer due to climate change and El Nino[86] and European Union scientists claimed that 2023 is likely to be *warmest in 125,000 years*[87]. The court said the efforts to check air pollution wasn't visible on the ground. But the court *omitted* the CAQM which was set up by the government in response to its concerns in 2021 or the MoEFCC – the central environment ministry. It also had nothing to say about the ruling BJP which generously contributes to the winter air pollutions in Delhi-NCR every Diwali by bursting firecrackers in *defiance* of the Supreme Court's *partial ban* (allowing low-emission firecrackers between 8-10 pm[88]) in the name of protecting and promoting Hindu culture. Days later, when the AQI level reached "very severe" level during Diwali and BJP ministers and Members of Parliament came for severe criticism (and police complaint) from other political parties for *leading* the firecracker bursting, the BJP and its senior leaders sprang to call the court's partial ban "unscientific, illogical, dictatorial" – and justified their action in the name of freedom and democracy, protecting the *Sanatan Dharma* traditions and celebrating Lord Ram's victory over Ravan in the mythological tale of Ramayana – putting the entire blame on the AAP governments of NCT and Punjab for failing to check air pollution.[89]

The air pollution control measures in Delhi-NCR – like higher standards for vehicular emissions (Bharat VI), automatic deregistration of old vehicles (10 years for diesel and 15 years for petrol run), free/subsidized LPG cylinders to cut down the use of firewood and cow dung etc. – are not working is evident from a recent study funded by the Ministry of Earth Sciences and helmed by Gulfan Beig, founding director of India's nodal agency SAFAR-India and current chair professor in the Bangalore's National Institute of Advanced Studies (NIAS), titled "Decadal growth in emission load of major air pollutants in Delhi".[90]

It traced the decadal changes (2010–2020) in emission patterns in Delhi-NCR and found all categories of air pollutants *growing*:

- Particulate matter PM2.5 (which kills) grew by 31% and PM10 by 3%. Delhi's PM2.5 level is 10 times the WHO's permissible limits.
- Killer gas Carbon monoxide (CO) grew by 13.6%.
- Black carbon (BC), organic carbon (OC) and nitrogen oxides (NO and NO2) grew by 34% to 91%.
- Contribution of the main sources of pollution, transport sector, grew the most, followed by the industrial and residential sectors.

The law also imposes a penalty of Rs 1 crore and/or five years of imprisonment for causing air pollution but exempts farmers for stubble burning (Section 14) – which was one of the grievances flagged during the farmers' protest against the new farm laws in 2021. Yet, Section 15 gives power to the commission to "impose and collect environmental compensation from farmers causing air pollution by stubble burning" the rate and manner to be specified later, thus keeping the sword on farmers' hanging[91] – reflecting illogical law making.

It needs to be pointed out that stubble burning is a *recent development* (post mechanization of harvesting) and is *forced on farmers* because of central and state government policies like: (a) asking primarily wheat consuming Punjab and Haryana to grow paddy for food security but (b) mandating a month delay in sowing of paddy (by Punjab and Haryana governments since 2009), a water guzzler, to prevent depletion of groundwater – which leads to late harvesting and leaves less than a month to prepare the fields for wheat and other winter crops and (c) government incentives to mechanized harvesting that leaves huge amounts of stubble – unlike manual harvesting – forcing farmers to burn stubble.[92]

Meanwhile, the state of pollution control across the country continues to be extremely poor. The secret was revealed in April 2023 when Delhi-based think tank CPR[93] (one of the NGOs targeted by the government for opposing the Adani's coal mining in the Hasdeo Arand's virgin and rich forests[94], see Chapter II) published its findings about *nine* state pollution control boards (SPCBs) and one pollution control committee (Delhi). These are some of the most polluted states, like Punjab, Haryana, Uttarakhand, Uttar Pradesh, Bihar, Jharkhand, Chhattisgarh, West Bengal and Delhi. It collected information through the RTI applications. It found:

- These are understaffed, lack technical expertise (most don't two expert members as the law requires) and finance to perform the assigned tasks.

- Conflict of interest as the boards are "largely" comprised of government servants and industry representatives – with "limited" representation to independent experts and civil society.

- "Little substantive discussion" on air pollution control or planning in board meetings.

- Many have no full-time chairpersons and member secretaries, but bureaucrats double up for this.

Water Woes

The state of water and soil are also grim but hasn't attracted as much attention in recent years.

That India's groundwater is fast depleting to alarming levels is known for long. A new report from the by United Nations University – Institute for Environment and Human Security (UNU-EHS)[95] – warned that India is close to reaching a tipping point. India is the world's largest user of groundwater, exceeding the use of the US and China together. It said 78% of wells in Punjab are overexploited and the north-western region as a whole is expected to hit critically low groundwater availability by 2025.

A 2018 NITI Aayog report ("Composite Water Management Index"[96]) pointed out that *600 million* face "high to extreme water stress" with "nearly 70% of water being contaminated", "about three-fourth of the households" do not have drinking water at their premise and India was placed at 120th amongst 122 countries in the water quality index. It warned that 21 major cities, including Delhi, Bangalore, and Hyderabad were heading for zero groundwater levels, affecting access for 100 million people. Two major river systems of north, the Ganges and Yamuna, are highly polluted with industrial affluents and sewage. Despite major rive cleaning programmes (the Ganges cleaning began in 1986 and the Yamuna cleaning in 1993), the progress has been very tardy. A few weeks into the pandemic lockdown of 2020 saw a dramatically clean sparkling blue waters of both the rivers.[97] What did the trick? It was the shutdown of industries which pollute these rivers.

Now, both are back to being polluted and this can't be checked because the decadal study of Delhi-NCR air pollution mentioned earlier made a damning revelation: "There is no comprehensive database for all industries with their technological details." Apart from contamination, indiscriminate sand mining is also causing extensive damages to rivers, as pointed out earlier. After having released the 2018 water index report (for 2015-16 and 2016-17), the NITI Aayog released the second report for 2017-18 but not the third one, for 2018-19 and 20219-20, marked it for "internal use" – which is reported to have said water scarcity was a "national problem"[98] – obviously to hide the ground realities.

The Green Revolution of late 1960s and 1970s made India food sufficient and reduced hunger but it also contaminated water and soil and depleted groundwater – particularly in Punjab and Haryana (together producing 50% of rice and 85% of wheat stocks) due to heavy use of chemical fertilizers and pesticides which high-yield hybrid seeds brought in their wake. As explained earlier, the stubble burning is an outcome of the delayed sowing of paddy – advanced by a month to prevent water depletion and make it entirely dependent on monsoon rain. The government's Jal Jeevan Mission (JJM) has increased supply of piped water to households, reaching 65.3% households in rural areas by July 2023.[99]

Extreme Weather and India's Poor response to Climate Change

The other big challenge is extreme weather events (frequent cyclones, floods, abnormal rainfall and above normal temperature) – causing enormous loss to humans, animals and the economy.

The RBI's May 2023 report, "Report on currency and finance: Towards a greener cleaner India"[100] provided an account of 2022 and early months of 2023. It said: "...the country experienced extreme weather events on 314 of 365 days of 2022, which claimed 3,026 lives, affected 1.96 million hectares of crop area and 4,23,249 houses, and killed over 69,899 animals" and: "India has faced its hottest February in 2023 since record-keeping began in 1901. In March, large parts of the country experienced hailstorms and torrents of unseasonal rain, leading to apprehensions of extensive damage to standing crops." It said up to 4.5% of India's GDP could be at risk by 2030 "owing to lost labour hours from extreme heat and humidity conditions".

Just as the case with air pollution, water pollution, extreme weather events caused by global warming and climate change has also not received attention from India. Its response is piecemeal and is limited to superficial declaration of targets – for reducing carbon emissions, creating carbon sinks, producing renewable energy etc. at international platforms. India's Nationally Determined Contribution (NDC) commitments "India's Long-Term Low-Carbon Development Strategy"[101] submitted to the UNFCC in November 2022, reflects this. The topmost government think tank, NITI Aayog's reports mapping progress in the Sustainable Development Goals (SDGs) doesn't even include mapping climate change mitigations. For, its 2018 baseline SDG report excluded the climate mitigation specific goal, "Goal Number 13: Take urgent action to combat climate change and its impacts" by saying[102]: "Progress on SDG 12, 13 and 14 could not be measured because relevant state level data could not be consolidated or found." So, even if the Finance Ministry's estimate of "cumulative" *investment needs* "for adapting to climate change", pegged this at Rs 85.6 lakh crore (at 2011-12 prices) by the year 2030[103], materializes, how will it be mapped is not clear.

Coal: Crony Capitalism and Energy

Notwithstanding lofty claims of "One Earth, One Family, One Future", "LiFE" and "Zero Emission", the government vigorously promotes coal energy – and cracks down on those who protest or dissent.

The attack on the CPR, LIFE and Environics Trust – IT raids, cancellation of FCRA license and tax exemption status etc. mentioned in Chapter II – for opposing the Adani group's coal mining in Chhattisgarh (which started digging 1,882 acre of virgin forest land in 2013) came in 2022. But the attack had begun with the Greenpeace in 2014.

In September 2014 – just four months after the new government came to power – Ben Hargreaves, a UK national and Greenpeace campaigner, was deported despite having a valid visa.[104] Greenpeace's India campaigner Priya

Pillai was offloaded from a London flight in January 2015. She had been named in a government circular as absconding criminal, despite having a valid visa and no criminal record – while more than a score of business tycoons facing banking fraud and money laundering charges fled and acquired foreign citizenship without trouble (Chapter VIII). Pillai was on her way to speak before the British Parliament against the Mahan coal mine in Madhya Pradesh – which was at the centre of controversy then. Pillai had been campaigning against the mine which was to affect thousands of villagers in and around the forest.[105]

In November 2015, the Greenpeace's FCRA license was cancelled, the ED seized its accounts and it was asked to close shop in India.[106] By February 2019 funds crunch had hit it hard and it was on the verge of complete shutdown.[107] It still runs from India but only on paper with no voice and presence. As part of this attack, the MHA even stopped funding by the US-based Hewlett Foundation for climate awareness campaigns in 2022, saying it wasn't permissible under the FCRA.[108]

This goes hand-in-hand with a new "Coalgate scam". In 2014, the Supreme Court had cancelled allocation of 214 coal mines (of 2018) between 1993 and 2010 declaring allocations made both under (a) the Screening Committee route and (b) the Government dispensation route as "arbitrary and illegal". This had happened despite the Congress-led UPA government's policy (2005) of competitive bidding. Following this, the auction route was used but in 2020, the government was back to the same old arbitrary and discretionary allocations of coal blocks.

The "screening committee" was replaced with "empowered committee of secretaries" which was given the discretionary/arbitrary power though an Office Memorandum (executive order) of May 28, 2020: "In case of single bid after successive rounds of auction for a coal mine, appropriate decision regarding allocation of mine." An investigating report of Shreegireesh Jalihal[109] revealed, this was used to allot "at least 12 cases of coal blocks to private companies after failing to attract competition". These firms include one belonging to the Adani group, Vedanta-owned firms, JSW Steel, Birla Corporation and other lesser-known companies. That there aren't many bidders showing interest reflect either cartelization or lack of interest. Jalihal's report pointed out that coal blocks allocated till 2017 were enough to produce 2,200 million ton of coal by 2030 – nearly double of the requirement of 1,200 million ton to meet the net demand for electricity by 2030!

Another investigating report of 2018 by Nileena MS[110] had alleged that separate sets of laws and rules were applied to the Adani group's coal and power projects in violation of the Supreme Court's 2014 ruling, thereby providing "benefits worth thousands of crores of rupees" to the group. There are many investigating reports[111] which point to undue advantages the Adani group received to produce the highly polluting coal and generate coal-based electricity.

India is the second largest coal consumer after China.[112] The government plans to export coal by 2025-26[113] – having claimed, in May 2023, that his nine years had seen coal production going up by 47% to a level which is "the highest in the history of the country."[114] After 2014, the government has rapidly opened coal mining, allowing 87 new coal mines by FY23[115] and proposes to open 25 more new coal mines in FY24[116]. It allowed 100% FDI for coal mining and sale of coal under the "automatic route" in 2019.[117] On June 7, 2023, the CCEA cleared an outlay of Rs 2,980 crore for further coal exploration[118] involving private sector[119].

In September 2023, Chief Economic Advisor (CEA) Anantha Nageswaran justified the contradiction between the push for polluting coal and other fossil fuel and climate mitigation: "In the short run, we need fossil fuels and more importantly we need our own resources to invest in green transition."[120] A few months later, a *review*[121] by the Power Ministry showed rising power demand was forcing states to commission new coal-based power projects and expand the capacity of the existing ones – reversing virtually signaling an end of the transition to clean energy.

The big picture, however, shows India's energy mix going in the right direction.

The Central Electricity Authority (CEA) reports[122] show a progressive fall in dependence on fossil fuel, including coal as renewable energy (RES, including hydropower) surges – since FY14. What, however, has to be kept in mind that the RES, particularly those on wind and solar, actual production of electricity is far less than the installed capacity because of heavy dependence on weather. At the end of FY23, the energy mix was:

- Coal – 49.3% (down from 51.9%)
- Fossil fuel (coal, lignite, gas, diesel) – 57% (down from 68.1% in 2019-20)
- Renewable, including hydropower – 41.4% (up from 38.1% in 2019-20)
- Nuclear power – 1.6% (down from 2.2% in 2019-20)

The trend certainly is positive, except actual power generation mix is not clear.

Graph: Sources of India's electricity

Installed capacity of electricity (as % of total) during 2015-2023

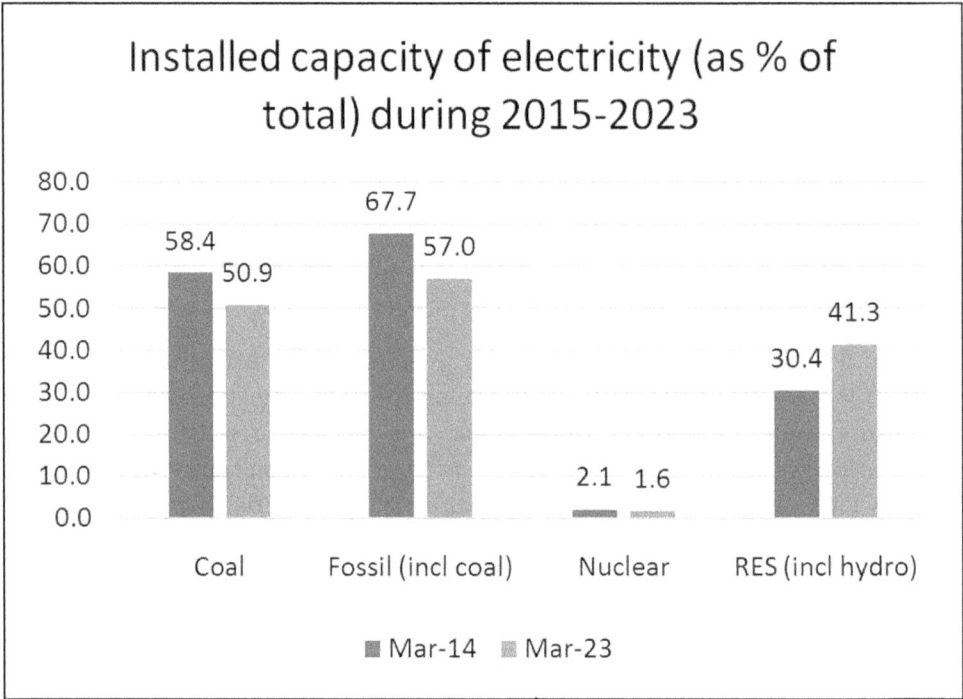

Source: Central Electricity Authority

Carbon Billionaires

At the Sharm el-Sheikh's COP27 conclave in November 2022, the Oxfam International's report "Carbon Billionaires"[123] came with some stunning disclosures about the contribution of wealthy individuals and corporations to pollution – pointing to the conflict of interest in controlling it.

It said new studies of *125 of the world's richest billionaires* shows that on average they are emitting *3 million ton a year – more than a million times the average* for someone in the bottom 90% of humanity – and unlike ordinary people, 50% to 70% of their emissions resulted from their *investments*. Their investments in polluting industries such as *fossil fuels and cement are double the average* for the Standard & Poor 500 group of companies.

It didn't mention India's richest, but the World Inequality Report of 2022[124] did so and showed a similar skewed carbon emission pattern: the top 1% contributed the maximum at 32.4 tCO2/per capita ('t' stands for metric ton), against the national average of 2.2 tCO2/per capita, in 2019. The top 10%, middle 40% and bottom 50% contribute 8.8, 2 and 1 tCO2/per capita, respectively.

How do countries at the forefront of climate mitigation negotiations fare in their carbon emission or consumption? The World Bank's database shows significant change: Developed countries are reducing their carbon footprints while developing and underdeveloped ones like India is increasing theirs – India by a smaller but China by a greater margin. This is on the expected line since development process needs higher energy consumption and therefore, the higher carbon emission numbers. This would explain why while the developed countries are committing to net-zero carbon emission by 2050, India and China are have set their targets to 2070 and 2060, respectively.[125]

NITI Aayog's Attack on Environment

The NITI Aayog not only doesn't map climate change mitigations in its SDG reports, in an apparent bid to support the government's cause of facilitating industries at the cost of environment and forests, it commissioned a study in January 2020[126] to *review the impacts* of five Supreme Court and NGT judgements relating to violation of environment pollution laws which it felt amounted to "judicial activism". These included three apex court judgements stopping iron ore mining in Goa, shutting down Sterlite's Thoothukudi copper plant in Tamil Nadu and halting consultation of Mopa Airport in Goa and two NGT decisions banning sand mining and halting construction activities in Delhi-NCR during mid-2018 to mid-2021.

The study came in a few months later, in June 2022[127] with the pre-set and predictable conclusions.

It said: "…at least about 75,000 persons were adversely impacted, and around 16,000 workers lost their jobs. The government did not receive revenues of around Rs 8,000 crores, which, if were received and invested as capital expenditure, could have resulted in economic impact of more than Rs 20,000 crore. The industry lost close to Rs 15,000 crore in revenues, and workers lost around Rs 500 crore of income…" While its disclaimer said the study was "purely an academic exercise and is nowhere intended to interfere with the decision-making process of the judiciary", a two-page brief it circulated lists "Will serve as useful training inputs for the training of judicial officers" as one of the "expected outcome".[128]

The objective was to discourage judiciary from considering the environmental impacts of project – as the study does. Annanya Mahajan[129] of the CPR pined out several flaws in the study, including a very partial "cost-benefit assessment" it set out to do by listing all benefits on the basis of incomplete studies and estimates but ignored all costs to environmental, health and finances of local communities; in three out of five cases, it excluded local communities and civil society, making it industry-centric. All these cases had emerged from public protests and posed serious danger to environment.

Whether that had any impact or not, the Supreme Court modified its 2022 order mandating a minimum 1-km eco-sensitive zone around national parks or wildlife sanctuaries in April 2023[130] – agreeing to the government's plea that it would prevent the government from building roads and other important infrastructure in those areas.

Premature Nod to GM food

While the government talks of sustainability, it has no respect for science and scientific rigour ensure that. The clearance to first genetically modified (GM) food – GM Mustard – in November 2022 amply reflected this lack of scientific temper – apart from opaqueness, lack of cost-and-benefit analysis and biosafety (human and environment) and institutional integrity in oversight mechanism.

Introduction of GM crop has a dubious history in India. The first GM crop, Bt Cotton, was clandestinely introduced in 1998[131], before being formally approved in 2002 – by the Vajpayee-led NDA government. The attempt to introduce the first GM food, Bt Brinjal, sparked a nation-wide protest, following which an indefinite moratorium was put on it in 2010. Then, in October 2022, suddenly the government allowed "environmental release" of GM Mustard – one step away from "commercial release". The government acted in *extraordinary hurry* – approving the environmental release on the very day, October 18, 2022, that the GEAC recommended it (disclosed in its affidavit of November 9, 2022[132]).

The development led to revival of the petitions challenging GM crop pending before the Supreme Court for 20 years – it was filed in *2004* after the Bt Cotton was approved for commercial use. The matter still remains pending before the court.

Everything that could go wrong went wrong in this case:

(a) The GM Mustard (technically called DMH-11), which was approved, is actually *herbicide-tolerant* (HT) crop – which is banned in India and farmers are not even allowed to use herbicides in their fields.

(b) The government's affidavit of November 9, 2022[133] said it was driven by three *commitments*: (i) increase in farm productivity (edible oil and legume) to make India self-sufficient (ii) increase in farmers' income and (iii) cut in import bill ("55-60% of edible in India is imported"). The DMH-11 *can't fulfil* any of these objectives – because there is *no evidence* to show.

It must be remembered that to fulfil the three objectives, the DMH-11 must have higher yield than the traditional and hybrid mustard varieties – which is not the case. Scientist Yaspal Singh Sodhi of the Delhi University's Centre for Genetic Manipulation of Crop Plants (CGMCP)[134] presented a comparative study in 2015 to show that *four non-GM hybrids* of mustard had higher yields and a fifth had nearly same yield as that of DMH-11.[135] His analysis was based on the 2013-14 yields of 14 mustard hybrids and non-hybrids – but not that of the DMH-11. The DMH-11 yield was taken from the disclosures made by the government in its 2016 affidavit to the apex court.[136] Incidentally, CGMP happens to be the current promoter of the DMH-11 – which carries the same three foreign genes *barnase, barstar and bar* with which M/s *Proagro* Seed Company of Gurgaon had first approached the Genetic Engineering Appraisal Committee (GEAC) – a statutory body for such approvals – way back in 2002.[137] At the time, the GEAC had *deferred* a decision because of incomplete studies and tests and unresolved concerns about health and environment issues involved.

Besides, around the time, on November 20, 2022, the government's nodal institute to carry out yield assessment – Indian Council of Agriculture Research (ICAR)'s Directorate of Rapeseed and Mustard Research (DRMR) at Rajasthan's Bharatpur – had denied claims of superior yield of DMH-11. Its director PK Rai had said that DMH-11 had "not been tested according to ICAR protocol" and that it had "just entered our system. Once trial and studies are over, one will not get a clear picture on actual yield of DMH-11".[138]

Other problems with the DMH-11's clearance:

(c) Biosafety data on DMH-11 is not available in public domain for scrutiny. The government's affidavit said, the dossier on "food and environmental safety (AFES)" was uploaded on the official website for *one month only*, between September 5, 2016 to October 5, 2016, and its scrutiny was allowed *in person* "at the premises of the MoEF&CC" *only*.

(d) *Conflicts of interests* in the testing, clearances and regulatory mechanism (GEAC) – which a parliamentary panel report of 2012 and the Supreme Court-appointed technical expert committee (TEC) report of 2013[139] had flagged – vis-à-vis the Bt Brinjal controversy.

Since, the DMH-11's yield is *lower* than traditional and widely used hybrids in India, it can't make India self-sufficient or increase in farmers' income (no known cost advantage is known) or cut in import bill. In fact, it will increase foreign exchange burden by way of the royalty outgo for using the technology and buying the herbicide. Ashwani Mahajan of the RSS affiliate Swadeshi Jagaran Manch (SJM) wrote to Minister in charge of MoEFCC Bhupender Yadav on October 28, 2022 pointing out that the DMH-11 had been developed by Germany company Bayer's subsidiary Proagro Seed Company (which had applied for approval in 2002) and that the *bar-barstar-barnase gene* is "a patented technology of Bayer Crop Science".[140]

The benefits from the Bt Cotton, is highly questionable. A large body of literature exists – apart from a parliamentary panel's report and the TEC report mentioned earlier – to show that the gains are far less than claimed; the costs are too high, leading to farmers' indebtedness and suicide; needs to buy fresh seeds every year at exorbitant prices; need for heavy pesticides toxic to environment and humans due to growing resistance; the farmers' suicide belt coinciding with the Bt Cotton growing areas; ad-hoc regulatory system in India; self-defeating bio-safety norms and worthless scientific data and complete absence of *post facto* scientific assessment.[141]

New Threats

A complete absence of scientific temperament and studies mean nobody is paying any attention to the bigger threats which are now known or are emerging.

Palm oil mission: In August 2021, *corporate monk* Ramdev aka Ramkrishna Yadav declared his foray into palm oil plantation in Assam, Tripura and other northeastern states. Seven days later, the government announced a Rs 11,040 crore National Mission on Edible Oils-Oil Palm (NMEO-OP)[142] to boost domestic production of palm oil in northeastern states and Andaman and Nicobar Islands.

This is when oil palm is known water guzzler, invasive and damaging to biodiversity and *despite red flags*[143] from top forestry institutes, Indian Council of Forestry Research & Education (ICFRE), Indian Council of Agricultural Research (ICAR) and Indian Institute of Oil Palm Research (IIOPR) to cultivate oil palm in rich biodiversity areas without "comprehensive" and "detailed" studies. Besides, *Mizoram experiment*[144] with oil palm has long shown how damaging it is for environment and farmers.

Methane Goes Unchecked: A 2021 UNEP paper said methane accounted for *30% of global warming* since pre-industrial times and it is *proliferating faster* since 1980s.[145] It is more dangerous than carbon emissions too. A Stanford University paper from November 2021 said[146]: "While carbon dioxide is more abundant and longer-lived, methane – the main component of natural gas – is far more effective at trapping heat while it lasts. Over the first two decades after its release, methane is over 80 times more potent than carbon dioxide in terms of warming the climate system.

The main sources of methane are: Agriculture (41%), energy (35%), sanitation and waste sectors (20%). Rice cultivation (flooded paddy fields prevent oxygen from penetrating the soil, creating ideal conditions for methane-emitting bacteria), agriculture waste burning, manure management and gas from cows and sheep; oil and gas extraction, pumping, transport and coal mining and from landfills and wastewater treatment are the activities which release methane.

The World Bank database shows[147], the US, India and China have seen a rise in methane emission while that of the UK and EU have fallen. But India is so wary of touching agriculture and livestock that it didn't sign the COP26

(Glasgow) pledge to cut methane (as also stop deforestation) by 2030.[148] Its Long-Term Low Emission Development Strategy report for COP27, submitted on November 14, 2022, is silent on curbing methane and agriculture is not in the list of strategic sectors (such as electricity, transport, urban development, industry and finance) to achieve net-zero by 2070.[149]

Electric Vehicles (EVs): India has joined the global race in promoting electric vehicles (EVs) – to replace fossil fuel-run vehicles. But its approach is ad hoc and without public consultations or debate. It has had a long and *utterly confusing* start.[150] India's EV share is just 2% in total light vehicles – two and three wheelers comprising 90% of it.[151] Its rapid transition presents two big concerns. One is the threat to *millions of auto sector jobs*[152] – at a time when the job crisis is chronic and severe. No attention has been paid to manage the transition with minimum job loss or training in new technology. The other is the China's *stranglehold*[153] on EV supply chain – starting with dominance in production of lithium and lithium-ion batteries to run EVs. India's trade and diplomatic relations have soured since 2020. More EVs would mean higher foreign exchange outgo, higher dependence on China and higher trade deficit with China – which accounted for 32% of India's total trade deficit in FY23, up from 29% in FY19[154] despite the past three years to attempt to discourage trade with China. The situation in semiconductor and mobile phones is no different.[155]

Hydrogen Fuel: India is yet to even consider the inherent dangers that hydrogen poses, let alone wake up, even as it goes on promoting hydrogen energy. Hydrogen is highly inflammable. Few seem to realise that the world's first aeroplanes (Zeppelin) were flown with hydrogen gas but then the fuel was abandoned after the Hindenburg disaster of 1937.[156] Sure, science and technology has made rapid progress but the government hasn't assured the public that India has the capacity to handle it safely and what safety measures would be put in place.

As mentioned in Chapter VII, the government launched a "National Green Hydrogen Mission"[157] on March 21, 2022 with an allocation of Rs 20,000 crore *without* a policy framework in place "to support establishment of Green Hydrogen ecosystem"[158]. India's most powerful business groups, the Adani group[159] and the Ambani group[160] have unveiled their plans to make India a hydrogen hub. But nothing more is known about the plans.

With such policies, nobody should be surprised if climate disaster strikes India harder than it has been foreseen until now – notwithstanding the UN's topmost environment award to the Prime Minister.

***

References

1   Ministry of environment and forests undergoes a nomenclature change; government serious to tackle climate change, May 28, 2014; https://economictimes. indiatimes.com/news/economy/policy/ministry-of-environment-and-forests-undergoes-a-nomenclature-change-government-serious-to-tackle-climate-change/ articleshow/35651292.cms?from=mdr

2   Unveiling of The Logo, Theme and Website of India's G20 Presidency, PMO, Nov 8, 2022; https://pib.gov.in/PressReleasePage.aspx?PRID=1874524

3   Living in harmony with nature will lead to better future: Modi, PTI, Jun 5, 2019; https://www.thehindu.com/news/national/living-in-harmony-with-nature-will-lead-to-better-future-modi/article27477486.ece

4   LiFE, MoEFCC, GOI, https://missionlife-moefcc.nic.in/

5   Supreme Court questions legality of National Board for Wildlife under Narendra Modi, Aug 26, 2014; https://www.downtoearth.org.in/news/supreme-court-questions-legality-of-national-board-for-wildlife-under-narendra-modi-45957

6   Apex court lifts its order restraining Wildlife Board, Nov 22, 2014; https:// indianexpress.com/article/india/india-others/apex-court-lifts-its-order-restraining-wildlife-board/

7   In 50 days, Modi govt gives environment clearance to 5 projects, Jul 18, 2014; https://www.business-standard.com/article/economy-policy/in-50-days-modi-govt-gives-environment-clearance-to-5-projects-114071800109_1.html

8   PMO asks green ministry to relax norms, speed up clearances for road projects, Aug 6, 2014; https://indianexpress.com/article/economy/pmo-asks-green-ministry-to-relax-norms-speed-up-clearances-for-road-projects/

9   TSR Subramanian panel proposes new law, institutions to fast track green clearances, Nov 20, 2014; https://www.downtoearth.org.in/news/t-s-r-subramanian-panel-proposes-new-law-institutions-to-fast-track-green-clearances-47482

10   Goldenberg Suzanne, Is Narendra Modi a climate sceptic? Sept 9, 2014; https:// www.theguardian.com/environment/2014/sep/09/narendra-modi-india-prime-minister-climate-change-sceptic

11   Narain Sunita, Green clearance test for NDA, Sept 15, 2014; https://www. downtoearth.org.in/blog/green-clearance-test-for-nda-45961

12   Narendra Modi receives UNEP Champion of the Earth award: A look at past laureates and their contributions, Oct 3, 2018; https://www.firstpost.com/india/ narendra-modi-receives-unep-champion-of-the-earth-award-a-look-at-past-laureates-and-their-contributions-5308371.html

13   Ban on identified Single Use Plastic Items from 1st July 2022, MoEFCC, Jun 28, 2022; https://pib.gov.in/PressReleasePage.aspx?PRID=1837518

14   Krishnan Murali, Why is India's single-use plastic ban failing? Nov 2, 2022; https:// www.dw.com/en/why-is-indias-single-use-plastic-ban-failing/a-63625217

15   "PARIVESH" – an environmental single window hub for Environment, Forest, Wildlife and CRZ clearances launched, MoEFCC, Aug 10, 2018; https://pib.gov.in/Pressreleaseshare.aspx?PRID=1542607

16   Inviting comments/suggestions on proposed amendments in Forest (Conservation) Act, 1980, Ministry of Environment, Forest and Climate Change, Oct 2, 2021; http://environmentclearance.nic.in/writereaddata/OMs-2004-2021/263_OM_02_10_2021.pdf

17   PM invokes Gandhi, Centre Sought Dilution of Forest Act on Oct 2, Oct 11, 2021; https://www.newsclick.in/PM-Invoked-Gandhi-Centre-Sought-Dilution-Forest-Act-Oct-2

18   Dutta Anisha, PM action plan: Single environment Act, birth certificate for citizenship, jobs clause in FTAs, Oct 19, 2021; https://indianexpress.com/article/india/pm-action-plan-environment-act-birth-certificate-citizenship-jobs-clause-ftas-7578973/

19   COP26 Summit: Key takeaways from PM Narendra Modi's historic speech, Zee News, Nov 2, 2021; https://zeenews.india.com/india/cop26-summit-key-takeaways-from-pm-narendra-modi-s-historic-speech-2407283.html

20   COP26: Did India betray vulnerable nations? Nov 16, 2021; https://www.bbc.com/news/world-asia-india-59286790

21   India's role in damaging climate negligible, says PM Modi in Denmark, May 4, 2022; https://www.business-standard.com/article/current-affairs/india-s-role-in-damaging-climate-negligible-says-pm-modi-in-denmark-122050301143_1.html

22   Wolf MJ, Emerson JW, Esty DC, de Sherbinin A, Wendling ZA et al, 2022 Environmental Performance Index, New Haven, CT: Yale Center for Environmental Law & Policy, Jun 2022; https://epi.yale.edu/downloads/epi2022report06062022.pdf

23   Goyal Prateek, 'Authorities indifferent': 90 days on, Adivasis from 70 villages protest against mining in Maharashtra's Surjagarh, Jun 15, 2023; https://www.newslaundry.com/2023/06/15/authorities-indifferent-90-days-on-adivasis-from-70-villages-protest-against-mining-in-maharashtras-surjagarh

24   Rohit Prajapati et al vs Union of India and others, NGT, Pune, Jan 8, 2016; http://www.indiaenvironmentportal.org.in/files/environment%20clearance%20United%20Phosphorous%20NGT%20order.pdf

25   Alembic Pharmaceuticals vs Rohit Prajapati and others, Supreme Court, Apr 1, 2020; https://main.sci.gov.in/supremecourt/2016/2562/2562_2016_0_1501_21582_Judgement_01-Apr-2020.pdf

26   Mohanty P, Rebooting Economy III: All that's wrong with India's environmental governance, Jul 6, 2020; https://www.businesstoday.in/opinion/columns/story/indian-economy-all-thats-wrong-with-indias-environmental-laws-green-clearances-climate-change-263217-2020-07-06

27   Puducherry Environment Protection Association vs Union of India, Madras High Court, Oct 13, 2017; https://www.livelaw.in/pdf_upload/pdf_upload-379865.pdf

28   The Government Is Effectively Helping Industries Bypass Environmental Safeguards, Jul 28, 2021; https://science.thewire.in/environment/the-government-is-effectively-helping-industries-bypass-environmental-safeguards/

29   Office Memorandum, Standard Operating Procedure (SoP) for identification and handling of violation cases under EIA Notification 2006 in compliance to order of Hon'ble National Green Tribunal in OA NO 34/2020 WZ – Regarding, Ministry of Environment, Forest and Climate Change, Jul7, 2021; http://environmentclearance.nic.in/DownloadPfdFile.aspx?FileName=5TkBfJOQLTysIW9ZJOLhCqf6iEW+g5k8COX/CPTzCuu5yxrs9Czm5hi13SOI4lt1i/rBdqyL/z03/sUgy3MkLAMoW 1fLIqrqhBHpRA6sYhNqrgQD- khj2USwwhVT35BL UxP06N1hEsp+JrSmg/64jSA==&FilePath=93ZZBm8LWEXfg+HAlQix2fE2t8z/pgnoBh- DlYdZCxzUlDadBGu7t8v4JoQvNU6UBE3S54TMuP1vF2oULmtt0ToST-mxDIXAn3/gYIdIZX+uf5Zk2mGYb/o+5J1tPJfIM097vT9VX25TsBqPe2rBKShQ==

30   The Government Is Effectively Helping Industries Bypass Environmental Safeguards, Jul 28, 2021; https://science.thewire.in/environment/the-government-is-effectively-helping-industries-bypass-environmental-safeguards/

31   Kapoor Meenakshi and Dinesh Krithika A, Throughout the Pandemic, Environmental Clearance Law Has Been Under the Chopping Block, May 23, 2011; https://thewire.in/environment/throughout-the-pandemic-environmental-clearance-law-has-been-under-the-chopping-block

32   Kapoor Meenakshi, Dinesh Krithika A, 2020 EIA Notification Remains a Draft, Yet MoEFCC Continues To Edit 2006 Version, Nov 29, 2022; https://science.thewire.in/environment/moefcc-eia-notification-modifications/#:~:text=in%20the%20gazette.-,By%20this%20change%2C%20the%20draft%20EIA%202020%20should%20have%20expired,notification%20to%20October%2011%2C%202022.

33   Nandi Jayashree, Recent environment rules mirror controversial draft, Jun 5, 2022; https://www.hindustantimes.com/india-news/recent-environment-rules-mirror-controversial-draft-101654367194857.html

34   PMO, Unveiling of The Logo, Theme and Website of India's G20 Presidency, Nov 8, 2022; https://pib.gov.in/PressReleaseIframePage.aspx?PRID=1874524

35   Congress protests decision to send forest Bill to select committee, Mar 29, 2023; https://www.thehindu.com/news/national/lok-sabha-sends-forest-conservation-amendment-bill-to-select-committee-congress-protests-decision/article66675096.ece

36   The Forest (Conservation) Amendment Bill, 2023, PRS Legislative Research's Bill Tracker; https://prsindia.org/billtrack/the-forest-conservation-amendment-bill-2023

37   The Forest Conservation (Amendment) Act, 2023, Aug 4, 2023; https://egazette.gov.in/WriteReadData/2023/247866.pdf

38   TN Godavarman Thirumulkpad vs Union Of India & Ors on 12 December, 1996; https://indiankanoon.org/doc/298957/

39   Statement of Clause by Clause consideration of the Forest (Conservation) Amendment Bill, 2023 by the Joint Committee on the Forest (Conservation) Amendment Bill, 2023; https://www.dropbox.com/scl/fi/ar1lkvjujlahaojtu0z8t/Clause-by-clause-JPC_Forest-Conservation-Act-2023.pdf?rlkey=mkz676g402jinyah4p10nz69r&dl=0

40   Forest Conservation Rule 2022, MoEFCC, Jun 28, 2022; https://parivesh.nic.in/writereaddata/FCRule2022Notificationdated28062022.pdf; Joshi Mukta, Sethi Nitin, Government to approve cutting down of forests without consent from tribals and forest dwellers, Jul 7, 2022; https://www.newslaundry.com/2022/07/07/government-to-approve-cutting-down-of-forests-without-consent-from-tribals-and-forest-dwellers; FC Rules 2022;

41   Nandi Jayashree, Govt stops portal to track green impact of projects, Apr 21, 2023; https://www.hindustantimes.com/india-news/indias-environment-ministry-stops-providing-project-impact-details-on-parivesh-website-citing-confidentiality-and-sensitivity-and-will-only-disclose-information-under-rti-act-101682024303352.htmls

42   Mohanty P, Draft Indian Forest (Amendment) Bill 2019: Arming state to undermine rights and wellbeing of tribals, India Today, Aug 7, 2021; https://www.indiatoday.in/news-analysis/story/draft-indian-forest-amendment-bill-2019-arming-state-to-undermine-rights-and-wellbeing-of-tribals-1578054-2019-08-07

43   Centre drops plan to bring in changes to Forest Act of 1927, Nov 16, 2019; https://www.thehindu.com/news/national/centre-drops-plan-to-bring-in-changes-to-forest-act-of-1927/article29986437.ece

44   MoEFCC notifications, Jul 1, 2022; https://moef.gov.in/wp-content/uploads/2022/07/EPA-Bill_compressed.pdf; Jun 30, 2022; https://moef.gov.in/wp-content/uploads/2022/06/Public-Notice-CP-Water_compressed.pdf; June 30, 2022; https://moef.gov.in/wp-content/uploads/2022/06/Public-Notice-CP-Air_compressed.pdf; Experts Divided as Government Moves to Decriminalise Environmental Offences, Jul 6, 2022; https://thewire.in/environment/environmental-offences-decriminalise-centre-experts-divided

45   The Jan Vishwas (Amendment of Provisions) Act, 2023, Aug 11, 2023; https://prsindia.org/files/bills_acts/bills_parliament/2022/Jan%20Vishwas%20(Amendment%20of%20Provisions)%20Bill,%202022.pdf; Highlights of the Bill, PRS India; https://prsindia.org/billtrack/the-jan-vishwas-amendment-of-provisions-bill-2022

46   India: Unlocking Opportunities for Forest-Dependent People in India, Volume 1, Main Report, World Bank, Dec 28, 2005; https://openknowledge.worldbank.org/entities/publication/4959ffbd-48b7-5c44-a1ea-4cbc3d5db669

47   Mohanty P, When the state denies livelihood rights, Governance Now, Aug 1-15, 2012; https://www.dropbox.com/preview/When%20state%20denies%20livelihood%20rights.pdf?role=personal

48   Govindwad Vishnukant and Sahu Geetanjoy, How A Family Of 5 Got Legal Rights Over 144 Hectares Of Forest & Why That Matters For 250 Million Indians, Oct 6, 2023; https://www.article-14.com/post/how-a-family-of-5-got-legal-rights-over-144-hectares-of-forest-why-that-matters-for-250-million-indians-651f78f56f039

49   Mohanty P, MSP for MFP: 15 years too late, Governance Now, Apr 16-30, 2011; https://www.dropbox.com/preview/msp%20for%20mfp%2C%2015%20yrs%20too%20late.pdf?role=personal

50   Kumar Brajesh, Minor forest produce in govt's major cold storage, Jan 4, 2012; https://www.governancenow.com/news/regular-story/minor-forest-produce-govts-major-cold-storage

51   Lakshman A, Titles given for just 50% of the total claims on forest land, Dec 14, 2022;   https://www.thehindu.com/news/national/only-half-of-44-lakh-claimants-to-forest-land-given-title-rights-under-fra/article66263125.ece

52   Nitnaware Himanshu, Experts irked over revised structure of Central Empowered Committee, Sept 8, 2023; https://www.downtoearth.org.in/news/environment/experts-irked-over-revised-structure-of-central-empowered-committee-91628

53   Mazoomdaar Jay, Lutyens' bungalows, RBI, encroachments are 'forests' in govt's forest cover map, Mar 4, 2023; https://indianexpress.com/article/express-exclusive/lutyens-bungalows-rbi-encroachments-forests-govt-forest-cover-map-8474137/

54   Tapasya and Sethi Nitin, Forests Deleted, Sept 21, 2023; https://www.reporters-collective.in/trc/forest-conservation-part-3

55   Sinha Amitabh, An Express Investigation – Part Four | Compensatory afforestation neither compensates nor forests: 60% funds unused, Mar 5, 2023; https://indianexpress.com/article/express-exclusive/express-investigation-compensatory-afforestation-funds-unused-8479513/

56   Chaitanya Krishna SV, NGT stays Rs 72,000 crore Great Nicobar Island project, Apr 7, 2023; https://www.newindianexpress.com/states/tamil-nadu/2023/apr/07/ngt-stays-rs-72000-crore-great-nicobar-island-project-2563459.html

57   89k hectares of forest land diverted for development projects in 5 years, Apr 7,   2023;   http://timesofindia.indiatimes.com/articleshow/99309089.cms?utm_source=contentofinterest&utm_medium=text&utm_campaign=cppst

58   2013 Kedarnath flood disaster: How a cloudburst killed 6,000 people 9 years ago, Jun 15, 2022; https://www.freepressjournal.in/india/2013-kedarnath-flood-disaster-how-a-cloudburst-killed-6000-people-9-years-ago

59   Uttarakhand Cloud Bursts in Monsoon 2019: No Doppler Radars Six Years Since 2013 Disaster, SNDRP, Dec 11, 2019; https://sandrp.in/2019/12/11/uttarakhand-cloud-bursts-in-monsoon-2019-no-doppler-radars-six-years-since-2013-disaster/

60   Cloudburst hits Devprayag in Uttarakhand, May 11, 2021; https://www.tribuneindia.com/news/nation/cloudburst-hits-devprayag-in-uttarakhand-251367

61   Sethi Narendra, Uttarakhand floods: Death toll climbs to 70, property worth Rs 1000

crore damaged, Aug 16, 2023; https://www.newindianexpress.com/nation/2023/aug/16/uttarakhand-floods-death-toll-climbs-to70-property-worth-rs-1000-crore-damaged-2605861.html

62   Mazoomdaar Jay, Explained: The Char Dham road debate, The Indian Express, Nov 12, 2021; https://indianexpress.com/article/explained/char-dham-road-debate-supreme-court-army-7618880/

63   Char Dham road: BrahMos needs to be taken to LAC, need wide roads, says govt, The Indian Express, Nov 12, 2021; https://indianexpress.com/article/india/char-dham-road-debate-lac-supreme-court-7618852/

64   Mohanty P, Rebooting Economy XXVI: Derailment of economy is not 'Act of God', it is 'Art of Misdirection', Sept 11, 2020; https://www.businesstoday.in/opinion/columns/story/india-derailment-of-indian-economy-is-not-an-act-of-god-it-is-art-of-misdirection-job-loss-unemployment-gdp-272743-2020-09-11

65   IAF positions BrahMos-armed SU-30MKIs at Thanjavur, Jan 20, 2020; https://www.thehindu.com/news/national/tamil-nadu/sukhoi-squadron-positioned-in-thanjavur/article30607625.ece

66   Why IAF has an edge over Chinese air force, Aug 22, 2021; https://www.theweek.in/theweek/current/2021/08/13/why-iaf-has-an-edge-over-chinese-air-force.html

67   Citizens for Green Doon & Ors vs Union of India and Ors, Supreme Court, Dec 14, 2021; https://main.sci.gov.in/supremecourt/2020/22369/22369_2020_4_1503_32125_Judgement_14-Dec-2021.pdf

68   Char Dham: How Much Will Wider, Landslide-Prone Roads in Uttarakhand Serve National Security? Dec 20, 2021; https://thewire.in/government/supreme-court-char-dham-highway-national-security-wider-landslide-prone-roads-uttarakhand

69   Chopra Ravi, Joshimath: An Avoidable Disaster, The India Forum, July 2023 issue; https://www.theindiaforum.in/environment/joshimath-avoidable-disaster; Joshimath sinking: National highway construction in 100-km range of border now has riders, Feb 15, 2023; https://www.downtoearth.org.in/news/urbanisation/joshimath-sinking-national-highway-construction-in-100-km-range-of-border-now-has-riders-87713

70   Joshimath: ISRO pulls down report, Govt tells top expert bodies not to speak to the media, Jan 15, 2023; https://indianexpress.com/article/india/joshimath-govt-run-bodies-media-ban-isro-land-subsidence-images-withdrawn-8382141/

71   Talwar Gaurav, Joshimath sinking: 'No reason to keep reports by experts secret', says Uttarakhand high court, Sept 22, 2023; https://timesofindia.indiatimes.com/city/dehradun/joshimath-sinking-no-reason-to-keep-reports-by-experts-secret-says-uttarakhand-high-court/articleshow/103851241.cms

72   Joshimath land subsidence: 5 other places in Uttarakhand that might sink in future, Jan 11, 2023; https://www.freepressjournal.in/lifestyle/joshimath-land-subsidence-5-other-places-in-uttarakhand-that-might-sink-in-future

73   Joshimath sinking: National highway construction in 100-km range of border now has riders, Feb 15, 2023; https://www.downtoearth.org.in/news/urbanisation/joshimath-sinking-national-highway-construction-in-100-km-range-of-border-now-has-riders-87713

74   Tapasya and Walia Aggam, As CM lobbied, Centre went against rules, courts to allow river mining in Uttarakhand, Jul 17, 2023; https://www.reporters-collective.in/trc/as-cm-lobbied-centre-went-against-rules-courts-to-allow-river-mining-in-uttarakhand

75   Bhanot Mallika and Rajendran CP, Himalayan blunders that are ravaging the Himalayas, Aug 28, 2023; https://www.thehindu.com/opinion/lead/himalayan-blunders-that-are-ravaging-the-himalayas/article67242063.ece

76   Joshi Hridayesh, 'River didn't come to us, we went to it': How NHAI's 'all-weather' highways eroded in Himachal, Aug 14, 2023; https://www.newslaundry.com/2023/08/14/river-didnt-come-to-us-we-went-to-it-how-nhais-all-weather-highways-eroded-in-himachal

77   Sand – A Priceless Resource? Sept 6, 2023; https://www.dw.com/en/sand-a-priceless-resource/a-65861239

78   39 out of world's 50 most polluted cities are in India: IQAir report, Mar 15, 2023; https://indianexpress.com/article/india/iqair-report-indian-worlds-most-polluted-cities-39-8498146/

79   Pollution and health: a progress update, Lancet Review, Vol 6, Jun 2022; https://www.thelancet.com/action/showPdf?pii=S2542-5196%2822%2900090-0

80   Health and economic impact of air pollution in the states of India: the Global Burden of Disease Study 2019, The Lancet Planetary Health, Vol 5, Jan 2021; https://www.thelancet.com/journals/lanplh/article/PIIS2542-5196(20)30298-9/fulltext

81   Parliamentary panel underlines lack of quality data on air pollution in smaller cities, Mar 9, 2021; https://www.downtoearth.org.in/news/pollution/parliamentary-panel-underlines-lack-of-quality-data-on-air-pollution-in-smaller-cities-75856

82   India Fact Sheet, Air Quality Life Index 2023, University of Chicago, Aug 2023; https://aqli.epic.uchicago.edu/wp-content/uploads/2023/08/India-FactSheet-2023_India-view_Final.pdf

83   The Commission for Air Quality Management in National Capital Region an Adjoining Areas Act, 2021, Gazette notification, Aug 13, 2021; https://egazette.nic.in/WriteReadData/2021/228982.pdf

84   Delhi Pollution : 'We Give You 24 Hours', Supreme Court To Create 'Task Force' If Air Quality Commission Doesn't Take Serious Measures, Dec 2, 2021; https://www.livelaw.in/top-stories/delhi-pollution-we-are-giving-you-24-hours-supreme-court-task-force-air-quality-commission-serious-measures-186770   &   Delhi Pollution : Supreme Court Directs Air Quality Commission To Invite Suggestions Of Public & Experts For Permanent Solution, Dec 16, 2021; https://www.livelaw.in/top-stories/supreme-court-delhi-air-pollution-air-quality-commission-suggestions-public-experts-solutions-187817

85   Efforts to curb air pollution in Delhi not reflecting on ground: SC seeks responses from Delhi, NCR states, Nov 1, 2023; https://indianexpress.com/article/cities/delhi/efforts-to-curb-air-pollution-in-delhi-not-reflecting-on-ground-sc-seeks-responses-from-delhi-ncr-states-9008186/

86   Gamio Lazaro, Levitt Zach, Shao Elena and Khurana Malika, Tracking Heat Across the World, Nov 1, 2023; https://www.nytimes.com/interactive/2023/world/global-heat-map-tracker.html

87   Abnett Kate and Dickie Gloria, This year 'virtually certain' to be warmest in 125,000 years, EU scientists say, Nov 8, 2023; https://www.reuters.com/business/environment/this-year-virtually-certain-be-warmest-125000-years-eu-scientists-say-2023-11-08/

88   No blanket ban, but SC puts checks on firecrackers this Diwali, Oct 23, 2023; https://www.hindustantimes.com/india-news/supreme-court-allows-less-polluting-crackers-between-8-pm-and-10-pm-on-diwali/story-gfseqs7YNrcp8P5qQsaajI.html#:~:text=People%20can%20burst%20low-emission%20firecrackers%20between%208%20pm,firecrackers%20should%20not%20be%20too%20noisy%20or%20polluting.

89   Kapil Mishra is 'proud of Delhi' for bursting crackers on Diwali; TMC MP writes to police over pollution, Nov 13, 2023; https://www.hindustantimes.com/india-news/kapil-mishra-is-proud-of-delhi-for-bursting-crackers-tmc-mp-saket-gokhale-slams-bjp-leaders-101699840756368.html; BJP defends firecracker use in Delhi, AAP calls its reasons 'absurd', Nov 15, 2023; https://indianexpress.com/article/cities/delhi/bjp-defends-firecracker-use-in-delhi-aap-calls-its-reasons-absurd-9026968/

90   Sahu Saroj Kumar, Mangaraj Poonam and Beig Gufran, Decadal growth in emission load of major air pollutants in Delhi, Jul 2023; https://essd.copernicus.org/articles/15/3183/2023/#:~:text=The%20decadal%20growth%20%282010%E2%80%932020%29%20in%20PM%202.5%20and,and%20NOx%20is%2057%E2%80%89%25%2C%2034%E2%80%89%25%2C%20and%2091%E2%80%89%25%2C%20respectively.

91   Explained: What the commission for air quality management in NCR aims to achieve and why are some opposing it? Aug 8, 2021; https://indianexpress.com/article/explained/delhi-air-quality-commission-explained-7444052/

92   Mohanty P, Rebooting Economy 40: Why Punjab farmers burn stubble? Business Today, Oct 26, 2020; https://www.businesstoday.in/opinion/columns/story/indian-economy-agriculture-why-punjab-farmers-burn-stubble-crop-residue-paddy-burning-276782-2020-10-26

93   The State of India's Pollution Control Boards, Centre for Policy Research, April 2023; https://cprindia.org/wp-content/uploads/2023/04/00-Executive-Summary_CPR-SPCB-study_27042023.pdf

94   India cracks down on critics of coal, Jun 5, 2023; https://www.washingtonpost.com/world/2023/06/05/india-coal-adani-modi-crackdown/

95   Interconnected Disaster Risks, United Nations University — Institute for Environment and Human Security (UNU-EHS) 2023; https://s3.eu-central-1. amazonaws.com/interconnectedrisks/reports/2023/UNU_Tipping-Points_231017_ no-watermark.pdf

96   Composite Water Management Index, NITI Aayog, June 2018; https://www. dropbox.com/scl/fi/lz5igz0cuy57bxpxa1lfs/NITI-Aayog-2018_Water-Index. pdf?rlkey=sqfk4cb1n00ietz7adqqysu2j&dl=0

97   Shukla Ravish Ranjan, How River Yamuna Cleaned Itself In 60 Days Of Coronavirus Lockdown, May 25, 2020; https://www.ndtv.com/india-news/coronavirus-lockdown-yamuna-cleanest-in-30-years-as-industrial-dumping-halts-2234790; Mani KAS, The Lockdown Cleaned the Ganga More Than 'Namami Gange' Ever Did, Apr 19, 2020; https://science.thewire.in/politics/government/ganga-river-lockdown-cleaner-namami-gange-sewage-treatment-ecological-flow/

98   Sharma Harikishan, NITI weighs discontinuing key water report launched 5 years ago, Nov 6, 2023; https://indianexpress.com/article/india/niti-weighs-discontinuing-key-water-report-launched-5-years-ago-9015084/

99   Piped water connections, Ministry f Jal Shakti, Aug 3, 2023; https://pib.gov.in/ PressReleaseIframePage.aspx?PRID=1945408

100   Report on currency and finance: Towards a greener cleaner India, RBI, May 3, 2023; https://rbidocs.rbi.org.in/rdocs/Publications/PDFs/ RCF03052023395FAF37181E40188BAD3AFA59BF3907.PDF

101   India's Long-Term Low-Carbon Development Strategy, UNFCC, Nov 14, 2022; https://unfccc.int/documents/623511

102   SDG India Index, NITI Aayog, 2018; https://www.niti.gov.in/sites/default/ files/2020-07/SDX_Index_India_Baseline_Report_21-12-2018.pdf

103   Report of the Sub-Committee for the Assessment of the Financial Requirements for Implementing India's Nationally Determined Contribution (NDC), Jun 202; https://dea.gov.in/sites/default/files/Sub%20Committee%20Report%20Final.pdf

104   Greenpeace campaigner Priya Pillai 'offloaded' at Delhi from flight headed to London, Jan 12, 2015; https://indianexpress.com/article/india/india-others/ greenpeace-campaigner-offloaded-at-delhi-from-flight-headed-to-london/

105   Greenpeace India campaigner prevented from travelling to the UK, Jan 12, 2015; https://www.theguardian.com/environment/2015/jan/12/greenpeace-india-campaigner-prevented-from-travelling-to-the-uk

106   Greenpeace says India has cancelled its legal registration, Nov 6, 2015; https:// www.theguardian.com/environment/2015/nov/06/greenpeace-says-india-has-cancelled-its-legal-registration

107   Greenpeace India shuts two offices, cuts staff after donations row, Feb 2, 2019; https://www.reuters.com/article/us-india-greenpeace-idUSKCN1PR0BT

108   Union Home Ministry places Hewlett Foundation under FCRA watchlist for climate

awareness funding, Mar 16, 2022; https://www.thehindu.com/news/national/mha-places-hewlett-foundation-under-fcra-watchlist-for-climate-awareness-funding/article65231578.ece

109   Jalihal Shreegireesh, Coal Reform Overturned: After Failed Auctions, Centre Hands Out Coal Blocks At Discretion, Oct 11, 2023; https://www.reporters-collective.in/trc/coal-forest-part-2

110   MS Nileena, Coalgate 2.0: The Adani Group reaps benefits worth thousands of crores of rupees as the coal scam continues under the Modi government, Mar 1, 2018; https://caravanmagazine.in/reportage/coalgate-2-0

111   The story of Gautam Adani's rise - from kidnapping & 26/11 survivor to Mukesh Ambani rival, The Print Dec 14, 2020; https://theprint.in/india/the-story-of-gautam-adanis-rise-from-kidnapping-26-11-survivor-to-mukesh-ambani-rival/566169/; Adani power project was on the brink of bankruptcy – but the BJP government in Gujarat saved it, Scroll, Mar 6, 2019; https://scroll.in/article/915109/adani-power-project-was-on-the-brink-of-bankruptcy-but-the-bjp-government-in-gujarat-saved-it; Modi Government's Rs 500-Crore Bonanza to the Adani Group, The Wire, Jun 19, 2017; https://thewire.in/business/modi-government-adani-group; Coal auctions: Modi govt's policy push to private miners will cost Chhattisgarh Rs 900 crore a year, Newslaundry, Aug 16, 2021; https://www.newslaundry.com/2021/08/16/coal-auctions-modi-govts-policy-push-to-private-miners-will-cost-chhattisgarh-rs-900-crore-a-year

112   Leading coal consuming countries worldwide in 2021; https://www.statista.com/statistics/265510/countries-with-the-largest-coal-consumption/#:~:text=The%20world's%20two%20largest%20coal,and%2020.1%20exajoules%20consumed%2C%20respectively.

113   India to start coal export by 2025-26: Coal minister Prahlad Joshi, Mar 29, 2023; https://timesofindia.indiatimes.com/business/india-business/india-to-start-coal-export-by-2025-26-coal-minister-pralhad-joshi/articleshow/99091162.cms

114   Ministry of Coal, India Achieves 47 % growth in Coal Production during last Nine Years, May 19, 2023; https://pib.gov.in/PressReleasePage.aspx?PRID=1925521#:~:text=During%20the%20last%20nine%20years,the%20history%20of%20the%20country.

115   Ministry of Coal, Timely Availability of Land and Clearances Crucial for Early Production of Coal-Coal Secretary Amrit Lal Meena, Apr 12, 2023; https://pib.gov.in/PressReleseDetailm.aspx?PRID=1915905

116   India Achieves 47 % growth in Coal Production during last Nine Years, May 19, 2023; https://pib.gov.in/PressReleasePage.aspx?PRID=1925521#:~:text=During%20the%20last%20nine%20years,the%20history%20of%20the%20country.

117   Ministry of Coal, Foreign Direct Investment in Coal Sector, Dec 12, 2022; https://pib.gov.in/PressReleasePage.aspx?PRID=1882739

118   Ministry of Coal, Union Cabinet approves continuation of Central Sector Scheme

of 'Exploration of Coal and Lignite Scheme', Jun 7, 2023; https://pib.gov.in/PressReleseDetailm.aspx?PRID=1930446

119   Cabinet clears Rs 2,980 crore coal exploration plan, Jun 8, 2023; http://timesofindia.indiatimes.com/articleshow/100834655.cms?from=mdr&utm_source=contentofinterest&utm_medium=text&utm_campaign=cppst

120   Dutt Ishita A, Global warming a problem but can't sacrifice growth, says CEA Nageswaran, Sept 29, 2023; https://www.business-standard.com/economy/news/global-warming-has-to-be-tackled-but-india-cannot-sacrifice-growth-cea-123092901147_1.html

121   Jai Shrya, Pillay Amritha and Jacob Shine, States ride coal wave in the time of renewables, Nov 15, 2023; https://www.magzter.com/stories/newspaper/Business-Standard/STATES-RIDE-COAL-WAVE-IN-THE-TIME-OF-RENEWABLES,

122   CEA Installed capacity report; https://cea.nic.in/installed-capacity-report/?lang=en

123   https://webassets.oxfamamerica.org/media/documents/bn-carbon-billlionaires-071122-en.pdf?_gl=1*1bg7usv*_ga*MTg1MzgwNjk2OS4xNjY3ODA1MDcw*_ga_R58YETD6XK*MTY2NzgwNTA2OS4xLjAuMTY2NzgwNTA42MC4wLjA.

124   https://wir2022.wid.world/www-site/uploads/2021/12/WorldInequalityReport2022_Full_Report.pdf

125   Mohanty P, COP27: Fighting climate crisis against carbon billionaires, Nov 24, 2022; https://www.fortuneindia.com/opinion/cop27-fighting-climate-crisis-against-carbon-billionaires/110508

126   Govt Think Tank Hand-Picked SC Rulings To Probe Judicial Activism, Jun 10, 2021; https://www.article-14.com/post/govt-think-tank-hand-picked-sc-rulings-to-probe-judicial-activism

127   Economic Impact of Select Decisions of the Supreme Court and National Green Tribunal of India, CUTS International, Jun 2022; https://cuts-ccier.org/pdf/synthesis-report-on-economic-impact-of-select-sc-and-ngt-decisions.pdf

128   CUTS Project Brief: Highlighting the Economic Impact of Judicial Decisions; https://www.cuts-ccier.org/pdf/project-brief-highlighting-the-economic-impact-of-judicial-decisions-DELFeb06-2021.pdf

129   Mahajan Annanya, Why a Niti Aayog study on the economic costs of 'judicial activism' must be viewed with scepticism, Aug 8, 2022; https://scroll.in/article/1029461/why-a-niti-aayog-study-on-the-economic-costs-of-judicial-activism-must-be-viewed-with-scepticism

130   G Ananthakrishnan, SC modifies order on eco-sensitive zone around national parks, sanctuaries, Apr 26, 2023; https://indianexpress.com/article/india/sc-modifies-order-on-eco-sensitive-zone-around-national-parks-sanctuaries-8577808/

131   Thomas G, De Tavernier, J, Farmer-suicide in India: debating the role of biotechnology, Life Sci Soc Policy 13, 8 (2017), May 2017; https://www.ncbi.nlm.nih.gov/pmc/articles/PMC5427059/

132 Centre's Affidavit_GM Mustard_Nov 9 2022; https://www.dropbox.com/s/oaxvzvuaf5ch5px/Centre%27s%20Affidavit_GM%20Mustard_Nov%209%202022.pdf?dl=0

133 Centre's Affidavit_GM Mustard_Nov 9 2022

134 Sodhi Yaspal Singh, Heterosis Breeding for Improvement of Indian Mustard, National Seminar on "Strategic Interventions to Enhance Oilseed Production in India", Indian Society of Oilseed Research, Feb 20, 2015; https://www.dropbox.com/scl/fi/mbz4xhf2c0juah344hzg9/YS-Sodhi_DU_Mustad-hybrids.ppt?dl=0&rlkey=0b7h85h5l22oomml8f5i1tuw2

135 Sharma Devinder, GM Mustard: India gearing up to be biggest dustbin for risky, harmful tech, Aug 1, 2017; https://www.business-standard.com/article/economy-policy/gm-mustard-india-gearing-up-to-be-biggest-dustbin-for-risky-harmful-tech-117051600321_1.html; Mohanty P, GM mustard: Where is data on biosafety and higher yield? Nov 29, 2022; https://www.fortuneindia.com/opinion/gm-mustard-where-is-data-on-biosafety-and-higher-yield/110559

136 Rodrigues Aruna, Rejoinder Affidavit GM Mustard Nov 2016; https://www.dropbox.com/s/k41xgtqbghmqgzd/Rejoinder%20Affidavit%20GM%20Mustard%20Nov%202016.pdf?dl=0

137 Brief record of the 34th Meeting of GEAC held on 7.11.2002.; https://geacindia.gov.in/Uploads/MoMPublished/2002-geac-34.pdf

138 Potential of GM mustard yield untested, says DRMR director P K Rai, Nov 20, 2022; https://www.business-standard.com/article/current-affairs/gm-mustard-yield-potential-untested-as-per-icar-rules-director-p-k-rai-122112000551_1.html

139 Final Report of the Technical Expert Committee (TEC), Supreme Court panel, 2013; http://indiagminfo.org/wp-content/uploads/2013/08/TEC-Main-Report-2.pdf

140 Mohanty P, GM food is back on the table, Oct 31, 2022; https://www.cenfa.org/gm-food-is-back/; Singh Shekhar, Interview| GM fundamentalists can't even give one valid argument, says SJM's Ashwani Mahajan, Dec 11, 2022; https://www.firstpost.com/opinion/interview-gm-fundamentalists-cant-even-give-one-valid-argument-says-sjms-ashwani-mahajan-11789141.html

141 Mohanty P, Marred by faith: GM debate, Governance Now, Feb 1-15, 2013; https://www.dropbox.com/preview/Public/GM%20Food_Lynas.pdf?role=personal; Thomas G, De Tavernier, J, Farmer-suicide in India: debating the role of biotechnology, Life Sci Soc Policy 13, 8 (2017), May 2017; https://www.ncbi.nlm.nih.gov/pmc/articles/PMC5427059/; Gruère Guillaume P, Mehta-Bhatt Purvi and Sengupta Debdatta Bt Cotton and farmer suicides in India: Reviewing the evidence, IFPRI Discussion Paper 2008; https://ebrary.ifpri.org/utils/getfile/collection/p15738coll2/id/14501/filename/14502.pdf; India's farmer suicides: are deaths linked to GM cotton? – in pictures, May 5, 2014; https://www.theguardian.com/global-development/gallery/2014/may/05/india-cotton-suicides-farmer-deaths-gm-seeds

142   Oil palm mission: Govt cleared despite red flags by top forestry institute, Aug 23, 2021; https://indianexpress.com/article/india/oil-palm-mission-govt-cleared-despite-red-flags-by-top-forestry-institute-7466071/

143   Oil palm mission: Govt cleared despite red flags by top forestry institute, Aug 23, 2021; https://indianexpress.com/article/india/oil-palm-mission-govt-cleared-despite-red-flags-by-top-forestry-institute-7466071/

144   Colney Kimi, Mizoram shows why centre's palm-oil plans will be disastrous for farmers, environment, Sept 28, 2021; https://caravanmagazine.in/agriculture/mizoram-shows-why-centres-palm-oil-plans-will-be-disastrous-for-farmers-environment; Srinivasan Umesh, Oil Palm Expansion: Ecological Threat to North-east India, Economic & Political Weekly, Sept 6, 2014; https://www.epw.in/journal/2014/36/reports-states-web-exclusives/oil-palm-expansion.html

145   Methane emissions are driving climate change. Here's how to reduce them. UN Environment Programme, Aug 20, 2021; https://www.unep.org/news-and-stories/story/methane-emissions-are-driving-climate-change-heres-how-reduce-them

146   Harthwaite Josie, Methane and climate change, Standford University, Nov 2, 2021; https://earth.stanford.edu/news/methane-and-climate-change#:~:text=While%20carbon%20dioxide%20is%20more,of%20warming%20the%20climate%20system.

147   Methane emissions (kt of CO2 equivalent), World Bank database, https://data.worldbank.org/indicator/EN.ATM.METH.KT.CE

148   Arora Neha and Bhardwaj Mayank, Fears for farming and trade stopped India signing COP26 forest, methane pledges, Nov 3, 2021; https://www.reuters.com/business/cop/fears-farming-trade-stopped-india-signing-cop26-forest-methane-pledges-2021-11-03/

149   India's Long-Term Low-Carbon Development Strategy, United Nations Climate Change, Nov 14, 2022; https://unfccc.int/documents/623511

150   Mohanty P, India's automotive fuel policy at a crossroads, India Climate Dialogue, Sept 19, 2018; https://indiaclimatedialogue.net/2018/09/19/indias-automotive-fuel-policy-at-a-crossroads/; Mohanty P, COP26: Why it's a long road ahead for India's tryst with climate change, Oct 18, 2021; https://www.fortuneindia.com/opinion/cop26-why-its-a-long-road-ahead-for-indias-tryst-with-climate-change/106112

151   India ripe target for EV companies but domestic take up slow: Report, PTI, May 16, 2023; https://energy.economictimes.indiatimes.com/news/power/india-ripe-target-for-ev-companies-but-domestic-take-up-slow-report/100263286

152   Yarlagadda Kavitha, India's Transition To EVs Threatens Millions Of Auto Sector Jobs, At A Time Of Rising Nationwide Unemployment; https://article-14.com/post/india-s-transition-to-evs-threatens-millions-of-auto-sector-jobs-at-a-time-of-rising-nationwide-unemployment--64740b579a7ce

153   China's Stranglehold on EV Supply Chain Will Be Tough to Break, Sept 26, 2023; https://www.bloomberg.com/graphics/2023-breaking-china-ev-supply-chain-dominance/#xj4y7vzkg

154   Export Import Data Bank: Country - wise, Department of Commerce; https://tradestat.commerce.gov.in/eidb/iecnt.asp

155   Mohanty P, 'COP27'

156   Hindenburg: German airship, Encyclopaedia Britannica; https://www.britannica.com/topic/Hindenburg

157   National Hydrogen Mission, Ministry of New and Renewable Energy, Mar 21, 2022;   https://static.pib.gov.in/WriteReadData/specificdocs/documents/2023/jan/doc2023110150801.pdf

158   Cabinet approves National Green Hydrogen Mission, MN &RE, Jan 4, 2023; https://pib.gov.in/PressReleasePage.aspx?PRID=1888547

159   Adani And TotalEnergies To Create The World's Largest Green Hydrogen Ecosystem, Jun 14, 2022; https://www.adani.com/newsroom/media-release/adani-and-totalenergies-to-create-the-worlds-largest-green-hydrogen-ecosystem

160   Ambani's $75 billion plan aims to make India a hydrogen hub, Jan 31, 2022; https://timesofindia.indiatimes.com/business/india-business/ambanis-75-billion-plan-aims-to-make-india-a-hydrogen-hub/articleshow/89236627.cms

Chapter X

Electoral Governance: Fall of Election Commission and the Bond

Elections are fundamental to democratic governance. After independence, India adopted first-past-the-post (FPTP) system – a representative form of elections in which all citizens above 21 years (lowered to 18 years in 1988) directly elect their representatives (universal franchise), from among the candidates fielded by different political parties, to legislative bodies at the central and state levels (Parliament and Assemblies). The political party winning maximum representatives (more than half seats) then elects its leader to head and form the government.

Electoral governance involves multiple laws and processes and multiple actors (voters, regulatory body, political party, executive, judiciary etc.). Once a model for the world for free and fair elections, Indian elections are now viewed with suspicion. This has happened simultaneously with its democracy slipping into "autocratisation" which is what Sweden's V-Dem Institute called it while downgrading India into "electoral autocracy" since 2020. India is not unique in this democratic backsliding and to understand it better we need to look at how this has happened in many countries around the world.

From Ballot Box to Autocracy

Harvard professors Steven Levitsky and Daniel Ziblatt in their 2018 book "How Democracies Die"[1] note that in the post-Cold War world, several democratic breakdowns have been caused by *elected governments,* unlike military coups and violent seizure of power in earlier periods. Elected leaders have subverted democratic institutions in Georgia, Hungary, Nicaragua, Peru, the Philippines, Poland, Russia, Sri Lanka, Turkey and Ukraine.

They explain how it happens: "Democratic backsliding today *begins at the ballot box*. The electoral road to breakdown is *dangerously deceptive*...Constitutions and other nominally democratic institutions remain in place. *People still vote.* Elected autocrats maintain *a veneer of democracy while eviscerating its substance.* Many government efforts to subvert democracy are "legal", in the sense that they are *approved by the legislature or accepted by the courts.* They may even be portrayed as efforts to improve democracy – making the judiciary more efficient, combating corruption or cleaning up the electoral process. Newspapers still publish but are *bought off or bullied into self-censorship.* Citizens continue to criticize the government but often find themselves facing *tax or other legal troubles.* This sows public confusion. People do not immediately realize what is happening. Many continue to believe they are living under a democracy. Because there is no single moment – no coup, declaration of martial law, or suspension of the constitution – in which the regime obviously "crosses the line" into dictatorship, nothing may set off society's alarm bells. Those who denounce government abuse may be dismissed as exaggerating or crying wolf. *Democracy's erosion is, for many, almost imperceptible." (Emphasis added)*

In short, countries *sleep-walk* from democracy to autocracy at the hands of *elected* governments. They didn't mention India, perhaps because the early trends of the democratic breakdown escaped their attention (on or before 2018). In 2021, at least *four global studies* pointed at India's fall in democratic polity and governance.

Sweden's V-Dem Institute (which tracks the state of democracy around the world)[2] downgraded India in its 2021 report (for 2020) from "electoral democracy" to "electoral autocracy" – just above the worst category regimes, "closed autocracy". It linked this fall directly to the *rise of* Prime Minister Modi and the BJP: "Narendra Modi led the Bharatiya Janata Party (BJP) to victory in India's 2014 elections and most of the decline occurred following BJP's victory and their *promotion of a Hindu-nationalist agenda.*" It said the sharp fall in India was "one of the *most dramatic shifts* among all countries in the world over the past 10 years", alongside *Brazil, Hungary, and Turkey. (Emphasis added)*

In its 2022 report (for 2021) the V-Dem Institute[3] said India's situation "worsened" along with Afghanistan, Bangladesh, Cambodia, Hong Kong, Thailand and the Philippines because "anti-pluralist parties are driving the autocratisation"; polarization was increasing to "toxic levels", contributing to electoral victories of anti-pluralist leaders and the empowerment of their autocratic agendas and such governments "increasingly use misinformation to shape domestic and international opinion".

The V-Dem Institute's report classifies countries into four types: two forms of democracy – electoral and liberal – and two types of autocracies – electoral and closed. To be minimally democratic, i.e., an "electoral democracy", a country has to meet sufficiently high levels of free and fair elections as well as universal suffrage, freedom of expression and association. Hence, it says, solely holding elections does not suffice for a country to be considered democratic. It defines "liberal democracies" as ones in which liberal aspects (executive constraint by the legislature and high courts, rule of law and individual rights) are respected on top of the requirements for electoral democracy. In electoral autocracies, in which India falls, "there are institutions *emulating democracy* but falling substantially below the threshold for democracy in terms of authenticity or quality". In closed autocracies, the lowest in the order, "an individual or group of people exercise power largely *unconstrained* by the people". *(Emphasis added)*

It uses five major indicators/indices for its Liberal Democracy Index: Electoral democracy index, liberal component index, egalitarian component index, participatory component index and deliberative component index. The significance of elections for India can be gauged from the act that of all five indices its 'democratic index' scored the highest – 0.44 for 2021 and 0.41 for 2020. Its graph shows a democratic rise in 1952 (first general elections were held), followed by a dramatic fall during the Emergency of 1975-77, a quick recovery and a sharp plunge in 2014. For 2021, there was, however, a marginal improvement in India's scores.

Image: V-Dem's tracking of India's democratic journey

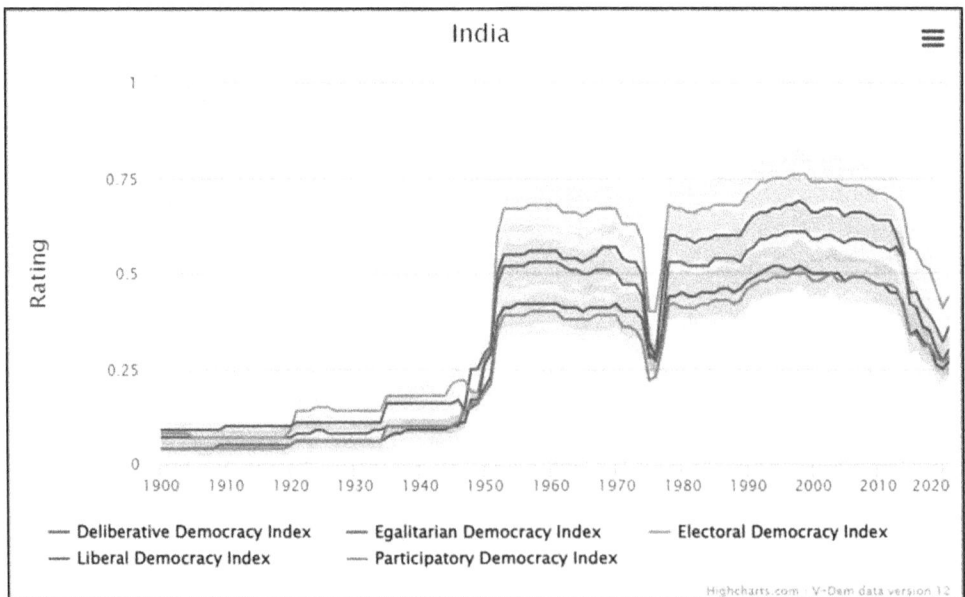

Source: V-Dem Institute, 2021

In addition to the V-Dem's reports, three other global agencies downgraded India's democracy in 2021.

- The US's Freedom House[4] downgraded India from "free" to "partly free" – just one rank above "not Free", stating much of the same things that the V-Dem had said (directly linking it to the rise of Modi and his BJP): Cracking down on critics, ham-fisted lockdown that resulted in the dangerous and unplanned displacement of millions of internal migrant workers, encouraging scapegoating of Muslims, who were disproportionately blamed for the spread of the virus and faced attacks by vigilante mobs. It also gave highest mark to India's "electoral process".

- The Economist Intelligence Unit (EIU), which held India earlier a "flawed democracy", pushed it further down in its Democracy Index stating "democratic backsliding".[5] In it too, India scored the highest in "electoral process and pluralism".

- Swedish think-tank The International Institute for Democracy and Electoral Assistance (International IDEA)[6] categorised India as a backsliding democracy and a "major decliner" in its Global State of Democracy 2021 (GSoD) report.

Jaffrelot[7] described India as "electoral authoritarianism" – which he defined as "a political system in which the rulers maximize their probability of winning by reducing the presence of their rivals in the media and by spending far more money than their opponents during the election campaign". The aptness of his description will be clear soon.

Sanctity of Elections in Question

Elections have lost sanctity in India for several reasons. Five major ones have been identified in earlier chapters.

- Even if the BJP loses state elections, it installs its government by stealing the mandate (through defections, misuse of the office of Governor and Lieutenant Governor).

- It subverts democratically elected governments (J&K and NCT of Delhi) through arbitrary laws. Four years down the line, there is no elections to the Assembly in J&K and the NCT of Delhi is ruled by the Centre's representative, Lieutenant Governor, despite having an elected government.

- Elections accompany raids on all political rivals by central agencies to damage their electoral prospects.

- After losing elections, the BJP tries to destabilise and unsettle state governments through riads, arrests and overnight transfers of key officials, discriminates and short-changes states in central assistances.

- The Centre encroaches in states' domain through a host of central schemes and laws.

This chapter focuses on how the electoral process has been compromised with the constitutionally empowered Election Commission of India (ECI) seemingly working to further the interests of government and the ruling party, the BJP, by allowing vitiations of level-playing fields and the Model Code of Conduct (MCC); increasing use of muscle (more candidates with criminal background) and money power (through the opaque Electoral Bond) and other omissions and commissions.

Executive Commission, Exit of Lavasa

The Pegasus investigations of 2021 revealed some aspects of the compromise in electoral processes. The Israeli military-grade spyware's targets included not just rival political leaders and governments (Karnataka in 2019) but also then Election Commissioner Ashok Lavasa. His case is chilling.

Lavasa was the only member of the three-member ECI to flag blatant and repeated violations of the MCC by Prime Minister Modi and then BJP president (now Home Minister) Amit Shah during the 2019 general elections. Lavasa protested when the ECI gave clean chits to them but his dissenting notes were excluded from the official communiques. His is a constitutional office, critical to ensure credibility of elections and yet his cell number showed up in the Pegasus snooping list[8].

Lavasa was persecuted by the government for this. His wife, sister and son were put under investigation. Eleven PSUs were asked to probe Lavasa's role in "undue influence" in decision making during his tenure in the Ministry of Power earlier.[9] His wife and sister were probed by the Income Tax Department(ITD) and the company in which his son was a director was probed by the Enforcement Directorate (ED). A few months thereafter, Lavasa resigned[10] from the office to join the Asian Development Bank (ADB) even as he was due to head the ECI in 2020.

Both the Prime Minister and then BJP president ran a highly communal campaign in 2019 and used armed forces to exploit voters' sentiments after the Pulwama terror attack in February 2019, in which 40 paramilitary Central Reserve Police Force (CRPF) personnel were killed. India launched a botched attack on Pakistan's Balakot – having declared Pakistan responsible for the bomb blasts but, as then Governor Satya Pal Malik alleged, multiple security lapses on part of the Indian establishment were to be blamed (Chapter V). India lost two planes, a pilot was captured and six Air Force personnel were killed in "a friendly fire"[11] and yet, fake claims of killing hundreds of terrorists in Balakot was made while the ground reports and forensic evidence[12] showed the strike killed a crow and inflicted minor injury on a civilian. The Prime Minister asked voters to dedicate their votes to the Pulwama martyrs and the non-existing heroes of the Balakot strike – against the written orders from the ECI not to invoke defence forces in election campaigns. Malik alleged that the Pulwama blasts and the Balakot strike were used by the government to win the 2019 elections and hence, he was asked by the Prime Minister and the NSA to keep quiet when he questioned the deliberate security lapses by India (multiple intelligence inputs, requests to airlift soldiers and keeping all roads linking to the one in which the CRPF convoy moved unmanned).[13]

Ironically, the ECI's own advertisements in newspaper and other media at the election time carried photographs of armed forces to ask people "Ready to vote in the Lok Sabha election 2019?" Such was the intensity of communalized campaign that Modi and Shah equated Congress leader Rahul Gandhi's Wayanad constituency in Kerala with Pakistan and a 'Hindu minority' area.[14] While similar communal transgressions from opposition leaders attracted swift action from the ECI, it gave clean chits to both in *five instances*[15] – to which Lavasa had objected. Later, encouraged by such complicity, the Central government would use defence forces for election campaigns in the run up to the Uttar Pradesh elections in November 2021: Once the Indian Air Force planes landed on a highway to showcase his party-ruled state's achievements in building good roads and then a mega military event ("Rashtriya Raksha Samarpan Parv") – both of which he attended.[16]

There were other violations during the 2019 general elections too. The BJP ran an *unauthorized and undeclared* "NaMo TV"[17], airing the Prime Minister's election speeches 24x7 on all DTH platforms – even during the silence (no-campaign) periods between different phases. The ECI didn't act nor did it pay heed to the complaints from the Opposition. Just as the final phase of no-campaign period began, the Prime Minister went on a highly publicized Kedarnath pilgrimage. All television channels and other media platforms widely covered it for two days with the chanting of mantras to give it a Hindu religious colour – again a gross violation of the poll code. But the ECI looked the other way and the Prime Minister duly acknowledged its role and profusely thanked it later – claiming that he had got the ECI's permission for the pilgrimage.[18]

Historian Ramchandra Guha[19] wrote the ECI's "complicity" was obvious "when the Election Commission allowed *falsehoods and communal poison to be spread* by ruling party candidates across India, even permitting the Prime Minister to shamelessly seek votes under the guise of a 'pilgrimage' to Kedarnath". He lamented: "In the past, some Chief Election Commissioners may have occasionally bowed a bit to ministerial or prime ministerial pressure. But never to such an extent as has occurred since 2014." *(Emphasis added)*

The ECI established its blatant *partisanship* during the Gujarat elections of 2017 by separating it from that of Himachal Pradesh. A delayed election for Gujarat was justified on the ground of incomplete flood relief – which turned out to be specious because before the election date for Himachal Pradesh was announced, entire flood relief fund had been distributed in Patan, most in Surendranagar and two-third for Banaskantha district (flood-affected Gujarat districts).[20] The separate schedule for Gujarat went against the convention of holding all state elections, due in the next six months, together. While Himachal Pradesh went to poll on November 9, Gujarat had two-phase poll on December 9 and 14. The extra time allowed the Prime Minister to keep announcing sops and campaign. Very cleverly, the road shows of the Congress and BJP in Ahmedabad were cancelled on the last day of campaigning[21] – citing law and order issue and public inconvenience. That this was a clever ploy was revealed soon as the Prime Minister staged a grand spectacle that day, which was televised live on TV. He flew in a seaplane, landed on the Sabarmati river and proceeded to Ambaji temple on pilgrimage while Rahul Gandhi of the Congres had to sit it out.

India Today described that inaugural *ferry* as a "grand hawa hawai stunt" and alleged it "flouted" several security norms "but what was more surprising is that DGCA gave its nod".[22] The violations included the Prime Minister riding a *hired* "single-engine seaplane"[23] while the security rule-book says he can fly only in "twin or multi-engine aircraft". The Prime Minister tweeted, "With air, roads & rail connectivity, our Government is making efforts for harnessing waterways. All this is for 125 crore Indians" to give a false impression that a seaplane service was being launched (no further seaplane flights took place, despite subsequent attempts[24]). It was during this campaign the Prime Minister alleged that Pakistan was interfering in the Gujarat elections and that Congress leaders, including his predecessor Manmohan Singh, had discussed the state polls with Pakistani guests at a dinner hosted by former diplomat and Congress leader Mani Shankar Aiyar. Aiyar was suspended from the party for his response to the Prime Minister allegations with a slur ("neech" or a lowlife) which was revoked a year later.[25]

During the November 2023 state elections in Madhya Pradesh, the Prime Minister reiterated his oft-repeated charge against the Congress of "openly conspires" against India and standing with foreign elements[26] – without providing evidence – and yet, national dailies had no qualms of turning these into headlines; the ECI didn't care to act.

Sanjay Kumar, Director of the Centre for the Study of Developing Societies (CSDS), listed five instances during 2017-19 when elections were *rescheduled* or advance information was shared to benefit the government and the BJP in his 2022 book "Elections in Indian: An Overview".[27] He wrote: "There have been at least five instances of the Election Commission being either accused of delaying the announcement of election dates to suit the BJP or of having shared the dates with individuals close to the ruling party prior to their announcement or having withdrawn its announced dates to suit the ruling party." The instances he listed were: Rescheduling of elections in Gujarat in 2017 (held *separately* and later than Hinachal Pradesh which went to polls at the same time) and also later in 2022), Karnataka elections in 2018 and byelections in 2019 and the 2019 general elections. Four of these were *rescheduled* to give the Prime Minister extra time to announce soaps and carryon his campaign.

In March 2022, the Delhi municipal (MCD) elections were put off even as the State Election Commission was about to announce the schedule[28] with the latter citing the Centre's communication about plans to merge the three municipalities into one single entity. The BJP faced the prospect of a near certain defeat from the Aam Admi Party (AAP); which it did when the elections were held later in the year after the merger of MCDs[29]). The MCD had been decentralized earlier to improve its efficiency. Even the Delhi government (GNCTD) was *unaware* of the merger plan and there were prior consultation with it. It was a political decision, the administrative and legal soundness of which are highly questionable and pending a judicial review. The Mumbai municipality (BMC) elections were also put on hold as the non-BJP alliance led by Udhav Thackeray was pulled down in 2022 but the rebel Shiv Sena-BJP government was unsure of its victory.[30] For the first time in its history, almost all municipalities in Maharashtra, including the BMC, remain without elected body since then.[31]

The West Bengal elections of 2021 showed the ECI's complicity again when an unprecedented eight-phase polling was scheduled for the state's 294 seats, amidst the rampaging second wave of the pandemic (from March 27 to April 29). In contrast, Tamil Nadu (234 seats but geographically larger in size than West Bengal) went to poll at the same time with one-day polling (April 6). This was for no other reason than letting the BJP leaders extended run of campaigning. The *phasing* of West Bengal elections was designed to benefit the BJP, as senior journalist Manini Chatterjee[32] explained: "An eight-phase election spread over a month has been carefully crafted in a way that the *BJP starts in its strongholds,* and with each passing phase, spreads the word that it is on a winning spree." *(Emphasis added)*

True, West Bengal had seen elections in several phases earlier (five in 2006 and six in 2011) but those were the times of heightened Maoist violence and boycott call for elections. There were genuine apprehensions about holding peaceful polling at one go – which wasn't the case in 2021. It is also true that the ECI justified the eight-phase polling citing the pandemic but the subsequent developments would show, that was as misleading as in the case of the Gujarat election of 2017.

The Prime Minister and Union Home Minister held massive rallies in the state spread over a month – completely ignoring the pandemic threat and *repeated reprimands* from the Madras and Calcutta high courts to the ECI to check the campaigning because of the pandemic. The Madras High Court was so enraged ("irresponsible" behaviour)[33] as to seek murder charges against the ECI for its criminal negligence. Its fears were found true and a BBC "reality check" [3] later showed a quantum jump in the cases.[4]

The Uttar Pradesh elections of 2022 saw the BJP and its Chief Minister run one of most vicious communal campaigns. Chief Minister Yogi Adityanath called it a "80% vs 20%" election (a reference to Hindu and Muslim population shares in the state), frequently used "abba jaan" and "bulldozer" as dog-whistles for Hindu supporters. The Wire's analysis found *more than 100*[35] distinct instances of "straightforward hate speech, anti-Muslim dog-whistling, an emphasis on anti-Muslim policy and legislation, the targeting of the opposition as a proxy for Muslims, and a chilling focus on Hindu supremacist rhetoric". No action was taken. Months earlier, in June 2021, Lavasa's place had been filled with Arup Chandra Pandey, retired chief secretary of Uttar Pradesh under Yogi. A political commentator said this was a "neat coincidence".[36]

The ECI had built up its reputation in conducting free and fair elections and was a global model, particularly since the days of TN Seshan in 1990s. During the three-decade-long coalition governments before 2014, it invoked fear in the minds of deviant politicians as a fiercely independent and impartial authority, which changed after 2014, which brought a majority government.[37] In order to check Seshan's "bulldog" days, then Congress government had turned the ECI into a three-member body in 1993 but that made no difference until 2014. It continued to be fiercely independent. Even then, there were incessant talks of its reforms, particularly since their appointment is exclusively done by the Central government. The proposal[38] then was to include Chief Justice of India (CJI) and Leader of Opposition in the selection/appointment committee and extend constitutional protections available to the Chief Election Commissioner to the two Election Commissioners.

In 2023, the Supreme Court ordered *inclusion of only CJI* (until appropriate law was made to ensure the ECI's independence)[39], while hearing the case of *post haste* appointment of the EC Arun Goyal in 2022 (Uttar Pradesh cadre officer who took voluntary retirement just six weeks prior to his retirement). A few months later, in August 2023, the government suddenly introduced a Bill[40] in the Rajya Sabha, proposing to undo the court order by replacing the CJI with a Prime Minister's nominee from the Union Cabinet, thereby giving complete control over the ECI appointments to itself. The Bill also proposed to downgrade the status of ECI and ECs from that of a Supreme Court judge to Cabinet Secretary. The Bill had remained pending in that monsoon session.

Mysterious Black Trunk

One election episode will remain forever etched in the memory for long.

During the 2019 general elections, a Karnataka cadre IAS officer Mohammad Mohsin was on election duty in Chitradurga. He was suspended by the ECI for ordering video-graphy of the Prime Minister's helicopter – which was his mandate. A video, which went viral, showed a few people running with a *black trunk* from the Prime Minister's helicopter and putting it into a waiting car without being stopped or checked.[41] The Central Administrative Tribunal (CAT), which overturned Mohasin's suspension order, observed that while the black trunk was suspected to contain cash but "apparently no action followed". The CAT order pointed to (i) non-existing directive not to inspect VIP or VVIP helicopter and (ii) non-existing privilege granted to VIPs during elections – the pleas that the ECI had made to suspend him. Though the ECI revoked the suspension order after thre CAT ruling, it sought disciplinary action[42] against Mohsin nontheless!

Former DGP of Uttar Pradesh AL Banerjee, who had actually carried out a *physical inspection* of former Prime Minister Rajiv Gandhi's aircraft during the state election of 1985, wrote[43] that he never faced any action for doing his job. Rajiv Gandhi had won 404 seats the previous year, in the 1984 general elections, against just two for the BJP then (101 seats more than the BJP's 303 in 2019) and led the last majority government before 2014 and 2019.

The ECI never tried course correction. During the November 2023 state elections, Chhattisgarh Chief Minister Bhupesh Baghel raised a red flag and *asked*[44] the ECI to check the CRPF vehicles coming to the state as he suspected cash was being brought in to influence the elections but nothing was heard from it.

Compromising Elections

There are various ways in which elections have been compromised after 2014:

(i) The decline in autonomy and integrity of the ECI – the dangers of which the Supreme Court pointed out in its 2023 order mentioned earlier (and included CJI in the selection panel for ECs).

(ii) The Prime Minister himself flouting the Model Code of Conduct (MCC) with impunity to run *communalize and polarize voting*.

(iii) The mysterious black trunk in the Prime Minister's helicopter reflects the ECI's unwilling to check black money or undeclared expenses of the ruling BJP.

(iv)   Incessant raids by central agencies on rival political parties during electioneering – which never happened since TN Seshan's days of 1990s. It helps the BJP to paint only its rivals as corrupt, derail their campaigns by seizing their cash while the ECI watches silently.

(v)   A *2023 study*[45] by Sabyasachi Das of Ashoka University said it found evidence of "electoral manipulation" in the 2019 general elections (a) at the stage of voter registration and (b) at the time of voting and counting (turnout manipulation) – both pointing to "strategic and targeted electoral discrimination against Muslims". This happened, the study said, through "deletion" of Muslim names from voter lists and "suppression" of their votes. It said the BJP "won a disproportionate share of closely contested elections" – which were "concentrated" in the BJP-ruled states at that time. It concluded that the evidence presents "a worrying development with potentially far-reaching consequences for the world's largest democracy". Incidentally, he had to quit (so much for academic autonomy)[46] days later due to protests from the BJP and the Intelligence Bureau (IB) officials (work under the MHA) visited the university to investigate who all were involved in this study – apparently to intimidate the academics there.[47]

(vi)   One of the key elements of electoral integrity and fair play is to match the EVM and VVPAT (paper trail) counts, particularly since complaints of EVMs recording only the BJP's symbol, irrespective of which button is pressed, has been common after 2014.

The ECI stopped matching the EVM and VVPAT counts. The government had *assured* the Parliament to provide information on the *discrepancies*, if any, in their counts during the 2019 general elections. Four years down the line, the Lok Sabha's Committee of Government Assurances disclosed (in July 2023) that "the requisite information from the EC is still awaited" despite five requests sent to it.[48]

This silence is disturbing since the ECI had pulled down[49] EVM counts of 373 of 543 seats after the 2019 general elections – after media *exposed serious discrepancies* with the ECI's two sets of data (in the EVM votes polled and the EVM votes counted) without explaining the discrepancies.

Meanwhile, 19 lakh EVMs were found missing in 2018[50] – through the RTI – which remains *unprobed* (see "investigation-mukt India" in Chapter V to know why). The ECI washed off its hand by stating that state election commissions also procured such EVMs. This only adds to the mystery over VVPAT cross checking.

Rising Criminals in Politics

It is known that the BJP has maximum number of Lok Sabha members with criminal antecedents – most with serious crimes attracting five years of imprisonment – and also that the number of such ministers in the Prime Minister's Cabinet has steadily increased (Chapter I). In the run-up to the 2014 general elections, he had vowed[51], as the prime ministerial candidate, to put all criminal politicians in jail and cleanse the politics and the Parliament *in one year*. It turned out to be an empty rhetoric.[52] Even the 2023 "Modi's guarantee" to do so turned out to be farce – as narrated in Chapter V.

In 2014, the Supreme Court had taken serious note of the growing criminalization (it did earlier too) and said 'criminal' politicians should not be in the government.[53] It hoped corrective measures would be taken with the observation that "corruption is an enemy of the nation" and "as a trustee of the constitution, the PM is expected not to appoint unwarranted persons as ministers." The Prime Minister ignored the court. He didn't drop any 'criminal' minister, not even when one of them, Nihal Chand Meghwal, was summoned by a court in a rape case. In 2018, when Meghwal was dropped during a cabinet reshuffle it was *not*[54] for his criminal background but for alleged poor performance – which is oxymoronic since most ministers are not even known to the people and count for little; the PM-PMO runs the entire government, save for the MHA (see Chapter V).

It may come as a shock to many that in the last cabinet reshuffle of July 2021, the Prime Minister added two MoSs in the MHA[55] – which is responsible for national security – Nisith Pramanik who had declared 21 "serious" criminal cases against himself, including murder, attempt to murder, theft, receiving stolen property etc. and Nityanand Rai, who had declared criminal cases ranging from extortion to promoting communal enmity, unlawful assembly armed with deadly weapons etc.

The third MoS in MHA, Ajay Mishra 'Teni', was already in the Union Cabinet – and is a known as a 'history sheeter" (rich in criminal background)[56] with many serious criminal cases pending against him. It was his car (he publicly admitted it), allegedly driven by his son (which he denied), mowed down four peacefully marching farmers in October 2021 in Lakhimpur Kheri of Uttar Pradesh.[57] After the alleged crime, Home Minister Amit Shah reportedly told him to continue in office.[58] His son was arrested only after the Supreme Court intervened.

A couple of months earlier in August 2021, the Supreme Court had expressed anguish at the growing criminalization and the Centre's inaction.[59] In sheer desperation (its hands are tied due to the constitutional separation of power) it lamented that "the political parties refuse to wake up from deep slumber" and "we can only appeal to the conscience of the law-makers and hope that they will wake up soon and carry out a major surgery for weeding out the malignancy of criminalization in politics." The context was non-compliance of its 2020 directive to all political parties to disclose and publicize criminal antecedents of their candidates ahead of the Bihar elections. It held the BJP and other political parties were guilty of not complying and fined Rs 1 lakh each.

For years, the apex court has been trying to break criminal-politician nexus by ordering Special Courts to be set up for speedy trials of 'criminal' politicians. Such courts are working for decades but the progress has been tardy with cases pending since 1980s. Many cases are yet to reach the trial stage. In 2020, a bench led by Justice Ramana was "shocked" to learn that *4,442 cases were pending*[60], of which *sitting* legislators figured in 2,556 cases. In 2021, the court upbraided the Central government for promising speedy trial but doing "nothing" about its three previous orders issued in September, October and November of 2020. It described the state of affair as "travesty of justice". [61] Nothing changed. In November 2023, the apex court again made a similar appeal – by which time the pending cases were *5,175* (as of November 2022).[62]

Another Supreme Court order of February 2020 had laid down six "mandatory" compliances[63] for the political parties fielding criminal candidates, which included not only declarations and wide publicity about the criminal cases but also (a) to provide "the reasons for such selection, as also as to why other individuals without criminal antecedents could not be selected as candidates" (ECI's Format C-7) (b) to submit compliance report to the ECI within 7 hours of such selection and (c) if political parties failed, the ECI "shall bring such non-compliance… to the notice of the Supreme Court as being in contempt of this Court's orders/directions". After the 2022 round of state elections in five states, the Association for Democratic Reforms (ADR) analyzed C-7 reports of political parties[64] to find that for 212 candidates (out of 1,178 candidates with criminal records it analyzed) political parties had offered no reason at all. "In most cases", the ADR said, "instead of giving cogent answers to the question, justification is given as to why the candidate in question has been selected. For some candidates it is mentioned that he/she is the best choice to win the election."

The ADR analysis of September 2023 showed[65], of 763 *sitting MPs* (Lok Sabha and Rajya Sabha), 306 MPs (40%) have have declared criminal cases against themselves, 194 (25%) of them serious criminal cases, including murder (11), attempt to murder (32), kidnapping, crimes against women (21) etc. Most of them (serious crime cases) are from Uttar Pradesh (37), Bihar (28), Maharashtra (22) and Kerala (10). The average assets of MPs are Rs 38.33 crore (the total of 763 MPs is Rs 29,251 crore) – while that of MPs with criminal records is Rs 50.03 crore and those with no criminal records Rs 30.5 crore. Another ADR analysis of October 2023 showed[66], 107 sitting MPs and MLAs (33 MPs and 754 MLAs) had declared registered cases of hate speech – of which 42 were from the BJP.

Such numbers, however, give an incomplete as well as misleading picture. Earlier we read former apex court judge Justice Ramana was "shocked" in 2020 to learn that *4,442 criminal cases were pending* against sitting and former legislators for long despite Special Courts for such cases. Here is another: Of 101 criminal cases against BJP legislator Raja Singh from Telangana, he was convicted only in one (one-year imprisonment for criminal assault on police); 18 cases relate to hate speeches but no conviction in any.[67]

BJP: Safe Haven for Tainted

After 2014, the BJP has proved a *safe haven* for criminal politicians. One of the firsts to join its rank was Congress leader Sukh Ram, former telecom minister who was found with Rs 3.6 crore of unaccounted cash in his home and was convicted in a telecom scam. He joined the BJP in 2017.[68] Many legislators with criminal background have publicly declared that after defecting to the BJP they were getting "sound sleep", "no (more) inquiries" and that "the ED won't come after me" after they joined the BJP.[69] It may have been said it in jest but when the Prime Minister's Cabinet colleague and MoS for Railways Raosaheb Danve compared, in 2019, the BJP with a "washing machine"[70] which cleanses taints it did sound very credible and convincing.

The BJP has a tainted legacy in the matter too.

In 2002, the BJP-led government under Vajpayee sought to protect politicians with criminal background, first through an ordinance, The Representation of People (Amendment) Ordinance, 2002[71], which was then passed as law. This was in response to the Supreme Court's order that all candidates must declare pending corruption cases, financial and educational backgrounds in their electoral affidavits. Ironically described as "electoral reforms", the Vajpayee era law overturned the order regarding disclosure of pending criminal cases and financial details (making it a "post-election matter") and allowed only the educational backgrounds to be declared. The court struck it down in 2003 as unconstitutional.[72]

Later, in 2013, the Supreme Court struck down, in the Lily Thomas case[73] (first filed decades earlier in 1952), a discriminatory provision in the Representation of People Act of 1951 (RP Act)[74] which provided immunity to lawmakers in criminal convictions and said a convicted legislator would be disqualified from the legislation *from the day of conviction* and *further disqualified* for elections for *six years* after the sentence is served – if the conviction carried "not less than two years of imprisonment". Until then, the law had denied ordinary citizens the right to contest elections if found convicted thus under Section 8(4) of the RP Act of 1951 but exempted convicted lawmakers – allowing them a three-month window to obtain a stay against such convictions from higher courts and thus, granted immunity from disqualification during the pendency of appeal (presumption of innocence until proven guilty). This apex court order led to the disqualification of RJD leader Lalu Prasad Yadav from the Lok Sabha in the same year[75] – the first of its kind – following his conviction in one of the fodder-scam cases.

The Congress-led UPA government too had sought to negate that order through an ordinance, later in 2013. But it was questioned by President Pranab Mukherjee (a former Congress minister) and thereafter, then Congress vice president Rahul Gandhi tore the ordinance[76] in a public display of righteous anger, putting an end to it. Later in 2023, Gandhi would be disqualified from the Lok Sabha hours after his conviction in a criminal defamation case (his membership was restored later as the apex court *stayed* the conviction (Chapter II).

The role of Election Commission is of utmost significance here – as the challenge to Gandhi's conviction process goes on. Constitutional expert PDT Achary says, post-disqualification, the Election Commission has the power to reduce or "remove" the disqualification under Section 11B of the RP Act of 1951 if "mitigating" circumstances are found.

This section reads: "The Election Commission may, for reasons to be recorded, remove any disqualification under sub-section (1) of section 11A" (Section 11 is "disqualification arising out of conviction and corrupt practices). It was this power which the Election Commission exercised in 2019[77] to roll back the six-year disqualification from contesting an election by Sikkim Chief Minister Prem Singh Tamang after his release from imprisonment in a corruption case – after he became an ally of the BJP.[78]

Tamang was also helped[79] because the government had, contrary to its public claims of "zero-tolerance" to corruption and the "Modi's guarantee" to put in jail all corrupt politicians, had actually removed convictions in corruption cases as a ground for disqualification!

In 2015, it had repealed the entire Act 9 of 2003[80] – or The Representation of the People (Amendment) Act, 2002 – which introduced Section 8(1)(m) to disqualify those found guilty under the Prevention of Corruption Act of 1988, Commission of Sati (Prevention) Act of 1987 and Prevention of Terrorism Act of 2002. By repealing the entire 2003 Amendment Act[81], the government made these offences not only not serious enough but also rolled back enhanced disqualification period – six years from the data of conviction and "further six years since release". It has also weakened the entire anti-corruption architecture over a period of time (Chapter V).

Honouring Terror Accused and Corrupt

Not just ordinary 'criminal' politicians, terror accused Pragya Thakur was fielded in the 2019 general elections after getting bail (in 2017) on health grounds – having spent eight years in jail in the 2008 Malegaon bomb blasts case. The blasts had killed six and injured many more. The Prime Minister personally endorsed and defended her candidature[82] saying that "Sadhvi is a symbol" against "those who branded a 5,000-year-old peaceful civilization a terrorist". His main argument was that Hindus can't be terrorists, notwithstanding many pending "saffron terror" cases listed in Chapter I.

The Prime Minister also picked BS Yeddyurappa to become Chief Minister of Karnataka twice, in 2018 (without the BJP having a majority in the legislature, leading to his resignation soon after being sworn in) and in 2019 after the JD(S)-Congress government was pulled down through "Operation Lotus" – after *six failed attempts in the interim year*. Yeddyurappa has the distinction of being the only serving Chief Minister convicted in corruption, resign and go to jail (in 2011).[83]

Deleting Crime Cases

Meanwhile, the BJP-ruled governments are known to remove criminal and corruption cases against their leaders. Uttar Pradesh Chief Minister Yogi Adityanath declared numerous pending criminal cases against himself in his election affidavit – attempt to murder, criminal intimidation, rioting, promoting enmity between different groups to defiling place of worship etc. After assuming office, he withdrew these cases against himself[84] through executive orders in his capacity as home minister. The Supreme Court was aghast to learn that 76 cases relating to the Muzaffarnagar riots of 2013 (ahead of the 2014 general elections) against sitting or former legislators had been withdrawn through executive orders, prompting then CJI Justice Ramana to direct that no state can withdraw criminal cases without high court's approval.[85]

In Karnataka, Chief Minister Yeddyurappa, himself an accused in many corruption cases, sought to withdraw 61 criminal cases against party MLAs; in Uttarakhand, a murder case against a legislator was sought to be withdrawn. It happened with non-BJP governments of Maharashtra and Andhra Pradesh too[86], but none of the non-BJP leaders had publicly avowed to cleanse politics in one year as the Prime Minister did and has to be held accountable by a higher standard. These are not healthy signs of BJP's electoral practices.

Growth of MPs' Assets

Before 2014, India was grappling with dramatic jump in the assets of politicians – disproportionate to their known income. An ADR study of 2011 had shown politics had become the *most profitable business* in India.[87] The following graph maps the trend in the average assets of *re-contesting MPs* of Lok Sabha in the 2019 elections.[88]

Graph 1: Average Assets of re-contesting Lok Sabha MPs

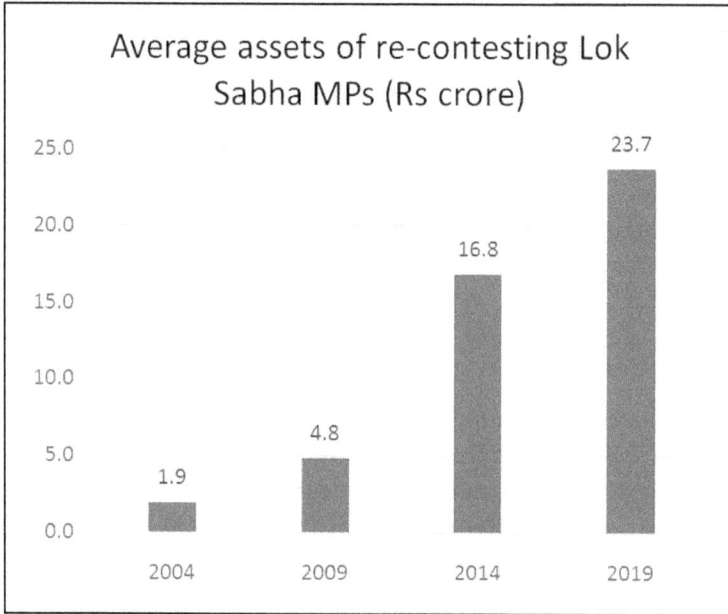

Average assets of re-contesting Lok
Sabha MPs (Rs crore)

Year	Value
2004	1.9
2009	4.8
2014	16.8
2019	23.7

Source: Association for Democratic Reforms (ADR)

In 2018, the Supreme Court was alarmed to find that the assets of some legislators, their kin and associates had gone up by more than 500% between two elections, sought a crackdown and constant monitoring of assets of not just lawmakers but their relatives.[89] It said such assets growth was a "sure indicator" of rampant corruption and beginning of a failing democracy, leading to "rule of mafia".

In 2019, the Supreme Court asked the Central government why no permanent mechanism had been created to monitor assets of lawmakers despite its repeated directives over the years. Last heard, the Law Ministry had written to the ECI[90] for its opinion to establish such a mechanism.

Presently, all MPs are required to declare their assets to the Speaker (Lok Sabha) and the Chairman (Rajya Sabha), which is confidential and can be revealed only with their special permission. As the ADR's September 2023 report showed[91] the average assets of *sitting MPs* of both Lok Sabha and Rajya Sabha are Rs 38.33 crore (the total of 763 MPs is Rs 29,251 crore) – while that of MPs with criminal records is Rs 50.03 crore and those with no criminal records Rs 30.5 crore.

There is yet another worrying new development: *Institutionalization* of political corruption through the Electoral Bond.

Electoral Bond: Structural Corruption

Electoral Bond is a bearer bond for political funding that allows *anonymous and unlimited* flow of *unaccounted money* from businesses and individuals in India and abroad – *without scrutiny* of the election watchdog ECI and *without accounting* for it in their financial statements. Thus, the bond compromises the very integrity of elections, policymaking and governance. Introduced in 2017, it marked a paradigm shift in India's fight against corruption. The Prime Minister promised a "corruption-free India" but saddled it with aruably the most corrupt method of political funding.[92]

Ironically, the bond was presented as a tool to "cleanse" political funding and ensure its "transparency".[93] The Prime Minister dismissed all objections to it saying "some people have issues if anything happens in the country to ensure transparency". Then Finance Minister Arun Jaitley wrote[94] it was a scheme "to enable clean money and substantial transparency".

Nothing can be more misleading. These are outright *lies* told by the high offices.

It's very genesis and design are shrouded in opacity and its constitutionality is suspect. It was first passed as 'Money Bill' through the Finance Act of 2017 (and notified in 2018) to bypass the Rajya Sabha where the BJP didn't have majority. Several laws were amended to facilitate this.

- The Representation of People Act of 1951 was amended to keep the Electoral Bond out of the ECI's scrutiny – undermining the existing transparency in political funding.

- The Income Tax Act was amended to disallow cash/anonymous donation exceeding Rs 2,000 but the cash limit for electoral donations remained untouched at Rs 20,000, thus making no material difference to accountability or transparency.

- The Companies Act of 2013 was amended to (a) remove limits placed on corporations on political funding and (b) make such donations anonymous (no disclosure in the profit and loss statement) – thus making the bond donations completely opaque and facilitating flow of black money flow into electoral funding.

The Law Ministry, Finance Ministry and the ECI – all of them objected to it.[95]

The government ignored all and lied to the Rajya Sabha saying that no concerns had been expressed by the ECI. In pre-2014 period, the ECI would have called press conferences, written multiple letters to the GOI and put its objections in public domain. This time around, its objections to the Law Ministry were unknown until responses to RTI queries revealed it. The ECI sought the bond's withdrawal on two grounds: (i) it described the move as "retrograde" for transparency as it hid donations from government-run corporations (PSUs) and foreign sources and (ii) "opens the possibility of shell companies being set up for the sole purpose of making donations" of black money.

The RTI queries later revealed[96] that even the RBI had strongly objected to it. The RBI had said: (i) the move would set "bad precedent", encourage money laundering and shell companies (ii) the bond had the "potential to become currency and if issued in sizeable quantities can undermine faith in banknotes issued by RBI", funnel money from Indian and foreign companies (including India's government companies or PSUs which is a cause of further worries) and that (iii) since these bonds were bearer bonds and "transferable by delivery", who "finally and actually contributes the bond to the political party will not be known". The government *summarily dismissed* all objections, with Revenue Secretary Hashmuk Adhia – the officer from Modi's Gujarat days who played *key roles*[97] in the implementation of disastrous demonetization and botched GST – telling the RBI that it "has not understood the mechanism". When the RBI sought to know if the secrecy of donor would bring transparency, it was bluntly told off by the Finance Ministry officials and the bond was rammed through the Parliament.[98]

True, the KYC norms were introduced for issuing such bonds and touted as a mechanism to ensure transparency, but that would only allow the largest public sector bank SBI, the issuing authority, to know the donor and by extension, the Central government which controls it, but not the ECI or the voters. Between March 2018 and April 2023, the Electoral Bond of Rs 12,979 crore had been sold through 26 rounds. The ADR's analysis of audited reports[99] showed, during FY18-FY22, the BJP got 57.4% while the next two, the Congress and Trinamool Congress got 10.4% and 8.4%, respectively (the top three beneficiaries). Besides, 94% of bonds were of Rs 1 crore denomination, indicating that these bonds were being purchased by corporations and HNIs, rather than ordinary mortals – again, as feared. Altogether, in 28 phases until October 2023, bonds worth *Rs 14,940.27 crore* had been sold to *unknown entities* (identity not revealed).[100]

It must, however, be pointed out that the bond provides only a fraction of the total electoral funding. Delhi-based think tank, the Centre for Media Studies, estimated that about Rs 100 crore was spent per Lok Sabha constituency in 2019 general elections – taking the total to about Rs 60,000 crore, double its estimate for the 2014 general elections at Rs 30,000 crore.[101]

There are two more shocking elements to the bond.

One, it is taxpayers who pay the *cost of printing* bond papers (Rs 25 apiece), *6% GST* on it charged by both the central and state governments and the *bank commission* on such transactions – not the donor or the receiver, who benefit from it.[102]

Two, this *secret donation* of *unaccounted money* to political parties is tax-exempt (reward) for both the doner as well as recipient. Since political parties are not under the RTI Act, it makes the whole bond affair a deeply reprehensible and who knows what happens to this money?

Lavasa asked in a 2023 article[103] another pertinent question: Why should contributions "to the cause of democracy be in secret"? It is a worthy cause and in countries like the US "people proudly and openly claim to provide donations to political parties". Why can't this be so in India?

The challenge to the constitutionality of bond has been pending with the Supreme Court, although it has heard these petitions multiple times and allowed its trading to go on. Former CJI Justice Ramana promised to take it up but didn't. As a consequence of this bond, the ADR analysis shows, political funding to national parties from *all unknown sources* – without giving source of income for donations below Rs 20,000 in IT Returns – went up again. This was a big cause of concern for decades prior to 2014 and which had come down from 71% during FY05-15 to 45.6% in FY17 – before the bond was introduced – but went up again to *71% in FY20* (fell to 31% in FY21, which was an unusual year as the sale of Electoral Bond too fell from the peak of Rs 2,555 crore in FY20 to a measly Rs 22.4 crore). The ADR found[104], in 18 years between 2004-05 and 2021-22, national parties collected Rs 17,250.201 crore funding from *unknown sources*.

Five CJIs retired during 2017-2022 while keeping the bond's constitutionality pending.

The sixth one, Justice Chandrachud, took it up on October 31, 2023, as head of five-judge bench (others being Justices Sanjiv Khanna, BR Gavai, JB Pardiwala and Manoj Misra). First Attorney General R Venkataramani submitted a statement to the court declaring that citizens *don't have the right to know the source of political funding*: "Firstly, there can be no general right to know anything and everything without being subjected to reasonable restrictions. Secondly, the right to know."[105] And then, Solicitor General Tushar Mehta personally appeared before the bench to justify the opacity and unaccountability of the bond/political funding by invoking the 2017 Puttaswamy (Aadhaar) judgement which declared privacy a fundamental right. He argued that the government was "constitutionally obliged" to respect and protect the right to privacy of citizens/voters – as "political self-expression, either through voting or donations to one's preferred party or candidate lies *at the heart of the zone of privacy…*"[106]

Duplicity on Privacy

These are breathtakingly duplicitous – for many reasons.

Firstly, it means protecting the donor's privacy over voters' rights to know and the government giving itself a waiver using the right to privacy as a pretext

– CJI Justice Chandrachud told the government plea[107] – and having completed the hearing, the court went to deep slumber by keeping the verdict *pending for an unspecified period*[108].

Second, when the Puttaswamy (Aadhaar) case was being heard, the government argued for years against privacy as a fundamental right.

- In 2015, then Attorney General Mukul Rohtagi said[109]: "Right to Privacy is not a fundamental right under our Constitution. It flows from one right to another right. Constitution makers did not intend to make Right to Privacy a fundamental right."

- In 2017, then Attorney General KK Venugopal[110] told the court, privacy can't be a fundamental right, not even a "generalised right"; privacy is "amorphous", "heterogeneous concept"; it "can't be absolute"; it is "elitist" and "meant more for developed countries but not for a country like India".

- In 2017, Attorney General Mukul Rohtagi[111] argued, "the right over one's body is not absolute", "bodily integrity is not absolute" and dismissed bodily intrusion to take biometric data for Aadhaar as "bogus".

The court dismissed all this.

Not a bit embarrassed, the government changed its position and went to town to take credit for the judgment. Then IT Minister Ravi Shankar Prasad made a series of tweets ('X') and called press conference to tell another lie: "Govt was of the view that #right to privacy should be a fundamental right" and that his government was "consistently been of the view that the right to privacy should be a fundamental right".[112]

Third, when it finally passed the Digital Personal Data Protection (DPDP) Act of 2023 *six years later* – without parliamentary scrutiny and parliamentary debate – as the Puttaswamy judgement warranted, the law *doesn't* recognize privacy as a fundamental right, *doesn't protect* privacy, gives *wholesale exemptions* to the government, the regulatory board and private companies dealing with personal data to *violate privacy* (see Chapters I and XI). The central agencies don't respect privacy when they go on *roving and fishing expeditions* to target political rivals (Chapter III), inconvenient journalists, academics and lawyers and seize their digital devices without following proper procedures and guidelines (Chapter XI).

Fourth, it used the privacy as fundamental right to *defang* the transparency law, the RTI Act of 2005, in the DPDPAct of 2023.[113]

Fifth, even after global investigations exposed the Israeli military-grade spyware Pegasus (which is sold only to governments and government agencies – as its maker has repeatedly said) against journalists, political rivals, rights activists, even top bureaucrats, then Election Commissioner Ashok Lavasa and a sitting Supreme Court judge, the government neither confirmed nor denied it. It didn't order any probe and didn't cooperate with the Supreme Court when the latter set up a probe panel – but the Supreme Court (i) didn't initiate contempt proceedings against the government for refusing to cooperate (ii) didn't make the probe report public and (iii) didn't take up further hearing after 2021 (not until December 2023). The SC probe panel report was evasive, it didn't answer any fundamental questions, made contradictory findings of having found evidence of snooping but couldn't prove that the Pegasus was used. (Details in Chapter XI)

After the Apple *alerted* through mail two dozen Indians using its iPhones, including selected political rivals and journalists, were being targeted by "state-sponsored attackers" on October 30, 2023 – days ahead of the November 2023 elections in five states – the possibility of the Pegasus (or another spyware *Predator* which was among the ones the Indian government was hunting for after the Pegasus scandal, as the London's Financial Times had alleged[114]) continued to be misused for political/electoral reasons seemed very real. Of course, the government denied it, calling the alert "vague and non-specific" and ordered a "technical kind of investigation".[115] Some TV anchors then shared a forward sent to them claiming that 'sources in Apple' had said an "algorithm malfunction triggered these mails" – which was later learnt to be from a senior government minister.[116]

Why Political Funding is a Concern

Why the bond *institutionalizes and centralizes structural corruption* in the hands of the government is easy to understand.

The anonymous individuals and companies who fund political parties will expect *quid pro quo* benefits, whether that can be proved or not. Only the government knows the donors because it is handled by the state-run State Bank of India (SBI). The benefits to donors can be in the forms of favourable policies, regulations, contracts, privatization of PSUs or something else. Since the major beneficiary is the party in power, as the data shows, the government's ability to make policies, regulate the economy or govern the country impartially and keeping public good in mind becomes highy suspect.

The Law Commission of India's 2015 report[117] listed three key reasons why political funding is always suspect.

1. *Money power disturbs level playing field* since richer candidates and political parties have a greater chance of winning elections.

2. *Quid pro quo corruption:* Widespread prevalence of black money, bribery and quid pro quo corruption mark India's electoral funding. The Supreme Court and the National Commission to Review the

Working of the Constitution (2002) concur that "the sources of some of the election funds are believed to be unaccounted criminal money in return for protection, unaccounted funds from business groups who expect a high return on this investment, kickbacks or commissions on contracts etc".

3. *State and regulatory captures:* Unregulated or under-regulated election financing leads to two types of captures: (i) regulatory capture: industry/private entities use the money to ensure less stringent regulation and (ii) state capture: money used to finance elections eventually leads to 'favourable policies'.

The Electoral Bond is an addition and an impossibility to manage.

Meanwhile, the ruling BJP has emerged as the biggest spender in elections. An analysis of the audit reports submitted to the ECI shows more than Rs 6,500 crore was spent on elections[118] by 18 political parties between 2015 and 2020. Of this, the BJP alone spent 55% (over Rs 3,600 crore) and Congress 21.4% (over Rs 1,400 crore). Its assets have registered dramatic rise over other national parties, particularly the Congress. The ADR's 2023 analysis[119] of declared assets by political parties shows, at the end of FY22, the BJP's assets were Rs 6,046.81 crore – as against the Congress' Rs 805.68 crore, the CPI (M)'s Rs 735.77 crore, the BSP's Rs 690.7 crore and the Trinamool Congress' Rs 458 crore. Come to think of it: The BJP's assets are 7.5 *times* more than the Congress which has ruled the New Delhi for over 50 years – as against the BJP's just about 15 years.

It isn't just money, the government uses multiple other ways to weaken electoral and democratic governance. Ineffective media and judiciary add to the *deadly cocktail* to derail the democracy (and *dismantle* it through other means explained in earlier chapters).

Foreign and PSU Funding to Political Parties

There is yet another disturbing development. Political donations are allowed for public sector companies (PSUs) and foreign sources. Section 29-B of the Representation of People Act of 1951 prohibits political parties from receiving funds from foreign and also from domestic government-run companies (PSUs). The Foreign Contribution (Regulation) Act (FCRA) of 2010, and its older version of 1976 had banned foreign contributions/donations to political parties to insulate Indian democracy and government from foreign influence. Section 4 of the FCRA 1976 and Section 3 of the FCRA 2010 said: "No foreign contribution shall be accepted by any political party or office bearer thereof."

The Modi government circumvented both.

In 2014, the Delhi High Court[120] found the BJP and Congress guilty of violating the two – FCRA and Representation of People Act – by accepting political funds from both foreign companies as well as PSUs (19 instances for the BJP and 15 instances from the Congress during FY04 and FY12). The court ordered punitive action within six months. Instead of honouring the order, the Modi government *legalized the violations*[121] by first amending the FCRA of 2010 to permit foreign donations by changing the definition of "foreign source" (through Finance Bill of 2016) and then extended it to the FCRA of 1976 (through Finance Bill of 2018) to give it retrospective effect from 1976 – which continues today. Several petitions challenging these amendments are pending before the Delhi High Court (and also the Supreme Court). The prohibition of the RP Act was made *infructuous through the Electoral Bond* – because the donor can't be identified.

Seeding Aadhaar with Voters Id

In December 2021, India woke up to the shocking news that the Chief Election Commissioner and two Election Commissioners had been summoned by the PMO to attend a meeting with the Principal Secretary to the PM and they did it.[122] There was widespread condemnation but the ECI was unapologetic. Days later, the government passed a law to link voters' identity card with Aadhaar, amidst strong protests from opposition parties who staged walk-outs demanding prior scrutiny of it by a parliamentary panel.[123] The ECI didn't object, making it evident that it had given its green signal at the meeting.

The ECI did propose such a linking since 2015 and had also tried it in some states to check duplications but the Supreme Court allowed Aadhaar seeding only for welfare schemes in 2018. In the meanwhile, the dangers of linking voters' identity card with the Aadhaar have been exposed by investigating reports. Kumar Sambhav[124] revealed how the BJP used this linkage to manipulate voting behaviour through "voter profiling", "targeted campaigning" *a la* Cambridge Analytica, during the Puducherry elections in 2021 and by other political parties in Andhra Pradesh and Telangana in 2019 – which saw massive "voter deletion". This threat remains.

In the meanwhile, the Aadhaar authentication has been found to be highly questionable. The CAG report of 2022[125] pointed out how 73% of Aadhaar cards carried "faulty biometrics" which were corrected by individuals "after payment of charges" and said "the quality of data captured to issue initial Aadhaar was not good enough to establish uniqueness of identity".

But shockingly, in September 2023, the ECI told the apex court that linking Aadhaar with the voters' identity card is "optional", not mandatory (in Rule 26B of the Registration of Electors (Amendment) Rules 2022). Assured by this and the promise by the ECI to tell voters about it, the court disposed of the petitions challenging the said linkage – *even when* the ECI told the court that it had already linked *662.3 million voters*[126] (that is nearly 100%) with their Aadhaar numbers and "already uploaded" the voters' list on their website.

Another instance of *arbitrary and illogical* institutional functioning in India after 2014.

No Transparency for Political Parties

The government certainly doesn't like transparency. When the Electoral Bond case was being heard, Attorney General KK Venugopal told the apex court in 2019 that "transparency cannot be the mantra" and that "my opinion is voters have a right to know about their candidates...Why should they know where the money of political parties is coming from".[127]

Political parties are also immune to the transparency law, the RTI Act of 2005, because the government doesn't allow it. In 2014 and 2015, the Central Information Commission (CIC) held that political parties are "public authority" and should come under the transparency law. When the case went to the Supreme Court, the government opposed it[128], saying, among other things, that (a) "if political parties are held to be political authority under the RTI Act, it would hamper their smooth internal working" and (b) "Political parties are not established or constituted by or under the Constitution or any other law made by the Parliament" and so can't be subjected to the RTI Act. The matter remains undecided.

A 2022 study by two ADR scholars[129] analyzed data to flag how political parties have undermined the integrity of elections in multiple ways. They concluded that "there are growing instances of disregard for transparency guidelines/laws by political parties, opacity in political funding, election expenditure underreporting, electoral malfeasance and lack of accountability for unfair practices…", listing limitations to ensuring election integrity in absence of long pending electoral reforms.

Votes Delinked from Performance

A *new marker* of elections (not listed in Introduction) is an apparent *delinking* of electoral outcomes from the performance of government. This became evident from 2017. Soon after the disastrous demonetization of November 2016 – which caused overnight loss of millions of jobs and businesses and cash was rationed – the BJP created history by winning an absolute majority in the most populous and politically important state of Uttar Pradesh.[130] The BJP emerged as the single largest party in Bihar in 2020, for the first time, months after the mass distress migration[131,] caused by the overnight national lockdown and a large number of these migrants were from Bihar. Again in 2022, the BJP won four of five state elections, including in Uttar Pradesh, after the devastating second wave of the pandemic (marked by lack of oxygen, hospital beds and essential medicines). Additionally, there were rising job crisis, poverty and inflation. None of it translated to anti-incumbency – as the post-poll surveys revealed [132]. In fact, the BJP used these electoral victories to claim success of the demonetization, national lockdown and pandemic mismanagement. In other words, electoral mandate is seen as an *excuse for reckless governance*.

Prannoy Roy and Dorab Sopariwala[133], eminent psephologists, have classified Indian elections since 1952 into three phases: (i) Pro-incumbency Era of 1952-1977 when marked continuity in the Congress running governments at the centre and in states (ii) Anti-incumbency Era of 1977-2002 which saw the emergence of rival political forces, galvanized by the Emergency of 1975-77 and "angry" voters frequently voting out governments and (iii) Fifty-Fifty Era of 2002-2019 when voters were more discernible and their votes went to governments that performed well.

Now they must add (iv) Delinked from Performance Era of 2014-.

Risks to Indian Elections

Several new risks have emerged to the electoral governance.

First, the Prime Minister's *renewed* advocacy of "One-Nation-One-Election" (ONOE) in 2023 – simultaneous polls to the Parliament and Assemblies. The *stated* objective is to minimizing election expenses and disruption in governance. This proposal finds support of a parliamentary panel, law ministry, NITI Aayog and ECI. But it strikes at the very root of India's electoral democracy. It was also the favourite hobby horse of the BJP in 1990s and early 2000s when Vajpayee towered over political rivals. It felt a US-style presidential election throughout the country at one go would work to its political advantage.

The *real motive* is to turn India into a US-style Presidential government. Jagdeep Chhokar[134], founding member of the ADR, has explained how it is flawed both conceptually and practically: (i) One-nation-one-election would entail extensive constitutional amendments, upsetting the balance of power between states and Centre in the latter's favour and potentially altering the basic structure of the Constitution and (ii) artificially cut short or extend the terms of elected Assemblies, which also strikes at the root of parliamentary democracy. He rightly argues that the objective of reforming electoral system should aim at making the democracy "most effective", rather than "least expensive" (ironical too since the BJP outspends others by a big margin). This is evidenced at all state elections as the Prime Minister has already re-written the rules of the game, becoming the *main campaigner-and-candidate* seeking votes in his own name[135], liberally distributing "Modi's guarantee"[136].

As for disrupting development work, this is misleading. The Model Code of Conduct imposes *no such restrictions*. Besides, the Prime Minister and his government are *permanently* in election campaign mode (24x7, 365 days) – with *public money*[137] by *combining official work with election campaigns*[138] in different states throughout the year in which he routinely runs down the Opposition and makes tall claims about his achievements – endlessly and without providing a shred of evidence. Some examples of such official functions:

- Apart from expenses by official agencies, additional public money is spent by outsourcing events to flag Vande Bharat trains – two such events cost the Railways Rs 2.6 crore in 2023 as per the RTI reply.[139]

- His monthly "Mann ki Baat" radio address costs Rs 8.3 crore per episode, as per the old 2015 RTI reply[140].

- Routinely launches or inaugurates mega projects, particularly ahead of elections, like in Telangana[141], Karnataka[142], Uttar Pradesh[143] and Gujarat[144].

On all such occasions, the Prime Minister forgets the dignity and responsibility of his office and perennially acts like a full-time *BJP pracharak*. The ECI never questions the Prime Minister or the BJP for such massive misuse of official machinery, public money and open violation of the election code (MCC).

Second, relentless campaign by the Prime Minister and his party to make India "Congress-mukt" (free of the Congress Party). Going by the record so far, the BJP's objective seems to impose one-party rule and remove all Opposition parties – save for state-bound regional parties to maintain the facade of elections. If they achieve their objective, India would lose the only other pan-Indian party which happens to be centrist and secular – the right foil for a communal and intrinsically governance-deficit BJP. The anti-democratic nature of this campaign is obvious in the way the Congress is targeted for defections and toppling of its governments in states. The ADR data[145] shows the BJP has gained the most from such defections since 2016 and the Congress lost the most. It seems India is ideology-free when it comes to defections and there is no taint or opprobrium from the voters.[146]

By *constantly branding* political rivals as enemies at the drop of a proverbial hat and without giving evidence – "anti-nationals", "in league with anti-nationals" and "like to talk about the enemies of the country and of terrorists' bosses" by the Prime Minister *of India*[147] – turns the Government-Opposition relations toxic[148], chokes space for competitive politics of ideas, policies and governance, besides creating an alt-reality to perpetuate power (generating fear and misleading voters through propaganda).

Graph 2: Back to Aaya Ram Gaya Ram era

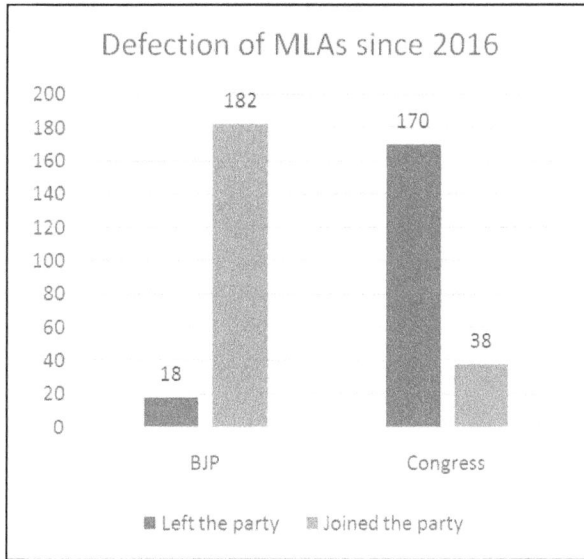

Defection of MLAs since 2016

BJP: Left the party 18, Joined the party 182

Congress: Left the party 170, Joined the party 38

Left the party · Joined the party

Source: ADR, March 11, 2021

Third, the government stands accused of using surveillance through the Israel spy-ware Pegasus, on rival political parties and governments. It was accused of pulling down the Karnataka government in 2019[149] by using the same military-grade spyware; the PMO was accused of pulling down the Bihar government in 2017 by using the CBI to frame RJD leader Lalu Prasad in the IRCTC scam by none other than CBI Director Alok Verma[150]. An investigation by an international consortium of 100 reporters[151] exposed Israel-based global disinformation unit called "Team Jorge" which allegedly meddled in elections in India and other countries, through disinformation campaigns. Led by Tal Hanan, a 50-year-old former Israeli special forces operative, "Team Geoge" sells hacking services and access to vast army of fake social media profiles. Despite demands, no probe was ordered by the government in these cases (more in Chapter XI).

Fourth, the Prime Minister's tight control over his own party poses a risk to the latter's democratic functioning – even if its presidents and office bearers are never elected (but nominated). Prof James Manor[152] warns that the Prime Minister's relentless drive for one-man show has already caused deep resentments in the party ranks and "has so undermined his party's organisation that its future and the future of his authoritarian project are in doubt".

Fifth, the Prime Minister has *obliterated* the difference between his government and his political party, the BJP, by institutionalized coordinated functioning in multiple ways – (a) targeted raids on rival political parties by central agencies (b) targeted delivery of government welfare schemes (c) turning government officials and the Army (detailed in Chapter XI) into the BJP's election agents ("rath prabharis") (d) raising party funds using the government schemes (e) use of surveillance and Aadhaar-linked voters' identity for perpetuating the BJP in power etc.

Sixth, the Prime Minister's *strategic silences*[153] on corruption (and induction of corrupt politicians to his party), communal attacks, economic and human crises etc. Prevalence of fake news and propaganda, generously helped by slavish (Godi) media, create a dystopian world in which truth, facts and evidence, good or effective governance have no place. The Prime Minister's silences *co-exist*[154] with his *incessant and one-way* talks (and tweets) at rallies, national addresses, daily TV appearances, public functions, "Mann Ki Baat" on radio – dumbing down citizens to virtual zombies.

Seventh, incessant politics of hate-and-violence by the ruling establishment – not just to dehumanize and disenfranchise Muslims, but also other minorities, Dalits, Adivasis and dissent (Chapter IV). The Prime Minister himself leads communal and polarizing campaigns. During the 2023 Karnataka elections, he supported malicious and anti-Muslim propaganda film 'Kerala Story'; defended right-wing group Bajrang Dal which indulges in violence by invoking monkey god Hanuman ('Bajrangbali') and asked voters to punish the Congress by shouting 'Jai Bajrangbali' while voting.[155] The ECI served no notice on it but served a notice to the Congress and asked it to provide "proof" of their corruption charges against the BJP-ruled state government stating that such accusation "had the potential of fermenting a feeling of distrust and undermining the legitimacy of the governance system".[156] This is when corruption was widespread in Karnataka, and visibly so, and played a key role in the BJP's defeat.[157]

Eighth, the Prime Minister has not only facilitated the politics of hate-and-violence to flourish, he continues to follow anti-social trolls[158] on Twitter ('X') who routinely threaten women, journalists and dissenting voices with rape, assault and murder (in spite of being repeatedly pointed out). He *personally felicitated* 150 such trolls at his official residence in 2015 and one of them Tejinder Bagga was appointed official *spokesperson of the BJP* – the public face of the party.[159] Such endorsement emboldens and legitimizes anti-social elements and sends a wrong signal to citizens about what is right and what is not. The Altnews – a fact-check website that routinely bursts fake news – has revealed that a significant number of people the *Prime Minister of India* follows are *serial abusers, sexist bigots and rumour mongers*[160]. Given that he is the most significant social and political influencer, healthy public debate on any issue is impossible. He and his ministers follow and amplify the BJP's propaganda unit known as the BJP's "IT Cell". The IT Cell has built up a formidable reputation for spreading hate and fake news. [161] It's insidious and incessant campaigns have been repeatedly exposed by insiders and outsiders, including by its former head Prodyut Bora[162], Altnews and others. Home Minister Amit Shah once declared with pride that his party was capable of making any news, real or fake, *go viral*[163] on social media.

This is a serious situation. When the top political executives are directly involved in spreading hate and misinformation and the mainstream media turns into a government mouthpiece/loudspeaker[164], there is a big danger to the very democracy and constitutional order. A 2014 study[165] by the Centre for the Study of Developing Societies (CSDS) found that in the 2014 general elections, "electorates with higher media exposure were more likely to vote for the Bharatiya Janata Party" and that "voters with higher media exposure were more likely to vote for the BJP in previous Lok Sabha elections as well". This is disconcerting given the kind of governance and socio-political order intrinsic to the BJP.

Nineth, rival parties are routinely run down as family-run dynastic parties and corrupt by none other than the Prime Minister. He calls family-run parties the biggest hurdle for a healthy democracy and against the spirit of the Constitution[166]. But his party and government outsrip all others in the number of people accused of being corrupt and known political dynasts[167] – some are homegrown and others are lured from other parties. His party routinely allies with others it accuses of being corrupt, like the JD(S) in Karnataka and the NCP in Maharashtra.[168] In the case of Ajit Pawar of the NCP and others, who joined the BJP-run Maharashtra government in 2023, the Prime Minister of India's public declaration of "Modi's guarantee" to put all the corrupt in jail (including those very leaders) had come *five days earlier*[169]. As for dynastiess, the BJP not only always nominates its party presidents and other office bearers, it protested the *loudest*[170] when former CEC TN Seshan attempted to make political parties democratic by honouring their party constitutions and holding internal elections in early 1990s. At one such occasion, the BJP claimed that it went by "consensus" and said consensus was also a "democratic process". Its ideological parent the RSS too does the same. Both are strictly hierarchical in approach. In contrast, Sonia Gandhi contested and won the post of Congress president in 2000 and Mallikarjun Kharge did the same in 2022.

A 2015 study by the Hindu Centre for Politics and Public Policies[171] found both the BJP and Congress have adopted a highly centralised and top-down approach in decision making. It also said the information provided to the ECI on internal elections for party positions was superfluous and did not help in drawing conclusions about the quality of these elections.

Democracy is more than winning elections and turning a political party into an election winning machine that the BJP has come to represent. Besides, the blatantly partisan role of ECI, highly communal campaigns, the spectre of Ayodhya temple (to be inaugurated by the Prime Minister of India in January 2024, just ahead of the general elections) becoming the focal point of the BJP's campaign for a third consecutive term – Union Home Minister Amit Shah has been promising "free" trips to Ayodhya[172] to voters if the BJP was voted to power in Madhya Pradesh – and a host of other issues flagged (skewed deployment of state machinery by a permanently electioneering Prime Minister, relentless attack on all rival political parties, repeated call to make India free of the only pan-Indian party, the delink of elections from performance of the governments and the threat of One-Nation-One-Election (ONOE) once the BJP wins another mandate with absolute majority in 2024 etc.) are pointers to a future when elections would be nothing more than just a charade.

***

References

1   Levitsky Steven and Ziblatt Daniel, How Democracies Die, Penguin, 2019; https://www.amazon.in/How-Democracies-Die-Steven-Levitsky/dp/0241381355; Levitsky & Ziblatt, This is how democracies die, The Guardian, Jan 21, 2018; https://www.theguardian.com/us-news/commentisfree/2018/jan/21/this-is-how-democracies-die

2   Autocratization Turns Viral, Democracy Report 2021, V-Dem Institute, Sweden, Mar 2021; https://www.v-dem.net/documents/12/dr_2021.pdf

3   Democracy Report 2022: Autocratization Changing Nature? V-Dem Institute, Mar 2022; https://v-dem.net/media/publications/dr_2022.pdf

4   Freedom in the world 2021: Democracy Under Siege, Freedom House, Washington, Mar 2021; https://freedomhouse.org/sites/default/files/2021-02/FIW2021_World_02252021_FINAL-web-upload.pdf

5   India falls to 53rd position in EIU's Democracy Index, Feb 3, 2021; https://www.thehindu.com/news/national/india-falls-to-53rd-position-in-eius-democracy-index/article33739128.ece

6   The Global State of Democracy 2021; International IDEA, Sweden, Nov 2021; https://www.idea.int/gsod/sites/default/files/2021-11/the-global-state-of-democracy-2021_0.pdf

7   Jaffrelot Christophe, Modi's India: Hindu Nationalism and the Rise of Ethnic Democracy, Princeton University Press, Aug 2021, https://www.amazon.in/Modis-India-Nationalism-Ethnic-Democracy/dp/0691206805

8   Ashok Lavasa Placed on Snoop List as EC After Flagging Modi's 2019 Poll Code Violations, Jul 19, 2021; https://thewire.in/government/pegasus-project-ashok-lavasa-narendra-modi-amit-shah-model-code-of-conduct

9   EC Ashok Lavasa, who dissented with poll code decisions on Modi & Shah, under Power Ministry scanner, Nov 5, 2019; https://scroll.in/latest/942708/ec-ashok-lavasa-who-dissented-with-poll-code-decisions-on-modi-shah-under-power-ministry-scanner

10   Ashok Lavasa quits as Election Commissioner; to join ADB as vice president, Aug 18, 2020; https://www.business-standard.com/article/current-affairs/ashok-lavasa-quits-as-election-commissioner-to-join-adb-as-vice-president-120081801062_1.html

11   Indian Air Force probe finds friendly fire caused February 27 Budgam chopper crash, 5 officers in dock, Aug 23, 2019; https://www.indiatoday.in/india/story/indian-air-force-budgam-chopper-crash-friendly-fire-officers-guilty-1590764-2019-08-23

12   An air strike and its aftermath, Mar 6, 2019; https://graphics.reuters.com/INDIA-KASHMIR/010090XM162/index.html; Surgical Strike in Pakistan a Botched Operation? DFR Lab, Mar 1, 2019; https://medium.com/dfrlab/surgical-strike-in-pakistan-a-botched-operation-7f6cda834b24

13   BJP used Pulwama attack, Balakot air strike to win 2019 LS polls: Ex-Tripura CM Manik Sarkar, PTI, Apr 23, 2023; https://www.thehindu.com/news/national/bjp-used-pulwama-attack-balakot-air-strike-to-win-2019-ls-polls-ex-tripura-cm-manik-sarkar/article66770170.ece

14   Mohanty P, Lok Sabha 2019: Why does Election Commission look weak in ensuring a level playing field? Apr 11, 2019; https://www.dailyo.in/politics/election-commission-lok-sabha-elections-2019-tn-seshan-namo-tv-2019-general-elections-model-code-of-conduct-narendra-modi-yogi-adityanath/story/1/30280.html

15   Election Commissioner Lavasa opposed five clean chits to Amit Shah, PM Modi, May 5, 2019; https://indianexpress.com/elections/lok-sabha-elections-lavasa-opposed-five-clean-chits-to-amit-shah-pm-modi-5710773/

16   Panag Lt Gen HS (retd), In two events, Modi added military into election engineering for UP. It's a bad sign, Nov 25, 2021; https://theprint.in/opinion/in-two-events-modi-added-military-into-election-engineering-for-up-its-a-bad-sign/771470/

17   Mohanty P, Lok Sabha 2019: Why does Election Commission look weak in ensuring a level playing field? Apr 11, 2019; https://www.dailyo.in/politics/election-commission-lok-sabha-elections-2019-tn-seshan-namo-tv-2019-general-elections-model-code-of-conduct-narendra-modi-yogi-adityanath/story/1/30280.html

18   PM Narendra Modi thanks EC for allowing Kedarnath visit, May 20, 2019; http://timesofindia.indiatimes.com/articleshow/69404503.cms?utm_source=contentofinterest&utm_medium=text&utm_campaign=cppst; related link: PM Modi's Kedarnath yatra: TMC alleges poll code violation, complains to EC, India Today, May 19, 2019; https://www.indiatoday.in/elections/lok-sabha-2019/story/modi-kedarnath-tmc-poll-code-violation-complains-ec-1528547-2019-05-19

19   Guha Ramachandra: Future of Indian democracy may hinge on Election Commission regaining credibility, May 09, 2021; https://scroll.in/article/994395/ramachandra-guha-has-the-credibility-of-the-election-commission-ever-been-so-low

20   Sharma Ritu and Nair Avinash, Gujarat elections 2017: Flood relief, before and after poll breather, Oct 27, 2017; https://indianexpress.com/elections/gujarat-assembly-elections-2017/gujarat-election-2017-flood-relief-before-after-poll-breather-bjp-congress-4906690/

21   Gujarat polls: Denied permission for roadshow, Modi travels in seaplane on last day of campaign, Dec 12, 2017; https://scroll.in/latest/861189/gujarat-polls-denied-permission-for-roadshow-modi-to-travel-in-sea-plane-on-last-day-of-campaign

22   Ganapatye Mayuresh, PM's Modi's seaplane ride: Private seaplane operator demands overhauling of industry rules, Dec 13, 2017; https://www.indiatoday.in/india/story/why-different-set-of-rules-for-pms-seaplane-ride-and-small-seaplane-operators-1106691-2017-12-13

23   V Manju, PM Narendra Modi's seaplane flight courts controversy, Dec 12,

2017;   http://timesofindia.indiatimes.com/articleshow/62036474.cms?utm_
source=contentofinterest&utm_medium=text&utm_campaign=cppst

24   Kumar Upendra and Goswami Madhusree, Failed Takeoff: Why India's First-Ever
Seaplane Service Stands Suspended, Mar 28, 2023; https://www.thequint.com/
explainers/seaplane-services-to-statue-of-unity-gujarat-discontinued

25   Choudhury Sunetra, PM Modi Flies On Seaplane In Gujarat, "Good Passenger",
Says Pilot, Dec 12, 2017; https://www.ndtv.com/india-news/pm-narendra-
modi-takes-seaplane-ride-to-temple-on-last-day-of-gujarat-campaign-1786747;
Congress revokes Mani Shankar Aiyar's suspension, Aug 18, 2018; https://www.
thehindu.com/news/national/congress-revokes-mani-shankar-aiyars-suspension/
article24727173.ece

26   Mohan Anand J, Congress stands with foreign elements that are against India: PM,
Nov 10, 2023; https://indianexpress.com/article/india/cong-stands-with-foreign-
elements-that-are-against-india-pm-9020906/

27   Kumar Sanjay, Elections in Indian: An Overview, Routledge 2021; https://www.
amazon.in/Elections-India-Overview-Sanjay-Kumar/dp/1032033134

28   Delhi civic election announcement deferred over 'plan' to merge 3 corporations,
Mar   9,   2022;   https://www.hindustantimes.com/cities/delhi-news/delhi-
civic-election-announcement-deferred-over-plan-to-merge-municipal-
corporations-101646831377821.html

29   Srinivasan C, AAP wins 134 seats in MCD election, secures big win and ends BJP's 15-
year reign, Dec 7, 2022; https://www.hindustantimes.com/cities/delhi-news/delhi-
mcd-election-results-aap-inches-ahead-of-bjp-in-see-saw-battle-101670392368619.
html

30   Gangan Surendra P, After SC verdict, Maha govt wary about holding local body
polls, May 13, 2023; https://www.hindustantimes.com/cities/mumbai-news/
political-crisis-in-maharashtra-delays-local-body-polls-pending-petitions-on-
wards-and-obc-reservation-must-be-cleared-first-sc-101683918404370.html

31   Acharya P and Bose N, BMC completes 18 months without corporators; no elected
reps in 24 municipal bodies in state, Sept 20, 2023; https://indianexpress.com/
article/cities/mumbai/bmc-completes-18-months-without-corporators-no-elected-
reps-in-24-municipal-bodies-in-state-8932683/

32   Chatterjee Manini, Bengal Assembly elections 2021: Floating voters, fluid loyalties
and change as new constant, Telegraph, Apr 10, 2021; https://www.telegraphindia.
com/west-bengal/bengal-assembly-elections-2021-floating-voters-fluid-loyalties-
and-change-as-new-constant/cid/1812154

33   Irresponsible… must perhaps face murder charge: Madras HC on Election
Commission, Apr 27, 2021; https://indianexpress.com/article/india/eci-responsible-
for-spreading-covid-19-says-madras-hc-7289824/

34   Menon Shruti and Goodman Jack, India Covid crisis: Did election rallies help

spread virus? Apr 29, 2021; https://www.bbc.com/news/56858980

35   Fatima Madeeha, Barton Naomi and Jafri Alishan, 100+ Instances of Hate Speech, Religious Polarisation, Hindutva Supremacy in Adityanath's Poll Speeches, Mar 3, 2022; https://thewire.in/communalism/100-instances-of-hate-speech-religious-polarisation-hindutva-supremacy-in-adityanaths-poll-speeches

36   Chishti Seema, Funding, the Election Commission, the Media—our electoral institutional framework needs scrutiny, Caravan, Mar 26, 2022; https://caravanmagazine.in/politics/funding-election-commission-media-electoral-framework-scrutiny

37   Ahuja Amit, Ostermann Susan, The Election Commission of India: Guardian of Democracy, Nov 13, 2020; https://link.springer.com/chapter/10.1007/978-3-030-51701-4_2

38   Mohanty P, Agenda for new government: A credible ECI, India Today, Jun 1, 2019; https://www.indiatoday.in/india/story/agenda-for-next-government-restoring-credibility-of-eci-1539929-2019-06-01

39   Anoop Baranwal vs Union of India, Supreme Court, Mar 2, 2023; https://main.sci.gov.in/supremecourt/2015/1458/1458_2015_3_1501_42634_Judgement_02-Mar-2023.pdf

40   The CEC and Other ECs (Appointment, Conditions of Service and Term of Office) Bill, 2023; https://prsindia.org/files/bills_acts/bills_parliament/2023/Bill_Text_Chief_Election_Commissioner_and_other_Election_Commissioners_Bill_2023.pdf

41   Congress complains to EC over 'suspicious black trunk' in PM Modi's helicopter, Apr 14,2019; https://indianexpress.com/elections/karnataka-congress-election-commission-suspicious-black-trunk-in-pm-modis-helicopter-5675081/; Suspension of Officer Who Inspected Modi's Chopper 'Questionable', Apr 18, 2019; https://thewire.in/government/ec-suspension-officer-modi-chopper-highly-questionable

42   'I Have Not Violated Any Rules', Says IAS Officer Suspended For Checking PM's Chopper, Apr 27, 2019; https://www.outlookindia.com/website/story/india-news-i-have-not-violated-any-rules-was-only-doing-my-duty-says-ias-officer-suspended-for-checking-pms-chopper/329405

43   Why I Searched Rajiv Gandhi's Aircraft in February 1985, May 2, 2019; https://thewire.in/politics/rajiv-gandhi-aircraft-al-banerjee-elections

44   Gupta Shobhit, Chhattisgarh CM asks Election Commission to check CRPF vehicles ahead of polls, Nov 2, 2023; https://www.hindustantimes.com/india-news/chhattisgarh-cm-asks-election-commission-to-check-crpf-vehicles-ahead-of-polls-101698907714256.html

45   Das Sabyasachi, Democratic Backsliding in the World's Largest Democracy, SSRN, Jul 2023; https://papers.ssrn.com/sol3/papers.cfm?abstract_id=4512936

46   Author of Paper on Possible 'Manipulation' in 2019 Polls Quits Ashoka University, Aug 14, 2023; https://thewire.in/education/author-of-paper-on-possible-manipulation-in-2019-polls-quits-ashoka-university

47   IB Team at Ashoka University Asked if Paper on 'Democratic Backsliding' Was a Solo Effort: Reports, Aug 23, 2023; https://thewire.in/education/ib-team-at-ashoka-university-asked-if-paper-on-democratic-backsliding-was-a-solo-effort-reports

48   4 yrs since LS polls, EC yet to give details of any discrepancy between EVM, VVPAT count, Jul 29, 2023; https://indianexpress.com/article/india/4-yrs-since-ls-polls-ec-yet-to-give-details-of-any-discrepancy-between-evm-vvpat-count-8865739/

49   Agarwal Poonam, EVM Vote Count Mismatch In 370+ Seats and EC Refuses to Explain, May 31, 2019; https://www.thequint.com/news/india/lok-sabha-election-results-2019-mismatch-in-votes-polled-and-counted-in-evm-on-multiple-seats#read-more

50   Whereabouts of 19 Lakh EVMs Not Known, Reveals RTI-Based Court Case, May 22, 2019; https://thewire.in/government/evm-missing-rti-court-case-frontline

51   Criminal-free Parliament top priority, says Modi, Apr 22, 2014; https://indianexpress.com/article/india/politics/criminal-free-parliament-top-priority-says-modi/

52   Modi's Report Card, Apr 17, 2019; https://graphics.reuters.com/INDIA-ELECTION-PROMISES/010091DR1ZR/index.html

53   India's supreme court says 'criminal' politicians should not be in government, Aug 27, 2014, https://amp.theguardian.com/world/2014/aug/27/india-supreme-court-criminal-politicians-government-ban

54   Modi's cabinet reshuffle: From Rajasthan, a Jat for a Jat, and SC for an SC balancing act, Aug 20, 2018; https://indianexpress.com/article/opinion/web-edits/modis-cabinet-expansion-from-rajasthan-a-jat-for-a-jat-and-sc-for-an-sc-balancing-act-2894929/

55   Analysis of Criminal, Financial, and Other background details of Union Council of Ministers Post Cabinet Expansion on 7th July, 2021; https://adrindia.org/content/17th-lok-sabha-analysis-criminal-financial-and-other-background-details-union-council & 17th Lok Sabha: Analysis of Criminal, Financial, and Other background details of Union Council of Ministers, May 31, 2019; https://adrindia.org/content/17-th-lok-sabha-analysis-criminal-financial-and-other-background-details-union-council

56   Kaur Jatinder, Kashyap Sunil, Murder, witness intimidation, evading arrest: The many allegations against Ajay Mishra Teni, Caravan, Dec 14, 2021; https://caravanmagazine.in/crime/the-many-allegations-against-ajay-mishra-teni-lakhimpur-kheri

57   Lakhimpur Kheri: MoS Ajay Mishra meets Amit Shah; told to resume his routine duties, Oct 7, 2021; https://indianexpress.com/article/cities/lucknow/lakhimpur-

kheri-ajay-mishra-amit-shah-meeting-7555495/

58   Lakhimpur Kheri: MoS Ajay Mishra meets Amit Shah; told to resume his routine duties, Oct 7, 2021; https://indianexpress.com/article/cities/lucknow/lakhimpur-kheri-ajay-mishra-amit-shah-meeting-7555495/

59   Brajesh Singh vs Sunil Arora and others, Contempt Petition, Supreme Court judgement, Aug 10, 2021; https://main.sci.gov.in/supremecourt/2020/24482/24482_2020_32_1502_29152_Judgement_10-Aug-2021.pdf

60   4,442 cases against MPs & MLAs still pending in courts across India, oldest dates back to 1983, Sept 10, 2020; https://theprint.in/judiciary/4442-cases-against-mps-mlas-still-pending-in-courts-across-india-oldest-dates-back-to-1983/500075/

61   SC asks Centre, states to set up more special courts to expedite trials against MPs and MLAs, Aug 27, 2021; https://theprint.in/judiciary/sc-asks-centre-states-to-set-up-more-special-courts-to-expedite-trials-against-mps-and-mlas/722878/

62   G Ananthakrishnan, Need benches for quick trial against MPs and MLAs, says Supreme Court, Nov 10, 2023; https://indianexpress.com/article/india/supreme-court-directs-high-courts-to-monitor-trials-against-mps-mlas-facing-criminal-cases-9019973/

63   Rambabu Singh Thakur vs Sunil Arora, Contempt petition of 2018, Supreme Court, February 13, 2020; https://main.sci.gov.in/supremecourt/2018/44369/44369_2018_4_1501_20493_Judgement_13-Feb-2020.pdf

64   Analysis of Format C7 - Publication of Reasons Given for Selection of Candidates with Criminal Cases by Political Parties, Jul 20, 2022; https://adrindia.org/sites/default/files/Analysis_of_FormatC7_Publication_of_Reasons_Given_for_Selection_of_Candidates_with_Criminal_Cases_by_Political_Parties_State_Assembly_Election_2022_Eng.pdf

65   Analysis of Sitting MPs from Lok Sabha and Rajya Sabha of India 2023, ADR, Sept 12, 2023; Analysis_of_Criminal_Background_Financial_Education_Gender_and_other_details_of_Sitting_MPs_2023_Final_Ver_English.pdf

66   Analysis of Sitting MPs/MLAs with Declared Cases Related to Hate Speech, ADR, Oct 3, 2023; https://adrindia.org/content/analysis-sitting-mpsmlas-declared-cases-related-hate-speech

67   Oommen Paul, 101 cases, just 1 conviction: How BJP's Raja Singh keeps getting away, Sept 22, 2022; https://www.thenewsminute.com/premium/101-cases-just-1-conviction-how-bjps-raja-singh-keeps-getting-away-168160

68   Sukh Ram, who once helped Dhumal form government, is no stranger to BJP, Oct 16, 2017; https://theprint.in/politics/snubbed-by-congress-sukh-rams-son-joins-bjp-in-poll-bound-himachal/12621/

69   ED will not come after me as I am BJP MP: Sanjay Patil, Oct 25, 2021; https://economictimes.indiatimes.com/news/politics-and-nation/ed-will-not-come-after-me-as-i-am-bjp-mp-sanjay-patil/articleshow/87249152.cms?utm_

source=contentofinterest&utm_medium=text&utm_campaign=cppst

70   BJP has washing powder from Gujarat to wash Opposition leaders before induction: Union minister Raosaheb Danve, Aug 30, 2019; https://www.indiatoday.in/india/story/raosaheb-danve-bjp-washing-powder-gujarat-opposition-leaders-incoming-1593409-2019-08-30

71   Salient features of Ordinance on Electoral Reforms, Ministry of Law and Justice, Aug 26, 2002; https://archive.pib.gov.in/archive/releases98/lyr2002/raug2002/26082002/r260820022.html

72   PUCL and others vs Union of India, Writ petition, Supreme Court, Mar 13, 2003; https://adrindia.org/sites/default/files/Supreme_Court's_judgement_13th_March_2003.pdf

73   Lily Thomas vs Union of India & Ors, Supreme Court, July 10, 2013; https://indiankanoon.org/doc/63158859/ e

74   The Representation of People Act of 1951; https://www.indiacode.nic.in/bitstream/123456789/2096/1/A1951-43.pdf

75   Jailed in fodder scam, Lalu Prasad Yadav disqualified from Lok Sabha, Oct 22, 2013; https://indianexpress.com/article/political-pulse/jailed-in-fodder-scam-lalu-prasad-yadav-disqualified-from-lok-sabha/

76   Rahul Gandhi trashes ordinance, shames government, Sept 28, 2013; https://timesofindia.indiatimes.com/india/rahul-gandhi-trashes-ordinance-shames-government/articleshow/23180950.cms

77   Application filed by Shri Prem Singh Tamang under Section 11 of the RP Act of 1951, Election Commission of India Sept 29, 2019; https://www.dropbox.com/s/m4puyk8llwqx8wf/EC_Tamang%20diswualification_2019.pdf?dl=0

78   Pisharoty Sangeeta Barooah, Total Recall: How Modi Government and Election Commission Provided Safety Net for Convicted Ally, Mar 26, 2023; https://thewire.in/politics/sikkim-golay-disqualification-rahul-gandhi

79   How the Modi Govt's Betrayal of a Key Vajpayee-Era Reform Helps Sikkim's New CM, Jun 7, 2019; https://thewire.in/law/sikkim-prem-singh-tamang-corruption

80   The repealing and amending Act, 2015, Ministry of Law and Justice, May 13, 2015; https://prsindia.org/files/bills_acts/acts_parliament/2015/the-repealing-and-amending-act,-2015.pdf

81   The RP (Amendment) Act, 2002, No. 9 of 2003, Jan 7, 2003; https://www.indiacode.nic.in/repealed-act/repealed_act_documents/A2003-9.pdf

82   Mody Anjali, Opinion: Pragya Thakur's candidacy is only one more building block in the BJP's Hindu rashtra, Scroll, Apr 24, 2019; https://scroll.in/article/921072/opinion-pragya-thakurs-candidacy-reaffirms-bjps-goal-to-turn-india-into-a-violent-hindu-rashtra

83   Kannaiah Venkatesh, Yeddyurappa: The man who never takes it easy, Jul 26, 2019;

https://indianexpress.com/article/opinion/karnataka-yeddyurappa-the-man-who-never-takes-it-easy-5850415/

84   How does Adityanath withdrawing criminal case against himself not count as 'jungle raj'? Dec 27, 2017; https://scroll.in/article/862892/how-does-adityanath-withdrawing-criminal-case-against-himself-not-count-as-jungle-raj

85   States cannot withdraw cases against MPs, MLAs without HC nod: SC, Aug 11, 2021;   https://www.hindustantimes.com/india-news/states-cannot-withdraw-cases-against-mps-mlas-without-hcnodsc-101628582060399.html

86   States cannot withdraw cases against MPs, MLAs without HC nod: SC, Aug 11, 2021;   https://www.hindustantimes.com/india-news/states-cannot-withdraw-cases-against-mps-mlas-without-hcnodsc-101628582060399.html

87   Mohanty P, Solution without Problem, Governance Now, May 2011; https://www.dropbox.com/s/i1k65rv0mg1y5d3/Solution%20without%20a%20problem.pdf?dl=0

88   Analysis of Assets Comparison of Re-Contesting MPs in the 2019 Lok Sabha Elections, Association for Democratic Reforms, May 13, 2019; https://adrindia.org/sites/default/files/Analysis_of_asset_comparison_of_Re-Contesting_MPs_in_Lok_Sabha_2019_elections_English.pdf; Analysis of Criminal and Financial Details of MPs of 15th Lok Sabha (2009), 2009; http://adrindia.org/files/High%20level%20criminal,%20financial%20&%20educational%20analysis%20LS%202009.pdf

89   Supreme Court cracks whip on 'rich' MPs, MLAs, orders constant monitoring of assets, Feb 17, 2018; https://www.indiatoday.in/mail-today/story/supreme-court-cracks-whip-on-rich-mps-mlas-orders-constant-monitoring-of-assets-1171502-2018-02-17

90   Election Commission view sought on ways to monitor lawmakers' assets, Dec 4, 2019; https://economictimes.indiatimes.com/news/politics-and-nation/election-commission-view-sought-on-ways-to-monitor-lawmakers-assets/articleshow/72357927.cms?from=mdr

91   Analysis of Sitting MPs from Lok Sabha and Rajya Sabha of India 2023, ADR, Sept 12, 2023; Analysis_of_Criminal_Background_Financial_Education_Gender_and_other_details_of_Sitting_MPs_2023_Final_Ver_English.pdf

92   Mohanty P, General Elections 2019: Who is funding the electioneering of our political parties? Part I, India Today, Mar 15, 2019; https://www.dailyo.in/politics/lok-sabha-elections-2019-party-funding-electoral-bonds-national-parties/story/1/29910.html

93   Electoral bonds: PM Modi says some people have problems with 'anything done to ensure transparency', Nov 26, 2019; https://scroll.in/latest/945012/electoral-bonds-pm-modi-says-some-people-have-problems-with-anything-done-to-ensure-transparency

94   Why Electoral Bonds are Necessary, Ministry of Finance, Jan 7, 2018; https://pib. gov.in/newsite/PrintRelease.aspx?relid=175452

95   Mohanty P, 'Who is funding'

96   Sethi Nitin, Electoral Bonds: Seeking Secretive Funds, Modi Govt Overruled RBI, Nov 17, 2019; https://www.huffpost.com/archive/in/entry/ rbi-warned-electoral-bonds-arun-jaitley-black-money-modi-government_ in_5dcbde68e4b0d43931ccd200?utm_hp_ref=in-paisapolitics

97   Siddhartha, Hasmukh Adhia: The man who changed the way we do business, Dec 31, 2017; https://economictimes.indiatimes.com/news/economy/policy/hasmukh- adhia-the-man-who-changed-the-way-we-do-business/articleshow/62314012.cms

98   Sethi Nitin, 'Electoral Bonds: Seeking Secretive Funds'

99   Electoral Bonds and opacity in political funding, Jun 5, 2023; https://adrindia. org/sites/default/files/Updated_Background%20Note_Electoral%20Bonds_ April_2023.pdf

100   Joy Shemin, Rs 1,148 cr worth of electoral bonds sold in latest round, Oct 31, 2023; https://www.deccanherald.com/india/rs-1148-cr-worth-of-electoral-bonds-sold- in-latest-round-2750591

101   Sarkar Gaurav, India just spent nearly Rs 60,000 crore on its election—but does this augur well for democracy?, Jun 4, 2019; https://www.newslaundry.com/2019/06/04/ india-just-spent-nearly-rs-60000-crore-on-its-election-but-does-it-augur-well-for- democracy

102   Taxpayers, Not Donors or Parties, Are Bearing the Cost of Printing Electoral Bonds: RTI, May 14, 2020; https://thewire.in/rights/electoral-bonds-tax-payers-cost- printing-bank-commission

103   Former Election Commissioner Ashok Lavasa on electoral bonds: Democracy, paid for in darkness, Nov 14, 2023; https://indianexpress.com/article/opinion/columns/ former-election-commissioner-ashok-lavasa-on-electoral-bonds-democracy-paid- for-in-darkness-9025492/

104   Analysis of Sources of Funding of National Parties, Mar 11, 2023; https://adrindia. org/content/analysis-sources-funding-national-parties-india-fy-2021-22

105   Sebastian Sheryl, Citizens Don't Have Right To Know Source Of Political Parties' Funds : Attorney General Tells Supreme Court In Electoral Bonds Case, Oct 30, 2023; https://www.livelaw.in/top-stories/citizens-dont-have-right-to-information- regarding-funding-of-a-political-party-centre-tells-supreme-court-in-electoral- bonds-case-241137

106   Vishwanath Apurva, Poll bonds anonymous since Govt protecting the citizen's right to privacy, SG tells SC, Nov 1, 2023; https://indianexpress.com/article/india/ poll-bonds-anonymous-since-govt-protecting-the-citizens-right-to-privacy-sg- tells-sc-9008256/

107   G Anathakrishnan, Slightly difficult to accept voter has no right to know source of funding: SC to Govt on electoral bonds, Nov 3, 2023; https://indianexpress.com/article/india/supreme-court-govt-electoral-bonds-9011003/

108   Supreme Court reserves verdict in the challenge to the electoral bonds scheme, Nov 2, 2023; https://www.thehindu.com/news/national/electoral-bonds-case-live-updates-from-supreme-court-on-day-3-november-2-2023/article67487720.ece

109   Right to Privacy not a fundamental right, cannot be invoked to scrap Aadhar: Centre tells Supreme Court, PTI, Jul 23, 2015; https://economictimes.indiatimes.com/news/politics-and-nation/right-to-privacy-not-a-fundamental-right-cannot-be-invoked-to-scrap-aadhar-centre-tells-supreme-court/articleshow/48178526.cms?utm_source=contentofinterest&utm_medium=text&utm_campaign=cppst

110   Anand Utkarsh, Privacy Neither Only About Aadhaar Nor an Elitist Concept: SC to Govt, Jul 26, 2017; https://www.news18.com/news/india/privacy-neither-only-about-aadhaar-nor-an-elitist-concept-sc-to-govt-1474013.html

111   Chaturvedi Aparna, Aadhaar Case: Right Over Your Body Not Absolute, Government Argues In Supreme Court, May 3, 2017; https://www.bqprime.com/law-and-policy/2017/05/02/aadhaar-case-right-over-your-body-not-absolute-government-argues-in-supreme-court

112   Modi Govt Makes U-Turn on Right to Privacy, IT Minister Calls AG's Statement 'Court Banter', Aug 24, 2017; https://thewire.in/law/right-to-privacy-narendra-modi-supreme-court

113   Mohanty P, Draft Data Protection Bill: Free pass to breach privacy, Nov 24, 2022; https://www.fortuneindia.com/opinion/draft-data-protection-bill-free-pass-to-breach-privacy/110505; Bhalla Vineet, How Modi government is using data privacy as an excuse to cripple the Right to Information, Aug 2, 2023; https://scroll.in/article/1053514/how-modi-government-is-using-privacy-as-an-excuse-to-cripple-the-right-to-information

114   Srivastava Mehul and Wiggins Kaye, India hunts for spyware that rivals controversial Pegasus system, Mar 30, 2023; https://www.ft.com/content/7674d7b7-8b9b-4c15-9047-a6a495c6b9c9

115   Lele Sourabh, Govt orders 'technical' probe as Opposition cites iPhone hacking alert, Oct 31, 2023; https://www.business-standard.com/india-news/government-launches-investigation-into-apple-s-snooping-attempt-alert-123103101112_1.html

116   Varadarajan Siddharth, Modi Government in Damage Control Mode As Apple Spyware Alert Revives Ghost of Pegasus, Nov 1, 2023; https://thewire.in/rights/modi-government-in-damage-control-mode-as-apple-spyware-alert-revives-ghost-of-pegasus

117   Electoral Reforms, Report 255, Law Commission of India, Mar 2015; https://lawcommissionofindia.nic.in/reports/report255.pdf

118   Big spenders: Election expenses cross Rs 6,500 crore, shows data, Dec 26, 2021;

https://www.business-standard.com/article/politics/big-spenders-election-expenses-cross-rs-6-500-crore-shows-data-121122600912_1.html

119   Analysis of Assets & Liabilities of National Parties for FY 2020-21 And 2021-22, Sept 4, 2023; https://adrindia.org/content/analysis-assets-liabilities-national-parties-fy-2020-21-and-2021-22

120   ADR vs Union of India, Delhi High Court, Mar 28, 2014; http://adrindia.org/sites/default/files/ADR%20vs.%20UOI%20%28Delhi%20High%20Court%20judgment%20on%20foreign%20%20funding%20received%20by%20INC%20and%20BJP%29.pdf

121   Mohanty P, General Elections 2019: Who is funding the electioneering of our political parties? Part II, DailyO, India Today Group, Mar 15, 2019; https://www.dailyo.in/politics/lok-sabha-elections-2019-party-funding-fcra-national-parties-general-elections-2019-political-funding-black-money/story/1/29913.html

122   Quraishi SY, Summoning CEC, EC to PMO is outrageous, Indian Express, Dec 18, 2021; https://indianexpress.com/article/opinion/columns/summoning-cec-ec-to-pmo-is-outrageous-7678391/

123   Electoral reform bill to link Aadhaar, Voter ID gets Rajya Sabha approval, Dec 21, 2021; https://www.hindustantimes.com/india-news/electoral-reform-bill-to-link-aadhaar-voter-id-gets-rajya-sabha-approval-101640082124479.html

124   Sambhav Kumar, Govt Has Cleared Linking Of Aadhaar & Voter Data. Past Experience Reveals How It Can Be Manipulated, Dec 27, 2021; https://article-14.com/post/govt-has-cleared-linking-of-aadhaar-voter-data-past-experience-reveals-how-it-can-be-manipulated-61c937a621c09

125   Audit report on 'functioning of Unique Authentication Authority of India'; Comptroller and Auditor General of India, Apr 6, 2022; https://cag.gov.in/uploads/PressRelease/PR-UIDAI-report-no-24-of-2021-in-English-0624d89a0e200e2-55589718.pdf

126   Not must to link Aadhaar with voter list, EC tells Supreme Court, Sept 22. 2023; https://indianexpress.com/article/india/clarificatory-changes-linking-aadhaar-voter-id-optional-ec-sc-8950543/

127   Mohanty P, Who is afraid of transparency in the functioning of our political parties? DailyO, India Today Group, Apr 13, 2019; https://www.dailyo.in/election/controversies/electoral-bonds-supreme-court-rti-lok-sabha-elections-2019-election-commission-rti-general-elections-2019/story/1/30307.html

128   Read gov't affidavit to SC: Political parties are really better off outside RTI, Aug 25, 2015; https://www.legallyindia.com/the-bench-and-the-bar/read-gov-t-affidavit-to-sc-political-parties-are-really-better-off-outside-rti-20150824-6481

129   'Electoral Malfeasance, Corruption and Unfair Practices: A Concern For India's Election Integrity, Chapter 6, page 95-132, International Journal of Transparency and Accountability in Governance (IJTAG) 2021-22, CTAG, National Law

University Delhi; https://adrindia.org/sites/default/files/International_journal_of_ transparency_accountability_and_governance_2021-22_compressed.pdf

130 All pro-poor initiatives including demonetisation led to victory in UP: Ravi Shankar Prasad, Mar11, 2017; https://economictimes.indiatimes.com/markets/ expert-view/up-election-result-all-pro-poor-initiatives-including-demonetisation-led-to-victory-ravi-shankar-prasad/articleshow/57592758.cms?utm_ source=contentofinterest&utm_medium=text&utm_campaign=cppst

131 Bihar elections: Modi's Covid-19 lockdown battered Indians – so why are they still voting BJP? Nov 11, 2020; https://scroll.in/article/978214/bihar-elections-modis-covid-19-lockdown-battered-indians-so-why-are-they-still-voting-bjp

132 Mohanty P, Modi's welfare offers: Extreme poverty led people to condone govt failures during polls, Centre for Financial Accountability, Apr 2, 2022; https:// www.cenfa.org/modis-welfare-offers-extreme-poverty-led-people-to-condone-govt-failures-during-polls/

133 Roy Prannoy, Sopariwala Dorab R, The Verdict: Decoding India's Elections, Penguin Ransom House, 2019; https://www.amazon.in/Verdict-Decoding-Indias-Elections/dp/0670092266

134 Chhokar Jagdeep S, Simultaneous Election: Striking at the Roots of Parliamentary Democracy, Issue Brief No. 8, The Hindu Centre for Politics and Public Policy and ADR, Apr 25, 2018; https://www.thehinducentre.com/publications/article23669303. ece/BINARY/Issue%20Brief%20No.8.pdf

135 P Chidambaram writes: Different states, Different strokes, Nov 19, 2023; https:// indianexpress.com/article/opinion/columns/p-chidambaram-assembly-elections-2023-modi-bjp-9032625/

136 In Madhya Pradesh rally, PM Modi assures people of 'Modi guarantee', PTI, Nov 13, 2023; https://economictimes.indiatimes.com/news/elections/assembly-elections/madhya-pradesh-assembly-elections/in-madhya-pradesh-rally-pm-modi-assures-people-of-modi-guarantee/articleshow/105189022.cms

137 Mukka Vikram, The Cost to the Nation of a Perpetually Campaigning Prime Minister, May 9, 2023; https://m.thewire.in/article/government/narendra-modi-inauguration-campaign-karnataka-election?utm_source=substack&utm_ medium=email; Lalwani Vijayta and Subramanian Nithya, Modi keeps combining official travel with BJP events, but who is paying the bills?, Feb 12, 2019; https:// scroll.in/article/912885/modi-keeps-combining-official-travel-with-bjp-events-but-who-is-paying-the-bills; Tewari Ruhi, How PM Modi transforms into campaigner Modi as he mixes official trips with politics, Feb 13, 2019; https://theprint.in/ politics/how-pm-modi-transforms-into-campaigner-modi-as-he-mixes-official-trips-with-politics/; Khan Hamza, Rajasthan Vande Bharat: PM Modi takes dig at him, past govts; Gehlot hits back, Apr 13, 2023; https://indianexpress.com/article/ india/pm-modi-swipe-ashok-gehlot-sachin-pilot-8552279/

138 Mohan J Anand, In MP, Modi links Opp to terror bosses, enemies, Oct 6, 2023;

https://indianexpress.com/article/india/in-mp-modi-links-opp-to-terror-bosses-enemies-8970478/; Khan Hamza, 'Ram Navami to Hanuman Jayanti — all festivals face stone pelting in Rajasthan': Modi, Oct 5, 2023; https://indianexpress.com/article/india/riots-red-diary-gang-wars-vaccine-war-modi-sharpens-attack-on-gehlot-govt-8970249/

139   Railways spent Rs 2.6 crore to arrange PM Modi events in Chennai, Thiruvananthapuram to flag off two Vande Bharat trains, Jul 12, 2023; https://timesofindia.indiatimes.com/city/chennai/railways-spent-rs-2-6-crore-to-arrange-pm-modi-events-in-chennai-thiruvananthapuram-to-flag-off-two-vande-bharat-trains/articleshow/101692374.cms?from=mdr

140   One-day message to the nation by PM cost Rs8.3 crore: RTI, Sept 13, 2015; https://www.dnaindia.com/mumbai/report-one-day-message-to-the-nation-by-pm-cost-rs83-crore-rti-2124666

141   Vadlapatla S, PM Narendra Modi launches projects worth Rs 13,500 crore in poll-bound Telangana, Oct 2, 2023; https://timesofindia.indiatimes.com/city/hyderabad/pm-modi-launches-projects-worth-13500-crore-in-poll-bound-telangana/articleshow/104092778.cms?from=mdr

142   Choudhury Shubhadeep, PM Modi launches Rs 10,863 cr projects in poll-bound Karnataka, Jan 19, 2023; https://www.tribuneindia.com/news/nation/pm-modi-launches-10-863-cr-projects-in-poll-bound-ktaka-471941

143   Srivastava Samarth, PM Modi launches projects worth Rs 3,200 crore in UP's Mahoba, Nov 19, 2021; https://www.indiatoday.in/elections/uttar-pradesh-assembly-polls-2022/story/up-elections-2022-narendra-modi-bundelkhand-mahoba-projects-worth-rs-3200-crore-1878691-2021-11-19; Shah Pankaj, PM Modi launches 80k crore projects at Uttar Pradesh investors' meet, Jun 4, 2022; PM Modi launches 80k crore projects at Uttar Pradesh investors' meet

144   PM Modi to pay three-day visit to Gujarat tomorrow; To launch several development projects worth over 14 thousand crore rupees, Oct 8, 2022; https://newsonair.gov.in/News?title=Gujarat-%3A-PM-Modi-to-inaugurate-%26-lay-foundation-stone-of-development-projects-of-over-3-thousand-crore-rupees-at-Mahesana&id=4490-38

145   Analysis of Re-contesting MPs and MLAs Who Changed Parties-Pan-India Since 2016, Association for Democratic Reforms, Mar 11, 2021; https://adrindia.org/content/analysis-re-contesting-mps-and-mlas-who-changed-parties-pan-india-2016

146   Kailash KK, Triumph of the Political Party in Public Office, India Forum, Nov 21, 2022; https://www.theindiaforum.in/politics/triumph-political-party-public-office

147   Naidu Jayprakash S, PM Modi hits back at Rahul Gandhi demand for caste census: 'Does Congress want to take away rights of minorities?', Oct 3, 2023; https://indianexpress.com/elections/congress-rights-abadi-muslim-minority-voters-chhattisgarh-speech-8966622/; Mohan J Anand, In MP, Modi links Opp to

terror bosses, enemies, Oct 6, 2023; https://indianexpress.com/article/india/in-mp-modi-links-opp-to-terror-bosses-enemies-8970478/; Khan Hamza, 'Ram Navami to Hanuman Jayanti — all festivals face stone pelting in Rajasthan': Modi, Oct 5, 2023; https://indianexpress.com/article/india/riots-red-diary-gang-wars-vaccine-war-modi-sharpens-attack-on-gehlot-govt-8970249/

148   Exclusive: BJP's 'Congress-mukt Bharat' slogan poisoned govt-Opposition ties, says P Chidambaram, Feb 10, 2017; https://www.firstpost.com/politics/exclusive-bjps-congress-mukt-bharat-slogan-poisoned-govt-opposition-ties-says-p-chidambaram-3275658.html

149   Mahaprashasta Ajoy Ashirwad, Leaked Snoop List Suggests Surveillance May Have Played Role in Toppling of Karnataka Govt in 2019, Jul 20, 2021; https://thewire.in/politics/karnataka-government-toppling-pegasus-spyware-surveillance

150   Rakesh Asthana, Sushil Modi and PMO Worked Together to Book Lalu: CBI Director, Nov 18, 2018; https://thewire.in/government/lalu-prasad-cbi-rakesh-asthana-alok-verma

151   Kirchgaessner Stephanie, Ganguly Manisha, Pegg David, Cadwalladr Carole and Burke Jason, Revealed: the hacking and disinformation team meddling in elections, Feb 15, 2023; https://www.theguardian.com/world/2023/feb/15/revealed-disinformation-team-jorge-claim-meddling-elections-tal-hanan

152   Manor James, Narendra Modi's Power and Cult Endanger the BJP, The Wire, Sept 3, 2021; https://thewire.in/politics/narendra-modis-power-and-cult-endanger-the-bjp

153   India's Modi has a strategy for dealing with controversies: Silence, Nov 18, 2018; https://www.washingtonpost.com/world/asia_pacific/indias-modi-has-a-strategy-for-dealing-with-controversies-silence/2018/11/27/ce7f6946-ed02-11e8-8b47-bd0975fd6199_story.html

154   Mohan Deepanshu, The Pandemic Has Yet Again Exposed Modi's Insidious Politics of 'Narrative Control', OP Jindal University, Apr 30, 2021; http://dspace.jgu.edu.in:8080/jspui/bitstream/10739/4884/1/The%20Pandemic%20Has%20Yet%20Again%20Exposed%20.pdf

155   Say 'Jai Bajrangbali' while casting vote, PM says in Karnataka; Cong defends stand on Bajrang Dal, PTI, May 4, 2023; https://www.hindustantimes.com/cities/bengaluru-news/say-jai-bajrangbali-while-casting-vote-pm-says-in-karnataka-cong-defends-stand-on-bajrang-dal-101683175731433.html

156   EC seeks proof from Cong for graft claims against BJP; Cong asks what about our complaints, May 7, 2023; https://indianexpress.com/elections/ec-asks-congress-for-empirical-evidence-for-corruption-rate-card-on-karnataka-bjp-8595497/

157   Shastri Sandeep, How the BJP lost Karnataka: Lacklustre leadership, corruption and dependence on Centre, May 13, 2023; https://indianexpress.com/article/opinion/bjp-lost-karnataka-leadership-corruption-dependence-centre-8607646/

158 Pandey Geeta, Why does Indian PM Narendra Modi follow trolls on Twitter? Oct 10, 2017; https://www.bbc.com/news/world-asia-india-41549756

159 Daniyal Shoaib, The age of trolls: What the BJP's new spokesperson signifies for Indian politics, May 17, 2017; https://scroll.in/article/832012/the-age-of-trolls-what-the-bjps-new-spokesperson-signifies-for-indian-politics

160 Jawed Sam, Hall of shame – Serial abusers, sexist bigots, rumour mongers followed by PM Modi on Twitter, Sept 7, 2017; https://www.altnews.in/hall-shame-serial-abusers-sexist-bigots-rumour-mongers-followed-pm-modi-twitter/

161 Chaudhuri Pooja, Amit Malviya's fake news fountain: 16 pieces of misinformation spread by the BJP IT cell chief, Feb 10, 2020; https://scroll.in/article/952731/amit-malviyas-fake-news-fountain-16-pieces-of-misinformation-spread-by-the-bjp-it-cell-chief; Yadav Jyoti, Indians are fighting against coronavirus and BJP IT cell is fighting against Indians, Apr 4, 2020; https://theprint.in/opinion/pov/indians-are-fighting-against-coronavirus-and-bjp-it-cell-is-fighting-against-indians/395058/

162 BJP under Modi went too far right, centrist politics needed: Prodyut Bora, BJP IT cell founder, Aug 25, 2020; https://caravanmagazine.in/interview/prodyut-bora-bjp-it-cell-rss-narendra-modi-amit-shah-vajpayee-right-wing

163 We Can Make Any Message We Want Go Viral, Real or Fake: Amit Shah, Sept 27, 2018; https://www.thequint.com/news/politics/amit-shah-real-fake-can-make-messages-viral

164 Goel Vindu and Gettleman Jeffrey, Under Modi, India's Press Is Not So Free Anymore; Apr 3, 2020; https://www.nytimes.com/2020/04/02/world/asia/modi-india-press-media.html; Baru Sanjaya, Narendra Modi used India's media elite for his own advantage, Apr 21, 2021; https://scroll.in/article/992808/narendra-modi-used-indias-media-elite-for-his-own-advantage-sanjaya-baru-explains-how-he-did-it

165 Verma Rahul, Sardesai Shreyas, Does Media Exposure Affect Voting Behaviour and Political Preferences in India? Economic and Political Weekly, Sept 27, 2014; https://www.lokniti.org/media/upload_files/Does%20Media%20Exposure%20Affect%20Voting%20Behaviour%20and%20Political%20Preferences%20in%20India.pdfie

166 Barman Sourav Roy, G Ananthakrishnan, Parties run by families are against the spirit of Constitution, biggest threat to democracy: PM, Nov 27, 2021; https://indianexpress.com/article/india/constitution-day-pm-modi-address-parliament-opposition-protest-congress-tmc-7642316/

167 BJP says it doesn't believe in dynastic politics, but its list of dynast leaders is ever-growing, Aug 2, 2021; https://theprint.in/politics/bjp-says-it-doesnt-believe-in-dynastic-politics-but-its-list-of-dynast-leaders-is-ever-growing/706764/

168 Joshi Kamal, JDS & Congress One, Parivarvadi And Corrupt: PM Modi Stings Kumaraswamy In His Home Turf, Apr 30, 2023; https://www.republicworld.com/elections/karnataka/jds-and-congress-one-parivarvadi-and-corrupt-pm-modi-stings-kumaraswamy-in-his-home-turf-articleshow.html

169   Ajit Pawar joins Shinde-Fadnavis Govt: From Chagan Bhujbal to Dilip Walse Patel - These NCP leaders 'defected' with him, Jul 2, 2023; https://www.livemint.com/politics/news/ajit-pawar-joins-shinde-fadnavis-govt-from-chagan-bhujbal-to-dilip-walse-patel-these-ncp-leaders-defected-with-him-11688288598779.html

170   Mohanty P, Solution without Problem, Governance Now, May 2011; https://www.dropbox.com/s/i1k65rv0mg1y5d3/Solution%20without%20a%20problem.pdf?dl=0

171   Singh Ruchika, Intra-party Democracy and Indian Political Parties, The Hindu Centre for Politics & Public Policy, 2015; https://www.thehinducentre.com/migration_catalog/article22981929.ece/BINARY/Intra_Party_Democracy_Ruchika_Policy_Report

172   New BJP government in Madhya Pradesh to arrange Ayodhya visit for residents of state: Amit Shah, PTI, Nov 13, 2023; http://timesofindia.indiatimes.com/articleshow/105185858.cms?utm_source=contentofinterest&utm_medium=text&utm_campaign=cppst

Chapter XI

When Society Gives Free Pass

This chapter seeks (in sheer desperation, one may add) both to understand and explain the new-found "Bhakti" culture in India which has seemingly made a significant chunk of its citizens, particularly the educated, empowered and vocal middle class, abjure its responsibility to hold the Prime Minister of India, his government and party to account – even in the face of all-round governance failures *seriously damaging* the economic and social wellbeing of the masses and also *dismantle* very constitutional democracy. Government is a part of society and as a 2011 UN document explained[1], governance "is the way society organizes itself to make and implement decisions" and comprises of "the mechanisms and processes for citizens and groups to articulate their interests, mediate their differences and exercise their legal rights and obligations".

The ultimate responsibility for good governance and welfare of people, thus, rests with the very people. When a society chooses to give a free pass to government it is inviting disaster on itself. In the case of India, it is more shocking because Indians never shied away from criticizing their governments or exercise their veto during elections to punish governments that failed to deliver. What changed after 2014? This needs to be understood and answered to find a way out of the current morass.

'Voluntary Servitude'

The previous chapter talked about Harvard professors Levitsky and Ziblatt writing about democratic breakdowns in the post-Cold War phase caused by elected governments. Another political scientist John Keane[2] narrowed down the focus to the new millennium in his 2020 book "The New Despotism". In this, Keane describes the degradation of democracies in countries like India,

Turkey, Hungary, Vietnam, the US and others as "New Despotism", rather than "tyranny", "autocracy" or "authoritarianism". In this New Despotism, elected demagogues come to power "spinning webs of confusion, lies, and unhinged talk of conspiracies".

In Keane's telling, the New Despotic mainstream politics is plagued by "post-truth", curbs on media freedom and disrespect for expertise and public service institutions; bitter cultural clashes occur over racial and religious identity which frames public discourse in terms of "us" and "them", "delight in humiliating others" and the governmental power is "wholly unaccountable to citizens and their elected representatives". These are "pseudo-democratic" governments with "phantom democratic qualities" that mask and legitimize the despots' arbitrary power. A remarkable feature of this New Despotism, Keane writes, is "voluntary servitude" which he explains as *unquestioned loyalty of people* towards their despotic rulers and this "servitude is chosen" – people don't lose their liberty, the new despotic rulers "win their enslavement". Such rulers are not blindly reckless, however; they are "skilled in the art of meddling with people' lives, marshalling their support and winning their conformity"; they are "masters of deception and seduction" and the cleverest of them "act as if they are magicians".

Here the reference to magicians is very apt. But what exactly magicians do?

Magicians and the Art of Misdirection

The job of magicians is to *entertain* a captive audience for which they employ a tool called "misdirection". In their 1911 classic book "Our Magic"[3], British magicians Nevil Maskelyne and David Devant explained this art of misdirection: "It consists, admittedly, in misleading the spectator's senses, in order to screen from detection certain details for which secrecy is required. It *militates* against the spectator's faculties of observation, not against his understanding. Broadly, it may be said to comprise three general methods, viz. – *Distraction, Disguise, and Simulation.* Every means employed by magicians for misdirecting the senses of an audience will be found allied to one or other of those elementary principles." *(Emphasis added)*

They go on to explain the words distraction, disguise and simulation. *Distraction* is from whatever the magician wishes to conceal from the captive audience, a "red herring drawn across the scent". *Disguise* consists of skillful blending of suspicious and innocent details in a manner that the former is overlooked, that is, making "fakey" things look as though they were free from sophistication. *Simulation* is "a form of pretence", making one thing look like another and entirely different thing, thereby, giving apparent existence to things "that do not exist, or presence to things that are absent".

The world of magicians and the art of misdirection is vastly different from government and governance. While a magic show is for entertainment, governance is not. When this distinction disappears, tragedies happen, as India is witness to, since 2014. The economy is down, job crisis is chronic and growing, poverty, hunger and inequality are growing, everyday political and social life is filled with hate-and-violence, institutions have collapsed for all practical purposes and yet, the Prime Minister of India and his government are hugely popular, enjoy unquestioned loyalty and admiration of a sizable chunk of educated and empowered middle-class – a trait that Keane called "voluntary servitude". This is *unique to India*, economist Pranab Bardhan points out[4], in that unlike other developing and developed countries where support for right-wing autocratic governments comes from "among less-educated, older, and more rural workers" in India it is "also the case for more educated, aspirational urban youth" – as is evident in much of the support coming from major metropolitan areas of New Delhi, Mumbai and Bangalore. Bardhan explained that these groups are "mobilised by resentment for what they perceive to be a Western liberal elite".

Headline & Perception Management

Media is key to distraction, disguise and simulation – at the heart of "misdirection". Arun Shourie, former BJP minister in the Vajpayee government and a critic of the current regime, was the first to flag this.

In 2015, Shourie said, while countering the government's claims about high growth with facts and evidence, that "they (the government) are managing headlines". He would prove right as the economy went into a tailspin before the pandemic hit and then collapsed in 2020 – the GDP growth plunged to -6.6% in FY21 (revised upward to -5.8% later) against the global average of -3.1%. The headline management was very obvious in the three consecutive announcements (2019, 2020 and 2021[5]) by the Prime Minister of India in his national addresses about gigantic infrastructure plans – Rs 100 lakh crore (trillion) or more – to boost growth and create jobs at his national addresses. He variously described those as "modern infrastructure" in 2019, "National Infrastructure Pipeline Project" in 2020 and "Gati Shakti" (power of speed) in 2021. This was when the real GDP in FY21 was Rs 135.13 lakh crore (trillion)![6] Finally, when he unveiled the "Gati Shakti" in October 2021, there was no mention of Rs 100 lakh crore investment at all[7]; it turned out to be just a *digital platform*[8] to coordinate and facilitate infrastructure development projects between 16 central ministries. It was in mid-2022[9] that state governments were taken on board.

The same is true in other cases too. In 2016, Shourie[10] drew public attention again: "…something bad happens in Kashmir, something bad happens in Gujarat, such as the Dalits doing this Gandhian leaderless protest, withdrawing cooperation, what does the government do? You plant another story or stories. Everybody runs these because you have a *tutored media.* Next morning you are not concerned about Kashmir or Gujarat, you are congratulating yourself on your success in diverting the media's attention. It compounds the problem. It means that you will not pay attention to the fire that you have set. You don't think there is a disaster there, you are busy celebrating a success. *Your obsession is the media, not the situation." (Emphasis added)*

Headline management got a new name later: "Perception management".

Some media reports began qualifying the Prime Minister of India and his government's acts as "perception management" – claims like making India a $5 trillion economy, past governments did nothing for "70 years", Muslims spread the Covid-19 virus etc., events like holding month-long Kumbh melas and electioneering in West Bengal bang in the middle of the far more devastating second wave of the pandemic in 2021, both proving to be "super spreader" events as forewarned or even the cabinet reshuffle of 2021.[11] The shock-and-awe spectacles like the overnight demonetization, overnight national lockdown are also part of building perceptions (of a strong and decisive leader).

The phrase is apparently inspired by the statement attributed to Gustave Flaubert: "There is no truth. There is only perception". Public relation (PR) profession seeks strength and justification from this concept for what they do. It has a military origin too. A 2001 US military document defined[12]: "Actions to convey and/or deny selected information and indicators to foreign audiences to influence their emotions, motives, and objective reasoning as well as to intelligence systems and leaders at all levels to influence official estimates, ultimately resulting in foreign behaviors and official actions favorable to the originator's objectives. In various ways, perception management combines truth projection, operations security, cover and deception, and psychological operations." Brigadier BM Kapoor identified six key tools of it[13]: (i) atrocity accusations (ii) hyperbolic inflations (iii) demonization and/or dehumanization (iv) polarization (v) claim of divine sanction and (vi) meta propaganda.

All these words and phrases ring true in today's India.

When scores of people were dropping dead in the second wave of 2021 due to the shortage of hospital beds and oxygen, the government denied shortages[14] and then denied such deaths[15]. When states complained of vaccine shortages, the Prime Minister asked Chief Ministers to micromanage (which he had overridden in March 2020 by imposing 24x7 curfew and national lockdown) and hold "tika utsav" (vaccine festival).[16] On September 17, 2021, when India was panned for low vaccination, a big headline hit[17]: "India sets record with 2.5 crore (25 million) COVID-19 jabs in one day: A gift to the Prime Minister, says Health Minister Mandaviya".

The "gift" is a reference to the Prime Minister's birthday (September 17). This record vaccination was a dramatic rise over 6.7 million a day earlier and 8.8 million a day later. This record was organized as a personal gift from the Prime Minister (like Modi's 'namak'). The following image of the official vaccination website CoWIN[18] best captures it.

Image: Record vaccination on the Prime Minister's birthday

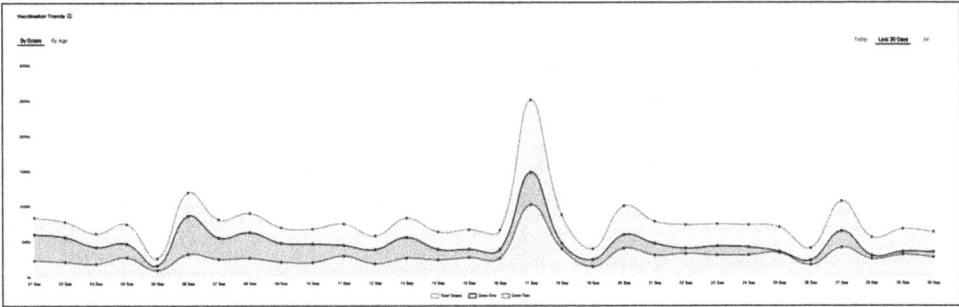

Source: CoWin dashboard

Perception management took such precedence that amidst the pandemic crisis, a prolonged Kumbh mela and electioneering, "bhoomi puja"[19] (ground breaking ceremony) for a grand temple in Ayodhya and several vanity projects like rebuilding the majestic Central Vista (by classifying it as "essential service" to bypass the lockdown restrictions) were staged to show that life was normal. The Central Vista's budget of Rs 20,000 crore could have built at least 40 major hospitals[20] which India desperately needed. The WHO said India lost 5.22 million lives in 2020 and 2021[21] to the pandemic.

Perception management is so systemic that bang in the middle of devastating pandemic in 2021, the government even organized a workshop to train its top 300 officers[22] to "create a positive image of the government", manage "perception through effectively highlighting positive stories and achievements", and ensure his government was "seen to be sensitive, bold, quick, responsive, hard-working etc." – called "Effective Communication".

It is also called "positivity" (positive spin in news reporting). Hours before the pandemic lockdown was declared in March 2020, the Prime Minister of India called owners and editors of several print and electronic media and asked them to publish positive stories and refrain from negative coverage; and they complied – an investigating report by the Caravan[23] revealed later. A Group of Ministers (GoM) too was set up to prepare strategies to "neutralize" journalists writing against the government and monitor "negative influencers"; it met *six times* during the pandemic lockdown of 2020 – another investigating report of Caravan[24] reveled. The actual pandemic management took a *back seat*[25] as the high deaths showed. And GoMs are never used for policymaking or governance.

During the pandemic calamity, the government was busy blaming it on Muslims and the Opposition. In the first wave, the Tablighi Jamaat, an Islamic organization which holds annual congregation in March in New Delhi every year *with government permission*, was blamed for spreading the pandemic. Their members were stuck in New Delhi due to the overnight 24x7 curfew and transport lockdown. Mainstream TV channels and right-wing troll armies worked incessantly, accusing the Jamaat members of deliberately spreading the infection through "Thook jihad"; the Jamaat members were arrested, jailed, mocked and harassed. Several high courts, including the Bombay High Court, severely reprimanded the Modi government, particularly the Ministry of Home Affairs (MHA) for a deliberate malicious campaign to target Muslims.[26] Since then, the right-wing trolls link virtually every calamity or accident to Muslims (Muslim angles and multiple fake jihad campaigns listed in Chapter IV).

More of the same followed during the far more devastating second wave in 2021 when scores were dropping dead every day due to lack of hospital beds and oxygen cylinders.[27] There was a twist too. More than a dozen senior BJP ministers and leaders got busy tweeting (Twitter is now rebranded as 'X') a manufactured toolkit named "Congress Toolkit"[28] (prepared using a forged Congress party's letterhead) to mount attacks on the Congress. These tweets accused the Congress of spreading negativity and hurting the national cause (of fighting the pandemic). The Twitter ('X') attracted raids[29] on its premises for calling these tweets "manipulated". A vernacular daily 'Dainik Bhaskar'[30] went through 1,110 tweets of 10 senior BJP ministers during May 1-14, 2021 – when thousands of desperate Indians were sending SOS for help to them and others on social media. It found *not one* tweet responded to the SOS messages, only one talked about Covid preparations and all tweets were devoted to *praising* the Prime Minister (who disappeared from public for a record *20 days*[31]) and his government's (non-existent) efforts to manage the pandemic. Dainik Bhaskar would soon pay a price for this (it was raided by the Income Tax department in July 2021[32]) for showing unaccounted deaths – numerous unidentified bodies floating in the Ganges in Uttar Pradesh and buried in its sand banks. This was worse than the Orwellian-Kafkaesque worlds.

The government had watched as millions of migrants marched on foot with family and luggage for their village homes hundreds of miles away during the pandemic lockdown in 2020 and hundreds perished on the way due to hunger, exhaustion and accidents. Many faced police brutality (for violating the 24x7 curfew). At the time, the newly appointed Chief of Defence Staff (CDS) and former Army chief General Bipin Rawat appeared on television with three service chiefs (a first in Indian history) to announce felicitating *health workers* with fly-pasts (showering rose petals from the sky) and band displays by mobilizing the Army, Air Force and Navy (to distract attention from the distress migration that no other country in the world witnessed).

It didn't occur to any of the worthies that dropping food packets and water bottles to help the hungry and exhausted migrants walking on foot for weeks or providing them transport would be a worthy cause.[33] At the time, China was denying India access to large swathes of territory in Ladakh (and later grabbed) – but not a word was said about it. Not just lack of humanitarian values and professionalism, this massive mobilization displayed gross incompetence and ineptitude in the basic task entrusted (to keep the border secure).[34] India had never witnessed such vanity projects – wasting time, energy and money.

And what happened to those who helped the migrants and poor during the pandemic? They faced raids and endless harassments from official agencies.

Income Tax officials raided film star Sonu Sood[35] after he arranged transports and finances for migrants in 2020 – which no BJP government, minister, leader or its "world's largest" political foot soldiers did (who display remarkable passion every single year in arranging food, camping sites for millions of "kanwarias" carrying 'Ganga jal' and shower rose petals on them from the sky with public money). Sood's credibility soared so high and that of the government and military establishment so low that during the second wave (May 2021) a senior Indian Army officer actually wrote to Sood for help in setting up a Covid hospital at the Jaisalmer military base – which, of course, attracted the Army's ire.[36]

The same fate befell to Rana Ayyub, investigating journalist and a critic of the government, who had worked tirelessly to provide relief to the poor and stranded for months during the pandemic. The ED and Tax officials raided her. This was after she was made to *pay Rs 1.05 crore* as income tax on the relief funds she had crowd sourced.[37] Youth Congress leader BV Srinivasan, who supplied oxygen cylinders and other assistance to ordinary patients and also to the embassies of New Zealand and Philippines during the second wave of the pandemic – to whom they turned to instead of the government – was questioned by the Delhi Police.[38] Delhi's DTC bus drivers faced 44 FIRs[39] for ferrying some of the migrants walking on foot on the orders of the Delhi government.

The farmers' agitation of 2021 saw more such perception management, along with strong arm treatments. The marching farmers (toward Delhi) were greeted with water cannons, baton charge, concertina wires, dug up roads, iron nails and sedition charges. The BJP and its supporters demonized and discredited them, calling them "Khalistanis", "terrorists" and "Pakistanis".[40] Central minister Ajay Mishra Teni's vehicle, allegedly driven by his son, mowed down peacefully marching farmers in Uttar Pradesh's Lakhimpur Kheri. Teni had threatened the farmers days earlier to withdraw their protests (see Chapter I).

When climate activists Greta Thunberg, singer Rihanna and US Vice President's niece Meena Harris tweeted supporting the farmers, the government and their supporters erupted in anger. Union Home Minister Amit Shah tweeted, "No propaganda can deter India's unity!".[41] Film and sports celebrities, like Lata Mangeshkar and Sachin Tendulkar (both awarded with the topmost civilian award, Bharat Ratna) were mobilized to tweet in protest.[42] They called the protests "internal matter" and cautioned that "India's sovereignty cannot be compromised". The Prime Minister of India dismissed the protesters as "andolanjibi" (professional protesters) influenced by "Foreign Destructive Ideology" from which India must protect itself.[43]

After more than a year of peaceful protests the Prime Minister apologized, and withdrew it (he never talked to them), in the usual double-speak: "With a true mind and a pure heart, I want to say that perhaps there was some *deficiency in our penance* because of which we were not able to explain to some of our farmer brothers a truth as clear as the light of an oil lamp."[44] *(Emphasis added)*

At that time, the crucial election in Uttar Pradesh was looming and the fear of BJP's defeat spread. By this time, *more than 700 farmers had lost their lives*, some committing suicide at the sit-in locations on Delhi's outskirts.[45] Just as the new farm laws had been brought without consultations with farmers and state governments (agriculture is a state subject and trade in farm produce is primarily state responsibility) and due diligence in the Parliament, it was withdrawn the same way. Then Meghalaya Governor Satya Pal Malik recalled his talks with Prime Minister: "He (Modi) was very arrogant. When I told him that 500 farmers had died, he said, 'Did they die for me?' I told him yes."[46] Some *tapasya* that was.

In 2022, when the Russia-Ukraine war broke out, thousands of Indian students were stranded in Ukraine for a prolonged period. As the local embassy failed to come to their rescue in time and bombing increased – while other countries had already evacuated their citizens – these students sent SoS on social media for help in sheer desperation, describing their ordeal. The Opposition raised strong objections to the delay in evacuation[47], forcing the government to admit the failure in the Parliament[48]. As the situation became embarrassing for the government, a vicious campaign was launched against those students by right-wing groups calling them "snakelings"[49] – meaning they will criticize the Prime Minister once they return to India – and falsely claimed that Ukraine and Russia were seeking India's help to resolve the war. Union Home Minister Shah and many senior BJP leaders repeatedly made *false claims[50]* that the Prime Minister had stopping the war for three hours[51] or three days[52] to evacuate them.

Worse, the Prime Minister of India advised students to "study in India", instead of going to "small countries"[53] – exposing either his ignorance or hypocrisy. Private medical colleges in India charge about Rs 1 crore and more[54] for a for medical degree while providing indifferent quality education – for both of which his own government is primarily responsible.[55] Ukraine provides world class medical education for Rs 20-25 lakh[56]. (Non-technical course don't come cheap in India either; private Indian universities of uncertain standards are charging

Rs 12-40 lakh for undergraduate courses in humanities – 100 times more than the known top-grade public universities[57] – and the IIMs are now charging more than Rs 30 lakh for a two-year course[58], from around Rs 4 lakh a few years ago[59]). One indication of the quality of medical education in India is what the National Medical Commission (NMC) found when it checked 246 medical colleges in the 2022-23 academic session: "Majority of the colleges had either ghost faculty and senior residents or had not employed the required faculty at all...*Zero attendance* (of the faculty) was common".[60] No wonder, more and more Indians are fleeing to foreign shores. In 2022-23, all-time high 268, 923 students landed in the US for study – 25% students of all landing there.[61] *(Emphasis added)*

Well, later Union Aviation Minister Jyotiraditya Scindia landed in Ukraine to lead the evacuation but not without first giving them a speech – to which the local mayor taking care of the students objected, leading to ugly spat.[62]

Perception management has become the official policy to counter multiple governance failures that global agencies and watchdogs routinely red-flag. Apart from denials, misleading claims and analysis (several instances given in the previous chapters), a large-scale media blitzkrieg was planned in 2022 to "shape India's perception for the domestic and global audience and publicise the problems, parameters and data sources of global indices".[63]

Even national security has fallen victim to perception management.

After it became public that China had intruded in and grabbed land on the Indian side of LAC in Ladakh, the Prime Minister of India called an all-party meeting and said: *"Na koi wahan hamari seema mein ghus aaya hai, na hi koi ghusa hua hai, na hi hamari koi post kisi dusre ke kabze mein hain"* (No one has intruded and nor is anyone intruding, nor has any post been captured by someone).[64] For years, as Gujarat Chief Minister Modi had gaven *free advice* to New Delhi to be brave and show "laal aankh" (red eye) to China. But he didn't even dare to name China then nor since then, despite cultivating an image of a strong leader (with "56-inch chest"[65]), which is endorsed[66] by his party. The Guardian had written in 2021: "Since Modi was first elected in 2014, his modus operandi has been that of a tough, unyielding, authoritarian strongman leader who does not bow to public pressure."[67] For years after becoming the Prime Minister he used to recite a poem at public rallies *"saugandh mujhe is mitti ki, main desh nahin jhukne doonga"*[68] (I vow to this soil of my country I will not let this country cow down).

China used the Prime Minister's very words ("*na koi...*") to turn the table on India and declare India as the aggressor. Former Prime Minister Manmohan Singh was forced to advise him to be "mindful" of his words for adverse implications on national security.[69] The official video of his denial was later truncated to give a misleading impression and the defence ministry document, acknowledging the Chinese intrusion, was removed from the official website.[70] There may not be any link but it shouln't be missed that less than a year before this, Union Home Minister Amit Shah had thundered in the Parliament to wrest 'Aksai Chin' (under Chinese control) on August 6, 2019[71] – without any apparent provocation – a day after abrogating Article 370 and downgrading J&K to two UTs.

Such is the timidity of the *strong* government that it asked the US not to even mention the China incursion into India in official communique.[72] Much later, in February 2023, Foreign Minister S Jaishankar explained the timidity: "Look, they (China) are the bigger economy. What am I going to do? As a smaller economy, I am going to pick up a fight with the bigger economy? It is not a question of being reactionary, it's a question of common sense...".[73] When Congress leader Rahul Gandhi called this "cowardice"[74] a fierce attack was mounted on him by the BJP supporters – who never demurred at the government's timidity or the Chinese land grab. Months earlier, at his UN address in December 2022, Jaishankar had talking about Pakistan, unprovoked and when the security threat from China was staring at the face. Security expert Sushant Singh put this bizarre act aptly: "The questions are about China. The answers are about Pakistan."[75]

This is understandable but surely gone are the days of false bravados and filmy discourse displayed in 2019 against a less powerful Pakistan – despite the failed Balakot strike, which backfired and apparent security failures which allowed the Pulwama terror strike to happen (Chapter V). The Prime Minister of India had declared then: *"Ye hamara siddhant hai, ki ghar mein ghus kar maarenge"* (It is our principle that we kill them in their home) and *"Chun chun ke hisaab lena meri fitrat hai"* (It is my nature to settle accounts one by one).[76]

End result of the timidity on display against China? The government has been outmanoeuvered[77] by China and it has failed to secure the national border. Though there have been *de-escalations* in some areas along the LAC, India keeps *pleading with* China (19th round of talk was held in August 2023) to give it back the patrolling rights in Ladakh and China *keeps refusing*.[78] Despite it, the Prime Minister hasn't withdrawn his statement, nor has the government refuted his statement or admitted that China has grabbed land earlier in the control of India. On the contrary, the Prime Minister told people in Pithoragarh of Uttarakhand – which has borders with China – in October 2023 that earlier governments feared enemies and didn't develop border areas but "New India" doesn't.[79] In the meanwhile, the Pentagon *confirmed* that China keeps *ramping up troops* and *infrastructure* along the LAC.[80]

There is yet another element at play.

'Low-Balling' and 'Mindless Consistency'

In marketing, "compliance professionals" use different tactics for producing compliance or 'yes' from people for buying products or services. These tactics are governed by fundamental psychological principles. Social psychologist Robert Cialdini listed seven such principles in his 2021 book "Influence: The Psychology of Persuasion"[81]. One of these, "commitment and consistency principle", he describes as the "hobgoblins of the mind" and elaborates several *tactics* used, two of which are of particular interest here since these tactics produce 'yes' *even when people know they have been short-changed*: "low-balling" and "automatic consistency".

On "low-balling", Cialdini says, most of us have experienced it at some point or other, with or without realizing it and it goes like this.

A customer is offered a "sweet deal", say, for a car, by a car dealer. The price offered is below that of competitors and good to coax out a deal – including overly generous trade-off for the customer's old car. Once the decision to buy the car is made, a flurry of activities follows – forms are filled, financing terms are arranged, customer is encouraged to drive the car for a day etc. All these activities reinforce personal commitment of the customer to buy. But something invariably happens before the deal is sealed. An "error" is discovered. The salesperson forgot to add the cost of the navigation package or a mistake is found in the financial arrangements or the deal is disallowed by the boss on the plea that the dealership would make a loss at that price. The price advantage offered is then withdrawn. Cialdini explains that this trick doesn't work on everybody but is "effective enough to be a staple compliance procedure" in many car showrooms in the US. This is despite the fact that the sweet deal was unscrupulous to begin with.

Why low-balling works?

Having watched this multiple times, Cialdini explains that "personal commitment" built up during the process provides its own support system of "new justifications" for buying – like the car price is still equal to what is available with other dealers, or the trade-off for old car was too generous and by agreeing to it the customer now feels guilty. These justifications provide so many strong legs that when the dealer pulls away the original leg (the sweet deal), there is no collapse. He writes: "The loss can be shrugged off by the customer who is consoled by the array of other reasons favouring the choice. It never occurs that those additional reasons might never have existed had the choice not been made in the first place." The impressive thing about low-ball tactic is *"its ability to make a person feel pleased with a poor choice"* and he writes, "those who *have only poor choices to offer* are especially fond of the technique". *(Emphasis added)*

On "automatic consistency", Cialdini narrates his experience with a "cult".

He once attended a cult's introductory lecture for selling a transcendental meditation (TM) programme. He took along a friend, a university professor specializing in statistics and logic. After the theory behind the TM was explained, his friend got up and demolished the presentation, pointing out where and why the arguments were contradictory, illogical and unsupportable. The effect was devastating on the presenters, who first offered weak reply and then, finally admit that his friend's points were good ones "requiring further study".

What followed was even more devastating for Cialdini and his friend.

They noticed that after the embarrassingly collapse of their presentation, the cult's meeting turned into a *huge success* and generated inexplicably high levels of compliance from the audience – sale of the admission form for the TM. The audience had understood his friend's argument "quite well, in fact, all too well", as they discovered after speaking to many of them. Then what happened? Cialdini writes "it was precisely the cogency of his (friend's) claims that drove them to sign up for it". He explains the apparent contradiction by arguing that those who bought the TM form were driven by *their need* and wanted to *believe* that the TM was their *answer*. His friend's voice of reason caused *panic* as it *left them without hope again*. This led to erecting walls against the voice of reason and subscribing to the TM to end their worries. He called this behaviour "the comforts of mindless consistency".

Cialdini explains how the mind works in such a situation: "It is our desire to be (and appear) consistent with what we have already said or done. Once we make a choice or take a stand, we encounter personal and inter-personal pressures to think and behave consistently with that commitment. Moreover, those pressures will cause us to respond in ways that justify our decision."

Such behavioural pattern is quite apparent in India.

The educated and empowered middle-class which never hesitated to find faults and criticize previous governments has suddenly turned loyalists and defenders of the government. They are willing to equate the Prime Minister and his government with 'nation' and no criticism is brooked. Many would praise him and his government for good works even while failing to cite an example or offer logic and evidence (plenty of videos in public to check). If a decision is indefensible (like the demonetization or untimely and unplanned pandemic lockdown), the failures would be shrugged off with statements like, "but the intention was good". These are now commonplace and didn't exist prior to 2014. Global experience tells us, consistent feeding of fake news, misinformation or disinformation, propaganda etc. play a big role in such behavioural change.

That probably explains the government's reliance on rhetoric and demonization of all protesters and critics as "anti-national", "terrorist", "tukde-tukde gang", "urban naxals" in which the attack is agitator-specific and all assets are mobilized (from Sachin Tendulkar and Lata Mangeskar to Mary Kom, PT Usha, ex-diplomats, ex-bureaucrats, ex-judges, God media etc.) and seeking resignations or actions against the accused (Anurag Thakur, Ajay Mishra Teni or Brij Bhushan Saran Singh) is no longer part of political lexicon.[82]

Fake News. Lies and Propaganda

Call it fake news, post-truth, alt-truth, half-truth, lies, misinformation, disinformation, propaganda or whatever suits you, these are now routine – more than ever before and employed by the government and its supporters more than ever in living memory. These are reprehensible as tools to *evade and avoid* responsibility, accountability or even answerability by distorting reality, undermining facts and evidence to mould public opinion in favour of the government.

It is known that the Prime Minister had acquired a formidable propaganda machinery from his Gujarat days, which he used to the hilt, using fair and unfair means (surrogate, secretive and sophisticated) to spread misinformation campaigns (fake news and false claims) in real and virtual worlds[83], going to the extent of floating an NGO on *women's empowerment*[84] to do so. Author Sonia Faleiro, who tracked this new phenomenon, writes in her 2021 essay "Fact-checking Modi's India"[85] that "when misinformation first started circulating widely across the country, it was the run-up to the 2014" and that, "misinformation is a challenge globally, but in India, it's practically baked into the ruling party's communications."

The Altnews[86] – pioneer fact-checking website in India started by Pratik Sinha and Mohammed Zubair (the one arrested for doing his job in 2022) – has steadfastly and virtually every single day exposed fake news and misinformation spread by the BJP's huge troll army, with its official IT Cell at the forefront. These are then shared and amplified by senior ministers, leaders and right-wing websites on social media and which gets into the mainstream media. Indian government is known for blocking websites, Facebook and Twitter (now 'X') accounts but not one of the right-wing hate-spewing ones – which are flourishing without check.

A global study on state-sponsored trolling[87] found eerie similarity between China's state-run disinformation machinery, "50 Cent Army", and the BJP's IT Cell, which is run by a mix of volunteer and paid amateur trolls. This study, like the Altnews, pointed out that the Twitter account of the Indian Prime Minister follows at least 26 troll accounts who are serial abusers, sexist bigots, rumour mongers, many of them have been hosted by him too – thus giving trolling legitimacy. Even Chief Justice of India Justice DY Chandrachud has been targeted by the BJP troll armies.[88]

As mentioned earlier, Union Home Minister Shah once boasted, as then BJP president, about his party's formidable troll army to his party's social media volunteers: "We can keep making messages go viral, whether they are real or fake, sweet or sour."[89] This troll army of the ruling establishment is not only formidable but innovative, insidious and toxic. It has created a world of fake profiles, of Muslims and Sikhs, on social media platforms. Pratik Sinha once exposed such fake Muslim profiles in 2017 and wrote[90]: "A Muslim name. That too a woman. Celebrates the recent success of Yogi Adityanath and constantly appreciates the 'greatness' of PM Modi. Very critical of Muslims. Repeatedly brands the entire Muslim community as extremist. Blind nationalism. Wouldn't that be a dream come true for the entire right-wing?" After the farmers' protest began in 2020, which was led by Punjab's Sikh farmers, a similar fake Sikh profile came up across social media platforms, 80 such accounts were found to be fake and suspended. A BBC report of 2021[91] explained what these accounts were doing by quoting the author: "The aim of the network appears to have been to "alter perceptions on important issues around Sikh independence, human rights and values."

Incessant communal violence, hate speech by leaders and workers alike keep the society on a perpetual boil, particularly peaking at election times to polarize votes in the BJP's favour. The mainstream Indian media has emerged as a major enabler of the disinformation campaigns and rhetoric, thereby undermining genuine journalists.[92]

Then there is this personality cult building operations – an expert on everything under the sun and a "Vishwaguru" (world teacher). The Prime Minister himself liberally contributes to this perception by airing his views in public on history[93], climate change[94], science[95], military affairs (cloud cover)[96] and even general technological matters[97], malnutrition[98] and even advises students every year (asking them to solve difficult questions first[99]) and has written a best-selling book titled "Exam Warriors"[100] even as legal battles[101] for verifying his *declared education degrees* go on for years. All these opinions and advises not just point to the Prime Minister of India's unfamiliarity with the subjects (and yet, endures) but are seemingly accepted unquestionably by his officials – explaining perhaps why policymaking since 2014 is *without logic, data and evidence* and invariably hurts the people and the economy (as explained in detail in earlier chapters).

Invariably this takes the shape of grand speeches and spectacles (in fact, former Deputy Prime Minister LK Advani from the BJP had called hisone-time protégé "a brilliant event manager"[102]), like claiming that his government stands for "Vasudhaiva Kutumbakam" (the world is one family) and "One Earth, One Family, One Future" – theeme of the *rotational* G20 summit in India in 2023 and everywhere else. (Entire New Delhi and other cities where G20 events were organized were covered with hoardings of "Vasudhaiva Kutumbakam" – quite ironical for the Hindu supremacist regime. In his Independence Day speech on August 15, 2023, the Prime Minister declared India a "Vishwamitr" (friend of the world)[103] – which he would keep *repeating*[104] even after siding with Israel in the Hamas-Israel conflict.) One of the government's former economic advisors Rathin Roy, described the grand staging of the G20 summit as "self-congratulating chest-thumping and celebratory entertainment"[105] – which cost more than Rs 4,100 crore – as against the budget of Rs 90 crore.[106] This is when India is at the bottom of G20 countries – in per capita income, hunger, human development, labour force participation (LFPR) and others.[107] But then, this not very ironically for a government which made India behave like a Third World country[108] during the second wave of the pandemic in 2021.

The Prime Minister also maintained his *unbroken record* of not opnely speaking to media or allowing other G20 leaders to hold an open press conferences. The grand summit ended up as a big publicity event for the Prime Minister[109] but it certainly didn't grant him the status of a "Vishwaguru"[110]. The Prime Minister, however, keeps telling at public rallies that the G20 showed *"Poori duniya me Bharat ka danka baj raha hai"* (India is being appreciated on global stage) and when he shakes hands with big leaders, he looks them in the eyes.[111]

A few other remarkable aspects of such propaganda are:

- The Prime Minister doesn't shy away from telling lies on but remains silent on every day communal hate and violence by his own party leaders and contributes to it by identifying Muslim protesters by their clothes and denying the discriminatory CAA.

- Huge spending on publicity (Rs 6,492 crore during FY15-FY23 (up to December 7, 2022)[112] and diverting money from genuine works to publicity (79% of the "Beti Bachao Beti Padhao", pension funds (NSAP) diverted for publicity of other schemes[113] etc.).

- Using celebrities like Lata Mangeshkar and Sachin Tendulkar to discredit protests (by farmers) and "nationalist" Hindi film narratives and targeting Muslims through propaganda films like 'Kashmir Files' and 'Kerala Story' – which are often crude and misleading.[114]

- The Prime Minister's biopic ahead of the 2019 general elections[115] and the NaMo TV's violations of election code during the (silence) period.

- 100th episode of his monthly radio monologue "Mann ki Baat" having "very low listenership"[116] was celebrated in 2023 with public money at 400,000 venues[117], including live-telecast abroad[118] for which Indian embassies were asked to mobilize crowd[119].

- The official façade[120] of invoking Mahatma Gandhi and Buddha in official functions in Indian and abroad while lionizing the Mahatma's assassin Nathuram Ram Godse and other Hindutva icons in India not known for advocating non-violence or search for peace and truth. In fact, when terror accused Pragya Thakur insulted Mahatma Gandhi in 2019, calling his assassin Nathuram Godse a "patriot", the Prime Minister merely said *"main unhey mann se kabhi maaf nahin kar paunga"* (I will never be able to forgive her from my heart).[121] The meaning of this remains unclear years later. This was around the time he endorsed her candidature as the BJP candidate for the Lok Sabha elections and she went on to win from Bhopal with a huge margin (days after insulting the Mahatma). She had also claimed that she had participated in the demolition of Babri masjid in 1992.[122]

- The Prime Minister's incessant talk of "Achche Din", "Amrit Kaal" (to make "developed" [123] or build "a prosperous and inclusive India"[124] by 2047) endures. In 2023, he mobilized *soil from 766 districts* with which he laid the foundation for a "Amrit Vatika" (golden garden) next to the India Gate in New Delhi.[125] By then, he had already rechristened "Amrit Kaal" as "Kartavya Kaal"[126] and renamed the Rajpath as "Kartavya Path" (Road of Duty). Then he said he was laying foundation for the *next 1,000 years*[127] – contrasting it with what he called 1,000 years of "slavery" under Muslim rulers. Endless rhetoric, bluff and bluster have replaced intelligent public debates.

A part of this propaganda, rather hate campaign, is the complicity of Big Tech companies.

Complicity of Facebook and Twitter ('X')

There is a long and ever-expanding list of investigating reports, including by global media (Time magazine, World Street Journal, Reuters [128]), exposing the social media platforms like Facebook, Twitter ('X'), WhatsApp, Reddit and GitHub hastening the proliferation of right-wing's toxic hate campaign with deadly consequences.

In March 2022, Kumar Sambhav and Nayantara Ranganathan revealed, in a four-part report[129], how the Facebook actively collaborated with the BJP to systematically undercut political competition; its members moonlighted for the BJP; its algorithm allowed and gave cheap rates to ghost and surrogate ads promoting the BJP; selectively targeted political rivals by blocking their sites – all to promote the BJP's politics of hate. They analyzed more than 5 lakh political advertisements on Facebook and Instagram between February 2019 and November 2020, which saw one general and nine state elections, to come to their conclusions.

In 2021, Facebook whistleblower Frances Haugen[130] pointed out how the pages of BJP IT Cell and those associated with the RSS promoting hate and violence against Muslims were not pulled down due to "political sensitivities". One Facebook's internal document revealed the toxic messages these pages spread: "Anti-Muslim narratives targeted pro-Hindu populations with [violent and incendiary] intent... There were a number of dehumanizing posts comparing Muslims to 'pigs' and 'dogs' and misinformation claiming the Quran calls for men to rape their female family members." The Facebook was warned and reminded repeatedly but it remained unmoved and let the ruling BJP and its supporters spread hate and violence even during the Delhi riots of 2020.

Another Facebook whistleblower Sophie Zhang[131] came out with more damning evidence that the microblogging site refused to act against fake accounts directly linked to a BJP MP after this link was discovered and sought permission to depose before a parliamentary committee. Lok Sabha Speaker Om Birla (from the BJP) refused her, dismissing it as a non-serious issue and her foreign nationality – although the rulebook doesn't disallow it and in 2019, the then Twitter CEO Jack Dorsey had done so. A 2018 BBC reported a study[132] showed the rise in "nationalism" as the driving force behind the fake news surge, the role of the Twitter and its direct link with the Prime Minister and concluded that there was "an overlap of fake news sources on Twitter and support networks of Prime Minister Narendra Modi". A study of the University of Michigan[133] found a noticeable rise in the spread of fake news and propaganda *baiting Muslims in the mainstream media.*

Ironically, however, the Meta which owns Facebook and WhatsApp, told the Delhi Police in November 2023 *to limit* its request for login or logout details to "cases of heinous nature or significant gravity" and provide a brief background of the case, explaining the relevance of the information sought – reflecting the frivolousness nature of demands on it.[134] The Twitter ('X') had also *challenged*[135] the Indian government's demand to block tweets and accounts all handles critical of the government's handling of the pandemic, farmers' protests etc. during 2020-2022 in various courts but got *no relief,* rather the Karnataka High Court imposed a fine of Rs 5 lakh[136].

True 'Make in India': Manufacturing Hate

The hate campaign continues unabated because it is systemic. Vidya Krishnan[137] captured this the dynamics at work to write, "Hate is the government's true "make in India" campaign" and has forced Indian citizens into self-censorship", adding: "Moderate citizens, now habituated to self-censorship, not only refuse to say out loud what they think of the violence but often do not know what to think about it. This is the greatest triumph of the Modi government: demolishing truth so entirely that it cannot be accused of lying."

The fact that the official mails of the Supreme Court and National Human Rights Commission (NHRC) – one a constitutional authority and the other a statutory body, both independent of the government – carried the Prime Minister's image and slogan "sabka saath, sabka vikas" as signature (mail footer) in 2021 wasn't accidental but part of the larger design (both were later withdrawn after public outcry).[138] In 2017, the Ministry of External Affairs (MEA) had uploaded a book on Jana Sangh (BJP's precursor) leader Deendayal Upadhyaya[139] stating that the BJP was the only political alternative in the country; Hindu thought is Bhartiya thought and only Hindu society can be spiritual etc. Since it is meant primarily for global audience, the Indian government pushing such a distorted view for the ruling party's propaganda defies logic and propriety. In 2022, the Ministry of Culture *equated* VD Savarkar, the man who wrote the Hindutva concept and one of the accused in the assassination of Mahatma Gandhi (later acquitted), with the Mahatma himself saying he was "no less" and dedicated a monthly magazine to him.[140]

In the official celebration for India@75, Savarkar found a place as a freedom fighter but not Pandit Nehru or any Muslim leader in the advertisements released by the Indian Council of Historical Research (ICHR), an autonomous body set up by the government, at the beginning of the year-long "Azadi ka Amrit Mahotsav" in 2021.[141] The Prime Minister put a seal of approval on it when he addressed the nation on August 15, 2022. He omitted Pandit Nehru from the frontline of freedom fighters, replacing him with Savarkar. Pandit Nehru's name figured in his *third set* of freedom fighters.[142]

The purpose of such citations is to show how such humongous state-sponsored propaganda, fake news, misinformation, hate campaigns and violence in which global tech companies like Facebook and Twitter have become integral part poses extraordinary risks to Indian social and political orders and imperils its very democracy (and sanity).[143]

The question that arises is: Why does hate work and used to win people's loyalty by political leaders?

American writer Eric Hoffer, who studied mass movements heralding the revolutionary changes in Europe, Asia and elsewhere during the early decades of 20th century (Russia, Germany, Italy etc.), provided insights in his 1951 classic "True Believer"[144]. He wrote, "hatred is the most accessible and comprehensive unifying agent" and "the ideal devil is a foreigner", adding: "It (hate) pulls and whirls the individual away from his own self, makes him oblivious of his weal (wellbeing) and future, frees him of jealousies and self-seeking. He becomes an anonymous particle quivering with a craving to fuse and coalesce with his like into one flaming mass." Another insight from him: People usually don't look for allies when they love, but they do when they hate.

There is yet another dimension to the new despotism that Keane pointed out: state-regulated surveillance. It is a tool to control and influence the minds of citizens to manipulate their behaviour and stifle dissent. The Pegasus surveillance scandal is a big example of this.

Pegasus and Surveillance Democracy

Surveillance does have a legitimate use in national security and public order emergencies but the Pegasus investigations of 2021[145] revealed that the Israeli military-grade spyware's use in India was to target civilians for perpetuating political power. Its targets were journalists (more than 40), academics, human rights activists, opposition leaders and governments, a scientist, businessmen, two cabinet ministers (including the IT Minister Ashwini Vaishnaw, who defended the government in the Parliament), senior CBI officers, a Supreme Court judge and other court officials and an Election Commissioner.

The use of Pegasus in India has been linked to the visit of Prime Minister and his National Security Adviser to Israel in 2016.[146] Their visit is also linked to an *extraordinary high budget allocation*[147] for the National Security Council Secretariat (NSCS) – a ten-fold increase from Rs 33 crore to Rs 333 crore in FY17. Shockingly 2017 was the year the Supreme Court declared the right to privacy a fundamental right. The New York Times investigation of 2022[148] revealed further that Pegasus was part of a "package of sophisticated weapons and intelligence gear worth roughly $2 billion" between India and Israel. The Prime Minister's visit to Israel is a first for an Indian, and so also the bonhomie, trade and diplomatic relations with Israel – a marked departure from India's traditional solidarity with Palestine in the Israel-Palestine conflicts. Th Prime Minister would confirm this departure by expressing solidarity with Israel when its conflict with Palestine flared up in October 2023 by taking to 'X': "Deeply shocked by the news of terrorist attacks in Israel. Our thoughts and prayers are with innocent victims and their families. We stand in solidarity with Israel at this difficult hour."[149] Later, he would add, "we strongly condemn the deaths of civilians in the conflict between Israel-Palestine"[150] but coming from the Prime Minister who never visited Manipur or condemned months' long violent ethnic clashes under his watch and under his "double-engine" government, nothing much (about human tragedy) should be read into such utterances.

The Pegasus surveillance violates the 1996 Supreme Court judgement[151], which disapproved indiscriminate snooping that violates rights to privacy. That pronouncement had come in response to the 1991 phone tapping of politicians. It is also an egregious violation of the fundamental right to privacy[152], the apex court had ruled in 2017. Besides, such surveillance is also *illegal*[153] according to the Information Technology Act of 2000. What did the government do when the scandal broke in 2021?

(i) It didn't allow questions and debates in the Parliament and blamed and branded Opposition as "anti-national" – having dismissed the charges as malicious, non-issue, international conspiracy etc.[154]

(ii) The Prime Minister asked his party to "expose the attitude of the Congress and some other Opposition parties".[155]

(iii) Several BJP Chief Ministers[156] issued statements to condemn the Opposition for disrupting the Parliament, calling it "unnecessary", display of "anti-national mindset" and sought ban on the Amnesty which investigated the use of Pegasus.

(iv) A parliamentary committee meeting, which was supposed to take up the issue, was sabotaged as 10 BJP members showed up but refused to mark attendance to cause lack of quorum; three government secretaries absented from this meeting but escaped punishment for such gross misconduct.[157]

(v) The government prevaricated before the Supreme Court for weeks, raising the *bogey of national security* and refusing a probe. The court set up a panel on its own to probe it in October 2021 to which it refused to cooperate.

The Supreme Court didn't make the panel's report public. It read out the main findings as: (i) malware found in five of 29 phones it examined but couldn't confirm it was Pegasus (ii) the Centre didn't cooperate (the NSO has categorically said it sold sell Pegasus only to governments) and (iii) the panel asked its report not to be made public on the plea that it carried sensitive information.[158] The court "resealed" the report and adjourned the hearing for a month – without taking the case to its logical conclusion. It remains stuck there (as of December 2023).

This was another failure of the apex court to uphold and protect citizens' fundamental rights to liberty and privacy and question the government. It didn't reveal anything about Pegasus or the origin and nature of the malware it detected and meekly accepted the government's non-cooperation – without going for *contempt proceedings*. The Wire's Siddharth Varadarajan (who led the Pegasus investigation in India)[159] wrote the court could have found the truth by taking two small steps: (a) let the panel report be peer reviewed for its methodology and findings by reputed international agencies to rule out Pegasus and (b) ask ministers and officials dealing with intelligence gathering to state on oath whether they are aware or unaware of the purchase and use of Pegasus in India. He also pointed out that India was an outlier since intelligence agencies of France and Belgium, as well as the European Commission and a United Kingdom court examined phones reported to have been infected and confirmed it.

In a series of reports, The Washington Post said[160] the governments of the US, France and Israel investigated and found evidence of the Pegasus misuse, but India didn't. The Israeli firm NSO supplying and operating Pegasus said it sold the tool only to "vetted government agencies". India is among the 10 top countries where the surveillance through Pegasus alleged to have taken place during 2016-2021. The leaked data base of *50,000* Pegasus with targets in more than *50 countries* was accessed by France's media outfit (non-profit) Forbidden Stories, investigated by a consortium of 17 media organizations across the world – *including The Wire from India* – supported by the Amnesty International's Security Lab and vetted by the University of Toronto's Citizen Lab. The other countries in the list aren't exactly shining examples liberal democracies: Azerbaijan, Bahrain, Hungary, Kazakhstan, Mexico, Morocco, Rwanda, Saudi Arabia and the United Arab Emirates.

This wasn't the first instance. In 2019 similar revelations about the use of Pegasus via WhatsApp had come to public notice when the latter alerted the targeted individuals. After having acknowledged it, the Indian government denied it, even when the WhatsApp CEO confirmed such attack in 2019 and many national dailies descried how dissent was turned into an act of terror by the Indian government.[161]

It (2021 expose) wasn't last either. On October 30, 2023, iPhone maker Apple alerted about two dozen Indians, including political rivals of the BJP and journalists, that "state-sponsored attackers" were targeting them – just ahead of the November 2023 round of state elections. This meant despite the Pegasus scandal, state-sponsored snooping was alive and kicking.[162] An investigation by the Financial Times had revealed in March 2023 that the India government was looking to spend up to $120 million (over Rs 986 crores) on *new spyware* sold by firms less exposed than Israel's NSO Group. It said: "Modi government officials have grown concerned about the "PR problem" caused by the ability of human rights groups to forensically trace Pegasus, as well as warnings from Apple and WhatsApp to those who have been targeted, according to two people familiar with the discussions."[163]

In August 2023, another investigating report by the Financial Times[164] alleged that the government was spying on 1.4 billion citizens through powerful surveillance tools from Israeli tech companies such as Cognyte and Septier. These are allegedly installed on *subsea cable landing stations*, which allows the security agencies to snoop on the personal data and communications. Israel-based Septier has reportedly sold such interception technology to major telecoms groups operating in India which can extract "voice, messaging services, web surfing and email correspondence" of targets. The other Israeli company Cognyte also provides surveillance products in India.

Such surveillance is part of a very wide network of systems in place.

At least 10 central agencies of India[165] are authorized to intercept communications under the IT Act of 2000 and snoop on people without parliamentary or independent oversight. These are: Intelligence Bureau (IB), Narcotics Control Bureau (NCB), Enforcement Directorate (ED), Central Board of Direct Taxes (CBDT), Directorate of Revenue Intelligence (DRI), Central Bureau of Investigation (CBI), National Investigation Agency (NIA), Cabinet Secretariat (RAW), Directorate of Signal Intelligence (for service areas of Jammu & Kashmir, North East and Assam only), and Commissioner of Police, Delhi.

Then there are mass surveillance projects like the National Technical

Research Organisation (NTRO) of the DoPT (under PMO); National Intelligence Grid (NatGrid) of the MHA itself; Crime and Criminal Tracking Network and Systems (CCTNS), a joint venture of Centre and states; Central Monitoring System (CMS) of the Ministry of Communications etc. Then there are many others under the MHA and Defence Ministry about which very little is known. Some are set up to collect and share (private) information (NatGrid, CCTN) with all other intelligence, security, and police agencies.[166]

The privacy law Digital Personal Data Protection (DPDP) Act of 2023 not only doesn't cover these agencies, it (i) doesn't even recognize right to privacy is a fundamental right (ii) *additionally* empowers surveillance (iii) grants *immunity* to government, adjudicating board and private business from prosecution (iv) the adjudicating board is unformed and executive controlled (v) keeps civil courts out of adjudication process.[167] The Post Office Bill of 2023, introduced in the Rajya Sabha[168], seeks to repeal the Indian Post Office Act of 1898 and allows post offices to violate privacy by empowering "any officer to cause any item in course of transmission by the Post Office to be *intercepted, opened or detained* in the interest of the security of the State, friendly relations with foreign states, public order, emergency, or public safety or upon the occurrence of any contravention of any of the provisions of this Act or any other law for the time being in force". *(Emphasis added)*

Such is the cavalier attitude to data privacy that once, then Attorney General KK Venugopal told the Supreme court (in 2018) that the Aadhaar data was very safe because it was protected by *13 feet high, 5 feet thick walls*[169]. This is when data theft is *rampant*[170] and so is *internet ban*[171]– wrecking lives, giving state control over news and creasing information asymmetry. Ironically, RS Sharma, then chairman of the Telecom Regulatory Authority (TRAI) who later launched the CoWin app for Covid-19 vaccination and used the Aadhaar numbers, had to face the ignominy of finding his own personal details in public hours after he threw a challenge and shared his Aadhaar number to how safe it was I 2018; hackers put his PAN and alternate phone numbers in public domain.[172] In October 2023, it was found that personal details like Aadhaar and passport numbers of 815 million were *on sale*[173] on the dark web – revealed to have been derived from the Indian Council of Medical Research (ICMR).

Britain-based Comparitech[174] found India to be one of the worst in privacy protection and surveillance – third from the bottom among 47 countries, above China and Russia. The countries that most respect privacy rights of individuals are also the ones that top press freedom indices and have a higher degree of free-market with moorings of a welfare state. Its 2021 profile on India[175] said the IT Rules of 2021 – which requires social media platforms to record connection information and on-demand from authorities, break the end-to-end encryption that provides complete privacy in chat apps, such as WhatsApp – ensures that "no matter what steps you take in India, you have no privacy on social media or chat apps". The IT Rules of 2023 which provides for setting up a *censorship board* by mandating the government to act as *fact-check body* on all information relating to itself. This makes the government the prosecutor, the jury and the judge as no accountability-based framework to protect privacy exists.

Developed democracies like Australia, Canada, New Zealand, the UK and the US have several tiers of oversight mechanisms: parliamentary accountability; judicial accountability; expert accountability and complaints mechanisms.[176] In contrast, India has none and two of the premier intelligence agencies empowered to snoop, the IB and RAW, are not even legal entities[177]; they have been created under executive orders and "at least one" of these bought the Pegasus spyware in the past[178]. During the UPA regime, there was a strong push to subject these intelligence agencies to parliamentary oversight. A private member's bill was introduced in 2011 for the purpose; after the Pegasus scandal, it was introduced again a decade later in 2021 but the government took notice.[179]

Another manifestation of this is the Aadhaar identity card and its 360-degree linkages with every aspect of Indians' life. Its linkage to voters' identity card makes it especially prone for electoral misuse through profiling and selective targeting of voters to influence voting (more in Chapter X) – which would be clearer soon.

Voters' Surveillance and Aadhaar Card

The Cambridge Analytica-Facebook episode of 2018 revealed why privacy laws must cover *political parties and big data harvesting firms* – another aspect Keane called "state-regulated surveillance capitalism" in democracies – for marketing and political purposes. The episode revealed that data can be harvested to manipulate people's behaviour to influence voting. The two best examples of it are the Brexit of 2016[180] – which saw the UK walking out of the European Union only to see the Brexit leaders, Nigel Farage, admit to making fake claims and leave the field after the referendum – and the US Presidential election of 2016[181] that brought Donald Trump as the US President. The Cambridge Analytica, a UK-based data firm, secretly harvested the data (profiles) of 87 million of Facebook users and built models to "to exploit what we knew about them and target their inner demons".[182] In India, it partnered with political parties like the BJP and Congress[183], although both denied it, to influence local elections. The government had then threatened action against the Facebook.

Does such demographic profiling work in influencing people's behaviour?

"Yes", said Michal Kosinski, a psychologist at the Stanford Graduate School of Business, who pioneered many of the original techniques that the Cambridge Analytica used. When the scandal broke, he said: "I've been warning about these risks for years...Our latest research confirms that this kind of psychological targeting is not only possible but effective as a tool of digital mass persuasion".[184] Kosinski *et al*[185] had explained the logic in their 2013 study paper: "We show that easily accessible digital records of behavior, Facebook Likes, can be used to automatically and accurately predict a range of highly sensitive personal attributes including: sexual orientation, ethnicity, religious and political views, personality traits, intelligence, happiness, use of addictive substances, parental separation, age, and gender...The model correctly discriminates between homosexual and heterosexual men...and *between Democrat and Republican...*" *(Emphasis added)*

Surveillance capitalism is a familiar word in the data-driven world of ours. Global giants like Google, Facebook, Amazon, Microsoft and others collect huge amounts of data on people's online behaviour to market products and maximize profits. As scientist Darshana Narayanan wrote[186]: "As a byproduct, their digital platforms have helped create echo chambers resulting in widespread *climate denialism, science skepticism, and political polarization.*" There is a fair bit of evidence that Indian elections are meddled with using Israel software, other than the Pegasus operations. A 2013 investigation by The Guardian[187] revealed that an Israel team of private contractors, code named "Team Jorge", was meddling around the world including India using Israeli software to operate fake social media campaigns to influence opinion on Twitter, LinkedIn, Facebook, Telegram, Gmail, Instagram and YouTube. *(Emphasis added)*

India is witnessing massive state-sponsored surveillance capitalism. The Aadhaar data is widely used by both government and private firms – for phone connections, banks accounts, filing income tax returns (ITR), school admissions, voters identity card, besides availing every single government welfare scheme – notwithstanding the fact that the Supreme Court had allowed it *only to avail government benefits* in 2018. It was first allowed as a statutory provision (in 2016) for identity authentication purposes, which sparked an uproar and the Supreme Court struck it down. The amendment that followed, retained the provision by allowing private use with "informed consent" in 2019 (for Aadhaar-based KYC verifications) by banks and telecom companies and in 2023, this was extended to 22 financial entities – including Amazon Pay (India) Pvt Ltd, Aditya Birla Housing Finance Ltd and IIFL Finance Ltd.[188] In the meanwhile, the government launched 'Ayushman Bharat Digital Mission' – not health service but a health database with unique health identity for all citizens – it was found that all those who availed Covid vaccines have already been assigned a unique identity without anyone knowing it, let alone giving "informed consent".[189] This scheme envisions sharing data with private healthcare providers and registries.

These are smart ways of making data of Indians freely available to private firms by the Indian government, except it is a blatant violation of the privacy right. An investigative report of 2020 by Huffpost had revealed that the government was creating a *360-degree database* [190], Aadhaar-linking "an all-encompassing, auto-updating, searchable database to track every aspect of the lives of each of India's over 1.2 billion residents" through a National Social Registry (NSR). It revealed the Indians were misled into believing that the NSR was a routine exercise by the government to update the 2011 Socio-Economic Caste Census (SECC) so as to prevent misuse of government schemes. This goal was achieved in 2023 when the Registration of Births and Deaths (Amendment) Act of 2023 was notified (see Chapter II).

In fact, the government's surveillance continues through CoWIN app for vaccination, Agristack for agriculture, e-SHRAM for migrant workers, Arogya Setu and Aysuhman Bharat Digital Health Mission for health and National Digital Education Architecture for school children – covering every area of life. Worse, the government proposes to sell such personal data to private companies, risking personal privacy for commercial interests through as yet a "draft", India Data Accessibility & Use Policy of 2022. The DNA Technology (Use and Application) Regulation Bill 2019 proposed to empower government to harvest citizens' DNA profiles even for civil cases. It evoked strong protest from the Opposition, a parliamentary panel and was withdrawn in 2023 – but *after having incorporated* such a provision in 2022 in the Criminal Procedure (Identification) Act of 2022[191] – which repealed the Identification of Prisoners Act of 1920 – amidst the Opposition's protests and demand for scrutiny[192] by the MHA-linked parliamentary standing committee. The later mentions "biological samples", instead of DNA, to bypass the objections.

There is yet another downside to it. As Chief Minister of Gujarat, Modi had strongly opposed the Aadhaar for compromising national security[193] but as Prime Minister, he not only implemented it rigorously, turned it from a voluntary identity marker (as originally drafted by the UPA government) to a mandatory one. His government often claims (without evidence) to save huge sums of money by eliminating duplications and checking corruption in welfare schemes but such claims don't stand to scrutiny[194]. It has also ended up not only enabling data theft but also denying people of welfare benefits. Development economist Reetika Khera's study[195] amply demonstrated this, forcing her to conclude: "Far from being inclusive and reducing corruption, Aadhaar is becoming a tool of exclusion, with little evidence of an impact on corruption in (MG)NREGA, PDS and pensions, etc. The government's estimates of savings are examined, but these do not stand scrutiny. What passes as 'savings' is often the result of denial of legal entitlements for lack of Aadhaar. In that sense, the Aadhaar project undermines the right to life."

One investigating report of 2023 showed, across India banks are enrolling account-holders in social security schemes (life insurance, accident insurance and pension schemes) *without their assent* ("deceitfully obtain customers' fingerprints for authentication via the Aadhaar-enabled Payment System, thus imposing the Narendra Modi government's welfare schemes on the rural poor").[196]

Personality Cult & Cult of Stupidity

Many experts have tried to explain the undiminished popularity of the Prime Minister and the fact that he doesn't pay political price for his series of disastrous economic and administrative decisions, endless communal strife and now the security threat from China. Some attribute these to his image of a 'saint', 'fakir', 'strong' leader.[197] Others have flagged emergence of two new cults – "cult of personality" around the Prime Minister and "cult of stupidity" – which better explains the new-found phenomenon called "Bhakti".

Author Kapil Komireddi explains[198] how a personality cult has been built around the Prime Minister: "An army of volunteers and keyboard warriors on the ruling party's payroll, devoted to pumping out lies about the prime minister's accomplishments, savaged those who disagreed, while digital evangelists deluged WhatsApp – the most effective propaganda medium in Modi's New India – with countless memes composed of doctored images portraying the prime minister as the weightiest of international statesmen..." He also adds: "The political, social and economic disasters of the past half-decade are inseparable from the cult of personality forged for Modi..."

A part of this cult building the Prime Minister's ubiquitous presence. His posters are at every petrol pump (withdrawn later as retail prices touched Rs 100), on highways, electric polls and buildings; every official website – even the Delhi Zoo.[199] His photo is on every Covid vaccine certificate, not that of the vaccinated. He appears on TV and newspapers ads and news coverage every day. He is always talking, tweeting, addressing rallies and inaugurating roads, bridges, underpasses, airports (even if already inaugurated and belongs to earlier regimes), flagging Vande Bharat trains and announcing new projects all across India. Even when appears with others local and even global leaders in posters (like it was during the G20 events for nearly a year) his face and persona towers over everyone else's. It is more like daily carpet bombing. There is an aspect of this which defies classification and yet is part of this cult building. Just one example of this kind for illustration: On the Diwali of 2023, the Prime Minister told the Indian Army that he spent *every Diwali* with the jawans in 30-35 years[200], but on the Diwali of 2019 he had said he spent *five days in jungle every Diwali* to reflect on life.[201]

Educator Rohit Kumar uses "cult of stupidity"[202] to explain the extraordinary change in people's attitude ('Bhakti' or 'voluntary servitude'): "The cult of stupidity…like any other cult worth its name, too, pledges unquestioning allegiance and absolute devotion to its leader – a demigod who can do no wrong, who despite his most glaring incompetencies and character flaws, is seen as the great answer to all the ills of the land…". To explain why this cult considers only itself wise and everyone else stupid, he cites the 1990s' experiment by two social psychologists known as 'Dunning-Kruger effect' – a cognitive bias in people with limited knowledge or competence who consider themselves smarter and more capable than they actually are because they lack the intelligence or awareness to know better. Commenting on the phenomenon, journalist Samar Halarnkar wrote[203]: "Too many of us are happy to swipe through and dismiss news of the gathering darkness (over our democracy), smile at falsehood and bigotry, and be narcoticised by the government and its fake-news factories into believing all is well."

German theologian Dietrich Bonhoeffer[204], who was executed by the Nazi government in 1945, explained "stupidity" of the Germans on display in 1930s and 1940s as a product of "certain circumstances" in which people with remarkable agile intelligence "are *made* stupid or that they allow this to happen to them" and thus, it is "not so much that stupidity is a congenital defect" and that such stupidity is "perhaps less a psychological than a sociological problem". He explained the circumstances such as "strong upsurge of power in the public sphere, be it of a political or a religious nature" which "*infects a large part of humankind with stupidity*". Such a stupid person "is *under a spell, blinded, misused, and abused in his very being*. Having thus become a *mindless tool*, the stupid person will also be *capable of any evil and at the same time incapable of seeing that it is evil*. This is where the danger of diabolical misuse lurks, for it is this that can once and for all destroy human beings". In conversation with such a person one feels "one is dealing *not at all with him as a person, but with slogans, catchwords, and the like that have taken possession of him*". The solution then is not to try and change him but wait for "external liberation" that turned him/her stupid. (*Emphasis added*)

Now that we are talking about Nazism and stupidity, Austrian author Robert Musil's celebrated lecture 'On Stupidity'[205], delivered during the Nazi ascendancy in 1937, distinguished between 'honourable' or 'simple' stupidity (lack of understanding, ability or deficiency) and 'intelligent' stupidity – the latter referring to intelligent people who know better but "can dress up in all the clothes of truth". About this latter category, Musil wrote, "is most lethal; a dangerous disease of the mind that endangers life itself". The allusion here is the intellectual debility or support to Nazism at the time.

Architect of India's Constitution BR Ambedkar[206] had warned Indians against both the types of cults (personality and 'Bhakti') long ago while addressing the Constituency Assembly in 1949. He said: "Bhakti in religion may be a road to the salvation of the soul. But in politics, Bhakti or hero-worship is a sure road to degradation and to eventual dictatorship."

Jason Stanley[207] of the Yale University provides an insight into why people prefer to follow others than apply their own mind (Cialdini's "mindless consistency") in his 2018 book "How Fascism Works": "...Socrates argues that people are not naturally led to self-governance but rather seek a strong leader to follow. Democracy, by permitting freedom of speech, opens the door for a demagogue to exploit the people's need for a strongman; the strongman will use this freedom to *prey on the people's resentment and fears*. Once the strongman seizes power, he will end democracy, replacing it with tyranny..." *(Emphasis added)*

The overall impact of grand spectacles the Prime Minister holds, his ubiquitous presence, grotesque display of money power by his government and party, constant criticism of the Opposition by the Prime Minister even when his own party is in power in a state for decades[208], blaming the Opposition or Nehru for all that ails India now, mass surveillance, all the lies, fake news etc. cloud citizens' minds and create an *alt-reality*[209] – helping in spreading the personality cult and the cult of stupidity. The net impact is dramatic change in the political culture of India which is making the Prime Minister, his government and their performance *unaccountable.* As political scientist Suhas Palshikar wrote[210], it is for social psychologists and theorists of democracy to ponder why this change has happened.

The Hindutva Factor

The role of the RSS – the fountainhead of 'Hindutva' ideology and the parent of ruling BJP – in bringing the extraordinary changes in social and political orders of India witnessing now is very significant. Andersen and Damle in their 2019 book "Messengers of Hindu Nationalism"[211] write, the RSS is arguably the largest civil society group in the world with close to 60,000 "shakhas" (branches, which hold daily indoctrination camps) and at least three dozen major platforms and organizations working in social, cultural and political spheres. There are innumerable associate organizations, militant and extremist groups ("saffron terror" in Chapter I) which are part of the larger right-wing Hindutva ecosystem spread across the country – about which Dhirendra Jha's "Shadow Army"[212] gives a detailed account. They are the foot soldiers; a huge committed cadre base the RSS has built since 1925 – for about 100 years. The BJP is the political wing of this ecosystem called the "Sangh Parivar" or RSS family; it runs the central and over a dozen state governments.

Just how deeply the RSS is entrenched in polity and society was revealed by Arundhati Roy, a strong critic of their politics, in her Sissy Farenthold lecture in the US on April 20, 2022. She said[213]: "In 2025, the RSS will mark its hundredth year. One hundred years of evangelical dedication has made it a nation within a nation. Historically the RSS has been tightly controlled by a coterie of west coast Brahmins. Today it has fifteen million members, among them Modi, several of his cabinet ministers, chief ministers, and governors. It is a parallel universe now, with tens of thousands of primary schools, its own farmer, worker, and student organizations, its own publishing wing, an evangelical wing that works among forest-dwelling tribes to "purify" them and "return" them to Hinduism, a range of women's organizations, a several-million-strong armed militia inspired by Mussolini's black shirts, and a plethora of unimaginably violent Hindu nationalist organizations that perform the role of shell companies and provide what is known as plausible deniability."

Now the Hindutva ideologues has spread into governments and institutions at all levels. Not just the Prime Minister but three out of four ministers in his Council of Ministers have roots in the RSS.[214] The Hindutva ideologues are in the PSUs boards (Chapter VII) and key institutions of accountability "to ensure their institutional capture", as Prof Khaitan wrote (Chapter V). Two key institutions, the National Commission for Women (NCW) and the National Commission for Protection of Child Rights (NCPCR) – both with wide powers to summon, probe and influence justice delivery – are now headed by individuals who have aligned the previously independent institutions to the Hindutva ideology and appointment rules were changed in 2022[215] to keep them in office. Once, while conceding that the Emergency was a "mistake", Congress leader Rahul Gandhi recalled[216] his conversation with former Congress Chief Minister of Madhya Pradesh Kamal Nath (before his government was overthrown in 2020 through defections). Nath reportedly told him that senior bureaucrats in his government would not listen to him as they belonged to the RSS.

Rewriting History: Capturing Intellectual Space and Young Minds through 'Saffronization'

'Saffronization' of education, particularly of history books, was started by the first BJP-led government by Atal Bihari Vajpayee's HRD (it was changed to 'Education' by the current regime) Minister Murli Manohar Joshi – sparking wider concerns and criticism.[217]

Hindutva ideologues particularly dominate education institutions, like the apex historical research body, Indian Council of Historical Research (ICHR)[218], apex grant and standard setting body for higher education, University Grant Commission (UGC)[219], leading university, Jawaharlal Nehru University (JNU)[220] and top civilian employment agency, Union Public Service Commission (UPSC)[221].

These ideologues are now leading the operation of rewriting school textbooks. Investigations by the Indian Express in 2022 revealed that 24 members with RSS links[222] are part of the national focus groups revising the National Curriculum Framework (NCF) for this purpose. The targets are social science books for class VI to XII – which are considered "facilitators of critical thinking" in students and thus, a threat to such development in the future generations. The investigative reports showed the revision seeks to *delete* important events and facts from the textbooks of the National Council of Educational Research and Training (NCERT) used extensively across the country, both in public and private schools. The deletions involve four sets of facts with clear social and political overtones: (i) content on the Delhi Sultanate and Mughal Empire (ii) content on the Emergency of 1975-77 and Gujarat pogrom of 2002 (iii) contents on inequities of the Hindu caste system and (iv) content on social and protest movements like the Narmada Bachao Andolan. These deletions go against the government's own National Economic Policy of 2021, which is ideologically agnostic.

The official reason for such deletion is to reduce the content to help students in "speedy recovery" in learnings disrupted by the pandemic (which is misleading because the rewriting continues in 2023). The deletions are clearly aimed at wiping out the history of Muslim rulers, state repressions and failures that the Emergency and Gujarat pogrom represent, oppressiveness and rigidity of the Hindu caste system and protest movements that challenge the established political order.

Palshikar[223] points out, the deletions reflect the ruling *establishment's idea of democracy and social sciences* and is driven by politics without academic rigour and objectivity. Others have commented that the Hindutva thinks the three big historic assaults on their idea of Hindu culture are "Muslim invasions, British capture and Gandhiji's rise to become the Father of Modern India" and rewriting of history is their attempt to hide their lack of contribution to India's freedom and establishment of modern India in 1947.[224] Palshikar was one of the chief advisors to the NCERT who withdrew himself, so did Yogendra Yadav protesting that the texts had been "mutilated beyond recognition"; strangely, the NCERT refused to remove their names saying that no "individual authorship is claimed" and "hence the withdrawal of association by anyone is out of question".[225] They were followed by 33 political scientists, including Peter Ronald de'Souza[226].

The NCERT first explained that many of the changes noticed *after* the books hit the market – which had been carried out without prior notifications (like removing sentences in Class XII relating to Hindu extremists' dislike for Gandhi and ban on the RSS after his assassination) was simply an "oversight" but later said those would *not be changed* ("will continue in 2023-24).[227] UGC chief M Jagadesh Kumar[228] dismissed the criticism saying the objective behind the "grumbling of protesting academicians was non-academic."

The pandemic disruption isn't the real reason; the rewriting is an ideological project. The *first round* had begun in 2017 when *additions* were made[229]: (a) the government's policies like the Swachh Bharat Abhiyan and demonetization (b) Rajput king Maharana Pratap (who fought and lost to Mughal emperor Akbar) and (c) additional information on Indian knowledge systems, like ancient Indian philosophy, yoga and Ayurveda. In the second round, in 2019, three chapters relating to caste struggles, history of cricket and impact of colonialism on rural communities were *deleted*.[230]. It continues well after the pandemic is over. Nor is it limited to the NCERT textbooks, which are used by most schools in India, but in the textbooks of BJP-ruled states as well. Here are a few examples to capture the magnitude of it.

(a) Food, poverty, inequality, Gujarat riots, understanding partition, cold war and reproduction in organisms etc. were found deleted from the NCERT textbooks in May 2022 in the name of reducing load and "rationalization".[231]

(b) Darwin's evolution theory and Periodic Table were deleted from Class X of NCERT book I 2022, but it came to be known that these would be taught in Class XI and XII when Education Minister Devendra Pradhan[232] said so a year later in 2023. What seemed to escape the minister's attention is that those joining non-science stream after Class X would be ignorant about these key scientific concepts.

(c) *Nehru out, Savarkar in*: In 2023, Karnataka's new Class VIII textbooks said Hindutva icon Savarkar *flew out* of the Andaman jail on *Bulbul birds* to visit motherland by the BJP-appointed committee, which justified it saying the flying out on Bulbul was "a figure of speech". The relevant sentence read: "There was not even a key hole in the cell where Savarkar was incarcerated. But bulbul birds used to visit the room and Savarkar used to sit on their wings and fly out and visit the motherland every day".[233] In June 2023, it was found the school textbooks of Uttar Pradesh would teach "50 great leaders of India" in which Pandit Nehru is missing but includes Hindutva leaders VD Savarkar and DD Upadhyay.[234] Savarkar got into the Madhya Pradesh textbooks in June 2023 with the state's Education Minister Inder Singh Parmar saying that Savarkar "became the *first writer* (note the missing 'participant') of the freedom movement and *called* the movement of 1857 as freedom struggle. He had an unprecedented contribution to India's independence, so he deserves the respect".[235]

(d) The BJP-run government had approved a drastic change in school textbooks in 2017 to teach that it was Maharana Pratap who had emerged victorious against Mughal emperor Akbar during the 16th-century Battle of Haldighati.[236]

(e) In 2020, textbooks in the BJP-ruled Karnataka dropped Tipu Sultan of Mysore who fought the British in their continued effort to demonize the Muslim ruler.[237]

Such changes come to public notice in drips because the exercise is carried out in *absolute secrecy*, not known to even advisors – as the protests by Palshikar and more than 30 other academics in the case of NCERT book shows. In August

2023, the NCERT set up a 19-member committee to develop final phase of developing new school textbooks for class III to XII which included the founding member of the RSS-affiliated Samskrita Bharati Chamu Krishna Shastry.[238] It promptly recommended study of mythological texts like the *Ramayan and Mahabharat* in school textbook – as part of history syllabi.[239] Which is not strange given the Hindutva take mythologies to be history – the assertion came from no less than Yellapragada Sudershan Rao, who was appointed as chairman of the Indian Council of Historical Research (ICHR) by the government immediately after Modi came to power in 2014.[240]

The rewriting of history is not limited to school textbooks.

Take the case of Delhi University. A "culture war"[241] is on – led by the Akhil Bharatiya Vidya Parishad (ABVP) and the National Democratic Teachers Front (NDTF), the students' and teachers' groups, respectively, linked to the RSS. It began with demand to remove lessons on the 2002 Gujarat pogrom, caste, sexuality and queerness, the 2013 Muzzafarnagar riots and anti-Muslim lynchings and the deletions continues. Unlike the NCERT, a mysterious censorship body called "oversight committee" was set up in 2019 for such deletions about which nothing is known. The teachings on Nehru, Tagore, Ambedkar, Raja Ram Mohan Roy and Muhammad Iqbal, the poet who wrote "*Saare jahan se achcha Hindostan hamara*", have been drastically cut. The new rising star is Savarkar who gets far more space. The rewriting of history and textbooks had begun with the first Prime Minister from the BJP, Atal Behari Vajpayee, in later 1990s and early 2000s. He also put Savarkar's portrait in the Parliament House in 2003, despite strong protests from the Opposition.[242] Now films have been made on Savarkar, Mumbai's new Varsova-Bandra sea link already named after him[243] and the new bridge in Mumbai is to be named after him[244]. Encouraged by such environment, non-academics and those with little training in history are now writing books on history[245].

Savarkar is a controversial historical figure. He wrote "Hindutva" which conceptualized the divisive "political" concept of Hindutva.[246] Mahatma Gandhi, in particular, remains an uneasy icon for Hindutva and its ambivalence towards him is more than evident. In 2023, the Gandhi Peace award was given to the Gita Press. Akshaya Mukul, who wrote an authoritative account of the Gita Press in 2015 ("Gita Press and the Making of Hindu India"[247]), pointed out the disconnect[248] between the Gandhian ideals and the values espoused by the publisher of Hindu texts.

However, the magnitude of Hindutva's infiltration into education and the government's involvement in the "culture war" in academic can't be complete without the following examples.

(i) A beginning was made with a two-day gathering in March 2017[249] in which more than 700 academics and vice chancellors from 51 state and central universities gathered in Delhi University to learn to bring the "true nationalist narrative" to academia. It was a closed-door event, called "Gyan Sangam" (knowledge summit) and one of its main speakers was RSS chief Mohan Bhagwat. The topics was "cultural onslaught on educational system", "colonisation" of intellectuals and the resurgence of nationalism in academia. You get the drift.

(ii) In 2023, the BJP-ruled Madhya Pradesh removed *actual candidates*, who had cleared written exams and interviews, and appointed RSS workers to public offices.[250] This is the same Shivraj Singh Chouhan-led BJP government which saw a massive recruitment scam called "VYAPAM" – which began with a test-fixing scandal so massive that it led to 2,000 arrests, including top politicians, academics and doctors. Then the suspects started turning up *dead*[251]. There is no closure to this scam yet.

(iii) In Delhi University, which have had close to 50% *ad hoc* teachers for more than a decade, new recruitment began in 2023 with those who are less qualified but "recommended" by certain "social and cultural organisations" (read the RSS and its sister organizations) – in place of adequately qualified and with 10-20 years of teaching experience in those very DU colleges.[252] That all permanent appointments are based on "ideological alignment rather than merit"[253] is an open secret.

(iv) The DU's Hansraj College has set up a *cow protection and research centre*.[254] The Indira Gandhi National Open University (IGNOU) introduced a Master's programme in *astrology* (which right-wingers equate with science) in 2021[255]; premier hospital AIIMS of Rishikesh is into clinical trials on yoga and chanting of gayatri mantra (religious hymn in Hinduism) for treating the Covid.[256] The IIT-Delhi was forwarded research proposals to promote cow urine and cow dung as medicines, under a programme called "SVAROP" – acronym for Scientific Validation And Research On 'Panchgavya' (concoction of cow dung, cow urine, milk, curd and ghee.[257]

The Orwellian erasure of inconvenient facts and history mentioned earlier extends to news media too. Inconvenient news reports are routinely taken down. Derogatory speeches of the Prime Minister are no longer available[258]; reports on assets and educational qualification of ministers have been deleted by national dailies[259]; even music legend Zubin Mehta was not spared and his observation that "I hope my Muslim friends can live in peace forever in India" was deleted – and restored after he complained[260]. In 2022, the Google told the Delhi High Court that it had removed contents relating to a controversial restaurant run by a Union Minister's daughter and promised to do more[261]. Facebook and Twitter are routinely asked to remove contents critical of the government – to which even the US objected[262]. Genocide follows erasure of history – warns Aditya Mukherjee[263] of the Jawaharlal Nehru University. He writes: "Whenever we have witnessed erasure of a particular community from our history, it is usually followed by a genocide of the community".

Hate trackers by news organizations, The Hindustan Times and IndiaSpend have been shut and their editors forced out[264]. While cancelling licenses of NGOs by abusing the FCRA is rampant, the information (data) on it has now been taken down[265] from the official website. So is the case with years of public records obtained through the RTI applications, although it is promised to be restored after recasting of the website[266]. Even a business conglomerate, the Adani group, stands accused of rewriting the entries about itself on Wikipedia using fake accounts and undeclared paid editors.[267] The risks of producing unthinking and ill-educated citizens are very real.

Rewriting history goes beyond textbooks.

What is on display is regressive ideas dominating politics and society – reflecting anti-intellectualism, anti-science, anti-modern and anti-liberal mindset. A few examples:

(a) The new ISRO chairman S Somnath – during whose term the Chandrayaan-3 landed on the moon in August 2023 – says[268] the principles of science originated in the Vedas, travelled to and adopted by the West. He is yet to explain which of these the Chandrayaan-3 or the ISRO has used in its space sciences. Later this expedition got into the NCERT school textbooks[269] – which credited the success of it to the Prime Minister, not the ISRO scientists or the Congress governments that set up the ISRO and built the scientific temperament or mindset in the first place. This isn't something new though. Better known astrophysicists Meghnad Saha and Jayant V Narlikar studied the Vedas to discover the link and rubbished the claims in earlier decades.[270]

(b) IIT-Mandi director Laxmidhar Behera told students in 2023 not to eat meat because that is what caused the devastating cloudbursts, landslides, environmental degradations in Himachal Pradesh. He has built a reputation preaching about exorcism and finding that people die from overeating, not hunger.[271]

These two examples are particularly disturbing because Nehru wanted India to develop scientific temper and established top grade scientific institutions, including the ISRO, BARC and also the IITs, IIMs, AIIMS and many others. This is not surprising. The incumbent Prime Minister and his government have been consistently trying to erase Nehru and discredit his legacy for long. The Prime Minister told the Parliament in 2018 that Nehru and the Congress *didn't bring democracy to India*[272]; Union Home Minister Shah said in 2019 that the Kashmir problems was a "Himalayan blunder" by

Nehru[273] etc. In 2023, Nehru's official residence, the Teen Murti Bhavan, which housed the Nehru Memorial Museum and Library (NMML), was renamed as Prime Ministers Museum and Library (PMML) – having converted into the memorial for all Prime Ministers of India.[274]

(c) Then Union Minister for Science and BJP leader Harsh Vardhan, a qualified medical practitioner, claimed in 2018 that Stephen Hawking had "emphatically said on record that our Vedas might have a theory which is superior to Einstein's theory of e=mc2"[275].

(d) Hindutva's beef with Darwin's evolution theory is very old. BJP MP Satyapal Singh (a retired IPS officer) had claimed in 2019: "Darwin's theory is scientifically wrong… Since man is seen on Earth, he has always been a man. Nobody, including our ancestors, written or oral, said they saw an ape turning into a man." He had added, humans were "children of rishis" without explaining where did rishis (ancinet sages) came from.[276]

(e) Then high court judge Justice Mahesh Chandra Sharma told media in 2017 that peacocka are 'brahmacharis' (celibates) and don't have sex; peahens get pregnant by drinking his tears (this was after seeking life imprisonment for cow slaughter and national animal status for cow in a judgement).[277]

(f) The incumbent Prime Minister and his government have promoted all kinds of rubbish for treatment of Covid-19 – like cow urine, sun-bathing, "Bhabhiji" papad, 'chyawanprash', 'kadha', Coronil etc.[278]

Odd balls always exist in any society but there is a deliberate attempt to create an alt-reality here. Here are two important examples.

- In Karnataka, where Tipu Sultan has been constantly demonized by the BJP and its support groups, fake historical characters and narratives have been created; one is to show that it wasn't the British who killed him in battle but two fictional characters Uri Gowda and Nanje Gowda.[279]

- In North India, similar fictional characters and exaggerated stories of valour against Muslims have been invented (particularly about Rampyari Gurjar) – both as part of the BJP's caste politics.[280]

Now 'saffronization' is rapidly spreading to other spheres.

West Bengal Chief Minister Mamata Banerjee strongly objected to saffron dress for the "Men in Blue" and paints for metro stations[281] in 2023. Sports writer Sharda Ugra wrote (2023)[282] about the saffron dress code for crickets: "Let's start with the plan (later cancelled) to have the Indians wear a one-time all-orange uniform in the match against Pakistan at the Narendra Modi Stadium. India vs Pakistan, Hindu orange vs Muslim green, pick your team. Get it? It was not the first time the Indians have dressed in sizeable orange. At the 2019 World Cup they wore a half-orange shirt (sleeves and back) against England on UNICEF's Day for Children, with the kit later donated for charity auction. Except UNICEF's CWC Day for Children this time was 2 November, when India played Sri Lanka. Where a saffron uniform would not have packed the punch as it would have had against Pakistan. That was the end of the all-orange kit."

The Cricket World Cup of 2023 (ODI) saw *unusual jingoism*, particularly at the main venue the "Narendra Modi Stadium" in Ahmedabad. Taunting Pakistani players, shouting slogans of "Jai Shri Ram" and "Bharat Mata ki Jai", a cop stopping Pakistani fans from shouting "Pakistan Zindabad" in Pakistan-Australia match (Bangalore) and advising him to shout "Bharat Mata Ki Jai" cheering their teams, delays in issuing visas to the Pakistani team, too few foreign fans, absolute lack of appreciation for foreign players, booed umpires after India lost, left the venue before the Australian team was handed over the trophy – and which culminated in the Prime Minister *walking out* of the stage immediately after handing over the trophy to the winning captain Pat Cummins, before the latter could lift the trophy to give a bemused, sheepish look as he was stranded alone on the stage, forcing the cricket magazine Wisden to call it "most awkward presentation of all time".[283] Kapil Dev, who had won the first World Cup for India in 1983 was not invited for the ceremonial welcome at the final, presumambly because of his support for women wrestlers protesting against the sexual harassment by BJP MP Brij Bhushan Saran Singh (Chapter IV).[284]

Rise of Militant Groups

The rise of Hindutva ideology is accompanied with the rise of militant groups associated with the Sangh Parivar. Dhirendra Jha, who traces the RSS activities and its Hindutva politics, lists the activities of "burgeoning" organizations such as the Vishwa Hindu Parishad (VHP), Bajrang Dal (BD), Sri Ram Sene, Hindu Yuva Vahini (HYV), Sanatan Sanstha, Hindu Aikya Vedi – the "shadow armies"[285]. Jaffrelot writes[286] "vigilantism" is "inherent" to the very mission of the RSS from its inception – but "outsourcing"coercion through violence" to its various affiliates like BD. The BD has spread violence from Gujarat to Karnataka to Uttar Pradesh, Haryana and indeed, most part of India – and openly gives *arms training*[287] to its cadre all over the country without the fear of law and despite court cases filed against this practice. The right-wing organizations routinely carry *deadly weapons*[288] during their religious processions, allowed by police even where they clamp prohibitory orders (Section 144), through the Muslim areas. In 2018, the US's CIA described the VHP and BD as "religious militant organizations" – in its "World Factbook".[289] It also named the RSS ("nationalist organization"), Hurriyat Conference ("separatist group") and Jamiat Ulema-e Hind ("religious organization"), among other political pressure groups in India.

Politicization of Police and Defence Forces

Far more insidious and dangerous is the ideological shift in police forces of the BJP-ruled states of Madhya Pradesh, Uttar Pradesh and Haryana – which are now allies of these militant groups[290] along with local Hindu community and panchayats[291]. Gujarat has a disturbing history of politicized police and in 2022, it staged a public flogging of Muslims in Kheda district despite court directives against such human rights violations and brutality.[292]

In Delhi (Delhi Police comes under the Central government), the role of police has been blatantly partisan – both during and after the Delhi riots of 2020. A particular video which went viral showed cops forcing five Muslim youths to sing "Vande Mataram" after beating them to pulp; one of them 23-year-old Faizan died. Such is the callousness and insensitivity of Delhi Police that three years later, the Delhi High Court (on May 8, 2023) had to order the recording of the statement of one of the five[293] (see more Chapters I and IV). There have been several incidents of police shouting "Jai Shri Ram"[294] – a Hindutva battle cry – while attacking Muslims. Communal poison has seeped so deep that even Indian Railways' security guard Chetansinh Chaudhary (acting alone, not in group) randomly pumped bullets into three Muslims in a moving train and thereafter gave a cool speech hailing Hindutva leaders.[295] Investigations later revealed that he had forced a burqa-clad (Muslim) woman to shout "Jai Mata Di" at gun point.[296]

Even more insidious and dangerous is the change in armed forces. Both serving and retired defence personnel attend RSS functions, visit temples associated with BJP leaders; Hindu rituals, like havans, totems, are now official part.[297] Defence Minister Rajnath Singh welcomed the Rafale jets in 2019 by applying "nimbu, mirchi and nariya" (lemon, chili and coconut)[298] – ironically, to ward off evil spirits from these planes. Defence expert Rahul Bedi wrote[299]: "It is no secret that many senior service personnel are increasingly identifying themselves with the Hindu nationalist BJP-led administration, that in turn unashamedly seeks to exploit military achievements for political gain."

An investigative report alleged that the Indian Army played a covert role in the hyper-nationalist protests in Kashmir aligned to promote the political interest of the BJP[300] – thereby endangering both Indian democracy and the Indian Army's standing as a professional force. In 2023, an Army major was accused of storming *two mosques in Pulwama* district in early hours and forcing (Muslim) worshippers to chant "Jai Shri Ram".[301] Around the same time, in Manipur, a mob of Hindu Meitei women led by a BJP legislator, *forced* the army to release 12 members of Kanglei Yawol Kanna Lup (KYKL), a terrorist organization during the civil war with Christian Kuki tribes – both severely denting the image and professionalism.[302] This was unprecedented in India.

Yet another unprecedented incident occurred when the state police and Assam Rifles (operationally under the Army and the oldest paramilitary force) had a public spat – following which the police filed a case (FIR) against the Assam Rifles for obstructing public servants. This damages not just the image of the army but the authoritative force of state. The apathy of both the political and military leadership (the FIR stands) creates a new vulnerability in the army's ability to manage and control internal security in future and also opens the space for future conflicts between police and army.[303]

On the other hand, this spat also brought to light the Army's lack of trust in the BJP-ruled Central and state governments. The Editors Guild of India (EGI)[304] facing an FIR by the Manipur police over its fact-finding report, told the apex court in September 2023 that it had gone to Manipur on the *invitation of the Army*. It presented a letter from a Colonel which said the local media had "been indulging in outright misrepresentation of facts that violate all norms of journalistic ethics and in the process may be one of the major contributors to the instigation of further violence". The helplessness of the Army reminds one of film star Sonu Sood, mentioned earlier, whose help an Army officer sought to set up a Covid-19 hospital in Jaisalmer in 2021 – instead of the Defence Ministry or the Central government. Both Jammu and Kashmir and Manipur are the BJP's double-engine-ruled states.

But then, the first Chief of Defence Staff (CDS) and former Army chief General Bipin Rawat[305] had made light of human rights (as narrated in Chapter I). On the other hand, in April 2023, the Modi government *denied permission*[306] to prosecute 30 Army personnel found guilty of killing 14 civilians in a fake encounter in Nagaland in 2021 – with the court martial concluding "a case of mistaken identity and error of judgement"[307]. This not only goes against multiple apex court verdicts and the Army's own rules[308] but makes mockery of human rights and widens the trust gap between people and the Army.

In September 2023, came another shocking news from Kerala's Kollam district. An Army soldier Shinekumar complained that he was attacked by six people who also wrote "PFI" on his back in green paint. The next day, his friend was arrested who revealed that it was fabricated case; the paint and brush were seized. The police said the soldier had done this to get national attention.[309] By then, the news had gone viral. 'PFI' stands for Popular Front of India, a radical Muslim group with a strong base in Kerala and Karnataka which was banned in September 2022 by the MHA for alleged unlawful activities and links with banned Islamist groups – the Students Islamic Movement of India (SIMI), Jamat-ul-Mujahideen Bangladesh (JMB) and Islamic State of Iraq and Syria (ISIS).[310] It had earned notoriety first in 2010 for attacking and severing the hand of Kerala professor TJ Joseph in 2010 over a Malayalam question paper on punctuation in which a person was named 'Mohammed'.[311]

In the meanwhile, in May 2023, the news of a letter from the Ceremonials and Welfare Directorate of the Adjutant General's Branch of Army Headquarters to all Command Headquarters hit the headlines. It directed[312] all soldiers going on annual leave to do "social service" to enhance "nation-building efforts". This "social service" entails talking to local community about the government's programmes like the Swachh Bharat Abhiyan, Ayushman Bharat, National Pension System (NPS), Atal Pension Yojana, Deendayal Grameen Kaushalya Yojana etc. and provide feeback. (NB: This was followed by a similar order from the DoPT under the PMO in October 2023 for all central services to appoint "rath prabharis" and take out "rath yatras" in all districts and all village panchayats to highlight the government's development works during November 20, 2023-January 25, 2024 – amidst the high-stake elections in five states and in the run-up to the 2024 general elections (April-May 2024) – as detailed in Chapter V.)

Defence expert Sushant Singh[313] pointed out, not one of the schemes listed included flagship schemes of the previous UPA government like the MGNREGS or others run by rival party-ruled states – making the political motive obvious. He also red-flagged the Air Force's silence when a BJP spokesperson made false allegations about its operations in Mizoram in 1966 and named and maligned wrongly two former IAF officers. He warned: "The military can be in politics if it behaves like its Pakistani counterpart but is equally politicized if it concurs to be used by the political leadership. A politicised military is scarcely professional." The move has caused consternation among other defence experts too. Lt Gen HS Panag wrote[314]: "Governments come and go. All ranks of the armed forces on enrolment/commissioning undertake an oath of allegiance to the Constitution and are duty-bound to remain apolitical. The "social warrior" scheme violates the terms and conditions of military service, impinges on domestic commitments and is likely to get soldiers involved in local politics. Soldiers should not become a tool for promoting the policies of the ruling party. The sooner, this scheme is withdrawn the better it would be."

The government's policy of inducting "Agniveers" under the "Agnipath" scheme of recruiting defence personnel for the Army, Navy and Air Force is another cause of serious concern.

"Agnipath" is a neoliberal contractual hiring system for the defence forces for a period of four years with minimal training (six months), at the end of which 75% will be retired without pension and social security ("Tour of Duty"). It poses systemic threats to the defence forces' professionalism and also to national security and society itself. Veterans, including Major General GG Dwivedi (retd) who called it "tourist soldiering[315], have expressed their strong opposition, arguing that it would adversely impact battle-readiness and professional ethos of soldiering. Admiral Arun Prakash (retd)[316] said the Army may not be so much burdened by the short training but for the Navy and Air Force would be as "at least 5-6 years are required" for to acquire enough experience to operate and maintain lethal weapon systems and complex machinery and electronics".

Sushant Singh[317] has repeatedly drawn attention to the "catastrophic" impact it may have for society once 75% "Agniveers" retire every four years. He argues that given the shrinking job market, it wouldn't be easy or smooth to absorb the influx of thousands of youths trained in inflicting violence in organized manner in the society – which is already in the grip of majoritarian violence. The retired "Agniveers" may end up as a "major recruiting pool" for groups wishing to use violence (which self-select themselves) to pursue their ideological goals. He draws attention to the critical role the World War II veterans played in the ethnic cleansing and violence during the partition riots of 1947 in India, and also elsewhere like Yugoslavia and Rwanda. Scholar Nayantara Sheoran Appleton calls the scheme a "Frankenstein Monster"[318] which may become a training ground for the next set of foot-soldiers for "hate-mongering organisations with no compunctions about public violence".

On the face of it, the compulsion for the hire-and-fire scheme is to cut the rising salary and pension bill of the defence ministry. The Army has declared to fill 50% of its force with "Agniveers" by 2032, beginning with 46,000 in 2022, in its attempt also to cut down the Army's strength.[319] In FY22, salary and pension bill alone accounted 54%, the largest portion of the defence budget.[320] On its part, the Supreme Court (bench led by CJI Justice Chandrachud and Justices PS Narasimha and JB Pardiwala) refused to examine the constitutionality of the short-term contract which had earlier been upheld by the Delhi High Court and dismissed all petitions saying that there is "no vested right" to get employed[321] – to emphasize that millions of youths preparing to join the defence forces but disappointed with the temporary nature of "Agnipath" could always opt out.

Hindutva's Intrinsic Governance-Deficit and Counter-attack

In 'Introduction', it has been explained that Hindutva is in conflict with the constitutional values and *intrinsically governance-deficit*. About the latter, as it was mentioned, political scientist Peter Ronald deSouza had explained that when their lack of skills, incompetence and ineptitude are exposed, the RSS-BJP members grown up in the RSS "shakhas" unleash shenanigans now manifest all around in India now – demonization of critics and truth tellers as "anti-nationals", weakening of autonomous institutions, propaganda and reliance on pseudo-science etc.

This aspect needs more attention because these shenanigans mark a new low in public life and reduce political accountability to a farce. While other aspects have been dealt with in some details in this chapter and earlier ones, one particular trait needs to be flagged here: Liberal use of intemperate languages and inanities as official response now so pervasive. A few examples.

In 2021, Union Minister Piyush Goyal[322] publicly called arguably India's most respected business house, the Tata group, that their business practices were anti-national for opposing the government's draft e-commerce rules. This was also criticized by others at the time, except the one known to be close to the government. Same year, Finance Minister Nirmala Sitharaman snubbed Congress leader Rahul Gandhi with a jibe on his "jijjaji"[323] (brother-in-law Robert Vadra) for objecting to the National Monetisation Pipeline (NMP) plan (handing over all brownfield public infrastructure to private businesses). Complaints against *unwarranted high fuel prices* (explained in Chapter VIII) provoked the most bizarre responses. In 2021, Sitharaman first blamed it on the "trickery" of the previous Congress-led UPA government[324] and later in 2022, on the Russian-Ukraine war[325] even as the import of substnatially cheap Russian oil was not passed on to consumers.[326] Another Union Minister Dharmendra Pradhan had said, in 2021, that high oil prices were due to "intense cold"[327]; a BJP legislator Arvind Bellad had blamed it on the Taliban take-over[328] of Afghanistan (Afghanistan doesn't export oil to India). Many BJP ministers and leaders have claimed high oil tax was to finance "free" Covid-19 vaccines, that it didn't matter to 95% of people or asked the questioning voices to go to Pakistan or Afghanistan etc.[329]

Political scientists Jyotirmaya Sharma wrote in his 2015 book "Hindutva: Exploring the Idea of Hindu Nationalism"[330] that "introduction of invective, abuse and contempt as legitimate tools of writing, conversation and public discourse" is one of the *six defining characteristics of Hindutva*. The other five characteristics he listed are: Transforming Hinduism to a rigid, codified, monochromatic entity; portraying the idea of Hinduism as masculine, aggressive and violent faith; reducing Hinduism into a story of confrontation and misfortune; victimhood, conspiracies and never-ending sense of threat to Hinduism, equating Hinduism with the nation or the very core of it and Hinduism had been perfected in the Vedas and Upanishads, the important thing was returning to the essential core of the Vedas and recreation of the Golden Age.

Now it is easier to understand why the current governance model is essentially about rhetoric, spectacles, fake news, propaganda, stealth, whataboutery, politics of hate-and-violence, undignified public discourses, a command-and-control economy meant for promoting cronies and crumbs for the impoverished millions.

Stanley in his book "How Fascism Works", mentioned earlier, lists 10 "distinct strategies" of Fascist regimes with a warning: "Fascist politics includes many distinct strategies: the mythic past, propaganda, anti-intellectualism, unreality, hierarchy, victimhood, law and order, sexual anxiety, appeals to the heartland, and a dismantling of public welfare and unity. Though a defense of certain elements is legitimate and sometimes warranted, there are times in history when they come together in one party or political movement. These are dangerous moments."[331]

In 2023, journalist Hartosh Singh Bal[332] cross-checked the "12-step authoritarian playbook"[333] of Standford University's Larry Diamond:

1. *Begin to demonize the opposition as illegitimate and unpatriotic, part of the discredited establishment, out of touch with the "true people."*

2. *Undermine the independence of the courts by forcing existing judges to retire or and then packing the courts.*

3. *Undermine the independence of the media, by denouncing them as partisan, mobilizing the intense populist following against them, taking over ownership of them through politically loyal businesses and party-linked political cronies, and so on.*

4. *If there is public broadcasting, gain control of it and politicize it.*

5. *Impose stricter control of the Internet, in the name of morality, security, counter-terrorism, but casting a chilling effect on free speech.*

6. *Subdue other elements of civil society—particularly NGOs and universities—by casting them as elitist, politically partisan and anti-government.*

7. *Intimidate the business community into ceasing support for opposition parties.*

8. *Use state control over contracts, credit flows, and other resources to enrich a new class of political crony capitalists who are tightly linked to and reliably supportive of the ruling party.*

9. *Extend political control over the state bureaucracy and security apparatus to purge the "deep state" of anyone not slavishly loyal. Use the state intelligence apparatus as a weapon against the opposition.*

10. *Gerrymander constituencies and otherwise rig electoral rules to make it much more difficult for opposition parties to win the next election.*

11. *Gain control over electoral administration to further tilt the electoral playing field and institutionalize competitive authoritarianism.*

12. *Repeat steps 1 to 11, ever more vigorously, deepening fear of opposing or criticizing the new political hegemony and thus demobilizing all significant forms of resistance.*

Guess what Hartosh found? Of the 12, 11 steps to be "true" and only one "untrue" – which was: Number 10. Reminding that the RSS would complete its 100th years in 2025, he observed: "…it should not be too much of a surprise if we move to *consecrate* what is already true de facto: India as a *Hindu nation in the image of the RSS*." (Emphasis added)

That says it all.

When Vajpayee led the BJP in late 1990s and early 2000s, the BJP was presented as a "natural party of governance" and a "party with a difference".[334] One doesn't hear any of it any more. The BJP certainly is a party with a difference – in the wrong sense as it has amply demonstrated – but certainly not a "natural party of governance". On the contrary, the BJP is *intrinsically unfit for governance*, which was not so evident during the Vajpayee years as Prime Minister – his being a coalition government with a good mix of centrist and secular parties as partners who kept the BJP's Hindu supremacist impulses in check (which is why the BJP kept aside its "core" divisive agenda of temple, Article 370 and UCC aside then).

Finally, to answer the question that remains unanswered: Why hasn't the Prime Minister paid a political price for his all-round failures?

The answer is a combination of factors highlighted in earlier chapters and this one:

(i)   Disillusionment of 'aspirational' Indians with the corruption and falling jobs in the second term of the Congress-led UPA government that led to excessive investment in the BJP ('low-bowling' and 'mindless consistency').

(ii)   Strong undercurrent of Hindutva and the manifest 'Bhakti' culture ('voluntary servitude') – which is reflected in the intellectual support to the government more than to any other in the past with CAs, ex-diplomats, ex-bureaucrats, ex-judges jumping in to support the government and its leadership. This is despite a decade of apparent incompetence, ineptness and damage to India's social, political and economic orders. The subservience of mainstream media and judiciary has accelerated the downward spiral of the nation.

(iii)   Keeping the communal pot boiling by feeding hate and violence against 'the enemy' – Muslims and other minorities, Dalits etc. ('hate' being the most accessible and comprehensive unifying agent).

(iv)   Creation of a new vote bank, the 'labharthi varg', and its constant harnessing by the government and the BJP through efficient delivery of welfare measures (through mainly cash transfers adn ration) – which helps alleviating the pains of worsening economic wellbeing and dents anti-incumbency.

(v)   Constant feeding of fake news and propaganda to create altered reality in which the Prime Minister is "Vishwaguru" and India a political and economic superpower because of him – which the mainstream media amplifies as a matter of routine and suppresses the harsh ground realities.

(vi)   Running a high-efficient 24x7 election-winning machinery – through institutionalized coordination between the government and the BJP leaders and cadre.

(vii)   Suppression of dissent and political rivals with all the state's might.

(viii) Enfeebled and ineffective Opposition.

(ix)   Use of majority in the Lok Sabha and enormous state power to breakdown institutions of accountability, checks and balances.

(x)   Failure of higher judiciary to uphold fundamental rights, rule of law and constitutional values.

(xi)   Economic policies oriented towards cronies and other private businesses to maximise their profits and win their affection (the opaque Electoral Bond being very helpful).

***

References

1   UNDP 2011: Governance principles, institutional capacity and quality, UNDP, 2011; https://www.dropbox.com/s/i5xf789xufnbk5o/UNDP%208%20Governance%20principles.pdf?dl=0

2   Keane John, The New Despotism, page 8-9 and 14, Harvard University Press, London, 2020; https://www.hup.harvard.edu/catalog.php?isbn=9780674660069

3   Maskelyne Nevil, Devant David, Our Magic: The art in magic, the theory of magic and the practice of magic, EP Dutton & Company, 1911; https://ia800900.us.archive.org/33/items/ourmagicartinmag00mask/ourmagicartinmag00mask.pdf

4   Bardhan Pranab, Working class politics: A global puzzle, Nov 21, 2022; https://www.business-standard.com/article/opinion/working-class-politics-a-global-puzzle-122112101073_1.html; Paidipaty Poornima, Interview | Fragile Democracies, the Global Shift Towards Right-Wing Populism, and Rising Inequality, Aug 4, 2023; https://thewire.in/politics/interview-fragile-democracies-the-global-shift-towards-right-wing-populism-and-rising-inequality

5   Modi repeats same Rs 100 lakh crore infrastructure plan in three I-Day speeches in a row, Scroll, Aug 16, 2021; https://amp.scroll.in/latest/1002917/modi-repeats-same-rs-100-lakh-crore-infrastructure-plan-in-three-i-day-speeches-in-a-row?__twitter_impression=true

6   Provisional Estimates of Annual National Income 2020-21, Ministry of Statistics and Programme Implementation, GOI, May 31, 2021; http://mospi.nic.in/sites/default/files/press_release/Press%20Note_31-05-2021.pdf

7   Prime Minister launches PM Gati Shakti, Prime Minister's Office, Oct 13, 2021: https://pib.gov.in/PressReleasePage.aspx?PRID=1763576

8   Singh Karunjit, Explained: Connecting ministries for infrastructure projects, Indian Express, Oct 16, 2021; https://indianexpress.com/article/explained/pm-gatishakti-infrastructure-development-projects-7574071/

9   States on board Gati Shakti, govt looks to cut project time, Jul 9, 2022; https://indianexpress.com/article/business/economy/states-on-board-gati-shakti-govt-looks-to-cut-project-time-8018273/

10   Chaturvedi Swati, 'It's a Decentralised Emergency... A Pyramidal Mafia State': Arun Shourie on Modi Sarkar, The Wire, Jan 14, 2017; https://thewire.in/politics/decentralised-emergency-pyramidal-mafia-state-arun-shourie-modi-sarkar

11   Singh DK, Something has changed for Modi. Perception management isn't working anymore, The Print, Apr 27, 2021; https://theprint.in/opinion/politically-correct/something-has-changed-for-modi-perception-management-isnt-working-anymore/646560/; Yadav Yogendra, Modi govt rejig has nothing to do with real governance, it's all about perception management, The Print, Jul 8, 2021; https://theprint.in/opinion/modi-govt-rejig-has-nothing-to-do-with-real-governance/692423/

12   Dictionary of Military and Associated Terms, Department of Defense, USA, 12 April 2001, Apr 12, 2001; https://www.cia.gov/library/abbottabad-compound/B9/B9875E9C2553D81D1D6E0523563F8D72_DoD_Dictionary_of_Military_Terms.pdf

13   Kapoor Brigadier BM, The Art of Perception Management in Information Warfare Today, The United Service Institute of India, Oct-Dec 2009; https://usiofindia.org/publication/usi-journal/the-art-of-perception-management-in-information-warfare-today-2/

14   No shortage of Covid vaccines, oxygen, medicines: Harsh Vardhan…New Indian Express, Apr 18, 2021; https://www.newindianexpress.com/states/karnataka/2021/apr/18/no-shortage-of-covid-vaccines-oxygen-medicinesharsh-vardhan-2291464.html

15   No deaths due to lack of oxygen reported during second Covid wave: Centre, Jul 21, 2021; https://www.indiatoday.in/coronavirus-outbreak/story/covid-second-wave-lack-shortage-liquid-medical-oxygen-lmo-deaths-health-ministry-response-parliament-1830549-2021-07-20

16   Coronavirus India Highlights: PM Modi asks CMs to focus on micro-containment, Indian Express, Apr 9, 2021; https://indianexpress.com/article/india/india-coronavirus-second-wave-live-updates-lockdown-curfew-rules-cases-deaths-vaccination-7262037/

17   India sets record with 2.5 crore COVID-19 jabs in one day, Sept 17, 2021; https://www.thehindu.com/news/national/india-administers-record-2-crore-50-lakh-covid-19-vaccine-doses-in-a-single-day-on-september-17-2021/article36512270.ece

18   CoWIN dashboard; https://dashboard.cowin.gov.in/

19   PM Narendra Modi performs 'bhoomi pujan' for Ram temple in Ayodhya, Aug 5, 2021; https://economictimes.indiatimes.com/news/politics-and-nation/pm-narendra-modi-performs-bhoomi-pujan-for-ram-temple-in-ayodhya/articleshow/77368092.cms?utm_source=contentofinterest&utm_medium=text&utm_campaign=cppst

20   The monstrous monument to Narendra Modi's ego, Daily Mail, UK, May 8, 2021; https://www.dailymail.co.uk/news/article-9547379/DAVID-JONES-millions-suffer-pandemic-Indias-narcissistic-leader-building-folly.html

21   Mohanty P, India has no data to challenge WHO excess Covid deaths, https://www.fortuneindia.com/opinion/india-has-no-data-to-challenge-who-excess-covid-deaths/108072

22   Top Central government officials attend session on boosting image, perception, May 5, 2021; https://www.hindustantimes.com/india-news/officials-attend-session-on-boosting-image-perception-101620153678959.html

23   Speaking Positivity to Power: Hours before lockdown, Modi asked print-media owners, editors to refrain from negative COVID coverage, Caravan, Mar 31, 2020; https://caravanmagazine.in/media/hours-before-lockdown-modi-asked-print-media-owners-editors-refrain-negative-covid-coverage

24   Bal Hartosh Singh, Paranoia about digital coverage led ministers to propose media clampdown, monitoring "negative influencers", Caravan, Mar 4, 2021; https://caravanmagazine.in/politics/paranoia-about-digital-coverage-led-gom-propose-media-clampdown-monitoring-negative-influencers

25   Rana Chahat, Culpable Carnage: How the Modi government's failure to act led to India's COVID-19 catastrophe, Caravan, Jun 1, 2021; https://caravanmagazine.in/health/modi-government-failure-led-india-covid-19-catastrophe

26   Mohanty P, Rebooting Economy XXVI: Derailment of economy is not 'Act of God', it is 'Art of Misdirection', Business Today, Sept 11, 2020; https://www.businesstoday.in/opinion/columns/story/india-derailment-of-indian-economy-is-not-an-act-of-god-it-is-art-of-misdirection-job-loss-unemployment-gdp-272743-2020-09-11

27   Tablighi Jamaat men India held for 'spreading COVID' share ordeal, Mar 25, 2021; https://www.aljazeera.com/news/2021/3/25/tablighi-jamaat-members-held-for-spreading-covid-stuck-in-india

28   Chaudhuri Pooja, Sinha Pratik, 'COVID toolkit' attributed to Congress created on forged letterhead, May 19, 2021; https://www.altnews.in/covid-toolkit-attributed-to-congress-created-on-forged-letterhead/

29   Delhi Police conducts raid at Twitter India offices over 'toolkit row', May 24, 2021; https://zeenews.india.com/technology/delhi-police-conducts-raid-at-twitter-india-offices-over-toolkit-row-2364108.html

30   May 2021; https://www.bhaskar.com/db-original/news/narendra-modi-ministers-covid-tweet-analysis-amit-shah-nitin-gadkari-rajnath-singh-s-jaishankar-harsh-vardhan-128502399.html; (For English) When Social Media Was Flooded With COVID SOS Calls, Union Ministers Only Praised Centre, The Wire, May 18, 2021; https://thewire.in/politics/india-second-covid-wave-bjp-tweet-analysis-sos-amit-shah-harsh-vardhan-modi

31   Patel Aakar 2021: Price of Modi Years, Westland Publications, page 361, 2021; https://www.amazon.in/Price-Modi-Years-Aakar-Patel/dp/9391234224

32   Taskin Bismeet, Income Tax dept raids Dainik Bhaskar media group, 'Modified Emergency', says Opposition, Jul 22, 2021; https://theprint.in/india/income-tax-dept-raids-dainik-bhaskar-media-group-modified-emergency-says-opposition/700585/

33   Food please, not flowers: As Armed Forces choppers drop petals on hospitals, Twitter users are angry, May 3, 2020; https://scroll.in/article/960896/food-please-not-flowers-as-armed-forces-choppers-drop-petals-on-hospitals-twitter-users-are-angry

34   Singh Amrit Pal (retd, Major General), Parallels Between India's Mishandling of COVID and the Chinese Incursion in Ladakh, May 5, 2021; https://thewire.in/government/parallels-between-indias-mishandling-of-covid-and-the-chinese-incursion-in-ladakh

35   Actor Sonu Sood Tweets After Tax Raids: "Every Rupee In My Foundation...", Sept

20, 2021; https://www.ndtv.com/india-news/sonu-sood-responds-after-income-tax-department-says-he-evaded-rs-20-crore-in-taxes-2546806

36   Army brass frowns as CO writes to Sonu Sood for help with Covid facility equipment, Indian Express, May 22, 2021; https://indianexpress.com/article/india/army-brass-frowns-as-commanding-officer-writes-to-sonu-sood-for-covid-facility-equipment-7324876/

37   Did not use public funds for self: Journalist Rana Ayyub after Enforcement Directorate attachment, New Indian Express, Feb 11, 2022; https://www.newindianexpress.com/nation/2022/feb/11/did-not-use-public-funds-for-self-journalist-rana-ayyub-after-enforcement-directorate-attachment-2418332.html

38   IYC president Srinivas BV questioned by Delhi police over his 'Covid assistance' to people, New Indian Express, May 14, 2021; https://www.newindianexpress.com/cities/delhi/2021/may/14/indian-youth-congress-president-srinivas-bv-questioned-by-police-over-his-covid-assistance-to-peop-2302534.html

39   FIRs against DTC drivers, ANI, April 2, 2020; https://www.dropbox.com/s/3351402aj2lrtac/FIR%20against%20DTC%20drivers.jpg?dl=0

40   Sen Jahnavi, Did Modi Repeal Farm Laws Out of 'Respect'? Here's 12 Times BJP Leaders Tried to Discredit the Protests, The Wire, Nov 19, 2021; https://thewire.in/politics/farm-laws-repeal-modi-bjp-leaders-comments

41   Farmers' protest: Why did a Rihanna tweet prompt Indian backlash? Feb 3, 2021; https://www.bbc.com/news/world-asia-india-55914858

42   By pitching Lata vs Rihanna, Narendra Modi is playing the wrong score, Feb 4, 2021; https://scroll.in/article/985890/by-pitching-lata-vs-rihanna-narendra-modi-is-playing-the-wrong-score

43   Modi profiles 'Andolan Jeevis', warns about 'Foreign Destructive Ideology', Feb 9, 2021; https://www.telegraphindia.com/india/farmers-protest/cid/1806126

44   Narendra Modi Surrenders to the Farmers, Nov 26, 2021; https://www.wsj.com/articles/modi-surrenders-to-the-farmers-narendra-laws-revoke-government-protests-11637810356

45   Farm laws repeal Highlights: Samyukt Kisan Morcha to decide future course of action during meet on weekend, The Indian Express, Nov 20, 2021; https://indianexpress.com/article/india/modi-address-to-nation-live-updates-7630350/

46   'Modi Asked If Farmers Died For Him': Decoding Satya Pal Malik's Rebellion, Jan 3, 2022; https://www.thequint.com/news/politics/satya-pal-malik-pm-narendra-modi-farmers-protest-amit-shah

47   Ukraine crisis: Opposition parties question Centre about delay in evacuating Indian students, Mar 2, 2022; https://scroll.in/latest/1018591/ukraine-crisis-opposition-parties-question-centre-about-delay-in-evacuating-indian-students

48   Sabarwal Harshit, Evacuation of Indian students from Ukraine got delayed due to...: EAM Jaishankar slams opposition, Mar 16, 2022; https://www.hindustantimes.

com/india-news/evacuation-of-indian-students-from-ukraine-got-delayed-due-to-eam-slams-oppn-101647396117769.html

49 Inside The Online Ecosystem Shielding Modi Govt & Mocking Indian Students In Ukraine, Mar 3, 2022; https://article-14.com/post/inside-the-online-ecosystem-shielding-modi-govt-mocking-indian-students-in-ukraine-62202d6db8a2c

50 Nayak Mahaprajna and Kumar Abhishek, Did Modi halt Ukraine war for evacuating Indians? BJP leaders' claim was refuted by MEA, Feb 24, 2023; https://www.altnews.in/j-p-nadda-falsely-claim-russia-stopped-war-at-pm-modis-phone-call/

51 Modi stopped Russia-Ukraine war for 3 hours to evacuate Indian students: Ravi Shankar Prasad, IANS, Jun 4, 2022; https://economictimes.indiatimes.com/news/politics-and-nation/modi-stopped-russia-ukraine-war-for-3-hours-to-evacuate-indian-students-ravi-shankar-prasad/articleshow/92000852.cms?utm_source=contentofinterest&utm_medium=text&utm_campaign=cppst

52 Cowper Amit, 'Russia, Ukraine tanks kept silent for 3 days after Modi's call': Amit Shah, Nov 22,2022; https://www.hindustantimes.com/elections/gujarat-assembly-election/modi-called-ukraine-pm-russian-prez-to-halt-war-for-3-days-amit-shah-in-gujarat-101669131711141.html

53 Study medicine in India, not smaller foreign nations, PM Modi says amid Ukraine crisis, PTI, Feb 26, 2022; https://www.deccanherald.com/india/study-medicine-in-india-not-smaller-foreign-nations-pm-modi-says-amid-ukraine-crisis-1085305.html

54 Rao Yogita, Navi Mumbai's D Y Patil Medical College's Rs 1.4 crore medical degree India's costliest, Aug 15, 2023; http://timesofindia.indiatimes.com/articleshow/102735626.cms?from=mdr&utm_source=contentofinterest&utm_medium=text&utm_campaign=cppst

55 Mohanty P, Coronavirus Lockdown XI: Why India's health policy needs a course correction, Apr 29, 2020; https://www.businesstoday.in/latest/economy-politics/story/coronavirus-lockdown-covid-19-india-health-policy-healthcare-private-hospitals-256789-2020-04-29; National Medical Commission Bill 2019: What is it and why is the medical fraternity opposed to it?, Aug 14, 2019; https://www.businesstoday.in/opinion/columns/story/national-medical-commission-bill-2019-medical-education-in-india-217724-2019-07-24

56 Explained: Why is Ukraine so popular among Indian medical students, Feb 28, 2022; https://www.cnbctv18.com/world/explained-why-is-ukraineso-popular-among-indian-medical-students-12652752.htm

57 Kishana Ravikant, Difference in Degree: The conservative vision of liberal education in India, Oct 1, 2023; https://caravanmagazine.in/education/ashoka-university-private-universities-caste-sabyasachi-das

58 Smart Pallavi, IIM Mumbai fixes 2-year course fee at Rs 21 lakh from next year, Oct 19, 2023; https://indianexpress.com/article/cities/mumbai/iim-mumbai-fee-at-

rs-21-lakh-highest-in-new-gen-institutes-8986416/

59   Over 570% rise in IIM-Ahmedabad fees in 15 years? Entrepreneur shares shocking receipt, Feb 26, 2023; https://www.livemint.com/news/india/over-570-rise-in-iim-ahmedabad-fees-in-15-years-maheshwer-perishares-shocking-receipt-11677384010416.html

60   Dutt Anonna, Most medical colleges have ghost faculty, all fail to meet 50% attendance requirement, says NMC, Oct 2, 2023; https://indianexpress.com/article/india/majority-medical-colleges-have-ghost-faculty-fall-short-of-50-attendance-requirement-nmc-study-8964561/

61   Zhou Marrian, Indian students in U.S. hit new high as foreign enrollment rebounds, Nov 14, 2023; https://asia.nikkei.com/Business/Education/Indian-students-in-U.S.-hit-new-high-as-foreign-enrollment-rebounds

62   Parent Deepa, 'He Had an Arrogant Tone': Romanian Mayor on Row With Scindia Over Evacuation, Mar 2022; https://www.thequint.com/news/world/romanian-mayor-mihai-anghel-interview-verbal-spat-with-aviation-minister-jyotiraditya-scindia

63   Modi govt plans media blitz for 'image correction' to boost India rank on global lists, Aug 20, 2022; https://theprint.in/india/governance/modi-govt-plans-media-blitz-for-image-correction-to-boost-india-rank-on-global-lists/486035/

64   Narendra Modi Didn't Watch His Words on Chinese Intrusion So PMO 'Censors' Official Video, Jun 25, 2020; https://thewire.in/government/narendra-modi-china-video-pmo-censor

65   Narendra Modi's talk of '56-inch chest' draws acerbic response from Sharad Yadav, Jan 24, 2014; https://www.ndtv.com/india-news/narendra-modis-talk-of-56-inch-chest-draws-acerbic-response-from-sharad-yadav-548777

66   Modi is the man with 56-inch chest: Amit Shah, Apr 28, 2019; https://www.thehindu.com/elections/lok-sabha-2019/modi-is-the-man-with-56-inch-chest/article26973945.ece

67   Ellis-Petersen Hannah, 'The strongman blinks': why Narendra Modi has backed down to farmers, Nov 9, 2021; https://www.theguardian.com/world/2021/nov/19/the-strongman-blinks-why-narendra-modi-has-backed-down-to-farmers

68   ০০০০০০০০০০০ ০০০০০০ ০০০০ ০০ ০০০ ০০০ ০০০০০ ০০০০ ০০ ০০০০০- ০০০০০ ০০০০ ০০ ০০০০০ ০০, Feb 26, 2019; https://www.aajtak.in/literature/poems/story/pm-narendra-modi-readout-prasoon-joshi-poem-main-desh-nahin-jhukane-dunga-644167-2019-02-26,

69   Ladakh face-off: Manmohan Singh asks PM Modi to be mindful of implications of his statements on national security, Jun 22, 2020; https://www.thehindu.com/news/national/ladakh-face-off-manmohan-singh-asks-pm-modi-to-be-mindful-of-implications-of-his-statements-on-national-security/article31886393.ece

70   Bhalla Abhishek, Defence Ministry removes report of Chinese intrusion from

website, looks at prolonged standoff at Pangong Tso, Aug 6, 2020; https://www.indiatoday.in/india/story/defence-ministry-report-chinese-transgression-website-lac-ladakh-remove-1708386-2020-08-06

71   Amit Shah tells Lok Sabha J&K also means PoK & Aksai Chin, ready to die for this, Aug 6, 2019; https://theprint.in/india/amit-shah-tells-lok-sabha-jk-also-means-pok-aksai-chin-ready-to-die-for-this/272875/

72   India asked Washington not to bring up China's border transgressions: Former US ambassador, Mar 2, 2022; https://scroll.in/latest/1018580/india-asked-washington-not-to-mention-chinas-border-transgressions-former-us-ambassador-to-india

73   Military veterans slam Modi's '56-inch chest' boast, S Jaishankar's comment on China, Feb 24, 2023; https://www.telegraphindia.com/india/military-veterans-slam-modis-56-inch-chest-boast-s-jaishankars-comment-on-china/cid/1918541

74   After Rahul's 'cowardice' jibe at Jaishankar, Congress demands his sacking over China issue, PTI, Mar 6, 2023; https://www.deccanherald.com/india/after-rahuls-cowardice-jibe-at-jaishankar-congress-demands-his-sacking-over-china-issue-1197823.html

75   Singh Sushant, Green Herring: Why India's political leadership is bragging about winning a war with Pakistan, Dec 26, 2022; https://caravanmagazine.in/security/india-war-pakistan-china

76   Singh Sushant, A Crumbling Façade: Modi unmasked amid rising tensions between India and Canada, Sept 23, 2023; https://caravanmagazine.in/politics/modi-unmasked-india-canada; Chun chun ke hisab lena fitrat hain, ghar mein ghus kar marenge: PM Modi's direct warning to terrorists, Mar 5, 2019; https://www.dnaindia.com/india/photo-gallery-chun-chun-ke-hisab-lena-fitrat-hain-ghar-mein-ghus-kar-marenge-pm-modi-s-direct-warning-to-terrorists-2726526/pm-modi-s-direct-warning-2726527

77   Singh Sushant, Out of Control: How China outmanoeuvred the Modi government and seized control of territory along the LAC, Oct 1, 2022; https://caravanmagazine.in/security/india-china-ladakh

78   Pandit Rajat, No concrete breakthrough in India-China military talks on resolving Ladakh confrontation, Aug 16, 2023; http://timesofindia.indiatimes.com/articleshow/102752667.cms?from=mdr&utm_source=contentofinterest&utm_medium=text&utm_campaign=cppst,

79   Singh Kautilya, Past governments feared enemy, ignored border areas: PM Modi, Oct 13, Oct 13, 2023; https://timesofindia.indiatimes.com/india/past-governments-feared-enemy-ignored-border-areas-pm-modi/articleshow/104381167.cms?from=mdr

80   Dutta Amrita N, Following Galwan clashes, China ramped up troop presence, infra along LAC in 2022, says Pentagon, Oct 22, 2023; https://indianexpress.com/article/india/following-galwan-clashes-china-ramped-up-troop-presence-infra-along-lac-in-2022-says-pentagon-8994076/

81   Cialdini Robert, Influence: The Psychology of Persuasion, , pages 296-299, HarperCollins, pages 296-99, 341-343, 2021; https://www.harpercollins.com/products/influence-new-and-expanded-robert-b-cialdini?variant=32903969996834

82   Sanghvi Vir, Modi isn't Manmohan, it'll take more than a media frenzy to fire Brij Bhushan, May 4, 2023; https://theprint.in/opinion/sharp-edge/modi-isnt-manmohan-itll-take-more-than-a-media-frenzy-to-fire-brij-bhushan/1554200/

83   Just the Right Image, Business Today, Jun 8, 2014 edition; https://www.businesstoday.in/magazine/case-study/case-study-strategy-tactics-behind-creation-of-brand-narendra-modi/story/206321.html

84   How Modi, Shah Turned A Women's NGO Into A Secret Election Propaganda Machine, Apr 4, 2019; https://www.huffpost.com/archive/in/entry/how-modi-shah-turned-a-women-s-rights-ngo-into-a-secret-election-propaganda-machine_in_5ca5962ce4b05acba4dc1819

85   Faleiro Sonia, Fact-checking Modi's India, Rest of World, May 12, 2021; https://restofworld.org/2021/fact-checking-modis-india/

86   Chaudhuri Pooja, Amit Malviya: How the ringmaster of BJP's propaganda machinery weaponises misinformation, Feb 10, 2020; https://www.altnews.in/amit-malviya-how-ringmaster-of-bjps-propaganda-machinery-weaponises-misinformation/; Fake News Round-up, November 2017 – BJP IT Cell head Amit Malviya is the star, Dec 6, 2017; https://www.altnews.in/fake-news-round-november-2017-bjp-cell-head-amit-malviya-star/; Who runs Kreately? – Alt News investigates the factory of hate and misinformation, Apr 10, 2021; https://www.altnews.in/who-runs-kreately-alt-news-investigates-the-factory-of-hate-and-misinformation/?utm_source=website&utm_medium=social-media&utm_campaign=newpost; The year that was: Misinformation trends of 2020, Jan 5, 2021; https://www.altnews.in/the-year-that-was-misinformation-trends-of-2020/; Hall of shame – Serial abusers, sexist bigots, rumour mongers followed by PM Modi on Twitter, Sept 7, 2017; https://www.altnews.in/hall-shame-serial-abusers-sexist-bigots-rumour-mongers-followed-pm-modi-twitter/

87   State-sponsored Trolling, Institute for the Future, California, 2018; https://www.iftf.org/fileadmin/user_upload/images/DigIntel/IFTF_State_sponsored_trolling_report.pdf

88   Explained: How BJP-supporting 'influencers' trolled CJI Chandrachud online, Jun 7, 2023; https://www.newslaundry.com/2023/06/07/explained-how-bjp-supporting-influencers-trolled-cji-chandrachud-online

89   Real or Fake, We Can Make Any Message Go Viral: Amit Shah to BJP Social Media Volunteers, Sept 26, 2018; https://thewire.in/politics/amit-shah-bjp-fake-social-media-messages

90   Sinha Pratik, Fake social media profiles with Muslim identities to bolster BJP: Case Study 1 (Gini Khan – @giniromet), Jun 22, 2017; https://www.altnews.in/fake-social-media-profiles-muslim-identities-bolster-bjp-caste-study-1-gini-khan-giniromet/

91   Fake social media profiles targeting Sikhs exposed, Nov 24, 2021; https://www.bbc.com/news/world-asia-india-59338245

92   Krishnan Vidya, To playing violins in the void, Dec 23, 2022; https://caravanmagazine.in/media/modi-media-2022-journalism-burden; Jaswal Srishti, Monitor reporter's trial opens: Why India treats journalists as terrorists, Apr 19, 2023; https://www.csmonitor.com/World/Asia-South-Central/2023/0419/Monitor-reporter-s-trial-opens-Why-India-treats-journalists-as-terrorists

93   Prime Minister Modi gets history wrong again, this time in Maghar, Jun 28, 2018; https://www.indiatoday.in/india/story/narendra-modi-maghar-uttar-pradesh-history-wrong-kabir-guru-nanak-baba-gorakhnath-1272424-2018-06-28; Narendra Modi must guard against more slip-ups, feels party, Nov 12, 2013; http://timesofindia.indiatimes.com/articleshow/25606731.cms?utm_source=contentofinterest&utm_medium=text&utm_campaign=cppst

94   Mehra Malini, The miseducation of Narendra Modi on climate change, Sept 8, 2014; https://www.climatechangenews.com/2014/09/08/the-miseducation-of-narendra-modi-on-climate-change/

95   Solomon Saskia, The false scientific claims made during Modi's first term, Jun 26, 2019; https://caravanmagazine.in/science/false-scientific-claims-modi-first-term; Can we build a Science in Motion: PM, Jan 3, 2020; https://twitter.com/PMOIndia/status/1212972603184275456; 'Liquid Nala Gas': Twitter cracks up on Narendra Modi's comment about making tea from gutter fumes, Aug 14, 2018; https://scroll.in/article/890416/liquid-nala-gas-twitter-cracks-up-on-narendra-modis-comment-about-making-tea-from-gutter-fumes; Modi trolled for claiming wind turbines can produce water, but is he wrong?, Oct 9, 2020; https://www.theweek.in/news/india/2020/10/09/modi-trolled-for-claiming-wind-turbines-can-produce-water-but-is-he-wrong.html

96   Row Over PM Modi's "Cloud Can Help Us Escape Radar" Comment On Air Strike, May 12, 2019; https://www.ndtv.com/india-news/controversy-over-pm-narendra-modis-cloud-can-help-us-escape-radar-comment-on-balakot-air-strikes-2036402

97   After "Cloud Cover", PM Fact-Checked On "1987-88 Digital Camera" Comment, May 13, 2019; https://www.ndtv.com/india-news/after-cloud-cover-pm-narendra-modi-fact-checked-on-email-in-1987-claim-2036793

98   Mishra Pankaj K, Dear PM Modi: Good Food Will Reduce the Burden of Malnutrition, Not Bhajans, Aug 30, 2022; https://science.thewire.in/health/narendra-modi-malnutrition-bhajan/

99   As Modi is mocked for advice to students on tough exam questions, PM's office, PIB delete tweet, Apr 8, 2021; https://scroll.in/latest/991746/pms-office-pib-delete-tweet-of-modi-advising-students-to-first-try-tough-questions-in-exams

100   'Exam Warriors' authored by Prime Minister Narendra Modi released by Goa Governor P.S Sreedharan Pillai & Union MoS Shripad Naik, Ministry of Education, Jan 19, 2023; https://pib.gov.in/PressReleaseIframePage.aspx?PRID=1892273

101   Ghosh Sohini, PM Modi degree row: Gujarat HC refuses priority hearing of Arvind Kejriwal, Sanjay Singh pleas for a third time, Sept 26, 2023; https://indianexpress.com/article/cities/ahmedabad/pm-modi-degree-row-gujarat-hc-refuses-hearing-arvind-kejriwal-sanjay-singh-pleas-8956745/

102   Narendra Modi not my protege, a brilliant events manager: L K Advani, Apr 6, 2014;   https://indianexpress.com/article/political-pulse/advani-modi-not-my-protege-a-brilliant-events-manager/

103   India has emerged as 'Vishwa Mitra,' says Prime Minister Modi in Independence Day speech, PTI, Aug 16, 2023; https://economictimes.indiatimes.com/news/india/india-has-emerged-as-vishwa-mitra-says-prime-minister-modi-in-independence-day-speech/articleshow/102741472.cms

104   India sees itself as 'Vishwamitra', world calls the country its friend, says PM Modi, PTI, NOv 26, 2023; https://www.deccanherald.com/india/india-sees-itself-as-vishwamitra-world-calls-the-country-its-friend-says-pm-modi-2785436

105   Rathin Roy, The darkness of trivialization, May 28, 2023; https://www.business-standard.com/opinion/columns/the-darkness-of-trivialization-123052800876_1.html

106   Anand Jatin, G20 India Summit: Over Rs 4,100 crore spent on Delhi for G20: where and by whom, Sept 7, 2023; https://indianexpress.com/article/cities/delhi/security-to-roads-lighting-to-signage-citys-expense-bills-for-g20-8928183/#:~:text=G20%20India%20Summit%202023%3A%20According,broadly%20under%20around%2012%20categories.&text=Over%20Rs%204%2C100%20crore%20was,which%20will%20kick%20off%20Saturday

107   P Chidambaram writes: Style, substance and slippery ice, Sept 17, 2023; https://indianexpress.com/article/opinion/columns/narendra-modi-g20-delhi-declaration-president-joe-biden-8943113/

108   Ninan TN, Is India back to being 'Third World'? Irony of an aspiring superpower exposed by Covid crisis, May 1, 2021; https://theprint.in/opinion/is-india-back-to-being-third-world-irony-of-an-aspiring-superpower-exposed-by-covid-crisis/649209/

109   The Observer view: Modi boosted his image, but the G20 summit looks set to achieve little else, Sept 10, 2023; https://www.theguardian.com/commentisfree/2023/sep/10/modi-boosted-image-but-g20-achieve-little-else

110   Singh Sushant, Unlikely Event: The G20 summit is not the crowning glory Modi hoped for, Aug 31, 2023; https://caravanmagazine.in/politics/g20-summit-not-crowning-glory-moment-modi-hoped; What is the G20 and what was achieved at the Delhi summit? Sept 11, 2023; https://www.bbc.com/news/world-48776664

111   Singh Kautilya, Past governments feared enemy, ignored border areas: PM Modi, Oct 13, Oct 13, 2023; https://timesofindia.indiatimes.com/india/past-governments-feared-enemy-ignored-border-areas-pm-modi/articleshow/104381167.cms?from=mdr

112   LS 2022: Advertisement expenditure, Lok Sabha, Question no.1143, Dec 13, 2022; https://sansad.in/ls/questions/questions-and-answers

113   Performance Audit of National Social Assistance Programme - Union Government (Civil), Ministry of Rural Development (Performance Audit), CAG, Aug 8, 2023; https://cag.gov.in/en/audit-report/details/119044

114   Bhatia Siddharth, Akshay Kumar's Hindu Samrat Goes Where No Other Bollywood Film Has Gone Before Jun 2, 2022; https://thewire.in/film/akshay-kumars-hindu-samrat-goes-where-no-other-bollywood-films-have-gone-before

115   PM Narendra Modi movie to re-release in cinema halls on October 15, Oct 11, 2020; https://indianexpress.com/article/entertainment/bollywood/pm-narendra-modi-movie-to-re-release-in-theaters-6719352/

116   Mann ki Baat's 100th Episode Promotion Blitzkrieg Hides 'Very Low Listenership' Findings, Apr 27, 2023; https://thewire.in/government/pm-narendra-modi-mann-ki-baat-100-episode

117   BJP plans 4-lakh venues for 100th episode of PM's 'Mann Ki Baat'; Apr 29, 2023; https://indianexpress.com/article/india/bjp-plans-4-lakh-venues-for-100th-episode-of-pms-mann-ki-baat-8581998/

118   'Mann Ki Baat' Highlights: 100th Episode Of PM Narendra Modi's Radio Programme, Apr 30, 2023; https://www.ndtv.com/india-news/mann-ki-baat-live-updates-pm-modis-mann-ki-baat-prime-minister-narendra-modi-radio-united-nations-un-3991830

119   Kapoor Coomi, Inside Track by Coomi Kapoor | Knock-out clout, May 7, 2023; https://indianexpress.com/article/opinion/columns/knock-out-clout-8595584/

120   Singh Sushant, A Crumbling Façade: Modi unmasked amid rising tensions between India and Canada, Sept 23, 2023; https://caravanmagazine.in/politics/modi-unmasked-india-canada

121   Tamang Sylvester, PM Narendra Modi Says He Will Never Forgive Sadhvi Pragya For Insulting Mahatma Gandhi, May 17, 2019; https://www.indiatimes.com/news/india/pm-narendra-modi-says-he-will-never-forgive-sadhvi-pragya-for-insulting-mahatma-gandhi-367441.html

122   Siddiqui Zeba, Terror-accused Hindu hardliner Pragya Thakur wins parliamentary seat in Bhopal, May 23, 2019; https://www.reuters.com/article/india-election-priestess-idUSKCN1ST1I9

123   Budget 2023-24 presents vision for Amrit Kaal, Ministry of Finance, Feb 1, 2023; https://pib.gov.in/PressReleaseIframePage.aspx?PRID=1895313; English rendering of PM's reply to the Motion of Thanks to President's address in Rajya Sabha, PMO, Feb 9, 2023; https://pib.gov.in/PressReleaseDetailm.aspx?PRID=1897766

124   English rendering of PM's reply to the Motion of Thanks to President's address in Rajya Sabha, Feb 9, 2023; https://pib.gov.in/PressReleaseDetailm.aspx?PRID=1897766

125 Mehra Anshita, PM unveils Amrit Vatika memorial, Oct 31, 2023; https://www.tribuneindia.com/news/delhi/pm-unveils-amrit-vatika-memorial-558472

126 "Amrit Kaal has been named as Kartavya Kaal": PM Modi, Kul 4, 2023; https://economictimes.indiatimes.com/news/india/amrit-kaal-has-been-named-as-kartavya-kaal-pm-modi/articleshow/101478517.cms?utm_source=contentofinterest&utm_medium=text&utm_campaign=cppst

127 English rendering of Prime Minister, Shri Narendra Modi's address from the ramparts of Red Fort on the occasion of 77th Independence Day, PMO, Aug 15, 2023; https://pib.gov.in/PressReleasePage.aspx?PRID=1948808#:~:text=My%20dear%20family%20members%2C,the%20independence%20of%20the%20country.

128 Facebook's Ties to India's Ruling Party Complicate Its Fight Against Hate Speech, Time magazine, US, Aug 27, 2020; https://time.com/5883993/india-facebook-hate-speech-bjp/; Facebook's Hate-Speech Rules Collide With Indian Politics, Wall Street Journal, Aug 14, 2020; https://www.wsj.com/articles/facebook-hate-speech-india-politics-muslim-hindu-modi-zuckerberg-11597423346; Exclusive: Facebook employees internally question policy after India content controversy - sources, memos, Reuters, Aug 9, 2020; https://www.reuters.com/article/us-facebook-india-exclusive/exclusive-facebook-employees-internally-question-policy-after-india-content-controversy-sources-memos-idUSKCN25F1VW; Kumar Abhishek, Exclusive: Network of shadow Facebook pages spending crores on ads to target Oppn are connected to BJP, Apr 4, 2023; https://www.altnews.in/exclusive-network-of-pseudo-entitles-running-political-ads-on-facebook-favoring-bjp-and-against-non-bjp-parties/; Twitter accused of censorship in India as it blocks Modi critics; Yashraj Sharma in Srinagar; Wed 5 Apr 2023 ; https://www.theguardian.com/world/2023/apr/05/twitter-accused-of-censorship-in-india-as-it-blocks-modi-critics-elon-musk?CMP=Share_iOSApp_Other; Purohit Kunal, How Meta, YouTube, Twitter & Instagram Ignored Their Own Hate-Speech Standards To Give Hindutva Its Latest Star, Apr 14, 2023; https://article-14.com/post/how-meta-youtube-twitter-instagram-ignored-their-own-hate-speech-standards-to-give-hindutva-its-latest-star-6438b8594afe3; Hindutva's Circulation of Anti-Muslim Hate Aided by Digital Platforms, Finds Report, Jan 31, 2022; https://thewire.in/communalism/india-anti-muslim-hate-twitter-facebook-whatsapp-hindutva-modi-bjp

129 Sambhav Kumar and Ranganathan Nayantara, How a Reliance-funded firm boosts BJP's campaigns on Facebook, Mar 14, 2022; https://www.aljazeera.com/economy/2022/3/14/how-a-reliance-funded-company-boosts-bjps-campaigns-on-facebook; Inside Facebook and BJP's world of ghost advertisers, Mar 15, 2022; https://www.aljazeera.com/economy/2022/3/15/inside-facebook-and-bjps-world-of-ghost-advertisers; Facebook charged BJP less for India election ads than others, Mar 16, 2022; https://www.aljazeera.com/economy/2022/3/16/facebook-charged-bjp-lower-rates-for-india-polls-ads-than-others; What helps India's BJP get lower Facebook rates? Divisive content, Mar 17, 2022; https://www.aljazeera.com/economy/2022/3/17/facebook-algorithm-favours-polarising-politics-helps-bjp

130 How Facebook neglected the rest of the world, fuelling hate speech and violence

in India, Oct 24, 2021; https://www.washingtonpost.com/technology/2021/10/24/india-facebook-misinformation-hate-speech/; The revelations from RSS, West Bengal and Duplicate Accounts: What the Facebook Whistleblower Complaint Touches Upon, Oct 5, 2021; https://m.thewire.in/article/tech/facebook-whistleblower-frances-haugen-complaints-sec-hate-speech-misinformation-india/amp?__twitter_impression=true

131   Abraham Arvind Kumar, Preventing Sophie Zhang from Testifying Is a Blow to Indian Parliamentary Democracy, The Wire, Jul 1, 2022; https://thewire.in/rights/preventing-sophie-zhang-from-testifying-is-a-blow-to-indian-parliamentary-democracy

132   Nationalism a driving force behind fake news in India, research shows, Nov 12, 2018; https://www.bbc.com/news/world-46146877

133   Akbar Syeda Zainab, Kukreti Divyanshu, Sagarika Somya, Pal Joyojeet, Temporal Patterns in COVID-19 misinformation in India, University of Michigan, http://joyojeet.people.si.umich.edu/temporal-patterns-in-covid-19-misinformation-in-india/

134   Manral Mahendra Singh, Limit requests for login/logout details to heinous cases: Meta to Delhi Police, Nov 7, 2023; https://indianexpress.com/article/india/limit-requests-for-login-logout-details-to-heinous-cases-meta-to-delhi-police-9016435/

135   Vengattil Munsif, Twitter seeks judicial review of Indian orders to take down content -source, Jul 6, 2022; https://www.reuters.com/world/india/twitter-pursues-judicial-review-indian-content-takedown-orders-source-2022-07-05/

136   Sarkar Indranil and Thomas Chris, Indian high court dismisses Twitter's plea against government; slaps 5 million-rupee fine, lawyer says, Jun 30, 2023; https://www.reuters.com/world/india/indian-high-court-dismisses-twitters-plea-against-govt-slaps-5-mln-rupees-fine-2023-06-30/

137   Krishnan Vidya, Hate is the Modi government's true "make in India" campaign, Caravan, Jun 26, 2022; https://caravanmagazine.in/politics/hate-modi-government-make-india-campaign

138   NHRC official aghast to find Modi photo and slogan in emails, Sept 30, 2021; https://www.telegraphindia.com/india/nhrc-aghast-with-modi-photo-and-slogan-in-their-emails/cid/1832827

139   Varadarajan Siddharth, MEA's Latest: BJP the 'Only Alternative', Only Hindus Are 'Spiritual', The Wire, Sept 30, 2017; https://thewire.in/diplomacy/mea-bjp-propaganda-hindutva-deendayal-upadhyaya-integral-humanism

140   Divya A, Culture ministry journal dedicates its latest issue to Savarkar: His place in history 'no less than' Gandhi's, Indian Express, Jul 17, 2022; https://indianexpress.com/article/india/culture-ministry-journal-dedicates-its-latest-issue-to-savarkar-his-place-in-history-no-less-than-gandhis-8033998/

141   George TJS, Azadi, Amrit Mahotsav and Savarkar, New Indian Express, Sept 5, 2021; https://www.newindianexpress.com/opinions/columns/t-j-s-george/2021/sep/05/azadi-amrit-mahotsav-and-savarkar-2354423.html

142   PM's address to the nation from ramparts of the Red Fort on the occasion of 76th Independence Day, PMIndia, Aug 15, 2022; https://www.pmindia.gov.in/en/news_updates/pms-address-to-the-nation-from-ramparts-of-the-red-fort-on-the-occasion-of-76th-independence-day/

143   Sircar Neelanjan, Disinformation: A New Type of State-Sponsored Violence, Sept 20, 2021; https://www.theindiaforum.in/article/disinformation-new-type-state-sponsored-violence?utm_source=facebook

144   Hoffer Eric, The True Believer: Thoughts on the Nature of Mass Movements (Perennial Classics) Paperback – January 19, 2010, first published in 1951; Harper Perennial Modern Classics, https://www.amazon.com/True-Believer-Thoughts-Movements-Perennial/dp/0060505915

145   Varadarajan Siddharth, Pegasus Project: 161 Names Revealed By The Wire On Snoop List So Far, The Wire, Aug 4, 2021; https://thewire.in/rights/project-pegasus-list-of-names-uncovered-spyware-surveillance

146   Varadarajan Siddharth, Revealed: How The Wire and Its Partners Cracked the Pegasus Project and What It Means for India, The Wire, Jul 30, 2021; https://thewire.in/media/revealed-how-the-wire-partners-cracked-pegasus-project-implications-india

147   Singh Vijaita, Security council secretariat gets Rs.333 crore, a tenfold hike, The Hindu, Feb 2, 2017; https://www.thehindu.com/news/national/Security-council-secretariat-gets-Rs.333-crore-a-tenfold-hike/article17148272.ece

148   The Battle for the World's Most Powerful Cyberweapon, Jan 28, 2022; https://www.nytimes.com/2022/01/28/magazine/nso-group-israel-spyware.html

149   India stands in solidarity with Israel at this difficult hour, says PM Modi after Hamas attack, Oct 7, 2023; http://timesofindia.indiatimes.com/articleshow/104241034.cms?from=mdr&utm_source=contentofinterest&utm_medium=text&utm_campaign=cppst

150   Roy Subhajit, New challenges emerging, condemn civilian deaths in Israel-Hamas conflict: PM Modi, Nov 18, 2023; https://indianexpress.com/article/india/israel-hamas-conflict-civilian-deaths-narendra-modi-9031340/

151   People's Union of Civil Liberties vs Union of India, Supreme Court, December 18, 1996; https://indiankanoon.org/doc/31276692/

152   Justice KS Puttaswamy and others vs Union of India and others, Supreme Court, Aug 24, 2017; https://main.sci.gov.in/supremecourt/2012/35071/35071_2012_Judgement_24-Aug-2017.pdf

153   Vishwanath A, Explained: The laws for surveillance in India, and concerns over privacy, The Indian Express, Aug 3, 2021; https://indianexpress.com/article/explained/project-pegasus-the-laws-for-surveillance-in-india-and-the-concerns-over-privacy-7417714/

154   Government disallows question on Pegasus, says matter is sub judice, Aug 6, 2021;

https://www.thehindu.com/news/national/government-disallows-question-on-pegasus-says-matter-is-sub-judice/article35768227.ece

155   House at a halt, PM says Cong behind it, tells MPs 'expose' Opp, Jul 28, 2021; https://indianexpress.com/article/india/house-at-a-halt-pm-says-cong-behind-it-tells-mps-expose-opp-7425702/

156   Anti-national, ban Amnesty, negative atmosphere: How BJP CMs, past and present, responded to charges, Indian Express, Jul 21, 2021; https://indianexpress.com/article/india/anti-national-ban-amnesty-negative-atmosphere-how-bjp-cms-past-and-present-responded-to-pegasus-charges-7414458/

157   No quorum as MPs spar at IT panel meet, secretaries skip it, Jul 29, 2021; https://timesofindia.indiatimes.com/india/no-quorum-as-mps-spar-at-it-panel-meet-secretaries-skip-it/articleshow/84845518.cms

158   No evidence, Govt didn't cooperate: SC panel on Pegasus, Aug 26, 2022; https://indianexpress.com/article/india/supreme-court-pegasus-spyware-case-8110566/

159   Varadarajan Siddharth, The Supreme Court on Pegasus: Two Short Steps Away From the Truth, The Wire, Aug 26, 2022; https://thewire.in/law/pegasus-spyware-supreme-court-truth

160   The spyware is sold to governments to fight terrorism. In India, it was used to hack journalists and others., Jul 19, 2021; https://www.washingtonpost.com/world/2021/07/19/india-nso-pegasus/; Private Israeli spyware used to hack cellphones of journalists, activists worldwide, Jul 18, 2021; https://www.washingtonpost.com/investigations/interactive/2021/nso-spyware-pegasus-cellphones/; On the list: Ten prime ministers, three presidents and a king, Jul 20, 2021; https://www.washingtonpost.com/world/2021/07/20/heads-of-state-pegasus-spyware/

161   Officials who are US allies among targets of NSO malware, says WhatsApp chief, Jul 24, 2021; https://www.theguardian.com/technology/2021/jul/24/officials-who-are-us-allies-among-targets-of-nso-malware-says-whatsapp-chief

162   Sebastian Meryl, Apple alert: India opposition says government tried to hack phones, Nov 1, 2023; https://www.bbc.com/news/world-asia-india-67269978

163   After Pegasus 'PR Problem', Modi Govt Looking for Spyware From Less Exposed Firms: Financial Times; https://thewire.in/government/pegasus-spyware-india-modi-quadream-cognyte

164   Heal Alexandra, Gross Anna, Parkin Benjamin, Cook Crish and Srivastava Mehul, India's communications 'backdoor' attracts surveillance companies, Aug 30, 2023; https://www.ft.com/content/adf1cbae-4217-4d7d-9271-8bec41a56fb4

165   MHA order for snooping to 10 agencies, Gazette notification, Dec 20, 2018; https://www.humanrightsinitiative.org/download/MHA-SO6227-Dec18.pdf

166   Mohanty P, DPDP Bill 2023: Question mark on privacy, more power to govt, Aug 10, 2023; https://www.fortuneindia.com/opinion/dpdp-bill-2023-question-mark-on-privacy-more-power-to-govt/113694

167   Mohanty P, 'DPDP Bill 2023'

168   Post Office Bill 2023; https://prsindia.org/files/bills_acts/bills_parliament/2023/Post%20Office%20Bill,%202023.pdf

169   'Aadhaar Data Protected by 13 Feet High, 5 Feet Thick Walls': Attorney General To SC, Mar 22, 2018; https://www.news18.com/news/india/aadhaar-data-protected-by-13-feet-high-5-feet-thick-walls-attorney-general-to-sc-1696269.html

170   Aadhaar Breach: Data Security Has Been Compromised Earlier Too, Jan 5, 2018; https://www.thequint.com/news/india/aadhaar-data-breach-glitches-data-security-compromised-earlier; Mohanty P, Why protecting privacy remains a challenge in India, Jun 21, 2023; https://www.fortuneindia.com/opinion/why-protecting-privacy-remains-a-challenge-in-india/113131#:~:text=It%20doesn't%20recognise%20privacy,Here%20is%20how.&text=breach%20of%20privacy--,The%20Digital%20Personal%20Data%20Protection%20Bill,does%20little%20to%20protect%20privacy.; Performance Audit of Ayushman Bharat-Pradhan Mantri Jan Arogya Yojana, CAG, Aug 8, 2023; https://cag.gov.in/en/audit-report/details/119060; Roy Esha, Govt finds 830 minority institutions on scholarship portal are fake, Aug 20, 2023; https://indianexpress.com/article/india/govt-finds-830-minority-institutions-on-scholarship-portal-are-fake-8900218/

171   Rajvanshi Astha, How internet shutdowns wreck havoc in India, Aug 15, 2023; https://time.com/6304719/india-internet-shutdowns-manipur/; Iyer Kavitha, In India, World's Internet Shutdown Capital, Blockades Undermine Livelihood, Food Security, Human Rights, Jun 14, 2023; https://article-14.com/post/in-india-world-s-internet-shutdown-capital-blockades-undermine-livelihood-food-security-human-rights--64892c096a39a; Dutta Alisha, Scarce news, fake news, Aug 18, 2023; https://www.thehindu.com/opinion/op-ed/scarce-news-fake-news/article67206976.ece; Apar Gupta writes: On Manipur, internet shutdown is no cure, Aug 4, 2023; https://indianexpress.com/article/opinion/columns/apar-gupta-writes-on-manipur-internet-shutdown-is-no-cure-8873758/

172   Personal details of TRAI chief RS Sharma 'leaked' after open challenge on Twitter, Aug 9, 2018; https://www.firstpost.com/tech/news-analysis/personal-details-of-trai-chief-rs-sharma-leaked-after-open-challenge-on-twitter-4844361.html

173   Sarkar Kanishka, Massive dark web data leak exposes India to digital identity theft and financial scams, warns Resecurity, Oct 31, 2023; https://www.cnbctv18.com/technology/massive-dark-web-data-leak-exposes-india-to-digital-identity-theft-and-financial-scams-warns-resecurity-18196331.htm

174   Data privacy laws & government surveillance by country: Which countries best protect their citizens? Comparitech, Oct 15, 2019; https://www.comparitech.com/blog/vpn-privacy/surveillance-states/

175   Cooper Stephen, India Cyber Profile, Aug 27, 2021; https://www.comparitech.com/blog/vpn-privacy/india-cyber-profile/

176   Oversight of the intelligence agencies: a comparison of the "Five Eyes" nations, UK Parliament, Dec 15, 2017; https://commonslibrary.parliament.uk/research-briefings/cbp-7921/

177   Daniyal Shoaib, Pegasus scandal shows that intelligence gathering urgently needs parliamentary oversight in India, Scroll, Jul 24, 2021; https://scroll.in/article/1000874/pegasus-scandal-shows-that-intelligence-gathering-urgently-needs-parliamentary-oversight-in-india

178   Datta Saikat and Venkatanarayanan, Israeli spyware: WhatsApp hack raises global fears, Nov 5, 2019; https://asiatimes.com/2019/11/israeli-spyware-whatsapp-hack-raises-global-fears/

179   Manish Tewari moves bill to 'regulate' intel snooping, seeks forum for complaints about RAW, IB, Dec 3, 2021; https://theprint.in/india/governance/manish-tewari-moves-bill-to-regulate-intel-snooping-seeks-forum-for-complaints-about-raw-ib/776167/; Tiwari Manish, Bill on Intelligence Agencies Reforms, 2011, ORF, https://www.orfonline.org/research/bill-on-intelligence-agencies-reforms/

180   Brexit is a reminder that some things just shouldn't be decided by referendum, Washington Post, Jun 27, 2016; https://www.washingtonpost.com/news/wonk/wp/2016/06/27/brexit-is-a-reminder-some-things-just-shouldnt-be-decided-by-the-people/; Menon Anand, Salter John Paul, Brexit: Initial Reflections, The Royal Institute of International Affairs, John Wiley & Sons, 2016; https://www.chathamhouse.org/sites/default/files/publications/ia/INTA92_6_01_Menon%20Salter.pdf

181   Everything you need to know about the Cambridge Analytica-Facebook debacle; Washington Post, Mar 19, 2018; https://www.washingtonpost.com/news/politics/wp/2018/03/19/everything-you-need-to-know-about-the-cambridge-analytica-facebook-debacle/

182   The scary truth that Cambridge Analytica understands, Washington Post, Mar 22, 2018; https://www.washingtonpost.com/news/worldviews/wp/2018/03/22/the-scary-truth-that-cambridge-analytica-understands/ & Whistleblower claims Cambridge Analytica's partners in India worked on elections, raising privacy fears, Mar 28, 2018; https://www.washingtonpost.com/world/asia_pacific/whistleblower-claims-cambridge-analyticas-partners-in-india-worked-on-elections-raising-privacy-fears/2018/03/28/1168c04c-328a-11e8-b6bd-0084a166-6987_story.html

183   As Congress, BJP Trade Blows Over Cambridge Analytica, Facts Go Out the Window, Mar 22, 2018; https://thewire.in/politics/congress-bjp-cambridge-analytica-controversy-facts

184   Andrews Edmund L, The Science Behind Cambridge Analytica: Does Psychological Profiling Work? Apr 12, 2018; https://www.gsb.stanford.edu/insights/science-behind-cambridge-analytica-does-psychological-profiling-work

185   Kosinski Michal, Stillwell David and Graepel Thore, Private traits and attributes are predictable from digital records of human behavior, Apr 9, 2013; https://www.pnas.org/content/pnas/110/15/5802.full.pdf

186   Narayanan Darshana, The Dangerous Populist Science of Yuval Noah Harari, Current Affairs, Jul 6, 2022; https://www.currentaffairs.org/2022/07/the-dangerous-populist-science-of-yuval-noah-harari

187   Kirchgaessner Stephanie, Ganguly Manisha, Pegg David, Cadwalladr Carole and Burke Jason, Revealed: the hacking and disinformation team meddling in elections, Feb 15, 2023; https://www.theguardian.com/world/2023/feb/15/revealed-disinformation-team-jorge-claim-meddling-elections-tal-hanan

188   Mohanty P, 'Why protecting privacy remains a challenge'

189   Rana Chahat, COVID-19 vaccine beneficiaries were assigned unique health IDs without their consent, The Caravan, Oct 1, 2021; Aadhaar amendment and private sector access, Mint, Jan 8, 2019; https://www.livemint.com/Opinion/jmxPkXXGWeEfiAsCsA1xnO/Opinion--The-Aadhaar-amendment-and-private-sector-access.html

190   Shrivastava Kumar Sambhav, EXCLUSIVE: Documents Show Modi Govt Building 360 Degree Database To Track Every Indian, Sept 15, 2020; https://www.huffpost.com/archive/in/entry/aadhaar-national-social-registry-database-modi_in_5e6f4d3cc5b6dda30fcd3462

191   The Criminal Procedure (Identification) Act 2022, Apr 18, 2022; https://www.mha.gov.in/sites/default/files/2022-11/CriminalPro_14112022%5B1%5D.pdf

192   Sharma Harikishan, Criminal Procedure (Identification) Bill, 2022: The dreaded thanedar vs empowerment of police, Apr 19, 2022; https://indianexpress.com/article/political-pulse/criminal-procedureidentification-bill-2022-7860934/

193   Rebelo Karen, Narendra Modi, From Aadhaar Critic To Champion: A FactCheck, Apr 11, 2017; https://www.boomlive.in/narendra-modi-from-aadhaar-critic-to-champion-a-factcheck/

194   Fact Check: Modi Claims His Govt Saved Rs 90,000 Crore. True or False? Jan 16, 2019; https://thewire.in/government/fact-check-modi-aadhaar-dbt-savings

195   Khera Ritika, Impact of Aadhaar in Welfare Programmes, Social Science Research Network, Oct 2 2017; https://papers.ssrn.com/sol3/papers.cfm?abstract_id=3045235s

196   Gairola Hemant, How An Aadhaar Fraud Forces The Poor Into Paying For Welfare Schemes They Do Not Want, Feb 22, 2023; https://article-14.com/post/how-an-aadhaar-fraud-forces-the-poor-into-paying-for-welfare-schemes-they-do-not-want-63f57eb9e8d15

197   Jaffrelot Christophe, What makes PM Modi immune to political accountability? Jun 24, 2021; https://indianexpress.com/article/opinion/columns/narendra-modi-popularity-2019-elections-india-covid-19-7372799/; Ali Asim, Modi faces no political costs for suffering he causes. He's just like Iran's Ali Khamenei, The Print, May 17, 2020; https://theprint.in/opinion/narendra-modi-no-political-costs-suffering-he-causes-iran-ali-khamenei/423355/; Patel Aakar, Who Are The People Attracted To Narendra Modi And His Style? His Followers Show A Clear Pattern, Dec 30, 2017; https://www.outlookindia.com/website/story/who-are-the-people-attracted-to-narendra-modi-and-his-style-his-followers-show-a/306179

198   Komireddi Kapil, India, the world's largest democracy, is now powered by a cult

of personality, The Washington Post, Mar 18, 2021; https://www.washingtonpost.com/outlook/modi-cult-of-personality/2021/03/18/dc7ee180-8773-11eb-bfdf-4d36dab83a6d_story.html

199   National Zoological Park, New Delhi; https://nzpnewdelhi.gov.in/?ln=en

200   "There has not been a single Diwali in the last 30-35 years, that I have not celebrated with you (Army jawans), Nov 12, 2023; https://twitter.com/PTI_News/status/1723618914574180664

201   Spent 5 days in jungle every Diwali to reflect on life, says PM Modi, PTI, Jan 23, 2019; https://theprint.in/politics/spent-5-days-in-jungle-every-diwali-to-reflect-on-life-says-pm-modi/182307/

202   Kumar Rohit, India and The Cult of Stupidity, The Wire, Mar 4, 2019; https://thewire.in/society/india-and-the-cult-of-stupidity

203   Halarnkar Samar, The lights begin to wink out in India's democracy, Scroll, Jul 24, 2021; https://amp.scroll.in/article/1000935/the-lights-begin-to-wink-out-in-indias-democracy?__twitter_impression=true.....cops

204   Dietrich Bonhoeffer's Letters and Papers from Prison; Christian Book Distributors; https://g.christianbook.com/ns/pdf/sample/402741.pdf;   https://ms.fortresspress.com/downloads/9781506402741_Prologue.pdf

205   The Collected Works of Eric Voegelin, Vol 31: Hitler and the Germans, edited by Detlev Clemens and Brendan Purcell page 102, University of Missouri Press, 1999; https://portalconservador.com/livros/Eric-Voegelin-Hitler-and-the-Germans.pdf

206   Ambedkar BR, Constituent Assembly Debates On 25 November, 1949; https://indiankanoon.org/doc/792941/

207   Stanley Jason, How Fascism Works: The Politics of Us and Them, Random House, New Work, 2018; https://www.penguinrandomhouse.com/books/586030/how-fascism-works-by-jason-stanley/

208   Choudhury Sunetra, PM Modi Flies On Seaplane In Gujarat, "Good Passenger", Says Pilot, Dec 12, 2017; https://www.ndtv.com/india-news/pm-narendra-modi-takes-seaplane-ride-to-temple-on-last-day-of-gujarat-campaign-1786747

209   Pamela Philipose: Backstory: In Karnataka, a New Poll Campaign Tool That Could Undermine Elections Forever; May 6, 2023; https://thewire.in/media/backstory-karnataka-elections-2023-undermine; Ninan TN, India's growing heft: The dichotomy between domestic and global opinion, Sept 1, 2023; https://www.business-standard.com/opinion/columns/india-s-growing-heft-the-dichotomy-between-domestic-and-global-opinion-123090101036_1.html

210   Suhas Palshikar writes on nine years of BJP government: Failures, Modi-proofed, May 30, 2023; https://indianexpress.com/article/opinion/columns/suhas-palshikar-writes-on-nine-years-of-bjp-government-failures-modi-proofed-8635584/

211   Andersen Walter, Damle Shridhar D, Messengers of Hindu Nationalism: How the RSS Reshaped India, C Hurst & Co Publishers, Apr 2019; https://www.amazon.in/Messengers-Hindu-Nationalism-Reshaped-India/dp/1787380254

212   Jha Dhirendra K, Shadow Armies: Fringe Oranisations and Foot Soldiers of Hindutva, Juggernaut, 2017; https://www.amazon.in/Shadow-Armies-Organizations-Soldiers-Hindutva/dp/9386228246

213   Roy Arundhati, The Battle to Save India Has to Be Waged By Every Single One of Us, The Wire, Apr 22, 2022; https://thewire.in/rights/arundhati-roy-india-democracy-communalism

214   RSS in Modi govt in numbers — 3 of 4 ministers are rooted in the Sangh, Jan 27, 2020; https://theprint.in/politics/rss-in-modi-govt-in-numbers-3-of-4-ministers-are-rooted-in-the-sangh/353942/

215   Jalihal Shreegireesh, How Modi Govt Tweaked Appointment Rules To Enable Second Terms For Heads Of 2 Powerful Commissions, Article14, Jul 13, 2022; https://article-14.com/post/how-modi-govt-tweaked-appointment-rules-to-enable-second-terms-for-heads-of-2-powerful-commissions-62ce2ec929636

216   'Emergency Was A Mistake': Congress Leader Rahul Gandhi, Mar 2, 2021; https://www.outlookindia.com/website/story/india-news-emergency-was-a-mistake-congress-leader-rahul-gandhi/375956

217   Muralidharan Sukumar, Challenging saffronisation, Sept 15, 2001; https://frontline.thehindu.com/other/article30251827.ece; Shrimankar Dishil, Hindu nationalism and education: Why vigilance is needed under a BJP government, London School of Economics; https://eprints.lse.ac.uk/66596/1/__lse.ac.uk_storage_LIBRARY_Secondary_libfile_shared_repository_Content_LSE%20India%20at%20LSE%20blog_2014_July_blogs.lse.ac.uk-Hindu%20nationalism%20and%20education%20Why%20vigilance%20is%20needed%20under%20a%20BJP%20government.pdf

218   Tiwari Ayush, One big family: The Hindutva takeover of ICHR is fuelled by nepotism, Jun 17, 2022; https://www.newslaundry.com/2022/01/17/one-big-family-the-hindutva-takeover-of-ichr-is-fuelled-by-nepotism

219   Controversial JNU Vice Chancellor Jagadesh Kumar appointed UGC chairman, Feb 4, 2022; https://www.business-standard.com/article/current-affairs/controversial-jnu-vice-chancellor-jagadesh-kumar-appointed-ugc-chairman-122020401003_1.html

220   History of toxic tweets confronts new JNU Vice-Chancellor, Feb 8, 2022; https://www.newindianexpress.com/nation/2022/feb/08/history-of-toxic-tweets-confronts-new-jnu-vice-chancellor-2416654.html

221   Bhatnagar Gaurav Vivek, New Chairman of UPSC, Manoj Soni, Shares Close Ties with BJP and RSS, The Wire, Apr 14, 2022; https://thewire.in/government/new-chairman-of-upsc-manoj-soni-shares-close-ties-with-bjp-and-rss

222   NCERT's textbook 'rationalisation' exercise raises questions of political intent, is at odds with progressive thrust of NEP, Jun 22, 2022; https://indianexpress.com/article/opinion/editorials/national-education-policy-nep-textbook-changes-7983024/

223   Palshikar Suhas, What school textbook deletions tell us about the ruling establishment's idea of democracy and its understanding of social sciences, Jun 23,

2022; https://indianexpress.com/article/opinion/columns/what-school-textbook-deletions-tell-us-about-ruling-establishment-idea-of-democracy-7982891/

224 Purandare Harshavardhan and Pandey Sandeep, Hindutva Fanatics Want to Rewrite History to Hide Their Lack of Contribution to India, Apr 20, 2023; https://thewire.in/communalism/hindutva-fanatics-want-to-rewrite-history-to-hide-their-lack-of-contribution-to-india

225 NCERT says no question of dropping Suhas Palshikar, Yogendra Yadav's names as textbook advisors, Jun 0, 2023; https://scroll.in/latest/1050680/ncert-says-no-question-of-dropping-suhas-palshikar-yogendra-yadavs-names-as-textbook-advisors

226 Chopra Ritika, 'Not in our name,' 33 political scientists join chorus, ask NCERT to drop their names from textbooks, Jun 15, 2023; https://indianexpress.com/article/education/remove-our-names-too-from-ncert-books-33-academicians-join-chorus-echo-yadav-and-palshikar-demand-8663737/; Peter Ronald deSouza writes: Why I withdrew my name from NCERT books, Jun 17, 2023; https://indianexpress.com/article/opinion/columns/peter-ronald-desouza-why-withdrew-name-ncert-books-8667205/

227 History textbook deletions: Why NCERT argument that it is trying to reduce pressure on students is weak, Apr 7, 2023; https://indianexpress.com/article/opinion/columns/history-textbook-deletions-ncert-argument-weak-8542044/; Oversight, should not be blown out of proportion: NCERT chief on missing texts in new school books, Apr 5, 2023; https://theprint.in/india/oversight-should-not-be-blown-out-of-proportion-ncert-chief-on-missing-texts-in-new-school-books-2/1499113/

228 UGC chief takes a jibe at academics criticising NCERT textbook revision, Jun 17, 2023; https://www.newindianexpress.com/nation/2023/jun/17/ugc-chief-takes-a-jibe-at-academics-criticising-ncert-textbook-revision-2585826.html

229 Modi govt plans NCERT syllabus change again, this time a major one, Aug 9, 2019; https://theprint.in/india/education/modi-govt-plans-ncert-syllabus-change-again-this-time-a-major-one/274854/

230 NCERT Removes 3 Chapters from Class 10 History Textbook, Apr 8, 2019; https://thewire.in/education/ncert-history-class-10-curriculum

231 Food, Poverty, Inequality Among Topics No Longer Part Of NCERT Textbooks, Jun 2, 2023; https://www.ndtv.com/education/food-poverty-inequality-among-topics-no-longer-part-of-ncert-textbooks-4084903

232 'Nothing of this sort has happened': Education minister on deletion of Darwin's theory of evolution from NCERT textbooks, Jun 21, 2023; https://indianexpress.com/article/education/nothing-of-this-sort-has-happened-education-minister-on-deletion-of-darwin-theory-from-ncert-textbooks-8676642/

233 Savarkar flew out of Andaman jail on bulbul birds to visit motherland, says Karnataka school textbook, Aug 26, 2022; https://www.thehindu.com/news/

national/karnataka/savarkar-flew-out-of-andaman-jail-on-bulbul-birds-to-visit-motherland-says-karnataka-school-textbook/article65815457.ece

234   Savarkar in, Nehru kept out from list of great leaders in UP syllabus, Jun 24, 2023; https://www.hindustantimes.com/india-news/up-board-s-new-syllabus-50-great-leaders-of-india-excludes-nehru-includes-savarkar-and-deen-dayal-upadhyay-101687549148759.html

235   Veer Savarkar to be taught in schools in MP, says education minister Inder Parmar, Jun 29, 2023; https://www.hindustantimes.com/cities/bhopal-news/veer-savarkar-to-be-taught-in-schools-in-mp-says-education-minister-inder-parmar-101688042073669.html

236   Rajasthan rewrites history: Maharana Pratap, not Akbar, won Battle of Haldighati, Jul 25, 2017; https://www.indiatoday.in/india/story/maharana-pratap-not-akbar-won-battle-of-haldighati-rajasthan-history-book-1026240-2017-07-25

237   After furore over dropping Tipu Sultan from textbooks, Karnataka govt puts decision on hold, Jul 29, 2020; https://theprint.in/india/education/after-furore-over-dropping-tipu-sultan-from-textbooks-karnataka-govt-puts-decision-on-hold/470832/

238   NCERT forms textbook panel for Classes 3-12; RSS affiliate founder, Fields medallist, Sudha Murty among 19 members, Aug 14, 2023; https://indianexpress.com/article/india/ncert-textbook-panel-rss-sudha-murty-niepa-chancellor-mc-pant-8889994/

239   NCERT panel recommends inclusion of Ramayana, Mahabharata in school textbooks, Nov 21, 2023; https://www.hindustantimes.com/india-news/ncert-panel-recommends-inclusion-of-ramayana-mahabharata-in-school-textbooks-101700567132062.html; Story, not history: NCERT must not include myths in history syllabi; myths have helped us endure; history divides us, Editorial, Nov 24, 2023; https://timesofindia.indiatimes.com/blogs/toi-editorials/story-not-history-ncert-must-not-include-myths-in-history-syllabi-myths-have-helped-us-endure-history-divides-us/

240   Mukhia Harbans, Between history and mythology, https://www.thehindu.com/opinion/op-ed/between-history-and-mythology/article6218099.ece;   'Ramayana, Mahabharata Are True Accounts Of The Period...Not Myths', https://www.outlookindia.com/magazine/story/ramayana-mahabharata-are-true-accounts-of-the-periodnot-myths/291363

241   Das Prabhanu Kumar, The Decline Of Nehru, Tagore & The Rise Of Savarkar: How Delhi University Got Itself A New Syllabus, Aug 30, 2023; https://article-14.com/post/the-decline-of-nehru-tagore-the-rise-of-savarkar-how-delhi-university-got-itself-a-new-syllabus-64eeaf5f94b31; Unit on Iqbal axed, nod for new course on Savarkar: DU's Academic Council approves changes to UG syllabi, May 28, 2023;   https://indianexpress.com/article/cities/delhi/unit-on-iqbal-axed-nod-for-new-course-on-savarkar-dus-academic-council-approves-changes-to-ug-syllabi-8632682/

242 President ignores Oppn, unveils Savarkar portrait, Feb 27, 2003; https://economictimes.indiatimes.com/president-ignores-oppn-unveils-savarkar-portrait/articleshow/38698461.cms?utm_source=contentofinterest&utm_medium=text&utm_campaign=cppst

243 Mumbai's Versova-Bandra Sea Link renamed as Veer Savarkar Setu, Jun 28, 2023; https://www.indiatoday.in/india/story/mumbai-versova-bandra-sea-link-renamed-veer-savarkar-setu-atal-bihari-vajpayee-2399036-2023-06-28

244 Swatantrya Veer Savarkar teaser: Randeep Hooda film gives glimpse of 'the most wanted Indian by the British', May 28, 2023; https://indianexpress.com/article/entertainment/bollywood/swatantrya-veer-savarkar-teaser-randeep-hooda-life-journey-most-wanted-indian-by-british-8633611/

245 Vishwanathan Meera, Against History: Sanjeev Sanyal's attempts to rewrite India's past, Oct 1, 2021; https://caravanmagazine.in/books/history-sanjeev-sanyal-attempts-rewrite-india-past; D'Souza Rohan, The Risks of Looking at India's History Through the Eyes of Pseudo-Historians, Oct 20, 2021; https://thewire.in/history/india-history-pseudo-historians-risks

246 Savarkar, Vinayak Damodar, Hindutva, 2020; https://www.amazon.in/Hindutva-Vinayak-Damodar-Savarkar/dp/9389982111

247 Mukul Akshyaya, Gita Press and the Making of Hindu India, Aug 2015, HarperCollins; https://www.amazon.in/Gita-Press-Making-Hindu-India/dp/9351772306

248 Akshaya Mukul writes: Gita Press founders and Gandhi – a relationship turned sour, Jun 21, 2023; https://indianexpress.com/article/opinion/columns/gita-press-founders-and-gandhi-a-relationship-turned-sour-8675362/

249 Bal Hartosh Singh, The Takeover: How the RSS is infiltrating India's intellectual spaces, Apr 1, 2019: https://caravanmagazine.in/reportage/how-rss-infiltrating-india-intellectual-spaces

250 Exclusive: Madhya Pradesh hired people close to RSS for govt jobs, skipping actual applicants, Mar 30, 2023; https://www.newslaundry.com/2023/03/30/madhya-pradesh-hired-people-close-to-rss-for-govt-jobs-skipping-actual-applicants

251 Sethi Aman, The mystery of India's deadly exam scam, Dec 17, 2015; https://www.theguardian.com/world/2015/dec/17/the-mystery-of-indias-deadly-exam-scam

252 Mahajan Shobhit, Delhi University ad hoc teacher suicide: Chronicle of a tragedy foretold, May 6, 2023; https://indianexpress.com/article/opinion/delhi-university-ad-hoc-teacher-suicide-chronicle-of-a-tragedy-foretold-8591129/; Mohanty P, Rebooting Economy XVIII: Does quality education really matter to India?, Aug 18, 2020; https://www.businesstoday.in/opinion/columns/story/indias-education-sector-quality-education-indian-economy-human-capital-workforce-270467-2020-08-18

253 'We will never forget this injustice': At DU, a protest and condolence meet for Samarveer Singh, Jun 3, 2023; https://www.newslaundry.com/2023/06/03/we-will-

never-forget-this-injustice-at-du-a-protest-and-condolence-meet-for-samarveer-singh

254   Baruah Sukrita, DU college sets up cow centre: 'Not just research, will give milk, curd to students', Jan 27, 2022; https://indianexpress.com/article/cities/delhi/du-college-sets-up-cow-centre-7743367/

255   Indians have great trust in science. So why is pseudoscience being promoted? Aug 24, 2021; https://indianexpress.com/article/opinion/columns/india-astrology-pseudoscience-state-of-science-index-7465949/

256   Centre funds AIIMS study to find if chanting 'gayatri mantra' can treat coronavirus, March 20, 2021; https://scroll.in/latest/990070/centre-funds-aiims-study-to-find-if-chanting-gayatri-mantra-can-treat-coronavirus

257   Lack of funds stalls research in cow-derivatives, Aug 11, 2019; https://www.thehindu.com/news/national/lack-of-funds-from-centre-stalls-research-in-cow-derivatives/article28982768.ece

258   Trivedi Deepal 2023: Of Narendra Modi, Gujarat and Rahul Gandhi: The Vulgarity of Speech, Mar 25, 2023; https://thewire.in/politics/of-narendra-modi-gujarat-and-rahul-gandhi-the-vulgarness-of-speech

259   Stories on Amit Shah's Assets, Smriti Irani's 'Degree' Vanish From TOI, DNA, Jul 30, 2017; https://thewire.in/media/amit-shah-assets-smriti-irani-degrees-toi-et-outlook

260   TOI removes, then restores, Zubin Mehta's quote on wanting peace for Indian Muslims, Aug 21, 2023; https://www.newslaundry.com/2023/08/21/toi-removes-then-restores-zubin-mehtas-quote-on-wanting-peace-for-indian-muslims

261   Give links, will disable: Google to Smriti Irani, Aug 9, 2022; http://timesofindia.indiatimes.com/articleshow/93441660.cms?utm_source=contentofinterest&utm_medium=text&utm_campaign=cppst

262   'Not aligned with our view of freedom of speech': US frowns over Modi government request to remove online posts, Apr 27, 2021; https://economictimes.indiatimes.com/news/india/not-aligned-with-our-view-of-freedom-of-speech-us-frowns-over-modi-government-request-to-remove-online-posts/articleshow/82269634.cms?utm_source=contentofinterest&utm_medium=text&utm_campaign=cppst

263   Indian government accused of rewriting history after edits to schoolbooks, The Guardian, Apr 6, 2023; https://www.theguardian.com/world/2023/apr/06/indian-government-accused-of-rewriting-history-after-edits-to-schoolbooks

264   FactChecker pulls down hate crime database (HT and IndiaSpend), IndiaSpend editor Samar Halarnkar resigns, Sept 12, 2019; https://scroll.in/latest/937076/factchecker-pulls-down-hate-crime-watch-database-sister-websites-editor-resigns

265   Ministry of Home Affairs removes data on NGO licences, funding from FCRA website, Jul 13, 2022; https://www.deccanherald.com/national/ministry-of-home-affairs-removes-data-on-ngo-licences-funding-from-fcra-website-1126240.html

266 Deep Aroon, Missing RTI info to be restored, website says, after years of data disappears, Aug 24, 2023; https://www.thehindu.com/news/national/missing-rti-info-to-be-restored-website-says-after-years-of-data-disappears/article67230977.ece

267 Adani Group 'almost certainly' manipulated its entries on Wikipedia, alleges site's newspaper, Feb 23, 2023; https://scroll.in/latest/1044453/wikipedia-newspaper-says-articles-on-adani-group-may-have-been-manipulated

268 'Principles of science originated in Vedas, but repackaged as western discoveries:' ISRO chairman S Somanath, May 25, 2023; https://www.hindustantimes.com/india-news/sanskrit-the-language-of-science-and-philosophy-uncovering-the-contributions-of-ancient-indian-scientists-to-modern-discoveries-101684953815696.html

269 Mohanty BK, NCERT module credits PM Modi for success of Chandrayaan-3, ignores ISRO's track record, Oct 18, 2023; https://www.telegraphindia.com/india/ncert-module-credits-pm-modi-for-success-of-chandrayaan-3-ignores-isros-track-record/cid/1974042?utm_source=substack&utm_medium=email

270 Bhattacharya Snigdhendu, How Scientists Meghnad Saha, J.V. Narlikar Rubbished Claim of Vedic Roots of Modern Science, Sept 5, 2023; https://science.thewire.in/the-sciences/how-scientists-meghnad-saha-j-v-narlikar-rubbished-claim-of-vedic-roots-of-modern-science/

271 Mullick Rohit, IIT-Mandi director blames Himachal Pradesh landslips on meateaters, Sept 8, 2023; http://timesofindia.indiatimes.com/articleshow/103482175.cms?from=mdr&utm_source=contentofinterest&utm_medium=text&utm_campaign=cppst,

272 Prime Minister Narendra Modi: Reply on Motion of Thanks to the President's Address (07-02-2018); https://eparlib.nic.in/bitstream/123456789/809843/1/pms_16_14_07-02-2018.pdf

273 Dutta Anisha, Kashmir letters cast doubt on claims Nehru blundered by agreeing ceasefire, Ma 8, 2023; https://www.theguardian.com/world/2023/mar/08/kashmir-letters-cast-doubt-claims-nehru-blundered-agreeing-ceasefire

274 Madhukulya Amrita, Nehru's name dropped, NMML renamed Prime Ministers' Museum and Library Society, Jun 17, 2023; https://www.deccanherald.com/india/nehrus-name-dropped-nmml-renamed-prime-ministers-museum-and-library-society-1228288.html

275 Science minister victim of fake news on Hawking's Veda comment, May 17, 2018; https://www.hindustantimes.com/india-news/science-minister-victim-of-fake-news-on-hawking-s-veda-comment-story-2Y84uI44WUr3b6PBNCLhTI.html

276 Nanda Meera, India's Long Goodbye to Darwin, Jun 28, 2023; https://thewire.in/education/indias-long-goodbye-to-darwin

277 Rajasthan High Court judge says peacocks don't have sex: How do you think peacocks reproduce? Jun 13, 2017; https://www.indiatoday.in/fyi/story/peacocks-mate-cow-national-animal-rajasthan-judge-sharma-980269-2017-05-31

278   Mohanty P, 'An Unkept Promise', Chapter V

279   Shivsundar, Who Killed Tipu? Why Twisting Historical Facts Is the BJP's Only Route to Victory in Karnataka., Feb 25, 2023; https://thewire.in/politics/tipu-history-twist-bjp-karnataka-politics

280   Deuskar Nachiket, Gurjar queens, Vokkaliga warriors: How BJP is inventing history for a new Hindutva caste politics, Mar 18, 2023; https://scroll.in/article/1045746/gurjar-queens-vokkaliga-warriors-how-bjp-is-inventing-history-for-a-new-hindutva-caste-politics

281   Team India practice jersey change a bid to saffronise cricket: Mamata, Nov 18, 2023; https://indianexpress.com/article/cities/kolkata/team-india-practice-jersey-change-a-bid-to-saffronise-cricket-mamata-9031580/

282   Ugra Sharda, A Cricket World Cup by India, for India, and about India, Nov 16, 2023; https://www.theindiaforum.in/society/cricket-world-cup-india-india-and-about-india?fbclid=IwAR3gj9-w3zFc5Y-uqj2av8bFj1UGT8XeDpRX5JIpulnUmWHUeoYs3FSWCz0

283   Rants&Roasts, Personally felt embarrassed just watching this happen. Nov 20, 2023; https://twitter.com/Sydusm/status/1726477322390581548 ; 'Most awkward presentation of all time' – Pat Cummins left standing with World Cup by himself before trophy lift, Nov 19, 2023; https://wisden.com/series-stories/cricket-world-cup-2023/most-awkward-presentation-of-all-time-pat-cummins-left-standing-with-world-cup-by-himself-before-trophy-lift ; Viral Video: Bengaluru cop stops Pakistani fan from cheering for team, Oct 21, 2023; https://timesofindia.indiatimes.com/viral-video-bengaluru-cop-stops-pakistani-fan-from-cheering-for-team/videoshow/104608987.cms ; Varadarajan Tunku, Cricket Mata Ki Jai: Jingoism Lost in Ahmedabad on Sunday, Nov 21, 2023; https://thewire.in/sport/cricket-mata-ki-jai-jingoism-lost-in-ahmedabad-on-sunday; Beyond a boundary: Overt nationalism marred the World Cup, editorial, Nov 21, 2023; https://www.business-standard.com/opinion/editorial/beyond-a-boundary-123112001179_1.html

284   @Advaidism, Kapil Dev was one of the first sportspersons to raise his voice for women wrestlers., Nov 20, 2023; https://twitter.com/Advaidism/status/1726451432797413412

285   Jha, Dhirendra K, Shadow Armies: Fringe Organizations and Foot Soldiers of Hindutva, Juggernaut, 2017; https://www.amazon.in/Shadow-Armies-Organizations-Soldiers-Hindutva/dp/9386228246

286   Christophe Jaffrelot writes: Bajrang Dal and making of the deeper state, Jun 5, 2023; https://indianexpress.com/article/opinion/columns/karnataka-election-result-poll-campaign-congress-bjp-8645595/

287   Case filed against Bajrang Dal for arms training in Assam to 'counter love jihad', Aug 1, 2023; https://www.indiatoday.in/india/story/case-filed-against-arms-training-assam-bajrang-dal-counter-love-jihad-2414937-2023-08-01; Arms training at Karnataka school draws flak, Bajrang Dal say only airguns used , May 17, 2023; https://indianexpress.com/article/cities/bangalore/bajrang-dal-arms-training-karnataka-school-7920733/

288 Siwach Sukhbir, 'Who gave weapons to the religious yatris at Nuh?' asks Union MoS Rao Inderjit Singh, Aug 2, 2023; https://indianexpress.com/article/political-pulse/rao-inderjit-singh-kanwar-yatras-nuh-violence-religious-yatris-at-nuh-8872070/

289 CIA names VHP, Bajrang Dal as 'religious militant organisations' in World Factbook, Jun 15, 2018; https://indianexpress.com/article/india/cia-names-vhp-bajrang-dal-as-religious-militant-organisations-in-world-factbook-5218249/

290 Jha, Dhirendra K, Are BJP-ruled states moving towards Nazi-style policing? May 26, 2022; https://caravanmagazine.in/politics/are-bjp-ruled-states-moving-towards-nazi-style-policing; Not just vigilantes: How gau rakshaks like Monu Manesar fuel Haryana govt's cow protection drive, Feb 21, 2023; https://theprint.in/india/not-just-vigilantes-how-gau-rakshaks-like-monu-manesar-fuel-haryana-govts-cow-protection-drive/1385848/

291 Not just vigilantes: How gau rakshaks like Monu Manesar fuel Haryana govt's cow protection drive, Feb 21, 2023; https://theprint.in/india/not-just-vigilantes-how-gau-rakshaks-like-monu-manesar-fuel-haryana-govts-cow-protection-drive/1385848/

292 High court frames contempt charges against four cops, Oct 5, 2023; https://timesofindia.indiatimes.com/city/ahmedabad/high-court-frames-contempt-charges-against-four-cops/articleshow/104173810.cms; India police flogging Muslims 'serious rights violation': Amnesty, Oct 6, 2022; https://www.aljazeera.com/news/2022/10/6/india-police-flogging-muslims-serious-rights-violation-amnesty

293 Roy Rohini, Record Statement of Muslim Man Beaten & Forced To Sing National Anthem: Delhi HC, May 9, 2023; https://www.thequint.com/news/law/northeast-delhi-riots-2020-muslim-man-delhi-police-national-anthem-court-latest-update#read-more

294 Report on AMU violence: 'Cops raised Jai Shri Ram slogans, admin failed in its duty', Dec 25, 2019; https://indianexpress.com/article/india/report-on-amu-violence-cops-raised-jai-shri-ram-slogans-admin-failed-in-its-duty/

295 Indian guard kills colleague and three passengers on train, then hails Modi, Jul 31, 2023; https://www.aljazeera.com/news/2023/7/31/indian-guard-kills-colleague-and-three-passengers-on-train-then-hails-modi

296 Yadav VK, Jaipur-Mumbai Train Killings: RPF constable forced woman in burqa to say 'Jai Mata Di' at gunpoint, finds probe, Aug 23, 2023; https://indianexpress.com/article/cities/mumbai/killings-on-train-rpf-constable-forced-woman-in-burqa-to-say-jai-mata-di-at-gunpoint-finds-probe-8894264/

297 Singh Sushant, Lock Step: The Modi government's dangerous politicisation of the Indian Army, Jul 19, 2023; https://caravanmagazine.in/security/modi-government-politicisation-indian-army; Raman P, By Supporting Politicised, Saffronised Barracks, Bipin Rawat Made Himself Modi's Perfect CDS, Jan 3, 2022; https://thewire.in/security/general-bipin-rawat-cds-saffronisation

298   #NimbuMirchi trends on Twitter, here's why, along with the reactions, Free Press Journal, Oct 10, 2019; https://www.freepressjournal.in/viral/nimbumirchi-trends-on-twitter-heres-why-along-with-the-reactions

299   Bedi Rahul, Why a Former Navy Chief is Right to Say 'Evil of Sycophancy' Will Undermine India's Military, The Wire, Aug 3, 2020; https://thewire.in/security/indian-military-leadership-politicisation

300   Tantray Shahid, False Flags: The Indian Army's secretive role in hyper-nationalist protests in Kashmir, Jun 1, 2022; https://caravanmagazine.in/conflict/indian-army-organises-aakhir-kab-tak-nationalist-protests-kashmir

301   Major accused of forcing worshippers to chant 'Jai Shri Ram' at Pulwama mosque, Jun 26, 2023; https://www.telegraphindia.com/india/pulwama-major-accused-of-forcing-worshippers-at-mosque-to-chant-jai-shri-ram-in-kashmir/cid/1947613

302   Panag Lt Gen HS (retd), Pulwama mosque, Manipur incidents bad for Army's image. There's need for course correction. Jul 6, 2023; https://theprint.in/opinion/pulwama-mosque-manipur-incident-bad-for-armys-image-theres-need-for-course-correction/1656958/; Singh Sushant, Lock Step: The Modi government's dangerous politicisation of the Indian Army, Jul 19, 2023; https://caravanmagazine.in/security/modi-government-politicisation-indian-army

303   Singh Sushant, Dangerous wedge, Aug 24, 2023; https://www.telegraphindia.com/opinion/dangerous-wedge-the-assam-rifles-humiliation-in-manipur/cid/1961116; Lt General Menon Prakash, Why Assam Rifles' vilification is a calculated, conniving move for revenge, Aug 15, 2023; https://theprint.in/opinion/why-assam-rifles-vilification-is-a-calculated-conniving-move-for-revenge/1715034/

304   'Bias of Manipur Media Towards a Community, Total Misrepresentation of Facts': Army's Letter to EGI,Sept 12, 2023; https://thewire.in/media/manipur-violence-imphal-media-army-letter-editors-guild

305   Kashmiris now share intel on terrorists, says Gen. Bipin Rawat, Nov 13, 2021; https://www.thehindu.com/news/national/kashmiris-now-share-intel-on-terrorists-says-gen-bipin-rawat/article37475888.ece?homepage=true

306   Khetan Ashish, Nagaland civilian killings: By refusing sanction for prosecution of army personnel, government promotes a culture of impunity, Apr 14, 2023; https://indianexpress.com/article/opinion/columns/nagland-civilian-killings-case-centre-prosecution-army-personnel-8556457/

307   Army concludes investigation into killing of 14 civilians in Nagaland's Mon district, May 17, 2022; https://scroll.in/latest/1024100/army-concludes-investigation-into-killing-of-14-civilians-in-nagalands-mon-district

308   Khetan Ashish, Nagaland civilian killings: By refusing sanction for prosecution of army personnel, government promotes a culture of impunity, Apr 14, 2023; https://indianexpress.com/article/opinion/columns/nagland-civilian-killings-case-centre-prosecution-army-personnel-8556457/

309   Soldier, friend arrested for faking 'PFI' assault: Kerala Police, Sept 27, 2023; https://

indianexpress.com/article/india/soldier-friend-arrested-for-faking-pfi-assault-kerala-police-8957377/

310 Natarajan S and Ali Faisal M, PFI ban: What is Popular Front of India and why has India outlawed it? Sept 28, 2023; https://www.bbc.com/news/world-asia-india-63004142

311 Vellaram S, Kerala professor whose hand was severed by PFI over a question, writes autobiography, Dec 30, 2019; https://www.thenewsminute.com/kerala/kerala-professor-whose-hand-was-severed-pfi-over-question-writes-autobiography-115012

312 Chhina MAS, Do social service on leave, be ambassadors for nation-building: Army to its soldiers, Sept 2, 2023; https://indianexpress.com/article/cities/chandigarh/do-social-service-on-leave-be-ambassadors-for-nation-building-army-to-its-soldiers-8920298/; When on leave... do social service, promote govt schemes: Army advises jawans, Sept 4, 2023; https://www.hindustantimes.com/india-news/army-encourages-soldiers-to-undertake-social-service-during-leave-contribute-to-nation-building-effort-101693765707394.html

313 Singh Sushant, Soldiers on leave now govt's marketing agents, by order of Army HQ! Sept 10, 2023; https://www.deccanherald.com/opinion/soldiers-on-leave-now-govts-marketing-agents-by-order-of-army-hq-2680096

314 Panag Lt Gen HS, Army can't ask soldiers to do social work on leave. It's beyond the 'call of duty', Sept 7, 2023; https://theprint.in/opinion/army-cant-ask-soldiers-to-do-social-work-on-leave-its-beyond-the-call-of-duty/1750131/

315 Dwivedi GG Major General (retd), Special to Express | Tour of Duty: Don't blunt our winning edge, Jun 14, 2022; https://indianexpress.com/article/cities/chandigarh/major-general-retd-g-g-dwivedi-tour-of-duty-dont-blunt-our-winning-edge-7969762/

316 Thapar Karan, Watch | 'Agnipath Timing Can Cause Turmoil, Naval Recruits Will Not Be Fully Trained', Jun 24, 2022; https://thewire.in/video/watch-agnipath-turmoil-naval-recruits-training-karan-thapar-admiral-arun-prakash

317 Singh Sushant, Analysis: New India army plan may have 'devastating consequences', Aljazeera, Jun 16, 2022; https://www.aljazeera.com/news/2022/6/16/analysis-new-india-army-plan-may-have-devastating-consequences & Tour of Duty model could add to majoritarian violence and affect army efficiency, The Caravan, Apr 21, 2022; https://caravanmagazine.in/security/tour-of-duty-pensions-lead-to-majoritarian-violence-hindutva-army-efficiency

318 Appleton Nayantara Sheron, Agnipath: A Frankenstein Monster of Demographic Anxieties and Neoliberal Solutions, The Wire, Jul 1, 2022; https://thewire.in/security/agnipath-demographic-anxieties-neoliberal-solutions

319 Bhalla Abhishek, Agnipath: Indian Army aims to reduce strength to under 11 lakh in a decade, India Today, Jun 25, 2022; https://www.indiatoday.in/

india/story/agnipath-indian-army-aims-reduce-strength-under-11-lakh-in-decade-1966451-2022-06-24

320   Mohanty P, 'Agnipath' ground realities harsh and unforgiving, Fortune India, Jun 23, 2022; https://www.fortuneindia.com/opinion/agnipath-ground-realities-harsh-and-unforgiving/108692

321   "Won't Interfere": Supreme Court Rejects Petitions Against High Court's Agnipath Verdict, PTI, Apr 10, 2023; https://www.ndtv.com/india-news/wont-interfere-supreme-court-rejects-petitions-against-high-courts-agnipath-verdict-3934838

322   Decoded: Why commerce minister Piyush Goyal is peeved at some in India Inc, Aug 16, 2021; https://www.business-standard.com/article/economy-policy/explained-why-piyush-goyal-is-peeved-at-some-in-india-inc-121081500994_1.html#; Reliance backs govt on proposed e-commerce rules as Tatas oppose, Aug 20, 2021; https://www.business-standard.com/article/companies/reliance-industries-backs-govt-on-the-proposed-e-commerce-rules-121081901415_1.html

323   'New Delhi Station Owned By Jijaji Now?': FM Sitharaman Taunts Rahul Gandhi Over Monetisation Plan, Aug 25, 2021; https://news.abplive.com/news/india/new-delhi-station-owned-by-jijaji-now-fm-sitharaman-taunts-rahul-gandhi-over-monetisation-plan-1478320

324   Oil bonds aim to 'insulate' customers: Experts see 'scope for fuel cess cuts', Aug 19, 2021; https://indianexpress.com/article/business/oil-bonds-aim-to-insulate-customers-experts-see-scope-for-fuel-cess-cuts-7460442/

325   Finance Minister Blames Ukraine War For Steepest Fuel Price Hike On Record, Mar 30, 2022; https://www.ndtv.com/business/finance-minister-blames-ukraine-war-for-steepest-fuel-price-hike-on-record-2851800

326   Mohanty P, West is vigilant about predatory pricing, India not, Jun 16, 2023; https://www.fortuneindia.com/opinion/west-is-vigilant-about-predatory-pricing-india-not/113069

327   Union Minister Dharmendra Pradhan says LPG prices rising due to 'intense cold', Deb 26, 2021; https://www.freepressjournal.in/india/uttar-pradesh-union-minister-dharmendra-pradhan-says-lpg-prices-rising-due-to-intense-cold

328   Rising fuel prices? A BJP MLA blames Taliban takeover of Afghanistan, Sept 5, 2021; https://www.hindustantimes.com/india-news/rising-fuel-prices-a-bjp-mla-blames-taliban-takeover-of-afghanistan-101630824495249.html

329   What is the best excuse for high petrol price? The DeshBhakt, Oct 22, 2021; https://www.facebook.com/178129355550407/posts/5013351595361468/

330   Sharma Jyotirmaya, Hindutva: Exploring the Idea of Hindu Nationalism, page xxiii, HarperCollins, 2015; https://www.amazon.in/Hindutva-Exploring-Idea-Hindu-Nationalism/dp/9351773973#:~:text=This%20revised%20edition%20of%20Hindutva,Vivekananda%20and%20Vinayak%20Damodar%20Savarkar.

331   Stanley Jason, 'How Fascism Works', page xiv

332   Bal Hartosh Singh, The Broken Compact: Modi's India replaces constitutional values with those of the RSS, Oct 20, 2023; https://caravanmagazine.in/politics/modi-india-constitutional-values-rss?utm_source=mailer&utm_medium=email&utm_campaign=current_issue&utm_id=157

333   Diamond Larry, Defending Liberal Democracy from the Slide Toward Authoritarianism, Stanford University, Nov 21, 2017; https://diamond-democracy.stanford.edu/speaking/speeches/defending-liberal-democracy-slide-toward-authoritarianism

334   Bharatiya Janata Party National Executive Meeting 12-13 June 2016, AllahabadResolution;   https://www.bjp.org/political-resolution/resolution-bjp-party-bharats-present-it-will-be-party-bharats-future-passed

Chapter XII

Food for Thought in 'Kartavya Kaal'

The previous chapters have shown the multiple challenges to the constitutional ideals – 'the idea of India' with which it began the journey as a modern democratic nation more than seven decades ago. A severe form of anti-democratic impulse has gripped it – which is far more insidious and enduring than the Emergency of 1975-77. This has spun dystopian political, economic and social orders which make the challenges intractable. How do you confront those challenges? Where do you begin? There are no easy answers or solutions. A beginning, however, must be made to understand the nature of these challenges and the options available with the hope that answers or solutions may emerge from them.

Saving the Constitution

Political scientist Christophe Jaffrelot offered four reasons, not mutually exclusive, to explain why there is an easy acceptance to the new authoritarianism in India in his book "Modi's India: Hindu Nationalism and the Rise of Ethnic Democracy"[1]. These are: (i) incremental assault on democracy – 'sleep-walk' into autocracy – in which the majority (Hindus) is safe (in the initial phase) and no reason to complain; the ones affected are minorities, be they religious minorities or activists (liberal, human rights activists and so on) (ii) "may be" democracy has lost its significance in India, compared to security (concerns over crime and terrorism) with the clamour for "strong leader", "military rule" etc. very high (iii) the political culture of India and the *traditional submission to hierarchy and acceptance of authority* and (iv) Modi's social background and projection as a man of the people who has suffered from class and caste hierarchies and who cultivate a sense of victimization that Indian plebians share.

These reasons help in narrowing down the challenges to the constitutional values – of justice, liberty, equality and fraternity, among others. Arguably, Ambedkar was even more specific. While handing over the Constitution of India to the Constituent Assembly in 1949, he had warned[2]: "…however good a Constitution may be, it is sure to turn out bad because those who are called to work it, happen to be a bad lot. However bad a Constitution may be, it may turn out to be good if those who are called to work it, happen to be a good lot. The working of a Constitution does not depend wholly upon the nature of the Constitution. The Constitution can provide only the organs of State such as the Legislature, the Executive and the Judiciary. The factors on which the working of those organs of the State depend are the people and the political parties they will set up as their instruments to carry out their wishes and their politics." Another of Ambedkar's observations is relevant here: "Constitutional morality is not a natural sentiment. It has to be cultivated. We must realise that our people have yet to learn it. Democracy in India is only a *top-dressing on an Indian soil which is essentially undemocratic.*"[3] *(Emphasis added)*

Ambedkar's cautions would make it clear that restoration of the constitutional values or order would call for dislodging the bad lot occupying the political power. That can happen only with an electoral defeat of the Prime Minister – which is distinct from the ones helmed by Vajpayee as the Prime Minister in the coalition era which tempered his actions and options. For this, the first line of political battle is for the political party/parties or alliance with the right ideological credentials – secular, pluralist, centrist and true belief in democracy and the Constitution of India – to fight. Here comes the problem. The only other pan-Indian party with such credentials, howsoever flawed and tainted may be, is the Congress (INC). It stands marginalized, after ruling India for most part after 1947. In August 2023, it was fighting for survival with its area of political and social influence shrunk to just two states (Himachal Pradesh and Karnataka). Its number in the Lok Sabha had dwindled to 44 in 2014 and 52 in 2019 – less than 10% of the total strength.

Of the regional or state-level parties, only the Aam Admi Party (AAP) rules more than one state – NCT of Delhi and Punjab. But its ideological commitment is suspect[4] for its support to the BJP's Hindu majoritarian politics. It silently watched as Muslims were attacked, killed and their houses/shops burnt and razed by bulldozers in Delhi – from the time of 2019-20 anti-CAA protests, to the Delhi riots of 2020 and the marauding bulldozers of 2022. It organizes pilgrimages for Hindu elders (especially to Ayodhya), holds Hindu rituals in public, endorses right-wings' battle cry of "Jai Shri Ram"[5], supported the abrogation of Article 370 in Jammu and Kashmir. This is not surprising given that it emerged out of the anti-corruption movement of 2011-14 against the Congress-led government (UPA) in which the RSS was an active collaborator.[6]

The Left parties, which were once a formidable force, are now restricted to Kerala (having lost its forts of Tripura and West Bengal). Odisha's ruling Biju Janata Dal (BJD) routinely sides with the BJP in contentious issues in the Parliament (disempowerment of Jammu and Kashmir and NCT of Delhi, CAA, triple talaq etc.).[7] Telangana's Bharat Rashtra Samithi (BRS), Andhra Pradesh's YSR Congress (breakaway group of the Congress) and Bahujan Samaj Party (BSP) show more inclination and support to the BJP.[8] Karnataka's JD(S) is on the BJP side. West Bengal's Trinamool Congress is a former BJP ally but now part of the 36-party anti-BJP alliance called INDIA (Indian National Developmental Inclusive Alliance). Tamil Nadu's DMK, Maharashtra's NCP, Bihar's RJD and JD(U) and Jharkhand's JMM are also part of this alliance.

One of the major reasons for many non-BJP parties to keep out of the anti-BJP alliance is multiple criminal cases registered against them by the central agencies like CBI, ED and Income Tax. These agencies are after the BRS (earlier called Tenagana Rashtra Samithi or TRS) chief and Telangana Chief Minister K Chandrashekar Rao's daughter K Kavitha (acused in the Delhi excise case, along with the AAP's former Deputy CM Manish Sisodia and Sanjay Singh).[9] The BJP allegedly offered to drop cases and make Sisodia the Chief Minister if he defected and joined the BJP[10]. This is not imaginary. It happened with Congress leader and now Assam Chief Minister Himanta Biswa Sarma, Shiv Sena's Eknath Shinde and NCP's Ajit Pawar and Narayan Rane, among many others who have been rewarded after defections (see Chapter I). The YSR Congress chief and Andhra Pradesh Chief Minister Jagan Mohan Reddy faces several corruption cases, pending with the CBI.[11] The BSP chief Mayawati too has many old pending CBI cases[12]; in 2023, she, her brother and sister-in-law got embroiled in a housing scam, allegedly for buying 261 flats in NOIDA through "fraudulent" means involving "deception" and "undervaluation"[13]. Mayawati (four-time Chief Minister) kept out of the 2022 Uttar Pradesh election campaigning and her party was wiped out from the state (winning just one of the 403 Assembly seats).[14]

As against this, the BJP has built up a formidable election winning machinery with an ideologically committed cadre (supplied by the RSS); it has considerably weakened political rivals by sending central agencies after them, seizing their cash, engineering defections in their ranks and pulling down their governments. It has too much money power, media and popular support to be easily dislodged at the Centre and in states. Such is the fear of Hindu majoritarianism that the Congress[15] and Samajwadi Party (SP)[16] have taken to "soft Hindutva" and seldom stand up for Muslims in public, except for odd gestures or statements. The Congress' dilemma was best captured during its three-day "chintan shivir" (brainstorming camp) in May 2022, when the party leaders couldn't come to a conclusion about whether to continue with "soft Hindutva" or abandon it. It belatedly claimed its secular credentials by announcing to *ban* right-wing militant group Bajrang Dal[17] and take tough against cow vigilantism[18] in Karnataka in

2023 but at the same time, its Madhya Pradesh chief Kamal Nath was merging a right-wing outfit, Bajrang Sena, with the Congress[19] ahead of the state elections.

It is the fear of Hindu backlash that neither the Congress nor other political parties strongly opposed the abrogation of Article 370 or downgrading of Jammu and Kashmir in 2019 – which was apparently undemocratic, unconstitutional (which was pending before the apex court since then) and aimed at hurting Muslims of the state. The AAP learnt its lessons too late as its government in the NCT of Delhi was delegitimized by the same Central government three years later in 2022 by declaring its nominee (LG) as the "government" there. Despite the pessimistic outlook, it must, however, be said that when all the Opposition partis are facing existential threats they are bound to join forces and fight back in the 2024 general elections. Whether that will work remains to be seen.

Challenges of Social Metamorphosis

The challenge is not just electoral and political but also societal – which adds another layer of complexity to the battle. Jaffrelot argued in his book cited earlier that an electoral defeat might be necessary but *not sufficient* to check to the march of Hindu supremacists because they are "deeply entrenched in the social fabric" and infiltrated institutions sufficiently enough to develop a "deep state". It was these deeper and wider political and societal roots of Hindutva which prompted author-activist Arundhati Roy to remark: "Elections will not reverse the tide. It's too late for that. This battle will have to be waged by every single one of us. The blaze is at our door."[20]

The onus then is on the people but how will they rise up and when? Who will lead them? These questions assume significance because India has witnessed significant mass movements fizzling out after 2014. The CAA was vigorously protested during 2019-20 by not just elderly Muslim women and students but Sikhs and civil society; the year-long farmers' protests against pro-corporate farm laws in 2020-2021 too had wider appeal and support. But both kept Opposition political parties out – falling for the BJP's malicious campaign and *wrongly assumed* that their agitation (to seek justice) was *apolitical activity* and politicization would delegitimize their cause. (*Seeking justice is a political act*.) The same happened with the women wrestlers' seeking justice and action against BJP MP Brij Bhushan Saran Singh for sexual harassment in January 2023 and it produced no result. They allowed the Opposition and civil society to join later.

None of these protests was, however, transformed into a larger social and political movements in the face of the BJP's sustained campaigns using state machineries, troll armies and physical attacks, demonizing and dismantling these protests with force without paying political or electoral price whatsoever. Multiple challenges to mass social and political mobilization have been identified. One is Hindu upper caste, mainly the educated and professional middle-class, who are far more influential than their numbers would suggest (for example, 75.8% high court judges appointed since 2018 (458 out of 604) are from upper castes[21]) and now form the *support base* of the Prime Minister, his BJP and their Hindutva project. In fact, development economist Jean Dreze wrote[22] that the growth of Hindutva or Hindu nationalism was a "quiet revolt of the upper castes against democracy" and was "now taking the form of a more direct attack on democratic institutions, starting with the freedom of expression and dissent". He described Hindutva as "a kind of lifeboat for the upper castes" who want "restoration of the Brahminical social order". Indeed, the dominance of upper caste has been undermined in various ways in post-independent India: Equal voting rights, irrespective of caste; abolition of zamindari system; green revolution; upliftment of socio-economically backward and underprivileged through reservation in education, jobs and legislations etc.

This division of Indian society is sharp, disturbing and calls for introspection by the elites. Intellectual dishonesty of economists in justifying the government's economic policies which have directly caused poverty, hunger and inequality to grow is pervasive. Three more instances to drive the point home. In 2019, 131 (chartered) accountants[23] joined issues with 108 economists and social scientists for questioning the quality of official statistics. In 2022, widespread condemnation of Muslim genocide call at the Haridwar "dharma sansad" (religious gathering) was met with 32 ex-diplomats[24] writing to dismiss it as "double standards" and "smear campaign" against the government even though hate speeches soared after he came to power. In 2022, more than 100 *retired judges and senior bureaucrats* issued a statement against a Supreme Court judge for criticizing BJP spokesperson Nupur Sharma for her blasphemous comments and police inaction; they said the judge had crossed "the Laxman Rekha" and left an "indelible scar on the justice system of the largest democracy".[25] Such instances were virtually unknown in pre-2014 India.

True, history does show leaders emerge out of political and societal crises but given the deep communal and ideological schisms and a general endorsement of the Hindu majoritarianism, it is as yet difficult to imagine that happening anytime soon. There is no Mahatma Gandhi to unite Hindus and Muslims, no Nehru and Ambedkar to set up a constitutional democratic order, no Jayprakash Narain to lead the fight against authoritarianism of the Emergency and no Vinoba Bhave (of 'Bhoodan Andolan') to attempt socio-economic parity. When Sri Lankan erupted with mass anger in early 2022 because of economic hardship, there was no mass leader and suddenly the possibility of change without a leader seemed possible and plausible. But it fizzled out in weeks after Ranil Wickremesinghe – political ally of ex-President Gotabaya Rajapaksa against whom the public uprising was targeted and who fled the country – assumed charge to complete the latter's term in office[26] and the Sri Lankans got busy rebuilding their lives.

When most Indians are fighting for mere survival, revolution is tough. Eric Hoffer wrote in his 1951 classic "The True Believer"[27]: "Where people toil from sunrise to sunset for a bare living, they nurse no grievances and dream no dreams. One of the reasons for the *un-rebelliousness* of the masses in China is the inordinate effort required there to scrape together the means of the scantiest subsistence. The intensified struggle for existence "is a static rather than a dynamic influence"." Dreze[28] echoed the same sentiment during the mass reverse migration in 2020 – which evoked no violent proests from the millions who walked home with luggage and family amidst the 24x7 national curfew: "Poor people are used to taking a lot of things lying down – when people are hungry and feeble, they are not necessarily well placed to revolt. But food riots could happen, who knows." No food riots happened either. The mass reverse migration saw 971 people perish, some to road and train accidents (how did these vehicles found their ways to roads and rail tracks?) and others to hunger and exhaustion.[29] The government denied any death saying it had no data and hence, refused to provide compensations. With 67% of population dependent on "free" ration, the hope for a mass anger bursting forth seems remote. *(Emphasis added)*

Recall how the US media talked about Plato and his prediction that too much democracy would lead to tyranny[30] after Donald Trump became the President. It resonated in India too. Books on how democracies die, how fascism works, the new despotism (all from the global perspectives) and also the democratic backsliding in India were written. The rise of right-wing demagogues, populism, nationalism or evoking nationalistic pride and attack on liberal and other democratic values were the focal points (political aspects) of such discourse and covered the US, India, the UK, Turkey, Hungary, Brazil, Poland and Philippines. (In the context of the Palestine-Israel conflict in 2023, this sort of nationalism got a new adjective, "putrid fumes"[31], from Israel newspaper Haaretz.) That brings to the other aspect (economic) of this right-wing tilt – the *neoliberal* shift – which adds another layer of complexity. There is now enough literature to show how neoliberal economics (radical capitalism or market fundamentalism – a "political doctrine" masquerading as economic concepts meant to serve certain private interests and not supported by economic theories or evidence as Nobel laureates Stiglitz, Krugman and others have extensively written[32]) has facilitated this right-wing transition of democracies and development of autocratic tendencies in several countries.[33]

These studies and research show neoliberal economics has increased *economic insecurities and globalized shocks*, fueling right-ward turn, not a left-ward turn, howsoever ironical this may sound, both *in politics and society*. This was particularly evident in the US and the UK. In the US, it was clear even before the 2016 elections that brought Republic President Donald Trump. In the UK, the 2016 Brexit referendum marked the beginning of its separation from the

European Union and the rise of Conservative Party (to which their premiers Boris Johnson Liz Truss and Rishi Sunak belong). These studies explained that economic insecurities and anxieties often work through *culture and identity*, and argued that long recession/stagnation following the implosion of global finance in 2007-09 acted as the *driving force* for this right-ward turn. These changes then cause politics to turned populist and economics "nationalist".[34]

In India, Hindutva and neoliberalism have blended – adding yet another layer of complexity. Political scientst Ajay Gudavarthy wrote[35]: "Today, there are two unmistakable strands to the aggressive mobilization of the Bharatiya Janata Party. One is instrumentalising religion and the second, weaponising the free market. Aggressive neoliberalism is hand in glove with militant imageries of religious figures..." Economist Prabhat Patnaik[36] advised India's 'liberal middle' the need to find "ways of transcending neo-liberal economics" for the Congress to re-acquire its political relevance in today's India. He argued that "the crisis of neo-liberalism provides a fertile soil for the growth of neo-fascism, as indeed it is doing, or of militant revolutionism, as it had done in the 1930s".

How are such challenges to be met?

Change in Education System?

Some have suggested changing the education system to address the growing *irrationality* and *uneduactedness* (degrees, yes; educated, no) in the society and popularity of the Hindutva's apparent obscurantism. Writing about the "cult of stupidity" (see Chapter XI), educator Rohit Kumar argued[37]: "A well-rounded education that encourages one to think, question, analyse and critique from childhood on up is really the only long-term cure – an education that, along with history, geography, language, science and mathematics, also teaches critical thinking, empathy, logic and genuine communication skills." Anurag Mehra[38] of IIT-Bombay wrote (in the context of educated young professionals targeting Muslim women) that "the contemporary education system seems to be completely ineffective in enabling people to screen out prejudices, bigotry and falsehoods". India's rote-learning system has created a worldview that has poor understanding of social and political issues and has created chauvinistic, amoral citizens. He captured the socio-economic context to the rabid worldview of educated youngsters, which has global relevance too: "We live in times when those stepping into adulthood are likely to face unemployment, financial insecurity and precarious futures; where authoritarian leaders provoke supporters to form vigilante mobs – digital and real – to destroy imagined enemies; where toxic discourses against such enemies provide "explanations" for social ills and personal misery; and, when this toxic polarization of views lives inside homes." His solution: An education policy that would infuse a liberal and multidisciplinary pedagogy into every level of education to enable deeper learning and thinking.

But the failure of Indian education system to produce individuals who question and think for herself/himself is also the failure of Hindu-dominated Indian society. Its traditions or culture inculcates obedience to authority, family elders and community leaders. Apart from the religious divide now so open and violently perpetuated, a large part of Indian society remains deeply feudal, rigidly caste-based, hierarchal, patriarchal, discriminatory and exploitative – none of which tolerate questioning or independent thinking. Loyalty to family, caste, village, khap (group of villages bound by caste/communities) and religion override individual choices and rights. One example of this is the rise[39] in "honour killing" without legal or social support in sight. It is difficult to keep the education system insulated as all the players come from the very same society. The Constitution of India does seek to undo these by empowering every individual through fundamental rights; the first Prime Minister Jawaharlal Nehru and others of the time actively promoted modern and scientific education and hoped this would produce a modern, scientific, rational and democratic society. For a long time, it seemed India was marching in the right direction until the Prime Minister and his party demonstrated for the world just how presumptuous that was. The biggest problem with changing the education system – howsoever unlikely that may seem, given the massive re-writing of school textbooks to prevent critical thinking and attack on universities displaying independent thinking and resisting Hindutva – the impact would be visible after a long time. What happens in the interim? India is witnessing a "self-repressing society" like China[40] here and now, with "Bhakts", right-wing militant organizations and sundry mobs establishing a Hindu supremacist order on the streets and institutions.

Nevertheless, education is an essential redeeming factor. Here is a clincher in support of education (howsoever defective). When the only BJP legislator from Kerala O Rajagopal (2016 to 2021) was asked in 2021 why his party was not growing in the state his answer was: "Kerala is a different state…Kerala has a literacy rate of 90%. They *think and communicate* and these are the habits of the educated. That is also a problem."[41] The other factor he listed was religious composition – 55% Hindus and 45% minorities. So, education is absolutely essential for India (which has a "literacy rate" of 74% as per 2011 Census) to get rid of the hate-and-violence spread by the Hindu supremacists. In this, India must reverse the debilitating attacks[42] on English. It is the English skills that drove India's IT industry, services exports and provided opportunities to Indians to migrate to the US and Europe.

Caste Curse: Legacy and Hindutva Push

The biggest evil besieging India society is its rigid caste system Brahminism has produced and perpetuated through the past 2,000 years (genetic study showing inter-mixing of population stopped around 100 CE in India[43]) and which Hindutva is now reinforcing. Economists Daron Acemoglu and James A Robinson trace the history of development across the world in the past 700-800 years in their book "Why Nations Fail: The Origins of Power, Prosperity and Poverty" and identify the key driving to be the development of "inclusive institutions" – political inclusion followed by economic institutions. The only worthwhile point they talked about India while explaining what held it back despite its rich civilizational (the Harappan urban revolution) and trading histories is its "uniquely rigid hereditary caste system".

They wrote: "In India, institutional drift worked differently and led to the development of a uniquely rigid hereditary caste system that limited the functioning of markets and the allocation of labour across occupations much more severely than the feudal order in medieval Europe. It also underpinned another strong form of absolutism under the Mughal rulers. Most European countries had similar systems in the Middle Ages. Modern Anglo-Saxon surnames such as Baker, Cooper and Smith are direct descendants of hereditary occupational categories. Bakers baked, coopers made barrels and smiths forged metals. But these categories were *never as rigid as Indian caste distinctions* and gradually became meaningless as predictors of a person's occupation. Though Indian merchants did trade throughout the Indian ocean, and a major textile industry developed, the *caste system and Mughal absolutism* were serious impediments to the development of inclusive economic institutions in India. By the nineteenth century, things were even less hospitable for industrialization as India became an extractive colony of the English." *(Emphasis added)*

The 'Mughal absolutism' (they explained elsewhere[44]) is the *hierarchical power structure* in which power is concentrated in the hands of a few, the ruling elites, and structured to extract resources from the majority for the benefit of a minority – not unusual for a king or a colonial power. The Indian caste system (which produced 'untouchability') has done the same for ages even without such a political structure at the top by exploiting and denying space to the majority of Indians who constitute lower castes (like the OBCs, Scheduled Castes and Scheduled Tribes). There are no OBC data at all-India level in the post-independent India but the government's Situation Assessment of Agricultural Households and Land Holdings of Households in Rural India, 2019, shows, 44.4% are OBCs, 21.6% SCs and 12.3% are SCs – taking the total to whopping *78.3% of rural population* (where about 70% Indians live) – while the rest 21.7% belong to other social groups (upper castes and non-Hindus).[45]

The impact of such caste division was visible during the pandemic. A study of 2023[46] showed, while all groups lost jobs in the first two months of national lockdown in 2020, the job losses for lowest-ranked caste were greater "by factor of more than two". The data also showed: "…caste gaps in employment outcomes remain sizeable, even when we compare groups within the same industry, occupations, or those who have completed secondary schooling. These findings suggest that *caste is not merely a proxy for class*, and identity-based policies might be essential to overcoming these disparities". The situation in higher education is no different. In fact, a Rajya Sabha answer of 2023 revealed that 25,593 students from the SC, ST, OBC and other minority categories dropped out[47] of Central Universities and IITs over the last five years – mostly the PG and PhD students. That such a large number of such students dropping out of Central Universities and IITs reflect gaping chasm[48] between the rhetoric of "inclusive" growth and reality.

Caste discriminations leading to suicides in IITs are no longer shocking. The IIT-Bombay is seeing food discrimination (separate mess and tables for veg and non-veg food).[49] The administration is supporting this wholeheartedly and promptly punished the protests by imposing a fine of Rs 10,000 on a student who objected to "veg only" table.[50] This is when most Indians eat non-veg food ("fish, chicken or meat") and their numbers are swelling – from 78.4% men and 70% women in the age group of *15-49 years* during the NHFS-4 survey period of 2015-16 to 83.4% men and 70.6% women in the NFHS-5 survey period of 2019-21.[51] If "egg" is added to the list, the number of men goes up to 84.7% and women to 72% (these numbers have risen too). The IIT-Bombay incident is a clear pointer to *imposing the Brahminical order on food* – although only some orthodox Brahmins are vegetarians, while Brahmins from Jammu and Kashmir, Bihar, West Bengal and Odisha are non-vegetarians.

Interestingly, in the supposedly vegetarian state of Gujarat and where Muslim vendors selling non-veg items were removed from public places/sight in the recent years, around *40% ate eggs or meat* (2014 survey) – proportionately more than Rajasthan, Haryana and Punjab.[52] As per the NHFS-5 of 2019-2021[53], 49% men and 37% women in the age group of 15-49 years eat non-veg food – a sharp rise from 41.7% men and 29.5% women from NHFS-4[54] of 2015-16. (NB: Gujarat where *alcohol is banned for more than six decades* but is available in plenty[55] and a RTI query revealed in 2023 that of 995 rail loco pilot who failed breathalyser tests (for drunkenness) in five years *104 were in Gujarat*[56]).

The BJP's ideological fountainhead RSS seeks to reinforce the rigid caste system and undo caste reservations ("affirmative actions"). Its occasional posturing about social harmony is a mere "strategy to get oppressed communities to accept that the caste system is for their own good and to not seek their welfare through sociopolitical assertions or constitutional safeguards".[57] It was in keeping with this duplicity that the RSS sought to deflect the Opposition's insistence on a nation-wide caste census – and the legitimacy of collecting the OBC data given that reservations to the OBC in jobs, education and local bodies are operational in the country since 1990 – during the November 2023 state elections (after Bihar made public its caste census report in October-November 2023) by declaring to float a social movement to spread "samajik samrasta" (social harmony) to foster "Hindu oneness"[58]. The Prime Minister accused the Opposition parties of *dividing*[59] the country on caste lines.

So long as a caste-ridden society – which is typical to Hindus and have spread to converts, but not practiced by tribal communities – continues there can be no inclusive growth. It is no rocket science to understand that, as one economist described it, caste system or caste inequality is "the mother of all other inequalities" to explain why poor nations like Nepal and Bangladesh have overtaken India in social indicators.[60] The BJP doesn't wish that.

Its 10% EWS quota for upper castes, which the Supreme Court upheld despite many flaws in the logic and approach, is one such step (explained in Chapter III). Another is not making public the OBC data collected for the first time in post-independence era, along with those of SCs and STs, through the ever Socio Economic and Caste Census (SECC) of 2011 – at the prompting of the Supreme Court. It may be afraid of giving a fresh sail to the 'Mandal' politics of 1990s (which brought the OBC quota and led to emergence of powerful regional parties like the Samajwadi Party and RJD). The RSS-BJP ran a parallel 'Kamandal' politics[61] (use of religion in politics, 'kamandal' is a water pot symbolizing Hindu asceticism) – which revived its religion-led political fortune that had sunk low after the demolition of Babri masjid in 1992. Therefore, no OBC data collection is contemplated in the 2021 Census (postponed to 2024-25) either. The government, in its affidavit[62] to the Supreme Court, made the usual excuses (OBC count in the Census) that it would be "administratively difficult and cumbersome" to collect OBC data and dismissed the SECC of 2011 data as "replete with technical flaws".

What India needs is not a Uniform Civil Code (UCC) but a Uniform *Caste* Code for Hindus – so that equal opportunity and social and economic mobility are available to the majority of (lower caste) Hindus. This will ensure the President of India Draupadi Murmu, a tribal and lower caste (Scheduled Caste), is not humiliated[63] again by sundry Hindu priests who barred her entry into the sanctum sanctorum of a Hindu temple in New Delhi in 2023 – which was, at the same time, accessed by sundry upper caste Hindus leaders. Former Panna 'maharani', a widow, can't be dragged out of a temple and arrested for performing rituals.[64] Nor a BJP man can dare to urinate on a tribal.[65]

Hindus carry their caste system everywhere – forcing the US institutions and states like California[66] to bring laws to *ban* caste discrimination. India needs to do that. There is also a dire need for an UCC to re-establish the constitutional secularism guaranteeing religious freedoms, gender parity, fundamental rights and equality of all individuals, irrespective of religion and caste. Ambedkar's warning, or a lesson if you may, at the Constituent Assembly in 1949 should always be kept in mind: "How long *shall we continue to deny equality in our social and economic life*? If we continue to deny it for long, we will do so only by putting our *political democracy in peril*. We *must remove* this contradiction at the earliest possible moment or else those who suffer from inequality will blow up the structure of political democracy..."[67] In a radio talk, he once said[68]: "Indians today are governed by *two different ideologies*. Their political ideal, set out in the preamble to the constitution, affirms a life of liberty, equality and fraternity. Their social ideal, embodied in their religion, denies them." *(Emphasis added)*

What Made India Tick in Past?

It would be worthwhile to look at how Indian institutions handled the tough transition from the colonial rule, communal orgies that marked the 1947 partition and the rigid hierarchical social order (caste system) – which has *corrupted* caste-neutral Islam and Christianity too but the government refused to recognize and allow affirmative actions for such Muslims and Christians.[69] Union Home Minister Amit Shah even vowed (in 2023) to end Muslim quota given by states in their list of Scheduled Castes[70]. Unlike the US institutions which stood up to President Trump[71], institutional failures in India have added to political and social crises and governance deficits.

Institutions did work in India in the past, save for the Emergency. None can claim otherwise. A big part of the explanations lies in political executive with strong commitment to democracy and the Constitution. The trouble arose under a "strong" leader, former Prime Minister Indira Gandhi then and now Prime Minister Narendra Modi – overwhelming established institutions, including the Supreme Court as Justice (retd) AP Shah has pointed out[72].

The years of multi-party coalition governments during 1989-2014 saw the reverse; institutions asserting their independence and autonomy from governments. This is understandable because no institution is more powerful than a government. It has huge resources at its disposal and it operates several levers of power in addition to law enforcing apparatus, intelligence agencies, paramilitary and military forces. For example, the Central government appoints or plays a big role in the appointments to all key offices, including the constitutional ones like the ECI, High Courts and Supreme Court; it can pass laws without resistance using its majority in the Parliament. But the dynamics change in coalitions. A part of the solution, therefore, could be a coalition government. Even the earlier BJP-led government under Vajpayee was "moderate" and put on hold all the three BJP's "core agenda" of its communal and divisive politics.

But now the first two goals have been achieved and the efforts are on to achieve the third (UCC). The Law Commission of India is working overtime (giving 30 days for public views[73]) to frame its recommendations. This is the second attempt by the government as its first "reference" to the Law Commission in 2016 had led to the 2018 consultation paper "Reform of Family Law"[74] which *rejected* the idea of UCC. It had said this was "neither necessary nor desirable at this stage"; a 'united' nation "need not necessarily have 'uniformity'"; the uniformity should be about "making diversity reconcile with certain universal and indisputable arguments on human rights" and "cultural diversity *cannot be compromised* to the extent that our urge for uniformity itself becomes a reason for threat to the territorial integrity of the nation" Its emphasis was reforming "laws that are discriminatory". The Law Commission should be very wary of not falling into the trap as the goal seems less about uniformity and equality and more about encroaching on the personal laws of minority and tribal communities.[75] Sure, further reforms are needed in personal laws but that requires national debate, consultations, not imposition or a dog whistle ahead of the 2024 general elections.[76] *(Emphasis added)*

The other challenge is what social scientists call "crisis of institutions" – state institutions seen as rent-seeking and corrupt, in decline or decay. One particular study of Indian institutions is very relevant here as it covers both the era of strong leader and coalition governments and also when institutions had already acquired the wrong qualifiers of being rent-seeking and corrupt. This study, "The Puzzle of India's Governance: Culture, Context and Comparative Theory"[77], was conducted by Subrata K Mitra of Heidelberg University and it was published as a book in 2006.

This is a comprehensive study, tracing the changes in governance between 1950 and 1998. Mitra's focus was on *communal riots and murders*, although he used other governance indicators like illegal strikes/lockouts, tax dodging, corruption and electoral frauds during 1950-1998 – using data and interviews (method: rational choice, neo-institutional model of political transactions). He analyzed data from six states (Bihar, Gujarat, Maharashtra, Punjab, West Bengal and Tamil Nadu) and found the overall level of governance kept rising after 1950 (dipped in 1975-77, went up thereafter and then fell in 1980s and 1990 but remained above 1950s and 1960s levels) and riots decreased, though not murders. He noted that the institutions of state (Parliament, Police, Army, Civil Service, Judiciary, federalism and the party system) were "singularly robust, vital and resilient" five decades after the independence.

The study attributed several factors for the success of governmental institutions: (i) the capacity of modern institutions to tap into the historical memory of the pre-colonial state tradition (ii) the political process that tends to cut across groups, rather than cumulating conflict in a manner that would deepen the chasm that divides them and (iii) the joint history of British rule and Indian resistance. It said the Indian government institutions had "relatively benign elasticity" because of "effective governance" (implying orderly rule) and "strategic thinking" of her elites. Why do people follow rules in some situations and not in others, and why do people in similar contexts behave differently with regard to specific rules? The study posed and answered this question: "... order ensues when both sides to a transaction decide for their own reasons to abide scrupulously by the letter and spirit of the rule, and that the decision by the actors to stick by the rules of transaction is not in any way determined by culture or context, but necessarily involves their *perception of potential rewards, risk and the comparison of likely outcomes, leading to a choice*...The motivations that underpin their decisions are guided by such basic concerns as *security, welfare and identity*, and, in the short run, by the tactical advantages of either abiding by rules, or contravening them in the myriad ways open to political men and women." *(Emphasis added)*

What happens when the choice of scrupulously abide by the letter and spirit of the rule is replaced by arbitrariness under a changed political culture? What happens when the motivating factors (security, welfare, identity, abiding or contravening the rule of law) overwhelmingly point towards establishing Hindu majoritarian state and good or effective governance is thrown out of the equations? Communal riots, that Mitra mapped, have seen a dramatic rise in post-2014 India. In 2020, the BJP members attacked the Congress in the Parliament by stating that *871 communal riots*[78] had occurred during Pandit Nehru (1947-64), India Gandhi (1966-77, 1980-84) and Rajiv Gandhi (1984-89) – in the span of 37 years. When the government was asked about the communal riots after 2014, the Parliament was told, in 2022[79], that during 2016-2020 (just five years), there were *3,399* communal riots. Notice the jump!

More such comprehensive studies are needed to understand the current dynamics and gather insights into the functioning of government institutions. Particularly keeping in mind recent administrative "reforms". There seems an attempt to build *committed bureaucracy*, which is aligned to the Prime Minister's vision of "New India"[80] – and involves forcible retirement of officers, a fresh pushed for lateral entry and attempt to break the IAS stranglehold. This is accompanied with a drastic fall[81] in appointment of civil servants through the Union Public Service Commission (UPSC) exams. The lateral entry into civil services is fraught with dangers as it increases further infiltration of Hindutva ideologues.[82] This fear is also caused by the proposed changes in recruitment process for top civil services posts with a 15-week foundation course[83] – without evidence of the efficacy of such a move. The reduction in intake and lateral entry into civil service means the shares of SCs, STs and OBCs gets reduced.

Diplomatic Fiascos and Moral Bankruptcy

The impact of a committed bureaucracy is evident in diplomacy. Indian diplomats now openly champion the Hindutva issues across the world[84], adopting the language of the nationalist government which is aimed more at domestic audience rather than furtherance of India's cause globally.[85] One account said Foreign Affairs Minister Jaishankar has created an image for himself as a Modi's messenger[86], rebranding the foreign policy, arguing that most tenets of diplomacy could be found in ancient Hindu texts and epics. Oxford scholar Kira Huju[87]called it "saffronization" of diplomacy, a departure from the "historically secular and relatively liberal bureaucracy" and is a cause of deep concern. The old and new diplomats and BJP affiliates working in the ministry now, Huju wrote, "follow the mandate of the 'Ayush' ministry, established in 2014, which, among other indigenous modalities, promotes Ayurveda and homoeopathy; yoga is accorded a particular centrality, with academic and physical classes to prepare future diplomats to promote yoga abroad".

Incidentally, the current China fiasco[88] – the Prime Minister repeatedly hosting Chinese President Xi Jinping during 2014-2020, describing his equation with him as "'plus one' friendship" and staging extravagant photo ops even as China undermined India's borders on multiple occasions and blocked India's membership in the Nuclear Suppliers Group (NSG), frustrated attempts to get Pakistan-based Jaish-e-Mohammed leader Masood Azhar as a global terrorist in the United Nations' list – is a reminder of the *Pakistan fiasco* (the Kargil war in 1999[89]) under former Prime Minister from the BJP, Vajpayee. Pakistan was busy staging the Kargil war when Vajpayee was taking the Lahore bus ride. Both Prime Ministers Modi and Vajpayee displayed rare exuberance that turned out to be quite embarrassing – displaying a kind *naivety* in diplomatic conduct.

The same embarrassment was visible when the diplomatic chill began with Canada in 2023 over the alleged killing of Hardeep Singh Nijjar on its soil by the Indian government agents and it was revealed that "Five Eyes" countries – one of the world's most cohesive and deep-rooted intelligence gathering group, led by the US and includes Canada, the UK, New Zealand and Australia – had provided the intelligence inputs. The Prime Minister's famous "2ab" special relations with Canada and "tu-taadi" pal US President Obama – nothing came to India's help. US President Biden[90] raised the issue on behalf of Canada at the G20 summit in September 2023; by now, the US, the UK and Australia had officially expressed their concerns over the allegation of India's involvement in the Nijjar's killing[91]. In a pique, India immediately stopped visas to Canadian citizens on the plea of "security threats" in September 2023 and then forced Canada to drastically cuts its diplomatic presence in the name of "parity". The US and the UK backed Canada that India was violating the Vienna Convention and asked India to cooperate with Canada in investigation instead[92] and India, on its part, decided to go back to resuming visa services a month later without actually spelling out what had changed in the security situation.[93] to Canadian citizens. India's diplomatic ineptitude was evident in the joint statement issued during and after

Prime Minister's US visit in June 2023. The joint statement spoke about cross-border terrorism despite there being no terror acts after the Pulwama incident of February 2019, and nothing about China's land grab which remains unresolved since 2020. Later, Defence Minister Rajnath Singh declared that India could wrest back the PoK without much ado[94] in response to Pakistan's routine and innocuous reply to the said joint statement. The PoK is under Pakistani control since 1947 and India has not attempted to take it back despite winning the 1965 and 1971 wars. Recall how the Chinese incursion happened about a year after Union Home Minister Amit Shah thundered in the Parliament (in 2019) "I am ready to give my life"[95] to wrest back "Aksai Chin" – the PoK territory under Chinese control since 1947.

This focus on Pakistan (proxy for domestic hate politics against Muslims) nearly caused a war in 2019 – following the Pulwama terror act which then Jammu and Kashmir Governor Satya Pal Malik blamed on gaping security lapses. A Big Brother attitude has already turned relations bad and India's influence has significantly wanned with its neighbours[96] like Nepal, Bhutan, Bangladesh, Maldives (which asked India to recall all its military staff in 2023[97]) and Sri Lanka after 2014 – allowing China to increase its presence in those countries. India's democratic backsliding also makes it an unreliable ally[98] for the western democracies. Such a situation is recipe for disasters. India has already opened up a two-front war (Pakistan and China), endangering external security, notwithstanding then Army chief General Bipin Rawat's 2017 statement declaring that India is "ready for two-and-half front war" (Pakistan, China and internal conflicts).[99] When China entered the Indian side of the LAC in Ladakh in 2020, General Rawat was Chief of Defence Staff (CDS) and busy mobilizing the Air Force and Navy to shower rose petals from the sky on healthcare professionals.[100] (And the Prime Minister of India kept Indians busy with clapping hands, banging 'thaalis' (utensils) and lighting candles on their balconies as millions of migrant workers walked by.)

Diplomacy calls for maturity which India had amply demonstrated in the past, and adherence to the Constitution of India, not Hindutva. Have you noticed how foreign dignitaries visiting India don't meet Opposition leaders after 2014? If you have, have you wondered why this happened? Do the visiting foreign dignitaries think there will be no end to the current government and hence they don't need to know or develop relations with the Opposition parties and leaders? You may not find anything in writing now (it did exist at one point) but look at the simple fact and you know denying such interactions is the silent policy of the government. The Opposition leaders of Lok Sabha (Adir Ranjan Chowdhury) and Rajya Sabha (Mallikarjun Kharge) – both from the Congress – were not even invited to the ceremonial dinner for the G20 delegations hosted by the President of India![101]

Now, India has not only lost courage but also its moral compass. This was amply demonstrated when the Russia-Ukraine war broke out in 2022 and then the Israel-Palestine conflict in 2023. India *never condemned* the Russian attack and *repeatedly abstained* from the UN resolutions to the effect[102]; even the G20 resolution of New Delhi removed "all references to Russia, Russian aggression and Russia's withdrawal in relation to the war in Ukraine that featured in last year's joint statement at the G20 summit in Bali", instead, it talked in generalities about "refrain from the threat or use of force to seek territorial acquisition" etc.[103] It condemned the Hamas attack on Israel as "terrorist attack"[104] but never condemned the carpet bombing of civilians in Gaza by Israel that followed for months skilling thousands of civilians (a larger number of which are kids); it even *refused to support* the UN resolution calling for "protection of civilians and upholding legal and humanitarian obligations" (which 120 countries supported and only 14 opposed (including Israel, the US, Hungary and five Pacific island states) and 45 opposed. India absented[105] on flimsy ground, which was: "The terror attacks in Israel on 7th October were shocking and deserve condemnation. Our thoughts are also with those taken hostages. We call for their immediate and unconditional release. Terrorism is a malignancy and knows no borders, nationality, or race. The world should not buy into any justification of terror acts. Let us keep aside differences, unite and adopt a zero-tolerance approach to terrorism." The government chose to forget the history of Palestine-Israel conflict and India's stand for decades until then. India probably was never seen so morally timid, for no strategic thinking or diplomatic pragmatism can stop denouncing war and violence or refuse to support ceasefires to violence.[106]

Going back to bureaucracy, there are plenty in the inbox from the Administrative Reforms Commissions to make it more responsive to people's need and accountable. But the big problem who cares? The incumbent ruling establishment is obssessed with centralization of power, perpetuating power and bringing 'transformative' changes to the very constitutional democracy – all this flowing from its regressive thinking.

Systemic Transformations

More ideas to improve institutions can be gleaned from the experience of the erstwhile Planning Commission. An attempt was made for its systemic transformation, led by then member Arun Maira, during 2004-14. Maira tried to transform from within by shifting the focus away from centralized planning and budgeting to governance, collaboration, coordination and building bridges with various stakeholders for inclusive growth and job creations – the two key concerns then. He met strong resistance and was, thus, forced to devise new methods to achieve his goals with varying degrees of success. When the NITI Aayog was set up in 2015, he endorsed its charter (in his 2015 book "An Upstart in Government"[107]), called it was "well in line" with the directions for change he had developed. He was impressed by the Union Cabinet resolution on the Aayog's objectives[108] emphasizing participative citizenry, shared vision, credible plans at local levels, encouraging partnerships, creating systemic processes for collaborations etc. But as we know by now, the Aayog has failed to live up to its promises.

One particular differentiation Maira made (in his 2015 book) "in the roles of public and private sectors in development is worth noting. He wrote: "... the scope of the government's responsibilities is much larger than that of any private sector company. To produce outcomes that are equitable, and not only efficient, in providing health services to all citizens, for example, is more difficult than selling medicines to only those who can pay the price that covers their cost of discovery and production. The government's job *is not to make profit*. It is to improve the world for everyone. 'Making profit is easy: changing the world is hard', was the poignant statement of a business management student at an international conference on business responsibility." *(Emphasis added)*

Surely, Maira knows what he is talking about, having spent a lifetime in private sector in India and abroad (including the US) and headed the Boston Consultancy Group in India before joining the Planning Commission. The future path for the Aayog is clear though. Instead of rushing to endorse government policies *post facto* – be it the mindless demonetization, botched GST, untimely, unplanned and mismanaged pandemic lockdown, pro-corporate farm laws etc. – it should revive National Development Council (NDC), Inter-State Council (ISC) and other consultative mechanisms to involve state governments, the Parliament, experts and people in planning and development process – which it doesn't. It shouldn't be promoting one-size-fits-all policies at all, given the wide divergence in infrastructure, human resources, geographic and climatic factors that characterize different states. It must switch to developing medium and short-term visions, objectives (growth, equity, sustainability etc.), list challenges and opportunities and accordingly designing strategies through wide consultations and discussions. It did produce such documents in the past but those were *rehashed* from the old Planning Commission reports and *copied* the new government's declared policies.[109]

Ready-to-use In-box Solutions

Going back to the beginning of this book (Introduction chapter), should the incumbent government decide to course correct on its own (optimism does help), there are plenty of inbox, ready-to-use good governance practices. Here are a few key ones.

First and most critical one is to *junk the top-down arbitrary policymaking*.

Instead, the government must follow the age-old standard operating procedures (SoPs) for policymaking: Identify the challenges; prepare blueprints of remedial measures with alternatives and cost-and-benefit analysis; consult experts, stakeholders and public, allow parliamentary scrutiny and debate to fine-tune the blueprint; run pilots to check how it works on the ground; prepare the ground before rolling out; review and course correct. The same goes for projects too: Prepare detailed project proposals and reports (DPR) with alternative and cost-benefit analysis, due diligence in administrative and legal clearances, budget approvals etc.

The reading of the Pre-legislative Consultation Process (PLCP) of 2014[110] must be made mandatory for both the political executive and bureaucracy before contemplating any legislative business: A draft or pre-legislative note giving justification for a legislation, essential elements, broad financial implications and assessment of the impact on environment, fundamental rights, lives and livelihoods of the concerned/affected people to be proactively shared and put up in public domain for 30 days. It is rather unfortunate that *after a meeting with the Prime Minister* in August 2017, the plans for PLCP, consultations with political parties and public debates before notifying the Electoral Bond was killed – which the file notings obtained through the RTI Act of 2005 revealed.[111] The Prime Minister must shun building the image of being a "Vishwaguru" (world teacher) and expert on everything under the sun (history, science, climate change, malnutrition, military etc. Or be seen to be unpredictable (the "madman theory" associated with US Presidents Richard Nixon and Donald Trump didn't really help[112]) or guided by "ilhaam"[113] (sudden revelations) or non-reader of official files[114] claiming to having photographic memory[115]. Then, there will be more trust in his decision making, particularly when he has been openly accused of being misled by vested interests[116]. No Prime Minister is not expected or supposed to be expert on everything, that is why experts, consultations, public debates and parliamentary scrutiny are the *de rigueur* in democratic polity. When a Prime Minister becomes expert on everything, all the SoPs get automatically junked and none dares to stand up or air differing opinion, at least not when dissent is treated as sedition and terror and when democratic impulses are almost dead.

Had the government followed the SoPs, there would have been no demonetization, the GST would have been better designed and implemented, the pandemic lockdown and management would have been more effective and less painful, the new Parliament and reconstruction of the majestic Central Vista projects could have been junked to prioritize containment of the pandemic (humanitarian and economic crises) and reconstruction and the regressive laws on privacy, forests and environment, Electoral Bond and wholesale replacement of criminal laws like the IPC, CrPC and Evidence Act wouldn't exist. Recall, China built 1,000 bed hospital in 10 days[117] when the pandemic struck, while India wasted money on vanity projects even while going to the world with a begging bowl for help. India could also have avoided bringing itself into the *brink of a nuclear war* in 2019 with Pakistan (after the failed Balakot strike) – as US Secretary of State Mike Pompeo[118] revealed in his book in 2023. The military top brass wouldn't have uncritically approved and gone by the Prime Minister's cloud-radar theory, which he himself revealed (positing that cloud can prevent radar detection of planes[119]) that ended in the Balakot strike fasco in 2019. Top top bureaucrats, advisers, ministers and others in the government perhap know better but can't and don't dare to stop.

Second, restore *respect for dissent and criticism* in public discourses to build trust with stakeholders and foster debate and scrutiny of policies and actions. Restore also the practice of prior public debate about policies – which is conspicuous by its complete obliteration after 2014. Recognize that constant feeding of fake news, misinformation, whataboutery, propaganda etc. damage, rather than help in good governance. The idea shouldn't be to create a surreal world fit only for *zombies,* but empowered and enlightened citizens of a modern democratic country. Use of intemperate and undignified language for rival political parties and dissenting voices – such as "anti-nationals", "tube lights", "tukde-tukde gang", "urban naxals" etc. turns public discourse toxic, prevents realistic assessments and dries out fresh and innovative ideas. A Prime Minister must work for all, not perpetually remain leader of a particular party, community and business interest.

Putting dissenting voices in jail or throwing out of legislatures on trumped-up charges is the very anti-thesis of the rule of law and democracy and ultimately, self-defeating because it ends up hurting the country and people. Civil society plays a key role in democratic governance; it reaches out to underprivileged communities in a big but poor and diverse country like India and must be promoted and protected, rather than disabled through misuse of draconian laws.

Third, decentralize fiscal, administrative and political powers to truly promote cooperative federalism. It improves relations with state governments ruled by rival parties. Political campaigns like "Operation Lotus" and "Congress-mukt Bharat" or Opposition-mukt Bharat are anti-thetical to any democratic polity or governance and must be junked immediately. So is the power grab by overnight scrapping of Article 370, declaring nominated LG as "government" in place of elected government and using the office of Governors to destabilize Opposition-ruled states.

Fourth, review of existing economic policies for efficacy. Several such policies are not supported by economic logic or evidence (pre or post facto), like the indiscriminate and *en masse* privatization of public assets, disproportionate faith in 'National Champions' and crony capitalims, manufacturing incentives like PLIs and DLIs, the failed import substitution policy, shunning mega trade treaties, routine write-off of corporate defaults (NPAs) without inquiry, failed

Insolvency and Bankruptcy Code (IBC), dubious "compromise settlements" with fraudsters and willful defaulters etc. Many policies have ended up increasing poverty, hunger and inequality, like corporate tax cut, disproportionate tax burden on poor (oil tax, GST) must be reversed and specific policies must be framed to create more jobs and raise income levels of the masses. As Nauriel Roubini said about India: "The country's long-term success ultimately depends on whether it can foster and sustain a growth model that is competitive, dynamic, sustainable, inclusive and fair."[120]

Fifth, there is no point in *living in denial, manufacturing data and narratives or creating a data vacuum* to create alt-truths. Blocking from view the pervasive poverty through clothes and walls, demolishing slums and relocating the poor to the city's fringe when G20 leaders came visiting in 2023[121] or US President Trump visited India in 2020[122] etc. are markers of abject governance failuresgovernance. Accepting failures is the first step to course correction. Relevant data must be collected to give right direction to policymaking. If a small private firm CMIE can collect extensive data on employment, investment, consumer expenditure etc. every week and month, the Government of India with huge resources at its disposal can do better. There is no reason not to conduct the Census 2021, economic census, MPCE and update CPI/WPI, poverty line for years. It is high time household "income" data is collected, rather than use consumption expenditure as a proxy. All policies must be pre-tested on economic logic, data and other evidence, reviewed and changed to achieve the intended goals. There is no scope for arbitrariness or personal likes and dislikes (or naivity), like the diplomatic and trade tensions with China which further jeopardizes national security and has skewed the trade balance even more. Remember, China is not only (a) the second largest economy it is also *the global leader* in (b) manufacturing (c) exports and (d) technological innovations. India stands to lose by confrontations and fear (like running out of the RCEP treaty in 2019).[123]

Sixth, immediate steps need to be taken to prevent demographic disaster by addressing the *chronic and severe job crisis.* Glib talks of "pakoda" selling as employment, job seekers turning "job creators" through start-ups or pushing GDP growth and 'Make in India' (for which huge tax incentives like the PLIs and DLIs are being given without even a *post facto* study to justify) to automatically create more jobs (contrary to more than sufficient evidence) reflect ineptitude and incompetence – not sincerity. More than half of Indian workforce (57.3%) is "self-employed" and vulnerable and 18.3% are "unpaid" workers – and half the workers are in informal and low-paying agriculture (45.8%). Filing of existing vacancies is only a small step. India needs a proper employment policy and a roadmap to create millions of jobs that are required. The "Agnipath" is a bad idea and must be scrapped immediately. Imagine the danger from the 75% "Agniveers" trained in organized killing getting into a communally divided and violent society (mob lynching, riots, ethnic cleansing).

Seventh, India needs to *invest more public funds* to build its human capital – on health and education. Remember, China could make rapid progress after it adopted capitalist model for economic development because it had a huge advantage[124] in terms of good education and health. Privatization of healthcare and gradual withdrawal of government have led to "catastrophic expenditure" pushing 60 million people into poverty every year in *normal times*.[125] It is time similar studies are carried out about the impoverishing impact of costly education – even daily wagers, maids and other poor are opting for private English-medium schools which are for-profit business. Lack of affordable and accessible quality education and healthcare is depriving millions from realizing their economic potential and growth.

Eighth, economic history offers two significant lessons. One is *inclusive political and economic institutions* are critical to growth and development of a nation and the process begins with political system that fosters "pluralism", not divisive and communal politics. Acemoglu and Robinson wrote in their book "Why Nations Fail" mentioned earlier: "Pluralism, the cornerstone of inclusive political institutions, requires political power to be widely held in society, and starting from extractive institutions that vest power in a narrow elite, this requires a process of empowerment." That is, empowerment of broader segments of society is key to development, followed by economic inclusiveness.

The other is, *both democracy and secularism are critical for growth* and development. One multi-country and multi-institutional study led by Acemoglu in 2019[126] – which looked at 184 countries from 1960 to 2010 (50 years) to see the impact of unprecedented spread of democracy around the world during which 122 cases of countries democratized and 71 cases of countries moved away from democracy to nondemocratic type – concluded that "democratizations increase GDP per capita by about 20 percent in the long run". Another multi-disciplinary study of 2018[127] – which looked at 109 countries spanning over 100 years by researchers from the Universities of Bristol (UK) and Tennessee (US) – found economic growth comes *after* secular polity, not the other way round.

There is no way India can grow and develop by persecuting nearly half, 44.5%, of its population – 19.3% minority communities (14.2% Muslims, 2.3% Christians, 1.7% Sikhs, 0.7% Buddhists, 0.4% Jains and 00.6% Parsis) and 25% Dalits (SCs) and tribals (STs) (16.6% and 8.6%, respectively), as per the 2011 Census. The history of attacks on minorities and genocides in neighbouring Sri Lanka, Pakistan and Myanmar (also in Rwanda and Germany) and the price they have paid or are paying, is evidence of how politics of hate-and-violence paralyzes a country. An end to divisive and corrosive politics of hate-and-violence would not only bring peace and harmony, it would strengthen and ensure internal security. That would save law enforcing agencies from frittering their energy in unproductive work, the people would have time to better their lives and the BJP's vast network of committed cadre would then be engaged in constructive work. Hindu majoritarianism is slowly but surely tearing apart India[128] and must be stopped before it is too late – as US President Obama warned ("we've seen what happens when you start getting those kinds of large internal (ethnic) conflicts)[129] in 2023.

As head of the government, a 'secular' state, the Prime Minister of India must abjure the lure of turning into a Hindu priest or champion of Hindus. He is bound by his oath not to discriminate on grounds of religion (or caste or gender) and preserve and protect the *constitutional values*. As head of government, his responsibility is welfare of the entire nation. He is not supposed to be *permanently in electioneering mode* either and certainly not to use public money for it by combing official programmes with party's campaigns and run down a community or political rivals ceaselessly.

India's problem isn't *too much democracy*. The claims of India being a "civilizational state", "Mother of Democracy", "democracy in our veins" etc. are empty rhetoric – *invisible* on the ground. Too much concentration of power with the PM-PMO ends up depreciating the expertise of civil servants. Yamini Aiyar of the CPR flagged how what Indian bureaucracy needs is "deliberative" norms that encourage bureaucrats to respond to the democratic impulses by working collectively, seeking inputs, consensus and participation from all stakeholders, particularly citizens, and where problem-solving aimed at being responsive to citizen needs are encouraged even if it means rule-bending. Rightly did she argue that it is through "deliberative" practices that "the real barriers – social divisions in our deeply unequal setting, power asymmetries that encourage bureaucratic misbehaviour such as absenteeism, corruption and an apathetic approach to tasks – can be overcome."[130]

But the question is how to *insulate* democratic institutions from excessive dominance of the government and hold the power to account when they are broken? This is a big imponderable and there are no readymade, in-box slutions – except actively seeking the way out through debates and explorations of ideas.

Nineth, 'the idea of India' can't survive without the Supreme Court upholding the constitutional values and individual rights in true sense. Its credibility and independence have taken a serious beating. It is clear that when a government is strong, judiciary bends. How does one insulate judiciary? That is another big imponderable. India was debating reforming the higher judiciary before 2014 by establishing an independent body to appoint the judges – a tri-partisan one in which citizens have as much as say as the ruling establishment and the Opposition. It is time that debate is revived.

Tenth, an independent and fearless media is a *pre-requisite* for creating aware and empowered citizenry. It is also the watchdog of democracy. Nobel laureate Amartya Sen once famously said[131], there had never been a famine in a democratic society or even in India since independence because famine was not even possible when the press was free as it would expose any shortage in time to force corrective measures. The political and social backsliding of India require a free and fearlessly fair media. It is also worth recalling in this context that Thomas Jefferson, one of the founding fathers of the US and its third President, had put the power of media at the very core of democracy. In a speech in Paris in 1787, he had said: "The basis of our government being *the opinion of the people, the very first object should be to keep that right…*And were it left to me to decide whether we should have a *government without newspapers, or newspapers without a government, I should not hesitate a moment to prefer the latter…*" So, glorification of pliant journalists and persecution of fearless ones who dare to tell truth to power must stop asap. Remember: News and journalism are what government or anyone powerful wants to hide, everything else is propaganda/advertisement or PR. But again, how does one make news media fearless and independent when big corporate houses with multiple business interests and vulnerabilities run it?

Eleventh, Eventually, India's redemption lies in an enlightened and empowered citizenry. Despite 70 plus years of freedom, rights, modern education, a large part of citizenry seem to revel in *regressive values and life choices*. What else could have made them rational and progressive?

A decade of the current regime has clearly shown that India needs nothing short of another freedom movement-like social and political metamorphosis to restore 'the idea of India' (or stop its dismantling) and finish the unfinished agenda of the founding fathers – which is to build a modern, liberal and developed nation. The time is running out fast. Another encore in the 2024 elections may turn out to be far too many and close the options for course corrections for ages to come.

***

References

1 Jaffrelot Christophe, Modi's India: Hindu Nationalism and the Rise of Ethnic Democracy, Princeton University Press, Aug 2021, https://www.amazon.in/Modis-India-Nationalism-Ethnic-Democracy/dp/0691206805

2 Ambedkar BR, Constituent Assembly Debates On 25 November, 1949; https://indiankanoon.org/doc/792941/

3 Writing and Speeches of Dr Baba Saheb Ambedkar, Volume No. 13, Government of India, Page No. 61; https://www.mea.gov.in/Images/attach/amb/Volume_13.pdf

4 Bhushan Bharat, Inclusive or communal? Dangers of Arvind Kejriwal's 'homely Hinduism', Business Standard, Nov 16, 2020; https://www.business-standard.com/article/opinion/inclusive-or-communal-dangers-of-arvind-kejriwal-s-homely-hinduism-120111600093_1.html

5 Manish Sisodia in Gujarat: "Jai Shree Ram ka naara hindustan me nahi lagega to kya pakistan me lagega", Feb 14, 2021; https://twitter.com/Rohit245_/status/1360945671503708161

6 Apoorvanand, AAP turning into one more version of BJP, Deccan Herald, Feb 18, 2022; https://www.deccanherald.com/opinion/aap-turning-into-one-more-version-of-bjp-1082858.html

7 Mohapatra Debabrata, BJD to support Modi govt over Delhi Services Bill, oppose no-confidence motion, Aug 1, 2023; https://timesofindia.indiatimes.com/india/bjd-to-support-modi-govt-over-delhi-services-bill-oppose-no-confidence-motion/articleshow/102316926.cms?from=mdr

8 Opposition vows to take on BJP unitedly in 2024; next meeting in Shimla to prepare common agenda, Jun 23, 2023; https://www.tribuneindia.com/news/nation/big-opposition-meeting-to-chart-roadmap-for-2024-lok-sabha-polls-begins-in-patna-519599

9 ED summons Telangana CM KCR's daughter K Kavitha in Delhi excise policy case, Mar 8, 2023; https://www.livemint.com/news/india/ed-summons-telangana-cm-kcr-s-daughter-k-kavitha-in-delhi-excise-policy-case-11678249293140.html

10 Approached with offer to drop cases if I join BJP, says Manish Sisodia; party seeks proof, Aug 23, 2022;http://timesofindia.indiatimes.com/articleshow/93717371.cms?utm_source=contentofinterest&utm_medium=text&utm_campaign=cppst

11 Jagan's affidavit shows 31 pending criminal cases, Mar 23, 2019; https://www.thehindu.com/news/national/andhra-pradesh/jagans-affidavit-shows-31-pending-criminal-cases/article26614165.ece

12 Taj corridor case: CBI gets sanction to prosecute the then NPCC GM, Apr 25, 2023; https://www.hindustantimes.com/cities/lucknow-news/taj-heritage-corridor-scam-haunts-mayawati-and-congress-leader-cbi-gets-prosecution-sanction-after-20-years-tajmahal-corruption-cbi-mayawati-101682431522056.html

13 Mayawati as CM, brother & wife got 261 flats at 46% discount, audit flags

'fraudulent' sale, Jun 16, 2023; https://indianexpress.com/article/express-exclusive/mayawati-as-cm-brother-wife-got-261-flats-at-46-discount-audit-flags-fraudulent-sale-8663414/

14   UP Election Results 2022: How Mayawati's BSP was decimated, Mar 11, 2023; https://www.moneycontrol.com/news/politics/up-election-results-2022-how-mayawatis-bsp-was-decimated-8220061.html

15   Call for taking soft Hindutva approach in Congress faces stiff opposition, Deccan Herald, May 15, 2022; https://www.deccanherald.com/national/national-politics/call-for-taking-soft-hindutva-approach-in-congress-faces-stiff-opposition-1109412.html

16   With havans and temple runs, SP's 'soft Hindutva' answer to the BJP challenge, May 30, 2023; https://indianexpress.com/article/political-pulse/havans-temple-runs-samajwadi-party-soft-hindutva-bjp-lok-sabha-polls-8635863/

17   Bal Hartosh Singh, The call for banning the Bajrang Dal shows rare electoral courage, May 9, 2023; https://caravanmagazine.in/politics/congress-banning-bajrang-dal-courage

18   Smarting under Priyank Kharge's warning against cow vigilantism, right-wing trolls twist his statement, Jun 25, 2023; https://www.nationalheraldindia.com/india/smarting-under-priyank-kharges-warning-against-cow-vigilantism-right-wing-trolls-twist-his-statement

19   Ahead of polls, Bajrang Sena merges with Congress in Madhya Pradesh, vows to defeat BJP, Jun 7, 2023; https://www.thehindu.com/news/national/other-states/ahead-of-polls-bajrang-sena-merges-with-congress-in-madhya-pradesh-vows-to-defeat-bjp/article66939315.ece

20   Roy Arundhati, The Battle to Save India Has to Be Waged By Every Single One of Us, The Wire, Apr 22, 2022; https://thewire.in/rights/arundhati-roy-india-democracy-communalism

21   Representation of Weaker Sections in High Court Judges, Lok Sabha, Jul 21, 2023; https://www.dropbox.com/scl/fi/rj9ayhexcgyx85ix4wlzg/LS_75-of-judges-upper-caste.pdf?rlkey=akk1jkc1l0jl11ye7uatkbzyu&dl=0

22   Dreze Jean, The Revolt of the Upper Castes, The India Forum, Feb 18, 2020; https://www.theindiaforum.in/article/revolt-upper-castes

23   131 CAs refute economists' claims on GDP base year revision, Mar 18, 2019; https://www.thehindu.com/business/Economy/cas-debunk-economists-claims/article26572154.ece

24   32 retired Indian diplomats back Modi govt amid hate speech controversy, Jan 5, 2022; https://www.indiatoday.in/india/story/retired-indian-diplomats-back-modi-govt-hate-speech-1896466-2022-01-05

25   SC observations in Nupur Sharma case unfortunate, unprecedented, say bureaucrats, Jul 5, 2022; https://www.thehindu.com/news/national/sc-observations-in-nupur-

sharma-case-unfortunate-unprecedented-say-bureaucrats/article65602789.ece

26   Sri Lanka: Ranil Wickremesinghe elected president by MPs, Jul 20, 2022; https://www.bbc.com/news/world-asia-62202901

27   Hoffer Eric, The True Believer: Thoughts on the Nature of Mass Movements (Perennial Classics) Paperback – January 19, 2010, first published in 1951; Harper Perennial Modern Classics, https://www.amazon.com/True-Believer-Thoughts-Movements-Perennial/dp/0060505915

28   Dreze Jean, When people are hungry and feeble, they are not well placed to revolt: Jean Drèze, The Caravan, Mar 30, 2022; https://caravanmagazine.in/policy/no-one-should-be-condemned-to-starvation-jean-dreze

29   No Data, No Problem: Centre in Denial about Migrant Worker Deaths and Distress, Sept 2020; https://thewire.in/rights/migrant-workers-no-data-centre-covid-19-lockdown-deaths-distress-swan

30   Torcello Lawrence, Plato was right. Democracy always creates tyrannical leaders, The Print, Nov 19, 2019; https://theprint.in/world/plato-was-right-democracy-always-creates-tyrannical-leaders/323059/

31   Haaretz, The public atmosphere is teeming with putrid fumes of nationalism... Nov 12, 2023; https://twitter.com/haaretzcom/status/1723743708213117182

32   Mohanty P, 'An Unkept Promise', Ch XII

33   Rodrik Dani, Why Does Globalization Fuel Populism? Economics, Culture, and the Rise of Right-Wing Populism, Annual Review of Economics; https://scholar.harvard.edu/files/dani-rodrik/files/why_does_globalization_fuel_populism.pdf; Bossert Walter, Clark Andrew E, D'Ambrosio Conchita and Lepinteur Anthony, Economic Insecurity and the Rise of the Right, London School of Economics, Oct 2019; https://cep.lse.ac.uk/pubs/download/dp1659.pdf; Siltala Juha, In Search of the Missing Links Between Economic Insecurity and Political Protest: Why Does Neoliberalism Evoke Identity Politics Instead of Class Interests? Apr 2020; https://doi.org/10.3389/fsoc.2020.00028

34   Ninan TN, Back to the new-old: West wind, East wind, or the warnings of a storm? Jul 14, 2023; https://www.business-standard.com/opinion/columns/back-to-the-new-old-west-wind-east-wind-or-the-warnings-of-a-storm-123071400864_1.html

35   Gudavarthy Ajay, In India, Religion and Neoliberal Individualism Have Converged, Apr 27, 2022; https://www.newsclick.in/India-Religion-Neoliberal-Individualism-Converged

36   Patnaik Prabhat, Futile consultation: The crisis in the 'liberal middle', May 6, 2022; https://www.telegraphindia.com/opinion/futile-consultation-the-crisis-in-the-liberal-middle/cid/1863780#

37   Kumar Rohit, India and The Cult of Stupidity, The Wire, Mar 4, 2019; https://thewire.in/society/india-and-the-cult-of-stupidity

38   Mehra Anurag, The failure of the Indian education system is creating chauvinistic,

Food for Thought in 'Kartavya Kaal' | **673**

amoral citizens, Scroll, Apr 7, 2022; https://scroll.in/article/1019349/opinion-the-failure-of-the-indian-education-system-is-creating-chauvinistic-amoral-citizens

39 Study Finds Rise in Reported Cases of Honour Killings, but No Legislative or Social Remedy in Hand, Apr 11, 2023; https://thewire.in/caste/caste-honour-killings-cases-laws

40 China builds a self-repressing society, May 14, 2022; https://www.economist.com/china/2022/05/14/china-builds-a-self-repressing-society

41 Kerala has a literacy rate of 90%, O Rajagopal reveals reasons why BJP is not growing in state, Mar 23, 2021; https://keralakaumudi.com/en/news/news.php?id=514982

42 Mohanty P, Future of Indian trade is in services exports, Apr 18, 2023; https://www.fortuneindia.com/opinion/future-of-indian-trade-is-in-services-exports/112303

43 Joseph Tony, Early Indians: The Story of Our Ancestors and Where We Came From, Dec 2018, Juggernaut; https://www.amazon.in/Early-Indians-Story-Ancestors-Where/dp/938622898X

44 Acemoglu Daron, Johnson Simon and Robinson James A, Institutions as the fundamental cause of long-run growth, Working paper 10481, National Bureau of Economic Research, Cambridge, May 2004; https://www.nber.org/system/files/working_papers/w10481/w10481.pdf

45 Sharma Harikishan, Amid census calls, data show nearly half of rural homes OBC, Sept 29, 2021; https://indianexpress.com/article/india/amid-census-calls-data-show-nearly-half-of-rural-homes-obc-7540637/

46 Deshpande Aswini and Ramachandran Rajesh, Covid-19 and caste inequalities in India: The critical role of social identity in pandemic-induced job losses, Jun 6, 2023; Applied Economic Perspectives and Policy, https://onlinelibrary.wiley.com/doi/epdf/10.1002/aepp.13384

47 Agrawal Soniya, 25,000 + SC/ST/OBC students quit IITs & central universities in last 5 yrs, shows Parliament data, Jul 26, 2023; https://theprint.in/india/25000-sc-st-obc-students-quit-iits-central-universities-in-last-5-yrs-shows-parliament-data/1687365/

48 Mhaske Deelip, 25000 SC/ST/OBC students have quit IITs & central universities but Modi is stuck on temples, Jul 31, 2023; https://theprint.in/opinion/isnt-it-incumbent-upon-the-ruling-party-to-draw-inspiration-from-global-citadels-of-learning-to-stop-sc-st-obc-students-from-dropping-out-of-iits/1692890/

49 Chatterjee Pushpita, IIT Bombay: 'Segregation Much Deeper,' After Caste, Food Choices Divide Mumbai Campus, Jul 30, 2023; https://www.freepressjournal.in/education/iit-bombay-segregation-much-deeper-after-caste-food-choices-divide-mumbai-campus

50 IIT-Bombay fines student Rs 10,000 for protest against mess table reserved for' Vegetarian food', Oct 3, 2023; https://www.newindianexpress.com/nation/2023/oct/03/iit-bombay-fines-student-rs-10000-for-protest-against-mess-table-reserved-for-vegetarian-food-2620460.html

51   Sharma Harikishan, More men eating non-veg than before: Health survey data, May 17, 2023; https://indianexpress.com/article/india/more-men-eating-non-veg-than-before-nfhs-data-7920932/

52   Kaushik Himanshu, 40% of Gujarat is non-vegetarian: Survey, Nov 17, 2021; https://timesofindia.indiatimes.com/city/ahmedabad/40-of-gujarat-is-non-vegetarian-survey/articleshow/87745555.cms; Shah Amirta, Big picture: who's eating meat in Gujarat, and why ban non-veg food stalls from public roads in Ahmedabad, Vadodara, Nov 17, 2021; https://www.moneycontrol.com/news/trends/current-affairs-trends/big-picture-why-ahmedabad-banned-non-veg-food-stalls-from-public-roads-7730021.html; Kothari Rita, Opinion: Gujarat is a vegetarian state only in the minds of its self-chosen custodians, Nov 25, 2021; https://scroll.in/article/1010984/opinion-gujarat-is-a-vegetarian-state-only-in-the-minds-of-its-self-chosen-custodians

53   NHFS-5, 2019-21, Gujarat, MoH&FW, Mar 2021; https://dhsprogram.com/pubs/pdf/FR374/FR374_Gujarat.pdf

54   NHFS-4, 2015-16, Gujarat, MoH&FW, October 2017; https://www.aidsdatahub.org/sites/default/files/resource/national-family-health-survey-4-2015-2016-india-gujarat.pdf

55   Jadeja Asha, Gujarat is anything but a dry state. Decriminalise liquor, use tax revenue for development, Jan 13, 2023; https://theprint.in/opinion/gujarat-a-dry-state-decriminalise-liquor-use-tax-revenue-for-development/1310697/;   Jha Vaibhav and Gosh Sohini, Gujarat prohibition law: Many a slip between the flask and lip, Jul 29, 2022; https://indianexpress.com/article/political-pulse/gujarat-prohibition-law-hooch-tragedy-bjp-8056523/

56   Jadeja Asha, Gujarat is anything but a dry state. Decriminalise liquor, use tax revenue for development, Jan 13, 2023; https://theprint.in/opinion/gujarat-a-dry-state-decriminalise-liquor-use-tax-revenue-for-development/1310697/;   Jha Vaibhav and Gosh Sohini, Gujarat prohibition law: Many a slip between the flask and lip, Jul 29, 2022; https://indianexpress.com/article/political-pulse/gujarat-prohibition-law-hooch-tragedy-bjp-8056523/

57   Sagar, Fraternal Sins: The deceptions behind the Sangh's concept of social harmony, Jun 1, 2023; https://caravanmagazine.in/politics/deceptions-sangh-concept-social-harmony; Yadav Shyamlal, RSS chief backs reservations: How Mohan Bhagwat's statement marks a departure from the Sangh's previous position, Sept 8, 2023; https://indianexpress.com/article/explained/explained-politics/rss-mohan-bhagawat-reservations-8929452/

58   Tiwari Deeptiman, To counter caste conundrum, RSS pushes for 'Hindu unity' via social harmony project, Nov 8, 2023; https://indianexpress.com/article/political-pulse/to-counter-caste-conundrum-rss-pushes-for-hindu-unity-via-social-harmony-project-9017758/

59   Opposition working to divide India on caste lines, says Modi, Oct 3, 2023; https://www.newindianexpress.com/nation/2023/oct/03/opposition-working-to-divide-india-on-caste-lines-says-modi-2620383.html

60   Aiyar SA, Why do Nepal, Bangladesh beat India in social indicators? Starts with caste, Nov 26, 2023; https://timesofindia.indiatimes.com/blogs/Swaminomics/why-do-nepal-bangladesh-beat-india-in-social-indicators-starts-with-caste/

61   Mohanty P, Why is the Centre afraid of caste data and the census? Jun 10, 2022; https://www.cenfa.org/why-is-the-centre-afraid-of-caste-data-and-the-census/

62   Centre's affidavit in Supreme Court on Caste Census, Sept 24, 2021; https://www.thehindu.com/news/resources/centres-affidavit-in-supreme-court-on-caste-census/article36643286.ece

63   Jun 26, 2023; https://www.bbc.com/hindi/articles/c9793pq9p2zo?xtor=AL-73-%5Bpartner%5D-%5Bbbc.news.twitter%5D-%5Bheadline%5D-%5Bhindi%5D-%5Bbizdev%5D&at_campaign=Social_Flow&at_link_origin=BBCHindi&at_ptr_name=twitter&at_link_id=478F6A3E-1422-11EE-9EA4-F703D872BE90&at_bbc_team=editorial&at_link_type=web_link&at_medium=social&at_format=link&at_campaign_type=owned

64   Mohan J Anand, Panna Maharani held for 'hurting religious sentiments' after trying to forcibly perform aarti inside temple: MP Police, Sept 9, 2023; https://indianexpress.com/article/india/panna-maharani-held-hurting-religious-sentiments-perform-aarti-temple-mp-8931968/

65   Tiwari Vishnukant, BJP MLA's Aide Arrested for Urinating on Tribal Man in MP After Video Goes Viral, Jul 5, 2023; https://www.thequint.com/news/india/madhya-pradesh-bjp-leader-urinates-tribal-kol-assembly-electios-2023

66   Beam Adam, California lawmakers vote to become first state to ban caste-based discrimination, Sept 5, 2023; https://www.washingtonpost.com/national/2023/09/05/california-caste-discrimination-legislation/2dae5f10-4c41-11ee-bfca-04e0ac43f9e4_story.html

67   Ambedkar BR, Constituent Assembly Debates On 25 November, 1949; https://indiankanoon.org/doc/792941/

68   Dr Babasaheb Ambedkar: Writings and Speeches, Vol 17, edited by Narake Hari, Kamble NG, Kasare ML and Godghate Ashok, page XXIII; https://www.marxists.org/archive/ambedkar/writings-and-speeches/Volume_17_01.pdf

69   Centre opposes reservation for Dalit Christians, Muslims, Nov 9, 2022; https://www.tribuneindia.com/news/nation/centre-opposes-reservation-for-dalit-christians-muslims-449293

70   Amit Shah vows to scrap 4% Muslim quota after Telangana poll win; Asaduddin Owaisi hits back, Apr 24, 2023; https://www.freepressjournal.in/india/amit-shah-vows-to-scrap-4-muslim-reservation-after-telangana-win

71   Our institutions didn't fail when Trump attacked them. Quite the opposite, Bai Matt, Feb 16, 2021; https://www.washingtonpost.com/opinions/2021/02/16/our-institutions-didnt-fail-when-trump-attacked-them-quite-opposite/

72   Shah AP 2022: From Lodha to Ramana, Sept 20, 2022; https://www.thehindu.

com/opinion/op-ed/from-lodha-to-ramana-the-chief-justices-of-the-modi-era/article65909662.ece

73   22nd Law Commission seeks views on UCC from public, religious organisations, Jun 14, 2023; https://www.business-standard.com/india-news/22nd-law-commission-seeks-views-on-ucc-from-public-religious-organisations-123061400975_1.html

74   Law Commission of India Consultation Paper on Reform of Family Law, Aug 31, 2018; https://archive.pib.gov.in/documents/rlink/2018/aug/p201883101.pdf

75   Rajalakshmi TK, Uniform Civil Code: BJP's proposal raises concerns of anti-minority measures, May 18, 2022; https://frontline.thehindu.com/the-nation/code-calculations-uniform-civil-code-bjp-proposal-raises-concerns-of-anti-minority-measures/article65428919.ece

76   P Chidambaram writes: Reform (not uniform) personal laws, Jul 9, 2023; https://indianexpress.com/article/opinion/columns/reform-not-uniform-personal-laws-8818777/

77   Mitra Subrata K, The Puzzle of India's Governance: Culture, context and comparative theory, Routledge, 2006

78   871 riots took place during your regimes, BJP tells Congress during Delhi violence discussion in Parliament, Mar 11, 2020; https://economictimes.indiatimes.com/news/politics-and-nation/871-riots-took-place-during-your-regimes-bjp-tells-congress-during-delhi-violence-discussion-in-parliament/articleshow/74576470.cms?utm_source=contentofinterest&utm_medium=text&utm_campaign=cppst

79   Riots and lynching incidents, Lok Sabha answer, Mar 29, 2022; http://164.100.24.220/loksabhaquestions/annex/178/AU4277.pdf

80   Modi govt is shaking the foundation of India's IAS-led civil service — one reform at a time, Sept 16, 2019; https://theprint.in/india/governance/modi-govt-is-shaking-the-foundation-of-indias-ias-led-civil-service-one-reform-at-a-time/291893/

81   UPSC recruitment has fallen 40% since 2014 while govt struggles to fill IAS-IPS vacancies, Apr 17, 2019; https://theprint.in/india/governance/upsc-recruitment-has-fallen-40-since-2014-while-govt-struggles-to-fill-ias-ips-vacancies/222023/

82   PM Modi wants to appoint officers of RSS' choice in civil services, alleges Rahul Gandhi, May 22, 2022; https://indianexpress.com/article/india/pm-modi-rss-civil-services-upsc-rahul-gandhi-5186702/

83   Service & cadre: Not just UPSC exam, score in foundation course may also matter, May 21, 2018; https://indianexpress.com/article/india/service-cadre-not-just-upsc-exam-score-in-foundation-course-may-also-matter-5184736/

84   Why Indian diplomats are now raising Hindutva issues across the world, Apr 9, 2023; https://scroll.in/article/1045744/why-indian-diplomats-are-now-raising-hindutva-issues-across-the-world

85   Singh Sushant, Paradigm Shift: Two recent articulations of Modi's "New India" paint a grim picture, Nov 1, 2022; https://caravanmagazine.in/politics/recent-articulations-modi-new-india-grim-picture

86   Agha Eram, Modi's Messenger: S Jaishankar as the voice of India's Hindu nationalist foreign policy Mar 1, 2023; https://caravanmagazine.in/government/jaishankar-modi-hindu-nationalist

87   Huju Kira, Saffronizing diplomacy: the Indian Foreign Service under Hindu nationalist rule International Affairs, Volume 98, Issue 2, March 2022, Pages 423–441; https://academic.oup.com/ia/article/98/2/423/6522060

88   Shukla Ajay, Modi, Xi Jinping and Six Years of Battle for the Psychological High Ground, Sept 17, 2020; https://thewire.in/diplomacy/modi-xi-jinping-six-years-summits-ladakh

89   Banerjee Rana, Special Commentary: The Military and Nawaz Sharif in Pakistan, IPCS, Jun 5, 2013; http://www.ipcs.org/comm_select.php?articleNo=3972

90   Joe Biden raised Canadian Sikh's death with India's Narendra Modi at G20, Sept 22, 2023; https://www.ft.com/content/54721d57-fe1b-4d28-ab9b-a664f110770b

91   What UK, Australia, US said on Canada accusing India of killing Sikh leader, Sept 19, 2023; https://www.aljazeera.com/news/2023/9/19/what-uk-australia-us-said-on-canada-accusing-india-of-killing-sikh-leader#:~:text=The%20United%20Kingdom%20says%20it%20is%20in%20close,leader%20in%20British%20Columbia%20province%20earlier%20this%20year.

92   Laskar Rezaul H, US, UK back Canada on diplomatic presence, ask India to cooperate, Oct 21, 2023; https://www.hindustantimes.com/india-news/us-uk-back-canada-on-diplomatic-presence-ask-india-to-cooperate-101697874070218.html

93   Yousif Nadine, India to resume visa services for Canadians, Oct 26, 2023; https://www.bbc.com/news/world-us-canada-67201932

94   Rajnath tells Pakistan: Don't need to work much to take back Pakistan-occupied Kashmir, Jun 27, 202; https://indianexpress.com/article/india/pm-modi-india-us-statement-pakistan-terrorism-rajnath-singh-8686711/

95   Amit Shah tells Lok Sabha J&K also means PoK & Aksai Chin, ready to die for this, Aug 6, 2019; https://theprint.in/india/amit-shah-tells-lok-sabha-jk-also-means-pok-aksai-chin-ready-to-die-for-this/272875/

96   Ganguly Sumit, India Is Paying the Price for Neglecting its Neighbors, Jun 23, 2020; https://foreignpolicy.com/2020/06/23/india-china-south-asia-relations/; Baru Sanjaya, Nijjar-Pannun episodes show India is a victim of its own Vishwaguru propaganda, Dec 2, 2023; https://indianexpress.com/article/opinion/columns/nijjar-pannun-killings-united-states-canada-india-vishwaguru-propaganda-9049917/

97   Roy Shubhajit, Recall military staff, Maldives President tells Indian Govt, Nov 9, 2023; https://indianexpress.com/article/india/maldives-president-asks-india-to-withdraw-military-personnel-from-island-9032515/

98   Tripathi Sali, India's Worsening Democracy Makes It an Unreliable Ally, Jun 20, 2023; https://time.com/6288505/indias-worsening-democracy-makes-it-an-unreliable-ally/

99   India Ready for 'Two-and-a-half Front War', Says Army Chief Bipin Rawat, Jun 10, 2017; https://www.news18.com/news/india/india-ready-for-two-and-a-half-front-war-says-army-chief-1426427.html

100   Mohanty P, Rebooting Economy XXVI: Derailment of economy is not 'Act of God', it is 'Art of Misdirection', Sept 11, 2020; https://www.businesstoday.in/opinion/columns/story/india-derailment-of-indian-economy-is-not-an-act-of-god-it-is-art-of-misdirection-job-loss-unemployment-gdp-272743-2020-09-11

101   Das Gupta Moushumi, G20 summit: Both LoPs not on guest list for presidential banquet, Adhir says 'unprecedented', Sept 8, 2023; https://theprint.in/politics/g20-summit-both-lops-not-on-guest-list-for-presidential-banquet-adhir-says-unprecedented/1752796/

102   Ukraine war: India abstains from UN vote on Russian invasion, Feb 24, 2023; https://www.bbc.com/news/world-asia-india-64753820

103   Ellis-Petersen Hannah, G20 leaders agree joint declaration after deal on Ukraine statement, Sept 9, 2023; https://www.theguardian.com/world/2023/sep/09/g20-leaders-agree-joint-declaration-after-deal-on-ukraine-statement

104   India condemns Hamas 'terrorist attack', reiterates backing for independent Palestine, Oct 13, 2023; https://www.reuters.com/world/india-condemns-hamas-terrorist-attack-reiterates-backing-independent-palestine-2023-10-12/

105   India Refuses to Back Landslide UN General Assembly Call for Humanitarian Truce in Gaza, Oct 28, 2023; https://thewire.in/world/india-refuses-to-back-landslide-un-general-assembly-call-for-humanitarian-truce-in-gaza

106   Choudhury Angshuman, Moral timidity: The contradictions in India's refusal to join the UN's call for a ceasefire in Gaza, Oct 29, 2023; https://scroll.in/article/1058267/why-has-india-refused-to-join-the-un-call-for-a-ceasefire-in-gaza

107   Maira Arun, An Upstart in Government, pages 216, 226, Rupa Publications, 2015 & Scenario Scenarios: Shaping India's Future, 2013; https://niti.gov.in/planningcommission.gov.in/docs/reports/genrep/rep_sce2307.pdf

108   Government constitutes National Institution for Transforming India (NITI) Aayog, GOI, Jan 1, 2015; https://pib.gov.in/newsite/PrintRelease.aspx?relid=114268

109   Mohanty P, An Unkept Promise: What Derailed the Indian Economy, Chapter I, Sage Publications, Dec 2021; https://www.amazon.in/Unkept-Promise-Derailed-Indian-Economy/dp/9354791867

110   Decisions taken in the meeting of the Committee of Secretaries (CoS) held on 10th January, 2014, Ministry of Law and Justice; https://lddashboard.legislative.gov.in/sites/default/files/plcp.pdf

111   Bhardwaj Anjali, In violation of Pre-legislative consultation policy, govt did not make draft of Electoral Bond Scheme public before notifying it. Info obtained under RTI suggests proposal to hold consultations with political parties & seek public comments was scrapped after a meeting with the PM, Oct 30, 2023; https://

twitter.com/AnjaliB_/status/1719028025763991968;   https://twitter.com/AnjaliB_/status/1719028025763991968

112   Naftali Tim, The Problem With Trump's Madman Theory, Oct 4, 2017; https://www.theatlantic.com/international/archive/2017/10/madman-theory-trump-north-korea/542055/

113   Arun Shourie Compares Demonetisation to Suicide, Calls It 'Largest Money-Laundering Scheme', Oct 4, 2017; https://thewire.in/economy/arun-shourie-demonetisation-modi-gst

114   Patel Aakar, Price of Modi Years, Westland Publications, 2021; https://www.amazon.in/Price-Modi-Years-Aakar-Patel/dp/9391234224

115   Swain Ashok, Modi claims he has a 'photogenic' memory! May 31, 2023; https://twitter.com/ashoswai/status/1663857352590630913?t=s5BbO3-zQYlwL6Yc7wdHWw&s=19

116   Aspirational youths of 21st century India want an "educated" PM, says Delhi CM Arvind Kejriwal, Apr 2, 2023; http://timesofindia.indiatimes.com/articleshow/99190155.cms?from=mdr&utm_source=contentofinterest&utm_medium=text&utm_campaign=cppst

117   Coronavirus: Built in 10 days, China's 1000-bed hospital opens. Takes 1st patients, Feb 3, 2020; https://www.indiatoday.in/world/story/coronvirus-built-10-days-china-1000-bed-hospital-1642855-2020-02-03

118   India, Pakistan came close to a nuclear war, claims former U.S. Secretary of State in new book, Jan 25, 2023; https://www.thehindu.com/news/national/india-pakistan-came-close-to-a-nuclear-war-claims-former-us-secretary-of-state-in-new-book/article66429650.ece

119   Row Over PM Modi's "Cloud Can Help Us Escape Radar" Comment On Air Strike, May 12, 2019; https://www.ndtv.com/india-news/controversy-over-pm-narendra-modis-cloud-can-help-us-escape-radar-comment-on-balakot-air-strikes-2036402

120   Mohanty P, National champions: Costs and benefits of India's new growth model, Mar 23, 2023; https://www.fortuneindia.com/opinion/national-champions-costs-and-benefits-of-indias-new-growth-model/112005#:~:text=Economist%20Amartya%20Lahiri%20lists%20four,systemic%20shocks%E2%80%9D%20(b)%20market

121   Mander Harsh, Glitz of G20 Brings in Its Trail the Suffering of Working and Destitute People, Sept 7, 2023; https://www.thequint.com/opinion/glitz-of-g20-demolitions-green-sheets-suffering-of-working-and-destitute-people

122   Wall hastily built ahead of Trump visit in India criticized as 'hiding poor people', AP, Feb 18, 2020; https://www.theguardian.com/world/2020/feb/18/trump-india-visit-wall-criticism-hiding-poor-people

123   Mohanty P, Paying for Russian oil in Yuan will hurt globalisation of Rupee, Jul 12, 2023; https://www.fortuneindia.com/opinion/paying-for-russian-oil-in-yuan-will-hurt-globalisation-of-rupee/113351

124   Mohanty P, Budget 2023: What gives China immunity from extreme poverty, but not India? Dec 28, 2022; https://www.fortuneindia.com/budget-2023/budget-2023-what-gives-china-immunity-from-extreme-poverty-but-not-india/110924

125   Mohanty P, Coronavirus Lockdown VI: How India's insurance-led private healthcare cripples its ability to fight COVID-19, Apr 17, 2020; https://www.businesstoday.in/latest/economy-politics/story/coronavirus-lockdown-india-health-insurance-private-healthcare-public-hospitals-covid19-254637-2020-04-14

126   Acemoglu Daron, Naidu Suresh, Restrepo Pascual, Robinson James A, Democracy Does Cause Growth, Journal of Political Economy, January 14, 2019; https://economics.mit.edu/files/16686

127   Ruck Damian J, Bentley Alexander R and Lawson, Daniel J, Religious change preceded economic change in the 20th century, American Association for the Advancement of Science, 2018; https://advances.sciencemag.org/content/advances/4/7/eaar8680.full.pdf

128   Subramanian Samantha, How Hindu supremacists are tearing India apart, Feb 20, 2020; https://www.theguardian.com/world/2020/feb/20/hindu-supremacists-nationalism-tearing-india-apart-modi-bjp-rss-jnu-attacks

129   Liptak Kevin, Obama warns democratic institutions are 'creaky' but Trump's indictment is proof rule of law still exists in US, Jun 23, 2023; https://edition.cnn.com/2023/06/22/politics/barack-obama-interview-cnntv/index.html

130   Democracy, bureaucracy, and State capacity: The false choices we make, Apr 1, 2023; https://www.deccanherald.com/opinion/democracy-bureaucracy-and-state-capacity-the-false-choices-we-make-1205814.html

131   Amartya Sen said no democracy, with a free press, has ever had major famines, Oct 31, 2020; https://theprint.in/pageturner/excerpt/amartya-sen-said-no-democracy-with-free-press-has-had-major-famines/534152/

Index

Black Eagle Books

www.blackeaglebooks.org
info@blackeaglebooks.org

Black Eagle Books, an independent publisher, was founded
as a nonprofit organization in April, 2019. It is our mission
to connect and engage the Indian diaspora and the world at
large with the best of works of world literature published
on a collaborative platform, with special emphasis on
foregrounding Contemporary Classics and New Writing.

www.ingramcontent.com/pod-product-compliance
Lightning Source LLC
Chambersburg PA
CBHW081142020426
42333CB00021B/2634